RECORDS

OF THE

MASSACHUSETTS VOLUNTEER MILITIA

Called out by the Governor of Massachusetts to suppress a Threatened Invasion during the War of 1812-14

PUBLISHED BY
BRIG. GENL. GARDNER W. PEARSON
The Adjutant General of Massachusetts
Under a Resolve of the General Court

CLEARFIELD COMPANY

Originally published 1913

Reprinted for
Clearfield Company, Inc. by
Genealogical Publishing Co., Inc.
Baltimore, Maryland
1993

NOTE.

This volume has been designated the "Massachusetts Volunteer Militia in the War of 1812." This was done in error, because by law the active militia of Massachusetts at the present day is so designated. During the War of 1812–14 the militia was simply called "Massachusetts Militia," and it should have been so termed in this volume.

Resolves of 1912, Chapter 81.

RESOLVE TO PROVIDE FOR PUBLICATION OF CERTAIN STATE MILITARY RECORDS OF THE WAR OF EIGHTEEN HUNDRED AND TWELVE.

Resolved, That the adjutant general is authorized and directed to prepare a compilation of the records of the militia who responded to the call of the governor of the commonwealth to repel a threatened invasion during the war of eighteen hundred and twelve, as the same are found in the archives in the office of the adjutant general. The said work shall be done solely under the direction of the adjutant general and shall be completed within one year after the passage of this resolve. [*Approved April 27, 1912.*]

The Commonwealth of Massachusetts.

THE ADJUTANT GENERAL'S OFFICE, STATE HOUSE, BOSTON, April 5, 1913.

Brig. Genl. GARDNER W. PEARSON, *The Adjutant General of Massachusetts.*

GENERAL: — In accordance with the foregoing resolve I received instructions to plan and compile, in proper form for publication, the records of the Massachusetts Volunteer Militia who responded to the call of the Governor of Massachusetts to suppress a threatened invasion during the War of 1812–14.

In the early part of May, 1912, I submitted for your approval the plan that was to be adopted in completing the work, and received final instructions to commence. The work being especially of a laborious kind, with your consent I called to my assistance Mrs. Ruth M. Bruce, clerk for the Service Schools, M. V. M., and Miss Mabel L. Cook, clerk in the indexing division of the archives of this office. The work during the whole year was done entirely outside of office hours, for the reason that the numerous interruptions that fall to my lot in my duties made it absolutely essential that correctness could only be assured in that way. No attempt has been made to make records or correct them, such as spelling, etc., except in cases where the ink is fading and the names are almost obliterated; then efforts were made to supply the missing letters in accordance with what the names might have been; for example, the name Abbott, Abott, Abot; the same with Barrett, Barret, Barett; also Clap, Clapp; Prescott, Prescot, etc.

The sources from which the records were obtained are unknown to this office other than that they were furnished during the term of office of Gen. A. Hun Berry, Adjutant General of Massachusetts in 1881, and accepted by him as coming from "reliable sources," the party furnishing them being Mr. Z. K. Harmon of Portland, Me.

Annexed will be found extracts pertaining to the actions of the British along the Massachusetts coast, from B. J. Lossing's "Pictorial Field Book of the War of 1812," pages 888 to 904; Williamson's "History of Maine;" Wheeler's "Castine, Past and Present;" Akin's "History of Halifax City," and Murdoch's "History of Nova Scotia."

Respectfully,

JOHN BAKER,
Custodian of Military Archives.

HISTORICAL NARRATIVE.

"New England experienced very little actual war within its borders, yet it felt its pressure heavily in the paralysis of its peculiar industries, the continual drain upon its wealth of men and money, and the wasting excitement caused by constantly impending menaces and a sense of insecurity. From the spring of 1813, until the close of the contest, British squadrons were hovering along our coasts, and threatening the destruction of our maritime cities and villages. The year 1814 was a specially trying one for New England. The British government had determined and prepared at the beginning of that year, to make the campaign a vigorous, sharp and decisive one on land and sea.

"Early in June the enemy commenced depredations on the coasts of Massachusetts. On the 13th a detachment of two hundred men in six barges, were sent from the SUPERB and NIMROD, then lying in Buzzard's Bay, to destroy the shipping at Wareham. The elevated rocky neck at the mouth of the Narrows concealed the approach of the barges, and the inhabitants were taken by surprise. The enemy fired a ship, brig, and several smaller vessels. The ship was partially saved, and so also was a cotton factory, which was set on fire by a congreve rocket. The estimated value of the loss was $40,000. Quite a number of the leading inhabitants were seized and carried away as hostages, so as to prevent the militia from firing on the barges. These were released when the barges arrived at their vessels. Similar destruction was inflicted at Scituate, and at Orleans. Sometimes the militia would meet the marauders and drive them away. At Orleans a sharp skirmish between the barges and the militia took place, wherein the enemy lost one killed and two wounded, besides nine taken prisoners at Yarmouth, where they had drifted on shore in a schooner laden with salt, which they had captured at Orleans.

"On the 16th of June the BULWARK, 74, Captain Milne, carrying about ninety guns, anchored off the mouth of Saco River, in Maine, and her commander sent one hundred and fifty armed men, in five large boats to destroy property on the Neck belonging to Captain Thomas Cutts. That gentleman met them with a white flag, and proposed a money commutation. The matter was referred to Captain Milne, who soon afterward came ashore in his gig. He assured Cutts that he had positive orders to destroy, and could not spare. The torch was then applied, and two vessels (one finished, the other on the stocks), valued at $15,000, were destroyed, and another one taken away, which the owner afterward ransomed for $6,000. They also plundered Mr. Cutts' store of goods to the amount of $2,000.

"At about the same time the NIMROD and LA HOGUE were blockading New Bedford and Fair Haven. Other places were menaced and some were attacked.

"Early on the morning of September 8th, the barges from the LEANDER, Sir George Collier, landed some seventy men at Sandy Bay in Gloucester; a dense fog favoring them, the sentinel on

x MASSACHUSETTS VOLUNTEER MILITIA IN THE WAR OF 1812.

the small fort was surprised, before an alarm could be given; they took the officer and ten privates of Capt. Haskell's company, prisoners, spiked the guns, set the guard-house on fire, and retreated to their boats. Meantime the alarm bell was rung, and the militia assembled, but not in time or sufficient numbers to obstruct their retreat. One of the barges after hauling off, commenced a fire on the houses, and more particularly at the meeting-house bell which was ringing, in order, as the officer said with an oath, 'to stop that church music'; the recoil of the gun caused the barge to spring a leak, and those who were in her were obliged to swim ashore, and by this means five of the privates who were taken in the fort were re-captured, and thirteen of the enemy were taken prisoners.

"As late as December 27th, 1814, the British brig NIMROD, Capt. —— ——, sixteen guns, came to anchor in Falmouth harbor, and sent a boat on shore with a flag of truce and a message to the officers of the town, demanding the field-pieces belonging to the Artillery Company, and, in case of refusal, threatening to fire upon the town. This was considered a mere ruse, to first get possession of their only means of defence, and then to land and help themselves to such supplies as they might want, and then plunder and destroy as they had done at other places, when once in their power. It is reported that the town officers called in Capt. Weston Jenkins, of the Artillery Company, and referred the message from the NIMROD to him for an answer; who at once told the messenger to inform his captain 'that if he wanted his field-pieces, to come and get them'. This was construed by the officers of the NIMROD as a challenge, who at once sent word that at 10 A.M. next day, they should bombard the town. Of course this caused great consternation among the inhabitants, who at once set about removing themselves and property to a place of safety. In the meantime Col. David Nye issued his orders calling out the militia of the town, and also a portion from Sandwich and Barnstable, who, during the night and early morning entrenched and posted themselves in such a manner as to prevent the enemy from landing, if such was his purpose. Promptly at the hour specified, the NIMROD opened fire upon the little town, and blazed away for two hours, but made no attempt to land; then quietly leaving the harbor, sailed for Halifax, no doubt with a parting blessing from the inhabitants, uttered at least from some of them in anything but a devotional spirit.

"Many of the dwellings and other buildings were badly riddled, and other property destroyed, which was the extent of the damage.

"A more serious invasion of the New England coast now occurred. Early in July, 1814, Sir Thomas M. Hardy sailed secretly from Halifax, with a formidable force for land and sea service. His squadron consisted of the RAMILLIES, seventy-four guns (his flagship), the sloop MARTIN, brig BOXER, the BREAME, the bomb-ship TERROR, and several transports with troops, under Col. Thomas Pilkington. Commodore Hardy came charged with a part of the duty enjoined in the terrible order of Admiral Cochrane, 'TO DESTROY THE COAST TOWNS AND SHIPPING, AND RAVAGE THE COUNTRY.' This squadron entered Passamaquoddy Bay on the 11th, and anchored off Fort Sullivan, at Eastport, which was then in command of Major Perley Putnam, (of the 40th U. S. Infantry) of Salem, with a garrison of fifty men and six pieces of artillery. The Commodore demanded an instant surrender of the post, giving the commander only five minutes for consideration. Putnam promptly refused compliance, but on account of the vehement importunities of the alarmed inhabitants who were indisposed to resist, he yielded his own judgment and gave up the post, on condition that while the British should take possession of all public property, private property should be respected. When this agreement was signed, a thousand men with women and children, a battalion of artillery, and fifty or sixty pieces of cannon were landed on the main, and formal possession was taken of the fort, the town of Eastport, and all the islands and villages in and around Passamaquoddy Bay. Declaration was made that these were in permanent possession of the British, and the inhabitants were called upon to take an oath of allegiance to the Crown, or leave the territory. The custom house was taken possession of and opened under British officials, who vainly endeavored to compel the collector to sign unfinished treasury notes to the value of $9,000. He refused, saying, 'Hanging would not compel him'. Trade was resumed, the fortifications around Eastport were completed, and sixty pieces of cannon were mounted, and an arsenal established. Several vessels, and goods valued at three hundred thousand dollars, accumulated there to be smuggled into the United States, were made prizes of by the British, who held quiet possession of that region until the close of the war.

"Having established British rule at Eastport, and left eight hundred troops to hold the conquered region, Hardy sailed westward with his squadron, spreading alarm along the coast. Preparations for his reception were made everywhere. Vigilant eyes were watching and strong arms waiting for the appearance of the foe. The forts at Bath, Portland, and Portsmouth were manned. Little Fort Lilly, at Gloucester, was armed, Fort Pickering, near Salem, and Fort Sewall at Marblehead, were strengthened and garrisoned; Fort Warren, on Governor's Island, and Fort Independence, in Boston harbor, were put in readiness for action, and well garrisoned by Massachusetts Militia.

"An attack upon the important City of Boston was confidently expected; it was the capital of New England, and the moral effect of its capture would be great. It was a place for the construction of American war vessels, which the enemy feared more than armies. On this account also its capture or destruction was desirable. It was also a wealthy town, and offered a rich harvest for plunderers. It was well known too that it was almost defenseless. Caleb Strong, then Governor, was, it was well known, intensely opposed to the war; and it was not until after all her territory east of the Penobscot river in the District of Maine, (then a part of Massachusetts,) was in possession of the enemy, that any energetic measures were taken for its defense. Then a public meeting was called to consider the matter, and a committee consisting of Harrison Gray Otis, and others, was appointed to wait on the Governor, and present to him an address on the defenseless state of the city. The Governor listened to this appeal, and at once instituted measures for the defense of the whole line of the coast of the State, and of the District of Maine. A heavy fort was at once commenced on Noddle's Island, (now East Boston,) under the supervision of Major Loammi Baldwin as chief engineer; a call was made for volunteers to work on the fortification, and the response was patriotic; large numbers of the citizens of all classes and trades might be seen day after day toiling like common laborers,

> With pickaxe, shovel, spade, crow-bar, hoe, and barrow.

"The towns of Concord and Lincoln sent in two hundred men in one day, and thus the work went bravely on and was completed and formally christened October 26, and named Fort Strong, in honor of the Governor. Water batteries were erected, and also on Forts Warren and Independence, and supplied with furnaces for heating shot. Fortifications were also erected at South Boston Point, and on Savin Hill. As a matter of precaution, to prevent the enemy's approach to the city in case he succeeded in passing the forts, vessels were purchased and made ready to be sunk in the channel, and providing all other means failed to prevent his approach by land, the bridges leading to the towns, Chelsea, Charlestown, Brighton and Cambridge, were placed under the care of two discreet men, each having fifty or sixty axe-men under them, who were as a last resort to destroy a portion of each bridge.

"On the 6th of September, Governor Strong had issued his orders for the whole of the State Militia of all arms, to be in readiness to march to Boston at a moment's notice, and on the same day some four thousand troops from the several divisions, consisting of Infantry, Artillery, and Riflemen were ordered to march at once for Boston. These troops began to gather September 8th, and were properly officered and formed into regiments and placed under the supervision of Major General Joseph Whiton. By the middle of September there were some five thousand State troops of all arms in service at Boston and on the forts and batteries in the harbor and vicinity, and all were retained in service until the middle of November.

"Hardy's easy conquest at Eastport and its vicinity encouraged the British to attempt the seizure of the whole country lying between Passamaquoddy Bay and the Penobscot River. For this purpose a British fleet consisting of the BULWARK, DRAGON, and SPENCER, seventy-four guns each, the frigates BACCHANTE and TENEDOS, sloops-of-war SYLPH and PERUVIAN, and schooner PICTOU, with ten transports sailed from Halifax on the 26th of August, 1814. The British troops consisted of the first company of Royal Artillery; two rifle companies of the 7th battalion of the Sixtieth Regiment; detachments from the Twenty-ninth, Sixty-second, and Ninety-eighth Regiments — the whole divided into two brigades, under command of General Sir John C. Sherbrooke, Governor of Nova Scotia, assisted by Major-general Gerard Gosselin and Colonel Douglass. The fleet was in command of Rear Admiral Edward Griffith. It was the intention of Sherbrooke and Griffith to stop and take possession of Machias, but learning that the United States corvette, JOHN ADAMS, twenty-four guns, Capt. Charles Morris, had gone up the Penobscot, they hastened to the mouth of that river to blockade her. Passing up the Green Island channel they arrived in the fine harbor of Castine on the morning of the first of September. Lieutenant Lewis, of the United States army, with about forty men, was occupying a half-moon redoubt, armed with four twenty-four pounders and two field-pieces. Lieutenant Colonel Nichols, of the Royal Engineers, sent a summons to Lewis at sunrise to surrender. Lewis saw that resistance would be vain, so he resolved to flee. He gave the enemy a volley from his twenty-four pounders as a parting salute, then spiked them, blew up the redoubt, and with the field-pieces he and the garrison fled over the high peninsula to its neck, and escaped up the Penobscot. Colonel Douglass immediately landed from the fleet with a detachment of Royal Artillery and two companies of

HISTORICAL NARRATIVE. xiii

riflemen and took quiet possession of Castine, and with that the control of Penobscot Bay. The number of troops landed was about six hundred.

"As soon as a landing had been completed, it was made known to Sherbrooke that the ADAMS had gone up the river, and he and Griffith immediately detached a land and naval force to seize and destroy that vessel, and treat the inhabitants of the towns on the Penobscot as circumstances might seem to require. The expedition consisted of the SYLPH and PERUVIAN, a small schooner as a tender, the transport brig HARMONY, and nine launches, commanded by Capt. Robert Barrie, of the Royal Navy, who acted as Commodore. 'In the midst of the rapine a committee waited on Barrie, and told him that the people expected at his hands the common safeguards of humanity, if nothing more, when the brutal officer replied, "I have none for you. My business is to burn, sink and destroy. Your town is taken by storm, and by the rules of war we ought both to lay your village in ashes and put its inhabitants to the sword. But I will spare your lives, though I don't mean to spare your houses."' — WILLIAMSON'S HISTORY OF MAINE, ii., 646. The land forces, seven hundred strong, were under the command of Lieut. Col. Henry John, assisted by Major Riddle. The expedition sailed in the afternoon of the day of the arrival at Castine (Sept. first),[1] and passing Bucksport at twilight, anchored for the night. There was no disposition among the inhabitants along the Penobscot to submit quietly, unless absolutely compelled to. On the day when the expedition sailed up the river, information of the fact was conveyed by express to Capt. Morris, of the ADAMS, at Hampden, and he at once sent word to Brig. Gen. John Blake, at his home in Brewer, asking him to call out the militia. Blake mounted his horse, and late in the afternoon was at Bangor, issuing orders for the assembling of the Brigade of the Tenth Massachusetts division, of which he was commander, and the same evening rode down to Hampden. There he found Capt. Morris engaged in preparations for defense. He had dismantled the JOHN ADAMS, dragged her heavy guns to the summit of the high right bank of the Soadabscook, fifty rods from the wharf, and placed them in battery there, so as to command the river approaches from below. On the following morning Blake held a consultation

---

[1] "Immediately after the capture of Castine, the British government there established a Custom-house, or excise house, and appointed a Collector of Customs, who from that time until the twenty-fourth of April 1815, continued to receive entries of vessels and merchandise, conformably to the laws and regulations in the province of Nova Scotia. During this period many merchants residing at Castine imported goods and entered them with the said British Collector paying duties thereon to the British government."— From Wheeler's "Castine," p. 175.

"The funds collected at this port by the British Custom-house authorities were used as an endowment for Dalhousie College, Halifax, N. S."— From "Castine; Past and Present," by George A. Wheeler, A.M., M.D., p. 53.

"The British authorities collected the Revenue of Maine while in occupation which amounted to a considerable sum of money. This fund was placed by the colonial minister in the hands of the Lieutenant-Governor of Nova Scotia who appropriated it in various ways as he thought most for the benefit of the country. It was from this fund that Dalhousie College was afterwards built."— From "History of Halifax City," by T. B. Akins, Vol. 8, Collections of the Nova Scotia Historical Society, p. 164.

"The sum of £9,750 was then remaining in the hands of the Governor from the revenues collected at Castine while the State of Maine was in the hands of the British troops. This sum Lord Dalhousie obtained the permission of the Colonial Secretary to appropriate towards the erection of a college in Halifax on the model of the Scotch Universities."— From "History of Halifax City," p. 179 (year 1817).

"1820, Monday 22d May, the Earl of Dalhousie laid the corner stone of Dalhousie College."— From Murdoch's "History of Nova Scotia," Vol. 3, pp. 401-2, 455.

with Morris, and citizens of Bangor and Hampden, on the best methods of defense, but opinions were so various that no specific determination was arrived at. Morris had not much confidence in the militia, and declined any immediate co-operation with them. He approved of a proposition to meet the foe at his landing-place, wherever that might be, and expressed his determination to destroy the ADAMS, should the militia retreat.

"On the morning of the 2d, Belfast on the western side of Penobscot Bay, was taken possession of by Gen. Gosselin, at the head of six hundred troops, without resistance, and, at the same time, the expedition under Barrie and John, after landing a detachment from the Sixtieth and Ninety-eighth Regiments at Frankfort, proceeded up the river. The detachment marched up the western side of the Penobscot unmolested, and the little squadron arrived at Bald Hill cove, near Hampden, at 5 o'clock in the evening. The troops and about eighty marines were landed, and bivouacked there during the night, in the midst of a drenching rain-storm.

"During the 2d, about six hundred raw militia, who had never seen anything more like war than their own annual parade, assembled at Hampden, and Gen. Blake posted them in an admirable position on the brow of the hill. He had been joined by Lieutenant Lewis and forty regulars who fled from Castine. The artillery company of Blake's brigade, commanded by Capt. Hammond was there with two brass three-pounders, and an eighteen pound cannonade from Morris' vessel was placed in battery in charge of Mr. Bent, of the artillery. Many of the militia were without weapons or ammunition, and these were supplied as far as possible by Capt. Morris. Such was Blake's position on the dark and gloomy morning of the 3d.

"Morris, in the meantime had mounted nine short eighteen-pounders from the ADAMS upon his redoubt on the high bank over Crosby's wharf, and placed the battery in charge of Lieutenant Wadsworth, first officer of the ADAMS, assisted by Lieutenants Madison and Purser. With the remainder of his guns he took position in person on the wharf with about two hundred seamen and marines, prepared to defend his ship to the last extremity.

"The whole region of the Penobscot was enveloped in a dense fog on the morning of the 3d. The British at Bald Hill Cove had been joined by the detachment which landed at Frankfort, and at five o'clock all were in motion toward Hampden. They moved cautiously in the mist, with a vanguard of riflemen. On the flanks were detachments of marines and sailors, with a six-pound cannon, and a six and one-half inch howitzer, and a rocket apparatus. The British vessels moved slowly up the river at the same time within supporting distance.

"Blake had dispatched two flank companies to watch and annoy the approaching enemy. Between seven and eight o'clock they reported them crossing the little stream below Hampden and ascending the hill to attack the Americans. The fog was so thick that no enemy could be seen; but Blake pointed his eighteen-pounder in the direction of the foe, and with his field-pieces blazed away with considerable effect, as was afterward ascertained. He had resolved to reserve his musket firing until the enemy should be near enough to be seriously hurt; but the ordeal of waiting without breastworks in front was too severe for the untried militia. The enemy suddenly advanced at a 'double-quick', firing volleys in rapid succession. The militia, panic stricken, broke and fled in every direction, leaving Blake and his officers alone. Lieut. Wadsworth, at Morris' upper battery, perceived the disaster in its full extent, and communicated the fact to his chief on the wharf. Morris knew the impending danger; his rear and flank were exposed, and he saw no other way for salvation than flight. He ordered Wadsworth to spike his guns, and with his men retreat across the bridge. Wadsworth did so, his rear gallantly covered by Lieut. Watson with some marines. The JOHN ADAMS was fired upon and blown up at the same time, the guns on the wharf were spiked, and the men under the immediate command of Morris retreated across the bridge. Their commander was the last to leave the wharf, and before he could reach the bridge the enemy were on the bank above him; he dashed across the stream arm-pit deep under a galling musket fire from the British, unhurt, and joining his friends on the other side, retreated with Blake, his officers, and a bare remnant of his command, to Bangor.

"The British took possession of Hampden without further resistance, and pushing on to Bangor entered that village and quartered on the inhabitants, where for thirty hours the soldiers and sailors were given tacit license by Barrie to plunder as much as they pleased. The inhabitants were compelled not only to bring in and surrender their arms and military stores, but to report themselves prisoners of war for parole. General Blake was compelled to come to Bangor, surrender himself as a prisoner, and sign the same parole.

"Having despoiled the inhabitants of property valued at $23,000, and destroyed several vessels, the marauders left Bangor, and spent the 5th in similar employment at Hampden. There the soldiers and sailors, unrebuked by Barrie, committed the most wanton acts of destruction. The total loss of property at Hampden, exclusive of a valuable cargo of brandy, wine, oil, and silk which they found on board the schooner COMMODORE DECATUR, was estimated at $44,000.

"The indignant sufferers charged a great portion of their misfortunes to the feeble resistance made by Gen. Blake at Hampden. His tardiness, his non-compliance with the wishes of Morris, and others to attack the enemy at their landing-place; his neglect to throw up breast-works on the ridge at Hampden, and other evidence of inefficiency, were regarded as crimes, and he was charged with cowardice and even treason. The clamor against him was vehement for some time, but the public indignation finally cooled, and sober judgment, on considering the crude materials of his little force, acquitted him of every other fault but a lack of competent military ability and experience for the extraordinary occasion. A court of inquiry investigated his conduct and acquitted him. On the 12th of September, Sherbrooke and Griffith, with most of the troops and a greater part of the fleet, left Penobscot Bay, and, after capturing Machias, returned to Halifax. The proclamation by the President, James Madison, of the Treaty of Peace, which was concluded on December 24, 1814, was made on the 18th of February 1815, and on the 25th of April the British sailed out of Penobscot Bay.

"Peace, joy, tranquillity, and prosperity came with the birds and blossoms in the spring of 1815, and from that day until now no foreign enemy has ever appeared on our coast."

MASSACHUSETTS VOLUNTEER MILITIA IN THE WAR OF 1812.

Gen. J. Bliss' Command.
From Sept. 10 to Nov. 8, 1814.

RANK AND NAME.	STAFF.	
Jacob Bliss, Brigadier General, Springfield	Noah D. Mattoon, Brigade Major, Amherst	Lyman Lewis, Brigade Quartermaster, Westfield George Bliss, Aide, Springfield

Captain Stall's Company of Artillery under General Goodwin.
From June 16 to Aug. 1, 1814. Service at New Bedford.

RANK AND NAME.	Privates.	
Samuel Stall, Captain	Barney, Griffin	Maxfield, Thomas
Frederic Mayhew, Lieutenant	Cannon, James	Maxfield, Warren
Hayden, Coggershall, Lieutenant	Caswell, Ira	Parker, Avery
	Coffin, Henry	Perry, Nathan
Thomas Earl, Sergeant	Coggershall, Charles	Pierce, Abraham
George L. Dunham, Sergeant	Cost, Nash D.	Place, Henry
Thomas Martin, Sergeant	Gifford, Jonathan	Reynard, John
Jesse Haskell, Sergeant	Hall, Henry	Shearman, Allen
David Kempton, Corporal	Hathaway, Martin	Smith, Barnabas
Thomas Ellis, Corporal	Heath, John R.	Smith, Isaac
Watson Ellis, Corporal	Howland, James	Smith, Josiah
Peleg Clark, Corporal	Howland, Lloyd	Soule, Sylvanus
George Carroll, Musician	Howland, Wing	Stetson, Smith
Russell Booth, Musician	Jackson, Edmund	Tripp, Ezekiel
	Jenney, Joseph L.	West, John P.
	Kempton, Isaac	West, Richard
	Macumber, Bryant	Wrightington, John

Capt. E. Jacob's Company of Artillery under Supervision of General Goodwin.
From Sept. 19 to Oct. 19, 1814. Service at Scituate and vicinity.

RANK AND NAME.	Eleazer Joslyn, Musician	Damon, Piam
Edward Jacobs, Captain	Levi Percy, Musician	Farrow, Nathaniel
Elisha Barrell, Lieutenant		Gross, John
Edmund Curtis, Lieutenant	Privates.	Gross, Lewis
	Bailey, Charles	James, John, Jr.
Stephen Jacobs, Sergeant	Bailey, Gad	Magowan, Elias
Amos Dunbar, Sergeant	Brooks, Joseph	Magowan, Elisha
Levi Curtis, Sergeant	Clapp, John	Pratt, Benjamin C.
Stephen Curtis, Sergeant	Clark, Benjamin H.	Silvester, Joseph
Calvin D. Wilder, Corporal	Curtis, Job	Stetson, Joshua
Reuben D. Wilder, Corporal	Curtis, John	Studly, Gideon
Oran Joslyn, Corporal	Curtis, Lemuel	White, Cyrus
Elias Barrell, Corporal	Curtis, Luther	Whiting, Justus
Luther Turner, Musician	Curtis, Nathaniel	Whiting, Ozias
Gideon Perry, Musician	Curtis, Robert	Wing, Barker
Benjamin L. Monroe, Musician	Damon, Joseph	

MASSACHUSETTS VOLUNTEER MILITIA IN THE WAR OF 1812.

Capt. E. Dyer's Company of Artillery, General Wells' Command.
From September to October, 1814. In service one month at Boston.

RANK AND NAME.		
Ebenezer Dyer, Captain	Cox, Thomas	Slade, Isaac
	Douglass, William	Spear, Lemuel B.
John Slade, Sergeant	Dunham, Josiah	Stevens, James
	Hammond, Timothy	Stowell, Thomas
Privates.	Jennings, John	Tate, William
Ames, Simeon	Jennings, Joseph	Thompson, Amasa T.
Barber, Oliver	Loring, Daniel	Tompkins, William
Benney, James	Lyms, Luther	Wade, Levi
Budge, Benjamin	Massy, Samuel	Webber, Daniel
Cannon, Cornelius	Moffat, Alvan	Wheeler, David
	Nichols, Henry	Whitcomb, Levi
Connor, John	Simpson, Benjamin	White, Thomas

Capt. J. E. Smith's Company of Artillery, General Wells' Command.
From September to October, 1814. In service one month at Boston.

RANK AND NAME.		
J. E. Smith, Captain	Fletcher, Timothy	Mallet, William
	Gabriel, John	Pitcher, David
	Grammar, Seth	Pratt, Edward
Zebina Monson, Sergeant	Hallis, Benjamin	Proctor, Uriah
	Hiler, Stephen G.	Seeman, Ebenezer
Privates.	Hiler, William H.	Shadbourn, Isaac
Alley, Richard	Hodge, Jacob	Speed, Robert
Caton, Rufus	Homes, Francis	Trueman, William
Cushing, David	Lambert, Gideon	Wilson, John
Duff, William	Littlefield, Frederic	
French, Othniel	Littlefield, John	

Capt. J. Thaxter's Company of Artillery, General Wells' Command.
From September to October, 1814. In service one month at Boston.

RANK AND NAME.		
Jonathan Thaxter, Captain	Elms, John	Reed, Quincy
	Fenno, John	Rickford, Lewis
	Fletcher, Henry	Robinson, Thaddeus
Jedediah Tuttle, Sergeant	Goodwin, Uriah	Rodman, Thomas
	Harris, Isaac	Shacksford, William
Privates.	Howe, Isaac	Sprague, Mathew
Bangs, Martin	Jenkins, Nathaniel	Sumner, Alexander B.
Bliss, Levi	Jones, Josiah	Thayer, Eli
Brigham, John	Lewis, Daniel	Tucker, Lyman
Bruce, Elijah	Long, John	Tufts, Gardner
Butler, Samuel	Lyons, Samuel	Vogle, John S.
Carry, Alpheus	McFarland, Thomas	White, Ebenezer
Clark, Atkins	Nelson, James	White, Thomas
Coy, Judson	Page, Daniel G.	Wilson, Jason
Crichet, Nathaniel	Rawson, George	

Lieut. Col. W. Edwards' Regiment of Artillery.
From Sept. 8 to Nov. 5, 1814. Service at Boston and vicinity.

FIELD AND STAFF.		NONCOMMISSIONED STAFF.
William Edwards, Lieutenant Colonel, Northampton	F. W. Ripley, Quartermaster, Greenfield	Elias Goodspeed, Sergeant Major
Solomon Warriner, Major, Springfield	Seth M. Maltby, Paymaster, Hatfield	John Brown, Sergeant Major
Zuriel Howard, Major, Milford	Samuel Elder, Surgeon, Northampton	George Bridgeman, Quartermaster Sergeant
Samuel Henshaw, Adjutant, Northampton	Abraham Burnham, Surgeon's Mate	
	Joseph Field, Chaplain, Weston	

Capt. E. Mattoon's Company of Artillery, Lieut. Col. W. Edwards' Regiment.
From Sept. 8 to Nov. 5, 1814. Raised at Northfield. Service at Boston.

RANK AND NAME.
Elijah Mattoon, Captain
Charles Bowen, Lieutenant
Isaac Gregory, Ensign

Calvin Stearns, Sergeant
King Harris, Sergeant
John Whiting, Sergeant
Samuel Alexander, Sergeant
James Hosley, Sergeant

Privates.
Ball, Josiah
Bissell, Jabez F.
Butler, Minor

Cotton, Richard
Field, Sharon
Fowler, Clark
Fowler, John
Groves, Ansel
Hall, William
Heminway, Micajah
Holton, Elias
Holton, John
Holton, Lucius
Hunt, Ellsworth
Lee, Reuben
Lyman, Thomas
Miller, Cyrus
Morgan, Apollus

Morgan, Obadiah
Morton, William
Nettleton, Edward
Prickard, John
Roberts, Alanson
Rockwood, Thomas
Sheperdson, Arema
Sheperdson, Elijah
Simonds, William
Smith, Adolphus
Stratton, Calvin
Stratton, Roswell
Wait, Elmer
Whiting, Ebner E.
Wright, Henry

Capt. S. Graves' Company of Artillery, Lieut. Col. W. Edwards' Regiment.
From Sept. 8 to Nov. 5, 1814. Raised at Worcester. Service at Boston.

RANK AND NAME.
Samuel Graves, Captain
Simeon Hastings, Lieutenant
Joshua Hale, Lieutenant

Abel Flagg, Sergeant
William Eaton, Sergeant
Andrew Slater, Sergeant
Joshua Gates, Sergeant
Ebenezer Hastings, Corporal
Moses Clements, Corporal
Joel Gleason, Corporal
Charles Putnam, Corporal
Sewall Goodridge, Musician
Benjamin F. Pierce, Musician
Caleb P. Stock, Musician
Edward Curtis, Musician

Privates.
Barber, Ebenezer
Brigham, Jabez

Campbell, James
Chadwick, Daniel
Chickering, Shubal
Clark, Leonard
Cook, Josiah
Eaton, Thomas
Elder, William
Flagg, Amos
Flagg, Elijah
Flagg, John, 2d
Foster, Peter
Gates, Joel
Gates, Levi
Gates, Levi, 2d
Gates, Oliver
Gleason, James
Gleason, Reuben
Goodale, Paul
Harrington, Seneca
Hastings, Joseph
Hewit, Daniel

Holt, Jonas
How, Edward F.
Knight, Elliott
Livermore, Stephen G.
Merryfield, Lewis
Morse, John G.
Newton, Daniel H.
Pierce, Hollis
Pierce, James
Reed, Benjamin
Rice, Josiah
Rice, Lovell
Sibley, Isaac
Slater, Samuel
Stearns, Artemas
Sturtevant, Samuel
Torrey, John
Totsman, John, Jr.
Willington, Edmund
Wilson, Hugh

Capt. S. Parker's Company of Artillery, Lieut. Col. W. Edwards' Regiment.
From Sept. 8 to Nov. 5, 1814. Raised at Lancaster and vicinity. Service at Boston.

RANK AND NAME.
Silas Parker, Captain
John Taylor, Lieutenant
Abraham Mallard, Lieutenant

Abijah Brown, Sergeant
Nathaniel Thayer, Sergeant
Hannibal Laughton, Sergeant
Artimas H. Brown, Sergeant

Privates.
Blood, Reuben
Brown, Edward
Brown, Odel
Churchill, Samuel

Damon, Samuel
Fisher, Ephraim C.
Godard, Asa
Gould, Nathaniel
Haskell, Israel
Hewson, Robert
Houghton, Henry
Johnston, Josias
Lynch, John
Lynn, John
Maynard, Gardner
McLelan, William
Messer, Samuel
Moses, Liberty B.
Osgood, Apollus

Osgood, Jonathan
Phelps, George
Phelps, Thomas
Randall, Alvin
Randall, Prosper
Rice, Benjamin S.
Safford, Thomas
Sawyer, Phinehas
Taylor, Ebenezer
Walden, Ephraim
Wheeler, Calvin
Wilder, Ebenezer
Wilder, Titus

MASSACHUSETTS VOLUNTEER MILITIA IN THE WAR OF 1812.

Capt. Q. Stebbins' Company of Artillery, Lieut. Col. W. Edwards' Regiment.
From Sept. 8 to Nov. 5, 1814.   Raised at Springfield.   Service at Boston.

RANK AND NAME.
Quartus Stebbins, Captain
Heber Hitchcock, Lieutenant
Ebenezer Burt, Lieutenant

Ithemer Stebbins, Sergeant
Richard Huntington, Sergeant
Asher Hitchcock, Sergeant
Henry Bates, Sergeant
John W. Dwight, Corporal
Walter Warriner, Corporal
Wells Lathrop, Corporal
Samuel Boylston, Corporal
Stephen Jones, Musician
Henry Stebbins, Musician

Privates.
Ashley, John
Aspinwall, William

Bliss, Ebenezer
Bliss, Stephen
Brewer, John
Buckland, Daniel
Burt, Henry
Calins, Ezra
Chapin, Enoch
Chapin, Philip
Cooley, Ariel
Cooley, Samuel
Cooley, Titus
Cooley, William
Currin, Jabin
Dunbar, Isaac
Harris, William
Hitchcock, Daniel
Hitchcock, Josiah
Hitchcock, Walter
Hunt, Josiah

Loomis, Russell
Marsh, Appollus
Meads, Ira
Moore, Eli
Perkins, Russell
Pringe, William
Rogers, William
Sacket, Gad
Shattuck, Calvin
Stebbins, Harvey
Thurber, Edward
Tufts, Benjamin S.
Vinton, David
Warriner, Justin
Wright, Calvin
Wright, Joel

Capt. Z. Stebbins' Company of Artillery, Lieut. Col. W. Edwards' Regiment.
From Sept. 8 to Nov. 5, 1814.   Raised at Belchertown.   Service at Boston.

RANK AND NAME.
Zenos Stebbins, Captain
Eliab Washburn, Lieutenant
Theodore Bridgeman, Lieutenant

Charles Dwight, Sergeant
Simeon Dwight, Sergeant
Hazo Parsons, Sergeant
Joseph Washburn, Sergeant
Bela Parker, Corporal
Hezekiah Walker, Corporal
William Phelps, Corporal
Joseph Graves, Corporal
Abram Allen, Musician
Joel Billings, Musician
Chester Allen, Musician
Elisha Fenton, Musician

Privates.
Ames, Gideon
Baker, Ivers
Barber, Lawrence
Billings, Benjamin
Bugbee, Nehemiah
Burnett, Bela
Chapin, Libbeus
Chase, Enos
Cowles, Enos
Dwight, John
Dwight, Peregrine
Dwight, Pliney
Ford, Daniel
Forward, George
Fox, Josiah
French, Leonard
Graves, Josiah D.
Hammon, Chester
Hammon, Gamaliel

Hammon, Pliney
Kent, Samuel
Lester, John
Mitchell, Thomas K.
Pope, Ichabod
Pratt, Micah
Preston, Samuel H.
Ramsdale, Joseph
Rice, Samuel H.
Sanford, Alonzo
Smead, Elihu
Squire, Benjamin
Stebbins, Samuel H.
Strong, Gennbeth
Taylor, Arial
Taylor, William
Towne, Israel
Underwood, Russell
Walker, Aaron
Walker, Horace

Capt. A. Strong's Company of Artillery, Lieut. Col. W. Edwards' Regiment.
From Sept. 8 to Nov. 5, 1814.   Raised at Northampton.   Service at Boston.

RANK AND NAME.
Asahel Strong, Captain
Julius Phelps, Lieutenant
Adolphus Patterson, Lieutenant

Joseph H. Clark, Sergeant
Marshall Flagg, Sergeant
Lucius Clark, Sergeant
Oliver Bridgeman, Sergeant
Samuel Williams, Corporal
Theodore Parsons, Corporal

Sidenham Clark, Corporal
Charles J. Allen, Corporal
George K. Hitchcock, Musician
Spencer Day, Musician

Privates.
Atley, William
Barlow, John
Bartlett, Benoni
Belding, Aretus
Belding, Hezekiah

Blanchard, Amos
Bryant, George
Clapp, Daniel
Clark, Alanson
Clark, Allen
Clark, Cephas
Clark, Christopher
Clark, Justin
Clark, Sereno
Clark, Thaddeus
Clark, William

MASSACHUSETTS VOLUNTEER MILITIA IN THE WAR OF 1812. 5

Capt. A. Strong's Company of Artillery, Lieut. Col. W. Edwards' Regiment — Concluded.

Privates — Concluded.
Coats, Elisha
Coats, Jesse
Cook, Justin
Curtis, Lebbeus
Dickinson, David
Folger, George F.

Gere (?), Silsby
Graham, Aretus
Laroke, William
Loveland, Thomas C.
Lyman, Horace
Phelps, John
Rogers, John J.

Sherman, Ephraim
Smith, Richard
Strong, Chester
Strong, Seth
Wilde, Calvin
Wilkie, George
Wilkie, Henry

Capt. J. Tenney's Company of Artillery, Lieut. Col. W. Edwards' Regiment.
From Sept. 8 to Nov. 5, 1814. Raised at Leominster. Service at Boston.

RANK AND NAME.
Joseph Tenney, Captain
Ephraim Carter, Lieutenant
William Snow, Lieutenant

John Stewart, Sergeant
Walter Johnson, Sergeant
Josiah Whitcomb, Sergeant
David Bigelow, Sergeant

Privates.
Allen, Henry
Bigelow, Isaac
Boutzell, William
Brabock, William
Brigham, Asa

Burdett, James
Capen, John
Carter, Joseph W.
Carter, Peter
Colburn, Nathaniel
Conant, Joseph
Divol, James
Fullam, Jacob
How, Amos
Johnson, Stephen, Jr.
Jones, Frederick W.
Joslyn, Elias, Jr.
Kendall, David
Maynard, John
Merriam, Amos
Newhall, Merritt

Nichols, Thomas
Parmenter, Silas
Platts, Moses
Polly, Luther
Rice, Horace
Rugg, William
Smith, Asa
Smith, Joseph
Stone, Windsor
Tell, Thomas M.
Tenney, William
Thompson, Joseph
Ware, James
Whitcomb, Joseph
Willard, David

Capt. R. Thayer's Company of Artillery, Lieut. Col. W. Edwards' Regiment.
From Sept. 8 to Nov. 5, 1814. Raised at Milford and vicinity. Service at Boston.

RANK AND NAME.
Rufus Thayer, Captain
Ezra Nelson, Lieutenant
Henry Nelson, Lieutenant

Levi Rockwood, Sergeant
Clark Ellis, Sergeant
Samuel Nelson, Sergeant
Leonard Chapin, Sergeant
Isaac Devenport, Corporal
Lewis Hayward, Corporal
Calvin Johnson, Corporal
Clark Sumner, Corporal

Privates.
Andrews, William
Baker, Silas
Barbor, James
Bathrick, Jonathan
Bliss, Hartwell
Bosworth, Stacy
Bowker, James
Chapin, Eli
Clarke, Lovell
Cleveland, Ira
Corbett, John
Daniel, Libeus
Farrington, Elijah
Gould, Silas

Kebbe, Isaac
Littlefield, Moses
Madden, James
Parkhurst, Alexander
Perry, Josiah
Pond, Jones
Pond, Preston
Rockwood, Peter
Sanders, Levi
Sumner, Emory
Taft, Amasa
Taft, Ellis
Taft, Leonard
Waston or Weston, Eaton
Woodward, Benjamin

Capt. R. Brown's Company, Lieut. Col. S. K. Chamberlain's Regiment.
From Sept. 10 to Oct. 30, 1814. Raised at Concord (Concord Artillery). Service at Boston.

RANK AND NAME.
Reuben Brown, Captain
Francis Wheeler, Lieutenant
Cyrus Wheeler, Lieutenant

Elisha Wheeler, Sergeant
Joseph Hosmer, Sergeant
Eli Brown, Sergeant

James F. Melvin, Sergeant
Abel Davis, Corporal
Jonathan Hildreth, Corporal
William Lee, Corporal
Cyrus Warren, Corporal
Jones French, Musician
Jacob Harrington, Musician

Privates.
Balcom, Thaddeus
Billings, Paul H.
Brooks, Benjamin
Clark, Joseph
Crops or Cross, John
Davis, Thomas H.
Heywood, Reuben

6   MASSACHUSETTS VOLUNTEER MILITIA IN THE WAR OF 1812.

Capt. R. Brown's Company, Lieut. Col. S. K. Chamberlain's Regiment—Concluded.

Privates—Concluded.
Hosmer, Charles
Hosmer, Jesse
Hosmer, John
Jones, James
Lock, Joel
Melvin, John

Melvin, Samuel
Meriam, Oliver
Miles, Reuben
Pratt, Reuben
Rogers, Luke
Seyross, Francis
Stacy, John

Stevens, Elijah
Walcut, Silas
Wheeler, Simeon H.
Willis, Jesse
Wright, Edward

Maj. B. T. Reed's Battalion of Artillery.
From June 14 to Aug. 5, 1814. Service at Marblehead. Different periods as a watch, 7, 12 and 14 days.

RANK AND NAME.
Isaac Story, Captain
Caleb Prentiss, Captain
John Traill, Adjutant
John Gilley, Lieutenant
Samuel Horton, Jr., Lieutenant
John H. Gregory, Lieutenant
Thomas Bridges, Lieutenant
Edmund Kimball, Lieutenant
William H. Reynolds, Ensign

William H. Reynolds, Sergeant
Nathaniel Chapman, Sergeant
Moses Goldthwait, Sergeant
John Reynolds, Sergeant
Benjamin Homas, Sergeant
Thomas Bridges, Sergeant
Lewis Girdler, Jr., Sergeant
Nathaniel Lindsay, Jr., Sergeant
Samuel D. Turner, Sergeant
Thomas Bailey, Sergeant
James S. Smith, Sergeant
Levi Langley, Sergeant
Joshua Prentiss, Sergeant
John Proctor, Sergeant
Samuel S. Trefry, Sergeant
Daniel Patten, Sergeant
Samuel Knight, Sergeant
Nathaniel Adams, Sergeant
Samuel Rogers, Corporal
Richard Lee, Corporal
John Proctor, 3d, Corporal
Daniel Patten, Corporal
Thomas Bailey, Corporal
Jacob Hooper, Corporal
Richard Cole, Corporal
Robert B. Chin, Corporal
John Lenan, Corporal
Benjamin Homan, Corporal
Thomas Martin, Corporal
William Elliot, Corporal
Bartholomew Francis, Corporal
Nehemiah Prible, Corporal
Samuel D. Turner, Corporal
Samuel Knight, Jr., Corporal
Charles Thompson, Corporal
Thomas Nicholson, Corporal
John Sparhawk, Jr., Corporal
Robert H. Curtis, Corporal
Richard Tutlow, Tate or Tuttle, Corporal
Joshua Prince, Corporal
Nicholas Tucker, Corporal
John Humphries, Musician

Joseph Gregory, Jr., Musician
Richard Philips, Musician
Samuel Homan, Musician
Ichabod S. Philip, Musician
Abel Gardner, Musician
Knott Martin, Musician
Cobb Bowler, Musician
William Bartlett, Musician
William Harris, Musician
William Dolibe, Musician

Privates.
Aborns, Benjamin
Adams, Samuel R.
Baily, Thomas
Barker, George, Jr.
Barley, John R.
Bartlett, Devereux D.
Bartlett, John
Bartlett, Joseph B.
Bartlett, Nathaniel
Bartlett, Robert
Bassett, Samuel T.
Bean, Henry, Jr.
Bliss, Elijah
Bonndy, Thomas
Bowler, James
Bray, Edmund
Bridges, Philip, Jr.
Bridges, Thomas
Brown, Abraham
Brown, Benjamin
Brown, Richard
Brown, Samuel, 3d
Brown, Thomas, 3d
Butman, Benjamin, Jr.
Butman, John
Butman, Joseph
Butman, Thomas
Caldwell, Ebenezer
Cash, James
Caswell, Richard
Clark, Porter
Clenne, John
Clough, Samuel
Cloutman, George
Cloutman, Henry
Clover, John
Cornish, Benjamin
Cox, James
Cruff, William
Curtis, Jesse
Curtis, Robert H.

Cushing, Joseph
Cutler or Cutter, Solomon
Davis, Thomas
Deacons, Jonathan
Dennis, Archibald S.
Dennis, Erasmus
Dennis, Jonas
Devereux, Benjamin
Devereux, Elisha S.
Dickman, Samuel
Dixie, John
Dixie, Woodward
Doak, Michael
Dobler, Benjamin
Dodd, Benjamin
Dodd, Thomas
Dook, John
Elliot, William
Farrder, Timothy
Felt, Thomas
Flint, David
Foss, Samuel
Francis, Bartholomew
French, John
Fretoe, James
Gale, Thomas
Gardner, Nicholas
Garney, Thomas
Goodwin, John
Goss, William
Grant, John
Grant, Thomas
Graves, Blaney
Graves, Christopher
Graves, John
Graves, Samuel
Graves, William
Green, Thomas
Gridler, Benjamin
Gridler, Lewis, Jr.
Hammond, Thomas P.
Hammonds, John, Jr.
Hampson, John
Hardy, John
Harris, John
Harris, Joseph
Harris, Robert, 4th
Hathaway, John
Hathaway, Joseph
Hathaway, Stephen
Hawkes, William, Jr.
Hibbard, Samuel
High, John

Maj. B. T. Reed's Battalion of Artillery — Concluded.

Privates — Concluded.		
Hitchins, Samuel	Norton, Simon	Smithers, Gamaliel
Holden, Daniel	Oaks, George	Snow, John P.
Holloway, James	Orne, Jonathan	Snow, Samuel, Jr.
Homan, Benjamin	Orne, Joshua	Snow, Thomas
Homan, Joseph	Paine, P. Francis	Sparhawk, John
Homan, William	Papoon, Solomon	Stacy, Samuel
Hooker, John	Pearson, Robert	Standley, S.
Hooker, Philip	Pedrick, Benjamin	Stone, Isaac
Hooper, John	Pedrick, John B.	Stone, Joseph
Humphries, Edward	Pedrick, William	Stone, Nathaniel
Hunt, William	Philips, David A.	Stone, Simeon
Ingalls, John	Philips, Joseph	Stone, Stephen
Ingalls, Joseph	Philips, Nathaniel	Story, Frederick W.
James, Thomas P.	Philips, Robert	Sweet, Stephen
Johnson, William W.	Philips, Thomas	Thompson, Amos
Kimball, Edmund	Philips, William	Thompson, John
Kinner, Richard	Pike, Benjamin	Thompson, Jonathan
Lackey, Azor O.	Porter, Job	Trask, John
Langley, Levi	Porter, Thomas	Tucker, John
Lecran, John	Preble, Nehemiah	Tucker, Thomas
Lindsey, Joseph	Prentiss, John	Tucker, William
Lindsey, Nathaniel	Prentiss, Joshua	Turner, Samuel D.
Lyon, James	Prichard, William	Tutt, Richard
Lyon, Thomas	Proctor, John	Valentine, Andrew
Mann, Frederick	Proctor, Joseph, Jr.	Valentine, Benjamin
Martin, Arnold, 3d	Randall, William	Vickery, Benjamin B.
Martin, James	Randlett, Daniel	Vickery, William
Martin, Oliver	Renow, Richard	Warner, John
Martin, Thomas	Reynolds, Joel	Weed, Warren
Matison, Mathew	Reynolds, John	Whitehouse, Hanson
Merritt, Francis	Rhodes, John	Widger, William
Morgan, Thomas	Roberts, George	Wilkins, Jacob
Moulton, Jonathan	Rogers, Peter	Wooldridge, John
Muk (?), Jacob	Rogers, Samuel	Wooldridge, Samuel G.
Newhall, Philip	Roundy, Jonathan	Wormstead, Benjamin
Nichols, John	Russell, John	Wright, Peter
Nicholson, Thomas	Sampreel, Simon	Wyman, Luke
	Shirley, John	

Capt. G. Sullivan's Company of Artillery, under Supervision of Commodore William Bainbridge.
From June 13 to June 23, 1814. Raised at Boston ("New England Guards"). Service at Charlestown Navy Yard.

Rank and Name.		
George Sullivan, Captain	Ballister, Joseph	Gibbs, Alex H.
Lemuel Blake, Lieutenant	Bangs, Isaac	Gore, Christopher
Benjamin T. Pickman, Ensign	Barnard, Jonah G.	Gore, Jeremiah
	Barnard, Robert M.	Gore, Watson
Aaron Peabody, Sergeant	Baxter, Thomas M.	Grafton, Joseph D.
Charles Tidd, Sergeant	Blake, Edwin	Grant, Moses
John Howe, Corporal	Blanchard, Hezekiah	Greenough, William
Abbott Lawrence, Corporal	Brown, John B.	Grovenor, Lewis
Lorenzo Draper, Corporal	Clapp, Jarvis	Gulliver, John
Richard Ward, Corporal	Clark, Benjamin F.	Hall, William
Daniel Simpson, Musician	Clark, John	Hall, William, 2d
Little Perry, Musician	Clark, Oliver	Henderson, Howard
	Cutter, Leonard	Hewes, William G.
Privates.	Cutting, Lewis	Horton, Samuel
Abbott, Samuel L.	Dalton, James	Hunt, Samuel
Allen, Samuel R.	Dana, George	Jarvis, Denning
Andrews, John	Dennis, Thomas	Jenney, Stephen
Athearn, Frederic	Ewing, Shirley	Lamson, John
Avery, James E.	Fiske, James J.	Lane, John
Bacon, Joshua B.	Freeman, William	Lewis, Henry
	Gallison, John	Littlehall, Sargent

Capt. G. Sullivan's Company of Artillery under Supervision of Commodore William Bainbridge — Concluded.

Privates — Concluded.
McFarland, John C.
Miller, John
Newell, Montgomery
Newhall, Seaver
Odin, George
Parkman, Elias
Pearce, Seth
Pope, Joseph
Putnam, Daniel

Putnam, John C.
Rice, Rufus
Richards, Reuben
Richardson, Andrew J.
Richardson, Jeffrey
Scudder, Charles
Sewall, Thomas R.
Swift, David
Swift, Henry
Taylor, Chester

Thompson, William
Tisdale, Barney
Todd, George
Ward, Benjamin C.
Wentworth, Hiram
West, Joseph
Whiting, Eben
Wild, Eben
Williams, Robert P.
Willis, Nathan

Maj. J. Lewis' Battalion of Artillery.
From Sept. 11 to Oct. 31, 1814. Service at Boston.

FIELD AND STAFF.
James Lewis, Major, Groton
Joseph Parker, Adjutant
James Brown, Quartermaster

NONCOMMISSIONED STAFF.
Thomas G. Gardner, Sergeant Major
William Belcher, Drum Major
Howard Frost, Fife Major

Waiters.
Darland, John
Johnson, James

Capt. W. Farnsworth's Company, Maj. J. Lewis' Battalion of Artillery.
From Sept. 11 to Oct. 31, 1814. Raised at Groton. Service at Boston.

RANK AND NAME.
William Farnsworth, Captain
William Dalrymple, Lieutenant

Asa Graves, Sergeant
Amos Brown, Sergeant
Edmund Longly, Sergeant
Jonathan Johnston, Sergeant
Artemas Wright, Corporal
John Williams, Corporal
Jonathan Pierce, Corporal
Danforth Shiple, Corporal
William Harem, Musician
Roswell Reed, Musician

Privates.
Crouch, Daniel
Crouch, Levi
Cutler, Liberty
Dadmun, Willard
Farnsworth, Jonathan
Farr or Tarr, Willard
Hall, Benjamin
Holden, Abel
Jewell, Joshua A.
Keyes, Imla
Laurence, Salmon
Laurence, Zadock
Lewis, Meric
Munro, George
Munro, John

Munro, Nathan
Parker, Jonas L.
Prescott, John
Prescott, Thomas
Scribner, Rufus
Spaulding, George
Spaulding, Samuel
Stevens, William
Stone, Levi, Jr.
Sylvester, William
Symms, William
Woodard, Theodore
Woods, Samuel
Wright, Bela
Wright, Parker

Capt. J. Farnum's Company of Artillery, under Command of Maj. James Lewis.
From Sept. 20 to Nov. 2, 1814. Raised at Andover and vicinity. Service at Boston.

RANK AND NAME.
Jedediah Farnum, Captain
Washington Parker, Lieutenant
Isaiah Silver, Ensign

Philip Howe, Sergeant
David Currier, Sergeant
Hazen Kimball, Sergeant
Enoch B. Hall, Sergeant
Benaiah Currier, Corporal
Jeremiah Palmer, Corporal
John Chamberlain, Corporal
John Underhill, Corporal
George Grant, Musician
Samuel Clark, Musician

Privates.
Abbott, David
Allen, Isaac
Aubin, Samuel
Ayer, Moses
Barnard, Jacob
Bell, Philip
Beverly, Joel
Bodwell, John
Bodwell, Samuel
Boswell, Isaac
Boynton, Elijah
Chandler, John
Chase, William J.
Clark, William

Cogswell, George
Daniel, Joseph G.
Duntlin, John
Eaton, Robert W.
Elliott, Andrew
Emerson, Jonathan
Emerson, Jonathan, 2d
Farnum, Edwin
Friets, Jacob
Furbush, Sylvester
George, Nathaniel
George, William
Gill, Nathan
Hardy, Benjamin
Hardy, Nathaniel

Capt. J. Farnum's Company of Artillery, under Command of Maj. James Lewis—Concluded.

Privates—Concluded.

Harriman, John
Hazelton, Leonard
How, Abraham
Johnson, William
Jones, Herman
Kilham, George W.
Kimball, Nathan
Little, Joseph
Millett, Isaac
Mills, Benjamin
Morse, Jonathan

Morse, William
Pace, David
Peabody, Francis
Peabody, Isaac
Pettee, Asa
Phelps, Theodore
Pike, Charles
Pike, Stephen
Poor, Thomas, 2d
Richardson, C. C.
Shattuck, Henry
Simmons, John

Simonds, Reuben
Smith, Benjamin
Smith, Eliphalet
Spafford, Henry
Stiles, Moses
Thurston, Daniel
Towns, Daniel
Trow, Charles
Tyler, Benjamin
Wheeler, Amos
Wood, Thomas

Capt. Z. Smith's Company, Maj. J. Lewis' Battalion of Artillery.
From Sept. 22 to Oct. 30, 1814. Raised at Abington. Service at Boston.

RANK AND NAME.
Zenas Smith, Captain
George Walker, Lieutenant

Daniel A. Ford, Sergeant
Joseph Holmes, Sergeant
Josiah Hedges, Sergeant
A. Lane, Sergeant
Daniel Alden, Corporal
Gridley Thaxter, Corporal
Calvin Lane, Corporal
Samuel Copeton, Corporal

Privates.
Alden, Isaac
Beal, Nathaniel

Bicknell, Randall
Bicknell, Samuel
Birt, Ebenezer
Branding, Noah
Brown, David
Crossman, Elisha
Curtis, John
Curtis, Rufus
Deane, Enos
Ford, Joseph
Gardner, Sanders
Harris, Abial
Hill, Leonard
Holmes, William
Hunt, Lawrence
Jenkins, Gridley

Jenkins, Merritt
Lincoln, Ebenezer M.
Morris, Daniel
Packard, Jedediah
Peck, Jonathan
Pitcher, Earle
Reed, Joseph
Reed, Samuel P.
Shaw, Charles
Smith, Stillman
Sweet, William
Terrell, Isaac
Townsend, Ezekiel, Jr.
White, Asa
Wild, John
Withen, George

Capt. J. S. Sayward's Company of Artillery, Lieut. Col. J. Appleton's Regiment.
Six days between Sept. 19 and Oct. 29, 1814. Raised at Gloucester. Service at Gloucester. In battle September 19 with the barges of the enemy.

RANK AND NAME.
Joseph S. Sayward, Captain

John Proctor, Sergeant
David Storey, Sergeant
John Haskins, Sergeant
William Dexter, Corporal
William Everden, Corporal
Benjamin Newman, Corporal
Nathaniel Pulcifer, Musician

Privates.
Bulkley, Samuel
Burroughs, Warner

Challis, Enoch
Choate, Solomon
Cogswell, David
Conter, William
Ellery, Benjamin
Everden, James
Foster, Elijah
Friend, Richard
Greenleaf, William
Hanck, Theophilus
Huffin, William
Lane, Jonathan D.
Parker, Andrew
Pearce, George W.

Perkins, Jonathan S.
Pew, William
Plummer, Henry
Plummer, Moses
Pool, Joshua
Rogers, Samuel
Sargent, Epes
Sargent, Winthrop
Sayward, William
Somes, Joseph
Stacey, Benjamin
Winchester, William D.
Woodbury, Obediah

Capt. J. Putnam's Company, Lieut. Col. J. Russell's Regiment.
From Sept. 22 to Oct. 31, 1814. Raised at Danvers (Artillery Company). Service at Salem and vicinity.

RANK AND NAME.
Jesse Putnam, Captain
David Foster, Lieutenant
Benjamin Goodridge, Lieutenant

Warren Porter, Sergeant
Amariah Prince, Sergeant
George Abbot, Sergeant
Aaron Tapley, Sergeant

Alfred Porter, Sergeant
Edward Perry, Corporal
Elisha Dana, Corporal
Saul Brown, Corporal

10   MASSACHUSETTS VOLUNTEER MILITIA IN THE WAR OF 1812.

Capt. J. Putnam's Company, Lieut. Col. J. Russell's Regiment—Concluded.

RANK AND NAME—*Concluded.*
Joseph Spaulding, Musician
William Been, Musician

Privates.
Abbot, John
Allen, Lewis
Butler, Richard
Chadbourn, Thomas
Dodge, Daniel
Dwinel, David
Flagg, Ephraim

Flint, Jeremiah
Floyd, George
Foster, Charles
Fowl, Saul
Frye, Eben
Glynn, Moses
Hesselton, John
Hooper, Edward
Hooper, Mathew
Knight, William
Lincoln, Abel
Munroe, Isaac

Nichols, Benjamin
Phelps, Joseph
Proctor, Perley
Reed, Nathaniel
Rushley, John
Russell, Asa
Smith, Nathaniel
Taylor, Eliphalet
Very, Saul
Whipple, Stephen
Wilkins, David
Wormstit, Saul

Capt. Isaac Lane's Company of Artillery, Lieut. Col. B. Lincoln's Regiment.
From June 29 to July 9, 1814. Raised at Norton and vicinity. Service at New Bedford.

RANK AND NAME.
Isaac Lane, Captain
David Lane, Lieutenant

George Walker, Sergeant
Thomas Brown, Sergeant
Josiah Hodges, Sergeant
Moses Hunt, Sergeant
Lemuel Perry, Corporal
Zophar Skinner, Corporal
Asa Danforth, Corporal
Allen Lane, Corporal

Privates.
Blandin, Noah
Bullock, Rufus
Burt, Ebenezer

Crossman, Elisha
Dary, Allen
Dean, Barzilla
Dean, Enos
Dean, Nathan
Dunbar, Amasa
Freeman, John
French, Alfred M.
Fuller, Joseph
Guill, Daniel
Hill, Leonard
Hodge, Stephen
Hodges, Adoniram
Hodges, George
Hodges, Joseph
Hunt, Joseph
Hunt, Oliver

Knapp, Abiather
Lane, Calvin
Lane, George
Lane, William
Lincoln, Ebenezer M.
Lincoln, Tisdal
Macumber, Ezra
Morey, Daniel
Peck, Oliver C.
Smith, Stillman
Sweet, Newton
Sweet, Thomas
Sweet, William
Wetherell, George
White, Walter
Willis, Sumner
Wilmarth, Benoni

Lieut. Col. J. Appleton's Regiment.
In service at Gloucester 4 days in September and October, 1814. In battle September 19.

FIELD AND STAFF.
James Appleton, Lieutenant Colonel, Gloucester
Ephraim Brown, Major, Gloucester
Henry Smith, Adjutant, Gloucester

Jacob Parsons, Quartermaster, Gloucester
William Saville, Paymaster, Gloucester
William Coffin, Surgeon, Gloucester
James Goss, Surgeon's Mate, Gloucester
Daniel Fuller, Chaplain, Gloucester

NONCOMMISSIONED STAFF.
Joseph Henderson, Sergeant Major

Capt. D. Elwell's Company, Lieut. Col. J. Appleton's Regiment.
From Sept. 19 to Oct. 12, 1814. Service at Gloucester. In battle September 19 with the barges of the enemy.

RANK AND NAME.
David Elwell, Captain
Joshua Clark, Lieutenant
William Low, Jr., Ensign

Moses I. Clark, Sergeant
John Foster, Sergeant
John Haskell, Sergeant
Asa Knowlton, Sergeant
William T. Abbott, Corporal

Henry White, Jr., Corporal
William Thurston, Corporal
Thomas York, Corporal
Eben Pool, Musician
Zebulon R. Davis, Musician

Privates.
Adams, William
Bagley, John
Blatchford, John

Bradstreet, Ezekiel
Bradstreet, Nathaniel
Chipman, Anthony
Clark, Abraham S.
Clark, Henry
Clark, Henry, Jr.
Clark, Samuel L.
Clark, Thomas L.
Clark, William C.

MASSACHUSETTS VOLUNTEER MILITIA IN THE WAR OF 1812.   11

Capt. D. Elwell's Company, Lieut. Col. J. Appleton's Regiment—Concluded.

Privates—Concluded.
Cunningham, John, Jr.
Dennin, Job
Doyl, Felix
Dunnaway, Daniel
Elwell, Caleb
Giles, William
Goss, William, Jr.
Grover, Ebenezer, Jr.
Haskins, Thomas
Haskins, William B.
Hodgkins, Henry
Jacob, Abraham
Knight, Charles
Knowlton, Azor
Lane, George, Jr.
Lee, Nathaniel B.
Leighton, Tobias
Low, David

Low, James
Low, Nathaniel
Lurvey, William
Morse, Essom
Parsons, John, 4th
Pool, Abram H.
Pool, Francis
Pool, John
Pool, John, 4th
Pool, Moses
Pool, Zebulon
Robards, George
Rowe, Benjamin, Jr.
Rowe, Daniel
Rowe, Eben
Rowe, George
Rowe, Isaac
Rowe, Job
Smith, John L.

Stockman, John
Tarr, David, Jr.
Tarr, Francis, Jr.
Tarr, Francis P.
Tarr, Jonathan, Jr.
Tarr, Joseph, Jr.
Tarr, Joshua
Tarr, Solomon
Thompson, Thomas
Thurston, Joseph
Wainright, Thomas
Webster, Joshua
Weeden, Daniel
Witham, Joseph

Waiters.
Brown, David
Clark, John

Capt. J. Harris' Company, Lieut. Col. J. Appleton's Regiment.
From Sept. 19 to Oct. 12, 1814.   Service at Gloucester.   In battle September 19 with the barges of the enemy.

RANK AND NAME.
John Harris, Captain
Ebenezer Tarr, Lieutenant
John Jumper, Ensign

Thomas Knutsford, Sergeant
Charles Sargent, Sergeant
Samuel Brookins, Musician
Amos Storey, Musician

Privates.
Anderson, Stephen
Bailey, Samuel
Barrett, David

Bassett, Daniel
Carter, Joseph
Dade, Isaac
Day, William
Fears, James
Gott, Solomon
Griffin, Amos
Harris, James, Jr.
Hoyt, Chase
Kimball, Jonathan
Knutsford, John
Knutsford, William
Lane, Joseph, 3d
Langsford, Andrew

Lufkin, Zebulon
Mander, Woodbery F.
Mann, William
Merchant, Daniel
Parsons, Ebenezer
Roberts, Theodore
Rowe, Benjamin, Jr.
Saunders, Simeon
Sergeant, David
Wheeler, Moses, Jr.
Woodbury, Epes, Jr.
Woodbury, Peter

Capt. B. Haskell's Company, Lieut. Col. J. Appleton's Regiment.
From Sept. 19 to Oct. 12, 1814.   Service at Gloucester.   In battle September 19 with the barges of the enemy.

RANK AND NAME.
Benjamin Haskell, Captain

Ebenezer James, Sergeant
Joseph Herrick, Sergeant
James Haskell, Sergeant
Joseph Herrick, Musician
Samuel Rust, Musician

Privates.
Bray, Edward
Bray, Edwin

Bray, Jeremiah
Choate, Adoniram
Clark, George, Jr.
Cole, William
Currier, Adoniram
Davis, John
Dodge, William
Gilbert, Benjamin
Gilbert, Samuel P.
Haskell, Jonathan
Haskell, Lemuel
Herrick, John

Honor, Oliver
Lufkin, Josiah
Lufkin, Michael
Proctor, Humphrey
Pulsifer, John
Roberts, Jacob
Roberts, Theodore
Rust, Israel, Jr.

MASSACHUSETTS VOLUNTEER MILITIA IN THE WAR OF 1812.

Capt. D. Sargent's Company, Lieut. Col. J. Appleton's Regiment.
From Sept. 19 to Oct. 12, 1814. Service at Gloucester. In battle September 19 with the barges of the enemy.

RANK AND NAME.
Dudley Sargent, Captain
Isaac Dennison, Jr., Lieutenant
Reuben Patch, Ensign

Jonathan Sargent, Sergeant
William Hodgkins, Sergeant
Enoch Carter, Musician
Samuel Lane, Musician

Privates.
Babson, James
Burnham, Andrew M.

Butler, E.
Butler, Walter
Clark, William
Davis, George
Dennis, William
Dodd, John
Griffin, Davis
Griffin, Henry
Harraden, Andrew
Jones, Samuel T.
Knowlton, John, Jr.
Lane, Mack
Lane, Solomon

Newman, John
Riggs, John
Robinson, Daniel A.
Sargent, Samuel, Jr.
Sylvester, Samuel
Woodbury, Asa, Jr.
Young, Elps

Waiter.
Dennison, David

Capt. J. Smith's Company, Lieut. Col. J. Appleton's Regiment.
Different periods from Sept. 19 to Oct. 12, 1814. Service at Gloucester. In battle September 19 with the barges of the enemy.

RANK AND NAME.
John Smith, Jr., Captain
Obediah Stoddard, Lieutenant

Charles Haskell, Sergeant
James P. Collins, Sergeant
Samuel Rush, Musician
Joseph Herrick, Musician

Privates.
Davis, Elias, Jr.
Davis, Francis H.
Davis, John H.

Elwell, Solomon
Flanders, Joseph
Goodrich, Joseph, Jr.
Grover, Josiah
Hales, William
Kinsman, Joseph
Lincoln, Perez W.
Lombard, James
Lifkin, Moses, Jr.
Lufkin, Samuel
Newcomb, William
Parsons, David
Plummer, Eber

Plummer, Micajah
Rogers, Nathaniel
Rogers, Timothy
Sayward, William
Smith, David
Somes, Isaac
Stacy, John, Jr.
Swinson, Peter
Williams, Abraham
Williams, John
Williams, Nathaniel
Witham, Mark
Witham, Nathaniel

Capt. C. Tarr's Company, Lieut. Col. J. Appleton's Regiment.
From Sept. 19 to Oct. 12, 1814. Service at Gloucester. In battle September 19 with the barges of the enemy.

RANK AND NAME.
Charles Tarr, Captain
George Lane, Lieutenant
Timothy R. Davis, Ensign

Henry Tarr, Sergeant
Eben Pool, Sergeant
Moses Tarr, Sergeant
John Davis, Musician
Edmund Haskins, Musician

Privates.
Bickford, Andrew
Brown, Charles
Cass, Robert
Davis, Daniel

Dodd, Asa
Gamage, Ebenezer
Gamage, Samuel G.
Giddings, Aarod
Gott, George
Gott, James
Grover, John
Grover, Nehemiah
Hooper, Robert
Hoyt, John H.
Lane, Andrew
Merrill, Daniel
Norwood, Daniel
Oakes, John
Parsons, Eben
Pool, Aaron

Pool, Francis
Pool, James, Jr.
Pool, Joshua
Pool, Solomon, Jr.
Pool, William
Putman, John
Robards, Thomas, Jr.
Stockman, John
Tarr, Jabez, Jr.
Tarr, James
Tarr, Nathaniel
Tarr, Robert
Todd, Nathan
Turner, John, Jr.
Webster, George
Witham, Henry, Jr.

MASSACHUSETTS VOLUNTEER MILITIA IN THE WAR OF 1812.

Capt. I. Tucker's Company, Lieut. Col. J. Appleton's Regiment.
Different periods from Sept. 19 to Oct. 12, 1814.   Service at Gloucester.   In battle September 19 with the barges of the enemy.

Rank and Name.	Privates.	
Isaac Tucker, Captain	Allen, Mack	Figes, William
Jacob Tucker, Lieutenant	Allen, William	Harvey, Benjamin
William Curtis, Ensign	Babson, Nathaniel	Harvey, Joseph
	Baker, William	Hodgkins, Isaac
John N. Edney, Sergeant	Brown, Nathaniel	Low, Isaac
Moses Palmer, Jr., Sergeant	Davis, Thomas	Pulsifer, John A.
Wintworth Riggs, Musician	Doggett, William	Riggs, Joshua
	Ellery, Joseph	Wharffey, William

Capt. C. Williams' Company, Lieut. Col. J. Appleton's Regiment.
Different periods from Sept. 19 to Oct. 12, 1814.   Service at Gloucester.   In battle September 19 with the barges of the enemy.

Rank and Name.		
Caleb Williams, Captain	Elwell, Elias, Jr.	Stevens, Samuel
Charles Sawyer, Lieutenant	Gaffney, William	Tappan, William
Charles Eaton, Ensign	Gray, William, Jr.	Tucker, William
	Hodgkins, John	Wallis, Jonathan
John W. Lowe, Sergeant	Lannanan, Barnard	Warner, William
Levi Haskell, Sergeant	Moore, John	Webber, Ignatius, Jr.
	Morse, Anthony	
Privates.	Parsons, Nicholas G.	*Waiters.*
Burnham, Benjamin M.	Parsons, Winthrop	Burnham, Joshua
Coffin, Tristram B.	Rust, William C.	Turner, Abel
	Smith, Nathaniel	

Capt. B. Haskell's Detached Company under General Hovey.
From June 21 to Sept. 18, 1814.   Service at Gloucester.

Rank and Name.	Bray, Daniel	Millett, Benjamin
Benjamin Haskell, Captain	Bray, Moses	Millett, Samuel R.
Benjamin C. Sargent, Lieutenant	Brookins, Samuel	Morse, Moses
Thomas Lufkin, Ensign	Brown, Ephraim	Norwood, Charles
	Brown, William	Norwood, Elias
Charles Collins, Sergeant	Choate, Humphrey	Norwood, James
Jacob Haskell, Sergeant	Cram, John	Parsons, John
James Dennison, Sergeant	Crowell, Samuel	Parsons, Jonah, 3d
Daniel Robbins, Corporal	Curtis, Benjamin	Parsons, Thomas
James W. Pierce, Corporal	Dennen, Samuel	Quimby, Daniel
Roger Sargent, Corporal	Elwell, William	Riggs, Thomas
John Wood, Corporal	Gammage, Stephen	Robbins, William
Denmark Proctor, Musician	Girdley, George	Roberts, James
Thomas Millett, Musician	Goady, William	Roller, Pisquale
	Griffin, Tristram	Roper, John
Privates.	Hall, John B.	Sargent, Andrew
Abbott, Nehemiah	Hodgkins, David	Sargent, Edward
Adams, Ezekiel	Ingersoll, Joshua	Sargent, Oliver
Adams, Isaac	Kemp, Joseph	Sawyer, William
Adams, Winthrop	Knight, James	Smith, Charles
Allen, Abner	Knight, James P.	Stillman, Daniel
Avery, Benjamin	Lane, Stephen	Turner, Leonard
Ayres, John	Lee, Aaron	Williams, William
Barrett, George S.	Lee, Nathan	Wilson, William
Barrett, John	Long, Charles	Witham, William
Bishop, John	McCartney, William	

Capt. B. Haskell's Detached Company, under Supervision of General Hovey.
From Sept. 21 to November, 1814. Service at Gloucester.

RANK AND NAME.
Benjamin Haskell, Captain
Benjamin C. Sargent, Lieutenant
Thomas Lufkin, Ensign

Charles Collins, Sergeant
Jacob Haskell, Sergeant
Nehemiah Abbott, Sergeant
Daniel Robbins, Sergeant
Roger Sargent, Corporal
John Wood, Corporal
William McCartney, Corporal
Thomas Millett, Corporal
Demmack Proctor, Musician
Oliver Sargent, Musician

Privates.
Adams, Ezekiel
Adams, Isaac
Adams, Winthrop
Allen, Abner
Avery, Benjamin
Ayres, John
Badger, Daniel
Barrett, George S.
Barrett, John
Bishop, John
Bray, Daniel

Bray, Moses
Brown, Ephraim
Brown, John
Brown, William
Choate, Humphrey
Crowell, Samuel
Curtis, Benjamin
Dennen, Samuel
Dennison, Jonah
Elwell, William
Girdler, William
Goday, William
Griffin, Eliphalet
Griffin, Tristram
Hall, John B.
Hodgkins, David
Ingersoll, Joshua
Kemp, Joseph
Knight, James
Knight, James P.
Lane, Stephen
Lang, Charles
Lee, Aaron
Lee, Nathan
Lloyd, John
Millett, Benjamin
Millett, Samuel
Morse, Moses

Norwood, Charles
Norwood, Elias
Norwood, James
Parsons, John
Parsons, Jonathan
Parsons, Thomas
Pew, Richard
Pulsifer, John
Quimby, Daniel
Riggs, Thomas
Roberts, James
Robinson, William
Roller, Pisquale
Roper, John
Roper, John, 2d
Rowe, William
Sargent, Andrew
Sargent, Edward
Sargent, George
Sawyer, James
Simonds, Andrew
Smith, Charles W.
Stillman, Daniel
Webber, Joseph
Williams, William
Wilson, William
Witham, William

Capt. M. Whittier's Company, Maj. R. Elwell's Regiment.
From Sept. 14 to November, 1814. Raised at Ipswich.

RANK AND NAME.
Moses Whittier, Captain
John Brown, Lieutenant
Robert Kimball, Ensign

Ebenezer Harwood, Sergeant
Joseph Lord, Sergeant
Abel Andrews, Sergeant
Havilah Dodge, Sergeant
Moses Knowlton, Corporal
Samuel Kinsman, Corporal
Samuel Andrews, Corporal
Joseph Hodgkins, Corporal
Moses Perkins, Musician
Moses Andrews, Musician

Privates.
Andrews, Benjamin
Andrews, Charles
Baker, Asa
Bickford, Silas
Bowden, Thomas
Burnham, Elisha
Burnham, Ezra
Burnham, Isaac
Burnham, Joshua
Butman, John
Champney, Joseph
Cheever, William
Clark, Edward
Clark, William

Clark, William, 2d
Davison, Pliney
Dennis, Thomas
Dickerson, Darius
Dodge, Israel
Dodge, John
Dodge, William
Durong, John
Ellery, William
Elwell, Isaac
Giddings, Henry
Goldsborough, Asa
Greenleaf, Edmund
Grush, Philip
Gurley, William
Hardy, Phineas
Hobson, Samuel
Hoyt, Daniel
Hull, William
Jewett, Eliphalet
Jewett, Thomas
Kimball, Nathaniel
Kimball, Stephen
Kneeland, Aaron
Kneeland, John
Lakeman, William
Lambert, Thomas
Leatherland, William
Lee, Andrew
Lee, Edward
Lord, Daniel

Lufkin, William
Lull, John
Lummus, John
Mace, John
Manning, Joseph B.
Ober, Daniel
Pearson, Amos
Perkins, Nathaniel
Perkins, Stephen
Pettingill, Moses
Phillips, James
Pickard, Nathaniel
Pickard, Samuel
Potter, Benjamin
Pulsifer, William
Ross, Frederick
Russell, William
Rust, Moses
Smith, Aaron, 3d
Smith, Thomas
Snelling, Moses
Stanwood, Robert
Thompson, John
Thompson, William
Vincent, Matthew
Welling, Michell
Wells, John
Wells, Joseph
Wells, Nathaniel B.
Wise, John
Wyatt, Simon

MASSACHUSETTS VOLUNTEER MILITIA IN THE WAR OF 1812.   15

Capt. S. Allen's Company, Lieut. Col. E. Hale's Regiment.
From Sept. 30 to Oct. 4, 1814.   Raised at Newbury.   Service at Newbury.

RANK AND NAME.
Samuel Allen, Captain
James Carey, Lieutenant
Asa Chamberlin, Ensign

Benjamin Lunt, Sergeant
Enoch Jaques, Sergeant
Elias Hunt, Sergeant
Henry C. Jaques, Sergeant

Privates.
Babb, Nathaniel
Bartlett, Moses
Battice, Joseph
Berry, George, 2d
Campbell, George

Carlton, John
Clifford, David
Farley, John D.
Floyd, Patrick
Floyd, Silas
Gould, John
Haysen, Daniel C.
Hoyt, Joseph
Ilsey, Wade
Jaynes, Charles
Lunt, Daniel A.
Noyes, John
Page, Richard
Pearson, Nathaniel
Pillsbury, Amos
Pillsbury, Daniel

Pillsbury, John
Rand, Daniel
Robertson, John
Rogers, Ezekiel
Rogers, Gideon
Rogers, James
Rogers, Joseph
Rogers, Oliver
Rogers, Theodore
Safford, Samuel
Sargent, Stephen
Sargent, William
Tenney, Benjamin T.
Thompson, John
Titcomb, John

Capt. E. Emery's Company, Lieut. Col. E. Hale's Regiment.
From Sept. 30 to Oct. 4, 1814.   Raised at Newbury.   Service at Newbury.

RANK AND NAME.
Eliphalet Emery, Captain
Benjamin Stanwood, Lieutenant
Nicholas Emery, Ensign

Cornelius C. Felton, Sergeant
Nicholas Durgen, Sergeant
Henry Mowatt, Sergeant
Stephen M. Emery, Sergeant

Privates.
Atwood, Saul
Baily, Abner

Baily, James
Bartlet, James
Bartlet, William
Burnham, Moses
Chase, John
Davis, James
Davis, Saul
Farrington, Ebenezer
Gould, Samuel
Greenleaf, Abner
Howell, Robert
Merrill, Charles
Moody, Charles

Morss, Joseph
Morss, Moses
Morss, Saul
Noyes, Thomas
Plummer, Nathaniel
Ridgway, Joseph
Rogers, Thomas
Sawyer, Saul
Tewksberry, Isaac
Tibbits, Aaron

Capt. R. Heath's Company, Lieut. Col. E. Hale's Regiment.
From Sept. 3 to Oct. 12, 1814.   Company served 2 and 4 days between these dates.   Service at Newbury.

RANK AND NAME.
Richard Heath, Captain
John Osgood, Lieutenant
Saul Tenney, Ensign

Benjamin Brown, Sergeant
George Gordon, Sergeant
Daniel Moulton, Sergeant
William Noyes, Sergeant
Moses Brown, Musician
Benjamin Caldwell, Musician
Thomas H. Chase, Musician

Privates.
Bailey, Daniel
Bailey, Samuel, 3d
Bailey, Tappan
Baily, Daniel C.
Baker, Gideon
Bootman, Elias
Brickett, Moody
Burrows, George
Chase, Daniel

Chase, Thomas
Clark, Henry
Dole, Enoch
Dole, Greenleaf
Downer, Daniel
Eaton, Jonathan
Emery, Jacob
Follansbee, Enoch
Follansbee, John
Follansbee, Newman
Goodrich, David
Greenough, Parker
Heath, Dudly
Hills, Edmun
Hills, Eliphalet
Horne, Ephraim B.
Ilsey, William
Jaynes, Moody
Jaynes, Moses
Ladd, John
Little, John
Little, Stephen M.
Lovejoy, Abiel

Marshall, John
McKinstry, William
Merrill, Laban
Morss, Amos
North, Edmund
Noyes, Enoch
Ordway, William
Richardson, David
Richardson, John, Jr.
Rogers, Abner
Rogers, David
Sanders, Jedediah
Sawyer, John
Sealy, Edward
Short, Sewell
Siloway, Daniel
Smith, Caleb
Smith, James
Smith, Saul W.
Titcomb, Benarah
Wadleigh, Benjamin

Capt. T. Lancaster's Company, Lieut. Col. E. Hale's Regiment.
From Sept. 30 to Oct. 4, 1814. Service at Newbury.

RANK AND NAME.	*Privates.*	
Thomas Lancaster, Captain	Adams, Richard	Merrill, Thomas, 3d
John Remick, Lieutenant	Babb, Solomon	Nichols, Edmund
John Merrill, Ensign	Brown, John O. W.	Page, Henry
	Coffin, John, 2d	Pellion, John
Jacob Merrill, Sergeant	Coffin, Joseph	Reed, David
Oliver Hall, Sergeant	Coleman, Daniel T.	Stiles, Joseph
Saul Woodman, Sergeant	Cresey, Michel	Tappan, Edward
Eliphalet Hall, Sergeant	Dix, Jonas	Webb, Nicholas B.
Timothy Gordon, Corporal	Emery, Paul	Wood, Amos
James Miltemore, Corporal	Kent, John	
John Miltemore, Corporal	Kinston, Abner	
Enoch Merrill, Musician	Kinston, Tappan	
Charles Flanders, Musician	Land or Sand, Saul	

Capt. S. Merrill's Company, Lieut. Col. E. Hale's Regiment.
From Sept. 30 to Oct. 4, 1814. Raised at Newbury. Service at Newbury.

RANK AND NAME.	Davis, Oliver	Nelson, D.
Samuel Merrill, Captain	Davis, Richard	Noyes, Joshua
Josiah Titcomb, Lieutenant	Dole, Enoch	Pearson, Abel
John Northond, Ensign	Dole, Jacob	Pearson, Henry
	Dole, Jedediah	Pike, Moses
Stephen Adams, Sergeant	Dow, James	Poor, Benjamin
Greenleaf Tilton, Sergeant	Dummer, Joshua	Poor, David
Charles Dennet, Sergeant	Dummer, Samuel	Poor, Eliphalet
Cookam T. Tenney, Sergeant	Floyd, Enoch	Poor, Enoch
Obadiah Hill, Corporal	Gray, Frederick	Ramsey, Charles
Samuel Scribner, Corporal	Hill, John	Roberts, John A.
Daniel Noyes, Corporal	Hills, Charles	Rogers, Daniel
	Jackman, Joseph N.	Shute, Aaron
Privates.	Jewet, David	Thurlow, John
Adams, Giles	Jewet, Isaiah	Thurlow, Parker G.
Burrill, Patrick	Jewet, Robert	Thurlow, Samuel
Cheaney, Abner N.	Low, David	Woodman, Stephen
Cheaney, Jonathan	McMaster, Adams	
Davis, John, 2d	Moody, William	

Capt. P. Ordway's Company, Lieut. Col. E. Hale's Regiment.
From Sept. 30 to Oct. 4, 1814. Raised at Newbury. Service at Newbury.

RANK AND NAME.	*Privates.*	Merrill, William, 3d
Peter Ordway, Captain	Bartlet, Charles	Moulton, William
George Little, Lieutenant	Bartlet, David	Ordway, Benjamin, 2d
Nathaniel Ordway, Ensign	Bartlet, Isaac	Ordway, James
	Bartlet, Israel	Ordway, Moses
Stephen R. Fox, Sergeant	Bartlet, William	Ordway, Richard
John Ordney or Ordward, Sergeant	Burrill, Anthony	Parsons, David
Eliphalet Rendal, Sergeant	Burrill, James	Parsons, Samuel
Jacob Chase, Sergeant	Chapman, Henry	Poor, Samuel
John Bouster, Corporal	Chase, Amos	Poor, Thomas
John England, Corporal	Chase, Josiah	Rogers, William
Henry Chase, Corporal	Jackman, Mathias, 3d	Severance, Rufus
Moses Low, Corporal	Jackman, Noah	Spendergast, Thomas
Eben Poor, Musician	Jackman, Samuel	Stevens, William
John Poor, Musician	Merrill, Enoch	Wicker, David

Capt. D. Smith's Company, Lieut. Col. E. Hale's Regiment.
From Sept. 30 to Oct. 4, 1814. Service at Newbury.

RANK AND NAME.
Daniel Smith, Captain
Stephen Plummer, Lieutenant
Stephen Little, Ensign

Aaron Rogers, Sergeant
Michael Little, Sergeant
William Brown, Sergeant

Privates.
Adams, Eben
Adams, Eli
Adams, Hanson H.
Adams, John
Adams, Joseph, 3d
Bartlett, Richard
Blake, Jespar
Bray, James
Buswell, John
Dole, Enoch

Floyd, Moses
Goodwin, Joseph
Halmer, Benjamin
Hewiston, Benjamin
Isley, Paul
Kent, Joseph, 2d
Knight, James
Knight, John
Knight, Joseph
Knight, Moses
Knight, Silas
Knight, William
Leigh, Benjamin
Leighton, Richard
Lunt, Richard
Lunt, Saul
Mace, Joshua
Magown, Joseph
Noyes, John
Noyes, Peter

Page, Insley
Pettengill, David
Pettengill, Moses
Plummer, David
Plummer, Isaiah
Plummer, Joseph
Plummer, William
Plummer, William, Jr.
Robbins, John
Rolf, Moses
Russell, Saul
Short, Henry
Smith, Lemuel, 3d
Smith, Richard
Stickney, Charles
Sweet, William
Taylor, Nathan
Thomas, Joseph M.

Capt. J. Woodwell's Company, Lieut. Col. E. Hale's Regiment.
From Sept. 30 to Oct. 4, 1814. Raised at Newbury. Service at Newbury.

RANK AND NAME.
John Woodwell, Captain
Enoch Hall, Ensign

David Pearson, Sergeant
Michell Stevens, Sergeant

Privates.
Atkinson, Benjamin
Ayers, David
Bayley, Thomas
Chase, Moses, 3d
Clark, John T.

Coffin, Saul
Coher, William
Collins, William
Floyd, Enos
Goodwin, Amos
Goodwin, Daniel
Goodwin, Josiah
Goodwin, Major
Goodwin, Nathaniel
Goodwin, Saul
Goodwin, Thomas
Greenleaf, Jacob
Griffin, Mark

Hall, Benjamin W.
Hall, William
Jackman, Richard
Janvim or Javim, Joseph
Morse, Joseph
Pettengill, Cuttin
Pettengill, Nathaniel
Pierce, Enoch
Stevens, Moses
Thurlow, James
Thurlow, Joseph
Willis, Daniel
Woodwell, Gideon

Capt. A. Caldwell's Company, Lieut. Col. P. Merrill's Regiment.
From Oct. 5 to Oct. 6, 1814. Service at Newburyport.

RANK AND NAME.
Alexander Caldwell, Captain
Reuben W. Rogers, Ensign

Eben Bradbury, Sergeant
Jacob Griffin, Sergeant
William Satchel, Sergeant

Privates.
Baker, Enos
Bassett, Nathaniel
Bradley, Harrison

Caldwell, John
Caldwell, William
Cass, Moses
Cross, Ralph
Glines, John
Hills, Joshua
Marden, William
Morse, Peter
Newman, Benjamin, Jr.
Peters, Richard
Putman, Joseph
Rogers, William

Skeels, Anias
Smith, Ephraim
Stone, Thomas B.
Sumner, Michel
Wadleigh, Benjamin H.
Welch, William
Wentworth, Joseph
Whitmore, William
Whood, Samuel
Wilson, Joseph, Jr.
Woodman, Joseph

18 MASSACHUSETTS VOLUNTEER MILITIA IN THE WAR OF 1812.

Capt. N. Coffin's Company, Lieut. Col. P. Merrill's Regiment.
From Oct. 5 to Oct. 7, 1814. Service at Newburyport.

RANK AND NAME.
Nathaniel Coffin, Captain
John Dodge, Jr., Lieutenant
Joseph H. Currier, Ensign

James Young, Sergeant

Privates.
Bricket, Nathan A.
Brown, Walter

Burk, William
Campbell, James
Cook, Thomas D.
Couch, William
Currier, Samuel
Davis, Charles
Kloot, William
Knap, Joseph, Jr.
Lasky, Joseph
March, Nathaniel

Ordway, Stephen
Pettingill, Jonathan
Piper, Joseph
Poor, Isaac
Post, Peter
Spiller, Daniel
Stanwood, William
Walch, Ebenezer

Capt. C. Greenleaf's Company, Lieut. Col. P. Merrill's Regiment.
From Oct. 5 to Oct. 7, 1814. Service at Newburyport.

RANK AND NAME.
Charles Greenleaf, Captain
Solomon Foster, Ensign

Thomas Brown, Sergeant
Henry Hudson, Sergeant

Privates.
Barber, Benjamin
Cole, Moses
Cook, Charles
Davenport, William
Davis, William
Doggett, Joseph
Donell, Frederic W.
Foreman, Amos

Huse, John
Middleton, William
Morse, Merrill
Page, John
Pike, Joseph
Stephens, John
Taylor, Joseph
Wilson, William K.

Capt. N. Pierce's Company, Lieut. Col. P. Merrill's Regiment.
From Oct. 5 to Oct. 7, 1814. Service at Newburyport.

RANK AND NAME.
Nicholas Pierce, Captain
Joseph Cook, Ensign

H. G. Britton, Sergeant
Saul Stevens, Sergeant
Silas Rogers, Sergeant

Privates.
Brown, John
Dodge, John
Hale, Moses
Hodge, Nathaniel
Hoyt, John
More, Moses

Moulton, Jonathan
Prince, Samuel
Smith, Daniel
Tabbott or Talbot, Nathaniel
Tenison, William
Woodman, Nathaniel

Capt. J. T. Pike's Company, Lieut. Col. P. Merrill's Regiment.
From Oct. 5 to Oct. 7, 1814. Service at Newburyport.

RANK AND NAME.
James T. Pike, Captain
Abner Pearson, Lieutenant
Benjamin Greeley, Ensign

Charles Hunt, Sergeant
Thomas B. White, Sergeant
Richard Evans, Sergeant
Jonathan Wood, Sergeant
John Butman, Musician
Joel Smith, Musician

Privates.
Berry, Edward
Burnham, William D.
Butler, Charles

Chase, Daniel
Chase, Saul
Coffin, John
Cross, Heaton
Edmunds, William
Elder, Joseph
Ellis, Helita
Foot, J. L.
Ford, Samuel D.
Frothingham, Henry
Furnald, Joseph
Gordon, Robert
Hastings, William
Kimball, William, Jr.
Mace, John
Peabody, George

Pearson, Thomas
Plummer, Joseph
Plummer, Thomas
Prichard, Jacob
Rand, Isaac
Shaw, William
Short, Charles
Short, George
Short, Joseph, Jr.
Smith, Tustin
Spring, Lewins
Spring, Samuel
Todd, Francis
Tupper, Joseph
Wheeler, Saul
Woodbridge, ——

MASSACHUSETTS VOLUNTEER MILITIA IN THE WAR OF 1812.   19

Capt. E. Plummer's Company, Lieut. Col. P. Merrill's Regiment.
From Oct. 5 to Oct. 7, 1814.   Raised at Newburyport.   Service at Newburyport.

RANK AND NAME.
Enoch Plummer, Captain
Jonathan Cooledge, Lieutenant

William Wood, Sergeant
Benjamin Pidgin, Corporal
Nathaniel Flanders, Corporal
Joseph T. Chase, Corporal
Benjamin Stearns, Musician
Charles F. Racklyft, Musician

Privates.
Bayley, Moses
Brown, J., Jr.
Brown, Joseph, 3d
Brown, Samuel
Burbant, Jonathan M.
Flanders, John
Flanders, Nehemiah
Flanders, William
Hobert, Thomas
Horton, J.
Moore, William
Morrison, Henry

Noyes, Ebenezer
Noyes, Robert
Packer, Edward
Packer, George
Pearson, Robert
Racklyft, Edmund
Silliway, Joseph
Somerby, Thomas, Jr.
Thompson, George
Titcomb, Edward
Trusdall, Artemas W.
Wells, Richard

Capt. P. Titcomb's Company, Lieut. Col. P. Merrill's Regiment.
From Oct. 5 to Oct. 7, 1814.   Service at Newburyport.

RANK AND NAME.
Paul Titcomb, Captain
John Chickering, Lieutenant
Charles H. Black, Ensign

Eleazer Johnson, Jr., Sergeant
Jonathan Johnson, Sergeant
Benjamin G. Sweetser, Sergeant
Joseph Gardner, Musician
John G. Stall, Musician
John Carlton, Musician
Leonard Philip, Musician

Privates.
Bartlett, Richard M.
Bishop, Paul
Black, William
Boardman, William
Call, Jonathan, Jr.
Coffin, George
Colley, ——
Davenport, Charles
Follansbee, Nathan
Gordon, Charles
Greenleaf, George
Greenleaf, John
Johnson, Abel
Johnson, Philip, Jr.
Johnson, William P.

Pardee, Benjamin
Perkins, Anthony
Porter, John
Rogers, George
Scott, John
Shaw, William
Smith, Anthony
Spaulding, Oliver
Stedman, Ebenezer
Street, Edmund
Swain, Jacob
Tappan, Jeremiah P.
Tilton, Stephen
Wheelright, Ebenezer
Whipple, Charles

Capt. A. Williams' Company, Lieut. Col. P. Merrill's Regiment.
From Oct. 5 to Oct. 11, 1814.   Company served 2 days between these dates.   Service at Newburyport.

RANK AND NAME.
Abraham Williams, Captain

Charles Pillsbury, Sergeant

Privates.
Batcheldore, Joseph
Brown, Orlando

Chase, J., Jr.
Emerson, Charles
Goodwin, Ephraim
Hervy, David
Kent, Benjamin
Lufkin, Caleb
Merrill, James
Mitchell, William

Moreson, Thomas
Ordway, Moses
Pearson, Charles
Plummer, Tristram
Stickney, Joseph
True, Ezekiel
Warner, Nathaniel
Wood, J.

Capt. J. Stickney's Company, Lieut. Col. P. Merrill's Regiment.
From Oct. 7 to Oct. 11, 1814.   Service at Newburyport.

RANK AND NAME.
Jacob Stickney, Captain
David Lufkin, Lieutenant
Charles Hodge, Ensign
Samuel Hoyt, Quartermaster

Jeremiah Wheelright, Sergeant
Green Johnson, Sergeant

Joseph Buntin, Sergeant
William Bartlet, Sergeant
William Young, Corporal
Joseph Aubin, Corporal
Charles Cok or Cook, Corporal
James Francis, Corporal
David Lake, Musician
John Putnam, Musician

Hoel Smith, Musician
Moses Bailey, Musician
Samuel Walter, Musician

Privates.
Adams, H.
Bassett, Christopher
Blanchard, Jeremiah

Capt. J. Stickney's Company, Lieut. Col. P. Merrill's Regiment — Concluded.

Privates — Concluded.
Boardman, Thomas
Boddely, John
Brown, Nathan
Coffin, David, Jr.
Couch, John
Cummings, James
Dennis, Amos
Dole, John
Friend, William
Furlong, Henry
Gerrish, Enoch
Gerrish, Mayo
Grind, Joseph

Hall, Charles
Haskell, David
Haskell, Enoch
Howard, William
Kilborne, George, Jr.
Kilborne, Robert
Knap, Jacob
Knight, Amos
Lattimore, Nicholas
Lawson, William
Livingston, Alexander
Lovell, Joseph
Nathan, Stephen
Norton, William B.

Nowell, Silas
Park, Isaac
Parsons, Joseph
Stallard, Thomas
Stone, John
Stover, Joseph
Swasey, Samuel
Tilton, Daniel
Titcomb, John H.
Titcomb, Jonathan
Toppen, Benjamin, Jr.
Welch, Jonathan C.
Young, John

Lieut. J. Moody's Company, Lieut. Col. P. Merrill's Regiment.

From Oct. 5 to Oct. 7, 1814. Service at Newburyport.

RANK AND NAME.
John Moody, Lieutenant

Jacob Noyes, Sergeant
Richard Hooker, Sergeant
Nathaniel Greely, Sergeant
Thomas Davis, Sergeant

Privates.
Atwood, Zacheriah
Boardman, Stephen

Chase, William
Clark, Saul
Currier, Edward
Currier, Mathew, Jr.
Dodge, Saul
Dunt, Micajah
Foster, Daniel, Jr.
Frye, Joshua
Green, John
Hall, Thomas
Hall, William

Haskell, Joseph
Hyatt, Benjamin, Jr.
Jackson, Henry
Pease, James
Perkins, John
Short, Nicholas
Somerby, Arthur
Tiney or Finney, John
Todd, Thomas
Wells, John, Jr.

Lieut. J. Chickering's Detachment.

From Oct. 8 to Nov. 7, 1814. Service at Newburyport.

RANK AND NAME.
John Chickering, Lieutenant

Franklin Gerrish, Sergeant
Nathaniel Flanders, Corporal
Joseph Morrell, Corporal
Richard Page, Musician

Privates.
Brown, John
Brown, Joseph

Call, Moses
Chase, John, Jr.
Emery, Moses
Farley, John Dennis
Gall, Daniel
Gardner, Robert
Goodwin, Levi
Hall, William
Kilburn, Jedediah
Kloot, William
Lasky, Joseph

Lunt, Samuel
Marden, William
Noyes, Amos, Jr.
Pearson, Henry
Pressey, John
Smith, Samuel
Smith, William
Somerby, Enoch
Stevens, Michel
Vickery, William

Lieut. J. Goodwin's Detachment, Lieut. Col. P. Merrill's Regiment.

From Nov. 7 to Dec. 7, 1814. Raised at Newburyport. Service at Newburyport.

RANK AND NAME.
John Goodwin, Lieutenant

Jacob Griffin, Sergeant
Stephen Bartlet, Corporal
Nathaniel Rogers, Musician
Charles Flanders, Musician
John Gerrish, Musician

Privates.
Adams, Ely
Bartlett, Charles

Blaisdell, John, 3d
Bush, William
Chase, Charles
Chase, William
Connor, William
Eaton, Jeremiah
Flanders, Enoch
Hoyt, Moses
Ilsey, Wade
Kent, Henry
Lowell, Joseph
Merrill, Jacob

Merrill, John, 4th
Nichols, James
Noyes, John M.
Ordway, Samuel
Parker, Edward
Pearson, Robert
Pickman, Levi
Racklifft, Charles F.
Robbins, James
Silloway, William
Wells, Daniel

MASSACHUSETTS VOLUNTEER MILITIA IN THE WAR OF 1812.   21

Lieut. G. Little's Detachment, Lieut. Col. P. Merrill's Regiment.
From Dec. 7 to Dec. 13, 1814. Raised at Newburyport. Service at Newburyport.

RANK AND NAME.	*Privates.*	
George Little, Lieutenant	Adams, Richard	Gall, Daniel
	Atwood, Samuel	Goodwin, Thomas
True G. Graves, Sergeant	Bartlet, Gideon	Lowell, Joseph
Walter Brown, Corporal	Burrell, James	McCrelles, Reuben
Philip Butler, Corporal	Chase, William, Jr.	Packer or Parker, George
John Morrell, Jr., Musician	Cotes, James S.	Reed, Caleb
Moses Brown, Jr., Musician	Donniel, Frederic	Rogers, Henry
	Emerson, Charles	Rogers, Michel
	Evans, John, Jr.	Saunders, William
	Flanders, Nehemiah	Wells, Daniel, Jr.
	Foot, James	Weston, Luther

Capt. S. Mudge's Company.
From Sept. 13 to Nov. 7, 1814. Raised at Lynn and vicinity. Service at Fort Lee, Salem. "The town of Lynn, with its accustomed liberality, voted to allow each officer and soldier detached from the town $10 a month in addition to the pay allowed by the government while in the service of the United States."

RANK AND NAME.	Chase, Charles	Noyes, John
Samuel Mudge, Captain	Clements, Ephraim	Odgson, Robert
Asa Tapley, Lieutenant	Clements, Henry	Orgin, Isaac
Amos King, Lieutenant	Collier, Isaac	Osgood, Robert B.
	Collier, John	Poor, James
Alonzo Lewis, Sergeant	Curtis, Nehemiah	Putnam, Elbridge
Peter Davis, Sergeant	Dix, John	Quiner, Benjamin
Michael Knowlton, Sergeant	Dodge, Enos	Ramsdale, Shadrack
David Day, Sergeant	Evans, James	Randall, John M.
George Atwell, Corporal	Foster, Stephen A.	Richards, Joseph
William Kelly, Corporal	Frothingham, Caleb	Robinson, George
David Hill, Corporal	Gardner, John	Ropes, Henry
Philip S. Segar, Corporal	Gardner, John, 4th	Safford, Thomas
Shadrach Ramsdell, Musician	Glidden, John	Sargent, Levi
Isaac Orgin, Jr., Musician	Henman, John	Smethhurst, Benjamin
	Higsbee, Lemuel	Stevens, Moses
Privates.	Hudson, Thomas B.	Steward, Joseph R.
Abbott, Nathaniel	Jackman, William	Tabor, David
Alley, Henry	Knowlton, Benjamin	Towns, Samuel
Bachelder, John	Lee, Benjamin	Turner, John
Barns, John	Lee, John	Twist, Joshua
Blanchard, Nathaniel	Long, Samuel	Webbs, John, 2d
Bright, Thomas	Mansfield, Nathaniel B.	Wilson, William
Brookhouse, Daniel W.	Mansise, John A.	Winchester, Bancroft
Brooks, Benjamin	Martin, Thomas	Woodberry, Moses
Brown, John	Masury, John	Wright, George
Buckman, John	McIntire, Jeremiah	
Bunker, Elisha	Noyes, Abraham	

Capt. I. Storey's Company, Colonel Reed's Regiment.
From June to August and Sept. 22 to Oct. 13, 1814. This company served as a watch at Marblehead and vicinity, mostly in the night, various times (7, 12 and 14 days).

RANK AND NAME.	Samuel D. Turner, Sergeant	*Privates.*
Isaac Storey, Captain	Benjamin Homan, Corporal	Adams, Nicholas G.
John H. Gregory, Lieutenant	Nathaniel Philips, Corporal	Adams, Samuel R.
William H. Reynolds, Ensign	Thomas Martin, Corporal	Barthol, John
	Jacob Hooper, Corporal	Bartlet, Eli
Moses Goldthwait, Sergeant	Abel Gardner, Musician	Bartlet, Joseph B.
Nathaniel Chapman, Sergeant	Ichabod Phillips, Musician	Bartlet, William
John Reynolds, Sergeant	Samuel Homan, Musician	Bray, Edward

Capt. I. Storey's Company, Colonel Reed's Regiment — Concluded.

Privates — Concluded.
Brown, Abraham
Carrol, John
Cask, James
Cole, Richard
Cole, William
Cuching, Joseph
Deveraux, Elisha S.
Dickerman, Samuel
Graves, Blaney
Green, John
Gregory, James
Harris, John
Harris, Robert, 3d
High, John
Homan, Nathaniel
Homan, Philip C.
Homan, William

Hooker, John
Hunt, William
Ingalls, John
Johnson, John
Johnson, William W.
Knight, Benjamin
Leeran, William
Lyons, Thomas
Martin, James
Martin, Knott
Merritt, Francis
Nicholson, Thomas
Nugan, Thomas
Pappoon, Solomon
Peach, John
Phillips, John
Prentis, John
Prince, John

Putman, John
Randall, Benjamin R.
Reynolds, Abel
Sevars, Benjamin
Skinner, John
Smith, James P.
Smithers, Gamaliel
Stone, Isaac
Stone, Simeon
Swisder, Eben T.
Thompson, Amos
Thompson, Charles D.
Thompson, John
Valentine, Benjamin T.
Wadder, Andrew C.
Wornestead, Benjamin

Lieut. S. Horton's Company, Lieut. Col. B. S. Reed's Regiment.
From Sept. 22 to Oct. 13, 1814. Service at Marblehead.

RANK AND NAME.
Samuel Horton, Captain
Thomas Bridges, Lieutenant

Nathaniel Adams, Sergeant
Daniel Patten, Sergeant
Joshua Prentiss, 3d, Sergeant
Samuel Rogers, Sergeant
Joseph Gregory, Musician
Richard Phillips, Musician

Privates.
Baker, George
Bartlett, John
Bartlett, Nathaniel
Bartlett, Peter
Bartlett, William
Boardman, Thomas
Bowler, Caleb
Bowler, James
Brown, Ailam
Brown, Peter
Brown, Thomas, 3d
Butnam, John
Caswell, Richard
Clough, Samuel
Cole, Richard
Cole, William
Cox, James
Curtis, Jesse
Davis, Thomas
Dennis, John
Doak, Michel
Dolibber, William
Elkins, Thomas
Elliot, William
Farrow, Timothy

Felton, Francis
Foss, Samuel
Francis, Bartholomew
Francis, James
Gale, Thomas
Grant, John
Graves, Blaney
Graves, Christopher
Graves, Samuel
Hardy, John
Harris, William
Hathway, James
Hathway, Joseph
Hathway, William
Hawks, William
Hitchins, Samuel
Hooper, John
Ingalls, Joseph
Ireson, Benjamin
Knight, Samuel
Lamprell, Simon
Laskey, James
Lemaster, George
Luckey, Azor
Luscomb, Andrew
Lyon, Thomas
Mallett, Thomas
Merritt, Francis
Moulton, Jonathan
Muckford, Samuel
Paine, Francis
Patten, John H.
Pearson, Robert
Pedrick, John B.
Pedrick, William
Perry, George
Phillips, Joseph

Phillips, William
Picket, Moses
Powers, John
Powers, Thomas
Preble, Nehemiah
Putnam, William
Quinn, John
Ramsdell, Benjamin
Roundy, Thomas
Russell, John
Russell, Joseph
Shirley, John
Snow, Thomas
Stone, Joseph
Stone, Nehemiah
Sweet, John
Sweet, Stephen
Swet, Richard
Thomson, Jonathan
Thomson, Richard L.
Thorner, Jacob
Tucker, John
Tucker, Joseph
Tucker, Nicholas
Tucker, Thomas
Twisden, Ebenezer L.
Valentine, Benjamin
Vickery, Benjamin
Warner, John
White, John
Widger, Thomas
Widger, William
Woodbridge, Samuel G.
Wornstead, Benjamin
Wright, Peter
Wyman, Luke

Lieut. Col. A. Binney's Regiment.
Ten days between Sept. 12 and Oct. 10, 1814. Service at Boston.

FIELD AND STAFF.
Amos Binney, Lieutenant Colonel, Boston
Barzilla Hudson, Major, Boston
Zachariah Hall, Major, Chelsea
Samuel Clark, Adjutant, Boston

Oliver Eldridge, Quartermaster, Boston
Stephen Cushing, Paymaster, Boston
William Ingalls, Surgeon, Boston
Benjamin Reed, Surgeon's Mate, Boston
J. A. Merrill, Chaplain, Boston

NONCOMMISSIONED STAFF.
Edward W. Haws, Sergeant Major
Samuel Withington, Quartermaster Sergeant

Capt. M. Ames' Company, Lieut. Col. A. Binney's Regiment.
From Sept. 12 to Oct. 10, 1814. Raised at Boston. Service at Boston.

RANK AND NAME.
Moses Ames, Captain
Levi Brigham, Lieutenant
Nathaniel Richards, Ensign

Joseph Randall, Sergeant
Daniel Hastings, Sergeant
Michael Thombs, Sergeant
Daniel Wood, Sergeant
Reuben Reed, Corporal
William Mitchell, Corporal
Isaac D. Richards, Corporal
Solomon Walker, Corporal
Sheldon Perry, Musician
Daniel Simpson, Musician

Privates.
Allen, Asa
Allen, Thomas
Bailey, John
Baker, Abel P.
Ballard, George
Bass, Charles
Bates, Ira
Beckland, Rodney

Beeton, John
Belcher, William
Billings, Jabez
Bissell, Harvey
Blanchard, Edward
Blanchard, Lemuel
Blanchard, Samuel
Bright, James
Bruce, George
Clapp, Edward
Clapp, Martin
Cutler, James
Dixon, Edward
Dunn, Jonathan
Field, Josiah
Fitz, William
French, William
Gordan, William
Gray, Asa
Hill, Samuel
Hobbs, John L.
Holbrook, Royal
Humphries, John
Humphries, Thomas
Jennison or Lennison, Asa

Lance, John
Lerow, Charles
Lingfield, William
McCurdy, Jesse
Mercy, Joseph
Miller, Joseph
Miltimore, James
Owen, Chauncey
Parker, Benjamin M.
Parker, Davis
Parris, John
Phelps, Lilly
Pollard, George
Raymond, Stephen
Rice, Solomon
Richards, Reuben
Sawtell, Calvin
Smith, Rufus
Standley, Phineas
Talbot, John
Thwing, Thomas
Whiting, Kimball
Wilson, Jesse
Wood, Nehemiah
Wright, Edmund, Jr.

Capt. D. Dunton's Company, Lieut. Col. A. Binney's Regiment.
Between Sept. 12 and Oct. 10, 1814. Service at Boston.

RANK AND NAME.
Daniel Dunton, Captain (3 days)
Jacob Howe, Lieutenant (10 days)
Joseph Lewis, Ensign (10 days)

Bartlett Stoddard, Sergeant
Richard Hosea, Sergeant
John Castle, Sergeant
Nathaniel Hobbs, Sergeant
Abraham Lambert, Corporal
Benjamin Dodd, Corporal
Horace Bernard, Corporal
George Andrews, Corporal
Sheldon Perry, Musician
Samuel Parsons, Musician

Privates.
Abbott, Joseph
Adams, Charles

Adams, Samuel
Atwood, Richard
Baldwin, Phineas P.
Barber, John
Barber, Samuel
Barnes, John
Bass, William W.
Beal, Isaac (10 days)
Berbeck, John
Berbeck, William
Blake, William
Boardman, Thomas
Bridge, Mathew
Brintnall, Charles
Cobb, William D.
Devens, John
Faxon, Nathaniel
Fisher, Benjamin (4 days)
Hall, Benjamin

Hastings, Nathaniel
Hasty, William
Holbrook, Joseph
Holden, Thomas
Hopkins, Freeman
Howe, John
Jay, William
Jones, George
Kepler, Jeremiah
King, Joseph
Lewis, Amos
Lewis, John
Lincoln, George
Lock, Jonathan
Loring, John (10 days)
Lovejoy, Perkins
Marsh, David
McFarland, Duncan
McLane, Joseph

Capt. D. Dunton's Company, Lieut. Col. A. Binney's Regiment—Concluded.

Privates — Concluded.
Newcomb, Charles
Osborn, George
Pach, William
Page, Benjamin (10 days)
Palfrey, George
Park, William
Parker, Samuel
Potter, David
Priest, Isaac D.
Putnam, Lewis

Ralph, Daniel (8 days)
Reed, Benjamin
Rodgers, William
Rumwell, Joseph
Sherman, James
Smith, Samuel
Snow, Amasa
Spead, Robert
Stedman, Calvin
Stickney, John
Stowell, Isaiah

Studley, Warren
Tompkins, Lemuel
Tucker, Woodard
Tuttle, John
Wade, John
White, Asa
Wilcot, Joseph
Williams, John
Williston, James
Williston, Samuel

Capt. G. Fairbanks' Company, Lieut. Col. A. Binney's Regiment.
Ten days between Sept. 12 and Oct. 10, 1814.   Raised at Boston.   Service at Boston.

RANK AND NAME.
Gerry Fairbanks, Captain
Caleb Hartshorn, Lieutenant
James Scott, Ensign

Isaac Rowse, Sergeant
Tisdale Lothrop, Sergeant
Samuel Aspinwall, Sergeant
Benjamin B. Carney, Sergeant
Samuel Hayward, Corporal
Charles Lincoln, Corporal
James Henery, Corporal
Abraham Call, Corporal
George Field, Musician
Samuel Wheelock, Musician

Privates.
Badger, Thomas
Ball, Ebenezer
Ballard, David C.
Barney, Jonathan
Bates, Stephen
Bender, Jacob
Brunett, John
Burrell, John
Burt, John M.
Cate, Joseph
Coolidge, Charles
Cormerais, John
Curtis, Nathaniel

Cutter, Samuel
Donnett, C. M.
Dow, Amos
Farnum, Thomas
Fearing, Cushing
Fillebrown, Asa
Fillebrown, James
Fish, Eliakim
Fisher, Jabez
Fisher, Oliver
Freeman, Philip
French, Charles
Gardner, Thomas
Gates, Sylvanus H.
Glover, William
Gold, Samuel
Gore, James
Green, Clark
Hall, William
Hartwell, Thomas
Hayden, Benjamin
Howe, Joseph N.
Howe, Richard
Howe, Thomas, Jr.
Hunt, Nathaniel P.
Hyde, Samuel
Jennings, Benjamin
Johnson, William H.
Kidder, Ephraim
Kneeland, Samuel

Laughton, William
Liscomb, John G.
Locke, William
Longley, Thomas
Martin, James P.
Mickell, Thomas
Muzzy, John
Norton, John
Palmenter, William
Pierce, John
Pollard, Amos F.
Reed, Benjamin
Reed, William
Rice, William
Ring, Nathaniel
Rugg, Elisha
Sargent, Solomon
Simonds, Joseph
Smith, Cyrus
Smith, Nowell
Spear, William
Taft, Elisha
Thayer, Loring
Torry, Ebenezer
Ward, Isaac J.
White, William
Whitehouse, Daniel O.
Wild, Frederic
Wyman, Simeon

Capt. S. Howes' Company, Lieut. Col. A. Binney's Regiment.
From Sept. 12 to Oct. 10, 1814.   Service at Boston.

RANK AND NAME.
Samuel Howes, Captain
Nathan Eaton, Lieutenant
Samuel Noyes, Ensign

Ezra Hawks, Sergeant
Daniel G. H. Haws, Sergeant
John Butterfield, Sergeant
Samuel Whittington, Sergeant
Peter Stephenson, Corporal
Asa Mayo, Corporal
Liberty Wiston, Corporal
Tilly Brigham, Corporal

Emanual Gordon, Musician
John Gordon, Musician

Privates.
Acres, George
Athearn, Cyrus
Austin, Thomas
Baily, Cushing
Bass, Moses
Beals, Alexander
Bemis, I.
Bennett, James H.
Blake, William

Bodlear, John
Bonner, John
Bruce, Cyrus
Bullard, Isaac
Caldwell, John
Chandler, Ebenezer
Crocker, Asa
Cummings, Samuel
Denton, William
Deverall, Samuel
Dillingham, Henry
Farnsworth, Oliver
Fessenden, Benjamin

MASSACHUSETTS VOLUNTEER MILITIA IN THE WAR OF 1812.   25

Capt. S. Howes' Company, Lieut. Col. A. Binney's Regiment—Concluded.

Privates — Concluded.
Field, Silas
Fisher, Jabez
Fitch, Amos
Flagg, William B.
Foss, Walter
French, William
Geyer, Frederick W.
Glover, Eaton
Goffield, Thomas
Gore, Christopher
Gould, Jacob
Gray, Samuel
Gridley, William, Jr.
Hancock, William
Harrington, Elisha
Hastings, Ezra
Hatch, Joshua
Haws, Joseph
Hays, Asa
Holbrook, John
Howe, Isaac
Hunt, Nathaniel P.
James, John

Jenkins, Solon
Johnson, Nath
Jones, David
Jones, John
Knight, Benjamin
Lane, Samuel
Lawrence, William
Leonard, Thomas
Lincoln, George
Loud, Asa
Mason, John
McDaniel, Michell
Merritt, Joshua
Mixter, Charles
Moulton, William
Mowry, Abraham
Nash, Alexander
Newcomb, Loring
Odion, George
Pool, Henry
Proctor, John
Reed, Lyman
Reynolds, William
Richardson, Nathan

Robinson, Lyman
Robinson, Smith
Russell, Edward
Scudder, Palmer
Shed, Samuel
Shepard, James
Smith, Martin
Snelling, Christopher
Stephens, Tilton
Stephenson, Martin
Taylor, Moses A.
Teel, Nathaniel
Thayer, Asaph
Thayer, Wyman
Tirrell, Loring
Townsend, David, Jr.
Treadwell, John
Tuttle, Edward
Wait, Thomas
White, Joseph
Wier, George
Willis, Abiel
Winship, Meyers
Winship, Stephen

Capt. T. Johnson's Company, Lieut. Col. A. Binney's Regiment.

Between Sept. 12 and Oct. 10, 1814.   Service at Boston.

RANK AND NAME.
Timothy Johnson, Captain (10 days)
Ezra Eaton, Lieutenant, (10 days)
Samuel Davis, Ensign (3 days)
Edward W. Haws, Sergeant (10 days)
Daniel C. Robinson, Sergeant (10 days)
Charles Mountford, Sergeant (2 days)
John Eliot, Sergeant (10 days)
John Snow, Corporal (10 days)
Joshua Pitman, Jr., Corporal (5 days)
Joel Nason, Corporal (10 days)
Edward Bell, Corporal (6 days)

Privates.
Acres, Thomas (3 days)
Andrews, Samuel (10 days)
Armstrong, William (10 days)
Austin, William (10 days)
Avis, Thomas (10 days)
Bacon, Judah (10 days)
Bailey, Daniel (9 days)
Baldwin, Cyrus (3 days)
Barnes, Charles (10 days)
Barnes, Thomas (10 days)
Bell, Samuel (10 days)
Bell, William D. (2 days)
Billings, Alanson (3 days)

Blackburn, Timothy (10 days)
Bond, William (1 day)
Broaders, John (9 days)
Burnham, Andrew (3 days)
Caswell, Lewis (10 days)
Claghorn, John W. (8 days)
Clark, Thomas (10 days)
Dana, William J. (10 days)
Darling, Elakin (10 days)
Dexter, James (10 days)
Dickey, Ephraim (3 days)
Dunton, John (3 days)
Fowell, John (10 days)
Hanson, Samuel (10 days)
Harris, William C. (10 days)
Hoar, Lot (4 days)
Ingeway, Philip (9 days)
Kendrick, Stephen (4 days)
Knowlton, Nathaniel (10 days)
Lincoln, Lewis (6 days)
Little, Ebenezer (6 days)
Lukin, Charles
Magown, N. S. (9 days)
Melcher, George (10 days)
Nelson, Peter (4 days)
Nicholas, Alexander (8 days)
Nichols, Samuel C. (2 days)
Pattee, Arthur S. (10 days)

Pearson, Thomas (4 days)
Peirce, Parker H. (10 days)
Porter, Thomas (3 days)
Pratt, Jotham (10 days)
Reed, George (1 day)
Richardson, John (10 days)
Ripley, Lorenzo (8 days)
Smith, Samuel (10 days)
Smith, Timothy (3 days)
Snow, John (2 days)
Snow, Larkin (3 days)
Snow, Royal (2 days)
Sprague, Isaac (10 days)
Stone, Ezra (3 days)
Sweetser, Joshua (10 days)
Tillinghast, George (10 days)
Torrey, Joseph (3 days)
Trowbridge, Henry (10 days)
Veasie, Eli (10 days)
Warrick, Paul (6 days)
White, Joseph (10 days)
Willard, Ephraim (8 days)
Willard, Simon (8 days)
Wilson, Caleb (10 days)
Wiswell, Thomas (3 days)
Woodard, John (5 days)

MASSACHUSETTS VOLUNTEER MILITIA IN THE WAR OF 1812.

Capt. E. Norcross's Company, Lieut. Col. A. Binney's Regiment.
Between Sept. 12 and Oct. 10, 1814. Raised at Boston. Service at Boston.

RANK AND NAME.
Elisha Norcross, Captain (10 days)
Christopher Lincoln, Lieutenant (10 days)
Ephraim Jones, Ensign (10 days)

John Snelling, Sergeant (10 days)
Ephraim Milton, Sergeant (10 days)
Rufus Baxter, Jr., Sergeant (10 days)
Lewis J. Bailey, Corporal (10 days)
Thomas Hiler, Corporal (10 days)
Nathaniel Clark, Corporal (10 days)
John B. Freeman, Corporal (10 days)
John Gordon, Musician (10 days)
Manly Gordon, Musician (10 days)

Privates.
Adams, Joseph (4 days)
Adams, Joseph, Jr. (8 days)
Adams, Joseph N. (10 days)
Alcock, John (10 days)
Baker, William M. (10 days)
Ball, Thomas (10 days)
Baxter, Solomon S. (10 days)
Belcher, John (2 days)
Benige, George (10 days)
Blake, Nathaniel (1 day)
Bridge, William (8 days)

Bromade, Abram (10 days)
Brown, Ebenezer (10 days)
Buckman, Joses (4 days)
Butler, Aaron (6 days)
Calder, William (6 days)
Capen, John (10 days)
Carnes, Edward (8 days)
Carter, John (10 days)
Chandler, Jacob (8 days)
Clark, Benjamin, Jr. (3 days)
Clark, Thomas (2 days)
Cutler, James (5 days)
Cutler, William (8 days)
Eaton, Ebenezer (7 days)
Fenno, John (2 days)
Freeman, Nathaniel (10 days)
Fuller, Ebenezer (8 days)
Goddard, Elias (4 days)
Goodrich, James T. (10 days)
Hart, Joseph (10 days)
Hemmenway, Benjamin (8 days)
Hiter, Stephen (2 days)
Howes, Loring (3 days)
Hutchinson, Joseph (3 days)
Hutchinson, Thomas (10 days)
Lilly, Jonathan W. (10 days)
Low, John (2 days)

Low, Samuel (8 days)
Mansir, Ebenezer B. (10 days)
Merry, Robert D. C. (10 days)
Nash, Levi (10 days)
Patch, Abijah (3 days)
Patten, Thomas (3 days)
Perry, George (3 days)
Pierce, Samuel (10 days)
Pitty, Joseph (10 days)
Pratt, Thomas (8 days)
Roberts, John (3 days)
Ross, William (8 days)
Sloan, Francis (2 days)
Southworth, Lewis (10 days)
Spurr, William (10 days)
Steele, Ephraim P. (3 days)
Thompson, Alexander (10 days)
Tolman, William F. (3 days)
Trull, Joel (3 days)
Tucker, David (10 days)
Tuckerman, John T. (10 days)
Tuttle, John W. (4 days)
Vinson, Samuel (10 days)
Whitney, Jacob (4 days)
Whittemore, Bernard (10 days)
Wild, John (8 days)

Capt. T. Page's Company, Lieut. Col. A. Binney's Regiment.
From Sept. 12 to Oct. 10, 1814. Raised at Boston. Service at Boston.

RANK AND NAME.
Thaddeus Page, Captain
Robert G. Mitchell, Lieutenant
David Henshaw, Ensign

W. D. Hill, Sergeant
George W. Armstrong, Sergeant
Lewis Lerow, Sergeant
Edward Bell, Sergeant
David Baker, Corporal
Ebenezer Oliver, Jr., Corporal
Thomas B. Sawyer, Corporal
Ephraim Snelling, Corporal
James Reed, Musician
Richard Clark, Musician
Sheldon Perry, Musician

Privates.
Appleton, William
Armstrong, James
Bannister, Samuel
Burrill, John
Butters, Joshua
Caldwell, Edward P.

Chandler, Benjamin
Cheever, William
Clark, James
Coolidge, James
Cooper, John
Cothel, Hosea
Cross, John
Curtis, David
Cutler, Amos
Cutler, Ezra
Cutler, John
Davis, Thomas
Dellawey, Samuel
Ellis, Elisha
Ellis, Moses
Forbisher, William
Foster, John
French, Othaniel
Gabriel, John
Gay, Timothy
Grammar, Seth
Hall, Timothy
Hillman, George
Hutchinson, Ephraim B.

Johnson, Edmund
Kelley, Andrew
Learnard, Elisha
Lewis, George
Lincoln, Ezekiel
Lord, Samuel
Noyes, Joseph
Perry, Ebenezer
Poor, Isaac
Pratt, Paul
Prince, Charles
Richardson, James P.
Rodgers, John
Smith, John, Jr.
Snelling, Nathaniel G.
Snelling, Samuel G.
Stebbins, Samuel
Stephens, Thomas
Terrill or Tirrell, George
Ward, Thomas
Wheeler, Joseph
Wolcott, Josiah

MASSACHUSETTS VOLUNTEER MILITIA IN THE WAR OF 1812.   27

Capt. J. Tewksbury's Company, Lieut. Col. A. Binney's Regiment.
From Sept. 12 to Oct. 10, 1814.   Raised at Chelsea.   Service at Boston.

RANK AND NAME.
John Tewksbury, 3d, Captain
John Pierce, Lieutenant
Jonathan Copeland, Ensign

Abner Gay, Sergeant
Stephen Green, Sergeant
Ebenezer Burrill, Sergeant
Thomas Tewksbury, Sergeant
Samuel Worcester, Corporal
John Wright, Corporal
Thomas O. Nichols, Corporal
James Willey, Corporal
Thomas Pratt, Musician

Privates.
Belcher, Samuel
Brackett, Richard
Brown, William
Brudin, Alnathan

Burrill, Bill
Burrill, Joseph, Jr.
Chambers, Prescott
Cheever, Joseph
Cheney, Moses
Edmunds, William
Floyd, Abijah
Floyd, John, 2d
Floyd, Samuel
Floyd, Thomas
Grant, Joseph
Green, John
Guilford, Samuel
Hall, Aaron
Hall, William
Hanes, Samuel
Jack, David
Jewett, Josiah
Needham, Joseph P.
Newman, Thomas

Nivens, William
Phlinn, John
Pratt, Oliver
Pratt, Samuel
Pratt, Washington
Shute, Jacob
Swift, Benjamin
Tewksbury, Bill
Tewksbury, H.
Tewksbury, Washington
Tufts, John, Jr.
Tupper, Lathrop
Tuttle, Israel
Wait, Oliver
Watson, Asa
Webster, John
Whicher, Ezekiel
Wilson, Benjamin
Wyman, Alpheus

Capt. I. Scott's Company, Lieut. Col. A. Binney's Regiment.
From Sept. 25 to Oct. 4, 1814.   Raised at Boston.   Service at Boston.

RANK AND NAME.
Isaac Scott, Captain
Geogre P. Hows, Lieutenant
E. O. Hows, Ensign

Ephraim Willard, Sergeant
William Barker, Sergeant
Edward Bannington, Sergeant
Nathaniel Bailey, Sergeant
Samuel Conant, Corporal
John Patten, Corporal
Pliney Smith, Corporal
Joseph Webb, Corporal
Marshall Conant, Musician
Moses Tyler, Musician
John Sylvester, Musician

Privates.
Allen, ———
Andrews, Stephen
Babcock, ———
Bacon, Robert
Barber, Fisher
Bates, Edmund
Baxter, Joseph
Beals, Lemuel
Bemis, Joel
Bennett, David
Billings, Elijah

Bradley, Thomas
Brown, John
Bush, Daniel W.
Capen, ———
Cheever, John
Cooper, John
Crane, George
Cummings, Alexander
Cummings, Luther
Curtiss, Elijah S.
Famington, Thomas
Field, Joseph
Foster, Ebenezer
Gillman, Thomas
Harvey, James
Homes, John
Humphries, Richard
Johnson, Willard
Johnson, Zacheriah
Jones, William
Kettle, Jonathan
Kimball, ———
Knowles, Nathan
Lathrop, James
Lathrop, Stillman
Lemon, David
Martin, John
McCluoley, Joseph
Mero, Jesse

Mero, Lemuel
Miles, Abner
Mosman, Rufus
Newcomb, Edward
Nutting, Samuel
Perry, Isaac
Phelps, Timothy
Pierce, Emery
Pierce, Silas
Plumer, Ezra
Plummer, Moses
Pond, Benjamin
Pratt, David
Ripley, Robert
Robinson, Jacob
Scott, James
Seymour, Friend
Smith, John
Snow, Tilley
Sweet, Jabez
Tenney, Moses
Thombs, William
Thurston, Benjamin
Veazie, Elijah
Vinton, Josiah
Wheelock, Cephas
White, Obediah
Williams, C. M.

Capt. A. Green's Company, Lieut. Col. A. Binney's Regiment.
October, 1814. Service at Boston. Detailed for special duty.

RANK AND NAME.
Andrew Green, Captain
Charles Hood, Lieutenant
Isaac Jenney, Ensign

William Blaney, Sergeant
Thomas Gay, Sergeant
James Rowse, Sergeant
Joseph Welch, Sergeant
Epaphras Bull, Corporal
Thomas G. Bangs, Corporal
William P. Tilton, Corporal
John R. Bradford, Corporal
John Sylvester, Musician
Sheldon Perry, Musician

Privates.
Badger, Thomas
Baker, Abel
Bass, George
Bell, William
Bourne, Ephraim

Chandler, Benjamin
Clapp, Galen
Copeland, John
Copeland, Seth
Corbett, Thomas
Crane, Lazra
Davis, William N.
Dow, Evan
Eaton, Samuel A.
Fox, Richard
French, Moses
Frothington, Charles
Gatley, Charles
Hailend, Henry
Hollis, Daniel
Kendell, Thomas
Laiton, John
Lamson, Benjamin
Lancey, Samuel F.
Learneard, William
Lewis, Edmund
Low, David

Low, George
Low, Samuel
Lyndes, Stephen
Mansin, Thomas
Mason, Aaron
Morrison, Henry
Newhall, John
Osborn, John
Parker, Nehemiah
Parks, William C.
Pearson, William
Rayner, John
Salmon, John
Snelling, Enoch H.
Spencer, Job
Warriner, W. B.
Watson, David
Wells, Ebenezer
Wheeden, John
Whitman, John
Williams, William C.

Sgt. Rouse's Guard from Capt. A. Green's Company, Lieut. Col. A. Binney's Regiment.
November, 1814. Service at Boston and vicinity. Detailed for special duty.

RANK AND NAME.
James Rouse, Sergeant
Thomas G. Banks, Corporal
Epaphras Bull, Corporal

Privates.
Armsby, Mathias
Atkins, Benjamin
Baker, Abel
Ball, Jonathan
Barnard, Josiah
Barnes, Thomas
Belcher, John H.
Bird, James
Bird, Robert L.
Blagge, T. W. T.
Bradford, William B.
Brown, Eldad
Brown, James B.
Burroughs, John
Burroughs, Stephen
Channing, Henry
Chapin, Aaron
Clapp, Frederic
Crane, Joshua
Davis, Timothy
Davis, William N.
Dow, Evan
Dow, Jones
Drake, Jesse
Eayres, Joseph

Edgar, George R.
Elliott, Ephraim L.
Elliott, Henry
Emmons, Thomas
Everett, Aaron
Fay, Winsor
Fisher, Alvin
Fowle, George M.
Furness, Nathaniel
Gibbens, Vassall
Gouch, James
Gray, Harrison
Gray, Henry
Guild, George
Hadoway, John T.
Hearsey, Caleb
Hopkins, Thomas R.
Hyde, Aaron
Laiton, John
Lathrop, John P.
Lilley, John
Lincoln, Hawks
Lincoln, Russell
Merry, Daniel
Messinger, Daniel
Mitchell, Gardner
Mitchell, Phineas
Morrison, Henry
Morse, Hazen
Newman, George L.
Osborn, John

Paine, Thomas
Parker, Edward W.
Pitman, John
Pope, Calvin J.
Porter, Charles
Proctor, William
Ripley, Charles
Sawyer, Moses
Smith, George W.
Smith, Joel
Smith, John
Spear, Daniel
Spear, Joseph C.
Stimpson, John
Swan, Timothy
Tannatt, Abram G.
Thayer, Gideon F.
Thompson, Archibald
Tileston, Ezra B.
Torrey, John
Towle, Jonathan
Tupper, Hiram
Vinton, M. M.
Vose, Isaac
Wentworth, James
Wetherbee, John H.
Wetherbee, Jonas
Williams, William C.
Withington, Joseph

MASSACHUSETTS VOLUNTEER MILITIA IN THE WAR OF 1812.   29

Lieut. Col. S. K. Chamberlin's Regiment.
From Sept. 10 to Oct. 30, 1814.   Stationed at Boston and vicinity.

FIELD AND STAFF.
Solomon K. Chamberlin, Lieutenant Colonel, Dalton
Thomas Stevens, Major, Sheffield
Erastus Rowley, Major, Richmond
Sherman Bosworth, Adjutant, Lenox

Henry Taylor, Quartermaster, Pittsfield
Henry Ashley, Paymaster, Sheffield
Asa Burbank, Surgeon, Lanesboro
Nathaniel Preston, Surgeon's Mate, Sheffield
Billy Hibbard, Chaplain

NONCOMMISSIONED STAFF.
Marcellus Sandes, Sergeant Major
Henry E. May, Quartermaster Sergeant
John Hamon, Fife Major

Capt. J. Temple's Company, Lieut. Col. S. K. Chamberlin's Regiment.
From Sept. 10 to Oct. 1, and Oct. 1 to Oct. 30, 1814.   Service at Boston.

RANK AND NAME.
John Temple, Captain
James Brown, Lieutenant
Adam Hemenway, Lieutenant

Leonard Arnold, Sergeant
Elisha Frost, Sergeant
Abel Eaton, Sergeant
Thomas Hastings, Sergeant
Amasa Kendall, Corporal
Thomas Arnold, Corporal
Richard Fiske, Corporal
Alexander H. Jones, Corporal

Privates.
Bacon, Michael
Belcher, Benjamin
Belcher, Curtis
Belcher, Joseph
Clap, Seth
Dadman, William
Dadman, William, 2d
Dalrymple, James
Forrester, Amariah
Frost, David
Frost, Horace
Gay, Joseph
Goodnow, Elisha
Goodnow, Jonas

Haven, Ashel
Hemenway, Elias
Jaquith, Josiah
Johnson, Amos
Johnson, Patten
Littlefield, Adams
McFarland, Robert
McFarland, Walter
Nurse, Newel
Parker, Artemas
Rice, Stephen
Stearnes, Amos
Twitchel, John
Warren, Samuel

Capt. D. Collins' Company, Lieut. Col. S. K. Chamberlin's Regiment.
From Sept. 10 to Oct. 30, 1814.   Raised at Lenox and vicinity.   Service at Boston.

RANK AND NAME.
Daniel Collins, Captain
Daniel Eames, Lieutenant
John Sherrill, Ensign

Calvin Kendal, Sergeant
John Matoon, Sergeant
Otis Barrett, Sergeant
Caleb Snow, Sergeant
Ebenezer Porter, Corporal
Daniel Sacket, Corporal
Henry Hollister, Corporal
Caleb I. Landers, Corporal
William Benton, Musician
Mydad Eames, Musician

Privates.
Andrews, Alonzo
Bangs, David
Barlow, Cornelius
Barnes, Russell
Beckwith, Chauncey
Bennet, Israel
Boone, Benjamin
Brooks, Anson
Brown, James
Burt, Francis

Butler, Daniel
Butler, Elijah
Butler, Stephen
Butmore, Jeremiah
Chapel, Jonathan
Clark, Harry
Clark, John
Clark, Oramel
Clark, Zenas
Cook, Moses
Crane, William
Curtis, Thomas S.
Dunbar, William
Durfry, Harvey
Evarts, John
Farley, John
Flowers, Enos
Flowers, James
Follet, Daniel
Francisco, Peter
Hall, Nathan
Hall, Oliver
Haskins, Orrin
Helmes, Peter Y.
Henry, Orrin
Henry, William
Hibbard, Billy

Jackson, Alexander
Lane, Lemuel
Leonard, Samuel
Lily, Gardner
Loveland, Joshua
Mateson, Amos, Jr.
Miller, Collins S.
Milliken, William
Morrell, Horace F.
Newbury, Isaac
Nicholson, Jonathan
Norris, Shepherd
Phelps, Leonard
Post or Rost, Horace
Richards, Phineas
Rost or Post, Horace
Sadder, Silas
Savory, Harvy
Segars, Martin
Sibly, Alva
Sikes, Shardat
Taylor, Dennis
Tyler, Chester
Walter, Harvey
Webber, William
Weller, Percy
Wood, Ebenezer

MASSACHUSETTS VOLUNTEER MILITIA IN THE WAR OF 1812.

Capt. J. Howland's Company, Lieut. Col. S. K. Chamberlin's Regiment.
From Sept. 10 to Oct. 30, 1814. Raised at Adams and vicinity. Service at Boston.

RANK AND NAME.
Joseph Howland, Captain
Silas Comstock, Lieutenant
Isaac Mason, Ensign

Townsend Waterman, Sergeant
Cornelius Basset, Sergeant
Alpheus Brown, Sergeant
Ephraim Willmoth, Sergeant

Privates.
Angel, Jeremiah
Ayers, Moses
Baker, George S.
Baker, Miles C.
Barber, Thomas, Jr.
Barton, William
Bassett, Adolphus
Bates, Simeon
Beach, Atwater
Beach, Henry
Beals, Caleb
Bird, Nelson
Bliss, Leonard
Briant, Alvin
Briant, Barton
Brown, John
Brown, Luther
Browning, Benjamin

Burlingame, Humphrey
Cadwell, Abel
Cady, Curtis
Carpenter, Elisha
Catlin, Hezekiah
Chamberlin, Gad
Claftin, Leonard
Clark, Russell
Comstock, Joshua
Crocker, Rodney
Curtis, Samuel
Davis, William
Demming, John
Dunham, Braddish
Fedwell, David
Fowler, James
Freeman, Jared, Jr.
Hall, Alva
Hall, Luman (D)
Harvey, Nathaniel
Harwood, William
Hathaway, Charles
Hathaway, Wilson
Holbrook, Josiah D.
Hosei, Clark
Howland, Isaac
Hunt, John
Hunt, Silas

Jenks, William
Jones, Nathan
Ketchum, Elihu
Ketchum, Solomon
Leonard, Jesse
Lewis, David
Mallery, Samuel
Mason, George
McFarland, Abel
Moore, George W. G.
Parkill, Stephen
Pierce, Thomas
Pomroy, Isaac
Pomroy, James
Randell, Joshua
Roberts, David W.
Robinson, Bonny
Ross, Zebulon
Sabine, Hezekiah
Sherman, Job
Short, Daniel
Slocum, Lemuel S.
Tyler, Isaac
Walker, Jacob I.
Waters, William D.
Wheeler, Milton
Whipple, John
Wilcox, Jeheel

Capt. N. Smith's Company, Lieut. Col. S. K. Chamberlin's Regiment.
From Sept. 10 to Oct. 30, 1814. Raised at Hancock and vicinity. Service at Boston.

RANK AND NAME.
Nathaniel Smith, Captain
Daniel Loomis, Lieutenant
Thomas Fincks, Ensign

Deodatus Hubbell, Sergeant
George Sweet, Sergeant
Eshon Gregory, Sergeant
Jestus Wheeler, Sergeant
Alpheus Jeffards, Corporal
Farman White, Corporal
Elias Thomas, Corporal
Hiram A. Mead, Corporal

Privates.
Arnold, Samuel
Baker, Matthew
Barrett, Royal C.
Bartlett, Jedediah
Bennett, Thomas
Bently, Caleb
Bently, Eliphalet
Boardman, Savillan

Brown, Alvin
Burlinham, Levi
Burnham, Nathan
Carpenter, Nathaniel
Cooley, Alvin
Cottrill, Oliver
Cowin, Charles
Dean, William
Debble, Sylvanus (D)
Edge, Asa
Ellis, Benjamin
Gilmore, Abraham
Goodrich, Aaron
Gregory, Esbon
Grove, Samuel
Guillam, Benjamin
Hall, Henry
Hand, Hollobert
Handley, James
Harrington, Jeremiah
Harrington, Nicodemus
Hill, Levi
Humphreville, Ambrose

Lasher, David W.
Minor, Noble F.
Olds, Luther
Osborn, Sylvester
Pettengale, Samuel
Potter, Peleg
Rogers, Gideon, Jr.
Sanders, Peter
Seaman, Job
Sheldon, Daniel
Shepherdson, Lovell
Smedly, Joseph
Smith, Enoch (D)
Sweet, Samuel
Taft, Lyman
Vincent, John
Walden, Benjamin
Washburn, Lettice
Waterman, George
Weed, Jonathan
Williams, Alpheus
Wilson, Samuel

MASSACHUSETTS VOLUNTEER MILITIA IN THE WAR OF 1812. 31

Capt. J. W. Rockwell's Company, Lieut. Col. S. K. Chamberlin's Regiment.
From Sept. 11 to Oct. 30, 1814.   Raised at New Marlborough.   Service at Boston.

RANK AND NAME.
Joseph W. Rockwell, Captain
Ira Owens, Lieutenant
Abner Heath, Ensign

Luther Banney, Sergeant
Edward Bush, Sergeant
John Brackinridge, Sergeant
John Pickett, Jr., Sergeant
Stephen Pope, Corporal
Hubbel Smith, Corporal
James Parks, Corporal
Jabez Howlan, Corporal
William Huggins, Musician
Elijah Ormsby, Musician

Privates.
Austin, Chester
Bosworth, Lyman
Bosworth, Oliver
Bowen, Chester
Bradford, Henry
Bradley, Samuel B.
Brown, Rex
Bush, Milo
Callender, Chester

Churchill, Moses
Cleveland, Josiah
Coe, Job
Dart, Elijah
Dunham, Gamaliel
Egleston, Frederic
Fargo, Thomas
Fox, Harvey
Frasier, Marvin
Fuller, Joseph
Goodrich, Anson B.
Grant, John
Gunn, Frederic
Hall, Arial
Hall, Benoni
Hall, George
Heath, Ebenezer
Heath, John
Hubbard, John
Hubbard, Orrin
Hubbard, Walter
Hubbard, Samuel
Hurd, Samuel
Knowles, Daniel
LeBarn, Roderic
Lockwood, (?) Stephen

Manley, Josiah B.
Noble, David
Noble, Henry
Noble, Paul
Palmeter, William
Pease, Elijah
Pickett, Benjamin
Pickett, Joseph
Reed, Zachariah
Rice, Elihu
Rich, George
Robinson, Timothy
Sage, Ira
Shaw, Samuel
Shaw, William W.
Snow, Loring
Stevens, Guy
Stevens, John
Vosburg, Nathaniel
Ward, Elihu
Waterhouse, Robert
Welden, Peter L.
Wilcox, Samuel
Woodworth, James
Worthy, Oramee
Wright, David

Capt. A. Jones' Company, Lieut. Col. S. K. Chamberlin's Regiment.
From Sept. 14 to Sept. 30, 1814.   Raised at Otis and vicinity.   Service at Boston.

RANK AND NAME.
Adonijah Jones, Captain
James Peck, Lieutenant
Plinny Karner, Ensign

Hezekiah Gear, Sergeant
Abiel Abbot, Sergeant
Ephraim Baldwin, Sergeant
Seymour Joiner, Sergeant
Ezra Heats, Corporal
Jonathan W. Boughton, Corporal
Edwin Brewer, Corporal
John Sherman, Corporal
Timothy Jones, Musician
William Kingsbury, Musician

Privates.
Allen, Daniel P.
Arnold, Elisha
Baker, Burton
Baldwin, Stephen
Ball, Milton
Bennet, John
Black or Blark, Bannon
Bolton, Gamaliel

Brooks, Lyman
Bullock, William
Burghart, Henry W.
Burghart, Josiah
Carter, Miles
Cline, Hugh
Curtis, Chauncey
Curtis, Leonard
Daily, Cornwell
Daily, William
Davis, Jabez
Dewey, Henry
Dexter, Leonard
Eels, Pitkin
Esty, David
Fowler, Calvin
Fray, Samuel
Fuller, Norman
Hail, William
Hooper, Leander
Hubbard, Hawly
Jacob, Francis
Loury, William
Mallon, James
McCarter, Solomon

Mills, Job
Mills, Simeon
Miner, Daniel
Morse, David
Noble, Ezekiel
Olds, Ephraim
Orcutt, Eber
Ormsby, Royal
Owen, Hiram
Paul, Michall
Phillips, Elisha
Pixley, Edmund
Porter, Aaron
Preston, Samuel
Richards, Benjamin
Scholdfield, Elisha
Skiff, Russell
Slater, Alanson
Smith, Harry
Still, William
Tuttle, John
Van Ness, Abraham
Winchel, Erastus
Worster, Nathan
Younglove, George

Capt. J. Hunt's Company, Lieut. Col. S. K. Chamberlin's Regiment.
From Sept. 19 to Oct. 30, 1814. Raised at Stockbridge and vicinity. Service at Boston.

RANK AND NAME.
John Hunt, Captain
Erastus Williams, Lieutenant
George Bacon, Ensign

William Williams, Sergeant
Benjamin Bacon, Sergeant
Philo Griswald, Sergeant
Otis Dresser, Sergeant
Heman Whittlesy, Corporal
Sunard Olmsted, Corporal
Daniel Barnes, Corporal
David P. Ingersoll, Corporal
Samuel Clark, Musician
Samuel F. Carter, Musician

Privates.
Allen, Harvey
Andrews, Luman
Bacon, Samuel
Baker, Walker
Belders, Silas
Bliss, Samuel
Bliss, Simeon
Brown, Isaiah
Carter, Charles
Churchill, Seymour
Curtis, Barnabas
Curtis, Jay
Dyer, Darius
Green, William
Hamilton, Luther
Hamilton, Patrick
Hill, George
James, George
Jostrum, Henry
Judd, Jabez
Landon, Luther
Manley, John
Nyles, Sands
Olmsted, Francis
Perry, Ezra
Phelps, Daniel
Phelps, Nathan
Pratt, Uri
Rathbon, Nathaniel
Rathbon, Samuel
Ripley, Phineas
Sage, John
Shinkle, John
Simonds, Ebenezer F.
Tollman, Timothy
Warner, George
Whittlesy, Charles
Whittlesy, Solomon
Wilcocks, Loven
Wilcocks, Lyman
Wilcocks, William
Williams, Horace
Williams, Isaac

Capt. J. Nye's Company, Lieut. Col. S. K. Chamberlin's Regiment.
From Sept. 14 to Oct. 30, 1814. Raised at Lee and vicinity. Service at Boston.

RANK AND NAME.
Joseph Nye, Captain
Hylon Toby, Ensign

Silas Gaspeld, Sergeant
Jonas Childs, Sergeant
Titus Thorp, Sergeant
James Burton, Sergeant
Arthur Buel, Corporal
Thomas Treat, Corporal
Elisha Whiton, Corporal
Calvin Wilson, Musician
Alfred Sears, Musician

Privates.
Allen, Hiram
Allen, John
Andrews, Elisha
Baird, Aaron S.
Baird, Samuel
Barnes, Elisha
Barnes, Elnathan
Barnes, Joseph
Benedict, Sylvester
Black, Samuel
Boughton, Joy C.
Boughton, Stephen
Bowen, John
Bradly, Ebenezer C.
Bradly, Monson
Brookins, Calvin
Budd, Nathaniel
Burr, Jehiel
Cannon, James
Carpenter, Levi
Childs, Benjamin
Childs, Stephen
Clark, Abijah
Covel, Elisha
Darling, Benjamin
Foot, Erastus
Ford, John
Fowler, Warham
Fox, Hubbard
Green, Lawson H.
Haddock, Henry
Hawk, John
Hewens, Elijah
Hewlet, Westly
Holdridge, Ira
Jones, James
Keep, James
Keith, Seth
Kemill, (?) John
Keyes, Albert
Lenolds, Joshua
Link, John
Mellen, James
Moon, Amos
Norcot, John
Ormsbury, Daniel
Ormsby, John
Osburn, Benjamin
Park, Caleb
Perry, Arthur
Phinney, Calvin
Rawson, Jonathan
Rood, Aaron
Sherman, Solomon
Sibly, John
Smith, Jesse
Spencer, Augustus
Spencer, Theron
Stanton, Peleg
Stone, John S.
Sturgis, Samuel
Sturgiss, Robert
Sweet, Sylvester
Thayer, Jesse
Tyler, John
Wadsworth, Kenophon
Webster, Lyman
Wilmarth, Foster
Woodruff, Henry
Woolly, Jonathan

Capt. H. Willmarth's Company, Lieut. Col. S. K. Chamberlin's Regiment.
From Sept. 14 to Oct. 30, 1814. Raised at Adams. Service at Boston.

RANK AND NAME.
Henry Willmarth, Captain
Silas A. Fobes, Lieutenant
Isaac Fisher, Ensign

William Maynard, Sergeant
Nathaniel Butts, Sergeant
Ira Stevens, Sergeant
Asa Cade, Sergeant
Allen Burlingame, Corporal
Seth Richmond, Corporal
Socrates Frissel, Corporal
Amos Tyler, Corporal
Phineas Atwood, Musician
William Lyman, Musician

Privates.
Abbot, Samuel
Allen, Josiah
Apthorp, James
Axdell, Thomas
Bacon, Benjamin
Barret, Archer
Barret, Elba C.
Bates, Dexter B.
Bennet, John, 2d
Bissel, Israel
Bonn, Caleb
Brown, Benjamin
Butts, Stephen

Cade, Daniel
Cain, Moses
Carpenter, Miles
Clark, Nathan T.
Coleman, Louden
Coleman, Samuel
Crosier, Andrew
Crosier, Jason
Cushing, Thomas
Cusick, Henry
Demoranois, Phineas
Dickinson, John
Estes, Thomas
Ferguson, James
Follet, Simon
Frink, Lyman
Frissel, Lemuel
Hardy, Jonathan
Harwood, Murvel
Hathaway, Benjamin
Hathaway, Chancy
Hathaway, Peleg
Haws, Daniel
Hemenway, Josiah
Idle, Harvey
Jones, Russell
Jones, Samuel
Kitteridge, Job
Latham, M.
Leland, Lemuel

Manchester, Joseph
Miller, Samuel, Jr.
Miller, William
Morgan, John
Negus, Aaron
Nelson, James
Payn, Burnell
Pierce, Josiah
Pierce, William
Pratt, Josiah
Raymond, Daniel
Russell, John
Shearman, James
Shearman, John
Shearman, Joseph
Shearman, Seth
Smith, Martin
Smith, William
Spencer, Erastus
Taylor, Augustus
Thomas, Richard
Tiffts, John
Torry, Nathan
Tucker, Pascal
Wait, Chester
Whitman, Jeptha
Witter, Abraham
Wright, Simeon W.

Capt. J. S. Catlin's Company, Lieut. Col. S. K. Chamberlin's Regiment.
From Sept. 30 to Oct. 30, 1814. Raised at New Marlborough. Service at Boston.

RANK AND NAME.
Joseph S. Catlin, Captain
Luke Harmon, Lieutenant
Sylvester Dowd, Ensign

Benjamin Smith, Sergeant
Harvey Wheeler, Sergeant
Samuel Wolcott, Sergeant
Hadlock Merry, Sergeant
Philo Smith, Corporal
Asa Stebbins, Corporal
Richard Roberts, Corporal
Hiram Case, Corporal
Jonathan Arnold, Musician
Eleze: Butler, Musician

Privates.
Agraull, Roswell
Arnold, Josiah
Ayers, Ebenezer
Baldwin, Jaheil
Barber, Samuel, Jr.
Barker, Jairus
Baxter, Francis
Bidwell, Barnabus

Brown, Averis M.
Brown, Isaac
Bullard, Eleazer
Bush, Hezekiah
Canfield, Roderick H.
Clark, Michael
Domony, John
Dowd, Asahel
Dowd, Noah, Jr.
Downs, Jabez
Emmons, John
Emmons, Lewis
French, Chancy
Hall, George
Harmon, Amos
Harmon, Hiram
Hulet, Lewis
Jackson, Solomon
Jones, Simon
Kellog, Auren
Kilber, David
Kilber, Phineas
King, Lyman
Knapp, Aurin K.
Lucas, William

Mabson, Ezra
Manley, Austin
Manley, Joseph N.
Moore, Pliny
Morley, William
Norton, Harvey
Phillips, Zacheus
Pratt, Aaron, Jr.
Reivry, Silas
Sacket, Thomas
Sage, Dennis
Smith, Amasa
Smith, Jabez
Smith, John P.
Smith, Sabinas
Smith, Warren
Stanmon, Gersham
Taylor, Ira
Thomas, Hezekiah
Thorpe, Aurin
Tillitson, Daniel
Townsend, Hosea
Walter, Sylvester
Wheeler, Abraham

MASSACHUSETTS VOLUNTEER MILITIA IN THE WAR OF 1812.

Lieut. Col. L. Dodge's Regiment.
Seventeen days, exact date not given (1814). Service at Beverly.

FIELD AND STAFF.
Levi Dodge, Lieutenant Colonel, Beverly.

Capt. N. Lamson's Company, Lieut. Col. L. Dodge's Regiment.
Different periods, 3 to 17 days, from June 21 to Aug. 22, 1814. Service at Beverly.

RANK AND NAME.
Nathaniel Lamson, Captain
John Davis, Lieutenant
Richard Pickett, Ensign

Jonathan Stickney, Sergeant
Stephen Baker, Sergeant
Thomas Farris, Sergeant
James Ford, Sergeant
Stephen Homans, Corporal
Levi Wallis, Corporal
James Creasy, Corporal
William Putnam, Corporal
Samuel Dodge, Musician
Ebenezer Trask, Musician

Privates.
Abbot, Nathaniel
Allen, Henry
Arbuckle, John
Barker, Nathan
Batchelder, George, 2d
Batchelder, Henry
Batchelder, Jonathan
Batchelder, Nathaniel
Batchelder, Winthrop
Bayles, Ichabod
Bennett, John
Bennett, Robert G.
Boyle, Ichabod
Bridge, Mathew
Brimmer, Daniel
Brimmer, William
Brown, Charles
Brown, Paul H.
Buckman, John
Buffington, John
Bunker, Benjamin
Burchstead, George
Campbell, Duncan
Carrol, William
Chamberlin, Silas
Chapman, Edward
Chapman, Isaac
Chase, Benjamin
Cheaver, Benjamin, 2d
Cheaver, Joseph
Cheaver, Nathaniel
Choate, Henry
Church, Stephen P.
Clayton, Joseph
Cole, Joseph
Cox, John
Dempsey, William
Dodge, Azor

Dodge, Jesse
Dodge, Jonathan, 3d
Dodge, Thomas
Eaton, William G.
Ellingwood, Ezra
Ellingwood, Herbert
Ellingwood, John
Elliot, Andrew
Endicott, Nathan H.
Farnes, John
Fielder, John
Fielder, Knott
Fielder, William
Foster, James
Foster, Joseph
Foster, Seth
Foster, Thomas
Gage, Asmon
Gage, William
Gardner, John
Gilman, Eliphalet F.
Givings, John
Gouldsberry, Joseph
Grush, Philip
Hall, John
Hammond, Andrew
Harris, Charles
Haskell, Samuel
Hatch, John
Herrick, George W.
Herrick, John, 2d
Herrick, Jonathan, 2d
Herrick, Thomas F.
Herrick, Thomas P., 2d
Herrick, William, 4th
Holt, William
Howard, Moses
Knowlton, Mark
Lakeman, Joseph
Lamson, George
Lamson, William
Larcom, Henry
Leach, William
Lefavour, Thomas
Leonard, John
Little, Ophert
Lord, Samuel D.
Loring, John
Lovett, Israel
Lovett, Jeremiah
Lovett, Joseph, 4th
Lovett, Pyam
Lovett, Samuel C.
Lovett, William B.
Meacom, Ebenezer

Meservy, Ephraim
Meservy, John
Mulliken, Alexander
Nichols, William
Nourse, Stephen
Ober, Oliver
Ober, Samuel
Pickard, Ephraim
Pickard, Thomas
Pickett, John
Pickett, Josiah
Pickett, Richard
Pickett, Thomas L.
Pierce, Thomas
Porter, Jeremiah
Porter, John
Pousland, John, 3d
Pousland, Joseph
Putman, Jeremy
Putman, William
Qunion, Abraham
Raymond, Benjamin, 2d
Raymond, Josiah
Raymond, William
Roundy, Israel W.
Roundy, Stephen
Rummonds, John
Rummonds, Robert
Smith, Nehemiah
Standley, Benjamin, 3d
Standley, Thomas
Stickney, Joseph
Stone, Ezra
Stone, Israel O.
Stone, Zacheriah
Thorndike, William
Tivers, Joshua
Trask, Benjamin, 2d
Trask, George
Trask, Israel
Trask, John
Trask, Nathaniel
Trask, Oliver
Wallis, Bartholomew
Wallis, Caleb
Wallis, Ebenezer, 2d
Wallis, Ebenezer, 3d
Wallis, Henry
Wallis, Israel
Wallis, Josiah H.
Wallis, Nathaniel
Ward, John
Webb, John, 2d
Webber, Israel
Webber, John P.

MASSACHUSETTS VOLUNTEER MILITIA IN THE WAR OF 1812. 35

Capt. N. Lamson's Company, Lieut. Col. L. Dodge's Regiment — Concluded.

Privates — Concluded.
Webber, Josiah
Weed, Moses
Whittridge, John
Wilkins, Jason
Wilson, John
Wood, George

Wood, William
Woodberry, George
Woodberry, Jacob
Woodberry, Joel
Woodberry, Joseph
Woodberry, Larkin
Woodberry, Moses

Woodberry, Peter
Woodberry, Robert
Woodberry, Samuel
Woodberry, Zebulon
Wright, James

Capt. A. Lord's Company, Lieut. Col. L. Dodge's Regiment.
Different periods, 3 to 17 days, from June 24 to Aug. 14, 1814. Service at Beverly.

RANK AND NAME.
Abraham Lord, Captain
William Ober, Lieutenant
Israel Trask, Ensign

Andrew Dodge, Sergeant
Benjamin Woodberry, Sergeant
Joseph Friend, Sergeant
William Gray, Sergeant
John Baker, Corporal
John Creasy, Corporal
Stephen Sands, Corporal
Stephen Abbot, Musician
Charles Buxton, Musician

Privates.
Bachelder, John
Blaisdell, John
Brown, Abraham
Brown, Robert
Burchstead, Allen

Coffin, Abner
Conant, Ezra
Creasy, Benjamin, 2d
Creasy, Jonathan, 2d
Creasy, Jonathan, 3d
Daniels, Moses
Dodge, Dudley
Dodge, John
Dodge, Robert
Edwards, Asa B.
Edwards, Benjamin
Edwards, Ezra
Edwards, Robert
Francis, George
Friend, Samuel
Fuliton, Benjamin
Grant, Joseph
Hill, Thomas
Lasky, James
Meservy, Joseph
Morris, Emery

Pearson, Ira
Piper, Gilman
Porter, John
Potter, Benjamin
Pousland, John
Quier, Benjamin
Raymond, James G.
Sands, Isaac
Shaw, Daniel
Sheldon, Joshua
Trask, Edward
Verry, James
Vincent, Thomas
Walley, John
Webb, Nathan
Wilkins, Sylvester
Woodberry, Thomas, 3d
Woodberry, William, 2d
Woodman, Timothy

Capt. A. Lord's Company, Lieut. Col. L. Dodge's Regiment.
From Sept. 21 to Oct. 11, 1814. Service at Beverly.

RANK AND NAME.
Abraham Lord, Captain
William Oliver, Lieutenant
Isaac Trask, Ensign

Andrew Dodge, Sergeant
Benjamin Woodbury, Sergeant
William Gray, Sergeant
Stephen Abbott, Musician
Charles Baxton, Musician

Privates.
Baker, John
Berry, Timothy
Blaisdell, John
Brown, Abraham
Brown, Robert

Burchstead, Allen
Conant, Ezra
Creasey, John, 2d
Creasey, Jonathan, 2d
Dodge, Dudley
Dodge, Robert
Dodge, William
Edwards, Asa B.
Edwards, Benjamin
Edwards, Robert
Friend, Samuel
Fulliton, Benjamin
Grant, Joseph
Hill, Thomas
Lasky, James
Masury, Joseph
Meservy, Ephraim

Norris, Emery
Porter, John
Pousland, John
Pousland, William
Raymond, John G.
Sands, Isaac
Sands, Stephen
Shaw, Daniel
Stanley, David, 3d
Trask, Edward
Verry, James
Webb, Nathan
Wheeler, Reuben
Wilkins, Sylvester
Woodberry, Thomas, 3d
Woodberry, William, 2d
Woodman, Timothy

MASSACHUSETTS VOLUNTEER MILITIA IN THE WAR OF 1812.

Capt. J. Hooper's Company, Lieut. Col. L. Dodge's Regiment.

Different periods, 3 to 59 days, from June 25 to Aug. 22, 1814.   Service at Beverly.

RANK AND NAME.
Joseph Hooper, Captain
Ebenezer Tappan, Jr., Ensign

Amos Knight, Sergeant
Benjamin Tappan, Sergeant
Asa Kitsfield, Sergeant
Eleazer Hooper, Corporal
John E. Bohonon, Musician

Privates.
Agers, John
Allen, Amos
Allen, Daniel
Allen, John P.
Allen, Joseph
Allen, Thomas
Anable, David
Andrews, John
Babcock, Joseph
Baily, Joshua
Bingham, Delwina L.
Brown, Andrew
Brown, James
Burges, Abial
Burges, Abial, Jr.
Burges, Amasa
Burges, David
Burges, David, Jr.

Carter, Benjamin
Cheaver, Samuel
Cladd, Peter
Cost, George
Crumby, Benjamin
Crumby, John
Currier, Daniel
Danford, Jeremiah
Danford, William
Dodge, John
Driver, Andrew
Driver, Solomon, 2d
Escot, John
Escot, Philip
Farr, John
Flowers, William
Fowler, Timothy
Goldsmith, John
Goldsmith, Samuel
Grant, Thomas
Gurdler, William
Hale, Daniel
Hildreth, Nathaniel
Hill, Amos
Hill, Benjamin
Hilton, Amos
Hooper, Eleazer
Hooper, John
Kinsman, Arnold

Kitsfield, Thomas H.
Knight, James
Knowlton, Benjamin
Knowlton, Caleb
Leach, Daniel
Lee, Andrew
Lee, I.
Lee, Nathaniel
Lul (?), Jonathan
Mann, William
Martin, Andrew
Martin, T.
May, Moses
Morgan, Jacob
Morse, Samuel
Norwood, Thomas
Norwood, William
Oriment, John
Preston, Isaac, Jr.
Proctor, Humphry
Pulsifer, Eps
Roberts, Andrew
Sargent, Montgomery
Simonds, Andrew
Smith, Stephen
Thompson, Benjamin
Tuck, Levi
Wallen, John
Wimbleton, Charles

Capt. A. Foster's Company, Lieut. Col. L. Dodge's Regiment.

Different periods, from Sept. 21 to Oct. 7, 1814.   Service at Beverly.

RANK AND NAME.
Aaron Foster, Captain
Jonathan Foster, Lieutenant
Zachariah M. Cole, Ensign

Isacker O. Foster, Sergeant
Joseph Williams, Sergeant
William Studley, Sergeant
Israel Foster, 2d, Sergeant
Hezekiah Foster, Corporal
William Young, Corporal
Zachariah M. Studley, Corporal
Andrew Woodbury, Corporal
Benjamin Butman, Musician
Benjamin Webber, Musician

Privates.
Andrews, Thomas
Appleton, Daniel
Bisson, Israel
Bradford, John
Bunker, Nathaniel
Clark, Israel
Claxton, Philip
Cleaves, William P.

Corning, Peter
Dodge, Thomas
Elliot, James
Elliot, John
Foster, Israel
Foster, Jeremiah
Foster, Jeremiah, 4th
Foster, Jonathan, 2d
Foster, Nathaniel
French, John
Hale, Henry
Haskell, James
Haskell, William
Herrick, Henry
Kelly, Shubal
Kent, Josiah
Knowlton, Ebenezer
Larcom, Andrew
Lee, Larkin F.
Lovett, Augustus
Lovett, Edmund
Lovett, Josiah, 2d
Marshall, John
Maxy, Elijah
Miller, James

Morse, Jeremiah
Ober, Joseph
Parker, William
Patch, William
Perkins, George
Pierce, William
Preston, Richard
Pride, Peter
Prince, John, 2d
Rea, Ebenezer, Jr.
Rea, Gideon
Roberts, David P.
Sewards, Nathaniel B.
Smith, Ezekiel
Standley, David
Standley, John
Studley, Andrew
Studley, Jonathan
Thistle, Nehemiah
Thistle, Samuel M.
West, Joseph
Woodberry, Gideon
Woodberry, Warren
Woodbury, Jeremiah
Woodbury, Stephen

Lieut. J. Foster's Detachment, Lieut. Col. L. Dodge's Regiment.

Different periods, 3 to 17 days, from June 20 to Aug. 22, 1814. Service at Beverly.

RANK AND NAME.
Jonathan Foster, Lieutenant

Joseph Williams, Sergeant
Israel Foster, Sergeant
William Standley, Sergeant
Isacker O. Foster, Sergeant
Hezekiah Foster, Corporal
William Young, Corporal
Asa Whiting, Corporal
Andrew Woodberry, Corporal

Privates.
Abbott, Stephen
Appleton, Daniel
Barker, William
Bayles, Alexander
Bisson, Israel
Bradford, John
Buck, Thomas
Bunker, Nathaniel
Butman, Benjamin
Cheaver, William P.
Clark, Israel
Clark, Jonathan
Claxton, Philip
Corning, Peter
Dodge, Thomas, 3d
Eldridge, West D.
Elliot, John
Elliott, James
Foster, Ezra
Foster, Israel
Foster, Jeremiah
Foster, Jonathan, 2d

Foster, Joseph L.
Foster, Josiah, 4th
Foster, Nathaniel
Foster, Samuel, 2d
Hale, James
Harris, Jonathan
Haskell, James
Haskell, John
Haskell, William
Herrick, Henry
Herrick, William, 3d
Kelly, Shubael
Knowlton, Benjamin
Knowlton, Ebenezer
Knowlton, Isacker
Larcon, Andrew
Lee, Larkin T.
Lefavour, Thomas
Lovett, Augustus
Lovett, Edmund
Lovett, Isaac
Lovett, Josiah, 2d
Marshall, James W.
Marshall, John
Maxy, Elijah
Morgan, John
Morse, Jeremiah
Ober, Isaac
Ober, Joseph
Ober, Samuel, 2d
Osborn, Asa
Patch, William, 2d
Perkins, George
Pierce, William
Prescott, Asa

Preston, Richard
Pride, Peter, Jr.
Prince, John, 3d
Ray, Gideon
Rea, Ebenezer, Jr.
Roberts, David P.
Roberts, James
Russell, Joseph
Sanderson, John
Seaward, Nathaniel B.
Smith, Isaac W.
Standley, Andrew
Standley, John, Jr.
Standley, Stephen
Standley, Zacheriah M.
Stuart, Joseph B.
Sumner, John W.
Thissell, Nehemiah
Thissell, Samuel M.
Tuck, John
West, Joseph
West, Thomas
Woodberry, Elisha
Woodberry, Elliot
Woodberry, Freeborn
Woodberry, Gideon
Woodberry, Jeremiah
Woodberry, Joseph
Woodberry, Mark
Woodberry, Richard
Woodberry, Samuel
Woodberry, Stephen
Woodberry, Willoughby

Lieut. J. Davis' Company, Lieut. Col. L. Dodge's Regiment.

From August 21 to September 21, 1814. Service at Beverly.

RANK AND NAME.
John Davis, Lieutenant

Thomas Farris, Sergeant
Benjamin Tappan, Sergeant
Ezra Stone, Corporal
Eleazer Hooper, Corporal
Charles Burton, Musician
Stephen Abbott, Musician

Privates.
Ames, Thomas
Bradford, John

Brown, Andrew
Butnam, William
Chapman, Isaac
Chase, Benjamin
Conant, Ezra
Cox, John
Edwards, Benjamin
Goldsmith, Samuel
Hammond, Andrew
Herrick, George W.
Hill, Amos
Howard, Moses
Leach, Daniel

Lovett, Edmond
Peart, Jacob
Rea, Gideon
Sands, Isaac
Standley, David
Tuck, Levi
Ward, John
Wilson, John
Wimbleton, Charles
Young, William

Lieut. D. Friend's Company, Lieut. Col. L. Dodge's Regiment.
From Sept. 21 to Oct. 21, 1814. Service at Manchester.

RANK AND NAME.
Daniel Friend, Lieutenant

Thomas Farris, Sergeant
Asa Richardson, Sergeant
Willoby Woodbury, Corporal
James Knight, Corporal
Benjamin Webber, Corporal
Asa Whiting, Corporal

Privates.
Ayers, Thomas
Bacheldor, George

Bachelor, Cornelius
Butnam, William
Carter, Nathan
Cheaver, Jacob
Creesy, Noah
Edward, Samuel
Ellingwood, Herbert
Herrick, William
Lee, John, 2d
Manning, William
Marshall, James W.
Peart, Jacob
Pollard, John

Roundy, Stephen
Stickney, Benjamin
Tuck, John
Tuck, John, 2d
Wallis, Nathaniel
Ward, John
Welch, John
Woodberry, Samuel
Woodbury, Gideon

Sergt. J. Ford's Detachment, Lieut. Col. L. Dodge's Regiment.
From June 14 to June 21, 1814. Service at Beverly.

RANK AND NAME.
James Ford, Sergeant
Jonathan Stickney, Sergeant
Thomas Farris, Sergeant
Stephen Homans, Corporal
James Creasy, Corporal
Jason Wilkins, Corporal
Samuel Dodge, Musician
Ebenezer Trask, Musician

Privates.
Abbot, Nathaniel
Allen, Henry
Baker, Stephen
Batchelder, Henry
Batchelder, Nathaniel
Bennet, John
Bennet, Robert G.
Bridge, Mathew
Burchstead, George
Cheever, Joseph
Choate, Henry
Cleaves, Benjamin
Cleaves, Nathaniel
Cox, John
Derrick, Thomas F.
Dodge, Jesse
Eaton, William G.
Ellingwood, Herbert

Ellingwood, John, Jr.
Elliot, Andrew
Fielder, Knott
Fielder, William
Foster, James
Gage, A.
Gardner, John
Gilman, Eliphalet F.
Gouldsberry, Joseph
Grush, Philip
Hall, John
Hammond, Andrew
Hatch, John
Herrick, George W.
Herrick, Jonathan, 2d
Howard, Moses
Knowlton, Mark
Lewis, John
Lovett, Joseph, 4th
Lovett, Pyam
Lovett, Samuel P.
Lovett, William B.
Meacon, Ebenezer
Nourse, Stephen
Ober, Samuel
Pickett, John, Jr.
Pickett, Richard
Pierce, Thomas
Pousland, John, 3d

Quinon, Abraham
Raymond, Benjamin, 2d
Raymond, Josiah
Raymond, William
Roundy, Israel W.
Rummonds, John
Samson, George
Smith, Nehemiah
Standley, Benjamin, 2d
Stone, Israel O.
Stone, Zachariah
Thorndike, William
Trask, Benjamin
Trask, John
Trask, Nathaniel
Wallis, Bartholomew
Wallis, Ebenezer
Wallis, Ebenezer, 2d
Wallis, Henry
Webb, John
Williams, Caleb
Wilson, John
Wood, George
Wood, William
Woodberry, Jacob
Woodberry, Joseph
Wright, James

Lieut. Col. J. Dudley's Regiment.
From Sept. 13 to Nov. 7, 1814. Service at South Boston.

FIELD AND STAFF.
Joseph Dudley, Lieutenant Colonel, Roxbury
Thomas Dean, Major, Boston
Loammi Kendall, Major, Charlestown

Lewis Pierce, Adjutant, Dorchester
George Ware, Quartermaster, Roxbury
Moses Kidder, Surgeon's Mate, Townsend

NONCOMMISSIONED STAFF.
Ralph Houghton, Sergeant Major
Enos Lake, Drum Major
John White, Fife Major

Capt. F. Davenport's Detached Company, Lieut. Col. J. Dudley's Regiment.
From Sept. 13 to Nov. 7, 1814.   Raised at Milton and vicinity.   Service at South Boston.

RANK AND NAME.
Francis Davenport, Captain
Robert S. Davis, Lieutenant
Asa Porter, Lieutenant
John C. Merriam, Lieutenant

Jason N. Houghton, Sergeant
Nathaniel Dinsmore, Sergeant
David Rice, Sergeant
Hopestill Willis, Sergeant
John Hobbs, Sergeant
Jesse Crane, Corporal
Cromwell Gibbs, Corporal
Samuel H. Boynton, Corporal
Emery Barnard, Corporal
John M. Hunt, Corporal
Timothy Bancroft, Musician
Moses Copeland, Musician
Joseph Alexander, Musician

Privates.
Alexander, John
Ayres, Joseph
Badger, Jonathan
Bancroft, Timothy
Billings, Ebenezer
Blanden, John
Blodgett, Enos
Bond, Phineas
Brick, Levi
Brick, Lewis
Cain, Edward
Chamberlain, Enoch
Cleverly, Ebenezer
Copeland, Moses

Crocker, John
Crossman, Benjamin
Cushing, David L.
Dedman, Jeduthan
Drury, Nathan
Eaton, Ebenezer
Emerson, William
Fairbanks, Pliney
Fay, John
Fowle, Joseph
French, Ebenezer
Gardner, Josiah
Garfield, Cooper
Gault, Benjamin
Gilchrist, Joseph
Green, Luther
Green, Thomas
Harrington, Charles
Harrington, William B.
Hayden, Artemas
Hayward, James
Heald, Thomas
Hollis, Ebenezer
Holton, Asaph
Hosmer, David
Hunt, Enoch
Hunt, John M.
Hunt, Thomas
Hunt, William
Jeffers, William
Jenkins, Charles
Jenkins, Noble
Kelly, John O.
Kenney, Edward
Lenant, William

Lincoln, Jaras
Lincoln, Nehemiah
Mann, Jacob
Marshall, Josiah
McDonald, Michael
McIntire, James
Merriam, Jacob P.
Morse, Samuel
Newton, Luther
Nichols, Jesse
Osborn, Luther
Pierce, Lambert
Pond, Moses
Prescott, Abel
Reed, Elisha
Richardson, Loammi
Richardson, Peter
Russell, Sylvanus
Shaw, John
Spooner, Abner
Stone, Samuel
Talbot, Joel
Thorning, Isaac
Turner, Fobes
Turner, Seth
Tyler, Richard
Underwood, Arad
Vial, James
Washburn, Eliab
Williamson, Calvin
Wilson, Charles
Wood, Edward
Wood, Jesse

Capt. N. Hastings' Company, Lieut. Col. J. Dudley's Regiment.
From Sept. 13 to Nov. 7, 1814.   Raised at Newton and vicinity.   Service at South Boston.

RANK AND NAME.
Nathan Hastings, Captain
John H. Reed, Lieutenant
Nathaniel Greggs, Lieutenant
Alvis Gearfield, Ensign
Joseph S. Waterman, Ensign
Samuel Davis, Ensign

John Cassell, Sergeant
William Hansell, Sergeant
Thomas Gookin, Sergeant
Edward Barrington, Sergeant
James S. Oliver, Sergeant
George Acres, Corporal
Joel B. Patten, Corporal
John Hunt, Corporal
James Armstrong, Corporal
William Stephenson, Corporal
Joshua Hatch, Musician
Samuel Lord, Musician
Jeremiah Kahler, Musician

Privates.
Abbott, William
Acres, Thomas
Ayres, Francis
Balch, William
Baldwin, Cyrus
Barnes, John
Barrill, Bill
Blake, Nathaniel
Bowker, Charles
Bradburn, Peter
Bright, Jonathan
Brown, John
Brown, William
Burchsted, John
Butler, Amos
Cheaver, John
Churchill, Joseph
Clapp, Artemus
Clark, Thomas B.
Clowes, Philip

Coffin, Charles
Complete, Dennis
Curtis, John
Damerell, Samuel S.
Damond, Josiah
David, James
Dean, Simeon
Everett, William
Ewing, Thomas A.
Fellows, Benjamin
Fenno, John
Flinn, John
French, Joseph
Hall, Benjamin
Harden, Charles
Harlow, Zacheus
Harrington, Wyman
Hayward, Independent
Hill, Ira
Holden, Ebenezer
Holland, John

Capt. N. Hastings' Company, Lieut. Col. J. Dudley's Regiment — Concluded.

Privates — Concluded.
Holland, John G.
Holland, William
Howe, Henry
Hurley, James
Jewett, Joseph
Johnson, John
Jones, David
Jorden, John
Mann, Thomas
Martin, Ezekiel
Merritt, Joshua
Miller, B. V. H.
Nelson, David
Norcross, Nathaniel
Parker, Eber

Parson, William
Peters, Horace
Peterson, John
Porter, Josiah
Sawyer, John
Smith, Andrew
Steele, Ephraim B.
Stephens, Hilton
Stevens, Thomas
Stowell, Isaiah
Tallman, William T.
Thomas, John
Tilden, Christopher
Tower, Benjamin C.
Tower, Jonas
Trueman, Samuel

Tucker, Chandler
Vincent, Joseph
Vose, William
Wait, Oliver
Ware, Thomas
Welch, John A.
White, Samuel
Wilcoat, Joseph
Williams, Joshua H.
Willis, Abial
Williston, James
Winston, John
Wiswell, Thomas
Woodfellow, James

Capt. M. L. Humphrey's Detached Company, Lieut. Col. J. Dudley's Regiment.

From Sept. 13 to Nov. 7, 1814. Raised at Hingham and vicinity. Service at South Boston.

RANK AND NAME.
Moses L. Humphrey, Captain
Alpheus M. Withington, Lieutenant
Thomas Griggs, Ensign

Ralph Houghton, Sergeant
John Benjamin, Sergeant
Josiah Babcock, Sergeant
Lot Stoddard, Sergeant
Laban Pratt, Sergeant
Thomas Stoddard, Sergeant
Nathaniel Wilder, Corporal
James B. Gill, Corporal
Benjamin Redman, Corporal
Benjamin Vinning, Corporal
Levi Chubbuck, Musician
Joseph Jordan, Musician

Privates.
Abbott, James
Airs, Jonathan S.
Atwood, William
Ayer, Joseph W.
Blake, Thomas
Blanchard, Nehemiah
Cheney, William
Clapp, John
Colburn, David
Colburn, William
Crehore, Lewis
Crossman, Abner
Cushing, Eleazer
Dove, George
Farnsworth, Thomas
Foster, Rufus
France, Stephen
Garden, Alpheus

Gardner, Anthony
Gening, Nathaniel
Gennerson, Samuel
Graves, John
Harding, Thomas
Hay, William
Herron, James
Hersey, Ebenezer
Howe, Thomas
Humphreys, Leavitt
Hunter, Ely
Jackson, Amasa
Johnson, Gerah
Johnson, Moses
Jones, Thomas
Joy, David
Keyes, Lewis
Kingman, Abner
Kingman, Asa
Knight, James
Landers, William
Lawrence, Isaac
Leavitt, Charles
Lincoln, Cornelius
Loring, Joshua
Lucas, Ephraim
Mace, John
Macuen, John
Marsh, William
Mason, Jabez
Masting, Edward
Masting, Richard
May, David
Merryfield, Arnold
Nutting, Buckley
Orcutt, Samuel
Otis, William

Percival, James
Pierce, Elijah
Pratt, Enoch
Pratt, Herriman
Reed, David
Reed, Isaac
Richards, Jacob
Richards, Jesse
Riley, David
Sanborn, David
Sparrowhawk, Charles
Stebbins, Timothy
Stoddard, Ichabod
Stoddard, Samuel
Stoddard, William
Sturdivant, Joshua
Sweet, Mark P.
Talbot, Nathaniel
Thayer, Bela
Thomas, John
Thompson, Samuel
Tower, Benjamin
Towns, John
Townsend, Samuel
Trumbull, Peter
Vose, John
Ward, John
Western, Henry
Whitney, James
Whitney, John
Whittemore, Amos
Wilkins, James C.
Williams, Noah
Williams, Tillson
Woodard, James

Capt. E. Kingman's Company, Lieut. Col. J. Dudley's Regiment.

From Sept. 13 to Nov. 7, 1814. Service at South Boston.

RANK AND NAME.
Edward Kingman, Captain
Jeduthan Tabor, Lieutenant

Henry Huttlestone, Sergeant
Nathaniel Rand, Sergeant
George Peck, Sergeant
Robert Robinson, Sergeant
Mark A. Johnson, Corporal
George Willis, Corporal
Turner Gilmore, Corporal
Gilbert French, Corporal
Martin Allen, Musician
John Dunham, Musician

Privates.
Beard, Stephen
Briggs, Peter
Carpenter, James
Carter, Dennis M.
Caswell, Noah
Cole, Joseph

Cook, John W.
Edson, Benjamin
Eldredge, Joseph
Elliott, Nathaniel
Evans, William
Forrester, John
Goof, Squier
Harding, Rufus
Harvey, James
Harvey, James, 2d
Haskell, Nathaniel
Haskell, Nathaniel, 2d
Hathaway, Anson
Hathaway, Enos
Hathaway, Gideon
Hathaway, Gideon, 2d
Ingalls, Royal
Lake, George
Lawton, Robert
Leonard, Elijah
Lincoln, John
Loring, Samuel

Lovell, Samuel
Macumber, O.
Mason, William C.
McFarlin, Elijah
Nickerson, Michel
Ormsby, George
Paine, Leonard
Perry, Caleb E.
Perry, Jabez
Phillips, Samuel
Read, Samuel
Richmond, John C.
Sampson, Philip
Sekins, Ezekiel
Snow, Ephraim
Sprague, James
Tabor, Lloyd
White, Eliot
Wilber, Jonathan
Williams, Silas
Wiswell, James

Capt. W. Knight's Company, Lieut. Col. J. Dudley's Regiment.

From Sept. 13 to Nov. 7, 1814. Raised at Boston and vicinity. Service at South Boston.

RANK AND NAME.
Wentworth Knight, Captain
Bela Hunting, Lieutenant
Castalio Hosmer, Ensign
David Moody, Ensign

Joseph Brown, Sergeant
Gardner Fletcher, Sergeant
Thomas Richardson, Sergeant
Eliphalet Weston, Sergeant
William Bell, Sergeant
Ebenezer Tirrell, Sergeant
Eli Chase, Sergeant
George Leighton, Corporal
Orin B. Sexton, Corporal
Harvey Crosby, Corporal
William Eaton, Corporal
Daniel Proctor, Corporal
Enos Lake, Musician
Ephraim Richardson, Musician
Cyrus Willis, Musician

Privates.
Abbott, Joshua
Angier, John
Austin, William
Babcock, Abel
Blodgett, Jacob
Boutwell, Sewall
Bowman, Samuel

Bradley, Caleb
Brooks, Barker
Burgess, William
Butterfield, Joseph
Carter, Enoch
Chubbuck, Henry
Colburn, Prescott
Cole, John
Cooley, John S.
Cutler, Leonard
Dean, Thomas
Deverall, Samuel
Dudley, Silas
Duren, John
Emerson, Ebenezer
Fossitt, Amaziah
Foster, Cyrus
Foster, Enoch
Fowle, Isaac
French, Nehemiah
Gibson, Isaac
Heath, Joshua
Holden, James
Hosmer, Nathaniel
Howard, Calvin
Howard, Johnson
Hunt, Sherabish
Jenkins, Solon
Johnson, Abel
Jones, Ephraim

Jones, James
Kittredge, Nahum
Lamb, William
Lincoln, Henry
Martin, Charles
McAlvin, William
Mears, Zebediah
Moore, John
Newton, Edward
Nichols, John
Pike, Moses F.
Pratt, Joseph
Reed, Isaac
Reed, Lott
Rex, John
Rich, Obediah
Richardson, Bodwell
Robbins, Henry
Siders, Martin
Smith, John
Somes, John G.
Sprague, Samuel
Stearns, Moses
Stevens, James
Upton, Reuben
White, George
Whittier, Peter
Winnick, William B.
Woods, Daniel
Worcester, Eldad

Capt. T. Munroe's Detached Company, Lieut. Col. J. Dudley's Regiment.
From Sept. 13 to Nov. 7, 1814. Raised at Dorchester and vicinity. Service at South Boston.

RANK AND NAME.
Thomas Munroe, Captain
Thomas Cheney, Lieutenant
Joseph Sanger, Lieutenant
Ebenezer Abbott, Ensign
John Fowle, Clerk

Samuel Savil, Sergeant
Samuel Newcomb, Sergeant
Benjamin Stone, Sergeant
Benjamin Dimond, Sergeant
James Taggart, Corporal
Charles Hersey, Corporal
Thomas R. Shepherd, Corporal
Isaac Wadsworth, Corporal
Garnet Hollis, Corporal
John Ward, Musician
John Vinton, Musician

Privates.
Alden, Hosea
Baggs, David
Bailey, John
Bates, Phineas
Beal, George
Billings, Nathaniel
Blanchard, Thomas
Briggs, Abner
Burrill, Robert
Churchill, Jesse
Clark, Shubal
Cushing, Adam
Cushing, Allen
Cushing, Ensign
Cushing, John

Cushing, John, 2d
Daniels, Isaac
Derby, Martin
Dunbar, Peleg
Dyer, Stephen
Field, Ebenezer
Gardner, Constant
Gardner, Perez
Gardner, Quincy
Hall, Judah
Hayden, Elijah
Hayden, Luther
Hayward, Samuel
Hicks, John
Hill, Jonathan
Holbrook, Dan
Holbrook, Elisha
Holbrook, James
Holbrook, William
Holbrook, Zadoc
Hooker, William
Hubbard, Benjamin
Hubbard, Silas N.
Hubbard, Thomas
Humphrey, Stephen
Hunt, Samuel
Leonard, Solomon
Lincoln, Zenas
Littleton, John
Loud, Alexander
Loud, Daniel
Loud, Eben
Loud, Perez
Lovell, Colton or Cotton
Mann, Joseph

Mcheren, Allen
Morey, Silas
Neal, John
Newcomb, Briant
Newcomb, Francis
Nichols, Isaac
Pratt, Aaron
Pratt, Caleb
Pratt, Gideon
Pratt, Mather
Pray, George
Prouty, Samuel
Reed, William
Richardson, Joshua
Sampson, Isaac
Simmons, Reuben
Souther, Asa
Souther, Nathan
Spear, Isaac
Sprague, Amos
Stoddard, Levi
Stowell, Eliakim
Sylvester, John
Thayer, David
Thayer, Job
Thayer, Randall
Tower, Alexander
Turrell, Kingman
Vinal, John
Wade, John
Whidden, Daniel
White, James
Wild, Elijah
Wise, William
Witherell, Joshua

Capt. S. Tolman's Detached Company, Lieut. Col. J. Dudley's Regiment.
From Sept. 13 to Nov. 7, 1814. Raised at Dorchester and vicinity. Service at South Boston. This company also appears under Lieut. Col. J. Page's regiment serving at Fort Warren, Boston harbor, under above dates.

RANK AND NAME.
Stephen Tolman, Captain
Ebenezer Humphrey, Lieutenant
L. Parker, Lieutenant
Newcomb Bates, Ensign

James Foster, Sergeant
Joseph Richards, Sergeant
Elias Holbrook, Sergeant
Joseph Battles, Sergeant
Bethuel Reed, Sergeant
Enos Tolman, Corporal
Jonathan Hamlet, Corporal
Ezra Swallow, Corporal
Jonas Hartwell, Corporal
Thomas Johnson, Corporal
Hosea Dunbar, Musician
Isaac Beal, Musician

Privates.
Adams, Casner
Allen, Tilly

Aubray, Benjamin
Bacon, Henry
Bailey, Henry
Barry, William
Barter, George
Belcher, Eliphalet
Belcher, Jeremiah
Bishop, James
Blackman, Jacob
Blanchard, Samuel
Bond, Thomas
Boxworth, Elijah
Bradshaw, Jesse
Briggs, James
Brocklebank, John
Callahan, Joseph
Chamberlain, Amos
Chamberlain, Obediah
Chamberlain, Stephen
Childs, Robert P.
Clark, Abner
Clary, Moses

Clay, Enoch
Codding, Josiah
Cook, James
Crane, Richard
Crosby, John
Dewing, Warren
Eddy, Sylvanus
Eddy, Zenas B.
Field, John
French, Reuben
Garland, Hiram R.
Green, Oliver
Hagar, Samuel
Hayden, Peter
Holbrook, Caleb
Hollis, Thomas
Hovey, Samuel
Hunting, Jabez F.
Hutchings, William
Lines, John
Lock, Benjamin B.
Lovell, James

Capt. S. Tolman's Detached Company, Lieut. Col. J. Dudley's Regiment — Concluded.

Privates — Concluded.
Magoon, James
Main, David
Marshall, Moses
Mastins, Joseph
McIntosh, Thomas
Minott, George
Muncy, Edward
Nightingale, Asa
Obrine, John
Orcutt, Micah
Packard, Buel
Packard, Othenial
Page, Charles

Paine, Barney
Paine, Samuel
Pender, Isaac
Perry, John
Pierce, Robert
Pierce, Thomas H.
Pinkham, Otis
Porter, Elijah
Reed, Seth
Roberts, Samuel
Salisbury, Abijah
Shumway, Ellis
Simmons, George
Stockbridge, Thomas

Tinkham, Ephraim
Tolman, Edward
Tolman, Elijah
Vinall, Simeon
Wheeler, Abraham
White, David
White, Nathaniel
Whitney, Stephen
Whittington, Samuel
Wild, Joseph
Williams, Samuel
Wood, Barnabus
Woodcock, Timothy

Lieut. J. Dyer's Detachment, Lieut. Col. J. Dudley's Regiment.
From Sept. 13 to Oct. 7, 1814. Raised at Hingham and vicinity. Service at South Boston.

RANK AND NAME.
James Dyer, Lieutenant

Micah Nash, Sergeant
Leonard Nash, Corporal
Joshua Curtis, Musician

Privates.
Bates, Jacob
Foster, Samuel
Joy, Cyrus
Leach, Eliphalet
Lowd, Nathaniel
Nash, Elias

Noyes, Merrit
Pool, William
Porter, Samuel
Pratt, Solomon
Shaw, Brackley
Stoddard, Jesse
Whiting, Ansel

Lieut. Col. Enos Foot's Regiment.
From Sept. 10 to Nov. 7, 1814. Service at Boston and vicinity.

FIELD AND STAFF.
Enos Foot, Lieutenant Colonel, Southwick
John Hoar, Major, Monson
David Mack, Jr., Major, Middlefield
Giles C. Kellog, Adjutant, Hadley
Edward Morris, Quartermaster, Wilbraham

Benjamin Stebbins, Paymaster, West Springfield
Otis Goodman, Surgeon, South Hadley
Reuben Champion, Surgeon Mate, West Springfield
Joshua Crosby, Chaplain, Greenwich

NONCOMMISSIONED STAFF.
Daniel Frost, Sergeant Major
O. Spelman, Quartermaster Sergeant
John Olds, Drum Major
Lemuel Gardner, Fife Major
John B. Cooley, Sergeant

Capt. J. Carew's Company, Lieut. Col. Enos Foot's Regiment.
From Sept. 10 to Nov. 7, 1814. Raised at Springfield. Service at Boston.

RANK AND NAME.
Joseph Carew, Captain
Ebenezer Russell, Lieutenant
David Chandler, Ensign

Owen Taylor, Sergeant
Olden Chapin, Sergeant
James Bennett, Sergeant
Theodore Chapin, Sergeant
Jesse Bellows, Corporal
Jacob Bliss, Corporal
Kenslow Ainsworth, Corporal
Jacob Cooley, Corporal
Otis Smith, Musician
Caleb Cooley, Musician

Privates.
Abbey, Abner
Baily, Adolphus
Bates, William
Beseley, Edward S.
Boman, Ransom
Booth, Elijah
Brainerd, Austin
Brainerd, Hosea
Burt, Francis
Cadwell, Stephen, Jr.
Chaffer, Alvin
Chapin, Aaron
Chapin, Asaph
Chapin, Isaac
Chapin, Quartus

Chapman, Elijah
Davis, Abel
Day, Porter
Dewey, Charles
Eaton, Justice
Eldredge, Freeman
Frink, Ichabod
Gardner, Lemuel
Gates, Saul
Grandey, Eri
Hanchet, Frederic
Hitchcock, Eleazer
Howard, John
Ingraham, Artemas
Jones, Solomon
Kellog, Hawley

Capt. J. Carew's Company, Lieut. Col. Enos Foot's Regiment — Concluded.

Privates — Concluded.
Kentfield, Smith
Kirkland, Ichabod, Jr.
Knight, Samuel
Lloyd, Peter
Lucas, George W.
Lyman, Joel M.
McNelly, Elijah
Mirrick, Jacob B.
Moody, Spencer

Morgan, Chancy
Morgan, Saul H.
Pease, Charles
Pilgrim, Israel
Pratt, Noah
Runville, Alexander
Sellars, John
Shaw, Walter
Smith, Amerith
Squires, Zebina

Talmage, Calvin
Tarbox, Adriel
Taylor, Levi E.
Taylor, Noah
Trask, John
Warriner, Warren
Webster, Owen
Wells, Otis
Winchester, Alden
Work, Stephen

Capt. H. Day's Company, Lieut. Col. Enos Foot's Regiment.
From Sept. 10 to Nov. 7, 1814. Raised at Springfield and vicinity. Service at Boston.

RANK AND NAME.
Hosea Day, Captain
Festus Cooley, Lieutenant
Amasa Smith, Ensign

Theodore Worthington, Sergeant
Joel Day, Sergeant
Ephraim Avery, Sergeant
William S. Bow, Sergeant
Joel Worthington, Corporal
George Phelps, Corporal
Eli Ball, Corporal
Thaddeus Warner, Corporal
Alfred Day, Musician
Jesse Whitman, Musician

Privates.
Ainsworth, Luther
Allen, Benjamin J.
Alvord, Sewall
Ball, Francis
Barnes, Harvey
Barnes, Nathan
Barton, Samuel
Bates, Sylvester
Bomphroy, Lewis

Bosworth, Elisha
Bosworth, Zadock
Boyd, Elisha
Brackett, Joshua
Brownson, William A.
Colley, Roger
Cook, James
Cooley, Charles
Danks, Eliakim
Davis, Amos
Day, Horace
Dunlap, Alexander
Ellis, John, Jr.
Ely, Henry
Ely, Osly
Farnham, Warren
Flower, Horner
Gillet, Cephas
Gorum, Charles
Hains, Daniel
Howard, Amasa
Kent, Gains
Knapp, Russel
Lad, John, Jr.
Lad, Nathan
Leonard, Juber, Jr.

Liswell, Thomas, Jr.
Meachum, Salalan
Miller, Hosea
Morley, Horatio
Munger, Daniel, Jr.
Newcomb, Lucius
Noble, Reuben
Norton, Simeon, Jr.
Olds, Zardeus
Pepper, Phiney
Prentice, Loammi
Prout, Harris
Richardson, Charles
Roberts, Joseph A.
Searl, Jerry
Shattuck, Jacob W.
Smith, Michel
Squire, Abel
Squire, Peter
St. John, Caleb
Underwood, Levi
Vanhorn, Harvey
Worthington, Ransford
Wright, Sylvester

Capt. I. Fuller's Company, Lieut. Col. Enos Foot's Regiment.
From Sept. 10 to Nov. 7, 1814. Raised at Monson and vicinity. Service at Boston.

RANK AND NAME.
Isaac Fuller, Captain
Abner Brown, Lieutenant
Robert Sessions, Ensign

Julius Ward, Sergeant
Erastus Lumbard, Sergeant
David H. Childs, Sergeant
Erastus Darley, Sergeant

Privates.
Allen, Lemuel
Allen, Sanders
Alvord, Luther
Barrows, William
Benchard, Seneca B.

Bennet, Calvin
Bennet, Eben
Bennett, Ralph R.
Blodget, William
Bradish, Henry
Bradway, William, 2d
Brown, Abner
Brown, James
Bunt, Sabin
Butler, Ebenezer
Butterworth, Shubal
Chaffer, Freeborn M.
Collins, Saniar
Cone, Mathew H.
Cooley, Aretus
Cooley, Asher

Cross, Lyman
Dangy, Martin
Dunbar, John
Ellingwood, Chester
English, Aaron
Fay, William
Fetton or Felton, Oliver
Gardner, Timothy
Hall, Bryant
Harvey, George
Hayrus, Jonathan
Hitchcock, Eaton
Lewis, Edward
Lumbard, Abiram
Lumbard, Lyman
Mexton, Daniel, Jr.

Capt. I. Fuller's Company, Lieut. Col. Enos Foot's Regiment.

Privates — Concluded.
Micholds, Zadock
Moore, John, 3d
Moulton, Abel
Moulton, Abiel
Moulton, Mace
Nichols, Daniel S.
Nichols, Joshua
Persons, Quartus
Reed, Jason

Richardson, Lewis
Rider, Elisha
Russell, Charles
Sherman, Joseph, Jr.
Smith, Martin
Squire, Charles, Jr.
Squire, John
Squire, Solomon, Jr.
Squire, William
Stacy, Alfred

Stanton, Palmer
Stebbins, Abiel
Stebbins, Erasmus
Stebbins, James
Switcher, Timothy
Thayne, Luther
Tupper, Spencer
Williams, Joshua
Wiswell, David

Capt. G. Gilbert's Company, Lieut. Col. Enos Foot's Regiment.

From Sept. 10 to Nov. 7, 1814. Raised at Belchertown and vicinity. Service at Boston.

RANK AND NAME.
George Gilbert, Captain
Thomas Field, Lieutenant
Samuel Rich, Ensign

Jonathan Olds, Sergeant
Joseph Winter, Sergeant
Ralph Morgan, Sergeant
Whitney Richardson, Sergeant
Sear Blackner, Corporal
Austin Ames, Corporal
Roswell Knowlton, Corporal
Noah Dyer Hubbard, Corporal
John Conkey, Musician

Privates.
Adams, Ichabod
Allen, Samuel
Alvord, Alvin
Arnold, Lewis
Ayers, Calvin
Barnaby, Nathan, Jr.
Bartlet, Alexander
Bartlett, Alva
Barton, Augustus
Boutwell, Levi
Chapin, James

Church, Jonathan
Clark, Eliphalet
Clark, Selah
Conant, Josiah
Currier, Samuel
Davis, Aaron
Davis, John
Davis, Rodney
Dunbar, Josiah, Jr.
Eastman, Peter
Elder, John
Eveleth, Asa
Fisher, Salem
Folk, Abraham
Forbes, Henry
Ford, Packard
Ford, Seth H.
Gray, Chester
Hamilton, Silas
Hannum, Sydney
Harwood, Benjamin B.
Hubbard, Elijah
Hunt, John
Jenks, Jeremiah
Kentfield, Elias
Kidder, Elkanah
Lathrop, Erastus

Marsh, Lemuel
Marsh, Moses
Moody, Enos, Jr.
Paine, Levi
Pepper, Abner
Phelps, Benjamin, Jr.
Phelps, Simeon
Randall, Lewis
Renmow, Thomas
Rice, Ransom
Rider, John
Shearer, Pierce
Smith, James, Jr.
Soal, Asa
Spring, John
Sprout, Ezra
Squire, Thomas
Stephenson, David
Taylor, Lucius
Titus, Horatio
Town, Solomon
Wheeler, Solomon
White, Saul
Whitney, Elisha
Willis, John
Wilson, Francis
Wright, Elan

Capt. W. Marvin's Company, Lieut. Col. Enos Foot's Regiment.

From Sept. 10 to Nov. 7, 1814. Raised at Granville and vicinity. Service at Boston.

RANK AND NAME.
William Marvin, Captain
Mathew Smith, Lieutenant
Saul Lyman, Ensign

Solomon Root, Sergeant
Samuel Pomroy, Sergeant
Salmon Belding, Sergeant
George W. Granger, Sergeant
Jeremiah S. Grove, Corporal
Simon Stewart, Corporal
James H. Birchard, Corporal
Charles Slayton, Corporal
George Taylor, Musician
Alpheus Bancroft, Musician
Morgan Deny, Musician

Privates.
Barlow, Heman
Barnes, Ebenezer
Bates, Phineas B.
Beach, Geriel
Booth, Elisha
Chandler, Samuel
Cheeseman, Abel
Cheeseman, Saul
Clampton, Samuel
Clark, Ralph C.
Cook, Russell
Darling, William
Day, Jacob
Dickson, Caleb W.
Durant, Clark

Elsworth, Hezekiah
Gilbert, Warren
Graves, Issacher
Hall, Elijah
Haskins, Elijah
Henry, Samuel
Hitchcock, Ebenezer M.
Meacham, Philip
Moore, Asa
Muffit, Abraham
Northway, Friend
Nott, Oliver
Parsons, John
Pheland, Gad
Pratt, Silas
Robinson, Chancy

Capt. W. Marvin's Company, Lieut. Col. Enos Foot's Regiment — Concluded.

Privates — Concluded.
Rogers, Joshua
Ronney, Sewall
Rose, Calvin
Rose, Christopher
Sanderson, Saul
Seagar, Charles H.
Skinner, John
Slocum, Charles C.

Smith, Abner
Smith, Anson
Smith, George
Smith, Jesse
Smith, Russell
Spelman, Lyman
Stedman, Edward P.
Still, Roger
Stone, Harvey

Taylor, William
Tillotson, Samuel
Waite, Thomas
Ward, Artemas
West, Lloyd
Witt, William
Wright, Erastus
Wright, William

Capt. A. G. Phelps' Company, Lieut. Col. Enos Foot's Regiment.
From Sept. 10 to Nov. 7, 1814.   Raised at Westfield.   Service at Boston.

RANK AND NAME.
Aaron G. Phelps, Captain
Nathan Morse, Lieutenant
Henry Tracy, Ensign

Royal Fowler, Sergeant
Abram Rising, Jr., Sergeant
Noah Bartlett, Sergeant
Logan Crosby, Sergeant
Robert Frazer, Corporal
Charles Parks, Corporal
Harvey Bosworth, Corporal
Ralph Dewey, Corporal
Amos Webster, Musician
Austin Stocking, Musician

Privates.
Allen, Alexander
Allen, Ziba
Bath, Daniel
Bath, Edmund
Blogett, Benjamin
Bond, Lucius
Brackett, John, Jr.
Brown, William
Brush, James, 2d
Buckmond, Jacob

Caldwell, Timothy
Carrington, John
Carter, Harry
Chapman, Asa
Chapman, Caleb
Chesbrock, Elihu
Clapp, Robert
Clark, Phiney
Clark, Roswell
Cooley, Festus
Corrin, Elijah
Cushman, Simeon M.
Danks, Ruel
Dewey, Paul
Dibble, Daniel, Jr.
Egleston, Eli
Field, Thomas, Jr.
Hayden, Jacob
Herrington, Asa
Hitchcock, Chancy
Holcomb, Edmund
Hombs, Lymond
Hubbard, Allen
Johnson, William
Leonard, Alanson
Lord, Samuel
Lownsbury, Benjamin

Morley, John
Noble, Alva
Noble, David
Noble, Edmund
Noble, Hezekiah
Olds, Moses, Jr.
Owen, Elijah
Parmer, Joseph
Quiles, Isaac
Richmond, John
Rowlen, Luther
Sacket, Israel
Shepherd, Theodore
Sikes, James
Smith, Joab
Stebbins, Asa
Stebbins, Obed W.
Steen, Elisha
Stephen, Jesse
Stephens, Solomon
Streeter, Kellog
Terry, Edmund S.
Upton, Sturgis
Ward, Simeon
Warfield, Horace
Williams, Saul

Capt. E. Scott's Company, Lieut. Col. Enos Foot's Regiment.
From Sept. 10 to Nov. 7, 1814.   Raised at Ware and vicinity.   Service at Boston.

RANK AND NAME.
Ephraim Scott, Captain
Joseph Shaw, Lieutenant
Ezekiel Boyden, Ensign

Allender Brackenridge, Sergeant
Jonathan Cooley, Jr., Sergeant
Evander Darby, Sergeant
Foster Marsh, Sergeant
Calvin Murray, Corporal
Heron Wright, Corporal
Phineas Converse, Musician
John Grant, Musician

Privates.
Abbey, Adolphus
Allen, Waters

Baldwin, King
Barton, Josiah
Boyden, Ozel
Carrier, Samuel
Cleveland, Benjamin
Collins, Sylvanus
Cutter, Eber
Cutting, Cyprian
Damon, Abel
Demon, Samuel, Jr.
Eaton, Darius
Eddy, Daniel
Eddy, Ira
Eddy, John
Fisk, Asa
Glazin, Perley
Graham, William

Harvey, Elijah, Jr.
Harwood, Andrew, Jr.
Hinckley, Stotham
Howlet, Sylvester
Kimball, Asa
Lake, Philip D.
Lamberton, James F.
Lamberton, Reuben
Lazell, Reuben
Levins, Charles
Lewis, Benjamin
Lumbard, Abial
Lumbard, David
Mason, William
May, Saul
Maynard, Jonathan
McIntosh, John

Capt. E. Scott's Company, Lieut. Col. Enos Foot's Regiment—Concluded.

Privates — Concluded.
Merrit, Isaac
Moulton, Perley
Needham, Abner
Needham, Jonathan
Nourse, Reuben
Osborn, Isaac
Osborn, Levi

Pratt, Ebenezer
Pratt, Jonathan
Richardson, Pliny
Richardson, Rufus
Ryder, Daniel
Sherman, Earl
Simmons, Joseph
Spear, William

Squire, Jesse
Stricklin, Emery
Thayer, Lyman
Thompson, Asa
Webber, Kimball
Woolcot, Lyman
Wright, Joel

Capt. J. Taylor's Company, Lieut. Col. Enos Foot's Regiment.
From Sept. 10 to Nov. 7, 1814. Raised at Pelham and vicinity. Service at Boston.

RANK AND NAME.
John Taylor, Captain
Enos Dickinson, Lieutenant
Abijah Dickinson, Ensign

Charles Billings, Sergeant
Chester Gray, Sergeant
Alpheus Osborn, Sergeant
Asa Brown, Sergeant
John A. Harris, Corporal
Luther Thompson, Corporal
Lyman Cutler, Corporal
Earl Wilds, Corporal
John Church, Musician
Horatio James, Musician

Privates.
Ayers, Lucius
Below, Leonard
Bennet, John
Billings, Christopher
Buckman, Arad
Conkey, John S.
Conkey, William
Cook, Asa
Cummings, Asa
Dana, Joseph

Davis, Levi
Dickinson, John, 3d
Dickinson, Jonathan
Dickinson, Leonard
Dillingham, Job
Eastman, Philip
Fisher, Loren
Goodall, Jacob
Goodall, Rufus
Gray, Patrick
Hannums, Gove
Hannums, Henry
Harlow, Lewis
Hawks, John
Hendrick, Stephen
Hooper, Gamaliel
Hubbard, Jonathan
Jannevar, George
Kellog, David
Kellogg, Joshua
Kenfield, Chester
Leach, Amasa
Lee, Ezra
Leonard, Watson
Lincoln, Luther
Marsh, Asa
Marsh, Joseph, 2d

Martin, Chester
Mason, William
McMaster, Henry
Newell, Reuben
Nobles, Walter
Packard, Elijah
Packard, Samuel
Parker, Saul
Pease, Lemuel
Pierce, Alden
Pike, Nathaniel
Prime or Prince, Saul
Randall, Elijah
Randol, Elisha
Root, Luther
Ruggles, Fordyce
Smith, James
Stanley, Samuel
Stockwell, Charles
Strong, Simeon
Thayer, Reuben
Turner, Jonathan
Wiley, Samuel
Wolcott, Francis
Wood, Alden
Wright, Gains
Wright, Saul

Capt. E. Goss' Detached Company of Mendon, Lieut. Col. W. Hasting's Regiment.
From Sept. 13 to Nov. 30, 1814. Service at Fort Warren.

RANK AND NAME.
Enos Goss, Captain
Asa Rogers, Lieutenant
Amasa Childs, Ensign
Isaac Wilkins, Ensign

Luther Davis, Sergeant
Artemas Prouty, Sergeant
—— Pond, Sergeant
Alexander White, Sergeant
Joseph Cook, Sergeant
Henry Lawrence, Sergeant
Jacob Whitney, Corporal
Lemuel Briggs, Corporal
Ebenezer Gears, Corporal
William Woodland, Corporal
Reuben Stoddard, Musician
Phinehas Barton, Musician

Privates.
Allen, Daniel
Allen, Otis
Amsden, David
Barton, Joseph
Battle, Ebenezer
Bowen, William C.
Briggs, Rufus
Brigham, Lambert
Brooks, Ebenezer
Brooks, Joseph
Brown, John
Brown, Rufus
Brown, William
Chittenden, Israel
Clemens, Luther
Cochran, James
Damon, George

Darling, John
Darling, Zelick
Davenport, Daniel
Dexter, Nathan
Doney, Benjamin
Elliot, Dummerston
Elwell, Thomas
Fish, Charles, Jr.
Flagg, Luke
Gage, Philip
Geer, Ebenezer
Gilman, James
Glazier, Reuben
Grinnell, Isaac
Hamilton, Squire
Hawes, Caleb
Hayward, John

Capt. E. Goss' Detached Company of Mendon, Lieut. Col. W. Hasting's Regiment—Concluded.

Privates — Concluded.

Holbrook, Otis
Holman, Richard
Holman, Samuel
Hunt, Horace
Keyes, Elisha
King, Samuel
Knight, George
Mann, Levi
McIntire, Jonathan
Meads, Freeman
Moores, Joseph A.
Murdock, Samuel
Newman, Ebenezer
Nichols, John, 3d
Parks, Artemas
Perry, Jeduthan

Pierce, William
Pond, Jeremiah
Prentice, George
Rawson, Allen
Rich, John
Russell, Job
Sawyer, John G.
Seaver, Joseph
Shepherd, Cheney
Shumway, Edward
Silsby, Phinehas
Smith, Phinehas
Smith, Sardius
Snow, Jonas
Staples, Charles
Stimpson, George
Stone, James

Stratton, Alpheus
Sweetser, Silas
Townsend, Henry
Tucker, Daniel
Tyler, Cutter
Walker, Orin H.
Walker, Samuel
Warner, Jonathan
Waters, Nathaniel
Wells, Albigence
Whalking, Jacob
White, Ancyl
White, Jeremiah
White, John
Wilson, Benjamin
Wood, John

Capt. Thomas Harrington's Roll of Detached Company of Shrewsbury and Vicinity, Lieut. Col. Walter Hasting's Regiment.

From Sept. 13 to Nov. 30, 1814.   Service at Fort Warren.

RANK AND NAME.
Thomas Harrington, Captain
Elisha Foster, Lieutenant
Thomas Hill, Ensign

Joshua N. Mellen, Sergeant
Joshua Sawyer, Sergeant
Rufus Ballou, Sergeant
Jonah Miles, Sergeant
Artemas Bowers, Corporal
John Bowers, Corporal
Reason Reed, Corporal
Jonah Goddard, Corporal
Stephen B. Brigham, Corporal
David Fisk, Musician
James Ball, Musician

Privates.
Boyden, Amos
Brewer, Abijah
Brewer, Henry
Brigham, Lovel
Brown, Charles
Bryant, Thomas
Butterfield, Stephen R.
Capron, Joshua
Carlton, Thomas
Chamberlain, Samuel J.
Chase, Daniel P.
Chickering, Oliver
Clark, Jason
Collis, Abel
Coolidge, Merrick
Cutler, Isaac
Davis, Abel
Davis, Oliver

Davis, Peter
Day, David
Dival, John, 3d
Duff, Royal
Dunster, Henry
Fenno, William
Flagg, Levi, Jr.
Furbush, Daniel
Gleason, Artemas
Goddard, Lyman
Gray, Abel
Hale, Otis
Hancock, William
Harrington, Emery
Harrington, Schuyler
Hart, Joseph
Hashley, Stephen S.
Haskell, Joseph
Hemenway, Martin
Holden, James
Houghton, Asa
Houghton, Millard
Houghton, Phinehas
Hunt, Frederic
Johnson, Joel or Jacob
Johnson, William
Kent, James
Lawrence, Millard
Leland, Lowell
Lincoln, Alanson
Mills, John
Moore, Henry
Murdock, Hollis
Murdock, James
Parker, Cyrus
Parks, Jesse

Partridge, Hiram
Partridge, Samuel
Perham, Hiram
Phelps, Asahiel
Polly, Amos
Polly, Jacob
Poore, Andrew
Priest, Libbeus
Randell, Edward
Reed, David
Rice, Loammi
Richardson, Thomas
Robbins, Jonathan
Robertson, James G.
Rogers, John
Sawtell, Henry
Sawyer, Jonas
Scott, Daniel
Sibley, Nathaniel
Simonds, Elijah
Small, Isaac
Spaulding, Maurice
Spring, Ephraim
Stowe, Samuel
Stowell, William E.
Taylor, Augustus
Taylor, Isaac
Tuttle, Simon
Vinica, Hiram
Wait, David
White, Amos
Whitman, William
Wiley, Samuel
Woodard, Jesse
Woods, John, Jr.

MASSACHUSETTS VOLUNTEER MILITIA IN THE WAR OF 1812.   49

Lieut. Col. C. Howard's Regiment.
From Sept. 2 to Oct 19, 1814.   Service at Plymouth.

FIELD AND STAFF.
Caleb Howard, Lieutenant Colonel, Bridgewater
Theodore Mitchell, Major, Bridgewater
Ephraim Ward, Major, Middleborough
Hector Orr, Adjutant, Bridgewater
Cyrus Keith, Adjutant, Middleborough

Jacob Dyer, Quartermaster, Abington
John Keith, Paymaster, Middleborough
James Thracker, Surgeon
James Kendall, Chaplain, Plymouth

NONCOMMISSIONED STAFF.
William Bonney, Sergeant Major
William Newhall, Quartermaster Sergeant

John Patty, Carpenter
Joshua Randall, Waiter

Capt. N. Edson's Company, Lieut. Col. C. Howard's Regiment.
From Sept. 20 to Oct. 12, 1814.   Raised at Bridgewater.   Service at Plymouth.

RANK AND NAME.
Nathaniel Edson, Captain
Nahum Leonard, Lieutenant
Ansel Hayward, Ensign

Benjamin B. Howard, Sergeant
Seth Keith, Sergeant
William Allen, Sergeant
Ansel Alger, Sergeant
Charles Howard, Corporal
Jonathan Copeland, Corporal
Simeon Taylor, Corporal
Apollos Randall, Corporal

Privates.
Alger, Howard
Ames, Charles
Bartlett, David
Briggs, Asa
Caldwell, Ebenezer
Caldwell, John

Churchill, Eleazer
Cook, Kingman
Copeland, Azel H.
Copeland, Charles
Dunbar, Charles
Dunbar, Martin
Edson, Jesse
Hartwell, Daniel
Hartwell, Daniel L.
Hayward, Jacob
Hayward, Luther
Haywood, Eli
Howard, David
Howard, Edward C.
Howard, Pliney
Howard, Sidney
Howard, Simeon
Howard, Ziba
Keith, Austin
Keith, Parden
Landis, Daniel W.

Lathrop, Beza
Orcutt, Gershom
Orcutt, Moses
Packard, Asa
Packard, Mayo
Packard, Samuel
Perkins, Edmund
Pool, John
Randall, Benjamin
Reed, Ezekiel
Snow, Charles
Snow, Daniel
Snow, David
Soule, John
Thayer, Abijah
Thayer, Earle
Wales, Nathaniel
Williams, Josiah
Williams, Perez
Willis, John
Willis, Martin

Capt. I. Keith's Company, Lieut. Col. C. Howard's Regiment.
From Sept. 20 to Oct. 15, 1814.   Raised at Bridgewater.   Service at Plymouth.

RANK AND NAME.
Isaac Keith, Captain
Waldo Ames, Lieutenant
Sylvester Keith, Ensign

Jared Pratt, Sergeant
Seth Leach, Sergeant
Thomas Whitmarsh, Sergeant
Jared Reed, Sergeant
Azor Howe, Corporal
Seth Gurney, Corporal
Joseph Chamberlin, Corporal
Ichabod Keith, Corporal

Privates.
Alden, Amasa
Alden, Ezra, 2d
Allen, Barziliel
Allen, Daniel
Ames, Nathaniel
Bates, Daniel
Beals, Asa

Bearce, Ford
Bellington, Nathaniel
Bisbee, Chandler
Blanchard, Eli
Brown, Emery
Brown, Isaac, Jr.
Chamberlin, Abija
Chamberlin, Louis
Conant, Andrew
Dunbar, Eliab
Dyer, Ezekiel
Eastburn, Peleg
Edson, Charles
Edson, Pliney
Fobes, Joshua, 2d
Gannet, Joseph
Hall, Barzilla
Hatch, Luther
Hathaway, Cushman
Hathaway, Seebra
Hobert, Joseph
Hooper, Simeon

Howard, Caleb
Howard, Lina
Hudson, Isaac
Hudson, Miles
Johnson, Lebina
Johnson, Sidney
Keith, Abner
Keith, Ephraim
Keith, Lewis
Keith, Oliver
Keith, Perez
Keith, Solomon
Keith, Zepheniah
Latham, D.
Lazell, Martin
Leach, Levi
Leach, Peleg
Mitchell, Simon W.
Parris, Orren
Parris, Thomas
Princin, William
Randall, Nathaniel

Capt. I. Keith's Company, Lieut. Col. C. Howard's Regiment — Concluded.

Privates — Concluded.
Rundell, Martin
Ruth, William, Jr.
Snell, Samuel
Standish, Miles
Sturdevant, Samuel

Stutson, Peleg
Washburn, Josiah
Waterman, Otis
Whitman, Nathan
Whitmarsh, Lot
Wilbur, Barrick

Wilbur, George
Wilbur, Isaac
Wiley, William
Willis, Daniel, Jr.
Wood, Philander

Capt. N. Lincoln's Company, Lieut. Col. C. Howard's Regiment.
From Sept. 20 to Oct. 16, 1814. Raised at Bridgewater. Service at Plymouth.

RANK AND NAME.
Nehemiah Lincoln, Captain
Ephraim Cole, Lieutenant
Silas Dunbar, Ensign

Gustavus Sylvester, Sergeant
Martin Kingman, Sergeant
Adam Packard, Sergeant
Simeon Dunbar, Sergeant
Daniel Packard, Corporal
Nathan Jones, Corporal
Jabez Kingman, Corporal
Galen Manly, Corporal

Privates.
Ames, Benjamin
Ames, John
Ames, Nathaniel
Ames, Theron
Battles, William
Brett, Lenos
Brett, Samuel
Bryant, Oliver
Bunnel, John
Carey, Lenos
Carey, Luther
Carey, Martin
Carey, Simeon
Cooley, Chester
Crocker, Ebenezer

Delano, John
Dickerman, Samuel
Dike, Bela C.
Dike, Samuel, Jr.
Drake, Martin
Dunbar, Simeon, 2d
Edson, Jonathan
Emes, Isaac
Field, John
Field, Waldo
French, Sylvanus
Glass, Charles
Hatch, James
Hayward, Ira
Hayward, Waldo
Howard, Austin
Howard, Cyrus
Howard, Gideon
Howard, Lewis
Howard, Oliver
Howard, Oliver, Jr.
Howard, Otis
Howard, Sidney
Jackson, Barnard
Kingman, Benjamin
Laning, James
Lincoln, Charles
Manly, Hayward
Manly, Solomon
May, John

Packard, Ambrose
Packard, David
Packard, David, 2d
Packard, Ezra
Packard, Galen
Packard, Hezekiah
Packard, Isaac
Packard, Jason
Packard, Jesse
Packard, Joseph S.
Packard, Lincoln
Packard, Luke
Packard, Sullivan
Phillips, Cyrus B.
Reynolds, Thomas
Shaw, N.
Smith, John
Snell, Jeremiah
Snell, Matthew
Snell, Oliver
Snow, Sprague
Sumner, Lemuel
Thomas, John
Warner, Simeon
Warren, Cyrus
Warren, Galen
White, Loring
Whiten, Isaac
Willis, Ephraim
Willis, James

Capt. J. Howe's Company, Lieut. Col. C. Howard's Regiment.
From Sept. 20 to Oct. 18, 1814. Service at Plymouth.

RANK AND NAME.
Joshua Howe, Captain
David Reed, Lieutenant
Benjamin King, Ensign

David Townsend, Sergeant
John Hunt, Sergeant
John Whiting, Sergeant
Spencer Gloyd, Sergeant
Robert Pratt, Corporal
Jacob Noyes, Corporal

Samuel Norton, Corporal
Joseph B. Smith, Corporal

Privates.
Brown, Daniel E.
Brown, Oak P.
Brown, Samuel N.
Burrill, Daniel
Erskine, Christopher
Gurney, Chandler R.
Humble, David

Nash, James
Norton, Benjamin, Jr.
Noyes, Alva
Noyes, Benjamin, Jr.
Pool, Daniel
Pool, William, Jr.
Reed, Abel
Shaw, Nathaniel
Vining, Ezra

MASSACHUSETTS VOLUNTEER MILITIA IN THE WAR OF 1812. 51

Capt. S. Washburn's Company, Lieut. Col. C. Howard's Regiment.
From Sept. 20 to Oct. 19, 1814. Raised at Bridgewater. Service at Plymouth.

RANK AND NAME.
Sears Washburn, Captain
Edward Southworth, Lieutenant
Shepherd Fales, Ensign

George Chipman, Sergeant
Abiel Rickman, Sergeant
Joseph Hooper, Sergeant
Jonah Benson, Sergeant
Caleb Bassett, Corporal
Elisha Richardson, Corporal
Joseph Hayward, Corporal
Lewis Harlow, Corporal
Elijah Pratt, Musician

Privates.
Alden, Oliver
Alden, Thomas
Andrews, Asaph
Bassett, Cyrus
Bassett, Jonathan
Bassett, Joseph
Bassett, Josiah
Bassett, Keith
Bassett, William
Benson, Cyrus
Benson, Jonathan
Benson, Nathan
Benson, Seth

Conant, Galand
Conant, Sylvanus
Copeland, Martin
Dyer, Daniel
Edson, Allen
Fobes, Alpheus
Fobes, Reed
French, Daniel
Fuller, William
Hall, Ebenezer
Hall, Reuben
Hall, Sylvanus
Harden, Jabez
Harden, Ward
Hayward, Calvin
Hayward, Edson
Hayward, Erastus
Hayward, Jeremiah
Hayward, Seth
Hayward, Tiba
Hill, Barnum
Hooper, Isaac
Jackson, John
Keith, Benjamin
Keith, Caleb
Keith, Orrin
Keith, Otis
Keith, Sylvanus
Leonard Ansel

Leonard, Charles F.
Leonard, Isam
Leonard, Samuel
Leonard, Seth
Leonard, Spencer
Leonard, William S.
Mitchell, Arthur
Mitchell, Caleb
Mitchell, Elisha
Mitchell, Jonathan
Packard, Pardon
Pierce, John
Pierce, Zadock
Pratt, Benjamin
Pratt, Nathan
Pratt, Seth
Richmond, James
Sanger, Samuel F.
Short, Samuel
Snell, Benjamin, Jr.
Sprague, Benjamin
Swift, Isaac
Swift, Ruel
Thompson, Abraham
Thomson, James
Washburn, Seth
Whitman, Daniel
Williams, George
Wintworth, Theophilus

Capt. N. Eddy's Company, Lieut. Col. C. Howard's Regiment.
From Sept. 21 to Oct. 12, 1814. Raised at Middleborough. Service at Plymouth.

RANK AND NAME.
Nathaniel Eddy, Captain
Croade Sturdevant, Lieutenant
John Trueman, Ensign

Simeon Wood, Sergeant
Micah Leonard, Sergeant
John Tinkham, Sergeant
Southworth Ellis, Sergeant
Isaac Soule, Corporal
William Cornish, Corporal
Bennet Briggs, Corporal
Samuel Bent, Corporal
Josiah Tinkham, Musician
Barnabus Eaton, Musician

Privates.
Atkinson, Samuel
Atwood, Francis
Atwood, Samuel
Baker, Joseph
Barrows, George
Bent, Zenos
Bosworth, Lewis
Briggs, S.
Bryant, Anchiel
Bryant, Isaac
Bryant, Levi
Bryant, Seth
Bumpus, Thomas
Burbank, Samuel

Burbank, Walter
Cobb, Otis
Cole, Freeman
Corrington, Jacob
Cushman, George
Donham, Daniel
Eaton, Ziba
Eddy, Ezra
Eddy, William S.
Everson, Timothy
Farmer, Joseph
Faunce, James
Freeman, Josiah
Fuller, John S.
Harlow, Ellis
Harlow, Josiah
Harlow, Stephen
King, Obed
Leonard, Samuel
Morse, Samuel
Norcutt, Ansell
Norcutt, Zebina
Pratt, Benjamin
Pratt, Zerubabel
Raymond, Levi
Reynolds, Joshua
Richmond, Allen
Robinson, Josiah
Shaw, Elijah
Shaw, Samuel
Shaw, Thomas

Sherman, Nathan
Soule, Ezra
Soule, Isaac
Soule, John, Jr.
Soule, Thomas
Soule, William
Standish, Joseph
Swift, Joseph
Thomas, Eliab
Thomas, Harvey C.
Thomas, Israel
Thomas, Jacob
Thomas, Jeremiah, Jr.
Thomas, Zenas
Tinkham, Asa
Tinkham, Ebenezer
Tinkham, Enos
Tinkham, George W.
Tinkham, Harvey
Tinkham, Levi
Tinkham, Sylvanus
Tucker, Nathan
Vaughan, Jabez
Warren, James
Washburn, Thomas
Weston, Daniel
Wood, Alba
Wood, Peter, Jr.
Wood, Ransom T.
Zall (?), Simon

Capt. J. LeBaron's Company, Lieut. Col. C. Howard's Regiment.
From Sept. 21 to Oct. 12, 1814. Raised at Middleborough. Service at Plymouth.

RANK AND NAME.
Joseph LeBaron, Captain
Gideon Haskins, Lieutenant
Jonathan Pierce, Ensign

Isaac Rider, Sergeant
James Cummins, Sergeant
Elisha T. Clark, Corporal
Ebenezer Smith, Corporal
John Benson, Corporal
Zenos Raymond, Corporal
William Shurtliff, Musician
Samuel Lovell, Musician

Privates.
Alden, Earl
Andrews, Zephaniah
Atwood, William
Barney, Jonathan
Bennett, Abraham
Benson, Ansel
Benson, Asa
Benson, Linus
Bishop, Zenos
Blackwell, Levi
Borden, Japtha
Bumpus, Samuel
Canady, Alexander
Carver, Josiah
Caswell, Benjamin
Caswell, Elijah
Caswell, Thomas

Chace, Benjamin
Crapo or Craps, Briggs
Edminster, John
Gammon, Ephraim
Gibbs, Andrew
Gibbs, Pelham E.
Griffith, Ellis
Hacket, George
Hall, Nathan
Hammond, John
Hammond, Shubal
Harlow, Benjamin
Haskell, Seth
Hatch, Samuel
Hathaway, Elijah
Hathaway, Noble E.
Holmes, Thomas
King, Isaac
LeBaron, Lazarus
LeBaron, Ziba
Macumber, Asa
Macumber, Joseph
Macumber, Josiah R.
Martin, Lindel
Miller, Loring
Musham, Caleb
Musham, Ebenezer
Musham, Joseph
Musham, Samuel
Parker, Joseph
Perry, Otis
Pierce, Eliphalet

Pierce, Elisha
Pierce, Freeman
Pierce, Gilbert
Pierce, Rowland
Pierce, Silas, 2d
Pratt, Elihu
Reddington, Joseph
Rider, Chapman
Rider, Robert
Rider, Samuel
Rider, Standish
Shaw, Benjamin
Shaw, John
Shaw, William
Sherman, Isaac
Sherman, Willis
Shurtliff, Abiel
Thomas, Andrew
Thomas, Eleazer
Thomas, Eliphalet
Thomas, Ephraim
Thomas, Lathrop
Thomas, Otis
Thomas, Perez
Thomas, Seneca
Thomas, William N.
Thomas, Winslow
Washburn, Roland
Wood, Harvey
Wood, Pelham
Wood, Thomas
Wood, Zenos

Capt. P. H. Pierce's Company, Lieut. Col. C. Howard's Regiment.
From Sept. 21 to Oct. 15, 1814. Raised at Middleborough. Service at Plymouth.

RANK AND NAME.
Peter H. Pierce, Captain
Luther Murdock, Lieutenant
Orren Tinkham, Ensign

Hercules Richmond, Sergeant
George Shaw, Sergeant
Enos Eaton, Sergeant
Ezra Wood, Sergeant
Daniel Hathaway, Corporal
Andrew Warren, Corporal
Abner Leonard, Corporal
Daniel Thomas, Corporal
Andrew Hopkins, Musician
Paddock Tinkham, Musician

Privates.
Alden, Rufus
Arms, Thomas C.
Atwood, Joshua
Bardon, Randolphus
Barrows, Sylvanus
Barrows, Thomas
Bennet, Jacob
Billington, Francis
Bosworth, Augustus
Bourne, East
Bourne, Leonard
Bump, Andrew
Bump, Josephus

Bump, Thomas
Bump, Warren
Burgess, Josiah D.
Caswell, George
Cole, James
Cole, Samuel
Cole, William
Doggett, Eliphalet
Dunham, Calvin
Ellis, George
Harlow, Ezra
Haskins, Levi
Howard, Abel
Keith, Cyrus
Keith, Israel
Kinsley, Unite
Leonard, Benjamin
Leonard, Gideon
Little, John William
Macumber, Gideon
Macumber, Nathaniel
McCully, Andrew
Nelson, Cyrus
Norcut, Daniel
Paddock, Joseph
Perkins, John C.
Perkins, Nathan
Pierce, Benajah
Pratt, Thomas

Reed, Nathan
Richmond, Elias
Richmond, William
Sears, Oliver S.
Shaw, Elisha
Southworth, Leonard
Southworth, Thomas
Thomas, Isaac
Thomas, Levi, 2d
Thomas, Walter
Tinkham, Caleb
Tinkham, Cornelius
Tinkham, John
Vaughan, Cushman
Vaughan, Daniel
Vaughan, Peter
Vaughan, Sylvanus
Waterman, Joseph
Weston, Daniel
Weston, Seth
White, Cyrus
Wilder, Beniah
Willis, William
Winslow, Edward
Wood, Ichabod, 2d
Wood, Jeremiah
Wood, Levi
Wood, Lorenzo
Wood, Sylvanus T.

Capt. G. Pratt's Company, Lieut. Col. C. Howard's Regiment.
From Sept. 21 to Oct. 15, 1814. Raised at Middleborough. Service at Plymouth.

RANK AND NAME.
Greenleaf Pratt, Captain
Ebenezer Vaughan, Ensign

Martin White, Sergeant
Benjamin Washburn, Sergeant
Malitiah H. Pearce, Sergeant
Anson Pearce, Sergeant
Henry Perkins, Corporal
Nathaniel Andrews, Corporal
Elias Parris, Corporal
John Clark, Corporal

Privates.
Alden, Daniel
Alden, Elijah, Jr.
Alden, Seth
Ashley, Luther
Baker, James
Baley, Winslow C.
Braley, Silas
Burgess, Stephen
Canady, Zebulon
Caswell, Nathaniel
Clark, Henry
Clark, Richard
Cole, Alden
Cole, Samuel
Coombs, Simeon
Drake, David

Drake, Enoch
Drake, Enos
Drake, William
Eaton, Alfred
Eaton, Barzilla
Eaton, Seth
Eaton, Solomon
Freeman, Stephen
Fuller, Elisha
Gifford, Jonah
Goodwin, Charles
Hammond, Elisha
Hathaway, Silas
Hawland, William
Hinds, Leonard
Hoar, Job, Jr.
Hoar, Stephen
Hoar, William
Keith, Aberdeen
Keith, Jeremiah
Lewis, Elijah
McAuly, Obed
Miller, Samuel
Nelson, John
Peirce, Isaac
Perkins, Zalli
Pickins, Silas
Pickins, Zacheus
Pierce, Eaton
Pierce, Joseph

Ramsden, Job
Reed, Elijah
Reed, Luke
Robbins, Lemuel
Robinson, Alvin
Rod, Solomon
Samson, John
Samson, Thomas
Shackley, Joseph
Shaw, Eben
Shaw, Ebenezer
Shaw, Eli
Shaw, Joel
Shaw, Joshua
Shaw, Sullivan
Shaw, Zephaniah
Skiff, Abraham
Standish, John C.
Strobridge, Ebenezer
Townsend, Avery
Washburn, Nathan
Washburn, Thomas
Westgate, Daniel
Westgate, Horace
Westgate, Obed
Westgate, William
Weston, Abner
White, Solomon

Capt. S. Cushman's Company, Lieut. Col. C. Howard's Regiment.
From Sept. 26 to Oct. 19, 1814. Raised at Attleborough. Service at Plymouth.

RANK AND NAME.
Samuel Cushman, Captain
Elijah Smith, Lieutenant
John A. Reed, Ensign

L. Hunt, Sergeant
Thacker Pierce, Sergeant
Andrew B. Blasdell, Sergeant
Daniel Burt, Sergeant
Seth Tisdale, Corporal
Jonathan French, Corporal
Zephaniah Briggs, Corporal
Barney Randall, Corporal
Seneca Wing, Musician

Privates.
Allen, Asa
Allen, Verona S.
Banny, Josiah
Barrows, Wheaton
Belcher, Solomon
Bicknell, William
Bowen, Uriah
Carpenter, Ebenezer
Chaffin, Comfort F.

Clark, Simeon
Cobb, Garvis
Codding, Abial
Cooper, Benjamin
Cushman, Richard
Dean, Charles
Drake, Isaac
Drew, John, Jr.
Dunkam, William
Field, Charles
Field, Solomon
Fisher, Daniel
Fuller, Jonathan
Goward, Israel
Hammond, Caleb
Howard, Asaph
Howard, Barnabas
Howard, Henry
Idle, Aruna
Jenks, George F.
Jillson, Amos
Jillson, David
Johnson, Oliver
Keith, Daniel
King, Benjamin

Lathrop, Cyrus
Morse, Swan
Newcomb, Thomas
Newland, John C.
Perry, Stephen
Phillips, Amasa
Pratt, Amasa
Quiggle, Elias
Randall, Caleb
Randall, Elvina
Randall, Nathan
Reed, Otis
Richards, George
Robbins, Moses
Sanford, Saul
Snow, Nathan
Thomas, Enoch, Jr.
Thompson, David, 3d
Tingley, Samuel
Tripp, Abel
Whipple, Larnard
White, Asa
White, Willis
Williams, Greenfield

Capt. E. Daggett's Company, Lieut. Col. C. Howard's Regiment.
From Sept. 26 to Oct. 19, 1814. Raised at Attleborough. Service at Plymouth.

RANK AND NAME.
Elihu Daggett, Captain
Alfred Skinner, Lieutenant
Jabel Ingraham, Ensign

Chester Bugbee, Sergeant
Benjamin Blandin, Sergeant
John Williams, Jr., Sergeant
Judson Blake, Sergeant
Fisher Blackinton, Sergeant
Joseph W. Hodges, Corporal
Nathaniel Danforth, Corporal
Elijah Eddy, Corporal
Charles Wetherell, Musician
Harmon Stanley, Musician

Privates.
Bates, Dexter
Bates, Ezekiel
Blackinton, David
Blackinton, Virgil
Blake, Samuel B.
Bramin, Andrew
Bramin, Sylvanus
Cooper, Noah

Crowley, Jacob
Dean, Abijah
Dean, Barnard
Dean, Simeon
Eddy, Lyman
Eldridge, Isaac
Everett, Joel
Everett, Silas
Gailor, Amhurst
Godfrey, David
Green, Simeon
Hall, George
Harden, Simeon
Hodges, Henry B.
Holmes, Eliphalet, Jr.
Hopkins, John
Ingraham, Elias
Keith, William
Lathrop, Salmon
May, Jully
May, Lemuel
Morse, Spencer
Norton, Asa
Penny, Ichabod
Penny, John

Richards, Thomas
Richardson, Benjamin
Robinson, Elijah
Skinner, Herbert
Skinner, Loring
Stanly, George
Stanly, Miller
Starkey, Cyrus
Starkey, Milton
Swan, Duty
Tailor, Ebenezer
Thayer, Ezra
Thayer, Jonathan
Thompson, Ebial
Thompson, Hiram
White, Augustus
White, Jonathan
Whiting, John T.
Whitmore, Edmund
Wilbur, Joel
Wilbur, Josiah
Williams, Joseph
Williams, Rufus
Wilmarth, Seth

Capt. N. Wilder's Company, under Gen. Goodwin's Command.
From June 24 to July 10, 1814. Raised at Middleborough. Service at New Bedford.

RANK AND NAME.
Nathaniel Wilder, Captain
Linus Washburn, Lieutenant
Coburn Shaw, Ensign

Joseph Haskell, Sergeant
Benjamin Richmond, Sergeant
Sylvanus Warren, Sergeant
Benjamin White, Sergeant
George Leonard, Corporal
Abner Leonard, Corporal
Hosea Leatch, Corporal
Apollus Richmond, Corporal
Joshua Haskins, Musician
Isaac Tinkham, Musician

Privates.
Alden, Oliver H.
Aldrich, Hosea

Barden, John
Barden, R.
Bennet, Jacob
Caswell, George
Cole, Samuel
Eaton, Israel
Eaton, Solomon
Eaton, Ziba
Hathaway, Silas
Hayford, Benjamin
Keith, Israel
Leonard, Samuel
Nelson, Cyrus
Paddock, Joseph
Perkins, Silva
Pinkham, Cornelius
Reed, Nathan
Reed, Solomon
Shaw, Elisha

Sherman, Willis
Snow, Daniel
Southworth, Leonard
Southworth, William
Stevens, Josiah
Tinkham, John
Vaughan, Andrew
Vaughan, Cushman
Vaughan, Daniel
Vaughan, George
Warren, Daniel
Washburn, Thomas
Winslow, Edward
Wood, Ichabod, 2d
Wood, Lorenzo
Wood, Sylvanus

Lieut. Col. Benjamin Lincoln's Regiment.
Different dates between June 13 and Oct. 18, 1814. Service at New Bedford.

FIELD AND STAFF.
Benjamin Lincoln, Lieutenant Colonel
Edward Pope, Major
John Coggshall, Major
Levi Pierce, Major
Ebenezer Hunt, Major

Elisha Toby, Adjutant
Daniel Lane, Adjutant
William Gordon, Engineer
William Kempton, Quartermaster
Samuel Perry, Surgeon

NONCOMMISSIONED OFFICER.
Elijah Wilber, Quartermaster Sergeant

MASSACHUSETTS VOLUNTEER MILITIA IN THE WAR OF 1812.

Capt. W. Nye's Company, Lieut. Col. B. Lincoln's Regiment.
From June 17 to June 29, 1814.   Raised at New Bedford.   Service at New Bedford.

RANK AND NAME.
William Nye, Captain
Jeduthan Taber, Lieutenant
Barnabas Hammond, Ensign

Freeman Pope, Sergeant
Loring Pope, Sergeant
Reuben Taber, Sergeant
William West, Sergeant
Allen Norton, Sergeant

Privates.
Alden, Ebenezer
Allen, John
Allen, Rufus
Allen, Warren
Bennet, Charles
Besse, Nathaniel
Blossom, Levi
Chandler, Ezekiel
Chase, Robertson
Church, James
Clark, Davis
Cunningham, Jesse
Delano, Ebenezer
Delano, Ephraim
Delano, Henry
Delano, Joseph
Delano, Reuben
Delano, Warren

Dillingham, Benjamin
Fitch, Hardy E.
Fuller, John
Gelatt, John
Gifford, Obed
Grinnell, Remington
Hamblin, Reuben
Hammond, James
Hammond, Michael
Hendricks, John
Hiller, Jonathan
Holmes, Oliver
Holmes, William
Howard, Benjamin
Howard, William
Huttlestone, Thomas
Jenne, Benjamin
Jenne, David
Jenne, Israel
Jenne, Jonathan
Jenne, Luther
Jenne, Nathaniel
Kelly, Amos
Kempton, Daniel
Kempton, Elijah
Kempton, Nathan
Kempton, Stephen
Kinney, Jonathan
Mitchell, Seth
Morton, Timothy

Nye, James
Peckham, William
Perkins, Alden
Pope, Enos
Pope, Silas
Russell, Lemuel
Shaw, Abraham
Shaw, George
Shaw, Thomas
Shaw, William
Sherkley, Ephraim
Spooner, Lemuel
Spooner, Noah
Stetson, Ansel
Stetson, Mitchell
Stevens, Seth
Stoddard, Henry
Swift, Charles D.
Taber, John
Taber, Joseph
Taber, Samuel
Tripp, James
Tripp, Sylvanus
Tripp, Thomas
Tripp, William
West, Samuel
West, Thomas
Whitefield, George
Wilson, Hammond
Wood, Elihu

Capt. R. Swift's Company, Lieut. Col. B. Lincoln's Regiment.
From June 17 to June 30, and July, 1814.   Raised at Fairhaven.   Service at Fairhaven.

RANK AND NAME.
Reuben Swift, Captain
Job Millard, Lieutenant
Seth Bumpus, Ensign

William Swift, Sergeant
James Ripner, Sergeant
Allen Bourne, Sergeant
Allen Chase, Sergeant
Zena Cowen, Sergeant
Nathaniel Spooner, Sergeant
Thomas Hathaway, Sergeant
Thomas Collins, Sergeant
James Purrington, Musician
Noah Waste, Musician
Thomas B. Smith, Musician

Privates.
Allen, Abraham
Allen, Gardner
Allin, John
Andrews, John
Arnoly, Lemuel M.
Babcock, Isaac
Brightman, Nathan
Burden, Holden
Burden, James
Burt, Simeon

Burt, Sylvester
Case, Isaac
Chase, Israel
Chase, Joseph
Cowen, William
Craps, Abel
Craps, Asa
Cummings, John
Davis, James
Demmings, Gordon
Douglass, George
Eddy, John
Edminster, John
Freeman, John
Gifford, Alden
Gifford, Jonathan
Gifford, Paul
Hammond, Samuel
Hathaway, Benjamin S.
Hathaway, Isaac
Hathaway, William
Higgins, Nathan
Hoard, Elias
Howland, Timothy
Hunter, John
Jackson, Edmund
Jenney, Joseph H.
Mosher, Gideon

Mosher, Holden
Mosher, Richard
Myrick, John
Omans, James
Parker, Elijah
Pettis, Silas
Philips, Ira
Pierce, Russell
Pool, Abiather
Pool, Major
Pope, Cornelius
Reed, Alden
Reed, Lemuel
Reed, Lemuel B.
Reynolds, Abraham
Reynolds, Benjamin
Reynolds, Noah
Reynolds, Philip
Reynolds, William
Rider, Henry
Russell, Humphrey
Russell, Stephen
Samson, Stephen
Shearman, Stephen
Shearman, Uriah
Snell, Abel
Snell, Leonard
Spooner, Joshua

Capt. R. Swift's Company, Lieut. Col. B. Lincoln's Regiment — Concluded.

Privates — Concluded.
Spooner, Micah
Strange, Lot
Taber, Peter
Thomas, Arnold
Tobey, Samuel F.
Tobey, William
Tripp, Ebenezer
Tripp, Rufus

Upham, James
Washburn, Stillman
Weston, Enoch
Whalen, Daniel
Whalen, Jonathan
Wheedon, Daniel
Wheeler, Calvin
White, Job
Williams, John

Wing, Stephen
Wing, Stephen, 2d
Winslow, Joshua
Winslow, Richard
Woddell, Nathaniel
Wolcott, Oliver
Wood, James

Capt. J. Davis' Company, Lieut. Col. B. Lincoln's Regiment.
From June 18 to June 28, 1814. Raised at Westport. Service at Westport.

RANK AND NAME.
Jonathan Davis, Captain
George Wood, Lieutenant
Wilson King, Ensign

Privates.
Allen, Jacob
Bert, Simeon
Bert, Sylvester
Besse, Lathrop
Borden, Biscum
Borden, Stephen
Borden, Thomas
Brown, George W.
Brownell, Daniel
Brownell, George
Buffington, Mason
Case, William
Chace, Levi
Cornell, James
Cornell, Solomon
Cornell, Thomas T.
Cornwell, Christopher
Craps, Reuben
Crocker, Canaan
Davis, Zebedee
Davol, Allen
Davol, Benjamin
Davol, Davis
Davol, Peter
Dennis, Peleg
Dwelling, Warren
Evans, William

Francis, Elisha
Gifford, Adams
Gifford, David
Gifford, George
Gifford, Isaac
Gifford, Job
Gifford, Pardon
Gifford, Peleg
Gifford, Warren
Gifford, Zacheus
Gray, Samuel
Handy, James H.
Hayden, Ebenezer
Howland, William
Kirby, Stephen
Kirby, William
Lincoln, Nathan
Macumber, Ephraim
Perry, Phineas
Petty, Asa
Petty, Benjamin
Petty, Elias
Petty, Moses
Petty, Nathan
Petty, Pardon
Petty, Philip
Petty, Silas
Petty, Stephen
Petty, Thomas
Pickham, Philip
Potter, George
Potter, Joshua
Potter, Philip

Reed, James
Reynolds, Thadeus
Sandford, Thomas
Sisson, Benjamin
Sisson, Daniel
Sisson, George
Smith, William
Snell, Henry
Snell, James
Snell, John
Strange, Joseph
Tripp, Benjamin
Tripp, Duray
Tripp, Elihu
Tripp, Howard
Tripp, Job
Tripp, Nathaniel
Tripp, Philip
Tripp, Stephen, 1st
Tripp, Stephen, 2d
Tripp, Stephen, 3d
Tripp, Weston
Tripp, William
Wate, Reuben
White, Alfred
White, George
White, Luther
Wordell, Benjamin
Wordell, George
Wordell, Gershom
Wordell, John
Wordell, Peleg
Wordell, Perry

Capt. S. Ashley's Company, Lieut. Col. B. Lincoln's Regiment.
From June 18 to June 30, 1814. Raised at Freetown. Service at New Bedford.

RANK AND NAME.
Simeon Ashley, Captain
Samuel Macumber, Ensign

Bishop Ashley, Sergeant
John Brownserville, Sergeant
Philip Taber, Sergeant
Gilbert Brownserville, Sergeant
Josiah Demoransville, Corporal

John Allen, Corporal
Benjamin Ellis, Corporal
Clark Haskins, Corporal
Ephraim Gurney, Musician
David F. Hathaway, Musician

Privates.
Ashley, Abraham
Ashley, Abraham, 2d

Ashley, Leonard
Ashley, Tabor
Ashley, Thomas
Braley, Job
Braley, Jonathan
Briggs, Abel
Brownserville, Joseph
Burt, John
Case, William

Capt. S. Ashley's Company, Lieut. Col. B. Lincoln's Regiment—Concluded.

Privates — Concluded.
Clark, Asa
Clark, Joseph
Cummings, George
Cummings, William
Downing, Frederic
Downing, John
Gorham, James
Haskell, Nathaniel
Hathaway, Philip

Jackett, Nathaniel
Lawrence, David
Lucas, Ansel
Mason, Hezekiah
Perkins, Noah
Pitsley, Abraham
Pitsley, Alexander
Pitsley, Francis
Pitsley, James
Reynolds, Micah, 2d

Reynolds, Wilbour
Rogers, Luther
Rounsville, Silas
Westgate, William
White, James
White, John
White, Malachi
White, Samuel, Jr.

Capt. L. Hathaway's Company, Lieut. Col. B. Lincoln's Regiment.
From June 20 to July 1, 1814. Raised at Freetown. Service at New Bedford.

RANK AND NAME.
Lynde Hathaway, Captain
Thomas Burbank, Lieutenant

Preserved Cotton, Sergeant
Joseph Evans, Sergeant
Joseph Evans, 2d, Sergeant
William Winslow, Musician
Calvin Payne, Musician

Privates.
Andrews, Zephaniah
Booth, Thomas S.
Bordon, Stephen
Briggs, John, Jr.
Briggs, Josephus
Burbank, Isaac, Jr.
Burr, William
Chace, Edmund
Chace, Gilbert, Jr.
Chace, Holden
Chace, James
Chace, Michael
Chace, Samuel
Chace, Simeon
Cudworth, John D.
Davis, Paul
Dean, Benjamin, Jr.
Dean, Ebenezer
Dean, John

Dean, John, 2d
Dean, King
Douglass, Daniel
Downing, Joshua
Edminster, Lemuel
Evans, William
Haskins, John
Hathaway, Bradford
Hathaway, Daniel
Hathaway, Ennis
Hathaway, Enoch
Hathaway, Ephraim
Hathaway, Henry P.
Hathaway, Jason
Hathaway, Joseph, 2d
Hathaway, Lot
Hathaway, Malbon
Hathaway, Michael
Hathaway, Noah
Hathaway, Philip P.
Hathaway, Silas
Howland, Malichi
Howland, Seth
Marble, Charles
Martin, Mason
Miller, Ebenezer
Nichols, John
Nichols, William
Paddock, Eddino
Payne, Abraham

Payne, Henry
Payne, Solomon
Perkins, George
Philips, Baytus
Philips, Pierce
Porter, Henry
Pratt, John N.
Randal, Thomas
Raymond, Benjamin
Read, Dean H.
Read, John
Reed, Joseph
Richmond, Abraham
Richmond, Isaac
Richmond, Samuel
Sepl, Joshua
Staples, Gilbert
Strange, John, Jr.
Terry, James
Terry, Joseph
Terry, Sials
Webster, James
Wilbour, Derius
Wilkinson, John
Winslow, Barnabas
Winslow, Ephraim
Winslow, Gilbert
Winslow, William

Capt. W. Nye's Command, Lieut. Col. B. Lincoln's Regiment.
From June 30 to July 10, 1814. Service at New Bedford and Fairhaven.

RANK AND NAME.
William Nye, Captain
Jeduthan Taber, Lieutenant
Barnabas Hammond, Ensign

NONCOMMISSIONED OFFICERS.
Freeman Pope
Reuben Taber
William West
Allen Morton

Privates.
Alden, Ebenezer
Allen, John
Allen, Rufus
Allen, Warren
Bennett, Charles
Besse, Nathaniel
Blossom, Levi
Chandler, Ezekiel
Chase, Robertson
Church, James

Clark, David
Cunningham, Jesse
Delano, Ebenezer
Delano, Ephraim
Delano, Henry
Delano, Joseph
Delano, Reuben
Delano, Warren
Dillingham, Benjamin
Fitch, Hardy E.
Fuller, John

MASSACHUSETTS VOLUNTEER MILITIA IN THE WAR OF 1812.

Capt. W. Nye's Command, Lieut. Col. B. Lincoln's Regiment — Concluded.

Privates — Concluded.

Gelatt, John
Gifford, Obed
Grinnell, Remington
Hamblin, Reuben
Hammond, James
Hammond, Michel
Hammond, Wilson
Hendricks, John
Hiller, Jonathan
Holmes, Oliver
Holmes, William
Howard, Benjamin
Howard, William
Huttlestone, Thomas
Jeune, Benjamin
Jeune, David
Jeune, Israel
Jeune, Jonathan
Jeune, Luther

Jeune, Nathaniel
Kelley, Amos
Kempton, Daniel
Kempton, Elijah
Kempton, Nathan
Kempton, Stephen
Kenney, Jonathan
Mitchell, Seth
Morton, Timothy
Nye, James
Peckman, William
Perkins, Alden
Pope, Enos
Pope, Silas
Russell, Lemuel
Shaw, Abraham
Shaw, George
Shaw, Thomas
Shaw, William
Shertley, Ephraim

Spooner, Lemuel
Spooner, Noah
Stetson, Ansel
Stetson, Michell
Stevens, Seth
Stoddard, Henry
Swift, Charles D.
Taber, John
Taber, Joseph
Taber, Samuel
Tripp, James
Tripp, Sylvanus
Tripp, Thomas
Tripp, William
West, Samuel
West, Thomas
Whitefield, George
Wood, Elihu

Capt. W. Nye's Command, Lieut. Col. B. Lincoln's Regiment.

From June 30 to July 10, 1814. Service at New Bedford.

RANK AND NAME.

William Nye, Captain
Jeduthan Taber, Lieutenant
Phineas White, Ensign

Robert B. Pratt, Sergeant
Thomas Adams, Sergeant
Joseph Keene, Sergeant
Ezra White, Sergeant
Henry Stoddard, Sergeant
Isaac S. Church, Sergeant
William Taber, Sergeant
Cornelius Brew, Sergeant
Stephen Merrihew, Corporal
Robert Cook, Corporal
Michael Bennet, Corporal
Ebenezer Keene, Corporal
Reuben Keene, Musician
Silas Stetson, Musician

Privates.

Alden, Seth
Allen, Alden
Allen, Anthony
Allen, Zacheus M.
Ashley, Abraham
Ashley, William
Bennet, Jeremiah
Bowen, Martin
Bradford, Mallone
Bryant, Bela
Clark, Ezekiel
Cushman, Isaac
Delano, John

Delano, Richard
Dillingham, Lemuel
Doane, Joshua
Gammon, William
Gifford, Reuben
Gifford, Shubal
Hammond, Caleb
Hammond, Daniel
Hammond, Elihu
Hathaway, Michael
Hathaway, Nicholas
Hiller, Jonathan
Hiller, Levi
Howard, Thomas
Jenney, Edward
Jenney, Jedutham
Jenney, Joseph
Jenney, Samuel
Kent, Noah
Kinney, Jacob
Kinney, Phineas
McNeal, Francis
Merrihew, Edmund
Moses, Joshua
Myrick, Ebenezer
Nye, James
Nye, Pardon
Omey, Wilbourn
Ornan, Thomas
Parker, John
Parker, Luther
Parker, Nathan
Perry, John
Pierce, Samuel

Pinkham, Ebenezer
Pratt, Andrew
Pratt, Luther
Proctor, Caleb
Randall, James
Sampson, Seth
Shaw, James
Snow, Loami
Spooner, Benjamin
Spooner, John
Spooner, Thomas
Staples, William
Taber, James
Taber, Pardon
Terry, Elias
Terry, Sanford
Tobey, Elisha
Tripp, Gilbert
Tripp, Lemuel
Tripp, Timothy
Tripp, William
Vincent, Abner
Vincent, Isaac
West, Edward B.
Wheeden, John
White, Ansel
White, William
Whitefield, Humphrey
Wilcox, Jonathan
Wood, Richard
Wood, Thomas
Wood, William
Woodcock, Manson

MASSACHUSETTS VOLUNTEER MILITIA IN THE WAR OF 1812.

Capt. G. G. Chace's Company, Lieut. Col. B. Lincoln's Regiment.
From July 8 to July 25, 1814. Raised at Berkley. Service at New Bedford.

RANK AND NAME.
Giles G. Chace, Captain
Enos Williams, Lieutenant
Job Dean, Ensign

William Garshee, Sergeant
Eliab Dean, Sergeant
Asa White, Sergeant
Biarush Hathaway, Sergeant
Thurston Brown, Sergeant
Andrew Backus, Corporal
Joel W. Dean, Corporal
Anson Hathaway, Corporal
John Perkins, Corporal
Chandler Dean, Musician
Daniel Howard, Musician
Isaac Paul, Jr., Musician

Privates.
Allen, Eaton
Bent, Joseph
Boodry, Benjamin S.
Bretton, Ira
Briggs, Bennet
Briggs, Peter
Caswell, Philip
Chace, Aaron, Jr.
Chace, James

Dean, Cornelius
Dean, Gilbert
Ellis, James
Evans, David
Fisk, David
Francis or Fraser, Charles
French, Joseph
Goff, Robert
Hacket, Joseph
Hathaway, Lemuel
Hathaway, Luther
Hervey, Darius
Hervey, Frederic
Hilliard, Henry
Hoard, Cromwell
Holmes, Abner
Holmes, Ebenezer
Horton, Simeon
Howland, Samuel
King, Isaac, Jr.
Levi, Morris
Luther, Royal
Newhall, Ebenezer
Newton, Arnold
Page, James B.
Palmer, David
Paul, Dean
Peckham, Silas

Philips, David
Philips, Ephraim
Philips, Serrannus
Pierce, Elisha
Pitts, John
Place, Joseph
Read, Gideon
Reading, Joseph
Richmond, Theodore
Robinson, Abial
Rose, Joseph
Simmons, Nathan
Snow, Ebenezer
Snow, Linus
Walker, George, Jr.
Walker, Robert
Walker, Saul
Warren, James
Westgate, Weston
White, Jarvis
Whitmore, John W.
Wilbour, Charles
Wilbour, Elkanah
Wilbour, Joshua
Williams, Thomas
Wright, John

Capt. S. Shepperd's Company, Lieut. Col. B. Lincoln's Regiment.
From July 8 to July 25, 1814. Raised at Taunton. Service at New Bedford.

RANK AND NAME.
Silas Shepperd, Captain
Nathan King, Lieutenant
Samuel Gulliver, Ensign

Oliver Soper, Sergeant
William Haskins, Sergeant
Zeph Walker, Sergeant
Benjamin King, Sergeant
James H. Blake, Corporal
Edward Knap, Corporal
Elisha Walker, Corporal
George S. Hood, Corporal
Ephraim Atwood, Corporal
Zera Wilbur, Musician
Lewis Wade, Musician
Solomon Austin, Musician
Gilbert Leonard, Musician

Privates.
Austin, Palmer
Bassett, David
Bisbey, Isaac
Briggs, Alanson D.
Briggs, Charles
Briggs, Edmund
Buffington, Benjamin
Burt, Alanson
Burt, Royal
Caswell, George, 2d

Coffin, Peleg
Coleman, Elijah B.
Crossman, John O.
Crossman, William
Crossman, William H.
Dean, Linus
Elliot, Asiel
Francis, Edward B.
Gilbert, Samuel
Godfrey, Albert
Harvey, David
Haskins, Eben
Haskins, Nathaniel
Haskins, William P.
Hathaway, Job
Hathaway, Leonard
Hewit, Richard
Holmes, Rufus
Kellock, James
King, Jonathan
King, Samuel
Knap, Job
Leonard, Alford
Leonard, Ebenezer
Leonard, Lewis
Lincoln, Abijah
Lincoln, Danforth
Lincoln, Elijah
Lincoln, Nephaniah
Lucas, William

Macumber, Bradford
McCumber, Ira
McFarland, Elisha
Mirrick, Ebenezer
Morcut, Benjamin
Paddelford, James
Park, William
Pierce, Clothier
Pratt, Enos
Reed, Amariah
Reed, George W.
Reed, Jonathan
Reed, William
Richmond, Beza
Shelby, Libeus
Staples, Allen
Staples, Daniel
Staples, Eliphalet
Staples, Noah
Thayer, Abiather
Thayer, Sylvester
Thrasher, Elkanah
Walker, Richmond
White, Abiather
Wilbur, William
Williams, Benjamin
Witherell, Nathaniel
Woodward, Robert
Woodward, Samuel

Capt. N. Reed's Company, Lieut. Col. B. Lincoln's Regiment.

From Aug. 1 to Sept. 20, 1814.   Raised at Taunton and Easton.   Service at New Bedford.

RANK AND NAME.
Noah Reed, Captain
Simeon Drake, Lieutenant
Jacob Williams, Ensign

John Allen, Sergeant
Joshua Hayward, Sergeant
Dexter Parmeter, Sergeant
Eddy Hardin, Sergeant
B. Ingalls, Corporal
George Derby, Corporal
Levi Bowen, Corporal
William Blake, Corporal
Martin Copeland, Musician
Jesse Blandin, Musician

Privates.
Angells, Asa
Barney, James O.
Boyden, Alexander
Britton, Joshua
Burk, Nathan
Carpenter, William
Carr, James
Caswell, Richard
Chaffin, Lester

Chaffin, Robert
Cole, Nathaniel
Crossman, Ebenezer S.
Curtis, John
Darra, Lewis
Dean, Gulliver
Dean, William
Dean, William I. or S.
Downing, Warren
Drake, Elijah
Drake, Jonathan
Field, Horace
Freeman, Asa
Freeman, Freeman or Trueman
French, Ephraim, Jr.
Gilson, Amos
Godfrey, Albert W.
Hapworth, William
Harden, Alfred
Hyer, John
Ide, Ebenezer
Kingman, Henry
Knowles, Jonathan, Jr.
Landers, Abiel
Leonard, Solomon
Lumber, Thomas

Macumber, John, Jr.
McGowns, Samuel
Metcalf, Junier
Negus, Abel
Packard, Jedediah
Peck, Jason
Peck, Jonathan
Phillips, Silas
Richardson, Moses
Richardson, Silas
Richardson, Varnum
Richman, Kingman
Rounds, Sylvester, Jr.
Russell, Francis
Russell, John
Skinner, Solon
Sparrow, Bradford
Thayer, M.
Thayer, Zacheriah
Turner, Stephen
White, Benjamin
White, Howe
Whiting, Caleb
Wilbour, Daniel
Wild, John, Jr.
Woodard, Zebra

Capt. J. Hood's Company, Lieut. Col. B. Lincoln's Regiment.

Twenty-five days in September and October, 1814.   Raised at Somerset.   Service at New Bedford.

RANK AND NAME.
John Hood, Captain
Lewis Walker, Lieutenant
Israel Pierce, Ensign

David W. Bucklin, Sergeant
Nathan Lewin, Sergeant
Joseph Cook, Sergeant
Samuel Place, Sergeant
John Davis, Corporal
Daniel Edson, Corporal
Ezra Bullock, Corporal
Ambrose Martin, Corporal
William Peck, Musician
Timothy Daggett, Musician

Privates.
Baker, Alexander
Baker, Daniel
Baker, Zenos
Bowen, Silas
Bowers, George
Boyle, Thomas
Bucklin, B.
Buffington, Stephen
Carpenter, Abijah

Carpenter, Calvin
Chace, Wanton
Chase, Sheffield
Cummins, Lloyd
Daggett, John, 2d
Daggett, Levi
Davis, Joseph
Fisk, George
Goff, Nathaniel
Handy, David
Handy, Otis
Hathaway, Clothier
Hix, Daniel
Holden, Jabez
Holmes, William
Hood, John
Horton, John
Hunt, Daniel
Ingalls, Samuel
Jones, Peleg G.
Kingsley, Hail
Lawton, Thomas
Lee, David
Lincoln, Seth
Luther, Abraham
Luther, David

Luther, John
Luther, Joseph
Luther, Levi
Luther, Obediah
Luther, Wheaton
Martin, Israel
Mason, Isaac
Ormsby, Samuel
Paine, Richard
Pearce, Jonah
Peck, Erasmus R.
Pierce, Comfort
Pierce, Darius
Pierce, Israel, 3d
Pierce, William
Ripley, Levi
Rodliff, William
Rood, Augustus
Sampson, Seth
Simmons, Russell
Thompson, James
Thrasher, Asahel
Trafton, Samuel G.
Wheeler, Wheaton
Wilmarth, Thomas, Jr.

MASSACHUSETTS VOLUNTEER MILITIA IN THE WAR OF 1812.   61

Capt. J. Reed's Company, Lieut. Col. B. Lincoln's Regiment.
From Sept. 6 to Oct. 6, 1814.   Raised at Taunton.   Service at New Bedford.

RANK AND NAME.
Joseph Reed, Captain
Edward Blake, Lieutenant

Barney Pratt, Sergeant
John King, Sergeant
James French, Sergeant
Gilbert Hoard, Sergeant
George Richmond, Corporal
William Stoddard, Corporal
John Curtis, Corporal
Jonathan Field, Corporal
Daniel Caswell, Musician
Ziba Wilbur, Musician

Privates.
Austin, Abiathar
Barrows, Gilford
Bent, Joseph
Bowen, Jonathan

Bradford, Davis
Briggs, Bennet
Caswell, Darius
Cummins, Howard
Dean, Allen
Dean, Linus
Dunham, Samuel
French, George G.
Godfrey, Rufus
Godfrey, William
Haskins, Henry
Haskins, William P.
Hathaway, Job
Hathaway, Lemuel
Hoard, Jarvis
King, Isaac
King, Nathan
Lewis, Aaron
Mirick, Ebenezer
Need, Amariah

Philips, David
Philips, Isacah
Reed, Gideon
Richmond, Henry
Richmond, William
Rider, Seth
Seckel, Job
Shaw, Oliver
Shaw, Samuel
Staples, Daniel
Staples, Eliphalet
Swazy, Stephen
Wescoat or Westgate, Weston
Whitacer, Nathaniel
White, Jarvis
White, William
Wilbur, Otis
Wilbur, Seth H.
Wilson, Eliphalet
Witherell, Nathaniel

Capt. Joseph Watson's Company, Lieut. Col. B. Lincoln's Regiment.
From Sept. 25 to Oct. 20, 1814.   Raised at Rehoboth.   Service at New Bedford.

RANK AND NAME.
Joseph Watson, Captain
John Midberry, Lieutenant
Stephen Bourn, Ensign

Simeon Walker, Sergeant
Thomas Pettis, Sergeant
Calvin B. Fuller, Sergeant
Isaac Pearce, Sergeant
Jonathan Wheaton, Corporal
Joseph Carpenter, Corporal
David P. Round, Corporal
Barney Davis, Corporal
Phileman Brown, Corporal
Nathan Carpenter, Musician
James Croswell, Musician

Privates.
Allen, Elisha, 2d
Armington, Ambrose
Armington, George
Armington, Joseph, 2d
Bliss, Alfred
Bliss, Caleb (Paschal Paine, substitute for)
Bliss, Oliver, 2d

Brayton, David
Brown, David
Brown, George
Bullock, Samuel W.
Carpenter, Jonathan
Carpenter, Samuel
Chaffee, Lewis
Chaffee, Walker
Chambers, Eli
Cole, William
Cotton, John S.
Daggett, Benjamin
Davis, Barney
Davis, Daniel
Davis, John
Drown, John J.
Earle, Joseph
French, Cyrus
Goff, Asahel
Haskins, Nathaniel
Horton, Asahel
Horton, Barnet
Humphrey, John
Kent, John
Kent, John, 2d
Lindsey, John

Martin, David
Mason, James
Munroe, Benjamin, Jr.
Newman, Nathan
Ormsby, William
Paine, Paschal (substitute for Caleb Bliss)
Peck, Edward
Peck, William
Pettis, Benjamin
Pettis, Daniel
Pettis, Ezekiel, 2d
Pierce, Preserved
Reed, Francis
Reed, Joshua
Reed, Noah
Reed, Thomas
Rice, Ephraim
Richmond, Nathaniel
Sisson, Benjamin
Tell, Warren
Wells, Allen
West, Amos, 2d
Wheaton, Samuel
Whitaker, Joel
Woods, Jonathan

Capt. S. Staples' Company, Lieut. Col. B. Lincoln's Regiment.
From Sept. 27 to Oct. 20, 1814. Raised at Taunton. Service at New Bedford.

RANK AND NAME.
Seth Staples, Captain
Crockett Babbitt, Lieutenant
Benjamin Dean, Ensign

Paul Staples, Sergeant
Seth Hart, Sergeant
Rufus Crossman, Sergeant
Seth Shelly, Sergeant
Elisha W. Tubbs, Corporal
Elijah B. Colman, Corporal
John Neall, Corporal
William C. Hood, Corporal
Abraham Caswell, Musician
Nathaniel Wheeler, Musician

Privates.
Baker, Davis
Barney, Lyman
Blake, Alfred
Briggs, Hathaway
Buck, Arimiah
Bullock, James
Burt, Nathaniel
Chace, Increase

Chase, Arnold
Clark, Willard
Clark, William
Cobb, Ebenezer
Dean, Abial F.
Field, Abiather
Gunsmith, John
Hach or Hatch, Daniel
Harvey, Barnabus
Harvey, Leonard
Haskins, Ebenezer
Hathaway, Job
Hathaway, William
Hood, James
Hood, Willard
Howard, John
King, Elijah, Jr.
Knapp, Ephraim
Leonard, Solomon
Leonard, Zadock
Lewis, Asa
Lincoln, Nicholas H.
Lincoln, Robert
Marvel, John
Mason, Philip

Paine, James
Paul, Micah
Philips, Nathaniel
Pierce, Nathan
Pratt, Ebenezer
Pratt, James
Presbrey, Asa
Reed, George W.
Reed, William
Richmond, King
Seaver, Benjamin
Seavery, Samuel
Seavey, David
Seekell, John, 2d
Thrasher, Elkanah
Thrasher, Noah
Wade, Amos
White, Abijah
White, Samuel
Wilber, Stephen
Wilber, William A.
Williams, Benjamin
Williams, William

Capt. S. Wilber's Company, Lieut. Col. B. Lincoln's Regiment.
From Sept. 27 to Oct. 18, 1814. Raised at Raynham. Service at New Bedford.

RANK AND NAME.
Samuel Wilber, Captain
Joseph Hall, Lieutenant
Daniel Wilber, Ensign

John D. Gilmore, Sergeant
Calvin Washburn, Sergeant
Isaac Goff, Sergeant
Benjamin D. Richmond, Sergeant
John Pierce, Corporal
Isaac Babbitt, Corporal
Cassine D. Shaw, Corporal
Hiram Pendleton, Corporal
Warren Lincoln, Musician
James Bosworth, Musician

Privates.
Atwood, Joseph
Babber, Abijah, 2d
Bassett, Jeremiah
Bolton, John
Boodry, Benjamin G.
Briggs, Frederick
Briggs, Silas P.

Burt, George
Chace, Aaron, Jr.
Chace, James, Jr.
Crabbe, Austin
Crane, Levi G.
Crocker, George
Dean, Jonathan
Deane, Asa
Deane, Daniel
Deane, Joseph
Deane, Samuel
Eddy, Apollus, Jr.
Fraser, Reuben
French, Benjamin C.
Goodwin, George
Hall, Isaac
Hathaway, Benjamin
Hathaway, Elkanah
Lewis, Timothy
Lincoln, Ambrose
Luther, Harron
Macumber, Venus
Miller, Nathan
Newell, Saul

Palmer, Jonathan
Perry, Edward
Philips, John
Philips, Surannus
Pidge, Palemon
Ricketson, Gilbert
Robinson, Godfrey, Jr.
Robinson, John, 2d
Robinson, Simeon
Shelley, Libeus
Simmons, Thomas
Smith, Wilber
Tabbot, John B.
Trafton, Benjamin, Jr.
White, Isaac
White, John
Williams, Eli
Williams, Enoch
Williams, Grusham
Williams, Philo
Williams, Stephen
Williams, Zebedee

Lieut. B. Howland's Company, Lieut. Col. B. Lincoln's Regiment.

From June to July, 1814. Raised at Dartmouth. Service at Dartmouth.

RANK AND NAME.
Bradford Howland, Lieutenant

Joseph Seagraves, Sergeant
John A. Shearman, Sergeant

Privates.

Allen, Benjamin
Allen, Charles
Allen, John
Allen, Major
Barker, Samuel
Bessey, Martin
Booth, Russ N.
Briggs, Weston
Brightman, Henry
Brightman, Jeremiah
Brownell, Perry
Butts, Stephen
Chace, John
Chandler, William
Cornell, Abner
Davis, Humphrey
Davol, Gideon
Davol, Joseph
Davol, Pardon
Gidly, Benjamin
Gidly, John
Gifford, Elihu
Grate, Samuel
Gridley, Jeremiah
Howland, Daniel
Howland, Eastman
Howland, John
Howland, Joshua
Howland, Pardon
Howland, Walter
Hull, Abraham
Hull, Robert C.
Hull, Samuel
Hull, William
Kirby, Noah
Lawrence, Freeman
Lawrence, Robert
Little, Isaac
Macumber, Allen
Mason, William B.
Mosher, Reuben
Pavol, David
Pearce, Pardon
Reed, Weston
Shearman, C.
Sherman, William
Simmons, Benjamin
Sisson, Edward
Sisson, Joseph
Slocum, Frederic
Slocum, Giles
Stafford, Lilly
Tallman, Stephen
Tripp, Benajer
Tripp, Henry
Tripp, James
Tripp, Joseph
Wead, Stephen
White, John
White, Nicholas
Wilcox, Abner
Wilcox, Henry
Wing, Charles
Wing, David
Wing, Latham

Lieut. N. Tompkins' Guard at Westport, Lieut. Col. B. Lincoln's Regiment.

From June to August, 11 days in September, 1814.

RANK AND NAME.
Nathaniel Tompkins, Lieutenant

Allen Tripp, Sergeant

Privates.

Allen, Green
Brightman, Jeremiah
Brightman, Samuel
Brownell, Benjamin
Brownell, Thomas
Case, Pardon
Davis, Christopher
Davis, George W.
Davis, Joseph
Davis, Philip
Drool, John
Dyer, Samuel
Gifford, Cook
Gifford, Pardon
Gifford, Reuben
Hicks, Joseph
Lincoln, Seth
Manchester, Calvin
Manchester, James
Manchester, William
Mannel, Samuel
Pall, Peter
Palmer, Gideon
Palmer, Isaac
Record, Owen
Seabury, Pearce
Sherman, Robert
Soule, Isaac
Towle, Israel
Tripp, Allen
Tripp, Carmi
Tripp, Job
Underwood, William
Wilcox, Abner

Lieut. Col. T. Longley's Regiment.

From Sept. 13 to Nov. 7, 1814. Service at Boston.

FIELD AND STAFF.
Thomas Longley, Lieutenant Colonel, Hawley
John Wilson, Major, Deerfield
Asa Howland, Major, Conway
Willis Carter, Adjutant, Buckland
John C. Hoyt, Quartermaster, Deerfield

Samuel or Saul Putnam, Paymaster, New Salem
George Rodgers, Surgeon, Conway
Stephen W. Williams, Surgeon's Mate, Deerfield
Alpheus Harding, Chaplain, New Salem

NONCOMMISSIONED STAFF.
Moses Ewers, Sergeant Major
Henry K. Newcomb, Quartermaster Sergeant
Ira Gleason, Drum Major

Capt. J. B. Brown's Company, Lieut. Col. T. Longley's Regiment.
From Sept. 13 to Nov. 7, 1814. Raised at Stow and vicinity. Service at Boston.

RANK AND NAME.
James B. Brown, Captain
Solomon Reed, Lieutenant
Calvin Peirce, Ensign

John Wilson, Sergeant
Ebenezer Morrill, Sergeant
William Burton, Sergeant
George Hall, Sergeant
Jesse Bosworth, Corporal
Daniel Fairwell, Corporal
Anson Bemant, Corporal
Ignatius Perkins, Corporal
Simeon Barr, Musician
Stephen Dowe, Musician

Privates.
Adams, Asa
Andrews, Rodolphus
Ayers, Benjamin
Barr, Phineas
Blodget, Lyman
Bolding, Asher
Bond, James
Bosworth, Benjamin
Boyden, David
Brown, Alfred
Brown, Henry

Chapin, Thomas
Churchill, Artemas
Cressey, John
Curry, Zenas
Dorrison, Levi
Eldridge, John
Gillson, Timothy
Gleason, Abijah
Gould, Joseph
Hartwell, Peter
Hillman, Justin
Hillman, Presberry
Hitchcock, Obed
Holmes, William
Howard, Amos
Jennings, Ira
Keyes, Luther
Knight, Abel
Knowlton, Ephraim
Lamson, Samuel
Marsh, Eliphaz
Maxwell, Alex P.
McCleod, Charles
McLintock, William
Nims, Samuel P.
Patterson, Sylvanus
Philips, Joel
Philips, Sawyer

Pike, Leonard
Potter, Ambrose
Sanderson, James
Shepherd, Samuel
Sherer, Joseph
Shippee, Amasa
Shippee, Reuben
Smith, Aaron
Stafford, William
Taft, John
Taggart, Rufus
Taylor, James
Temple, Benjamin
Temple, Solomon
Thompson, Joseph
Thompson, Stephen
Vincent, David
Vincent, Joseph, Jr.
Wait, Abraham
Ward, Roswell
Warner, Newton
Wells, Pliny
Whitcomb, John
White, Gardner
White, Joseph
Wilcox, Cyrenus
Willis, Alden
Wilson, Otis

Capt. S. Jenkins' Company, Lieut. Col. T. Longley's Regiment.
From Sept. 13 to Nov. 7, 1814. Raised at Williamsburg and vicinity. Service at Boston.

RANK AND NAME.
Southworth Jenkins, Captain
Artemas Knight, Lieutenant
Elijah Sanderson, Ensign

Jonathan Porter, Sergeant
Serano Lyman, Sergeant
Julius Cook, Sergeant
Harvey Phillips, Sergeant
James Nichols, Musician
Horatio Strong, Musician

Privates.
Attis, Daniel
Attis, George
Badger, Daniel
Bennery, Luke
Bird, Eli
Bridgman, Spencer
Bunce, Frederic
Bunce, Richard
Burnal, Newton
Chapman, Jedediah
Childs, Jonathan
Claghorn, Ahaz
Clapp, Amasa
Clapp, George L.
Clapp, Richard
Clapp, Zebediah

Coats, Erastus
Cole, Consider
Cowen, Job
Crafts, Thomas
Demmean, Louis
Demmean, Zenas
Demnien, Nathan
Dickenson, Giles
Dickenson, Jonathan
Dohl, Benjamin
Faerman, Orrin
Fisher, Aaron
Gillet, Jonathan A.
Graves, Lomous
Green, Daniel P.
Haley, Seth
Hastings, Oliver
Hatch, John
Hemenway, Jason
Hemenway, William
Ingraham, Nathaniel
Leonard, William
Litchfield, Ensign
Luffingwell, Andrew
McCoy, Daniel
Morris, Hezekiah
Nims, James
Perkins, John
Pitcher, Robert P.

Pitsinger, John
Pitsinger, Jonathan
Reswick, Field
Rogers, Joshua
Sanderson, Allen
Scott, David
Shaw, Zachariah
Smith, Ashley
Smith, Mager
Smith, Phineas
Smith, Samuel
Souther, Daniel
Sparks, David
Strong, Paul
Tery, Reuben
Thayer, Silas
Vinlon, Lothrop
Wait, Enos
Wait, Joel
Warner, Alvin
Wells, Israel
White, Freeborn
White, Harris
Wight, Willard
Williams, Abner
Williams, Isaac, 3d
Williams, Kanson
Williams, Warren
Wright, Almond

MASSACHUSETTS VOLUNTEER MILITIA IN THE WAR OF 1812.   65

Capt. T. Lyman's Company, Lieut. Col. T. Longley's Regiment.
From Sept. 13 to Nov. 7, 1814. Raised at Goshen and vicinity. Service at Boston.

RANK AND NAME.
Timothy Lyman, Captain
Daniel Whitman, Lieutenant
William Rice, Ensign

Asa Billings, Sergeant
William Knapp, Sergeant
Levi Olds, Sergeant
Ouvin Towner, Sergeant
Thomas Hayden, Corporal
William Abel, Corporal
Alfred Brown, Corporal
Milton Brewster, Corporal
Pearley Healey, Musician
Benjamin Tyrrel, Musician

Privates.
Anable, Barnabas
Barrows, Robert
Bartlet, Lazarus
Bartlet, Luther
Bates, Daniel
Bates, James
Bates, Nathan
Bates, Orrick
Brewster, William
Briggs, Thomas
Buck, Abner
Buck, Isaac

Buck, Jesse
Burr, Elijah
Burwell, Jason
Cathcart, Oliver T.
Claghorn, Benjamin
Cole, Joseph
Colson, Bolter
Crosby, John
Cushing, John
Daily, Joseph
Drake, Stimson
Dyer, Jacob
Fitch, Solomon P.
Ford, John
Fuller, John
Hall, Thomas
Hatch, James
Higerman, Ira
Higgins, Luther
Hollis, Stephen
Hosford, Arad
James, Enoch
Jordan, Elijah
Lee, Harmon B.
Mason, Nathan
Metcalf, Harvey
Mungo, Elias
Olds, Nathaniel
Parish, Daniel

Parmely, Benjamin
Parsons, Davis
Parsons, Stephen
Parsons, Timothy
Pratt, Josiah
Shaw, Leonard
Shaw, Solomon
Snow, Jacob
Starkweather, Joseph
Sterns, Ezra
Stowel, Davis
Streeter, Samuel
Taylor, Rufus
Terrell, Orrin
Thayer, Samuel
Thayer, Simeon
Tilton, William
Tinker, Nehemiah
Tirrell, Henry
Tirrell, Thomas, Jr.
Tower, Ezekiel
Tower, Luther
Tower, Obediah
Tubbs, Isaac
Warner, Henry
Wheeler, Dewey
Whitmarsh, Nathan
Williams, Abisha
Wing, Saul

Capt. E. Mayo's Company, Lieut. Col. T. Longley's Regiment.
From Sept. 13 to Nov. 7, 1814. Raised at Shutesbury and vicinity. Service at Boston.

RANK AND NAME.
Enos Mayo, Captain
Ebenezer Allen, Lieutenant

Paul Macumber, Sergeant
Otis French, Sergeant
Medad Devett, Sergeant
Louis Reed, Sergeant
Rodolphus Taylor, Sergeant
Chester Lamb, Corporal
Thomas Keet, Corporal
Amasa Brush, Corporal
James Pratt, Corporal
Seth Fisk, Corporal

Privates.
Anderson, Daniel
Anderson, David
Ball or Bull, George
Ball, Stephen
Bartlett, Alfred
Beach, Apolus
Benson, Henry
Bruge, Isaac

Burnham, Ruel
Butterfield, Thomas
Caldwell, James
Carpenter, George W.
Clark, Freeman
Collerton, William W.
Ellis, Moses
Ellis, William
Esterbrook, Henry
Field, Rowlin
Fish, Alexander
Fisk, Dexter
Freeman, Rodolphus
Fuller, James
Gale, David
Gale, Stephen
Goodenough, Thomas
Groves, Merritt
Gunn, Willard
Hosman, Nathan
Joseph, George
Kemp, Laurence
Kindell, Elisha
Lamb, John

Long, David
Macumber, Nathaniel
Mallard, Moses
Mitchell, Dolphin
Paine, Ira
Permenter, Joseph
Philips, William B.
Pierce, Thomas
Pierce, Zadoc
Prindel, John
Reed, Charles
Shepherd, Sterry
Shepherdson, Amos
Simpson, Robert
Smith, Daniel
Spear, Stephen
Stratton, Henry
Taylor, Chester
Taylor, David
Turner, Zadoc
Whelock, Manning
Wood, Ezekiel
Woodward, Mark

Capt. A. Powers' Company, Lieut. Col. T. Longley's Regiment.
From Sept. 13 to Nov. 7, 1814. Raised at New Salem and vicinity. Service at Boston.

RANK AND NAME.
Asa Powers, Captain
Silas Osgood, Lieutenant
Abner Goodell, Ensign

Elisha Shaw, Sergeant
Luther Ford, Sergeant
William Putman, Sergeant
James Clark, Sergeant
Joseph Williams, Corporal
Jonas Ward, Corporal
Amos King, Corporal
Thomas Walkup, Corporal
Noah Wallis, Musician

Privates.
Alber, Samuel
Bancroft, Lyman
Benson, Consider
Briggs, Elkanah
Bruce, James
Butterfield, Levi
Childs, Saul
Clark, John
Crossman, Daniel
Day, Samuel

Farr, Samuel
Fisk, Martin
Forgate, John
Forgett, Aseph
Gall, Abraham
Giles, Magra
Grigg, Stephen
Hager, Martin
Hager, Reuben
Haskins, John
Holt, Jonathan
Holt, Saul, 2d
Jinkot, Asa
Johnson, Hugh M.
Kidder, Jonathan, Jr.
Marble, Jones
Mason, Jonathan
Needham, Joseph
Osgood, Luther
Perkins, Caleb
Perry, Benjamin
Perry, Samuel
Pierce, Ebenezer, Jr.
Rand, Joseph
Reynolds, Alden
Rich, Elisha

Ripley, Ezra
Robinson, Asa
Sampson, Samuel
Sawyer, Thomas
Scranton, Amos
Shaw, Eber
Shaw, John
Smith, Bradwell, Jr.
Smith, William
Stutson, Thaddeus
Thayer, Elijah
Thayer, Savil
Thompson, Willard
Upton, Stephen
Weeks, Caleb
Wheeler, Daniel
Wheeler, Zacheus
Wheelock, Josiah
Whitaker, Paul
Whitcomb, Silas
Williams, Drury
Williams, Stephen
Wilmouth, David
Winship, Benjamin
Wiswell, Edward
Wood, Benjamin, Jr.

Capt. D. Strickland's Company, Lieut. Col. T. Longley's Regiment.
From Sept. 13 to Nov. 7, 1814. Raised at Greenfield and vicinity. Service at Boston.

RANK AND NAME.
David Strickland, Captain
Samuel Coolidge, Lieutenant
Thomas Gilbert, Ensign

Timothy Hall, Sergeant
Alpha Ryther, Sergeant
Augustus Baldwin, Sergeant
Briggs Potter, Sergeant
Elijah Tryon, Musician
James Barry, Musician
Zelotes Ballard, Musician

Privates.
Aldrich, Hosea
Allen, David
Arms, Ralph
Babcock, James
Bacon, Jonathan
Ballard, Alva
Ballard, Orin
Barber, Robert
Billings, Zebina
Bissell, John W.
Bissell, Oliver
Bliss, David
Boyden, David
Caul, Ira

Chapin, Gorham
Clark, Ralph
Coolidge, Rufus
Dennison, John
Dennison, Nathan
Eason, Alden
Foskitt, Robert M.
Foster, Rufus
Gant, Ira
Graves, Newell
Guillow, David
Hastings, Orrissimus
Haynes, Josiah
Horsley, Oralana
Javery, Ephraim
Kendall, Calvin
King, William
Kinyon, Charles
Lamphear, Robert S.
Mann or Munn, Seth
Martindale, Cyrus
Metcalf, John
Morgan, Horace
Nelson, Ichabod
Newcomb, Samuel
Newton, Asahel
Newton, Henry
Nightingale, Ebenezer

Nutting, Zacheriah
Parsons, Amos
Pratt, Ephraim
Presson, Emerson
Rice, Moses
Ripley, Elijah
Russell, Pliny
Ryther, Erastus
Scott, Lewis
Scott, Zorah
Shattuck, Thomas
Sheldon, Alva
Sheldon, Israel
Smith, Stephen
Smith, Walter
Stanhope, Asahel R.
Starr, Samuel
Stevens, Ephraim
Stewart, Amos
Stone, Theophilus
Tiffany, Henry
Towne, Arad
Walker, Ripley
Walker, Samuel
Wells, Abner
Wheeler, Simeon
Wilbur, John

Capt. E. Strong's Company, Lieut. Col. T. Longley's Regiment.

From Sept. 13 to Nov. 7, 1814. Raised at Northampton and vicinity. Service at Boston.

RANK AND NAME.
Elisha Strong, Captain
Thaddeus Persons, Lieutenant
Stephen Woolcott, Ensign

Noah Dailey, Sergeant
Joseph Allen, Sergeant
Thaddeus Clark, Sergeant
Benjamin W. Edgarton, Sergeant
James Clapp, Corporal
Gershom Dunks, Corporal
Elisha Edwards, Corporal
Moses Brick, Corporal
Elihu Strong, Musician
Russell Strong, Musician

Privates.
Alvord, Elisha
Alvord, Samuel
Avery, Worster
Bailey, Otis
Barns, Nathaniel
Bates, Asa
Brockway, Simelious
Brown, Elihu
Brown, Rowland G.

Burk, Franklin
Chapin, Frederic
Chapman, David
Chapman, Isaac
Clap, Eleazer
Clap, Joel
Clap, Luther C.
Clap, Quartus
Clapp, Azariah
Clark, Abner
Clark, Amasa
Clark, Anson K.
Clark, Edward
Clark, Philip
Couch, Moses
Day, Eli
Edwards, Ralph
Hamilton, Adam R.
Hastings, Mitchell
Hendrick, Stephen
Holt, Amasa
Horton, James M.
Levens, Elkanan W.
Lyman, Joel
Mark, Abel
Palton, David

Perkins, Horace
Pierce, Luther
Pomroy, Spencer
Ring, Jesse
Rowley, Thomas
Russell, Samuel
Russell, Solomon L.
Scurl, Wareham
Smith, Chester
Smith, Lebina
Stephens, Cyrus
Strong, Huit S.
Strong, Job S.
Strong, Jonathan
Temple, Ebenezer
Tyler, Elijah
Wait, Ashial
Wait, James
Warlow, Benjamin
Warren, William
Wight, Harris
Wood, Collins
Wood, Ebenezer
Woolcott, Hasall

Capt. J. White's Company, Lieut. Col. T. Longley's Regiment.

From Sept. 13 to Nov. 7, 1814. Raised at Charlemont and vicinity. Service at Boston.

RANK AND NAME.
Joseph White, Captain
Elisha Smith, Lieutenant
Jonathan Comstock, Ensign

William Oaks, Sergeant
Holmes Mayhew, Sergeant
Justus Smith, Sergeant
David Morrison, Sergeant
Erastus Andrews, Sergeant
Anthon Riddle, Corporal
Loren Longley, Corporal
Asa Blood, Jr., Corporal
Amos Brooks, Corporal
Amos Bangs, Musician

Privates.
Alden, Jonathan
Belding, Amos
Belding, Samuel
Boyden, Israel
Boyden, Nathaniel
Brunsen, Smissen
Carter, Brigham
Carter, John
Case, B.
Cobb, David
Cobb, John

Crosby, Theophilus
Crowell, Ebenezer, Jr.
Davis, Nathaniel
Dickinson, Epaphras
Dodge, Thomas
Drake, Jehiel
Eddy, Zebulon
Eldridge, Eli
Flagg, Chandler
Fox, Israel
Gilford, Samuel
Graves or Groves, Orlando
Grover, Josiah, Jr.
Hall, Atherton
Hall, John
Harding, Abijah
Hart, Charles
Hawks, Isaac
Hawks, Rufus
Holden, Obed
Howard, Jonathan
Howes, William
Johnson, William
Kelly, Josiah
Knowlton, Friend
Lazell, Alvah
Leonard, John
Longley, Luther

Look, John
Loverage, Ethan
Lyon, Nathan
Merrill, James
Miller, James
Nelson, Moses
Olis or Otis, Rodolphus
Phipps, James
Pike, Elisha
Pomroy, Aaron
Pratt, Silas
Rice, Colver
Risley, Chester
Sears, Abner
Sears, Sylvester
Smith, Glisson
Sprague, John
Stocking, Herod
Strong, Noble
Taylor, Ansel
Upton, Elias, Jr.
Upton, Josiah, Jr.
Vibber, William
Washburn, Benjamin
Weatherhold, John
Wilcox, David
Woodman, Peter

Lieut. Col. D. Messinger's Regiment.
From Sept. 16 to Oct. 10, 1814. Service at Boston.

FIELD AND STAFF.		NONCOMMISSIONED STAFF.
Daniel Messinger, Lieutenant Colonel, Boston	Jechonias Thayer, Quartermaster, Boston	John Heard, Sergeant Major
Samuel Curtis, Major, Boston	Ferdinand E. White, Paymaster, Boston	
Charles Curtis, Major, Boston	Asa Buckman, Surgeon, Boston	
Stephen Fairbanks, Adjutant, Boston	Samuel Reeves, Surgeon's Mate, Boston	
	Horace Holley, Chaplain, Boston	

Capt. B. B. Appleton's Company, Lieut. Col. D. Messinger's Regiment.
From Sept. 10 to Oct. 10, 1814. Raised at Boston. Service at Boston.

RANK AND NAME.		
B. B. Appleton, Captain	Childs, Jonathan	Lyon, Abner
Luke Richardson, Lieutenant	Chubbuck, Henry	Martis, Anthony
John Parks, Ensign	Clap, Artemus	Merritt, Noah
	Cook, Seth B.	Mills, George
David Firmin, Sergeant	Cruse, John	Moody, Samuel
Henry K. Appleton, Sergeant	Curtis, Charles	Morgan, Daniel L.
George Wheelright, Sergeant	Darling, Samuel	Oliver, Charles
Samuel Farmer, Sergeant	Dearborn, Math	Powers, Francis
	Demming, Jonathan E.	Powers, Levi
Privates.	Dunsmore, Samuel	Richards, John
Appleton, Thomas	Emerson, George S.	Ruddock, Amos
Ayers, Moses	Fay, Joel	Russell, Samuel
Ayers, Will	Felton, Luther	Sargent, James
Baldwin, Abel	Foster, James	Simmons, Luke
Ball, Russell	Francis, Math	Southworth, Thomas
Belcher, John	Gale, John	Stebbins, Judah
Blackburn, Benjamin	Gale, Will	Ward, Royal
Blaney, Benjamin	Hadley, Charles	Weston, Asahel
Bowker, Charles	Hadley, Samuel	Wethercox, Jacob
Brown, John	Hatch, John	Whiting, David
Buckingham, Joseph F.	Hendley, Henry W.	Williams, Josiah
Burkis, Lewis	Hoard, Stephen	Wishington, Newell
Burnham, Isaac	Hosmer, Hammond	Wiswall, Andrew
Chamberlain, David	Kennard, Aleut	Wright, Will
	Knight, George	Young, Joseph

Capt. E. O. Fifield's Company, Lieut. Col. D. Messinger's Regiment.
From Sept. 16 to Oct. 10, 1814. Raised at Boston. Service at Boston.

RANK AND NAME.		
E. O. Fifield, Captain	Carey, Josiah D.	Leroy, Job
Benjamin Huntington, Lieutenant	Carlton, Isaac	Loring, William
Joseph Williams, Ensign	Davis, Frederick	Lyman, Thadeus
	Decoster, James	Marshall, Samuel
William B. Willis, Sergeant	Dodd, Benjamin	Maynard, Joseph
Nathaniel Healey, Sergeant	Fessenden, Moses	McClure, Bartholomew
Daniel Hill, Sergeant	Fowle, William	Morse, Jesse
Charles Callender, Sergeant	French, Joseph	Parker, Eber
Silas Dodd, Corporal	Fullman, Samuel	Pierce, John
William Kerr, Corporal	Geyer, John J.	Porter, William L.
William Blake, Corporal	Geyer, Joseph	Sanford, Samuel
James Powers, Corporal	Geyer, Samuel	Shumway, Asa
Sheldon Perry, Musician	Hagar, James	Snow, Thomas
Samuel Pearson, Musician	Hagar, William	Sweetser, Charles B.
	Harlow, Zacheus	Tufts, Fitch
Privates.	Harrington, Wyman	Welch, John A.
Abbott, Nathaniel	Holbrook, Samuel	Wheeler, Cyrus
Ames, Jacob	Hollis, William	Whitton, Robert
Barry, Thomas, Jr.	Jewett, Solomon	Wilder, Eleazer
Billings, Ebenezer	Kensly, Henry	Worcester, Alpheus
Blackman, Thomas	Kettle, Andrew	Wyman, Marbick
Bowdly, Samuel	Kidder, Stephen	
	Laughton, John	

MASSACHUSETTS VOLUNTEER MILITIA IN THE WAR OF 1812.   69

Capt. R. Hartshorn's Company, Lieut. Col. D. Messinger's Regiment.
From Sept. 16 to Oct. 10, 1814.   Raised at Boston.   Service at Boston.

RANK AND NAME.
Rolin Hartshorn, Captain
Thomas A. Drayton, Lieutenant
James Hendley, Ensign

John Drayton, Sergeant
Joseph Hartshorn, Sergeant
Rufus G. Amory, Jr., Sergeant
Lewis B. Davis, Corporal
Benjamin Horton, Jr., Corporal
Robert Emerson, Corporal
James Topliff, Corporal
Joseph Champney, Musician

Privates.

Allen, Marston
Anderson, John
Badgers, Samuel
Capen, Edmund

Cory, Avory
Cox, Samuel
Davidson, John
Dow, Stephen
Emmons, Jonathan
Emmons, Samuel F.
Everett, William
Foster, John H.
Garland, Francis
Hawes, William
Hovey, Aaron
Hurland or Ireland, James
Jenkins, Samuel
Kimball, Abel
Mason, Comer
Parker, Isaac
Parsons, William
Phillips, Samuel
Pierce, Hach

Potter, David
Raymond, Francis
Richards, Joseph
Robinson, Ebenezer
Savage, Edward
Shattuck, Jesse
Smith, Mark
Somerby, Profit
Sprague, J.
Stowell, Benjamin
Stowell, John
Thorndike, Jeremiah
Vinton, Abel
Ware, Joshua
Waters, Clark
West, Benjamin
Worthington, Anthony

Capt. W. Knight's Company, Lieut. Col. D. Messinger's Regiment.
From Sept. 16 to Oct. 10, 1814.   Raised at Boston.   Service at Boston.

RANK AND NAME.
Winthrop Knight, Captain
Joseph Jenkins, Lieutenant
D. Moody, Ensign

William Symonds, Sergeant
Aaron Merrett, Sergeant
Sylvester Morse, Musician
Jabez Conant, Musician

Privates.

Baker, Francis
Beals, Levi
Bean, Simeon
Blasland, Gideon
Bowers, Charles
Brown, Isaac
Bruce, David
Cassell, James
Champney, William I.
Chapin, D.
Cobb, Enos
Cowing, Cornelius

Dane, Nathan
Ditson, John
Emmerston, Jeremiah
Fellows, Benjamin
Francis, John
Frothingham, Thomas, Jr.
Green, Jeremiah
Hapgood, Samuel
Hathwait, Francis
Heath, John
Hill, Samuel B.
Howard, Barnard
Howe, Henry
Irving, Edward
Jewett, Nathaniel
Johnson, John
Lewis, William R.
Lincoln, Ezekiel
Lincoln, Ezra
Lincoln, Lemuel
Lyon, Benjamin
Mace, James
Marsters, Robert

Mason, John
Miller, Jesse
Murdock, Isaac
Payne, William
Pitts, Lindall
Reynolds, William
Safford, Daniel
Sprague, Hosea
Steel, Robert
Trask, James
Trumbull, James
Vose, James W.
Vose, Reuben
Waterman, Levi
Wells, Charles
Wells, Theodore
Wheelock, Paul
Whelwell, William
Wood, Lewis
Woodward, Joseph
Wyett, George

Capt. J. B. Marston's Company, Lieut. Col. D. Messinger's Regiment.
From Sept. 16 to Oct. 11, 1814.   Raised at Boston.   Service at Boston.

RANK AND NAME.
James B. Marston, Captain
Joshua Simmonds, Lieutenant
Christopher Gore, Jr., Ensign

Jeremiah Smallidge, Sergeant
Samuel Jewett, Sergeant
Peter Seaver, Sergeant
Ebenezer Tirrell, Sergeant

Robert Jenks, Corporal
William Butler, Corporal
George Hagerty, Corporal
Thomas Holland, Corporal

Privates.

Alden, John A.
Appleton, Charles J.
Bannia, David

Bickford, John
Black, William
Blanchard, Nathaniel
Bryant, Thomas
Chardon, James, Jr.
Churchwell, Levi
Cobb, Josiah
Cook, Corey
Cutter, Oliver

Capt. J. B. Marston's Company, Lieut. Col. D. Messinger's Regiment — Concluded.

Privates — Concluded.
Dame, Abraham
Davis, Ebenezer
DeForest, Sydney
Durwage, Francis S.
Goff, Robert S.
Gray, Jeremiah
Gulliver, Stephen
Hale, Nathan
Harris, Ephraim
Harris, Robert
Hay, Thomas
Hitchborn, Alexander
Holland, Thomas, 2d
Johnson, Milton
Keith, Nathaniel

LaRogue, Benjamin
Lena, Ebenezer
Lloyd, Frederic
Loring, Josiah
Malcomb, Michael
Merrill, James C.
Mott, Joshua
Nelson, David
Page, John
Parker, Amos B.
Payne, Ezra
Pennyman, James
Richards, Peter
Richardson, Benjamin
Robbins, William
Robbinson, John

Scott, Nathaniel
Smith, Cicero
Smith, Oliver
Stephens, Oliver
Stockwell, Joseph
Tirrell, Gideon
Tirrell, Joseph
Tolman, Robert P.
Tucker, John
Tucker, John, Jr.
Weller, Andrew
Wendall, Jacob, Jr.
Wheelwright, John
Whitcomb, Laban

Capt. J. Fairbanks' Company, Lieut. Col. D. Messinger's Regiment.
From Sept. 28 to Oct. 4, 1814. Raised at Boston. Service at Boston.

RANK AND NAME.
John Fairbanks, Captain
Bela Hunter, Lieutenant
James Blake, Ensign

Josiah Blanchard, Sergeant
Amos Sumner, Sergeant
Esekiel Sawin, Sergeant
Ephraim Harrington, Sergeant
Amos Coolege, Corporal
Washington Thayer, Corporal
Thomas Dascomb, Corporal
George Willard, Corporal
Jonas Emery, Musician

Privates.
Abbott, William
Adams, Charles
Ayling, Thomas
Ball, Daniel
Bennett, Moses
Bent, Adam
Blanchard, Elisha
Brett, William, Jr.
Briggs, John
Cabot, John O.

Chapman, John
Cole, Seth
Curtis, Benjamin
Curtis, Samuel
Curtis, Theophilus
Dewey, William
Dimond, David
Eggleston, Elisha
Estey, Joseph
Field, Charles
Fisher, William, Jr.
Ford, Burnett
Godfrey, Joseph
Gould, Asa
Gould, Reuben
Gove, Stephen
Green, Isaac
Hammond, Thomas
Hammond, William
Hancock, Henry
Harris, Elijah
Harris, Isaac
Harris, James
Harris, Joseph
Hayward, Cyrus
Hewins, Abel

Hewins, Whiting
Hunt, William H.
Jackson, Stephen W.
Jones, Samuel
Kingsley, Ellis
Leadbetter, Gurdon A.
Long, Joseph
Looker, Marshall
Meade, Nathaniel
Nolen, Spencer
Phinney, Joseph
Pratt, Joseph W.
Richardson, John
Rowe, Anthony
Sanderson, Amos
Sawyer, Asaph
Searle, Ephraim
Skinner, Charles
Talbott, George
Thomas, John
Tilestone, Euclid, Jr.
Tisdale, Mace
Upham, Amos
Whiting, George
Whitmore, Nathaniel
Williams, Joshua H.

Capt. P. Bonner's Company, Lieut. Col. D. Messinger's Regiment.
From Oct. 23 to Oct. 30, 1814. Raised at Boston. Service at Boston.

RANK AND NAME.
Philip Bonner, Captain
Micah B. Bacon, Lieutenant
William H. Ireland, Ensign

J. Farriter, Sergeant
Thomas Stowell, Sergeant
Samuel Edes, Sergeant
David Claflin, Sergeant
Henry Weyer, Corporal

Jeremiah Sprague, Corporal
Thomas Ayers, Corporal
Joshua Cheevers, Corporal
——— Park, Musician
J. Nutting, Musician

Privates.
Ayling, Henry
Bass, Elias
Beck, Frederick

Blake, Henry
Cambridge, Frederick
Capen, Thomas
Childs, Thomas
Conder, Joseph
Copeland, Elias, Jr.
Corry, George
Crane, William
Cunningham, Thomas
Cutler, Nahum

Capt. P. Bonner's Company, Lieut. Col. D. Messinger's Regiment — Concluded.

Privates — Concluded.
Detson, William
Foster, Adams
Gordon, Jonathan
Gray, Benjamin
Haskins, Thomas
Holbrook, Edmund
Holden, Ebenezer
Howes, William
Hunt, John
Ireland, Jonathan
Jordan, Jonathan
Lovell, William
Newman, Andrew

Patten, Joel B.
Powers, Jonathan
Russell, George
Sawyer, Jonathan
Shaites, Edmund
Shoates, William
Sprague, Charles
Sprague, Jonathan
Stanwood, William
Stowell, John
Sumner, Seth
Teel, George
Tileston, Charles
Tolman, William

Vincent, Samuel, Jr.
Vose, William
Webber, John
Wetherbee, Simon P.
Wheeler, Nathaniel
Wheeler, Samuel
Wheeler, William
White, John
Whitmore, John
Whitney, Elisha
Wilder, Lewis
Willes, George

Capt. H. Rice's Company, Lieut. Col. D. Messinger's Regiment.[1]
October, 1814. Service at Boston. Detailed for special duty.

RANK AND NAME.
Henry Rice, Captain
David Francis, Lieutenant
George Bond, Ensign

Samuel Adams, Sergeant
Samuel Blake, Sergeant
Benjamin Stevens, Sergeant
Andrew Bradshaw, Sergeant
Charles Ellis, Corporal

William Gilman, Corporal
Joseph W. Holmes, Corporal
Benjamin Seaver, Corporal
John Wetherbee, Musician
Jedediah Barker, Musician

[1] List of privates, if any, not found.

Lieut. Col. David Nye's Regiment.
A few days each in January, February, June, September and October, 1814, at alarms, 14 days in all. Service at Falmouth and Barnstable.

FIELD AND STAFF.
David Nye, Lieutenant Colonel, Falmouth

John Freeman, Major, Sandwich
James or John Toby, Adjutant, Sandwich

Nathaniel Nye, Paymaster, Falmouth

Capt. T. Swift's Company, Lieut. Col. D. Nye's Regiment.
From Jan. 20 to Jan. 31, and Oct. 3 to Oct. 5, 1814. Raised at Sandwich. Service at Falmouth.

RANK AND NAME.
Thomas Swift, Captain
Nathan B. Gibbs, Lieutenant
Benjamin Battles, Ensign

Levi Swift, Sergeant
Luman Swift, Sergeant
William King, Sergeant

Privates.
Bassett, Thomas
Bennett, Thomas
Blackwell, Benjamin
Blackwell, Ellis
Bourne, Alvin
Bourne, Elisha
Bourne, Lemuel
Bourne, Nathan
Bumpus, Braddock
Burgess, Anson
Burgess, Jacob
Cobb, Allanson

Colman, Ebenezer
Cook, John
Dimmick, David, Jr.
Dimmick, Frederick
Dunham, Samuel
Ellis, Abner
Ellis, Bartlett
Ellis, Jesse
Ellis, Josiah
Ellis, Levi
Ellis, Micah
Ellis, Thomas
Ellis, William
Gibbs, Barnabus
Gibbs, Caleb, Jr.
Gibbs, Freeman
Gibbs, Jonathan
Gibbs, Josiah
Gibbs, Pitham, Jr.
Gibbs, Robert
Gibbs, Rufus
Gifford, Silas

Gurnsey, Thomas
Handy, Calvin
Harriss, James
Harriss, Joseph
Human, John, Jr.
Keen, Abraham
Keen, John
Keen, Trueman
Kinkley, Edward
Lawrence, David
Lawrence, Owen
Lumbard, Thomas, Jr.
McGowns, Lot
Nightingale, Ellis
Nightingale, William
Nye, Daniel B.
Nye, Samuel
Nye, Solomon
Perry, Arthur
Perry, Heman
Perry, James
Perry, Mitaliah

Capt. T. Swift's Company, Lieut. Col. D. Nye's Regiment — Concluded.

Privates — Concluded.
Perry, Phineas
Perry, Prince
Perry, Silas
Perry, Solomon
Perry, Stephen
Perry, Zacheus
Phinney, Edward
Phinney, Elisha

Phinney, Jabez
Phinney, John
Phinney, Josiah
Swift, Abraham
Swift, Alden
Swift, Clark
Swift, Ellis
Swift, James
Swift, Thomas, Jr.

Swift, William
Toby, Tristram
Willis, Wendell D.
Wing, Alvin
Wing, Lot
Wing, Nathaniel
Witherell, John

Capt. S. Hamlin's Company, Lieut. Col. D. Nye's Regiment.
From Jan. 28 to Jan. 31, June 13 to June 14, and Oct. 3 to Oct. 9, 1814. Service at Falmouth.

RANK AND NAME.
Seth Hamlin, Captain
Joshua Nye, Lieutenant
Joshua Jenkins, Ensign

Walter Turner, Sergeant
John Robinson, Sergeant
Francis Nye, Sergeant
Barnabus Hamlin, Musician
Jarvis Green, Musician

Privates.
Baker, Barnabus
Baker, Edmund
Baker, Jabez
Baker, Nathaniel
Bourne, Barnabus
Bourne, David
Bourne, Elijah
Bourne, Jarvis
Bourne, Nathaniel
Bradford, David
Butler, Davis
Cahoon, Smalley
Chadwick, Barnabus
Chadwick, David
Chadwick, Elijah
Chadwick, Oliver
Chadwick, Samuel
Childs, Barnabus
Childs, Calvin
Childs, John
Childs, Joseph
Childs, Thomas
Crocker, Alexander
Crocker, Henry
Crowell, Adinah
Crowell, Benjamin
Crowell, William
Davis, Isaiah, Jr.
Davis, Job
Davis, Joseph, 3d
Davis, Malorhia, Jr.

Davis, Samuel
Davis, Thomas
Davis, Walter
Edwards, Asa, Jr.
Edwards, John
Eldridge, Benjamin
Eldridge, Ezekiel
Eldridge, Nathaniel
Eldridge, Samuel
Eldridge, Simeon
Eldridge, Ward
Ellis, Nathan
Fish, Edward
Fish, Nathan
Fish, Nathan, 2d
Fish, Rufus
Fish, Timothy
Fisk, Calvin
Fisk, James
Fuller, Daniel
Fuller, Eleazer
Green, Edward
Green, Thomas
Hamlin, Reuben
Hamlin, Silvanus
Hamlin, Solomon
Harding, Simeon
Hatch, Benjamin
Hatch, Colman
Hatch, Dunham
Hatch, Ebenezer
Hatch, Eliphalet
Hatch, Isaac
Hatch, Isaiah
Hatch, John
Hatch, Moses, Jr.
Hatch, Reuben
Hatch, Silvanus
Head, William
Himer, Joseph A.
Hinkley, Abner
Hinkley, Elijah
Jenkins, Joseph

Jenkins, Samuel
Landers, Bathuel
Lawrence, Shubel
Lewis, Isaiah
Lewis, James
Lewis, Thomas
Lombard, Edward
McLane, Thomas
Nickerson, Enos
Nye, Alvin
Nye, Benjamin
Nye, Ervin
Nye, James
Nye, Paul
Nye, Prince
Nye, Samuel
Nye, Shubal
Nye, Stephen
Parker, Benjamin
Parker, Calvin
Parker, George
Parker, Isaac
Parker, Silvanus
Phinney, Abner
Phinney, Asa
Phinney, Braddock
Phinney, Ebenezer
Phinney, Robinson
Robinson, Braddock
Robinson, Ezekiel
Robinson, Peter
Robinson, Seth
Sanders, Abiel
Smalley, Anthony
Smalley, James
Snow, Ezekiel
Sturdley, Ebenezer
Swift, Allen
Swift, Ezekiel
Swift, John, Jr.
Swift, Nathaniel
Swift, Thomas
Tobey, John

Capt. W. Jenkins' Company, Lieut. Col. D. Nye's Regiment.

From Jan. 28 to Jan. 31, June 13 to June 18, and Oct. 3 to Oct. 15, 1814. Service at Falmouth.

Rank and Name.
Weston Jenkins, Captain
William Nye, Lieutenant
Thomas Lawrence, Lieutenant

William Eldred, Sergeant
Ebenezer Nye, Sergeant
Nathaniel Shiverick, Sergeant
Alfred Gifford, Sergeant

Privates.
Allen, Willard
Allen, William
Butler, David, Jr.
Butler, John
Crocker, John
Davis, Stephen
Dimmick, Henry
Dimmick, John
Gifford, Asa
Gifford, Bassett
Gifford, Rossiter
Green, Ebenezer
Hatch, Allen
Hatch, Ebenezer
Hatch, Elihu
Hatch, Elisha
Hatch, Foster
Hatch, Silas
Lawrence, John
Lawrence, Silas, Jr.
Lewis, Fletcher
Lewis, Thatcher
Marchant, Barua
Noble, Jesse
Nye, Nathan
Nye, Warren
Parker, Ephraim
Peas, Barzilla
Robinson, Joseph
Shiverick, William
Wicks, John

Capt. O. B. Nye's Company, Lieut. Col. D. Nye's Regiment.

From Jan. 28 to Feb. 3, 1814. Raised at Sandwich. Service at Falmouth.

Rank and Name.
Obed B. Nye, Captain
Nathan B. Gibbs, Lieutenant
Edward Nye, Lieutenant
Henry Lawrence, Ensign
Thomas S. Nye, Ensign

James Stewart, Sergeant
Ezra L. Bourne, Sergeant
Herman Swift, Sergeant
Zenas Nye, 2d, Sergeant
Bethuel Nye, Sergeant

Privates.
Allen, Alden
Bacus, Herman
Bassett, John
Bassett, Nathan
Bassett, William, Jr.
Blossom, Benjamin
Blossom, Samuel
Bourne, Elisha
Bourne, Elisha, 2d
Bourne, Elisha, 3d
Bourne, Samuel
Burgess, James
Burgess, Perez
Crocker, George
Crocker, John
Dean, Alonzo
Dean, Monroe
Dillingham, John B.
Dillingham, Lemuel
Dillingham, Simon
Drody, Allen
Drody, Samuel
Ellis, Abner
Ellis, Josiah, Jr.
Ewer, Alvin
Ewer, Lemuel
Faunce, William
Fessenden, Samuel
Fessenden, Thomas
Fessenden, William
Fish, Abraham
Fish, Chipman
Fish, Daniel
Fish, Ephraim
Fish, Isaiah
Fish, James
Fish, Lemuel, Jr.
Fish, Moody
Fish, Silas
Freeman, Edmund
Fuller, Benjamin
Fuller, Joseph, Jr.
Fuller, Samuel
Gibbs, Josiah
Gibbs, Pitham, Jr.
Gibbs, Robert
Gifford, Alden
Goodspeed, Harrison
Goodspeed, Luther
Hall, Joseph
Hall, Winslow
Hamlin, Thomas
Harris, Joseph
Heman, Joshua
Heman, William
Holway, William
Howland, James
Hoxie, John
Jones, Francis
Jones, Francis F.
Keen, Abraham
Keen, Freeman
King, William
Knowland, James
Lawrence, Peleg
Lawrence, Solomon
Meiggs, Jonathan
Newcomb, Samuel
Nightingale, Ellis
Nye, Abraham
Nye, Abraham W.
Nye, Bethuel
Nye, Charles
Nye, Edmund
Nye, Edward
Nye, Heman
Nye, Holmes
Nye, Isaac
Nye, Joseph, 3d
Nye, Joshua
Nye, Josiah
Nye, Nathaniel
Nye, Paul
Nye, Samuel
Nye, Thomas S.
Nye, Zenas, 2d
Percifal, Freeman
Percifal, John
Perry, Stephen
Phinny, Gersham
Phinny, Josiah
Pope, Lervin
Pope, Seth
Smith, Joseph
Toby, Ezra
Truman, Joshua
Truman, William
Wetherell, John

74 MASSACHUSETTS VOLUNTEER MILITIA IN THE WAR OF 1812.

Capt. B. Hamlin's Company, Lieut. Col. D. Nye's Regiment.
From Jan. 29 to Jan. 31, and Oct. 3 to Oct. 12, 1814. Raised at Sandwich. Service at Falmouth.

RANK AND NAME.
Benjamin Hamlin, Captain
Anson R. Fish, Lieutenant
Henry Lawrence, Ensign

Ellis Hamlin, Sergeant
Theodore Fish, Sergeant
Lot Adams, Sergeant

Privates.
Adams, Samuel
Ames, William
Bearse, Thomas
Chadwick, James
Doty, James
Eldridge, Ephraim
Ewer, Abram
Ewer, Benjamin
Ewer, Lemuel
Ewer, Shubel

Fish, Asa
Fish, Braddock
Fish, Chipman
Fish, David
Fish, Ephraim
Fish, Jesse
Fish, Lemuel
Fish, Prince
Fish, Simeon
Fish, Simeon, Jr.
Fish, Thomas
Gifford, Adam
Goodspeed, Rowland
Goodspeed, Walley
Hallet, Ezekiel
Hamlin, Charles
Hamlin, Nathaniel
Hamlin, Seth
Jones, John
Jones, Micajah

Lawrence, Peleg
Lawrence, William
Lawrence, Zeno
Lombard, William
Lowell, David
Meigs, Eliphalet
Meigs, Asa
Meigs, Jonathan
Meigs, Josiah
Meigs, Seth
Notway, Joseph
Percifal, John
Percifal, Timothy
Percival, Trueman
Phinney, Thomas
Sanders, Abraham
Tanner, Joshua
Townsend, Ellis
West, Samuel
West, Stephen, Jr.

Capt. C. Crocker's Company, Lieut. Col. D. Nye's Regiment.
Various dates from Jan. 28 to Oct. 5, 1814. Raised at Falmouth. This company was in battle at Falmouth, Jan. 28, 1814, at the time the British brig "Nimrod" bombarded the town.

RANK AND NAME.
Calvin Crocker, Captain, Jan. 28 to Oct. 5
Joseph Hamblin, Lieutenant, Jan. 28 to Oct. 5
Ebenezer Bodfish, Ensign, Jan. 28 to Oct. 5

Allen James, Sergeant, Jan. 28 to Oct. 5
Lemuel Jenkins, Sergeant, Jan. 28 to Oct. 5
William Lamson, Sergeant, Jan. 28 to Oct. 5
Joseph Goodspeed, Sergeant, Jan. 28 to Oct. 5

Privates.
Backus, Calvin, Jan. 28 to Oct. 5
Backus, Heman, Feb. 2 to Oct. 5
Backus, Joshua, Jan. 28 to Oct. 5
Backus, Joshua, Sept. 18 to Oct. 5
Backus, Thomas, Sept. 18 to Oct. 5
Bassett, Charles, Jan. 28 to Oct. 5
Bassett, John, Jan. 28 to Oct. 5
Black, David, Jan. 28 to Oct. 5
Blish, Charles, Sept. 27 to Oct. 5
Blish, George, Jan. 28 to Oct. 5
Blossom, Josiah, Jan. 28 to Oct. 5
Bodfish, Alvin, Sept. 27 to Oct. 5
Bodfish, David, Jan. 28 to Oct. 5
Bodfish, Joseph, Jan. 28 to Oct. 5
Bodfish, Josiah, Jan. 28 to Oct. 5
Bodfish, Oliver, Sept. 18 to Oct. 5
Bodfish, Prince, Jan. 28 to Oct. 5
Bussby, Heman, Jan. 28 to Oct. 5
Bussby, Josiah, Jan. 28 to Oct. 5
Coombs, Ephraim, Sept. 18 to Oct. 5

Cotelle, John, Jan. 28 to Oct. 5
Crocker, Abiather, Jan. 28 to Oct. 5
Crocker, Abner, Jr., Feb. 2 to Oct. 5
Crocker, Alvin, Jr., Feb. 2 to Oct. 5
Crocker, Arthur, Jan. 28 to Oct. 5
Crocker, Barnabas, Jan. 28 to Oct. 5
Crocker, Bethuel, Feb. 2 to Oct. 5
Crocker, David, Jan. 28 to Oct. 5
Crocker, David, 2d, Jan. 28 to Oct. 5
Crocker, Enoch, Jan. 28 to Oct. 5
Crocker, Ezra, Jan. 28 to Oct. 5
Crocker, George, Jan. 28 to Oct. 5
Crocker, Hamlin, Jan. 28 to Oct. 5
Crocker, Heman, Jan. 28 to Oct. 5
Crocker, Isaac, Jan. 28 to Oct. 5
Crocker, Joseph, 3d, Jan. 28 to Oct. 5
Crocker, Josiah, Jr., Jan. 28 to Oct. 5
Crocker, Lemuel, Jan. 28 to Oct. 5
Crocker, Moses, Sept. 18 to Oct. 5
Crocker, Nimphus, Jan. 28 to Oct. 5
Crocker, Prince, Jan. 28 to Oct. 5
Crocker, Rufus, Jan. 28 to Oct. 5
Crocker, Thacker, Jan. 28 to Oct. 5
Crocker, Watson, Jan. 28 to Oct. 5
Crocker, Zacheus, Jan. 28 to Oct. 5
Crocker, Zacheus, Feb. 2 to Oct. 5
Crocker, Zenas, Jan. 28 to Oct. 5
Fish, David, Sept. 18 to Oct. 5
Fish, Reuben, Jan. 28 to Oct. 5
Fish, Theodore, Sept. 18 to Oct. 5
Fish, Zenas, Jan. 28 to Oct. 5
Fuller, James, Jr., Jan. 28 to Oct. 5
Fuller, Matthias, Jan. 28 to Oct. 5
Fuller, Thomas, Jan. 28 to Oct. 5
Goodspeed, Benjamin, 2d, Jan. 28 to Oct. 5

Goodspeed, Charles, Jan. 28 to Oct. 5
Goodspeed, Charles H., Jan. 28 to Oct. 5
Goodspeed, Ervin, Jan. 28 to Oct. 5
Goodspeed, Ezra, Jan. 28 to Oct. 5
Goodspeed, John, Feb. 2 to Oct. 5
Goodspeed, Jonathan, Jan. 28 to Oct. 5
Goodspeed, Joseph, 2d, Sept. 18 to Oct. 5
Goodspeed, Levi, Jan. 28 to Oct. 5
Goodspeed, Silas, Jan. 28 to Oct. 5
Goodspeed, Thomas, Jan. 28 to Oct. 5
Green, David, Jan. 28 to Oct. 5
Hamlin, Daniel, Jan. 28 to Oct. 5
Hamlin, John, Jr., Jan. 28 to Oct. 5
Hamlin, Shubael, Sept. 18 to Oct. 5
Hamlin, Winslow, Jan. 28 to Oct. 5
Hinkle, Abraham, Jan. 28 to Oct. 5
Hinkly, James, Jan. 28 to Oct. 5
Hinkly, William, Jan. 28 to Oct. 5
Howland, Jason, Feb. 2 to Oct. 5
Howland, Joseph, Jan. 28 to Oct. 5
Jenkins, Baily, Jan. 28 to Oct. 5
Jenkins, Charles, Jan. 28 to Oct. 5
Jenkins, Eliphalet, Jan. 28 to Oct. 5
Jenkins, Ellis, Jan. 28 to Oct. 5
Jenkins, Nathan, Jan. 28 to Oct. 5
Jenkins, Nathaniel, Jr., Feb. 2 to Oct. 5
Jenkins, Perez, Jan. 28 to Oct. 5
Jenkins, Samuel, Jan. 28 to Oct. 5
Jones, Asa, Jr., Jan. 28 to Oct. 5
Jones, Benjamin, Jan. 28 to Oct. 5
Jones, Benjamin, Jr., Sept. 18 to Oct. 5
Jones, Henry, Jan. 28 to Oct. 5
Jones, Jedediah, Jan. 28 to Oct. 5
Jones, Joseph, Jan. 28 to Oct. 5
Jones, Joseph Q., Jan. 28 to Oct. 5
Jones, Merena, Jan. 28 to Oct. 5

MASSACHUSETTS VOLUNTEER MILITIA IN THE WAR OF 1812.

Capt. C. Crocker's Company, Lieut. Col. D. Nye's Regiment — Concluded.

Privates — Concluded.
Jones, Nathan, Jan. 28 to Oct. 5
Jones, Stephen, Jr., Jan. 28 to Oct. 5
Jones, Thomas, Jan. 28 to Oct. 5
Kelly, Jeremiah, Sept. 18 to Oct. 5
Kelly, Warren, Jan. 28 to Oct. 5
Lavell, Benjamin, Jan. 28 to Oct. 5
Lawrence, Joseph, Jan. 28 to Oct. 5
Lovell, Charles, Sept. 18 to Oct. 5
Marston, Charles, Jan. 28 to Oct. 5
Marston, Clement, Jan. 28 to Oct. 5
Marston, Nimphus, Jan. 28 to Oct. 5
Marston, Prentice, Jan. 28 to Oct. 5

Nye, L., Jan. 28 to Oct. 5
Nye, Parker, Jan. 28 to Oct. 5
Parker, David, Jan. 28 to Oct. 5
Parker, Joseph, Feb. 2 to Oct. 5
Parker, Joshua, Jan. 28 to Oct. 5
Parker, Josiah, Jr., Jan. 28 to Oct. 5
Parker, Seth, Jan. 28 to Oct. 5
Parker, Sturges, Jan. 28 to Oct. 5
Percival, Isaac, Jan. 28 to Oct. 5
Phinny, David, Jan. 28 to Oct. 5
Sampson, Josiah, Jr., Jan. 28 to Oct. 5
Saunders, Joseph, Sept. 18 to Oct. 5
Smith, Charles, Jan. 28 to Oct. 5

Smith, Isaac, Jan. 28 to Oct. 5
Smith, Joseph, Jr., Sept. 18 to Oct. 5
Smith, Mathias, Jan. 28 to Oct. 5
Snow, Hercules, Jan. 28 to Oct. 5
Stevens, Samuel, Jan. 28 to Oct. 5
Taylor, Simeon, Jan. 28 to Oct. 5
Thomas, Elisha, Jan. 28 to Oct. 5
Vowland, Jabez, Jan. 28 to Oct. 5
Weeks, Zenos, Jan. 28 to Oct. 5
Whitman, Joseph, Sept. 18 to Oct. 5
Willard, Bartlet, Jan. 28 to Oct. 5
Wood, Waterman, Feb. 2 to Oct. 5
Wright, Benjamin, Sept. 18 to Oct. 5

Lieut. N. Gibbs' Company, Lieut. Col. D. Nye's Regiment. Under Capt. Thomas Swift, with 20 miles' travel twice.
Six days in January and 6 days from Sept. 6 to Sept. 12, 1814. Raised at Sandwich. Service at Falmouth.

RANK AND NAME.
Nathan B. Gibbs, Lieutenant
Benjamin Battles, Ensign

Othniel Onions, Sergeant
Heman Swift, Sergeant
James Ellis, Sergeant
William King, Sergeant

Privates.
Barton, Solomon N.
Bennet, Thomas
Bourne, Elisha
Bourne, Henry
Bourne, John
Bourne, Lemuel
Bourne, Timothy
Burgess, Anson
Burgess, Covel
Burgess, Jabez
Burgess, Peter
Burgess, Thomas
Cook, John L.

Covell, Eli
Dimmick, David
Dimmick, Frederic
Dunham, Samuel
Ellis, Abner
Ellis, Bartlet
Ellis, Gideon
Ellis, Jesse
Ellis, Micah
Ellis, Thomas
Gibbs, Barnabus
Gibbs, Caleb
Gibbs, Josiah
Gibbs, Pelham, Jr.
Gibbs, Robert
Gibbs, Samuel
Gurney, Heman
Harris, Joseph
Hinkley, Edmund
Keen, Abraham
Keen, John
Lovell, Ezekiel
McGowen, Lot

Nightingale, Ellis
Nye, Daniel B.
Perry, Ather
Perry, Heman
Perry, Phinheas
Perry, Prince
Perry, Solomon
Phinney, Edward
Phinney, Isaiah
Phinney, Jabez
Swift, Alden
Swift, Alvan
Swift, Ellis
Swift, James
Swift, William
Tobey, Tristram
Trueman, John
Trueman, Keen
Willis, Wendall
Wing, Alvan
Wing, Lot
Wing, William
Witherell, John

Lieut. James Fisk's Company, Lieut. Col. D. Nye's Regiment.
From Oct. 7 to Oct. 15, 1814. Raised at Falmouth. Service at Falmouth.

RANK AND NAME.
James Fisk, Jr., Lieutenant
Ephraim Dexter, Ensign

David Eldred, Sergeant
Mathew Hatch, Sergeant
Isaac Robinson, Sergeant
Luriel Hatch, Musician

Privates.
Allen, Alden
Allen, Zacheus
Bourne, Barah
Butler, Obed
Crouch, Elwin
Davis, Francis, Jr.
Davis, John, Jr.
Davis, Nathaniel
Davis, Noah
Davis, Thomas, 3d

Deriggs, Marvel
Donaldson, George
Fish, Francis
Fish, Otis
Gifford, Bethuel
Gifford, Jesse, Jr.
Hammond, Isaiah
Hammond, Samuel
Hatch, Allen
Hatch, Davis
Hatch, Silvanus
Hatch, Thacher L.
Jenkins, Abner
Jones, Silvanus
Jones, Thomas
Lawrence, Ephraim
Lawrence, Peleg
Lawrence, Shadrack
Lewis, David
Lewis, Nathaniel

Nye, Francis
Nye, Timothy
Nye, Willard
Parker, Ward M.
Price, David
Robinson, Calvin
Robinson, Davis
Robinson, Elijah
Robinson, Rowland
Robinson, Sylvanus
Sampson, Micah
Sanders, Robinson G.
Sanford, Samuel
Swift, Oliver
Tobey, Zimri
Wicks, Charles
Wicks, Henry
Wicks, Thomas
Wicks, William, 3d
Wooderson, James

MASSACHUSETTS VOLUNTEER MILITIA IN THE WAR OF 1812.

Capt. T. Parker's Company, Lieut. Col. B. Noyes' Regiment.

From Jan. 28 to Jan. 31, 1814. Raised at Falmouth. Service at Falmouth. This company was in battle Jan. 28, 1814.

RANK AND NAME.
Timothy Parker, Captain
James Fish, Lieutenant
Ephraim Dexter, Ensign

Job Hatch, Sergeant
William Laurence, Sergeant
David Eldred, Sergeant
Hatch Mayhew, Sergeant

Privates.
Allen, Zacheus
Bourne, Freeman
Bourne, Isaac
Butler, Obed
Davis, Luther
Davis, Nathaniel
Davis, Noah
Davis, Thomas
Davis, William
Demmick, Lot
Driggs, Manual
Gifford, Abiather

Gifford, Bethuel
Gifford, Jesse
Green, Benjamin
Green, Elisha
Hammond, Isaiah
Hammond, Robert
Hammond, Samuel
Hatch, Anslem
Hatch, Foster
Hatch, Robinson
Hatch, Roswell
Hatch, Silvanus
Jenkins, Abner
Jones, Cyrus
Jones, Robinson
Jones, Silvanus
Lawrence, Ephraim
Lawrence, Peleg
Lewis, David
Lewis, Nathaniel
Nye, Francis
Nye, Nathaniel
Nye, Timothy

Price, Isaac
Robinson, David
Robinson, Elisha
Robinson, Isaac
Robinson, Joseph
Robinson, Nathaniel
Robinson, Silvan
Robinson, Thomas
Sampson, Micah
Sanford, Charles
Sanford, William, Jr.
Shiverick, Foster
Shiverick, Nathaniel
Swift, Asaph
Swift, John
Swift, Thomas
Tobey, Zimri H.
Wicks, Charles
Wicks, Henry
Wicks, Thomas
Wicks, William, 3d
Young, Andrew

Lieut. E. Nye's Company, Lieut. Col. B. Noyes' Regiment.

From Jan. 29 to Jan. 31, 1814. Oct. 3 to 12, under Capt. Obed B. Nye. Raised at Sandwich and Falmouth. Service at Sandwich and Falmouth.

RANK AND NAME.
Edward Nye, Lieutenant
Thomas Nye, Ensign

Zenas Nye, Sergeant
Bethuel Nye, Sergeant

Privates.
Bassett, Nathan
Bassett, William, Jr.
Blossom, Saul
Bourne, Elisha, 3d
Burgess, James
Crocker, George
Dean, Alonzo
Dillingham, John B.
Dillingham, Simeon

Drody, Allen
Droely, Samuel
Fessenden, William
Fish, Abraham
Fish, Daniel
Fish, Isaiah
Fish, Moody
Freeman, Edward
Fuller, Benjamin
Fuller, Joseph, Jr.
Fuller, Samuel
Goodspeed, Luther
Hall, Joseph
Hall, Winslow
Hamlin, Thomas
Heman, Joshua
Heman, William

Holway, William
Howland, James
Hoxie, John
Jones, Francis F.
Lawrence, Solomon
Nye, Abraham
Nye, Abraham W.
Nye, Charles
Nye, Edmund
Nye, Heman
Nye, Holmes
Nye, Josiah
Nye, Paul
Nye, Samuel
Phinney, Gershom
Pope, Lewin
Tobey, Ezra

Lieut. Col. P. Osgood's Regiment.

From July 1 to July 30, 1814. Service at Boston.

FIELD AND STAFF.
Peter Osgood, Lieutenant Colonel, Boston
Samuel Curtis, Major, Boston
Barzilla Hudson, Major, Boston
Abner Bourne, Adjutant, Boston

Henry S. Waldo, Quartermaster, Boston
Samuel B. Ford, Paymaster, Boston
George Parkman, Surgeon, Boston
George B. Doane, Surgeon's Mate, Boston
Charles Lowell, Chaplain, Boston

NONCOMMISSIONED STAFF.
Moses B. Foster, Sergeant Major
John Peabody, Quartermaster Sergeant

MASSACHUSETTS VOLUNTEER MILITIA IN THE WAR OF 1812. 77

Lieut. Col. P. Osgood's Regiment.

Ten days between Sept. 11 and Oct. 10, 1814. Service at Boston.

FIELD AND STAFF.
Peter Osgood, Lieutenant Colonel, Boston
Thomas Dean, Major, Boston
Jonathan Whitney, Major, Boston
Abner Bourne, Adjutant, Boston.

Henry L. Waldo, Quartermaster, Boston
Samuel B. Ford, Paymaster, Boston
George B. Doane, Surgeon's Mate, Boston
Charles Lowell, Chaplain, Boston

NONCOMMISSIONED STAFF.
Moses B. Foster, Sergeant Major

Capt. M. Ames' Company, Lieut. Col. P. Osgood's Regiment.

From July 1 to July 30, 1814. Raised at Boston. Service at Boston.

RANK AND NAME.
Moses Ames, Captain
Ezra Eaton, Lieutenant
Nathaniel Richards, Ensign

Ezra Hawks, Sergeant
Joseph Randall, Sergeant
Daniel Hastings, 2d, Sergeant
Daniel G. Davis, Sergeant
Peter Lincoln, Corporal
Samuel Richardson, Corporal
John Bayley, Corporal
Benjamin Dodd, Corporal

Privates.
Acres, George
Allen, Edward F.
Baker, Abel P.
Barnard, Horace
Beales, Isaac N. C.
Berry, Joseph
Blanchard, David
Blanchard, Samuel
Bouetlier, John
Brannum, Stephen
Brooks, Theodore
Bullard, George

Clap, Benjamin
Clap, Martin
Clap, Nehemiah
Cooper, William P.
Davis, William
Dickinson, Obediah
Dillingham, Asa
Duff, Royal
Duff, William
Eaton, Thaddeus
Gilman, Thomas
Hall, Stephen
Hill, Samuel
Hill, William
Hollis, Joseph
Holman, Richard
Howe, John
Hunt, Timothy
Hunting, John
Hyde, Michel S.
Jenkins, Elijah
Jorden, William
Lambert, Abraham T.
Lawton, Abel
Litchfield, Abner
Mason, Joel
McCurdy, Jesse

Nance, John W.
Page, John
Reynolds, William
Robinson, Jacob G.
Rolph, Daniel
Savill, John
Seymour, Friend
Simpson, Andrew
Singer, Jesse
Smith, Daniel
Smith, Ira
Smith, Martin
Smith, Phineas
Snelling, Christopher
Southwarth, Lewis
Taylor, Daniel
Tirrell, Ezra
Townsend, Henry
Waters, James
Weston, Liberty
Wheelright, James
Willis, Benjamin
Williston, James
Wilson, Jesse
Wyer, George

Capt. J. Fairbanks' Company, Lieut. Col. P. Osgood's Regiment.

From July 1 to July 30, 1814. Raised at Boston. Service at Boston.

RANK AND NAME.
John Fairbanks, Captain
Luke Richardson, Lieutenant
James Blake, Ensign

Josiah Blanchard, Sergeant
Aaron Merritt, Sergeant
Robert Omond, Sergeant
Joseph Brown, Sergeant
Thomas Ayers, Corporal
John Foster, Corporal
Thomas Foye, Corporal
Nathan Dame, Corporal
Ezekiel C. Hall, Musician
Benjamin Perkins, Musician

Privates.
Ball, Thomas
Barney, John C.
Barter, George
Blanchard, Elisha
Blanchard, James T.
Bright, Samuel
Carlton, Martin
Chapman, John
Chase, Luther
Childs, Timothy
Cleaver, John
Cole, Seth
Collidge, Aaron
Crandall, Caleb

Davis, William N.
Emerson, Phineas
Farnsworth, David B.
Fellows, Benjamin
Ferry, Thomas
Fife, Nathan
Foster, Benjamin
Francis, John
Frothingham, Thomas
Godfry, Joseph
Goodrich, Joseph
Gormin, John D.
Gould, Asa
Hager, Joseph
Hammond, Thomas

78   MASSACHUSETTS VOLUNTEER MILITIA IN THE WAR OF 1812.

Capt. J. Fairbanks' Company, Lieut. Col. P. Osgood's Regiment — Concluded.

Privates — Concluded.
Harrington, Charles
Hayward, Ansel
Hobart, Calvin
Hosea, Samuel
Josslyn, Samuel
King, William
Laurence, Henry
Lawton, James
Lee, Cyrel
Lowe, Joseph
Mason, John

Mead, Nathaniel
Nudd, Moses
Oliver, Robert
Pearsons, William
Potter, Asa
Rand, Aaron
Richardson, John
Rowe, Anthony
Saunders, Kendal P.
Spear, Joshua
Sprague, Hosea
Sprague, Isaac S.

Stimpson, Reuben
Talbot, George
Train, Oliver
Turner, Calvin
Washburn, Samuel
Webb, Walter
Welles, Theodore S.
Wheeler, David
Whitney, Theodore
Wilkinson, Thomas
Willard, George
Woodward, Smith

Capt. R. Hartshorn's Company, Lieut. Col. P. Osgood's Regiment.
From July 1 to July 30, 1814.   Raised at Boston.   Service at Boston.

RANK AND NAME.
Rolan Hartshorn, Captain
Philip Curtis, Lieutenant
James Hendley, Ensign

James Hartshorn, Sergeant
David Fermin, Sergeant
Thomas Stowell, Sergeant
Samuel Leeds, Sergeant
Henry Wier, Corporal
Joseph Blany, Corporal
Benjamin Topliff, Corporal
John Stowell, Corporal
Joshua Hardy, Musician
William Paddock, Musician

Privates.
Andrews, George
Baker, James
Baker, William
Blackman, Samuel
Bryant, Job
Burbeck, Henry
Burrage, George H.
Cambridge, Frederic
Capen, John
Chandler, Jacob

Childs, Caleb
Clark, Nathaniel
Cook, Seth B.
Cously, Caleb C.
Cunningham, Thomas
Davis, Lewis B.
Deming, John E.
Ditson, William
Dorr, Nathan
Druherst, Henry
Emes, Clark
Foster, John
French, Charles
Goddard, Elias
Goldsbuck, Adam
Goodrich, James T.
Hapgood, Ephraim
Hatch, Allen
Hawes, William B.
Hoffman, Peter
Holbrook, Sylvanus
Hollis, William
Ireland, Jonathan
Keun, James
Lalley, Daniel
Loring, William
Lovett, John

Lummis, Warren
Mace, John
Macy, Samuel
McIntire, Nathaniel
Merrick, William
Nichols, Alexander H.
Parker, John A.
Pearson, Amos
Pollard, Clark
Rand, Charles
Ridgway, Joseph
Shales, William
Sprague, Charles
Sprague, Jonathan
Stowell, Isaiah
Tolman, William
Topliff, James
Vincent, Joseph
Vincent, Saul
White, John
Whitney, Elisha
Wilder, Lewis
Wilson, Henry
Wise, John
Wyman, John

Capt. E. G. House's Company, Lieut. Col. P. Osgood's Regiment.
From July 1 to July 30, 1814.   Raised at Boston.   Service at Boston.

RANK AND NAME.
Eleazer G. House, Captain
John Dodd, Lieutenant
James N. Staples, Ensign

Charles Appleton, Sergeant
William K. Phillip, Sergeant
Isaac K. Brazier, Sergeant
Thomas Dillaway, Sergeant
George Haynes, Corporal
Charles Goff, Corporal
William Endicott, Corporal
Joshua Hardy, Corporal
Samuel Littlefield, Musician

Privates.
Adams, Henry K.
Aikin, John
Barton, Henry
Bearce, Saul
Bennet, David
Blake, James H.
Boardman, William
Boynton, Stephen
Bradly, Thomas
Brasier, Thomas
Brooks, Nathaniel W.
Brumade, Abraham
Butler, Merrill

Carlton, William
Carter, Timothy
Church, William
Clapp, Ezekiel
Conden, Saul
Cushing, Leavitt
Darling, Joseph
Dillaway, John
Fairfield, John
Fitzgerald, William
Furness, Nathaniel H.
Geyer, George
Gilbert, John
Gove, John

Capt. E. G. House's Company, Lieut. Col. P. Osgood's Regiment — Concluded.

Privates — Concluded..
- Hamilton, John
- Harrington, Elisha
- Howe, Alvin
- Ingalls, Benjamin
- Jackson, Daniel
- Jenkins, Samuel
- Johnson, Zacheriah
- Lane, Anthony
- Loring, Henry
- Loring, Joseph
- Lovis, Calvin
- McClure, Robert
- McLemer, William
- Myrick, Joseph
- Nutter, George
- Parker, Robert H.
- Parsons, Thomas
- Perry, Charles
- Porter, John
- Rich, John
- Rich, Obediah
- Roberts, John
- Shorey, Samuel
- Smith, Robert
- Spear, Gershorn
- Summers, Ezra
- Teel, Nathaniel
- Tower, Rufus
- Turnbull, John
- Vaughan, James
- Ward, John
- West, John
- Williams, James
- Withington, Enos

Capt. T. Johnson's Company, Lieut. Col. P. Osgood's Regiment.
From July 1 to July 30, 1814. Raised at Boston. Service at Boston.

RANK AND NAME.
- Timothy Johnson, Captain
- Jacob Howe, Lieutenant
- Joseph Lewis, Ensign

- Edward W. Hawes, Sergeant
- William Hansell, Sergeant
- William Parker, Sergeant
- Nathan Hobbs, Sergeant
- Joshua Pitman, Corporal
- John Snow, Corporal
- Isaac Bemis, Corporal
- William D. Bell, Corporal

Privates.
- Baker, William
- Barker, David
- Bayley, Job
- Bell, David
- Bell, Edward
- Braders, John B.
- Caldwell, James
- Chandler, Benjamin
- Coolidge, James
- Cushman, Alexander
- Cutler, Amos
- Cutler, Ezra
- Davis, Amos
- Davis, Ethan
- Dexter, Aaron
- Dillaway, Samuel
- French, Othniel, Jr.
- Gibson, Nathaniel
- Goldsmith, George W.
- Horton, John
- Hunt, Solomon
- Hutchins, Purley
- Johnson, John
- Joy, Samuel
- Lewis, George
- Lincoln, James M.
- Litchfield, Hersey
- Mayo, Samuel
- Mero, Lemuel
- Messenger, Timothy
- Morse, Dana
- Nash, James
- Otherman, Henry
- Parker, Thomas G.
- Petty, Joseph
- Pratt, David, Jr.
- Reed, George
- Roberts, John
- Sawyer, Thomas B.
- Smith, Samuel
- Snelling, Ephraim
- Snow, Royal
- Southack, Ciprian
- Stebbins, Saul
- Thistle, Andrew
- Thompson, Alexander
- Thurston, Benjamin
- Tuckerman, John T.
- Vincent, Samuel
- Webb, Joseph
- Wilson, John
- Woods, Nehemiah

Capt. J. B. Marston's Company, Lieut. Col. P. Osgood's Regiment.
From July 1 to July 30, 1814. Raised at Boston. Service at Boston.

RANK AND NAME.
- James B. Marston, Captain
- Micah B. Bacon, Lieutenant
- Arnold Hayward, Ensign

- Henry K. Appleton, Sergeant
- Peter Seaver, Sergeant
- Nathaniel Healey, Sergeant
- John G. Somes, Sergeant
- Lewis Burches, Corporal
- James Powers, Corporal
- William Jewitt, Corporal
- Seth Grammer, Corporal
- William Hardy, Musician
- Edward Harrington, Musician
- Samuel Russell, Musician

Privates.
- Abbott, Nathaniel
- Alden, John
- Balch, William
- Baldwin, Abel
- Bell, William
- Bishop, James
- Blackman, Thomas
- Bowden, Simeon
- Briggs, Seth
- Brown, Isaac
- Butler, William
- Chandler, Henry
- Cobb, Josiah
- Cook, Cory
- Cutter, Oliver
- Darling, John
- Davis, Ebenezer
- Davis, Frederic
- Davis, Reuben
- Decoster, James
- Downs, Jesse
- Dyer, George
- Fessenden, Moses
- Geyer, James W.
- Gregg, Stephen
- Grossman, Henry
- Hale, Nathan
- Hayden, John
- Hayward, John
- Henley, Henry
- Hitchborn, Alexander

Capt. J. B. Marston's Company, Lieut. Col. P. Osgood's Regiment — Concluded.

Privates — Concluded.
Hobbs, Daniel
Holbrook, Samuel
Holmes, Oliver
Hopkins, Constant
Hosmer, Hammon
Jewitt, Joseph
Kenard, Aleut
Lloyd, Frederic

Martin, Isaac
Nowell, James
Parker, David
Pelfrey, Jonathan
Purkitt, Henry
Reed, Quinsey
Robertson, John
Rose, Gideon
Ruddock, Amos

Sanford, Samuel
Shed, James
Stephen, Oliver
Sweetser, Charles B.
Tirrell, Gideon
Vilner, Peter
White, Josiah
Wilder, Eleazer
Winslow, William P.

Capt. J. Whitney's Company, Lieut. Col. P. Osgood's Regiment.
From July 1 to July 30, 1814. Raised at Boston. Service at Boston.

RANK AND NAME.
Jonathan Whitney, Captain
Joshua Preston, Lieutenant
Zachariah G. Whitman, Ensign

Nathaniel Philips, Sergeant
John R. Moor, Sergeant
Alexander Mitchell, Sergeant
George Singleton, Sergeant
John Adams, Corporal
Robert Smith, Corporal
William Holland, Corporal
Atherton H. Stevens, Corporal
Miles Perry, Musician
Asa Lee, Musician

Privates.
Barnes, John
Bass, Gillam
Beals, Martin
Bennett, James
Bull, William
Burr, Theophilus
Campbell, John
Converse, Joshua
Coolridge, Lewis
Curtis, Benjamin

Curtis, John
Cushing, Martin
Daniels, Nathaniel
Davenport, Israel
Davis, Henry
Davis, William
Dunton, Peter
Emery, Peter
Fulton, Samuel B.
Gardner, Oakman
Gerand, Peter
Gill, Michel
Haskell, Luther
Hayden, Henry
Herrick, Samuel
Hollis, David
Hunt, John
Hunt, Simon
Kent, Martin
Lamb, William
Leighton, George
Lillie, Daniel
Loud, Asa
Lufkin, Jacob
Merriam, Jacob
Milcher, George
Miller, John

Oliver, Charles
Perry, John
Plummer, Joshua
Pollard, Amos F.
Porter, Edward
Reding, Joseph
Rex, John
Roberts, Richard S.
Rummey, Benjamin
Rupp, Adam
Russell, Solomon
Sargent, James
Scott, Daniel
Sears, Peter
Sinclair, Robert
Smith, Jonathan
Stoddard, Hosea
Sumner, Benjamin
Swan, Amos M.
Tirrell, Ebenezer
Trask, Daniel
Wells, Caleb T.
White, George
Whitney, Salmon
Williams, Ambrose
Wyman, David
Wyman, Maverick

Capt. S. Whitney's Company, Lieut. Col. P. Osgood's Regiment.
From July 1 to July 30, 1814. Raised at Boston. Service at Boston.

RANK AND NAME.
Silas Whitney, Captain
Elna Hoyt, Lieutenant
Ira Brown, Ensign

Jonas Amus, Sergeant
Nathaniel Bryant, Sergeant
Daniel Brown, Sergeant
Lemuel Clark, Sergeant
Daniel Whitney, Corporal
Reuben Allen, Corporal
James G. Southack, Corporal
Levi Beals, Corporal
Leonard Parks, Musician
Daniel Simpson, Musician

Privates.
Adams, Charles
Barney, Jonathan
Bemis, Reuben
Bouse, Benjamin
Brigford, James
Brown, Eliab
Brown, John
Carpenter, Samuel
Clapp, Francis W.
Clark, George W.
Collar, Aaron
Conant, Asa
Cook, David
Crane, Nathan

Cushing, Levi L.
Cushing, William
Dearborn, Edward
Dugate, David
Fisk, Jonas
George, William
Grossman, John G.
Hammatt, Abraham
Haskell, Calvin
Hatch, Clift
Heald, Josiah
Hollis, Daniel
Howland, Benjamin I.
Hutchinson, Joseph
Jones, David

Capt. S. Whitney's Company, Lieut. Col. P. Osgood's Regiment — Concluded.

Privates — Concluded.
Kendall, Thomas
Kenney, John H.
Leach, Henry
Lincoln, Daniel
Loring, Freeman
Low, Lewis
Master, George L.
Merriam, Artemas
Morrow, James
Murray, John
Oliver, Ebenezer

Parks, Leonard
Parks, Royal M.
Payson, Leonard
Perkins, Enos
Pike, William
Quimby, Benjamin M.
Rice, Abner
Rich, David
Seaver, William
Sherman, James
Smith, Nowell
Stephens, William

Stimpson, George
Strong, Cotton
Tenney, Moses
Todd, John
Trueman, William
Tufts, Edmund
Valentine, Jonathan
Wallis, Jeremiah
Wetherbee, William B.
Wilkins, Asa
Willard, John
Wood, Wyman

Capt. L. Colburn's Company, Lieut. Col. P. Osgood's Regiment.
Ten days between Sept. 11 and Oct. 10, 1814.   Raised at Boston.   Service at Boston.

RANK AND NAME.
Lemuel Colburn, Captain
Job Drew, Lieutenant
Sylvanus Packard, Ensign

Alex Mitchell, Sergeant
Edmund Reed, Sergeant
Christopher Tilden, Sergeant
Levi Haskell, Sergeant
Thomas Spear, Corporal
David Hollis, Corporal
Jonathan Forrester, Corporal
Charles Colburn, Corporal
Stephen Ingalls, Musician
Alpheus Gurney, Musician
William Waldo, Musician

Privates.
Blodgett, Isaac
Brown, Phineas
Carnes, David G.
Coburn, Hiram
Conwise, Joshua
Foster, Isaac

Fulton, Samuel B.
Gardner, William
Gould, Thomas
Gurney, Alpheus
Harrington, Elisha
Hatchman, John
Hayden, Henry
Hayden, Peleg
Headley, Joseph
Holland, William
Keen, Nathan
Kennard, Michael
Kilham, Eliab
Kingman, Elias H.
Kittredge, William
Knight, Mannasseh
Leighton, Charles
Litchfield, Simeon
Loring, Caleb
Mead, William
Merriam, Jacob
Millis, Charles
Orne, John
Page, Jacob

Perry, John
Philips, Benjamin C.
Pratt, Obed
Pratt, Phineas
Ramsdell, Reuben
Ray, Levi
Remick, Samuel H.
Rice, Nathaniel
Rowe, Benjamin
Ruff, Adam
Rumney, Benjamin
Sanders, John
Sears, Peter
Severens, Rodney
Sinclair, Robert
Stearnes, Curtis
Stearnes, John
Taylor, Solomon
Tilden, Thomas
Veizey, George
Wallis, Mordecai L.
Williams, Ambrose

Capt. E. G. Howe's Company, Lieut. Col. P. Osgood's Regiment.
Ten days between Sept. 11 and Oct. 10, 1814.   Raised at Boston.   Service at Boston.

RANK AND NAME.
Eleazer G. Howe, Captain
Daniel L. Gibbons, Lieutenant
Zacheriah G. Whitman, Ensign

Ezekiel Jones, Sergeant
Charles Appleton, Sergeant
Sylvanus Reed, Sergeant
Isaac K. Brazier, Sergeant
George Haynes, Corporal
Isaac McCleary, Corporal
James Williams, Corporal
Gershom Spear, Corporal
James Putnam, Musician

Privates.
Allen, William
Blake, James H.
Bowdoin, Simpson
Brazier, William G.
Brooks, Nathaniel W.
Brown, Nathaniel
Bruce, Calvin
Carter, Timothy
Clapp, Benjamin
Clapp, Ezekiel
Clough, Aaron
Codman, George
Cowden, Samuel

Crocker, Robert
Cushing, Samuel
Cutler, Pliny
Dean, Samuel
Dickinson, Ira
Dillingham, Seth
Gates, Lemuel
Glover, James
Gore, John
Gorham, George
Gorham, Thomas
Hamilton, William
Hawes, Prince
Hayden, John

Capt. E. G. Howe's Company, Lieut. Col. P. Osgood's Regiment — Concluded.

Privates — Concluded.
Hudson, Thomas
Hurley, John L.
Loring, William
Lovis, Calvin
Lovis, Thomas
Low, Joseph H.
Manning, Samuel
Merrill, Moses

Page, John
Park, Moody
Pierce, John
Pratt, George
Sanderson, Lodi
Searles, Joseph
Shepherd, Edward
Taylor, Samuel
Tilden, Christopher

Trumbull, John W.
Valentine, Jonathan
Vaughn, James
Warner, Theodore S.
Wentworth, John
Whiting, Jabez
Wilkins, Jeremiah
Wilkins, John
Wyman, Joseph

Capt. B. Loring's Company, Lieut. Col. P. Osgood's Regiment.
Ten days between Sept. 11 and Oct. 10, 1814. Raised at Boston. Service at Boston.

RANK AND NAME.
Benjamin Loring, Captain
John Dodd, Lieutenant
James N. Staples, Ensign

John Webb, Sergeant
Moses Jaquith, Sergeant
William K. Phipps, Sergeant
William Grubb, Sergeant
Joshua Colman, Corporal
William Fenno, Corporal
William Callendar, Corporal
Joshua Brinney, Corporal
—— Hardy, Musician
Sheldon Perry, Musician

Privates.
Abbott, Joshua
Adams, Levi
Armin, William B.
Austin, Abner
Austin, Richard
Barnet, Josiah M.
Basson, John
Bemis, Samuel
Bisbey, J.
Boardman, William
Bowans, Jonas
Bowker, Gershom
Boynton, Stephen
Buffum, Henry
Butler, Merrill
Campbell, John
Cardeff, Philip
Carlton, William

Clapp, Francis
Clapp, Nehemiah
Coit, Thomas C.
Conant, John
Cushing, George
Cushing, Samuel
Cutting, Samuel
Dalton, John
Darling, John
Davenport, Isaac
Fessenden, Stephen
Forrester, Levi
Fowle, Charles
Fowle, Parker
French, Noah
Gerry, Samuel
Gilbert, John
Hall, Jason
Hamilton, William
Haskell, R.
Hastings, Charles
Hayward, Thomas C.
Hickey, Dennis
Hilton, Peter
Ingalls, David
Jaques, E.
Jennings, William
Johnson, James
Lane, Anthony
Lee, Oliver
Lincoln, Anslen
Lincoln, Elijah
Lord, R.
Loring, Henry
Lowe, John

Lyman, George
Marsters, Andrew
Martin, William
Matthews, George
Miles, William
Nash, Nathaniel
Nichols, Thadeus
Norris, Jesse
Nowell, James
Pealer, David
Phillips, Thomas
Pollock, George
Pollock, Neal
Raymond, Thomas
Richardson, George
Richardson, Josiah
Russell, Ephraim
Sanderson, Nathan
Smith, Nathaniel
Smith, Ralph
Stoddard, John
Stoddard, John, 2d
Sweet, Stephen
Sweet, William B.
Tarbell, Thomas
Thompson, James
Tolman, Jesse
Wendell, Charles J.
Wheeler, Jona
Whiting, Nathan
Winton, John
Wiswell, Payne
Withington, E.
Wyman, William

Capt. A. Richardson's Company, Lieut. Col. P. Osgood's Regiment.
Ten days between Sept. 11 and Oct. 10, 1814. Raised at Boston. Service at Boston.

RANK AND NAME.
Asa Richardson, Captain
Elna Hayte, Lieutenant
Ira Brown, Ensign

Elias Davis, Sergeant
George Singleton, Sergeant

Lemuel Clark, Sergeant
Francis Addington, Sergeant
Tristram Vose, Corporal
Obediah Dickinson, Corporal
John Ward, Corporal
Noah Gale, Corporal
Edward Harrington, Musician

Privates.
Aiken, John
Ashton, Elisha V.
Auben, Greenleaf
Babcock, Alpheus
Babcock, Samuel H.
Bates, Henry

MASSACHUSETTS VOLUNTEER MILITIA IN THE WAR OF 1812. 83

Capt. A. Richardson's Company, Lieut. Col. P. Osgood's Regiment — Concluded.

Privates — Concluded.
Broughton, Charles
Brown, Charles
Brown, Jonas
Chadwick, Thomas A.
Clough, Benjamin
Conner, Richard C.
Cunningham, Henry
Cunningham, James
Dearborn, Richard
Dearborn, Samuel
Dewing, Timothy
Dunttin, Nathaniel
Eckley, David
Foster, Charles
Foster, William
Fowle, William
Goff, William

Hapgood, Ephraim
Hastings, Lewis
Hobbs, Daniel
Hollis, William
Hope, George S.
Howe, Alvin
Hyde, Amasa
Jordan, Henry
Long, William
Masters, William
McIntosh, Francis
McLane, Edward
Parker, Jonathan
Peabody, Ebenezer
Porter, Benjamin
Reed, Amos
Reynolds, Samuel
Sanderson, Luther

Scott, Daniel
Shed, Samuel A.
Somerby, Robert
Stevens, Joshua B.
Stone, Joshua
Swift, William
Thorndike, Israel
Town, Jonathan
Tufts, Caleb
Webster, Nathan
Wheeler, Henry
Whitney, Jacon
Whitney, Levi
Whitwell, Samuel
Witham, Jonathan
Woodbury, Edward
Woodbury, John

Capt. G. Wells' Company, Lieut. Col. P. Osgood's Regiment.
Between Sept. 11 and Oct. 10, 1814. Raised at Boston. Service at Boston.

RANK AND NAME.
George Wells, Captain
Israel Whitney, Lieutenant
Otis Howe, Ensign

Leonard Goss, Sergeant
Nathaniel Bryant, Sergeant
Daniel Brown, Sergeant
Cornelius Briggs, Sergeant
John Crofts, Corporal
James Seaton, Corporal
Hugh Gelston, Corporal
Nathan Crane, Corporal
Daniel Simpson, Musician
Benjamin Strow, Musician
Miles Perry, Musician

Privates.
Adams, William D.
Bailey, Joseph
Belknap, Samuel A.
Berry, Isaac
Bowers, Levi
Bowers, Luther
Bradbury, Charles
Brown, John
Coleman, James
Colley, Johnson
Collins, James
Cook, David

Copeland, William
Cushing, Henry
Darling, Joseph
Edes, Benjamin F.
Frost, Coleman
Fullam, Boylston
Fullam, Daniel
Fullam, Jacob
Gale, Isaac
Hammett, William B.
Harris, Oliver
Henry, William
Homer, William
Howe, George
Howland, Benjamin J.
Hunt, Simon
Kelley, William
Kendall, Artemas
Kneeland, Samuel
Laughton, Samuel
Leach, Thomas
Lee, Washington
LeMaster, George
Lincoln, Amos
Lincoln, Daniel
Lincoln, Elijah
Lock, Nathan
Lufts, Edmund
Mann, Isaiah
McClure, David

Moore, Joshua
Murry, Thadeus
Newton, Martin
Nicholas, George
Parsons, Henry
Pattey, William
Parker, Peter
Parker, William
Pike, Richard
Pray, David P.
Ripley, Samuel
Roach, Samuel
Royse, Silas
Russell, Benjamin G.
Shepard, Thomas
Smith, Joseph
Snow, Martin
Snowden, William
Taggerd, Henry
Taylor, Daniel
Thayer, Isaac
Tidd, Jacob
Weatherbee, William B.
Webster, John
Weld, William
Widen, John
Wild, Benjamin
Willard, John
Williams, Isaac

Capt. S. Whitney's Company, Lieut. Col. P. Osgood's Regiment.
Ten days between Sept. 11 and Oct. 10, 1814. Raised at Boston. Service at Boston.

RANK AND NAME.
Silas Whitney, Captain (absent)
Joshua Preston, Lieutenant (in command)
John Whitney, Ensign

Jonas Ames, Sergeant
Daniel Whitney, Sergeant
Reuben Allen, Sergeant
Levi Beale, Sergeant
Moses Hadly, Corporal
Joel Conant, Corporal

Luther Farwell, Corporal
Benjamin Rowe, Corporal
Edward T. Parker, Musician
Pearley Holmes, Musician
Josiah Heald, Musician

Capt. S. Whitney's Company, Lieut. Col. P. Osgood's Regiment — Concluded.

Privates.

Adams, Charles
Adams, Etheiner
Allen, James
Bacon, John
Billings, Ezekiel F.
Blaney, Ambrose
Bradford, Nelson
Bradlee, Ebenezer
Cheever, William
Clark, Ebenezer
Clesley, Joseph
Conant, Joel
Coverly, Samuel
Cushing, John
Cushing, Levi L.
Dean, Thaddeus
Dennis, Foster S.
Dodge, Isaac
Donnell, Charles
Dugate, David
Emerson, John
Farwell, Luther

Fay, Silas
Folsom, Samuel
Gansley, Andrew
Gould, Silas
Gray, Francis
Grinnell, William F.
Hadley, Moses
Haskell, Abiah
Hatch, Clift
Hersey, Lewis
Hobbs, John L.
Holton, Henry
Hull, George
Hunt, John
Hurley, George
Jacob, John
Jacobs, David C.
Jacobs, Thomas N.
Jones, Daniel
Joy, Elisha
Kimball, John
Kinsbury, Benjamin
Mayhew, Augustus

Meeker, Medad
Morrow, James
Newton, Foye
Perrin, George
Powers, John G.
Prouty, Jonas
Robbins, Thomas
Rowe, Benjamin
Ruggles, Levi
Russ, Robert
Sawtell, Joseph
Simonds, Shepherd
Smallpeace, Robert
Souther, Isaiah
Stedman, Elijah
Stoddar, Thomas
Stoddard, Bela
Tent, Isaac
Tileston, Otis
Wenzell, Henry
Wilder, John N.
Wright, Simon

Lieut. G. King's Company, Lieut. Col. P. Osgood's Regiment.

From July 1 to July 30, 1814. Raised at Boston. Service at Boston.

RANK AND NAME.
Gedney King, Lieutenant
Henry Codman, Ensign

John N. Hinkley, Sergeant
Eleazer F. F. Richardson, Sergeant
Peter Mackentosh, Sergeant
Thomas Mason, Corporal
James D. Ross, Corporal
George Palmer, Corporal
Samuel Dunn, Corporal
—— Parks, Musician
S. Perry, Musician

Privates.

Austin, William B.
Banister, John B.
Bartlet, George
Bonner, John
Bowen, Jonathan
Braynard, Gelden
Burdaken, Joseph
Burdett, Ebenezer
Burdit, Henry
Burdit, James W.

Cabot, Richard C.
Carey, George
Clark, G. W.
Clark, James
Cooper, Jesse
Danforth, Isaac
Dawes, Harrison
Elwell, Robert
Eustis, Joseph
Fanning, John B.
Fessenden, Arthur
Finch, Eleen
Folsom, Samuel
Fowle, John
Gamage, Nathaniel
Gardner, Simon
Grant, Charles
Grant, John
Greenough, Jonathan M.
Hammot, Consider H.
Haven, Calven
Heath, John
Holbrook, Charles
Ingersoll, James
Kittle, John

Kittle, Porter
Lane, George
Leverett, John
Mackay, William
Moore, Augustus
Oliver, Daniel
Parker, R. H.
Peterson, Thomas
Pope, Ebenezer
Pope, Ralph
Richardson, James B.
Rogers, David
Rogers, Eldred
Russell, John
Russell, Otis
Smith, William G.
Tileston, James
Tileston, O. C.
Vila, Joseph
White, Stephen B.
Whitney, Joseph
Williams, Eleazer W.
Winship, Amos
Winslow, Charles
Woods, Samuel

Lieut. C. Beale's Company, Lieut. Col. P. Osgood's Regiment.

Ten days between Sept. 11 and Oct. 14, 1814. It is claimed that this was the Ancient and Honorable Artillery Company of Boston (incorporated 1638). Service at Boston.

RANK AND NAME.
Caswell Beale, Lieutenant
Jesse Shaw, Ensign

Nathaniel Philips, Sergeant
John W. Hyde, Sergeant
Atherton H. Stevens, Sergeant
Henry Davis, Sergeant

Robert Smith, Corporal
Thomas Magroth, Corporal
George Noble, Corporal
John Holman, Corporal

Lieut. C. Beale's Company, Lieut. Col. P. Osgood's Regiment — Concluded.

Privates.

Adams, Isaac
Adams, Isaac, 2d
Atkins, Edward
Austin, Samuel
Barker, Wendell R.
Bell, David W.
Blodgett, William
Bowdage, Horace
Bull, Briggs
Bull, William
Capen, Phineas
Clark, Julius
Coller, Aaron
Cook, Otis
Cummings, Thomas
Cushing, Martin
Davis, Thomas
Dole, John

Dunbar, Peter
Dunbar, Seth
Ellis, Ebenezer
Emerson, Jeremiah
Foster, Thomas W.
Fowle, John
Fowle, William B.
Goodrich, John
Green, Samuel R.
Hammett, Charles
Hayden, Ezekiel
Hunnewell, Peter
Hyde, Nathaniel
Larrabee, John
Libby, Daniel
Lowe, John
Merriam, Abraham
Merrill, Sidney
Nichols, Aaron

Pike, Benjamin
Preston, Michael
Reed, Augustus
Ring, Samuel
Roberts, Richard S.
Silloway, Joseph
Simpson, Charles
Smith, James C.
Sprague, William
Stodder, Hosea
Sumner, Benjamin
Tinney, William
Towne, Edmund B.
Wade, George F.
Waterhouse, Daniel
Whitney, Salmon
Wyman, David

Lieut. Col. J. Page's Detached Regiment.

From Sept. 13 to Nov. 7, 1814. Service at Fort Warren, Boston Harbor.

FIELD AND STAFF.
Jonathan Page, Lieutenant Colonel, Charlestown
Loammi Kendall, Major, Boston
Joseph Stone, Adjutant

NONCOMMISSIONED STAFF.
Francis Jackson, Sergeant Major
Asa Stone, Quartermaster Sergeant

Capt. J. Tucker's Company, Lieut. Col. J. Page's Regiment.

From Sept. 13 to Nov. 7, 1814. Raised at Canton and vicinity. Service at Fort Warren, Boston Harbor.

RANK AND NAME.
John Tucker, Captain
James B. Brown, Lieutenant
Joseph Bachelder, Lieutenant
Benjamin Hapgood, Ensign
Nathaniel Owen, Ensign

Asa Moore, Sergeant
Reuben Cook, Sergeant
Nathaniel Stone, Sergeant
Jabez Boyden, Sergeant
Zacheus Wyman, Sergeant
Amos Miller, Sergeant
Benjamin Foster, Corporal
James B. Puffer, Corporal
Joshua Caswell, Corporal
Alpheus Bird, Corporal
Davenport Shaw, Corporal
Lewis Muzzy, Corporal
Benjamin Goldthwait, Musician

Privates.

Alexander, Robert
Allen, Thompson
Ayers, Joseph
Babb, James
Bachelder, Josiah
Ballou, Ebenezer M.

Ballou, James
Bardon, Amos
Black, Asa
Blake, William
Blanchard, Abel
Blanchard, Josiah
Broad, William
Bryant, Thomas
Bullen, Joseph
Capers, Simeon
Chubb, Thomas
Clisby, Samuel
Crocker, James
Crosby, Isaac
Daniels, Jeremiah
Davis, Joseph W.
Ellingwood, Abraham
Ellis, Simeon
Fairbanks, Silas
Farrell, Laurence L.
Farrington, Daniel S.
Farrington, Nathan
Fife, Silas
Fuller, Daniel
Gay, Ichabod
Gay, Phineas
Gerry, James
Gerry, Samuel

Giddings, Francis
Goldthwait, George W.
Gulliver, Spencer
Gulliver, Stephen
Hagen, Joseph
Harrin, Oliver
Harris, John
Hastings, Thaddeus
Henderson, Luther
Henshaw, Ebenezer
Hunt, Martin
Jerald, John
Johnson, Amory
Kennard, William
Leavers, John
Lord, Mark (D)
Marble, Elijah
Merrick, Joseph
Messinger, Ebenezer
Noble, Isaac
Prescott, Levi
Puffer, Otis
Reed, George, M.D.
Rhoads, Ellis
Rich, Isaac
Richards, Rufus
Rickford, Abraham
Right, Timothy

Capt. J. Tucker's Company, Lieut. Col. J. Page's Regiment — Concluded.

Privates — Concluded.
Rockwood, Benjamin
Sanderson, Amos
Sargent, Thomas
Scott, Elhanan
Smith, Asa
Smith, Elijah
Snelling, Henry
Southworth, Apollos

Stevens, Timothy
Stewart, Charles
Thayer, Charles
Tolly, Daniel
Tombs, Dexter
Turrill, Job
Vial, Burrill
Vincent, Joseph
Vose, John

Walcott, Silas
Wallis, Chancey
Wentworth, Oliver
Wentworth, Spencer
Whittemore, Joshua
Winslow, Isaac
Wiswell, Lovell

Capt. T. Page's Company, Lieut. Col. J. Page's Regiment.
From Sept. 13 to Nov. 7, 1814. Raised at Bedford and vicinity. Service at Fort Warren, Boston Harbor.

RANK AND NAME.
Timothy Page, Captain
Oliver Shaw, Lieutenant
Amos Holt, Lieutenant
Phineas Withington, Lieutenant
Eliphalet Holbrook, Lieutenant

Nathaniel Harrington, Sergeant
James Vining, Sergeant
Seth Pettee, Sergeant
Amos B. Gay, Sergeant
Elisha Harrington, Sergeant
John Barber, Sergeant
Isaac Alden, Corporal
David Capen, Corporal
Vincent Turrill, Corporal
Royal Oliver, Corporal
Eliphas Pratt, Corporal

Privates.
Adams, Thomas
Baker, Ruel
Bates, James
Beers, John B.
Blanchard, David
Blanchard, Nathan
Blanchard, Nathaniel
Blood, Richard
Brigham, Jonathan
Brooks, Thomas
Clapp, Jonathan
Collie or Collier, Edward
Collier, Jonathan

Convis, Rufus
Cook, Abijah
Curtis, Benjamin
Cushing, Abner
Cutler, Amos
Daniels, Joel, Jr.
Davis, Charles
Dean, Timothy
Eddy, William
Ellis, Jason
Falls, Hiram
Field, James
Fisher, Elias
Gale, Luther
Gay, Willard
Gilbert, Judson
Hall, Elijah
Harding, Pliny
Hastings, Oliver
Hawes, Caleb
Hawes, James
Hawes, Joseph
Hobert, William
Holbrook, Henry
Horton, Aseph
Humphries, John
Jay, Charles
Johnson, Ellis
Johnson, Lewis
Kelton, Elihu
Kelton, Jason
Laurence, Jonas
Laurence, Samuel

Lasell, Warren
Livermore, Nathaniel
Lock, Low
Lord, Lemuel
Lord, William
Lovering, John
Lower, John
Orcutt, Benjamin
Page, Larkin P.
Payen, Lemuel
Pond, Jemotis, Jr.
Pond, Lewis
Pratt, Elijah
Rion, Nathaniel
Shaw, John
Shaw, Nathaniel T.
Smith, Josiah
Thayer, David
Thayer, John W.
Thomas, John
Tirrell, David
Tolbert, Enoch
Tolbert, Joseph
Torry, Benjamin
Torry, Saul
Tufts, Thomas
Ware, George
Weatherby, Henry C.
White, Jeremiah
Williams, John, Jr.
Winship, William

Capt. M. Roulston's Company, Lieut. Col. J. Page's Regiment.
From Sept. 13 to Nov. 7, 1814. Raised at Boston. Service at Fort Warren, Boston Harbor.

RANK AND NAME.
Michel Roulston, Captain
Daniel L. Gibbons, Lieutenant

John Biglow, Clerk
Sylvanus Reed, Sergeant
Michel Tombs, Sergeant
Martin Kent or Keint, Sergeant
Francis M. Addington, Sergeant

John Brown, Corporal
Samuel Barber, Corporal
Robert Somersby, Corporal
Charles Brown, Corporal
Joseph King, Corporal
William Starr, Corporal
William Andrews, Corporal

Privates.
Baker, William
Ballard, George
Barber, Fisher
Barmester, Samuel
Barron, Oliver
Bass, Gilman, Jr.
Bell, David
Bemis, Joel

Capt. M. Roulston's Company, Lieut. Col. J. Page's Regiment — Concluded.

Privates — Concluded.
Bennet, Barzillai
Bennet, Jesse
Bent, Avery
Blair, M. D.
Blake, William
Boden, Simpson
Bracket, Richard
Brazer, William G.
Brooks, Abijah
Brooks, Michel L.
Brooks, Nathaniel W.
Brown, Thomas
Buffum, H. F.
Cambell, Charles
Carnes, David G.
Connor, Richard C.
Dean, Lemual
Dewing, Timothy
Dow, Moses
Edwards, Benjamin
Emerson, Jeremiah
Estes, Samuel G.
Farsar, Adoniram
Favor, Isaac
Foster, Rufus
Freeman, Benjamin B.

French, Amos
Fuller, Elisha D.
Fuller, Joseph
Gates, Eneas
Gilman, George G.
Gorman, John
Graham, George
Green, John
Hall, Aaron
Hatch, Allen
Hayden, John
Hayden, Peleg
Hillman, George
Hollis, David
Hoverman, Peter
Howes, Loring
Hunt, John
Hutchinson, Joseph
Jennings, William
Jones, John
Jones, John R.
Kemp, Francis
King, Seth
Kingsbury, Samuel
Leland, Aaron
Lilly, Daniel
Mannings, Samuel B.

Merchant, Chester
Newcomb, Charles
Nickerson, James
Parker, William A.
Peabody, Ebenezer
Pike, Elisha
Purkett, Henry F.
Ramsdale, Reuben
Redding, Joseph
Rich, David
Richardson, Nathan
Ripley, Samuel
Robertson, Smith
Roulston, Michel, Jr.
Sanders, John
Simons, Silas
Smith, Thomas
Speed, Amos
Stone, Ezra
Thayer, Wyman
Thomas, William
Trull, Joel
Vincent, Samuel
Wallis, Jeremiah
Williston, Caleb
Woodbury, John

Capt. N. Shattuck's Company, Lieut. Col. J. Page's Regiment.

From Sept. 13 to Nov. 7, 1814. Raised at Groton and vicinity. Service at Fort Warren, Boston Harbor.

RANK AND NAME.
Noah Shattuck, Captain
Thomas Pearsons, Lieutenant
Samuel Warren, Lieutenant
Archelaus C. Bennet, Ensign

James Going, Sergeant
Micajah Rice, Sergeant
Calvin Shattuck, Sergeant
Thomas Dunton, Sergeant
Noah Gates, Sergeant
Israel Richardson, Corporal
Joel Wright, Corporal
Jesse Wiswell, Corporal
Zenas Brown, Corporal
Cyrus Buttrick, Corporal
Alden Wood, Corporal
Joseph Handson, Corporal
Eleazer Kemp, Corporal

Privates.
Abbott, James
Atkins, Edward
Ayers, Charles
Bartlett, Martin
Bennet, Jacob
Bixby, Asa
Blanchard, Samuel
Blaney, Benjamin
Bottom, Eliab
Brown, James

Brown, Joseph
Brown, Willard
Cabbott, John C.
Campbell, Nathaniel
Carr, John
Childs, Nathaniel
Cole, Seth
Cook, Jonathan
Davenson, Peter
Davis, James
Dole, Joseph
Dudley, John
Edes, Benjamin
Egleston, George (D)
Farnsworth, Rufus
Fuller, Charles
Gilson, James
Gilson, Jonas
Gleason, Josiah
Gragg, Jacob
Groves, John
Hardin, Joseph
Hardy, Noah
Harris, William
Harrod, William
Hayson, John
Hearsey, Jacob
Heart, Elias
Homer, John
Hudson, Charles (D)
Jewett, Solomon

Johnson, George W.
Kehew, Aaron
Kemp, Jonas
King, Nathan
Lynfield, William V.
Lynfield, Zeno
Maguire, Patrick
Marvin, Whitman
Mecom, Robert
Mitchell, William
Mitts, Samuel
Moore, Cephas
Osburn, Cyrus
Parker, Lemuel
Pearsons, Joseph
Phelps, John
Pierce, Jonathan
Puffer, Jesse
Puffer, Josiah
Ramsdell, William
Rice, John
Rich, David
Richardson, Sheron
Richardson, William
Riley, Micah
Sanburn, Daniel
Sheldon, William
Sherman, Reuben
Shipley, Oliver
Simons, James
Souther, Moses

Capt. S. Shattuck's Company, Lieut. Col. J. Page's Regiment — Concluded.

Privates — Concluded.
Stoder, Elijah
Swift, William
Taylor, Calvin
Taylor, Elisha
Townsend, Samuel
Trull, Elijah

Viat, Elias
Williams, Luther
Wilson, Abel
Wilson, Andrew
Woorster, Benjamin
Wright, Ebenezer
Wright, Joel

Wyman, Richard
Young, Joseph

Waiters.
Parker, William
Shattuck, Noah
Shattuck, Walter

Capt. A. Tarbell's Company, Lieut. Col. J. Page's Regiment.
From Sept. 13 to Nov. 7, 1814. Raised at Groton and vicinity. Service at Fort Warren, Boston Harbor.

RANK AND NAME.
Abel Tarbell, Captain
Jedediah Wood, Lieutenant
William McIntosh, Ensign
William Clough, Ensign

James Draper, Sergeant
Otis Reed, Sergeant
Francis Leighton, Sergeant
Eldridge Gerry, Sergeant
Benjamin Walker, Sergeant
Lyman Hayden, Corporal
Elijah G. Wetharbee, Corporal
Joseph Childs, Corporal
William Tufts, Corporal
Peter C. Conant, Corporal
Ezekiel O. Hall, Musician
Abraham A. Edwards, Musician
Jesse Brown, Musician

Privates.
Abbott, Jonathan
Arnold, Samuel
Atherton, Marshall
Babon, Reuben
Baily, Zebina
Baldwin, Davis, Jr.
Barnam, David
Billings, John
Blood, Faron
Brooks, Jacob
Brown, Jonas
Brown, Samuel
Burly, Josiah
Butler, Amos
Butler, Simeon
Chickering, Hartshorn

Childs, Benjamin
Clark, Warren
Coburn, Blanchard
Conant, Daniel
Corning, Samuel
Cowin, Isaac
Curtis, Thaddeus
Cuttings, Mark
Daggett, Carlos
Danforth, Isaac (died)
Darling, David
Davis, Joshua, Jr.
Ditson, William
Emery, Joel
Farmer, Asa
Farnsworth, James D.
Fletcher, Phineas P.
Fletcher, Porter
French, Daniel
Gilman, John T.
Gleason, Joel
Goodnow, Rufus
Green, Abel
Hall, Daniel
Harley, Joseph
Haskell, Joseph (D.)
Hastings, John
Hayood, Josiah
Hemingway, Israel
Hopping, William
Hubbard, Darius
Hunt, William
Hurd, Abel
Jones, John
Kendall, Peter
Kendall, Samuel
Laurence, Edmund

Leverett, Gad
Manning, James, Jr.
Marble, John
Marshall, James
Mellen, Joseph
Morse, Lyman
Newell, Harrington
Parker, Josiah
Parker, Walter
Petingill, Asa
Pratt, Jonathan
Rand, Nathaniel
Read, George
Read, Howard
Read, Nathaniel
Read, William
Richardson, Josiah
Roberts, Samuel
Robings, Jedediah
Roe, Benjamin
Russell, James
Sabells, Thomas
Sanders, Asa
Sargent, Hall B.
Sawyer, Simon
Stephens, Sampson
Stone, Abraham
Swallow, Thomas
Thrasher, James
Trobridge, Luther
Tufts, Asa
Tufts, William
Van Sailor, Jarret
Weston, Daniel
Whitcomb, Samuel

Capt. S. Tolman's Company, Lieut. Col. J. Page's Regiment.
From Sept. 13 to Nov. 7, 1814. Raised at Dorchester. Service at Fort Warren, Boston Harbor. This company also appears under Lieut. Col. Joseph Dudley's regiment, raised at Dorchester and vicinity and serving at South Boston.

RANK AND NAME.
Stephen Tolman, Captain
Ebenezer Humphry, Lieutenant
Levi Parker, Lieutenant (died)
Newcomb Bates, Ensign

James Foster, Sergeant
Joseph Richard, Sergeant
Elias Holbrook, Sergeant
Joseph Battles, Sergeant
Bethuel Reed, Sergeant
Enos Tolman, Corporal

Jonathan Hamlet, Corporal
Ezra Swallow, Corporal
Jonas Heartwell, Corporal
Thomas J. Holman, Corporal
Hosea Dunbar, Musician
Isaac Beall, Musician

Capt. S. Tolman's Company, Lieut. Col. J. Page's Regiment — Concluded.

Privates.

Adams, Casner
Allen, Tilly
Amby, Benjamin
Bacon, Henry
Bailey, Henry
Barry, William
Barter, George
Belcher, Eliphalet
Belcher, Jeremiah
Bishop, James
Blackman, Jacob
Blanchard, Samuel
Bond, Thomas
Bosworth, Elijah
Bradshaw, Jesse
Briggs, James
Brocklebank, John
Calahan, Joseph
Chamberlain, Amos
Chamberlain, Obediah
Chamberlain, Stephen
Childs, Reuben P.
Clapp, Enos
Clapp, Moses
Clapp, Silas
Clark, Abner
Codding, Josiah
Cook, James
Crane, Richard
Crosby, John
Dewing, Warren

Eddy, Sylvanus
Eddy, Zenos D.
Field, John
French, Reuben
Garland, Hiram R.
Green, Oliver
Harvey, Samuel
Hayden, Peter
Holbrook, Caleb
Hollis, Thomas
Huger, Samuel
Hunting, Jabez F.
Hutchings, William
Jackson, Antyrhas
Lines, John
Lock, Benjamin B.
Lovell, James
Magoon, James
Maine, David
Maintosh, Thomas
Marshall, Moses
Mastings, Joseph
Minott, George
Muney, Edward
Nightingale, Asa
Olvine, John
Orcutt, Micah
Packard, Bewel
Packard, Othniel
Page, Charles
Paine, Parney
Paine, Samuel

Pender, Isaac
Perry, John
Pierce, Thomas H.
Porter, Elijah
Prine, Robert
Reed, Seth
Roberts, Saul
Saulsbury, Abijah W.
Shumway, Ellis
Simmons, George
Stockbridge, Thomas
Tinkham, Ephraim
Tinkham, Otis
Tolman, Edward
Tolman, Elijah
Vinal, Simeon
Weld, Joseph
Wheeler, Abraham
White, David
White, Nathaniel
Whitney, Stephen
Williams, Samuel
Withington, Samuel
Wood, Barnabas
Woodcock, Timothy

Waiters.

Bates, Nathaniel N.
Cushing, Harvey
Vose, Samuel

Capt. A. Williams' Company, Lieut. Col. J. Page's Regiment.

From Sept. 13 to Nov. 7, 1814. Raised at Newburyport and vicinity. Service at Fort Warren, Boston Harbor.

RANK AND NAME.
Abraham Williams, Captain
David Walker, Lieutenant
Joseph Picket, Ensign
Jonathan Sargent, Ensign

William S. Mason, Sergeant
Joseph Follansbee, Sergeant
Levi Knowlton, Sergeant
Caleb Dudley Morris, Corporal
Thomas Robinson, Corporal
David S. Silloway, Corporal
Moses Ross, Musician
William Stickney, Musician

Privates.

Adams, Thomas
Adams, William
Andrews, Ebenezer
Bailey, Abner R.
Bartlett, Cutting
Batchelder, Winthrop
Bowers, Dennison T.
Boyington, Methuselah

Bradlee, Hezakiah
Brown, William
Butler, Philip
Cheevers, Aaron
Cheevers, Philip
Coffin, Enoch
Follansbee, William
Foot, Barnard
Goodhue, James S.
Goodwin, Thomas
Gray, Ezekiel
Harris, John
Hervey, Eliphalet
Hervy, James
Hill, John
Lewis, Mark
McCrillis, Andrew
Morrison, Michel
Morse, Robert
Nichols, Thomas
Norton, George, Jr.
Norton, Moses
Pecker, George W.
Pettingill, Benjamin, Jr.

Pike, Jabez
Pilsbury, William C.
Pritchard, Stephen
Richardson, John
Richardson, Marzite
Robie, Joseph
Rogers, Beniah
Sawyer, Abel
Smith, Daniel
Smith, Samuel
Somersby, William
Stanwood, Saul
Stevens, Daniel W.
Tappan, Thomas P.
Tilden, Robert
Todd, Wallingford
Walker, Gideon
Warner, Joseph H.
Whitmore, Joseph
Woodman, David

Waiter.

Barrington, Henry

MASSACHUSETTS VOLUNTEER MILITIA IN THE WAR OF 1812.

Capt. G. Fisher's Detached Company from Dover and Vicinity, Lieut. Col. J. Page's Regiment.
From Sept. 13 to Nov. 30, 1814. Service at Fort Warren.

RANK AND NAME.
George Fisher, Captain
Aaron Hill, Lieutenant
James Paine, Ensign
Edmund Rice, Ensign

Peter Fisher, Jr., Sergeant
George M. Shaw, Sergeant
James Sleet, Sergeant
Amasa Weeks, Sergeant
Clark Holbrook, Sergeant
Reuben Newell, Corporal
John Haynes, Corporal
Francis Carpenter, Corporal
Amos Hill, Corporal
Jacob Thomas, Corporal
―――― Byran, Corporal
Jesse Houghton, Musician
John Hewes, Musician

Privates.
Adams, Whiting
Allen, Lewis
Allen, Ophie
Amsden, Ephraim
Ayers, Fisher
Bacon, Bela
Barnard, Joel
Baxter, John C.
Bemis, David
Berry, George W.
Besse, Elijah
Brown, William D.
Buckman, Asahel
Butler, Eliphalet
Carpenter, Samuel
Childs, Caleb

Claflen, Otis
Clark, Cephas
Cole, Nathaniel S.
Coolidge, Francis
Cutter, Benjamin
Davis, John
Davis, William
Deane, Edward
Dunklee, Jesse
Durant, Charles
Edson, Robert
Ferdinan, Samuel
Fisher, James, 2d
Fisher, Luther
Foster, William
Frost, Antipas
Gay, Leonard
Gerry, John O.
Goldthwaite, John
Guild, James
Hall, John
Hardy, John
Harford, Ira
Hart, Daniel
Hart, Martin
Hastings, Josiah
Haynes, John
Holmes, Samuel, Jr.
Hopkins, John
Horrey, Calvin
Horton, John
Johnson, Reuben
Kimball, Clark
Kimball, Henry
Leathers, Benjamin
Leonard, David
Lincoln, Leonard

Martin, Isaac
Martin, Petty
Merrill, Edmund
Morse, Justin
Morton, Amasa
Nelson, David
New, Jesse
Orcutt, Hosea
Packer, James, Jr.
Parker, Benjamin
Peck, Samuel
Petty, Martin
Phillips, Daniel H.
Plimpton, John
Plummer, Joshua
Pratt, Lemuel
Richards, Abel, Jr.
Shearman, Emery
Smith, Luke
Stimson, John
Stone, Isaac
Sylvester, James
Sylvester, Richard
Thayer, Aaron
Thompson, Jacob
Thurston, Philo
Tinkham, Seth
Tor, Vincent
Turner, Hezekiah, Jr.
Upton, Eliab
White, Asa
Whitney, Lewis
Williams, William, Jr.
Winship, Oliver
Woodward, Caleb
Wyman, Daniel
Wyman, John

Lieutenant Pritchard's Company, Lieut. Col. J. Page's Regiment.
From Sept. 13 to Nov. 7, 1814. Service at Fort Warren, Boston Harbor.

RANK AND NAME.
Thomas Pritchard, Lieutenant
Nathaniel Stevens, Ensign
Ira Preston, Ensign

Saul Bassett, Sergeant
William Isley, Sergeant
Dean Chadwick, Sergeant
John Ross, Corporal
David Boynton, Corporal
Saul Stevens, Corporal

Privates.
Abbott, Stephen
Adams, Nehemiah
Ames, Peter
Aubin, John
Begram, Charles
Bixley, David
Bray, Eli
Burley, Jonathan
Burnam, Nathaniel
Caldwell, James
Chase, Edmund

Cheever, William
Cogswell, Moody
Crowell, Ariel
Day, Nathaniel
Fielder, Knott
Fielder, William
Flagg, Edward
Francis, George
Frye, Samuel
Gale, John
Galee, Ephraim
Glidden, Robert
Greaves, John
Harlow, John
Harriden, Robert
Hawkes, Thomas
Holt, Enoch
Hudson, John
Ingalls, Nathaniel
Josslyn, William
Kent, Charles
Kimball, Benjamin
Linsey, James M.
Lovett, Stephen

Masting, John B.
Merrick, Joseph
Odell, William
Palmer, John
Panchard, Benjamin
Phillips, Richard
Pierce, Thomas
Pousland, Joseph
Ross, William
Runnels, Eliphalet
Russell, Thomas
Silver, John P.
Simons, Thomas
Smith, Thomas
Sollanus, Francis
Soule, Nathaniel
Stephens, Lewis
Wallace, John
Wells, Stephen

Waiters.
Goodwin, William
Peters, Joseph

Lieut. E. Whitman's Company, Lieut. Col. J. Page's Regiment.

From Sept. 13 to Nov. 7, 1814. Service at Fort Warren, Boston Harbor.

RANK AND NAME.
Ebenezer Whitman, Lieutenant
Gurney Azel, Ensign

George Keith, Sergeant
Salmon Dunbar, Sergeant
Isaac Cook, Corporal
Alexander Nash, Corporal

Privates.
Aldrich, Eaton
Ames, Charles
Arnold, Nathaniel T.

Brown, Lewis
Conant, Jacob
Dickerman, Benjamin
Dunphe, Elvin
Edson, Barnabas
Edson, David
Garner, Abner
Harsey, Sylvanus
Hayward, Otis
Hobert, Nehemiah
Howard, Barnabas
Joy, Thomas
Keith, Benjamin H.

Keith, Thaxter
Leonard, Azza
Loud, Esau
Shaw, John
Snow, George
Thrasher, Cyrus
Tribeau, Francis
Washburn, Nahum
Weston, Enoch
Whitmarsh, Jacob
Wood, Samuel M.

Lieut. Col. Salem Town's Regiment.

From Sept. 9 to Oct. 30, 1814. Service at Boston and vicinity.

FIELD AND STAFF.
Salem Town, Lieutenant Colonel, Charlton
John Murray, Major
Holland Forbes, Major, Westborough
Lorenzo Draper, Adjutant, Boston

Henry W. Taylor, Quartermaster
Daniel Denny, Paymaster
Parley F. Groves, Surgeon
James Trowbridge, Surgeon's Mate
Daniel Oliver, Chaplain, Salem

NONCOMMISSIONED STAFF.
Liberty Baninster, Sergeant Major
Luther Bigelow, Quartermaster Sergeant
Horace Kendall, Drum Major
Benjamin Bennett, Fife Major

Capt. L. Abbott's Company, Lieut. Col. S. Town's Regiment.

From Sept. 8 to Oct. 30, 1814. Raised at Brookfield and vicinity. Service at Boston.

RANK AND NAME.
Lewis Abbott, Captain
Nathaniel Lynde, Lieutenant
Daniel Drake, Ensign

William Hastings, Sergeant
Benesley Davis, Sergeant
Pliny Upham, Sergeant
Jonathan Moore, Sergeant
Seth B. Otis, Corporal
Benjamin Adams, Corporal
Cheney Rice, Corporal
Foster Newton, Corporal
Nathan Dane or Done, Musician

Parker Johnson, Musician
Samuel Stevens, Musician
Samuel Spooner, Musician

Privates.
Barrett, William
Barrows, Rufus
Brigham, Sylvanus
Dewing, Cheney
Dewing, Ephraim
Folds, Solomon
Forbes, Dexter
Gilbert, Coleman
Gilbert, Reuben

Harwood, Nathaniel
Mathews, David
Olds, Cheny
Olds, George
Olds, Jonathan
Potter, Edward
Segers, Henry
Smith, Lewis
Upham, Joel
Waite, Otis
Wilder, George
Winslow, Leonard

Capt. P. Brigham's Company, Lieut. Col. S. Town's Regiment.

From Sept. 8 to Oct. 30, 1814. Raised at Westborough, Northborough and vicinity. Service at Boston.

RANK AND NAME.
Pierpont Brigham, Captain
Charles Parkman, Lieutenant

Elijah Morse, Sergeant
Elias Forbes, Sergeant
Asa Godfrey, Sergeant
Eli Chamberlin, Sergeant
Otis Brigham, Corporal
Nathaniel Brigham, Corporal
Jesse Rice, Corporal
Ephraim Maynard, Corporal

John Warren, Musician
Horace Kendall, Musician
Newell Bellows, Musician
John Rice, Musician

Privates.
Andrews, John
Bird, Bayley
Blake, Barnum
Bowman, John
Brigham, Benjamin
Brigham, Dexter

Brigham, Joseph
Brigham, Samuel
Chamberlin, Edward
Chamberlin, Jason
Chamberlin, Samuel
Fay, Elihu
Fay, William
Fisher, Nahum
Gloves, Levi G.
Goodnow, William
Green, Joseph
Harrington, Dana

Capt. P. Brigham's Company, Lieut. Col. S. Town's Regiment — Concluded.

Privates — Concluded.	Maynard, Leonard	Sibley, Jonas
Harrington, Eli	Maynard, Moses Gill	Stone, Abijah
Hawes, Luther	Maynard, Silas	Stone, Thomas
Kendall, Samuel	Miller, Rodolphus	Warren, Willard
Maynard, Ebenezer	Morn, Thomas	Wesson, Russell

Capt. J. Cushing's Company, Lieut. Col. S. Town's Regiment.
From Sept. 8 to Oct. 30, 1814. Raised at Abington and vicinity. Service at Boston.

RANK AND NAME.	Richard Holbrook, Musician	Reed, Goddard
John Cushing, Captain	Lemuel Jenkins, Musician	Shaw, Brackly
Thomas V. Totman, Lieutenant	Simeon Reed, Musician	Shaw, Daniel
William Wales, Ensign	Reuben Holbrook, Musician	Shaw, Ebenezer, 2d
		Sprague, Zebedee
Melvin Gurney, Sergeant	*Privates.*	Stetson, Oliver
Joseph Wilkes, Sergeant	Cushing, Brackly	Thayer, Benjamin
David Beal, Sergeant	Harris, Nathaniel S.	Vining, Ebed
Cyrus Wales, Sergeant	Lane, Isaiah	Vining, Joseph
Oliver Blanchard, Corporal	Loud, John	Wales, Samuel
Daniel Alger, Corporal	Phillips, Thomas	Whiting, Eleazer
Joseph Jenkins, Corporal	Pratt, Noah	
James Noyes, Corporal	Reed, Abiah	

Capt. W. W. Partridge's Company, Lieut. Col. S. Town's Regiment.
From Sept. 8 to Oct. 30, 1814. Raised at Northampton and vicinity. Service at Boston.

RANK AND NAME.	*Privates.*	Parsons, George W.
William W. Partridge, Captain	Bartlet, Edward M.	Pilkin, Edward
John Hutchins, Lieutenant	Bridgman, Cephas	Pope, Thomas
John Stewart, Ensign	Clapp, Lemuel	Pratt, Thomas
	Coolridge, William	Stebbins, Samuel
John S. Partridge, Sergeant	Crane, Silas	White, Job
Howard Bosworth, Sergeant	Dickinson, Josiah	Wilcox, Benjamin B.
Joseph Hutchins, Sergeant	Edmunds, Elijah	Wilmer, David
Nathan Pratt, Sergeant	McDonald, Alexander	

Capt. S. Woodward's Company, Lieut. Col. S. Town's Regiment.
From Sept. 8 to Oct. 30, 1814. Raised at Hadley and vicinity. Service at Boston.

RANK AND NAME.	Lewis Marsh, Musician	Galord, Israel
Samuel Woodward, Captain	Dennis Smith, Musician	Herrington, Ebenezer
Sylvester Goodman, Ensign	Elijah Smith, Musician	Hodge, Benjamin
	Samuel Dickinson, Musician	Hodge, George
William Smith, Sergeant		Marsh, Moses
Stephen Montague, Sergeant	*Privates.*	Montague, Heman
Spencer Goodman, Sergeant	Dickinson, Elihu	Porter, Elisha
Oliver Warner, Sergeant	Dickinson, Elisha	Quance, Thomas
Oliver Barney, Corporal	Dickinson, Sylvanus	Smith, Lorenzo
Daniel Cook, Corporal	Eastman, Joseph	Wallis, Levi
Roswell Cook, Corporal	Eastman, Saul	White, David
Reuben Cook, Corporal	Edson, Noah	

MASSACHUSETTS VOLUNTEER MILITIA IN THE WAR OF 1812.

Capt. B. Brown's Company, Lieut. Col. S. Town's Regiment.
From Sept. 9 to Oct. 30, 1814. Raised at Royalston and vicinity. Service at Boston.

RANK AND NAME.	Privates.	
Benjamin Brown, Captain	Bemis, Luke	Peck, Chancy
Benoni Peck, Lieutenant	Bliss, Benjamin W.	Pierce, James
Willard Newton, Ensign	Brewer, Joseph	Prescott, John
	Chamberlin, John	Richardson, Stephen
Isaac Yale, Sergeant	Chase, William	Rogers, Thomas
Elmer Newton, Sergeant	Dexter, John	Stockwell, Isaac
Alanson White, Sergeant	Eaton, John	Stockwell, Jonathan
Josiah Walker, Sergeant	Emerson, Elias	Stockwell, Joseph
Thomas Norton, Corporal	Forbush, Chancy	Stockwell, Reuben
Josiah Wheeler, Corporal	Garfield, Moses	Stockwell, Simeon
Moses Tyler, Corporal	Godard, Nathaniel	Stockwell, Tarrant
David Thurston, Corporal	Hill, John	Walker, Asa
Joseph Pierce, Musician	Leathe, Benjamin	Walker, John B.
Silas Pierce, Musician	Lewis, Hiram	Wilson, Nathaniel
Edson Clark, Musician	Morse, Russell	
Silas Metcalf, Musician	Peabody, Chandler	

Capt. W. Crawford's Company, Lieut. Col. S. Town's Regiment.
From Sept. 9 to Oct. 30, 1814. Raised at New Braintree. Service at Boston.

RANK AND NAME.	Privates.	
William Crawford, Captain	Bars, Ebenezer N.	Howard, Ebenezer
James Allen, Lieutenant	Bars, Hiram	Marsh, Elias
Michell Lincoln, Ensign	Blake, Jonathan	Marsh, Richard K.
	Brinkall, Jonas	Pepper, Ashbel
Stephen Lincoln, Sergeant	Clark, Mason	Pepper, Jacob
Edward Wodis, Sergeant	Converse, Boswell	Stone, Isaac
James Conant, Sergeant	Dow, Daniel	Stone, Seth
Lot Conant, Corporal	Dow, Zenas	Thrasher, Harlow
George Mullet, Corporal	Flint, Daniel	Thrasher, Samuel
Parly Ayers, Corporal	Granger, Parley	Tomlinson, Fabian
Sylvester Marn, Musician	Hall, Percival	Warner, Daniel
John Thompson, Musician	Holmes, Charles I.	

Capt. I. Jewett's Company, Lieut. Col. S. Town's Regiment.
From Sept. 9 to Oct. 30, 1814. Raised at Ashburnham and vicinity. Service at Boston.

RANK AND NAME.	Privates.	
Ivers Jewett, Captain	Adams, Stephen	Laws, James
Timothy Crehore, Lieutenant	Bigelow, Luther	Marble, Joel
Walter B. Adams, Ensign	Billings, James	Marble, Stephen
	Blodgett, Elias	Maynard, Edward
Ebenezer Adams, Sergeant	Brooks, Dickerson	McIntire, Flint
John Gates, Sergeant	Butler, Joseph	Miller, James
Reuben Townsend, Sergeant	Carey, Archer	Munroe, Charles
Elijah Booth, Sergeant	Garfich, Elisha	Munroe, Ebenezer
James Adams, Corporal	Green, Hosea	Philips, Asa
Benjamin Barrett, Corporal	Harris, Heman	Polly, Joseph
Amos Stone, Corporal	Harris, Humphrey	Rice, Joseph
Laban Cushing, Corporal	Hastings, John	Sampson, Abraham
Josiah White, Musician	Holden, Jonas	Smith, Ebenezer
Ephraim Taylor, Musician	Hunting, John	Stimpson, Reuben
Enoch Whitmore, Musician	Hunting, Joseph	Ward, Jacob
Reuben Rice, Musician	Lampson, Jonathan	Willard, Caleb
		Wither, George

Capt. R. S. Chappell's Company, Lieut. Col. S. Town's Regiment.
From Sept. 10 to Oct. 30, 1814.   Raised at Pittsfield and vicinity.   Service at Boston.

RANK AND NAME.		
Richard S. Chappell, Captain	Demon, Jeremiah	Palmeter, Calvin D.
Eaton Janes, Lieutenant	Fanning, Chester	Parker, Elias
Amos Barnes, Ensign	Gates, Henry	Parker, Giles
	Gay, William	Sherwood, Orson
Henry W. Taylor, Sergeant	Graves, Rodney	Smith, Samuel
Thomas Lawrence, Sergeant	Holmes, Horace	Squires, Josiah
Enos White, Sergeant	Howland, Joseph	Stocking, Ralph
Henry Janes, Sergeant	Hunnewell, Jonathan	Storey, Miles
	Ingersoll, Jonathan	Stow, Stephen
Privates.	Kilburn, Alva	Strong, James
Bosworth, Hezekiah F.	Lawrence, Horatio G.	Taylor, Daniel G.
Brattle, William W.	May, Chauncy	Tracy, Horace
Bush, Henry W.	Merrill, Justus	Waite, Josiah
Casey, John	Mosley, Thomas D.	Wovel, Silas
Delano, John R.	Munroe, Thaddeus	Wright, Woodbridge S.
	Nelson, Calvin	

Capt. E. Williams' Company, Lieut. Col. S. Town's Regiment.
From Sept. 10 to Oct. 30, 1814.   Raised at Gardner and vicinity.   Service at Boston.

RANK AND NAME.		
Ephraim Williams, Captain	Edward Loud, Musician	Kendall, Hubbard
Samuel Swain, Lieutenant	William Fenno, Musician	Leland, Amasa
Joel Covell, Ensign	Levi Divol, Musician	Moore, Phinehas
		Newell, Joseph L.
Ebenezer Botten, Sergeant	*Privates.*	Perly, David
Charles Hoar, Sergeant	Bennet, Thomas	Reed, David
Benjamin Stone, Sergeant	Brick, Jonas	Wheeler, Joel
Reuben Wheeler, Sergeant	Conant, Farwell	Whiting, Joseph
Aaron Conant, Corporal	Coolridge, James	Whitney, Luke
Phinny Billings, Corporal	Eaton, Josiah	Whitney, Seth
Josiah Hilder, Corporal	Edgell, Benjamin	Wilder, David
George Davis, Corporal	Glazier, Abram F.	Wilder, Isaac
	Jackson, Isaac	Wright, Nathaniel

Capt. J. W. Lincoln's Company, Lieut. Col. S. Town's Regiment.
From Sept. 11 to Oct. 30, 1814.   Raised at Worcester and vicinity.   Service at Boston.

RANK AND NAME.		
John W. Lincoln, Captain	*Privates.*	Perry, Jonah
Sewall Hamilton, Lieutenant	Alexander, William T.	Perry, Luke
John Coolridge, Ensign	Ball, Phinehas	Rice, Peter
	Brown, Warren	Rice, Timothy R.
Levi Wellington, Sergeant	Butler, Abijah	Rutman, Austin R.
Luther Johnson, Sergeant	Carle, Dexter	Smith, Levi
Edward D. Bangs, Sergeant	Curtis, Aaron	Stowell, Samuel
Samuel Green, Sergeant	Deland, Joseph	Tracy, William
Jeremiah Healy, Corporal	Drury, Joseph	Tucker, Isaac
Lincoln Fenring, Corporal	Dunean, Jason	Tufts, Walter
Charles Bridge, Corporal	Fenno, Joseph	Warren, Charles W.
James Thompson, Corporal	Flagg, Asa	Webb, Daniel
Jason Mann, Musician	Fletcher, Eleazer	Wheeler, William D.
Oliver Cajer, Musician	Johnson, Gardner	White, Benjamin
Rufus Paine, Musician	Mann, Arnold	Wilder, Nahum
	Paine, Wales	Witt, Archibald

MASSACHUSETTS VOLUNTEER MILITIA IN THE WAR OF 1812.

Capt. A. Thompson's Company, Lieut. Col. S. Town's Regiment.
From Sept. 12 to Oct. 30, 1814. Service at Boston.

RANK AND NAME.
Asa Thompson, Captain
Nehemiah Thompson, Lieutenant

Isaiah Ripley, Sergeant
Cephas Thompson, Sergeant
Adam Thompson, Sergeant
Giles Thompson, Sergeant
Jabez P. Thompson, Corporal
Oran Freeman, Corporal
Zadoc Churchill, Corporal
Eliab Thompson, Corporal
Samuel Bryant, Musician

Zebulon Thompson, Musician
Jabez Soule, Musician
Zadoc Thompson, Musician

Privates.
Bearce, Benjamin
Bourne, Newcomb
Bradford, John
Briggs, Lewis
Bryant, Cephas
Hall, Joseph
Johnson, Elijah
Joslin, Marquis F.

Lyons, Joshua
Pratt, Stillman
Richmond, Oliver
Rider, Ezra
Sears, Josiah
Sturtevant, Caleb
Sturtevant, Ward
Thompson, Nehemiah
Thompson, Ward
Tillson, Ephraim
Wood, John

Capt. I. Lothrop's Company, Lieut. Col. Town's Regiment.
From Sept. 19 to Oct. 31, 1814. Raised at Easton and vicinity. Service at Boston.

RANK AND NAME.
Isaac Lothrop, Captain
Seth Williams, Lieutenant
Melvin Gilmore, Ensign

Howard Lothrop, Sergeant
Oliver Pool, Sergeant
Simeon Leach, Sergeant
Dwelly Williams, Sergeant
George Alger, Corporal
Lewis Williams, Corporal
Charles Wilber, Corporal
Silas H. Britt, Corporal
John Pool, Musician
Ethan Howard, Musician

Thomas Howard, Musician
Asel Pratt, Musician

Privates.
Cobble, Alanson
Copeland, Horatio
Dickerman, Daniel T.
Drake, Lincoln
Drake, Reuben
Drake, Zenas
Guild, Nathaniel
Harlow, Asa
Harlow, Tisdale
Hayward, Nahum
Howard, Charles

Howard, George
Howard, Warren
Keith, Lemuel
Lothrop, Joshua
Mitchell, Eliphalet
Mitchell, Leonard
Randall, Elijah
Thayer, Simeon
Ward, Joseph
White, Alanson
Wilber, Isaiah
Wilber, Jason
Wilber, Joseph
Williams, Larned

Lieut. W. Whitaker's Company, Lieut. Col. Town's Regiment.
From Sept. 12 to Oct. 30, 1814. Raised at New Salem and vicinity. Service at Boston.

RANK AND NAME.
William Whitaker, Lieutenant
Simon Tenny, Ensign

David Twitchell, Sergeant
James Whitaker, Sergeant
Jesse Merriam, Sergeant
William H. Carey, Sergeant
John Powers, Corporal
John Twitchell, Corporal
Nahum Curtis, Corporal
Silas Whitaker, Corporal
Jonathan Kellogg, Musician
James Day, Musician
Joseph Shaw, Musician

Privates.
Bond, John
Brooks, Amos
Curtis, William
Day, John
Fay, Nehemiah
Fisher, Everett
Fiske, Abijah
Garrison, Joseph
Gay, Ebenezer
Goodnow, Elmer
Goodnow, Isaac
Hascall, Benjamin
Hascall, Saul
Kimball, Phineas
Leach, Stephen
Macumber, Ebenezer
Merriam, Benjamin

Merriam, Rubus
Morning, Samuel
Morse, Oliver
Orcutt, John
Phinney, Jason
Putnam, Samuel
Shaw, Samuel
Stow, Benjamin
Thayer, Jesse
Thompson, Daniel
Thompson, Ezra
Thompson, Jesse
Twitchell, Benjamin M.
Twitchell, George
Washburn, Joseph
Whitney, Abner
Whitney, Jacob

Capt. D. McB. Thaxter's Company, Major Maltby's Battalion.

From Sept. 22 to Oct. 31, 1814. Raised at Hingham. Service at Boston.

Rank and Name.	*Privates.*	
Duncan McB. Thaxter, Captain	Amedy, John	Ray, Thomas
Jairus Sprague, Lieutenant	Bicknell, Lovell	Ripley, Peter
Daniel Basset, Ensign	Burrell, John	Stoddard, Joshua
	Churchill, Rufus	Stoddard, Luther
Daniel Stoddard, Sergeant	Gurney, Gridley	Stowell, Seth
Charles Fearing, Sergeant	Hammond, Loring	Thayer, Jairus
Charles Lane, Sergeant	Leavitt, Samuel, Jr.	Waters, John
Calvin Gardner, Sergeant	Lewis, Elijah W.	Whiton, Job S.
Justin Ripley, Corporal	McDurmit, George W.	
Martin Sprague, Corporal	Pennington, Elisha	*Waiter.*
Martin Leavitt, Corporal	Pittee, Nathaniel, Jr.	Ray, Caleb
Stephen Stoddard, Jr., Corporal	Ray, Charles	

Capt. E. Cobb's Company, Maj. W. Ward's Battalion of Rifles.

From Sept. 22 to Oct. 31, 1814. Raised at Bellingham. Service at Boston.

Rank and Name.	Eli Thompson, Corporal	Dewing, Elijah
Eaton Cobb, Captain	John McWales, Corporal	Hill, Jonathan
Amos Hill, Lieutenant	Levi Allen, Corporal	Holbrook, Aaron, 2d
Seth Holbrook, Ensign		Holbrook, Ellis
	Privates.	Lee, Henry
Hamlet Barber, Sergeant	Adams, Joseph	Luke, George
Cephas Holbrook, Sergeant	Briggs, John	Partridge, Philip
John Cook, 2d, Sergeant	Chilson, Ichabod	Thayer, Martin
Peter Adams, Sergeant	Chilson, John, Jr.	Thompson, Zeba
Laban Burr, Corporal	Chilson, Joshua, Jr.	Williams, Martin

Capt. J. Hay's Company, Maj. W. Ward's Battalion of Rifles.

From Sept. 22 to Oct. 31, 1814. Raised at Stoneham. Service at Boston.

Rank and Name.	Jeddo Brown, Musician	Geary, Saul
Jonathan Hay, Captain	William Holden, Musician	Hays, Pierpont
John H. Wright, Lieutenant	Joseph Mathews, Musician	Howard, Amos
William Richardson, Ensign	Thomas Parker, Musician	Jones, Simon
	Nathaniel Richardson, Musician	Knight, Henry
William Deadman, Sergeant		Leathe, James
Benjamin Geazy, Jr., Sergeant	*Privates.*	Lewis, Charles
Samuel Richardson, Sergeant	Brown, James	Pierce, Timothy
William Bryant, Sergeant	Converse, Jeremiah	Porter, Asahel
Abraham Marshall, Corporal	Eaton, Joseph	Richardson, Alpheus
Ephraim Pearce, Corporal	Emerson, James	Rowe, Jonas W.
Samuel Wiley, Corporal	Evans, Samuel	Slocumb, Frederic
Jesse Converse, Corporal	Flint, Benjamin	Sweezer, Samuel

Capt. A. Pratt's Company, Maj. W. Ward's Battalion of Rifles.

From Sept. 22 to Oct. 31, 1814. Raised at Whately. Service at Boston.

Rank and Name.	Arnold Morton, Corporal	Larrabee, Benjamin
Amos Pratt, Captain	Gad Smith, Jr., Corporal	Phelps, Edward
Asa Parker, Lieutenant	Simeon Reed, Musician	Scott, Aretus
Phinna Graves, Ensign	Sylvester Morton, Musician	Smith, Justin
		Smith, Robert
Martin Wood, Sergeant	*Privates.*	Stark, Justus
Jonathan C. Loomis, Sergeant	Belding, Chester	Thompson, Azel W.
Perez Graves, Sergeant	Graves, John	Warner, Luther
William Graves, Sergeant	Graves, Justus	Wood, Jonathan, Jr.
John Monson, Corporal	Graves, Rolin	
Erastus B. Hillman, Corporal	Graves, Wrotus	

Lieut. Col. J. Valentine's Regiment.
From Sept. 10 to Oct. 30, 1814. Service at Boston.

FIELD AND STAFF.		NONCOMMISSIONED STAFF.
Joseph Valentine, Lieutenant Colonel, Hopkinton	Elial W. Metcalf, Adjutant, Cambridge	George Woodward, Quartermaster Sergeant
Aaron Pearson, Major, Wilmington	Moses Morton, Quartermaster, Hatfield	Leonard Messer, Drum Major
Edward Pope, Jr., Major, New Bedford	Harvey Nolan, Paymaster	John Kimball, Fife Major
Edward Foster, Jr., Major, Dorchester	Benjamin Pond, Surgeon, Hopkinton	Nathaniel Mune, Musician
	John W. Webster, Surgeon's Mate	
	Nathaniel How, Chaplain, Hopkinton	

Capt. C. Alden's Company, Lieut. Col. J. Valentine's Regiment.
From Sept. 10 to Oct. 30, 1814. Raised at Bridgewater and vicinity. Service at Boston.

RANK AND NAME.	*Privates.*	
Cyrus Alden, Captain	Alden, Ezra	Keith, Parley
Cushing Mitchell, Lieutenant	Alden, Jonathan, Jr.	Lincoln, Pruel
Bartholomew Trow, Ensign	Bryan, Robert	Mitchell, George
	Cary, Francis	Newhall, Samuel P.
Ephraim Carey, Sergeant	Edson, Jonah	Osborn, Martin
Benjamin Robertson, Sergeant	Faxton, Luther	Pineer, Benjamin
Levi Washburn, Sergeant	Field, Amasa	Pratt, William
Jonathan Chamberlain, Sergeant	Harden, John C.	Reynolds, David P.
Alexander Whitman, Corporal	Harden, Noah	Roberson, Marcus
Welcom Otis, Corporal	Harden, Thomas	Soule, Nathan
Alvin Shaw, Corporal	Harris, Asa	Washburn, Herman
Thaxter Norton, Corporal	Harris, William	White, Thomas
Thomas Dunbar, Musician	Hill, Bela	Whitman, Gilbert
Daniel Holbrook, Musician	Hill, Bezar	Whitman, Martin
John A. Conant, Musician	Howland, Ichabod	Whitman, Thomas
Joseph Dunbar, Musician	Keith, Heman	

Capt. W. Clapp's Company, Lieut. Col. J. Valentine's Regiment.
From Sept. 10 to Oct. 30, 1814. Raised at Walpole and vicinity. Service at Boston.

RANK AND NAME.	*Privates.*	
Warren Clapp, Captain	Allen, Daniel	Hartshorn, Richard
Samuel Mason, Lieutenant	Allen, Reuben	Hill, Josiah
Daniel Hartshorn, Ensign	Allen, Samuel	Lewis, Aaron
	Allen, Warren	Lewis, Isaac
Harvey Boyden, Sergeant	Boyden, Jason	Lewis, Jason
Henry Plimpton, Sergeant	Boyden, Warren	Lewis, John
Otis Hartshorn, Sergeant	Clapp, Bradish	Mann, Samuel
Pitts Smith, Sergeant	Clapp, Curtis	Mann, William
Daniel Boyden, Musician	Day, Jeremiah, Jr.	Plimpton, Daniel
Horace Guild, Musician	Day, Josiah	Plimpton, Elias
Lewis Guild, Musician	Ellis, Willard	Plimpton, Ziba
Joseph W. Gray, Musician	Fales, Abijah	Pond, John A.
Jason Williams, Musician	Fales, Lewis	Robbins, Joseph
	Hall, Josiah	Smith, Jeremiah
	Hall, Willard	Turner, Daniel

Capt. S. Childs' Company, Lieut. Col. J. Valentine's Regiment.

From Sept. 10 to Oct. 30, 1814. Raised at Cambridge and vicinity. Service at Boston.

RANK AND NAME.
Samuel Childs, Captain
Jonathan C. Prentiss, Lieutenant
Eliab W. Metcalf, Ensign

John Ruggles, Sergeant
William Hunnewell, Sergeant
Oliver L. Childs, Sergeant
Rufus Roberts, Sergeant
Jacob H. Bates, Corporal
Asa Wyman, Corporal
David Boutell, Corporal
Nathaniel Munro, Musician

Privates.
Bates, William
Bellows, Elijah
Brackett, John
Brown, William
Child, James
Colburn, Nathaniel
Everett, Charles
Fillebrown, John
Flagg, Timothy
Gould, Abraham J.
Greenwood, Henry
Hadley, Sewell
Herrick, Isaac
Hollis, William

Kilburn, Isaac
Larabee, Richard
Morse, Cyrus
Munroe, Harris
Sanderson, Seth
Stone, Buckley
Thompson, Moses
Walton, Charles
Ware, Galen
Wythe, Jones, 3d

Waiters.
Adams, Saul
Burdish, William
Child, John W.

Capt. W. Curtis' Company, Lieut. Col. J. Valentine's Regiment.

From Sept. 10 to Oct. 30, 1814. Raised at Mendon and vicinity. Service at Boston.

RANK AND NAME.
Wright Curtis, Captain
Isaac Silsby, Lieutenant
Jared Benson, Ensign

Eaton Tourtellot, Sergeant
Daniel Southwick, 3d, Sergeant
Thaddeus Curtis, Sergeant

Privates.
Aldrick, Willis
Boyden, David
Capron, Collins

Cass, John, Jr.
Cook, Stephen W.
Daniels, Amos
Daniels, Elbridge G.
Daniels, Moses, Jr.
Daniels, Riley
Daniels, Smith
Darling, Newton
Gillson, Sutton
Kingman, Ebenezer
Mann, Richard
Merriam, George
Merriam, John

Paine, Alva
Parkhurst, Horace
Rhodes, Washington
Richardson, Allen
Sienett, Stephen
Thayer, Thompson
Tourtellot, Stephen
Wilson, Willard

Waiters.
Brown, Samuel
Cook, Noah

Capt. L. Cushing's Company, Lieut. Col. J. Valentine's Regiment.

From Sept. 10 to Oct. 30, 1814. Raised at Rehoboth and vicinity. Service at Boston.

RANK AND NAME.
Loring Cushing, Captain
Wooster Carpenter, Lieutenant
Ephraim W. Walker, Ensign

Ezra French, Sergeant
Newman Ide, Sergeant
Christopher Blanding, Sergeant

Darius Carpenter, Musician
Abel Carpenter, Musician

Privates.
Allen, Isaiah
Barney, John
Campbell, Joshua T.
Chaffee, Noah

Drown, Royal P.
Ide, Ephraim
Pearce, Robert
Smith, Samuel
Walker, George
Wheaton, John

Capt. S. W. Duncan's Company, Lieut. Col. J. Valentine's Regiment.

From Sept. 10 to Oct. 30, 1814. Raised at Haverhill and vicinity. Service at Boston.

RANK AND NAME.
Samuel W. Duncan, Captain
Nathan Burrill, Lieutenant
Thomas Newcomb, Ensign

Joseph Coffin, Sergeant
Samuel M. Johnson, Sergeant
John Atwood, Sergeant

John Trumbull, Sergeant
Leonard Messer, Musician
Frederick Sayer, Musician
William Brown, Musician

Privates.
Ames, Isaac
Bartlett, Bailey, Jr.

Briggs, Henry
Curwen, Samuel
Davis, John
Emerson, Henry
Emerson, Nathan
Follansbee, John
Frink, Andrew
Greenough, Thomas M.

Capt. S. W. Duncan's Company, Lieut. Col. J. Valentine's Regiment — Concluded.

Privates — Concluded.
Hale, Christopher
Hale, Saul
Hall, Charles B.
Hall, Ezekiel, Jr.
Hovey, Rufus P.

Howe, Calvin W.
Lake, Ephraim E.
Loring, William P.
Nesmith, John
Noyes, Saul
Porter, Eleazer A.

Smith, Peter
Stickney, Jeremiah
Sweet, William
Townsend, William
West, Thomas, Jr.
White, William

Capt. D. Everett's Company, Lieut. Col. J. Valentine's Regiment.
From Sept. 10 to Oct. 30, 1814. Raised at Foxborough and vicinity. Service at Boston.

RANK AND NAME.
Daniel Everett, Captain
Asa Plimpton, Lieutenant

Amos Morse, Sergeant
James Wilber, Sergeant
Calvin Grover, Sergeant
Henry Hobert, Sergeant
Oliver Pettee, Musician
Simon Pettee, Musician
Edwin Stearns, Musician

Privates.
Belcher, Comfort
Billings, Dudley
Boyden, Alexander
Brayton, B.
Carpenter, Daniel
Childs, Willard
Comee, Aaron
Comee, Lyman
Durphy, Peleg
Everett, George
Fields, Libbeus

Guild, Freedom
Hall, David
Hartshorn, Fisher
Hartshorn, George
Hevins, Nathan
Hodges, Otis
Plimpton, Elijah
Rhodes, Stephen
Shaw, Levin
Titus, Samuel
Torry, Martin
Wilbur, Abiathar

Capt. N. Flint's Company, Lieut. Col. J. Valentine's Regiment.
From Sept. 10 to Oct. 30, 1814. Raised at Concord and vicinity. Service at Boston.

RANK AND NAME.
Nehemiah Flint, Captain
John Brown, Lieutenant
Artemus Wheeler, Ensign

Cyrus Hubbard, Sergeant
Edward Flint, Sergeant
Nehemiah Flint, Jr., Sergeant
Artemus Brown, Sergeant
Nathan Munroe, Corporal
Joseph Dailey, Corporal
Isaac Brooks, Corporal
Perez Blood, Corporal
Cyrus Farwell, Musician
John Hayward, Jr., Musician

Privates.
Allen, John P.
Banett, Daniel
Blanchard, John R.
Cogswell, Henry T.
Connant, Ebenezer
Connant, Silas
Farrar, Amos D.
Flint, Daniel
Flint, Silas
Harrington, Jonas
Hayward, Joseph
Hosmer, Cyrus, Jr.
Hosmer, Pearley
Hubbard, Jonathan

Jarvis, Francis, Jr.
Lee, Cyrus
Minott, William
Ray, Heman
Wheeler, Noah, Jr.
Wheeler, Phineas
Wheeler, Thomas, 2d
Wheeler, Timothy
Wood, Ebenezer
Wood, Nathan
Wyman, Samuel

Capt. A. Guild's Company, Lieut. Col. J. Valentine's Regiment.
From Sept. 10 to Oct. 30, 1814. Raised at Dedham and vicinity. Service at Boston.

RANK AND NAME.
Abner Guild, Captain
Joshua Fales, Lieutenant
Pliney Bingham, Ensign

Jesse Farrington, Sergeant
Samuel Lewis, Sergeant
Noah Hersey, Sergeant
Jabez Weatherbee, Sergeant
Joel Richards, Musician
James Fales, Musician

Privates.
Bullard, Chester
Cobbert, Joseph

Crehone, Elisha, Jr.
Everett, Joel
Everett, Leonard
Everett, Nathan
Fales, Nehemiah
Fales, Stephen
Fuller, Calvin
Gouch, Russell
Gragg, Moses
Hansel, Robert
Leland, Ebenezer
Mann, Joseph
Marston, John C.
Mason, Cyrus
McIntosh, Elisha

Noyes, Nathaniel
Noyes, Samuel
Richards, Mason
Richards, William
Sherman, Samuel
Smith, Oliver
Tilden, Jonathan
Whiting, Isaac
Whiting, John
Wright, Jason

Capt. S. Jones' Company, Lieut. Col. J. Valentine's Regiment.
From Sept. 10 to Oct. 30, 1814. Raised at Acton and vicinity. Service at Boston.

RANK AND NAME.
Silas Jones, Captain
James Jones, Lieutenant
Aaron Haywood, Ensign

Jonathan Hosmer, Sergeant
John Fletcher, Sergeant
Samuel Conant, Sergeant
John Hendly, Sergeant
Luther Haywood, Corporal
James Fletcher, Corporal
Jonathan B. Davis, Corporal
James Hayward, Corporal
Silas Piper, Musician
Paul Conant, Musician
Abner Wheeler, Musician

Privates.
Adams, Josiah H.
Barber, James or Joseph, Jr.
Billings, Ephraim, Jr.
Bright, Josiah, Jr.
Chaffen, John
Chamberlin, Ezekiel
Chamberlin, Joseph B.
Conant, James
Conant, Joel
Conant, John
Davis, Ebenezer
Davis, Luther
Fletcher, John S.
Forbush, Abel
Hapgood, Nathaniel

Harris, John, Jr.
Hayward, Moses
Hosmer, Silas
Keyes, James
Reed, William
Richardson, Allen
Robbins, George
Robbins, George W.
Robbins, Joseph
Weatherbee, Oliver
Wheeler, Jonathan
Whitney, Samuel

Capt. H. Poor's Company, Lieut. Col. J. Valentine's Regiment.
From Sept. 10 to Oct. 30, 1814. Raised at Andover. Service at Boston.

RANK AND NAME.
Henry Poor, Captain
Benjamin Abbott, Lieutenant
Joseph Bradley, Ensign

Timothy Poor, Sergeant
Thomas E. Foster, Sergeant
Samuel Frye, Sergeant
John Chickering, Sergeant
Jacob Abbott, Corporal
Amos Flint, Corporal
Benjamin Boynton, Corporal
Jeduthan Abbott, Corporal
Timothy Barley, Musician
Timothy Foster, Musician

Uriah French, Musician
Daniel Poor, Musician

Privates.
Abbott, Nathan, Jr.
Austin, Aaron
Barker, Jacob W.
Boynton, Amos
Carlton, Benjamin
Chickering, Daniel
Chickering, Isaac
Frye, Samuel, 3d
Johnson, Timothy
Lovejoy, Orlando
Mason, Daniel

Movars, Jacob
Needham, Samuel
O'Neal, Joseph
Pilsbury, Enoch
Richards, Thomas
Simonds, Solomon
Spofford, Henry
Spofford, Thomas
Stevens, Enoch
Stickney, John
Summers, Samuel
Towns, Daniel

Waiter.
Chickering, Samuel

Capt. T. Tirrell's Company, Lieut. Col. J. Valentine's Regiment.
From Sept. 10 to Oct. 30, 1814. Raised at Quincy and vicinity. Service at Boston.

RANK AND NAME.
Thomas Tirrell, Captain
Elihu Thayer, Lieutenant
John Whitney, Ensign

Elisha Marsh, Sergeant
Josiah Glover, Sergeant
James Green, Sergeant
Benjamin Page, Sergeant
Josiah Brigham, Corporal
William James, Corporal
John Savil, Corporal
George Nightingale, Corporal
Eliphalet Chandler, Musician
William Wheeler, Musician
John Talbott, Musician
William A. Field, Musician

Privates.
Adams, Josiah
Arnold, Joseph
Belcher, William
Burrell, Joseph
Burrell, Seth, 2d
Chandler, Charles
Chandler, Ebenezer
Cleverly, Lewis
Cook, Jonathan
Damon, Ezra
Dexter, Nathaniel
Gay, Benjamin
Glover, Elisha
Hayden, Samuel
Hayden, Solomon
Newcomb, John

Nightingale, Solomon
Osborn, John
Pratt, James
Pray, James
Pray, Peter
Putnam, Henry
Spear, Daniel B.
Tirrill, George
Vezie, Stephen
Wales, Joseph
White, Thomas

Capt. S. Townsend's Company, Lieut. Col. J. Valentine's Regiment.

From Sept. 10 to Oct. 30, 1814. Raised at Waltham and vicinity. Service at Boston.

Rank and Name.
Samuel Townsend, Captain
Saul Green, Lieutenant
Abraham Willing, Ensign

Isaac Stearns, Sergeant
Jacob Farwell, Sergeant
John Kimball, Sergeant
Ephraim Allen, Sergeant

Privates.
Bryant, Jacob
Bryant, John
Bryant, Lyman
Bryant, Saul
Cutler, Richard
Emerson, Daniel
Farwell, Isaac
Fisk, Henry
Goss, William
Harrington, Amasa
Harrington, Asa
Hastings, James
Hoar, Joseph
Lawrence, Elijah
Lawrence, Jacob
Lawrence, Jonas
Piper, Alexander H.
Sanderson, John
Stearns, Nathaniel
Symonds, John
Tidd, Ebenezer G.
Treat, William
Warren, Josiah
Wellington, Darius

Capt. S. Wheeler's Company, Lieut. Col. J. Valentine's Regiment.

From Sept. 10 to Oct. 30, 1814. Raised at Cambridge and vicinity. Service at Boston.

Rank and Name.
Stephen Wheeler, Captain
Stephen Laske, Lieutenant
John Perry, Ensign

Joshua S. Robbins, Sergeant
Thomas Hutchinson, Sergeant
Stephen P. Day, Sergeant
Thomas Hathaway, Sergeant
James Cutter, Musician
Joseph Dickson, Musician
William Wilson, Musician
Thomas H. Teele, Musician
Samuel Ames, Musician

Privates.
Adams, Jonas
Adams, Samuel
Butterfield, Benjamin
Butterfield, John
Cook, Simeon
Cutler, Artemus
Cutter, Levi
Cutting, William
Davidson, Thomas
Estabrooks, Endor
Fillebrown, Leonard
Frost, Asa
Frost, Isaac
Frost, Joel
Hall, Ebenezer, Jr.
Hill, Samuel
Hovey, Ebenezer
Locke, Abel
Locke, Davis
Locke, Peter
Perry, James
Prentis, Amos
Russell, Philemon R.
Russell, William
Swan, Henry
Swan, Stephen
Teele, Ammi
Teele, Benjamin
Teele, Samuel P.
Weston, Ephraim
Whittemore, Gershom
Whittemore, Joseph

Waiters.
Blaney, Joseph
Hall, William

Capt. J. Cleverly's Company, Lieut. Col. S. Webb's Regiment.

From June 15 to July 16, 1814. Raised at Weymouth.

Rank and Name.
Jonathan Cleverly, Captain
Samuel Loud, Lieutenant
Noah Torry, Ensign

William Wittington, Sergeant
Rufus Curtis, Sergeant
James Wilder, Sergeant
Thomas Stoddard, Sergeant
Isaiah Corthill, Corporal
Charles Leach, Corporal
Theophilus Whiton, Corporal
John Holbrook, Corporal
Charles Pratt, Musician
Benjamin Torry, Musician

Privates.
Ayer, Samuel
Basley, John
Bates, Ezekiel
Bates, Mordicai
Beale, Charles
Beale, George
Blanchard, Ezra
Boggs, David
Briggs, Joseph
Burr, John
Cain, Daniel
Chubbuck, Eleazer
Churchill, Rufus
Cushing, Adam
Cushing, John
Cushing, John, 2d
French, David
Gardner, Perez
Garney, Gridley
Gross, Jacob
Hayward, Samuel
Hobart, Hawks, 2d
Holbrook, D.
Hollis, Hosea
Jacobs, Peter
Jones, Moses
Joy, David
Leavitt, Aaron
Leavitt, Isaac

Capt. J. Cleverly's Company, Lieut. Col. S. Webb's Regiment — Concluded.

Privates — Concluded.
Leavitt, John C.
Lewis, Elijah N.
Lincoln, Zenas
Marble, Abner P.
Nash, Levi
Neale, John
Nichols, David F.
Piatt, Laban
Piatt, Matthew

Piatt, William
Pitte, Joseph
Pratt, Caleb
Pray, George
Ray, Caleb
Richards, James
Shaw, John
Sprague, Amos
Stoddard, Ichabod
Stoddard, Isaiah

Stoddard, Luther
Stoddard, Matthew
Stodder, Caleb
Sturtevant, Joshua
Stutson, Oliver
Thayer, David
Thompson, John
Tyrrel, Benjamin
Wallis, Ezekiel
Whiton, Isaiah

Capt. J. Cleverly's Company, Lieut. Col. S. Webb's Regiment.
From July 16 to Aug. 16, 1814. Raised at Weymouth.

RANK AND NAME.
Jonathan Cleverly, Captain
Ebenezer Humphrey, Lieutenant
Lemuel Humphrey, Ensign

Hanks Whiton, Sergeant
Charles Leach, Sergeant
Cotton Lovell, Sergeant
John Thompson, Sergeant
John Nash, Musician
David Cushing, Musician
Caleb Bates, Musician
Peter Howard, Musician
Ziba Cushing, Musician

Privates.
Bates, Benjamin
Bates, Benjamin, 2d
Bates, Cotton
Bates, Elnathan
Bates, James
Bates, Jesse, Jr.
Bates, John
Bates, William

Bicknell, Thomas
Bigelow, David
Binney, Elkanah
Blanchard, William
Bucknell, Stephen
Burrell, Asa
Cushing, John
Cushing, Thomas, 2d
Cushing, Thomas, 3d
Dyer, David
Dyer, Stephen
Ford, David
French, David
French, Isaac
French, Stephen, Jr.
Hingman, Samuel
Holbrook, Dan
Holbrook, Elisha
Holbrook, Joshua
Humphrey, William
Hunt, Asa
Hunt, Samuel
Loud, Ebenezer
Loud, Joseph

Lovell, David
Nash, Amasa
Nash, Asa
Nash, John P.
Nash, Martin
Nash, Timothy
Nash, Zichri
Pratt, Abner
Pratt, Asa
Pratt, Enoch
Pratt, Gideon
Pratt, Laban
Pratt, Lewis
Pratt, William
Reed, Thomas
Reed, William
Stoddard, Ananias
Thomas, James
Tirrell, Noah
Torrey, James
Torrey, John
Torrey, Silas
Vinal, John S.
Williams, Isaac

Capt. G. Shaw's Company, Maj. Levi Pierce's Battalion.
From June 24 to July 8, 1814. Raised at Middleborough. Service at New Bedford.

RANK AND NAME.
Gains Shaw, Captain
Aulden Miller, Lieutenant
Abiather Briggs, Ensign

Warren Clark, Sergeant
Jonathan Cobb, Sergeant
Abiel P. Booth, Sergeant
Jepthah LeBarron, Sergeant
Earl Alden, Corporal
Caleb Maxum, Corporal
James Sturdevant, Corporal
Zenos Raymond, Corporal
Martin Keith, Jr., Musician
Foster A. Keith, Musician

Privates.
Allen, Clother
Alwood, William

Barrows, Stillman
Briggs, Judson
Briggs, Melbone
Cole, Samuel, 2d
Coombs, Elnathan
Cushman, Isaac, 3d
Gifford, David
Hall, Samuel
Harlow, Branch
Hathaway, Nobles E.
Hathaway, Salathiel
Keith, Aberdeen
LeBarron, Joshua
LeBarron, Ziba
Lewis, Elisha
Lovell, Samuel
Nelson, William
Parris, Enos
Pierce, Eli

Pierce, Eliphalet
Pierce, Enos
Pratt, Elihu
Rickens, Henry
Rickens, James
Rider, Robert, Jr.
Shaw, Silas
Shurtliff, Abiel
Smith, Ansel
Strobridge, Henry
Thomas, Winslow
Westgate, Jonathan
Westgate, Joseph
Wood, Samuel

MASSACHUSETTS VOLUNTEER MILITIA IN THE WAR OF 1812.   103

Capt. J. Cushman's Company, Maj. Levi Pierce's Battalion.
From June 24 to July 10, 1814. Raised at Middleton. Service at New Bedford.

Rank and Name.	Privates.	
James Cushman, Captain	Bobbins, Samuel	Pierce, George
Pelham Atwood, Lieutenant	Bosworth, Lewis	Pratt, Zerobabel
Ebenezer Vaughan, Ensign	Briggs or Bennett, Isaac	Richard, Thomas
	Bryant, Isaac, 2d	Robinson, Josiah
Zenas Cushman, 2d, Sergeant	Bryant, Levi	Sampson, Thomas
Nathan Bodrey, Sergeant	Cobbington, Jacob	Shaw, Joshua, Jr.
Ezra Thomas, Sergeant	Cushman, George	Shaw, Marshall
Joseph Barker, Jr., Sergeant	Darling, Darius	Shaw, Samuel
Levi Tinkham, Corporal	Eddy, Ezra	Standish, Joseph
John Soule, Jr., Corporal	Ellis, Cyrus	Swift, Joseph
Cyrus Tinkham, Corporal	Everson, Timothy	Thomas, James, Jr.
John T. Fuller, Corporal	Fanie, Joseph	Thomas, Jeremiah, Jr.
Samuel Bent, Musician	Fuller, Consider	Tinkham, Caleb
George Thompson, Musician	Hinds, Edward	Tinkham, Enoch
	Hinds, Leonard	Thrasher, Cyrus
	King, Obed	Washburn, Luther
		Wood, Ransom T.

Capt. J. Bowker's Company, Lieut. Col. C. Turner's Regiment.
At different periods, 6 and 13 days, between June 20 and Nov. 6, 1814. Service at Scituate.

Rank and Name.	Privates.	
Joshua Bowker, Captain	Bowker, Benjamin	Jacobs, James H.
Edward Curtis, Lieutenant	Brooks, Nathaniel	Magown, Elias
Enoch Collomore, Ensign	Clapp, Nathaniel	Simmons, Charles W.
	Corthell, Theophilus	Studley, Gideon, Jr.
Levi Curtis, Sergeant	Curtis, Nathaniel	Tolman, Isaac
Gideon Perry, Musician	Curtis, Seth	Turner, Elijah B.
	Damon, Elijah	Whiting, Justus
	Goddard, Cyrus	Wing, Baker

Capt. D. Elmes' Company, Lieut. Col. C. Turner's Regiment.
At different periods, 6 and 13 days, between June 2 and Nov. 6, 1814. Service at Scituate.

Rank and Name.	Clark, Benjamin H.	Mann, Thomas
Daniel Elmes, Captain	Cole, Braddock	Otis, Howland
William Vinall, Ensign	Cudworth, Israel	Tolman, Benjamin
	Curtis, John	Wade, Nathaniel
Amos Dunbar, Sergeant	Curtis, Shadrach B.	Webb, Stephen
	Elmes, John	White, Cyrus
Privates.	Elmes, William	Whiting, Ozias
Alden, Isaiah	Hammond, Frederick	Young, Ephraim
Bailey, Charles	Jacobs, Edward	
Bailey, Gad	Jenkins, Perez T.	

Capt. W. Peaks' Company, Lieut. Col. C. Turner's Regiment.
At different periods, 6 and 13 days, between June 20 and Nov. 6, 1814. Service at Scituate.

Rank and Name.	Damon, Gale	Merritt, Dexter
William Peaks, Captain	Grass, John	Merritt, James L.
Elisha Barrell, Lieutenant	Joyce, David T.	Pratt, Benjamin C.
William Vinall, Ensign	Litchfield, Barnard	Pratt, Thomas
	Litchfield, Perez	Sheverick, Turner
Reuben Curtis, Jr., Corporal	Litchfield, Isaac	Sylvester, Joseph
Eleazer Joslin, Musician	Litchfield, James	Vinall, Levi
	Litchfield, Marshall	
Privates.	Litchfield, Milton	
Cole, Augustus	Litchfield, Stephen	
Curtis, Robert	Magoun, Elisha	

Capt. L. Tilden's Company, Lieut. Col. C. Turner's Regiment.

At different periods, 6 and 13 days, between June 20 and Nov. 6, 1814. Service at Scituate.

Rank and Name.
Luther Tilden, Captain

Joshua James, Sergeant
Calvin Wilder, Corporal
Levi Penny, Musician

Privates.
Briggs, Bartlett
Briggs, Henry
Curtis, Lemuel

Damon, James
Damon, Priam
Ellms, Nathaniel
Farrow, Nathaniel
Grass or Gross, Lewis
Harris, Abraham
Hatch, Samuel
Jacobs, Benjamin R.
James, John, Jr.
Jenkins, Bailey
Judkins, Calvin

Merrett, Benjamin
Merrett, Consider
Morthy, Joseph
Pincin (?), Elias
Pincin (?), Perez
Sampson, John
Turner, Abel
Turner, Benjamin
Turner, Samuel

Capt. S. Tolman's Company, Lieut. Col. C. Turner's Regiment.

At different periods between June 20 and Nov. 6, 1814. Raised at Scituate. Service at Scituate.

Rank and Name.
Samuel Tolman, Captain
Thomas Waterman, Lieutenant

Michael Ford, Sergeant
Luther Turner, Musician

Privates.
Brooks, Joseph, Jr.
Clapp, John
Copeland, William
Curtis, Job
Curtis, Luther
Lapham, William
Leavitt, Cushman

Munroe, Benjamin S.
Randall, Samuel
Stetson, Joshua
Stetson, Melzar
Tolman, Joseph C.
Torrey, David
Torrey, George
Town, Solomon D.

Lieut. Col. Jonathan Snow's Regiment.

From Sept. 15 to Sept. 16 and Oct. 3 to Oct. 4, 1814. Service at Orleans and Barnstable.

Field and Staff.
Jonathan Snow, Lieutenant Colonel, Brewster
Elijah Cobb, Major, Brewster

Joseph Sampson, Major, Brewster
Simeon Kingman, Adjutant, Orleans
Nathan Winslow, Quartermaster, Brewster

Noncommissioned Staff.
Samuel Snow, Sergeant Major.

Capt. M. Higgins' Company, Lieut. Col. J. Snow's Regiment.

From Dec. 19 to Dec. 20, 1814. In battle at Orleans.

Rank and Name.
Moses Higgins, Captain
Isaac Sparrow, Lieutenant
Benjamin Linnell, Ensign

Thomas Higgins, Clerk
Jonathan Freeman, Sergeant
James Rogers, Sergeant
Ebenezer Rogers, Sergeant
Benoni Baker, Sergeant
Isaac Linnell, Corporal
Joshua Freeman, Corporal
Sylvanus Higgins, Musician
Zoath Taylor, Musician

Privates.
Adams, Isaac A.
Arey, Joseph
Cole, Elisha
Cole, Ephraim
Cole, Joel

Cole, John
Crosby, Abel
Crosby, Joseph
Crosby, Nathaniel
Crosby, Obed
Doane, Beriah
Doane, Joshua
Doane, Lewis
Doane, Timothy, Jr.
Freeman, Benjamin
Freeman, Edmund
Gould, James
Gould, Thomas
Gould, Thomas, Jr.
Hayden, Freeman
Higgins, Abiather
Higgins, Asa
Higgins, Charles
Higgins, Eliakim
Higgins, Hezekiah
Higgins, Jabez

Higgins, James, Jr.
Higgins, Knowles
Higgins, Richard
Higgins, Simon
Hopkins, Asa
Hopkins, Curtis
Kenrick, John
Linnell, Benjamin
Linnell, Jonathan
Linnell, Josiah
Linnell, Russell
Linnell, Solomon
Mayo, Abner
Mayo, Asaph
Mayo, Robert
Mayo, Theophilus
Rogers, Israel
Rogers, Jonathan
Rogers, Timothy
Snow, Dean S.
Snow, Edmund, Jr.

Capt. M. Higgins' Company, Lieut. Col. J. Snow's Regiment — Concluded.

Privates — Concluded.		
Snow, Elnathan	Sparrow, Harvey	Taylor, Amasa
Snow, Jesse	Sparrow, Joel	Taylor, David
Snow, Jonathan	Sparrow, Joshua R.	Taylor, John
Snow, Luther	Sparrow, Josiah	Taylor, Richard
Sparrow, Godfrey	Sparrow, Samuel	Young, Nathaniel
	Sparrow, Seth	

Capt. M. Higgins' Company, Lieut. Col. J. Snow's Regiment.

From June 10, 1814. Service at Orleans.

RANK AND NAME.		
Moses Higgins, Captain	Crosby, Joseph	Kenrick, John
Isaac Sparrow, Lieutenant	Crosby, Joshua	Linnell, Josiah, Jr.
Benjamin Linnell, Ensign	Crosby, Nathaniel	Mayo, Abner
	Doane, Beriah	Mayo, Robert
Thomas Higgins, Clerk	Doane, Joshua	Mayo, Theophilus
Jonathan Freeman, Sergeant	Doane, Lewis	Rogers, Israel
James Rogers, Sergeant	Doane, Timothy, Jr.	Rogers, Thomas, Jr.
Ebenezer Rogers, Sergeant	Freeman, Benjamin	Seabury, George
Benoni Baker, Sergeant	Freeman, Edmund	Seabury, George, Jr.
Joshua Freeman, Corporal	Freeman, Joseph	Snow, Edmund, Jr.
Isaac Linnell, Corporal	Hayden, Freeman	Snow, Jonathan
Sylvanus Higgins, Musician	Higgins, Aaron	Snow, Thatcher
	Higgins, Asa	Sparrow, Harvey
Privates.	Higgins, Benjamin	Sparrow, Joel
Arey, Joseph	Higgins, Carney	Sparrow, Joshua R.
Baker, Abijah	Higgins, Elisha	Sparrow, Samuel
Cole, Elisha	Higgins, Hezekiah	Taylor, John
Cole, Ephraim	Higgins, James	Twining, Barnabus, Jr.
Cole, Joel	Higgins, Knowles	Twining, Prince, Jr.
Cole, John	Higgins, Richard	Young, Nathaniel
Crosby, Abial	Higgins, Simon, Jr.	
	Hopkins, Curtis	

Capt. M. Higgins' Company, Lieut. Col. J. Snow's Regiment.

From July 4 to July 5, 1814. Service at Orleans.

RANK AND NAME.		
Moses Higgins, Captain	Cole, Joel	Linnell, Benjamin
Isaac Sparrow, Lieutenant	Crosby, Abial	Linnell, Josiah, Jr.
Benjamin Linnell, Ensign	Crosby, Joseph	Linnell, Russell
	Crosby, Joshua	Mayo, Abner
Thomas Higgins, Clerk	Crosby, Obed	Mayo, Robert
Jonathan Freeman, Sergeant	Doane, Beriah	Mayo, Theophilus
James Rogers, Sergeant	Doane, Joshua	Rogers, Israel
Ebenezer Rogers, Sergeant	Doane, Timothy	Rogers, Thomas, Jr.
Benoni Baker, Sergeant	Freeman, Benjamin	Seabury, Dodge
Isaac Linnell, Corporal	Freeman, Edmund	Snow, Edmund, Jr.
Joshua Freeman, Corporal	Hayden, Freeman	Snow, Jonathan
Sylvanus Higgins, Musician	Higgins, Benjamin	Snow, Thatcher
	Higgins, Carney	Sparrow, Harvey
Privates.	Higgins, James, Jr.	Sparrow, John
Arey, Joseph	Higgins, Knowles	Sparrow, Joshua R.
Baker, Abijah	Higgins, Richard	Taylor, John
Cole, Elisha	Higgins, Simon, Jr.	Twining, Barnabus, Jr.
Cole, Ephraim	Hopkins, Curtis	Twining, Prince, Jr.
	Kenrick, John	Young, Nathaniel

MASSACHUSETTS VOLUNTEER MILITIA IN THE WAR OF 1812.

Capt. H. Knowles' Company, Lieut. Col. J. Snow's Regiment.
From July 4 to July 5, 1814. Service at Orleans.

RANK AND NAME.
Henry Knowles, Captain
Joseph Atkins, Lieutenant

Joshua Rogers, Sergeant
Judah Higgins, Sergeant
John Young, Sergeant
John Jarvis, Sergeant
Benjamin Hurd, Corporal
Seth Freeman, Corporal
Samuel Doane, Corporal
Taylor Smith, Corporal
Mathew Kingman, Musician
Edmund Crosby, Musician

Privates.
Eldridge, Obediah
Eldridge, Thomas
Freeman, Hezekiah
Freeman, Josiah
Higgins, James
Hopkins, Joshua
Hurd, Alvin
Hurd, Luther
Kenrick, Henry
Knowles, Seth
Linnell, Israel
Mayo, Jonathan
Mayo, Thomas
Mayo, Uriah, Jr.
Myrick, Samuel
Nickerson, Nathaniel

Rogers, Asa
Rogers, Foster
Rogers, Samuel
Rogers, Seth
Rogers, Shubel
Rogers, Tully
Rogers, Uriah
Rogers, Zenas
Smith, Elisha
Smith, Joseph
Smith, William
Snow, Abiather
Snow, Gideon S.
Swain, Walter P.
Walker, Nathan
Young, Jonathan
Young, Jonathan F.

Capt. H. Knowles' Company, Lieut. Col. J. Snow's Regiment.
From July 10, 1814. Service at Orleans.

RANK AND NAME.
Henry Knowles, Captain
Joseph Atkins, Lieutenant

Joshua Rogers, Sergeant
Judah Higgins, Sergeant
John Young, Sergeant
John Jarvis, Sergeant
Benjamin Hurd, Corporal
Seth Freeman, Corporal
Edmund Crosby, Musician
Mathew Kingman, Musician

Privates.
Eldridge, Obediah
Freeman, Josiah
Higgins, James
Hurd, Alvin
Hurd, Luther
Hurd, Zenas
Kenny, John
Kenrick, Henry
Knowles, Seth
Linnell, Israel
Linnell, Samuel
Myrick, Samuel
Nickerson, Nathaniel
Rogers, Foster

Rogers, Hezekiah, Jr.
Rogers, Seth
Rogers, Tully
Rogers, Zenas
Small, Isaac
Small, Zachariah
Smith, Elisha
Smith, Josiah
Smith, William
Snow, Abiather
Snow, Gideon S.
Snow, Prince
Walker, Nathan
Young, Jonathan
Young, Jonathan F.

Capt. M. Higgins' Company, Lieut. Col. J. Snow's Regiment.
From Sept. 13, 1814. Service at Orleans.

RANK AND NAME.
Moses Higgins, Captain
Isaac Sparrow, Lieutenant
Benjamin Linnell, Ensign

Thomas Higgins, Clerk
Jonathan Freeman, Sergeant
James Rogers, Sergeant
Ebenezer Rogers, Sergeant
Benoni Baker, Sergeant
Joshua Freeman, Corporal
Isaac Linnell, Corporal
Zoath Taylor, Musician
Sylvanus Higgins, Musician

Privates.
Arey, Joseph
Cole, Elisha
Cole, Ephraim
Cole, Joel
Cole, John
Crosby, Joshua

Doane, Beriah
Doane, Joshua
Doane, Lewis
Doane, Zenas
Freeman, Abner
Freeman, Benjamin
Freeman, Edmund
Freeman, Joseph
Hayden, Freeman
Higgins, Aaron
Higgins, Asa
Higgins, Benjamin
Higgins, Charles
Higgins, Eliakim
Higgins, James
Higgins, Richard
Higgins, Simon, Jr.
Hopkins, Curtis
Kenrick, John
Linnell, Josiah
Linnell, Solomon
Mayo, Abner

Mayo, Robert
Mayo, Theophilus
Rogers, Israel
Rogers, Thomas, Jr.
Rogers, Timothy
Snow, Edmund
Snow, Elnathan
Snow, Jonathan
Snow, Thatcher
Sparrow, Harvey
Sparrow, Joshua R.
Sparrow, Josiah
Sparrow, Samuel
Sparrow, Seth
Taylor, David
Taylor, John
Taylor, Richard
Twining, Barnabas
Twining, Prince
Zenas, John

Capt. H. Knowles' Company, Lieut. Col. J. Snow's Regiment.
From Sept. 14 to Sept. 15, 1814. Service at Orleans.

RANK AND NAME.
Henry Knowles, Captain
Joseph Atkins, Lieutenant

John Jarvis, Sergeant
Judah Higgins, Sergeant
Joshua Rogers, Jr., Sergeant
Walter P. Swain, Sergeant
Benjamin Hurd, Corporal
Seth Freeman, Corporal
Edmund Crosby, Musician

Privates.
Cole, Asa
Eldridge, Obediah
Eldridge, Thomas
Freeman, Hesekiah
Freeman, Nathaniel

Higgins, James
Hopkins, Joshua, Jr.
Hurd, Alvin
Hurd, Luther
Hurd, Zenas
Kenny, John
Knowles, Seth
Linnell, Elisha
Linnell, Israel
Linnell, Samuel
Mayo, Simon
Nickerson, Absalom
Nickerson, Nathaniel
Pepper, Simon
Rogers, Asa
Rogers, Foster
Rogers, Hezekiah, Jr.
Rogers, Samuel

Rogers, Shubal
Rogers, Tully
Rogers, Uriah
Rogers, Zenas
Small, Zachariah
Smith, Elisha
Smith, Isaac
Smith, Joseph
Smith, Josiah
Smith, Taylor
Smith, William
Snow, Gideon S.
Snow, Herman, 3d
Taylor, Isaac
Walker, Nathan
Young, Jonathan
Young, Jonathan F.

Capt. M. Higgins' Company, Lieut. Col. J. Snow's Regiment.
From Oct. 2, 1814. Service at Orleans.

RANK AND NAME.
Moses Higgins, Captain
Isaac Sparrow, Lieutenant
Benjamin Linnell, Ensign

Thomas Higgins, Clerk
Jonathan Freeman, Sergeant
James Rogers, Sergeant
Ebenezer Rogers, Sergeant
Zoath Taylor, Sergeant
Isaac Linnell, Corporal
Joshua Freeman, Corporal
Sylvanus Higgins, Musician
Amasa Taylor, Musician

Privates.
Arey, Joseph
Baker, Abijah
Cole, Elisha
Cole, Ephraim
Cole, Joel
Cole, John
Crosby, Joshua

Doane, Beriah
Doane, Joshua
Doane, Lewis
Doane, Timothy, Jr.
Freeman, Benjamin
Freeman, Edmund
Freeman, Joseph
Gould, James
Gould, Thomas
Hayden, Freeman
Higgins, Aaron
Higgins, Abisha
Higgins, Asa
Higgins, Carney
Higgins, Elisha
Higgins, James, Jr.
Higgins, Richard
Higgins, Richard, Jr.
Higgins, Simon, Jr.
Hopkins, Curtis
Kenny, Jesse
Kenrick, John
Linnell, Joseph, Jr.

Linnell, Russell
Mayo, Abner
Mayo, Asaph
Mayo, Robert
Mayo, Theophilus, Jr.
Rogers, Israel
Rogers, Thomas, Jr.
Rogers, Timothy
Snow, Edmund, Jr.
Snow, Elnathan
Snow, Fletcher
Snow, Jesse
Snow, Jonathan
Sparrow, Harvey
Sparrow, Joel
Sparrow, Joshua R.
Sparrow, Samuel
Taylor, Joshua
Taylor, Richard
Twining, Barnabas
Twining, Prince, Jr.
Young, Nathaniel
Young, Zenas

Capt. H. Knowles' Company, Lieut. Col. J. Snow's Regiment.
From Oct. 2 to Oct. 3, 1814. Service at Orleans.

RANK AND NAME.
Henry Knowles, Captain

Joshua Rogers, Sergeant
John Jarvis, Musician

Privates.
Crosby, Edmund
Eldridge, Obediah
Eldridge, Thomas
Freeman, Hesekiah
Freeman, Seth

Higgins, James
Hurd, Alvin
Hurd, Benjamin
Hurd, Luther
Hurd, Zenas
Kenny, John
Kenrick, Henry
Knowles, Seth
Linnell, Israel
Mayo, Simon
Nickerson, Nathaniel
Rogers, Hezekiah, Jr.

Rogers, Shubal
Rogers, Zenas
Small, Zacheriah
Smith, Elisha
Smith, Isaac
Smith, Josiah
Snow, Gideon S.
Taylor, Asa
Young, Jedediah
Young, Jonathan

Capt. H. Knowles' Company, Lieut. Col. J. Snow's Regiment.

From Dec. 19 to Dec. 20, 1814. Raised at Orleans. In battle at Orleans, December 19.

RANK AND NAME.
Henry Knowles, Captain
David Crowell, Lieutenant
Joseph L. Rogers, Ensign

John Jarvis, Sergeant
Judah Higgins, Sergeant
Walter P. Swain, Sergeant
Benjamin Hurd, Corporal
Edmund Crosby, Musician

Privates.
Eldridge, Obediah
Eldridge, Thomas
Freeman, Hezekiah
Freeman, Josiah

Higgins, James
Hopkins, Joshua, Jr.
Hurd, Alvin
Hurd, Luther
Hurd, Zenas
Kenny, John
Kenrick, Henry
Knowles, Seth
Linnell, Israel
Linnell, Samuel
Myrick, Samuel
Nickerson, Nathaniel
Rogers, Asa
Rogers, Eleazer, Jr.
Rogers, Isaac
Rogers, Sears

Rogers, Seth
Rogers, Shubel
Rogers, Uriah
Rogers, Zenas
Small, Zachariah
Smith, Elisha
Smith, Joseph
Smith, Josiah
Smith, William
Snow, Abiather
Snow, Gideon S.
Young, Jedediah
Young, Jonathan
Young, Jonathan F.
Young, Zenas

Sergt. J. A. Shaw's Guard.

From May 22 to May 29, 1813. Service at Boston, guarding a park of artillery in gun house on Common.

RANK AND NAME.
John A. Shaw, Sergeant
Ansell Fobes, Corporal
Lyman Tucker, Corporal

Privates.
Bliss, Levi
Butler, Samuel
Fletcher, Henry
Jackson, Francis
Lynes, Samuel
Myer, Timothy

Sherwin, Richard
Sprague, Matthew
Sumner, Alexander B.
Tilden, Joseph
White, Ebenezer
White, Thomas

Sergt. J. Slade's Guard.

From May 29 to June 4, 1813. Service at Boston, guarding a park of artillery in gun house on Common.

RANK AND NAME.
John Slade, Sergeant
Philip Curtis, Corporal
John Farmer, Corporal

Privates.
Bodge, Benjamin
Hammon, Timothy
Jennings, Joseph
Pillsbury, Tristram
Simpson, Benjamin
Soyer, Joseph

Stevens, Simeon
Tewksbury, Andrew
Thompson, Amasa T.
Tompkins, William
Tufts, Matthias
Wade, Levi

Sergt. Z. Rawson's Guard.

From June 5 to June 12, 1813. Service at Boston, guarding a park of artillery in gun house on Common.

RANK AND NAME.
Zebina Rawson, Sergeant
Benjamin Brintnall, Corporal
James Cole, Corporal

Privates.
Alley, Richard
Cushing, Bela
Duff, William
Eaton, Rufus
Fletcher, Timothy
Hayden, Robert

Hiler, Simeon
Hiler, William H.
Lambert, Gideon
Parkman, Nathaniel
Watts, Samuel L.
Wilcott, George

Sergt. J. N. Hinkley's Guard.

From June 12 to June 19, 1813. Service at Boston, guarding a park of artillery in gun house on Common.

Rank and Name.	Privates.	
John N. Hinkley, Sergeant	Barnard, Edward	Grant, John
David Lamb, Corporal	Coolidge, William C.	Ingersoll, Isaac P.
Thomas Mason, Corporal	Cremer, Edward	Moore, Augustus
	Day, James	Oliver, James T.
	Fowle, John	Ridley, Thomas
	Gamage, Nathaniel	Spofford, Enoch W.

Sergt. N. Phillips' Guard.

From June 19 to June 26, 1813. Service at Boston, guarding a park of artillery in gun house on Common.

Rank and Name.	Privates.	
Nathaniel Phillips, Sergeant	Barker, Wendal R.	Nichols, Ebenezer B.
Robert Smith, Corporal	Cummings, Thomas	Parsons, John
Thomas B. Magrath, Corporal	Holden, Moses	Potter, David
	Holman, John	Shaw, Jesse
	Hyde, Nathaniel	Town, Edmund
	Larrabee, Richard	Zumon, Levi

Sergt. C. Appleton's Guard.

From June 26 to July 3, 1813. Service at Boston, guarding a park of artillery in gun house on Common.

Rank and Name.	Privates.	
Charles Appleton, Sergeant	Adams, Isaac	Loring, Benjamin
Isaac K. Brasier, Corporal	Bailey, Gideon	Marshall, Samuel
Asaph Harlow, Corporal	Daniels, Nathaniel	Page, John
	Hay, Thomas	Perkins, John H.
	Hollis, William	Valentine, Jonathan
	Learned, William	Vaughan, James

Sergt. D. Whitney's Guard.

From July 3 to July 10, 1813. Service at Boston, guarding a park of artillery in gun house on Common.

Rank and Name.	Privates.	
Daniel Whitney, Sergeant	Bass, Charles	Jones, Daniel
Lewis Low, Corporal	Bradford, Nelson	Meeker, Medad
Silvanus Gates, Corporal	Chandler, Thomas	Nichols, John
	French, John	Prouty, Jonas
	George, William	Washburn, Samuel
	Hyde, Asa	Williams, Harvey

Sergt. J. R. Moore's Guard.

From July 10 to July 17, 1813. Service at Boston, guarding a park of artillery in gun house on Common.

Rank and Name.	Privates.	
John R. Moore, Sergeant	Beal, Martin	Fuller, Seth
John Ridgway, Corporal	Colting, Elijah D.	Hollis, William
Elijah R. Brasier, Corporal	Cotton, William	Nichols, George
	Davison, John	Rust, Robert
	Dole or Doll, Joseph	Symmes, Thomas
	Eaton, Rufus	Vaughan, James

Sergt. J. Glynn's Guard.

From July 17 to July 24, 1813. Service at Boston, guarding a park of artillery in gun house on Common.

Rank and Name.	Privates.	
John Glynn, Sergeant	Aubin, Joshua	Sanders, Stephen
Isaac Childs, Corporal	Bradley, Joseph T.	Sanderson, Elisha
William Joy, Corporal	Dewing, Timothy	Smallpeace, Robert
	Floyt, Charles	Towne, Jonathan
	Gale, Noah	Waters, John
	Grice, Caleb E.	Whitney, Jason

Sergt. C. Tilden's Guard.

From July 24 to July 31, 1813. Service at Boston, guarding a park of artillery in gun house on Common.

Rank and Name.	Privates.	
Christopher Tilden, Sergeant	Aiken, James G.	Hartson, Preston
Seth Fuller, Corporal	Beale, Lewis	Mentzer, Andrew
Leonard Parks, Corporal	Bennett, James	Robertson, Robert
	Briggs, Daniel	Rupp, Adam
	Colburn, Charles	Sears, Peter
	Cook, Seth B.	Shaw, Thomas

Sergt. J. Peabody's Guard.

From July 31 to Aug. 7, 1813. Service at Boston, guarding a park of artillery in gun house on Common.

Rank and Name.	Privates.	
John Peabody, Sergeant	Carlton, William	Hollis, William
Isaac K. Brasier, Sergeant	Darling, John	Jones, Daniel
James Vaughan, Corporal	Dean, Faxon	Keith, James
	Geyer, Frederick W.	Myer, William Otis
	Grubb, William	Pelham, Thomas
	Hall, Jason	Stacey, John

Sergt. D. Brown's Guard.

From Aug. 7 to Aug. 14, 1813. Service at Boston, guarding a park of artillery in gun house on Common.

Rank and Name.	Privates.	
Daniel Brown, Sergeant	Bennett, John	Kimball, Jonathan
Levi Beale, Corporal	Chamberlain, David	Low, Lewis
Jonas Wetherbee, Corporal	Crane, Nathan	Merriam, Artemas
	Foster, Eliab	Muzzy, John
	Humphrey, Levi	Pratt, Joseph W.
	Hunt, Timothy	Wiswell, Benjamin

Sergt. J. Dalton's Guard.

From Aug. 14 to Aug. 21, 1813. Service at Boston, guarding a park of artillery in gun house on Common.

Rank and Name.	Privates.	
James Dalton, Sergeant	Allen, Samuel R.	Oden, George
Charles Tidd, Corporal	Athean, Frederick W.	Rice, Rufus
Abbott Lawrence, Corporal	Dennie, Thomas	Richards, Reuben
	Hewer, William Y.	Todd, George
	Miller, John	Ward, Richard
	Newell, Montgomery	Williams, Robert P.

MASSACHUSETTS VOLUNTEER MILITIA IN THE WAR OF 1812. 111

Sergt. R. G. Amory's Guard.
From Aug. 21 to Aug. 28, 1813. Service at Boston, guarding a park of artillery in gun house on Common.

RANK AND NAME.	*Privates.*	
Rufus G. Amory, Sergeant	Allen, Marston	Parker, Samuel
Lewis Dupee, Corporal	Bowker, Lemuel	Patten, David
Jonathan Jackson, Corporal	Carman, John	Powers, Levi
	Cunningham, Charles	Sargent, David
	Davis, Isaac D. or James D.	Topliff, James
	Marshall, William	Wise, Jonathan

Sergt. A. Sumner's Guard.
From Aug. 28 to Sept. 4, 1813. Service at Boston, guarding a park of artillery in gun house on Common.

RANK AND NAME.	*Privates.*	
Amos Sumner, Sergeant	Blaney, Joseph	Looker, Marshall
Thomas R. Dascomb, Corporal	Brown, Samuel L.	Mead, William
Washington Thayer, Corporal	Bullard, Charles	Topliff, James
	Farrington, Joshua	Warren, Stephen
	Hollis, William	Watkins, Andrew
	Lewis, Moses	Wiswell, Benjamin

Sergt. J. G. Davis' Guard.
From Sept. 4 to Sept. 11, 1813. Service at Boston, guarding a park of artillery in gun house on Common.

RANK AND NAME.	*Privates.*	
Joseph G. Davis, Sergeant	Adams, William D.	Parkman, Samuel
Joshua Crane, Sergeant	Davidson, John	Porter, Edward J.
Joseph Geyer, Corporal	Forrester, J.	Stevens, Alexander
	Hay, Thomas	Tufts, Aaron
	Keith, James	Vaughan, James
	Mann, William B.	Wiswell, Benjamin

Sergt. J. Heard's Guard.
From Sept. 11 to Sept. 18, 1813. Service at Boston, guarding a park of artillery in gun house on Common.

RANK AND NAME.	*Privates.*	
John Heard, Sergeant	Blaney, Joseph	Merritt, Aaron
Isaac K. Brazier, Corporal	Davidson, John	Piper, Moses
Robert Omond, Corporal	Hollis, William	Steele, James, Jr.
	Keith, James	Stimpson, Reuben
	Mann, William B.	Warner, Stephen
	Merrill, Sidney	Wiswell, Benjamin P.

Sergt. D. Felt's Guard.
From Sept. 18 to Sept. 25, 1813. Service at Boston, guarding a park of artillery in gun house on Common.

RANK AND NAME.	*Privates.*	
David Felt, Sergeant	Blaney, Joseph	Lewis, Moses
Jeremiah Vose, Corporal	Davis, William	Mann, William B.
Alfred Curtis, Corporal	Davison, John	Parkman, Samuel S.
	Farrington, Joshua	Topliff, James
	Hollis, William	Warner, Stephen
	Jones, Daniel	Wiswell, Benjamin P.

Sergt. S. Adams' Guard.

From Sept. 25 to Oct. 2, 1813. Service at Boston, guarding a park of artillery in gun house on Common.

RANK AND NAME.	*Privates.*	
Samuel Adams, Sergeant	Burroughs, Edward	Gray, Harrison
Charles Ellis, Corporal	Drake, Jesse	Hersey, Noaman
William Gilman, Corporal	Everett, Aaron	Holmes, Josiah N.
	Faxon, Nathaniel	Lewis, Henry
	Gibson, Simeon	Merry, Daniel
	Gould, George	Thompson, Archibald

Sergt. W. B. Willis' Guard.

From Oct. 2 to Oct. 9, 1813. Service at Boston, guarding a park of artillery in gun house on Common.

RANK AND NAME.	*Privates.*	
William B. Willis, Sergeant	Allen, Nathan	Mann, William
T. K. Brazier, Corporal	Blaney, Joseph	Peterson, John
William Hollis, Corporal	Burns, Michael	Raymon, William
	Farrington, Joshua	Topliff, James
	Gear, Joshua W.	Ward, Wiswell
	Lewis, Moses	Wiswell, Payne

Sergt. H. K. Appleton's Guard.

From Oct. 9 to Oct. 13, 1813. Service at Boston, guarding a park of artillery in a gun house on Common.

RANK AND NAME.	*Privates.*	
Henry K. Appleton, Sergeant	Clark, Isaac	Howes, Loring
Samuel Parkman, Corporal	Farrington, Joshua	Oliver, Charles
William Holly, Corporal	Ford, Stephen	Peterson, John
	Geyer, Joseph W.	Porter, Benjamin
	Growman, Henry F.	Stowell, William
	Holmes, Stephen	Wiswell, Payne

Sergt. T. Tewksbury's Guard, Lieut. Col. P. Osgood's Regiment.

From July 1 to July 30, 1814. Raised at Chelsea. Service at Boston.

RANK AND NAME.	Floyd, Abijah	Pray, Joseph
Thomas Tewksbury, Sergeant	Floyd, John, 2d	Tewksbury, Henry
Privates.	Floyd, Thomas	Webster, John
Bumpus, Lenus	Jack, David	Willey, James
Cheever, Henry	Nichols, Thomas P.	
	Pratt, Isaac	

Sergt. A. Peabody's Guard, Capt. G. Sullivan's Company.

From Oct. 6 to Oct. 13, 1814. Service at Boston, guarding Faneuil Hall, where arms were stored. ("New England Guards.")

RANK AND NAME.	*Privates.*	
Aaron Peabody, Sergeant	Dana, George	Hunt, Samuel
Richard Ward, Corporal	Denning, Thomas	Lewis, Henry
	Gore, Watson	McFarland, J. C.
	Greenough, William	Miller, John
	Hall, William	Wentworth, Hiram
		West, James

Ensign B. S. Pickman's Guard, Capt. G. Sullivan's Company.

From Oct. 14 to November, 1814. Service at Boston. ("New England Guards.")

RANK AND NAME.		
Benjamin S. Pickman, Ensign	Dana, George	Putnam, John J.
	Fiske, Eben	Rice, Rufus
Charles Tidd, Sergeant	Gibbs, Alex H.	Simpson, Daniel
John Howe, Sergeant	Gore, Jeremiah	Spooner, William
Abbott Lawrence, Corporal	Hay, Joseph	Thompson, William
Richard Ward, Corporal	Hayward, Nathaniel H.	Warren, Henry
	Hopkins, Samuel	Wentworth, Hiram
Privates.	Keating, Charles	West, Joseph
Bangs, Isaac	Lewis, Henry	
Cheever, Charles	Miller, John	
	Pope, Joseph	

S. H. Parker's Company.

Raised at Boston. In service various times at Boston and vicinity in September, October and November, 1814. ("Winslow Blues.")

RANK AND NAME.		
Samuel H. Parker, Captain	Cotton, Alex	Marsh, Ephraim
Benjamin Darling, Lieutenant	Curtis, William T.	McAllister, James
	Darracott, George	McCleary, John
Nathaniel D. Stevenson, Sergeant	Dearborn, John M.	McClemen, William
Samuel Avery, Sergeant	Dupee, Lewis	Murch, Ephraim
Thomas B. Kendall, Sergeant	Durrell, Daniel	Oliver, Henry J.
John D. Howard, Sergeant	Eliot, John	Rand, William M.
Aaron Reed, Jr., Corporal	Farrie, John	Richardson, Samuel
John Bannister, Corporal	Felt, David	Russell, Joseph
John David, Corporal	Fowle, Henry	Saunders, William
Nathaniel Brintnall, Corporal	Gould, Frederick	Smith, George G.
	Green, Job W.	Southack, Joseph G.
Privates.	Hardy, Joshua	Southack, Robert G.
Badger, Barber	Harris, John	Stuart, Silas
Bradley, Thomas	Hill, John W.	Topliff, Benjamin
Burge, Lorenzo	Hill, Samuel	Torrey, Nathaniel
Burroughs, William	Holmes, Nathaniel B.	Truman, Thomas
Cain, John P.	Hull, George	Turner, Henry
Calton, Frederic M.	Kettle, Samuel	Williams, Charles
	Low, Solomon	Williams, Thomas

Sergt. S. Avery's Guard, Capt. S. H. Parker's Company.

From Sept. 22 to Sept. 29, 1814. Service at Boston, guarding Faneuil Hall, where arms were stored. ("Winslow Blues.")

RANK AND NAME.		
Samuel Avery, Sergeant	Cotton, Alex	Richardson, Samuel
John Bannister, Corporal	Darracott, George	Saunders, William
	Dearborn, John M.	Williams, Charles
Privates.	Felt, David	
Badger, Barber	Gould, Frederick	
Carlton, Roderick M.	Green, Job W.	
	Marsh, Ephraim	

Sergt. J. D. Howard's Guard, detached from Capt. S. H. Parker's Company.

Guarding Faneuil Hall, September 29 to October 6. ("Winslow Blues.")

RANK AND NAME.		
John D. Howard, Sergeant	Dupee, Lewis	Smith, George G.
John David, Corporal	Durrell, Daniel	Torrey, Nathaniel
	Harris, John	Turner, Henry
Privates.	Hill, Samuel	
Bradley, Thomas	Holmes, Nathaniel B.	
Cain, John P.	McAllister, James	
	McClemen, William	

Lieut. B. Darling's Guard, detached from Capt. S. H. Parker's Company.

From Oct. 19 to Oct. 26, 1814. Service at State Arsenal, Charlestown. ("Winslow Blues.")

Rank and Name.		
Benjamin Darling, Lieutenant	Curtis, William T.	McAllister, James
	Dearborn, John M.	McCleary, John
John D. Howard, Sergeant	Eliot, John	Rand, William M.
Nathaniel D. Stevenson, Sergeant	Felt, David	Russell, Jonas
Nathaniel Brintnall, Corporal	Hardy, Joshua	Southack, Joseph D.
Aaron Reed, Jr., Corporal	Hill, Samuel	Topliff, Benjamin
	Hill, William	Tower, Henry, Jr.
Privates.	Hull, George	Trueman, Thomas
Burroughs, William	Kettle, Samuel	Williams, Thomas
Carlton, Roderick M.	Low, Solomon	
	Marsh, Ephraim, Jr.	

Corp. J. Snow's Guard, detached from Lieut. Col. A. Binney's Regiment.

Three days in October, 1814. Service at Boston.

Rank and Name.	Burbeck, William	Mowing, Abraham
John Snow, Corporal	Burrill, John	Plummer, Moses
Sheldon Perry, Musician	Butler, Aaron	Ponno, John
	Capen, John	Priest, Isaac D.
Privates.	Cummings, Luther	Proctor, John
Andrews, Stephen	Denton, John	Ross, Charles
Babcock, ——	Dickey, Ephraim	Stevens, Thomas
Baldwin, Phineas P.	Fessenden, Benjamin	Thomb, William
Banister, John B.	Gridley, William	Tillinghast, George
Bifling, Alanson	Hopkins, Freeman	Trull, Joel
Blake, William	Jack, David	Webb, Joseph
Blanchard, Lemuel	Jennison, Asa	

Lieut. C. Hartshorn's Guard, detached from Capt. G. Fairbanks' Company, Lieut. Col. A. Binney's Regiment.

October and November, 1814. Service at Boston and vicinity.

Rank and Name.	*Privates.*	Longley, Thomas
Caleb Hartshorn, Lieutenant	Barney, Jonathan	Martin, James P.
	Bates, Stephen	Muzzy, John
Isaac Rowse, Sergeant	Burt, John M.	Reed, Benjamin
Benjamin B. Carney, Sergeant	Cutter, Samuel	Reed, William
Charles Lincoln, Corporal	Donnett, C. M.	Ring, Nathaniel
Samuel Hayward, Corporal	Fearing, Cushing	Rugg, Elisha
Samuel Wheelock, Musician	Gates, Sylvanus H.	Smith, Cyrus
	Gore, James	Smith, Nowell
	Hartwell, Thomas	Taft, Elisha
	Howe, Richard S.	

Sergt. J. Francis' Guard, detached from Lieutenant Colonel Page's Regiment of Charlestown, under Supervision of Major Jaques.

From Sept. 25 to Oct. 2, 1814. Service at State Arsenal.

Rank and Name.	Calf, Thomas	Tufts, Aaron
James Francis, Sergeant	Dexter, Timothy	Wyman, Jonathan
William Henry, Corporal	Dunham, Thomas	Young, Benjamin
	Fowle, William	
Privates.	Hadley, Samuel D.	
Bancroft, Ebenezer	Haskell, Jeremiah	
Bucknam, Spencer	Russell, Samuel	

Sergt. D. Smith's Guard, detached from Lieutenant Colonel Page's Regiment of Charlestown, under Supervision of Major Jaques.

From Oct. 9 to Oct. 16, 1814. Service at State Arsenal.

RANK AND NAME.		
Daniel Smith, Sergeant	Childs, Charles H.	Niles, Jesse
Nathan Warren, Corporal	Fiske, Sewall	Pierce, Luther
	Gregory, Uriah	Sanderson, Jacob
Privates.	Harrington, Moses	
Bigelow, Thomas	Hill, Woodbury	
Bigelow, William H.	Kent, Hezekiah	
	Morse, Charles	

Sergt. D. Bucknam's Guard, detached from Lieutenant Colonel Page's Regiment of Charlestown, under Supervision of Major Jaques.

From Oct. 3 to Oct. 9, 1814. Service at State Arsenal.

RANK AND NAME.	*Privates.*	
David Bucknam, Sergeant	Clark, Jacob	Reed, Amos
Abiel Kimball, Corporal	Davis, Joshua	Simonds, Isaac W.
	Davis, Zimri	Symmes, Edmund
	Fowle, Samuel	Tufts, Samuel
	Johnson, Samuel	Tufts, Seth
		Vinal, Seth

Sergt. C. Russell's Guard, detached from Lieutenant Colonel Page's Regiment of Charlestown, under Supervision of Major Jaques.

From Oct. 16 to Oct. 23, 1814. Service at State Arsenal.

RANK AND NAME.		
Cyrus Russell, Sergeant	Jones, Isaac	Stratton, Henry
Charles Bemis, Corporal	Loring, Hollis C.	Stratton, Thomas
	Niles, David	Warren, Nehemiah
Privates.	Pepper, Benjamin	
Colburn, Charles	Stearns, Jonas	
Jones, Cyrus	Stearns, Silas	
	Stratton, Elisha	

Sergt. J. Deblois' Guard, detached from Lieutenant Colonel Page's Regiment of Charlestown, under Supervision of Major Jaques.

From Oct. 24 to Oct. 25, 1814. Service at State Arsenal.

RANK AND NAME.		
James Deblois, Sergeant	Edmonds, Nathaniel	Stimpson, George
John Mullett, Corporal	Emerson, Benjamin	Sweetser, John
	Frothingham, Isaac C.	Turner, Barnabas
Privates.	Hoppin, Daniel	
Allison, Walter H.	Leonard, James B.	
Butts, Samuel	Raymond, Joel	
	Sisson, Charles	

Sergt. H. K. Appleton's Guard.

From Dec. 1, 1814, to Feb. 15, 1815. Service at Fort Strong (Noddle Island).

RANK AND NAME.		
Henry K. Appleton, Sergeant	Douglass, William	Pratt, Thomas
Josiah Blanchard, Corporal	Ears, Charles (to January 1st)	Robertson, Jacob G.
John Powers, Corporal	Gray, Francis (to January 1st)	Stowell, George
	Harrington, Leonard	Stowell, John (from January 1, 1815)
Privates.	Martin, Isaac	
Conner, John	Newhall, Thomas (from January 1, 1815)	
Davison, John	Park, William	
	Plummer, Joshua	

Sergt. J. Noyes' Detachment of Videttes, Lieut. Col. J. Coleman's Regiment of Cavalry.

From Oct. 5 to Oct. 22, 1814. In service between Salem and Newburyport.

RANK AND NAME.		
Jacob Noyes, Sergeant	Emery, Eliphalet H.	Prince, Daniel N.
	Frost, Samuel A.	Webster, Charles
Privates.	Hood, John	
Blunt, Isaac	Jaquith, Parker	
Bradstreet, Nathaniel	Lovejoy, Boswell	
	Pearly, John	

Sergt. J. Tapley's Guard, detached from Capt. B. Mudge's Company, Lieut. Col. S. Brimblecom's Regiment.

Three to 9 days, from June 29 to Aug. 15, 1814. Service at Lynn. Night Guards.

RANK AND NAME.		
Jesse Tapley, Sergeant	Hallowell, John	Phelps, Jacob, Jr.
Otis Newhall, Sergeant	Hawks, John	Proctor, John
	Hawks, Thomas	Randell, William P
Privates.	Hinfield, Richard L.	Richardson, Israel
Alkerson, Joseph	Hughs, James	Richardson, John
Alley, Solomon, Jr.	Ingalls, Jacob, Jr.	Rowe, William D.
Alley, William	Ingalls, John	Segar, Henry
Atwill, Jesse L.	Ingalls, Jonathan B.	Segar, John
Bachelder, Amos	Jackson, Bartholomew	Shepard, Jonathan
Bachelder, James	Levit, Charles B.	Skinner, Jacob
Blanchard, Nathaniel	Lewis, Aaron	Smith, Benjamin
Bowker, John	Lewis, Blaney	Southwick, James
Burrell, Ebeneser, Jr.	Lewis, Henry	Stone, Benjamin
Burrell, Nathaniel	Mansfield, Daniel	Stone, John
Cavendish, John	Mansfield, William	Stone, Joshua
Chase, John	Marshall, William	Townsend, Daniel, Jr.
Clark, Theophilus	McFarley, Robert	Townsend, Jacob
Coates, Benjamin	Mudge, Joseph	Townsend, John
Danforth, John	Needham, David	Turner, Burrell D.
Davis, Lanson	Newhall, James	Watson, Jonathan
Delands, David	Newhall, Josiah	Wellman, Bartholomew
Glidden, Robert	Ober, Samuel	Wheeler, Josiah
Goldsmith, Joseph	Patterson, James, Jr.	Williams, John
	Perley, Henry	Withey, John

Sergt. I. Perkins' Guard, detached from Capt. E. Duntley's Company, Lieut. Col. S. Brimblecom's Regiment.

Three to 9 days, from June 29 to Aug. 15, 1814. Raised at Lynn. Service at Lynn. Night Guards.

RANK AND NAME.		
Israel Perkins, Sergeant	Damon, Samuel	Newhall, Allen, 3d
William Abbott, Sergeant	Fairfield, Abraham	Questrom, Oliver
Samuel Batchelder, Sergeant	Forest, Francis	Reed, Ephraim
William Brown, Musician	Frothingham, James	Richardson, Ebenezer
	Gifford, Rufus	Richardson, Henry
Privates.	Gilson, John	Smith, Simon
Alley, James, Jr.	Hallowell, James	Stacey, George
Alley, Lewis	Houghton, John	Stoker, George
Batchelder, Nathaniel	Johnson, Benjamin B.	Tarbox, William, 3d
Breed, Amos	Johnson, John R.	Tufts, Samuel
Burdett, Stephen	Johnson, Legree	Warren, George
Coats, John	Johnson, Samuel	
	Munrad, Edmund	

MASSACHUSETTS VOLUNTEER MILITIA IN THE WAR OF 1812. 117

Sergt. T. Richardson's Guard, detached from Capt. W. Skinner's Company, Lieut. Col. S. Brimblecom's Regiment.
Three to 9 days, from June 29 to Aug. 15, 1814. Raised at Lynnfield. Service at Lynn. Night Guards.

RANK AND NAME.	*Privates.*	
Thomas Richardson, Sergeant	Aborn, Samuel	Gardner, Giles
George Parsons, Corporal	Carter, George	Hart, Hartfield
Joseph Burnham, Musician	Cox, Benjamin	Richardson, Moses
	Emerson, David	Stoddard, Obediah
	Flagg, Edward	Townsend, Daniel
		Wiley, Jacob

Sergt. E. Aborn's Guard, detached from Capt. B. Mudge's Company, Lieut. Col. S. Brimblecom's Regiment.
Three to 9 days, from June 29 to Aug. 15, 1814. Service at Lynn. Night Guards.

RANK AND NAME.	*Privates.*	Newhall, Wright
Ebenezer Aborn, Sergeant	Emerson, Ephraim	Norwood, James
John Nichols, Corporal	Emerson, Loring	Sanderson, Benjamin
Oliver Emerson, Musician	Fay, John	Smith, William
George Newhall, Musician	Holmes, George	Swaine, Nathaniel
	Larrabee, Josiah	Upton, John S.

Sergt. J. Newhall's Guard, detached from Capt. D. Capen's Company, Lieut. Col. S. Brimblecom's Regiment.
Three to 9 days, from June 29 to Aug. 15, 1814. Service at Lynn. Night Guards.

RANK AND NAME.	Bartlett, Samuel K.	Hitchings, Jesse
John Newhall, Sergeant	Blanchard, Daniel	Ives, Peter S.
David S. Oliver, Sergeant	Blaney, Jonathan	Jacob, Benjamin H.
Benjamin Alley, Sergeant	Boynton, Ellis	Johnson, Albert
Thomas Dowley, Corporal	Brown, Josiah	Mansfield, John
Josiah Hayward, Corporal	Burp, Joseph	Newhall, Joseph, Jr.
Charles Sweetser, Corporal	Chamberlin, William	Parker, Timothy, Jr.
Richard H. Post, Corporal	Cheever, Frederick	Payne, Ebenezer
Ephraim Mansfield, Corporal	Cheever, Joshua	Rowe, Allen
Nathan Alley, Musician	Davis, William	Rowe, Amos
Privates.	Downing, John, Jr.	Segars, Philip L.
Alley, Benjamin	Evans, James	Slocum, Otis
Annis, Moses	Gage, Nathaniel	Sweetser, Charles
Barnes, John	Gilman, John	Tuttle, Samuel
Barrett, Nathaniel	Grover, Asa	
	Hall, James	

Sergt. S. Newhall's Guard, detached from Capt. C. Robie's and Mudge's Companies, Lieut. Col. S. Brimblecom's Regiment.
Three to 9 days, from June 29 to Aug. 15, 1814. Raised at Lynn. Service at Lynn. Night Guards.

RANK AND NAME.	Bowler, Samuel	Mudge, Daniel L.
Samuel Newhall, Sergeant	Breed, Allen	Newhall, Edward
William G. Newhall, Sergeant	Breed, Amos	Perkins, Edward
Thomas Rhodes, Sergeant	Breed, Andrew, Jr.	Randell, Joseph
Nathan Hudson, Sergeant	Breed, Joseph	Reynolds, Andrew
Josiah Newhall, Sergeant	Breed, William	Rhodes, Allen
Smith Downing, Sergeant	Cheever, John	Robinson, George
Isaac Orgins, Musician	Crane, Elisha C.	Russell, John
Joshua Batchelder, Musician	Ellingwood, Benjamin	Selange, James
	Frasier, Hugh	Snow, Daniel
Privates.	Green, James	Thomas, Cyrus
Allen, Ezra, Jr.	Johnson, George	Tucker, Peter
Ashton, William	Johnson, Samuel	Tufts, David, Jr.
Atwill, Amos	Lewis, Edward C.	Warren, George
Bowler, John	Lye, Joseph	Wiely, John
Bowler, Nathaniel	Mansfield, John	Wipphen, Joseph B.

Sergt. D. C. Watt's Guard, detached from Captain Latham's Company, Lieut. Col. S. Brimblecom's Regiment.
Three to 9 days, from June 29 to Aug. 15, 1814. Service at Lynn. Night Guards.

RANK AND NAME.		
Daniel C. Watts, Sergeant	Joseph Skinner, Corporal	Mansfield, Rufus
William Ingalls, Sergeant	Jedediah Newhall, Jr., Corporal	Martin, Jonathan B.
Benjamin Parrott, Sergeant	Ezra Rand, Corporal	Moulton, Moses
John W. Haskell, Sergeant	Henry Coutman, Musician	Newhall, Benjamin
Richard L. Henford, Sergeant	Isaac M. Newhall, Musician	Newhall, Ebenezer
William Liscom, Sergeant		Newhall, Frederick
John F. Gardner, Sergeant	*Privates.*	Newhall, James
Alonzo Lewis, Sergeant	Abon, James	Newhall, John B. L.
John B. Newhall, Sergeant	Atkins, Rowland W.	Newhall, Samuel
Levi Orcutt, Sergeant	Ball, John	Norwood, Thomas
Ebenezer Martin, Corporal	Bird, Daniel	Oliver, Benjamin P.
Marshall Brown, Corporal	Brown, Joseph, Jr.	Oliver, John B.
Isaac Watts, Corporal	Burrell, James	Pratt, Joseph
Benjamin Ireson, Corporal	Cox, Benjamin	Smith, James
Nathaniel Pratt, Corporal	Currier, Jonathan	Stevens, John H.
Joseph Ingalls, Corporal	Fern, James	Symonds, Daniel
Samuel Chase, Corporal	Haskell, Edward	Tarbox, Samuel
Bartlett Jennings, Corporal	Haskell, Mathew	Walden, Abijah
John Townsend, Corporal	Hudson, John	Whitmore, William
John Doak, Corporal	Kingsbury, Fisher	Wood, Henry
Henry Eayrs, Corporal	Lewis, Daniel	
	Mansfield, Jonathan	

Sergt. T. Mansfield's Guard, detached from Capt. D. Capen's Company, Lieut. Col. S. Brimblecom's Regiment.
Three to 9 days, from June 29 to Aug. 15, 1814. Service at Lynn. Night Guards.

RANK AND NAME.		
Thomas Mansfield, Sergeant	*Privates.*	Mansfield, Amos
David Newhall, Sergeant	Bailey, Aaron	Mansfield, John
Bachus N. Stokes, Sergeant	Boardman, Jeremiah	Mansfield, Nathaniel, Jr.
William Nelson, Sergeant	Boardman, William	Newhall, James
Daniel Hawks, Sergeant	Burrill, Samuel	Parker, Timothy
Samuel H. Damon, Sergeant	Burrill, William	Parker, William
Samuel Sargent, Corporal	Chase, Josiah	Roddin, Joseph
Peter S. Lewis, Corporal	Cheever, William	Sewell, Samuel
Amos Adams, Corporal	Cole, Amos	Slocken, Amos
Nathaniel Tarbell, Corporal	Crasbury, Samuel B.	Smith, William
Alex Nelson, Corporal	Davis, Timothy	Southwick, John
Nathan Hawks, Jr., Corporal	Dixon, Francis	Staples, Peter
Benjamin B. Hitchins, Corporal	Eames, Joseph	Stone, Aaron
Daniel Abbott, Musician	Eames, Peter	Sweetser, Oliver
John Hitchins, Musician	Eames, Robert	Tuttle, Thomas
Ebenezer Parker, Musician	Edmunds, Lot	Van Esch, Simon Zward
Ephraim Mansfield, Musician	Florence, Charles	Weston, Ephraim
John Burrill, Musician	Fox, Joseph, Jr.	Weston, Samuel
	Gowdey, John	White, Samuel F.
	Hall, John B.	Wilson, Asa
	Hitchins, Benjamin T.	Wilson, Samuel
	Howard, Joshua	

Corp. E. Higbee's Guard, under General Hovey.
From Nov. 9, 1814, to Jan. 7, 1815. Service at Fort Lee, Salem.

RANK AND NAME.		
Lemuel Higbee, Corporal	*Privates.*	Dodge, Josiah
	Blanchard, Samuel J.	Low, Richard
	Chamberlin, Nathaniel	Silsbee, Nathaniel
	Davis, John	

Lieut. M. R. Lancton's Guard, under Colonel Dearborn.

From Nov. 14, 1814, to Feb. 15, 1815. Stationed at Salem.

RANK AND NAME.		
Matthew R. Lancton, Lieutenant	Bentlet, John	Isham, L.
	Blankenship, Stephen	Kellogg, Phineas
	Brand, Abel	King, Ebenezer
Hezekiah Gear, Sergeant	Cadwell, Daniel	Parker, Elinda
Thomas Ensign, Sergeant	Clark, John	Pike, Barnabus
Kensalear Taylor, Corporal	Donion, Henry	Powers, Joel C.
William Lord, Corporal	Fuller, Oliver	Root, Whiting
Giles Parker, Musician	Hase, Benjamin J.	Row, Joseph
Pierce Heavens, Musician	Hicock, George	Sacket, Roy
	Hicock, Moses	Spencer, Jesse
Privates.	Holmes, John	Williams, Tyler
Allen, Rufus	Hubbard, Daniel W.	
Bation, Mula	Hunt, Arad	

Sergt. C. Pilsbury's Guard.

From June 21 to June 28, 1814. Raised at Newburyport. Service at Newburyport.

RANK AND NAME.	Davids, John	Pingree, Daniel R.
Charles Pilsbury, Sergeant	Emerson, Charles	True, Ezekiel
	Goodwin, Ephraim	Webster, Washington
Privates.	Kent, Benjamin	
Bacheldor, Joseph	Knight, Winchester	
Blasdell, Nicholas		

Sergt. J. Young's Guard.

From June 28 to July 5, 1814. Raised at Newburyport. Service at Newburyport.

RANK AND NAME.	Choate, Jonathan	March, Nathaniel
James Young, Sergeant	Colby, Philip	Norton, George, Jr.
	Davis, Charles	Norton, Moses
Privates.	Goodhue, James S.	Perkins, Nathaniel
Bagley, Samuel	Kimball, Moses	Poor, Isaac
Burk, William	Knapp, Samuel	Stanwood, Daniel
Campbell, James	Leigh, Robert	Yatte, Thomas

Sergt. J. Griffin's Guard.

From July 5 to July 12, 1814. Raised at Newburyport. Service at Newburyport.

RANK AND NAME.	*Privates.*	
Jacob Griffin, Sergeant	Newman, John	
	Prichard, Stephen	
	Somerby, Thomas	

Sergt. R. Griffin's Guard.

From July 5 to July 12, 1814. Service at Newburyport.

RANK AND NAME.	Danforth, Enoch	Pilsbury, William C.
Robert Griffin, Sergeant	Demars (?), John	Smith, Ephraim I.
	Gibson, Samuel	Tolman, Benjamin
Privates.	Libbey, Theodore	Whittemore, Joseph
Burnham, Jeremiah	Packard, George	Wyatt, Thomas
Butler, Philip	Pilsbury, Daniel	

Sergt. W. S. Mason's Guard.
From July 12 to July 19, 1814. Service at Newburyport.

Rank and Name.	Privates.	
W. S. Mason, Sergeant	Call, Charles	Somerby, William
James Campbell, Sergeant	Dennison, William, Jr.	Somerby, William, Jr.
George Moulton, Jr., Musician	Dodge, John	Stanwood, Daniel
Jonathan Moulton, Jr., Musician	Gerrish, Joseph	Sweet, Jonathan
	Hodge, Nathaniel	Wheelright, Ebenezer
	Morton, Moses	Whittemore, Joseph
	Prince, Samuel	Wyatt, Thomas

Sergt. T. B. White's Guard.
From July 25 to July 30, 1814. Service at Newburyport.

Rank and Name.	Privates.	
Thomas B. White, Sergeant	Butler, Philip	Shaw, William
James Campbell, Corporal	Call, Charles	Smith, Ephraim I.
Samuel Gibson, Musician	Cross, Hector	Somerby, Thomas
Charles Butler, Musician	Evans, Richard	Somerby, William
	Hastings, William	Stanwood, Daniel
	Mason, Samuel	Wheeler, Samuel, Jr.
	Pilsbury, Daniel	Wyatt, Thomas

Sergt. C. Gordon's Guard.
From July 30 to Aug. 6, 1814. Service at Newburyport.

Rank and Name.	Privates.	
Charles Gordon, Sergeant	Allen, William	Haskell, Humphrey B.
James Campbell, Corporal	Chase, Joseph F.	Noyes, Robert H.
Moses Bayley, Musician	Flanders, John	Pidgin, Benjamin
Nathaniel S. Flanders, Musician	Flanders, Nehemiah, Jr.	Pike, Daniel
	Furnald, Thomas	Smith, Ephraim I.
	Gardner, Robert	Truesdale, A. W.
	Hall, Charles	Woodman, Joseph, 3d

Sergt. T. Brown's Guard.
From Aug. 6 to Aug. 14, 1814. Service at Newburyport.

Rank and Name.	Privates.	
Thomas Brown, Sergeant	Burnes, James	Huse, John
Daniel Stone, Corporal	Campbell, James	Middleton, William
William Mason, Musician	Clark, Amos	Morse, Merrill
John Flavers or Havers, Musician	Cole, Charles	Packer, George
	Davenport, William	Silloway, Joseph
	Davis, William	Swasey, Samuel
	Ham, Joseph	Wyatt, Thomas

Sergt. W. Wood's Guard.
From Aug. 20 to Aug. 27, 1814. Service at Newburyport.

Rank and Name.	Carr, John	Pidgin, Benjamin
William Wood, Sergeant	Cressey, Samuel	Pilsbury, Charles
James Campbell, Corporal	Fitz, Nathaniel	Silloway, Joseph
Moses Bayley, Musician	Griffin, Jacob	Smith, Ephraim I.
Joseph Knapp, Musician	Hardy, Dudly	Warner, Nathaniel
	Lasky, Joseph	Wood, James
Privates.	Morrison, Henry	Wyatt, Thomas
Anderson, William	Ordway, Moses	
Call, Charles	Packer, George	

Sergt. J. Griffin's Guard.

From Aug. 27 to Sept. 3, 1814. Service at Newburyport.

RANK AND NAME.
Jacob Griffin, Sergeant
Ephraim I. Smith, Corporal
Thomas B. Stone, Musician
John Butler, Musician

Privates.
Bassett, Joseph
Call, Charles
Campbell, James
Currier, Edward
Finney, John
Flanders, Nehemiah
Gardner, Robert
Gibson, Samuel
Marden, William
Mason, William
Morton, James

Newman, Benjamin, Jr.
Somerby, Arthur
Truesdall, Artemas W.
Wadleigh, Benjamin H.
Wilson, Joseph
Wood, Samuel
Wood, Thomas

Sergt. R. Evans' Guard.

From Sept. 3 to Sept. 10, 1814. Service at Newburyport.

RANK AND NAME.
Richard Evans, Sergeant
John Putnam, Corporal
Moses Bayley, Musician
Robert Gordon, Musician

Privates.
Anderson, William
Campbell, James
Carr, John
Dodge, Samuel
Flanders, Nehemiah, Jr.
Kloot, William

Laskey, Joseph
Morrison, Henry
Pidgin, Benjamin
Pike, Daniel
Prichard, Jacob
Wood, James

Sergt. W. Stone's Guard.

From Sept. 10 to Sept. 17, 1814. Service at Newburyport.

RANK AND NAME.
William Stone, Sergeant
Amos Foreman, Corporal
Tristram Plummer, Musician
Orlando Brown, Musician

Privates.
Coffin, Moses
Cook, Charles
Cressey, Samuel
Flanders, Nehemiah, Jr.
Gardner, Robert
Merrill, James

Packer, George
Peabody, Stephen H.
Pearson, Charles
Pike, Joseph, Jr.
Stickney, Joseph
Wood, James
Wood, Thomas

Sergt. J. Wood's Guard.

From Sept. 14 to Sept. 24, 1814. Service at Newburyport.

RANK AND NAME.
Jonathan Wood, Sergeant
Ebenezer Noyes, Corporal
Charles F. Rockliff, Musician
Joseph Knapp, Musician

Privates.
Balch, William
Bayley, Moses
Butler, John
Clark, Samuel
Currier, Edward
Elder, Joseph
Hull, William

Johnson, Thomas
Kloot, William
Packer, George
Pearson, Thomas, Jr.
Reed, David
Smith, Ephraim I.
Walker, Charles

Sergt. N. Greeley's Guard.

From Sept. 24 to Oct. 1, 1814. Service at Newburyport.

RANK AND NAME.
Nathaniel Greeley, Sergeant
William Kloot, Corporal
Artemas W. Truesdall, Musician
Charles Rogers, Musician

Privates.
Brown, Samuel, Jr.
Flanders, William
Furnald, Joseph
Gardner, Robert
Howard, Nathaniel
Hoyt, John

March, Nathaniel
Packer, Edward
Pease, James
Robinson, Alexander
Silloway, Joseph
Wells, Richard
Woodman, Nathaniel

MASSACHUSETTS VOLUNTEER MILITIA IN THE WAR OF 1812.

Sergt. S. S. Hodge's Guard.
From Oct. 1 to Oct. 8, 1814. Service at Newburyport.

RANK AND NAME.	Privates.	
S. S. Hodge, Sergeant	Brackett or Prescott, Nathan A.	Knapp, Joseph
Daniel Balk, Corporal	Brooking, John	Loring, Henry
Enoch Stickney, Musician	Campbell, James	Lunt, Joseph, Jr.
Benjamin G. Johnson, Musician	Carter, George	Plummer, Nathan
	Devenport, Anthony	Prescott, Oliver, Jr.
	Francis, James	Prince, William H.
	Johnson, Thomas	Tyler, William H.
		Wyer, Nathaniel, Jr.

Sergt. C. Presbury's Guard, from Lieut. Col. P. Merrill's Regiment of Newburyport.
From June 21 to June 28, 1814. Service at Plum Island.

RANK AND NAME.	Privates.	
Charles Presbury, Sergeant	Batchelder, Joseph	Kent, Benjamin
Samuel Cressy, Musician	Blaisdell, Nicholas	Knight, Winchester
Jacob Griffin, Musician	Daniel, John	Ordway, Moses
	Emerson, Charles	Pingrey, David R.
	Foot, Bernard	True, Ezekiel
	Goodwin, Ephraim	Warner, Nathaniel
		Webster, Washington

Sergt. J. Young's Guard, from Lieut. Col. P. Merrill's Regiment of Newburyport.
From June 28 to July 5, 1814. Service at Plum Island.

RANK AND NAME.	Privates.	
James Young, Sergeant	Bagley, Samuel	Leigh, Robert
James Campbell, Corporal	Choate, Jonathan	Marsh, Nathaniel
George Morton, Musician	Colby, Philip	Morton, Moses
William Buck, Musician	Davis, Charles	Perkins, Nathaniel
	Goodhue, James	Poor, Isaac
	Kimball, Moses	Stanwood, David
	Knapp, Samuel	Wyatt, Thomas

Sergt. J. A. Griffin's Guard, from Lieut. Col. P. Merrill's Regiment of Newburyport.
From July 5 to July 12, 1814. Service at Plum Island.

RANK AND NAME.	Privates.	
Jacob Griffin, Sergeant	Butler, Philip	Packer, George
John Newman, Corporal	Danford, Enock	Pillsbury, Daniel
Thomas Somerby, Musician	Demares, John	Pillsbury, William C.
Stephen Pritchard, Musician	Gibson, Samuel	Smith, Ephraim
	Griffin, Robert	Whittemore, Joseph
	Lilly, Theodore	Wyatt, Thomas

Sergt. W. J. Mason's Guard, from Lieut. Col. P. Merrill's Regiment of Newburyport.
From July 12 to July 19, 1814. Service at Plum Island.

RANK AND NAME.	Privates.	
William J. Mason, Sergeant	Call, Charles	Prince, Samuel
James Campbell, Corporal	Dodge, John	Somerby, William
George Norton, Musician	Gerrish, Joseph	Stanwood, Daniel
Jonathan Moulton, Musician	Hodge, Nathaniel	Sweet, Jonathan
	Jennison, William	Wheelright, Ebenezer
	Norton, Moses	Whittemore, Joseph
		Wyatt, Thomas

Sergt. T. W. White's Guard, from Lieut. Col. P. Merrill's Regiment of Newburyport.

From July 19 to July 26, 1814. Service at Plum Island.

Rank and Name.	Privates.	
Thomas B. White, Sergeant	Butler, Philip	Shaw, William
James Campbell, Corporal	Call, Charles	Smith, Ephraim
Samuel Gibson, Musician	Cross, Hector	Somerby, Thomas
Charles Butler, Musician	Evans, Richard	Somerby, William
	Hastings, William	Stanwood, Daniel
	Nason, Samuel	Wheeler, Samuel
	Pillsbury, Daniel	Wyatt, Thomas

Sergt. C. Gordon's Guard, from Lieut. Col. P. Merrill's Regiment of Newburyport.

From July 26 to Aug. 2, 1814. Service at Plum Island.

Rank and Name.	Privates.	
Charles Gordon, Sergeant	Allen, William	Haskell, H. B.
James Campbell, Corporal	Call, Charles	Noyes, Robert K.
Moses Bagley, Musician	Chase, Joseph	Pidgin, Benjamin
Nathaniel Flanders, Musician	Flanders, John	Pike, Daniel
	Flanders, Nehemiah	Smith, Ephraim
	Furnald, Thomas	Truesdale, A. W.
		Woodman, Josiah

Sergt. T. Brown's Guard, from Lieut. Col. P. Merrill's Regiment of Newburyport.

From Aug. 2 to Aug. 9, 1814. Service at Plum Island.

Rank and Name.	Privates.	
Thomas Brown, Sergeant	Burnes, James	Huse, John
Daniel Stone, Corporal	Call, Charles	Middleton, William
William Mason, Musician	Campbell, James	Morse, Merrill
John Stevens, Musician	Clark, Enos	Packard, George
	Davenport, William	Silloway, Joseph
	Davis, William	Swasey, Samuel
	Ham, Joseph	Wyatt, Thomas

Sergt. J. Noyes' Guard, from Lieut. Col. P. Merrill's Regiment of Newburyport.

From Aug. 9 to Aug. 16, 1814. Service at Plum Island.

Rank and Name.	Privates.	
Jacob Noyes, Sergeant	Barrett, Joseph	Jackson, Henry
Samuel Clark, Corporal	Campbell, James	Norton, Daniel
Samuel Dodge, Musician	Currier, Edward	Norton, James
Charles Davis, Musician	Currier, Matthew	Phinney, John
	Gardner, Robert	Somerby, Arthur
	Green, John	Todd, Thomas
	Hale, William	Wyatt, Thomas

Sergt. J. Noyes', Jr., Guard.

From Aug. 13 to Aug. 20, 1814. Raised at Newburyport. Stationed at Plum Island.

Rank and Name.	Privates.	
Jacob Noyes, Jr., Sergeant	Campbell, James	
Samuel Clark, Corporal	Currier, Nathaniel, Jr.	
Samuel Dodge, Musician	Gatt or Yatt, Thomas	
Charles Davis, Musician	Green, John	
William Hall, Musician	Jackson, Henry	
Daniel Morton, Musician	Ladd, Thomas	

Sergt. W. Wood's Guard, from Lieut. Col. P. Merrill's Regiment of Newburyport.
From Aug. 16 to Aug. 23, 1814. Service at Plum Island.

Rank and Name.	Privates.	
William Wood, Sergeant	Anderson, William	Morrison, Henry
James Campbell, Corporal	Brickett, Nathan A.	Packer, George
Moses Bailey, Musician	Call, Charles	Pidgin, Benjamin
Joseph Knapp, Musician	Carr, John	Silloway, Joseph
	Fitz, Nathaniel	Smith, Ephraim J.
	Hardy, Dudley	Wood, James
	Laskey, Joseph	Wyatt, Thomas

Sergt. J. Griffin's Guard, from Lieut. Col. P. Merrill's Regiment of Newburyport.
From Aug. 23 to Aug. 30, 1814. Service at Plum Island.

Rank and Name.	Privates.	
Jacob Griffin, Sergeant	Call, Charles	Mason, William
Ephraim J. Smith, Corporal	Campbell, James	Newman, Benjamin
Thomas B. Stone, Musician	Flanders, Nehemiah	Truesdale, Artemas W.
John Butler, Musician	Gardner, Robert	Wadleigh, Benjamin H.
	Gibson, Samuel	Wilson, Joseph
	Marden, William	Wood, Samuel
		Wood, Thomas

Sergt. R. Evans' Guard, from Lieut. Col. P. Merrill's Regiment of Newburyport.
From Aug. 30 to Sept. 6, 1814. Service at Plum Island.

Rank and Name.	Privates.	
Robert Evans, Sergeant	Anderson, William	Laskey, Joseph
John Putnam, Corporal	Campbell, James	Morrison, Henry
Moses Bailey, Musician	Carr, John	Packer, Edward
Robert Gorden, Musician	Dodge, Samuel	Pidgin, Benjamin
	Flanders, Nehemiah	Pike, Daniel
	Kloot, William	Pritchard, Jacob
		Wood, James

Sergt. W. Stone's Guard, from Lieut. Col. P. Merrill's Regiment of Newburyport.
From Sept. 6 to Sept. 13, 1814. Service at Plum Island.

Rank and Name.	Privates.	
William Stone, Sergeant	Coffin, Moses	Packer, George
Amos Foreman, Corporal	Cook, Charles, 3d	Peabody, Stephen H.
Tristram Plummer, Musician	Cresy, Samuel	Pearson, Charles
Orlando Brown, Musician	Flanders, Nehemiah	Pike, Joseph
	Gardner, Robert	Stickney, Josiah
	Merrill, Joseph C.	Wood, James
		Wood, Theo

Sergt. J. Wood's Guard, from Lieut. Col. P. Merrill's Regiment of Newburyport.
From Sept. 13 to Sept. 20, 1814. Service at Plum Island.

Rank and Name.	Privates.	
Jonathan Wood, Sergeant	Bagley, Moses	Johnson, Thomas
Ebenezer Noyes, Corporal	Balch, William	Kloot, William
Charles Racklyft, Musician	Butler, John	Packer, George
Joseph Knapp, Musician	Clark, Samuel	Pearson, Thomas
	Currier, Edward	Reed, David
	Elder, Joseph	Smith, Ephraim J.
	Hale, William	Walker, Charles

MASSACHUSETTS VOLUNTEER MILITIA IN THE WAR OF 1812.   125

Sergt. N. Greeley's Guard, from Lieut. Col. P. Merrill's Regiment of Newburyport.

From Sept. 20 to Sept. 27, 1814. Service at Plum Island.

Rank and Name.	Privates.	
Nathaniel Greeley, Sergeant	Brown, Samuel	March, Nathaniel
William Kloot, Corporal	Flanders, William	Packer, Edward
A. W. Truesdale, Musician	Furnald, Jacob	Pease, James
Charles Rogers, Musician	Gardner, Robert	Robinson, Alexander
	Howard, Nathaniel	Silloway, Joseph
	Hoyt, John	Wells, Richard
		Woodman, Nathaniel

Sergt. S. S. Hodge's Guard, from Lieut. Col. P. Merrill's Regiment of Newburyport.

From Sept. 21 to Oct. 8, 1814. Service at Plum Island.

Rank and Name.	Privates.	
S. S. Hodge, Sergeant	Brookings, John	Loring, Henry
Daniel Balch, Corporal	Campbell, James	Lunt, Joseph
Enoch Stickney, Musician	Carter, George	Plummer, Nathan
Benjamin G. Johnson, Musician	Davenport, Anthony	Prescott, Oliver
	Francis, James	Prince, William H.
	Johnson, Thomas	Tyler, William H.
	Knapp, Joseph	Wyer, Nathaniel

Sergt. J. Griffin's Guard.

From Dec. 13, 1814, to Feb. 11, 1815. Service at Newburyport.

Rank and Name.	Privates.	
Jacob Griffin, Sergeant	Brewster, John	Jackson, Samuel
Joshua Mace, Corporal	Butler, Philip	Morrison, Thomas
Charles Flanders, Musician	Campbell, James	Silloway, Joseph
Stephen Gordon, Musician	Gardner, Robert	Stoddard, Thomas
	Graves, Truel G.	Wells, Daniel

Sergt. J. Griffin's Guard.

From Feb. 11, 1815, to March 15, 1815. Service at Newburyport.

Rank and Name.	Privates.	
Jacob Griffin, Sergeant	Brewster, John	Jackson, Samuel
Joshua Mace, Corporal	Butler, Philip	Morrison, Thomas
Charles Flanders, Musician	Campbell, James	Silloway, Joseph
Stephen Gordon, Musician	Gardner, Robert	Stallard, Thomas
	Graves, True G.	Wells, Daniel, Jr.

Sergt. J. Lewis' Detachment.

From July 17 to Nov. 11, 1814. This detachment was a coast guard and stationed at different points in Barnstable, Yarmouth, Sandwich, Brewster and Harwich.

Rank and Name.		
Jesse Lewis, Sergeant	Crocker, Rufus	Horsefield, Timothy
Zoath Berry or Perry, Sergeant	Doan, Joseph, Jr.	Jeffers, Ebenezer
David Loring, Corporal	Dunbar, John W.	Lambert, Solomon
S. Whelden, Corporal	Eldridge, John	Miller, Parker
Lewis Hawes, Corporal	Ettis, Levi	Nye, Joseph, 3d
	Fessenden, Thomas	Nye, Stephen
Privates.	Foster, Nathan	Phillips, George
Baker, Sylvanus	Freeman, Barnard	Pitcher, Samuel
Bean or Bears, Moses	Gage, Prince	Pope, Joseph H.
Bourne, Benjamin	Gorham, John	Raymond, Solomon
Bragg, William	Hallets, Hansard	Rider, Ebenezer
	Hinkley, S.	Rogers, Zacheus

Sergeant Savery's Guard.
From June 24 to July 24, 1814. Service at Wareham.

Rank and Name.	Privates.	
Samuel Savery, Sergeant	Besse, Asa	Gibbs, Joshua
Valentine C. Coffin, Corporal	Bumpus, Eliphalet	Gibbs, Seth
Benjamin Nye, Corporal	Claflin, Hartford	Howard, Calvin
	Everett, Noble, Jr.	Savery, Phineas
	Fearing, Moses T.	Soule, Josiah
	Galt, John	Tupper, Enoch

Lieut. D. Lane's Guard.
From August to November, 1814. Stationed at Fairhaven.

Rank and Name.		
Daniel Lane, Lieutenant	Danforth, Charles	Noyes, Moses
	Drew, Nicholas	Reed, Thomas
Thomas Braman, Sergeant	Dyer, Henry B.	Stacy, Charles C.
Peres Pool, Sergeant	French, Ephraim	Sweet, William
Joseph Fuller, Corporal	Gay, Martin	Wetherell, Zelotes
	Glody, David	White, Asaph
Privates.	Hodges, Barnam	Whiting, Ephraim
Andrews, Philip	Holbrook, Daniel	Wilbour, Ziba
Bennett, George	Macumber, Ezra	Wilmot, Benoni
	Macumber, Josiah	

Sergt. J. Jarvis' Guard, from Lieut. Col. J. Snow's Regiment.
From Oct. 5 to Nov. 24, 1814. Service at Orleans. Shore guard from Captain Knowles' company.

Rank and Name.	Privates.
John Jarvis, Sergeant	Smith, Elisha
	Young, Jonathan
	Young, Jonathan S.

Sergeant Savery's Guard.
From July 25 to Oct. 28, 1814. Service at Wareham.

Rank and Name.	Privates.	
Samuel Savery, Sergeant	Briggs, Spencer	Hathaway, Thomas
William Gibbs, Corporal	Bumpus, Admiral	Leonard, Ichabod
Rufus Lincoln, Corporal	Bumpus, Benjamin	Perry, Salathiel
	Doty, Nathaniel	Tobey, Curtis
	Gibbs, Joshua	Wridington, Thomas
	Hamblin, Nathaniel	Young, John
		Young, Thomas

Sergt. J. Craw's Guard, from Lieut. Col. B. Lincoln's Regiment.
From June to July, 1814. Service at Dartmouth.

Rank and Name.		
John Craw, Sergeant	Gifford, Paul	Sherman, Peleg
	Haffords, James	Slocum, Charles
Privates.	Kerby, Every	Trafford, Joseph
Baxter, Robert	Kerby, George	Tripp, William
Dunum, Charles	Ricketson, Cook	
	Shearman, Stephen	

Sergt. F. Pope's Guard, from Capt. W. Nye's Company, Lieut. Col. B. Lincoln's Regiment.
Over 14 days in July, 1814. Stationed at New Bedford.

RANK AND NAME.
Freeman Pope, Sergeant

Privates.
Allen, Warren
Bismore, David
Blossom, Levi

Delano, Joseph
Dillingham, Benjamin
Gelatt, John
Hammond, Freeman
Hammond, James
Hutlesom or Hutlestone, Henry
Myrick, Ebenezer

Russell, Prince
Sampson, Seth
Taber, Edward, Jr.
Tripp, Aaron
Wood, Elihu, Jr.

Sergt. I. Welden's Guard, from Lieut. Col. B. Lincoln's Regiment.
Over 14 days in July, 1814. Service at Dartmouth.

RANK AND NAME.
Isaac Welden, Sergeant

Privates.
Allen, John
Eldridge, Richard
Evans, William

Faunce, James
Gifford, George
Hathaway, Ezra
Hefford, James
Kerby, Eleazer
Lapham, Thomas
Macumber, Elisha

Taber, Gideon
Tripp, Ishmael
Wadey, Henry
Wilbour, Stephen
Wilcox, Allen

Sergt. B. Gifford's Guard, from Lieut. Col. B. Lincoln's Regiment.
July and August, 1814. Service at Dartmouth.

RANK AND NAME.
Benjamin Gifford, Sergeant
James Akens, Corporal

Privates.
Akens, Elihu
Cushman, Obed

Hathaway, Charles
Haws, Lot
Lawton, James
Mathews, Charles
Reed, William
Sanford, Paul
Smith, Increase

Snow, Knowles
Stafford, James
Wellborn, Stephen

Corp. J. Akins' Guard, from Lieut. Col. B. Lincoln's Regiment.
From July to October, 1814. Service at Westport.

RANK AND NAME.
Job Akins, Corporal

Privates.
Akins, Benjamin
Akins, Job, Jr.

Bismore, David
Delano, Henry
Huttlesom or Huttlestone, Henry

Lieut. Ebenezer Simmons' Guard, under General Goodwin.
From Oct. 12, 1812, to May, 1813. Service at Plymouth.

RANK AND NAME.
Ebenezer Simmons, Lieutenant

Levi Curtis, Sergeant
John Ramsdell, Corporal

Privates.
Bates, Clement
Bishop, Daniel

Boslear, Jesse
Clark, David
Cole, Joseph
Damon, Abiah
Howard, John
Munro, John
Oldham, John
Osborn, John
Perry, John

Ramsdell, Bartholomew
Rand, William
Stetson, Elisha C.
Stetson, Nathaniel
Thomas, Ebenezer S.
Walker, John

Sergt. Finney Leach's Guard, under General Goodwin.

From Oct. 12, 1812, to May, 1813. Service at Plymouth.

RANK AND NAME.		
Finney Leach, Sergeant	Clark, Consider	Finney, Seth
	Clark, Nathaniel	Holmes, Bartlet
Privates.	Finney, Clark	Howland, Charles
Burgess, John	Finney, Elkanah	Howland, William
Cassidy, Henry	Finney, Ephraim	Leach, Samuel
Churchill, Hosea	Finney, George	
	Finney, Robert	

Sergt. H. Torry's Guard, under General Goodwin.

From June to July, 1814. Service at Pembroke.

RANK AND NAME.	Cook, Peleg B.	McLaughlin, Miller
Haviland Torry, Sergeant	Cudworth, Elijah	Monroe, Cyrus
Elijah Perry, Sergeant	Curtis, Samuel	Nash, Zebulon
Levi Thomas, Corporal	Cushing, Benjamin	Pratt, Nathaniel
Zadoc Fish, Corporal	Everson, Levi	Ramsdell, Isaac
	Foster, Micah	Smith, Christopher
Privates.	Howe, Samuel	
Barney, Ezra	Joslyn, Waterman	
Bearce, Homer	Mann, Thomas	

Capt. A. Drew's Detached Company, by Order of Major General Goodwin.

From June 19 to Aug. 30, 1814. Service to mount guard in Plymouth, Duxbury and Kingston; also to row guard at Beach Point.

GUARD ON DUTY AT PLYMOUTH.
RANK AND NAME.
Atwood Drew, Captain (68 days)
Prince Bradford, Lieutenant (68 days)
Coomer Weston, Ensign (68 days)

Charles Goodwin, Sergeant (66 days)
Stephen Rogers, Sergeant (66 days)
Nathan Holmes, Sergeant (54 days)
Stephen Doten, Sergeant (72 days)
Benjamin W. Bradford, Corporal (66 days)
Isaac Torry, Corporal (66 days)
John B. Bates, Corporal (48 days)
Ephraim Whiting, Musician (66 days)
Benjamin Whiting, Jr., Musician (66 days)

Privates.
Bagnall, Joseph (66 days)
Bartlett, Elkanah (65 days)
Brigs, Samuel (46 days)
Cassidy, Henry (72 days)
Chamberlin, Thomas (53 days)
Churchill, Lewis (66 days)
Clark, John H. (72 days)
Cosset, Lothrop (66 days)
Cotton, Thomas J. (42 days)
Davee, William (66 days)
Dennis, William (53 days)
Dunan, David, Jr. (66 days)
Dunham, Jacob (66 days)
Dunham, John F. (62 days)
Farmer, Thomas (52 days)
Finney, Elkanah (72 days)
Harlow, Amariah (45 days)

Harlow, Nathaniel (66 days)
Hathaway, Joshua (66 days)
Holmes, Peter (66 days)
Howard, James (66 days)
Howland, Henry, Jr. (72 days)
Hueston, Nathaniel (66 days)
Lane, Marshall (66 days)
Lanman, Nathaniel (66 days)
LeBaron, Isaac (66 days)
Lewis, Samuel (66 days)
Lucas, Alden (66 days)
Lucas, Ivory (46 days)
Manlon, Henry (65 days)
Morey, Ichabod (72 days)
Nicholson, John (48 days)
Pratt, Joshua (66 days)
Robbins, Charles (66 days)
Robbins, Henry (66 days)
Robbins, John A. (66 days)
Robbins, Rufus (66 days)
Rogers, Sylvanus (66 days)
Seamore, Benjamin (66 days)
Sears, Eleazer (66 days)
Sherman, Thomas B. (66 days)
Simmons, Lemuel (38 days)
Thrasher, George, Jr. (46 days)
Thurston, John B. (46 days)
Whiting, Joseph (72 days)
Woodard, Elkanah (66 days)

GUARD ON DUTY AT DUXBURY.
RANK AND NAME.
Weston Simmons, Sergeant (12 days)
Nathan Chandler, Sergeant (12 days)

Luther Sturtavant, Sergeant (18 days)
Nehemiah Thompson, Sergeant (18 days)
Peleg Churchill, Sergeant (34 days)
Zenas Winslow, Corporal (61 days)
Levi Loring, Corporal (34 days)
Peleg Churchill, Corporal (30 days)
Martin Waterman, Musician (63 days)
Martin Simmons, Musician (63 days)

Privates.
Appling, William (16 days)
Atwood, Levi (19 days)
Atwood, Warren (16 days)
Barnes, Stephen (19 days)
Barrows, Charles (19 days)
Barrows, Joseph (16 days)
Bates, Caleb (13 days)
Bosworth, William (19 days)
Bradford, James, Jr. (13 days)
Bradford, Luther (16 days)
Brewster, Martin, Jr. (13 days)
Briant, Micah (19 days)
Briggs, Lewis (18 days)
Chandler, Ephraim (13 days)
Chandler, Ira (11 days)
Churchill, Alfred (19 days)
Churchill, Jacob (16 days)
Churchill, Seth (18 days)
Cole, James (16 days)
Cook, John, 3d (13 days)
Cook, Robert, Jr. (13 days)
Cooper, Richard (16 days)
Cushing, Seth, Jr. (13 days)
Cushman, Daniel (13 days)
Doten, Ebenezer (16 days)

Capt. A. Drew's Detached Company, by Order of Major General Goodwin — Concluded.

GUARD ON DUTY AT DUXBURY — Concluded.

Privates — Concluded.

Drew, Ebenezer (13 days)
Drew, Reuben, Jr (61 days)
Edson, Josiah (19 days)
Ellis, Joseph (16 days)
Everson, Ephraim (19 days)
Faunce, Allen (19 days)
Faunce, Ezra (16 days)
Faunce, Zenas (13 days)
Fuller, Ebenezer (19 days)
Fuller, Josiah, Jr. (13 days)
Fuller, Samuel (19 days)
Fuller, Thomas (18 days)
Hammond, Benjamin (19 days)
Harlow, Gideon (61 days)
Higgins, Nathaniel (11 days)
Holmes, Bradford (13 days)
Holmes, Francis (16 days)
Holmes, Nathaniel, Jr. (18 days)
Howland, John, Jr. (63 days)
Jostlin, Marquis F. (19 days)
Leach, Thomas (18 days)
Lobdell, George (18 days)
Loring, Joshua (11 days)
Lucas, Abijah (13 days)
Lucas, Isaac (19 days)
Maxim, Thomas (16 days)
Munroe, Benjamin, Jr. (18 days)
Nye, Isaac (19 days)
Oldham, Thomas (11 days)
Parrish, Ambrose (16 days)
Peterson, Charles (61 days)
Peterson, Clark (11 days)
Pierce, Benjamin (18 days)
Pratt, Tillson (16 days)
Richards, Isaac, Jr. (18 days)
Richmond, Oliver (16 days)
Ripley, David (18 days)
Ripley, Sylvanus (18 days)
Ripley, Zenas (18 days)
Saul, Zabel, Jr. (16 days)
Savory, William (16 days)
Shaw, Benjamin, 2d (19 days)
Shaw, Joseph (19 days)
Sherman, Ebenezer (16 days)
Sherman, Zacheus (18 days)
Shurtliff, Barnabas (19 days)
Shurtliff, Ebenezer (16 days)
Simmons, James (13 days)
Smith, Benjamin (13 days)
Sprague, Luther (16 days)
Standish, Thomas (18 days)
Sturdavant, Samuel (18 days)
Sturdavant, Winslow (19 days)
Sturdavant, Zedock (18 days)
Thomson, Isaac (18 days)
Thomson, Jacob, 3d (18 days)
Thomson, Ward (19 days)
Tilton, John (16 days)
Tiltson, Ephraim, Jr. (19 days)
Vickery, Daniel (18 days)
Ward, Benjamin (19 days)
Ward, Eliab (19 days)
Washburn, Reuel (63 days)
Waterman, Benson (18 days)
Weston, John (13 days)
Weston, Melzar (11 days)
Weston, Stephen (11 days)
Weston, Thomas F. (63 days)
White, Isaac, Jr. (18 days)
White, Levi (16 days)
Williams, Jabez (13 days)
Wood, L. (16 days)
Wright, Zebedee (19 days)

GUARD ON DUTY AT KINGSTON.

RANK AND NAME.
Ichabod Harlow, Sergeant (12 days)
Josiah Holmes, Sergeant (52 days)
Melzar Whiting, Sergeant (52 days)

Privates.
Adams, Gamaliel (52 days)
Cook, Asa (12 days)
Cushman, Elkanah (52 days)
Cushman, Robert (12 days)
Drew, Lazarus (12 days)
Fisk, Perez (52 days)
Fuller, Eleazer (52 days)
Simmons, William (52 days)
Stranger, Edward (12 days)
Wadsworth, Cephas (12 days)

Capt. N. Nelson's Company, under Command of General Goodwin.

From June 16 to July 5, 1814. Raised at New Bedford. Service at New Bedford.

RANK AND NAME.
Nathaniel Nelson, Captain
Job Gray, Lieutenant
George Clark, Ensign

Benjamin Warren, Sergeant
Gamaliel Hart, Sergeant
Thomas Reddell, Sergeant
Nathaniel Perry, Sergeant
David Howland, Corporal
James Proud, Corporal
Robert Trickerman, Corporal
Charles Covel, Corporal
Alanson Caswell, Musician
Charles Pratt, Musician

Privates.
Akins, John
Albert, Ivory C.
Allen, David
Babcock, James
Bassett, Nathaniel
Birtch, Stanton
Bliss, Josiah S.
Bliss, William, Jr.
Briggs, Elisha
Brownell, Benjamin
Chase, Gardner
Clark, Elisha
Covel, Benjamin B.
Cudworth, William
Cushman, Heman
Douglass, Benjamin
Durfer, Thomas
Frederick, Henry
Gardner, Edward
Gilbert, Charles
Hafford, James
Hammond, Benjamin
Hathaway, Charles
Hathaway, Ezra
Hathaway, Morrell
Head, Uriah
Hill, Richard
Holmes, Nye
Howland, Jonathan
Howland, Stephen
Jennings, Perry
Kempton, Thomas
Kempton, William N.
Lane, William
Merrit, Joseph
Mosher, Elihu
Mosher, Rauen
Napp, Elijah
Parker, Avery
Price, Stephen
Prowd, Samuel
Randal, Michel
Russell, Thomas
Seabury, Millet
Sisson, John
Smith, Israel
Stafford, Jonathan
Taber, Noel
Tompkins, Tillinghast
Towle, Abner
Tuckerman, William
Washburn, Moses
West, Stephen
Wilcox, Joseph
Winslow, Josiah
Wood, Charles
Wood, Russell

Ensign J. Vaughan's Guard, under General Goodwin at Rochester.
June and July, 1814.

RANK AND NAME.		
Jonathan Vaughan, Ensign	Bishop, Joseph	Hitchman, Solomon
Thomas Ashley, Sergeant	Blackwell, Micah	King, Jonathan
Tillotson Duncan, Sergeant	Briggs, Elijah	Lombard, Joseph
Joseph Doty, Corporal	Clark, Peleg	Pratt, Jesse
Azel Bryant, Corporal	Corning, Samuel	Rider, Benjamin
	Cornwell, John	Sears, John
Privates.	Corsing, Richard	Shearman, John, 3d
Avery, Philip	Crapo, Briggs	Snow, Ephraim
Bates, Moses	Douglas, Barnabas N.	Stetson, William
Bennett, Joseph	Hammond, Charles	Stevens, Micah
	Hathaway, Peleg	

Ensign M. Mendall's Guard, under General Goodwin.
From September to October, 1814.

RANK AND NAME.		
Moses Mendall, Ensign	Blankenship, James, Jr.	Freeman, James
	Boston, George, Jr.	Handy, Jabez
Dennis Pierce, Sergeant	Cannon, Cable L.	Hillis, Francis
Israel Hammond, Sergeant	Cobb, Josiah	Lain, Samuel W.
Peres Bassett, Corporal	Crapo, Briggs	Mendall, Samuel
Jared Blankenship, Corporal	Crapo, William	Snow, Benjamin
	Cushing, Benjamin	Snow, Ephraim
Privates.	Cushing, Nathaniel	Snow, James
Bates, Paddock	Dexter, Gideon	Tinkham, Ephraim
Blankenship, George	Dexter, Jonathan	
	Dexter, Luke	

Sergt. C. Jones' Guard, under Supervision of Gen. N. Goodwin.
From September to October, 1814. Service on seashore, Plymouth County.

RANK AND NAME.	*Privates.*	Merritt, Daniel
Charles Jones, Sergeant	Benson, Artemas	Mitchell, Samuel H.
Luther Little, Sergeant	Bowker, David	Ranell, Joseph
	Cudworth, Benjamin	Silvester, Thomas
	Curtis, Samuel	Tilden, John
	Jacobs, Walter	Young, Gideon

Sergt. D. C. Chadwick's Guard at Falmouth, under General Goodwin.
From September to December, 1814.

RANK AND NAME.	Chadwick, Thatcher	Hamblin, Simeon
Samuel C. Chadwick, Sergeant	Edwards, Asa	Parker, Calvin
	Fish, Calvin	Snow, Robinson
Privates.	Fish, Edward	
Brown, Uziel	Gifford, Prince	
Chadwick, Charles	Hamblin, Barnabus	

Sergt. S. Smith's Guard, under General Goodwin.

One month or over, in October and November, 1814. Service at Plymouth.

Rank and Name.		
Sylvanus Smith, Sergeant	Drew, Charles	Lamson, Alfred
Elijah Baker, Sergeant	Drew, Reuben, Jr.	Morton, Josiah
	Frazer, John	Peterson, George
Privates.	Fuller, George	Peterson, Nathaniel
Baker, Daniel	Glass, Consider	Simmons, Noah
Bates, Benjamin	Glass, Nathaniel	Smith, Benjamin, Jr.
Delano, William	Goodspeed, David S.	Smith, Jacob
	Jameson, Levi	

Sergt. N. Chandler's Guard, under General Goodwin.

From October to November, 1814. Service at Kingston.

Rank and Name.	*Privates.*	
Nathaniel Chandler, Sergeant	Cook, Levi	
	Faunce, Tilden	
	Tupper, Peleg	

Sergt. C. Goodwin's Guard, under Supervision of Gen. N. Goodwin.

From October to November, 1814. Service at Plymouth.

Rank and Name.	Churchill, Nathan	Norton, John L.
Charles Goodwin, Sergeant	Davis, Joseph	Richmond, Alpheus
Lemuel Simmonds, Corporal	Donham, John F.	Robbins, Anselm
	Harlow, Amaziah	Robbins, Benjamin
Privates.	Hathaway, Joshua	Robbins, Jesse
Allen, William	Holmes, Andrew	Robbins, John A.
Bagnall, Benjamin	Lauman, Samuel	Rogers, Silvanus
Barnes, Elkanah	Marston, Henry	Sherman, Thomas
Bates, Isaac	Mayo, Seth	Smith, Abiather
Bradford, David	Milford, Joshua	Turner, Jesse
Bradford, Josiah	Mitchell, Ebenezer	Whiting, Ephraim
Bradford, Lemuel	Nelson, Ebenezer, Jr.	

Capt. E. Lathrop's Company, under Supervision of General Lathrop.

From Feb. 2 to Feb. 4, Sept. 17, Oct. 2 to Oct. 7, 1814. Raised at Barnstable. Service at Falmouth.

Rank and Name.	Brown, Sylvanus	Ewer, Barnabas
Ebenezer Lathrop, Captain	Childs, Samuel	Gorham, Charles
Gorham Hall, Lieutenant	Chipman, Barnabas	Gorham, John
John Barsley, Jr., Ensign	Chipman, Walter	Gorham, John, Jr.
	Cobb, Benjamin	Gorham, Nathaniel
Asa Young, Sergeant	Cobb, Eleazer, Jr.	Gorham, Sylvanus
William Cobb, Sergeant	Cobb, Isaac	Hall, Ezekiel
James Childs, Sergeant	Cobb, Jonathan	Hall, John
Joseph Barsley, Sergeant	Cobb, Matthew	Hallett, John, Jr.
	Cobb, Prentiss	Hinckley, Benjamin
Privates.	Cobb, Richard	Hinckley, Charles
Allen, Charles	Crocker, Asa	Hinckley, Isaac
Allen, Joseph	Crocker, Cornelius	Hinckley, Josiah
Bacon, Ebenezer	Crocker, Loring	Hinckley, Lot
Bacon, Henry	Davis, Barzilla	Hinckley, Otis
Bacon, Oris, Jr.	Davis, Edward S.	Hinckley, William
Baker, Davis	Davis, George	Jenkins, Charles
Baker, Sylvester	Davis, John, Jr.	Larkin, John
Barnes, William	Davis, Nymphus	Lewis, Seth
Baxter, Charles	Eldridge, Bartlett	Loring, Elijah
Bragg, William	Estabrook, Charles G.	Loring, Joshua

Capt. E. Lathrop's Company, under Supervision of General Lathrop — Concluded.

Privates — Concluded.		
Marston, Edward	Smith, James	Swift, Eben
Marston, John	Smith, Nathaniel	Thatcher, James
Sears, Thomas	Smith, Reuben	Thatcher, John, Jr.
Smith, Caleb	Sturgis, David	Thatcher, Peleg
	Sturgis, Jackson	Tupper, Lothrop, Jr.

Lieut. Col. J. White's Regiment.

Service at Salem. The several companies of this regiment were ordered to assemble 2 days in each week for military instruction and discipline, and it was not, properly speaking, military service.

FIELD AND STAFF.
Joseph White, Lieutenant Colonel, Salem.

Capt. J. C. King's Company, Lieut. Col. J. White's Regiment.

From June 10 to Aug. 1, Sept. 22 to Oct. 5, 1814. Service at Salem. This service was for military instruction only, from 2 to 10 days.

RANK AND NAME.	Chamberlin, Timothy	Mansfield, James, Jr.
James C. King, Captain	Choate, John	Newhall, George
Edward Lander, Lieutenant	Cloutman, Joseph	Norris, Jeremiah
Abel Lawrence, Jr., Ensign	Cross, Henry	Orne, Edward
	Dean, George, Jr.	Page, Saul
Joseph Peabody, Sergeant	Derby, Richard	Palfrey, Thomas
Benjamin Dow, Sergeant	Endicott, Samuel	Pitman, Michel
Convers Tilden, Sergeant	Eveleth, Joseph, Jr.	Potter, Elijah
George A. Ward, Sergeant	Farless, James	Potter, Thomas
Thomas Farless, Corporal	Felt, Ephraim	Proctor, William
Samuel B. Dudley, Corporal	Fenno, John W.	Rogers, Richard S.
Samuel B. Derby, Corporal	Gardner, John, 3d	Rogers, William A.
Joseph Dalton, Musician	Gerard, Peter	Safford, Nathaniel
	Goodale, Nathan	Saltonstall, Richard
Privates.	Goss, Joseph	Sandey, Edward A. H.
Andrews, Isaac W.	Gould, James	Saunders, Edward
Andrews, Nathaniel	Grafton, George W.	Shillaber, John
Babbidge, Benjamin	Hawkes, Benjamin, Jr.	Smith, Jesse, Jr.
Brooks, Saul	Hodges, George A.	Smith, Thomas
Brooks, Thomas, Jr.	Holman, Samuel	Warner, Caleb
Brown, Edward T.	Ireland, Thomas	Warner, John
Buffum, James R.	Leach, George	Webb, William
Bullock, James	Leach, Hardy	West, Edward
Chamberlin, Saul	Low, William H.	

Capt. T. R. Williams' Company, Lieut. Col. J. White's Regiment.

From June 20 to Aug. 5, 1814. Service at Salem. This service was for military instruction only, from 2 to 10 days.

RANK AND NAME.	Babbidge, Benjamin	Fox, Ebenezer
Thomas R. Williams, Captain	Ballard, Henry	Galland, Robert
James Goodhue, Ensign	Beckett, John	Garrett, Joseph
Jeremiah Goodhue, Ensign	Bott, Linch	Glover, George
	Bray, Daniel	Gray, John
John Quarter, Sergeant	Chamberlin, Henry	Gray, Saul
Joseph Dalton, Musician	Chandler, Benjamin	Hammond, John
Henry Herbon, Musician	Chrispin, William	Hart, Joseph
	Collier, Isaac	Harvey, John
Privates.	Davenport, Thomas	Henderson, Samuel
Abbot, Ephraim	Dodge, A.	Henman, John
Abbott, Saul	Duncan, William	Hill, David
Adams, George	Fishley, Benjamin	Hobbs, Jeremiah
Alcher, Daniel	Foster, Stephen A.	Hodgden, Saul

Capt. T. R. Williams' Company, Lieut. Col. J. White's Regiment — Concluded.

Privates — Concluded.
Hutson, Thomas B.
Jewett, John
Johnson, Saul
Kehew, John
Knight, Aaron
Knight, Daniel
Lamson, Rufus
League, William
Mansfield, Benjamin
Miller, Job
Nichols, Henry

Pens, Robert
Petty, John
Phippen, Abraham
Pierce, Ephraim
Rogers, Richard
Saul, Joseph
Sawyer, Nathaniel
Seague or Teague, Nathaniel
Seague or Teague, Thomas
Smith, Elliot
Smothers, Benjamin
Southwick, John

Trask, Joseph
Trask, Joshua
Upton, Robert
Wakefield, William
Webb, Thomas B.
Webber, Henry
White, Henry
Williams, John
Willis, Benjamin
Wilson, Robert
Wood, Stephen

Capt. S. Mansfield's Company, Lieut. Col. J. White's Regiment.
From June 24 to Aug. 5, 1814. Service at Salem. This service was for military instruction only, from 2 to 10 days.

RANK AND NAME.
Samuel Mansfield, Captain
Benjamin A. Dix, Lieutenant
Samuel Fabins, Ensign

Bryant Newcomb, Sergeant
John Bradshaw, Sergeant
Jonathan Whipple, Sergeant
William Kimball, Sergeant
Joseph Dalton, Musician
Joseph Chamberlin, Musician

Privates.
Agge, Jacob
Akins, John
Arrington, Joseph
Bader, Charles
Batchelder, William
Berry, Oliver
Boynton, Nathaniel
Brookhouse, Benjamin
Brookhouse, Daniel
Brown, Ephraim
Callum, Ebenezer
Carner, William
Chamberlin, Hazen
Cilly, Cuttin
Clark, Ebenezer
Clough, William
Colley, William
Collins, Dixy
Cross, Isaac
Daland, John
Erving, Joseph
Eustis, Joseph
Fabins, Benjamin

Fabins, William
Felt, Joseph
Felt, Nathaniel
Fletcher, Amos
Flint, Elias
Florance, John
Foster, Jesse
Frothingham, Caleb
Gibson, John
Gilman, Henry
Glover, John H.
Goodhue, Isaac
Hall, Benjamin
Hamilton, Alexander
Hamsted, Nathaniel
Hardy, Temple
Hathaway, William
Hibbard, Joseph
Hill, Henry
Hunt, David
Ingalls, James
Ingalls, Nathaniel
Ingalls, Thomas
Ingersoll, George H.
Johnson, Samuel
Joslin, William
Kilby, Nathaniel
Kingman, Thomas
Larrock, John
Little, Daniel
Low, Richard
Luscomb, Andrew
Mansfield, Nathaniel B.
Marrow, William
Morton, David
Moulton, Joseph

Nichols, John
Norwood, William
Perce, Jonathan
Perkins, Jacob
Pierce, George P.
Pike, Jacob
Pomroy, Arad
Preston, David
Preston, Jonathan
Price, William
Radford, John
Richards, John
Richards, Walter
Richardson, Edmund
Richardson, Isaac
Richardson, Stephen
Russell, William
Searls, Stephen
Sibly, Joseph
Smith, George
Smith, William
Sparhawk, John
Stanwood, Saul
Stetson, William
Thompson, Andrew
Thompson, Joseph A.
Upton, Saul
Vanderford, Charles
Vent, James
West, Nathaniel
Wiggins, John D.
Wiggins, Thomas D.
Wilson, Jonathan
Winn, Erastus

Capt. William B. Dodge's Company, Lieut. Col. J. White's Regiment.
From June 27 to Aug. 5, 1814. Service at Salem. This service was for military instruction only, from 2 to 10 days.

RANK AND NAME.
William B. Dodge, Captain
William Stearnes, Lieutenant
Dudley Kimball, Ensign

David M. Prince, Sergeant
John Chipman, Jr., Sergeant
Saul Randall, Sergeant
Charles Hill, Sergeant

Jonathan Barry, Musician
Aaron Wood, Musician

Capt. William B. Dodge's Company, Lieut. Col. J. White's Regiment — Concluded.

Privates.

- Adams, Joseph
- Allen, John
- Berry, John, Jr.
- Berry, Oliver
- Berry, William
- Carey, John
- Carey, Thomas
- Chamberlin, Daniel
- Chandler, William H.
- Cook, John M.
- Cox, Joseph
- Cushing, John
- Davis, John
- Davis, William
- Fowler, Abraham
- Fuller, Nathan
- Gerry, Nathaniel
- Hensler, George
- Hitchings, Benjamin
- Hodgkins, Thomas
- Hutchinson, John
- Johnson, Mathew
- Joye, Joseph
- Kilham, Daniel
- Patch, David
- Peel, Robert, Jr.
- Peirce, Henry
- Perkins, John
- Prince, William H.
- Randall, William
- Reed, Holtin
- Richards, Joseph
- Saltmarsh, Seth
- Skerry, John
- Smith, Joseph
- Snelling, John
- Stickney, John
- Swan, Aaron
- Swan, Benjamin
- Swan, John
- Swan, Joseph
- Swan, Nathaniel
- Swan, Samuel, Jr.
- Swan, Saul
- Swan, Thomas
- Symonds, Ebenezer
- Symonds, Ephraim
- Symonds, John
- Symonds, John D.
- Symonds, Joseph
- Symonds, Nathaniel
- Symonds, Samuel
- Symonds, Stephen
- Symonds, Thomas, Jr.
- Symonds, Thorndike
- Town, Elijah
- Town, Samuel
- Treadwell, Samuel
- Ward, Stephen
- Wheeler, Thomas
- Wilkins, John G.
- Willy, James

Capt. T. Oaks' Company, Lieut. Col. J. White's Regiment.

From June 30 to July 18, 1814. Service at Salem. This service was for military instruction only, from 2 to 10 days.

Rank and Name.
- Thomas Oaks, Captain
- John Clark, Lieutenant
- William Stickney, Ensign

- Ebenezer Slocum, Sergeant
- Richard Hay, Sergeant
- Nathaniel Kimball, Sergeant
- Jonathan Webb, Sergeant
- Henry Roper, Corporal
- John Harris, Corporal
- John Sage, Corporal
- Joseph Kittredge, Corporal

Privates.
- Beach, Joseph
- Bickford, David
- Brown, Abraham
- Brown, Benjamin, Jr.
- Brown, Enoch
- Caldwell, John
- Clemens, Saul
- Cloutman, Joseph
- Collins, Barnard
- Dean, Thomas
- Dodge, Josiah, Jr.
- Edwards, Joshua
- Endicott, Samuel, Jr.
- Forbes, Charles
- Gardner, John
- Givum, James
- Hall, Israel
- Haywood, Aaron
- Hazelton, Saul
- Hersey, Abel
- Hobson, Moses
- Horton, Benjamin
- Jacobson, Mathias
- Kelly, Christopher
- Kennister, Edward
- King, Nathaniel
- Knapp, Isaac
- Lampson, Benjamin
- Lefavor, Thomas
- Lord, Ammi
- Lord, Philip
- Marker, Philip
- Moody, James
- Noyes, Abraham
- Noyes, John
- Noyes, Lincoln
- Palfrey, Richard
- Peabody, Webster
- Pedrick, John
- Pierce, George
- Prince, Ebsaphon
- Roper, Benjamin
- Rue, Benjamin
- Sawyer, Saul
- Silsbee, Zachariah F.
- Skerry, Chipman
- Southworth, Richard
- Stickney, William
- Stone, Benjamin
- Sweeney, William
- Teague, Richard
- Underwood, George
- Walden, Daniel
- Walden, Joseph
- Warner, Daniel
- Waters, John
- Wells, Moses
- Wells, Nathaniel
- Williams, Stephen
- Willison, John
- Wittemore, Stephen

Capt. T. Oaks' Company, Lieut. Col. J. White's Regiment.

From June 30 to July 18, 1814. Service at Salem. This service was for military instruction only, from 4 to 10 days.

Rank and Name.
- Thomas Oaks, Captain
- John Clark, Lieutenant
- William Stickney, Ensign
- Ebenezer Slocum, Jr., Sergeant
- Richard Hay, Sergeant
- Nathaniel Kimball, Sergeant
- Jonathan Webb, Sergeant
- Henry Ropes, Corporal
- John Harris, Corporal
- John Sage, Corporal
- Asaph Kittredge, Corporal

Capt. T. Oaks' Company, Lieut. Col. J. White's Regiment — Concluded.

Privates.

Bench, Joseph
Bickford, David
Brown, Abraham
Brown, Benjamin, Jr.
Brown, Enoch
Caldwell, John
Clemens, Saul
Cloutman, Joseph
Collins, Barnard
Dean, Thomas
Dodge, Josiah, Jr.
Edwards, Joshua
Endicott, Samuel
Forbes, Charles
Gardner, John
Gwinn, James
Hall, Israel
Hayes, Abraham
Hayes, John
Hayward, Aaron

Hazelton, Saul
Hersey, Abel
Hobson, Moses
Horton, Benjamin
Jacobson, Mathias
Kelly, Christopher
Kenester, Edward
Knapp, Isaac
Lampson, Benjamin
Lefavour, Thomas
Lord, Ammi
Lord, Philip
Markoe, Philip
Moody, James
Noyes, Simeon
Palfrey, Richard
Peabody, Webster
Pedrick, John
Pierce, George
Prince, Elsaphan
Roper, Benjamin

Rue, Benjamin
Sawyer, Saul
Silsbee, Zacheus F.
Skerry, Ephraim
Southworth, Richard
Stickney, William
Stone, Benjamin
Sweeney, William
Teague, Richard
Underwood, George
Walden, Daniel
Walden, Joseph
Wales, John
Warner, Daniel
Wells, Moses
Wells, Nathaniel
Whittemore, Stephen
Williams, Stephen
Wilson, John

Capt. B. Morgan's Company, Lieut. Col. J. White's Regiment.

From July to August, 1814. Service at Salem. This service was for military instruction only, from 4 to 10 days.

RANK AND NAME.
Benjamin Morgan, Captain
George Brown, Lieutenant
Dana Linus, Ensign

David Ellsworth, Sergeant
Joseph B. Smith, Sergeant
Aaron Porter, Sergeant
James Gale, Sergeant
Rufus Wetherell, Musician
John Jones, Musician

Privates.
Abbot, George
Andrews, John H.
Balch, Benjamin
Barr, John, Jr.
Barr, Robert
Barr, William
Bowker, Joel
Bradly, William
Butchmore, Stephen
Chapman, Benjamin
Cilly, Cutting
Clark, Francis G.

Clark, John
Crowell, David
Deland, Jonathan T.
Derby, George
Derby, James
Field, Stephen
Frye, John W.
Gardner, Benjamin
Garet, Edward
Garet, Jonathan
Garet, W. M.
Glover, Ichabod
Gould, Edmund
Hale, Jonathan
Johnson, Charles
Johnson, Edmund
Johnson, John
Joy, John
Kinsbury, Daniel
Lakeman, Robert M.
Lamson, Asa
Lamson, Joseph
Lander, William
Lord, Benjamin
Moore, Elisha

Newhall, Dudley
Nordiss, Edward
Nordiss, Henry
Odell, James
Odell, Thomas
Osborn, Jonathan
Page, Samuel L.
Parth, Abraham
Patterson, H.
Perkins, Daniel
Perkins, Jonathan
Prescott, Peter
Quillon, John P. M.
Richardson, James
Rope, Joseph
Sanborne, Mark
Sanborne, Moses
Scates, Joseph
Sergent, Levi
Shillaber, Benjamin
Smith, Benjamin W.
Smith, Charles
Waldow, Edward
Waters, John
Welden, Solomon

Capt. J. Edwards' Company, Lieut. Col. J. White's Regiment.

From July 20 to Aug. 5, 1814. Service at Salem. This service was for military instruction only, from 2 to 10 days.

RANK AND NAME.
Joseph Edwards, Captain
Josiah Lord, Lieutenant
David Robbins, Ensign

Jabez Treadwell, Sergeant
David Lord, Sergeant
William Haskell, Sergeant
William Nicholas, Musician
Sergent Ingalls, Musician

Privates.
Bachelder, Nathaniel
Bickford, Joshua
Blanchard, Saul T.
Boardman, John
Cook, James

Capt. J. Edwards' Company, Lieut. Col. J. White's Regiment — Concluded.

Privates — Concluded.

Doart, Samuel	Johnson, Saul	Putnam, William
Felt, Joseph	Kimball, Jonathan C.	Robbins, David
George, Benjamin	Kimball, Josiah	Roberts, William
Hall, Moses	Lord, Ammi	Runnalls, Valentine
Hard, Daniel	Lord, Philip	Slemmon, Andrew
Harris, Moses	McIntire, Daniel	Spiller, Moses
Haselton, Jonathan	Neal, Jonathan, 4th	Stickney, Richard
Haslett, William	Neal, Joseph	Symons, Saul
Hobson, Moses	Peabody, Webster	Trumbull, Nathaniel
Howard, Aaron	Pearson, Joseph	Tucker, Joseph
	Pierce, George P.	Webber, Henry

Capt. J. Howard's Company, Lieut. Col. J. White's Regiment.

From July 6 to July 27, 1814. Service at Salem. This service was for military instruction only, from 2 to 10 days.

RANK AND NAME.

John Howard, Captain
Ephraim Treadwell, Ensign

Joshua Grout, Sergeant
William Treadwell, Sergeant
William M. Brooks, Corporal
Charles Hill, Corporal

Privates.

Adams, Ira	Churchward, Timothy	Leavitt, Charles
Alden, Lott	Cloutman, George	Lee, Joshua
Ames, Peter	Cook, James	Needham, Benjamin
Barstow, Joseph	Cross, Aaron	Oaks, Joshua
Batchelder, Joshua	Cross, Joseph	Pervin, Meshack
Boynton, Joshua	Crowninshield, Benjamin W.	Prime, Henry
Brooks, Charles	Curtis, Nathaniel	Roper, Saul
Brooks, Samuel	Deveroux, Thomas	Russell, Benjamin
Carlton, Joseph	Doland, Benjamin	Sanders, Thomas M.
Chapman, Saul	Doland, Benjamin, 2d	Saul, Thomas
Chase, Jacob	Emery, Saul	Shannon, M.
	English, Philip	Shelden, Saul
	Eveleth, Francis	Strout, Joshua
	Farley, James	Swasey, Joseph
	Forrester, Charles	Talum, Henry
	Forrester, Thomas H.	Teague, Jonathan
	Fry, William	West, Thomas
	Glidden, Jonathan	Wilson, Jonathan
	Hare, James S.	Wood, Benjamin
	Hutchinson, Israel	
	Lander, Warren	

Capt. S. Mansfield's Company, Lieut. Col. J. White's Regiment.

From Sept. 9 to Oct. 10, 1814. Service at Salem. This service was for military instruction only, from 2 to 10 days.

RANK AND NAME.

Samuel Mansfield, Captain
Benjamin A. Dix, Lieutenant
Samuel Fabins, Ensign

Bryant Newcomb, Sergeant
James Bradshaw, Sergeant
Jonathan Whipple, Sergeant
William Kimball, Sergeant
Joseph Chamberlin, Musician
Andrews Shuman, Musician

Privates.

Barry, Oliver	Clough, William	Keen, Shadrick
Batchelder, William	Cross, Isaac	Kinsman, Thomas
Bodin, Charles	Daland, John	Larock, John
Burdon, Thomas	Davis, William	Little, Daniel
Callum, Ebenezer	English, Philip	Low, Richard
Carnes, William	Erving, Ernest A.	Luscomb, Henry
Clark, Ebenezer	Eustace, Joseph	Martin, John
	Fabins, Benjamin	Moulton, Joseph
	Felt, Joseph	Osborn, Ezra
	Felt, Nathaniel	Osgood, Jeremiah
	Fletcher, Amos	Peirce, Jonathan
	Gilman, Henry	Pike, Jacob
	Glover, Cook O.	Pomroy, Arad
	Hall, Benjamin	Prenton or Preston, Jonathan
	Hamilton, Alexander	Preston, David
	Hobbard, Joseph	Price, William
	Hunt, Daniel	Radford, John
	Ingalls, James	Richards, John
	Ingalls, Nathaniel	Richards, Walter
	Ingalls, Thomas	Russell, William

MASSACHUSETTS VOLUNTEER MILITIA IN THE WAR OF 1812. 137

Capt. S. Mansfield's Company, Lieut. Col. J. White's Regiment — Concluded.

Privates — Concluded.
Sandwood, Samuel
Satchwell, William
Searls, Stephen
Sibley, Joseph
Smith, George

Smith, William
Sparrowhawk, John
Stetson, William
Thompson, Andrew
Thompson, Joseph A.
Upton, Samuel

Vanderford, Charles
Ware, Arstus
Waters, John
Wiggin, James D.
Wiggin, Thomas D.
Wilson, Jonathan

Capt. B. Morgan's Company, Lieut. Col. J. White's Regiment.

From Sept. 9 to Oct. 10, 1814. Service at Salem. This service was for military instruction only, from 2 to 10 days.

RANK AND NAME.
Benjamin Morgan, Captain
George Brown, Lieutenant
Dana Lewis, Ensign

Joseph B. Smith, Sergeant
Aaron Porter, Sergeant
James Gale, Sergeant
Benjamin Gardner, Musician
John Jones, Musician

Privates.
Balch, Benjamin
Barker, Jeremiah
Barr, William
Bowker, Joel
Brown, Jonathan
Burchmore, Stephen
Chamberlin, Hazen

Cilly, Cutting
Clark, Francis G.
Clark, John
Crowell, David
Frothingham, Nathaniel
Frye, John N.
Garet, Edward
Garet, William
Gould, Emerson
Johnson, Charles
Johnson, E.
Joy, John
Lamson, Asa
Larder, William
Lovett, Benjamin
Moore, Elisha
Newell, Dudley
Nichols, Joseph P.
Norris, Edward, 3d

Norris, Henry
Odell, James
Patterson, Hans
Perkins, Daniel
Perkins, John
Phippen, Robert
Prescott, Peter
Quillon, John P. M.
Richardson, James
Roberts, Joseph
Sanborne, Mark
Scates, Joseph
Shillaber, Benjamin
Shorey, Benjamin
Smith, Benjamin W.
Symonds, George
Waldo, Edward

Capt. J. Howard's Company, Lieut. Col. J. White's Regiment.

From Sept. 10 to Oct. 10, 1814. Service at Salem. This service was for military instruction only, from 2 to 10 days.

RANK AND NAME.
John Howard, Captain
Ephraim Treadwell, Lieutenant
John Choate, Ensign

Joseph Grant, Sergeant
Francis Pulsifer, Musician
Benjamin Horton, Musician
Jacob Chase, Musician

Privates.
Adams, Ira
Alden, Lot
Ames, Peter
Archer, George
Bachelder, Joshua

Barstow, Joseph
Brooks, Charles
Brooks, William
Carlton, Joseph
Chipman, Saul
Churchward, Timothy
Cloutman, George
Cook, James
Cross, Aaron
Cross, Charles
Cross, Joshua
Cross, Saul
Daland, Benjamin
Devereaux, Thomas
Emery, Saul
Farley, James

Fry, Jonathan
Greeley, Philip
Hare, James S.
Hill, Charles
Leavitt, Charles
Lekeman, Richard M.
Manning, Robert
Morrong, Jonathan
Needham, Benjamin
Patrick, William
Sheldon, Samuel H.
Swazy, Joseph
Treadwell, William
Ward, Nathaniel
Wilson, Jonathan

Capt. N. Blood's Company, Lieut. Col. J. White's Regiment.

From Sept. 16 to Oct. 10, 1814. Service at Salem. This service was for military instruction only, from 2 to 10 days.

RANK AND NAME.
Nathan Blood, Captain
Robert Hill, Lieutenant
Joshua Chase, Ensign

Saul Balch, Sergeant
Thomas L. Wiggins, Sergeant
Pierce L. Wiggins, Sergeant
William Babbidge, Sergeant

Richard Gale, Sergeant
Richard Ward, Sergeant
Joseph Hodge, Corporal
Joseph Gardner, Corporal

138 MASSACHUSETTS VOLUNTEER MILITIA IN THE WAR OF 1812.

Capt. N. Blood's Company, Lieut. Col. J. White's Regiment — Concluded.

RANK AND NAME — Concluded.
Jacob Wood, Corporal
William Foye, Corporal
Timothy Wellman, Corporal
John Beckett, Corporal
Richard Hill, Musician
Benjamin Balch, Musician
Hugh Pike, Musician

Privates.
Abbot, Elias
Adams, Amos
Allen, William
Andrews, Daniel
Andrews, Saul
Andrews, Thomas
Austin, William
Babbidge, John P.
Battin, John
Becket, William
Beson, Saul
Bickford, Thomas
Blanchard, Daniel
Boardman, John
Boynton, Stephen
Bright, Thomas
Brown, David
Brown, John, 3d
Brown, William
Chase, Plummer
Cheaver, James
Clafford, Peter
Cliff, James
Clough, Andrew
Cloutman, Saul
Colfield, Anthony D.
Collins, Robert
Crandall, John
Davis, John
Davis, Richard

Dix, John
Dockhan, Stephen B.
Dodge, Judah
Donaldson, Alexander
Durant, Edward
Fairfield, Samuel
Foster, Isaac P.
Fuller, James
Gale, Stephen
Gilmour, Joseph
Goss, Francis
Griffin, Nathaniel
Hall, Spencer
Hammond, John L.
Hill, Henry
Hill, Simon
Hitchings, Nathaniel
Hodgdon, Robert
Hodges, George
Hulin, William
Hutchinson, William
Isaacs, James
Kenny, Jesse
Kimball, Ebenezer
Kimball, Nathaniel
King, Samuel
Lambert, Saul
Lane, John
Lawrence, Lewis
Lebetter, Daniel
Marque, Philip
Millet, Charles
Millet, Jonathan
Nesmith, Adam
Nichols, John
Ober, William
Oliver, William
Palfrey, Andrew
Peel, Robert
Phippen, Hardy

Poland, Oliver
Polin, David
Read, Robert
Richards, Stephen
Richardson, Asa
Richardson, Ephraim
Richardson, Robert
Ring, Daniel
Ropes, Ebenezer
Sabor or Tabor, David
Safford, Joshua
Shehan, Daniel
Silsbee, Nathaniel S.
Silsbee, Samuel
Silsbee, William
Skeery, William
Smith, James
Southwick, Joseph
Stickney, Charles
Sumner, George
Surner or Turner, John
Swasey, John
Taylor, Andrew
Taylor, George
Town, Joshua
Towzer, William
Ward, Andrew
Ward, George H.
Webb, Thomas
Webb, William
Wellman, Timothy
Welsh, James
Whittemore, John
Whittle, James
Williams, George
Williams, John, Jr.
Wilson, Charles
Wright, George
Wynn, Sylvanus

Capt. S. White's Company, Lieut. Col. J. White's Regiment.
From Sept. 17 to Oct. 10, 1814. Service at Salem. This service was for military instruction only, from 2 to 10 days.

RANK AND NAME.
Stephen White, Captain
John Dodge, Lieutenant
Saul Chadwick, Ensign

Samuel Webb, Sergeant
S. W. Shepard, Sergeant
Jonathan Ward, Sergeant
David Becket, Sergeant
John Jameson, Musician
Benjamin Horton, Musician

Privates.
Atkins, John
Auker, John, 3d
Barr, John S.
Besson, Jonathan
Boardman, Francis
Brace, James, Jr.
Bray, John

Briggs, Abner
Briggs, Saul
Burrill, Elijah G.
Burrill, Josiah G.
Chadwick, John
Cheever, Joseph
Dowst, Samuel
Driver, Stephen
Forbes, Charles
Foster, John B.
Gardner, Robert
Gavitt, Jonathan
Hammond, Daniel
Hutchinson, Thomas
Lee, Joseph L.
Macintyre, Joseph
Mansfield, John
McCarthy, James
Millet, Jonathan
Palfrey, Warwick

Pettyplace, William
Potts, William H.
Proctor, Thorndike
Purviss, J.
Raines, Miles
Rantoul, William
Richardson, John
Silver, James
Story, Franklin
Todd, Jeremiah
Townsend, Penn
Upton, Edward
Wallace, Elisha F.
Ward, Andrew
Ward, Saul
Warner, Joseph
Webb, Jonathan
Wellington, Thaddeus
Whittidge, Henry T.
Winn, John

Capt. D. Davis' Company, Lieut. Col. J. White's Regiment.

From July 1 to Aug. 2, 1814. Service at Salem. This service was for military instruction only, from 4 to 10 days.

Rank and Name.
David Davis, Captain
David Safford, Lieutenant
Benjamin Hawes, Ensign

Stephen Hawes, Sergeant
Benjamin Nichols, Sergeant
William Harris, Sergeant
Samuel Cleves, Sergeant

Privates.
Annable, Benjamin
Atkins, James
Bancroft, Stephen
Bancroft, Thomas
Batchelder, Nathaniel
Bradley, H.
Brown, Saul
Burbank, Caleb
Carlton, Francis
Chamberlin, Joseph
Cheever, William
Clark, Charles C.
Dalton, Eleazer
Davis, John
Deveraux, Humphrey
Dodge, P.
Easty, Jeremiah
Fabins, John
Fernal, William
Foster, John
Foster, John B.
Frothingham, Richard S.
Fry, Ebenezer
Gardner, John
Gillet, Marcus
Grant, John
Green, Nathan
Griffin, Dudly
Ham, Moses
Harrington, Jonas
Hentry, Saul F.
Hopkins, Daniel
Ingersoll, Sargent
Kenny, Moses
Lurch, Hardy
Moulton, Bartholomew
Neal, Joseph
Noble, Joseph
Page, Woodberry
Phipps, Joseph
Pickering, Stephen
Pillsbury, Silas
Pitman, Benjamin
Potter, Jesse
Potter, Nathaniel
Proctor, Ebenezer
Proctor, Hadley
Proctor, Willoughby
Putman, Saul
Richardson, Parker
Robbins, Thomas
Shreve, Isaac
Smith, William
Trask, Enoch
Town, Elijah
Twist, William
Very, Robert
Very, William
Waring, James
Wellman, Samuel E.
Wellman, Stephen
White, Moses
Wilson, Nathaniel
Winchester, Bancroft

Capt. D. Davis' Company, Lieut. Col. J. White's Regiment.

From Sept. 19 to Oct. 10, 1814. Service at Salem. This service was for military instruction only, from 2 to 10 days.

Rank and Name.
David Davis, Captain
David Safford, Lieutenant
Benjamin Hawes, Ensign

Stephen Haws, Sergeant
Isaac Shreve, Sergeant
Elijah Towne, Sergeant
Woodbury Page, Sergeant
John Batchelder, Musician
Aaron Guilford, Musician
Moses Renney, Musician

Privates.
Allen, Otis
Annable, Benjamin
Bancroft, Stephen
Bancroft, Thomas
Brown, Saul
Burbank, Caleb
Clark, Charles C.
Davis, John
Dickerman, Caleb
Dole, Benjamin
Dole, William
Easty, Jeremiah
Farrington, Ebenezer
Foster, John
Gardner, John
Gillet, Marcus
Griffin, Dudly
Ham, Moses
Harrington, John
Harris, William
Hopkins, Daniel
Ingersoll, Sargent
McEntire, Samuel F.
Moulton, Bartholomew
Osborn, James
Palmer, George
Parks, Ebenezer
Phipps, Joseph
Pickering, Stephen
Pitman, Saul
Potter, Jesse
Potter, Nathaniel
Proctor, Benjamin
Proctor, Ebenezer
Proctor, George
Proctor, Willoughby
Richardson, Parker
Stone, Isaac
Trask, Enoch
Twist, William
Very, James
Very, William
Vicory, Robert
Walch, Abraham
Waring, James
Wellman, Oliver
Wellman, Samuel E.
Wellman, Stephen
White, Moses
Whittington, Francis
Wilson, Nathaniel

Capt. W. B. Dodge's Company, Lieut. Col. J. White's Regiment.

From Sept. 19 to Oct. 10, 1814. Service at Salem. This service was for military instruction only, from 4 to 10 days.

Rank and Name.
William B. Dodge, Captain
William Stearns, Jr., Lieutenant
Dudley Kimball, Ensign

David N. Prince, Sergeant
John Chipman, Sergeant
Samuel Randall, Sergeant
Charles Hill, Sergeant

Jonathan Berry, Musician
Aaron Wood, Musician

140 MASSACHUSETTS VOLUNTEER MILITIA IN THE WAR OF 1812.

Capt. W. B. Dodge's Company, Lieut. Col. J. White's Regiment — Concluded.

Privates.
Adams, Joseph
Adams, Saul
Allen, John
Berry, John
Berry, John, Jr.
Berry, Oliver
Berry, William
Bott, Linch
Carey, John
Carey, Joseph W.
Carey, Thomas
Chamberlin, Daniel
Cook, John M.
Cox, Joseph
Cushing, Caleb
Cushing, John
Davis, William
Fuller, Nathan
Gerry, Nathaniel

Hensler, George
Hodgkins, Thomas
Hutchingson, John
Joye, Joseph
Patch, Abraham
Peel, Josiah
Perkins, John
Pope, Jesper
Prince, William H.
Randall, William
Rodgers, Nathaniel
Saltmarsh, Seth
Skerry, John, Jr.
Smith, Joseph
Snelling, John
Swan, Aaron
Swan, Benjamin
Swan, John
Swan, Joseph
Swan, Nathaniel

Swan, Samuel
Swan, Thomas
Symonds, Ebenezer, Jr.
Symonds, Ephraim
Symonds, John, 3d
Symonds, Jonathan, Jr.
Symonds, Joseph
Symonds, Nathaniel
Symonds, Samuel
Symonds, Stephen
Symonds, Thomas
Symonds, Thorndike
Town, Elijah
Town, Samuel
Trumbull, W.
Tucker, Joseph
Ward, Stephen
Wiley, James
Wilkins, John G.

Capt. J. Edwards' Company, Lieut. Col. J. White's Regiment.
From Sept. 19 to Oct. 10, 1814. Service at Salem. This service was for military instruction only, from 2 to 10 days.

RANK AND NAME.
Joseph Edwards, Captain
Josiah Lord, Lieutenant
David Robbins, Ensign

Jabez Treadwell, Sergeant
David Lord, Sergeant
William Haslett, Sergeant
William Nichols, Sergeant
Sergent Ingalls, Musician
James Boardman, Musician

Privates.
Batchelder, Nathaniel
Bickford, Joshua
Blanchard, Samuel T.
Bright, William

Converse, Robert
Cook, James
Far, Samuel
Felt, Joseph
Fox, Ebenezer
George, Benjamin
Hall, Benjamin
Hall, Moses
Heard, Daniel
Hobson, Moses
Howard, Aaron
Johnson, Saul
Kimball, Jonathan C.
Kimball, Josiah
Larrabee, Samuel
Lord, Ammi
Lord, Philip

McEntire, Daniel
Morey, John
Neal, Jonathan
Neal, Joseph
Peabody, Webster
Pearson, Joseph
Pierce, George T.
Putman, William
Roberts, William
Russell, Valentine
Semond, Samuel
Spiller, Moses
Sticky, Richard
Turnbull, Nathaniel
Webber, Henry

Capt. T. R. Williams' Company, Lieut. Col. J. White's Regiment.
From Sept. 19 to Oct. 10, 1814. Service at Salem. This service was for military instruction only, from 2 to 10 days.

RANK AND NAME.
Thomas R. Williams, Captain
John Adams, Lieutenant
Jeremiah Goodhue, Ensign

John Quarles, Sergeant

Privates.
Abbott, Saul
Bott, Lynch
Botton, William
Burpee, Joseph
Chamberlin, Henry
Chandler, Benjamin
Cowell, Saul
Crispin, William

Crowninshield, Benjamin
Davenport, Thomas
Deland, Robert
Duncan, William
Fishley, Benjamin
Garrett, Joseph
Gavitt, Saul
Gray, John, 3d
Gray, Saul
Hart, Joseph
Henderson, Saul
Hodgdon, Saul
Hodges, Gamaliel
Knight, Aaron
Mansfield, Benjamin
Nichols, Henry

Nichols, William
Perkins, Thomas
Phippen, Abraham
Price, Ephraim
Rider, Joseph
Saul, Joseph
Sawyer, Nathaniel
Smith, Eliott
Southwick, John
Spiller, Job
Teague, John G.
Teague, Thomas
Teague, William
Trask, Joseph
Willis, Benjamin

Capt. P. Wells' Company, Lieut. Col. J. Russell's Regiment.

From Sept. 19 to Oct. 7, 1814. Service at Salem. Artillery Company, 4 to 10 days.

Rank and Name.		
Philip Wells, Captain	Carlton, Daniel	Manning, Richard
John Brooks, Lieutenant	Carter, Asa	Marks, John
Henry Whipple, Lieutenant	Cleveland, George	Merrill, Jonathan
	Cleverly, Saul	Moriarty, John
	Darlin, Michel C.	Moulton, David
Thomas Brown, Sergeant	Devereux, Humphrey	Nichols, George
Jacob Town, Sergeant	Edgerly, Peter	Noyes, Michel
Joseph D. Chandler, Sergeant	Emerson, Cyrus B.	Palfrey, Warwick
Saul Eveleth, Sergeant	Flint, Joseph	Palmer, Enoch
Jonathan M. Farnham, Corporal	Gardner, Benjamin	Perkins, Elisha
John C. Thayer, Corporal	Glidden, Joseph	Rand, Ebenezer
Aaron Osborne, Corporal	Goldthwait, Ezekiel	Seaver, Thomas
Ebenezer Himman, Corporal	Goldthwait, Luther	Town, Stephen
Benjamin Foster, Musician	Hale, John	Waldo, Jonathan
Luther Spaulding, Musician	Hardy, Temple	Webster, Peter E.
	Hildreth, Alvan	Wiggin, Asa
Privates.	Hunt, Benjamin B.	Wolcott, Calvin
Allen, David	Jones, John	
Bean, Jude	Knight, William	*Drivers.*
Berry, Jonathan	Lee, Andrew	Breed, Josiah
Brown, Saul	Lord, Joseph H.	Boynton, Joshua
		Moreland, James

Capt. S. P. Lewis' Company, under General Stanton, Jr.

Service 3½ days in August, 1812. There is doubt by the compiler of the correctness of the fact of this company having rendered any service in the War of 1812-14, for the reason that, though Simon P. Lewis, captain, Welcome Horsey, lieutenant, and Benjamin Congdon, ensign, are given as serving from Charlestown in Third Regiment, Third Brigade, under Gen. Joseph Stanton, Jr., none of these "officers" are found of record to have been in service or in any way connected with the Massachusetts Volunteer Militia previous to and subsequent to 1814.

Rank and Name.		
Simon P. Lewis, Captain	Browning, John	Crandall, John
Welcome Hersey or Horsey, Lieutenant	Browning, John (or Stephen)	Cross, Joseph
Benjamin Congdon, Ensign	Burdish, Lodowick	Cross, William
	Card, Achus	Green, Azel
Simeon Perry, Sergeant	Card, Jeffrey	Grinol, Wilson
Littlebridge Green, Sergeant	Card, Jelly	Lewis, Augustus I., Jr.
	Card, William	Moon, Robert
Privates.	Church, Charles	Noyes, Joshua
Babcock, Elisha	Clark, Christopher	Shingon, Elisha
Browning, Clark	Clark, Elias	Worden, Isaac
Browning, George	Clark, Gardner	
	Clark, Stephen	

MAINE.

Massachusetts Volunteer Militia in the War of 1812.

Division and Brigade Staff.

From Sept. 8 to Nov. 9, 1814. Service at Portland.

Division and Brigade Staff Officers.	Brigadier General and Staff.[1]	Band.
Alford Richardson, Major General, North Yarmouth Abel W. Atherton, Aid-de-camp, Portland Edward Russell, Aid-de-camp, North Yarmouth William B. Sewall, Judge Advocate, Portland Barnabas Bartol, Division Quartermaster, Freeport	James Irish, Jr., Brigadier-General, Gorham Francis Osgood, Brigade Major, Portland Nathaniel Thomes, Brigade Quartermaster, Gorham	Henry Knowlton, Band Master, Portland Samuel Clark, Deputy Band Master William Davis, Musician Mark Johnson, Musician Stephen Field, Musician Joseph Frye, Musician Thomas C. Wood, Musician

Capt. Jacob Auld's Company of Artillery.

From Aug. 1 to Nov. 1, 1814. In the service of United States at the forts and garrisons at Damariscotta, St. George, Edgecomb and Phipsburg.

Rank and Name.

Jacob Auld, Captain
David Hodgkins, Lieutenant
Jeremiah Holton, Lieutenant
John Robinson, Ensign

Daniel Newcomb, Sergeant
John Foye, Sergeant
Bela Packard, Sergeant
Daniel Oliver, Sergeant
Joseph Adams, Sergeant
John Fullerton, Corporal
Samuel Houston, Corporal
Daniel Sandford, Corporal
Jacob Sidelinger, Corporal
William Suller, Corporal
Thomas McIntire, Musician
William Marshall, Musician

Privates.

Bailey, John
Barlow, Samuel
Bean, Isaac
Blackwell, Alfred
Boldin, Sargent
Boyd, James
Bradford, Charles
Brice, William, 3d
Brown, John, 3d
Brown, William
Caine, John
Campbell, James
Chappels, James
Coombs, Samuel
Dalton, Jesse
Dogett, Frederick
Dow, Thomas
Erskine, George
Erskine, John
Farnham, Ebenezer
Farnham, Samuel
Fitch, Timothy
Gould, Edward
Guy, Jesse
Hall, John
Hall, William
Hariden, Andrew
Hurd, Moses
Hustin, Josiah
Jones, John
Jones, Shadrack
Kelloch, Benjamin
Kelly, Isaac
Knight, John A.
Light, James
Little, Jacob T.
Little, Samuel
Little, William M.
McFarland, John
McFarland, John, 2d
McKenney, George
Montgomery, Nathaniel
Moses, Timothy, Jr.
Mossman, Aaron
Noyce, Enoch
Oliver, Jacob
Overlock, Godfrey
Poland, John
Reed, Henry
Richards, Daniel
Roak, Daniel
Roe, Rufus
Rogers, Enoch
Royal, Jacob
Sheldon, Nathaniel W.
Spear, Mark
Spear, William
Stahl, Jacob
Stebbins, Thomas
Stephens, Samuel
Stoddard, Jacob T.
Suckforth, Philip
Tibbets, Giles
Tilson, Gilbert
Tool, Andrew
Trask, William
Trask, William, 2d
Tyler, Timothy
Varnum, William
Vining, Daniel
Walker, George
Warren, Phineas
Watson, James
Weeks, David S.
Welch, Lawrence
Wire, James
Worthing, Benjamin
Wylie, Alex

Maj. A. Blossom's Battalion of Artillery.

From Sept. 12 to Sept. 24, 1814.

Field and Staff.

Alden Blossom, Major, Turner
Hiram Bradford, Adjutant, Turner
James Perry, Quartermaster, Paris

---

[1] September 7 to September 20.

Capt. J. Bemis' Company, Major Blossom's Battalion of Artillery.

From Sept. 12 to Sept. 24, 1814. Raised at Paris. Service at Portland.

RANK AND NAME.	Privates.	
Jonathan Bemis, Captain	Barrows, Asa	Fuller, Isaiah
	Bemis, Francis	Hall, Cyprian
David Bemis, Sergeant	Besse, Anthony	Jackson, Jacob
Amos Armsby, Sergeant	Bird, John	Jackson, Lemuel
Jonathan Bemis, Sergeant	Bird, John, 2d	Jackson, Sylvanus
James Bemis, Sergeant	Bullen, Daniel	Morse, Seth
Benjamin Jackson, Corporal	Bullen, John R.	Pratt, Jedediah
Frederic N. Hall, Corporal	Churchill, Sprague	Pray, Abraham
Benjamin Hammon, Corporal	Cushman, Ebenezer	Rawson, Emor
Isaiah Willis, Corporal	Daniels, James	Rawson, Nathaniel W.
Joseph Jackson, Musician	Daniels, Joseph	Shaw, Solomon
Moses Hammon, Musician	Deane, Asa	Stevens, Benjamin
	Durell, Peter	Stout, Peter B.
	Durell, William	Stout, Peter B., 2d
	Field, Ansel	Woodbury, John

Maj. J. Chandler's Battalion of Artillery.

From Sept. 14 to Sept. 24, 1814. Awaiting orders at Hallowell. Stationed at Vassalborough.

FIELD AND STAFF.
Joseph Chandler, Major, Monmouth
Jonathan G. Huntoon, Adjutant, Readfield
John S. Kimball, Quartermaster, Augusta

Capt. S. G. Ladd's Company, Major Chandler's Battalion of Artillery.

From Sept. 12 to Sept. 24, 1814. Raised at Hallowell. Service at Wiscasset.

RANK AND NAME.	Branscomb, James	Lakeman, Thomas, Jr.
Samuel G. Ladd, Captain	Clark, Joel	McCausland, Charles
Jedediah Lakeman, Lieutenant	Cottrill, John	McCausland, Jeremiah
Joseph S. Smith, Lieutenant	Couch, George	Norcross, Thomas
	Crane, John, 2d	Norris, Jonathan C.
Abraham Thurle, Sergeant	Cross, William	Nye, Charles
Samuel Tenney, Sergeant	Dana, Thomas	Pollard, George
Daniel Norcross, Sergeant	Dennis, Thomas	Pray, Jonathan
David Stickney, Sergeant	Devenport, Nathaniel	Rallings, John W.
Ezekiel Goodall, Corporal	Dummer, Joseph O.	Read, John
Richard Dana, Corporal	Fowl or Towl, Robert L.	Robinson, Asa
William Livermore, Jr., Corporal	Freeman, Ebenezer	Sewall, Moses
Cromwell Aldrich, Corporal	French, Edmund	Shaw, George
John Woods, Musician	Gardiner, John	Smith, Henry
Levi Johnson, Musician	Goodwin, John	Stickney, Amos
Aaron Bickford, Musician	Greeley, Eben B.	Stickney, Benjamin, Jr.
Harvey Porter, Musician	Haskins, Samuel	Stickney, Paul
John Dennet, Musician	Hinkley, Benjamin	Sweet, Samuel, Jr.
	Hinkley, Holmes	Talpy, Oliver
Privates.	Hodges, Benjamin	Trask, James
Alexander, Joseph	Kent, Frederick A.	Woodbury, William A.
Bardotte, Joseph	Kimball, Cook	Wyman, Jacob

MASSACHUSETTS VOLUNTEER MILITIA IN THE WAR OF 1812. 147

Capt. S. Ranlett's Company, Major Chandler's Battalion of Artillery.
From Sept. 14 to Sept. 23, 1814. Raised at Monmouth. Service at Wiscassett, awaiting orders.

Rank and Name.	Privates.	
Samuel Ranlett, Captain	Allen, Eliab	Hamm, Robert
Dudley Moody, Lieutenant	Allen, Luther	Kimball, Heber
Eleazer Smith, Lieutenant	Andrews, Arthur	King, Bernard
	Beal, David	Ladd, Paul
Ebenezer Freeman, Sergeant	Billington, Isaac	Marshall, John
Jacob Miller, Jr., Sergeant	Bingham, Preston	Morse, Aaron
Joseph Kelly, Sergeant	Butler, Samuel	Noyes, Samuel
James Fairbanks, Sergeant	Fairbanks, Dennis	Prescott, Newell
Asa Robbins, Jr., Corporal	Fairbanks, Enos	Prescott, Stephen
Jason Prescott, Corporal	Fairbanks, Jesse	Robbins, Cyrus
Phineas Killy, Corporal	Fairbanks, John	Smith, Clark
Marcus Gilbert, Corporal	Fogg, Peleg B.	Welch, Otis
Levi Gilbert, Musician	Foster, Freeman	Whittier, Nathaniel
Benjamin Berry, Musician	Fowle or Towle, Benjamin, Jr.	

Capt. S. Randlett's Company of Artillery, detached from Maj. J. Chandler's Battalion and attached to Lieut. Col. E. Sherwin's Regiment.
From Sept. 24 to Nov. 8, 1814. Raised at Monmouth and vicinity. Service at Wiscassett and vicinity.

Rank and Name.	Privates.	
Samuel Randlett, Captain	Adams, Solomon	Foster, Freeman
Dudley Moody, Lieutenant	Allen, Eliab	Gould, Nathaniel W.
Henry Butterfield, Lieutenant	Allen, Luther	Green, Guy
Eleazer Smith, Lieutenant	Andrews, Arthur	Kimball, Heber
	Bartlett, Edward	King, Bernard
Ebenezer Freeman, Sergeant	Bartlett, Flavel	Ladd, Paul
Jacob Miller, Sergeant	Beal, David	Maxwell, James B.
Joseph Kelley, Sergeant	Billington, Isaac	Mercy, Leonard, Jr.
James Fairbanks, Sergeant	Bingham, Parsons	Morse, Aaron
William Talcott, Sergeant	Blake, Nathaniel	Morton, Ephraim, Jr.
Benjamin Butler, Sergeant	Butler, Moses	Morton, George
Asa Robbins, Corporal	Butler, Moses S., 2d	Morton, Zebulon
Jason Prescott, Corporal	Butler, Samuel	Noyes, Samuel
Phineas Kelley, Corporal	Butler, William	Pinkham, Nathan
Marcus Gilbert, Corporal	Butterfield, Joseph	Prescott, Newell
Levi Gilbert, Musician	Chandler, Moses	Prescott, Stephen
Benjamin Berry, Musician	Clark, Smith	Smith, Samuel
Peleg B. Fogg, Musician	Corey, Daniel	Spooner, Benjamin
Jesse Fairbanks, Musician	Dodge, John	Spooner, Shubal
John Marshall, Musician	Fairbanks, Dennis	Towl, Benjamin, Jr.
	Fairbanks, Enos	Wethern, Benjamin
	Fairbanks, John	Whittier, Nathaniel
		Winslow, Nicholas

Maj. D. Holden's Battalion of Artillery.
From June 20 to June 22, and Sept. 10 to Sept. 29, 1814. Service at Bath.

Field and Staff.	Noncommissioned Staff.	Waiters.
Daniel Holden, Major, Topsham	Daniel Foster, Quartermaster Sergeant	Mimey, Peter
Seth Trufant, Adjutant, Bath		Loring, David R.
Irvin C. Loring, Quartermaster, Bath		Casdiff, William

Capt. P. O. Alden's Company, Maj. D. Holden's Battalion of Artillery.

From June 20 to June 22, and Sept. 10 to Sept. 29, 1814. Raised at Brunswick. Service at Bath.

RANK AND NAME.
Peter O. Alden, Captain
Robert Eastman, Lieutenant
Thomas Pennell, Lieutenant
Harvey Stutson, Lieutenant

Edward Welch, Sergeant
Johnson Dunham, Sergeant
Charles Stutson, Sergeant
George Hedge, Musician

Privates.
Carey, James, Jr.
Cumings, Samuel S.
Danforth, Isaac

Dunlap, Joseph
Gray, Uriah (D.)
Gwin, William, Jr.
Hall, Robert
Hunt, Jeremiah
Hunt, John
Kimball, Dean
Kincaid, Patrick
Littlefield, Moses
Lunt, John
Merrill, James
Morse, Ephraim
Morse, Lemuel
Murry, Trueworthy
Nelson, James

Osgood, Eliphalet
Owen, John, 2d
Owen, Philip, Jr.
Potter, William S.
Powers, Paul
Pray, Edmund
Simpson, Thomas
Stanwood, Thomas
Todd, John
Toothaker, Charles
Toothaker, William
Welch, Reid
Wilmot, Orlando
Wing, Allen

Capt. N. Sprague's Company of Artillery, Maj. D. Holden's Battalion.

From June 20 to June 22, and Sept. 10 to Sept. 29, 1814. Raised at Bath. Service at Bath.

RANK AND NAME.
Nathaniel Sprague, Captain
Samuel Noble, Lieutenant

Edward H. Page, Sergeant
Philip Owen, Sergeant
Dunham or Durham Witham, Sergeant
Samuel Hodgkins, Sergeant
David Dexter, Corporal
William Stinson, Corporal
William Winslow, Musician

Privates.
Averill, Daniel I.
Bennett, William L.
Brown, Consider
Brown, Nathaniel

Cleavis, William P.
Coller, David
Davis, John
Dexter, David
Fassett, John
Foster, James
Getchell, Peter
Hinkley, Matthew
Hodgkins, Samuel B.
Huff, Samuel
Hutchins, William
Littlefield, Joseph
McGill, Benjamin
McKenney, Brooks
Mitchell, Eliphalet
Mitchell, Joseph
Morrison, Nathaniel

Morrison, Richard
Osgood, Jonathan
Osgood, Samuel
Owens, Benjamin
Pettingill, David
Pettingill, Summers
Robinson, Bryant
Sprague, Peleg
Stinson, Samuel
Stinson, William
Turner, Fobes
Wakefield, James
Weeks, William
Whittemore, Gamaliel
Whittemore, William D.
Witham, Samuel
Woodward, Cyra

Capt. N. Walker's Company, Maj. D. Holden's Battalion of Artillery.

From June 20 to June 22, and Sept. 10 to Sept. 29, 1814. Raised at Topsham. Service at Bath.

RANK AND NAME.
Nathaniel Walker, Captain
James Cook, Lieutenant
Nahum Perkins, Lieutenant

Samuel Perkins, Sergeant
John Wentworth, Sergeant
Moses Plummer, Corporal
Abner Haley, Musician

Privates.
Alexander, David
Baker, Jonathan
Brown, Robert

Crosby, Ebenezer
Dennett, William
Gray, Solomon
Green, Gardner
Haley, James
Hanes or Harris, Reuben
Harding, Richard C.
Hinkley, Ezekiel
Hunneford, William
Jack, John
Plummer, Lemuel D.
Plummer, Nathaniel
Rollings, Aaron
Thomas, Consider

Thomas, George
Townes, Samuel
Tuttle, Josiah
Wager, William
Weymouth, Moses

Hostlers.
Hinkley, James
Holbrook, Jesse
Wilson, John, 4th

Waiters.
Cook, Lincoln
Stone, Alfred

MASSACHUSETTS VOLUNTEER MILITIA IN THE WAR OF 1812. 149

Capt. C. Barnes' Company, Lieut. Col. M. Nichols' Regiment.
From Sept. 7 to Sept. 19, and Sept. 28 to Oct. 27, 1814. Raised at Portland. Service at Portland. Portland Artillery Company.

RANK AND NAME.
Cornelius Barnes, Captain
Amos S. Webber, Lieutenant
George Hill, Ensign

David Brown, Sergeant
Aaron Stamford, Sergeant
James Crocker, Sergeant
Ephraim Wilbour, Sergeant
Samuel Chase, Sergeant
John Green, Jr., Corporal
Richard Mason, Corporal

John Baker, Corporal
Joshua F. Weeks, Corporal
Benjamin Green, Corporal

Privates.
Baker, John
Barter, Benjamin A.
Bridges, John
Field, John
Foye, Henry
Hall, Ebenezer
Merrill, Jonathan

Poole, Abijah, Jr.
Powell, John
Rolfe, Benjamin
Sutton, Richard
Todd, Samuel
Tucker, David

Waiters.
Haskins, William
Johnson, Thomas
Whipple, Jonathan

Capt. P. Varnum's Company, Lieut. Col. M. Nichols' Regiment.
From Sept. 7 to Sept. 19, and Sept. 28 to Oct. 27, 1814. Service at Portland. Portland Artillery, organized June 17, 1812.

RANK AND NAME.
Phineas Varnum, Captain
Nathan Babcock, Lieutenant

John Leach, Sergeant
Eliphalet Farrington, Sergeant
Carrol Staples, Sergeant
John Corry, Sergeant
William Parker, Sergeant

Hugh Stanly, Corporal
William Parker, Corporal

Privates.
Bailey, Joseph
Carlton, Charles C.
Coolbroth, Edward
Davis, Saul
Davis, William

Dyer, Sylvanus
Farwell, Absalom
Green, Daniel
Little, Stephen
Roberts, Reuben
Tukey, Daniel
Tukey, David
Webster, Benjamin
Young, John

Capt. J. Howard's Company, under Maj. Simon Nowell.
From Oct. 8 to Nov. 19, 1814. Service at Kittery and York. Drafted company of artillery.

RANK AND NAME.
Josephus Howard, Captain
Seth S. Fairfield, Lieutenant
Nathan Merrill, Lieutenant

John Thompson, Sergeant
Jacob Ayer, Sergeant
Benjamin W. Hall, Sergeant
William Tarbox, Sergeant
George Southerlin, Corporal
Nehemiah Butler, Corporal
Timothy Donnell, Corporal
Charles Snowman, Musician
Jonathan Pollard, Musician
Woodman Beal, Musician

Privates.
Adams, John
Babb, Samuel
Bradbury, Ezra
Davis, Edward

Discom, Thomas
Drew, Aaron
Drew, Asa
Dyer, Abijah
Edgcomb, Thomas
Emery, William
Fall, Ebenezer
Farnham, Moses
Floyd, Samuel
Goodwin, Edmund
Goodwin, Simeon
Gowin, Nathan
Grant, William
Guilford, Benjamin
Haley, Abraham
Hazeltine, Samuel
Howard, Samuel B.
Hubbard, Joseph
Huzzy, John
Kimball, Daniel
Kimball, John

Lang, John
Linscot, Elisha
Low, Besulah
March, John S.
Mason, Stephen
Mills, Elligood
Parsons, Samuel
Preble, John
Roberts, Samuel
Rumery, Edward
Sandburn, Jonathan V.
Smith, Aaron
Smith, Nathan
Thompson, John
Trafton, George
Walker, Dependence
Warren, William
Welch, Jonathan
Young, Hezekiah

MASSACHUSETTS VOLUNTEER MILITIA IN THE WAR OF 1812.

Capt. J. Bemis' (Artillery) Company, Lieut. Col. W. Ryerson's Regiment.
From Sept. 25 to Nov. 7, 1814.   Raised at Paris and vicinity.   Service at Portland.

RANK AND NAME.
Jonathan Bemis, Captain
Samuel Rawson, Lieutenant
Ebenezer Fessenam, Lieutenant

James Bemis, Sergeant
Jonathan Bemis, Jr., Sergeant
James Hutchinson, Sergeant
Frederic N. Hall, Sergeant
Abraham Pray, Corporal
Peter Droell or Dwell, Corporal
Anthony Besse, Corporal
John R. Bullen, Corporal
James Jackson, Musician
Jacob Emerson, Musician

Privates.
Abbott, Abel B.
Abbott, Stephen
Anderson, Timothy
Ayer, Asa
Barrows, Asa

Bemis, Francis
Bracket, Peter
Bragdon, Daniel
Brown, Jonas A.
Bucknell, Andrew R.
Bullen, Daniel
Churchill, Sprague
Davis, Isaac
Dennet, John
Dovell or Dwell, William
Elder, William
Evans, Jacob
Fessenden, William
Field, Ansel
Frye, Frederic
Gamage, Joshua
Gordan, John
Greenleaf, William
Grover, Josiah
Grover, William
Hall, Ephraim
Heath, John W.

Hersey, Moses
Hodgkins, Chipman
Jackson, Jacob
Jordan, Elijah
Morse, Seth
Osgood, Isaac
Osgood, James
Page, John
Pratt, Jedediah
Rawson, Nathaniel W.
Shaw, Solomon
Shirley, Jonathan
Spencer, William
Sterling, John
Stevens, John
Thompson, Samuel
Townsend, Thayer
Tufts, Simeon
Ward, Jonathan
Whitham, Benjamin

Capt. L. Richmond's (Artillery) Company, Lieut. Col. W. Ryerson's Regiment.
From Sept. 25 to Nov. 7, 1814.   Raised at Turner and vicinity.   Service at Portland.

RANK AND NAME.
Leonard Richmond, Captain
Henry Jones, Lieutenant
Hezekiah Bryant, Lieutenant

Dura Bradford, Sergeant
Israel Lasell, Sergeant
Nathaniel Brackett, Sergeant
Charles Staples, Sergeant
Benjamin Conant, Corporal
Ira Jones, Corporal
Caleb Snell, Corporal
Burt Townsend, Corporal
Galen Jones, Musician
Alfred Jones, Musician
Amos Shaw, Musician

Privates.
Allen, Isaac, 1st
Allen, Isaac, 2d

Allen, John
Batten, John
Bean, Thomas
Berry, Mial
Berry, Thomas
Bradford, Ethelbert
Brett, Simeon
Burgen, Isaac
Caswell, William
Chamberlin, Philip
Delano, Seth, Jr.
Dillingham, Cornelius
Dow, Joseph
Fairbanks, Joel
French, Henry
Gibson, Samuel
Harlton, Ebenezer
Harris, John
Harvey, Stephen
Hood, Billings

Hood, Otis
Janes, Libbeus
Johnson, Asa
Jones, Barnum
Leavit, Albert
Lumber, William
Merrill, Calvin
Poor, William
Sheafe, William
Sweat, John
Thayer, Abner
Thurlow, Robert
Townsend, Solomon
Tyler, Saul
Warren, Isaiah
Webster, Josiah
Whitman, Samuel

Maj. J. Steele's Battalion of Artillery.
From June 13 to June 24, 1814 (3 days' travel).   Service at Portland.

FIELD AND STAFF.
James Steele, Major, Brownfield
Josiah Heald, Adjutant, Lovell
William or Richard Russell, Quartermaster, Fryeburg

Moses Chandler, Surgeon, Fryeburg
Samuel S. Hadley, Surgeon's Mate, Brownfield

Peter Walker, Quartermaster Sergeant

MASSACHUSETTS VOLUNTEER MILITIA IN THE WAR OF 1812.   151

Capt. P. Eastman's Company of Artillery, attached to Major Steele's Battalion.
From Sept. 11 to Sept. 24, 1814. Raised at Fryeburg. Service at Portland.

RANK AND NAME.
Philip Eastman, Captain
Ebenezer Fessendon, Lieutenant
John Evans, Lieutenant

Abiel Farnham, Sergeant
Isaac Frye, Sergeant
Noyes Knight, Sergeant
William Shirley, Sergeant
Thomas Davy, Corporal
Abel Gibson, Corporal
James Atwood, Corporal
Thomas Farrington, Corporal
John Page, Musician
Jacob Emerson, Musician

Privates.
Abbot, Stephen
Brooks, George
Brown, Jonas A.
Carter, Samuel F.
Chase, Enoch
Colby, Robert
Evans, Jacob
Farrington, Jacob
Fessenden, Jonathan
Fessenden, William
Frye, William
Hardy, Jonathan
Hardy, Stephen G.
Haseltine, Ebenezer
Hatch, John

Head, Asa
Heath, John W.
Howe, Seneca
Hutchins, John
Knight, John
Lassell, Israel
McIntire, Ebenezer
Osgood, Isaac
Osgood, James
Richardson, Philip
Shirley, Jonathan
Stirling, John, Jr.
Walker, Benjamin
Ward, Jonathan
Warren, Isaiah

Capt. Stephen Barry's Company, Maj. James Steele's Battalion of Artillery.
From Sept. 13 to Sept. 24, 1814. Raised at Denmark. Service at Portland.

RANK AND NAME.
Stephen Barry, Captain
William Davis, Lieutenant
Aaron Ingalls, Ensign

William Pengrea, Sergeant
Daniel Hill, Sergeant
Daniel How, Sergeant
George Murphy, Sergeant
James Warren, Corporal
David Porter, Corporal
John Ames, Corporal
Moses Peary, Corporal
Stephen Peary, Musician
Jacob Frost, Musician

Privates.
Abbot, Joel
Alexander, Jeduthan
Allen, William
Berry, Henry
Berry, William
Blake, Edward
Blanchard, Farwell
Boston, John
Brigham, Samuel

Colcord, David
Deering, James
Emerson, George W.
Flint, Nathaniel
Fox, Nathaniel
Gilman, John
Goodwin, Joseph
Gray, Daniel
Green, William
Hall, Perley
Hamden, Benjamin
Hamden, Ebenezer
Head, Nathaniel
Hill, William
Hilton, Daniel
Hilton, Nathan
Hilton, Nathaniel
Jewett, Daniel
Jewett, Ephraim
Jewett, William
Johnson, Asa
Johnson, John
Jordan, James H.
Kinison, David B.
Kinison, John, Jr.
Lord, James

Lord, Job
Matthews, Thomas
Patrick, Benjamin
Pease, Mark
Pike, Job K.
Pike, Samuel
Pingree, Parker
Porter, Asael
Powers, Calvin
Richardson, Amos
Richardson, George
Roberts, John
Sanderson, Stephen
Smith, Joseph
Smith, Theophilus
Snow, James
Symonds, Jesse
Trull, Micah
Trumbull, J.
Trumbull, Samuel
Walker, Robert
Warren, Caleb
Whiden, David
Whiden, John
Whitman, Eli
Wilson, Joseph

Capt. J. Charles' Company, Maj. James Steele's Battalion of Artillery.
From Sept. 13 to Sept. 24, 1814. Raised at Fryeburg. Service at Portland.

RANK AND NAME.
James Charles, Captain
Joseph Colby, Lieutenant
Benjamin Woodman, Ensign

Nathaniel G. Jewett, Sergeant
Jeremiah Bradley, Sergeant
Isaac Charles, Sergeant
Hull Chase, Sergeant

Jeremiah Chandley, Sergeant
Nehemiah C. Dresser, Sergeant
Benjamin Wylie, Corporal
Seth S. Chase, Corporal
Moses Abbott, Corporal
John Stevens, Corporal
William Stevens, Corporal

Privates.
Abbot, Asa
Abbot, Isaac
Abbot, Micah
Abbot, Silas
Bemis, Amos
Bradley, David
Burgen, Isaac
Chandler, Isaac

Capt. J. Charles' Company, Maj. James Steele's Battalion of Artillery — Concluded.

Privates — Concluded.

Chandler, John	Fox, Ephraim	Marden, John
Chandler, Nathan	Frye, Frederic	Mason, John
Charles, John, Jr.	Gamage, John	Richardson, Joshua
Charles, Simeon	Gamage, Joshua, Jr.	Richardson, Luther
Charles, Timothy	Gordon, Henry, Jr.	Stacy, Jordan
Coombs, David	Gordon, John, Jr.	Stacy, Oliver
Dresser, Job	Gordon, Joseph	Stearns, John S.
Dutch, Samuel	Hapgood, William	Stevens, Joseph
Eaton, William	Hill, Amos	Smith, Asa
Evans, Jonathan	Hill, Daniel	Thompson, William
Farrington, Jonathan	Hitchins, Ichabod	Tibbitts, Samuel
Farrington, Philip	Huntress, Samuel D.	Walker, John, Jr.
Farrington, Samuel	Irish, Stephen	Warren, Nathaniel
Farrington, Stephen	Johnson, Andrew	Whiting, Oliver, Jr.
Fifield, Benjamin	Johnson, James	Wiley, America
Fifield, Jonathan F.	Knight, Eliphalet	Wiley, John
	Lewis, Jesse	

Capt. A. Mansfield's Company, Maj. James Steele's Battalion of Artillery.

From Sept. 13 to Sept. 24, 1814. Raised at Brownfield. Service at Portland.

RANK AND NAME.

Asa Mansfield, Captain	Boynton, William	Kimball, William
Eber Rice, Lieutenant	Bradbury, Elijah	Linsey, Ephraim
	Bragdon, Daniel	Littlefield, Peletiah
	Brickett, Jonathan	McAllister, Isaac
Amos Poor, Sergeant	Bridges, Josiah	McAllister, John
Moses Merrill, Sergeant	Broad, Amos	McOldpine, Moses
Robert H. Miller, Sergeant	Butters, Timothy S.	Merrill, Isaiah
Isaac Spring, Musician	Chamberlain, John	Merrill, John
Page Knox, Musician	Colby, Jacob	Parker, Joseph
Joseph Kilgore, Musician	Day, Jabez	Patterson, Robert
Joseph Kimball, Musician	Day, Samuel	Poor, William
	Dresser, Frederic	Ricker, Ichabod
Privates.	Dresser, Jonathan	Rounds, Stephen
Andrews, Amos	Dresser, Levi	Sands, Thomas
Andrews, Isacher	Dresser, Stephen, Jr.	Sands, William
Andrews, Jacob	Eastman, James	Small, Samuel
Banford, Jeremiah	Eastman, Joseph	Snow, Joseph
Bartlett, J. W.	Eastman, Solomon	Snow, Silas
Bean, Nathan	Eaton, Simeon	Sterns, Benjamin
Bean, Nathaniel	Edgcomb, Walter	Tyler, Samuel
Bean, Samuel, 2d	Gibson, Samuel	Waite, Abraham
Bean, Saul	Goodnow, William	Walker, Ebenezer
Bean, Thomas, Jr.	Hazelton, Saul	Webster, Josiah
Bemis, Thaddeus, Jr.	Heald, Samuel	Wentworth, Samuel
Berry, Levi	Hill, Nathaniel	Whiting, James
Blake, John	Hubbard, Warwick	Whitney, Ephraim
Blake, William	Hutchins, Moses, Jr.	

Capt. A. Spring's Company, Maj. James Steele's Battalion of Artillery.

From Sept. 13 to Sept. 24, 1814. Raised at Hiram. Service at Portland.

RANK AND NAME.

Alpheus Spring, Captain	Benjamin Bucknell, Corporal	Boston, William
Asa Burbank, Lieutenant	Daniel Cram, Corporal	Bothwell, James
	Asa Osgood, Jr., Corporal	Brooks, William
	J. Storer, Musician	Bucknell, Andrew B.
Thomas G. Watson, Sergeant	James McLucas, Musician	Burbank, Israel, Jr.
John W. Chadbourn, Sergeant		Chadbourn, Humphrey A.
Ephraim Kimball, Sergeant	*Privates.*	Chase, Gideon
John Bucknell, Sergeant	Allen, Joseph	Clark, Jacob
Josiah Maybery, Corporal	Bickford, William	Coolrath, James

MASSACHUSETTS VOLUNTEER MILITIA IN THE WAR OF 1812. 153

Capt. A. Spring's Company, Maj. James Steele's Battalion of Artillery — Concluded.

Privates — Concluded..
Cotton, William
Cram, John
Cross, Aaron
Davis, Ephraim
Durgin, John
Durgin, Joseph
Eastman, John
Fillbrock, Jonathan
Fillbrock, Simon
Floyd, Michael
Fox, John, Jr.
Fox, Jonathan
French, Benjamin
French, Jacob
Gray, Abraham
Gray, Joseph
Harford, Solomon
Hayes, John

Howard, Henry
Jack, James
Lewis, Edward
Lewis, Morgan
Lewis, Noah
Libby, Elisha
Libby, Hanson
Libby, John
Libby, Stephen, Jr.
Libby, Thomas
Libby, Tobias
Lord, Jacob
Lord, Levi
Lowell, Moses
Lowell, Reuben
Lowell, Thomas
McKissick, Aaron
McKissick, Moses
Merryfield, Richard

Moulton, John
Nutter, Charles
Pearl, Dimon
Pierce, Benjamin I.
Pierce, John, Jr.
Pierce, Josiah
Richardson, Aaron
Robbins, Joshua
Stanley, Elisha
Storer, John
Thompson, Caleb
Tibbets, Ephraim
Trafton, Jeremiah
Truett, George
Vainey, Andrew
Wadsworth, Peleg, Jr.
Wadsworth, Peleg, 3d

Capt. D. Bang's Company of Artillery, under Command of General Sewall, awaiting Orders.

From Sept. 13 to Sept. 23, 1814. Raised at Vassalborough. Service at Augusta.

RANK AND NAME.
Dean Bangs, Captain
Lemuel Pullen, Lieutenant
Abraham Smith, Lieutenant

Jabez Dow, Sergeant
Artemas Smith, Sergeant
William McFarland, Sergeant
William Marston, Sergeant
Alexander McKechnie, Corporal
Abiel Moore, Corporal
James Bragg, Corporal

Henry Richardson, Corporal
Bernard Sturdevant, Musician
William Bates, Musician

Privates.
Blackwell, Dennis
Blackwell, Eli
Blish, William
Bradford, Andrew
Bradford, Martin
Freeman, Charles
Gulliver, Joseph

Hastings, Samuel
Jackson, Godfrey
Marston, Joseph
Morrill, Josiah
Page, Newell
Rines, Benjamin
Shorey, James
Smiley, Joseph
Smith, Jeremiah
Tozier, Jeremiah, 3d
Tozier, Jonathan E.
Trask, Alvin

Capt. W. Haskell's Company of Artillery, under Maj. Lemuel Weeks, under Supervision of United States Officers.

From Aug. 5 to Nov. 5, 1814. Raised at New Gloucester. Service at forts in Portland harbor.

RANK AND NAME.
William Haskell, Captain
Samuel Emery, Lieutenant
Oliver Bray, Lieutenant

John Lowell, Sergeant
Charles Rogers, Sergeant
Loammi Cushing, Sergeant
Samuel Simmons, Corporal
Moses Stinchfield, Corporal
Bela Hammond, Corporal
Joseph Yetten, Musician
Levi Leighton, Musician

Privates.
Ames, John
Ardeton, Nathaniel B.
Bartol, Ammi
Beals, Jarvis
Blair, Robert

Bond, John
Briggs, Thomas
Burns, William
Card, William
Carter, Nathan
Choate, Josiah
Cobb, George
Cobb, Joseph
Coffin, Tristram
Elliott, Josiah
Erskine, Asa
Erskine, George
Fannin, Daniel
Foss, Samuel
Gilman, John
Haley, James
Hammond, Jacob
Haskell, Nathan
Knight, Thomas
Knight, Winslow

Lamb, Seth
Leighton, Reuben
Libbey, Theophilus
Lincoln, John M.
Lowell, John P.
March, Samuel
McLelland, Joseph
Meguire, Nathaniel
Mitchell, John
Mitchell, Nathaniel
Mitchell, Samuel
Morris, John
Nichols, William
Noice, Joseph C.
Norwood, Joshua
Parker, Caleb E.
Penny, Ephraim
Pierce, Samuel
Pike, John
Pride, Henry

Capt. W. Haskell's Company of Artillery, under Maj. Lemuel Weeks, under Supervision of United States Officers — Concluded.

Privates — Concluded.
Prince, John
Riggs, Jeremiah
Riggs, Stephen
Rogers, John, Jr.
Smith, Joseph

Smith, William
Tobey, Lemuel
Tobey, William
Townsend, Jacob
Wait, Edward
Wait, Solomon

White, Job
Wilson, George
Woodman, Joshua
Wyer, Peter
Wyman, John
Young, Anson

Capt. I. Leighton's Company of Artillery, under Major Weeks.
From Sept. 9 to Sept. 17, 1814. Raised at Falmouth. Service at Portland.

RANK AND NAME.
Isaac Leighton, Captain
Isaac Mason, Lieutenant

Thomas Hodsdon, Sergeant
Nathan Morrell, Sergeant
William Knight, Sergeant
Peter M. Knight, Sergeant
Joseph Quimby, Corporal

David Barbour, Corporal
John Batchelder, Corporal
Robert Huston, Corporal
Thaddeus Leighton, Musician
Edward Leighton, Musician

Privates.
Baker, Elijah
Cobb, Enoch

Cobb, Isaac
Elder, William
Knight, Alexander
Knight, Richard
Knight, Stephen
Lord, William G.
Morse, Nathaniel, 2d

Muster Roll of Lieut. S. S. Fairfield's Company, Lieut. Col. J. Spring's Regiment.
From June 20 to June 30, 1814. Raised at Saco. Service at Saco. Saco Artillery Company.

RANK AND NAME.
Seth S. Fairfield, Lieutenant
George Thacher, Jr., Ensign

William Waterhouse, Sergeant
Joseph Hammond, Sergeant
Joseph H. Randall, Sergeant
James Wood, Musician
Edwin Lapsell, Musician

Privates.
Bangs, Ezekiel
Benson, William
Bright or Knight, Coleman W.
Davis, George

Davis, Israel
Durgin, Benjamin
Elwell, Jabez
Gillpatrick, Jacob
Harmon, John
Hill, Josiah, Jr.
Justin, Phineas W., Jr.
Kenny, Edward
Kidlon or Ridlon, Charles
Kimball, Daniel
Kindricks, Seth
Knight, John
Marshall, Isaac
McKunnison, Lemuel
Patten, Nathaniel

Patterson, William
Pearster, William
Perkins, Noah
Rounds, Mark
Runnels, Isaac
Sawyer, Tristram
Scammon, Samuel
Shehan, Benjamin
Smith, Thomas, Jr.
Tibbets, Eli
Tibbetts, Timothy
Timpson, George
Tornning, Thomas
Wentworth, Daniel
Young, Lewis

Lieut. S. S. Fairfield's Detachment.
From June 30 to July 30, 1814. Raised at Saco. Service at Saco. Saco Artillery.

RANK AND NAME.
Seth S. Fairfield, Lieutenant

Michael Plummer, Sergeant
Nathaniel Patten, Musician
Marshall Maxwell, Musician

Privates.
Andrews, Isaac
Bragdon, Simeon

Dow, Abram
Dyer, James
Goodwin, Edmond
Grant, Benjamin
Hally, James
Hierl, John
Kimball, Caleb
Lord, Samuel
Mounts, Stephen
Sands, Isaac

Smith, Joseph
Smith, Noah
Stannels, John
Thompson, Joshua
Young, Richard

Lieut. S. S. Fairfield's Detachment of Artillery.

From July 31 to Aug. 31, 1814. Raised at Saco. Service at Saco.

Rank and Name.		
Seth S. Fairfield, Lieutenant	Chicks, James S.	Patten, Nathaniel
	Davis, Ezra, 3d	Pitts, Benjamin
James Mann, Jr., Sergeant	Durgin, Benjamin	Robinson, George
	Edgcomb, John	Smith, Israel
Privates.	Furlong, Patrick	Strout, George
Bradin, Isaac	Knox, Chadwick	Webber, Edmund
Chase, Abel	Lord, Daniel	
	Meeds, Artemas	

Capt. E. Small's Company, under Supervision of General Goodwin.

From Sept. 20 to Oct. 17, 1814. Service on seacoast at Kennebunk. Limington Light Artillery Company.

Rank and Name.	*Privates.*	Libby, Stephen
Edward Small, Captain	Black, Aaron	Libby, William
Benjamin Small, Lieutenant	Blake, Benjamin	Man, Isaac
David Otis, Ensign	Blake, Seth	McKenney, Humphrey
	Boothby, Arthur	Meserve, Silas
James Staples, Sergeant	Boothby, Asa	Moody, Daniel
William Staples, Sergeant	Brackett, Joseph	Moody, Simon
Samuel Larrabee, Sergeant	Bragdon, Arthur	Mulloy, Edward
James Libbey, Sergeant	Clark, Nathaniel	Mulloy, Thomas
Humphrey Small, Corporal	Cousens, Abraham	Parker, Kendall
Jonathan Atkinson, Corporal	Douglass, Elisha	Richardson, Isaac
David Small, Corporal	Douglass, John	Richardson, Thomas
Joshua Small, Corporal	Hasty, Benjamin	Small, Nathaniel C.
Isaac Small, Musician	Hasty, Dominicus	Small, Samuel
Francis Small, Musician	Libby, James, Jr.	Small, William
	Libby, Parmenio	Thompson, William

Capt. A. Boynton's Company, Maj. B. Ames' Company of Cavalry.

From June 20 to June 22, and Sept. 12 to Sept. 29, 1814. Raised at Bath. Service at Bath.

Rank and Name.	Robert Sagar, Saddler	Morse, Francis
Abel Boynton, Captain	Joseph Dyer, Smith	Morse, Richard
Daniel Baker, Lieutenant		Russell, Stoddard
William Frost, Lieutenant	*Privates.*	Small, James
Stephen Winship, Cornet	Adams, Charles	Weston, Jacob, Jr.
	Batchelder, Samuel E. (4 days)	Worray, John
Abeizer Matthews, Sergeant	Eaton, Joseph	
William Morse, Sergeant	Frost, Jacob	*Waiters.*
Daniel Peterson, Sergeant	Jordan, Robert	Ferrin, Rufus
Jesse P. Mitchell, Sergeant	Jordan, Samuel	Lombard, John
Ebenezer Stimpson, Trumpeter	Marston, John	

Capt. S. Jack's Company, Maj. B. Ames' Battalion of Cavalry.

From Sept. 10 to Sept. 29, 1814. Raised at Bowdoin. Service at Bath.

Rank and Name.	Thomas Power, Trumpeter	Gobert, John
Samuel Jack, Captain	Jacob Fletcher, Smith	Hall, Luther
Andrew Cushman, Lieutenant		Harwood, Thomas
George Rogers, Lieutenant	*Privates.*	Henry, George
Martin Hall, Cornet	Adams, Nathan	Henry, James
	Allen, Jesse	Kelly, David H.
James Alexander, Sergeant	Blanchard, Benjamin	Lancaster, Christopher
Stephen Gould, Sergeant	Brierhurst, Thomas	Malee, Philip
Andrew Dinsmore, Sergeant	Cowing, Calvin	Maxwell, Robert
John Alexander, Sergeant	Dinsmore, Thomas	

Capt. S. Jack's Company, Maj. B. Ames' Battalion of Cavalry — Concluded.

Privates — Concluded.
Mustard, James
Parks, Daniel
Parks, James
Parks, Richard
Perry, Otis

Potter, Stephen
Sanford, William
Springer, John
Springer, Stephen
Williams, George
Williams, James

Waiters.
Card, Seth
Low, John
Low, William
Parker, Fry

Detachment of Capt. A. Boynton's Company, Maj. B. Ames' Battalion of Cavalry.
From Sept. 29 to Oct. 5, 1814.

RANK AND NAME.
William Frost, Lieutenant

Abiezer Matthews, Sergeant

Privates.
Adams, Nathan
Allen, Jesse
Bryrehurst, Thomas

Frost, Jacob
Hall, Luther
Jordan, Samuel
Lancaster, Christopher
Maxwell, Robert
Morse, Richard
Parks, Daniel
Parks, Richard
Potter, Stephen

Sanford, William
Small, James
Springer, John
Weston, Jacob, Jr.
Williams, James
Worray, John

Waiter.
Ferrin, Rufus

Maj. Thomas McCrate's Battalion of Cavalry.
From Sept. 10 to Oct. 5, 1814. Stationed at Wiscasset.

FIELD AND STAFF.
Thomas McCrate, Major, Wiscasset
Charles Spofford, Adjutant, Thomaston
Samuel E. Smith, Quartermaster, Wiscasset

Capt. I. Bernard's Company, Maj. T. McCrate's Battalion of Cavalry.
From Sept. 4 to Sept. 9, 1814. Raised at Thomaston. Service at Thomaston, Wiscasset and vicinity.

RANK AND NAME.
Isaac Bernard, Captain
Philip Ulmer, Lieutenant
David Tolman, Cornet

Calvin Tolman, Sergeant
Elliot Tolman, Sergeant
William Butler, Corporal
Charles Harrington, Corporal

Privates.
Barnes, Benjamin
Barnes, Edmund
Brewster, Benjamin
Cooper, George B.
Crawford, Lawrence
Fales, James, 3d
Fales, Waterman
Flagg, Adonijah

Gerrish, Rufus B.
Godding, John
Hewett, Samuel
Killsa, John K.
Perry, Henry
Rankin, Samuel
Smith, Abiather
Tolman, Josiah
Walsh, William, Jr.

Capt. J. Chism's Company, Maj. T. McCrate's Battalion of Cavalry.
From Sept. 5 to Sept. 6, 1814. Raised at Alna. Service at Wiscasset.

RANK AND NAME.
John Chism, Jr., Captain
Charles Rundlet, Lieutenant
George Hondlett, Lieutenant
James Hodge, Cornet

Charles Hondlett, Sergeant
Snow Baker, Sergeant
Briggs Turner, Sergeant
Turner Barker, Sergeant
Enoch Heath, Musician

Privates.
Ames, Phineas
Austin, Edward
Bickford, George
Blanchard, Nathan
Call, Nathan
Carlton, Benjamin
Carlton, Jonathan
Chism, Ephraim
Chism, William
Clark, James

Clough, Samuel or Saul
Gilman, Jonathan
Goodwin, Samuel or Saul
Gould, Daniel
Heath, Aaron
Hilton, Andrew
Hondlett, Francis
Hondlett, James
Hondlett, Philip
Jewett, James
Jewett, John

Capt. J. Chism's Company, Maj. T. McCrate's Battalion of Cavalry — Concluded.

Privates — Concluded.
Johnson, John
Lithgow, Alfred
Mayers or Moyer, John
Plummer, John

Poltusky, John
Potter, Daniel
Richardson, Smith
Rondlet, Philip
Simpson, Robert

Theobald, George
Trask, Jonathan
White, Joseph
Woodbridge, Hodge

Capt. J. Chism's Company, Maj. T. McCrate's Battalion of Cavalry.
From Sept. 10 to Sept. 24, 1814. Raised at Alna. Service at Wiscasset.

RANK AND NAME.
John Chism, Jr., Captain
Charles Rundlett, Lieutenant
George Hondlett, Lieutenant
James Hodge, Cornet

Charles Hondlett, Sergeant
Snow Baker, Sergeant
Briggs Turner, Sergeant

Turner Barker, Sergeant
Enoch Heath, Musician

Privates.
Ames, Phineas
Blanchard, Nathan
Carlton, Benjamin
Chism, William
Clark, James

Heath, John
Hilton, Andrew
Jewett, James
Jewett, John
Johnson, John
Simpson, Robert
Woodbridge, Hodge

Sergt. C. Hoadlett's Guard, Maj. T. McCrate's Battalion of Cavalry.
From Sept. 25 to Oct. 4, 1814. Raised at Alna. Service at Wiscasset.

RANK AND NAME.
Charles Hoadlett, Sergeant

Privates.
Austin, Edward
Barker, Turner
Bickford, George

Call, Nathan
Carlton, Jonathan
Clough, Samuel
Goodwin, Samuel
Gould, Daniel
Heath, Aaron
Hilton, Andrew

Hondlett, Francis
Jewett, James
Johnson, John
Mayers or Moyer, John
Plummer, John
Theobald, George
White, Joseph

Sergt. C. Tolman's Guard, Maj. T. McCrate's Battalion of Cavalry.
From Sept. 25 to Oct. 5, 1814. Service at Wiscasset.

RANK AND NAME.
Calvin Tolman, Sergeant

Privates.
Barnes, Edward
Fales, Waterman
Harrington, Charles

Johnson, Josiah
Lincoln, Luther
Ruth, Josiah

Sergt. Snow Baker's Guard, Maj. T. McCrate's Battalion of Cavalry.
From Oct. 3 to Oct. 25, 1814. Raised at Alna. Service at Wiscasset.

RANK AND NAME.
Snow Baker, Sergeant

Privates.
Ames, Phineas
Barnard, Edward
Blanchard, Nathan
Chism, William

Clark, James
Gerrish, Rufus H.
Heath, Enoch
Heath, John
Hondlett, James
Jewett, John
Johnson, John
Lithgow, Alfred

Poltusky, John
Potter, Daniel
Richardson, Smith
Simpson, Robert
Trask, D.
Woodbridge, Hodge

Capt. T. Eastman's Company of Cavalry, Maj. Peter Grant's Battalion, under the Supervision of Maj. Gen. Henry Sewall and William King.

From Sept. 11 to Nov. 6, 1814. Raised at Hallowell, Winthrop and vicinity. Service at Wiscasset as express and videttes between Wiscasset and Bath, and at Camden and Augusta.

Rank and Name.	Privates.	
Thomas Eastman, Captain	Andrews, Samuel	Morrow, Milton
Francis Morris, Lieutenant	Barrows, John	Perkins, Joseph H.
William Winslow, Lieutenant	Blackman, Henry B.	Philbrick, Benjamin
Henry D. Morrill, Cornet	Chandler, Levi	Philbrick, David
	Day, Daniel	Prescott, Elisha
Parsons Smith, Clerk	Day, Francis	Pullen, Greenleaf
Benjamin Prince, Sergeant	Follett, Otis	Reed, George
Alvin Hayward, Sergeant	French, James	Rice, William
Jonathan Matthews, Sergeant	Getchell, Otis	Robinson, James
Samuel Blake, Corporal	Gould, Robert	Robinson, Kilburn G.
John Savage, Corporal	Haskell, Rufus	Rollins, Enoch W.
Albert Hayward, Corporal	Hewins, James	Shaw, Abisha M.
Richard Belcher, Corporal	Lombard, Allen	Shaw, Eliab, Jr.
Ebenezer Mathews, Musician	Lothrop, David	Shaw, Orin
	Lyon, Tabor	Stone, Daniel
	Marshall, William	Webber, Daniel, Jr.

Detachment of Cavalry, under Maj. J. Trowbridge.

From Sept. 12 to Sept. 26, 1814. Raised at Falmouth. Service at Portland and vicinity as express and videttes.

Rank and Name.	Privates.	
John Trowbridge, Major	Abbott, Nathaniel	Freeman, Daniel
Nathaniel Leighton, Lieutenant	Baker, Solomon	Frye, James
William Thomes, Cornet	Blake, Daniel	Leighton, George
	Brackett, Zacheriah	Libby, Joseph
James Smith, Sergeant	Chase, David	Pettingill, Benjamin
Andrew Leighton, Sergeant	Cochran, Timothy	Stevens, Harvey
John Phinney, Corporal	Crockett, Samuel	Webb, William
Levi Wilson, Corporal	Deering, Joshua L.	Wilson, Cyrus
	Fields, John	Winslow, Adam

Detachment of Cavalry, under Maj. J. Trowbridge.

From Sept. 26 to Oct. 29, 1814. Raised at Cape Elizabeth, Gorham and Falmouth. Service at Portland and vicinity as express and videttes.

Rank and Name.	Privates.	
John Trowbridge, Major	Alden, Jesse	Smith, William H.
Clark Dyer, Lieutenant	Bacon, Stephen	Sweat, Samuel
Nathaniel Hall, Cornet	Blake, Samuel	Weeks, William
	Frye, James	Whitney, Adam
William Brackett, Sergeant	Frye, John	
Joseph Wescott, Sergeant	Hustin, Rufus	
Nathaniel Abbott, Corporal	Johnson, Isaac	
William Warren, Corporal	Libbey, Joseph	
Benjamin F. Johnson, Musician	Phinney, John	

Maj. J. Greenwood's Battalion of Cavalry, attached to Lieut. Col. Wm. Ryerson's Regiment.

From Sept. 13 to Sept. 24, 1814; 3 days additional for travel. Raised at Portland.

Field and Staff.	Noncommissioned Staff.	
John Greenwood, Major, Hebron	Levi Bartlett, Quartermaster Sergeant	
Thomas Brown, Adjutant, Minot		
Ezra Brett, Quartermaster, Paris		

MASSACHUSETTS VOLUNTEER MILITIA IN THE WAR OF 1812.   159

Capt. William B. Bray's Company of Cavalry.

From Sept. 13 to Sept. 24, 1814; 3 days additional for travel. Raised at Turner, Minot and New Gloucester. Service at Portland.

Rank and Name.		
William B. Bray, Captain	Samuel Hayes, Corporal	Martin, William
Isaac Currin, Lieutenant	Moses Rollins, Musician	Mason, William
Edmund Chase, Lieutenant		Packard, Nehemiah
William Allen, Cornet	*Privates.*	Perry, Dimon
	Austin, Jacob	Pollard, Stephen
Jacob S. Rollins, Sergeant	Braley, Hattel	Pottle, Moses
Henry Hatch, Sergeant	Clark, Jona	Pottle, Richard
Sampson Foss, Sergeant	Cole, John	Sampson, John
Joseph Crooker, Sergeant	Crooker, Isaac	Seabury, Josiah
Quincy Keith, Corporal	Dwinal, Isaac	Waterhouse, Richard
Moses Bailey, Corporal	Dwinal, Jacob	Welcomb, John
Andrew Dwinal, Corporal	Hackett, Barnabus	Woodbury, Willard H.
	Kilbourn, Ira	Yeaton, Joseph

Sergt. A. Lemond's Detachment of Cavalry, acting as Express.

From Oct. 6 to Oct. 10, 1814. Service at Thomaston.

Rank and Name.	*Privates.*	Lemond, Oliver
Alexander Lemond, Sergeant	Cooper, George B.	Smith, Abiather
	Crawford, Lawrence	

Lieut. Col. O. Shead's Regiment.

From July to Sept. 12, 1812. Service at Eastport.

Field and Staff.		
Oliver Shead, Lieutenant Colonel, Eastport	John Balcomb, Major, Robinstown	Benjamin D. Prince, Paymaster, Eastport
Joseph Whitney, Lieutenant Colonel, Calais	Thomas Vose, Major, Robinstown	John Barstow, Surgeon, Eastport
	John Wood, Adjutant, Eastport	Henry A. Clark, Chaplain, Eastport
	Stephen Jones, Quartermaster, Eastport	

Capt. T. Vose, Jr.'s Company, Lieut. Col. O. Shead's Regiment.

From July 2 to Aug. 5, 1812. Raised at Robinstown. Service at Eastport.

Rank and Name.	Dudley, Moses	Potter, Solomon
Thomas Vose, Jr., Captain	Felt, Jonathan W.	Pottle, Benjamin
Amos Davis, Ensign	Frost, Thomas	Pottle, John
	Garey, Elbridge	Pottle, William
Martin Byrnes, Sergeant	Golding, Peter	Seeley, Joseph
George Phelps, Sergeant	Hubbard, Thomas	Spaulding, Robert
Seth Gayney, Sergeant	Johnson, Hezekiah	Springer, Samuel
William Nutt, Sergeant	Johnson, Job, Jr.	Stanhope, Rudolphus
Isaac Parker, Musician	Johnson, John	Stephenson, Priest P.
Nathaniel D. Snow, Musician	Johnson, Samuel	Stickney, Samuel
	Kellogg, Ezekiel F.	Stickney, Timothy
Privates.	Loring, Isaac	Stovers, Experiance
Bonds, Samuel	Loring, Peter, Jr.	Temple, Isaac
Bugbee, Robert	McField, Duncan	Tuttle, Cyrus
Bugbee, William, Jr.	Mesemel, John	Webber, Asa
Cox, John	Morrison, John	
Davis, Joseph	Morrison, William	

Capt. J. Keene's Company, Lieut. Col. O. Shead's Regiment.
From July 15 to Sept. 5, 1812. Raised at Calais. Service at Eastport.

RANK AND NAME.
Jarius Keene, Captain

Lebee G. Spring, Clerk
Jeremiah Robbins, Sergeant
Coffin Sanborn, Sergeant
Robert Webb, Sergeant
Elijah G. Wetherbee, Corporal
Joshua Whitney, Corporal
Thomas Paine, Corporal
Ephraim Sands, Corporal

Privates.
Allen, Noah
Barker, Timothy
Beliter, Thomas
Bohanan, Amariah
Bohanan, Daniel
Brooks, John
Chandler, Stephen
Christopher, George

Clark, William, 27 July
Crockett, William
Dunning, Andrew
Dyer, Samuel
Dyer, Stephen, Jr.
Eastman, Joseph
Frost, Aaron
Hill, Thomas
Hodgman, Thomas
Hopkins, Redfield
Hutchings, John
Kilburn, John
Knight, Henry
Knight, Joel
Knight, Westbrook
Nights, George
Lamb, James, Sept 5
Lane, John
Lane, Nathan
Lane, William
Nevers, Jonathan

Noble, Daniel
Paine, Richard
Pettegrow, Francis
Pettegrow, Nahun
Pike, Robert
Reading, Ebenezer
Reading, Joseph
Rhoads, Daniel
Russell, Elijah
Scott, Samuel
Shillaber, William
Spencer, John
Sprague, James
Sprague, John
Thomhill, Thomas
Townson, Abijah
Townson, Robert
Williams, Johnson
Young, David I.

Capt. J. W. Raynolds' Company, Lieut. Col. O. Shead's Regiment.
From July 15 to Aug. 28, 1812. Service at Eastport.

RANK AND NAME.
John W. Raynolds, Captain
Jotham G. Raynolds, Ensign

William Phelps, Clerk
Benjamin Raynolds, Sergeant
William Lawrence, Sergeant
Joseph Roberson, Sergeant
Benjamin Small, Corporal
William Runney, Corporal
Ebenezer Rice, Corporal

Privates.
Bornwell, Timothy
Bundell, Daniel
Case, William

Clark, Benjamin R.
Coggin, Benjamin W.
Eaton, Henry M.
Fay, Briah
Grace, Richard P.
Guptil, Nathaniel
Guptil, Robert
Guptil, Thomas
Hardy, Daniel
Hart, William
Hasking, Samuel
Janes, Robert
Kelly, William
Leighton, Hatwell
Lyon, Mathew
Maroney, Joseph

Maroney, Peter
Maroney, Samuel
McDaniel, John
Nezenby, John
Nutter, George
Nutter, James
Nutter, John
Phelps, Jonah
Ramsdell, Isaac
Raynolds, Jonathan
Stearns, Elijah
Wilson, Samuel N.
Woodward, Josiah
Yerbey, John

Capt. W. Hill's Company, Lieut. Col. O. Shead's Regiment.
From July 21 to Sept. 1, 1812. Service at Eastport and Lubec.

RANK AND NAME.
William Hill, Captain
John Swett, Lieutenant
Thomas Rice, Quartermaster

Robert Dutch, Sergeant
Samuel Leighton, Sergeant
Jeremiah F. Young, Sergeant
Jesse Stephenson, Sergeant
Lewis F. Delesdiner, Jr., Corporal
Hiram Earle, Corporal
Alexander Capen, Musician
James Perkins, Musician

Privates.
Baker, Edward
Bell, George, Jr.
Briant, William
Brooks, Anthony
Brown, Walter B.
Buckman, Ben, substituted by Hoppin, John B.
Clark, Nathaniel, substituted by Rogers, John
Clark, Nathaniel, Jr.
Cochran, Samuel, substituted by Lunt, John
Hatch Stephen, substituted by Trim, John
Hill, Miles

Hill, Oliver C.
Jones, Lemuel H.
Keys, Jonas T.
Leighton, John, substituted by Lunt, Joseph
Lincoln, John C.
McGlauflin, David
McGlauflin, William
McQuillin, David P.
Morgan, James
Morton, Nathaniel
Powers, Daniel, substituted by Hood, Peter
Small, Nehemiah
Stetson, Gideon
Todd, John M.

Capt. J. N. Peary's Company, Lieut. Col. O. Shead's Regiment.

From July 21 to Sept. 1, 1812. Service at Eastport.

RANK AND NAME.
John N. Peary, Captain
Sherman Leland, Lieutenant

Leonard Peirce, Clerk
Franklin Gould, Sergeant
Thomas Lesure, Sergeant
Enoch Freeman, Sergeant
Barney Allen, Corporal
Henry Newcomb, Corporal
Henry G. Archer, Corporal
William Wortman, Corporal
John Rogers, Musician

Privates.
Andrews, Ebenezer
Bacon, Thomas
Bean, Ira A.
Beeman, Charles

Blatchford, Joseph
Buck, Asa
Buskirk, L. V.
Carson, Aaron
Chalmer, Peter
Crane, Robert, substituted by Pruttlebury, Thomas
Delesderwin, William, substituted by Blackwell, James
Fiket, Nathaniel
Folsom, Joseph
Fuller, Moses, substituted by McDonald, Michael
Gilman, Warren
Gleason, Silas
Hill, Ralph
Johnson, Paul, Jr., substituted by Buswell, John
Kelly, William

Kimball, James
Mason, John
McMiller, Fryling
Morton, Elkanah
Norwood, Moses, substituted by Burnes, Patrick
Norwood, Nathaniel, substituted by Barnaby, Benjamin
Norwood, William, substituted by Smith, John
Olds, James
Palmer, John
Rich, James
Russell, Abraham
Tuttle, Worster, substituted by Lunt, John
York, Archibald

Capt. T. George's Company, Lieut. Col. O. Shead's Regiment.

From Aug. 11 to Aug. 31, 1812. Raised at Eastport. Service at Eastport.

RANK AND NAME.
Thomas George, Captain, Aug. 11 to Aug. 31
Seth Rider, Lieutenant, Aug. 11 to Aug. 31
Joseph Bridgham, Jr., Ensign, Aug. 11 to Aug. 31

James Webster, Sergeant, Aug. 11 to Aug. 31
James Jackman, Sergeant, Aug. 11 to Aug. 31
Daniel Kimball, Sergeant, Aug. 11 to Aug. 31
Daniel Burt, Sergeant, Aug. 11 to Aug. 31
James Dunning, Corporal, Aug. 14 to Aug. 31
James Anderson, Corporal, Aug. 14 to Aug. 31
Abram Chick, Corporal, Aug. 14 to Aug. 31
Levi Torrence, Corporal, Aug. 14 to Aug. 31
John Allen, Musician, Aug. 14 to Aug. 31
Clark Peak, Musician, Aug. 14 to Aug. 31

Privates.
Black, Edward, Aug. 21 to Aug. 31
Bridges, Moses, Aug. 21 to Aug. 31
Butler, William, Aug. 14 to Aug. 31
Carter, David K., Aug. 21 to Aug. 31
Carter, Isaac, Aug. 21 to Aug. 31
Chamberlain, Pickman, Aug. 14 to Aug. 31
Clark, Josiah, Aug. 14 to Aug. 31
Clay, Benjamin, Aug. 21 to Aug. 31
Clay, George, Aug. 21 to Aug. 31
Coggins, Samuel, Aug. 21 to Aug. 31
Conhord, James, Aug. 14 to Aug. 31
Davis, John, Aug. 14 to Aug. 31
Dodge, Hezekiah, Aug. 21 to Aug. 31
Dodge, William, Aug. 21 to Aug. 31
Douglas, Randal, Aug. 14 to Aug. 31
Eddy, William, Aug. 14 to Aug. 31
Ellis, Stephen, Aug. 21 to Aug. 31
Fruthy, James, Aug. 21 to Aug. 31
Gage, John, Aug. 21 to Aug. 31
Gilpatrick, John, Aug. 31 to Aug. 31
Godfrey, Albert W., Aug. 14 to Aug. 31
Grant, Elijah, Aug. 14 to Aug. 31
Gray, Aaron, Aug. 21 to Aug. 31
Gray, John, Aug. 21 to Aug. 31

Gross, James, Aug. 14 to Aug. 31
Heath, John G., Aug. 14 to Aug. 31
Heath, Jonathan, Aug. 14 to Aug. 31
Herrick, Amos, Aug. 21 to Aug. 31
Holt, William, Aug. 14 to Aug. 31
Hutchins, Jonathan, Aug. 31 to Aug. 31
Inman, Allin, Aug. 14 to Aug. 31
Inman, Marcy, Aug. 31 to Aug. 31
Jackman, John, Aug. 14 to Aug. 31
Johnson, Ebenezer, Aug. 14 to Aug. 31
Low, Thomas, Aug. 14 to Aug. 31
McCaslin, Adam, Aug. 21 to Aug. 31
McCaslin, Reuben, Aug. 21 to Aug. 31
McPheters, William, Aug. 14 to Aug 31
Oakes, Eli, Aug. 14 to Aug. 31
Page, Joseph, Aug. 14 to Aug. 31
Phillips, James, Aug. 14 to Aug. 31
Pishon, Isaac, Aug. 14 to Aug. 31
Prisher, Joel, Aug. 14 to Aug. 31
Tibbetts, Ichabod, Aug. 21 to Aug. 31
Tibbetts, John, Aug. 14 to Aug. 31
Tozer, William, Aug. 14 to Aug. 31
White, William, Aug. 14 to Aug. 31
Wilson, John, Aug. 21 to Aug. 31

Lieut. B. Wilder's Detachment, Lieut. Col. O. Shead's Regiment.

From July 15 to Aug. 7, 1812. Raised at Lubec and Eastport. Service at Eastport.

RANK AND NAME.
Bela Wilder, Lieutenant

Privates.
Blackwood, James, Jr.
Blankinburgh, John
Bosworth, Daniel
Bridge, Jesse C.

Brown, Christopher, Jr.
Gardner, A., Jr.
Harrison, James W.
Heath, Hows
Kilby, Daniel
Kilby, John
Kilby, William, Jr.
Leighton, George W.

Mahen, William
Mahoon, James
Oraston, William
Orvin, William
Parrot, William
Smith, Thomas
Wilder, Oren
Wilder, T., 3d

Capt. J. Chamberlain's Detached Company of Militia, Maj. J. Ulmer's Battalion.

From Sept. 1 to Dec. 31, 1812. Raised at Brewer. Mustered into the United States service and stationed at Eastport.

Rank and Name.		
Joshua Chamberlain, Captain	Clark, James	Loud, Ephraim
Peter Newcomb, Lieutenant	Cobb, William	Lowell, Benjamin
Samuel Freeman, Ensign	Cole, Seth	Mayo, Joseph
	Colson, David	Merrill, Davis
Robert Thompson, Sergeant	Craig, George	Michaels, William
Daniel Nickerson, Sergeant	Curtis, James	Milvin, Benjamin
Joshua Sparrow, Sergeant	Dean, Obadiah	Mudgett, Levi
Lemuel Hamilton, Sergeant	Dean, Robert	Murch, Walter
Emery Bradbury, Corporal	Dean, William	Murray, Benjamin
John Boohr, Corporal (died)	Dearborn, Jacob	Nutter, James
William Kendall, Corporal	Dunbar, Isaac	Odell, John
John Sanborn, Corporal	Dyer, David	Palmer, Silas
Zenos Dexter, Musician	Fisher, Gardner	Pomery, William (D)
Mark Fernald, Musician	Freeman, Thomas	Pratt, Seth
	Frost, Samuel	Rice, David
Privates.	Furbush, Elisha	Rinds, Samuel
Baker, Jeremiah	Galen, Richard	Smith, Josiah
Ballard, William	Henderson, Nathan	Smith, Lemuel
Booder, William	Hews, Elihu	Snow, Henry C.
Bottom, Solomon	Higgins, Josiah	Sparrow, Benjamin
Buzzell, Daniel	Humes, John	Stuts, Eben
Carr, Richard	Jackson, David	Stuts, Edad
Chadbourn, John	Kenney, Edward	Turrier, John B.
Chadburn, Daniel G.	Kenney, Levi	West, William
Chase, Abner	Kenniston, David (D)	
	Knowles, Abiather	

Lieut. Col. J. Black's Command.

March and April, 1813; 7 to 9 days only. Service at Mount Desert. Lieut. Col. John Black's Second Regiment, Second Brigade, Tenth Division, called out to defend Mount Desert, Dec. 28, 1813.

Rank and Name.	Staff.	
John Black, Lieutenant Colonel	Moses Adams, Adjutant	Jonathan Madden, Sergeant
Labin Pond, Major	Samuel Dutton, Quartermaster	John Tinker, Sergeant
John Jellison, Major		
	Noncommissioned Officers.	Love Joy, Musician
John G. Dean, Lieutenant Colonel Commanding	David G. McCobb, Sergeant	Daniel Monarch, Musician
Simeon Milliken, Captain	Joseph Morrison, Sergeant	John G. Joy, Musician
Daniel Adams, Captain	Samuel Milliken, Sergeant	Sewall E. Tuttle, Musician
Nathaniel Truwargy, Ensign	John Clark, Sergeant	Alfred Joy, Musician
Nathan Clark, Ensign	Richard Heath, Sergeant	Temple Joy, Musician
	Nathaniel Smith, Jr., Sergeant	

Lieut. Col. J. Black's Command.

March and April, 1813; 7 to 9 days. Raised at Ellsworth. Service at Mount Desert.

Rank and Name.	Joseph Morrison, Sergeant	*Privates.*
John Black, Lieutenant Colonel	Samuel Milliken, Sergeant	Alley, Isaac
Labin Pond, Major	John Clark, Sergeant	Atherton, Peter
John Jellison, Major	Richard Heath, Sergeant	Atherton, Thomas
Simeon Milliken, Captain	Nathaniel Smith, Sergeant	Barker, James
Daniel Adams, Captain	Jonathan Maddox, Sergeant	Beal, Edward
John G. Seame, Lieutenant	John Tinker, Sergeant	Bennet, Daniel
Nathaniel Turwagry, Ensign	Love Joy, Musician	Card, Dominicus
Nathan Clark, Ensign	Daniel Monarch, Musician	Card, Jeremiah
Moses Adams, Adjutant	Sewall E. Tuttle, Musician	Carter, James
Samuel Dutton, Quartermaster	John G. Joy, Musician	Colby, Eli
(David George Washington Cobb) (?)	Alfred Joy, Musician	Davis, Ezra
	Temple Joy, Musician	Day, Moses

Lieut. Col. J. Black's Command — Concluded.

Privates — Concluded.
Day, Thomas
Fish or Fisk, James C.
Freeman, George
Freeman, Reuben
Freeman, Reuben, Jr.
Freeze, Abraham
Freeze, George
Freeze, Isaac
Fullerton, Henry
Garland, Benjamin
Garland, Edward
Garland, Josiah
Gilley, William
Gilman, Eliphalet
Ginn, William R.
Gott, Eliab
Gott, Nathaniel
Gove, Peter
Harmon, George
Harper, William
Herbert, George
Hodgdon, John
Holt, Stephen
Hopkins, Allen
Jackson, John
Jellison, Zacharius
Jones, Charles
Jones, Theodore
Jordan, Benjamin
Jordan, Isaac

Jordan, John G.
Jordan, Joseph
Jordan, Solomon
Jordan, Stephen T.
Jordan, Walter
Joy, Ivory H.
Joy, Samuel
Kelly, Nathaniel
Leavy, John
Maddocks, Amos
Maddocks, Benjamin
Maddocks, Benjamin, Jr.
Maddocks, Samuel
Manchester, John
McKenzie, John
McKenzie, William
Medar, Daniel
Milliken, Allen
Moon, Abner
Moore, Benjamin
Moore, Cornelius
Moore, Edward
Moore, Jotham
Moore, Wyatt
Murch, William
Nason, Joseph
Nutter, Alexander
Parsons, Amos
Peters, Andrew
Phillips, Henry
Pond, Asa A.

Pond, Jasper
Reed, William
Richardson, Benjamin
Richardson, David
Richardson, George
Richardson, Hugh
Richardson, Isaac
Richardson, James
Richardson, Nathaniel
Richardson, Richard
Richardson, Stephen
Richardson, Stephen, Jr.
Roberts, William
Sear, John
Semes, John
Sevey, Jacob
Smith, Daniel
Smith, Elijah
Stratton, David
Tinker, Joseph
Townsend, Gara
Tucker, Nicholas
Wallis, John
Wargatt, Asa
Wargatt, David
Wargatt, Davis
Wargatt, Moses
Warwell, Joseph
Woodworth, Stephen G.

Capt. D. Adams' Company, Lieut. Col. J. Black's Regiment.

March and April, 1813; 7 to 9 days only. Raised at Ellsworth. Service at Mount Desert.

RANK AND NAME.
Daniel Adams, Captain

Privates.
Barker, James
Beall, Edward
Card, Jeremiah
Carter, James
Davis, Ezra
Fish, James C.
Freese, Abraham
Freese, George
Freese, Isaac
Fullerton, Henry
Garland, Benjamin
Garland, Edward
Garland, Josiah, Jr.
Gilman, Eliphalet
Gove, Peter
Holt, Stephen
Hopkins, Allen

Jellison, Jack
Joy, Samuel, Jr.
Kelly, Nathaniel
Maddox, Benjamin
Maddox, Benjamin, Jr.
Maddox, Samuel, Jr.
Margatt or Wargatt, Asa
Margatt or Wargatt, David, Jr.
Maxwell, Joseph
Moore, Abner
Moore, Benjamin, Jr.
Moore, Edward, Jr.
Moore, Jotham
Moore, Wyatt, Jr.
Mulliken or Milliken, Allen
Nason, Joseph
Nutter, Alexander
Parsons, Amos
Phillips, Henry
Reed, William
Richardson, Benjamin

Richardson, David
Richardson, George
Richardson, Hugh
Richardson, Isaac
Richardson, James
Richardson, Nathaniel
Richardson, Richard
Richardson, Stephen, Jr.
Richardson, Stephen, 3d
Richardson, Stephen, 4th
Roberts, William
Sleavry, John
Smith, Daniel
Smith, Elijah
Stratton, David
Tourtellot, Nathaniel
Townsend, Jerva
Tucker, Nicholas
Wallis, John
Wargatt or Margatt, David
Wargatt or Margatt, Moses

Capt. Simeon Milliken's Company, Lieut. Col. J. Black's Regiment.

March and April, 1813; 7 to 9 days only. Raised at Ellsworth. Service at Mount Desert. Captain Milliken volunteered and rendered service, having resigned and being discharged Dec. 11, 1812.

RANK AND NAME.
Simeon Milliken, Captain

Privates.

Alley, Isaac
Atherton, Peter
Atherton, Thomas
Bennet, Daniel
Card, Dominicus
Colby, Eli
Day, Moses
Day, Thomas
Freeman, George
Freeman, Reuben, Jr.
Freeman, Reuben, Sr.
Gilley, William

Gott, Eliab
Gott, Nathaniel
Harman, George
Harper, William
Hodgdon, John
Hubert, George
Jackson, John
Jones, Charles
Jones, Theodore, Jr.
Jordan, Benjamin, Jr.
Jordan, Isaac
Jordan, John G.
Jordan, Joseph
Jordan, Solomon, Jr.
Jordan, Stephen F.
Jordan, Walter, Jr.

Joy, Ivory H.
Lean, John
Lewey, Jacob
Maddocks, Nathan
Manchester, John
McKenzie, John
McKenzie, William
Medar, Daniel
Murch, William
Nason, Robert
Peters, Andrew
Pond, Asa A.
Pond, Jasper
Tinker, Joseph
Woodman, Stephen G.

Capt. J. Farmer's Company, Lieut. Col. M. Nichol's Regiment.

From Oct. 17 to Dec. 6, 1813. Service at Jordan's Point and Portland Harbor.

RANK AND NAME.
James Farmer, Captain (31 days)
Hollibut Herrick, Lieutenant (31 days)
Enoch Moody, Ensign (31 days)

Samuel Gookin, Sergeant (30 days)
Caleb Brown, Sergeant (31 days)
Robert Evans, Sergeant (31 days)
Gain Robinson, Sergeant (38 days)
Alvan Dillingham, Corporal (31 days)
Richard Skilton, Corporal (35 days)
William Curtis, Corporal (37 days)
John J. Jennings, Corporal (40 days)
Stephen Knight, Musician (25 days)
Joseph Bailey, Musician (35 days)

Privates.

Adams, Henry (35 days)
Bailey, James P. (36 days)
Barret, Benjamin (35 days)
Benskins, Thomas (36 days)
Berry, Levi (41 days)
Bracket, Daniel (37 days)
Bracket, Ephraham (36 days)
Bragdon, Solomon (36 days)

Cash, Stephen (34 days)
Chamberlain, Joshua (36 days)
Choate, Benjamin (42 days)
Cobb, Joseph (42 days)
Conant, Edward (35 days)
Doan, Edward (34 days)
Dodge, John (36 days)
Dyer, Chadbourne (35 days)
Edgcumb, Daniel (41 days)
Edgcumb, Gideon, Jr. (37 days)
Fickett, Samuel (41 days)
Field, Josiah (41 days)
Foss, John S. (42 days)
Gillman, John (36 days)
Hall, Josiah (42 days)
Hanscomb, Moses (38 days)
Harmon, Jonathan (36 days)
Harmon, Thomas (36 days)
Hersey, Israel (38 days)
Howard, Abiazer (36 days)
Johnson, William (35 days)
Jones, Butler (49 days)
Jones, Jonathan (35 days)
Knight, William (36 days)
Leighton, Andrew (36 days)

Leighton, Ezekiel (41 days)
Libby, Joseph (36 days)
Lilley, John (48 days)
Long, Lemuel (38 days)
Lord, Nathan (42 days)
Maxwell, Stephen (38 days)
McCorrison, William (36 days)
Merrill, Levi (37 days)
Merrill, Timothy (42 days)
Nason, Abraham, Jr. (35 days)
Noble, Isaac (35 days)
Paine, Alexander (36 days)
Quinby, Hiram (42 days)
Randall, Benjamin (37 days)
Skillings, Lemuel (34 days)
Staples, Richard (34 days)
Thrasher, Robert (34 days)
Warren (?), Robert (42 days)
Waterhouse, Joseph H. (36 days)
Weymouth, Robert (41 days)
Wheeler, Joseph (38 days)
Wheeler, Nathaniel (38 days)
Whitney, Luther (35 days)
Woodman, Jeremiah (37 days)
Woodsom, Daniel (42 days)

Muster Roll of Capt. J. Farmer's Company, Lieut. Col. Nichols' Regiment.

From Oct. 17 to time of discharge, 1813. Stationed at, and from Portland. This appears to be a consolidation of two companies, giving the number of days served.

RANK AND NAME.
James Farmer, Captain (31 days)
Hallibut Herrick, Lieutenant (31 days)
Enoch Moody, Ensign (31 days)

Samuel Gookin, Sergeant (30 days)
Caleb Brown, Sergeant (31 days)
Robert Evans, Sergeant (31 days)

Gain Robinson, Sergeant (38 days)
Alvin Dillingham, Corporal (31 days)
Richard Skilton, Corporal (35 days)
William Curtis, Corporal (37 days)
John H. Jennings, Corporal (40 days)
Stephen Knight, Musician (20 days)
Joseph Bailey, Musician (35 days)

Privates.

Adams, Henry (35 days)
Bailey, James P. (36 days)
Banskins, Thomas (36 days)
Barrett, Benjamin (35 days)
Berry, Levi (41 days)
Brackett, Daniel (37 days)
Brackett, Ephraim (36 days)

Muster Roll of Capt. J. Farmer's Company, Lieut. Col. Nichols' Regiment — Concluded.

Privates — Concluded.
Bragdon, Solomon (36 days)
Cash, Stephen (34 days)
Chamberlain, Joshua (36 days)
Choate, Benjamin (42 days)
Cobb, Joseph (42 days)
Conant, Edward (35 days)
Doane, Edward (34 days)
Dodge, John (36 days)
Dyer, Chadbourn (35 days)
Edgcomb, Daniel (41 days)
Edgcomb, Gideon, Jr. (41 days)
Fickett, Samuel (41 days)
Field, Josiah (41 days)
Foss, John S. (42 days)
Gillman, John (36 days)
Hall, Josiah (42 days)

Hanscomb, Moses (38 days)
Harmon, Jonathan (36 days)
Harmon, Thomas (36 days)
Hersey, Israel (38 days)
Howard, Abiazer (36 days)
Johnson, William (35 days)
Jones, Butler (49 days)
Jones, Jonathan (35 days)
Knight, William (36 days)
Leighton, Ezekiel (41 days)
Libby, Joseph (36 days)
Lilly, John (48 days)
Long, Lemuel (38 days)
Lord, Nathan (42 days)
Maxwell, Stephen (38 days)
McCorison, William (36 days)
Merrill, Levi (37 days)

Merrill, Timothy (42 days)
Nason, Abram, Jr. (35 days)
Noble, Isaac (35 days)
Paine, Alexander (36 days)
Quimby, Hiram (42 days)
Randall, Benjamin (37 days)
Skillings, Lemuel (24 days)
Staples, Richard (34 days)
Thrasher, Robert (34 days)
Warren, Robert (42 days)
Waterhouse, Joseph H. (35 days)
Weymouth, Robert (41 days)
Wheeler, Joseph (38 days)
Wheeler, Nathaniel (38 days)
Whitney, Luther (34 days)
Woodman, Jeremiah (37 days)
Woodson, Daniel (42 days)

A Consolidated Muster Roll of Capt. A. W. Atherton's Company, from Time of Entry to Oct. 17, 1813, and from October 17 to Date of Discharge.
Service at Portland.

RANK AND NAME.
Abel W. Atherton, Captain
Henry Smith, Lieutenant (31 days)
John Watson, Ensign (31 days)
Benjamin Tukey, Adjutant (30 days)
James Chase, Adjutant (31 days) (substituted Benjamin Tukey)
John Chadwell, Commissary (30 days)

George Stacy, Sergeant (30 days)
Samuel Shattuck, Sergeant (28 days)
James Gammon, Sergeant (26 days)
Sherburn Libby, Sergeant (25 days)
Timothy Chadburn, Corporal (30 days)
Jonathan Wares, Corporal (30 days)
Benjamin Carter, Corporal (26 days)
Benjamin Clough, Corporal (26 days)
Abram Jordan, Corporal (24 days)
Josiah Long, Musician (26 days)
Joshua Chadburn, Musician (26 days)

Privates.
Bacon, Timothy, Jr. (27 days)
Baxton, Edward (27 days)
Berry, John (30 days)

Bolton, Royal (26 days)
Bolton, Thomas (26 days)
Burns, George, Jr. (30 days)
Chase, David (26 days)
Cotton, Joseph (2 days)
Crockett, Henry (26 days)
Dresser, Joseph (30 days)
Elwell, Joseph (27 days)
Emery, Elijah (1 day)
Emery, William (26 days)
Foss, John (26 days)
Freeman, Henry (30 days)
Gould, Thomas F. (24 days)
Gray, Samuel (26 days)
Harding, Joseph (30 days)
Harmon, James (26 days)
Heath, Samuel (26 days)
Hodges, Ezra (24 days)
Jones, Edward (30 days)
Jumper, Joseph (26 days)
Knight, Winslow (23 days)
Leighton, Robert (8 days)
Libby, Enos (27 days)
Love, Alva, Deserted Oct. 3
Lowell, Jonathan, Jr. (28 days)

Martin, Josiah (21 days)
McDetton, Hugh (30 days)
Moody, Lemuel, 2d (30 days)
Morton, Major (26 days)
Nason, Uriah (26 days)
Philbrick, Caleb P. (26 days)
Phillips, Charles E. (30 days)
Pierce, Joseph (30 days)
Plummer, Moses (30 days)
Prince, Sewell (26 days)
Rogers, Edward (26 days)
Sanborn, James, Jr. (11 days)
Sculley, William (30 days)
Stewart, Wentworth (26 days)
Stimpson, Amos (26 days)
Stimpson, John (26 days)
Sweet, Benjamin (26 days)
Thomas, Amos (21 days)
Treat, Richard (30 days)
Twombly, Amos (11 days)
Williams, Joseph (26 days)
Williams, Joseph L. (30 days)
Williams, Peter (26 days)
Wood, William (26 days)
York, Joseph (26 days)

Pay Roll of Capt. A. W. Atherton's Company, Lieut. Col. Nichols' Regiment.
From Sept. 16 to Nov. 24, 1813. Service at Portland.

RANK AND NAME.
Abel W. Atherton, Captain (69 days)
James Farmer, Captain (62 days)
Henry Smith, Lieutenant (62 days)
Hollibut Herrick, Lieutenant (62 days)
John Watson, Ensign (62 days)
Enoch Moody, Ensign (62 days)
Benjamin Tukey, Adjutant (30 days)
John Chadwell, Commissary (61 days)

George Stacy, Sergeant (61 days)
Samuel Gookin, Sergeant (61 days)
Samuel Shattuck, Sergeant (78 days)
Caleb Brown, Sergeant (61 days)
Robert Evans, Sergeant (61 days)
James Gammon, Sergeant (61 days)
Sherburn Libbey, Sergeant (61 days)
Gaine Robinson, Sergeant (61 days)
Timothy Chadburn, Corporal (68 days)

Jonathan Wares, Corporal (61 days)
Oliver Dillingham, Corporal (61 days)
Benjamin Carter, Corporal (61 days)
Benjamin Clough, Corporal (68 days)
Richard Shilton, Corporal (61 days)
William Curtis, Corporal (61 days)
Abram Jordan, Corporal (61 days)
John H. Jenning, Corporal (61 days)
Josiah Ling or Long, Musician (68 days)

MASSACHUSETTS VOLUNTEER MILITIA IN THE WAR OF 1812.

Pay Roll of A. W. Atherton's Company, Lieut. Col. Nichols' Regiment — Concluded.

RANK AND NAME—*Concluded.*
Joshua Chadburn, Musician (68 days)
Joseph Bailey, Musician (61 days)
Stephen Knight, Musician (25 days)

Privates.
Adams, Henry (61 days)
Bacon, Timothy, Jr. (61 days)
Bailey, James P. (61 days)
Banskins, Thomas (61 days)
Barret, Benjamin (61 days)
Baxton, Edward (61 days)
Berry, John (61 days)
Berry, Levi (61 days)
Bolton, Royal (61 days)
Bolton, Thomas (61 days)
Bracket, Ephraim (61 days)
Brackett, Daniel (61 days)
Bragdon, Solomon (61 days)
Burns, George, Jr. (61 days)
Cash, Stephen (61 days)
Chamberlain, Joshua (61 days)
Chase, David (61 days)
Chase, James (31 days)
Chote, Benjamin (68 days)
Cobb, Joseph (61 days)
Conant, Edward (61 days)
Cotton, Joseph (44 days)
Crockett, Henry (61 days)
Doan, Edward (61 days)
Dodge, John (61 days)
Dresser, Joseph (61 days)
Dyer, Chadburn (61 days)
Edgecomb, Daniel (61 days)
Edgecomb, Gideon, Jr. (61 days)
Elwell, Samuel (61 days)
Emery, Elijah (43 days)
Emery, William (68 days)
Fickett, Samuel (41 days)

Fields, Josiah (61 days)
Foss, John (61 days)
Foss, John S. (61 days)
Freeman, Henry (68 days)
Gilman, John (61 days)
Gould, Thomas F. (61 days)
Gray, Samuel (61 days)
Hall, Josiah (59 days)
Hanscomb, Moses (61 days)
Harding, Joseph (61 days)
Harmon, James (61 days)
Harmon, James, 2d (61 days)
Harmon, Thomas (61 days)
Heath, Samuel (61 days)
Hersey, Israel (61 days)
Hodges, Ezra (61 days)
Howard, Abijah (61 days)
Johnson, William (61 days)
Jones, Butler (57 days)
Jones, Edward (61 days)
Jones, Jonathan (61 days)
Jumper, Joseph (61 days)
Knight, William (61 days)
Knight, Winslow (61 days)
Leavis, Hugh M. (61 days)
Leighton, Andrew (61 days)
Leighton, Ezekiel (53 days)
Leighton, Robert (49 days)
Libbey, Enos (61 days)
Libby, Joseph (61 days)
Lilley, John (74 days)
Long, Demuel (61 days)
Lord, Nathan (67 days)
Lowell, Jonathan (61 days)
Mareun, Josiah (61 days)
Maxwell, Stephen (61 days)
Mayson, Uriah (61 days)
McCorriston, William (61 days)
Merril, Levi (61 days)

Merrill, Timothy (61 days)
Moody, Samuel, 2d (67 days)
Morton, Major (61 days)
Nayson, Abraham, Jr. (61 days)
Noble, Isaac (61 days)
Paine, Alexander (61 days)
Philbrick, Caleb P. (61 days)
Phillips, Charles E. (61 days)
Pierce, Joseph (61 days)
Plummer, Moses (61 days)
Prince, Sewell (74 days)
Quimby, Hiram (68 days)
Randall, Benjamin (61 days)
Rogers, Edward (61 days)
Sanborn, John, Jr. (53 days)
Sculley, William (61 days)
Skillin, Lemuel (61 days)
Staples, Richard (61 days)
Stimpson, Amos (61 days)
Stimpson, John (61 days)
Stuart, Wentworth (61 days)
Sweet, Benjamin (61 days)
Thomas, Amos (61 days)
Thrasher, Robert (61 days)
Treat, Richard (61 days)
Twombly, William (61 days)
Warren, Robert (66 days)
Waterhouse, Joseph (61 days)
Waymouth, Robert (61 days)
Wheeler, Joseph (61 days)
Wheeler, Nathaniel (61 days)
Whitney, Luther (61 days)
Williams, Joseph (74 days)
Williams, Joseph, 2d (61 days)
Williams, Peter (61 days)
Wood, William (61 days)
Woodman, Jeremiah (61 days)
Woodsom, Daniel (56 days)
York, Joseph (61 days)

Lieut. Col. W. R. Blaisdell's Regiment.
From Sept. 13 to Sept. 27, 1814. Service at Bath. Rendezvous at Gardiner, awaiting orders.

FIELD AND STAFF.
William R. Blaisdell, Lieutenant Colonel, Greene
Josiah Libby, Major, Wales
Jotham Thompson, Major, Monmouth

Jonathan Marston, Adjutant, Monmouth
Joseph Mitchell, Quartermaster, Leeds
Thomas W. Bridgham, Surgeon, Leeds

NONCOMMISSIONED STAFF.
Josiah Larrabee, Sergeant Major
David Dunning, Quartermaster Sergeant
Joel Small, Drum Major
Amos Woodman, Fife Major

Capt. N. Pettingill's Company, Lieut. Col. W. R. Blaisdell's Regiment.
From Sept. 13 to Sept. 20, 1814. Raised at Lewiston. Service in camp at Gardiner, awaiting orders.

RANK AND NAME.
Nathaniel Pettingill, Captain
Nathan Sleeper, Lieutenant
Zacheus Litchfield, Ensign

Phineas Wright, Sergeant
Davis Nevins, Sergeant
Luther Litchfield, Sergeant
Samuel R. Reed, Sergeant

Lang Wright, Corporal
Thomas Ham, Corporal
Stephen Wilkins, Corporal
John Wright, Corporal
Amaziah Merrill, Musician
John Ham, Musician
Freeman Skinner, Musician

Privates.
Anderson, Robert
Barker, David
Barnes, Peletiah
Batten, Abraham
Cole, Jeremiah
Cole, Samuel, Jr.
Dill, William

Capt. N. Pettingill's Company, Lieut. Col. W. R. Blaisdell's Regiment — Concluded.

Privates — Concluded.
Downing, John
Graffam, David
Hackett, John
Harris, Richard
Hooper, Isaac S.
Jepson, Ebenezer
Landfest, Abraham
Lowell, James

Merrill, Jedediah, Jr.
Merrill, Richard
Moore, Nathan
Pearce, William
Perham, Seled
Randall, Ezra, Jr.
Randall, James
Ray, Jonathan
Read, Ichabod

Read, Jacob H.
Read, Oliver
Sawyer, Ezra
Stetson, Elijah
Stetson, Stephen
Taylor, Thomas
Winslow, John
Witham, Ebenezer

Capt. M. Sprague's Company, Lieut. Col. W. R. Blaisdell's Regiment.
From Sept. 13 to Sept. 25, 1814. Raised at Greene. Service in camp at Gardiner, awaiting orders.

RANK AND NAME.
Moses Sprague, Captain
Gershom Curtis, Lieutenant
Otis Anderson, Ensign

John Beals, Sergeant
Turner Stetson, Sergeant
Jacob Hatch, Sergeant
William Sprague, Jr., Sergeant
Luther Robbins, Corporal
James Chadbourn, Corporal
Nathaniel Harris, Corporal
Joseph Herrick, 2d, Corporal
Reuben Robbins, Musician
Isaac Sprague, Musician

Privates.
Austin, Stephen
Bailey, Joseph
Bates, Reuben

Booker, Jacob
Briggs, David
Briggs, William
Brown, Richard
Chadbourne, John
Chick, Elias
Coburn, Isaiah
Coburn, Phineas
Coffin, James
Curtis, Robert
Cushman, Artemas
Day, Jacob
Firbish, Abraham
Firbish, John
Grant, Stephen
Griffin, Isaac
Hatch, Josiah
Hatch, Samuel
Herris, John, Jr.
Herris, Joseph

Jackson, Michael
Layne, Samuel
Littlefield, Ephraim
Littlefield, Ivory
Littlefield, Laphael
Littlefield, Story
Mower, Isaac
Mower, Thomas
Pere, Charles
Pere, James, Jr.
Quimby, Benjamin
Quimby, John
Reed, Russell H.
Richardson, Silas
Richardson, Zacheriah
Shipley, Jonathan
Stevens, Rufus
Weld, Timothy
Wilkins, David

Capt. S. Howard's Company, Lieut. Col. W. R. Blaisdell's Regiment.
From Sept. 10 to Sept. 26, 1814. Raised at Leeds. Service in camp at Gardiner, awaiting orders.

RANK AND NAME.
Stillman Howard, Captain (Absent)
Levi Foss, Lieutenant (Commanding)
Samuel Brown, Ensign

Benjamin Willett, Sergeant
Daniel Parcher, Sergeant
Hoten Sumner, Sergeant
Israel Herrick, Sergeant
Orthnell Pratt, Sergeant
Thaddeus Foss, Sergeant
Isaac Boothby, Corporal
Cyrus Foss, Corporal
Amos Phillips, Corporal
Nathaniel Huse, Jr., Corporal
Jonathan Gould, Musician
Naphtali Hanson, Musician
Seth Fish, Musician
Ebenezer Hanson, Musician

Privates.
Andrews, John
Bailey, Ebenezer
Bailey, Joseph

Bailey, Whitman
Berry, Joseph
Boothby, Cyrus
Boothby, Stephen
Brown, Abner
Carver, Eleazer
Carver, John
Carver, William
Cushman, Andrew
Dean, Zebulon
Ellis, Oran
Fish, Benjamin
Fish, I. or J., Jr.
Fish, William
Francis, John
Francis, Thomas, Jr.
Freeman, Allen
Freeman, Isaac
Freeman, Samuel
George, Francis, Jr.
Gould, Asa
Gould, Eli
Gould, Peltiah
Gould, Robert

Gould, Rufus
Gould, Simeon
Gould, William
House, H.
Jennings, Alexander
Jennings, Franklin
Jennings, John
Knapp, Charles
Knapp, Elijah
Knapp, Elijah, 2d
Knowlton, John
Lane, Alpheus
Lane, John
Leadbetter, Luther
Lincoln, Rufus
Lindsey, James
Lothrop, Ira
Lothrop, Thomas
Mason, John
Mason, Martin
Millett, John
Millett, Zebulon P.
Moore, Samuel
Moulton, William

Capt. S. Howard's Company, Lieut. Col. W. R. Blaisdell's Regiment — Concluded.

Privates — Concluded.
Otis, Ensign
Parker, Zacheriah
Paul, Samuel
Pettingill, Harvey
Pettingill, John

Pratt, Charles
Ramsdell, Joshua
Ramsdell, William
Richards, Daniel
Richards, John
Richards, Nathaniel

Robbins, William
Stinchfield, Ebenezer
Stinchfield, Ezekiel G.
Stinchfield, Ezra
Witham, Daniel

Capt. A. Daggett's Company, Lieut. Col. W. R. Blaisdell's Regiment.
From Sept. 13 to Sept. 26, 1814. Raised at Greene and vicinity. Service in camp at Gardiner, awaiting orders.

RANK AND NAME.
Aaron Daggett, Captain
Jabez Pratt, Lieutenant

Thadeus Sawyer, Sergeant
Benjamin Rackley, Sergeant
Ambris Brown, Sergeant
Massey Sylvester, Sergeant
Levi Merrill, Jr., Corporal
Samuel Merrill, Corporal
Stephen Rackley, Corporal
Thomas Graffam, Corporal
Solomon Brown, Musician
Joseph H. Clark, Musician

Privates.
Additon, John
Alden, Benjamin, Jr.

Allen, Ichabod
Berry, John
Cary, Anslem
Caswell, John, Jr.
Cummins, Ebenezer
Cummins, John
Evans, Nathaniel
Fogg, Walter
Getchell, Daniel
Ham, Rufus
Landers, Ansel
Landers, Freeman
Larrabee, Ammi
Larrabee, John, Jr.
Longley, Thomas
Merrill, Amos
Merrill, Benjamin, 3d
Merrill, Jacob

Merrill, John
Merrill, Levi, 3d
Muloon, Samuel
Parker, Jacob
Pettingill, John, Jr.
Robertson, John
Rose, Asa, Jr.
Rose, Seth
Safford, Nathan
Sampson, Abel
Sinclair, James
Stevens, Thomas, Jr.
Thomas, Isaac
Thomas, Martin
Wheeler, Simeon
White, Linus

Capt. D. Lindsey's Company, Lieut. Col. W. R. Blaisdell's Regiment.
From Sept. 13 to Sept. 26, 1814. Raised at Leeds and vicinity. Service in camp at Gardiner, awaiting orders.

RANK AND NAME.
David Lindsey, Captain
Codding Drake, Lieutenant
Stephen Welcome, Ensign

Joseph Turner, Sergeant
Alpheus Turner, Sergeant
Charles D. Gilbert, Sergeant
Joseph Pettingill, Sergeant
James Wing, Corporal
Oliver Sampson, Corporal
Libeus Curtis, Corporal
Obediah Turner, Corporal
William Mitchell, Musician

Privates.
Bates, Henry
Bates, Joseph
Bates, Levi, Jr.
Bishop, James
Bishop, Joseph
Brewster, Morgan, Jr.
Cary, Luther

Crockett, Richard
Curtis, Abner
Curtis, Lincoln
Curtis, William B.
Day, William
Day, William A.
Foster, Timothy
Foye, Nathaniel
Gilbert, Alvah
Gilbert, Bailey
Gordon, George
Gordon, Jonathan
Hoit, Samuel
House, John
Hutchinson, Isaac
Jones, Israel
Lane, Elias
Leathers, Aaron
Libbey, Ebenezer
Libbey, Philip
Libbey, Reuben
Libbey, Thomas
Lindsey, Ira

Lindsey, Robert B.
Lothrop, Lovet
Lothrop, Solomon
Lothrop, Sullivan
Manes, William
Mitchell, Thomas
Morse, Jonathan
Murray, Amos
Owen, Gideon
Pettingill, Arcadus
Pettingill, Real
Rowe, John
Sampson, Hazel
Sampson, Robert
Sanborn, Jonathan
Southard, Constant
Stinchfield, Solomon B.
Turner, Benjamin
Turner, Simeon
Wallis, Levy
Whitney, Joseph
Wing, Caleb

Capt. N. Jewell's Company, Lieut. Col. W. R. Blaisdell's Regiment.
From Sept. 13 to Sept. 26, 1814. Raised at Wales and vicinity. Service in camp at Gardiner, awaiting orders.

RANK AND NAME.
Nathaniel Jewell, Captain
Ebenezer Given, Lieutenant

Benjamin Thompson, Sergeant
Reuben Andrews, Sergeant
Samuel Libbey, Sergeant
Smith Ricker, Sergeant
Samuel Pierce, Corporal
Daniel Foss, Corporal
Freeman Watts, Corporal
John Colby, Corporal
John Hawes, Musician

Privates.
Adams, Benjamin
Austin, Henry

Chase, Nathaniel
Clerk, James
Clerk, Samuel
Dammen, Nisbet
Dickson, Shedrick
Fogg, Benjamin
Fogg, William
Given, John
Gray, Joseph
Gray, Stephen
Hamilton, John
Hannon, Philip
Hodgdon, James
Lombard, Harding
Lombard, Wentworth
Marr, Rufus
Marvel, Joseph

Mills, Jeremiah
Mitchell, Emeziah
Plummer, David
Plummer, William
Small, Ebenezer
Strout, William
Sweat, William
Thompson, Aaron
Thompson, Thomas
Watts, Nathaniel
Weymouth, Walter
Witherell, William

Capt. J. A. Torsey's Company, Lieut. Col. W. R. Blaisdell's Regiment.
From Sept. 13 to Sept. 26, 1814. Raised at Monmouth. Service in camp at Gardiner, awaiting orders.

RANK AND NAME.
John A. Torsey, Captain
Pascal P. Blake, Lieutenant
Frederic W. Dearborn, Ensign

Martin Cushing, Sergeant
Jacob Smith, Sergeant
Robert Gilman, Sergeant
Thomas Witherell, Sergeant
John Plummer, Corporal
Samuel Titus, Corporal
Josiah Towle, Corporal
James Merrill, Corporal
Henry Day, Musician
John Merrill, Musician

Privates.
Adams, Nathaniel
Allen, William

Andrews, Ichabod
Andrews, Otis
Blake, Samuel S.
Brimison, William
Brown, Abraham
Campbell, Xerxes
Cinklee, Ebenezer
Coombs, John
Dearborn, David
Eaton, James
Foss, Hiram
Gilman, John
Gove, Caleb
Gray, Aaron
Gray, Jesse
Gray, Robert
Hall, Isaac
Hinkley, Aaron
Hinkley, Benjamin

Hutcherson, John
Jewett, David
Jones, John
King, Jason
Merrill, Abraham
Murch, Aaron
Norris, George W.
Otis, Simon
Quinn, George
Shaw, John
Smith, Abial
Smith, George
Spears, Asa
Swift, Jiah
Tilton, Josiah
Welch, Edward
Williams, Thomas
Wright, Jonathan

Capt. G. Williams' Company, Lieut. Col. W. R. Blaisdell's Regiment.
From Sept. 13 to Sept. 26, 1814. Raised at Lewiston. Service in camp at Gardiner, awaiting orders.

RANK AND NAME.
George Williams, Captain
Joseph Dill, Lieutenant
William Garcelon, Ensign

Thomas Piper, Sergeant
John Golden, Sergeant
Samuel Staten, Sergeant
Samuel Garcelon, Sergeant
Daniel Garcelon, Corporal
Aaron Lander, Corporal
Ezekiel Merrill, Corporal
William Davis, Corporal
James Garcelon, Musician
Mark Garcelon, Musician

Privates.
Anderson, James
Brooks, William
Bubier, Mark
Carroll, John
Carvill, Joseph
Carvill, Sewell
Coburn, Reuben
Davis, John
Dill, Josiah
Dyer, Barzilla
Dyer, Elkanah
Field, James
Field, Joseph
Ford, Stephen

Garcelon, Ammi
Gilpatrick, Samuel
Golder, William
Haley, Samuel
Ham, James
Hatch, John
Hinkley, Jacob
Hodgkins, Jonathan
Holland, John
Jones, William
Jordan, Nathaniel
Litchfield, Noah
Lowell, Edward
Lowell, William
Merrill, Asa

Capt. G. Williams' Company, Lieut. Col. W. R. Blaisdell's Regiment — Concluded.

Privates — Concluded.
Merrill, Joshua
Merrill, Stephen
Mitchell, James
Mitchell, Joshua
Mitchell, Josiah, Jr.

Morse, Joel
Pettingill, Benjamin
Pettingill, John
Proctor, John
Rand, Barzilla
Ray, William

Thompson, David
Thompson, Samuel
Ware, Lewis
Wright, James
Wright, Zebulon

Capt. M. Boynton's Company, Lieut. Col. W. R. Blaisdell's Regiment.

From Sept. 13 to Sept. 27, 1814. Raised at Monmouth. Service in camp at Gardiner, awaiting orders.

RANK AND NAME.
Moses Boynton, Captain
Royal Fogg, Lieutenant
Benjamin Sinclair, Ensign

Joseph Prescott, Sergeant
Joseph B. Allen, Sergeant
Jedediah B. Prescott, Sergeant
John S. Blake, Sergeant
Newell Fogg, Corporal
Hugh M. Boynton, Corporal
Ivory Towl, Corporal
George W. Fogg, Corporal
Levi Tozier, Musician
John Richardson, Musician

Privates.
Allen, Ichabod
Arno, Ezekiel
Arno, Isaac
Arno, Zacheus
Arnold, John, Jr.
Bartlett, John
Basford, Reuben
Batchelder, William

Bates, Elijah
Blanchard, Joseph
Blew, John
Blossom, Ansel
Boynton, Ebenezer A.
Clough, Asa
Cousins, Alexander
Dearborn, Ebenezer S.
Edgcomb, John
Fogg, Jonathan
Fogg, Nathan
Gilman, John H.
Gray, James
Gray, Joshua
Gray, Nathan
Gray, Thomas N.
Holmes, Samuel
Jackson, Benjamin
Jenkins, Abner
Jenkins, Philip, Jr.
Jenkins, Samuel
Jewell, Robert
Johnson, Daniel
Jones, James
Kimball, Benjamin, Jr.

King, Samuel
Knight, John
Lothrop, Daniel, 3d
Manton, Lewis
Merrill, Joseph
Mitchell, James
Pierce, Oliver
Pinkham, Andrew
Randlett, Moses
Reed, George
Richardson, William
Rowell, Moses
Small, Isaac
Smith, James
Sprague, Elkanah
Thurston, Ebenezer
Tinkham, Amasa
Towle, Robert
True, Thurston W.
Walker, John
Warren, Nathaniel W.
Warren, Peltiah, Jr.
Witherell, James

Lieut. Col. J. Burbank's Regiment.

From Sept. 7 to Sept. 20, 1814. Service at Portland.

FIELD AND STAFF.
John Burbank, Lieutenant Colonel, Standish
John Waterhouse, Major, Scarborough
John T. Smith, Major, Gorham
Daniel Hasty, Adjutant, Standish

Nathan Chadbourne, Quartermaster, Gorham
Joseph Hasty, Paymaster, Gorham
Dudley Folsom, Surgeon, Gorham
Asa Heath, Chaplain, Scarborough

NONCOMMISSIONED STAFF.
Samuel McLellan, Sergeant Major
David Cobb, Quartermaster Sergeant
Thomas Paine, Jr., Fife Major
Peter Sanborn, Drum Major

Capt. E. Andrews' Company, Lieut. Col. J. Burbank's Regiment.

From Sept. 7 to Sept. 20, 1814; 1 day additional for travel. Raised at Scarborough. Service at Portland.

RANK AND NAME.
Ebenezer Andrews, Captain
Eli Leavy, Lieutenant
Jonathan Jose, Ensign

John Andrews, Sergeant
Joseph Meservey, Sergeant
Jacob Milliken, Sergeant
William Foss, Sergeant
Nathaniel Boothby, Corporal
Benjamin Fenderson, Corporal

Timothy Libby, Corporal
John McKenney, Musician
John Pillsbury, Musician

Privates.
Anderson, John
Banks, James
Boothby, George
Boothby, Nathaniel, 2d
Bryant, Eliphalet
Burnham, Ebenezer

Burnham, John
Burnham, Richard
Burnham, Samuel
Burnham, Thomas, 2d
Carter, Benjamin
Carter, Richard, 2d
Carter, Rufus
Carter, Thomas
Coolbroth, Joseph
Coolbroth, Rufus
Dearborn, Josiah

Capt. E. Andrews' Company, Lieut. Col. J. Burbank's Regiment — Concluded.

Privates — Concluded.
Dearing, John, Jr.
Edgcomb, Gibbens, 2d
Edgcomb, Robert
Emery, Isaac
Fabins, Ilar
Fenderson, James
Foss, Jonathan
Foss, Pelatiah
Grace, Thomas
Harmon, Dummer
Harmon, Elias
Harmon, Zachariah, 2d
Hight, Humphrey
Holmes, John, 2d

Holmes, William
Leavitt, Abraham
Leavitt, Edward
Leavitt, Hinskin
Leavitt, James, 2d
Leavitt, Mark
Lovett, Rufus
Marshall, Jonathan
Marshall, Nathaniel
McKenney, Benjamin
McKenney, Philemon
Merrill, Reuben
Milliken, Abraham
Milliken, Benjamin
Milliken, Isaac

Milliken, Joseph
Milliken, Simeon
Pillsbury, David
Pillsbury, Tristram
Rice, Samuel, Jr.
Seavey, Nathaniel
Seavey, Solomon
Seavey, William, 2d
Shute, Samuel
Snow, Phares
Stevens, Calvin
Stuart, Niles
Thurston, Daniel
Wheaton, Elisha

Capt. J. Bailey's Company, Lieut. Col. J. Burbank's Regiment.
From Sept. 7 to Sept. 20, 1814; 1 day additional for travel. Raised at Standish. Service at Portland.

RANK AND NAME.
Joseph Bailey, Captain
Aldrich Paine, Lieutenant
Daniel Cram, Ensign

Robert Mitchell, Sergeant
Samuel Mitchell, Sergeant
Joshua Paine, Sergeant
Abraham Tibbetts, Sergeant
Jabez Dow, Jr., Corporal
Samuel Hasty, Corporal
Jonathan Lowell, Jr., Corporal
Joseph Paine, Corporal
James Moody, Jr., Musician
James Philbrick, Musician

Privates.
Butler, Ivory
Davis, Josiah
Davis, Nathaniel
Dow, Joseph
Green, Joseph
Hasty, Hiram
Linnell, Elisha, Jr.
Lowell, Stephen
Marean, John
McGill, William
Moody, Daniel
Moody, William
Paine, John K.
Paine, Jonathan

Paine, Richard
Paine, Stephen
Paine, William
Paine, Zebulon A.
Shaw, Daniel
Spencer, William
Thompson, William J.
Thorn, John
Wescott, John, Jr.
Whitney, Levi

Capt. J. Bettes' Company, Lieut. Col. J. Burbank's Regiment.
From Sept. 7 to Sept. 20, 1814; 1 day additional for travel. Raised at Gorham. Service at Portland.

RANK AND NAME.
Jacob Bettes, Captain
Levi Hall, Lieutenant
Oliver Johnson, Ensign

James Emery, Sergeant
Clark Swett, Sergeant
Ezekiel Ward, Sergeant
James Wescott, Sergeant
William Bolton, Corporal
Benjamin Irish, Corporal
Uriah Wason, Jr., Corporal
Josiah Waterhouse, Corporal
Robert Walker, Musician
John Walker, Musician

Privates.
Baker, Levi
Bolton, Thomas
Brackett, Daniel
Clay, William
Cole, Joseph
Crockett, John, Jr.
Elder, Reuben, Jr.
Elder, Samuel, Jr.

Emery, Elijah
Files, Nathaniel
Files, Robert, Jr.
Flood, Joseph
Fogg, David
Getchell, Samuel H.
Harding, James
Harding, William
Hicks, Ephraim
Hicks, Nathaniel
Irish, Jacob
Johnson, George
Kemp, David
Kemp, Jonathan
Libby, James
Libby, Jethro, Jr.
Libby, Sewall
Libby, Walter
Lilly, John, Jr.
March, Mathias, Jr.
Mason, Ephraim
Mason, James
Mason, Joseph
Mason, Richard
Mason, Samuel, Jr.

McDonald, James
McDonald, Joseph
Millions, Ebenezer
Mitchell, Matthew
Mitchell, Zachariah
Morton, David, Jr.
Morton, John
Noble, Webber
Pennington, Daniel
Plummer, Christopher
Plummer, Isaac, Jr.
Roberts, Joseph, Jr.
Sanborn, Joseph
Smith, Samuel
Sweet, David
Thomas, William
Tyler, Daniel, Jr.
Tyler, James
Warren, James, 3d
Webb, Seth
Williams, Daniel
Williams, Joseph
Winship, Daniel
Young, Enos

Capt. H. V. Comston's Company, Lieut. Col. J. Burbank's Regiment.

From Sept. 7 to Sept. 20, 1814; 1 day additional for travel. Raised at Scarborough. Service at Portland.

RANK AND NAME.
Henry V. Comston, Captain
Oliver Staples, Lieutenant

William McLaughlin, Sergeant
Jonathan Harmon, 3d, Sergeant
John Meservey, Jr., Sergeant
Robert Moulton, Sergeant
Nathaniel Berry, Corporal
Reuben S. Moulton, Corporal
Luther S. Jewett, Corporal
James McLaughlin, Corporal
Ai Waterhouse, Musician
Joseph Waterhouse, Musician

Privates.
Avery, Thomas
Berry, Abraham
Berry, John
Berry, John, Jr.
Berry, Levi
Berry, Robert
Berry, Zebedee
Berry, Zebulon, Jr.
Bragdon, James

Brown, David
Burnham, Jonathan
Chamberlain, William
Coombs, Benjamin
Davis, Daniel
Evens, Josiah
Fogg, Joseph or Josiah
Fogg, Moses
Foss, Ezekiel
Graffam, James
Graffam, Jeremiah
Harmon, Daniel, 3d
Harmon, John M.
Harmon, John S., Jr.
Harmon, Levi M.
Harmon, Moses, Jr.
Harmon, Richard
Harmon, Robert
Harmon, Zacheus, 3d
Haselton, Asel
Jewett, Joseph S.
King, Cyrus
Libby, Andrew, Jr.
Libby, Benjamin
Libby, Daniel, 3d

Libby, Ephraim
Libby, John, Jr.
Libby, Luther, Jr.
Libby, Moses, Jr.
Libby, Richard, 3d
Libby, Robert, Jr.
Libby, Samuel K.
McLaughlin, Robert, Jr.
Meservey, Andrew
Meservey, Nathaniel
Meservey, Thomas, Jr.
Meservey, William, Jr.
Milliken, Alexander
Milliken, Allison
Milliken, Cyrus
Milliken, John M., Jr.
Milliken, Thomas, Jr.
Milliken, William
Mitchell, Josiah
Moulton, Daniel, 4th
Moulton, John, 3d
Moulton, Thomas
Rice, Phineas
Sawyer, Dean
Stine or Stone, Isaac

Capt. J. Fogg's Company, Lieut. Col. J. Burbank's Regiment.

From Sept. 7 to Sept. 20, 1814; 1 day additional for travel. Raised at Scarborough. Service at Portland.

RANK AND NAME.
John Fogg, Captain
Daniel Larrabee, Lieutenant
Richard Libby, Ensign

John A. Libbey, Sergeant
Sherborn Libbey, Sergeant
Benjamin Sweetser, Sergeant
Joseph Watson, Sergeant
Samuel Hagen, Corporal
Reuben Libbey, Corporal
George Libbey, Corporal
Joshua Chamberlain, Corporal
Israel Perry, Musician

Privates.
Blake, Nathaniel
Bragdon, Enoch
Chamberlain, Joshua
Cobb, John
Crockett, Silas
Dyer, Timothy
Fickett, Ezra
Fly, Nathaniel
Fogg, Abner, Jr.
Freeman, Josiah
Goldthwait, Samuel
Gustin, Thomas
Harmon, Daniel
Harmon, Stephen

Hasty, Joseph
Hunnewell, Josiah
Jones, John
Jones, Samuel
Larrabee, Isaac
Larrabee, Joseph
Lary, John
Libbey, Abner
Libbey, Amos, Jr.
Libbey, Andrew
Libbey, Cyprus
Libbey, Daniel
Libbey, Daniel, 3d
Libbey, Dennis
Libbey, Eliakim
Libbey, James
Libbey, Joseph, 3d
Libbey, Luke
Libbey, Morris
Libbey, Nathaniel
Libbey, Parker
Libbey, Rufus
Libbey, Sewall
Libbey, Shirley
Libbey, Simon, Jr.
Libbey, Stephen
Libbey, Thomas, Jr.
Libbey, Zenos
Matthews, Samuel
Maynard, Cornelius D.

McKenney, Moses
Milliken, Thomas, 3d
Moody, John, Jr.
Moody, Joseph
Moody, Rufus
Moses, Silas
Plaisted, Roger
Plummer, Abraham
Plummer, Joshua
Plummer, Moses
Plummer, Moses, Jr.
Prout, Dominicus I.
Rand, Philemon
Randall, James
Robertson, John
Sawyer, Henry
Skillin, Dennis
Skillin, Enoch
Skillin, Josiah B.
Skillings, Josiah
Small, Reuben
Smith, William
Smith, William, Jr.
Stanford, William
Sweet, George
Sweetser, John, Jr.
Thomas, Job
Walker, Isaac I.
Webb, Stephen

MASSACHUSETTS VOLUNTEER MILITIA IN THE WAR OF 1812. 173

Capt. B. Higgins' Company, Lieut. Col. J. Burbank's Regiment.
From Sept. 7 to Sept. 20, 1814; 1 day additional for travel. Raised at Gorham. Service at Portland.

RANK AND NAME.
Barnabus Higgins, Captain
Ephraim Blake, Lieutenant
Cyrus Hamblin, Ensign

Samuel C. Higgins, Sergeant
John B. Rand, Sergeant
Andrew Crockett, Sergeant
James Thombs, Sergeant
William Weeks, Corporal
Samuel Blake, Corporal
Timothy Bacon, Jr., Corporal
Major Moreton, Corporal
Rufus Rand, Musician
Andrew Plaisted, Musician

Privates.
Adams, Joseph
Babb, John
Bacon, James
Bryant, Abel
Clements, Ebenezer
Clements, John
Cotton, Joseph
Creesy, Joseph, Jr.

Files, Ebenezer, Jr.
Files, Ebenezer S. S.
Frost, Benjamin
Frost, Charles
Frost, Dominicus
Gibbs, Heman
Gilkey, Reuben
Gilkey, Samuel
Green, Stuart
Hall, Isaac
Hall, John
Hamblin, Charles
Hamblin, Enoch
Hamblin, Isaac
Hamblin, Nathaniel
Hunt, James
Kimbol, Daniel
Knight, Colman W.
Lewis, Samuel H. B.
Libby, Benjamin
Libby, Daniel, Jr.
Libby, Solomon
Lincoln, John
Mann, Edmund
McCrusen, Lemuel

Merton, Nathaniel
Moody, John
Paine, Richard
Phinney, Coleman
Phinney, Nathan
Rand, Henry J.
Rolfe, Benjamin
Smith, Caleb
Smith, George T.
Snow, William, Jr.
Stimpson, Amos
Stimson, John
Stone, Jonathan, Jr.
Sturgess, Ebenezer G.
Sturgess, Joseph
Thombs, Eli
Thombs, George, Jr.
Treat, Richard
Wescott, Reuben, Jr.
Whitney, Edmund
Whitney, Eli
Whitney, Luther
Woods, William, Jr.

Capt. R. McLellan's Company, Lieut. Col. J. Burbank's Regiment.
From Sept. 7 to Sept. 20, 1814; 1 day additional for travel. Raised at Gorham. Service at Portland.

RANK AND NAME.
Robert McLellan, Captain
Jacob S. Smith, Lieutenant
Greenleaf C. Watson, Ensign

Nathaniel Phinney, Sergeant
Samuel Edwards, Sergeant
Frederick Colman, Sergeant
Calvin Edwards, Sergeant
Samuel Bartlett, Musician
Samuel Woodard, Musician

Privates.
Clark, John R.
Elder, Simon
Fiskett, Joseph

Freeman, David
Freeman, Nathan
Frost, Luther
Frost, Mason
Gammon, James
Hamblin, Joseph, 3d
Hanscom, Lewis
Harding, David
Harmon, Benjamin
Higgins, Enos F.
Hunt, Joseph
Jordan, Allen
Lakeman, Solomon
McLellan, David
McLellan, John
McLellan, Thomas

McQuillan, William
Merrill, Nahum
Paine, Thomas
Paine, William, Jr.
Patrick, Charles, Jr.
Patrick, Stephen
Sawyer, Isaac
Skillings, Benjamin
Staples, Samuel, Jr.
Stevens, John
Stone, Archellus
Tole, Benjamin
Waterhouse, William H.
Webster, Nathaniel
Williams, Peter

Capt. T. Robie's Company, Lieut. Col. J. Burbank's Regiment.
From Sept. 7 to Sept. 20, 1814; 1 day additional for travel. Raised at Gorham. Service at Portland.

RANK AND NAME.
Toppan Robie, Captain
Nathaniel Hatch, Lieutenant
William Frost, Ensign

James Babb, Sergeant
Philip Larrabee, Sergeant
Thomas Robie, Sergeant
Caleb Seaver, Sergeant
Seward Merrill, Corporal

Moses Rice, Corporal
Perez Burr, Corporal
Alexander Phinney, Corporal
Josiah Jenkins, Musician
George Knight, Musician

Privates.
Alden, Gardner
Blanchard, William
Bragdon, Ephraim

Brown, Levi
Brown, Samuel
Burnell, David
Cash, Jacob
Colbrook, Isaac
Creasy, John
Crockett, Nathaniel
Darling, George L.
Davis, Luther
Edwards, William

Capt. T. Robie's Company, Lieut. Col. J. Burbank's Regiment — Concluded.

Privates — Concluded.
Eldridge, Ebenezer
Farnam, John
Fogg, Daniel
Fogg, George
Freeman, Joshua
Frost, Daniel H.
Gammon, Edmund
Gibbs, Alrich
Hanscom, John
Hanson, Nathan
Harding, John, 3d
Harding, Joseph
Harding, Robert
Harding, Seth, Jr.
Hunt, Daniel

Huston, Robert
Irish, Elisha
Johnston, William
Libby, Darius
Libby, Elliott
Libby, Lemuel
Lincoln, Cotton
Lombard, Joseph, Jr.
Lord, Nahum
March, Moses
McDougal, Thomas
McLellan, James, Jr.
McLellan, William, Jr.
McQuillium, John
Mosher, Samuel F.
Paine, Samuel

Penfield, Nathan
Rice, John
Rice, Joseph
Rice, Lemuel
Rice, Nathaniel
Roberts, Joshua
Roberts, Samuel
Scribner, Samuel G.
Staples, Ai
Strout, George, Jr.
Towle, Abner
Warren, David
Waterhouse, David
Worster, Thomas

Capt. M. White's Company, Lieut. Col. J. Burbank's Regiment.
From Sept. 7 to Sept. 20, 1814; 1 day additional for travel. Raised at Standish. Service at Portland.

RANK AND NAME.
Mark White, Captain
William Wescott, Lieutenant
Levi Haskell, Ensign

Israel Harmon, Sergeant
John Moulton, Sergeant
Solomon Newbegin, Sergeant
Enoch Shaw, Sergeant
James Newbegin, Corporal
Benjamin Haskell, Jr., Corporal
William Hoar, Corporal
Abraham Nason, Corporal
Solomon White, Musician
Joshua Chamberlain, Musician

Privates.
Butterfield, Jesse
Crockett, Henry

Cummings, John
Cummings, Simeon
Davis, Isaac
Elder, Francis
Gilman, Ebenezer
Gray, Charles
Gray, George
Green, Ware
Hall, Moses
Hall, Oliver
Harmon, Daniel
Harmon, Rufus
Knight, George
Larrabee, Benjamin
Larrabee, Isaac, Jr.
March, Benjamin
Mayberry, Abraham
Morton, Caleb
Morton, Jacob

Morton, James
Morton, Thomas
Parker, Benjamin
Proctor, Ebenezer
Rand, Benjamin
Rich, Israel
Sawyer, John
Shaw, Ebenezer, Jr.
Shaw, Peter
Smith, John
Smith, Mack
Smith, Thomas
Stewart, Wentworth
Stuart, Solomon
Whittemore, Major

Capt. J. York's Company, Lieut. Col. J. Burbank's Regiment.
From Sept. 7 to Sept. 20, 1814; 1 day additional for travel. Raised at Standish. Service at Portland.

RANK AND NAME.
John York, Captain
George Rackliff, Ensign

Sargent Shaw, Jr., Sergeant
William Whitmore, Jr., Sergeant
John S. Edgecomb, Sergeant
Joseph York, Sergeant
Reuben Whitney, Musician
Benjamin Sanborn, Musician

Privates.
Anderson, Samuel
Berry, Benjamin
Boothby, Samuel
Boothby, Samuel, 2d
Boulter, Daniel
Boulter, John
Boulter, Nathaniel

Boulter, Samuel
Bradbury, Andrew
Brown, Josiah
Chase, Amos
Cram, Wear
Crane, Ashabel
Davis, Noah
Decker, John, Jr.
Dennett, Samuel
Foss, Ebenezer
Foss, John
Hasty, William
Higgins, Zacheus
Hill, Chase
Hutchinson, Matthew
Libby, Joel
Lowell, Richard
Marean, Enoch
Martin, Abner

Mason, Moses
Mayo, Edmund
McGill, Joseph
Moody, Enoch
Morton, Joseph
Morton, William
Moulton, Benjamin F.
Muzzy, Daniel
Muzzy, William
Parker, Samuel
Philbrick, John
Pierce, Samuel
Rand, Nathaniel
Rich, Moses
Richardson, David
Rogers, Edward
Sanborn, Asa
Sawyer, James
Thombs, Amos, Jr.

MASSACHUSETTS VOLUNTEER MILITIA IN THE WAR OF 1812.

Capt. J. York's Company, Lieut. Col. J. Burbank's Regiment — Concluded.

Privates — Concluded.
Thombs, George
Thombs, Stephen
Thombs, Thomas
Thompson, Jacob

Thorn, Israel, 3d
Thorn, Joseph
Wescott, John
Whitney, Adam
Whitney, William, Jr.

Wood, Edward
Yates, Josiah
York, Jacob, Jr.
York, Joshua

Lieut. Col. C. Clark's Regiment.
From Sept. 13 to Sept. 24, 1814. Stationed at Portland.

FIELD AND STAFF.
Cyrus Clark, Lieutenant Colonel, Minot
Henry Farwell, Major, Buckfield
Levi Merrill, Jr., Major, Turner

Joseph Keith, Adjutant, Minot
Nathaniel Cushman, Quartermaster, Hebron
Benjamin Bradford, Surgeon, Turner

NONCOMMISSIONED STAFF.
Samuel Decoster, Sergeant Major
Calvin Bridgham, Quartermaster Sergeant
Levi Briant, Jr., Drum Major
Alden Bumpus, Fife Major

Capt. I. Bearce's Company, Lieut. Col. C. Clark's Regiment.
From Sept. 13 to Sept. 24, 1814. Raised at Hebron. Service at Portland.

RANK AND NAME.
Isaac Bearce, Captain
Stephen Myrick, Lieutenant
Alvan Turner, Ensign

Gideon Cushman, Jr., Sergeant
Jabez Barrows, Sergeant
Silas Bumpas, Sergeant
Timothy Morton or Norton, Corporal
David Bicknell, Corporal
Elias Tubbs, Corporal
Ebenezer Dunham, Corporal
William Bumpas, Musician
Ezekiel Merrill, Musician

Privates.
Barrows, Cornelius
Barrows, George
Barrows, Job C.
Barrows, Buel or Ruel
Bearce, Gideon, Jr.
Bearce, Levi
Benson, Caleb
Besse, Seth
Bicknell, Cyrus
Bogart, Amos

Bryant, Amos
Bumpas, Jesse
Bumpas, Samuel
Carmon, Luther
Crafts, Samuel, Jr.
Curtis, Ashley, Jr.
Cushman, Isaac, Jr.
Cushman, Reuben
Davis, Simeon
Davis, Solomon
De Coster, Jacob
De Coster, Roger
Drake, Alpheus
Dudly, Nathan
Dunham, James, Jr.
Farris, William
Fuller, Barnabus
Fuller, Robert, Jr.
Glover, Joseph
Gurney, Lemuel
Hutchinson, Henry
Irish, Simeon
Keene, Nathaniel
Keene, Snow, Jr.
Marshall, Aaron
Marshall, John

Merrill, Giles, Jr.
Merrill, Moses
Morgan, Solomon
Morton, Job
Morton, John
Packard, Isaac
Packard, Lewis
Perkins, Ebenezer or Eleazer
Pratt, Barnabus
Pratt, William
Richardson, Stephen
Rowe, Benjamin
Rowe, Joseph
Rowe, Samuel
Stedman, John
Stedman, Samuel W.
Sturdevant, Francis, Jr.
Sturdevant, John
Sturdevant, Joseph
Sturdevant, Nathaniel
Washburn, Peleg
Washburn, Stephen
Whittemore, John
Whittemore, Levi
Whittemore, Samuel, Jr.
Whittemore, William

Capt. L. Bridgham's Company, Lieut. Col. C. Clark's Regiment.
From Sept. 13 to Sept. 24, 1814. Raised at Minot. Service at Portland.

RANK AND NAME.
Luther Bridgham, Captain
James Murdock, Lieutenant
Henry Coy, Ensign

Merrill Woodman, Sergeant
Daniel Freeman, Sergeant
Thomas Gurney, Sergeant

Amos Hersey, Sergeant
Peter Noyes, Corporal
Samuel Bridgham, Corporal
Samuel Bailey, Corporal
Jacob Davis, Corporal
Samuel Davis, Musician
Benjamin Davis, Musician

Privates.
Allen, Benjamin
Allen, William
Bartlett, Jonathan
Bates, John
Beals, Zenas
Bearce, Asa, Jr.
Berry, Timothy

Capt. L. Bridgham's Company, Lieut. Col. C. Clark's Regiment — Concluded.

Privates — Concluded.
Bonner or Bonney, John
Bradbury, Enos
Bradford, Samuel
Bradman, George
Bridgham, Cyrus
Campbell, Charles
Chandler, Ichabod
Chandler, John F. or T.
Chandler, Jonathan
Chandler, Nathaniel
Chandler, Phineas
Chandler, Reuben
Chandler, Stephen
Chandler, Zebedee
Chase, Charles
Crooker, Alden
Crooker, Comfort
Crooker, William
Currier, Benjamin

Davis, William
Dinsmore, James
Evans, Benjamin
Hackett, Salmon
Harlow, Asa
Harris, Amos
Hasey, Jacob
Hasey, Joseph
Haskell, William
Hassam or Hassum, John
Hawks, Dan or Daniel
Hill, William
Hodge, Joseph
Howard, William
Hutchins, Isaiah
Hutchins, Jonathan
Jackson, Henry
Jackson, Joseph
Kilborn, Samuel
Leach, Elijah

Littlefield, Enoch
Marston, Samuel
Millet, David
Millet, Samuel
Millet, Simeon
Millet, Solomon
Philips, Thomas
Pool, David
Sampson, Isaiah
Shaw, Samuel
Stocken, Samuel
Verrill, John
Verrill, Samuel, 4th
Washburn, James
Washburn, Joseph
Wolcott, Solomon
Wolcott, William
Woodman, Jabez

Capt. D. Chase's Company, Lieut. Col. C. Clark's Regiment.
From Sept. 13 to Sept. 24, 1814. Raised at Buckfield. Service at Portland.

RANK AND NAME.
Daniel Chase, Captain
David Record, Lieutenant
Dominicas Record, Ensign

Tobias Ricker, Sergeant
Nathaniel Gammon, Sergeant
Moses Packard, Sergeant
Samuel Record, Sergeant
James N. Pate, Corporal
Ephraim Ricker, Corporal
Lewis Record, Corporal
John Packard, Musician
Pelham Bryant, Musician

Privates.
Berry, Obadiah
Berry, Peter
Briggs, Daniel
Bryant, George
Buck, Simeon
Chase, Joseph
Cole, William
Dagget, Daniel D.
Davis, Joseph H.
Davis, Stephen

Day, George
Doble, Aaron
Drake, Martin
Drew, Cornelius
Drew, Josiah
Drew, Lewis
Ellis, Isaac
Ferrald, Samuel
Forbes, Azra
Foster, Abijah
Foster, Michael
Gammon, Robinson
Gammon, Thomas
Hall, Andrew
Hall, John
Hodgdon, Israel
Hodgdon, John
Homes, Miles
Hutchinson, Daniel
Hutchinson, Stephen
Irish, Joseph
Jewett, James
Latham, Barzillia
Lovell, Mark
Martin, Robert, Jr.
Matthews, Constine

Matthews, John, Jr.
Matthews, Samuel
Merrill, David
Milliken, John
Packard, Elathan
Packard, Jonathan
Packard, Samuel
Person, Aaron
Record, Ebenezer
Record, Ezekiel
Record, Jonathan, Jr.
Record, Simon, Jr.
Record, Thomas
Record, Timothy
Roberts, Seth
Rogers, Levi, Jr.
Shaw, Amos
Sweet, Joseph
Taylor, Elias
Thompson, Gilmore
Thompson, Jonathan
Whitman, Joshua
Young, Benjamin
Young, Isaac
Young, Moses

Capt. J. Harlow's Company, Lieut. Col. C. Clark's Regiment.
From Sept. 13 to Sept. 24, 1814. Raised at Minot. Service at Portland.

RANK AND NAME.
James Harlow, Captain
Ruel Phillips, Lieutenant
Ebenezer Whitehouse, Ensign

Hannibal Thompson, Sergeant
Eliphalet Packard, Sergeant
Ira Beal, Sergeant

Levi Allen, Sergeant
Timothy Welcome, Corporal
Samuel P. Pool, Corporal
John Dillingham, Jr., Corporal
James Perkins, Corporal
Zapher Reynolds, Musician
Luther Tirrell, Musician

Privates.
Allen, Libbeus
Berry, Charles
Bird, Shippen
Bird, William
Bradbury, Jacob
Bradford, Calvin
Bradford, David

Capt. J. Harlow's Company, Lieut. Col. C. Clark's Regiment — Concluded.

Privates — Concluded.
Bradford, Martin, Jr.
Caswell, Noah
Caswell, Otis
Chamberlin, Aaron, Jr.
Chase, Abner
Crooker, Isaac, 3d
Drake, Enos
Freeman, Samuel
Harlow, Hosea

Hatch, Chesley
Hersey, John
Holmes, Asa
Howard, Asaph
Keith, Phiny
Kingsley, Asahel, Jr.
Kingsley, Justin
Landers, Lot
Mitchell, Nahum
Nason, Samuel

Packard, Matthew
Packard, Stephen
Perry, Gad
Perry, Thomas
Tirrel, William
True, Philip
Worcester, James
Young, Christopher

Capt. I. Reynold's Company, Lieut. Col. C. Clark's Regiment.
From Sept. 13 to Sept. 24, 1814. Raised at Minot. Service at Portland.

RANK AND NAME.
Ichabod Reynolds, Captain
Charles Briggs, Lieutenant
Lemuel Nash, Ensign

Benjamin Johnson, Sergeant
Daniel Merrill, Sergeant
John Briggs, Sergeant
Amos Downing, Sergeant
Ezekiel Verrill, Corporal
John Verrill, Corporal
James Willis, Corporal
Jonah Waterman, Corporal
Thomas Dill, Musician
James Goff, Musician

Privates.
Alden, Daniel
Allen, Alpheus
Berry, William
Bradbury, David
Bray, Daniel

Bray, Libbeus
Briggs, Daniel
Caswell, Job
Chase, Peter
Crafts, Moses
Crafts, Zibeon
Davis, Isaac
Drake, Nathaniel
Eaton, Samuel
Frank, Thomas
Gowell, James
Haskett, Isaiah
Herrick, Moses
Hersey, Noah, Jr.
Hodgkins, Ebenezer
Hutchins, Jonathan
Knowlton, Joshua
Lane, Benjamin
Lappand, Abial, Jr.
Leavitt, Jesse
Libby, David
Littlefield, Joshua

Merrill, Jabez
Merrill, Jeremiah
Moody, Nathaniel
Nason, Nathaniel
Nason, Nathaniel, Jr.
Nason, Samuel, Jr.
Niles, Nathan
Pennell, Joseph
Perkins, Moses
Perry, Levi
Pettengill, Eaton
Record, Elisha
Record, Thomas
Reed, Jacob, Jr.
Small, James
Smith, Hatevil H.
Stacy, John
Staples, Josiah
Starling, Solomon
Stetson, Hervey
Verrill, Samuel, 3d

Capt. A. Soule's Company, Lieut. Col. C. Clark's Regiment.
From Sept. 13 to Sept. 24, 1814. Raised at Turner. Service at Portland.

RANK AND NAME.
Aaron Soule, Captain
Isaac Leavitt, Lieutenant
Jabez Merrill, 2d, Ensign

Caleb House, 2d, Sergeant
Daniel Pratt, Sergeant
Josiah Keen, Sergeant
James Allen, 2d, Sergeant
Zelotes Haskell, Corporal
Luther Merrill, Corporal
James Allen, Musician
John C. Young, Musician

Privates.
Austin, John
Bourne, Caleb
Bradford, Ephraim

Brown, Aaron
Brown, Moses
Burt, William
Hall, David
Harlow, Ebenezer
Harris, Martin
Haskell, Asa
Hinds, Chipman
Hine, Thaddeus
House, Joshua
Jones, Abijah
Jones, Benjamin, Jr.
Jones, Isaac
Jones, Tilden
Keen, Jacob
Keen, John, Jr.
King, Grinfill H.
Lucas, David

Ludden, Jacob
Lumber, Peter
Mason, Willard
Merrill, Humphrey
Merrill, Zeriah
Morse, Henry
Pratt, Church
Ross, Jesse
Sawtell, Nathaniel, 2d
Shaw, Jesse
Smith, Israel
Soule, Samuel W.
Turner, Abiel, Jr.
Tuttle, Daniel
Tuttle, William
Waterman, Grey

Capt. S. Staples' Company, Lieut. Col. C. Clark's Regiment.
From Sept. 13 to Sept. 24, 1814. Raised at Turner. Service at Portland.

RANK AND NAME.
Seth Staples, Captain
John Briggs, Lieutenant
Ezra Carey, Ensign

Marcus Conant, Sergeant
Tyrus Dresser, Sergeant
Ichabod Bonney, Jr., Sergeant
Asa Jones, Sergeant
Abner Thayer, Corporal
Clement Randall, Corporal
Otis Phillips, Corporal
Luther Staples, Corporal
Benajah Niles, Musician

Privates.
Adation, Joseph
Bailey, Aretas
Bailey, Luther
Barrell, Pascal
Barrell, William
Bonney, Moses
Bradford, Asa
Bradford, Freeman
Bradford, Stephen
Briggs, Hart
Brown, Artemas
Bryant, Nehemiah
Carey, Cassander
Caswell, William
Cole, Nathan
Conant, Hooper
Dresser, John
Evans, Gilbert
French, Charles
Gilbert, Josiah
Gorham, William
Hall, Sylvanus
Hatch, Levi
Hutchinson, John, Jr.
Jones, Abner
Jones, Richmond
Jones, Sylvester
Loring, Thomas
Loring, William
Manuel, James
Maxim, Abraham
McLaughlin, Daniel
Merrill, Abel, Jr.
Moors, Jonathan
Newell, Gustavus
Packard, Josiah
Patch, Levi
Prescott, Solomon
Ramsey, Blanchard
Records, Calvin E.
Russell, Daniel
Smith, Elliot
Snell, Eleazer
Snell, Moses, Jr.
Thorp, Reuben
Turner, Oliver
Washburn, Cyrus
Wightman, Melvin
Williams, Philip

Lieut. E. Stevens' Company, Lieut. Col. C. Clark's Regiment.
From Sept. 14 to Sept. 24, 1814. Raised at Sumner. Service at Portland.

RANK AND NAME.
Ezra Stevens, Captain
Jesse How, Ensign

Simeon Hersey, Sergeant
Zenas Stetson, Sergeant
Joseph Robinson, Jr., Sergeant
Zenas Hall, Sergeant
John Benney, Sergeant
Israel Held, Corporal
Leonard Benson, Corporal
Elijah C. Hall, Corporal
Alvin Robinson, Jr., Corporal
Amasa Tucker, Musician
William Allen, Musician

Privates.
Abbott, Daniel
Baird, John
Barnes, James
Barrett, Joseph
Barrows, Ansel
Bates, Cyrus
Beard, Samuel, Jr.
Benson, Joseph
Bisbee, Calvin
Bisbee, Daniel
Bisbee, Luther
Bonney, Thomas
Bosworth, William
Briggs, Nathaniel
Briggs, Samuel
Bryant, James
Butterfield, John
Clark, William
Cobb, Stephen
Coburn, Peter
Coburn, Samuel
Coburn, Silas
Con or Cox, John
Crockett, Joseph
Crockett, Samuel
Cummings, Oliver, Jr.
Cushman, Levi
DeCoster, Thomas
Doble, Phineas
Drake, Ephraim
Dutton, David
Elliot, Moses
Fletcher, Benjamin
Ford, Joshua
Ford, Seth
Fry, Jonathan
Fuller, Artemas
Glover, Nathaniel
Gowell, Joseph
Held, Benjamin
Held, Benjamin, Jr.
Hersey, James, Jr.
How, Jeremiah
Keen, Andrew
Keen, Cyrus
Keen, Daniel
Keen, Edward
Keen, Freeman
Keen, Judah
Keen, Meshack
Mason, Reuben
Merrill, David
Merrill, Enoch
Moore, William
Newman, William
Oldham, Daniel
Oldham, Thaddeus
Parlen, Almond
Parlen, Ira
Parlen, Oliver
Robbins, Oliver
Robinson, Asa, Jr.
Robinson, Stephen
Rowe, Zacheus
Stetson, Abel
Stetson, Ephraim
Stetson, Hezekiah, Jr.
Swift, Joseph, Jr.
Tuell, Gilbert
Woodman, William

Lieutenant Col. J. Commings' Regiment.

From Sept. 3 to Sept. 20, 1814. Service at Belfast.

FIELD AND STAFF.
John Commings, Lieutenant Colonel, Beaver Hill
Mark Hatch, Major, Putnam
Joseph Gowin, 2d, Major, Montville
Michael Crowel, Adjutant, Palermo

Jesse Martin, Chaplain, Palermo
Elias Davis, Quartermaster, Freedom
Ebenezer Broadstreet, Paymaster, Freedom
Samuel C. Hito or Kito, Surgeon's Mate, Palermo

NONCOMMISSIONED STAFF.
Edmund Black, Sergeant Major
Benjamin Commings, Quartermaster Sergeant

Capt. Gideon Barton's Company, Lieutenant Col. J. Commings' Regiment.

From Sept. 3 to Sept. 20, 1814. Raised at Windsor. Service at Belfast.

RANK AND NAME.
Gideon Barton, Captain
George Marson, Lieutenant
John Page, Ensign

William Baroler, Sergeant
Jacob Jewett, Sergeant
Clement Moody, Sergeant
Michel Lane, Sergeant
Robert Hutchinson, Corporal
Luther Pierce, Corporal
Walter Dockindoff, Corporal
Thomas Harriman, Corporal
Lot Chadwick, Musician
Joseph Wright, Musician

Privates.
Bowdin, Frank
Choat, Rufus
Clary, David
Clary, James

Cottle, John
Foster, Joseph, Jr.
Givins, James
Gol, Edward
Gordon, Daniel
Gustin, Robert M.
Hallowell, James
Hallowell, Joel
Hallowell, John
Hallowell, William
Hillen, Benjamin
Jordan, Elias
Keene, Prince
Lawton, Jonathan
Lebalister, Thomas
Linn, James
Linscott, Joseph
Livin, Samuel B.
Marsh, Henry
Moody, John
Ostin, John

Philbrick, Joseph
Pike, Elisha
Plummer, Daniel
Pratt, James
Prebble, Jeremiah
Rines, Thomas
Rockton, Jonas
Rogers, Enoch
Rogers, Joseph, Jr.
Rollins, Ichabod
Sekins, Benjamin
Speed, Joseph
Stickney, Benjamin
Stickney, Thomas
Taylor, Samuel, 3d
Trask, David
Trask, John
Tylor, Timothy
Wright, Elias
Wright, Warren

Capt. Moses Burley's Company, Lieutenant Col. J. Commings' Regiment.

From Sept. 3 to Sept. 20, 1814. Raised at North Palermo. Service at Belfast.

RANK AND NAME.
Moses Burley, Captain
David Sylvester, Lieutenant
Jonathan Nelson, Ensign

John Foye, Sergeant
Silas Hamilton, Sergeant
Henry Sanford, Sergeant
Nathaniel Broadstreet, Sergeant
John Spiller, Musician
Joseph Spiller, Musician

Privates.
Arnold, Spencer
Arnold, William
Baily, John W.
Baily, Thadeus
Belding, Stephen
Bishop, Hersey
Black, Joshua
Blake, William
Brasure, Joseph
Bryant, Jacob
Bryant, Nehemiah

Bryant, William
Bryant, Zimrie
Carlisle, George
Carr, Richey
Clary, Timothy
Crowell, Asa
Davis, Elias
Dean, John, Jr.
Dennis, Amos, Jr.
Foster, Aaron
Foye, Hollis
Foye, Joseph
Foye, William
Gillpatrick, Riggs
Hamilton, William F.
Hoyt, John
Ledbetter, Samuel
Lelan, Lewis, Jr.
Longfellow, Green
Longfellow, Stephen
Magregory, Alpheus
Marden, James, Jr.
Marden, Jonathan
Morry, Ichabod

Nelson, John
Parkhurst, Jonathan
Perkins, Nathaniel
Pullen, Gilbert
Robinson, Charles, Jr.
Robinson, Nathaniel B.
Rowe, James
Sanford, Daniel
Shoney, Benjamin
Shoney, Edmund
Shoney, James
Soule, Ezekiel
Soule, John
Soule, Joseph
Tuck, Hugh
Tuck, Saul G.
White, Joseph
Whittier, Joseph
Whittier, Reuben
Worthen, John
Worthen, Jonathan
Worthen, Nathan
Young, Benjamin

Capt. J. Daggett's Company, Lieut. Col. J. Commings' Regiment.
From Sept. 3 to Sept. 20, 1814. Raised at Washington. Service at Belfast.

RANK AND NAME.
James Daggett, Captain
Daniel McCardy, Lieutenant
William Witt, Sergeant
Calvin Starrett, Sergeant
William Priest, Sergeant
John Gilpatrick, Sergeant
John Bowman, Sergeant
John Clark, Sergeant

Privates.
Clark, Elisha
Cooland, Daniel, Jr.
Cunningham, John
Cunningham, Samuel
Cunningham, Simon
Cunningham, Timothy
Davis, Daniel
Dearing, John
Dearing, William
Dodge, Peter
Dor, Samuel

Eastman, Enos
Farrow, Thomas
Fish, John
Fitch, Henry
Gane, Enoch
Gilpatrick, David
Gilpatrick, Thomas
Grenald, Philip
Heaton, Isaac
Hibbard, Daniel
Hopkins, Robert
Jones, Kinsley, Jr.
Lawton, James
Layer, Henry
Layer, Martin
Light, Peter
Lisner, Charles
Lisner, George
Maining, John
Marr, John, Jr.
Montgomery, Robert
Moody, John

Overlock, Jacob
Overlock, John
Overlock, Joseph, Jr.
Overlock, Martin
Pelton, Joel
Pinkham, Amos
Pinkham, John
Randall, Nelson
Razor, Charles, Jr.
Razor, Jacob
Riggs, Thomas M.
Rollins, Eliphalet
Speed, Benjamin
Speed, Robert
Taylor, John S.
Tibbetts, Benjamin
Toby, Joseph
Walker, Henry
Wilson, Amos
Wilson, Walter H.
Winchempan, Jacob
Witt, Sewell

Capt. Job Lord's Company, Lieut. Col. J. Commings' Regiment.
From Sept. 3 to Sept. 20, 1814. Raised at Palermo. Service at Belfast.

RANK AND NAME.
Job Lord, Captain
John Treat, Lieutenant
John Brown, Ensign

Stephen Baker, Sergeant
Stephen Greely, Sergeant
Jonathan Towl, Sergeant
Moses Bradstreet, Sergeant
Jacob Greely, 3d, Musician
John Edwards, Musician

Privates.
Benton, Burnham
Berry, Joseph

Bowler, Joseph
Boynton, Oliver
Bradstreet, Aaron
Brown, Benjamin
Brown, Isaac
Cain, David
Cain, Henry
Cunningham, Asa
Day, Elihu
Dennis, Benjamin
Dow, Joseph
Fish, John
Glidden, David
Greeley, Daniel
House, Eleazer

Jones, William
Landers, James, Jr.
Lanfer, James
Lewis, Andrew
Lewis, William
Longfellow, Jonas
Man, Benjamin
Nelson, Charles
Turner, Benjamin, Jr.
Turner, David, 2d
Turner, Hollis
Turner, Nathan
Warf, Oliver
Worthen, Samuel

Capt. J. M. Sinclair's Company, Lieut. Col. J. Commings' Regiment.
From Sept. 3 to Sept. 20, 1814. Raised at Montville, Beaver Hill (now Freedom) and vicinity. Service at Belfast.

RANK AND NAME.
John M. Sinclair, Captain
Amos Sylvester, Lieutenant
John Robinson, Ensign

Thomas Broadstreet, Sergeant
Thomas Penny, Sergeant
Stephen P. China, Sergeant
Richard Gerry, Sergeant
John M. Perkins, Corporal
Reuben Abbott, Jr., Corporal
John S. Ayer, Corporal
Joseph Robinson, Corporal
Anson Barlow, Musician
David Ranlett, Musician

Privates.
Abbott, John
Ayer, Benjamin, Jr.
Banton or Bowton, Joseph
Bickmore, Samuel
Brown, John
Carr, Josiah
Chase, Job, Jr.
Clay, Jonathan
Clay, Stephen
Coffin, Grindal
Cookson, Abram
Cookson, John
Cookson, Joseph
Danforth, Josiah

Danforth, Nathaniel
Danforth, Stephen
Davis, Daniel
Emmons, John
Gerry, John
Glidden, Moses
Going, Samuel
Gould, Aaron
Gould, Moses
Harryman, Eliakim
Huff, Noah
Lathrop, Samuel
Leatherby, Samuel
Loring, Lemuel
Lowell, Jonathan A.

Capt. J. M. Sinclair's Company, Lieut. Col. J. Commings' Regiment — Concluded.

Privates — Concluded.
Lowell, Rufus
Plummer, Aaron
Prebble, John
Reigns, Samuel
Robinson, Charles
Robinson, Robert M.
Rollins, Aaron

Russell, Joseph
Sidelinger, Charles
Sidelinger, John
Smart, Jacob
Smart, Jonathan
Smith, James A.
Smith, John, Jr.
Spencer, William

Stubborn, John
Sylvester, Ebenezer
Sylvester, Luke
Tibbets, Henry
White, John B. or R.
Wiggin, John
York, Abel
York, Simon

Capt. R. Thompson's Company, Lieut. Col. J. Commings' Regiment.
From Sept. 3 to Sept. 20, 1814. Raised at Montville. Service at Belfast.

RANK AND NAME.
Robert Thompson, Captain
Jonathan Carter, Lieutenant
Asa Taylor, Ensign

Asa Gowin, Sergeant
Nathaniel Gowin, Sergeant
Thomas Foster, Sergeant
Abiel Pearce, Sergeant
Jonathan Bean, Musician
Joseph Barton, Musician

Privates.
Ames, Doyal
Beal, Henry
Bean, Jeremiah
Catlin, John
Catlin, Richard
Choat, Robert
Clement, Job
Cobb, Thomas
Cox, Ezra

Curtis, Charles
Cushman, Thomas
Doty, Paul
Dyer, Henry
Ellis, Joseph
Evans, Ephraim
Foster, Nathan
Gamage, William
Gilchrist, Hugh
Gilchrist, William
Gilman, Smith
Gorton, James
Gowin, Ebenezer, Jr.
Hall, Isaac
Jackson, William
Jones, William
McFarland, Andrew
McFarland, John
McLaughlin, Thomas
Nash, David
Pearce, Elius
Pearson, Andrew, Jr.

Perry, John
Pierce, Nathan, Jr.
Pollan, John
Ranlet, Henry
Ripley, Naum
Rockleff, Samuel
Rogers, Samuel
Rowell, Jacob
Shed, Pierce
Simmons, Levi
Temple, Levi
Temple, Stephen
Thatcher, Elisha
Thompson, Ichabod
Thompson, Israel or Isaac
Thompson, Joshua
Thompson, Moses
Thompson, Thomas
Thompson, William
Whitten, Ebenezer, Jr.
Whitten, Paul, Jr.

Capt. James Wallace's Company, Lieut. Col. J. Commings' Regiment.
From Sept. 3 to Sept. 20, 1814. Raised at South Montville. Service at Belfast.

RANK AND NAME.
James Wallace, Captain
John Twitchell, Lieutenant
Macarus Carr, Ensign

Moses Sargent, Sergeant
Joseph Carr, Sergeant
George Roberts or Robertson, Sergeant
Paul True, Sergeant
Richard McAllister, Corporal
Joshua Davis, Corporal
Thomas Robertson, Corporal
Nathan French, Corporal
Joseph Bean, Musician
Ebenezer Demerit, Musician

Privates.
Atkinson, James
Ayer, Hazen
Bagley, Levi
Barker, Stephen
Bartlett, David
Bartlett, Jonathan
Bean, Nathan
Cram or Crane, James
Davis, Israel
French, Joseph
Fry, Robert
Harriman, Dudley
Hatch, Abiel
Joy, Benjamin
Keith, Friend

Keys, Tyler
Laiten, Saul or Samuel
Ledbetter, James
Ledbetter, John
McAllister, Archibald
Milliken, Moses
Robbins or Rollins, Edward
Small, Joseph
Stevens, Ebenezer
Taft, Wales
Thomas, John
True, Ezekiel
True, Moses
Wheaton, Humphrey
White, John

Lieut. Col. E. Cutter's Regiment.
From June 20 to June 24, June 30 to July 5, and Sept. 10 to Sept. 28, 1814. Service at Boothbay.

FIELD AND STAFF.
Ezekiel Cutter, Lieutenant Colonel, Wiscasset
John McKown, Major, Boothbay
Daniel Cate, Major, Dresden
Joel Howe, Major, Nobleboro
Philip E. Theobald, Surgeon, Wiscasset

Benjamin L. Howe, Surgeon's Mate, Wiscasset
Joshua Hilton, Adjutant, Wiscasset
Daniel Quinnam, Quartermaster, Wiscasset
Calvin Pratt, Paymaster, Wiscasset
Hezekiah Packard, Chaplain, Wiscasset

NONCOMMISSIONED STAFF.
Tilly H. Cleasby, Drum Major, Wiscasset
Nehemiah Somes, Fife Major, Wiscasset
Solomon Holbrook, Quartermaster Sergeant, Wiscasset

Capt. J. Hunnewell's Company, Lieut. Col. E. Cutter's Regiment.
From June 20 to June 24, 1814. Raised at Wiscasset. Service at Wiscasset.

RANK AND NAME.
James Hunnewell, Captain
Nathaniel Robinson, Lieutenant

Robert Trevett, Sergeant
Oliver Dickinson, Sergeant
Spencer Greenleaf, Sergeant
William Elmes, Musician

Privates.
Baker, Henry A.
Bayley, Charles
Bolden, Joseph
Boynton, Jeduthan
Briggs, John W.
Crane, Abijah

Cushman, Kenelam
Dickinson, Abijah
Dickinson, John
Dickinson, Joseph
Frith, Joseph
Greenough, Moses
Harris, John
Heard, James
Holbrook, Solomon
Jackins, David
Linch, Daniel
Linch, John
Lovel, John
McKenney, Daniel, Jr.
Morland, John
Noyes, Thomas

Otis, Thomas
Porter, Ezra, Jr.
Pottle, Jordan
Savage, Abraham
Sevey, James
Sevey, Michel
Sheldon, John
Stevens, William
Stuart, Robert
Wheelright, Robert
White, Bartlett
White, Jesse
White, Joseph G.
Young, John, Jr.

Capt. J. Hunnewell's Company, Lieut. Col. E. Cutter's Regiment.
From June 20 to June 24, and Sept. 10 to Sept. 28, 1814. Raised at Wiscasset. Service at Wiscasset.

RANK AND NAME.
James Hunnewell, Captain

Robert Trevett, Sergeant
Oliver Dickenson, Sergeant
Spencer Greenleaf, Sergeant
William Stevens, Sergeant
William Elmes, Musician

Privates.
Baker, Henry
Bolden, Joseph
Briggs, Benjamin
Brooks, John

Crane, Abijah
Cushman, Kineland
Dickenson, John
Dickinson, Abijah, Jr.
Dickinson, Joseph
Greenough, Moses
Harris, John
Holbrook, Solomon
Jackins, David
Linch, Daniel
Linch, John
Noyes, Thomas
Parsons, Guy
Porter, Ezra, Jr.

Pottle, Jordan
Ross, Benjamin
Savage, Abraham
Sevey, James
Sevey, John
Sevey, Michel
Sevey, Solomon, Jr.
Sheldon, John
Stevens, William
Stuart, Robert
Wheelright, Robert
White, Bartlett
White, Jesse, Jr.
White, Joseph G.

Capt. Henry Whitney's Company, Lieut. Col. E. Cutter's Regiment.
From June 20 to June 24, and Sept. 10 to Sept. 28, 1814. Raised at Wiscasset. Service at Wiscasset.

RANK AND NAME.
Henry Whitney, Captain
Barker Neal, Lieutenant
Warren Rice, Ensign

Elisha T. Taylor, Sergeant
Benjamin Sewall, Sergeant
Ezra Clark, Sergeant
Dutty Ladd, Sergeant
Jason Sewall, Musician
Samuel Sewall, Musician

Privates.
Anderson, William
Babson, John, Jr.
Bartlett, Seth
Carleton, William
Cook, Jonathan
Doane, Isaac W.
Dodge, Endicott F.
Fowle, Henry
Harding, Daniel F.
Hodge, John
Lowell, John

Nutter, John
Payson, Silas
Prentiss, George W.
Roby, Henry
Stacy, John
Stacy, William
Weathern, Arthur
Weed, Henry
Wilder, Darius
Winchester, Solomon W.
Young, Bradford
Young, Joshua

Capt. W. M. Reed's Company, Lieut. Col. E. Cutter's Regiment.

From June 20 to June 23, June 24 to June 26, June 29 to July 5, and Sept. 10 to Sept. 28, 1814. Service at Boothbay.

RANK AND NAME.
William M. Reed, Captain
Joseph McCobb, Lieutenant
John Pinkham, Ensign

John Baker, Sergeant
Samuel Montgomery, Sergeant
Joseph Morse, Sergeant
Ephraim McCobb, Sergeant
Joseph Tibbetts, Sergeant
John B. Booker, Sergeant
William Thompson, Sergeant
Paul M. Reed, Musician
William Rust, Musician
Samuel Bush, Musician
Israel Gardner, Musician

Privates.
Abbott, George
Alley, Ephraim, Jr.
Alley, Jacob
Alley, John, Jr.
Alley, John, 3d
Alley, William
Babcock, Benjamin
Barter, John, 4th
Bennett, Daniel
Bennett, John
Booker, Joseph, Jr.
Boyd, George M.
Boyd, Samuel
Brattle, Jesse
Breen, Joseph
Brewer, Samuel
Brier, Elihu, Jr.
Brier, Jesse
Brier, Samuel
Brown, Samuel
Buck, Simon I.
Campbell, John
Clifford, William, 3d
Crooker, Francis
Cunningham, Rufus
Cunningham, William
Dodge, Ebenezer
Dodge, John
Dodge, John, 2d
Dodge, Samuel
Dole, Cyrus
Durang, Daniel
Farnham, John
Farnham, Joseph
Grant, Thomas
Grimes, Joseph
Grover, John, Jr.
Huff, Moses, 2d
Hutchings or Huckings, Jonathan
Hutchings, Samuel
Jennes, Joseph
Kelly, John
Kennedy, William
Knight, John
Lampson, Ephraim
Landerkin, John
Landerkin, Richard, 2d
Lewis, Gills
Lewis, John, 2d
Lewis, Joseph, 2d
Mathews, William
Merry, David
Montgomery, James
Montgomery, William
Morrison, Jonathan
Murray, James
Murray, Samuel
Page, Daniel
Perkins, Jacob
Race, George, Jr.
Radcliff, William
Reed, James
Riggs, Samuel
Robbinson, Micah
Sargent, Thomas
Sherman, Elisha
Sherman, John
Sherman, Joseph
Smith, Francis
Springer, Abraham
Tibbetts, Mark
Trask, Daniel
Trask, William
Wylie, John, Jr.
Wylie, Robert, 3d

Capt. D. R. Adams' Company, Lieut. Col. E. Cutter's Regiment.

From June 20 to June 24, 1814. Raised at Boothbay. Service at Boothbay.

RANK AND NAME.
David R. Adams, Captain
William Clark, Lieutenant
Ebenezer Decker, Ensign

William Thompson, Sergeant
Samuel Thompson, Jr., Sergeant
John Southward, Jr., Sergeant
Stephen Lewis, Jr., Sergeant
Nathaniel Tibbets, Musician
John Lewis, Jr., Musician

Privates.
Abbott, George
Adams, James
Adams, Samuel, Jr.
Barter, Benjamin
Barter, John
Barter, Samuel
Barter, Samuel, 2d
Barton, John, Jr.
Cameron, John
Cameron, William
Cunningham, William
Decker, Abraham, Jr.
Decker, James
Decker, John
Decker, Thomas, Jr.
Dexter, Thomas
Farmer, William
Floyd, John
Gray, Henry
Gray, Saul
Harris, Samuel, Jr.
Harris, William
Hodgden, Benjamin
Hutchings, Andrew
Hutchings, John
Kenney, John
Kent, Joseph
Knight, Daniel
Lewis, Samuel, Jr.
Lewis, Saul
Love, George
Love, John
Lundy, Ebenezer
Maddox, Pelagrave
Mathews, Daniel
Mathews, Joseph
Merrill, George U.
Orn, William
Pierce, David
Pierce, Edward B.
Pierce, George W.
Pierce, Sylvester
Pierce, Thomas
Pinkham, Ichabod
Pinkham, Isaac
Pinkham, Nathan
Pinkham, Samuel
Pinkham, Solomon
Pinkham, Thomas
Pribble, Aris
Pribble, David
Pribble, Joseph
Rand, John, Jr.
Rand, Stephen
Rand, William
Reed, Andrew
Reed, John
Reed, John M.
Reed, Paul
Reed, Paul, Jr.
Rino, Joseph, Jr.
Rowell, Thomas
Smith, Saul G.
Stover, John
Stover, Saul
Thompson, David
Tibbets, Mark
Tibbetts, Isaac
Webber, John
Webster, Stephen
Wilie, Alexander, Jr.
Wilie, Robert
Williams, James

Capt. R. McLean's Company, Lieut. Col. E. Cutter's Regiment.
From June 21 to June 25, 1814. Raised at Alna. Service at Wiscasset.

RANK AND NAME.
Robert McLean, Captain
Jotham Donnell, Ensign

Edward Robinson, Sergeant
Abram Walker, Sergeant
James Peva, Sergeant
James Averill, Sergeant
Ezekiel Averill, Musician

Privates.
Averill, William
Ayer, James
Ayer, William
Bailey, Richard
Boyd, Thomas
Boynton, John
Boynton, John, Jr.
Brack, Benjamin
Carlton, Jeremiah

Clough, Joseph
Cooper, James N.
Decker, Israel
Dole, John, 2d
Dunlap, Ezekiel
Erskine, Thomas
Fairservice, John
Farnham, Benjamin
Heath, James
Hilton, Joseph
Hunt, David
Hutchins, John
Jewett, Jeremiah
Jewett, Nathaniel
Kimball, George
Laiton, Joseph
Lowell, Abner
Lowell, Charles
Lowell, John
Moffett, James

Neaton, Harvey
Nelson, David
Nelson, Eli
Newell, Nathan
Noyes, Daniel
Palmer, Elisha
Palmer, John
Palmer, Jonathan
Palmer, William
Pearson, Paul
Perkins, Samuel
Plummer, Jeremiah
Simpson, William
Somes, Simeon
Tobey, Isaac
Toby, Sylvester
Tomlison, John
Woodbridge, William

Capt. R. McLean's Company, Lieut. Col. E. Cutter's Regiment.
From June 24 to June 25, 1814. Raised at Alna.

RANK AND NAME.
Robert McLean, Captain
Nathaniel Robinson, Lieutenant
Dudley Smith, Ensign

Nathan Clark, Jr., Sergeant
John W. Briggs, Sergeant
William Cargill, Sergeant
Ezra Clark, Sergeant
Nehemiah Somes, Musician
Spencer Tinkham, Musician

Privates.
Anderson, William
Austin, Josiah
Babb, Nathaniel
Blagdon, Alexander
Boland, John
Boland, Joseph
Campbell, John
Campbell, Thomas
Cochran, David
Cochran, William
Coffin, Stephen
Cook, David

Crane, Abijah
Crane, Joseph
Cunningham, Thomas
Cushman, Wendam
Davis, Heald
Decker, Isaac
Dickinson, Joseph
Dodge, Moses
Dow, John
Dow, Joseph
Given, David
Glass, John
Gray, Thomas, Jr.
Greenleaf, Benjamin, Jr.
Greenough, Moses
Haggett, Daniel
Hussey, Richard
Kennedy, Thomas, Jr.
Leathers, Asa
Lenox, Patrick, Jr.
Linch, Daniel
Lynch, John
McKenney, Daniel
Moore, Jonathan
Munsey, Isaac

Noyes, Thomas
Pottle, Jordan
Rundlet, Oak
Seavey, James
Seavey, Michel
Seavey, Solomon, Jr.
Sheldon, Webb
Simpson, Robert
Simpson, Robert, Jr.
Simpson, William
Soames, David
Stearns, Ezekiel
Stewart, Robert
Stinson, William, Jr.
Turner, Gideon
Viney, Samuel
Waters, William, Jr.
West, John
Wheelwright, Robert
White, Bartlett
Woodbridge, Benjamin
Woodbridge, Harry
Woodbridge, James
Young, Bradford
Young, Joshua

Capt. D. R. Adams' Company, Lieut. Col. E. Cutter's Regiment.
From June 30 to July 5, 1814. Raised at Boothbay. Service at Wiscasset.

RANK AND NAME.
David R. Adams, Captain
William Clark, Lieutenant
Ebenezer Decker, Ensign

William Thompson, Sergeant
Samuel Thompson, Sergeant

John Southward, Sergeant
Stephen Lewis, Sergeant

Privates.
Abbott, George
Adams, James
Adams, Samuel, Jr.

Ball, Levi
Barter, Benjamin
Barter, John
Barter, John, 4th
Barter, Samuel
Brice, Edward, 2d
Burley, Paul

Capt. D. R. Adams' Company, Lieut. Col. E. Cutter's Regiment — Concluded.

Privates — Concluded.
Cameron, John
Carlton, Stephen
Crocker, Benjamin
Cunningham, William
Currier, William
Decker, John
Decker, Thomas, Jr.
Decker, William
Farmer, William
Floyd, John
Gray, Henry
Gray, Samuel
Harris, Samuel, Jr.
Harris, William
Hodgdon, Benjamin
Hutchings, Andrew
Hutchings, John
Ingraham, John
Kent, Ebenezer
Kent, Joseph
Kimball, Henry
Kinney, Edward
Kinney, John
Knight, Dan
Lewis, Giles

Lewis, Lemuel, Jr.
Lewis, Samuel
Love, George
Love, John
Love, John, Jr.
Lunds, Ebenezer
Mathews, Dan
Mathews, John
Mathews, Joseph
McCobb, John
McKown, William
Orn, James
Orn, William
Pierce, David
Pierce, George W.
Pierce, Jacob
Pierce, Sylvester
Pinkham, Ichabod
Pinkham, Isaac
Pinkham, Nathaniel
Pinkham, Samuel
Pinkham, Thomas
Prebble, David
Pribble, Joseph
Rand, John, Jr.
Reed, Andrew

Reed, Andrew, 2d
Reed, Andrew, 4th
Reed, Frederic
Reed, John
Reed, John, 2d
Reed, John M.
Reed, Joseph
Reed, Paul
Reed, Paul, 2d
Reed, Robert, 3d
Reed, Robert, 4th
Rowell, Thomas
Smith, Samuel G.
Stover, John
Stover, Samuel
Thompson, David
Tibbets, Isaac
Tibbets, James
Tibbets, Nathaniel
Webber, John
Webster, Stephen
Wiley, Alexander, Jr.
Williams, James
Wotten, Samuel
Wylie, Robert

Capt. S. G. Wilson's Company, Lieut. Col. E. Cutter's Regiment.
From June 30 to July 5, and Sept. 10 to Sept. 28, 1814. Service at Edgecomb.

RANK AND NAME.
Samuel G. Wilson, Captain
Rufus Sewall, Lieutenant
Enoch Dodge, Ensign

Samuel Patterson, Sergeant
Israel Harrington, Sergeant
John Baker, Sergeant
David Webster, Sergeant
Saul Huff, Musician

Privates.
Baker, Azariah
Brown, Elijah
Brown, Ephraim
Burnham, Solomon
Clifford, Ebenezer
Clifford, John
Clifford, Spencer

Cothern, Robert
Cunningham, Rufus
Dodge, Daniel
Dodge, John
Dodge, John, 2d
Dodge, Samuel
Dodge, Warren
Doll, Cyrus
Emerson, Joseph
Fly, William, Jr.
Gove, Elijah
Gove, James
Hagget, Amos
Haggett, William
Harrington, John
Huff, Daniel
Huff, George
Huff, Moses, 2d
Huff, Moses, 3d

Hutchings, Saul
Jemes, Joseph
Light, Andrew
Lowers, Nathaniel
Merry, Joseph
Moore, William
Patterson, David
Patterson, William
Pool, Isaac
Riggs, Saul
Ring, Aaron
Shearman, Joseph
Shearman, William
Tiller, James
Trask, Daniel
Trask, William, Jr.
Webster, Stephen
Williams, Saul

Capt. A. Potter's Company, Lieut. Col. E. Cutter's Regiment.
From July 2 to July 31, 1814. Service at Wiscasset and Boothbay.

RANK AND NAME.
Aaron Potter, Captain
Nathaniel Robinson, Lieutenant
Dudley Smith, Ensign

Joseph Morse, Sergeant
Jonathan Heath, Sergeant
James Thomas, Sergeant

Ruel Smith, Sergeant
Joseph Brooks, Corporal
Jordan Tarbox, Corporal
Louis Mayer, Corporal
James Pickard, Corporal
Abram Choat, Musician
Rufus Brawn, Musician

Privates.
Adams, Samuel
Allen, George
Alley, John
Ayer, William
Babson, John
Barker, John W.
Barker, Samuel

Capt. A. Potter's Company, Lieut. Col. E. Cutter's Regiment — Concluded.

Privates — Concluded.
Barter, John
Barter, John, Jr.
Bates, Israel
Bennett, John
Blagdon, Charles
Blinn, Gilmore
Brown, Samuel
Carlisle, Amos
Clifford, Ebenezer
Clough, Joseph
Cookson, William
Crooker, Hatch
Cunningham, William
Decker, John
Decker, Thomas, Jr.
Densmore, Ephraim
Fowler, Ebenezer

Goodwin, Daniel
Groves, Joseph
Hailey, Matthew
Heard, James
Hutchins, Andrew
Keating, James
Kenney, Edward
Kettle, John
King, Benjamin
Larrabee, Seth
Lewis, Joseph
Lewis, Samuel
Munsey, Reuben
Palmer, William
Partridge, Ichabod
Patterson, David
Peasley, Oliver
Pottle, David

Race, George
Reed, Paul
Rittall, James
Sampson, William
Simpson, William, Jr.
Stilfin, James T.
Stover, Samuel
Wadleigh, William
Ware, Everett
Ware, Joseph
Webb, Joshua
Weed, Henry
Whittier, James
Wilson, Moses
Woodbridge, Benjamin, Jr.
Woodward, Levi
Yeaton, Harvey

Capt. J. Erskine's Company, Lieut. Col. E. Cutter's Regiment.
From June 18 to June 24, 1814. Raised at Wiscasset. Service at Wiscasset.

RANK AND NAME.
John Erskine, Captain
Phineas Wellam, Lieutenant
Dudley Smith, Ensign

Nathan Clark, Jr., Sergeant
John M. Decker, Sergeant
William Bradley, Sergeant
Daniel Carr, Sergeant
Joseph Clark, Corporal
Benjamin Allbee, Corporal
William Perkins, Corporal
Oliver Whitcomb, Corporal
Richard M. Barker, Musician
Spencer Tinkham, Musician

Privates.
Allbee, John
Blagden, Alexander
Blagden, Charles
Blagden, James
Burding, Winslow
Clark, Samuel
Coffin, Stephen
Crane, Joseph
Decker, Isaac
Dow, John
Dunnell, Moses
Fegan, Joseph I.
Glass, John
Greenleaf, Benjamin, Jr.

Haggett, Daniel
Huntoon, John
Hussey, Richard
Munsey, Isaac
Munsey, Samuel
Nute or Mute, John
Place, Charles
Stinson, William, Jr.
Thompson, John
Thompson, William
Tucker, Richard H.
Vincy, Samuel
West, John
Whittier, James

Capt. J. Erskine's Company, Lieut. Col. E. Cutter's Regiment.
From June 21 to June 24, 1814. Raised at Wiscasset. Service at Wiscasset.

RANK AND NAME.
John Erskine, Captain
Nathaniel Robinson, Lieutenant
Dudley Smith, Ensign

William Bradley, Sergeant
Daniel Carr, Sergeant
Spencer Greenleaf, Sergeant
William Cargill, Sergeant
Oliver Whitcomb, Corporal
Joseph Church, 2d, Corporal
Richard M. Barker, Musician
Spencer Tinkham, Musician

Privates.
Blagden, Alexander
Blagden, Charles
Blagden, James
Cargill, Donald
Chandler, Stephen

Chase, William
Clark, Samuel
Cochrane, David
Cochrane, William
Coffin, Stephen
Crane, Abijah
Crane, Joseph
Cunningham, Alexander
Cunningham, Charles
Decker, Isaac
Dickerson, John
Dodge, Moses
Dow, John
Duncan, Joseph
Fairservice, Thomas
Given, David
Glass, John
Gray, Thomas
Greenleaf, Benjamin, Jr.
Greenough, Moses

Haggett, Daniel
Harley, Robert
Huntoon, John
Hussey, Richard
Jackins, David
Kennedy, Robert
Kennedy, William, 3d
Lacy, Patrick
Laiton, George
Leathers, Asa
Lynch, John
Malcomb, David
McKenney, Daniel
McNear, Samuel
Morse, James
Munsey, Isaac
Nichols, John
Nute or Mute, John
Otis, Thomas
Rundlet, Oaks

MASSACHUSETTS VOLUNTEER MILITIA IN THE WAR OF 1812.

Capt. J. Erskine's Company, Lieut. Col. E. Cutter's Regiment — Concluded.

Privates — Concluded.		
Scovy, Solomon, Jr.	Stearns, Ezekiel	Woodbridge, Benjamin
Shattuck, David	Stinson, William	Woodbridge, Henry
Sheldron, Fred	Turner, Gideon	Woodbridge, James
Simpson, William	Waters, William, Jr.	Woodbridge, Thomas
Somes, David	Webb, Joshua	
	Wilson, Moses	

Capt. J. Erskine's Detachment, Lieut. Col. E. Cutter's Regiment.
From Aug. 1 to Aug. 5, 1814. Service at Wiscasset.

RANK AND NAME.	*Privates.*	
John Erskine, Captain	Burding, Winslow	Hobert, Seth
	Dow, John	Tucker, Richard H.
William Bradley, Sergeant	Fickett, Nathaniel	Viney, Samuel

Capt. J. Erskine's Company, Lieut. Col. E. Cutter's Regiment.
From Sept. 6 to Sept. 12, 1814. Raised at Wiscasset. Service at Wiscasset.

RANK AND NAME.	*Privates.*	
John Erskine, Captain	Allbee, John	Munsey, Isaac
Phineas Wellam, Lieutenant	Backliff, Benjamin, Jr.	Munsey, Samuel
Dudley Smith, Ensign	Blagden, Charles	Nute or Mute, John
	Blagden, James	Rollins, Nathaniel
Nathan Clark, Sergeant	Coffin, Stephen	Stinson, William
John M. Decker, Sergeant	Decker, Isaac	Thompson, William
William Bradley, Sergeant	Dow, John	Viney, Samuel
Daniel Carr, Sergeant	Dow, Joseph	West, John
Oliver Whitcomb, Corporal	Fegan, Joseph J.	Whittier, James
Joseph Currier, Corporal	Fickett, Nathaniel	
William Perkins, Corporal	Glass, John	
Richard M. Barker, Musician	Huntoon, John	
Spencer Tinkham, Musician	Hussey, Richard	

Capt. J. Johnson's Company, Lieut. Col. E. Cutter's Regiment.
From Sept. 6 to Sept. 12, 1814. Raised at Dresden. Service at Wiscasset.

RANK AND NAME.	*Privates.*	
Joseph Johnson, Captain	Allen, Jesse	Hathorn, John, Jr.
Benijah Cate, Lieutenant	Barker, Caleb, Jr.	Meserve, Daniel
William Bowerman, Ensign	Bickford, William, 2d	Meserve, Reuben
	Call, Philip	Myer, William
Daniel C. Howard, Sergeant	Call, Richard	Myers, Louis
Stephen Myers, Sergeant	Call, Samuel	Patterson, Samuel
Elisha Meserve, Sergeant	Call, William	Sewall, David
John Bickford, Sergeant	Call, William, Jr.	Smith, Rind
Jabez Blanchard, Musician	Groves, Joseph	Stone, Nathaniel
		Woodward, Levi

Capt. B. Goodwin's Company, Lieut. Col. E. Cutter's Regiment.
From Sept. 6 to Sept. 28, 1814. Raised at Dresden. Service at Wiscasset.

RANK AND NAME.		
Benjamin Goodwin, Captain	William G. Johnson, Sergeant	James Turner, Musician
Samuel G. Johnson, Ensign	Samuel Barker, Sergeant	William Rittal, Musician
	Zebediah Perkins, Corporal	
James White, Sergeant	Francis White, Corporal	*Privates.*
Benjamin Webb, Sergeant	David Call, Corporal	Allen, George
	John Seigars, Jr., Corporal	Allen, John

Capt. B. Goodwin's Company, Lieut. Col. E. Cutter's Regiment — Concluded.

Privates — Concluded.
Allen, Samuel
Allen, Samuel, 2d
Barker, Gideon
Barker, John W.
Barrett, Henry
Bickford, Charles
Blair, Alexander
Blair, John
Blair, Joshua
Blair, Samuel
Blen, Gilmore
Blen, Harrison
Blen, John
Call, Jonathan

Colburn, William
Costelow, John
Densmore, Ephraim
Fisher, Mathias
Fogg, Joseph
Goodwin, Daniel
Goodwin, David S.
Goodwin, Samuel
Hinton, John
Hinton, William
Johnson, Rowland
Marson, Stephen
Mayer, Charles
Mayer, George
Obrine, Charles

Obrine, James
Obrine, William, Jr.
Pushard, John G.
Rittal, Francis
Rittal, James
Rittal, John
Robbins, Abither
Robbins, Elias
Rollins, Elias
Sanborne, John
Seigars, Ebenezer
Stilphin, Cornelius
Stilphin, James L.
Stilphin, Louis
Wadleigh, William

Capt. R. McLean's Company, Lieut. Col. E. Cutter's Regiment.
From Sept. 6 to Sept. 28, 1814. Raised at Alna. Service at Wiscasset.

RANK AND NAME.
Robert McLean, Captain
Jonathan Dannel, Ensign

Edward Robinson, Sergeant
Abram Walker, Sergeant
James Perd, Sergeant
James Averill, Sergeant
William Ayer, Corporal
James Ayer, Corporal
Richard Bailey, Corporal
Ezekiel Averill, Musician
Benjamin Black, Musician

Privates.
Averill, William
Boyd, Thomas
Boynton, John, Jr.
Boynton, John, 3d

Carlton, Jeremiah
Clough, Joseph
Cooper, James A.
Dole, John, 2d
Dunlap, Ezekiel
Erskine, Thomas
Heath, James
Hilton, Joseph, Jr.
Hunt, David
Hutchins, John
Jewett, Benjamin
Jewett, Jeremiah
Jewett, Nathaniel
Kimball, George
Laiton, Joseph
Lowell, James
Moffatt, James
Nelson, David
Nelson, Elis

Palmer, Elisha
Palmer, John
Palmer, Jonathan
Palmer, William
Pearson, Paul
Philbrooks, John
Plummer, Jeremiah
Plummer, Nathaniel
Rowe, Rufus
Simpson, William
Somes, Simeon
Stevens, James
Toby, Sylvanus
Tomlinson, John
Viney, David
Walker, William
Woodbridge, William
Yeaton, Harvey

Capt. D. R. Adams' Company, Lieut. Col. E. Cutter's Regiment.
From Sept. 10 to Sept. 28, 1814. Raised at Boothbay.

RANK AND NAME.
David R. Adams, Captain
William Clark, Lieutenant
Ebenezer Decker, Ensign

William Thompson, Sergeant
Samuel Thompson, Jr., Sergeant
John Southward, Jr., Sergeant
Stephen Lewis, Jr., Sergeant
Nathaniel Tibbetts, Musician
John Lewis, 3d, Musician

Privates.
Abbot, George
Adams, James
Adams, Samuel, Jr.
Barter, Benjamin
Barter, John
Barter, John, 4th

Barter, Samuel
Barter, Samuel, 3d
Cameron, John
Cameron, William
Cunningham, William
Decker, Abraham, Jr.
Decker, James
Decker, John
Decker, Thomas, Jr.
Decker, Thomas, 3d
Farmer, William
Floyd, John
Gray, Henry
Gray, Samuel
Harris, Samuel
Harris, William
Hodgdon, Benjamin
Hutchings, Andrew
Hutchings, John

Kent, Joseph
Kinney, John
Knight, Daniel
Lewis, Saul
Lewis, Saul, Jr.
Love, George
Love, John
Lundy, Ebenezer
Maddox, Pelsgrave
Mathews, Daniel
Mathews, Joseph
Merrell, George W.
Orn, William
Pierce, David
Pierce, Edward B.
Pierce, George W.
Pierce, Sylvester
Pierce, Thomas
Pinkham, Ichabod

Capt. D. R. Adams' Company, Lieut. Col. E. Cutter's Regiment — Concluded.

Privates — Concluded.
Pinkham, Isaac
Pinkham, Nathan
Pinkham, Samuel
Pinkham, Solomon
Pinkham, Thomas
Pribble, Aris
Pribble, David
Pribble, Joseph
Rand, John, Jr.

Rand, Stephen
Rand, William
Reed, Andrew
Reed, John
Reed, John M.
Reed, Paul
Reed, Paul, Jr.
Rino, Joseph, Jr.
Rowell, Thomas
Smith, Samuel G.

Stover, John
Stover, Samuel
Thompson, David
Tibbetts, Isaac
Tibbetts, Mark
Webber, John
Webster, Stephen
Williams, James
Wylie, Alexander, Jr.
Wylie, Robert, 4th

Capt. S. Johnson's Company, Lieut. Col. E. Cutter's Regiment.
From Sept. 10 to Sept. 28, 1814. Raised at Newcastle.

RANK AND NAME.
Samuel Johnson, Captain
Timothy Page, Lieutenant

William Kennedy, Sergeant
Robert Murry, Sergeant
Thomas Kanservice, Sergeant
David Malcom, Sergeant
Joshua Webb, Corporal
William Waters, Corporal
Benjamin Woodbridge, Corporal
Royal Copeland, Corporal

Privates.
Babb, George
Barker, Bamos
Campbell, John
Cargill, Daniel
Chase, William
Cochran, David

Cooper, Leonard
Cothern, John
Cunningham, Alexander
Cunningham, Charles
Cunningham, Henry
Cunningham, Isaac
Cunningham, Samuel
Cunningham, Thomas
Dodge, Daniel
Dodge, Joseph
Dodge, Moses
Duncan, Joseph
Gray, Thomas
Gwin, David
Haggett, Ebenezer
Harley, Caleb
Harley, Robert
Hopkins, William
Kennedy, Robert
Laman, Henry

Lenox, Patrick
Lenox, Thomas
McNear, Samuel
Nichols, George
Patterson, Elias
Rundlett, Oaks
Sherman, Aaron
Simpson, Robert
Simpson, William
Smith, Francis
Stearns, Ezekiel
Stevens, Mark
Tukey, William
Turner, Gideon
Turner, Nathaniel
Waters, Nathaniel B.
Wilson, Moses
Woodbridge, Henry
Woodbridge, Thomas

Capt. Samuel Tarbox's Company, Lieut. Col. E. Cutter's Regiment.
From Sept. 10 to Sept. 28, 1814. Service at Squam Island and Edgecomb.

RANK AND NAME.
Samuel Tarbox, Captain
Benjamin Knight, Ensign

Abner Duncan, Sergeant
James Thomas, Sergeant
Jonathan Fowler, Sergeant
Benjamin Wills, Sergeant
J. Colby, Musician
Simon Crumbell, Musician

Privates.
Brooks, Charles
Brooks, Thomas, Jr.

Colby, Henry, Jr.
Crumbell, Moses
Decker, Spencer, Jr.
Duncan, Andrew
Duncan, Daniel, Jr.
Duncan, John, Jr.
Duncan, Simon
Duncan, Stephen
Fowles, Ebenezer
Greenleaf, Ebenezer
Greenleaf, Westbrook
Heal, James
Hodgdon, Caleb
Hodgdon, John

Hodgdon, John, Jr.
Hodgdon, Joseph
Hodgdon, Joseph, 2d
Hodgdon, Thomas
Jewett, Moses
Knight, Stephen
Knight, Thomas
McCarty, James
Tarbox, Jordan
Thomas, William
Warden, William P.
Webber, John

MASSACHUSETTS VOLUNTEER MILITIA IN THE WAR OF 1812.

Capt. J. Erskine's Company, Lieut. Col. E. Cutter's Regiment.
From Sept. 13 to Sept. 26, 1814. Raised at Wiscasset. Service at Wiscasset.

RANK AND NAME.
John Erskine, Captain
Phineas Kellum, Lieutenant
Dudley Smith, Ensign

Nathan Clark, Jr., Sergeant
John M. Decker, Sergeant
William Bradley, Sergeant
Daniel Carr, Sergeant
Oliver Whitcomb, Corporal
Joseph Currier, Corporal
William Perkins, Corporal
Isaac Decker, Corporal
R. M. Barker, Musician
Spencer Tinkham, Musician

Privates.
Alber, John
Backliff, Benjamin, Jr.
Blagden, Charles
Blagden, James
Burding, Thomas
Burding, Winslow
Coffin, Stephen
Crane, Joseph
Dow, John
Dow, Joseph
Fegan, Joseph I.
Fickett, Nathaniel
Gibson, Peter
Glass, John

Hunter, John
Hussey, Richard
Lincoln, Isaac
Munsey, Isaac
Munsey, Saul
Mute, John
Robinson, John
Rollins, Nathaniel
Stimson, William, Jr.
Thompson, William
Viney, Saul
West, John
Whittier, James

Capt. Joseph Johnson's Company, Lieut. Col. E. Cutter's Regiment.
From Sept. 13 to Sept. 28, 1814. Raised at Dresden. Service at Wiscasset.

RANK AND NAME.
Joseph Johnson, Captain
Benijah Cate, Lieutenant
William Bowerman, Ensign

Daniel C. Howard, Sergeant
Stephen Myers, Sergeant
Elisha Meserve, Sergeant
John Bickford, Sergeant
Jabez Blanchard, Musician

Privates.
Allen, Jesse
Barber, Caleb, Jr.
Barker, Gideon
Bickford, William
Call, James, Jr.
Call, Philip
Call, Richard
Call, Saul
Call, William
Getchell, George, Jr.

Groves, Joseph
Hartshorn, John, Jr.
Lowell, David
Meserve, Daniel
Meserve, Reuben
Myers, Lewis
Myers, William
Patterson, Saul
Smith, Revel
Stone, James
Woodward, Levi

Capt. A. Potter's Company, Lieut. Col. E. Cutter's Regiment.
From Sept. 13 to Sept. 28, 1814. Raised at Whitefield.

RANK AND NAME.
Aaron Potter, Captain
Roger Northey, Lieutenant
Simeon Whealor, Ensign

Seth Larrabee, Sergeant
Jonathan Hatch, Sergeant
Nathaniel Carlton, Sergeant
Christopher Tarr, Sergeant
Abram Choat, Musician

Privates.
Askins, John
Bates, Jared
Carlton, Samuel, Jr.
Cookson, William
Cooper, Alexander
Decker, John

Dunton, Israel
Finn, James
Glidden, Charles
Gray, James
Heath, Isaac
Heath, Isaac, Jr.
Herriman, John
James, William
Jewett, Joseph
Jewett, Moses
Jones, George
Kincaid, Samuel, Jr.
Kincaid, William
Krating or Keating, James
Munsey, Reuben
Partridge, Ichabod
Peasby, Abial
Peasby, John

Peasley, Ezekiel
Peasley, James
Peasley, Nathan, Jr.
Peasly, Daniel, Jr.
Philbrook, Ebenezer, Jr.
Philbrook, James
Potter, Ezekiel
Pottle, David
Priblet, Abraham
Reed, Joseph
Sweet, Lemuel
Ware, Benjamin
Ware, Everett
Ware, Joseph
Ware, Nathan, Jr.
Ware, Timothy

Capt. D. R. Adams' Company, Lieut. Col. E. Cutter's Regiment.

From Sept. 28 to Oct. 12, 1814. Raised at Boothbay. Service at Squam Island, erecting a battery.

RANK AND NAME.
David R. Adams, Captain
Barker Neal, Lieutenant
Jotham Donnell, Ensign

William Thompson, Sergeant
Samuel Thompson, Sergeant
Abraham Walker, Sergeant
Benjamin Williss, Sergeant
Nathaniel Tibbetts, Musician
John Lewis, Musician

Privates.
Ayers, James
Barter, Benjamin
Barter, John
Bartlett, Seth
Baxter, Samuel, 3d
Bickford, William
Boynton, John, Jr.
Boynton, John, 3d
Bruce, Barnard
Call, James
Call, Philip
Call, Samuel
Charlton, Jeremiah

Chase, William
Cochran, David
Cochran, William
Cooper, James M.
Cunningham, Thomas
Doan, Isaac W.
Dodge, Moses
Floyd, John
Givens, David
Grey, Francis
Grey, Henry
Grey, Thomas, Jr.
Hagget, Ebenezer
Hagget, Ebenezer, Jr.
Harris, John
Harthern, John
Heath, James
Hodgdon, Benjamin
Horn, Joseph
Jewett, Benjamin
Jewett, Jeremiah
Jewett, Nathaniel
Jones, Simon
Kennedy, Robert
Leighton, George
Lenox, Robert

Lowell, David
Mattocks, Pelsgrove
McNear, Samuel
Merrill, George W.
Nelson, David
Nutter, John
Paison, Paul
Parsons, Guy
Patterson, Elias
Payson, Silas
Pinkham, Nathan
Porter, Ezra
Roby, Henry, Jr.
Savage, Abraham
Sevey, John
Sheldon, John
Smith, Samuel G.
Stacy, John
Stacy, William
Tobey, Sylvanus
Waters, Nathaniel B.
Webber, John
White, Jesse
Woodbridge, Henry
Woodbridge, William

Capt. B. Goodwin's Company, Lieut. Col. E. Cutter's Regiment.

From Sept. 28 to Oct. 12, 1814. Raised at Dresden. Service at Wiscasset.

RANK AND NAME.
Benjamin Goodwin, Captain
Rufus Savage, Lieutenant
Simeon Wheeler, Ensign

Richard Berry, Sergeant
William G. Johnson, Sergeant
John Baker, Sergeant
Jonathan Heath, Sergeant
James Turner, Musician

Privates.
Baker, Asa
Barker, John W.
Binney, Samuel
Blair, Joshua
Chase, Andrew
Clifford, Andrew
Clifford, William
Cochran, Samuel
Colby, Henry, Jr.
Cooper, Alexander
Cromwell, Moses
Cunningham, Rufus
Dow, John
Dow, Joseph

Dunton, Daniel
Dunton, Simon
Glidden, Arnold
Goodwin, Samuel
Gould, William, 2d
Gove, Elijah
Gray, Josiah
Haggett, William
Harrington, James
Harrington, Job
Hintoon, John
Hodgdon, John
Hodgdon, Thomas
Huff, George
Huff, Saul
Hussey, Richard
James, William
Jewett, Joseph
Jewett, Moses, Jr.
Kincaid, William
King, Moses
Lampson, Ephraim
Mason, Daniel
Merrill, Simon
Moore, J.
Munsey, Samuel

Noyes, Thomas
Obrine, Charles
Obrine, William
Palmer, James
Peaslee, Abiel
Peaslee, Nathan, 2d
Philbrick, James
Place, Charles
Preble, William
Rittal, Francis, Jr.
Rittal, William
Robbins, Elias
Robinson, John
Sanborn, John
Seigars, John, Jr.
Stilphin, Cornelius
Stilphin, Lewis
Thomas, William
Tilton, Abraham
Towers, Nathaniel
Ware, Benjamin
Ware, David
West, Joseph
Whitcomb, Oliver

Capt. B. Flint's Company, Lieut. Col. E. Cutter's Regiment.
From Sept. 30 to Nov. 8, 1814. Raised at Nobleborough. Service at Bristol.

RANK AND NAME.
Benjamin Flint, Captain
William Hiscock, Ensign

George Yeates, Sergeant
William Elliot, Sergeant
James Hackelton, Corporal
Arad Hazeltine, Corporal
Isaac Rust, Musician
Alexander Palmer, Musician

Privates.
Burns, William
Chapman, Israel

Chapman, Jesse
Chapman, John
Chapman, Thomas
Fossett, Henry, 3d
Greenlow, Alexander
Greenlow, Joseph
Hall, James, 3d
Hall, Timothy
Hatch, Alexander
Hatch, Oaks
Hodgdon, Benjamin
Hussey, Job, Jr.
Knowlton, David
Knowlton, Joseph

McFadden, Abraham
Milcher, William
Palmer, Ephraim
Poland, Nehemiah
Reed, Abel
Rollins, Frank
Russell, Robert
Sidelinger, Peter
Sprowl, James
Sprowl, William
Studson, Elisha
Turnbull, Robert

Capt. John Sprowl's Company, Lieut. Col. E. Cutter's Regiment.
From Oct. 1 to Oct. 15, 1814. Raised at Bristol.

RANK AND NAME.
John Sprowl, Captain
Nathan Boynton, Lieutenant
Isaac Noyes, Ensign

William Cox, Sergeant
Samuel Fossett, Sergeant
Henry Folsom, Sergeant
Henry Bond, Jr., Sergeant
Henry McGuire, Musician
Thomas Calderwood, Musician
John Foster, Musician

Privates.
Barton, John
Boynton, Richard
Bryant, Benjamin
Bryant, George
Carter, Ephraim
Clark, Nicholas
Cleary, John
Coggins, Simon
Crafts, David
Curtis, Samuel

Day, Elijah
Dow, John
Fish, Nathaniel
Fish, Simeon
Folsom, James
Ford, Gideon
Grimage, William
Gunlan, Ebenezer
Hall, Jesse
Hall, Joseph
Hinds, Benjamin
Humphreys, Jacob
Hutton, Joseph
Johnson, Ephraim
Jones, Alexander
Jones, Rufus
Keen, Mark
Kennedy, Alexander
Layton, Thomas
Marcy, Thomas
McGuire, James
Meeks, Benjamin
Meeks, Ephraim
Meeks, John

Morton, James
Morton, Thomas
Peasly, Jonathan, Jr.
Plummer, John
Poland, John
Revice, Isaac
Revice, William
Richards, James
Richards, Paul
Richardson, Ezra
Ripley, James
Robinson, William
Robison, Robert
Sheppard, Davis
Simonton, Benjamin
Sprowl, William
Thompson, Benjamin
Tole, Samuel
Trask, Enos
Whitehouse, John
Winslow, Reuben
Witham, Josiah
Wright, Josiah

Lieut. Col. Robert Day's Regiment.
From June 30 to July 1, and Sept. 6 to Sept. 23, 1814. Service at Wiscasset, Bristol and vicinity.

FIELD AND STAFF.
Robert Day Lieutenant Colonel, Bristol
Charles Clark, Major, Newcastle
Daniel Cate, Major, Nobleborough
Joel How, Jr., Major, Nobleborough
William Jones, Adjutant, Bristol

Ephraim Rollins, Quartermaster, Nobleborough
Daniel Day, Paymaster, Nobleborough
Lot Myrick, Surgeon, Newcastle
Harry Hazeltine, Surgeon's Mate, Nobleborough

NONCOMMISSIONED STAFF
Joseph Glidden, Sergeant Major
Ephraim Clark, Quartermaster Sergeant
Daniel Quinnam, Quartermaster Sergeant
Simon Dodge, Fife Major
Samuel H. Pool, Drum Major

MASSACHUSETTS VOLUNTEER MILITIA IN THE WAR OF 1812. 193

Capt. John Sprowl's Detachment, Lieut. Col. R. Day's Regiment.
From June 20 to June 22, June 30 to July 1, and Sept. 10 to Sept. 15, 1814. Raised at Bristol. Service at Bristol and vicinity.

RANK AND NAME.
John Sprowl, Captain
Arthur Cox, Lieutenant
James Sprowl, Ensign

John Clark, Sergeant
Jerry Bean, Sergeant
William Cox, Sergeant
Thomas Foster, Sergeant
Henry McGuire, Musician
Thomas Calderwood, Musician

Privates.
Avery, John
Barton, John
Blunt, Samuel
Brackett, Joshua
Bradley, Jesse
Brewer, John
Calderwood, John
Clark, Samuel, Jr.
Curtis, Peter
Curtis, Rufus
Curtis, William
Davis, Nicholas
Davis, William

Fossett, Alex
Fossett, George
Fossett, Henry
Fossett, James
Fossett, Thomas
Foster, Alex
Foster, John
Gamage, Daniel
Gamage, Joshua
Gamage, Thomas
Gamage, William
Greenlaw, Eben
Greenlaw, Thomas Alexander
Hackelton, James
Harding, Joseph
Hervey, Robert
Humphries, Jacob
Johnson, William
Libby, Joel
Little, Hugh
Little, John
McCobb, William
McKown, William
Miller, George
Miller, William
Morton, James, Jr.

Morton, Thomas
Morton, William
Nichols, Charles
Nickels, Thomas
Otis, John
Pool, Ebenezer
Rogers, Moses
Russell, George
Russell, James
Russell, Robert
Russell, William
Simonton, Benjamin
Sprowl, Amos
Sprowl, James
Sprowl, John
Sprowl, John, Jr.
Sprowl, William
Thompson, Benjamin
Thompson, Daniel
Tibbetts, David
Tibbetts, Ephraim
Tibbetts, Samuel B.
Tibbitts, Samuel, Jr.
Tukey, Benjamin
Young, Edward

Capt. James Robinson's Company, Lieut. Col. R. Day's Regiment.
Four days, June 21, 22, 30, July 1, and from Sept. 6 to Sept. 23, 1814. Raised at Newcastle. Service at Newcastle and vicinity.

RANK AND NAME.
James Robinson, Captain
Robert Catland, Lieutenant
Ephraim Taylor, Ensign

Eben D. Robinson, Sergeant
Ebenezer Webb, Sergeant
Jesse Jones, Corporal
Thomas Little, Corporal
Richard Wilkinson, Musician
Abner Stetson, Musician

Privates.
Barstow, Alexander
Barstow, Nathaniel
Clark, Benjamin
Clark, Elisha

Clark, John
Clark, Nathaniel
Codd, Thomas
Dodge, Alexander
Dodge, Benjamin
Dodge, Francis
Dodge, Isaac
Dodge, James
Dodge, John, Jr.
Dodge, Josiah
Dodge, Washington
Elliott, Andrew
Farley, Ebenezer
Glidden, William
Gorham, David
Hall, Ezekiel
Hatch, Frederic

Hatch, Zacheus
Hutchins, Solomon
Jackson, Thomas
Kavanaugh, Edward
Little, Alexander, Jr.
Little, Henry, Jr.
Moody, David
Moony, William
Morgan, Paul
Otis, William
Perkins, Daniel
Perkins, Ebenezer, Jr.
Siders, Daniel
Teague, Joseph
Tilton, John
Whitehouse, Stephen
Young, Stephen

Capt. R. Hiscock's Company, Lieut. Col. R. Day's Regiment.
Four days, June 21, 22, 30, July 1, and from Sept. 7 to Sept. 23, 1814. Raised at Bristol. Service at Bristol.

RANK AND NAME.
Richard Hiscock, Captain
James McNear, Lieutenant
Alexander Cox, Ensign

James Woodward, Sergeant
Patrick Hanby, Sergeant
Isaac Howland, Sergeant

John Harris, Sergeant
William Hunter, Fifer
Isaac Rust, Drummer

Privates.
Askins, James
Askins, John
Askins, Richard

Askins, William
Bearce, Ebenezer
Bearce, John
Bearce, Samuel
Chamberlain, William
Chapman, Israel
Curtis, James
Davis, James

Capt. R. Hiscock's Company, Lieut. Col. R. Day's Regiment — Concluded.

Privates — Concluded.
Farnham, David
Hall, Harvey
Harden, Charles
Hatch, Thomas
Hiscock, James
Huston, Daniel
Huston, James
Huston, John, Jr.
Huston, Robert
Huston, William
Hutchings, Baker
Hutchings, Thomas, Jr.
Jones, James

Jones, John
Killsy, John
Knowlton, Washington
Little, Thomas
McMichel, David
McMichel, James, Jr.
McNear, John
Page, James W.
Page, John
Richards, John
Sidelinger, John
Sidelinger, Samuel
Sprowl, Cornelius
Sprowl, James

Sprowl, Thomas
Sprowl, William
Stratter, George W.
Sykes, Artemas
Thompson, Benjamin
Thompson, Ephraim
Tomlinson, Paul, Jr.
Wiley, John
Wintworth, James
Wintworth, John
Wintworth, John, 2d
Wintworth, Samuel
Woodbery, Israel
Woodward, John

Capt. J. Winslow's Company, Lieut. Col. R. Day's Regiment.

From June 29 to July 1, and Sept. 7 to Sept. 23, 1814. Raised at Nobleborough. Service at Bristol and vicinity. In skirmish at Bristol June 29, 1814.

RANK AND NAME.
John Winslow, Captain
Nathaniel Bryant, Ensign

Nathaniel Winslow, Sergeant
Daniel Moody, Sergeant
Nathaniel Webber, Sergeant
James Waters, Sergeant
Asa Densmorr, Sergeant
Snow Winslow, Fifer
Timothy Hall, Drummer

Privates.
Benner, James
Benner, Joshua
Borland, Samuel
Chapman, Nathan
Chapman, William
Clark, David
Clark, West
Dunbar, Joseph
Engby, Jacob

Genthmer, Samuel
Goodenow, Nathan
Hall, Daniel
Hall, Daniel, Jr.
Hall, Elijah
Hall, Isaac
Hall, James, Jr.
Hall, Mark
Hall, Stephen
Hatch, David
Hatch, Elijah
Hodgdon, Samuel
Hodgkins, Frank
Hodgkins, James
Hussey, Benjamin
Hussey, John
Hussey, Nathaniel
Hussey, Samuel
Jameson, Samuel
Keen, Ephraim
Keen, James
Keen, Samuel

Knowlton, John
Merrill, Enoch
Merrill, John
Merrill, Samuel
Merrill, Thomas, Jr.
Moody, Ezekiel
Moody, John, Jr.
Moody, Richard, Jr.
Morgan, Tolford
Nash, Church
Nash, Samuel
Ross, Daniel
Ross, John
Ross, Samuel
Ross, William
Varner, George
Varner, Henry
Varner, John
Whitehouse, David
Wols, Benjamin

Capt. J. Glidden's Company, Lieut. Col. R. Day's Regiment.

From Sept. 7 to Sept. 23, 1814. Raised at Newcastle. Service at Newcastle.

RANK AND NAME.
John Glidden, Jr., Captain
James Barstow, Lieutenant
John Hussey, Ensign

Daniel Flint, Sergeant
Joseph Glidden, Sergeant
James Turnbull, Sergeant
Moses Tibbits, Sergeant
Daniel Purkins, Corporal
Jeremiah Russell, Corporal
Nathaniel Merservey, Musician
Josiah Winslow, Musician

Privates.
Brown, John H.
Chapman, Daniel
Chapman, Stephen
Dunbar, Jesse
Dunbar, John
Fly, Daniel
Folinsby, Charles
Genthmer, John
Glidden, Nathaniel, Jr.
Groton, Zenas
Grunlow, Joseph
Hall, James
Hall, Timothy
Hatch, Oakes

Hiscock, Perez
Hussy, Job, Jr.
Knowlton, Joseph
McFadden, Abner
Milcher, William, Jr.
Myrick, Josiah
Oliver, Jonathan, Jr.
Sidelinger, Jacob
Stetson, Elisha H.
Turnbull, Robert
Turnbull, William
Varner, Charles
Walts, Samuel
Weeks, Daniel
Winslow, Joseph

Capt. J. Yeates' Company, Lieut. Col. R. Day's Regiment.
From Sept. 7 to Sept. 24, 1814. Raised at Bristol. Service at Bristol.

RANK AND NAME.
James Yeates, Captain
Joseph Richards, Lieutenant
James Yeates, 2d, Ensign

Samuel Bryant, Sergeant
Charles Wilmanhouser, Sergeant
Barker Ozier, Sergeant
James Elliott, Sergeant
Wait Keen, Corporal
Jonas Woodbury, Corporal
William Elliott, Corporal
Thomas Brackett, Corporal
James Blen, Musician
Alexander Palmer, Musician

Privates.
Barton, Enoch
Brown, Peter
Bryant, George
Bryant, John
Bryant, Reuben
Burns, Thomas
Collamer, Davis
Collamer, Nathaniel
Dockindorf, Thomas

Eggan, Simmons
Elliott, Simon
Farrow, Edward
Farrow, William
Fountain, John
Fuller, Samuel
Genthners, John
Hastings, William
Hinds, Benjamin
Horn, Frederick
Humphrey, Ebenezer
Humphrey, Jesse
Hyer, George
Johnson, James
Johnston, James
Johnston, William
Keen, Howlen
Keen, Mark
Kimball, Timothy
Lanter, John
Little, Charles
Martin, William, Jr.
Morton or Norton, Thomas
Nash, Oliver
O'Res, David N.
Ozier, Thomas

Poland, Nehemiah
Richards, Benjamin
Richards, James
Richards, Paul
Richards, Timothy
Smith, Joseph
Stephens, John
Stephens, Thomas
Studly, Nathaniel
Stutson, John
Trowent, Samuel
Webber, Benjamin
Wellman, Gilbert
Wellman, Samuel
Weston, Eliphas
Weston, Joshua
Wibly or Wilby, William
Willmanhouser, Frederick
Wilton, James
Wilton, Joseph
Yeates, George
Yeates, George W.
Yeates, John
Yeates, Thomas
Yeates, Zinas

Capt. Benjamin Flint's Company, Lieut. Col. R. Day's Regiment.
From Sept. 10 to Sept. 23, 1814. Raised at Nobleborough. Service at Nobleborough.

RANK AND NAME.
Benjamin Flint, Captain
Robert Chapman, Lieutenant
William Hiscock, Jr., Ensign

Lucas Barnard, Sergeant
Anthony Chapman, Sergeant
Nathaniel Clapp, Sergeant
Joseph Flint, Sergeant
Ephraim Palmer, Corporal
Michael Chapman, Corporal
Jesse Chapman, Corporal
Frank Rollins, Corporal
Ephraim Chapman, Musician
William Rollins, Musician

Privates.
Barstow, Benjamin
Chapman, Abraham
Chapman, Israel
Chapman, Jacob
Chapman, John
Chapman, Joseph, Jr.
Chapman, Nathaniel
Chapman, Nathaniel, Jr.
Chapman, Orris
Chapman, Robert, Jr.
Chapman, Thomas, Jr.
Dennis, David, Jr.
Flint, Jesse, Jr.
Haseltine, Arad
Hatch, Crowell
Hiscock, Benjamin

Hiscock, John
Hiscock, William
Hussey, Joseph
Knowlton, David
Linscot, William
Merrill, Joseph
Oliver, Samuel
Palmer, John
Perkins, Joseph
Place, Joshua
Plummer, John
Prichard, Thomas
Reed, Abiel
Rollins, John, Jr.
Rollins, Robert
Sidelinger, Charles
Tufts, Francis

Capt. A. Richardson's Company, Lieut. Col. R. Day's Regiment.
From Sept. 10 to Sept. 23, 1814. Raised at Jefferson. Service at Wiscasset.

RANK AND NAME.
Abiathar Richardson, Captain
Elias Hasket, Ensign

John Waters, Sergeant
Henry Bond, Jr., Sergeant
Abiel Noyes, Sergeant
Henry Folsom, Sergeant

Ephraim Packard, Corporal
Ezra Richardson, Corporal
John Eames, Corporal
William Bond, Corporal
Joseph Weeks, Musician
Alexander Jackson, Musician

Privates.
Clark, Alexander
Clark, John
Clark, John, Jr.
Day, Alpheus
Day, Eben
Day, Elijah
Day, William

Capt. A. Richardson's Company, Lieut. Col. R. Day's Regiment — Concluded.

Privates — Concluded.		
Dow, John	Kennedy, John	Sheppard, Cullever
Folsom, James	Kennedy, Nicholas	Sheppard, Francis
Hall, Abiel	Kennedy, William	Sheppard, James, Jr.
Hall, Alexander	Linscot, Elijah	Sheppard, Samuel
Hall, Ebenezer	Linscot, Ephraim	Sheppard, William, Jr.
Hall, Joseph	Linscot, Jeremiah	Weeks, Benjamin
Hall, Robert	Linscot, Thomas	Weeks, Daniel, Jr.
Hatch, Charles	Linscot, William	Weeks, Ephraim
Hilton, James	McCobb, Andrew	Weeks, John
Jackson, Nathaniel	Morey, Philip	Weeks, Joseph
Jackson, Samuel	Noyes, John	Weeks, Joseph, Jr.
Jones, Alexander	Partridge, Joseph	Weeks, Josiah G.
Jones, Alexander, Jr.	Ripley, James	Weeks, Thomas, Jr.
Jones, Gardner	Robinson, Archibald	Whitehouse, James
Jones, Hawkes	Robinson, Charles	Whitehouse, John
Jones, James	Robinson, James, Jr.	Whitehouse, William
Jones, Michael	Robinson, Robert	Witham, Josiah
Kennedy, Alexander	Robinson, William	Young, Johnson
	Rowell, Jesse	

Capt. David Boynton's Company, Lieut. Col. R. Day's Regiment.
From Sept. 11 to Sept. 23, 1814. Raised at Jefferson. Service at Wiscasset and vicinity.

RANK AND NAME.	*Privates.*	
David Boynton, Captain	Boynton, John	King, Benjamin
Nathan Boynton, Lieutenant	Clary, John	Knight, Daniel
Isaac Noyes, Lieutenant	Clary, Robert, Jr.	Noyes, Benjamin
	Clifford, Peter	Noyes, Daniel
John Murphy, Sergeant	Cunningham, Daniel	Peaslee, Jonathan, Jr.
Charles Gray, Sergeant	Cunningham, William	Reeves, Isaac
Nathan Fourd, Sergeant	Decker, Joseph	Tole, Samuel
Jonathan Berry, Corporal	Ford, Gideon	Trask, Enos
Enoch Plummer, Corporal	Ford, William	Trask, Jonathan
David Trask, Corporal	Hayward, Israel	Trask, Thomas
Enoch Wicks, Musician	Henry, Robert	
Joseph Henry, Musician	Hopkins, Bradford	
Rufus Boynton, Musician	How, Marcus	

Capt. J. Winslow's Company, Lieut. Col. R. Day's Regiment.
From Sept. 30 to Nov. 15, 1814. Raised at Nobleborough. Service at Bristol.

RANK AND NAME.	Curtis, James	Hall, Stephens
John Winslow, Captain	Davidson, William	Hall, Zenas
Robert Catland, Lieutenant	Davis, James	Harding, Charles
James Yates, Ensign	Dodge, Francis	Hatch, Elijah
	Dodge, Josiah	Hatch, Frederic
Thomas Little, Sergeant	Doyle, Patrick	Hodgkins, Francis
Nathaniel Winslow, Sergeant	Dunbar, Joseph	Humphrey, Ebenezer
Daniel Moody, Sergeant	Dunsmore, Asa	Hussey, Benjamin
David Varnum, Sergeant	Engley, Jacob	Hussey, Lemuel
Alexander Jackson, Musician	Erskins, John, 3d	Hutchings, Henry
Joseph Weeks, Musician	Erskins, William	Hutchings, Thomas
	Follansbee, Charles	Hutchings, William
Privates.	Gates, John	Jamerson, William
Barstow, Alexander	Gentner, Samuel	Jones, Benjamin, Jr.
Briant, Reuben	Hall, Daniel, Jr.	Jones, John, 2d
Chamberlain, William	Hall, Ephraim	Jones, Shadrack
Chapman, Benjamin	Hall, Isaac	Knowlton, John
Chapman, Nathan	Hall, James, Jr.	Little, William
Clark, Amasa	Hall, Jesse	Merrill, John
Collomore, Nathaniel	Hall, Marks	Moody, David

Capt. J. Winslow's Company, Lieut. Col. R. Day's Regiment — Concluded.

Privates — Concluded.	Ross, Samuel	Stratton, George W.
Osyer, Thomas	Ross, Saul	Thompson, Ephraim
Parmer, Elnathan	Siders, Daniel	Varner, George
Perkins, Daniel	Sprowl, Thomas	Wall, Benjamin
Richards, Isaac	Sprowl, William	Willmanhouser, Frederick
Ross, John	Stephens, John	Wintworth, John

Ensign James Yates' Detachment, Lieut. Col. R. Day's Regiment.
From June 29 to June 30, 1814. Raised at Bristol. Service at Bristol.

Rank and Name.	Brackett, Thomas	Osgood, Joseph
James Yates, Ensign	Burnes, Thomas	Richards, Daniel
	Burnes, William, Jr.	Stetson, John
James Elliott, Sergeant	Collomore, Davis	Webber, Benjamin
	Elliott, Simon, Jr.	Weston, Daniel
Privates.	Elliott, William	Weston, Eliphas
Barton, Enoch	Fuller, Samuel	Yates, George
Blen, James	Hinds, Benjamin	Yates, Thomas

Lieut. Col. E. Foot's Regiment.
From Sept. 2 to Sept. 9, and Nov. 2 to Nov. 7, 1814. Service at Wiscasset.

Field and Staff.	Archelaus J. Coombs, Major, Thomaston	William Stearns, Surgeon, Camden
Erastus Foot, Lieutenant Colonel, Camden	William Carleton, Adjutant, Camden	Enoch Lovejoy, Surgeon's Mate, Thomaston
John Spear, Major, Thomaston	James W. Blackington, Quartermaster, Thomaston	Samuel Baker, Chaplain, Thomaston
Jonathan Wilson, Major, Hope	Samuel Jacobs, Paymaster, Camden	

Capt. A. G. Coombs' Company, Lieut. Col. E. Foot's Regiment.
From June 22 to June 26, 1814. Service at Thomaston.

Rank and Name.	Everett, David	Pilsbury, Nathaniel
A. G. Coombs, Captain	Gray, Leverett	Post, Enoch
George Coombs, Lieutenant	Hall, Anthony	Post, Ezekiel
Ralph Chapman, Ensign	Herd, Moses	Post, Zacheus
	Hix, Samuel	Sayward, James
John Keating, Sergeant	Ingraham, Barnard	Sayward, Joseph
Nathan Pilsbury, Corporal	Ingraham, Coit	Sherman, Nathan
Joseph Bridges, Corporal	Ingraham, Isaac	Simonton, Abraham
Ephraim McLean, Corporal	Ingraham, Josiah	Simonton, John
Anthony Matthews, Musician	Jameson, Robert	Sleeper, Jesse
Elisha Snow, Musician	Jordan, Eben	Small, Jonathan
	Jordan, Ebenezer, Jr.	Snow, Ambrose
Privates.	Jumper, Joseph	Snow, Israel
Amberry, Thomas H.	Lovett, Ephraim	Snow, John M.
Bartlett, Knot	Lowell or Lovell, Archibald C.	Snow, William
Bartlett, Richard	McAllister, Joseph	Thompson, Eben
Bradbury, Wyman	Packard, Benjamin, Jr.	Wade, Leonard
Brewer, Isaac	Packard, David	Walter, George
Bridges, Kingsbury	Perry, David	Whitham, Jerry
Bunker, Isaac	Philbrook, Jerry	Williams, Benjamin
Crockett, Asa	Pierce, Bezzilla	Williams, Jonathan
Emery, John	Pilsbury, John	
Emery, Jonah	Pilsbury, Joseph, Jr.	

198   MASSACHUSETTS VOLUNTEER MILITIA IN THE WAR OF 1812.

Capt. C. Curtis' Company, Lieut. Col. E. Foot's Regiment.
From June 22 to June 25, 1814. Raised at Camden. Service at Camden.

RANK AND NAME.
Calvin Curtis, Captain
Edward Hanford, Lieutenant
Arthur Pendleton, Ensign

William Brown, Sergeant
John Harkness, Sergeant
Amos Foster, Sergeant
Jesse Fay, Sergeant
Israel Thorndike, Musician

Privates.
Blake, William
Crosby, Ephraim G.
Hodgman, Buckley
Hosmer, Anthony
Mirrick, Joseph
Ogier, Joseph
Sherman, Almarine
Start, Ebenezer
Thorndike, Ebenezer

Thorndike, J. W.
Tyler, Abel
Tylor, Simeon
Tyson, Saul

Capt. A. Palmer's Company, Lieut. Col. E. Foot's Regiment.
From June 22 to June 23, Sept. 3 to Sept. 10, and Sept. 21 to Sept. 23, 1814. Service at Camden.

RANK AND NAME.
Asher Palmer, Captain
Noah Brooks, Lieutenant

Henry Bowers, Sergeant
Henry Pendleton, Sergeant
David Ring, Sergeant
Josiah Harrington, Sergeant
Josiah Dillingham, Jr., Corporal
Job Hodgman, Jr., Corporal
Samuel Farr, Corporal
Parley F. Pike, Corporal
John Hewett, Musician
Nathan Fales, Musician

Privates.
Barnes, Abel
Barrett, Daniel, Jr.
Barrett, Nathan
Carle, James
Carle, John

Cloutman, John
Cooper, Nicholas
Cothrell, Jonathan
Cothrell, Robert
Dary, Jesse
Davis, Thomas
Dillingham, Barnard
Fogler, Charles
Harrington, James
Heal, Peter
Higgins, Jonathan
Hilt, Freeman
Hilt, William
Hobbs, Ebenezer
Hopkins, Charles
Hopkins, Nathan
Hopkins, Richard
Hosmer, Charles
Lindsey, Alfred
Maryfield, William
McKeller, Isaac

Melvin, John
Metcalf, James
Molineax, John
Parker, Moses
Perry, Israel
Richard, Robert
Richards, William
Robason, Charles
Rollins, David
Russell, Saul, Jr.
Sargent, Leonard A.
Sawtell, Elnathan
Sherman, Joseph
Tarr, John
Thomas, Edward
Ulmer, Martin
Wagg, James
Wentworth, Tobias
Wheeler, Jonas
Wood, Zacheus

Capt. S. Tolman's Company, Lieut. Col. E. Foot's Regiment.
From June 22 to June 23, 1814. Service at Camden.

RANK AND NAME.
Samuel Tolman, Captain
Joseph Ross, Lieutenant
Isaac Orbeton, Ensign

James Andrew, Sergeant
William Brewster, Sergeant
John Packard, Sergeant
Daniel Packard, Sergeant
Moses Prescott, Musician
John George, Musician

Privates.
Barnes, Amos
Barrows, Saul
Barrows, Stephen
Beckett, John
Bradford, Abraham

Brewster, Ira
Brown, James P.
Bucklin, Mark
Bucklin, Robert
Clough, David
Elmes, John
Fiske, John
Harkness, William
Hathorne, James
Hewett, Waterman
Hewitt, Harvey
Johnson, George
Jones, Benjamin
Jones, Crowel
Keen, Daniel
Keen, Elisha
Keen, James
Manning, John

Newell, Ebenezer
Nutt, William
Oxton, William
Packard, James
Packard, Saul
Perry, John
Perry, Thomas
Pilsbury, Johnson
Post, Stephen
Rollins, Daniel
Ross, Stephen
Simmons, George
Simonton, William
Smith, Abiather
Waterman, Henry
Waterman, Jonah
Watton, John

MASSACHUSETTS VOLUNTEER MILITIA IN THE WAR OF 1812.

Capt. S. Tolman's Company, Lieut. Col. E. Foot's Regiment.
From Sept. 2 to Sept. 9, 1814. Service at Camden.

Rank and Name.	Privates.	
Samuel Tolman, Captain	Barnes, Amos	Nutt, Ashley
Joseph Ross, Lieutenant	Beckett, John	Nutt, William
Isaac Orbeton, Ensign	Bowers, Samuel	Oxton, William
	Bradford, Abraham	Oxton, William, Jr.
Daniel Packard, Sergeant	Bucklin, Robert	Packard, James
John Packard, Sergeant	Clough, David	Perry, Thomas
James Andrews, Sergeant	Elmes, John	Pilsbury, Johnson
William Brewster, Sergeant	Harkness, William	Post, Stephen
Harvey Heart, Corporal	Hathorne, James	Rankins, Constance
Jonathan Brown, Corporal	Johnson, George	Rollins, Daniel
Crowel Jones, Corporal	Jones, Benjamin	Simmons, George
Stephen Burrows, Corporal	Keen, Daniel	Simonton, William
John Fiske, Corporal	Keen, James	Waterman, Henry
Samuel Packard, Musician	Manning, John	Waterman, Jonah
John George, Musician	Norwood, Abraham	Waterman, Joseph
		Watton, John

Capt. C. Curtis' Company, Lieut. Col. E. Foot's Regiment.
From Sept. 3 to Sept. 10, 1814. Raised at Camden. Service at Camden.

Rank and Name.	Privates.	
Calvin Curtis, Captain	Blake, William	Start, Ebenezer
Edward Hanford, Lieutenant	Crosby, Ephraim G.	Thorndike, Ebenezer
Arthur Pendleton, Ensign	Gregory, William, 3d	Thorndike, J. W.
	Hodgman, Buckley	Tyler, Abel
William Brown, Sergeant	Hunt, Simon	Tyler, Coburn
Amos Foster, Sergeant	Mirrick, Joseph	Tyler, Dudley
Jesse Fay, Sergeant	Ogier, Joseph	Tyler, Samuel
John Harkness, Sergeant	Prichard, Asa	Tyler, Simeon, Jr.
Israel Thorndike, Musician	Sherman, Almarine	

Capt. N. Payson's Company, Lieut. Col. E. Foot's Regiment.
From Sept. 3 to Sept. 9, 1814. Raised at Hope. Service at Camden.

Rank and Name.		
Noyes Payson, Captain (absent)	Graham, John	Pease, Palatiah
William Collins, Ensign (in command)	Gwiney, Elisha	Peavey, John
	Hart, James	Perkins, Thomas S.
Benjamin Simmons, Sergeant	Humphrey, John	Proctor, Jeremiah
John Fuller, Sergeant	Irish, Levi	Richards, Robert
George Pease, Sergeant	Jacobs, McCowan	Ripley, Aaron
Shubal M. Pease, Sergeant	Jones, Thomas, Jr.	Ripley, Archalaus
Ephraim Perkins, Corporal	Jordan, Ephraim	Ripley, Peter
Daniel Lincoln, Corporal	Kating, John	Ripley, Thomas
William McLain, Musician	Kinsell or Lassell, John	Robbins, Harvey
Martin Meservey, Musician	Lassell or Kinsell, John	Robbinson, George
	Lincoln, Lemuel	Robinson, Joshua
Privates.	Lincoln, Peleg	Royal, Peter
Arnold, John	Martin, John	Shaw, Samuel
Arnold, William	Maxfield, James	Simmons, Jedediah
Barker, Samuel	Maxfield, William	Simmons, Oliver, Jr.
Brown, Benjamin	McClain, John	Sprague, Noah
Bryant, Henry	McComber, John	Suckforth or Luckforth, Robert
Bryant, William	McLain, Alexander	Sumner, Samuel
Clark, James, Jr.	Merservey, Barnet	Thomas, William
Clark, Josiah	Merservey, George	Thomson, John
Collins, Aaron	Newlet, John, Jr.	Wagner, Jacob
Davis, William	Payson, Ephraim, Jr.	Welman, Jedediah
Drake, James	Pease, Alexander	Wentworth, Lemuel
Gowers, John	Pease, Henry M.	
	Pease, Nathan, Jr.	

Capt. A. Palmer's Detached Company, Lieut. Col. E. Foot's Regiment.
From Sept. 12 to Oct. 11, 1814. Service at Camden.

RANK AND NAME.
Asher Palmer, Captain
John Watts, Lieutenant
Arthur Pendleton, Ensign

John Packard, Sergeant
Asa Payson, Sergeant
Henry Pendleton, Sergeant
John Keating, Sergeant
Samuel Norwood, Corporal
Ebenezer Thorndike, Corporal
Shubal M. Pease, Corporal
George Lindsey, Corporal

Privates.

Acorn, Michel
Bowley, George
Bowley, Michel
Bradford, Abraham
Bucklin, Robert
Butler, George
Butler, Samuel
Carle, James
Carle, Rufus
Conway, Frederic
Coombs, Asa
Copeland, Nathaniel
Crabtree, Saul

Crockett, Knot
Crockett, Robert
Crosby, Ephraim G.
Dean, William
Fales, Atwood
Fogerty, Dennis
Fogler, Charles
Foster, Jeremiah
Gentner, David
George, John
Graffan, Jacob
Graham, John
Hall, Anthony
Hall, Peter, Jr.
Handly, Henry
Hart, James
Haynes, William
Healey, James H.
Humphrey, John
Jenks, Henry
Johnson, George
Jones, Thomas, Jr.
Jordan, Ebenezer
Lincoln, Isaac W.
Lincoln, Lemuel
Marshall, John
Martin, Thomas
Mason, Abraham

Maxfield, William
McLean, Alexander
McLellan, George
Melvin, John
Nutt, William
Packard, David
Packard, Samuel
Palmer, Nathaniel
Parker, Moses
Perry, Thomas
Pierce, Bezaleel
Post, Stephen
Ripley, Thomas
Robbins, Henry
Robertson, George
Russell, Samuel
Sartell, Amos
Sherman, Joseph
Snow, Israel
Spear, Rufus
Spearer, Reuben
Starte, Ebenezer
Stephenson, Francis
Ulmer, Martin
Watts, George
Watts, Moses

Capt. N. Payson's Company, Lieut. Col. E. Foot's Regiment.
From Sept. 21 to Sept. 23, 1814. Raised at Hope. Service at Camden.

RANK AND NAME.
Noyce Payson, Captain
William Collins, Ensign

John McLain, Sergeant
John Fuller, Sergeant
George Pease, Sergeant
Peabody Simmons, Sergeant
Ephraim Perkins, Corporal
Daniel Linckin, Corporal
William McLain, Musician
Martin Meservey, Musician

Privates.

Arnold, John
Brown, Benjamin
Bryant, Henry
Bryant, William
Clark, James, Jr.
Clark, Josiah
Collins, Aaron

Conclin, Isaac
Davis, William
Fairbanks, John, Jr.
Gower, John
Gurney, Elisha
Irish, Levi
Jacobs, McConn
Jordan, Ephraim
Kating, John
Lincoln, Peleg
Martin, John
Maxfield, James
McCumber, John
Meservey, Barrett
Meservey, George
Meservey, John
Newbert, John, Jr.
Payson, Ephraim, Jr.
Pease, Henry M.
Pease, Nathan, Jr.
Peavey, John

Perkins, Thomas S.
Proctor, Jeremiah
Reen, Robert
Richards, Robert
Ripley, Aaron
Ripley, Archelaus
Ripley, Peter
Roakes, James
Robbinson, Joshua
Shaw, Samuel
Simmons, Jedediah
Sinclair, William
Sprague, Noah
Suckforth, Robert
Sumner, Samuel
Thompson, John
Thomson, William
Wagner, Jacob
Wellman, Jedediah

MASSACHUSETTS VOLUNTEER MILITIA IN THE WAR OF 1812. 201

Capt. J. Weed's Company, Lieut. Col. E. Foot's Regiment.
From Sept. 3 to Sept. 9, 1814. Raised at Hope. Service at Camden.

RANK AND NAME.
James Weed, Captain
William Hewett, Lieutenant
Boyce Crane, Ensign

Asa Payson, Sergeant
Nathaniel Kendall, Sergeant
Reuben Safford, Jr., Sergeant
John Bartlett, Corporal
Jonathan Laughton, Corporal
James Tolman, Corporal

Privates.
Athan, Benjamin
Athan, John
Blood, Abel
Boardman, Stephen
Bowly, Ephraim, Jr.

Bowly, George
Bowly, William
Brown, William
Burwell, Benjamin
Conant, Abraham
Conant, Isaac
Copeland, Nathaniel
Cotton, Eliphalet
Crabtree, Samuel
Fiske, Abel
Flagg, Isaac, Jr.
Gilmore, Samuel
Haynes, Willliam
Hilt, Daniel
Hilt, Philip
Howard, Richard
Jamison, Peter
Jordan, James

Kendall, Charleville
Kendall, Samuel
Lassell, John
Lassell, Joshua, Jr.
Mayson, Abraham
Metcalf, Jesse
Noyce, Daniel
Petingel, Holmes
Richards, Dodipher
Richards, Pearl
Simmons, George
Stephenson, Francis
Stinson, Nathaniel
Sweetland, James
Webster, Thomas
Whitcomb, Ebenezer, Jr.

Capt. S. Tolman's Company, Lieut. Col. E. Foot's Regiment.
From Sept. 21 to Sept. 23, 1814. Service at Camden.

RANK AND NAME.
Samuel Tolman, Captain
Joseph Ross, Lieutenant
Isaac Orbeton, Ensign

Daniel Packard, Sergeant
James Andrews, Sergeant
William Brewster, Sergeant
Harvey Hewit, Corporal
James Brown, Corporal
Crowell Jones, Corporal

John Fiske, Corporal
Stephen Barrows, Musician
Henry Waterman, Musician

Privates.
Barnes, Amos
Barrows, Saul
Becket, John
Clough, David
Harkness, William
Jones, Benjamin

Keen, Daniel
Manning, John
Nutt, William
Oxton, William
Packard, James
Rollins, Daniel
Simmons, George
Walton, John
Waterman, Jonah

Capt. J. Weed's Company, Lieut. Col. E. Foot's Regiment.
From Sept. 21 to Sept. 23, 1814. Raised at Hope. Service at Camden.

RANK AND NAME.
James Weed, Captain
William Hewett, Lieutenant
Boyce Crane, Ensign

Isaac Dunton, Sergeant
John Bartlett, Corporal
James Tolman, Corporal

Privates.
Athan, Benjamin
Athan, John
Blood, Abel
Boardman, Stephen
Bowly, Ephraim, Jr.
Bowly, William

Brown, William
Burwell, Benjamin
Conant, Abraham
Conant, Isaac
Cotton, Eliphalet
Farrar, John
Fiske, Abel
Flagg, Isaac, Jr.
Hilt, Daniel
Hilt, Philip
Howard, Richard
Jamison, Peter
Jordan, James
Kendall, Charleville
Kendall, Daniel
Lassell, John

Lassell, Joshua, Jr.
Metcalf, Jesse
Noyce, Daniel
Payson, Sion
Petingel, Holmes
Richards, Dodipher
Richards, Pearl
Simmons, George
Stinson, Nathaniel
Sweetland, James
Sweetland, Wade
Webster, Thomas
Whitcomb, Ebenezer, Jr.
Wingate, Simon
Young, Harvy

Capt. C. Curtis' Detached Company, Lieut. Col. E. Foot's Regiment.
From Oct. 11 to Nov. 19, 1814. Service at Camden.

RANK AND NAME.
Calvin Curtis, Captain
Noah Brooks, Lieutenant
William Collins, Ensign

Jesse Fay, Sergeant
David King, Sergeant
George Pease, Sergeant
Isaac Dunton, Sergeant
J. W. Thorndike, Corporal
Harvey Hewett, Corporal
James Brown, Corporal
Jonathan Laughton, Corporal
Martin Mescrvey, Musician
Nathan Barrett, Musician

Privates.
Arnold, William
Athan, Benjamin
Barnes, Amos
Barrett, Daniel
Barrows, Samuel
Blake, William
Boardman, Stephen
Bowers, Joseph
Bowley, William

Brown, William
Carle, John
Clark, Josiah
Collins, Aaron
Conant, Isaac
Cotterill, Jonathan
Cotterill, Robert
Dean, Samuel
Derry, Jesse
Dillingham, Barnard
Dyer, Brackett
Elmes, John
Gilmore, Samuel
Gurney, Elisha
Harrington, James
Hobbs, Ebenezer
Hopkins, Nathan
Hosmer, Josiah W.
Hunt, Simon
Keen, James
Kendell, Charleville
Lassall, Joshua
Lincoln, William L.
Manning, John
Martin, John
Maxfield, James

McLane, John
Mescrvey, George
Metcalf, James
Ogil, Joseph
Oxton, William
Payson, Sion
Pease, Henry M.
Pilsbury, Johnston
Porter, Benjamin
Richards, Robert
Robbins, John G.
Robinson, Joshua
Rollins, Daniel
Rollins, David
Royal, Peter
Ruswell, Benjamin
Shaw, Samuel
Tarr, John
Thomas, Edward
Thompson, William
Tolman, Nathan
Tyler, Coburn
Tyler, Dudley
Wagner, Jacob
Waterman, Jonah
Wellman, Jedediah

Capt. A. Palmer's Company, Lieut. Col. E. Foot's Regiment.
From Nov. 2 to Nov. 7, 1814. Service at Camden.

RANK AND NAME.
Asher Palmer, Captain

Henry Bower, Sergeant
Henry Pendleton, Sergeant
David Ring, Sergeant
Josiah Harrington, Sergeant
Samuel Farr, Corporal
Parley F. Pike, Corporal
Zacheriah Wood, Corporal
John Hewett, Musician
Nathan Fales, Musician
Robert Annis, Musician

Privates.
Barnes, Abel
Carle, James
Carle, Rufus
Cooper, Nicholas
Curtis, James
Dillingham, Benjamin P.
Fogler, Charles
Hall, Frye
Higgins, Jonathan
Hilt, William
Hobbs, Charles
Hodgman, Thomas
Hopkins, Richard
Hosmer, Charles

Lindsey, Alfred
Melvin, John
Molineax, John
Morse, Charles
Morse, Isaac
Ogier, Peter
Palmer, Nathaniel
Parker, Moses
Robason, Charles
Sherman, Joseph, Jr.
Simonton, John
Ulmer, Martin
Wagg, James
Wentworth, Tobias

Capt. S. Tolman's Company, Lieut. Col. E. Foot's Regiment.
From Nov. 2 to Nov. 7, 1814. Service at Camden.

RANK AND NAME.
Samuel Tolman, Captain
Joseph Ross, Lieutenant
Isaac Orbeton, Ensign

John Packard, Sergeant
Daniel Packard, Sergeant
James Andrews, Sergeant
John Fiske, Corporal
Crowel Jones, Corporal
Henry Waterman, Musician

Privates.
Barrows, Stephen
Bradford, Abraham
Bucklin, Mark
Clough, David
George, John
Harkness, William
Hathorn, James
Johnston, George
Jones, Benjamin
Keen, Daniel

Nutt, Ashley
Nutt, William
Oxton, William
Packard, James
Packard, Samuel
Post, Stephen
Simmons, George
Waterman, Joseph

Capt. J. Weed's Company, Lieut. Col. E. Foot's Regiment.
From Nov. 2 to Nov. 7, 1814. Raised at Hope. Service at Camden.

RANK AND NAME.
James Weed, Captain
William Hewett, Lieutenant
Boyce Crane, Ensign

Asa Payson, Sergeant
Nathan Kendal, Sergeant
Reuben Safford, Sergeant
John Bartlett, Corporal
James Tolman, Corporal

Privates.
Athan, John
Blood, Abel
Bowly, Ephraim, Jr.
Bowly, George
Conant, Abraham
Copeland, Nathaniel
Cox, John
Crabtree, David
Crabtree, Samuel
Fiske, Abel
Flagg, Isaac
Harwood, Richard
Haynes, William
Hilt, Daniel
Hilt, Philip
Hobbs, Micah
Jamison, Peter
Jordan, James
Kendal, Samuel
Lassel, John
Mattocks, James
Mayson, Abraham
Metcalf, Jesse
Noyes, Nathaniel
Pendleton, Alexander
Richards, Dodipher
Richards, Pearl
Simmons, George
Smith, Joseph
Stephenson, Francis
Stimson, Nathaniel
Sweetland, James
Webster, Thomas
Whitcomb, Ebenezer, Jr.
Whitcomb, Ira
Whitcomb, John
Wingate, Simon

Capt. N. Payson's Company, Lieut. Col. E. Foot's Regiment.
From Nov. 3 to Nov. 7, 1814. Raised at Hope. Service at Camden.

RANK AND NAME.
Noah Payson, Captain

John Fuller, Sergeant
Benjamin Simmons, Sergeant
Peabody Simmons, Sergeant
Shubal M. Pease, Corporal
Archelaus Ripley, Corporal
Thomas Ripley, Corporal
Barrett Merservey, Corporal
Daniel Lincoln, Musician

Privates.
Arnold, John
Bryant, Henry
Bryant, William
Clark, Joseph, Jr.
Davis, William
Gowen, John
Graham, John
Humphrey, John
Irish, Levi
Jacobs, McCowan
Jones, Thomas, Jr.
Kating, John
Keen, Robert M.
Kinsel, John
Maxfield, William M.
McLain, Alexander
Meservey, John
Newlet, John, Jr.
Payson, Ephraim
Pease, Nathan, Jr.
Richards, Robert
Ripley, Aaron
Ripley, Abraham
Ripley, Peter
Roakes, James
Robinson, George
Simmons, Jedediah
Sprague, Noah
Suckforth or Luckforth, Robert
Summer, Samuel
Thomson, John

Maj. A. G. Coombs' Battalion and Staff, Lieut. Col. E. Foot's Regiment.
From Sept. 21 to Sept. 27, 1814. Service at Thomaston.

RANK AND NAME.
A. G. Coombs, Major, Thomaston
James W. Blackington, Quartermaster
Enoch Lovejoy, Surgeon's Mate

Capt. George Coombs' Company, Lieut. Col. E. Foot's Regiment.
From Sept. 3 to Sept. 9, 1814. Raised at Thomaston. Service at Camden and Thomaston.

RANK AND NAME.
George Coombs, Captain
Asa Crockett, Lieutenant
Ralph Chapman, Ensign

John Keating, Sergeant
Joseph Sayward, Sergeant
Benjamin Packard, Sergeant
Thomas Bartlett, Sergeant
Nathan Pilsbury, Corporal
Joseph Bridges, Corporal
Ephraim McLean, Corporal
Leonard Wade, Corporal
Benjamin Dean, Musician

Privates.
Bartlett, Knot
Bartlett, Richard
Bradbury, Wyman
Bridges, Kingsbury
Brown, Isaac
Bunker, Isaac
Carney, James
Coombs, Abizer
Dean, William
Dyer, Charles
Emery, Jonah

Capt. George Coombs' Company, Lieut. Col. E. Foot's Regiment — Concluded.

Privates — Concluded.
Everett, David
Graffan, Jacob
Gray, Leverett
Hall, Anthony
Hambelly, Thomas
Haskell, John
Haskell, Thomas
Herd, Oliver
Herd, Robert
Hix, Samuel
Ingraham, Barnard
Ingraham, Coit
Ingraham, Isaac
Ingraham, John
Ingraham, Josiah, 3d
Jameson, John

Jordan, Eben
Jumper, Joseph
Lindsey, John
Lovett, Ephraim
McCalister, Joseph
McLenan, George
Packard, David
Packard, Isaac
Perry, David
Philbrook, Jeremiah
Pierce, Bezzilla
Pilsbury, John
Pilsbury, Joseph, Jr.
Pilsbury, Nathaniel
Post, Enoch
Post, Ezekiel
Post, Zachariah

Sayward, James
Sherman, Nathan, Jr.
Simonton, John
Simonton, John, 2d
Sleeper, Jere
Sleeper, Jesse
Small, Jonathan
Snow, Ambrose
Snow, Israel
Snow, William
Thomas, Eben
Williams, Benjamin, Jr.
Williams, Jonathan
Williams, Peter
Witham, Benjamin

Capt. G. Coombs' Company, Lieut. Col. E. Foot's Regiment.
From Sept. 20 to Sept. 25, 1814. Raised at Thomaston. Service at Camden and Thomaston.

RANK AND NAME.
George Coombs, Captain
Asa Crockett, Lieutenant
Ralph Chapman, Ensign

Benjamin Packard, Jr., Sergeant
Joseph Sayward, Sergeant
Thomas Bartlett, Sergeant
Nathan Pilsbury, Sergeant
Joseph Bridges, Corporal
Ephraim McLenan, Corporal
David Perry, Corporal
Benjamin Dean, Corporal
Isaac Brewer, Musician

Privates.
Amberry, Thomas H.
Bartlett, Richard
Bradbury, Wyman
Bridges, Kingsbury
Bunker, Isaac
Carney, James
Coombs, Abizer

Dean, William
Dyer, Charles
Eastman, John
Emery, John
Emery, Josiah
Everett, David
Haskell, John
Haskell, Thomas
Herd, Moses
Herd, Robert
Hix, Samuel
Ingraham, Barnard
Ingraham, Coit
Ingraham, Isaac
Ingraham, John
Ingraham, Josiah
Jumper, Joseph
Kellock, Joseph
Linsey, John
Lovett, Ephraim
Lowell or Lovell, Archibald C.
McAllister, Joseph
Merriman, Nathaniel

Munroe, William
Packard, Isaac
Paul, James
Pilsbury, John
Pilsbury, Joseph, Jr.
Post, Enoch
Post, Ezekiel
Sayward, James
Sherman, Nathan, Jr.
Simonton, John
Sleeper, Jerry
Sleeper, Jesse
Snow, Ambrose
Snow, Israel
Snow, William
Stackpole, ——
Thompson, Eben
Wade, Leonard
Williams, Benjamin
Williams, Jonathan
Williams, Peter
Witham, Jerre

Capt. E. Spear's Company, Lieut. Col. E. Foot's Regiment.
From Sept. 3 to Sept. 9, 1814. Raised at Thomaston.

RANK AND NAME.
Elkhanah Spear, Captain
Solomon Dwight, Lieutenant
Jeremiah Berry, Ensign

Aaron Austin, Sergeant
Elisha Fales, Sergeant
Iddo Kimbel, Sergeant
Richard Smith, Sergeant
Ensebins Fales, Corporal
George Lindsey, Corporal

John Ulmer, Corporal
Joel Blood, Corporal
John Jenks, Corporal
James Spear, Corporal

Privates.
Achorn, John
Achorn, Michel
Achorn, Philip
Blackington, Benjamin
Brewster, Benjamin

Butler, Briggs
Butler, George
Butler, George, 2d
Champus, John D.
Crockett, David, Jr.
Crockett, Knot
Crockett, Oliver
Crockett, Robert
Crockett, Thomas
Cutler, Abner
Edmunds, Walter

MASSACHUSETTS VOLUNTEER MILITIA IN THE WAR OF 1812.   205

Capt. E. Spear's Company, Lieut. Col. E. Foot's Regiment — Concluded.

Privates — Concluded.
Fales, Alwood
Gentner, Benjamin
Gentner, David
Gibbs, Daniel
Gilchrist, Joseph L.
Harden, Freeman
Hasty, Joseph
Havener, Joseph
Healey, James H.
Healy, Tildton
Ivry, Elijah
Jameson, Paul
Jenks, Henry
Kellock, Moses
Kenniston, Henry

Kenniston, Theodore
Kilsa, William
Lincoln, Isaac W.
Mankin, Andrew
Manning, Sylvester
Miner, Robert
Mitchell, Stuben
Mobbins or Robbins, Arunah
Mobbins or Robbins, Isaac C.
Mobbins or Robbins, Shepherd
Morse, James
Mossman, William
Munroe, Martin
O'Brian, John, Jr.
Palmer, Daniel
Partridge, James

Shearer, Reuben
Shibles, Simon
Simonton, Abraham
Spear, Rufus
Stevens, George W.
Stevens, Nathaniel
Tolman, Joseph
Tolman, Shepherd
Ulmer, Andrew
Washburn, Job
Whitney, Calvin
Whitney, Hains
Willes, Preserved
Williamson, Samuel S.

Capt. E. Spear's Company, Lieut. Col. E. Foot's Regiment.
From Sept. 22 to Sept. 23, 1814. Service at Thomaston.

RANK AND NAME.
Elkanah Spear, Captain, absent
Solomon Dwight, Lieutenant, in command
Jeremiah Berry, Ensign

Aaron Austin, Sergeant
Elisha Fales, Sergeant
Iddo Kimball, Sergeant
Richard Smith, Sergeant
Ensebins Fales, Corporal
John Ulmer, Corporal
Joel Blood, Corporal
James Spear, Corporal

Privates.
Achorn, John
Achorn, Philip
Batles, Briggs
Blackinton, Benjamin
Brewster, Benjamin
Cogswell, Stephen

Crockett, David
Crockett, Oliver
Crockett, Thomas
Cutler, Abner
Edmunds, Walter
Fales, Nathaniel, Jr.
Gentner, Benjamin
Gibbs, Daniel
Gilchrist, Joseph L.
Harden, Freeman
Havener, Joseph
Healy, Tildston
Ingraham, Joseph
Jenkins, Henry
Kellock, Moses
Kenniston, Theodore
Killsa, William
Kinniston, Henry
Manning, Sylvester
Mero, Martin
Mitchel, Stuben
Morse, James

Mossman, William
Obrian, John
Palmer, Daniel
Partridge, James
Rivers, Robert
Robbins, Arunah
Robbins, Isaac C.
Robbins, Shepard
Simonton, Abraham
Stevens, George W.
Stevens, Nathaniel
Tolman, Joseph
Tolman, Shepard
Torry, Elijah
Tucker, Benjamin
Twichel, Josiah
Ulmer, Andrew
Washburn, Job
Whitney, Calvin
Whitney, Hains

Lieut. S. Dwight's Company, Lieut. Col. E. Foot's Regiment.
From June 22 to June 27, 1814. Raised at Thomaston. Service at Thomaston.

RANK AND NAME.
Solomon Dwight, Lieutenant
Jeremiah Berry, Ensign

Aaron Austin, Sergeant
Elisha Foles, Sergeant
Joel Blood, Corporal
Ensebins Foles or Fales, Corporal

Privates.
Butler, Briggs
Butler, George
Butler, Leonard B.

Butler, Levi
Cogswell, Stephen
Foles or Fales, Asa
Foles or Fales, Atwood
Foles or Fales, Nathaniel
Gibbs, Daniel
Jenks, Henry
Jenks, John
Kinneston, Theodore
Lincoln, Isaac W.
Mitchell, Stuben
Munroe, James
Munroe, Martin

Palmer, Daniel
Prine, John O.
Robbins, Avery
Robbins, Isaac C.
Robbins, Shepard
Shibles, Simon
Stevens, George W.
Stevens, Nathaniel B.
Tucker, Benjamin
Welch, William
Whitney, Hanes

Capt. T. Kenney's Company, Lieut. Col. E. Foot's Regiment.
From Sept. 3 to Sept. 9, and Nov. 2 to Nov. 5, 1814. Raised at St. George. Service at Thomaston.

Rank and Name.		
Thomas Kenney, Captain	Foster, Richard	Long, Michel
John Watts, Lieutenant	Fountaine, Barna	Marshall, John
William Watts, Ensign	Gilchrist, Alexander	Martin, Thomas
	Gilchrist, Robert	Mathews, Daniel
	Gilchrist, Saul	McMurphy, Robert
John Robinson, Sergeant	Hall, Archibald	Mills, James
John Montgomery, Sergeant	Hall, Isaac	Norwood, Isaac
James Linekin, Sergeant	Hall, Peter	Norwood, Jacob
John Leeds, Sergeant	Hall, Samuel	Reeves, Richard
William Kellock, Corporal	Hanly, Henry	Robinson, Andrew
Saul Norwood, Corporal	Harris, James	Robinson, Ephraim
Luther Bryant, Corporal	Hart, Ephraim	Seavery, Nathaniel
David Wall, Corporal	Hart, Samuel	Seavey, Daniel
Joseph Robinson, Musician	Hart, William	Smalley, Archelaus
	Haskell, Charles	Smalley, Isaac
Privates.	Hawes, Robert	Stover, Caleb
Allen, John	Henderson, Joseph	Sweetland, James
Bickmore, Benjamin	Hupper, William	Wall, Ephraim
Chaples, John	Jones, Samuel	Watts, George
Clark, John	Jones, William	Watts, Moses
Clark, William	Kellock, Haunce	Wheeler, David
Colby, Thomas	Kellock, John	Wiley, Adam
Fogerty, Dennis	Kellock, John, 2d	Wilson, William
Foster, Francis	Kiff, Ephraim	
Foster, Jeremiah	Linekin, Benjamin	

Capt. T. Kenney's Detachment, Lieut. Col. E. Foot's Regiment.
From July 21 to Aug. 10, 1814. Raised at St. George. Service at Camden.

Rank and Name.		
Thomas Kenney, Captain	*Privates.*	Harris, James
	Bickmore, Benjamin	Hathorn, Alexander
John Robinson, Sergeant	Clark, William C.	Jones, John
John Leeds, Sergeant	Gilchrist, Alexander	Kellock, Matthew
	Hall, Isaac	Smalley, Isaac
	Hall, Samuel	

Capt. T. Kenney's Detached Company, Lieut. Col. E. Foot's Regiment.
From Oct. 1 to Nov. 9, 1814. Raised at St. George. Service at Camden.

Rank and Name.		
Thomas Kenney, Captain	Cutler, Abner	Kellock, Hance
Solomon Dwight, Lieutenant	Dean, Benjamin	Kellock, Joseph
Ralph Chapman, Ensign	Dean, Israel	Kellock, Moses
	Dean, Jonas	Killser, William
John Montgomery, Sergeant	Dyer, Charles	Kinneston, Henry
Elisha Fales, Sergeant	Eastman, John	Kinneston, Theodore
Iddo Kimball, Sergeant	Edwards, Walter	Lehorn, John
Thomas Bartlett, Sergeant	Emery, John	Lovett, Ephraim
Nathan Pilsbury, Jr., Corporal	Foster, Francis	Lovett, Jordan
William Kellock, Corporal	Fuller, James	Lowell, Archibald C.
John Ulmer, Jr., Corporal	Gilchrist, Alexander	Manning, Sylvester
David Perry, Corporal	Gilchrist, Samuel	McKellock, Archibald
	Hall, Archibald	McMurphy, Henry H.
Privates.	Harlow, Freeman	McMurphy, Robert
Blackinton, Benjamin	Hart, John, 3d	Mills, James
Brown, Isaac	Henderson, William	Moore, James
Butler, Briggs	Herd, Robert	Munroe, William
Clark, John, Jr.	Ingraham, Coit	Packard, Isaac
Coombs, Albion	Ingraham, Isaac	Pilsbury, John
Crockett, David, Jr.	Ingraham, Joseph, Jr.	Post, Ezekiel
	Jones, Samuel	Rankins, Andrew

Capt. T. Kenney's Detached Company, Lieut. Col. E. Foot's Regiment — Concluded.

Privates — Concluded.
Rivers, Robert
Robins, Shepherd
Robinson, Andrew
Sayward, James
Seavey, Nathaniel
Sherman, Nathan, Jr.

Shibles, Simon
Simonton, John, Jr.
Smally, Joshua
Snow, William
Stevens, George W.
Thompson, Ebenezer
Torry, Elijah

Trafton, Jacob
Ulmer, Henry
Wall, Ephraim
Wheeler, David
Whitney, Haynes
Young, James
Young, William

Lieut. E. Hanford's Detachment, Lieut. Col. E. Foot's Regiment.
From Aug. 8 to Aug. 19, 1814. Service at Camden.

RANK AND NAME.
Edward Hanford, Lieutenant

Benjamin Packard, Jr., Sergeant
Tilson Healy, Musician

Privates.
Bradford, Joseph
Bridges, Kingsbury

Calderwood, Ezekiel
Crocker, James
Crocker, Thomas
Dyer, Charles
Gibbs, Samuel
Hall, Frye
Haskell, Charles
Jamerson, Paul
Luckforth, Robert

Molineax, John
Noyes, Daniel
Ogier, Robert
Oxton, William
Richards, Asa
Ripley, Peter
Spear, Rufus
Sweetland, James
Wheeler, David

Lieut. E. Hanford's Guard, Lieut. Col. E. Foot's Regiment.
From Sept. 21 to Sept. 23, 1814. Service at Camden.

RANK AND NAME.
Edward Hanford, Lieutenant

Amos Foster, Sergeant
John Harkness, Sergeant
Jesse Fay, Sergeant
Simeon Tyler, Jr., Corporal
J. W. Thorndike, Corporal

Privates.
Blake, William
Hosmer, Anthony
Hunt, Simon
Mirick, Joseph
Ogier, Joseph
Sherman, Almarine
Tyler, Abel

Tyler, Coburn
Tyler, Dudley
Tyler, Saul

Lieut. E. Hanford's Detachment, Lieut. Col. E. Foot's Regiment.
From Nov. 3 to Nov. 9, 1814. Service at Camden.

RANK AND NAME.
Edward Hanford, Lieutenant
Arthur Pendleton, Ensign

William Brown, Sergeant
John Harkness, Sergeant
Simeon Tyler, Jr., Corporal
Ebenezer Thorndike, Corporal
Israel Thorndike, Musician

Privates.
Annis, John
Gregory, Israel
Gregory, William, 3d
Hodgman, Buckley
Hosmer, Anthony
Mirick, Joseph
Richards, Asa
Sartell, Amos

Start, Ebenezer
Tyler, Abel
Tyler, Samuel

Lieut. N. Brooks' Company, Lieut. Col. E. Foot's Regiment.
From June 22 to June 23, 1814. Service at Camden.

RANK AND NAME.
Noah Brooks, Lieutenant
Joseph Hall, Ensign

Henry Pendleton, Sergeant
Henry Bowers, Sergeant
David King, Sergeant

Josiah Herrington, Sergeant
John Hewit, Musician
Nathan Barrett, Musician

Privates.
Annis, Robert
Barnes, Abel

Bowers, John, Jr.
Brackett, Jeremiah
Brown, Paul
Calderwood, Ezekiel
Carle, James
Carle, John
Cloutman, John

Lieut. N. Brooks' Company, Lieut. Col. E. Foot's Regiment—Concluded.

Privates — Concluded.
Cooper, Nicholas
Cothrel, Robert
Curtis, James
Dillingham, Benjamin
Dillingham, Josiah
Gerry, Jesse
Hall, Frye
Herrington, James
Higgins, Jonathan
Hilt, William
Hobbs, Ebenezer
Hodgman, Job
Hopkins, Charles
Hopkins, Nathan
Hopkins, Richard

Hosmer, Charles
Hosmer, Josiah W.
Joslyn, Peter
Lassel, Jeremiah
Lindsey, Alfred
Mansfield, William
McKeller, Isaac
Metcalf, Joseph
Molineax, John
Morse, Isaac
Nicholson, John
Ogier, Peter
Ogier, Robert
Palmer, Nathaniel
Parker, Moses
Pike, Perley F.

Richards, Robert
Robinson, Charles
Rollins, David
Russell, Nathaniel
Russell, Samuel
Sargent, Leonard A.
Tarr, John
Tarr, Nathaniel
Thomas, Edward
Ulmer, Martin
Wagg, James
Wentworth, Tobias
Wheeler, Jonas
Wood, Zachariah
Young, John

Lieut. N. Brooks' Company, Lieut. Col. E. Foot's Regiment.
From June 24 to June 25, 1814. Service at Camden.

RANK AND NAME.
Noah Brooks, Lieutenant
Joseph Hall, Ensign

Amos Foster, Sergeant
Henry Bowers, Sergeant
Josiah Herrington, Sergeant
John Packard, Sergeant
Robert Bucklin, Musician
Saul Packard, Musician

Privates.
Barnes, Abel
Barrett, Nathan
Becket, Jeremiah
Bradford, Abraham

Brown, James P.
Calderwood, Ezekiel
Carle, James
Carle, John
Clough, David
Crosby, Ephraim G.
George, John
Gregory, Israel
Gregory, William
Harkness, William
Herrington, James
Hewit, Waterman
Hilt, William
Hodgman, Job
Hosmer, Anthony
Keene, Elisha

Nutt, William
Ogier, Joseph
Ogier, Robert
Perry, Thomas
Robeson, Charles
Ross, Stephen
Sargent, Leonard A.
Smith, Abiathar
Tarr, John
Tarr, Nathaniel
Thomas, Edward
Thorndike, J. W.
Tyler, Simeon
Waterman, Henry
Wood, Zachariah

Lieut. N. Brooks' Company, Lieut. Col. E. Foot's Regiment.
From Sept. 21 to Sept. 23, 1814. Service at Camden.

RANK AND NAME.
Noah Brooks, Lieutenant

Henry Bowers, Sergeant
David King, Sergeant
Josiah Herrington, Sergeant
Josiah Dillingham, Jr., Corporal
Samuel Tarr, Corporal
Perly F. Pike, Corporal
Zacheus Wood, Corporal
Nathan Barrett, Musician

Privates.
Annis, Robert
Barnes, Abel
Barrett, Daniel, Jr.

Carle, John
Cloutman, John
Cooper, Nicholas
Curtis, James
Dean, Saul
Heal, Peter
Herrington, James
Higgins, Jonathan
Hilt, Freeman
Hilt, William
Hobbs, Ebenezer
Hopkins, Charles
Hopkins, Nathan
Hopkins, Richard
Hosmer, Charles
Kent, Ezekiel

Lindsey, Alfred
McKeller, Isaac
Metcalf, James
Molineax, John
Morse, Isaac
Richards, Robert
Robison, Charles
Rollins, David
Sargent, Leonard A.
Simonton, John
Thomas, Edward
Wagg, James
Wentworth, Tobias
Wheeler, Jonas

MASSACHUSETTS VOLUNTEER MILITIA IN THE WAR OF 1812.

Ensign J. Hall's Detachment, Lieut. Col. E. Foot's Regiment.
From June 25 to June 30, 1814. Service at Camden.

RANK AND NAME.
Joseph Hall, Ensign

Henry Bowers, Sergeant
Josiah Harrington, Sergeant
Henry Pendleton, Sergeant
John Hewett, Musician
Nathan Barrett, Musician
Andrew Ogier, Musician

Privates.
Corthel, Robert
Dillingham, Benjamin P.
Hosmer, Josiah W.
Martin, Nathaniel
Nicholson, John
Ogier, Peter
Palmer, Nathaniel
Parker, Moses

Parkman, William
Perry, Oaks
Pike, Perley F.
Russell, Samuel, Jr.
Sartel, Amos
Wagg, James
Wilson, Leonard

Ensign J. Hall's Detachment, Lieut. Col. E. Foot's Regiment.
From July 1 to July 30, 1814. Service at Camden.

RANK AND NAME.
Joseph Hall, Ensign

Henry Bowers, Sergeant
Stephen Barrows, Musician

Privates.
Annis, Robert
Arnold, John

Bucklin, Jonas
Hopkins, Charles
Hopkins, Richard
Keen, Daniel
Keen, Robert S.
Kendal, Samuel
Lincoln, Peleg
Lindsey, Ichabod
Mansfield, William

Mirick, Joseph
Ogier, Abraham
Richards, Dodipher
Richards, Pearl
Simmons, Oliver
Sumner, Samuel
Waterman, Joseph, Jr.
Wentworth, Tobias
Wheeler, Jonas

Lieut. Col. J. E. Foxcroft's Regiment.
From Sept. 10 to Sept. 24, 1814. Service at Portland.

FIELD AND STAFF.
Joseph E. Foxcroft, Lieutenant Colonel, New Gloucester
Seth Mitchell, Major, North Yarmouth
John Perley, Major, Bridgton
William Bradbury, Adjutant, New Gloucester

Samuel Laurence, Quartermaster, North Yarmouth
William Bridgham, Surgeon, New Gloucester
Gad Hitchcock, Surgeon's Mate, North Yarmouth

NONCOMMISSIONED STAFF.
Saul Cushman, Sergeant Major
Benjamin Mayberry, Quartermaster Sergeant

Capt. E. Brewer's Company, Lieut. Col. J. E. Foxcroft's Regiment.
From Sept. 10 to Sept. 24, 1814. Raised at Brewer and Freeport. Service at Portland.

RANK AND NAME.
Edward Brewer, Captain
James Brewer, Lieutenant
John Laurence, Ensign

John Dennison, Sergeant
Thomas R. Dellingham, Sergeant
Rufus Cushing, Sergeant
Simeon Jones, Sergeant
Gideon Edes, Corporal
Timothy Soule, Corporal
Theodore Curtis, Corporal
George Anderson, Corporal
George Hicks, Musician

Privates.
Allen, Paul
Bartol, Samuel
Bennet, Andrew H.
Blackstone, Samuel
Brown, Samuel
Carver, Isaac
Chandler, Joel
Chandler, William
Clark, Francis
Coffin, Thomas

Curtis, James
Curtis, Samuel
Curtis, Stephen
Davis, Saul
Dennison, Caleb
Deven, Francis
Fitz, Richard
Fogg, Abel
Fogg, Saul
Grant, Watts
Holbrook, Reuben
Jordan, William
Kilby, Thomas
Knight, Abner
Libbey, Josiah
Lincoln, Daniel
Mann, Andrew
Marston, Daniel
McGray, Samuel
McKenney, Jedediah
Merrill, Edward
Mitchell, Ammi
Mitchell, Edward
Mitchell, Joel
Mitchell, Nathaniel
Mitchell, Robert

Noyes, John
Osgood, Silas
Paine, Charles
Rice, Calvin
Rice, Rufus
Richardson, Joseph
Rogers, John
Sanborn, Paul
Small, Daniel
Soule, Barnabas
Soule, Cornelius
Soule, Daniel
Soule, Emory
Soule, Isaac
Soule, James
Soule, Joseph E.
Staples, David
Sylvester, Abner, Jr.
Talbot, Simeon
Thoyts, Simeon
Townsend, William
Tukesbury, Benjamin
Tuttle, William
Ward, Nehemiah
Webster, Benjamin
Witherspoon, Robert

Capt. E. Cobb's Company, Lieut. Col. J. E. Foxcroft's Regiment.
From Sept. 10 to Sept. 24, 1814. Raised at Gray. Service at Portland.

RANK AND NAME.
Ebenezer Cobb, Captain
William Coff, Lieutenant

Nicholas Low, Jr., Sergeant
Robert Starbird, Sergeant
Josiah Frank, Sergeant
Joseph Scribner, Sergeant
Samuel Skillings, Corporal
Samuel Ramsdel, Corporal
John Dolly, Corporal
William Webb, Corporal
Ezekiel Crague, Musician

Privates.
Adams, Robert
Cole, George
Cummings, Joseph
Davis, Gideon
Doe, Charles
Dunn, Daniel
Elder, Morrill
Fletcher, Zachariah
Foster, Moses
Foster, Saul
Frank, Alpho

Frank, James, Jr.
Gibbs, Ezra, Jr.
Gillson, Alexander
Harmon, Elias
Haskell, Daniel
Hunt, David, Jr.
Hunt, Israel
King, Adverdas
Laurence, Ephraim
Libbey, Andrew
Libbey, Benjamin
Libbey, James
Libbey, Jedediah
Libbey, Jedediah C.
Libbey, Joab
Libbey, William
Maybury, Foster
Maybury, Jordan
McDonald, Charles
Mitchell, Job
Morse, Benjamin
Muchmore, John
Mumfad, Edmund
Pennel, James
Pennel, Thomas
Perley, Abraham

Perley, Isaac
Plummer, Elliot
Skilling, Edward, Jr.
Skillings, Joseph
Skinner, Peter
Small, Daniel
Small, Levi
Small, Simeon
Smith, Benjamin
Smith, James
Staples, Josiah
Starbird, William
Stiles, Stephen
Strout, Ebenezer
Strout, Saul
Thayer, Stephen
Thurlo, Richard
Tinny, Henry
Ward, Jonathan
Webster, Thomas
Weeks, Isaac
Weeks, Joseph
Weston, John
Weymouth, John S.
White, Horatio

Capt. S. Fessenden's Company, Lieut. Col. J. E. Foxcroft's Regiment.
From Sept. 10 to Sept. 24, 1814. Raised at New Gloucester. Service at Portland.

RANK AND NAME.
Samuel Fessenden, Captain
Moses Rowe, Lieutenant
Nathan Knight, Ensign

William Tarbox, Sergeant
Jonathan True, Sergeant
John Witham, Sergeant
Joseph T. Parson, Sergeant
Jonathan Chase, Jr., Corporal
William Stockman, Corporal
Charles P. McKenney, Corporal
Josiah Davis, Corporal
James Tyler, Musician
Osgood Bradbury, Musician

Privates.
Allen, David
Allen, Joshua C.
Barron, John
Bearce, Oliver
Bradbury, John
Brooks, John
Chase, Moses
Clark, Joseph
Cobb, Chandler

Cobb, Silvanus, Jr.
Davis, Elias
Davis, John
Davis, Lane
Dyer, Benjamin
Eveleth, Moses
Eveleth, Perkins
Finsome, Thomas
Glass, Ezekiel
Godding, Andrew R., Jr.
Grover, Jonathan
Harmon, Robert
Haskell, Charles C.
Haskell, James
Haskell, William
Hodge, David
Hollis, Solomon
Jackson, Lemuel
Jones, Joel
Jordan, James, Jr.
Kingman, William
Lane, Josiah
McKenney, Jonathan
Merrill, Giles
Mitchell, Israel
Morgan, John

Morton, Simon
Nevens, Hugh
Nevens, Robert
Pierce, Daniel
Plummer, Edward
Prince, Isaac
Rowe, Jonathan
Rowe, Joshua
Rowe, Saul
Rowe, Zebulon
Royal, Samuel
Saur, Moses
Soule, Robert
Starbird, Robert
Tufts, John, Jr.
Tyler, Isaac
Tyler, Simeon
Vickery, Nathaniel
Vosmus, Isaac
Walker, James P.
Waterhouse, Zebulon
Winslow, Philip
Witham, Aaron
Witham, William C.
Woodbury, Philemon
Woodward, Davis

MASSACHUSETTS VOLUNTEER MILITIA IN THE WAR OF 1812. 211

Capt. N. Gould's Company, Lieut. Col. J. E. Foxcroft's Regiment.
From Sept. 10 to Sept. 24, 1814. Raised at Windham. Service at Portland.

RANK AND NAME.
Nathan Gould, Captain
Noah S. Santer, Lieutenant
William Legrove, Ensign

Elias Baker, Sergeant
Nathaniel Knight, Sergeant
John Crague, Jr., Sergeant
Jesse Brown, Sergeant
Benjamin Baker, Corporal
Isaac Powers, Corporal
Ezra Anderson, Corporal
Elijah Long, Corporal
Levi Merrill, Musician

Privates.
Anderson, Abraham
Anthoyn, John
Austin, Jonah, Jr.
Austin, William
Bodge, John
Bolten, Daniel
Bolten, Saul
Bracket, Anthony
Brown, Ephraim, Jr.
Brown, James

Brown, John
Brown, Joseph
Cobb, Philip
Crague, James
Crague, Josiah
Crocket, Joseph
Crocket, Mark
Davis, Benjamin
Delly, Joseph E.
Freeman, Jonathan
French, John
Goodall, John, Jr.
Goold, Abner
Gould, Jonathan
Graffam, Caleb
Hamblin, Samuel
Hanscomb, Aaron
Hanscomb, Nathan
Haynes, Timothy
Hearsey, Isaac
Hodsdon, Israel, Jr.
Hunewell, Nathaniel
Jackson, Francis
Jordan, Benjamin
Jordan, Roger, Jr.
Knight, Daniel

Knight, John, Jr.
Knight, Peter
Lamb, Richard
Leighton, Thomas
Lombard, James
Lovell, John
Low, Justus
Lunt, John
Manchester, Stephen
Maybury, Francis
Maybury, Oliver
Maybury, Robert M.
Maybury, Thomas
Morrell, Benjamin
Mugford, Ezra
Pettingill, Jacob
Proctor, David
Rogers, Joshua
Skillings, John
Smith, Ebenezer
Stephens, Thomas
Waterhouse, Daniel
Whitmore, Benjamin
Wier, Robert
Worthington, William
Young, William

Capt. A. Ingalls' Company, Lieut. Col. J. E. Foxcroft's Regiment.
From Sept. 13 to Sept. 24, 1814. Raised at Bridgton. Service at Portland.

RANK AND NAME.
Asa Ingalls, Captain
Isaiah Ingalls, Lieutenant
Joseph McIntosh, Ensign

James Flint, Sergeant
Theodore Emerson, Sergeant
Ahira Sampson, Sergeant
Oliver Spurr, Sergeant
Simeon Haywood, Corporal
Seth Oarsley or Carsley, Corporal
Edward Stanley, Corporal
Samuel Anderson, Corporal
Saul Knight, Musician
Stephen Beeman, Musician

Privates.
Bracket, Enoch
Bracket, William
Bray, Edward
Butler, Samuel
Carsley, William C.
Chadborn, James
Currill, David
Douglass, John

Dutch, George
Edwards, Caleb
Emmerson, Mirick
Emmerson, Nathaniel
Emmerson, Seth
Flint, Farman
Fogg, Joseph
Garner, Richard
Gibbs, Jesse
Goodhue, Manassah
Hale, Nathaniel, Jr.
Harmon, Leander
Ingalls, Spofford
Jordan, David
Jordan, Saul
Knight, Apollus
Leach, James
Libbey, Thomas
Lombard, Richard
Maybury, Harvey
Millet, John
Morse, Calvin
Morse, John
Newcomb, Elisha
Noble, John

Noble, Joseph
Packard, Ephraim
Paul, William
Perley, Daniel
Perley, Saul
Pike, Jacob
Ross, Jonathan
Sanborn, Benjamin
Sawyer, Levi
Scribner, Harvey
Scribner, Jonathan
Scribner, Joseph
Smith, Abiel
Smith, Silas
Staples, James
Stevens, Jonathan
Stewart, Joseph
Stewart, Solomon
Stiles, Enoch
Stiles, Jacob
Thompson, Nathaniel
Trafton, Joshua
West, Thomas
Weston, James
Weymouth, Stephen

Capt. J. Kilborn's Company, Lieut. Col. J. E. Foxcroft's Regiment.
From Sept. 10 to Sept. 24, 1814. Raised at Bridgton. Service at Portland.

RANK AND NAME.
John Kilborn, Captain
Thomas Perley, Lieutenant
Saul Richardson, Ensign

Jeremiah Hall, Sergeant
Richard Larabee, Sergeant
Eleazer Mans or Mars, Sergeant
Joseph Brown, Sergeant
Nathaniel Martin, Corporal
Thomas Burnell, Corporal
Mathew Dodge, Corporal
Jonathan Dodge, Corporal
Jesse Vlezie, Musician
Josiah C. Earline, Musician

Privates.
Andrews, Samuel
Bennet, Jeremiah
Black, Saul
Brigham, Aaron
Brigham, Daniel
Broadstreet, David
Brown, David
Brown, Levi
Brown, Reuben, Jr.
Bucknell, John, Jr.

Burnall, William
Burns, William
Caswell, Libbeus
Chace, John
Dearing, Saul
Dresser, Elijah
Dyke, Samuel
Edwards, Nathaniel, Jr.
Fitch, George
Goold, James
Graffam, Peter
Gray, James, Jr.
Green, Jonathan
Griffin, Simon
Ingalls, Saul, 3d
Johnson, Asa, Jr.
Jordan, Curtis
Jordan, George
Leavit, Josiah
Lord, Abraham
Martin, David
Martin, John
McKenneson, William
Milliken, Benjamin
Milliken, Ezekiel
Morrell, Jonathan
Muffitt, Aquila

Oliver, John
Porter, Tyler
Riggs, William S.
Ripley, Joseph
Ripley, Thomas
Robison, Eli
Robison, Joseph
Rounds, John
Rowe, Daniel
Sanborn, Daniel, Jr.
Sanborn, David, Jr.
Sawyer, Joseph
Stone, William
Tappin, Luther
Thoms, Benjamin
Thoms, John
Trott, John
Watchman, Ebenezer
Webb, William
Whitney, George W.
Whitten, Daniel
Wiggins, John
Wiggins, Samuel
Wilson, Ephraim
Woodman, Samuel
Woodson, Abijah

Capt. D. Mitchell's Company, Lieut. Col. J. E. Foxcroft's Regiment.
From Sept. 10 to Sept. 24, 1814. Raised at Yarmouth. Service at Portland.

RANK AND NAME.
Daniel Mitchell, Captain
Amasa Baker, Lieutenant
Benjamin Herrick, Ensign

Jeremiah Mitchell, Sergeant
Jacob Blanchard, Sergeant
John Trus, Sergeant
Nathaniel Bacon, Sergeant
William Wescot, Sergeant
John Soule, Corporal
Cushing Prince, Jr., Corporal
Reuben Brewer, 3d, Corporal
John M. Russell, Corporal
Phineas Soule, Musician
Asa Bishop, Musician

Privates.
Allen, Elisha
Allen, Isaac
Bachelder, Ephraim
Bachelder, Rufus
Beals, Saul
Blanchard, Cyrus
Bosworth, David
Brackett, John
Brewer, James, Jr.
Buxton, Joseph
Clough, John
Collins, Joseph W.
Corliss, Ebenezer, Jr.

Delano, Benjamin
Delant, Ezekiel
Dennison, Ammi
Drinkwater, John R.
Drinkwater, Tristram
Favot, Jacob
Fogg, Benjamin
Gray, David
Griffin, Joseph
Hall, Stephen
Hall, Willard
Jordan, Ebenezer
Kelly, John
Lambert, Seth
Lang, Levi
Leighton, William
Lincoln, Gershon
Lord, Joseph
Loring, Charles
Lufkin, Seth S.
Marston, Thomas
Mason, Thomas
Maxfield, Robert C.
Merrill, Saul
Meservey, John
Mitchell, Daniel, Jr.
Mitchell, Timothy
Newbegin, John
Porter, Benjamin
Reed, Daniel
Reed, Reuben

Ring, Martin
Royal, Winthrop
Sawyer, Enos
Shaw, David
Skillings, Isaac
Skillings, James
Skillings, Reuben
Smith, William
Snell, John
Soule, Benjamin
Soule, Isaac
Soule, Samuel
Staples, Daniel, Jr.
Swasey, Ambrose
Sweetser, Levi
Sweetser, Salathiel
Sweetser, Saul
Talbot, Bailey
Taylor, William
Taylor, Zebulon
Thompson, Edward, Jr.
Thompson, William
Titcomb, Bendiah, Jr.
Titcomb, Enoch
Tribou, Alpha
Whitcomb, John
Whitehouse, John
Whitney, James
Winslow, Jacob
Wyman, Lemuel
Young, John

Capt. M. Woodman's Company, Lieut. Col. J. E. Foxcroft's Regiment.
From Sept. 10 to Sept. 24, 1814. Raised at New Gloucester. Service at Portland.

RANK AND NAME.
Moses Woodman, Captain
Amos Toms, Lieutenant
John Webber, Ensign

James Dunn, Sergeant
William Twombly, Sergeant
David McIntyre, Sergeant
Josiah Dunn, 3d, Sergeant
Jabez Cushman, Corporal
William Hammond, Corporal
Ephraim Harris, Corporal
Daniel Waterman, Corporal
Timothy Waterhouse, Musician
Joseph Davis, Musician

Privates.
Acly, Saul
Allen, William
Atwood, Isaac
Bailey, Amos
Bailey, John
Bailey, Levi
Bailey, Reuben
Barton, William
Bennet, Henry

Bennet, Moses
Bennet, Noah
Blake, Ephraim
Bray, Aaron
Bray, Benjamin
Bray, Nathaniel
Cotton, Asa
Davis, Benjamin
Davis, Gideon
Davis, Timothy
Davis, William
Dennin, Peter
Eveleth, David
Fogg, Saul
Foss, Shepherd
Frazier, Joseph
Frazier, Thomas
Hacket, Elijah
Harris, Enos
Haskell, John
Hearsey, Levi
Jordan, Josiah
Keith, Timothy
Lane, Nathaniel
Lane, Nehemiah
McIntyre, Solomon

Merrill, Jeremiah
Mury, Benjamin
Nash, John
Nute, Saul
Pierce, David
Pierce, Samuel
Pulsifer, Jonathan
Sawyer, Moses
Sawyer, Reuben
Snell, Job
Snell, Robert
Spilinger, Jeremiah
Staples, Frost
Stenchfield, Ephraim
Stenchfield, William
Stephens, Benjamin
Strout, Nehemiah
Tarbox, Daniel
Toby, Thomas H.
Varell, Jeremiah
Walker, John
Waters, John
Wentworth, William
Whitham, Thomas
Whitney, Frost
Whorf, Nathaniel

Gen. John Blake's Brigade, 3d Regiment, 2d Brigade, 10th Division.
Service at Hampden. This regiment in battle at Hampden, Sept. 3, 1814.

GENERAL OFFICER.
John Blake, Brigadier General, Bangor

FIELD AND STAFF.
Andrew Grant, Lieutenant Colonel, Hampden
Joshua Chamberlin, Major, Orrington
Rufus Gilmore, Adjutant
Ebenezer Brewer, Quartermaster, Orrington

Andrew Tyler, Jr., Paymaster, Frankfort
Edmund Abbott, Surgeon's Mate, Frankfort
Enoch Mudge, Chaplain, Orrington

Capt. Samuel Butman's Company, Lieut. Col. Andrew Grant's Regiment.
From Aug. 31 to Sept. 3, 1814. Raised at Dixmont. Service at Hampden. Company in battle at Hampden.

RANK AND NAME.
Samuel Butman, Captain
Richard P. Clarkson, Lieutenant
Frederick B. Butman, Ensign

Edmund Wingate, Sergeant
John Shadman, Jr., Sergeant
Lemuel Drake, Sergeant
Jonathan Ferguson, Sergeant
William Ferguson, Sergeant
Nathaniel Nanscomb, Corporal
John Oddell, Corporal
Simeon Obeon, Corporal

Privates.
Barker, Henry
Barker, John
Barker, Stephen
Basford, Jonathan
Basford, Joseph
Buckman, John

Chase, Eliphalet
Check, Moses
Cook, George
Cook, James
Craige, George
Dodge, Samuel
Emery, Joseph
Ferrald, Edmund
Freeman, Timothy
Garland, John
Godfrey, Benjamin
Goodhue, Ira
Goodspeed, Reuben
Higgins, Samuel
Johnson, David
Johnson, David, 2d
Kuscot, Jeremiah W.
Merrell, James W.
Mitchell, Charles
Mitchell, Christopher
Mitchell, John

Mitchell, Milby
Morse, Barnet
Morse, George
Mudgett, Abraham
Mudgett, Edmund
Mudgett, Nathaniel
Pierce, David
Pierce, Samuel
Porter, David
Porter, Tyler
Smith, Elijah
Smith, John
Staples, Richard
Taylor, Rowland
Thurston, John
Tucker, Ebenezer
Williams, Cornelius
York, Joseph
York, Stephen

Capt. J. Patton's Company, Lieut. Col. Andrew Grant's Regiment.
From Sept. 1 to Sept. 3, 1814.   Raised at Hampden.   Service at Hampden.   Company in battle at Hampden.

RANK AND NAME.		
James Patton, Captain	Cowan, Jacob	Miller, Henry
Abel Ruggart, Lieutenant	Cowan, Jonathan	Miller, James
John Miller, Jr., Ensign	Dunham, George	Miller, Timothy
	Dunham, Jesse	Patton, John
	Dunham, John	Pickard, Daniel
Robert Miller, Jr., Sergeant	Emerson, Daniel	Pomroy, Andrew
William Potter, Jr., Sergeant	Emerson, Stephen	Pomroy, Joseph, Jr.
Nathaniel Gevlin, Sergeant	Farnum, Samuel	Pomroy, William
Richard Gevlin, Sergeant	Gevlin, Peter	Read, William V.
	Hewes, David	Robinson, Isaac
Privates.	Hewes, Elijah	Robinson, John
Benson, Samuel	Hinkley, Ebenezer C.	Swan, Jeremiah
Blagdon, John	Hunt, Asa	Taylor, James
Cole, Seth	Jennis, Francis	
Cowan, George	Miller, Benjamin	

Capt. Solomon Blake's Company, attached to Lieut. Col. Grant's Regiment.
From Sept. 1 to Sept. 4, 1814.   Raised at Brewer.   Service at Hampden.   Company in battle at Hampden.

RANK AND NAME.	*Privates.*	
Solomon Blake, Captain	Blake, Billing	Hart, Jacob
Emmons Kingsbury, Lieutenant	Blake, Charles	Hart, Russell
Charles Levans, Ensign	Blasdell, Sanbourn	Holbrook, Calvin
	Burr, Alanson	Jones, Elijah
William Copeland, Sergeant	Campbell, Abijah	Kingsbury, Nathan
Joseph Copeland, Sergeant	Coombs, Benjamin	Man, Jacob
David Sibly, Musician	Farmington, Daniel	Pond, Loring
Benjamin Farrington, Musician	Farmington, Silas	Torrener, Levi
Ezekiel More, Musician	Field, Elias	Trueworthy, Jeremiah
	Field, Peter	White, Augustine
	Fish, Russel	Winchester, Benjamin
	Fisher, Alexander R.	Winchester, Charles

Capt. J. Emery's Company, Lieut. Col. Andrew Grant's Regiment.
From Sept. 1 to Sept. 3, 1814.   Raised at Hampden.   Service at Hampden.   Company in battle at Hampden.

RANK AND NAME.	*Privates.*	
John Emery, Jr., Captain	Cobb, William	Higgins, Seth
William H. Reed, Lieutenant	Cornish, William	Hopkins, Allen
Daniel Emery, Ensign	Covell, Solomon	Jones, Samuel F.
	Dean, Isaiah	Mayo, Hayes, Jr.
Samuel Libbey, Sergeant	Dean, Jesse S.	Murch, Walter
Jacob Jones, Sergeant	Dean, Trueman	Myrick, Solomon
Daniel Grant, Sergeant	Dow, Amos	Perkins, John
Bango Young, Sergeant	Dudley, James	Pomroy, Arad H.
Simeon Stone, Musician	Flagg, William	Rogers, John
Zenas Dexter, Musician	Hamilton, Lemuel	Smith, Daniel
Benjamin Higgins, Musician	Harding, Reed	Smith, John
	Hardy, Benjamin	Snow, Micajah
	Higgins, Cyrus	Young, Reuben
		Young, Zebulon, Jr.

Capt. Abram Hill's Company, Lieut. Col. Andrew Grant's Regiment.

From Sept. 1 to Sept. 4, 1814. Raised at Bucksport. Service at Hampden. Company in battle at Hampden.

Rank and Name.		
Abram Hill, Captain	Crosby, James	Reed, Littleton
Josiah Chapin, Lieutenant	Fisher, Joel	Rich, Isaiah
	Freeman, Reuben	Rich, Sylvanus
	Higgins, Elisha	Smith, Jacob, Jr.
Abisha Bottom, Sergeant	Higgins, James, 2d	Smith, James
James Hariman, Sergeant	Hoxie, John	Smith, Joseph
	Lowell, Benjamin, Jr.	Smith, Lemuel
Privates.	Lowell, James	Wood, Manning
Baker, Samuel	Lowell, Samuel	
Colvard, James, Jr.	McDaniel, Jeremiah	

Capt. J. Nealley's Company, Lieut. Col. Andrew Grant's Regiment.

From Sept. 1 to Sept. 4, 1814. Raised at Monroe. Service at Hampden. Company in battle at Hampden.

Rank and Name.		
Joseph Nealley, Captain	Curtis, Samuel	Nickerson, Huberd
James Manson, Lieutenant	Curtis, Simeon	Parker, Luther
	Davison, James G.	Perry, David
	Dicky, Elijah	Plummer, Timothy
Archibald Woodman, Sergeant	Dicky, William	Potter, Philip
Daniel Buckes, Sergeant	Dodge, Benjamin	Putman, Silas
Daniel Putman, Sergeant	Douglass, Abraham	Real, Michael
Ezekiel York, Sergeant	Douglass, Elisha	Robison, Richard
Solomon Twambly, Musician	Durham, James	Sanbourn, Abiather
Gilman Roberts, Musician	Emery, Hosea	Smith, Daniel
	Emery, Simon	Smith, Samuel, Jr.
Privates.	Ford, William	Sterns, David
Avery, Jeremiah	Frost, Josiah	Sterns, Levi
Barns, Samuel	Frost, Winthrop	Sumner, Benjamin
Bartlett, Jeremiah	Gage, John	Thistle, Ezra
Bartlett, Rufus	Gipson, William	Twambly, Arch, Jr.
Bottons, Solomon	Goodin, Moses	Twambly, Samuel F.
Chase, Noah	Grant, Stephen	Wallby, Ichabod
Chase, Thomas	Hinkly, William	Ward, Benjamin
Clemens, Hill	James, Elisha	Ward, John
Clemens, John	Jewell, Samuel	Ward, Jonathan
Colson, David	Lolson, John	Ward, Nathaniel
Coulson, Jonathan J.	Mason, Nathaniel	West, Enos
Crowell, William	McDaniel, Matthew	Whitman, James
Curtis, David	Mitchell, Jeremiah	Winshall, William
Curtis, Lemuel	Nealley, John	

Capt. P. Newcomb's Company, Lieut. Col. Andrew Grant's Regiment.

From Sept. 1 to Sept. 3, 1814. Raised at Hampden. Service at Hampden. Company in battle at Hampden.

Rank and Name.		
Peter Newcomb, Captain	Cobb, Samuel H.	Hopkins, James
Jonathan Knowles, Lieutenant	Doan, Edward	Hopkins, Josiah
Stephen Dallas, Ensign	Doane, Amos	Knowles, Abiather
	Doane, Dennis	Linning, Bryant
Allen Rogers, Sergeant	Dunning, Robert	Mayo, Israel, Jr.
Josiah Sparrow, Sergeant	Dunton, James	Mayo, James, Jr.
Josiah Ware, Sergeant	Emerson, Benjamin	Mayo, Joseph
Jonathan Kendall, Sergeant	Emerson, Nathan	Mayo, Nathaniel, Jr.
Thomas Willman, Musician	Emery, Jonas	Mayo, Simeon
	Emory, William	Mayo, Thomas
	Gould, John	Murch, John
Privates.	Harding, Austen	Myrick, Joseph
Atwood, Ebenezer	Higgins, Misha	Myrick, Reuben
Baker, Jeremiah	Higgins, William	Patton, Samuel
Blasdil, Sanbourn	Hopkins, Benjamin	Perkins, John

Capt. P. Newcomb's Company, Lieut. Col. Andrew Grant's Regiment — Concluded.

Privates — Concluded.
Piper, David
Porter, Asa
Porter, Benjamin
Rider, Francis
Smith, Henry
Snow, Freeman
Snow, William
Stubbs, Eben
Stubbs, Edward
Stubbs, Richard
Tarr, Andrew
Turner, Barker
Ward, John
Webber, Samuel
West, Bartlett
Wiley, Aaron

Capt. Lot Rider's Company, attached to Lieutenant Colonel Grant's Regiment.
From Sept. 1 to Sept. 4, 1814. Raised at Eddington. Service at Hampden. Company in battle at Hampden.

RANK AND NAME.
Lot Rider, Captain
John Holyoke, Lieutenant

William Rider, Sergeant
Joseph Severance, Sergeant
Asa Howard, Musician

Privates.
Bond, Hollis
Brown, William
Cobb, Lemuel
Johnson, Daniel
Johnson, Ephraim
Lovel, David
Severance, Benjamin

Snow, Benjamin
Snow, Israel
Stearns, Daniel
Tainter, Benjamin
Tibbits, John
Weed, Benjamin
Wood, Jonathan

Capt. Elisha Thayer's Company, Lieutenant Colonel Grant's Regiment.
From Sept. 1 to Sept. 4, 1814. Raised at Frankfort. Service at Hampden. Company in battle at Hampden.

RANK AND NAME.
Elisha Thayer, Captain
Robert Thompson, Lieutenant
Saul Trevett, Ensign

John Lain, Sergeant
James Curtis, Sergeant
Joseph Nickerson, Sergeant
Nathaniel Grant, Musician

Privates.
Baker, Moses
Bowlin, John
Bowlin, Peter
Campbell, Daniel
Clark, John
Cole, Joseph
Curtis, James, Jr.
Curtis, John
Downs, Joshua
Downs, Paul

Ellingwood, Ralph
Goodwin, Francis L. B.
Goodwin, William
Grant, William
Hobin, Richard
Idle, Rowland
Idle, Stephen
Johnson, Isaac
Johnson, Thomas
Keene, William
Kenney, Benjamin
Kingsbury, John
Kingsbury, William
Lain, Charles
Lain, Daniel
Lain, Elijah
Lain, Silas
Nichols, George
Nickerson, Aaron
Nickerson, Jesse
Oakman, Tobias

Page, James
Page, William
Parker, Oliver
Patten, Moses B.
Pickard, Joshua
Rogers, Knowles
Sedgly, Daniel, Jr.
Shaw, William H.
Sparrow, Benjamin
Sparrow, Joshua
Treadwell, Jacob
Treat, Ezra
Trivett, Benjamin
Wardwell, Jeremiah
Weed, Moses
Weed, Nathan
Wentworth, Gant
West, William
Wintworth, Joshua
Witham, Jotham
Woodman, Benjamin

Capt. W. Ware's Company, Lieut. Col. Andrew Grant's Regiment.
From Sept. 1 to Sept. 4, 1814. Raised at Orrington. Service at Hampden. Company in battle at Hampden.

RANK AND NAME.
Warren Ware, Captain

Simeon Fowler, Sergeant
Theophilus Nickerson, Sergeant
John Brooks, Sergeant
Warren Nickerson, Sergeant

Privates.
Atwood, Benjamin
Atwood, Jesse, Jr.
Baker, David

Baker, Nathaniel
Baker, Richard
Bartlett, Amasa
Boddershall, Doan
Boddershall, Fredoni
Doane, Elihu
Doane, Ephraim
Doane, Joseph
Doane, William
Downs, Phineas
Dyer, Nathaniel
Eldridge, Hereziah, Jr.

Eldridge, Seth
Freeman, James, Jr.
Freeman, Thomas
Gould, Nathaniel, Jr.
Harden, Jesse
Hopkins, Ephraim
Kent, Richard
Kent, Stillman
Kent, William
Marston, William
Nickerson, Eliphalet
Nickerson, John

Capt. W. Ware's Company, Lieut. Col. Andrew Grant's Regiment — Concluded.

Privates — Concluded.
Nye, Paul
Pierce, David
Pierce, Nathaniel
Rice, Cyrus
Rider, Atkins
Rider, Richard
Rider, Samuel, Jr.
Rider, Stephen

Rogers, Henry
Rogers, Smith
Rooks, Joseph
Severance, John
Severance, Reuben
Severance, Samuel
Smith, Zenas
Snow, Daniel
Snow, Ephraim

Snow, Harry C.
Snow, Joseph
Varrell, William M.
Weeks, Edward
Wheeldon, Ebenezer
Willard, John
Wintworth, John
Wiswell, Thomas

Capt. A. Weston's Company, Lieut. Col. Andrew Grant's Regiment.
From Sept. 1 to Sept. 4, 1814. Raised at Frankfort. Service at Hampden. Company in battle at Hampden.

RANK AND NAME.
Amos Weston, Captain
Samuel White, Lieutenant
James Rowell, Lieutenant

Robert Littlefield, Sergeant
Samuel Hosmer, Sergeant
James Sawyer, Sergeant
Andrew Ritcher, Sergeant
Daniel Littlefield, Musician

Privates.
Carlton, John
Chase, John
Clark, James
Clark, Robert
Clemmons, Prentice
Courllard, Henry
Ellingwood, Joseph
Grant, Josiah
Grant, Samuel
Hall, Amos

Littlefield, Jeremiah
Low, Asa
Low, Elijah
Mugridge, William
Ritchie, Thomas
Sedgley, Samuel
Snow, Edward
Tibbetts, William
Twambly, Nathaniel

Capt. Timothy Sibley's Company, attached to Lieutenant Colonel Grant's Regiment.
From Sept. 2 to Sept. 4, 1814. Raised at Eddington. Service at Hampden. Company in battle at Hampden.

RANK AND NAME.
Timothy Sibley, Captain
Samuel Call, Lieutenant

Billings Clapp, Sergeant
Ebenezer Eddy, Sergeant
Jesse Cousens, Sergeant

Privates.
Anderson, James
Barnes, Benjamin
Blackman, Bradley
Burton, Davis
Burton, Joel
Butler, Joshua

Chick, Abraham, Jr.
Collins, Daniel
Collins, Moses
Comins, Charles
Crane, Allen
Davis, Joseph
Douglass, Randal
Goodwin, Nehemiah
Grant, Judin
Grant, Stephen, Jr.
Gulliver, Lemuel
Gulliver, Thomas
Jones, Cyrus
Knapp, Moses
Lancaster, William

Little, Joseph
Nichols, James
Oliver, Ephraim
Orcutt, Elijah
Orcutt, John
Penny, Benjamin
Raviel, Ebenezer
Rowe, Elisha
Sibley, Benjamin F.
Spencer, Andrew
Spencer, Benjamin
Spencer, Isaac
Spencer, Moses
Stockwell, Caleb

Capt. Daniel Webster's Company, attached to Lieutenant Colonel Grant's Regiment.
From Sept. 2 to Sept. 4, 1814. Raised at Bangor. Service at Hampden. Company in battle at Hampden.

RANK AND NAME.
Daniel Webster, Captain
Robert McPhetres, Lieutenant

Lynde Valentine, Sergeant
Robert Boyd, Sergeant
Marks McBurns, Sergeant
Elijah Webster, Sergeant
John Hook, Musician
Sasson Weston, Musician

Privates.
Adams, Samuel G.
Boynton, Joseph W.
Boynton, Nathaniel

Boynton, Robert
Clark, John
Dresser, Daniel
Dutton, Gideon
Freeman, Allen
Freeman, Samuel
George, Henry
Gross, Andrew
Ham, John
Hartshorn, Ashbel
Hartshorn, David
Hartshorn, David, 2d
Hartshorn, Joseph
Hartshorn, Josiah
Hartshorn, Silas

Howard, John
Jarvis, Edward
Kenney, John
Lambert, Daniel
Lambert, Joseph
Lancaster, John
Lancaster, Levi
Liscomb, Thomas D.
McGrath, Richard
Perkins, Stephens
Randell, William
Spencer, Isaac
Thompson, Warren
Webster, John

Lieut. J. Stevens' Company, Col. A. Hastings' Regiment.
From Sept. 13 to Sept. 17, 1814. Service at Andover.

RANK AND NAME.
James Stevens, Lieutenant
Ingalls Bragg, Ensign

James F. Bragg, Sergeant
Jacob Farrington, Sergeant
Winthrop Newton, Sergeant
Moses Adams, Sergeant

Privates.
Abbot, Enos
Abbot, Holtin

Abbot, J.
Abbot, John
Abbot, Moses
Abbot, Nathaniel F.
Abbot, Timothy
Arnold, S.
Badcock, J.
Benning, Joseph
Bragg, Thomas
Burnham, Ira
Burnham, John
Farrington, Benjamin

Farrington, Philander
Homan or Hornan, John
Lovejoy, Benjamin
Marstin, Samuel
Merrill, Moses
Newton, Holdworth
Poor, Edward
Smith, John
Stevens, Enoch
Stricking, Oliver

Lieut. Col. J. Hobbs' Regiment.
From Sept. 8 to Sept. 20, 1814. Stationed at Portland.

FIELD AND STAFF.
Josiah Hobbs, Lieutenant Colonel, Falmouth
Thomas Hammond, Major
Ezekiel Dyer, Major, Cape Elizabeth
Arthur Dyer, Adjutant
Peter Lunt, Adjutant, Falmouth

Joseph Chamberlin, Quartermaster, Falmouth
Stetson Lobdell, Paymaster, Westbrook
William Sanborn, Surgeon, Falmouth
Jacob Hunt, Surgeon's Mate, Falmouth
Caleb Bradly, Chaplain, Falmouth

NONCOMMISSIONED STAFF.
Josiah R. Clough, Sergeant Major
Stetson Lobdell, Sergeant Major
Hezekiah Slemmon, Quartermaster Sergeant
James Porterfield, Fife Major
Charles Walker, Drum Major

Capt. J. Bailey's Company, Lieut. Col. J. Hobbs' Regiment.
From Sept. 8 to Sept. 20, 1814. Raised at Westbrook. Service at Portland.

RANK AND NAME.
Jeremiah Bailey, Captain
John Babb, Lieutenant
Charles Jordan, Ensign

John L. Johnson, Sergeant
Robert C. Rand, Sergeant
Thomas Broad, Sergeant
Benjamon Remick, Sergeant
Joshua Starbird, Corporal
Peter O. Clark, Corporal
Thomas Riggs, Corporal
Levi Starbird, Corporal
James B. Rand, Musician
David Horn, Musician

Privates.
Alden, Leustin
Bailey, Samuel, Jr.
Bartlett, Charles
Bradberry, John
Broad, Joseph
Broad, Silas
Broad, William
Chase, Abel

Davis, James W.
Field, Michael
Frost, Andrew P.
Furguson, Charles
Gould, Samuel
Gould, William
Greenwood, Thaddeus
Harper, Samuel
Hayes, David
Jones, Jeremiah R.
Jordan, John
Knight, Asa
Lowell, George
Maddocks, James
Mitchell, Andrew
Mitchell, Peleg
Osgood, Alexander
Palmer, Braddock S.
Plummer, Moses
Porterfield, James
Porterfield, William
Pratt, Asa
Pratt, Cushing, Jr.
Pratt, Henry
Pride, John, Jr.

Rice, Baxter
Richmond, Atwood
Roberts, Vinson
Sargent, Joel
Starbird, William
Stevens, Charles
Stevens, Tristram C.
Storer, Joseph
Tait, George
Thombs, George W.
Thombs, Job
Trickey, David
Trickey, William
Warren, Robert
Waterhouse, Joseph H.
Webb, Eli
Webb, George
Westcot, Charles
Young, John

Waiters.
Babb, Samuel
Bailey, Frederic
Jordan, Charles

Capt. E. Dyer's Company, Lieut. Col. J. Hobbs' Regiment.
From Sept. 8 to Sept. 20, 1814. Raised at Cape Elizabeth. Service at Portland.

RANK AND NAME.
Ezekiel Dyer, Captain
Simon Cutter (?), Lieutenant

Samuel Dyer, Sergeant
Elliot Dyer, Sergeant
John Mariner, Sergeant
Zebulon Skillen, Sergeant
Caleb Dyer, Corporal
Henry Frickett, Corporal
John Emery, Corporal
Nathaniel Frickett, Corporal
Reuben Roberts, Musician
Alexander Skillen, Musician

Privates.

Babb, James, Jr.
Berry, Thomas
Bowe, Nathaniel
Brown, Elisha, Jr.
Brown, Jackson
Brown, Stephen
Cash, Francis
Cash, Stephen
Cummings, William
Doane, Asa
Dyer, Christopher

Dyer, Israel
Dyer, James
Dyer, Jesse
Dyer, Reuben
Frickett, Moses
Frickett, Samuel
Graham, John
Hatch, John
Hunnewell, Joseph
Jackson, Thomas
Jumper, Ezekiel
Jumper, Joseph
Knight, Solomon
Lear, Philip
Libby, John T.
Liscom, John
Majory, John
Manner, Joseph
Mitchell, Christopher
Pillsbury, Joshua
Pillsbury, Tobias
Plummer, Daniel
Ricker, Winthrop
Sawyer, David F.
Sawyer, Elisha
Sawyer, Ephraim
Sawyer, Ivory

Sawyer, John, Jr.
Sawyer, Moses
Sawyer, Nathaniel
Simonton, Thomas
Skillen, Daniel, Jr.
Skillen, Isaac
Skillen, Lemuel
Skillen, Rufus
Skillen, William
Stanford, Israel
Stannard, Winthrop
Stanwood, Samuel
Stout, Christopher
Strout, George
Strout, Jonathan
Thompson, Asa
Thrasher, Ebenezer
Thrasher, Robert
Waterhouse, Samuel
Welch, James
Welch, Joseph
Welch, Lemuel
Willard, John
Willard, Samuel
Woodberry, Peter
Woodbury, Israel

Capt. A. Field's Company, Lieut. Col. J. Hobbs' Regiment.
From Sept. 8 to Sept. 20, 1814. Raised at Falmouth. Service at Portland.

RANK AND NAME.
Alpheus Field, Captain
Robert Hall, Lieutenant
Robert Anderson, Ensign

Samuel Richards, Sergeant
Frederick Merrill, Sergeant
William Frank, Sergeant
John Lunt, Sergeant
Josiah Field, Corporal
Ezekiel Leighton, Corporal
Josiah Hall, Corporal
Henry Hall, Corporal
Ephraim Marston, Jr., Musician
Nathaniel Field, Musician

Privates.

Acass, Benjamin
Adams, Isaac
Adams, Moses, Jr.
Allen, William
Blanchard, Ozias
Blanchard, Samuel
Brackett, Silas
Colley, John, Jr.

Colley, William, Jr.
Crabtree, Agreen
Crabtree, Eleazer
Cresey, John
Dill, Enoch
Dolly, Daniel
Dolly, William
Field, Hanson
Field, Simeon
Field, Stephen
Gilman, John
Goodell, Samuel
Green, Jesse
Hadlock, William
Hall, George
Hall, Moses
Hicks, Samuel
Hobbs, Jonathan
Huston, William
Ilsley, Nathaniel
Knight, Simon
Lambert, John
Leighton, Daniel
Leighton, Thomas
Libby, Isaac

Lock, Nathaniel
Lunt, Joshua
Lunt, Lane
Lunt, Nathan
Marston, Ebenezer
McKellar, Archibald
Merrill, Charles
Merrill, Edmund
Merrill, Joseph
Merrill, Lane
Merrill, Luther
Merrill, Solomon
Merrill, Timothy
Merrill, William
Mountford, George
Noyes, Amos
Noyes, Nathaniel
Noyes, Reuben
Prince, Reuben
Shaw, Joseph
Sweet, Adam
Sweet, Samuel
Weymouth, Robert
Woodsom, Daniel
Woodsom, Gideon

Capt. C. Knight's Company, Lieut. Col. J. Hobbs' Regiment.
From Sept. 8 to Sept. 20, 1814. Raised at Falmouth. Service at Portland.

RANK AND NAME.
Charles Knight, Captain
Jonathan Bartlett, Lieutenant
James Sweet, Ensign

Ephraim Merrill, Jr., Sergeant
Jeremiah Merrill, Sergeant
John Bucknam, Jr., Sergeant
Ebenezer Pool, Sergeant
Reuben Knight, Corporal
Reuben Merrill, Corporal
Alexander Merrill, Corporal
Reuben Merrill, 3d, Corporal
Peter Marston, Musician
John Waite, Jr., Musician

Privates.
Adams, John
Blackstone, Benjamin
Blackstone, Robert
Bucknam, Asa
Butterfield, Leonard
Chase, Thomas
Colley, Joshua
Davis, Edward
Dennet, Joseph
Dobbins, James, Jr.
Dobbins, William

Higgins, Thomas
Huston, Lewis
Huston, Paul
Jones, Stephen
Knight, Ephraim
Knight, Jacob
Knight, Nathaniel
Knight, Oliver
Knight, Samuel
Knight, Zebulon
Lock, Ebenezer
Lord, James
Lunt, Nathaniel
Merrill, Ephraim
Merrill, Ezra
Merrill, Giles
Merrill, Joshua, Jr.
Merrill, Josiah
Merrill, Zachariah
Meservy, Curtis
Moody, Jonathan
Moody, Samuel
Nolen, Christopher
Noyes, David
Noyes, Merrill
Noyes, Nathan
Noyes, Silas
Pittee, John

Pomroy, Richard
Prince, George
Prince, Noyes
Richards, William
Sandborn, Jonathan
Sawyer, John
Sweet, Joshua
Sweet, Moses, 3d
Tewksbury, James
Thomas, Benjamin
Titcomb, Benjamin
Titcomb, George
Titcomb, Reuben
Titcomb, Samuel
Titcomb, William, Jr.
Underwood, John
Webber, Aaron
Williams, Gustavus
York, Ebenezer G.
York, Reuben G.
York, Samuel G.
York, William
York, William, Jr.

Waiter.
Sweet, Lewis

Capt. P. Pride's Company, Lieut. Col. J. Hobbs' Regiment.
From Sept. 8 to Sept. 20, 1814. Raised at Falmouth. Service at Portland.

RANK AND NAME.
Peter Pride, Captain
Richard Cobb, Lieutenant
Daniel Handy, Ensign

Samuel Pride, Sergeant
Josiah R. Clough, Sergeant
William Reed, Sergeant
George Bishop, Sergeant
William Winslow, Corporal
James P. Bailey, Corporal
Zacheriah B. Stevens, Corporal
Ephraim Brackett, Corporal
Elisha Higgins, Musician
John Lunt, Musician

Privates.
Babb, George, Jr.
Barbour, John
Berry, Samuel
Blake, Samuel
Blake, William
Brackett, Zacheriah
Brackett, Zacheriah, Jr.
Campbell, Benjamin
Clark, John
Cobb, Asa
Cobb, James, Jr.
Cobb, Levi
Cobb, Peter, Jr.
Cobb, William, Jr.
Crawford, William
Davis, Christopher S.

Forbus, Amasa
Frink, Samuel
Frost, William
Gowen, James, Jr.
Gowen, Levi
Gowen, Moses
Graffam, Peter
Grant, Joseph
Graves, Andrew
Hale, George
Hicks, James
Higgins, John, Jr.
Hinkly, Samuel
Howard, Abner
Husten, Alexander
Husten, Thompson
Ingersoll, Peter
Knight, Aaron
Knight, Abner
Knight, Amos
Knight, Isaac
Knight, John
Knight, John T., Jr.
Knight, Josiah
Knight, Levi
Knight, Stephen
Lord, Samuel
Lunt, Batholomew
Lunt, Joshua
Merrill, Nathaniel W.
Minot, John
Newman, Ebenezer
North, Elijah

Pride, John
Pride, Thomas
Proctor, Frederic
Sampson, Joshua
Sawyer, Asa
Sawyer, Benjamin
Sawyer, James
Sawyer, John, Jr.
Sawyer, Joseph M.
Sawyer, Joshua
Sawyer, Mark
Sawyer, Thomas, Jr.
Shaw, Bela
Small, Asa
Small, Peter
Stevens, Benjamin
Stevens, Isaac
Stevens, Joseph
Stevens, Joshua A.
Thurston, William
Townsend, George
Trafton, Joseph
Waldron, Nathaniel
Walker, Samuel
Webb, Benjamin
Wilson, Goen
Wilson, Henry
Wilson, Increase
Winslow, Ebenezer
Woodbury, Ebenezer
Woodbury, Larken
Woodford, Chauncy

Capt. W. Slemon's Company, Lieut. Col. J. Hobbs' Regiment.
From Sept. 8 to Sept. 20, 1814. Raised at Falmouth. Service at Falmouth.

RANK AND NAME.
William Slemon, Captain
William Kenney, Lieutenant
Daniel Broad, Ensign

Josiah Stevens, Sergeant
Benjamin Burnham, Sergeant
John M. Milliken, Sergeant
David Stevens, Sergeant
David Knight, Musician
Samuel Kenney, Musician

Privates.
Bailey, Richard G.
Bell, William
Blake, Henry
Blake, James, Jr.
Broad, Ephraim
Choate, Benjamin
Cobb, George
Davis, Frederick
Fly, Isaac, Jr.
Haskell, Nathaniel, Jr.
Hicks, William

Jordan, John
Knight, Henry
Knight, Rowland
Knight, Theophilus
Nichols, Eaton
Ray, Jonathan
Stevens, Nathaniel
Stevens, William

Waiters.
Jeffords, Rufus
Strout, George

Capt. J. Valentine's Company, Lieut. Col. J. Hobbs' Regiment.
From Sept. 8 to Sept. 20, 1814. Raised at Westbrook. Service at Portland.

RANK AND NAME.
Joseph Valentine, Captain
Henry Babb, Lieutenant
John Bixby, Ensign

Levi Tole or Towle, Sergeant
Josiah Gould, Sergeant
Benjamin Quimby, Sergeant
Jeremiah Clements, Sergeant
James Webb, Musician
Joseph Bailey, Musician

Privates.
Adams, Henry
Babb, Alexander
Babb, David
Babb, George
Babb, Henry, Jr.
Babb, Mark
Bailey, Samuel
Bixby, William
Brown, Samuel
Burnett, Nathan
Chesley, Isaac
Conant, Edward

Conant, Daniel, Jr.
Conant, Samuel
Dyer, Sherborn
Elder, Reuben
Elwell, Hezekiah
Freeman, Nathaniel
Freeman, Nathaniel, Jr.
Galvin, George I.
Haskell, George
Haskell, Nathaniel
Ingalls, Nehemiah
Johnson, William
Jordan, Thomas
Lamb, John
Moody, William
Newcomb, Archelaus
Newcomb, Samuel
Patridge, Joseph
Pease, Lewis
Pike, Samuel D.
Plummer, Major
Pratt, Charles
Proctor, Charles
Proctor, Richard
Proctor, Samuel A.

Quinby, Benjamin F.
Quinby, Charles
Quinby, Simeon
Roberts, William
Sloper, Noah
Small, John
Small, Joseph
Smith, Tyng
Starbird, John, Jr.
Sweet, Stephen, Jr.
Thurlow, James
Valentine, Lowell
Walker, Gardner
Wallis, John
Wallis, Levi
Warren, Nathaniel
Webb, Kier
Winslow, David
Winslow, Miles

Waiters.
Freeman, James
Libby, Daniel
Valentine, Gilbert

Lieut. H. Dyer's Company, Lieut. Col. J. Hobbs' Regiment.
From Sept. 8 to Sept. 20, 1814. Raised at Cape Elizabeth. Service at Portland.

RANK AND NAME.
Henry Dyer, Lieutenant
Joshua Mitchell, Ensign

Robert Dyer, Jr., Sergeant
Woodbury Jordan, Sergeant
Ebenezer Dyer, Sergeant
Henry M. Kenney, Sergeant
Nathaniel Wheeler, Corporal
James Marrs, Corporal
Joseph Wheeler, Corporal
Richard Jordan, Corporal
John S. Small, Jr., Musician
Enos H. Dyer, Musician

Privates.
Armstrong, John
Briggs, Ezra
Bryant, Abraham
Clark, John, Jr.
Cobb, Lemuel
Davis, James
Davis, Simeon
Delano, Ebenezer
Delano, Nathaniel
Dresser, Joseph P.
Dresser, Richard
Duren, James
Duren, John

Dyer, Benjamin
Dyer, Clement J.
Dyer, Edward
Dyer, Jonah
Dyer, Leonard
Dyer, Reuben
Dyer, Reuben H.
Foss, Nathaniel
Gammon, John
Haskins, Ebenezer
Hatch, Joseph
Jordan, Abraham
Jordan, Clement
Jordan, Daniel

Lieut. H. Dyer's Company, Lieut. Col. J. Hobbs' Regiment — Concluded.

Privates — Concluded.
Jordan, Elliot
Jordan, Ignatius
Jordan, Israel
Jordan, James
Jordan, Nathaniel, Jr.
Jordan, Nathaniel, 4th
Jordan, Nathaniel, 5th
Jordan, Rufus
Jordan, Samuel
Jordan, Thomas
Jordan, Walter

Jordan, William
Jordan, Winter
Marrs, Cyrus
Maxwell, James
Maxwell, Matthew
Maxwell, Stephen
Maxwell, William
Miller, Apollus
Pebbles, Charles, Jr.
Pebbles, James
Richard, John
Stanford, Jeremiah

Staples, Nathaniel
Strout, Anthony
Strout, James
Trundy, William
Waterhouse, Alexander
Wheeler, John
Willard, Daniel

Waiter.
Dyer, Silas G.

Lieut. Col. S. Holland's Regiment.
From Sept. 14 to Sept. 24, 1814. Stationed at Portland.

FIELD AND STAFF.
Samuel Holland, Lieutenant Colonel, Jay
Moses Stone, Major, Jay
James Chase, Adjutant, Livermore
Henry Wood, Quartermaster

John Briggs, Paymaster, Sumner
Cornelius Holland, Surgeon, Livermore
Joshua Sole, Chaplain, Livermore

NONCOMMISSIONED STAFF.
Ebenezer Ellis, Sergeant Major
Daniel Austin, Quartermaster Sergeant
John Henry, Drum Major

Adam Knight, Waiter

Capt. J. Barnard's Company, Lieut. Col. S. Holland's Regiment.
From Sept. 13 to Sept. 24, 1814. Raised at Dixfield. Service at Portland.

RANK AND NAME.
Joel Barnard, Captain
Jonathan Holman, Ensign

Gersham Wait, Sergeant
Isaac Waters, Sergeant
Joshua Park, Sergeant
Silas Barnard, Sergeant
Harvey Wait, Corporal
David Tucker, Corporal
James Mitchell, Corporal
Thomas Morse, Corporal
Thomas Burgess, Musician
Thomas Townsend, Musician

Privates.
Abbot, John
Childs, Amos
Clausen, Luther J.
Cooledge, Moses
Hall, Josiah R.
Holman, Ebenezer
King, Henry
Marble, Baldwin
Marble, Ira
Marsh, David
Mitchell, Charles
Newman, Josiah
Newton, Abraham

Newton, Jacob
Newton, Levi, Jr.
Park, Caleb, Jr.
Richmond, Israel
Savery, Aaron
Savery, Archibald
Thomas, Micah
Thomas, Nathaniel
Torry, Isaac
Tucker, Jonas
Wait, Tyler
Waters, Gardner
White, James

Capt. E. Morse's Company, Lieut. Col. S. Holland's Regiment.
From Sept. 13 to Sept. 24, 1814. Raised at Livermore. Service at Portland.

RANK AND NAME.
Elias Morse, Captain
Henry Aldrich, Ensign

Nathaniel Soper, Sergeant
Thomas Haskell, Sergeant
Daniel Child, Sergeant
Hardwick Griffin, Sergeant
John Fisher, Corporal
John Hayes, Corporal
John Griffith, Corporal
Bradish Turner, Corporal
Nezer Bailey, Jr., Musician
Seth Ballan, Musician

Privates.
Ames, Samuel
Andrews, Lescom
Andrews, Lucius
Beals, Luther
Beals, Samuel
Bigelow, John
Boothby, Samuel
Brown, Simeon
Bryant, Thomas
Campbell, Joshua
Chandler, George
Daily, Warren
Edgcomb, Daniel

Edgcomb, Dedymus
Fisher, Elijah
Fisher, Grinsell
Foss, Joseph
Foster, Seth
Fuller, Samuel
Graffan, Daniel
Hathaway, Eli
Hobbs, Josiah
Jackson, Joseph
Jones, Stephen
Lovewell, Luther
Merrill, Jonathan
Morse, David, Jr.

Capt. E. Morse's Company, Lieut. Col. S. Holland's Regiment — Concluded.

Privates — Concluded.	Safford, Daniel	Soper, Gad
Morse, Oris	Safford, John	Starbird, James
Putnam, Simeon	Sanders, William	Strickland, John
Rich, David	Savery, Abijah, Jr.	
Robinson, Fall	Soper, Alexander	

Capt. I. Bartlett's Company, Lieut. Col. S. Holland's Regiment.
From Sept. 14 to Sept. 24, 1814. Raised at Hartford. Service at Portland.

Rank and Name.	Corliss, David	Soule, Joseph
Ira Bartlett, Captain	Edgcomb, James	Stetson, Elisha
Joshua Carpenter, Lieutenant	Ellis, Arden	Stubbs, Nathan
Joseph Tobin, Ensign	Foster, Nathaniel	Thomas, Daniel
	Glover, Joshua	Thomas, Elisha
Thomas Towns, Sergeant	Irish, Ebenezer	Thomas, William
William Sparrow, Sergeant	Lowell, John	Thompson, Uzza
Uriah Proctor, Sergeant	Moulton, James	Tilson, John
Morse Sampson, Sergeant	Parker, Joseph	Tilson, Robert
Nathaniel Thomas, Corporal	Parks, Edward	Washburn, James
Charles Burgess, Corporal	Parsons, George	Washburn, Martin
Ephraim Russell, Corporal	Richardson, Adam	Woodman, Rufus
Jacob Russell, Corporal	Russell, Jeremiah	Young, Benjamin
Thomas Allen, Musician	Russell, John	Young, Isaac
Joshua Barrows, Musician	Sampson, Jacob	
	Shaw, Daniel	
Privates.	Shaw, Job	
Allen, Otis	Skinner, David	
Brown, James	Soule, Bezai	

Capt. M. M. Craft's Company, Lieut. Col. S. Holland's Regiment.
From Sept. 14 to Sept. 24, 1814. Raised at Jay. Service at Portland.

Rank and Name.	*Privates.*	Manuel, John
Moses M. Craft, Captain	Alden, Alexander	Merrit, John S.
Joseph Cooledge, Lieutenant	Bean, Israel	Morse, Daniel
Elijah Lothrop, Ensign	Bean, Samuel	Noyes, Stillman
	Benson, Asa	Pike, James
Josiah Bennet, Sergeant	Benson, Hosea	Stevens, Aaron
Joshua Strout, Sergeant	Capen, Uriah	Strout, Nathaniel
Elijah Kees, Sergeant	Dyke, Nathaniel	Tucker, John
William Harlow, Sergeant	Ellis, Gideon	Wadsworth, Jesse
William Chenery, Corporal	Ellis, Jonathan S.	Warren, Marshall
Joel White, Corporal	Eustis, George	White, Henry
Jeremiah Stevens, Corporal	Eustis, Thomas	Wood, Timothy
Nathaniel Jackson, Corporal	Fuller, Oliver	
Isaac Harlow, Musician	Hatch, William	
Ivory Harlow, Musician	Hill, James	

Capt. W. Morrison's Company, Lieut. Col. S. Holland's Regiment.
From Sept. 14 to Sept. 24, 1814. Raised at Livermore. Service at Portland.

Rank and Name.	Timothy Eastman, Sergeant	*Privates.*
William Morrison, Captain	John Clark, Corporal	Allen, Datus T.
Thomas Davis, Lieutenant	Samuel Randall, Corporal	Bartlet, David
Billy Benjamin, Ensign	Nehemiah Noles, Corporal	Benjamin, Charles
	Jacob Lovejoy, Corporal	Burgess, Ebenezer
Alden Wellington, Sergeant	Francis Haynes, Musician	Burgess, Samuel
Martin Farrington, Sergeant	Daniel Daley, Musician	Carver, Amos
Obed Wing, Sergeant		Dunn, Samuel

Capt. W. Morrison's Company, Lieut. Col. S. Holland's Regiment — Concluded.

Privates — Concluded.
Dutton, Stephen
Farmington, Benjamin
Freeman, Stephen
Fuller, Abraham
Hammond, Paul
Hobbs, Amos
Hodgsdon, Abraham
Hodgsdon, John
Hodgsdon, Samuel C.
Knox, Jeremiah
Leadbetter, Thomas

Libby, Jonathan
Lyford, Joseph
Lyford, Oliver S.
Lyford, Samuel
Morrill, Elijah
Morrill, Joseph
Norris, Samuel
Norris, Simeon
Norris, William
Page, Moses
Philips, Edward
Smith, Mace

Smith, William
Stenchfield, William
Tanner, Ebenezer
Walker, George
Weldbore, Adam
Wellington, Elijah
White, Lewis
Wyman, John
Young, Moses
Young, Moses, Jr.

Capt. G. Paget's Company, Lieut. Col. S. Holland's Regiment.
From Sept. 14 to Sept. 24, 1814. Raised at Jay. Service at Portland.

RANK AND NAME.
George Paget, Captain
James Bean, Lieutenant
Uriah H. Gray, Ensign

Ezekiel Richardson, Sergeant
Eliphalet Dunn, Sergeant
Ebenezer West, Sergeant
Joseph Brow or Brown, Sergeant
Asa Austin, Corporal
Howland Childs, Corporal
Moore Powers, Corporal
Joseph Fuller, Corporal
Solomon Aush, Musician
Hilton Fuller, Musician

Privates.
Alden, Alexander
Allen, Asa
Allen, Stephen
Atkinson, Enoch

Barry, Aaron
Bean, Greenleaf
Bell, Robert
Blackwell, William
Brown, Charles
Bryant, Timothy
Childs, Ephraim
Childs, William
Dean, Thomas
Drout, John
Dyke, Fuller
Ellis, Martin
Ellis, Philip
Farrington, Jabez
French, William
Fuller, Charles
Fuller, Ezra
Fuller, Jackson
Fuller, John B.
Gross, William
Harris, Leach

Hayden, Lewis
Hunnaford, William
Jackson, Elijah
Jones, Silas
Kimball, Nathan
Lawrence, Noah
Luke, Eleazer
Lumber, Calvin
Merrit, Daniel
Moore, Asa
Richardson, Josiah
Rowell, John
Smart, Jeremiah
Taylor, James
Thorn, Thomas
Uland, Edmund C.
Wait, Niles
Wentworth, Thomas
Whiting, Samuel, Jr.
Wilson, Mark

Lieut. J. Elliot's Company, Lieut. Col. S. Holland's Regiment.
From Sept. 14 to Sept. 24, 1814. Raised at Livermore. Service at Portland.

RANK AND NAME.
John Elliot, Lieutenant
Philip Pitts, Ensign

Gilbert Hathaway, Sergeant
Jason Walker, Sergeant
John Fuller, Sergeant
Frank Gibbs, Sergeant
Samuel Morrison, Corporal
Seth Nelson, Corporal
Gardner Child, Corporal
Hobson Norton, Corporal
Calvin Delano, Musician

Privates.
Bartlett, Ozias
Bumpus, Calvin
Clark, John
Clark, Samuel
Coffin, Naphtali

Darr or Dorr, Ebenezer
Darr or Dorr, Ebenezer, Jr.
Delano, Abel
Delano, Abiel
Delano, Leonard
Delano, William
Gibbs, John
Gooding, Isaac
Hamlin, Isaac
Haskell, Amasa
Hathaway, Bailey
Hawkins, Henry
Hayes, George H.
Hinkley, Alanson
Holman, Abner
Holman, Daniel
Howard, Penos
Jones, Apollus
Knox, Eli
Knox, James

Knox, Joshua
Merrill, Richard
Merrill, Samuel
Neal, Samuel
Norton, Zebulon
Record, Isaac
Robinson, West
Snow, Levi
Stone, John
Vaughn, Zenos
Walker, Elijah
Washburn, David
Waterman, Noah
Waters, Lewis
Webb, Winslow
Whitaker, Stewart F.
Winslow, Gilbert
Winslow, Thomas, 2d
Wyman, William

Lieut. C. Thompson's Company, Lieut. Col. S. Holland's Regiment.

From Sept. 14 to Sept. 24, 1814. Raised at Hartford. Service at Portland.

Rank and Name.		
Cyrus Thompson, Lieutenant	Ames, Ralph	Irish, Stephen
	Baird, William	Irish, William
Isaac Fuller, Jr., Sergeant	Banks, John	Jackson, Abraham
Willard Lucas, Sergeant	Banks, Richard	Leighton, Chesley
James Kilbreth, Sergeant	Bosworth, Noah	Parsons, Daniel
Benjamin Dearborn, Corporal	Briggs, George	Pinkham, William
Oliver Lucas, Corporal	Churchill, Jabez	Poland, Sylvanus
Robert Peirce, Corporal	Decoster, Chandler	Sampson, Nathaniel
Joshua Taylor, Corporal	Dunham, Lemuel	Thompson, John
Jedediah Thomas, Musician	Elwell, Isaac	Tobin, Benjamin
Joshua Irish, Musician	Farron, Samuel	Turner, Enos
	Gammar, Perkin	Warner, Johnson
Privates.	Hayford, Gustavus	Wood, Heman
	Hodge, John M.	Young, Richard
Allen, Edmund	Holmes, Caleb	
Allen, John	Holmes, Jonathan	

Staff of Brig. Gen. J. McMillan, Second Brigade, Thirteenth Division.

From Sept. 13 to Sept. 23, 1814 (3 days travel). Service at Portland.

General and Staff.	James Starr, Brigade Major, Jay	Oliver Pollard, Brigade Quartermaster, Turner
John McMillan, Brigadier General, Fryeburg	James W. Ripley, Brigade Quartermaster, Fryeburg	Enoch Lincoln, Aid-de-Camp, Fryeburg
Joshua B. Osgood, Brigade Major, Fryeburg		

Capt. W. Rand's Company, under Maj. George Rogers, and under Supervision of United States Officers.

From Aug. 5 to Nov. 5, 1814. Raised at Cape Elizabeth. Service at forts in Portland Harbor.

Rank and Name.	Bray, Henry	Gray, Samuel
Watson Rand, Captain	Brigham, Artemas	Green, John, 3d
Caleb Haskell, Lieutenant	Brigham, Athemar	Hancock, Lewis
Samuel Knight, Lieutenant	Brown, John, 3d	Harmon, James
Robert Dunning, Ensign	Brown, Reuben	Harmon, William
	Chase, John	Haskell, Seth L.
George Stacey, Sergeant	Clark, John	Hays, John, 3d
Andrew Dennison, Sergeant	Coffin, Simeon	Howard, Almond
Thomas Foss, Sergeant	Crockett, Richard	Howard, Joshua
Isaac Small, Sergeant	Cummings, William	Hutchins, Samuel
John J. Simonds, Sergeant	Davenport, Darius	Johnson, George
James Swett, Corporal	Davis, Benjamin	Jones, Hiram
John H. Jennings, Corporal	Davis, Robert	Jordan, Levi
Joel Merrill, Corporal	Davis, Samuel	Knight, Daniel
Jasper Johnson, Corporal	Dawes, Bela	Knight, Ebenezer
Nathaniel Kimball, Corporal	Delano, Rufus	Knight, Nathaniel
John Preston, Corporal	Dennison, Abner	Knight, Stephen
Joseph Leighton, Corporal	Dodge, John	Knight, William
Isaac Cummings, Musician	Dole, Richard	Larrabee, Benjamin
Joseph Waterhouse, Musician	Dyer, James	Leighton, Daniel
	Dyer, Willis	Leighton, Jeremiah
Privates.	Edward, Richard	Long, Darius
	Eels, William, Jr.	Maibury, Isaac
Adams, Isaac	Gammon, Samuel	Mann, Fisher
Allen, John	Goodwin, Samuel	Manson, James
Allen, Otis	Goold, Robert	Marble, David
Allen, Paul	Goold, Thomas F.	Maservy, Roger
Andrews, Daniel H.	Grace, Aaron	Merrill, Samuel
Areas, James	Grant, Asa	Mitchell, Edmund
Blake, Samuel		

MASSACHUSETTS VOLUNTEER MILITIA IN THE WAR OF 1812.

Capt. W. Rand's Company, under Maj. George Rogers, and under Supervision of United States Officers — Concluded.

Privates — Concluded.

Moody, Charles	Redlen, Charles	Tobin, John
Moses, Daniel	Rogers, Thomas	Todd, William
Nason, John	Sandburn, Joseph	True, Jonathan
Nevins, Amaziah	Sandburn, Seth	Tuttle, Lebbeus
Noble, George	Sawyer, John	Tuttle, Reuben
Noble, Stephen	Shane, William	Twitchell, Mark
Paine, Josiah	Shaw, Samuel	Twombly, Solomon
Pierce, Isaac	Simonds, Samuel	Waite, Daniel
Pote, Samuel	Skillings, Simon	Ward, Lemuel
Potter, Alexander	Snow, Paul M.	Weeks, Ezra
Potter, David	Soule, Barnabas	Weeks, Samuel
Prince, Amos	Stevens, Samuel	West, Joseph
Pulcifer, Jonathan	Stevens, William	Whitney, Alexander
Purington, Elisha	Stimpson, Charles	Witham, John
Quimby, Hiram	Stubbs, Bradbury S.	Woodman, Benjamin
Rand, Bradbury	Thorn, Benjamin	Woodman, Nathaniel
	Thorn, Simeon	York, Stephen

Lieut. Henry Little's Drafted Company.
From Aug. 26 to Nov. 26, 1814. Stationed at Edgecomb, in the service of the United States.

RANK AND NAME.		
Henry Little, 1st Lieutenant	Bird, William	Jones, John
John Wales, 2d Lieutenant	Black, Henry	Lawney, Nathaniel
	Brebner, Archibald	Mudgett, Stephen
Samuel R. Gilbert, Sergeant	Campbell, Collins	Nickerson, Yates
Perkins Hull, Sergeant	Campbell, Samuel	Palmer, Joseph
John Wilson, Corporal	Covell, Israel	Partridge, David
Darius Dickey, Corporal	Crocker, Samuel	Reed, Thomas
	Davis, William	Smart, Nehemiah
Privates.	Drew, John	Smart, Winthrop
Alexander, James	Flagg, William	Snow, Harding
Batchelder, George	Frost, Samuel J.	West, Asa
Bates, Nathan	Frost, Thomas	West, Luther
Bird, Samuel S.	Gardner, Benjamin	Woodbridge, Oliver
	Hersey, Jesse	

Lieut. Col. D. McGaffey's Regiment.
From Sept. 12 to Sept. 26, 1814. Regiment rendezvoused at Hallowell, awaiting orders.

FIELD AND STAFF.		NONCOMMISSIONED STAFF.
David McGaffey, Lieutenant Colonel, Rome	John Russ, Quartermaster, Farmington	Varnum Cram, Sergeant Major
Moses Sanborn, Major, Vienna	John P. Shaw, Paymaster, Wilton	Shearabiah Dakin, Quartermaster Sergeant
Francis Mayhew, Major, New Sharon	John Barker, Surgeon, Wilton	Timothy Woodward, Fife Major
John Gilbreth, Adjutant, Rome	John Ring, Surgeon's Mate, Wilton	Jotham Sewall, Jr., Drum Major

Capt. D. Baker's Company, Lieut. Col. D. McGaffey's Regiment.
From Sept. 12 to Sept. 26, 1814. Raised at New Sharon. Service at Hallowell.

RANK AND NAME.		
Daniel Baker, Captain	Oliver Baily, Sergeant	George Hovey, Musician
Ezekiel Gilman, Lieutenant	Samuel Prescott, Jr., Corporal	Jesse L. Tibbetts, Musician
Ebenezer Weeks, Ensign	Oliver Gould, Corporal	Werborn A. Sweet, Musician
	George Sanders, Jr., Corporal	
	Abraham Williamson, Corporal	*Privates.*
Chase S. Sleeper, Sergeant	James Dyer, Jr., Musician	Ames, Noyes
Daniel K. Follinsbe, Sergeant	John S. Dyer, Musician	Arnold, Samuel
Samuel Sleeper, Sergeant	Isaac Teague, Musician	Baker, Abel

Capt. D. Baker's Company, Lieut. Col. D. McGaffey's Regiment — Concluded.

Privates — Concluded.
Baker, William
Baldwin, Nahum
Blackstone, Ebenezer
Blackstone, William, Jr.
Bradley, Wingate
Brainard, Josiah
Brown, Daniel C.
Cochran, Nathaniel

Dyer, Gideon B.
Foster, Ebenezer
French, Abel
Gordon, Daniel
Hale, John
Kelly, Jacob
Kelly, Moses
Lancaster, Thomas
Leeman, Jacob

McIntire, Henry
Ramsdel, Abner
Robbins, Joseph
Shaw, Joseph
Soule, Rufus
Williamson, Warren
Wingate, Harrison
Winslow, Prince

Capt. D. Beale's Company, Lieut. Col. D. McGaffey's Regiment.
From Sept. 12 to Sept. 26, 1814. Raised at Farmington. Service at Hallowell.

RANK AND NAME.
Daniel Beale, Captain
Silas Perham, Lieutenant
Lemuel Bursly, Ensign

John Bailey, Sergeant
Ebenezer Hutchinson, Sergeant
Joseph Gennings, Sergeant
John Morrison, Sergeant
James Cummings, Musician
John Branscomb, Musician

Privates.
Allen, Winthrop
Arnold, Thomas
Bailey, William
Berry, Rufus
Brainerd, William
Brown, Jeffry B.

Brown, John
Butler, Joseph
Butterfield, Jacob W.
Case, John
Cottle, Lot
Dwinel, David
French, Nehemiah
Goddard, Ebenezer
Hamilton, Asa
Hamilton, William
Hamlin, Solomon
Knowlton, Joseph
Knowlton, Samuel
Lovell, Oliver
Norton, George W.
Norton, Joseph, Jr.
Norton, Mayhew
Norton, Samuel B.
Parker, James

Parsons, Jeremiah
Pease, Warren
Presson, Tristram
Rice, Oliver
Rice, Samuel
Roby, Samuel
Russ, Henry
Sewell, Joshua
Shaw, Ebenezer
Stinchfield, John
Stinchfield, Thomas
Stowers, John
Thompson, John
Tufts, William
Walker, Bartoll
Willard, Asa
Withum, Joshua
Young, John

Capt. J. Gould's Company, Lieut. Col. D. McGaffey's Regiment.
From Sept. 12 to Sept. 26, 1814. Raised at Wilton. Service at Hallowell.

RANK AND NAME.
John Gould, Captain
Ephraim Woodward, Lieutenant
Benjamin Walker, Ensign

Hosmer Powers, Sergeant
Gideon Powers, Jr., Sergeant
Samuel Eames, Sergeant
Samuel Chandler, Corporal
Jeremiah Fletcher, Jr., Corporal
Noah Davenport, Corporal
John Scales, Corporal
Philip Butterfield, Jr., Musician
J. P. Butterfield, Musician

Josiah Gould, Musician
Jacob Sawyer, Jr., Musician

Privates.
Adams, Jepthah H.
Bragdon, Stephen
Brown, Elijah
Butterfield, Ebenezer
Caunnet, Peter
Chandler, Daniel
Eaton, Topham
Fletcher, Lemuel
Hardy, Moses
Harper, Elliot

Hunt, Noah I.
Knowles, Amos
Millet, Samuel
Mosher, Brise
Price, Jonathan
Rodberd, Thomas S.
Smith, Jasiel
Sweet, Jesse
Tufts, John
Welch, Elijah
Wilson, David
Wood, James L.

MASSACHUSETTS VOLUNTEER MILITIA IN THE WAR OF 1812.

Capt. W. Hussey's Company, Lieut. Col. D. McGaffey's Regiment.
From Sept. 12 to Sept. 26, 1814. Raised at Rome. Service at Hallowell.

RANK AND NAME.
William Hussey, Captain
Robert Hussey, Lieutenant
Ezekiel Page, Ensign

Enoch Knight, Sergeant
Samuel Mitchell, Sergeant
Elijah K. Hussey, Sergeant
Richard Forbush, 2d Sergeant
Benjamin White, Corporal
Rufus Clements, Corporal
Jonathan Butterfield, Corporal
Moses Choate, Corporal
Elijah Mosher, Musician
Samuel Grant, Musician

Privates.
Blaisdell, Ivory
Blanchard, Moses
Blasdell, Samuel
Blunt, Jesse
Danford, Moses
Davis, James
Ellis, Ivory
Furbush, Stephen
Gordon, Daniel
Hussey, Richard, 2d
Jordan, Elijah
Lain, Abraham C.
Mosher, Elisha
Mosher, Ephraim

Mosher, George W.
Rankin, Thomas
Stevens, Elihu
Tracy, Nathaniel
Tracy, Solomon, Jr.
Turner, Daniel
Turner, Lemuel
Wentworth, Mark
White, Asa

Capt. M. Laine's Company, Lieut. Col. D. McGaffey's Regiment.
From Sept. 12 to Sept. 26, 1814. Raised at Rome. Service at Hallowell.

RANK AND NAME.
Matthias Laine, Captain
Peletiah Leighton, Ensign

Peter Reed, Sergeant
James Colbath, Jr., Sergeant
William Blye, Sergeant
Benjamin Folsom, Sergeant
James Wells, Corporal
Joseph Gordon, Corporal
John Allen, Corporal
Peter Folsom, Corporal

John Jewell, Musician
Joseph Jewell, Musician

Privates.
Allen, Daniel
Allen, Moses
Chesley, Jonathan
Chesley, Sawyer, Jr.
Gilman, Moses
Gordon, Joseph
Hammon, Samuel
Leighton, Daniel

Leighton, Levi
Leighton, Mordecai
Leighton, Peter
Philbrick, Joseph
Prescot, Simon M.
Prescott, Jonathan
Scribner, Jonathan
Turner, Solomon
Webber, Samuel
Whittier, Clark

Capt. S. Linscott's Company, Lieut. Col. D. McGaffey's Regiment.
From Sept. 12 to Sept. 26, 1814. Raised at Chesterville. Service at Hallowell.

RANK AND NAME.
Samuel Linscott, Captain
Oliver Sewall, Lieutenant
Jotham Bradbury, Ensign

Nathaniel Maddocks, Sergeant
Barnabus Merrick, Sergeant
William Chancy, Sergeant
Levi Perry, Sergeant
John Fellows, Musician
Henry Sewall, Musician

Privates.
Alexander, Campbell
Ames, Jacob
Baker, Clark
Batchelder, Phineas
Bean, Lyman
Bennet, Elisha, Jr.
Bennet, William
Billings, Joel
Blake, Bradbury
Bradbury, Joseph
Bragden, Jeremiah

Butterfield, John
Carr, John
Chaney, John, Jr.
Chaney, Josiah
Chandler, Moses
Day, Jonathan F.
Dudley, Joseph
Eaton, Isaac
Eaton, Jeremiah
Eaton, John
Eaton, Rowell
Fellows, Aaron
Fellows, Isaac
Flint, Daniel
French, Dearborn
Gordan, Newell
Gordan, Simeon
Gordan, Thomas, 2d
Heath, Abram
Hutchinson, Asa
Knowles, John C.
Knowles, Samuel L.
Knowlton, Ebenezer
Lane, Berchwell B.

Linscott, Andrew D.
Linscott, Jacob
Margrige, William
Merriman, Timothy
Mitchell, Jonathan
Mitchell, Lovell
Perry, Elisha
Pierce, Cyrus
Porter, James
Quimby, John
Sewell, Dummer, Jr.
Soper, Jesse
Staples, Nathaniel
Stickney, William
True, John
Walton, Moses
Wheeler, Edward T.
Wheeler, George
Whittier, Benjamin
Whittier, David W.
Whittier, Josiah
Wing, David
Wymard, William

MASSACHUSETTS VOLUNTEER MILITIA IN THE WAR OF 1812. 229

Capt. C. Morse's Company, Lieut. Col. D. McGaffey's Regiment.
From Sept. 12 to Sept. 26, 1814. Raised at Wilton. Service at Hallowell.

RANK AND NAME.
Charles Morse, Captain
Asa Walker, Lieutenant
Elisha Clark, Ensign

John Pickens, Jr., Sergeant
Ignatius Allen, Sergeant
Daniel Butterfield, Sergeant
Hammon Brown, Sergeant
Benjamin Learned, Corporal
Benjamin Gould, Corporal
John Hiscock, Corporal
Moses Adams, Jr., Corporal

Privates.
Butterfield, Aaron
Butterfield, James
Dunn, Joshua, Jr.
Fletcher, Abner
Fosdick, Willard
Hall, Richard
Hathaway, Braddock
Hathaway, Ezra
Hill, Ezekiel
Hiscock, Jesse
Law, Reuben
McCully, John
Pickens, David
Pickens, Leonard

Randell, Timothy, Jr.
Robbins, Hildreth
Robbins, John
Sarter, David B.
Stone, Ephraim
Stone, Ephraim, Jr.
Towns, Elisha
Walker, Jonathan
Walker, Joseph
Walker, Osgood
Wright, Isaac

Waiter.
Brown, Eliphalet

Capt. J. Trask's Company, Lieut. Col. D. McGaffey's Regiment.
From Sept. 12 to Sept. 26, 1814. Raised at New Sharon. Service at Hallowell.

RANK AND NAME.
John Trask, Captain
Christopher Dyer, Lieutenant
Nathaniel Parsons, Ensign

Jeremiah Bean, Sergeant
Ebenezer Bean, Sergeant
Benjamin Brainard, Sergeant
Ivory Bean, Sergeant
William Dill, Corporal
Frederic Swan, Corporal
Benjamin C. Goss, Corporal
Moses P. Bradly, Corporal
Saul Blaming, Musician
James Davis, Musician
Asa Reed, Musician

Privates.
Ames, Isaac
Ames, Rufus
Baker, Elisha
Bean, Nathaniel
Bent, Isaac
Berry, Allen
Blacksten, Benjamin
Bowley, Benjamin
Boynton, Joshua
Bradbury, Samuel
Bullen, Warren

Bulling, Joshua
Burwell, Thomas
Coburn, Jephtha
Coburn, Manly
Cowing, Isaac
Dyer, Reuben
Floyd, Nathaniel
Floyd, Samuel
Folsom, Samuel
Ford, Forbes
French, Ebenezer, Jr.
Gage, Daniel
George, John
George, William
Gove, Solomon, Jr.
Greenleaf, Joseph
Harding, Nathaniel, Jr.
Holdes, Steven
Hollis, Samuel
Hollis, Thomas
Hopkins, Joshua
Hopkinson, Theophilus
Hord, Nehemiah
Hovey, Isaac
Jones, John
Luce, Samuel
Morrel, John
Morrel, Joseph
Norcross, James B.

Page, John
Page, Moses
Page, Saul
Paul, James
Paul, Oliver
Pease, Elijah
Pratt, Paul
Prescott, Abel
Preston, Hiram
Prews, Alfred
Proctor, Isaac
Rollings, John
Sawyer, Leonard
Sevens, Nathaniel
Shaw, Gilman
Small, Elisha
Small, James
Smith, Elijah
Smith, Nathan
Teague, Asa
Tibbetts, John
Trask, John, Jr.
Welch, Charles
Willard, Nathaniel
Willets, John
Witham, Ebenezer
Works, Henry
Yeaton, Philip, Jr.

Capt. N. Whittier's Company, Lieut. Col. D. McGaffey's Regiment.
From Sept. 12 to Sept. 26, 1814. Raised at Vienna. Service at Hallowell.

RANK AND NAME.
Nathaniel Whittier, Captain
Orem Dow, Lieutenant
Enoch M. Moore, Ensign

Abel Whittier, Sergeant
John Raynes, Sergeant

True Hodgkins, Sergeant
Adonijah Prescot, Sergeant
Andrew Neal, Corporal
Benjamin Kimball, Corporal
J. P. Boswort, Corporal
Calvin Lapham, Corporal
Jesse Snow, Musician

Stephen Sandburn, Musician
Joseph Dow, Musician
David Cassin, Musician
Eliphalet Brown, Musician

MASSACHUSETTS VOLUNTEER MILITIA IN THE WAR OF 1812.

Capt. N. Whittier's Company, Lieut. Col. D. McGaffey's Regiment — Concluded.

Privates.

Brown, Jesse
Burrell, Jacob
Con, James
Con, Joseph
Currier, Edmund
Folsom, Eliphalet
Folsom, Jacob
French, William
Harris, Pliny

Hoyt, George
Hubbard, John
Ireland, Samuel
Johnson, Jacob
Kimball, William
Lane, David
Mitchell, Robert
Moore, Henry F.
Moore, Josiah
Morrell, Daniel, Jr.

Morrell, Stephen
Porter, John
Porter, Stephen
Prescot, Jedediah
Sandburn, Stephen
Smart, Robert
Webber, Israel
Webber, Joseph
Wood, Eliphalet

Lieut. Col. A. Merrill's Regiment.

From June 20 to June 23, and Sept. 10 to Sept. 25, 1814. Service at Bath.

FIELD AND STAFF.
Abel Merrill, Lieutenant Colonel, Topsham
James McRogers, Major, Bowdoin
Charles Pray, Major, Lisbon
Charles Thompson, Adjutant, Topsham

William G. Sandford, Paymaster, Topsham
James Purrington, Quartermaster, Topsham
Benjamin H. Mace, Surgeon's Mate, Lisbon

NONCOMMISSIONED STAFF.
Hezekiah B. Thompson, Sergeant Major
Robert Jack, Quartermaster Sergeant
Hugh Wilson, Drum Major
Henry Sampson, Fife Major

Capt. H. Getchell's Company, Lieut. Col. A. Merrill's Regiment.

From June 20 to June 22, and Sept. 10 to Sept. 28, 1814. Raised at Litchfield. Service at Bath.

RANK AND NAME.
Hugh Getchell, Captain
William Randall, Lieutenant

James B. Smith, Sergeant
Cornelius Richardson, Sergeant
Cyrus Bourk, Sergeant
Adam Johnson, Corporal
Isaac Smith, Corporal
Thomas Springer, Corporal
William Towns, Corporal
Cornelius Thompson, Musician
Isaac Shirtliff, Musician

Privates.
Ashford, Robert
Baker, Abner
Basset, Abner
Basset, Heli
Basset, Lewis

Bourk, Charles
Bourk, Thomas
Brown, James
Brown, Saul
Campbell, Adam
Cook, Saul
Dunlap, Ezekiel
Dunlap, John
Dunlap, Robert
Farren, Richard
Farrin, William
Gatchell, John S.
Gatchell, Simmons
Goldsmith, Zacheus
Gower, William
Hall, Timothy
Ham, Thomas
Hanscomb, Benjamin
Hodgman, Amos
Hodgman, Asa

Huntington, Timothy
Hutchinson, James
Lydstone, John
Miles, Caleb
Morgridge, John
Nickerson, Esdras
Potter, David
Potter, Reuben
Potter, Robert
Randall, John
Richardson, Abijah
Richardson, Amos
Shirtliff, William
Smith, John
Smith, Myrick
Smith, Samuel W.
Smith, Thomas
Thurrell, John
Walker, Joshua
Williams, William

Capt. E. Hatch's Company, Lieut. Col. A. Merrill's Regiment.

From June 20 to June 22, and Sept. 10 to Sept. 28, 1814. Raised at Bowdoinham. Service at Bath.

RANK AND NAME.
Ebenezer Hatch, Captain
Job Jelason, Lieutenant
Caleb Baker, Ensign

Jeremiah Preble, Sergeant
William P. Oliver, Sergeant
George Maxwell, Corporal
John I. Hosnal, Corporal
Zenas Baker, Musician

Privates.
Allen, Daniel
Baker, John
Blanchard, Solomon
Blanchard, William
Dinsmore, Samuel
Farrow, Jacob
Ganbert, Nicholas
Hatch, Elihu
Holmes, J. G.

Jelason, William
Mains, John
Matoon, Isaac
Maxwell, John
Maxwell, William
McFadden, John
Parks, Chetham
Parks, Thomas I.
Pottle, David, Jr.
Pratt, Benjamin

Capt. E. Hatch's Company, Lieut. Col. A. Merrill's Regiment — Concluded.

Privates — Concluded.	Raymond, James	Thomas, John
Pratt, Samuel	Sedgley, Joseph	Tolman, Elias
Preble, Joseph	Sedgley, Stephen	Whitmore, Abraham
Preble, Richard	Speed, David	Wilson, Samuel
Preble, William	Springer, Elisha	Wilson, Samuel, 2d
Purrington, Isaac	Taylor, Benjamin	Woodward, Samuel

Capt. N. McLellan's Company, Lieut. Col. A. Merrill's Regiment.

From June 20 to June 22, and Sept. 20 to Sept. 28, 1814. Raised at Bowdoin. Service at Bath.

RANK AND NAME.	Bryre, John	Lydston, William
Nathaniel McLellan, Captain	Buker, David	Mullen, Stephen
Abiazer Purrington, Lieutenant	Campbell, George	Percy, William
Joseph Carr, Jr., Ensign	Campbell, James	Persley, John
	Campbell, Nathaniel	Potter, James B.
Samuel Smith, Jr., Sergeant	Chace, James	Potter, Saul
Ebenezer Temple, Jr., Sergeant	Cox, Nathaniel	Sampson, Rufus
Samuel Clark, Jr., Sergeant	Davis, James	Small, Jonathan
Judah Chase, Sergeant	Davis, Saul	Smith, James
David Story, Corporal	Dunlap, Ebenezer	Smith, Nathaniel
Andrew Jack, 3d, Corporal	Flagg, John	Starboard, Samuel
William Verney, Corporal	Forbus, Thomas	Story, Stephen
George Ridley, Jr., Corporal	Grover, James	Tarr, Paul
Jacob Ellet, Musician	Grover, John	Thurrell, Jacob
Stephen Ellet, Musician	Grover, Joseph	Townes, Abner
	Hanscom, Joseph	Towns, Thomas
Privates.	Huff, Nathaniel	Wheeler, John
Alexander, James	Huff, Samuel	Wheeler, Simon
Alexander, William	Jack, Andrew, Jr.	Wheeler, William
Blackman, James	Jackson, William	White, Gideon
Booker, Beniah	Jones, John	White, Isaac
Bower, Alexander	Knight, Daniel	Williams, James

Capt. G. F. Patten's Company, Lieut. Col. A. Merrill's Regiment.

From June 20 to June 22, and Sept. 10 to Sept. 28, 1814. Raised at Topsham. Service at Bath.

RANK AND NAME.	Graves, Jacob	Patten, Adams
George F. Patten, Captain	Graves, Levi	Patten, James B.
George Rogers, Lieutenant	Graves, Moses	Patten, Matthew
James M. Perry, Ensign	Graves, Samuel	Patten, William
	Gwin, Saul	Perry, Robert
Charles Hunter, Sergeant	Heal, Gilbert	Potter, Jesse
Ezekiel M. Brown, Sergeant	Howland, Abraham	Randall, William, Jr.
David Thompson, Sergeant	Howland, Benjamin	Rideout, Jacob
Hugh Rogers, Sergeant	Howland, George	Rogers, John, Jr.
Henry Sampson, Musician	Howland, John	Rogers, William
	Hunter, Adams	Sampson, James, Jr.
Privates.	Hunter, Alexander	Sandford, John, Jr.
Abell, Jehiel	Hunter, Arthur, Jr.	Small, Francis
Berry, Josiah	Hunter, Benjamin	Smith, Joseph
Brown, Jeremiah	Hunter, David	Stockman, Jesse
Card, Francis	Hunter, Lithgo	Taylor, John
Chase, John, Jr.	Hunter, Samuel	Wade, Abner
Cummins, Jacob	Hunter, Thomas, 3d	Wade, Luther
Fog or Foy, Henry	Hunter, William	Winshell, Robert
Foster, Joseph, 3d	Mallet, Collamore	Work, David
Foster, Philip H.	Mallet, William, Jr.	
Fox, Joshua	Mustard, Joseph	*Waiter.*
Graves, Daniel	Nichols, Benjamin	Combs, Abner
Graves, Eben	Owen, John	

MASSACHUSETTS VOLUNTEER MILITIA IN THE WAR OF 1812.

Capt. H. Purrinton's Company, Lieut. Col. A. Merrill's Regiment.
From June 20 to June 22, 1814. Raised at Bowdoin. Service at Bath.

RANK AND NAME.
Humphrey Purrinton, Captain
Abel Thompson, Ensign

John Snow, Sergeant
Benjamin Townsend, Sergeant
Actor Willson, Sergeant
Joshua Coombs, Sergeant

Privates.
Adams, Adam
Adams, James
Alexander, Elisha
Barker, Caleb
Barnes, Henry
Barnes, Robert
Beel, Zacheus
Brannigum, Samuel
Conant, Oliver
Coombs, Zebulon
Cornish, Henry
Dugen, Thomas

Emerson, Asa
Ewin, William
Foster, Benjamin
Getchell, John
Getchell, Winslow
Gowell, John
Gowell, William
Grover, Samuel
Hall, John, 2d
Hall, Lemuel
Hanscomb, James
Hodgman, Amos
Hogan, John
Hogan, William
Hopkins, John
Jaques, Aaron
Jaques, Johnson
Maxwell, Thomas
Polley, Asahel
Potter, Benjamin
Potter, James
Potter, Jesse

Potter, John, 2d
Potter, Joseph
Purrinton, Charles
Rideout, John H.
Rideout, Johnson
Rolins, John
Small, John
Small, Mark
Small, Stephen
Small, Tailor
Smart, William, 2d
Snow, Isaac
Snow, Jonathan
Stover, Charles
Thompson, Abijah
Townsend, Jesse
Townsend, Terize
Ward, Josiah
Willson, Andrew
Willson, James
Wire, Joseph

Capt. H. Snow's Company,[1] Lieut. Col. A. Merrill's Regiment.
From June 20 to June 22, and Sept. 10 to Sept. 28, 1814. Raised at Bowdoin. Service at Bath.

RANK AND NAME.
Henry Snow, Captain
Humphrey Purrington, Lieutenant
Abel Thompson, Ensign

John Snow, Sergeant
Benjamin Townsend, Sergeant
Actor Wilson, Sergeant
Perez Townsend, Sergeant
John Hopkins, Corporal
Abijah Thompson, Corporal
James Potter, Corporal
Samuel Brinngion, Corporal
William Rideout, Musician
Asa Emerson, Musician

Privates.
Adams, Adam
Adams, James
Alexander, Elisha
Barker, Caleb
Barns, Henry

Beals, Zacheus
Combs, Zebulon
Conant, Oliver
Cornish, Humphrey
Duggin, Thomas
Ewen, William
Foster, Benjamin
Getchell, John
Getchell, Winslow
Gowel, John
Gowel, William
Grover, Samuel
Hall, John, 2d
Hanscomb, James
Hogan, Charles
Hogan, John
Hogan, William
Jaquis, Aaron
Jaquis, Johnson
Mallet, John
Maxwell, Thomas
Polly, Asahel

Polly, William
Potter, Benjamin
Potter, John, 2d
Potter, Joseph
Rideout, John H.
Rideout, Johnson
Ring, Thomas
Rollins, John
Small, John, 2d
Small, Stephen
Small, Tailor
Smart, William
Snow, Isaac
Snow, Jonathan
Stover, Charles
Townsend, Jesse
Ward, Joshua
Willson, Andrew
Willson, James
Wire, Joseph

Capt. J. White's Company, Lieut. Col. A. Merrill's Regiment.
From June 20 to June 22, and Sept. 10 to Sept. 28, 1814. Raised at Bowdoinham. Service at Bath.

RANK AND NAME.
John White, Captain
Charles Jennings, Lieutenant
Josiah Sandford, Ensign

Enoch Libby, Sergeant
William Willson, Sergeant
Joseph Totman, Sergeant

Benjamin Randall, Sergeant
George Jackson, Corporal
William White, Corporal
John Starbird, Corporal
Dunmer Mitchell, Jr., Corporal
Daniel Plummer, Musician
Samuel Harlow, Musician

Privates.
Aderton, John
Bates, Frederic
Bates, James
Bragdon, Daniel
Brown, Matthew
Buker, Samuel
Collier, William

---

[1] This is the way the companies appear in the records, but there is doubt as to the correctness of the dates.

MASSACHUSETTS VOLUNTEER MILITIA IN THE WAR OF 1812. 233

Capt. J. White's Company, Lieut. Col. A. Merrill's Regiment — Concluded.

Privates — Concluded..
Curtis, Obediah
Dingley, John
Dinsmore, Charles
Hershel, Ebenezer D.
Jack, Joseph
Lancaster, Joseph, Jr.
Meder, Edward
Mitchell, Charles
Newel, Zebulon
Pain, Samuel
Plummer, Aaron

Plummer, Isaac
Raymond, Benjamin
Ridley, Daniel
Ridley, William
Rollins, David
Sandford, James
Scarles, Sylvester
Shaw, Thomas
Stimson, John
Stinson, Abiel
Tibbets, John
Toothaker, Joseph

Varman, Ralph
Waterhouse, Benjamin
Waterhouse, Elias
Waterhouse, James
Waterhouse, Zenus
Watson, Saul
Webber, Loring
Webber, Samuel
Webber, Stephen
Webber, Stephen, Jr.
Williams, Samuel

Capt. P. Whitney's Company, Lieut. Col. A. Merrill's Regiment.
From June 20 to June 22, and Sept. 10 to Sept. 28, 1814. Raised at Lisbon. Service at Bath.

RANK AND NAME.
Peter Whitney, Captain
David Green, Lieutenant
William Blake, Ensign

Gideon Curtis, Sergeant
Benjamin Southerland, Sergeant
Benjamin Whitney, Sergeant
John Godfrey, Sergeant
John A. Thompson, Corporal
Job Bleathen, Corporal
Zebulon Blake, Corporal

Privates.
Beal, William
Blethen, Increase
Blethen, Reuben
Coombs, Joseph
Coombs, William
Dain, Ebenezer
Dain, William, Jr.
Green, James
Kimbal, Phineas
Lambert, Thomas
Neal, William

Peterson, Benjamin
Pierce, Daniel
Sawyer, Joseph
Smith, Isaac
Smith, Nathan
Southerland, Alexander, Jr.
Stackpole, Cornelius
Stanwood, Samuel
Warren, Edmund
Webber, Joseph

Capt. A. Dwinal's Company, Lieut. Col. A. Merrill's Regiment.
From Sept. 10 to Sept. 28, 1814. Raised at Lisbon. Service at Bath.

RANK AND NAME.
Aaron Dwinal, Captain
Thomas Henderson, Lieutenant
Abel Curtis, Ensign

William Bucknam, Sergeant
Stephen Foss, Sergeant
Samuel Moody, Sergeant
William Woodard, Sergeant
Thomas Small, Corporal
John B. Dyer, Corporal
Thomas Owen, Corporal
Lemuel Woodard, Corporal
Dudley D. Young, Musician
Nathaniel Eames, Musician
Edward Woodbury, Musician

Privates.
Andrews, Ephraim
Arras, James
Arras, Thomas L.
Arzas, Patrick
Atwood, John
Baker, Saul
Bickford, Aaron
Bickford, William
Blake, Jacob
Boothbay, John
Cowing, Thomas
Crowley, Jeremiah

Cushing, John
Cushman, Isaac
Cushman, Lewis
Davis, Jonathan
Denerson, Solomon
Donnell, Benjamin
Dunning, Joshua
Dwinal, Simeon
Frasier, James
Gilbert, Lee
Goold, John
Goold, Moses
Ham, Israel
Hanson, Hiram
Harmon, Levi
Heath, Samuel
Henderson, Moses
Henry, Samuel, Jr.
Higgins, Dyer
Hinkley, Edmund
Hinkley, John
Hinkley, Thomas
Hinkley, Thomas W.
Hinkley, William
Hopkins, Isaac
Jackson, Aaron
Jordan, Andrew
Kelgore, Caleb
Littlefield, Samuel
Mayall, John

Metcalf, Tuel
Moody, Nathan
Morefield, Eliakim
Nowell, John
Parker, John
Sinclair, John
Sinkley or Hinkley, Nathaniel
Small, James
Smith, Archibald
Smith, Charles, Jr.
Smith, George
Smith, James
Smith, William
Smullen, Joseph
Stafford, Edward
Staple, Hosea
Stinson, Mark
Thompson, Phineas
Tibbets, Enoch
Tibbets, Paul
Toothaker, Ephraim
Vosmas, John
Whitmore, Jacob
Whitney, Nathan
Wilson, William
Woodard, Joseph

Waiters.
Staple, Isaac
Wales, Samuel

Capt. D. Haynes' Company, Lieut. Col. A. Merrill's Regiment.
From Sept. 10 to Sept. 28, 1814. Raised at Bowdoinham. Service at Bath.

RANK AND NAME.
David Haynes, Captain
Samuel Coombs, Lieutenant

William Brooker, Jr., Sergeant
Jeremiah Mallay, Sergeant
John Prebble, Sergeant
Enoch Elliot, Musician
James Woodworth, Musician

Privates.
Barnes, Benjamin
Cobb, Cyrus
Cobb, Saul

Curtis, Barstow
Curtis, Levi
Eaton, Enoch
Fisher, John, Jr.
Fisher, Thomas
Fisher, William
Graves, Johnson
Graves, Thomas
Heddon, George
Henry, John
Jack, Saul
Jordan, Samuel
Keith, Asa
Littlefield, Calvin A.

Orr, Gershom
Page, John
Paine, Joshua
Purrington, Nathaniel
Purrington, William
Reed, James B.
Sampson, William
Spear, Robert
Spear, Thomas
Stanforth, Warren
Staples, Robert
Stewart, Joseph
Tarbox, Philip
Welch, Mark

Capt. S. True's Company, Lieut. Col. A. Merrill's Regiment.
From Sept. 10 to Sept. 28, 1814. Raised at Lisbon. Service at Bath.

RANK AND NAME.
Samuel True, Captain
Thomas Hewey, Lieutenant
Samuel Mallet, Ensign

J. Londborn, Sergeant
John Smith, Sergeant
Peter Garcebon, Sergeant
David Spofford, Sergeant
Elias Colby, Musician
John Hanscomb, Musician

Privates.
Anderson, Jacob
Bassford, Nathaniel
Brown, David
Chase, Nahum
Cherrne, Abner
Colby, James, Jr.
Crocket, John
Dalton, William A.
Dearing, Samuel
Dennat, Samuel
Eaton, William
Farrow, James
Farrow, John

Farrow, Josiah
Farrow, Nathan
Farrow, Reuben
Firbush, Isaac
Firbush, John
Frost, Gardner
Gilpatrick, Christopher
Gilpatrick, Nathaniel
Gilpatrick, Timothy
Gould, Nathan
Grant, Benjamin
Gray, James
Haley, Joshua
Hamilton, Aaron
Harlow, Josiah
Hewey, David
Hewey, Joseph, Jr.
Hewey, Samuel
Higgin, Timothy
Jack, Jacob
Jack, Samuel
Jones, Belcher
Jones, Isaac
Jordan, Benjamin
Jordan, Dominicus
Jordan, Robert

Jordan, Valentine
Libby, Rufus
Marr, John
Maxwell, Richard
Maxwell, Solomon
McFarland, William
McKinney, Lot
Moody, Elias
Niles, Jeremiah
Niles, Robert H.
Noble, Stephen
Orrs, John
Potter, Joseph
Potter, Thomas
Prebble, Zebulon
Robinson, Samuel
Spofford, Greenlief
Spofford, Moody
Storer, Jedediah
Temple, Joseph
Thompson, Samuel
Weymouth, H.
Weymouth, Nathan
Weymouth, Nathaniel
Weymouth, Thomas

Capt. J. Wilson's Company, Lieut. Col. A. Merrill's Regiment.
From June 20 to June 22, 1814. Raised at Topsham. Service at Bath.

RANK AND NAME.
John Wilson, Jr., Captain
Nathaniel Sandford, Lieutenant

Hugh Patten, Sergeant
Daniel E. Tucker, Sergeant
Benjamin Thompson, Sergeant
Thomas Wilson, Sergeant
Nathaniel Bunker, Sergeant
John Dearborn, Musician

Privates.
Barron, Charles
Coombs, David
Coombs, John
Coombs, John, 2d
Coombs, Thomas
Dinsmore, Prince
Dudley, Elihu
Dunlap, John I.
Fall, Stephen

Farrin, John
Farrin, William
Flagg, David
Gray, Daniel
Haley, Peletiah, Jr.
Hewey, Jonathan, Jr.
Higgins, Jeremiah
Hinckley, Samuel
Huley, John
Jameson, John

Capt. J. Wilson's Company, Lieut. Col. A. Merrill's Regiment — Concluded.

Privates — Concluded.
Littlefield, Moses
Lord, John
Marrs, John, Jr.
Melcher, Abner
Metcalf, Benjamin
Patten, Actor
Patten, William, Jr.
Pennel, Joshua
Perkins, Enoch

Perkins, Enoch, 2d
Perkins, Levi
Roberts, Mark
Sergeant, John
Tarr, Clark
Tate, William
Thompson, Alexander
Thompson, Saul
Thurlow, Joshua
Varney, Enoch

Welsh, Daniel
Whitten, Joseph
Wilson, Adam
Wilson, Humphrey
Wilson, James
Wilson, John H.
Wilson, Samuel
Wood, Samuel

Capt. J. Wilson's Company of Drafted Militia, in Service of United States, under Command of Lieut. Col. Abel Merrill.
From Aug. 1 to Nov. 1, 1814. Stationed at Bath, Hunewell's Point and Georgetown.

RANK AND NAME.
John Wilson, Captain
Moses M. Marsh, Lieutenant

Samuel S. Cummings, Sergeant
Benjamin Owen, Sergeant
Joseph Jack, Sergeant
Benjamin Thompson, Sergeant
Hugh Rogers, Sergeant
Matthew Hinckley, Corporal
Dean Kimball, Corporal
John McManus, Jr., Corporal
Davis Hanniford, Corporal
Isaac Hopkins, Corporal
John Dearborn, Musician

Privates.
Adams, Daniel
Bassett, Lewis
Beal, Ebenezer
Brown, Matthew
Coombs, Asa, Jr.
Coombs, Joseph
Coombs, Thomas

Danforth, Isaac
Dunlap, Isaac
Dunlap, Martin
Eaton, Abel
Foster, John
Frasure, James
Gammon, Samuel
Gardner, John
Gatchell, John
Gowell, Charles
Haley, James
Hall, William
Hallet, Avory
Hanniford, William
Harwood, Otis
Hinckley, Edmund
Hinckley, John
Hinckley, Samuel W.
Hodgkins, Samuel B.
Huff, Samuel
Jordan, Benjamin
Kilgore, William
Kilpatrick, Joseph
Lane, William

Maxwell, Thomas
McDaniel, Major
McIntosh, Nathan
Mitchell, Ammi
Morrison, Nathaniel
Oliver, James
Oliver, John
Osgood, Hazen
Pettingill, Sumner
Pray, Edmund
Radcliff, Henry
Ridley, Mark
Rollins, David
Rollins, Joseph
Sanborn, Bradbury
Smith, Benjamin
Smith, Jeremiah
Spinney, Ephraim
Stanwood, James
Stinson, Samuel
Toothaker, Gideon
Weymouth, Archibald
Wilson, James

Lieut. R. Hunter's Company, Lieut. Col. A. Merrill's Regiment.
From Sept. 10 to Sept. 28, 1814. Raised at Topsham. Service at Bath.

RANK AND NAME.
Robert Hunter, Lieutenant
Nathaniel Potter, Ensign

Elisha Patterson, Sergeant
Thomas Lewis, Sergeant
Ezekiel Raymond, Sergeant
Wanton Rideout, Sergeant
Leonard Eaton, Musician

Privates.
Allen, John
Campbell, Moses
Conant, Oliver
Crocker, Waldron
Dunham, James
Haiden, William
Hathorn, Samuel
Hogen, Charles
Lydstone, Roby
McFellan, Warren

Noyes, John
Powers, Robert
Sampson, Thomas
Small, James
Snow, Isaac
Spears, George
Stinson, William
Thompson, James
Whitney, Abiezer
Whitney, Abraham
Whitney, Jonathan

Lieut. N. Sandford's Company, Lieut. Col. A. Merrill's Regiment.
From Sept. 10 to Sept. 28, 1814. Raised at Bowdoin. Service at Bath.

RANK AND NAME.
Nathaniel Sandford, Lieutenant
Saul Veasie, Ensign

Thomas Wilson, Sergeant
Hugh Patton, Sergeant
Daniel Tucker, Sergeant
John Haley, 2d, Sergeant

Privates.
Akley, William
Banan, Charles
Bunker, Nathan
Cole, James
Doughty, Elijah
Dunlap, John, 2d

Eaton, Charles
Fall, Stephen
Ferrin, Eben, 2d
Ferrin, John
Ferrin, William
Fuller, Constant
Gray, Solomon
Haley, Peletiah, 2d
Hamblin, Saul
Hewey, Jonathan
Higgins, Jeremiah
Hinckley, Samuel
Jameson, John
Libby, Nahum
Lord, John
Mans, John, 2d

Melcher, Abner
Metcalf, Benjamin
Patten, William
Pennel, Joshua
Perkins, Levi
Robert, Mark
Tarr, Clark
Thompson, Samuel, 2d
Varney, Enoch
White, Elijah, 2d
Whitten, Joseph
Wilson, Humphrey (?)
Wilson, James
Wilson, John H.
Wood, Saul
Work, William

Lieut. Col. H. Moore's Regiment.
From Sept. 12 to Sept. 27, 1814. Service at Wiscasset.

FIELD AND STAFF.
Herbert Moore, Lieutenant Colonel, Winslow
Nathan Stanly, Major, Harlem
Daniel Stevens, Major, Fairfax
Joseph Clark, Adjutant, Clinton

Daniel Hayden, Quartermaster
Stephen Thayer, Surgeon, Vassalborough
Whiting Robinson, Surgeon's Mate, Plimpton

NONCOMMISSIONED STAFF.
Henry Johnson, Sergeant Major
Asher Hinds, Quartermaster Sergeant
James Crosby, Drum Major
William Crosby, Fife Major

Capt. J. L. Child's Company, Lieut. Col. H. Moore's Regiment.
From Sept. 12 to Sept. 27, 1814. Raised at Winslow. Service at Wiscasset.

RANK AND NAME.
James L. Child, Captain
Washington Heald, Lieutenant
William Getchell, Ensign

William Harvey, Sergeant
James Heald, Sergeant
Joel Crosby, Sergeant
Abram Bean, Sergeant
Alvin Blackwell, Corporal
Richard V. Hayden, Corporal
Simeon Heald, Corporal
Elisha Ellis, Corporal

Privates.
Abbott, George
Abbott, Stephen
Barton, Hernand C.
Bates, Samuel

Dingley, Nathan
Drummond, Clark
Fife, James
Fletcher, William
Getchell, Asa
Getchell, Stephen
Gould, John
Ham, William
Hayden, Charles, Jr.
Heald, Joseph
Howard, Zepheon
Libby, Daniel
Paine, Frederick
Pilsbury, George
Pollard, Levi
Pollard, William
Pressey, Thomas J.
Reynolds, Adna
Rhodes, Rufus

Richards, Daniel
Richardson, Ebenezer
Richardson, Samuel
Ross, Wentworth
Small, Phineas
Spring, William
Swift, Joseph
Thompson, Jeremiah B.
Wilson, Ephraim, Jr.
Wilson, Luke
Wilson, Samuel
Winship, Benjamin
Wood, Butler
Wyman, William

Waiter.
McIntyre, Samuel

Capt. D. Crowell's Company, Lieut. Col. H. Moore's Regiment.
From Sept. 12 to Sept. 27, 1814. Raised at Harlem (now China). Service at Wiscasset.

RANK AND NAME.
Daniel Crowell, Captain
Nathaniel Spratt, Lieutenant
Zalmana Washburn, Ensign

Jonathan Furber, Sergeant
Elisha Clark, Sergeant
Jabish Crowell, Sergeant
Thomas Ward, Jr., Sergeant
Samuel Branch, Corporal
David Spratt, Corporal
Samuel Ward, Corporal
James Wiggins, Corporal
Ephraim Clark, 3d, Musician
Jonathan Doe, Musician

Privates.
Burgess, David, 2d
Burgess, Richard
Chase, Moses
Crowell, David
Crowell, John, Jr.
Doe, David
Hamlin, Isaiah
Hamlin, Josiah
Hanson, Joshua
Lancaster, James, Jr.
Lancaster, Joseph
Lancaster, Robert
McLaughlin, Benjamin
McLaughlin, Jacob
Monk, William, Jr.
Pratt, William
Rundel, Reuben
Spratt, George
Spratt, James
Tarbell, Josiah
Ward, Nehemiah
Webber, Sylvanus
Woodbridge, Paul D.
Wyman, Ezekiel, Jr.

Waiter.
Crowell, Elbridge

Capt. J. Farwell's Company, Lieut. Col. H. Moore's Regiment.
From Sept. 12 to Sept. 27, 1814. Raised at Vassalborough. Service at Wiscasset.

RANK AND NAME.
Jeremiah Farwell, Captain
Aaron Garlin, Lieutenant

Charles Webber, Sergeant
Eli French, Sergeant
John G. Hall, Sergeant
Elijah Morse, Sergeant
Benjamin Basset, Corporal
Nathaniel Marchent, Corporal
Heman Sturgiss, Corporal
Luke Shaw, Corporal
John Lovejoy, Musician

Privates.
Basset, Jabez
Basset, Joseph
Chadburn, Francis
Cowen, Thomas
Davis, Asa
Farnsworth, Chephas
Farwell, Hannibal
Faught, James
Faught, Nathaniel
Garlin, Thomas
Gould, James
Hacker, Edmund
Hallet, Soule
Hallet, William S.
Haws, David
Hedge, Seth
Horne, William
Howard, Libbeus
Lovejoy, Nathaniel, Jr.
Matthews, Winslow
Niebbs, Moses
Nottage, Henry
Nubbs, Amos
Packard, Nathaniel
Pollard, William
Randall, Caleb
Risly, John
Rollins, James
Snell, Edward
Wiggin, James

Capt. R. Fletcher's Company, Lieut. Col. H. Moore's Regiment.
From Sept. 12 to Oct. 1, 1814. Raised at Harlem (now China). Service at Wiscasset.

RANK AND NAME.
Robert Fletcher, Captain
Nathaniel Bragg, Lieutenant
Caleb Palmeter, Ensign

John Weeks, Sergeant
John Whetely, Sergeant
William Bradford, Sergeant
Jedediah Fairfield, Sergeant
Nathaniel Evens, Corporal
Daniel Fowler, Corporal
Daniel Bragg, Corporal
Ephraim Weeks, Corporal
Thomas Burrell, Musician
Timothy Waterhouse, Musician

Privates.
Baker, Jonathan
Balcomb, Lima
Bean, Daniel
Bragg, David
Bragg, Isaac
Bragg, Nathan
Bryant, David
Burrell, Abram, Jr.
Chadwick, Sylvanus
Crummet, John
Doe, Andrew
Evens, Thomas
Getchell, David
Givens, Ebenezer
Gray, Daniel
Gray, Jonathan
Gray, Nathaniel
Gray, Samuel
Hammon, Frederick
Hanson, Andrew H.
Hanson, Caleb, Jr.
Hanson, Samuel
Haskell, Benjamin
Haskell, William
Hatch, Ezra
Haws, James
Lombard, John
McLaughlin, Abraham
McNull, Vryling S.
Moore, Oliver
Moore, Robert
Morrell, Jedediah
Mosher, William
Norton, Jacob
Norton, Joseph
Norton, Thomas
Norton, Zachariah
Palmeter, Joseph
Prentice, Jesse
Prentice, Philo
Prentice, Saul
Purkins, Ephraim
Stewart, George

Capt. R. Fletcher's Company, Lieut. Col. H. Moore's Regiment — Concluded.

Privates — Concluded.
Stutley, Daniel
Thompson, John
Varney, Jedediah
Ward, William

Weeks, Braddock
Whitley, Benjamin
Whitley, William, Jr.

Waiters.
Bragg, Nathaniel, 3d
Bragg, Royal
Norton, Nathaniel

Capt. I. Hall's Company, Lieut. Col. H. Moore's Regiment.
From Sept. 12 to Sept. 27, 1814. Raised at Clinton. Service at Wiscasset.

RANK AND NAME.
Irial Hall, Captain
James Gray, Lieutenant
Israel Richardson, Ensign

Saul Haywood, Sergeant
Nathaniel Brown, Sergeant
John Fitzgerald, Sergeant
William M. Carr, Sergeant
William Richardson, Corporal
Peter Robinson, Corporal
David Gray, Corporal
George Flagg, Corporal
Rufus Bartlett, Musician
Saul Gibson, Musician

Privates.
Barton, Nathan
Brackett, Moses
Brown, Asa, Jr.
Brown, Isaac, Jr.
Brown, Jonathan
Brown, Luke
Burton, Ebenezer
Carl, Jonathan
Davis, Samuel
Ferguson, John
Fitzgerald, William
Foss, Joel
Fox, Israel
Heald, Odiorne
Hinds, Benjamin

Hudson, Samuel
Hunter, David
Hunter, James
McNelly, James
Michels, James
Rand, William
Richardson, Andrew
Richardson, Robert
Richardson, Samuel
Roundy, Amos
Roundy, David
Small, Nathan
Spaulding, Andrew
Spiner, Rex
Winn, Japheth

Capt. J. Moore's Company, Lieut. Col. H. Moore's Regiment.
From Sept. 12 to Sept. 27, 1814. Raised at Clinton. Service at Wiscasset.

RANK AND NAME.
John Moore, Captain
William Spearen, Lieutenant
Nathan Brackett, Ensign

Isaac Holt, Sergeant
Amos Decker, Sergeant
Joseph Spearen, Sergeant
William Eames, Sergeant
Caleb Goodwin, Corporal
Samuel Peavey, Corporal
Asa Pratt, Corporal
James Ford, Corporal
Henry Ford, Musician
Timothy Chase, Musician

Privates.
Bagley, Green
Barrett, Thomas

Boston, Joseph
Cain, David
Cone, David
Cone, Isaac
Cone, Oliver
Cone, Samuel, Jr.
Cozens, Nathaniel
Decker, Joshua, Jr.
Dunbar, Jacob
Freeze, Abraham
Gifford, John
Gilman, Samuel
Goodrich, Noah
Goodwin, Jedediah
Goodwin, Miles
Hutchinson, Samuel
Jaquith, Andrew
Joy, James
Leavitt, David

Lewis, Ebenezer
Lewis, Ebenezer, 2d
Libby, Levi
Merrill, Eliphalet
Morrison, Dependence
Nelson, William
Pratt, James, Jr.
Priest, Joel
Reynolds, Parmenas
Shaw, Advardis
Shaw, Francis
Smith, James
Smith, John M.
Smith, Moses
Thornton, Joshua
True, Abner
Varnum, Samuel, Jr.
Wing, Jabez
Winn, William

Capt. B. Robinson's Company, Lieut. Col. H. Moore's Regiment.
From Sept. 12 to Sept. 27, 1814. Raised at Fairfax. Service at Wiscasset.

RANK AND NAME.
Benjamin Robinson, Captain
Thomas Harlow, Lieutenant
Benjamin Lewis, Ensign

Warren Drake, Sergeant
Hiram Brackett, Sergeant
Stephen Bragg, Sergeant
Ebenezer Shaw, Sergeant
Washington Drake, Corporal
Richard Handy, Corporal
Oliver Baker, Corporal
Moses Dow, Corporal
Zebulon Morse, Musician
Asa Burrell, Musician

Privates.
Baker, Benjamin
Baker, Zachariah
Bean, Simon
Bessey, Ephraim
Brackett, James
Dexter, Gideon
Fry, John
Handy, Lemuel
Hanson, James
Harlow, Sylvanus, Jr.
Hawley, William
Hussey, William
Lewis, Charles
Lewis, Samuel

Libby, Ebenezer
McLaughlin, John
Morse, Bezaleel
Shorry, Daniel
Stackpole, William
Sturteford, Jonas
Wiggins, Charles
Wing, Ezekiel
Wing, Stephen
Woodsman, Daniel, Jr.

Waiter.
Weeks, Charles

Capt. J. Wellington's Company, Lieut. Col. H. Moore's Regiment.
From Sept. 12 to Sept. 27, 1814. Raised at Fairfax. Service at Wiscasset.

RANK AND NAME.
Joel Wellington, Captain
Saul Kidder, Lieutenant
Ebenezer Stratton, Ensign

Saul Libby, Sergeant
James Chalmers, Sergeant
James Skillin, Sergeant
Charles Stratton, Sergeant
Saul Tarbell, Corporal
John Jackson, Corporal
John Kidder, Jr., Corporal
Samuel Stackpole, Jr., Corporal
Benjamin Reed, Jr., Musician
Thaddeus Broad, Musician

Privates.
Abbot, John
Barnard, Josiah
Briant, Nehemiah
Broadstreet, John
Brown, John
Buxton, Ebenezer

Cally, William
Cammett, Jonathan
Chalmers, Scotland
Clark, Thomas
Farnham, Benjamin
Farnham, Joshua
Farnham, Rufus
Glidden, John
Hawes, Seth
Kimball, Charles
Lessett, Robert
Libby, David
Marden, George
Murdough, Robert
Phillips, Sutherland
Piper, Silas
Plummer, Aaron
Plummer, John
Pollard, Henry D.
Pratt, Vincent
Reed, Perrin
Reed, Samuel W.
Rollins, George

Rollins, Nathaniel
Rollins, Samuel
Rollins, Thomas
Spencer, James
Spiller, Samuel
Stackpole, Joseph
Stratton, Austin
Stratton, James
Stratton, Paul
Sylvester, Joseph
Tarbell, Benjamin
Taylor, Elnathan
Varney, Silas
Walker, Joseph
Wentworth, Timothy
Woodcock, Isaac

Waiters.
Barnard, John
Chalmers, John
Stratton, Ness

Capt. J. Wing's Company, Lieut. Col. H. Moore's Regiment.
From Sept. 12 to Sept. 27, 1814. Raised at Vassalborough. Service at Wiscasset.

RANK AND NAME.
James Wing, Captain
Levi Maynard, Lieutenant
Nehemiah Gould, Ensign

Elijah Robinson, Sergeant
Moses Rollins, Sergeant
Stephen Low, Sergeant
Josiah Priest, Sergeant
Levi Chadburn, Corporal
Amasa Starkey, Corporal
John Fly, Corporal
Reuben Priest, Corporal
Enoch Marshall, Musician
Stephen Townsend, Musician

Privates.
Boswell, William, Jr.
Bragg, William
Buckminster, William
Burgess, Samuel
Burgess, Zadock
Carlton, Thomas
Clement, Cyrus
Coburn, George
Dickey, William
Doe, John
Doe, John, 2d
Doe, Jonathan
Doe, Nathaniel, Jr.
Ewer, John, Jr.

Farriss, Benjamin
Field, George
Freeman, Richard
Getchell, Abial
Getchell, Edmund, Jr.
Getchell, Elihu, Jr.
Getchell, Howard H.
Jackson, Alexander, 2d
Kates, Edmund
Law, John
Lewis, Elisha
McKenney, George
Merrill, Peter, Jr.
Parker, Simeon
Pease, Thomas

Capt. J. Wing's Company, Lieut. Col. H. Moore's Regiment — Concluded.

Privates — Concluded.
Priest, Timothy
Sewall, Daniel
Stewart, Charles
Studley, John
Taylor, Abner

Taylor, Abram
Taylor, John, Jr.
White, John
Williams, Benjamin, Jr.
Worthen, Lewis

Parker, Joseph   *Waiter.*

Capt. D. Wyman's Company, Lieut. Col. H. Moore's Regiment.
From Sept. 12 to Sept. 27, 1814. Service at Wiscasset.

RANK AND NAME.
Daniel Wyman, Captain
Alexander Jackson, Lieutenant
William Tarbell, Ensign

Thomas Hawes, Sergeant
Daniel Whitehouse, Sergeant
Zenas Perseval, Sergeant
Rolen Frye, Sergeant
John Clay, Corporal
Gershom Clark, Corporal
Thomas Whitehouse, Corporal
Jonathan Smart, Corporal
George Webber, Musician

Privates.
Austin, Robert
Brown, John, Jr.
Clark, Thomas
Coleman, John
Cross, Nathaniel
Cross, Saul
Cross, William
Dearborn, Asa
Dearborn, John
Freeman, Nathaniel
Freeman, Reuben
Gifford, Joseph
Hawes, Ebenezer
Lord, Peter

Randall, Thomas
Richardson, Seth
Samson, David
Seward, John, Jr.
Smart, Levi
Smart, Richard
Smith, William
Stevens, Jacob
Warren, John
Warren, Richard, Jr.
Wentworth, Jonathan
Willey, Charles
Wyman, Fairfield
Wyman, William
Wyman, Zebedee

Lieut. B. J. Radcliff's Company, Lieut. Col. H. Moore's Regiment.
From Sept. 12 to Sept. 27, 1814. Service at Wiscasset.

RANK AND NAME.
Benjamin J. Radcliff, Lieutenant
Zadock Gould, Ensign

Daniel Small, Sergeant
Aaron McKenney, Sergeant
Amariah Hardin, Jr., Sergeant
Enoch Stout, Sergeant
Charles Bickmore, Corporal
William Swan, Corporal
Josiah Cookson, Corporal
Benjamin Melvin, Corporal
Benjamin Bither, Musician
Elisha Bither, Musician

Privates.
Basto, Israel
Bickmore, John
Bither, Peter
Briggs, Enos
Brooks, Francis
Burnham, John
Call, Reuben
Carl, Asa
Carl, Nathaniel

Carl, Robert
Comfort, Richard
Connor, Jeremiah
Cookson, Reuben
Drake, Richard
Drake, William
Elder, Hanson
Farwell, Ebenezer
Force, Nathaniel
Fowler, Nathan
Fowler, Thomas
Glidden, John C.
Ham, Enoch
Hardy, Stephen
Hopkins, Chandler
Hopkins, Richard
Hopkins, Theodore
Hurd, Hiram
Kelley, Samuel
Kirk, William
Larabee, John
Libby, Dean S.
McDonald, John
McManners, Daniel
Mitchell, Benjamin

Mitchell, Joseph
Mitchell, Joseph, 2d
Murch, Ebenezer
Murch, Josiah
Nickery, David
Nickery, Joel
Paine, John
Parkhurst, Elisha
Parkhurst, Nathan
Rickerson, Nehemiah
Runnels, Daniel
Small, Isaac
Sparrow, Stephen
Spring, Jacob
Stevens, Ebenezer
Stone, Zachariah
Trueworthy, Daniel
Trueworthy, Jacob
Webb, John
Webb, Pearson
Wilson, Lemuel
Wood, George
Wood, Henry

MASSACHUSETTS VOLUNTEER MILITIA IN THE WAR OF 1812.

Lieut. Col. M. Nichols' Regiment.
From Sept. 7 to Sept. 19, 1814.

FIELD AND STAFF.
Martin Nichols, Lieutenant Colonel, Portland
John Pratt, Major, Portland
John Storer, Major, Portland

John Sampson, Adjutant, Portland
Edward Barneywell, Adjutant, Portland
Christopher Wright, Quartermaster, Portland
William Swan, Paymaster, Portland

Nathaniel Coffin, Surgeon, Portland
John Merrill, Surgeon's Mate, Portland
George Hall, Chaplain, Portland

Muster Roll of Capt. A. W. Atherton's Company.[1]
April 16, 1814. Service at Portland.

RANK AND NAME.
Abel W. Atherton, Captain
Henry Smith, Lieutenant
John Watson, Ensign

William B. Sewall, Sergeant
Arthur Shirley, Sergeant
Joseph M. Gerrish, Sergeant
William P. Davis, Sergeant
John Adams, Corporal
Thomas Chadwick, Corporal
Henry Jones, Corporal
Abiel W. Tinkham, Corporal
John P. Thurston, Corporal
Benjamin Tukey, Corporal
Charles Atherton, Corporal
Enoch Moulton, Corporal
Seth Clark, Corporal
Stewart Porter, Corporal
Nathaniel Morton, Corporal
Benjamin Butman, Corporal
Thomas Todd, Musician

Privates.
Bowman, Joshua
Butman, Henry
Chase, Caleb S.
Clark, George
Cobb, Smith W., Jr.
Codman, Edward P.
Cross, Amos H.
Cross, Leonard
Curry, Edward
Dana, Luther
Field, Stephen
Griffin, Leonard
Hartshorn, Oliver T.
Hersey, Elias
Hill, George
Horle, Joseph
Hyde, Jonathan L.
Irving, John
Jewett, Joseph
Kenney, Benjamin W.
Kent, Justin, Jr.

Kimball, Charles
Kimball, James
Lelland, Joseph M., Jr.
Lewis, Thomas
Maxwell, Joseph
Merrill, Joseph
Mitchell, Reuben
Myltic or Myttic, James
Pearson, Henry S.
Phillips, Seth
Rachlyeft, Nelson
Sawyer, Joseph
Shirley, Joshua
Smith, William
Stover, George D.
Thurston, Ezekiel
Tucker, James B.
Walker, Ezekiel
Warren, Henry
Warren, Thomas
Webber, Amos
Wheaton, Godfrey

Capt. J. How's Company, Lieut. Col. M. Nichols' Regiment.
From Sept. 2 to Sept. 19, and Sept. 26 to Oct. 3, 1814. Raised at Portland. Service at Portland.

RANK AND NAME.
Joseph How, Captain
Nathan Nutter, Lieutenant
Robert Noyes, Ensign

William Dinsdell, Sergeant
Nathaniel Griffin, Sergeant
John How, Sergeant
George Bangs, Sergeant
George Cross, Corporal
Charles Parsons, Corporal
Josiah Gage, Corporal
Kinicum Randal, Corporal

Privates.
Anderson, Thomas
Bean, John

Beeman, Samuel
Chadwick, Richard
Chadwick, William
Cobb, Elisha
Cobb, Robert
Day, Abraham
Dolley, Ammizabad
Dorset, Samuel
Dresser, Mark
Fluent, Nathan
Frothingham, J. M.
Fuller, Adam
Gardner, David
Hays, George
How, Daniel
Hoyt, William
Kellog, James M.

Ketson, Richard
Kilbourn, Ivory
Leavitt, William
Mason, Jeremiah
Mitchell, Joshua
Moses, Henry
Robie, Joseph
Ross, Thomas
Seavy, Rufus
Tole, Theophilus
Welch, George
Wiswell, Richard

---
[1] The record of this company is a muster roll for pay, but time for which is not specified.

Capt. A. Atherton's Company, Lieut. Col. M. Nichols' Regiment.

From Sept. 7 to Sept. 19, 1814. Five days subsequent for vidette duty. Portland Rifle Corps, organized June 12, 1812.

RANK AND NAME.
Abel Atherton, Captain
Henry Smith, Lieutenant
John Watson, Ensign

William B. Sewall, Sergeant
Arthur Shirley, Sergeant
J. M. Gerrish, Sergeant
William P. Davis, Sergeant
Thomas Chadwick, Corporal
Henry Jones, Corporal
Benjamin Tukey, Corporal
Abiel W. Tinkham, Corporal

Privates.
Adams, John
Atherton, Charles
Bowman, Joshua
Brooks, Charles
Butman, Benjamin

Chase, Caleb S.
Clark, Seth
Cross, Amos H.
Cross, Leonard
Curry, Cadwalder
Dana, Luther
Field, Stephen
Fox, George
Griffin, Leonard
Hartshorn, Oliver S.
Heath, Justin
Hoole, Joseph
Hyde, Jonathan L.
Kimball, Charles
Kimball, James
Lane, Alphonso F.
Lewis, Thomas, Jr.
Martin, Nathaniel
Maxwell, Joseph
McLellan, Joseph, Jr.

Merrill, Joseph
Mitchell, Reuben
Moulton, Enoch
Noble, Joseph
Noyes, John P.
Pearson, Henry S.
Philips, Seth
Potter, John
Radcliff, Nelson
Sanger, Joseph
Scott, John
Shirley, Joshua
Smith, William
Thurston, Ezekiel
Thurston, John P.
Tucker, James B.
Walker, Ezekiel
Wheaton, Godfrey

Capt. T. Baker's Company, Lieut. Col. M. Nichols' Regiment.

From Sept. 7 to Sept. 19, and Sept. 26 to Oct. 3, 1814. Raised at Portland. Service at Portland.

RANK AND NAME.
Thomas Baker, Captain
Benjamin I. Chase, Lieutenant
John W. Chase, Ensign

William Warner, Sergeant
Edward Pope, Sergeant
Ezekiel Loring, Sergeant
William Coolige, Sergeant
Stephen Tarbox, Musician

Privates.
Beeman, Daniel
Beeman, Ezra

Burns, George, Jr.
Carlton, Albert
Chase, Daniel
Corry, Ebenezer M.
Cross, Nathaniel, Jr.
Dawsett, John
Drinkwater, Bradford
Drinkwater, Sewall
Gilford, Elijah
Gilford, James
Harlow, Henry
Harmon, George (D.)
Harris, Stephen
Hassack, Daniel

Jordan, Ezekiel
Knight, James
Love, James
Mayhew, Thomas
Merrill, Francis
Miller, George
Richard, Edward
Ryanson, Ebenezer (D.)
Sawyer, Anthony
Sheafe, William
Simonton, John
Virgin, Jeremiah W.

Capt. E. Moody's Company, Lieut. Col. M. Nichols' Regiment.

From Sept. 7 to Sept. 19, and Sept. 26 to Oct. 3, 1814. Raised at Portland. Service at Portland.

RANK AND NAME.
Enoch Moody, Captain
Dudly Cammett, Lieutenant
William Pollyes, Jr., Ensign

Eleazer Gould, Sergeant
Stephen Wait, Jr., Sergeant
J. S. Jewett, Sergeant
Lemuel Moody, Jr., Sergeant
John Cammett, Corporal

Privates.
Baker, Alexander
Barnes, James

Clark or Clerk, James
Coolbroth, Edward
Emery, William
Goodhue, Richard
Hammond, Thomas B.
Hanson, Josiah
Hodgkins, Nathaniel
Hudson, Benjamin
Knight, Robert
Knight, Samuel
Lord, Benjamin
McLellen, Elihu
Moody, William, Jr.
Mountford, Daniel, Jr.

Mountford, James
Pond, Caleb
Porter, Jonathan
Richardson, Luther
Robinson, Woodberry
Runnels, Saul
Sawyer, William
Stanton, John
Staples, Isaac
Weeks, Daniel
Witherton, William

Capt. J. Remick's Company, Lieut. Col. M. Nichols' Regiment.

From Sept. 7 to Sept. 19, and Sept. 26 to Oct. 3, 1814. Raised at Portland. Service at Portland.

Rank and Name.		
John Remick, Captain	Bryant, James, Jr.	Lilla, Caleb
Thomas Osgood, Lieutenant	Burnham, Amos	Loring, Calvin
Bradbury C. Atwood, Ensign	Buzzel, Nathaniel	McFarlin, Robert
	Chadwick, George	McKenney, Enoch
	Deland, Ezekiel	Owen, Ebenezer, Jr.
Joseph Very, Sergeant	Dudly, Joseph	Patterson, Benjamin
Nathaniel Le Favor, Sergeant	Elder, Jacob	Smart, Anthony
William Norton, Sergeant	Flint, James	Smith, Joseph
Joseph Cushing, Sergeant	Green, Robert S.	Stickney, Nicholas
	Harden, William	Stockman, John
Privates.	Hask, Samuel	Thomas, John W.
Berry, John	Knight, Abraham	Tisdale, Dean
Boston, Timothy	Lewis, Hugh M.	Todd, George

Capt. N. Shaw's Company, Lieut. Col. M. Nichols' Regiment.

From Sept. 7 to Sept. 19, and Sept. 26 to Oct. 3, 1814. Raised at Portland. Service at Portland. Portland Light Infantry, organised June 6, 1803.

Rank and Name.	*Privates.*	McLaughlin, John
Nathaniel Shaw, Captain	Bradberry, Andrew	Milikin, Phinehas
John H. Hall, Lieutenant	Briggs, John	Moyes, James
James Poole, Jr., Ensign	Chadwell, John	Neale, Benjamin
	Chamberlin, William	Rice, Samuel
Moses I. Plummer, Sergeant	Cobb, Stephen	Roberts, Nathaniel
Augustus Adams, Sergeant	Dresser, John	Ryers, John
James Henly, Sergeant	Ham, Jeremiah	Spiller, Amos
Stephen Noyes, Corporal	Ingram, Joseph	Treats, James
James Tukey, Corporal	Insly, Benjamin	Warren, M.
William Shaw, Corporal	Lasley, Richard	Whitmarsh, Charles
John Foy, Musician	Libby, Simon	Wiswell, Joseph
Rufus Porter, Musician	Lunt, Isaac	

Capt. J. Skillings' Company, Lieut. Col. M. Nichols' Regiment.

From Sept. 7 to Sept. 19, and Sept. 26 to Oct. 3, 1814. Raised at Portland. Service at Portland.

Rank and Name.	Fickett, Ephraim	Mariner, James
John Skillings, Captain	Glazier, Joseph	Marsh, George
John Crocker, Lieutenant	Gore or Gove, John	McLelland, Alexander
Henry Mange, Ensign	Gould, Abner	Morrison, Samuel
	Haggett, William	Osgood, Thomas D.
Eleazer Holmes, Sergeant	Hamblet, John P.	Plummer, Thomas
Joshua Dyer, Sergeant	Hanson, Moses	Roberts, Joseph
John T. Hoyt, Sergeant	Hasty, Nathaniel	Scott, Peter
Daniel Herrick, Sergeant	Hilton, Samuel	Seavy, David
	Hodges, George	Simonton, James
Privates.	Huchins, Daniel	Smith, Jonathan
Bartlet, Robert	Ingraham, G. T.	Townsend, Nathaniel
Bell, William	Jones, Cyrus	Twambley, William
Bradford, Andrew	Jordan, Asa	Warren, Abraham
Causwell, Allen	Lane, Ezekiel	Webster, Nathaniel
Crockett, Joseph	Larrabee, Joseph	Winship, Jonas
Degno, John	Libby, Enos	
Fessenden, John	Libby, Hugh	

Capt. J. W. Smith's Company, Lieut. Col. M. Nichols' Regiment.
From Sept. 7 to Sept. 19, and Sept. 26 to Oct. 3, 1814. Service at Portland, Portland Mechanic Blues. Organized June 24, 1807.

Rank and Name.	Privates.	
John W. Smith, Captain	Alexander, Jeremiah	Niles, Stephen H., Jr.
Friend Loring, Lieutenant	Belford, Davis	Richard, Willard
Francis Douglass, Ensign	Canney, Benjamin	Runnels, Job
	Clough, David	Smith, Benjamin
John Ricker, Sergeant	Farley, Charles	Smith, Moses
Eliphalet Wharf, Sergeant	Hamblin, Ichabod	Todd, Thomas
Nathan Hubbard, Sergeant	Horn, James	
Josiah Pennell, Corporal	Loring, George	
James Seavey, Corporal	Merrill, Enos	
Joseph Benny, Corporal	Mitchell, James	
Henry Green, Musician	Moody, John	

Lieut. T. Capen's Company, Lieut. Col. M. Nichols' Regiment.
From Sept. 7 to Sept. 19, and Sept. 26 to Oct. 3, 1814. Raised at Portland. Service at Portland.

Rank and Name.	Carter, Amos H.	Hilton, Moses
Thomas Capen, Lieutenant	Carter, Peter	Jackson, Samuel
Lazarus Harlow, Ensign	Collins, Charles	Johnson, David
	Cook, Horatio G.	McLelland, Alexander
Daniel Radford, Sergeant	Coolbroth, Edward	Parsons, George W.
William Marsh, Sergeant	Day, Robert	Pease, Lewis
John Bruce, Sergeant	Day, William	Riggs, Jacob
William Ingraham, Sergeant	Dix, John	Smith, Nicholas
Nathan How, Corporal	Edgcomb, Eliphalet C.	Tibbetts, Ephraim
Loring Varney, Corporal	Foster, Isaac	Townsend, James
Ward Boney, Corporal	Fowler, Joseph	Tukey, Charles
Charles Baker, Corporal	Fowler, Philip	Waterhouse, Elias
	Furnald, Thomas	Whitman, John
Privates.	Gallison, Henry	
Averill, John	Gardner, David M.	
Bell, William B.	Hall, Abiel	

Capt. James Ayers' Drafted Company, under Maj. Simon Nowell's Command.
From October to November, 1814. Service at Kittery and York.

Rank and Name.	*Privates.*	Danielson, Otis S.
Simon Nowell, Major	Abbott, Joseph	Davis, Daniel
James Ayers, Captain	Applebee, Hawley	Day, Dependence
James W. Roberts, Lieutenant	Bachelder, Ephraim	Day, Ebenezer
Joseph Morrow, Ensign	Barker, Ezra	Day, Ezekiel
John Crockett, Ensign	Bennett, Joseph	Day, Henry
	Bickford, Gideon	Day, Henry, 2d
John Sinderson, Sergeant	Blasdell, Abner	Day, James
John Thomas, Sergeant	Branchder, John	Doe, Dearborn
Joseph Merrill, Sergeant	Chadburn, Levi	Doe, Henry
Daniel Shackley, Sergeant	Cleek, James	Drew, Robert
Isaac Cowell, Sergeant	Cluff, Nathaniel	Eastman, William
John Drew, Corporal	Cole, Asahel	Edgcomb, Isaac
Stephen Piper, Corporal	Cole, Daniel	Edgcomb, Levi
George Whales, Corporal	Cole, Eli	Eldredge, Daniel
Hiram Ricker, Corporal	Cole, John	Emery, George
John Drew, Musician	Cook, James M.	Evans, John
John Hobbs, Musician	Cooper, Richard	Frye, Benjamin
William Perry, Musician	Copps, William	Furbush, David
Peletiah Moore, Musician	Cousens, Jeremiah	Furnald, Tristram

Capt. James Ayers' Drafted Company, under Maj. Simon Nowell's Command — Concluded.

Privates — Concluded.
Gentleman, Joseph
Gerry, Morgan
Getchell, Isaac
Goodwin, Henry
Goodwin, Hiram
Goodwin, Thomas
Goodwin, William
Goulder, Arnold
Gowen, Alpheus
Gowen, John
Ham, Samuel
Harris, Nathaniel
Hartford, William
Heard, John
Hibbard, John
Hill, Jeremiah
Hobbs, Nathaniel

Hodgdon, Joshua
Hodgdon, Samuel
Horsum, Oliver
Hubbard, Stephen
Huntress, James
Huntress, Nathaniel
Huzzey, Richard
Jacobs, William
Johnston, Jotham
Jones, Ebenezer
Keniston, Daniel
Knight, Samuel
Libbey, Jeremiah
Libbey, Solon
Linscot, Jacob
Littlefield, Nathaniel
Lord, Ichabod
Lord, Samuel

Lose, William
McLelan, George
Mighalls, Jesse
Newbegin, Jonathan
Piper, Peletiah
Shackley, Joseph
Smith, James
Smith, Joseph
Sovernigh, Joseph
Stewart, Stephen
Tanner, Anthony
Tebbetts, Greenleaf
Tefferin, William
Thompson, Joshua
Tripe, Thomas
Waterhouse, John
Wormwood, Ithamar

Capt. B. Thompson's Company.

From October to November, 1814, one month. Stationed at Kittery. This is a roll of a company of drafted militia in service at Kittery under command of Major Simon Nowell.

RANK AND NAME.
Bartholomew Thompson, Captain
Alexander Worcester, Lieutenant
Ephraim Low, Lieutenant
Wentworth Butler, Ensign

Elias Libbey, Sergeant
Samuel Drew, Sergeant
Samuel Frost, Sergeant
Reuben Dennett, Sergeant
Thomas Abbott, Sergeant
Alpheus Hanson, Corporal
Temple Lord, Corporal
Joseph Spinney, Corporal
James Pray, Corporal
Jacob Hamilton, Musician
Phineas Morrell, Musician

Privates.
Abbott, John
Boston, Joseph
Brackett, David
Brackett, Ebenezer
Bragdon, J. R.
Brooks, Gideon
Carlisle, George
Chadbourn, Benjamin
Chick, Samuel
Chick, Thomas
Clement, Tilly
Courson, Isaac
Cutts, Oliver
Emery, Joel
Estes, William
Fall, John
Ferguson, Alexander
Fogg, William
Goodwin, Benjamin
Goodwin, Benjamin, 2d

Goodwin, John
Grant, Thomas
Hanscom, Samuel
Hare, Mack
Heart, James
Hill, Nelson
Horn, Mishach
Jellison, Stephen
Keag, Thomas
Kennard, Alpheus
Kennison, Hugh
Leathers, Obednego
Libbey, John
Linscott, John
Linscott, William
Lord, Jeremiah
Low, Nathaniel
Marrs, Oliver
Mason, Nathan
Mason, Peletiah
Maxwell, Seth
Miller, Caleb
Muchmore, Joseph
Murray, Adam
Murray, Hiram
Murray, Ivory
Nock, David
Nowell, Mack
Penny, John
Perkins, Jesse
Perkins, Naham
Pierce, Hopkins
Pierce, Stephen
Pike, Nathaniel
Raitt, Alexander
Raitt, John
Randall, William
Ranking, Joshua
Remick, Enoch

Remington, Hutchins
Ricker, Jacob
Ricker, Levi
Ricker, Nathaniel
Ricker, Richard
Ricker, Theodore
Roberts, John
Roberts, Thomas
Round, Theodore
Sherburn, George
Smith, Joseph
Smith, Stephen
Snow, Hiram
Spinney, John
Spinney, S. R.
Stackpole, Absalom
Stackpole, Stephen
Stanley, Thomas H.
Staples, Oliver
Staples, Timothy
Staples, William
Stebbins, Rook
Taylor, Jotham
Taylor, Obediah
Thompson, Oliver
Thunnell, George or John
Thunnell, Samuel
Trafton, Ivory
Trafton, Zacheus
Twombly, Ezekiel
Varney, James
Welch, Moses
Wentworth, Enoch
Weymouth, John
Whitehouse, John
Wilkinson, Samuel
Worcester, Clement
Young, Richard

Capt. E. Andrew's Detached Company, under Supervision of Gen. Alford Richardson.

From July 4 to Sept. 2, 1814. Raised at Scarborough and vicinity. Service at Portland.

RANK AND NAME.
Ebenezer Andrews, Captain
William Wescott, Lieutenant
William Frost, Ensign

Benjamin Tukey, Sergeant
Lemuel Moody, Jr., Sergeant
Isaac Frost, Jr., Sergeant
Hugh McLeavis, Sergeant
William Chamberlain, Corporal
Joshua Howard, Corporal
William Winslow, Corporal
Albert Carleton, Corporal
James Bacon, Musician
John Moody, Musician
Sylvanus Dyer, Musician
Abraham McLucas, Musician

Privates.
Anderson, Abel
Babb, Charles
Babb, Henry
Barry, John
Beeman, Ezra
Blake, Samuel
Blanchard, William

Boothby, Nathaniel
Brackett, Alfred
Brackett, Elijah
Brown, John
Cahoon, Asa
Campbell, John
Chamberlain, Earle
Damerin, Samuel
Dearborn, John
Dearborn, Josiah
Deering, John
Dobbin, William
Evans, Josiah
Fenderson, Benjamin
Foss, Nichols
French, John
Gray, George
Hall, Henry
Harding, Joseph
Harmon, Jonathan, 3d
Hersey, Israel
Jones, Jeremiah
Jumper, Joseph
Knight, George
Leavitt, Joseph
Libby, Thomas

Linnell, Samuel
Liscomb, John
Lombard, Joseph
Long, Elijah
Lunt, John
Maxwell, Stephen
Merrill, Levi
Merrill, Reuben
Morton, Jacob
Moulton, Reuben T.
Nason, Abraham
Patterson, Benjamin
Pierce, Joseph
Prince, George
Rogers, Edward
Russell, Nathaniel
Sanger, John
Smith, John
Smith, William
Swett, Joshua
Webb, David
Whittemore, Major
Willard, Daniel
Withington, William
Wood, William, Jr.
Young, Enos

Lieut. O. Bray's Detached Company, under Supervision of Maj. Gen. Alford Richardson.

From Nov. 5 to Nov. 25, 1814. Raised at Portland. Service at Fort Burrows, Fish Point, Portland, "for the protection of the forts, ordnance, and munitions of war and other property belonging to the Commonwealth."

RANK AND NAME.
Oliver Bray, Lieutenant
Amos S. Webber, Lieutenant

George Stacey, Sergeant
Timothy Chadbourne, Sergeant
Hugh Leavis, Sergeant
Asa Erskine, Corporal
Abner Gould, Corporal
Rufus Porter, Musician
Joshua Chadbourne, Musician

Privates.
Brown, Jacob
Butterfield, Leonard
Chamberlain, Earle
Claridge, Stephen
Coolbroth, Rufus
Crockett, Richard
Davis, John, Jr.
Doane, Asia
Dobbins, James

Dobbins, William
Donald, Henry M.
Dresser, Joseph
Elliott, Josiah
Emery, Elijah
Harding, Joseph
Harmon, James
Harmon, John M.
Harmon, Jonathan
Harmon, Stephen
Harmon, William
Hartshorn, William
Henly, John
Hunnewell, Josiah
Huston, Robert
Hutchins, John
Johnson, Thomas
Jordan, Abraham
Knight, Charles
Lamb, Seth
Leighton, Daniel
Leighton, Reuben

Libby, Richard
Miller, George
Milliken, John M.
Morrison, Samuel
Newburn, James
Pierce, Joseph
Roberts, Daniel
Ross, John
Sargent, Benjamin
Smith, John
Sweat, Gardner
Sweat, Joshua
Sweat, Moses, 3d
Sweat, Moses, 4th
Sweat, Samuel
Thombs, Joseph
Treat, Richard
True, William
Weymouth, Robert
Wiggin, Eaton
Wise, Peter M.

Lieut. Col. A. Reed's Regiment.

June 22 and Sept. 10 to Oct. 10, 1814. Service at Bath.

FIELD AND STAFF.	NONCOMMISSIONED STAFF.	
Andrew Reed, Lieutenant Colonel, Georgetown	Seth Hathorn, Sergeant Major	Porterfield, J.
William Bourk, Major, Bath	Charles D. Loring, Quartermaster Sergeant	Reed, John
Zina Hyde, Adjutant, Bath	Thomas B. Seavey, Fife Major	Thompson, John
Charles Clapp, Quartermaster, Bath		
Thomas D. Robinson, Paymaster, Bath	*Waiters.*	
William Jenks, Chaplain, Bath	Burk, Charles	
Timothy W. Waldron, Surgeon, Bath	Cobb, John	
Nathaniel Weld, Jr., Surgeon's Mate, Bath	Foster, Benjamin	
	Othcoor, John H.	

Capt. B. Davenport's Company, Lieut. Col. A. Reed's Regiment.

From June 20 to June 22, and Sept. 5 to Oct. 1, 1814. Raised at Bath. Service at Bath.

RANK AND NAME.	*Privates.*	
Benjamin Davenport, Captain	Bloom, William	Purrington, Nathaniel
Enoch Foote, Lieutenant	Crooker, Noah	Richardson, William
	Donnell, Jeremiah	Roberts, Aaron
Benjamin Randall, Sergeant	Edgcomb, Joseph	Rouse, William
John Lane, Sergeant	Fitts, Ephraim	Sanford, John, Jr.
Thomas H. Gage, Sergeant	Foy, Samuel	Sewell, Charles
David Foot, Corporal	Haley, James	Snow, Benjamin
Timothy Rairdon, Corporal	Haley, Thomas	Stow, William M.
Kingsbury Donnel, Corporal	Ham, Joel	White, Isaac
Caleb Mitchell, Musician	Innis, Samuel	
	Little, Nathaniel	*Waiters.*
	Parshly, Ezekiel	Eames, Daniel
	Purrington, John, Jr.	Parker, William

Capt. J. Fisher's Company, Lieut. Col. A. Reed's Regiment.

From June 20 to June 22, and Sept. 10 to Oct. 1, 1814. Raised at Georgetown. Service at Bath.

RANK AND NAME.		
Jeremiah Fisher, Captain	Hall, Samuel	Shipe or Snipe, Charles
James C. Whitmore, Lieutenant	Higgins, Simeon	Snipe, John, Jr.
Charles Potter, Ensign	Laurence, John	Stinson, Eben
	Manson, Robert	Stinson, Eben, Jr.
John White, Sergeant	Parker, Robert	Stinson, James
Collins Potter, Sergeant	Pattee, Benjamin	Stinson, James, Jr.
John Potter, Sergeant	Pattee, Samuel	Stinson, John, 3d
David Potter, Sergeant	Potter, William	Stinson, John, 4th
James Hogan, Musician	Preble, John, Jr.	Stinson, Samuel
	Riggs, Moses	Stinson, Stephen
Privates.	Ruirdon, Samuel	Tibbetts, Isaac
Beel, James	Ruirdon, William	Webber, John
Bell, Jeremiah	Rush, John	White, James
Cowllard, Joseph, Jr.	Rush, Peleg	White, William
Drummond, Ezekiel	Salby, James	Whitmore, Francis
Hagan, John	Sewall, William	Whitmore, William
Hagan, Michael	Shea, David	
	Shea, Nicholas	

Capt. R. Heagen's Company, Lieut. Col. A. Reed's Regiment.
From June 20 to June 22, July 3 to July 5, and Sept. 10 to Oct. 1, 1814. Raised at Georgetown. Service at Bath.

RANK AND NAME.
Richard Heagen, Captain
Nathaniel Todd, Lieutenant
David Oliver, 2d, Ensign

William Hinkly, Sergeant
William Hunt, Jr., Sergeant
Alexander Campbell, Sergeant
Wadsworth Oliver, Sergeant
James Remick, Musician
Seth Tarr, Jr., Musician

Privates.
Beel, Samuel H., Jr.
Campbell, Elijah
Campbell, Robert
Carey, Edward
Emmons, Thomas
Gott, William, Jr.
Hall, Isaac
Harford, George
Harford, Lewis
Harford, William
Hinkly, John

Hunt, John
Keel, Luther
Linen, Andrew
Linen, James
Mahoney, Thomas
Manes, Sargent
Mars, Alexander
Mars, Dennis
Mars, Isaiah
Mars, James
Mars, Richard
Mars, Thomas
McFadden, Saul
McFadden, Thomas
McInney, Benjamin
McInney, Matthew
McInney, Matthew, Jr.
McMahon, Thomas
Oliver, David
Oliver, Ensebius
Oliver, Henry, Jr.
Oliver, Isaiah
Oliver, Jacob
Oliver, Nathaniel, Jr.

Oliver, Richard
Oliver, Thomas, Jr.
Oliver, Turner
Oliver, William
Oliver, William Y.
Power, Robert, Jr.
Radcliff, William
Rogers, Francis
Rogers, George
Rogers, Nathaniel
Spinney, Caleb
Spinney, David
Spinney, Nicholas
Spinney, Richard
Swombly or Twombly, John
Tarr, Aaron
Tarr, Benjamin, Jr.
Tarr, Benjamin, 3d
Tarr, James
Tarr, Jordan
Tarr, Joseph, Jr.
Trafton, Thomas
Williams, Elijah
Williams, Thomas

Capt. E. Percy's Company, Lieut. Col. A. Reed's Regiment.
From June 20 to June 25, and Sept. 10 to Oct. 1, 1814. Raised at Georgetown. Service at Bath.

RANK AND NAME.
Ellis Percy, Captain
James Cushing, Lieutenant
Jotham Crosby, Ensign

Thomas Cushing, Sergeant
Thomas Kelly, Sergeant
James Cushing, Sergeant
John Kelly, Sergeant
Patrick Duley, Corporal
Loring Cushing, Corporal
George Oliver, Corporal
Thomas Oliver, Corporal
John Oliver, Musician
Jacob Oliver, Musician

Privates.
Bleathen, Levi
Campbell, William
Duley, James

Hutchins, John
Lowell, Abner
Lowell, Stephen
McIntire, Henry
McIntire, Isaiah
Morse, Elijah
Morse, Esdias
Morse, Francis
Morse, Winslow
Oliver, Alexander
Oliver, David
Oliver, Henry
Percy, Arthur
Percy, Gilmore
Percy, Nathaniel
Reed, Denny
Shaw, James
Spinney, Jeremiah
Sprague, Nelson
Sylvester, Turner

Wallace, Alexander
Wallace, Eli
Wallace, Francis
Wallace, John
Wallace, William
Wallace, Zachariah
Wilder, Ephraim
Wilder, John
Wilder, Samuel, Jr.
Wyman, David
Wyman, Ephraim
Wyman, F.
Wyman, Percy

Waiters.
Kirky, John
Mains, Joseph
McKinney, Henry
Wildes, Francis

Capt. J. Pettes' Company, Lieut. Col. A. Reed's Regiment.
From June 20 to June 22, and Sept. 10 to Oct. 1, 1814. Service at Bath.

RANK AND NAME.
John Pettes, Captain
Alden Winter, Lieutenant
Samuel D. Crooker, Ensign

David Drummond, Sergeant
William Snow, Sergeant
John Barton, Sergeant

James Williams, Sergeant
Joseph Higgins, Corporal
William Brown, Jr., Corporal

Privates.
Athern, William
Bailey, Philip
Brown, Elisha

Coombs, David
Dow, Aaron
Flanders, John C.
Flanders, Samuel, Jr.
Higgins, Levi
Higgins, Philip, Jr.
Higgins, Samuel
Higgins, Simeon, Jr.

MASSACHUSETTS VOLUNTEER MILITIA IN THE WAR OF 1812.   249

Capt. J. Pettes' Company, Lieut. Col. A. Reed's Regiment — Concluded.

Privates — Concluded.
Hogan, Thomas
Holbrook, Abizur
Holbrook, Jesse
Jewel, Thomas
Leavitt, William
Lumbard, Thomas

Mitchell, Benjamin
Parks, John D.
Small, Ephraim
Swanton, William
Weeks, Henry
Winslow, Consider
Winslow, Samuel

Waiters.
Brown, Henry
Crooker, William
Parshley, William

Capt. W. Torrey's Company, Lieut. Col. A. Reed's Regiment.
From June 20 to June 22, 1814. Service at Bath.

RANK AND NAME.
William Torrey, Captain
Thomas Agry, Lieutenant
William Emerson, Ensign

J. M. Marsh, Sergeant
William H. Webb, Sergeant
Christian A. Brown, Corporal
Rufus K. Porter, Corporal

Privates.
Allen, Micah
Bowman, Samuel G.
Harding, Nehemiah
Hatch, Darius
Lemont, Robert
Marston, Daniel
Robinson, Jeremiah
Smith, John
Sprague, Oakman

Springer, David T.
Tallman, Scott J.
Todd, Thomas
Walker, David
Whitmore, Isaiah C.
Wormwood, Jotham

Waiters.
Card, Joshua, Jr.
Crooker, Robert

Capt. T. Motherwell's Company, Lieut. Col. A. Reed's Regiment.
From Sept. 5 to Oct. 1, 1814. Service at Woolwich.

RANK AND NAME.
Thomas Motherwell, Captain
William D. Leonard, Lieutenant
John W. Stinson, Ensign

Peleg Bradford, Sergeant
Peleg Delano, Sergeant
Bradford Delano, Sergeant
John C. Delano, Sergeant
Albert Delano, Corporal
Joshua Delano, Corporal
Moses Gray, Corporal
Joseph Shaw, Corporal
Joshua Baker, Musician

Privates.
Bayley, Joseph
Blair, James, Jr.
Blair, Thomas
Bolden, John

Brookins, Nathan
Card, Joseph
Card, Thomas
Card, Thurston
Card, Walter
Carlton, John
Carlton, John G.
Delano, Ebenezer
Farnham, Joshua
Gahan, John
Grover, Benjamin, Jr.
Harnden, Lemuel W.
Hathorn, Seth, Jr.
Hilton, Alfred
Hodgkins, Benjamin
Hodgkins, John, Jr.
Knowlton, Benjamin
Mains, James McCobb
McCown, Robert
McKinney, Alexander

McMurphy, Neill
Mitchell, Nathaniel
Reed, Charles
Reed, Joel
Reed, John M.
Reed, Robert, Jr.
Reed, Samuel
Reed, Ulrich
Savage, Joseph
Soul, David
Stinson, Alfred
Stinson, Frederick
Stinson, Thomas, Jr.
Trott, Charles
Trott, David
Trott, Samuel, Jr.
Wade, Caleb
Witham, Amnon
Wright, Reuben
Wyman, Stephen

Capt. F. D. A. Foster's Company, Lieut. Col. A. Reed's Regiment.
From Sept. 10 to Oct. 1, 1814. Raised at Phippsburg. Service at Bath.

RANK AND NAME.
Forris D. A. Foster, Captain
William David, Ensign

James Bowker, Sergeant
Isaac M. Corbett, Sergeant
Nicholas Nichols, Sergeant
Joseph Morse, Sergeant
Patrick Davis, Corporal

Lazarus Bowker, Corporal
William Owen, Corporal
Andrew Hogin, Corporal

Privates.
Batchelder, Levi
Blasdell, Christopher
Burgess, Seth, Jr.
Butler, George

Butler, John
Butler, Thomas, Jr.
Chisam, James
Cotton, Ebenezer
Cowing, Francis
Drummond, Alexander
Drummond, Parker
Emmons, Benjamin
Ford, William

Capt. F. D. A. Foster's Company, Lieut. Col. A. Reed's Regiment — Concluded.

Privates — Concluded.
Gardner, William
Hamond, David
Jackson, Samuel
Lee, Charles
Lee, William C.
Lovell, Benjamin
Lovell, John
Malcolm, Robert
McKinney, Matthew
Merrill, Joseph

Morrison, John
Morrison, Parson
Nichols, John, Jr.
Nichols, Joseph
Perry, Joseph
Perry, Mark
Perry, Thomas
Rogers, James G.
Rogers, Samuel L.
Small, Daniel
Spalding, John

Spinney, George
Walker, John
Wallace, Isaac
Wallace, John, Jr.
Wallace, Samuel, Jr.
Welch, John
Welch, Richard

Waiters.
Batchelder, Samuel
Pearsey, Gilmore, Jr.

Lieut. S. H. Rogers' Company, Lieut. Col. A. Reed's Regiment.
From June 20 to July 5, 1814. Service at Bath and Cox's Head.

RANK AND NAME.
Saul H. Rogers, Lieutenant
William Davis, Ensign

James Bowker, Sergeant
James Crisam, Sergeant
Nicholas Nichols, Sergeant
Patrick Davis, Musician

Privates.
Bachelder, Jordan P.
Bachelder, Levi
Bachelder, Timothy, Jr.
Blasdell, Christian, Jr.

Bowker, Lazarus
Burge, Seth, Jr.
Butler, James
Butler, John
Butler, Thomas, Jr.
Cotton, Ebenezer
Cowing, Francis
Drummond, Alexander, Jr.
Drummond, Patrick
Elwell, John
Foard, William
Hammond, David
Hogan, Andrew
Jackson, Samuel

Lee, Charles
Lee, William C.
Malcomb, Robert
Morrison, John
Morse, Joseph
Nicholas, John, Jr.
Nichols, Joseph
Perry, Joseph
Perry, Mark
Rogers, James G.
Small, Daniel
Walker, John
Welch, John
Welch, Richard

Lieut. Col. William Ryerson's Regiment.
From Sept. 14 to Sept. 24, 1814. Service at Portland.

FIELD AND STAFF.
William Ryerson, Lieutenant Colonel, Paris
Ebenezer Rawson, Major, Paris
Simeon Cummings, Major, Paris
Henry Rust, Jr., Captain, Paris
Enoch Burnham, Adjutant, Paris

Benjamin Chesley, Quartermaster, Paris
Alanson Mellon, Paymaster, Paris
Benjamin Chandler, Surgeon, Norway
William Brigham, Surgeon's Mate, Buckfield
James Hooper, Chaplain, Paris

NONCOMMISSIONED STAFF.
Bartholomew Cushman, Quartermaster Sergeant
Lewis Stowell, Drum Major
Abner Pratt, Fife Major
George Brigham, Waiter

Capt. I. Flint's Company, Lieut. Col. W. Ryerson's Regiment.
From Sept. 13 to Sept. 24, 1814. Three days additional for travel. Raised at Greenwood. Service at Portland.

RANK AND NAME.
Isaac Flint, Captain
John Small, Lieutenant
Amos Young, Ensign

Frederic Coburn, Sergeant
Cyprian Cole, Sergeant
John Sanborn, Sergeant
John Cummings, Sergeant
Rufus Richardson, Corporal
Jonathan Cole, Corporal

Privates.
Bacon, Benjamin
Berry, William
Caldwell, Elijah
Cole, Levi
Cross, Jesse
French, James
Frost, Edmond
Furlong, Thomas
Gurney, Samuel B.
Hicks, Benjamin
Hill, Charles
Lane, John

Morgan, Samuel D.
Nutting, James
Packard, Asa
Sanborn, David
Stevens, Josiah
Swan, Foxwell
Wentworth, Paul
Work, William
Yates, William
Yeates, William, Jr.
Young, Asa
Young, Charles

MASSACHUSETTS VOLUNTEER MILITIA IN THE WAR OF 1812.

Capt. J. Perham's Company, Lieut. Col. W. Ryerson's Regiment.
From Sept. 13 to Sept. 24, 1814. Three days additional for travel. Raised at Woodstock. Service at Portland.

RANK AND NAME.
Jotham Perham, Captain
Lemuel Perham, Lieutenant

Alexander Day, Sergeant
Samuel Bryant, Sergeant
Seth Curtis, Sergeant
Josiah Dudley, Sergeant
Gideon Swan, Musician

Privates.
Briggs, Luther
Bryant, Christopher
Bryant, Solomon
Clifford, Jonathan F.
Colton, William
Curtis, Morton
Curtis, Noah, Jr.
Davis, Aaron, Jr.

Dudley, Moses
Dunham, Samuel
Fuller, Consider
Hammond, Enoch
Rand, David
Swan, William, Jr.
Thurlow, Amos
Townsend, Otis
Whitman, Jacob

Capt. Jesse Turner's Company, Lieut. Col. W. Ryerson's Regiment.
From Sept. 13 to Sept. 24, 1814. Three days additional for travel. Raised at Buckfield. Service at Portland.

RANK AND NAME.
Jesse Turner, Captain
Moses Buck, Lieutenant
Richard Waldron, Ensign

Isaac Turner, Sergeant
Jonathan Buck, Sergeant
John Warren, Sergeant
Job Prince, Sergeant
Collins Woodbury, Corporal
Richard Hathaway, Corporal
David Farrow, Corporal
Noah Hall, Corporal
Elisha Buck, Musician
Jonas Spaulding, Musician

Privates.
Allen, Jacob
Andrews, Samuel
Besse, Warren
Bisby, Ansel
Bisby, Hopstill

Bowker, Cyprian
Brock, John, Jr.
Brock, Leonard
Buck, James
Buck, John, 3d
Buck, Samuel
Chaffin, John
Churchill, Bela
Churchill, Mathew
Churchill, Shepherd
Cole, James
Cole, Sampson
Cushman, Caleb
Damon, Jonathan, Jr.
Damon, Joseph
Drake, John or Joseph
Drake, Stephen
Farrow, Bela
Farrow, Nathan
Gardner, Ira
Jordan, Benjamin
Jordan, Elijah, Jr.

Leighton, Robert
Leonard, Jacob
Lewis, James
Lord or Low, David
Maxim, Nathan
Mayhew, John
Mayhew, Nathaniel
Monk, Alfred
Packard, Stephen
Packer, Samuel, Jr.
Rounds, Abner
Spaulding, William
Stevens, Moses
Thayer, John
Tucker, Samuel
Tucker, Samuel, Jr.
Turner, Joseph
Turner, Levi
Turner, Luther
Warren, Samuel, Jr.

Capt. U. Ripley's Company, Lieut. Col. W. Ryerson's Regiment.
From Sept. 14 to Sept. 24, 1814. Raised at Paris. Service at Portland.

RANK AND NAME.
Uriah Ripley, Captain
Eleazer Stevens, Lieutenant
Joel Fuller, Ensign

William Walker, Sergeant
Moses Allen, Sergeant
John Carpenter, Sergeant
Aaron Fuller, Sergeant
Francis Keene, Corporal
Eleazer Dunham, Corporal
Daniel Cummings, Corporal
Levi Gray, Corporal
George W. Cummings, Musician
Daniel Cummings, Jr., Musician

Privates.
Allen, Isaac
Bartlet, Tilden
Basford, David
Benson, Seth
Bent, Otis

Berry, Levi
Colburn, Jeraghmeel
Cole, Calvin
Cole, Job
Cole, Joseph
Curtis, Charles
Dasy, Daniel
Dean, Edmund
Deering, John
Deering, Robert
Dunham, Selva
Field, Galen
Field, Zibron
Fuller, Freeman
Fuller, Harvey
Greenleaf, William
Hall, Kimball
Harris, Amariah
Hill, Alexander
Keene, Shadrack
Kilgore, Andorus
Knight, Isaac

Labroke, Jacob
Labroke, Nicholas
Moody, Robert
Packard, Shepard
Porter, Charles
Porter, John
Rawson, Mark B.
Ripley, William
Sawyer, Reuben
Smith, Nicholas, Jr.
Stearnes, Phineas
Stevens, Samuel, Jr.
Sturdevant, Joseph, Jr.
Swift, John
Titcomb, Isaac
Truell, Abiather
Truell, Ebenezer
Videto, Jasper
Walker, Daniel
Watson, Simeon
Wyman, Baily
Young, Joshua

Capt. Stephen Blake's Company, Lieut. Col. W. Ryerson's Regiment.

From Sept. 14 to Sept. 24, 1814. Three days additional for travel. Raised at Paris. Service at Portland.

RANK AND NAME.
Stephen Blake, Captain
Thomas Hill, Jr., Lieutenant
Thomas Crooker, Ensign

Daniel Stowell, Jr., Sergeant
Micah Walker, Sergeant
Caleb Besse, Sergeant
Alexander Robinson, Sergeant
Charles Jordan, Corporal
Moses Hodgden, Corporal
John Hill, Corporal
Reuben Hill, Corporal
Seneca Brett, Musician
Isaac Record, Jr., Musician

Privates.
Andrews, Lloyd
Austin, Buck
Barker, Jonathan
Bartlett, Sylvanus
Besse, John
Blake, Eliphalet
Blake, Richard
Bolster, Alvin
Brett, Martin
Bryant, Arodus
Bryant, Ichabod
Bryant, Ichabod, Jr.
Bryant, Zebulon

Bullard, Joseph
Cardwell, Francis
Carey, John S.
Chipman, Simeon
Churchill, Perez
Churchill, William
Cloudman, Nathan
Cobb, Cyrus
Daniels, Simeon
Dudley, Daniel
Dwelly, Barzilla
Ellenwood, Jacob
Farrar, Thomas
Fobes, Billings
Forbes, Daniel
Frank, Levi
Frost, Enoch
Gammon, Moses
Gammon, Stephen
Hall, Abijah
Hall, Stephen or Solomon
Harlow, David
Hathaway, Lazarus
Hodgdon, Stephen
Leach, Mark
Lebanon, William
Maxim, Silas
Merrill, Humphrey
Mixer, William
Needham, John

Noble, Daniel
Noyes, John
Pendley, James
Perkins, Simeon
Perry, Caleb
Perry, James or Joseph
Prince, Isaac
Record, Andrew
Ripley, Ransom
Royal, John
Shirtliff, Alva
Smith, Antipas
Smith, William H.
Stearns, John
Stearns, Theodore or Thomas
Stowell, Rufus
Swift, Caleb
Swift, Jonathan
Swift, Samuel
Thomas, John
Tribou, Adna
Twitchell, David
Twitchell, John
Twitchell, Moses
Valentine, John
Walker, Charles
Weeks, Samuel P.
Whitehead, John
Willis, Seth

Capt. Bailey Bodwell's Company, Lieut. Col. W. Ryerson's Regiment.

From Sept. 14 to Sept. 24, 1814. Three days additional for travel. Raised at Norway. Service at Portland.

RANK AND NAME.
Bailey Bodwell, Captain

John Pike, Jr., Sergeant
Enoch Knight, Sergeant
William Frost, Sergeant
Moses Horton, Sergeant
Moses Cummings, Corporal
William Corson, Corporal
Samuel Pike, Corporal
John Witt, Corporal
John Quinby, Musician
Nathaniel Young, Musician

Privates.
Atwood, Job
Bartlett, Lemuel
Bartlett, Lemuel, 2d
Bartlett, Mailchi
Bartlett, Rufus, Jr.

Bennett, Isaac
Bodwell, Nathaniel
Bonney, Marshall
Buck, Daniel
Cleaves, Charles
Cleaves, Humphrey
Clifford, John
Cobb, Churchill
Coy, Cyrus
Crockett, Ephraim
Crockett, Lewis
Crockett, Samuel
Davis, Samuel
Delano, Ezekiel
Dolly, Joseph
Everett, John B.
Frost, Peter
Frost, Robert
Gorham, Benjamin
Gould, Andrew

Gould, Noah
Greenleaf, Stephen
Greenwood, Thadeus
Hill, Consider
Jordan, Elijah
Jordan, Samuel
Lord, Samuel
Marston, James M.
Monroe, James
Noble, Daniel or David
Perry, John
Perry, Joshua, Jr.
Pierson, John, Jr.
Pike, Nathaniel
Rowe, Samuel
Sawyer, James D.
Tubbs, Samuel
Watson, Ebenezer
Witt, Daniel
Young, William

MASSACHUSETTS VOLUNTEER MILITIA IN THE WAR OF 1812. 253

Capt. S. Robinson's Company, Lieut. Col. W. Ryerson's Regiment.
From Sept. 14 to Sept. 24, 1814. Three days additional for travel. Raised at Hebron. Service at Portland.

RANK AND NAME.
Samuel Robinson, Captain
Stephen Pratt, Lieutenant
Andrew Cushman, Ensign

Stephen Penny, Sergeant
Oliver Perkins, Sergeant
Ebenezer Holmes, Sergeant
Dean Andrews, Sergeant
Nathan Wright, Corporal
Abraham Dean, Corporal
Alexander Nelson, Corporal
Jennet Holbrook, Corporal
Artemus Turner, Musician

Privates.
Allen, Samuel
Allen, Solomon
Andrews, Loved
Bean, Abiather
Benson, Samuel
Blair, Reuben
Brown, Samuel
Chadborn, Zebedee

Cushman, Zebedee, Jr.
Dean, Henry C.
Dean or Dunn, Isaiah
Emery, William
Farris, Hezekiah
Fuller, Ira
Fuller, Nathaniel, Jr.
Gammon, Wilmot
Hamden or Handen, Levi
Hayes, Dennis
Herring, John
Hilbourn, Robert
Holmes, Solomon
Keene, Joshua
Keene, Seth
Littlefield, Samuel
Maddox, Henry
Mixter, Joseph
Moore, John
Moreton, Mathias
Moreton, Richard
Penley, William
Perkins, Isaiah
Perkins, Joseph, Jr.

Perkins, Luther
Perry, Benjamin F.
Pratt, Benajah
Pratt, Zebedee
Richmond, Eliab
Riggs, John L.
Robbins, Calvin
Robbins, Lebbeus
Rowe, Joseph
Russell, Solomon
Shaw, Francis
Shepherd, Green
Soule, James, Jr.
Staples, Andrew
Staples, David
Staples, Simon
Tarbox, Lemuel
Thayer, Peter
Washburn, Eli
Washburn, Isaac
Waterman, John
Weston, Josiah
Wood, Absalom
Wright, Samuel

Capt. Amos Town's Company, Lieut. Col. W. Ryerson's Regiment.
From Sept. 14 to Sept. 24, 1814. Three days additional for travel. Raised at Norway. Service at Portland.

RANK AND NAME.
Amos Town, Captain
William Persons, Jr., Lieutenant
Chad F. Jones, Ensign

Thomas Hall, Sergeant
John Whitmarsh, Sergeant
Isaac Lovejoy, Sergeant
John Needham, Sergeant
Joseph Stevens, Corporal
Joshua Crockett, Corporal
Simeon or Simon Noble, Corporal
Bela Noyes, Corporal
Daniel Leighton, Musician
Jonathan Stevens, Musician

Privates.
Bancroft, Jacob or Joseph
Bartlett, Clement
Bradbury, A.

Case, John
Flint, Elijah
Foster, Amos
Foster, Nathan, Jr.
French, Benjamin
Hall, David
Hill, Josiah, Jr.
Hobbs, Jeremiah
Hobbs, Jeremiah, Jr.
Hobbs, Robinson
Jordan, Abraham
Jordan, John
Judkins, Thomas
Lovejoy, Isaac F. or T.
Merrill, Edmund
Merrill, Enoch
Merrill, John
Merrill, William
Millett, Israel
Needham, Evi

Noble, Nathan, Jr.
Pierce, Joseph
Pingrey, Hezekiah
Pingrey, Hoyt
Pingrey, Samuel
Pingrey, Stephen, Jr.
Pingrey, William
Poole, Asa
Prentis, Henry
Shed, Silas
Small, James
Staples, Jeremiah
Stevens, Joel, Jr.
Upton, Francis
Upton, Micah
Watson, Stephen P.
White, Hosea
Wilkins, Darius

Lieut. Col. W. Ryerson's Regiment.
From Sept. 25 to Nov. 7, 1814. Service at Portland.

FIELD AND STAFF.
William Ryerson, Lieutenant Colonel, Paris
James Steele, Major
Peletiah Smith, Major, Pejepscot
James Chase, Adjutant, Livermore
Joshua Carpenter, Adjutant, Hartford
Ruel Phillips, Adjutant, Minot
Billy Benjamin, Quartermaster, Livermore
John Briggs, Paymaster, Sumner
Benjamin Chandler, Surgeon, Norway
Cornelius Holland, Surgeon's Mate, Livermore

NONCOMMISSIONED STAFF.
Henry Rust, Sergeant Major
Moses Plummer, Sergeant Major
Saul Ames, Quartermaster Sergeant
William Swan, Drum Major
Elisha Buck, Drum Major
Pelham Bryant, Fife Major
Alvan Robinson, Fife Major

Waiters.
Dusenbury, James
Folsom, George
Hanson, Humphrey
Jackson, Boston
McKenney, William
Merrill, Edward
White, John

Capt. H. Bickford's Company, Lieut. Col. W. Ryerson's Regiment.
From Sept. 25 to Nov. 7, 1814. Raised at Porter. Service at Portland.

RANK AND NAME.
Hezekiah Bickford, Captain
John Evans, Lieutenant
Benjamin Woodman, Ensign

Moses Merrill, Sergeant
Daniel Howe, Sergeant
Jeremiah Chandler, Sergeant
Moses Hutchins, Sergeant
Nehemiah C. Dresser, Sergeant
John Chandler, Corporal
James Warner, Corporal
Robert Patterson, Corporal
Benjamin Fifield, Corporal
William Berry, Musician
Amos P. Knox, Musician

Privates.
Adams, Henry
Andrews, Amos
Bean, James
Bean, Nathaniel
Bemis, Amos
Bemis, Joseph
Bemis, Thaddeus, Jr.
Blake, John
Blake, William
Boynton, William, Jr.
Charles, Simeon
Charles, Timothy
Clay, Benjamin
Day, Jabez C.
Dresser, Elijah

Dresser, Frederic
Dresser, Levi
Dresser, Stephen, Jr.
Dutch, Samuel
Eastman, Joseph
Emery, James
Farnum, Joseph
Gardner, David
Gerrish, Obediah
Gordon, Joseph
Hapgood, William
Harnden, Benjamin
Harnden, Elbridge
Hartshorn, William
Head, Nathaniel
Heaton, Samuel
Hubbard, Warwick
Huntress, Saul D.
Hutchins, Ichabod
Irish, Stephen
Jewell, John
Johnson, David
Kennister, John
Kimball, Isaac
Knight, Tristram
Knowles, Aaron
Libbey, James
Lord, Job C.
Low, Justin
Mason, Gideon
McAllister, John
Merrill, John
Osgood, Dean

Osgood, Robert
Palmer, Moses
Parker, Joseph
Pike, Saul
Porter, Asahel
Porter, David
Quimby, Jacob
Record, Saul
Richardson, Joshua
Sargent, Joseph F.
Snow, Joseph
Snow, Silas
Travers, Saul
Treadwell, Jonathan
Trull, Micah
Walker, Supply
Warren, Nathaniel
Wentworth, William
Whiting, Clement
Whiting, James
Whiting, Oliver, Jr.
Whitney, Ephraim
Winship, Thomas
Woodman, Enoch (died)
Wyly, America
Wyly, John, Jr.

Waiters.
Evans, Henry H.
Pearl, Joseph
Shed, John

Capt. S. Blake's Company, Lieut. Col. W. Ryerson's Regiment.
From Sept. 25 to Nov. 7, 1814. Raised at Paris. Service at Portland.

RANK AND NAME.
Stephen Blake, Captain
Thomas Hill, Lieutenant
Thomas Crocker, Ensign
James Sweet, Ensign

Thomas Hall, Sergeant
John Warren, Sergeant
Elijah Long, Sergeant
Josiah Dudley, Sergeant
Alexander Robinson, Sergeant
Francis Keene, Corporal
Daniel Witt, Corporal
Rufus Richardson, Corporal
Amos Thurlow, Corporal
Lloyd Anderson, Corporal
Seneca Pratt, Musician
Isaac Record, Musician

Privates.
Allen, Elisha
Allen, Joshua
Barron, William L.
Bartlet, Sylvanus
Bassford, David (D)
Benson, Seth
Bent, Otis
Berry, Levi
Blake, Richard
Boker, Cyrian
Brett, Martin
Briggs, John
Brooks, Jacob L.
Bryant, Christopher
Bryant, Ichabod
Bryant, Samuel
Bryant, Solomon, Jr.
Bryant, Zebulon

Buck, James
Caldwell, Elijah
Chesley, Jonathan
Churchill, Benjamin
Churchill, William
Clifford, Jonathan F.
Cobb, Cyrus
Coburn, Jeremiah
Cole, James (D)
Cole, Joseph
Cole, Levi
Cotton, William
Curtis, Charles
Dammon, Jonathan
Dean, Edmund
Doten, Silas
Drake, Stephen
Dudley, Moses
Dunham, Eleazer
Dwelley, Barzaleel
Farrar, Thomas
Frost, Edmund
Graffan, Thomas
Gurney, Edward
Gurney, Samuel B.
Hall, Abijah
Hall, Kimball
Hill, Charles
Hodgdon, Moses
Hodgkins, Israel
Jordan, Elijah
Keene, Shadrack
Kilgore, Andrew
Knight, Isaac
Lambert, John L.
Lane, John
Leach, Mark
Leighton, Robert

Leonard, Jacob
Libbey, Enos
Marshall, Moses
Maxim, Silas, Jr.
Needham, John
Packard, Shepherd
Packard, Stephen
Parsons, George
Penley, James
Perry, Joseph, Jr.
Porter, John
Prince, Job
Sanborn, David
Serill, William
Shirtliff, Alva
Simonton, James
Smith, William H.
Stearns, John
Stearns, Phineas
Swan, Farwell
Swift, John
Swift, Samuel
Townsend, Otis
Tucker, Saul
Twitchell, John
Valentine, John
Videto, Jasper
Walker, Charles
Walton, Simeon
Wentworth, Paul
Work, William
Yates, William
Young, Asa

Waiters.
Dresser, James
French, James
Green, John

Capt. B. Bodwell's Company, Lieut. Col. W. Ryerson's Regiment.
From Sept. 25 to Nov. 5, 1814. Drafted and in service at Portland.

RANK AND NAME.
Bailey Bodwell, Captain
William Ingalls, Lieutenant
Stephen Pratt, Ensign
Richard Cook, Ensign
Daniel Stevens, Ensign

Nathan Pettingill, Sergeant
James Stewart, Sergeant
Samuel Wiggins, Sergeant
Alexander Merrill, Sergeant
Reuben Merrill, Corporal
William Greeley, Jr., Corporal
Nathan Sawyer, Corporal
William Corson, Corporal
Simeon Noble, Corporal
Peletiah Berry, Musician
John Quinby, Musician
Nathaniel Bodwell, Musician

Privates.
Abbott, Micah
Anderson, Montgomery
Anthoine, Amos
Atwood, Job
Bancroft, Jacob
Banford, Jeremiah
Bartlett, Lemuel, 2d
Bartlett, Malachi
Burbank, Isaiah
Clifford, John
Cobb, Churchill
Cole, Joseph
Coy, Cyrus
Davis, John
Dawbin, James
Dawbin, William
Delano, Ezekiel
Drinkwater, William

Flood, Luther
Flood, Samuel
Gilman, Ebenezer
Goold, Jonathan
Goold, Noah
Gorham, Benjamin
Gould, Andrew
Graffam, Peter
Greenwood, Thaddeus
Harmon, Jonathan
Hawk, Sheppard
Hersey, Israel
Hill, Consider
Hill, Josiah, Jr.
Hooper, Henry
Hunter, Robert
Ingalls, Loammi
Ingersoll, Daniel B.
Irish, Samuel

Capt. B. Bodwell's Company, Lieut. Col. W. Ryerson's Regiment — Concluded.

Privates — Concluded.
Jackson, Thomas
Jewett, Daniel
Johnson, Andrew
Johnson, James
Jordan, Abraham
Kemp, Eben
Kennison, David
Kezer, Luther
Lamb, Solomon
Lamb, William
Lewis, Joseph
Lock, Nathaniel
Lombard, Richard
Lord, David
Mackie, Andrew
Martin, Nathaniel
Maybury, Ezekiel
McKenney, Daniel

Means, Nicholas
Merrill, John
Millet, Israel
Milliken, Josiah
Noble, Christopher
Noble, David
Parsons, John, Jr.
Patrick, Benjamin
Perry, John
Perry, Maish
Pingree, Hezekiah
Pingree, Hoyt
Porter, Rufus
Pray, Alexander
Prince, Joseph
Royal, William
Sanborn, John
Sanborn, Lewis
Sawyer, Ebenezer

Smith, Asa
Snow, James
Strout, Isaac
Swet, Josiah
Thomb, John
Thorn, Eleazer
Thorn, William
Thurston, David, Jr.
Tubbs, Samuel
Tukey, Samuel
Turner, Charles
Usher, Robert
Wardwell, Samuel, Jr.
Waterhouse, Samuel, Jr.
Weeks, John
Whitehouse, Ephraim
Whitmore, Major
Winn, John

Capt. H. Frost's Company, Lieut. Col. W. Ryerson's Regiment.

From Sept. 25 to Nov. 7, 1814.   Drafted from Poland, Gray, New Gloucester and Danville.   Service at Portland.

RANK AND NAME.
Henry Frost, Captain
Moses Rowe, Lieutenant
Elijah Huston, Lieutenant
Samuel True, Ensign

Samuel H. Haskell, Sergeant
John Humphrey, Sergeant
Moses Plummer, Sergeant
Thomas Waterman, Sergeant
Ephraim Stenchfield, Sergeant
Benjamin Weeks, Corporal
John Stenchfield, Corporal
Walter Johnson, Corporal
Jabez Waterman, Corporal
Nathan Allen, Corporal
Derring Johnson, Musician
James Eveleth, Musician

Privates.
Allen, John
Allen, Zadock
Austin, Minion
Babb, Charles
Bennet, Isaac
Berry, Morrill
Blake, Ephraim
Blake, Richard
Brooks, Charles
Brown, Jacob
Chipman, Seth
Crockett, David
Davis, Benjamin
Davis, Moses
Davis, William
Dennin, Samuel
Dennison, Simeon
Doubty, John M.

Dyer, Charles
Estes, William
Eveleth, Moses
Fernald, Joseph
Fogg, Daniel
Fowler, Hugh
Gammon, Nathaniel
Goss, George
Goss, Philemon C.
Goss, William
Gould, William
Grant, Isaac
Grover, Zebulon P.
Hackett, James
Hammond, William
Harris, Martin
Haskell, Ebenezer (died)
Haskell, Peleg
Hollis, David
Houston, Joseph
Humphrey, John, 3d
Jordan, Charles
Jordan, William
Jordan, William, Jr.
Knight, Abraham
Knight, Moses
Larabee, Dennis
Leach, James
Leach, Mark
Libbey, Jedediah C.
Libbey, William
Libbey, William, Jr.
Loring, David
Martin, John
Mason, Nathaniel
McGuire, John
McKenney, William
Paine, Charles

Parce, Jabez W.
Patterson, Abraham
Pearce, Crocker
Penny, Aaron
Pierce, Abraham
Pratt, Eberdeen
Preble, John
Prince, William
Ramsdell, Robert
Roach, James K.
Roberts, Daniel
Rogers, Edward
Rowe, Gilbert A.
Rowe, Samuel
Small, Jeremiah
Small, John
Smith, John
Stenchfield, John
Trickey, Joseph
True, Jacob L.
Verril, John
Wagg, William P.
Waite, George
Walker, John
Wharf, Nathaniel
Whitham, Asa
Whitham, Ebenezer, Jr.
Wiggins, Nathaniel
Winslow, Jacob
Woodbury, Benjamin
Woodbury, William

Waiters.
Frost, George D.
Preble, Ebenezer
Roberts, Reuben

MASSACHUSETTS VOLUNTEER MILITIA IN THE WAR OF 1812. 257

Capt. J. Harlow's Company, Lieut. Col. W. Ryerson's Regiment.
From Sept. 25 to Nov. 7, 1814. Raised at Minot and vicinity. Service at Portland.

RANK AND NAME.
James Harlow, Captain
Reuel Phillips, Lieutenant
John Small, Lieutenant
Andrew Cushman, Ensign
William Frost, Ensign

Eliphalet Packard, Sergeant
Nathaniel Gammon, Sergeant
Ebenezer Holmes, Sergeant
Asia Jones, Sergeant
David Corliss, Sergeant
Samuel P. Poole, Sergeant
William Chenery, Corporal
Ephraim Ricker, Corporal
Peter Noyes, Corporal
Jennet Holbrook, Corporal
Pelham Bryant, Musician
James Goff, Musician

Privates.
Alden, Alexander
Andrews, Loved
Austin, Ebenezer
Bean, Abiather
Bearce, Asa, Jr.
Berry, Obediah
Bird, William
Bonney, John
Bradbury, Jacob
Buck, Elisha
Buck, Simeon
Capen, Uriah
Caswell, John
Caswell, Noah
Chamberlain, Aaron, Jr.
Chase, Abner
Cox, Edward

Cushman, Zebedee, Jr.
Dauble, Elijah
Davis, Joseph
Davis, Stephen
Day, George
Drake, Enos
Drake, Martin
Drew, Lewis
Drew, Stephen
Eustace, George
Eustace, Thomas
Foster, Abijah
Foster, Michel
Freeman, Saul
Fuller, Nathaniel
Fuller, Oliver, Jr.
Gammon, Robertson
Gammon, Wilmot
Hall, Andrew
Hall, John
Hamblin, Eliphalet
Hayden, Lewis G.
Hayes, Dennis
Hennaford, William W.
Hill, William
Hisey, John
Holmes, Alvah
Holmes, Miles
Holmes, Salmon
Howard, Asaph
Jackson, Elijah
Keith, Pliney
Kilborn, Robert
Knowlton, Alvin
Landers, Lot
Latham, Barzilla
Matthews, Constant
Matthews, Jabez

Matthews, John, Jr.
Mitchell, Zenas
Morse, Daniel
Packard, Jonathan
Park or Parks, Caleb
Penly, William
Perkins, Joseph
Perkins, Luther
Perry, Gad
Phillips, Thomas
Pratt, Zebedee
Robbins, Calvin
Rounds, Abner
Soule, Alexander
Staples, Moses
Staples, Simon
Stout, Nathaniel
Sweet, Josiah
Thompson, Gilmore
Treat, Richard
True, William
Turner, Levi
Washburn, Eli
Witt, John
Wood, Absalom
Wood, Earl
Wood, Israel
Wright, Nathan
Wright, Samuel
Young, Christopher
Young, Isaac

Waiters.
Stanford, David
Thrasher, Joseph
Webb, Gustavus

Capt. J. Holt's Company, Lieut. Col. W. Ryerson's Regiment.
From Sept. 25 to Nov. 7, 1814. Raised at Albany and Bethel. Service at Portland.

RANK AND NAME.
Joseph Holt, Captain
Jonathan Powers, Lieutenant
Aaron Cummings, Lieutenant
Eleazer Twitchell, Ensign

Isaac Kilburn, Sergeant
John Atherton, Sergeant
Norman Clark, Sergeant
Herman Holt, Corporal
Daniel Scribner, Corporal
Daniel Chaplin, Jr., Corporal
Josiah Brown, Corporal
Ebenezer Colby, Corporal
Joseph Willis, Corporal
George W. Longley, Musician
Nathan F. Twitchell, Musician

Privates.
Amis, Solomon, Jr.
Andrews, William
Atherton, Ezra
Barker, Samuel, 3d
Barker, William
Bartlett, Ebenezer
Bean, Daniel, Jr.
Bean, Jesse
Bean, Kimball
Bean, Nathaniel
Beckley, Francis
Beebe, Robert
Bell, John, Jr.
Billings, Daniel
Bisbee, Moses
Blake, Benjamin

Brigham, Briant
Brigham, Levi
Brigham, Luther
Brown, Asaph
Brown, Herman
Brown, Jabez
Capen, Timothy
Case, John
Chamberlain, John
Chapman, Timothy
Coffin, Naphtali
Cross, Ebenezer, Jr.
Cummings, Francis
Cushman, John
Dustin, Farnham
Estes, John
Foster, Jeremiah

Capt. J. Holt's Company, Lieut. Col. W. Ryerson's Regiment — Concluded.

Privates — Concluded.
French, John
Frisbee, Austin S.
Frost, Peter
Greenwood, Nathaniel, Jr.
Grover, Asahel
Grover, Elias
Grover, James
Grover, James, Jr.
Grover, Peter
Hall, Benjamin, Jr.
Hall, Charles
Hall, Israel
Hapgood, Oliver, Jr.
Hapgood, Sprout
Haskell, Parsons
Haskell, Samuel, Jr.
Hersey, Caleb
Holt, Timothy A.
Jewell, John, Jr.
Jewell, Lewis

Jones, Sullivan
Jordan, Wales
Kendall, Bezaleel
Kendall, Joseph
Kilgore, Elihu
Kilgore, Gabriel
Kimball, Isaiah, Jr.
Kimball, Jeremiah
Libbey, Samuel
Lock, Luther
Moffat, Stephen
Morse, Marner
Page, Samuel
Peabody, Asa
Plummer, Josiah
Pride, Josiah
Proctor, John
Russell, Chandler
Sanborn, Nathaniel
Sanders, George W.
Shed, John

Shorry, Urban
Smith, Amos
Sotherly, William
Sprague, Elbridge
Stearnes, Charles, Jr.
Stiles, Nathan
Swift, William
Trull, Silas
Twitchell, Asa
Twitchell, Sylvanus
Walker, Joseph C.
Warren, Abijah
Warren, Peleg
Wetherbee, Jude
Wheeler, Samuel
Whitcomb, Paul

Waiters.
Greenwood, Mason
Pierce, Levi
Turrell, Francis

Capt. J. Kilbourn's Company, Lieut. Col. W. Ryerson's Regiment.
From Sept. 25 to Nov. 7, 1814. Raised at Bridgton and vicinity. Service at Portland.

RANK AND NAME.
John Kilbourn, Captain
John Smith, Lieutenant
Daniel Hall, Lieutenant
Robert Andrews, Jr., Ensign

Jonathan Bernard, Sergeant
John Skillings, Sergeant
John Whitmarsh, Sergeant
Stephen Edwards, Sergeant
Joshua Goodridge, Sergeant
Ithamar Brigham, Sergeant
William Stone, Corporal
Richard T. Smith, Corporal
Samuel Hermon, Corporal
Edward Jordan, Corporal
Marks Jordan, Corporal
Daniel Clute, Corporal
Porter Perley, Musician
Rufus Harmon, Musician

Privates.
Baker, Samuel
Barker, Nathan
Barton, Jacob
Bean, Abner
Bearce, John
Blake, Nathaniel
Brackett, Enoch
Brown, Simeon
Burnall, William
Burnett, Samuel
Burnham, Simeon
Califf, Jedediah T.
Carrol, David
Carsley, Ebenezer
Cash, John, Jr.
Caswell, Libbeus
Center, Jacob

Chadbourn, Benjamin
Chaplin, Jacob
Chase, Joseph
Colby, Israel
Cook, John
Dawes, Bela
Decker, David
Dyer, Andrew
Edwards, Ephraim
Elwell, John
Emerson, Isaac
Emerson, Joshua
Fowler, David
Gay, David
Graham, John
Haynes, William
Hill, John
Hill, Thomas
Hobbs, Isaac
Hobbs, John
Ingalls, Francis, 3d
Ingalls, Gardner
Ingalls, Samuel, 2d
Jackson, William
Jordan, James
Jordan, Nathaniel, Jr.
Kimball, Israel, Jr.
Kneeland, Moses
Kneeland, Simeon
Knight, Abraham
Knight, Thomas
Lane, Levi
Latham, Galen
Laurence, Simon S.
Leach, Jonathan
Lombard, Joseph (D.)
Long, Darius
Marsh, Peletiah
Mayo, Thomas

Montford, David
Montford, Joshua
Moors, Solomon
Morrison, James
Morse, John, Jr.
Newcomb, Elisha
Noble, John
Oliver, John
Porter, Nehemiah
Potter, Asa
Purvis, William
Scribner, Joseph
Shaw, Richard, Jr.
Skillings, John
Small, Francis
Smith, James
Smith, Joseph (D.)
Smith, Marshall
Spiller, John, Jr.
Stinchfield, Stephen
Strout, Prince
Symonds, Joseph
Tenney, John
Thrasher, Robert
Titcomb, Jeremiah
Tukey, John
Tyler, Abraham
Tyler, Joseph
Usher, Scilly G.
Watkins, Jacob S.
Webster, Whitely
Weston, John
Whitney, George W.
Wilson, Earl

Waiters.
Kilborn, Ebenezer
Roberts, Benjamin
Smith, Benjamin, Jr.

Capt. W. Morrison's Company, Lieut. Col. W. Ryerson's Regiment.
From Sept. 25 to Nov. 7, 1814. Raised at Livermore. Service at Portland.

RANK AND NAME.
William Morrison, Captain
Thomas Davis, Lieutenant
Billy Benjamin, Ensign
Jesse Howe, Ensign

Zenas Hall, Sergeant
William Harlow, Sergeant
Israel Waters, Sergeant
Alding Willington, Sergeant
Nathaniel Dyke, Sergeant
John Clark, Corporal
David Ducker, Corporal
James Waite, Corporal
Jacob Lovejoy, Corporal
Joseph Fuller, Corporal
Francis F. Haynes, Musician
William Spaulding, Musician

Privates.
Abbott, John
Abbott, William
Allen, Asa
Allen, Datus T.
Allen, Reuben
Alley, Thomas
Atkinson, Enoch
Barber, Elias
Barrows, Simeon
Bartlett, David
Bell, Robert
Benson, Joseph
Bisbee, Luther
Bonney, Asa
Bosworth, William
Brown, James
Bryant, James
Burgess, Ebenezer

Carver, Amos
Clark, John
Clark, Saul
Clauson, Luther, Jr. (D.)
Cobb, Stephen
Coburn, Jonas, Jr.
Cox, John
Crockett, John
Cummins, Oliver
Cushman, Levi
Dally, Daniel
Dike, Fuller
Doane, Asa
Doane, Charles
Doane, Edward
Doble, Solomon
Drout, John
Eastman, Timothy
Edgcomb, Didimus C.
Ellis, Ardin
Eustace, William
Fletcher, Benjamin
Frye, Jonathan
Fuller, Aaron
Fuller, Abraham
Fuller, Charles
Fuller, Ezra, Jr.
Fuller, John B.
Gowell, William
Hodgdon, Abraham
Irish, Ebenezer
Keene, Judah, Jr.
Kimball, Nathan
King, Henry
Knowles, Silas
Laroach, Stephen
Leadbetter, Thomas
Lyford, Samuel

Marble, Ira
Marsh, David
Merrill, Joseph
Mitchell, Charles
Moore, Asa
Morrell, Elijah
Page, Elijah
Paine, Thomas
Parker, Edward
Phillips, Edmund
Randall, Samuel
Robinson, Stephen R.
Sampson, Jacob
Sargent, Benjamin
Shaw, Job
Skinner, David
Smart, Jeremiah
Soule, Beza
Steele, Samuel
Stubbs, Nathan
Thomas, Levi, Jr.
Thomas, Nathaniel
Thompson, Galen
Townsend, Thomas
Uland, Edmund C.
Waite, Tyler
Washburn, Martin
Wellington, Elijah
Wentworth, Thomas
Wilson, Gowen
Winter, Joseph
Woodruff, John
Young, Moses, 2d

Waiters.
Bennett, William
Johnson, John
Vose, William

Capt. E. Morse's Company, Lieut. Col. W. Ryerson's Regiment.
From Sept. 25 to Nov. 7, 1814. Raised at Livermore. Service at Portland.

RANK AND NAME.
Elias Morse, Captain
Ezra Stevens, Lieutenant
Stephen Pratt, Lieutenant
Hendrick Aldrich, Ensign

Hezekiah Griffith, Sergeant
Isaac Fuller, Sergeant
Thomas Towns, Sergeant
Zenas Stetson, Sergeant
John Cummings, Sergeant
John Griffiths, Corporal
Oliver Lucas, Corporal
Ezra Anderson, Corporal
Leonard Benson, Corporal
Jacob M. Russell, Corporal
Abner Holman, Musician
John Lunt, Musician

Privates.
Allen, James
Andrews, Lucius
Andrews, Manassah
Beals, Luther
Benson, Sullivan
Birt, William
Bosworth, Noah
Bourn, Caleb
Brown, Moses
Brown, Simeon
Bumpas, Calvin
Cole, George
Decoster, Chandler
Deland, Abial
Deland, William
Delano, Samuel
Dorn, Ebenezer, 1st

Dorn, Ebenezer, 2d
Dutton, David
Edgcomb, Daniel
Elwell, David
Fairbanks, Elias
Farrar, Saul
Fisher, Elijah
Ford, Obadiah
Gammons, Perkins
Gibbs, John
Gilkey, James
Graffum, Daniel
Gross, William
Haines, William
Haskell, Asa
Hathaway, Eli
Hawkins, Henry
Hind, Chapman

Capt. E. Morse's Company, Lieut. Col. W. Ryerson's Regiment — Concluded.

Privates — Concluded.
Hinkley, Alanson
Hobbs, Robinson
Hodge, John M.
Irish, Elkanah
Irish, Joshua
Irish, William
Jackson, Joseph
Keene, Edward
Keene, John, Jr.
Kenny, Elisha
Knox, James
Knox, Joshua
Kranska, Jason
Lovewell, Luther
Lucas, David
Ludden, Jacob
Luther, Chelsey
Mason, Reuben

Merrill, Abel, Jr.
Merrill, David
Morrill, Humphries
Morse, David, Jr.
Morse, Henry
Noble, Nathan
Packard, Josiah
Parlin, Almond
Parlin, Oliver
Persons, Daniel
Pingree, William
Poland, Sylvanus
Pratt, Church
Rich, David
Robinson, Asa
Simmons, Daniel
Smith, Elliot
Snell, Moses
Snow, Levi

Soper, Alexander
Soper, Gad
Soule, Samuel
Stacy, John
Starboard, James
Stetson, Ephraim
Thompson, John
Tobin, Benjamin
Tucker, John
Vaughn, Zenas
Waterman, Noah, Jr.
Waters, Gardner
Wood, William
Wyer, William

Waiters.
Strout, Daniel
Strout, James
Strout, Lemuel

Capt. I. Reynold's Company, Lieut. Col. W. Ryerson's Regiment.
From Sept. 25 to Nov. 7, 1814. Raised at Minot and vicinity. Service at Portland.

RANK AND NAME.
Ichabod Reynolds, Captain
Charles Briggs, Lieutenant
Joshua Carpenter, Lieutenant
Samuel Nash, Ensign

Joseph Sampson, Sergeant
Abel Allen, Sergeant
Asa Harlow, Sergeant
Daniel Pratt, Sergeant
Silas Bumpas, Sergeant
Stephen Maxwell, Corporal
Nathaniel Flint, Corporal
John Ferrill, Corporal
Otis Phillips, Corporal
Zelotes Haskell, Corporal
Erastus Miles, Musician

Privates.
Alden, Daniel
Allen, Benjamin
Baily, Aretus
Baily, Hudson
Baily, Luther
Barrows, Cornelius
Barrows, Job H.
Bartlett, Jonathan
Bates, John
Bradbury, Andrew
Bradford, Benjamin
Bradford, Samuel
Briggs, Daniel
Brown, Artemus
Bryant, Abel
Bryant, Amos
Bumpas, Jesse
Campbel, Alexander
Carman, Luther
Caswell, Job

Chandler, Jonathan
Chandler, Phineas
Chandler, Seth
Chandler, Stephen
Chase, Peter
Cole, Nathan
Collins, Daniel D.
Crocker, Charles
Currier, Benjamin
Cushman, Isaac
Davis, Lane
Davy, Solomon
Drake, Nathaniel
Dresser, John
Eaton, Samuel
Folsom, Samuel
Fuller, Barnabus
Gardner, John
Goff, James
Gowell, James
Gurney, Levi
Hasey, Jacob
Hasey, Joseph
Hasty, Nathaniel
Hesum or Hersum, John
Hodge, David
Hodge, Joseph
Hutchins, Jonathan
Hutchinson, Daniel
Irish, Joseph
Jackson, Joseph
Jones, Abner
Jones, Richard
Kingsly, Martin
Lane, Amos
Latham, Abial
Littlefield, Enoch
Lord, James
Mallet, Solomon

Marshall, Aaron
Mason, Nathaniel
McLaughlin, Daniel
Merrill, Edward
Merrill, Rufus
Millet, David
Minon, Reuben
Moody, Nathaniel
Morgan, Solomon
Packard, Cyrus
Perkins, Moses
Pettingill, Ethan
Philips, Saul
Potter, Daniel
Prescot, Solomon
Record, Calvin E.
Record, Elisha
Reed, Jacob
Richardson, Stephen
Rowe, Benjamin
Runnel, Isaac
Runnels, Isaac E.
Shaw, Edward
Small, Saul
Sturdevant, James
Turner, Oliver
Varrell, John
Washburn, Stephen
Whittemore, Levi
Wood, Solomon
Woodman, Jabez
Woolcot, Solomon

Waiters.
Boney, Lebbeus
Hasty, John
Hasty, Nathaniel

Capt. W. Wheeler's Company, Lieut. Col. W. Ryerson's Regiment.
From Sept. 25 to Nov. 7, 1814. Raised at Rumford and vicinity. Service at Portland.

RANK AND NAME.
William Wheeler, Captain
Asa Burbank, Lieutenant
Ingalls Bragg, Ensign
Henry Floyd, Ensign

Jesse Duston, Sergeant
Thomas B. Watson, Sergeant
Winthrop Newton, Sergeant
Moses Frost, Sergeant
Isaac Spring, Sergeant
Samuel Knight, Corporal
Josiah Mayberry, Corporal
Benjamin Farrington, Corporal
Daniel Crane, Corporal
Ebenezer Bergin, Musician
Joseph Kilgore, Musician

Privates.
Abbott, Ebenezer
Abbott, Enos, Jr.
Abbott, Farnum
Abbott, Moses
Abbott, Nathaniel
Adams, Nathan
Allen, Joseph
Bailey, Joseph
Baker, Nathaniel
Bartlet, Freeborn
Baston, William
Bell, William
Bothwell, James (D.)
Burbank, Stephen
Burnham, Bohemia
Burnham, Ira
Burnham, Jedediah

Chadburn, Humphrey A.
Chatty, John
Coburn, Moses
Coolbroth, Ebenezer
Crane, John
Dolloff, David
Durgen, Leavit
Eames, Saul
Eastman, Haynes
Estes, George
Farnum, Merrill
Farnum, Samuel
Farrington, Philander
Fillbrooks, Simpson
Foster, Asa
Foster, Nathan
Frost, John
Glines, Daniel
Glines, Timothy
Goddard, David
Godfrey, Joseph
Graham, George
Hanford, Solomon
Haynes, John
Henley, John
Henry, John
Hodsden, Daniel
Howard, John
Howe, John
Howe, Otis
Jewell, Enoch
Lewis, Noah
Lock, Thomas
Lovell, Moses
Lovell, Thomas
Merryfield, Richard

Moore, Humphrey
Moulton, S.
Newton, Hollsworth
Newton, Lambert
Nutter, Charles
Osgood, Asa
Pearl, Benjamin
Pearl, Dimond
Pierce, Benjamin T.
Pierce, William
Poor, Edward L. or S..
Putman, Jacob
Putman, Jesse
Putman, Stephen
Randall, Ezra
Ripley, Joseph
Rolf, Nathaniel
Rolf, Samuel
Simpson, Paul R.
Simpson, William
Smart, Ira
Smith, Peter
Snow, Joshua
Stanley, Elisha
Stevens, Enoch
Tripp, Nathaniel
Truett, George
Varney, Andrew
Virgin, John
Warren, Gilbert
White, Aaron

Waiters.
Burbank, Samuel S.
Mason, Ebenezer
Webster, Andrew

Lieut. Col. Elnathan Sherwin's Regiment.
From Sept. 13 to Sept. 24, 1814. Service at Wiscasset.

FIELD AND STAFF.
Elnathan Sherwin, Lieutenant Colonel, Waterville
Richard M. Dorr, Major, Waterville
Abraham Brackett, Major, Sidney

John Cleveland, Major, Fairfield
Ephraim Gatchell, Adjutant, Waterville
Joseph B. Hallett, Quartermaster, Waterville
David Wheeler, Paymaster, Waterville

Moses Appleton, Surgeon, Winslow
John Wright, Surgeon's Mate, Waterville
Zedekiah Belknap, Chaplain, Waterville

Capt. L. Barret's Company, Lieut. Col. E. Sherwin's Regiment.
From Sept. 13 to Sept. 24, 1814. Raised at Fairfield. Service at Augusta.

RANK AND NAME.
Levi Barret, Captain
Robert Hathaway, Lieutenant
William Bodfish, Ensign

Prince Clifford, Sergeant
George Dogget, Sergeant
John Burrell, Sergeant

Privates.
Atwood, Nathaniel
Beales, George
Buck, Zebediah
Burrell, Benoni
Burrell, Josiah
Burrell, Noah
Chase, Arthur

Colcord, Wilson
Cook, Joseph, Jr.
Cook, Nathaniel
Decker, Stephen
Emery, Caleb
Emery, James
Emery, Samuel
Emery, Samuel, 2d

Capt. L. Barret's Company, Lieut. Col. E. Sherwin's Regiment — Concluded.

Privates — Concluded.
Fall, Ebenezer
Fisk, Peleg
Gifford, Joseph, Jr.
Gray, Samuel
Guffield, Abraham
Gullifer, David
Gullifer, John, Jr.
Gullifer, Peleg
Higgins, Nathan
Higgins, Thomas
Hubbard, Leroy

Kendall, Jonas
Kendall, Saul
Mackay, James
McKeckner, John M.
Noble, Eleazer
Noble, Joseph
Noble, Thomas
Nye, Sturgis
Osborn, William
Page, Ebenezer
Page, Francis
Page, Peter

Pishon, Reuben
Poshard, Abraham
Poshard, David
Snell, Appleton
Spaulding, Sylvester G.
Tuttle, Reuben
Witham, Jesse
Wyman, Starkey

Waiter.
Bodfish, William, Jr.

Capt. A. Lesley's Company, Lieut. Col. E. Sherwin's Regiment.
From Sept. 13 to Sept. 25, 1814. Raised at Sidney. Service at Augusta.

RANK AND NAME.
Amasa Lesley, Captain
Bethure Perry, Lieutenant
David Daniels, Ensign

Ebenezer Perry, Sergeant
Rufus Emerson, Sergeant
Francis Smiler, Sergeant
John Bragg, Sergeant
John Davis, Sergeant
Zenas Perry, Sergeant
Robert Packard, Corporal
Abel Sawtelle, Corporal

Woodis Royal, Corporal
Seth Perry, Musician

Privates.
Bacheler, Samuel
Blasdell, Daniel
Blasedell, Samuel
Bragg, Shubal
Chamberlin, William
Chase, James
Church, Randall
Davis, Charles
Day, Benjamin

Dowty, Elias
Ellis, Robert
Emmerson, Hazen
Handy, James
Moore, Collins
Moore, Nathan
Morse, Newbury
Scudder, William
Thomas, John
Thomas, Jonah
Townsend, Daniel
Townsend, Samuel

Capt. S. Lovejoy's Company, Lieut. Col. E. Sherwin's Regiment.
From Sept. 13 to Sept. 24, 1814. Raised at Sidney. Service at Augusta.

RANK AND NAME.
Stephen Lovejoy, Captain
John Ellis, Ensign

John Pinkham, Sergeant
John Sawtelle, Sergeant
Joseph Hastings, Sergeant

Privates.
Baker, Amariah
Beck, Thomas
Branch, Benjamin, Jr.
Branch, Palmer
Branch, Tibbetts

Cummings, Samuel
Dutton, John
Dyer, Moses
Ellis, Samuel
Faught, Philip
Faught, Samuel
Field, Benjamin
Hamlin, Perez
Hastings, Matthew
Heath, Asa
Howard, Zenas
Hutchason, John
Libbey, Daniel
Lovejoy, Joseph

Matthews, John
Moore, Ebenezer
Pinkham, Abraham
Pinkham, Walter
Porter, James
Reynolds, Edward
Reynolds, Luther
Reynolds, Thomas
Robison, Samuel
Shaw, James
Thayer, Barnabas
Thayer, Daniel

Capt. S. Morrell's Company, Lieut. Col. E. Sherwin's Regiment.
From Sept. 13 to Sept. 24, 1814. Raised at Dearborn.

RANK AND NAME.
Stephen Morrell, Captain
Oliver Richardson, Lieutenant
Solomon Varney, Ensign

John Penny, Jr., Sergeant
Henry Bickford, Sergeant
Moses Bickford, Sergeant

Samuel Bickford, Sergeant
Robert Whitehouse, Corporal
Levi Wade, Corporal
Samuel Bickford, Corporal
Henry Richardson, Jr., Corporal
Joseph Howland, Musician
Ezra Page, Musician

Privates.
Blake, John
Brooks, William
Chote, James
Clark, Josiah
Clark, Samuel
Decker, William
Ellis, Ebenezer

MASSACHUSETTS VOLUNTEER MILITIA IN THE WAR OF 1812.   263

Capt. S. Morrell's Company, Lieut. Col. E. Sherwin's Regiment — Concluded.

Privates — Concluded.
Ellis, John
Ellis, Jonathan
Green, Daniel
Hall, Aaron, Jr.
Holmes, Ebenezer
Homer, John
Hussey, Reuben
Hussey, Samuel
James, Benjamin
Kineson, Job

Libby, Peter
Lord, William
Maine, Jacob
Merry, Stephen
Mosher, Caleb
Murry, Joshua
Osborn, Cyrus
Penny, George
Penny, Nehemiah
Purkins, Daniel
Rowe, William Jr.,

Richardson, Anthony W.
Thayer, Alvin
Tuttle, John
Whitehouse, Isaac
Whitehouse, Nathaniel
Whitehouse, Thomas
Wickford, Hilles
Witham, James
Young, Asa

Capt. R. Smith's Company, Lieut. Col. E. Sherwin's Regiment.
From Sept. 13 to Sept. 24, 1814. Raised at Sidney. Service at Augusta.

RANK AND NAME.
Richard Smith, Captain
John Robinson, Ensign

Privates.
Abbott, Abial
Abbott, Samuel
Bickford, Abijah
Bolton, William
Craig, Freeman
Crosby, William
Cummings, Joseph
Cummings, Samuel
Dillanse, Caleb

Dillingham, Anson
Dinsmore, Samuel
Dyer, Jonathan
Ellis, William
Emerson, Isaac
Gifford, William
Hammond, Paul
Hubbard, Noah
Jacobs, Daniel
Jones, Samuel C.
Langley, Edmund
Leonard, Caleb
Lincoln, William
Nash, Joseph

Pitt, Adam
Pitts, Ichabod
Savage, James
Savage, John
Sawtelle, Asa
Smith, Samuel
Stanley, Leonard
Trask, Ebenezer
Ward, Thomas
Weeks, David
Wilbur, Caleb
Wilbur, David
Wood, Obadiah
Wood, Ralph

Capt. Ansel Toby's Company, Lieut. Col. E. Sherwin's Regiment.
From Sept. 13 to Sept. 28, 1814. Raised at Sidney. Service at Augusta.

RANK AND NAME.
Ansel Toby, Captain

Elias Burgess, Sergeant, 11 days' service
Joseph Nye, Corporal, 8 days' service

Privates.
Allen, Ansel, 11 days' service
Allen, Moses
Bates, Elijah
Bates, James
Bates, Silas
Cannon, Nathan

Cleveland, Timothy
Coffin, Charles
Davis, Joseph, 8 days' service
Fish, Elisha
Gibbs, Reuben, 11 days' service
Nye, Ezra
Tibbitts, George, 11 days' service

Capt. J. Hitchings' Company, Lieut. Col. E. Sherwin's Regiment.
From Sept. 14 to Sept. 25, 1814. Raised at Waterville. Service at Augusta.

RANK AND NAME.
Joseph Hitchings, Captain
Samuel Webb, Lieutenant
Thomas McFarland, Ensign

Josiah Jacobs, Sergeant
Solomon Berry, Sergeant
Abraham Butts, Sergeant
Abraham Merrill, Sergeant
Calvin L. Getchell, Sergeant
Peletiah Soule, Corporal
William Watson, Corporal
Lewis Tower, Musician
David Low, Musician

Privates.
Bacon, Columbus
Bennett, John
Blanchard, Jonas
Clifford, John
Clifford, Richard
Cool, Jacob
Getchell, Abel
Hume, William
Parker, David
Parker, Zacheus
Phillips, William
Priest, David
Readington, Samuel

Readington, Silas
Readington, William
Riker, Moses
Smith, Benjamin
Smith, William
Soule, David
Stagpole, John
Sweetser, Richard
Sweetser, William
Tower, Stephen

Capt. J. Minot's Company, Lieut. Col. E. Sherwin's Regiment.
From Sept. 14 to Sept. 25, 1814. Raised at Belgrade. Service at Augusta.

RANK AND NAME.
James Minot, Captain
John Page, Lieutenant

Lewis Page, Sergeant
Samuel Page, Sergeant
Richard Mills, Sergeant
Lemuel Lombard, Corporal
Charles Lombard, Corporal
Wentworth Stewart, Corporal
James Black, Corporal
David Wyman, Musician

Privates.
Barry, Daniel
Brailey, Amos
Brailey, James

Brailey, Russel
Brailey, William
Brownell, George
Burbank, Eleazer
Burbank, Silas
Clark, Joseph
Damaron, Samuel
Dudley, Gilman
Dutton, Asa
Farnham, Samuel
Gould, Lemuel
Hancock, John
Merchant, Ebenezer
Merchant, Edward
Moshier, David
Page, Charles
Page, James

Penney, Daniel
Richardson, Silas
Rogers, John
Rowe, Asa
Rowe, Caleb
Rowe, Elisha
Stevens, Jonathan
Stevens, Thomas
Taylor, Elias
Taylor, John
Tilton, Jeremiah
Townsend, Robert
Welman, James
Welman, John
Yeaton, James

Capt. W. Pullen's Company, Lieut. Col. E. Sherwin's Regiment.
From Sept. 14 to Sept. 25, 1814. Raised at Waterville. Service at Augusta.

RANK AND NAME.
William Pullen, Captain
Leonard Cornforth, Ensign

Ichabod Smith, Sergeant
Rufus Ricker, Sergeant
John Hallet, Sergeant
Isaiah Hallett, Sergeant
Samuel Merry, Corporal
James Gilbert, Corporal
Wiman Sherry, Corporal
Thomas Stephens, Corporal
Isaac Gay, Musician
Dexter Pullen, Musician
Asa Bates, Musician

Privates.
Badger, Philip
Bassey, Thomas
Burgess, James
Cobb, John
Combs, David
Crowell, Hiram
Crowell, Isaiah
Crowell, Miller
Crowell, Seth
Gage, Seth
Gibbs, Dennis
Gleason, Bryant
Hallett, Elisha
Hayward, Timothy
Hodgdon, Elijah
Hussey, Ebenezer

Lander, Abraham
Lander, Moody
Lewis, Asa
Lewis, William
Low, Ivory
Merrifield, William
Rice, James
Ricker, George
Ricker, George, 2d
Soule, Philander
Stephens, Benjamin
Terrell, Isaac
Tupper, Samuel
Wade, Lorin
Wheeler, Cyrus
White, James

Captain J. Sylvester's Company, Lieut. Col. E. Sherwin's Regiment.
From Sept. 14 to Sept. 25, 1814. Raised at Belgrade. Service at Augusta.

RANK AND NAME.
Joseph Sylvester, Captain
Levi Bean, Lieutenant
Isaac Lord, Ensign

Daniel Stevens, Sergeant
Samuel Smith, Sergeant
William Stevens, Jr., Sergeant
John Sylvester, Sergeant
Jonathan Hill, Corporal
Ephraim Tibbitts, Corporal
William Wells, Corporal
Samuel Tupper, Corporal
Samuel Littlefield, Musician
Isaac Farnham, Musician

Privates.
Appleton, Joseph
Austin, John
Austin, Nahum
Burks, Thomas
Crain, Samuel
Damaron, Joshua
Downs, Thomas
Dunn, Jeremy
Dunn, Nathaniel
Farnham, Moses
Farnham, Samuel
Fitch, William
Frost, Samuel
Hanson, Nehemiah
Holmes, John
Jewett, John
Jones, Richard

Jones, Samuel
Littlefield, Frost
Lord, John
Mills, Richard
Penney, John
Rollins, John
Rollins, Jonathan
Rollins, Valentine
Rollins, William
Sylvester, David
Tibbitts, John
Tibbitts, John, 2d
Tibbitts, Moses
Towles, Thomas
Turner, Asa
Wells, Robert
Yeaton, Samuel

MASSACHUSETTS VOLUNTEER MILITIA IN THE WAR OF 1812.   265

Lieut. Col. E. Sherwin's Regiment of Drafted Militia.
From Sept. 24 to Nov. 10, 1814. Service at Wiscasset and Edgecomb.

FIELD AND STAFF.		NONCOMMISSIONED STAFF.
Elnathan Sherwin, Lieutenant, Waterville	Joseph M. Hallett, Quartermaster, Waterville	Charles Hayden, Jr., Sergeant Major
Richard M. Dorr, Major, Waterville	David Wheeler, Paymaster, Waterville	Benjamin Foster, Quartermaster Sergeant
Nathan Stanley, Major, China	Moses Appleton, Surgeon, Winslow	David Low, Drum Major
Ephraim Getchell, Adjutant, Waterville	Joseph Bachellor, Surgeon's Mate, Norridgewock	Thomas Leeman, Fife Major

Capt. J. Collins' Company, Lieut. Col. E. Sherwin's Regiment.
From Sept. 24 to Nov. 9, 1814. Service at Wiscasset.

RANK AND NAME.		
James Collins, Captain	Curtis, Stephen	Lindsay, James
James Manton, Lieutenant	Daggett, Henry	Lowry, Calvin
Daniel Leighton, Ensign	Dows, Kennel	Moody, James
	Ellis, Benjamin	Moore, Daniel
	Everett, John	Moore, Heman
John Moore, Sergeant	Getchell, Benjamin	Moore, Samuel
Luther Quint, Sergeant	Getchell, Howard	Mullin, Daniel
John Henderson, Sergeant	Goodridge, John	Patten, Joseph
Moses Ayres, Sergeant	Gould, Samuel	Peabody, Oliver
John Holbrook, Corporal	Graham, Jeremiah	Pennell, Joseph
Hartley Colby, Corporal	Gray, Joshua	Richardson, Eben
James Walker, Corporal	Green, John	Robbins, Leonard
Nathaniel Merchant, Corporal	Hannell, John	Rowe, Stephen
Nimrod Eames, Musician	Hayden, James	Rowell, Jonathan
William Lowry, Musician	Hayden, Jonathan	Savage, Charles
	Hilton, Ebenezer	Savage, Robert
Privates.	Hilton, Elisha	Sawyer, Luke
Annis, Rollins	Hilton, Simeon	Stevens, Jonathan
Barker, Jonah	Hooper, Levi	Sweet, Arnold
Bray, Ezekiel	Hutchins, David	Walker, John
Cleaves, Abraham	Lane, Moses	Witham, Asa
Colby, Harry	Lincoln, Ezekiel	Wyman, James

Capt. J. Farwell's Company, Lieut. Col. E. Sherwin's Regiment.
From Sept. 24 to Nov. 10, 1814. Raised at Vassalboro. Service at Wiscasset.

RANK AND NAME.	Bran, Simon	Lancaster, Thomas
Jeremiah Farwell, Captain	Brown, John, Jr.	Larrabee, John
Nathaniel Spratt, Lieutenant	Bryant, Seth	Lewis, Charles
Nehemiah Gould, Ensign	Cone, Isaac	McLaughlin, George
	Cown, Thomas	McLaughlin, John
Charles Webber, Sergeant	Crosby, Manson	McManus, Hugh
Amariah Hardin, Jr., Sergeant	Crosby, William	McNally, Arthur
Jabez Crowell, Sergeant	Dearborn, Asa	Meservey, Charles
Elijah Morse, Sergeant	Doe, David	Michaels, George, Jr.
Rowland Frye, Corporal	Farwell, Ebenezer	Mitchell, Joseph, 4th
Samuel Brand, Corporal	Farwell, Hannibal	Monk, William, Jr.
Benjamin Malone, Corporal	Freeman, Reuben	Morrison, Elijah
Thomas Whitehouse, Corporal	Frees, Abraham	Morse, Zebulon, Jr.
Washington Drake, Musician	Frye, John	Nickerson, Nehemiah
Timothy Waterhouse, Musician	Gould, Crowell	Palmer, William
	Hallett, Watson F.	Parker, Joseph
Privates.	Ham, Enoch	Reynolds, Parmenus
Bagley, Green	Handy, Lemuel	Roundy, Samuel
Bartlett, Rufus	Hawes, Burnard	Shaw, Advertis
Bassett, Jabez	Hood, Christopher	Shaw, Freeman
Bassett, Joseph	Hunter, David	Smart, Jonathan
Brackett, Moses	Jaquith, Andrew	Smith, James

MASSACHUSETTS VOLUNTEER MILITIA IN THE WAR OF 1812.

Capt. J. Farwell's Company, Lieut. Col. E. Sherwin's Regiment — Concluded.

Privates — Concluded.
Smith, John M.
Sparrow, Jonathan
Spratt, George
Stevens, John
Thombs, William
Vickery, Joel
Ward, Nehemiah
Webb, John
Webber, John
Webber, Sylvanus
Weymouth, Solomon
Whittemore, Hill
Wilson, John
Wing, Ezekiel
Winn, Joseph
Wood, George
Wood, Jordan
Wyman, Fairfield

Capt. I. Holt's Company, Lieut. Col. E. Sherwin's Regiment.
From Sept. 24 to Nov. 10, 1814. Raised at Canaan and vicinity. Service at Wiscasset.

RANK AND NAME.
Isaac Holt, Captain
James Thompson, Lieutenant
Josiah Blackstone, Ensign

John Pooler, Sergeant
John W. Moore, Sergeant
Benjamin Fairbanks, Sergeant
Valentine Look, Sergeant
David Lambert, Corporal
Nathaniel Sawyer, Corporal
Jonas Wheeler, Corporal
Lemuel Adams, Corporal
Benjamin McDaniels, Musician
Phineas Hunnewell, Musician

Privates.
Ames, Eliakim
Ames, Isaac F.
Ames, Jonas
Annis, George
Booker, Charles
Burrell, Joseph
Buzzell, Elisha
Church, James
Collins, Barnett

Combey, David C.
Davis, Robert
Dowe, Levi
Fairbrother, James
Gerald, David F.
Grant, Christopher
Graves, William
Hanson, Thomas
Harding, Benjamin
Hart, John
Hayden, James
Hill, Amos S.
Hinds, Nimrod
Hobbs, George
Horn, Benjamin
Hoxie, Barrett
Jenkins, Joseph
Jewett, Joshua
Kidder, Isaac
Lambert, Solomon
Laughton, Asa
Laughton, Luther
Lewis, Isaac
Lyford, Levi
Mason, Abijah
Mayo, Seth

Mitchell, Andrew
Oakes, Simeon
Osborne, George
Pishon, Frederic
Pratt, Jacob
Pratt, Joseph
Rines, George
Russell, Luther
Russell, Ziba
Sanborn, Levi
Sanborn, Newell
Shorey, Samuel
Smith, John
Smith, William
Titcomb, Benjamin
Tucker, Stephen
Watson, Jonathan
Weymouth, Samuel
Whidden, James
Whidden, James, 2d
Whitcher, Artemas
Whitman, John
Whitney, John
Wyman, John, 2d
York, Lewis

Capt. A. Lesley's Company, Lieut. Col. E. Sherwin's Regiment.
From Sept. 24 to Nov. 10, 1814. Raised at Sidney and vicinity. Service at Wiscasset.

RANK AND NAME.
Amasa Lesley, Captain
Benjamin Sawtelle, Lieutenant
William Bodfish, Ensign

Elias Doughty, Sergeant
Samuel Page, Sergeant
David Guilford, Sergeant
John Bragg, Jr., Sergeant
Wentworth Stewart, Corporal
Daniel Jones, Corporal
Robert Packard, Corporal
Ebenezer Trusk, Corporal
Nathaniel Dunn, Musician
Richard Jones, Musician

Privates.
Appleton, Joseph
Bates, Asa
Berry, Daniel
Blaisdell, Daniel
Bodfish, William, Jr.
Brailey, Amos
Brailey, Russell

Burbank, Silas
Burke, Thomas
Burrill, Benoni
Burrill, Josiah
Chamberlain, William
Chase, Arthur
Cook, Nathaniel
Craig, Freeman
Cummings, Joseph
Davis, Charles S.
Decker, Steven
Dinsmore, Samuel
Downs, Thomas
Dudley, Gilman
Dunbar, John
Dyer, Jonathan
Ellis, Robert
Fish, Peleg
Gaffield, Abram
Handy, James H.
Hubbard, Luroy
Hubbard, Noah
Kendall, Jonas
Kingsley, Silas

Lord, John
Morse, Newbury
Moshier, Stephen
Page, Ebenezer
Page, James
Pishon, Reuben
Pitts, Adam
Rollins, Freeman
Rollins, John
Rowe, Caleb
Rowe, Elisha
Sawtelle, Moses, Jr.
Smiley, Lemuel
Spaulding, Sylvester
Stevens, Jonathan
Stilson, Lemuel
Taylor, Elias, Jr.
Thomas, John
Towle, Thomas
Wellman, James
Wood, Thomas
Woodcock, George
Woodworth, Benjamin

MASSACHUSETTS VOLUNTEER MILITIA IN THE WAR OF 1812. 267

Capt. S. Lovejoy's Company, Lieut. Col. E. Sherwin's Regiment.
From Sept. 24 to Nov. 10, 1814. Raised at Sidney and vicinity. Service at Wiscasset.

RANK AND NAME.
Stephen Lovejoy, Captain
Joseph Warren, Lieutenant
Ebenezer Lawrence, Ensign

Palmer Branch, Sergeant
John Bates, Sergeant
Jabez Harlow, Sergeant
Joshua Grant, Sergeant
Levi Meade, Corporal
Ebenezer Morse, Corporal
Winthrop Robinson, Musician

Privates.
Bickford, Abijah
Bickford, Henry
Blanchard, Ellis
Blanchard, Jonas
Burgess, Ellis
Cannon, Nathan
Carsen, Seward
Chamberlain, John
Cleveland, Timothy
Clifford, John
Coombs, David

Cowan, James
Crowell, Seth
Davis, Benjamin
Davis, Walter
Ellis, John
Ellis, Jonathan
Fall, Aaron, Jr.
Faning, Pliney
Fish, Eliab, Jr.
Gage, Reuben
Green, George
Hallett, Joseph M.
Haskins, Matthew
Hayward, Timothy B.
Hodgdon, Joseph
Holway, Joseph
Homer, John
Howard, Zenas
Hume, William
Hussey, Samuel
Hutchinson, John
Lander, James
Lawrence, Henry
Lawrence, James
Lawrence, William

Lewis, William, Jr.
Lovejoy, Albert
Lovejoy, Samuel
Magoon, Joseph
Mains, Jacob
Nye, Alden
Nye, Ezra
Parker, David
Parker, Joseph
Penney, Aiba
Pinkham, Reuben
Richardson, Joel
Ricker, Moses
Robinson, Wentworth
Shorey, James
Sloan, John
Snell, Bezar
Soule, George
Thayer, Alvin
Thayer, Barnabus
Tozier, Simeon
Tozier, William
Whelden, Peter
Young, Moses

Capt. J. Wellington's Company, Lieut. Col. E. Sherwin's Regiment.
From Sept. 24 to Nov. 10, 1814. Raised at Albion and vicinity. Service at Wiscasset.

RANK AND NAME.
Joel Wellington, Captain
Washington Heald, Lieutenant
Israel Richardson, Ensign

Robert Richardson, Sergeant
Charles Stratton, Sergeant
William Eames, Sergeant
Samuel Ward, Sergeant
Richard V. Hayden, Corporal
Nathaniel Merchant, Corporal
Andrew S. Perkins, Corporal
Benjamin Reed, Jr., Corporal
Odiorne Heald, Musician
John Kidder, Jr., Musician
Samuel Gibson, Musician

Privates.
Ally, John
Andrews, Samuel, Jr.
Arlean, James
Bangs, Alkanah
Barker, Jotham
Barton, Herman C.
Bates, Samuel
Bean, Daniel
Bixby, John
Brown, John
Bryant, David
Burgess, Samuel
Burgess, Zadoc

Clifford, David
Crowell, David
Doe, Andrew
Doe, Jonathan
Evans, Thomas
Ewer, John, Jr.
Farnham, Rufus
Faught, Nathaniel
Field, George
Ford, James
Fowler, Nathan
Getchell, Abial
Gibson, Andrew
Hanson, Caleb
Haskell, Benjamin
Hawes, David
Hawes, Ebenezer
Hawes, Isaiah
Hawes, James
Hawes, Seth
Heald, Jonas
Jackson, John
Lambert, John
Low, John
McKenny, William
McLaughlin, Abraham
Moore, Oliver
Moore, Samuel
Nichols, Stephen
Parker, Simeon
Pollard, Barton

Pollard, Henry D.
Pollard, Levi
Pollard, William
Pressy, Thomas, Jr.
Randall, Reuben
Richardson, Andrew
Richardson, Ebenezer
Richardson, Seth
Richardson, Seth, 2d
Rollins, George
Rollins, Nathaniel
Rollins, Thomas
Sewall, Daniel
Small, Phineas
Snell, David
Spiller, Samuel
Stackpole, William
Studley, John
Thatcher, Edmund
Walker, Timothy
Ward, William
Warren, Andrew
Wellington, Erastus
Whitly, William
Whitten, Israel
Wilson, Ephraim
Wilson, Samuel
Winship, Benjamin
Withee, Samuel
Woodson, Daniel, Jr.
Worthen, Samuel

Capt. A. Fletcher's Company, Lieut. Col. E. Sherwin's Regiment.

From Sept. 25 to Nov. 10, 1814. Raised at Bingham and vicinity. Service at Wiscasset.

RANK AND NAME.
Asa Fletcher, Captain
John Neal, Lieutenant
Benjamin Goodridge, Ensign

James Baker, Sergeant
Joseph Maynard, Sergeant
Israel Drew, Sergeant
Samuel Leighton, Sergeant
Reuben Smith, Corporal
David Whipple, Corporal
Joseph Moses, Corporal
Francis Bunker, Corporal
Abel Parlin, Musician
John Moore, Musician

Privates.
Baker, David
Ball, John
Benjamin, John
Blagden, Charles
Brown, Amaziah
Brown, Jeremiah
Brown, Nicholas
Bunker, Joseph
Bunker, Robert
Card, Simeon
Chase, Joel
Cook, Joseph
Corson, Samuel
Drew, Benjamin
Durell, Joseph
Dyer, Asa
Emery, Silas
Fellows, Isaac
Folsom, Samuel
Frost, Joseph
Gibson, John
Goldsmith, David
Gould, Elijah
Grant, John
Hall, Jeremiah
Haskell, Joshua
Hatch, Nehemiah
Heald, Thatcher
Howes, Edmond
Hunnewell, Barnabas
Jackman, James
Kelliher, Samuel
Knight, Solomon
Knowles, William
Lambert, Solomon
Leighton, John
Maynard, Simon
Moore, Aaron
Pierce, Nathaniel
Russell, Calvin
Smith, David
Smith, Zenos
Stafford, Amherst
Stafford, Isaac
Stinson, David
Tebbitts, James
Temple, Luther
Town, Samuel
Tuttle, Jonathan
Watson, Jonathan
Wentworth, John
Woodman, Nathan

Capt. J. Greenleaf's Company, Lieut. Col. E. Sherwin's Regiment.

From Sept. 26 to Nov. 10, 1814. Raised at Stark and vicinity. Service at Wiscasset.

RANK AND NAME.
John Greenleaf, Captain
Abram Greenleaf, Lieutenant
Mathew Taylor, Ensign

Thomas Williamson, Sergeant
Thomas Greenleaf, Sergeant
Edgar Hilton, Sergeant
Martin Burns, Sergeant
Samuel Albra, Corporal
William Ladd, Corporal
Robinson Gilman, Corporal
Joseph Ames, Corporal
Benjamin Rollins, Musician
William Johnson, Musician

Privates.
Arnold, James
Bates, Isaac
Beal, Harvey
Beede, Aaron
Boyd, John
Boynton, George
Boynton, John
Boynton, William
Bradbury, John S.
Burns, John
Chandler, Daniel
Chapman, Amasa
Chapman, Samuel
Corkins, Ephraim
Crandall, Soltner
Crompton, George
Dean, Ebenezer
Dickerson, James
Drew, Elisha
Dudley, James
Dutton, Josiah
Ellis, John
Eveleth, Joseph
Fish, Eleazer
Fish, John
Frederick, Valentine
Frederick, William
Gray, Ebenezer
Gray, John
Green, Stephen
Green, Stephen, 2d
Groton, Leonard
Hawes, Lemuel
Hilton, John
Hobbs, Joseph
Jacobs, Theodore
Johnson, Doremus
Lovejoy, William
Luce, Benjamin
Martin, David
Meade, Henry
Morse, Caleb
Ohlin, John
Pierce, Isaac
Qurley, Stephen
Riggs, Stenford
Robbins, Ammial
Rowe, Ebenezer
Stanley, James
Swift, Ebenezer
Taylor, James
Taylor, Joel
Taylor, Josiah
Vose, Eben
Washburn, Hosea
Wells, David
Whitcomb, Levi
Williams, Thomas
Williamson, Sylvanus

Lieut. Col. J. Spring's Regiment.
Stationed at Saco.

FIELD AND STAFF.
John Spring, Lieutenant Colonel, Standish
Samuel Merrill, Major, Biddeford

William Waterman, Major, Buckston
John F. Scammon, Adjutant, Saco
Enoch Moody, Quartermaster, Saco
Josiah Calef, Paymaster, Saco

Thomas Thornton, Surgeon, Buckston
John Cogswell, Chaplain, Saco

Maj. S. Merrill's Command, Lieut. Col. J. Spring's Regiment.
From Sept. 19 to Oct. 12, 1814. Stationed at Saco.

RANK AND NAME.
Samuel Merrill, Major
David Coffin, Adjutant
Joseph Stimpson, Captain
James Woodman, Jr., Captain
Isaac Felch, Lieutenant
David Coffin, Lieutenant
Asa Johnson, Ensign
Moses Dunn, Ensign

Charles Alden, Sergeant
Samuel Gilpatrick, Sergeant
Thomas Foster, Sergeant
James Pierce, Sergeant
Ebenezer Sawyer, Sergeant
Samuel Hill, Sergeant
Stephen Lane, Sergeant
William Woodman, Sergeant
Moses Dale, Musician
John N. Stinson, Musician
Thomas Wentworth, Musician
Stephen Hanson, Musician

Privates.
Adams, Joseph
Allen, Elijah
Allen, Theophilus
Andrews, Elisha, Jr.
Barker, Simeon
Boothby, Samuel
Burlingham, C. F. or T.
Chadbourne, Ira
Clark, Artherton
Clark, Joshua
Cole, Robert
Day, Jonathan
Dinger, Jeremiah
Dole, Daniel
Dunnell, Joseph, Jr.
Durgin, Joshua
Eaton, Aaron
Elwell, Otheil
Field, John
Gordan, Jabez
Harmon, Jonathan

Harper, Samuel, Jr.
Hill, Daniel, Jr.
Kinsman, Thomas F.
Lane, Silas
Lord, Daniel
Miles, Joel
Miles, John
Morrill, John A.
Norris, Ezra
Norris, John
Perkins, John
Perry, William
Philpot, Andrew
Philpot, Moses
Philpot, Richard
Pierce, Nicholas
Spencer, D. S.
Spencer, John
Tarbox, Stephen
Tucker, Devenport
Woodman, Isaac

Capt. J. Woodman's Company, Lieut. Col. J. Spring's Regiment.
From Sept. 19 to Oct. 12, 1814. On the sea shore as guard under Lieut. Col. J. Spring. Buxton Light Infantry Company.

RANK AND NAME.
James Woodman, Captain
David Coffin, Lieutenant
Moses Dunn, Ensign

Ebenezer Sawyer, Sergeant
Samuel Hill, Sergeant
Stephen Lane, Sergeant
William Woodman, Sergeant
Stephen Hanson, Musician
Thomas Wentworth, Musician

Privates.
Andrews, Elisha
Berry, Ephraim

Boothby, Enoch
Burlingham, Carpenter J.
Davis, Moses
Dunnell, Joseph, Jr.
Elwell, Athiel
Hanson, Daniel, Jr.
Hanson, Elijah
Hanson, Michael
Harmon, Jonathan
Harmon, Pelatiah
Hill, Daniel, Jr.
Jordan, Jabez
Lane, Silas
Lord, James
Lord, John

Lovett, Benjamin
Merrill, John
Moulton, John
Owen, William
Palmer, Richard
Pennell, Jabez
Plaisted, Joseph
Sands, James
Sands, Samuel
Severs, Henry
Spencer, D. S.
Spencer, John
Towle, Samuel
Woodman, Isaac

Muster Roll of Capt. D. Appleton's Company, Lieut. Col. J. Spring's Regiment.
From Oct. 10 to Nov. 11, 1814. Raised at Buxton. Service at Saco.

RANK AND NAME.
Daniel Appleton, Jr., Captain
Thomas Sands, Lieutenant
Joel Marshall, Ensign

Lemuel Foss, Sergeant
Rufus Foss, Sergeant
Samuel G. Bennett or Dennett, Sergeant
James Thompson, Musician
William Goodwin, Musician

Privates.
Berry, David
Berry, Rufus
Bond, Samuel
Boynton, Isaac
Cousins, Joseph
Dean, D. E.
Derham, Joseph
Dresser, Edmund
Emery, Haven
Fast, Walter

Flood or Hood, William
Fogg, Hezekiah
Goldthwight, Thomas
Gordon, Amos
Haley, William
Hanscomb, John, Jr.
Hanscomb, Joseph
Harding, Simon
Harmon, James, Jr.
Harmon, Stephen
Henson, Moses

Muster Roll of Capt. D. Appleton's Company, Lieut. Col. J. Spring's Regiment — Concluded.

Privates — Concluded.
Hill, Samuel, Jr.
Hobson, Samuel
Hobson, William
Hooker, Benning
Ladd, Thomas
Ladd, William
McCornison, Isaac
Miller, Nathaniel
Nutter, Jacob

Owen, Elijah
Patterson, Aaron
Patterson, John M.
Patterson, Nathan
Patterson, Richard
Patterson, William
Ridlen, Joseph
Sawyer, Justum
Simpson, Joshua
Smith, William, Jr.

Staples, Joseph
Tarbox, John
Tarbox, Jonathan
Tarbox, Samuel
Tarbox, Samuel, Jr.
Watson, Alexander
Wood, James
Woodman, Levi
Woodman, William

Muster Roll of Capt. S. Strout's Company, Lieut. Col. J. Spring's Regiment.
From Oct. 30 to Nov. 13, 1814. Raised at Limington. Service at Saco.

RANK AND NAME.
Solomon Strout, Captain
Henry Dole, Lieutenant
Elijah Chadbourn, Ensign

William Mills, Sergeant
William P. Mew (?), Sergeant
Elisha Strout, Sergeant
Richard Hamilton, Sergeant
Solomon McKinney, Musician
Moses Chase, Musician

Privates.
Anderson, William
Bangs, Silvanus
Brooks, Samuel
Carpenter, Andrew
Carpenter, Samuel
Chase, James

Darling or Furlong, Edmund
Durgin, Abraham
Foster, Brad
Gould, Ebenezer
Grant, Benjamin
Haggens, Aaron
Hamilton, Edward
Hanson, Thomas
Heard, John
Hopkins, John
Hopkins, Samuel
Imbener, Edward
King, David
Knight, Jonathan
Knock, Reuben
Leavitt, Bracet
Lewis, Henry
Manson, Joseph
Mesener, Joseph

Mesener, Rufus
Nason, Simon
Pitts, John
Randell, William
Richard, James
Robinson, Thomas
Sawyer, Michael
Small, Ebenezer
Small, Ephraim
Smith, Clement
Smith, John
Smith, John, 2d
Strout, Joseph
Strout, Samuel
Sutton, George
Walker, Simeon
Woodward, Joseph

Lieut. Col. J. Stone's Regiment.
From Sept. 11 to Sept. 25, 1814. Stationed at Wiscasset and vicinity.

FIELD AND STAFF.
John Stone, Lieutenant Colonel, Gardiner
Ruell Howard, Major, Augusta
Henry W. Fuller, Major, Augusta
Enoch Hale, Jr., Adjutant, Gardiner
Gideon Farrell, Quartermaster, Hallowell
Rufus K. Page, Paymaster, Hallowell
Eliphalet Gillet, Chaplain, Hallowell

Ariel Mann, Surgeon, Hallowell
Joel B. Ellis, Surgeon's Mate, Augusta

NONCOMMISSIONED STAFF.
Benjamin Davenport, Sergeant Major
James Tarbox, Quartermaster Sergeant
Roswell Whittemore, Drum Major
John Wadsworth, Fife Major

Waiters.
Davison, John
Wentworth, John
Young, Servant

MASSACHUSETTS VOLUNTEER MILITIA IN THE WAR OF 1812. 271

Capt. D. P. Bailey's Company, Lieut. Col. J. Stone's Regiment.
From Sept. 11 to Sept. 25, 1814. Raised at Pittstown. Service at Wiscasset.

RANK AND NAME.
David P. Bailey, Captain
John Blanchard, Lieutenant
Jacob Bailey, Ensign

Joseph Follansbee, Sergeant
Elihu Lord, Sergeant
Joseph Kidder, Sergeant
George Williamson, Sergeant
William Troop, Corporal
Nathaniel Brown, Corporal
George Jewett, Corporal
Tristram Folsom, Corporal
James Bailey, Musician
Alexander Blanchard, Musician

Privates.
Ballard, Daniel
Bean, John
Blair, Eben
Blake, Ebenezer
Blanchard, Leonard
Bliss, Obed
Brown, Joseph
Colburne, John
Colburne, Joseph
Culvert, Richard
Cutts, Samuel
Eastman, Benjamin
Eldred, Michell
Fitch, Andrew
Flitner, Thomas
Freeman, Charles
Freeman, William
Fuller, Thomas
Grant, Charles
Hanover, William
Hill, Josiah
Hill, Nathaniel
Jackson, Benjamin
Jewett, Moses
Lapham, James
Lord, Charles
Mason, Stephen
Moore, Robert
Moores, Thomas
Moores, Tristram
Noyes, Isaac
Robinson, Stephen
Scott, Daniel
Scott, John
Shepherd, Charles
Stevens, John
Stevens, William
Stiffin, Charles
Troop, Alexander
White, Benjamin

Capt. B. Burbank's Company, Lieut. Col. J. Stone's Regiment.
From Sept. 11 to Sept. 25, 1814. Raised at Augusta. Service at Wiscasset.

RANK AND NAME.
Benjamin Burbank, Captain
Nathan Wood, Lieutenant
David Church, Ensign

Ephraim Dutton, Sergeant
Benjamin Ross, Sergeant
Ebenezer B. Williams, Sergeant
Philip W. Peck, Corporal
John Hamlin, Corporal
William B. Johnson, Corporal
Thomas Elmes, Corporal
Bartlet Lancaster, Corporal

Privates.
Babcock, William
Bates, Solomon
Bond, John
Briggs, John
Burton, James, Jr.
Coffin, David N. B.
Conn, John
Conner, David Y.
Cowan, Isaac, Jr.
Dillingham, Albert A.
Dillingham, Joseph P.
Elmes, Abner
Elmes, Elijah
Goldthwait, Jacob
Hebard, Davison
Hilton, Daniel, Jr.
Jones, John, 2d
Lovejoy, Samuel
Lunt, Simeon I.
Mason, Samuel R.
Niles, John
Page, David
Perkins, Jonathan
Prescott, Jonathan
Ranlett, Daniel
Safford, Moses
Savage, David B.
Savage, Isaac
Sewell, William
Shurts, Moody
Soule, Abraham
Smith, Joel
Sullivan, Dennis
Thwing, James

Capt. D. C. Burr's Company, Lieut. Col. J. Stone's Regiment.
From Sept. 11 to Sept. 25, 1814. Raised at Litchfield. Service at Wiscasset.

RANK AND NAME.
David C. Burr, Captain
Nathaniel Marston, Lieutenant
Ebenezer Colby, Ensign

Andrew Goodwin, Sergeant
Daniel Herrick, Sergeant
Jesse Tucker, Sergeant
James Parker, Sergeant
William Hutchinson, Corporal
John Sears, Corporal
Joshua Ritchinson, Jr., Corporal
Daniel Cram, Corporal
Cypron I. Edwards, Musician
David Fuller, Musician
William Brown, Musician
James Goodwin, Musician

Privates.
Batchelder, Abraham
Batchelder, Philip
Briggs, Simeon
Brown, James
Chamberlin, Benjamin
Cole, Abel
Cram, Stephen
Day, Levi
Doe, Joshua
Doe, Simeon, Jr.
Douglass, Joseph
Dyer, Paul
Fuller, William, Jr.
Gelusha, Abijah
Glass, Moses
Glass, Nehemiah
Goodwin, Daniel
Goodwin, Simeon, Jr.
Gordon, Thomas
Hanscom, Charles
Hanscom, Henry
Haskell, Isaac
Hildreth, Robert
Jewell, Gould
Judkins, Abraham
Judkins, Zacheus
Larned, Abel
Marston, James
Merrill, Daniel
Nash, Samuel
Nash, William, Jr.
Neal, Joseph, Jr.
Pike, Jesse

Capt. D. C. Burr's Company, Lieut. Col. J. Stone's Regiment — Concluded.

Privates — Concluded.
Pinkham, Nathaniel
Potter, Bailey
Potter, Hugh, Jr.
Potter, Simeon
Richardson, Jonathan
Richardson, Thomas
Roberts, Joseph
Robinson, Ezekiel

Sampson, William
Spear, Israel
Spear, Thomas
Stevens, Aaron, Jr.
Stoddard, Amos
Stoddard, Calvin
Taylor, James
Tibbets, James
Tibbets, William

True, John
Wadsworth, Aaron, Jr.
Waterhouse, Ezekiel
Williams, James
Woodberry, Amos
Woodberry, Hugh
Woodberry, True

Capt. J. Davis' Company, Lieut. Col. J. Stone's Regiment.
From Sept. 11 to Sept. 25, 1814. Raised at Gardiner. Service at Wiscasset.

RANK AND NAME.
Jacob Davis, Captain
Ebenezer Moore, Jr., Lieutenant
Arthur Plummer, Ensign

William Partridge, Clerk

Privates.
Adams, David
Alden, Silas
Andrews, Jonathan
Atkins, Eleck
Atkins, John
Ball, Daniel
Bartlett, James
Booker, James
Booker, Nicholas
Byram, Charles
Clay, Daniel
Clay, Richard
Cox, George
Cram, William
Crowell, Benjamin
Crowell, Elisha
Douglas, Zebedee
Eastman, Nathaniel
Edgcomb, Thomas
Fall, Samuel
Gay, Harvey
Gay, Seth, Jr.

Gay, Thomas
Gooding, Nathaniel
Goodwin, Ebenezer
Goodwin, Levi
Gray, Pardon
Hardin, Harlow
Hardin, Pelham
Haseltine, John
Hooker, Revercius
Hopkinson, William
Huntington, John
Jones, John
Jordan, Abraham
Jordan, Benjamin
Jordan, Jeremiah
Laurence, James
Leighton, Nathaniel
Leman, David
Libby, Asa
Libby, Samuel
Libby, Solomon
Marston, James
McCauslin, Henry
McCauslin, James
McLellan, Elkanah
Meader, Benjamin
Merrifield, Samuel
Merrill, William
Miller, Daniel
Moore, John

Moore, John, 2d
Morgan, Ammi
Newell, George
Niles, John
Osgood, Stephen
Peacock, Benjamin
Peacock, Edward
Peacock, James
Perkins, Eliphalet
Plaisted, Ichabod, Jr.
Pratt, Oliver
Randall, Benjamin
Richardson, John
Roberts, Lemuel
Robinson, John
Robinson, William E.
Smith, Amasa
Smith, Hugh
Sprague, Josiah
Tarbox, Eleazer, Jr.
Tarbox, Nathaniel
Tarbox, Saul B.
Tarbox, Zachariah
Towne, John (D.)
Towne, Thomas
Tuck, Samuel
Wentworth, Noah
Wilson, Robert

Capt. B. Dearborn's Company, Lieut. Col. J. Stone's Regiment.
From Sept. 11 to Sept. 25, 1814. Raised at Hallowell. Service at Wiscasset.

RANK AND NAME.
Benjamin Dearborn, Captain
Thomas B. Coolidge, Lieutenant
William Clark, Ensign

Isaac Smith, Sergeant
Enoch Marshall, Sergeant
Ebenezer White, Sergeant
Shephard H. Norris, Sergeant
Ephraim Mayo, Corporal
Thomas Fillebrown, Corporal
John Folsom, Corporal
Benjamin Plummer, Corporal

Seth Sturdevant, Musician
James Batchelder, Musician
Elias Webber, Musician
Bradbury C. Folsom, Musician

Privates.
Blunt, John W.
Clark, Peter, Jr.
Clark, William M.
Davis, John
Dow, Ebenezer
Eastman, David
Fillebrown, William

Goodwin, James
Griffin, William
Hinds, Owen
Hinkley, Levi
Hinkley, Owen
Hussey, James
Hussey, John
Hussey, Obed
Kanavan, John
Lyon, Alpheus, Jr.
McCausland, Alexander
Metcalf, Gorham
Metcalf, Joseph

Capt. B. Dearborn's Company, Lieut. Col. J. Stone's Regiment — Concluded.

Privates — Concluded.
Morrill, Pelatiah
Morse, William, Jr.
Norton, Ebenezer
Nye, Robinson
Palmer, John

Sargent, Lewis
Smith, Daniel
Smith, John
Sweetland, Seth
Thing, Isaiah
Thing, Jonathan

Thing, Joseph
Tuckerman, Stephen
West, Charles C.
West, William
White, Lazarus
White, Timothy

Capt. J. Dennis' Company, Lieut. Col. J. Stone's Regiment.
From Sept. 11 to Sept. 25, 1814. Raised at Litchfield. Service at Wiscasset.

RANK AND NAME.
John Dennis, Captain
Daniel Stevens, Lieutenant
Joseph Jewell, Ensign

Samuel Hutchinson, Sergeant
William Robinson, Sergeant
Joseph Wharff, Sergeant
Israel Hutchinson, Sergeant
Robert Crawford, Corporal
Ebenezer Harriman, Corporal
Moses Williams, Corporal
William Spears, Corporal
John Rollins, Musician
James Hutchinson, Musician
Elijah Palmer, Musician

Privates.
Babb, Joseph
Batchelder, Asa

Berry, Andrew
Butcher, Daniel
Chick, Joseph
Crawford, John
Cunningham, Mark
Harriman, Levi
Huntington, John
Huntington, William
Hutchinson, James
Hutchinson, William
Johnson, Robert
Lincoln, Christopher
Lord, Joseph
Lunt, Joseph
Magoon, Ephraim
Magoon, John
More, Levi
Neal, Samuel
Nelson, Samuel
Owen, Shimmel

Pennel, Isaac
Potter, Alexander
Potter, Amos
Potter, Jeremiah
Potter, William
Richardson, Henry
Richardson, Rufus
Ring, Daniel
Ring, William
Sawyer, Samuel
Spears, Ivory
Springer, James
Stevens, Moses
Towns, Joseph
True, William
Washburn, Benjamin

Capt. A. Fairbanks' Company, Lieut. Col. J. Stone's Regiment.
From Sept. 11 to Sept. 25, 1814. Raised at Winthrop. Service at Wiscasset.

RANK AND NAME.
Asa Fairbanks, Captain
Solomon Easty, Lieutenant
Jonathan Whiting, Ensign

Benjamin Prichard, Sergeant
Wadsworth Foster, Sergeant
Oliver Foster, Sergeant
John Richards, Corporal
Eliphalet Stevens, Corporal
Thomas Stevens, Corporal
Samuel Chandler, Corporal
Columbus Fairbanks, Corporal
Nathan Bishop, Musician
Bezer Snell, Musician

Privates.
Bramhead, James
Bramhead, Orin
Bramhead, Reuben, Jr.
Cahn, James
Day, Moses
Day, Nathaniel
Estey, Aaron
Fosse, William
Foster, Moses
Freeman, Joseph
French, Isaac
Gurney, David
Jameson, William, Jr.
Joy, Abijah
Keizer, John, Jr.
Lovering, Nathaniel
Phinney, John

Prescott, Benjamin B.
Pullin, James
Richards, Samuel
Richards, William, Jr.
Ripley, Simeon
Robbins, Benjamin
Robbins, Oliver
Shaw, Isaac, Jr.
Sturdevant, David
Tompson, Robert
White, Ambrose
White, George
White, Moses
Wood, Obed
Woodcock, Ari
Woodcock, James
Woodcock, Matthew

Capt. S. Jewett's Company, Lieut. Col. J. Stone's Regiment.
From Sept. 11 to Sept. 25, 1814. Raised at Augusta. Service at Wiscasset.

RANK AND NAME.
Stephen Jewett, Captain
Oliver Wyman, Lieutenant

Benjamin Swan, Sergeant
William Stone, Sergeant
Timothy Goldthwait, Sergeant
George Hamlin, Sergeant
William Pilsbury, Corporal
John Goldthwait, Corporal
Dela F. Ballard, Corporal
Ansel Stone, Musician

Privates.
Bennet, Jonathan
Brackett, Abraham
Branch, Nathaniel
Brown, David
Burden, William
Burges, Josiah
Butterfield, Josiah
Chote or Choate, Aaron, 2d

Claver, John
Con, John
Field, Joseph
Foster, Seth
Foye, James
Gill, William
Goldthwait, William
Hall, Oliver, Jr.
Haws, Moses
Hodge, Ezra
Keen, Charles
Kennedy, James
Lyon, Elon
Marshall, Isaac
Marshall, Samuel
Mason, Asa
Mason, Asa, Jr.
Maxwell, David
Norris, Otis
Norton, Milford B.
Owen, Abisha, Jr.
Pain, Nathaniel

Pearce, Pason
Perkins, Andrew L.
Reed, Jason
Reed, Luther
Savage, Isaac, Jr.
Shaw, John
Shed, Josiah
Sprague, Peter
Springer, Gideon
Springer, James
Springer, John
Springer, Stephen
Springer, Tillinghast
Stone, Moses
Taylor, Saul G.
Tolman, Samuel
Wade, James
White, Benjamin
White, Thomas
Williams, Asa, Jr.
Woodard, Daniel

Capt. S. Norris' Company, Lieut. Col. J. Stone's Regiment.
From Sept. 11 to Sept. 25, 1814. Raised at Hallowell. Service at Wiscasset.

RANK AND NAME.
Simeon Norris, Captain (absent)

Isaac Leonard, Lieutenant (commanding)
Stephen Smith, Ensign

James B. Starr, Sergeant
William B. Littlefield, Sergeant
Samuel Merrill, Sergeant
James Kean, Sergeant
Samuel Carr, Jr., Corporal
John Greeley, Corporal
George Waterhouse, Corporal
Joshua Carr, Corporal
Robert Childs, Musician

Privates.
Agrey, John, Jr.
Barrett, Calvin
Boler, Bebani
Bragdon, Joseph
Carr, Wingate
Chisholm, Daniel B.

Church, Rufus
Couch, Elijah
Crummet, Saul
Currier, Morrel
Doll, Ebenezer
Downs, Elisha
Dudley, James
Gardiner, Luke
Gray, Joseph Y.
Hagget, Isaac
Hall, Cyrus
Hand, Joseph
Hinkley, Ariel
Hinkley, Barnard
Hinkley, Shubel, Jr.
James, Daniel S.
Kean, John, Jr.
Kilbourne, Nathaniel
Littlefield, Jeremiah
Mayo, Ebenezer
Mayo, Obed
Mills, Asa C.
Monsul, John

Moulton, Oliver
Mulliken, Jonathan
Need, Ivory
Newman, Daniel
Nye, Ansel
Palmer, William
Parker, Elisha
Parker, Thomas
Phelps, William B.
Philbrick, William
Pratt, Nathan G.
Prebble, James
Slade, William
Smiley, Dean M.
Southard, Joslin
Stevens, Daniel
Waterhouse, Isaac
Whitten, Thomas
Wingate, Frederick
Wymer, Oliver, Jr.
Yetton, Ebenezer

MASSACHUSETTS VOLUNTEER MILITIA IN THE WAR OF 1812. 275

Capt. E. Swan's Company, Lieut. Col. J. Stone's Regiment.
From Sept. 11 to Sept. 25, 1814. Raised at Gardiner. Service at Wiscasset.

RANK AND NAME.
Edward Swan, Captain
Daniel Woodard, Lieutenant
William Norton, Ensign

William B. Grant, Sergeant
Thomas Gilpatrick, Sergeant
Michael Woodard, Sergeant
Arthur Berry, Sergeant
Benjamin Lewrader, Corporal
William Bradstreet, Corporal
Charles M. Dustin, Corporal
Jonathan Perkins, Musician
John Palmer, Musician
Edward Bowman, Musician

Privates.
Berry, Andrew B.
Berry, David
Berry, Josiah
Blake, Ira
Blanchard, Theophilus
Brown, Daniel
Caldwell, Stephen
Clay, Samuel
Crowell, Arnold
Eastman, William
Follinsbee, Benjamin, Jr.
Fuller, Samuel
Grant, Samuel
Hanscomb, Moses
Jack, Thomas
Jackson, Elijah
Johnson, Daniel
Johnson, Joseph
Kimball, Henry
Lapham, Isaac
Laurence, Charles
Laurence, Simeon
Laurence, William
Law, John
McCausland, Andrew
McCausland, John
Moore, Charles
Moore, William
Noys, Samuel
Prey, Eliphalet
Shaw, William
Smith, John W.
Springer, Jacob
Springer, Mark
Springer, William, 2d
Stuart, Richard, Jr.
Wakefield, Jeremiah
Wells, Nathaniel
Wentworth, Andrew
Wentworth, David
Woodard, Amos
Woodard, Daniel, 2d
Worcester, Lemuel

Capt. W. O. Vaughn's Company, Lieut. Col. J. Stone's Regiment.
From Sept. 10 to Sept. 25, 1814. Raised at Hallowell. Service at Wiscasset.

RANK AND NAME.
William O. Vaughn, Captain
Pettey Vaughn, Lieutenant
William Cobb Wilde, Ensign

Abisha Handy, Sergeant
Nathaniel Brown, 2d, Sergeant
Levi Thing, Jr., Sergeant
George Carr, Sergeant
Benjamin Perry, Corporal
Charles Kenney, Corporal
Joseph Richards, Corporal
Daniel Dyer, Musician
Zebulon Sanger, Musician
Samuel Howard, Musician
John Movers, Musician

Privates.
Atherton, Ebenezer
Atkins, Ansel
Atkins, Thomas N.
Ballard, Calvin
Blanchard, Asa
Bowman, James
Boynton, Joseph
Brown, Andrew
Brown, James
Brown, William
Bugnon, George
Burns, James
Carter, Jacob
Caskman, William
Clark, Solomon
Collins, James
Collins, Samuel
Davis, Aaron A.
Davis, John
Doe, Asa
Faxon, Charles
Fitch, David
Greeley, Samuel
Hall, Luther
Hinkley, Ebenezer
Hinkley, Obed
Hodsdon, Samuel
Kenney, Gilman
Kenney, Woodman
Kinsman, Daniel
Laughton, Ebenezer
Lord, Hiram
Lord, Isaac
Mason, Moses
McCurdy, Robert
McGoon, Josiah
McPherson, Paul
Morgan, David
Movers, Timothy
Mudgett, Thomas, Jr.
Neall, Lemuel
Noble, Benjamin
Norcross, Robert C.
Ormsby, Daniel
Owen, John
Page, John C.
Page, Timothy, Jr.
Pilsbury, Amos
Pilsbury, Isaac
Pollard, Charles
Prescott, Stephen
Richards, Jacob
Rollins, Job
Sargent, John
Sherburn, James
Simmons, Daniel
Smith, John
Smith, Samuel
Springer, Benjamin
Springer, James
Springer, William, 3d
Sturdevant, Zenos
Thing, John
Ward, William
West, Shubal
Whidden, Asa
Whidden, Rendol
White, Asa
White, Stephen
Wood, Alonzo
Wood, John
Wooster, John
Young, Rowland

Capt. D. Wall's Company, Lieut. Col. J. Stone's Regiment.

From Sept. 11 to Sept. 25, 1814. Raised at Augusta. Service at Wiscasset.

RANK AND NAME.
David Wall, Captain
Charles Sewall, Ensign

Luther Church, Sergeant
William Fellows, Sergeant
Nathan Stackpole, Sergeant
Elias Stackpole, Sergeant
Jeremiah Tolman, Corporal
Jesse Babcock, Corporal
Elisha Bolton, Corporal

Privates.
Allen, Ezra
Allen, Lewis
Anderson, Ephraim

Babcock, David
Babcock, Jonathan
Bolton, Elijah
Bolton, James, 3d
Bolton, Walter
Brooks, John
Brown, Nathaniel
Caldwell, Daniel
Childs, Oliver
Church, Samuel, Jr.
Clark, Charles
Deniston, Joseph
Fletcher, David, Jr.
Fletcher, Joseph, Jr.
Fletcher, Robert D.
Gilley, James

Hoyt, Stephen
Page, Samuel
Pettingill, Ansel
Pettingill, Howard
Pierce, Asa
Robinson, Nathaniel
Savage, Daniel, Jr.
Savage, James
Smith, William
Stackpole, Joseph, Jr.
Swanton, William
Toby, Elias
Waldron, Daniel
Waters, Gardner
Williams, Daniel

Capt. J. Young's Company, Lieut. Col. J. Stone's Regiment.

From Sept. 11 to Sept. 25, 1814. Raised at Pittstown. Service at Wiscasset.

RANK AND NAME.
Jonathan Young, Captain
Eli Young, Lieutenant
Dudley Young, Ensign

Jonathan Clark, Sergeant
Leonard Cooper, Jr., Sergeant
James Gray, Jr., Sergeant
Henry Benner, Musician
Nathaniel Benner, Musician
Reuben Lewis, Musician
Frederick Lewis, Musician

Privates.
Averit, Asa
Baily, John, Jr.
Baily, Micajah
Baily, Nathan
Blackman, Eliphalet
Blair, Lemuel
Blish, Joseph
Blodget, David
Blodget, Nathaniel

Brookings, James
Brookins, Henry
Clark, Isaac, Jr.
Cooper, Henry
Cooper, Peter
Crocker, Avery
Crocker, Barret
Davis, Jonathan
Dudley, Aaron
Eldred, Levi
Gray, Mark
Hatch, Ephraim, Jr.
Hatch, Sylvanus
Heal, James
Johnson, James
Johnson, Levi
Kincade, James
Lee, Stephen
Longfellow, Dearborn
Manson, George W.
Marson or Maxson, Benjamin
Marson or Maxson, James
Marson or Maxson, Samuel

Moody, Jeremiah, Jr.
Moody, John
Moody, Levi
Moody, William
Nash, Peter
Palmer, Samuel, 1st
Palmer, Samuel, 2d
Pickard, David
Pickard, Thomas, Jr.
Pottle, Samuel
Prebble or Pribble, Daniel
Prebble or Pribble, Joseph
Reed, Daniel
Reed, Isaac
Richard, Turner
Scammon, Eliakim
Smith, Samuel
Smith, Stinson
Weighmont, Timothy
Young, John
Young, Joseph
Young, Oliver

Lieut. Col. E. Sweet's Regiment.

From Sept. 12 to Sept. 24, 1814. Stationed at Wiscasset.

FIELD AND STAFF.
Ellis Sweet, Lieutenant Colonel, Wayne
Samuel Currier, Major, Readfield
Moses Wing, Jr., Major, Wayne
Daniel Campbell, Adjutant, Readfield

Joseph H. Underwood, Quartermaster, Fayette
Charles Smith, Paymaster, Fayette
Jesse Tuck, Paymaster, Fayette
Robert Low, Chaplain, Readfield

NONCOMMISSIONED STAFF.
Isaac Bonney, Sergeant Major
Richard Gower, Quartermaster Sergeant
Charles Robbins, Fife Major
Ferdinand LaCrois, Drum Major

MASSACHUSETTS VOLUNTEER MILITIA IN THE WAR OF 1812.

Capt. N. Pettingill's Company, Lieut. Col. E. Sweet's Regiment.
From Sept. 2 to Nov. 8, 1814. Raised at Lewiston and vicinity. Service at Bath.

RANK AND NAME.
Nathaniel Pettingill, Captain
Levi Foss, Lieutenant
Zacheus Littlefield, Ensign

John S. Blake, Sergeant
Thomas S. Piper, Sergeant
Luther Littlefield, Sergeant
Othniel Pratt, Sergeant
George W. Frogg, Corporal
Thomas Ham, Corporal
Thomas Taylor, Jr., Corporal

Privates.
Anderson, James
Arno, Isaac
Arnold, John
Arns or Arus, Ezekiel
Baily, Joseph
Baily, Whitman
Barker, David
Barrees, Peletiah
Blossom, Ansel
Boothby, Stephen
Boynton, Ebenezer A.
Carver, Eleazer, Jr.
Carver, John
Carvil, Joseph

Carvil, Sewel
Cushman, Andrew, Jr.
Davis, John
Dearborn, Dudly
Dill, William
Dyre, Bezilla
Dyre, Elkanah
Fish, William, Jr.
Ford, Stephen
Foss, Cyrus
Freeman, Allen
Freeman, Isaac
Gareslon, Mark
Gellinan, John
Gould, Eli
Gould, Peletiah
Gray, James
Hackett, John
Harris, Richard D.
Jarulson, Mark, Jr.
Jenkins, Abner
Jenkins, Samuel
Johnson, Daniel
Jones, William
Knowlton, John
Lane, Eliphalet
Lane, John
Lanford, Abraham

Martin, Lewis
Merrill, Asa
Merrill, John
Mitchell, Josiah
Morrell, Amariah
Otis, Ensign
Pettingill, Harvy
Ramsdel, Joshua
Randall, James
Ray, Jonathan
Reed, George
Reed, Ichabod
Reubier, Mark
Richards, Daniel
Richardson, John
Small, Isaac
Sprague, Elkanah
Stetson, Elisha
Stetson, Stephen
Stinchfield, Ezekiel G.
Taylor, James
Walker, John
Ware, Lewis
Warren, Nathaniel M.
Witherell, Ivory
Wright, Zebulon

Capt. E. Davenport's Company, Lieut. Col. E. Sweet's Regiment.
From Sept. 12 to Sept. 25, 1814. Raised at Winthrop. Service at Wiscasset.

RANK AND NAME.
Elijah Davenport, Captain
Samuel Benjamin, Lieutenant
Herman Harris, Ensign

Jabez Bacon, Sergeant
Levi Fairbanks, Sergeant
Joseph Haselton, Sergeant
Francis Perly, Sergeant
Stephen Sewall, Corporal
Benjamin King, Corporal
Daniel C. Haselton, Corporal
Caleb Harris, Corporal
Waterman Stanley, Musician
Josiah Bacon, Musician
Stephen Abbott, Musician
Thomas Fuller, Musician
Simon Clough, Musician

Privates.
Atkins, John
Atkinson, Henry
Bears, Hezekiah

Bears, Josiah
Besser, David
Bonney, James
Bradbury, Silas
Carr, Daniel
Chandler, Alfred
Chase, Welcome U.
Cole, Gale
Currier, John
Currier, Jonathan, Jr.
Decker, William
Fairbanks, David
Fairbanks, Franklin
Fellows, Moses
Fowler, Samuel R.
Frost, Edmund
Harris, Obediah
Hentton, William
Jackson, John
Johnson, Saul
King, Amasa
King, Isaac
Luce, Helron

Luce, Shubal, Jr.
Marrows, Daniel
Marvin, Benjamin
Maxim, Seth
McCrillis, Andrew
Morrill, John
Morrill, Saul
Morton, Cornelius B.
Nelson, Jacob
Newman, Thomas
Perkins, Nathan
Rideout, Johnson
Robbins, Nathaniel
Sedgly, James
Shepherd, Artemas
Stevens, Timothy
Stinson, Charles
Thornton, William
Thurston, William
Wing, Joshua
Wing, Noah
Wood, John
Young, Benjamin

Capt. J. Haskell's Company, Lieut. Col. E. Sweet's Regiment.
From Sept. 12 to Sept. 28, 1814. Raised at Wayne. Service at Wiscasset and vicinity.

RANK AND NAME.
Jacob Haskell, Captain
William Burgess, Lieutenant
Levi Roberts, Ensign

William Knight, Sergeant
Jesse Bishop, Sergeant
Eliakim Foss, Sergeant
Gustavus Foss, Sergeant
Warren Crocker, Corporal
James Wing, Corporal
Asa Tapley, Corporal
James Burgess, Corporal
Asa Foss, Musician
Joshua Norris, Musician

Privates.
Atkins, Nathaniel, Jr.
Besse, Woodin
Billington, Job
Blackwell, Sylvanus
Burgess, Elisha
Dinsmore, Samuel
Erskine, Robert
Felch, Samuel
Foss, George
Frost, Noah
Gott, William, Jr.
Gould, Levi
Gould, Samuel
Jenkins, Dennis

Jennings, Henry
Jennings, Lewis
Jennings, Samuel, Jr.
Judkins, Jacob
Knight, Francis
Maxim, Jacob
Norris, Grafton
Ridley, Daniel
Ridley, Matthias
Ridley, Samuel
Wallis, Joseph
Williams, Lewis
Wing, Calvin
Wing, Obed

Capt. J. Judkins' Company, Lieut. Col. E. Sweet's Regiment.
From Sept. 12 to Sept. 28, 1814. Service at Monmouth.

RANK AND NAME.
John Judkins, Captain
Thomas Anderson, Lieutenant
Luther Bumpus, Ensign

John Jack, Sergeant
Gilman Barhall, Sergeant
Jonathan Knowles, Sergeant
Andrew Sturdevant, Sergeant
Cyrus Baldwin, Jr., Corporal
Amos Tilton, Corporal
Samuel Jack, Jr., Corporal
William Billings, Corporal
John A. Page, Musician
Reuben Crane, Musician

Privates.
Bean, Asa
Bean, Smith
Davis, Thomas
Jack, Joseph
Jones, Nathaniel F.
Jones, Sylvester, Jr.
Judkins, David
Judkins, Joel, Jr.
Judkins, Moses
Lane, Elijah
Lane, John
Marston, Philbrick
Morrison, Montgomery
Quinby, John

Richards, Jeremiah
Richards, Oliver
Ross, Joseph
Russell, Isaac
Tuck, Levi
Watson, Joseph
Watson, Richard
Watts, Andrew
Woodworth, John
Young, Aaron

Capt. J. Smith's Company, Lieut. Col. E. Sweet's Regiment.
From Sept. 12 to Sept. 25, 1814. Raised at Readfield. Service at Wiscasset.

RANK AND NAME.
John Smith, Captain
Eli Adams, Lieutenant

Daniel Campbell, Sergeant
James Fillebrown, Jr., Sergeant
Lary Bacon, Sergeant
Jethro Hillman, Sergeant
James Smith, Sergeant
Jacob Turner, Corporal
David Huntoon, Corporal
Jacob Cochran, Corporal
William Simpson, Corporal
Thomas Pierce, Musician
Charles Pierce, Musician
John Turner, Musician

Privates.
Armstrong, Elias
Atkinson, Benjamin
Bean, Franklin
Bean, Manly
Bean, Milton

Bean, Oliver
Bearse, David
Cochran, Osgood
Craig, John O.
Craig, Peter
Dunn, Richard
Dutton, James
Fillebrown, Luther W.
Fillebrown, Thomas
Fling, Nathan
Ford, James, Jr.
Ford, John
Gordon, Alexander
Gray, William
Hains, Peleg
Hunt, Francis
Jackins, Saul
Johnson, Alfred
Johnson, Calvin
Johnson, Daniel
Judkins, Asa
Kent, Barker
Kent, Elisha

Kent, Nathaniel
Kittredge, Ingalls
Ladd, Simeon, Jr.
Luce, Alsatt
Luce, Thomas
Macomber, William
Morrison, Alexander
Nickerson, Constant, Jr.
Packard, Caleb, Jr.
Packard, Joshua, Jr.
Packard, Nathaniel
Pullen, Larnead
Smith, Bowen
Smith, Carpenter
Smith, George
Smith, John H.
Smith, William
Stevens, Ezra
Stone, Thomas, Jr.
Taylor, Saul, Jr.
Turner, Christopher
Waugh, John

Capt. T. L. Stevens' Company, Lieut. Col. E. Sweet's Regiment.
From Sept. 12 to Sept. 25, 1814. Raised at Mt. Vernon. Service at Wiscasset.

RANK AND NAME.
Timothy L. Stevens, Captain
George McGaffy, Lieutenant
Ansel Kimball, Ensign

James McGaffy, Sergeant
William Whittier, Sergeant
Levi Fletcher, Sergeant
John Brown, Sergeant
Joseph Greeley, Corporal
Edward Griffin, Corporal
Moses Carson, Corporal
Bezoled Bullard, Corporal
Abel Whittier, Musician
Squire Bishop, Jr., Musician

Privates.
Bean, Edward
Blank, Franklin
Brown, Nathan
Brown, Samuel
Bullard, David
Carson, James
Cleary, Caleb
Clough, Daniel
Dolloff, David
Dolloff, John
Gilman, Benjamin
Gilman, Nathan
Gorden, Ithnal
Jewell, Jesse
Jewell, Jesse, Jr.
Ladd, Benjamin
Laighton, David
Laighton, Joseph
Laighton, Samuel
Laighton, Silas
Laighton, Simeon
Laighton, Thomas
Laighton, Timothy
Lyford, Dudly
McGaffy, Andrew
Morse, Elijah
Morse, Joseph
Perkins, Nathaniel T.
Pinkham, James
Quimby, James
Robinson, Daniel
Robinson, Jonathan
Robinson, Moses
Smith, Samuel
Trask, James
Wells, Stephen
Wiggins, Daniel

Capt. H. Watson's Company, Lieut. Col. E. Sweet's Regiment.
From Sept. 12 to Sept. 25, 1814. Raised at Fayette. Service at Wiscasset.

RANK AND NAME.
Henry Watson, Captain
Alden Josselyn, Lieutenant
David Knowles, Ensign

Elisha Marston, Sergeant
Richard Hubbard, Sergeant
Thomas Fuller, Sergeant
Benjamin P. Winchester, Sergeant
James Watson, Corporal
Moses Hubbard, Corporal
David Knowles, 2d, Corporal
Moses Sturdevant, Corporal
William Sturdevant, Musician
John D. Josselyn, Musician
Jesse Lovejoy, Musician

Privates.
Bissel, William B.
Clough, Jonathan
Craig, Elias, Jr.
Drew, John B.
Elkins, Josiah
Elkins, Saul
Ford, Isaac
Ham, Reuben
Harmon, Simon
Hill, William
Hutchinson, Joseph
Hutchinson, Luther
Jewett, John
Josselyn, Harvey
Josselyn, Martin
Judkins, Elisha
Lane, Jeremiah
Lane, William H.
Lovejoy, Ebenezer
Lovejoy, Peter
Palmer, Amos
Pettingill, Elisha
Poke, Benjamin
Sargent, William
Stevens, Benjamin
Swift, Alfred
Walton, Rufus
Walton, Saul
Watson, David
Watson, Joseph, 3d
Woodman, Amos
Woodworth, John
Young, Jacob
Young, Jonathan

Capt. G. Waugh's Company, Lieut. Col. E. Sweet's Regiment.
From Sept. 12 to Sept. 25, 1814. Raised at Readfield. Service at Wiscasset.

RANK AND NAME.
George Waugh, Captain
Alden Josselyn, Lieutenant
Herman Harris, Ensign

Elisha Marston, Sergeant
William Whittier, Sergeant
Richard Hubbard, Sergeant
Gilman Bachelor, Corporal
Samuel Tuck, Corporal

Privates.
Bean, Asa
Besse, Samuel
Brown, Saul, Jr.
Bullard, David
Clough, Daniel
Dolloff, David
Griffin, Edward
Ham, Reuben
Jewett, Washington
Josselyn, Martin
Judkins, Elisha
Judkins, Joel
Knowles, William
Ladd, Benjamin
Ladd, Jesse
Lane, William H.
Laton, David
Laton, Simeon
Lovejoy, Ebenezer O.
Morrison, Montgomery
Morse, Elijah
Page, John A.
Page, Sewal
Peterson, Alfred
Pettingill, Elisha
Quimby, John
Richards, Oliver
Robinson, Moses
Rogers, John
Rolinger, Jonathan
Sargant, William
Scott, William
Swift, Alfred
Tuck, Levi
Watson, David
Watson, Joseph
Wiggins, Daniel
Woods, Henry

Capt. T. Nickerson's Company, Lieut. Col. E. Sweet's Regiment.
From Sept. 13 to Sept. 25, 1814. Raised at Mt. Vernon. Service at Wiscasset.

RANK AND NAME.	*Privates.*	
Thomas Nickerson, Captain	Bartlet, Joshua	Lane, John
John Stevens, Lieutenant	Bartlet, Saul	Philbrook, Elias
John Blake, Ensign	Covel, Caleb	Philbrook, John
	Crane, Obediah	Porter, Amasa
Joseph Gilman, Sergeant	Crane, Shadrack	Porter, Calvin
Daniel Gordon, Sergeant	Currier, John	Rasebrook, Eleazer
Nathaniel S. Philbrook, Sergeant	Davis, Jonathan	Russell, Abram G.
Ephraim Nickerson, Sergeant	Fletcher, Atwood	Sherburn, Elias
W. W. Philbrook, Corporal	Folsom, Jeremiah	Smith, Bradbury
Nathan Smith, Corporal	Folsom, Warren	Smith, Joseph
Levi French, Jr., Corporal	Gilman, Dennis	Smith, Walden
Bela Gilman, Corporal	Gorden, Robert	Stain, Emerson
John Stone, Musician	Gould, David	Stain, Saul
Jesse Ladd, Musician	Ham, William	Taylor, John
	Ingham, Amasa	Thomas, Nathan, Jr.
	Kent, John T.	Whittier, Levi
		Wood, Sampson

Capt. E. Butler's Company, Lieut. Col. E. Sweet's Regiment.
From Sept. 18 to Nov. 8, 1814. Raised at New Vineyard. Service at Bath.

RANK AND NAME.		
Elijah Butler, Captain	Barker, Jacob	Gray, Saul
John Davis, Lieutenant	Batts, John	Hackett, Simeon
Mark Pettingill, Ensign	Batts, Robert	Haskell, Israel
	Brackly, William	McLain, Jesse
	Burbank, Jesse S.	Merry, Joseph
Andrew Whitney, Sergeant	Butler, Joseph	Morton, William
Ebenezer French, Sergeant	Clark, Chandler	Norton, Isaac
Ebenezer Ames, Sergeant	Clark, Eli	Norton, Saul
Joseph Viles, Sergeant	Clough, Daniel	Ridgway, James
Leonard Boardman, Corporal	Collier, Ebenezer	Saul, Joshua
John Brackly, Corporal	Cony, Hartson	Stevens, Joshua
Daniel Howard, Corporal	Coombs, Joshua	Sylvester, John
David Hodgman, Corporal	Crawford, Benjamin T.	Thompson, Isaac
James Battle, Musician	Cutler, Nathan	Tuttle, Saul
James Jacob, Musician	Daggett, Plemington	Weymouth, Samuel
	Dollbier, Charles	Whitney, Christopher A.
Privates.	Farr, Simeon	Whitney, Ebenezer
Ames, Isaac	Fassett, Alexander	Whitney, James
Badry, Joseph	Gilkey, John	Williams, Stephen

Lieut. E. Norris' Company, Lieut. Col. E. Sweet's Regiment.
From Sept. 12 to Sept. 25, 1814. Raised at Wayne. Service at Wiscasset.

RANK AND NAME.	*Privates.*	
Ebenezer Norris, Lieutenant	Bean, Moses	Marvin, Reuben
	Billington, Nathaniel, Jr.	Morrison, John
Amasa Dexter, Sergeant	Billington, Seth	Norris, Ephraim
Seth Billington, Sergeant	Blackwell, Ansel	Norris, Woodin, Jr.
Benjamin Norris, Sergeant	Chandler, John	Perry, Edmund
Samuel Besse, Corporal	Chandler, Noah	Perry, Franklin
Allen House, Corporal	Crocker, James	Perry, John
Samuel Wing, Corporal	Cummer, John	Raymond, Thomas
Elisha Besse, Corporal	Foss, Charles	Raymond, William, Jr.
Nathan Sturdevant, Musician	Frost, Aaron, Jr.	Smith, John, Jr.
Seth Hammond, Musician	Frost, George	Stevens, Jacob
	Frost, Richard M.	Stevens, John, 2d
	Hammond, Sylvanus	Sturdevant, John
		White, John

Lieut. Col. E. Sweet's Regiment.

From Sept. 24 to Nov. 14, 1814. Service at Bath.

FIELD AND STAFF.
Ellis Sweet, Lieutenant Colonel, Wayne
Moses Sanborn, Major, Vienna
Moses Wing, Major, Wayne
Daniel Campbell, Adjutant, Readfield

Jabez Gay, Quartermaster, Farmington
Thomas W. Bridgham, Surgeon, Leeds
Charles Smith, Surgeon's Mate, Fayette
Jesse Tuck, Paymaster, Fayette
Robert Low, Chaplain, Readfield

NONCOMMISSIONED STAFF.
Isaac Banney, Sergeant Major
Elias Craig, Jr., Sergeant Major
Reuben Robbins, Drum Major

Capt. M. Sprague's Company, Lieut. Col. E. Sweet's Regiment.

From Sept. 24 to Nov. 8, 1814. Service at Bath.

RANK AND NAME.
Moses Sprague, Captain
Codding Drake, Lieutenant
Stephen Welcome, Ensign

Joseph Turner, Sergeant
Benjamin Rackley, Sergeant
William Sprague, Jr., Sergeant
Thomas Witherell, Sergeant
Joseph Herrick, Jr., Sergeant
John Colbey, Corporal
William Brimejohn, Corporal
Ammi Larrabee, Corporal
William Mitchell, Corporal

Privates.
Adams, Nathaniel
Allen, Ichabod
Andrews, Otis
Bates, Joseph
Booker, Jacob
Brown, Abram
Chase, Nathaniel
Clark, Joseph H.
Clark, Samuel
Coburn, Isaiah
Coburn, Phineas
Cousins, Ebenezer

Curtis, William B.
Day, William
Fogg, William
Foss, Daniel
Foss, Hiram
Furbish, John
Gatchell, Daniel
Gilbert, Bailey
Gordon, Jonathan
Gray, Jesse
Gray, Stephen
Hall, Isaac
Hamilton, Oliver
Harris, Joseph
Hatch, Samuel
Hinkley, Benjamin
Hodsdon, James
Hutchinson, Isaac
Jackson, Michael
Jewett, David
Jones, Isaac
King, Jason
Lander, Ansel
Layne, Elias
Libby, Ebenezer
Littlefield, Ephraim
Lothrop, Lovit
Lumbard, Harding

Maines, William
Maloon or Matoon, Samuel
Maloon or Matoon, Simon
Maxwell, Joseph
Merrill, John, 2d
Merrill, Levi, 3d
Mower, Isaac
Murry, Amos
Parker, Jacob
Perea (?), James
Pettingill, Arcadus
Pettingill, John
Plummer, John
Plummer, William
Quimby, Benjamin
Quinby, John
Read, Russell H.
Rowe, John
Shaw, John
Sinclair, Ebenezer
Sinclair, William
Southard, Constant
Strout, William
Sturdivant, William
Thomas, Martin
Tilton, Josiah
Wild, Timothy
Wilkins, David

Capt. J. Smith's Company, Lieut. Col. E. Sweet's Regiment.

From Sept. 25 to Nov. 8, 1814. Raised at Readfield. Service at Bath.

RANK AND NAME.
John Smith, Captain
Samuel Benjamin, Lieutenant
Eli Adams, Ensign

Joseph Gilman, Sergeant
Nathan S. Philbrick, Sergeant
Joseph Haselton, Sergeant
James McGaffey, Sergeant
Walter W. Philbrick, Corporal
Benjamin King, Corporal
David Huntoon, Corporal
Warren Crocker, Corporal
Joshua Bartlett, Musician
Josiah Bacon, Musician
Stephen Abbot, Musician
John M. Shaw, Musician

Privates.
Atkinson, Henry
Bartlett, O. Timothy
Bean, Joshua
Bean, Manly
Bearse, David
Besse, David
Besse, Woodin
Blackwell, Sylvanus
Bradbury, Silas
Chace, Welcome W.
Chandler, Alfred
Craig, John O.
Dinsmore, Samuel
Dudley, Benjamin
Dutton, James
Fairbanks, David

Fairbanks, Levi
Fletcher, Atwood
Folsom, Jeremiah
Ford, John
Foss, George
Fuller, William C.
Ham, William
Hunt, Francis
Jennings, Samuel
Johnson, Saul
Judkins, Jacob
Kent, Barker
Kent, John S.
Kent, Nathaniel
Knight, Francis
Ladd, Simeon, Jr.
Leru, Shubal, Jr.

Capt. J. Smith's Company, Lieut. Col. E. Sweet's Regiment — Concluded.

Privates — Concluded.
Low, O. Thomas
Maxim, Benjamin
Morrison, Alexander
Morron, Daniel
Packard, Joshua, Jr.
Philbrick, Elias
Rideout, Johnson
Ridley, Daniel

Sedgley, James
Simpson, William
Smith, Carpenter
Smith, John H.
Stain, Samuel
Stanly, Lemuel
Stanly, Morrell
Stevens, Timothy
Taylor, John

Taylor, Samuel
Thomas, Nathan
Turner, Christopher
Wallis, Joseph
Williams, Lewis
Wing, Joshua
Woods, Sampson

Capt. G. Waugh's Company, Lieut. Col. E. Sweet's Regiment.
From Sept. 25 to Nov. 8, 1814. Raised at Readfield. Service at Bath.

RANK AND NAME.
George Waugh, Captain
Samuel Page, Lieutenant
Reuben Smith, Ensign

Jeremiah Page, Sergeant
William Taylor, Sergeant
Christopher Adle, Sergeant
Joseph Hutchinson, Sergeant
Moses Simmons, Corporal
Sewal Page, Corporal
Elijah Clough, Corporal
Nathan Coy, Corporal
Henry Carlton, Musician
William Fuller, Musician
Levi Howill, Jr., Musician

Privates.
Bean, Nathaniel
Brown, Jacob
Brown, Samuel G.

Case, Ambrose
Clough, James I.
Day, Jacob
Dudly, Henry
Dudly, Saul
Fifield, Ebenezer, Jr.
Fifield, Wire
Gordon, Daniel
Gordon, Luther
Greely, Henry
Greely, Samuel
Hall, Nathan
Hinkly, Joseph
Hows, David
Hoyt, John H.
Hoyt, Levi
Jewett, Washington
Joss, Oliver
Judkins, Richard
Knowls, John
Knowls, Jonathan, Jr.

Knowls, Joseph
Knowls, William
Melvin, John
Morrill, Josiah
Morrill, Samuel
Morse, Leonard
Neal, John
Prescot, Joseph
Prescot, William
Rowe, Lewis
Sawyer, John
Volage, Nathaniel
Watson, Josiah M.
Waugh, Samuel
White, Aaron
Whittier, Benaiah
Whittier, Jonathan
Whittier, Joseph
Whittier, Josiah

Capt. D. Beale's Company, Lieut. Col. E. Sweet's Regiment.
From Sept. 26 to Nov. 8, 1814. Raised at Farmington. Service at Bath.

RANK AND NAME.
Daniel Beale, Captain
Robert Hussey, Lieutenant
Nathaniel Parsons, Ensign

Ebenezer Hutchinson, Sergeant
Moses P. Bradley, Sergeant
Elijah K. Hussey, Sergeant
William Blye, Sergeant

Privates.
Allen, John
Allen, Winthrop
Ames, Rufus
Arnold, Samuel
Arnold, Thomas
Baker, William
Battle, Daniel
Berry, Rufus
Blackstone, Benjamin
Blackstone, Ebenezer
Blasdell, Samuel
Blaswell, Thomas
Blunt, Jesse
Boyington, Joshua

Bradbury, David, Jr.
Brainerd, Josiah
Brown, Daniel C.
Buss, Henry
Coburn, Manly
Cottle, Lott
Covall, Joshua
Dyer, Reuben
Ellis, Ivory
Floyd, Nathaniel
Floyd, Saul
Foster, Ebenezer
French, Nehemiah
Furbush, Stephen
Gordan, Daniel
Goss, Benjamin C.
Gove, Solomon
Greenleaf, Joseph
Hale, John
Hamilton, William
Harding, Nathaniel, Jr.
Harding, Nehemiah
Jordan, Elijah
Kent, Henry
Knowlton, Jonathan, Jr.

Lancaster, Thomas
Lovell, Oliver
Luce, Ezekiel
Parker, James
Parson, Hiram
Pratt, Paul
Prescot, Abel
Presson, Tristram
Rollins, Joseph, Jr.
Sanborn, Stephen, Jr.
Shaw, Joseph
Silsbee, John
Smith, Nathan
Soule, Rufus
Stevens, John
Sweet, Winborn A.
Tibbets, Jesse L.
Turner, Daniel
Welch, Charles
Wilson, David
Winslow, Prince
Witham, Joshua
Wright, Isaac
Young, John

Capt. J. Gould's Company, Lieut. Col. E. Sweet's Regiment.
From Sept. 26 to Nov. 5, 1814. Raised at Wilton. Service at Bath.

RANK AND NAME.
John Gould, Captain
Ozum Dowst, Lieutenant
Jotham Bradbury, Ensign

Nathaniel Maddocks, Sergeant
Thomas Baker, Sergeant
John Hubbard, Sergeant
Hammond Brown, Sergeant
Rufus Dresser, Musician
Josiah Gould, Musician

Privates.
Adams, Jeptha H.
Barker, Clark
Benet, Elisha
Bragdon, Jeremiah
Brown, Elijah
Butterfield, Aaron
Butterfield, Asa
Butterfield, James

Carr, James
Carr, John
Chandler, David
Chandler, Moses
Chany, Josiah
Eaton, Lowell
Eaton, Tappan
Flint, Daniel
French, William
Gordon, Newal
Hammond, Samuel H.
Hardy, Moses
Harper, Eliot
Hathaway, Ezra
Hill, Ezekiel
Hutchinson, Asa
Johnson, Joseph
Knowls, John C.
Lapham, Calvin
Learnard, Benjamin
Leighton, Mordecai

McCulley, John
Mitchell, Jonathan
Peckham, David
Prescott, Adonijah
Prescott, Jedediah
Randell, Timothy, Jr.
Reed, Jonathan
Sewall, Henry
Soper, Jesse
Stickney, William
Stone, Ephraim
Sweet, Jesse
True, John
Walker, John
Walker, Osgood
Wheeler, George
Whittier, Benjamin
Whittier, David W.
Whittier, Josiah

Capt. N. Russell's Company, Lieut. Col. E. Sweet's Regiment.
From Sept. 28 to Nov. 11, 1814. Raised at Farmington and vicinity. Service at Bath.

RANK AND NAME.
Nathaniel Russell, Captain
John F. Wood, Jr., Lieutenant
James Hearsey, Ensign

James Stephens or Stevens, Sergeant
James Norton, Sergeant
Jedediah K. Conant, Sergeant
Edward Oakes, Sergeant
John Howe, Corporal
William Cothran, Corporal
David Reed, Corporal
John Paine, Corporal
Isaac Chace, Musician
Enos Hiscock, Musician

Privates.
Baker, William
Ballard, Frederick
Battle, William
Butler, Ezra A.
Claiton, John, Jr.
Conan, Samuel

Craig, Enoch, Jr.
Daggett, William
Davis, Daniel
Durphy, Elijah
Elsworth, Joseph
Foot, Stephen
Hackett, Richard
Hatch, Reuben
Hersey, Abisha
Hinkley, Enoch
Hiscock, Daniel
Hiscock, Thomas, Jr.
Hodgdon, John
Huston, Saul
Kennedy, Andrew
Kennedy, William
Lambert, Levi G.
Mace, Fayette
Mayhew, Andrew B.
Norton, Bassett
Norton, Peter
Norton, Winthrop
Peterson, William

Pettingill, Abraham
Pool, George P.
Porter, Jeremy
Riant, Joseph, Jr.
Richards, Edward
Russell, Thomas
Sawyer, Nathaniel
Smith, David P.
Smith, George
Smith, Jonathan
Sprague, Stephen G.
Staple, Daniel
Staple, William
Steward, William M.
Stewart, Daniel
Sweet, Zebediah
Thompson, Daniel O.
Tuck, Enos
Tuck, William
Welch, Jacob
Worthley, Daniel
Wright, Josiah

Lieut. J. Vickere's Company, Lieut. Col. E. Sweet's Regiment.
From October to November, 1814. Raised at Norridgewock. Service at Bath.

Rank and Name.		
Joseph Vickere, Lieutenant	Bixby, Rufus	Tarbelly, Joseph
	Blunt, Mark S.	Taylor, Ansel
	Bridges, Jesse	Turner, Silas
Thomas Heald, Sergeant	Ellis, Freeborn	Walker, Simeon
Asa Clark, Sergeant	Fletcher, Joel	Weston, Cyrus
William Sylvester, Sergeant	Gilinan, Zebulon	Weston, Stephen
Cyrus Kidder, Corporal	Harding, Isaac	Wetherell, Samuel B.
Thomas Densmore, Corporal	Harding, Jesse	White, James
Vintin Streeter, Corporal	Haynes, John	White, William
	Heald, Cyrus	Withee, Zachariah
Privates.	Kenny, Henry	
Bairon, Joseph	Spaulding, Daniel	
Bixby, Amasa	Spaulding, Otis	

Lieut. Col. E. Thatcher's Regiment.
From Sept. 10 to Sept. 29, 1814.

Field and Staff.		Noncommissioned Staff.
Ebenezer Thatcher, Lieutenant Colonel, Thomaston	David Fales, Adjutant, Thomaston	Kalsey Healy, Quartermaster Sergeant, Warren
Samuel Adams, Surgeon, Wiscasset	William McLellan, Quartermaster, Warren	

Capt. M. Robinson's Company, Lieut. Col. S. Thatcher's Regiment.
From June 2 to June 25, and Sept. 4 to Sept. 8, 1814. Raised at Cushing. Service at Cushing.

Rank and Name.	*Privates.*	Norton, Jabez
Moses Robinson, Captain	Barton, Isaac	Nutting, George
Job Gay, Lieutenant	Burton, Matthew	Nutting, Silas B.
	Davis, Robert	Robinson, Alexander
Dunbar Henderson, Sergeant	Elwell, Saul	Robinson, Charles
Darius Norton, Sergeant	Gay, Isaac J.	Robinson, Henry
Ephraim Robinson, Sergeant	Hartshorn, Saul	Robinson, Jacob
Yarby Robinson, Sergeant	Hyler, Hannce	Robinson, John
Benjamin Robinson, Sergeant	Hyler, Jacob	Robinson, John, 3d
Cornelius Robinson, Sergeant	Hyler, John	Robinson, Simon
Thomas Smith, Corporal	Hyler, William	Seavey, Thomas
Archibald Robertson, Corporal	Jamerson, Thomas	Smith, Joseph
Mabbry Robinson, Corporal	Malcom, Andrew	Wiley, John
William Vose, Corporal	McCaller, James	Wiley, Robert
John Vose, Corporal	McCarther, Robert	Young, James
	McIntire, Robert	

Capt. J. Auld's Company, Lieut. Col. E. Thatcher's Regiment.
From June 20 to June 24, and June 29 to July 5, 1814. Raised at Boothbay. Service at Boothbay.

Rank and Name.	*Privates.*	Pinkham, John
Jacob Auld, Captain	Auld, James	Reed, Alexander
William McCobb, Lieutenant	Auld, William	Reed, Henry
Jeremiah Holton, Lieutenant	Brown, John, 3d	Reed, William
	Campbell, James	Robinson, William
William Reed, Sergeant	Currier, William	Sherman, Robert
John Fuller, Sergeant	Favours, Peters	Tibbets, Giles
Paul McCobb, Sergeant	Fullerton, James	Tool, Andrew
Joel Thompson, Sergeant	Kelly, Isaac	Wylie, William
Samuel Tibbets, Corporal	Keniston, Thomas	
John Fullerton, Corporal	Knight, John A.	
Henry Williams, Corporal	McFarland, Ephraim	
Robert Reed, Corporal	McFarland, John	
William Bragg, Musician	Montgomery, Nathaniel	
Tilly H. Cleasby, Musician	Pinkham, Benjamin	

MASSACHUSETTS VOLUNTEER MILITIA IN THE WAR OF 1812.   285

Capt. N. Morse's Company, Lieut. Col. E. Thatcher's Regiment.
From June 20 to June 22, 1814. Raised at Wiscasset. Service at Wiscasset.

RANK AND NAME.
Nathaniel Morse, Captain
William Pitt, Lieutenant

James Gibbs, Sergeant
Moses Hilton, Sergeant
John Faye, Sergeant
Joshua Damon, Sergeant
Nehemiah Somes, Musician

Privates.
Allen, Benjamin
Bazlin, Sargent
Boyle, John
Burton, Frederic

Chick, Silas
Coames, Josiah
Damon, Israel
Dane, Asa
Farnham, Ebenezer
Farnham, John
Farnham, Samuel
Farnham, William
Garry, Benjamin
Gray, William
Hedge, Barria
Hilton, Daniel
Hilton, Ellis
Hilton, Rufus
Holmes, John

Hutchinson, John
Lazell, James
Lazell, Saul
Leeland, Abner
Light, James
Marshall, William
Noyes, Henry
Robbins, Cheney
Savage, Daniel
Smith, William
Smith, William, 2d
Stinson, James
Vincent, William
Warren, John

Capt. S. Parker's Company, Lieut. Col. E. Thatcher's Regiment.
From June 21 to June 25, and Sept. 3 to Sept. 10, 1814. Service at Friendship.

RANK AND NAME.
Simon Parker, Captain

Frederic Bradford, Sergeant
Jonah Morse, Sergeant

Privates.
Bickmore, Solomon
Brown, Abraham
Card, John
Chadwick, James W.
Condee, George
Conden, William

Conden, William, 2d
Conner, Charles
Cook, Cornelius
Davis, Benjamin
Fernald, Solomon
Gay, Jonah
Gyer, Martin
Gyer, Martin, Jr.
Jameson, Jeremiah
Jamison, Thurston W.
Loury, Benjamin
Morse, Ebenezer
Morse, Elijah

Morse, Jonah
Morse, Oliver
Morse, Saul
Morton, Cornelius
Morton, Isaac
Morton, James
Morton, Josiah, 2d
Parker, Oliver
Thomas, Melzer
Watson, Nathaniel
Wolsgrover, George
Woltzgrover, Christopher

Capt. J. Haskell's Company, Lieut. Col. E. Thatcher's Regiment.
From June 22 to June 27, and Nov. 3 to Nov. 7, 1814. Raised at Thomaston. Service at Thomaston.

RANK AND NAME.
John Haskell, Captain
Alexander Lammond, Lieutenant
John D. Ryder, Lieutenant

James Wilie, Sergeant
Ivory Hovey, Sergeant
Aaron S. Benson, Sergeant
Saul Kellock, Sergeant
David Vose, Corporal
Gideon Seavey, Corporal
Franklin Sterns, Corporal
Benjamin Kellock, Corporal
Peaslee Wells, Musician
James Cox, Musician

Privates.
Anderson, James
Andrews, Seth
Barnard, John
Beamos, Elisha
Bennett, Asa
Blood, Simon
Boggs, Ephraim
Bosworth, Zenas
Butler, Brackett
Chaples, John
Creighton, John
Fales, Noyes
Hall, Benjamin
Hawkes, John B.
Lovejoy, John

Mallett, James B.
McIntosh, Henry
McIntyre, Palmer
McIntyre, Thomas
Roakes, David
Robinson, William
Slover, Charles
Spafford, John
Spear, Edward
Stall, Jacob
Stover, John
Tilson or Felson, Gilbert
Woodcock, Nathan
Woodcock, Patrick
Young, Benjamin

Capt. J. Haskell's Company, Lieut. Col. E. Thatcher's Regiment.
From Aug. 21 to Aug. 22, 1814. Raised at Thomaston. Service at Thomaston.

Rank and Name.	Privates.	
John Haskell, Captain	Anderson, James	Mallett, James G.
Alexander Lammond, Lieutenant	Andrews, Seth	McIntosh, Henry
	Barnard, John	McIntyre, Palmer
John D. Rider, Sergeant	Blood, Simon	McIntyre, Thomas
Daniel Newcomb, Sergeant	Boggs, Ephraim	Robinson, William
Joseph Copeland, Sergeant	Butler, Brackett	Spafford, John
James Wilie, Sergeant	Creighton, John	Spear, Edward
Ivory Hovey, Sergeant	Fales, Noyes	Spear, Gideon
George Larmond, Corporal	Felson or Tilson, Gilbert	Stall, Jacob
Aaron L. Benson, Corporal	Hall, Benjamin	Storer, Elias
William Stackpole, Corporal	Hawkes, John B.	Storer, John
Franklin Sterns, Corporal	Kellock, Benjamin	Vose, David
Peaslee Wells, Musician	Kellock, Saul	Woodcock, Nathan
James Cox, Musician	Lovejoy, John	Woodcock, Patrick
		Young, Benjamin

Capt. D. Grafton's Company, Lieut. Col. E. Thatcher's Regiment.
From Sept. 3 to Sept. 8, 1814. Raised at Union. Service at Camden.

Rank and Name.	Butler, Martin	Leniken, Daniel
David Grafton, Captain	Butters, Daniel	Libbey, William
Rufus Gilmore, Lieutenant	Butters, Flavel	Litchfield, Benjamin
Bailey Moore, Ensign	Carriel, Nathaniel	Luce, Thadeus
	Clark, Abner	Maddock, George
John M. Thorndike, Sergeant	Clark, Ezekiel	March, Henry
John Batchelder, Sergeant	Collamore, Alpheus	Miller, Joseph
Phillip Cummings, Sergeant	Cutting, John	Miller, Joseph, 2d
Jonathan Carrul, Sergeant	Dagget, Henry	Mitchell, Thomas
Lewis Batchelder, Corporal	Dagget, William	Morse, Walter
Noah Rice, Corporal	Daggett, Saul	Payson, Hartwell
John Stevens, Corporal	Drake, Jesse	Peabody, Stephen
Nathaniel Tobey, Corporal	Drake, John	Reed, Joel
Edmund Daggett, Musician	Fosset, Henry	Rice, Nathan D.
Miller Gilmore, Musician	Fuller, Simon	Robbins, John P.
	Grinnel, Daniel B.	Shepherd, Nathan
Privates.	Grinnel, Samuel S.	Sibley, Jacob
Adams, Ebenezer W.	Hager, Ezekiel	Sinclair, James
Bartlet, Jason B.	Hager, Saul	Sleeper, Nathaniel
Bennet, Saul	Hager, Sewel	Snell, Chadrick
Bills, Jason	Hart, John F.	Thompson, James
Blake, Walter	Haskell, David	Townsend, Isaac
Blunt, Ebenezer	Hawes, Otis	Ware, Vinal
Boothe, Isaac	Hills, Josiah	Whetten, Thomas
Bowen, Amos	Holton, Euclid	Whitcomb, John
Bowen, Ezra	Irish, Cornelius	Wiley, Peleg
Burns, John	Larmond, James	

Capt. J. Haskell's Company, Lieut. Col. E. Thatcher's Regiment.
From Sept. 5 to Sept. 9, 1814. Raised at Thomaston. Service at Thomaston.

Rank and Name.	Privates.	
John Haskell, Captain	Anderson, James	Seavry, Gideon
John B. Rider, Lieutenant	Barnard, John	Spear, Edward
	Butler, Bracket	Stearns, Franklin
James Wiley, Sergeant	Fales, Noyes	Storer, Elias
Joseph Copeland, Sergeant	Hall, Benjamin	Tilson, Gilbert
Aaron S. Benson, Corporal	Hawks, John B.	Vose, David
Peaslee Wells, Musician	Kellock, Saul	Woodcock, Nathan
James Cox, Musician	McIntosh, Henry	Woodcock, Patrick
	Robinson, William	Young, Benjamin

Capt. M. Howe's Company, Lieut. Col. E. Thatcher's Regiment.
From Sept. 10 to Sept. 29, 1814. Raised at Bristol.

RANK AND NAME.
Marius Howe, Captain
Barry G. Pomroy, Lieutenant
John Goudy, Lieutenant

A. Blany, Sergeant
Alexander Houston, Sergeant
John Hanly, Sergeant
James Blunt, Sergeant
Samuel Miller, Corporal
Amos Goudy, Corporal
James Jones, Corporal
Joseph T. Huston, Musician
Henry Erving, Musician
George Mars, Musician

Privates.
Askins, Henry
Baker, Andrew
Bearce, Isaac
Cox, John
Crooker, Philip
Dockendorf, Solomon
Fossett, Alexander
Hanly, Roger
Hatch, Alexander
Hatch, John
Huston, William
Killsea, Enoch
Killsea, Moses
McCobb, William

Mears, Jeremiah P.
Mears, John
Paul, Jacob W.
Sproul, John
Sproul, William
Varny, Isaac W.
Varny, James

Waiter.
Dockendorf, Solomon

Capt. N. Morse's Company, Lieut. Col. E. Thatcher's Regiment.
From Sept. 10 to Sept. 29, 1814. Raised at Wiscasset.

RANK AND NAME.
Nathaniel Morse, Captain
Thomas Brentnall, Lieutenant
William Pitt, Lieutenant

Moses Hilton, Sergeant
Joshua Damon, Sergeant
Asa Dane, Sergeant
William Farnham, Corporal
James Lovell, Corporal
Samuel Lovell, Corporal
John McKenney, Corporal
Benjamin Gerry, Musician

Tilly H. Chesly, Musician
Burley Somes, Musician
Nehemiah Somes, Musician

Privates.
Burton, Frederic
Chamberlin, Ira
Chick, Silas
Damon, Israel
Farnham, John
Gray, William
Heard, James
Hedge, Barna

Hilton, Daniel
Hilton, Ellis
Hilton, Rufus
Leeland, Abner
McKenny, Daniel
Melvin, Daniel
Robbins, Chaney
Smith, Nathan
Stinson, James
Warren, John
Young, John

Lieut. J. Hunt's Detachment, Lieut. Col. E. Thatcher's Regiment.
From July 6 to Aug. 5, 1814. Service at Waldoboro.

RANK AND NAME.
John Hunt, Lieutenant

David Rivers, Sergeant
Charles Hebner, Sergeant

Privates.
Bradford, Josiah
Burnes, Jacob

Chase, Perkins
Clark, John
Clark, Joseph
Currier, James S.
Daggett, Frederick
Genthner, Charles
Hall, James
Howard, Caleb
Keizer, George

Maxey, Smith
Morton, Isaac
Palmer, Charles
Parsons, William
Snow, Ansel
Willey, John
Young, James

Lieut. W. McCobb's Company, Lieut. Col. E. Thatcher's Regiment.
From Sept. 12 to Sept. 28, 1814. Raised at Boothbay. Service at Boothbay.

RANK AND NAME.
William McCobb, Lieutenant
Jeremiah Holton, Lieutenant

William Reed, Sergeant
John Fuller, Sergeant
Paul McCobb, Sergeant
Joel Thompson, Sergeant
Samuel Tibbets, Corporal
John Fullerton, Corporal
Henry Williams, Corporal

Robert Reed, Corporal
William Bragg, Musician
Tilly H. Cleasby, Musician

Privates.
Auld, James
Auld, William
Briar, William
Favours, Peter
Fullerton, James
McCobb, Ephraim

McFarland, Ephraim
McFarland, John
Montgomery, Nathaniel
Morse, Joseph
Pinkham, John
Reed, Alexander
Reed, Henry
Robinson, William
Wylie, William

Ensign J. H. Becket's Detachment, Lieut. Col. E. Thatcher's Regiment.
From June 26 to July 15, 1814. Service at Friendship.

RANK AND NAME.		
Joseph H. Becket, Ensign	Condon, Saul	Morse, Ebenezer
	Condon, William	Morse, Elijah
Frederick Bradford, Sergeant	Cook, Elijah	Morse, Oliver
Edward Guy, Sergeant	Cook, Francis	Morton, Isaac
	Cook, James	Winchenpan, Daniel
Privates.	Cook, James, 2d	
Barton, John	Davis, Benjamin	
Card, George	Gyer, John	
	Lowry, Benjamin	

Ensign J. H. Becket's Detachment, Lieut. Col. E. Thatcher's Regiment.
From Nov. 3 to Nov. 5, 1814. Service at Camden.

RANK AND NAME.		
Joseph H. Becket, Ensign	Condin, William	Moote, William
	Cook, Cornelius	Morse, Jonah
Frederic Bradford, Sergeant	Cook, Elijah	Morse, Samuel
Solomon Bickmore, Sergeant	Guy, Jonah	Winchenpan, Henry
Adam Brause, Corporal	Horton, James	Winchenpan, John
	Horton, Joshua	Woltzgrove, Christopher
Privates.	Jamison, Thurston W.	
Card, George	Jones, Ezekiel S.	
Chadwick, James W.	Lathrop, John	
	Marble, James	

Capt. M. Robinson's Company, Lieut. Col. S. Thatcher's Regiment.
From June 2 to June 25, 1814. Service at Cushing.

RANK AND NAME.		
Moses Robinson, Captain	Elwell, Saul	Rivers, Thomas
	Fogerty, Saul	Robinson, Archibald
William Burton, Sergeant	Gay, Eleazer	Robinson, Benjamin
Benjamin Grafton, Sergeant	Gilchrist, James	Robinson, Charles
Dunbar Henderson, Sergeant	Gilchrist, James, 2d	Robinson, Charles, 2d
Darius Norton, Corporal	Gilchrist, Joseph	Robinson, Edward
	Hartshorn, Samuel	Robinson, Jacob
Privates.	Hartshorn, Saul	Robinson, John
Bradford, Isaiah	Henderson, William	Robinson, John L.
Burton, Isaac	Hyler, William	Robinson, Robert V.
Burton, Matthew	Killeran, Arthur S.	Robinson, Simon
Carby, Robert	Jameson, Thomas	Robinson, Yardley
Carter, John M.	Norton, Jabez	Scavy, Thomas
Davis, Francis	Nutting, Silas B.	Vose, John
Davis, Francis, 2d	Page, William	Willey, Robert
Davis, George	Page, William, Jr.	Willey, William
Davis, Richard	Parsons, James	Young, James
Davis, Robert	Parsons, William	
	Rivers, David	

Capt. J. Haskell's Company, Lieut. Col. S. Thatcher's Regiment.
From June 22 to June 27, Aug. 21 to Aug. 22, and Nov. 3 to Nov. 7, 1814. Raised at Thomaston. Service at Camden.

RANK AND NAME.		*Privates.*
John Haskell, Captain	Joseph Copeland, Jr., Sergeant	Anderson, James
Alexander Larmond, Jr., Lieutenant	George Larmond, Corporal	Barnard, John
John B. Rider, Lieutenant	Aaron L. Benson, Corporal	Blood, Simon
	William Stackpole, Corporal	Boggs, Ephraim
Daniel Newcomb, Sergeant	Franklin Sterns, Corporal	Butler, Brackett
James Willis, Sergeant	Pensley Wells, Musician	Creighton, John
Ivory Hovey, Sergeant	James Cox, Musician	Fales, Noyes

Capt. J. Haskell's Company, Lieut. Col. S. Thatcher's Regiment — Concluded.

Privates — Concluded.	McIntyre, Palmer	Storer, Elias
Hall, Benjamin	McIntyre, Thomas	Storer, John
Hawks, John B.	Robinson, William	Tilson, Gilbert
Kellock, Benjamin	Seavey, Gideon	Vose, David
Kellock, Samuel	Spear, Edward	Woodcock, Nathan
Lovejoy, John	Stafford, John	Woodcock, Patrick
McIntosh, Henry	Stall, Jacob	Young, Benjamin

Lieut. Col. S. Thatcher's Regiment.
From Sept. 3 to Sept. 18, 1814. Service at Camden.

FIELD AND STAFF.	James Head, Paymaster, Warren	NONCOMMISSIONED STAFF.
Samuel Thatcher, Lieutenant Colonel, Warren	Alfred Hovey, Quartermaster, Warren	William Crane, Sergeant Major
Isaac G. Reed, Major, Waldoboro	Edmund Buxton, Surgeon, Warren	Thomas S. Mallett, Quartermaster Sergeant
Herman Hawes, Major, Union	Joseph Huse, Surgeon's Mate, Camden	
Jesse Page, Adjutant, Warren	Jonathan Huse, Chaplain, Warren	

Capt. G. Clouse's Company, Lieut. Col. S. Thatcher's Regiment.
From Sept. 3 to Sept. 10, 1814. Raised at Waldoboro. Service at Camden.

RANK AND NAME.	Cromer, Charles	Riply, Daniel
George Clouse, Captain	Cromer, Cornelius	Roler, Jacob
Levi Soule, Lieutenant	Cushman, Seneca	Roler, Jacob, 2d
John Wagner, Ensign	Dolhiner, Paul	Roler, Jacob L.
	Flanders, Daniel	Roler, John
Godfrey Ludwing, Sergeant	Genthnor, John	Roler, John W.
William Close, Sergeant	Hager, Charles	Roler, Paul
George Kuhn, Sergeant	Hasses, Charles	Sidelinger, George
Charles Belnap, Sergeant	Hasses, William	Sides, Charles
Eleazer Nash, Corporal	Hock, Jacob	Sides, Philip
Jacob Roler, 3d, Corporal	Hock, John	Sprague, Abijah
Joseph Ludwing, Corporal	Kennedy, William	Turner, John
Henry Winchenpaw, Musician	Lash, Jacob	Wagner, William
	Light, Adam	Wallice, John
Privates.	Light, George	Wallice, William
Acron, George	Ludwing, James	Warner, John
Acron, Joseph	Moore, Richard	Wellman, Benjamin
Arf or Orf, George	Overlock, George	Winslow, Henry
Boardman, Saul	Overlock, John	Witt, Charles
Close, Jacob	Overlock, John, 2d	Witt, John W.

Capt. J. Fuller's Company, Lieut. Col. S. Thatcher's Regiment.
From Sept. 5 to Sept. 8, 1814. Raised at Warren. Service at Camden.

RANK AND NAME.	John Jamison, Corporal	Brackett, Joshua, 2d
Jonathan Fuller, Captain	Joel Robbins, Musician	Conce, Rufus
Marshall Wilber, Lieutenant	Ephraim Standish, Musician	Condy, Daniel
John M. Paskell, Ensign		Copeland, Amasa
	Privates.	Copeland, Bois
Alexander Kellock, Sergeant	Anderson, Archibald	Copeland, John
James Dickey, Sergeant	Anderson, Joshua	Copeland, Moses
Joseph Bucklin, Sergeant	Benson, Jonathan G.	Copeland, Rufus
James Paskell, Sergeant	Blake, John W.	Crawford, James
Charles Robinson, Corporal	Boggs, James	Cushman, Ezra
Hugh Anderson, Corporal	Boggs, James, 2d	Damoth, Jacob
Alexander Anderson, Corporal	Brackett, Joshua	Davis, Israel

Capt. J. Fuller's Company, Lieut. Col. S. Thatcher's Regiment — Concluded.

Privates — Concluded.
Dickey, David
French, Saul
French, William
Fuller, James
Hall, James
Hall, William
Hysler, Peter
Kellock, Adam
Kimball, George
Libbey, Alexander
Libbey, George
Libbey, Hatwil
Libbey, Henry
Libbey, Isaac

Libbey, James
Libbey, Oliver
Lincoln, Lot
McCollum, Andrew
McCollum, Andrew, 2d
McCollum, Archibald
McCollum, John
Robinson, Richard
Robinson, William
Rokes, John
Sidensparder, George
Sidensparder, John
Skinner, John
Spear, Alexander
Spear, Isaac

Standish, David
Standish, John
Standish, William
Standish, William, 2d
Summer, Saul
Summer, Seth
Vaugh, Daniel
Vose, John
Vose, Seth
Walton, William
Weston, George
Weston, Theodore
Young, Alexander
Young, William

Capt. D. Grafton's Company, Lieut. Col. S. Thatcher's Regiment.
From Sept. 3 to Sept. 7, and Nov. 3 to Nov. 7, 1814. Raised at Union. Service at Camden.

RANK AND NAME.
David Grafton, Captain
Baly Moore, Ensign

John M. Thorndick, Sergeant
Elisha Bennet, Sergeant
John Bachelor, Sergeant
Noah Rice, Sergeant
David Snell, Corporal
John Stevens, Corporal
Nathaniel Toby, Corporal
Willard Gilmore, Corporal
Ebenezer W. Adams, Musician
James Adams, Musician

Privates.
Barnard, Thomas
Bartlett, Jason
Bennet, Saul
Bills, Jason
Blunt, Ebenezer
Boothe, Isaac
Bowen, Amos
Bowen, Ezra

Burns, John
Butler, John
Butler, John, 2d
Carver, Nathan
Clark, Ezekiel
Clark, Joseph
Collamore, Alpheus
Dagget, Henry
Dagget, Samuel
Dagget, William
Drake, Jesse
Drake, John
Fossitt, Henry
Grinat, Daniel B.
Hagar, Ezekiel
Hagar, Sewel
Hascall, David
Hawes, Noyes P.
Hawes, Whiting
Hill, Josiah
Houghton, Evelio
Howard, Caleb
Hutler, Simon
Irish, Cornelius

Lathrop, Howard
Libbey, Jacob
Libbey, William
Lincoln, Daniel
Litchfield, Benjamin
Luce, Thadeus
March, Henry
Miller, Joseph
Mitchell, Thomas A.
Morse, Moses
Peabody, Stephen
Piper, Samuel
Rice, Nathan
Robbins, John P.
Sincklar, James
Sleeper, Nathaniel
Snell, Shadrack
Thompson, James
Thompson, John
Titus, Conly
Townsend, Isaac
Whitney, John
Wood, Saul

Capt. J. W. Lindley's Company, Lieut. Col. S. Thatcher's Regiment.
From Sept. 3 to Sept. 8, 1814. Raised at Union. Service at Camden.

RANK AND NAME.
John W. Lindley, Captain
Harvy Maxey, Lieutenant
Saul Stone, Ensign

David Robbins, Sergeant
Peter W. Robbins, Sergeant
Fisher Hart, Sergeant
Reuben Hills, Sergeant
Spencer Mero, Musician
Thomas Arnold, Musician

Privates.
Carrid, Nathan
Chase, Calvin
Cobb, Ebenezer
Cumins, David
Fogler, John
Gay, David
Gay, Obed
Hills, Joel
Hills, Saul
Irish, Ichabod
Law, Benjamin L.

Litterall, James
Maxey, Waterman
Robbins, Ebenezer
Sheperd, Thaddeus
Simons, Moses
Simons, Ziba
Stone, Ebenezer
Taylor, Thomas
Wentworth, Saul
Young, Anson
Young, David

Capt. S. Parker's Company, Lieut. Col. S. Thatcher's Regiment.
From Sept. 3 to Sept. 10, 1814. Raised at Friendship. Service at Friendship.

RANK AND NAME.		
Simon Parker, Captain	Card, George	Geyer, Saul
John Studley, Lieutenant	Card, John	Horn, Andrew
Joseph H. Becker, Ensign	Chadwick, James W.	Jones, Ezekiel S.
	Cook, Cornelius	Lothrop, John
	Cook, Elijah	Lowry, Benjamin
Frederic Bradford, Sergeant	Cook, Francis	Marble, Jerome
Solomon Bickmore, Sergeant	Cook, James	Morse, Ebenezer
Zenas Cook, Sergeant	Cook, James, 2d	Morse, Jonah
Edward Gay, Sergeant	Coudin, Saul	Morse, Oliver
James Bradford, Corporal	Coudin, William	Morse, Saul
James Frye, Musician	Davis, Benjamin	Morton, John
	Davis, Robert	Morton, Joshua
Privates.	Davis, Robert, 2d	Parker, Oliver
Bennet, Asa	Davis, Thomas	Winchenpaw, Henry
Burnet, Almond	Gay, Jonah	

Capt. P. Keizor's Company, Lieut. Col. S. Thatcher's Regiment.
From Sept. 4 to Sept. 10, 1814. Raised at Waldoboro. Service at Camden.

RANK AND NAME.	Castner, Charles	Newbit, Christopher
Philip Keizor, Captain	Clark, John	Newbit, John
John Hunt, Lieutenant	Coll, Abram	Newbit, Michel, 2d
Frederic Castner, Ensign	Coll, James	Newbit, Michel, 3d
	Cushman, Abel	Overlock, Jacob
George Fooler or Fuller, Sergeant	Ewell, Nathan	Palmer, Nathaniel
Gardner Davis, Sergeant	Farnsworth, John	Pitcher, James
Zebedee Simmons, Sergeant	Farnsworth, Robert	Pitcher, John
Joseph Vinal, Sergeant	Fish, Church	Russell, Peleg
George Keiler, 2d, Sergeant	Fish, Saul	Schwartz, Jacob
Joseph Overlock, Corporal	Fitzgerald, Andrew	Schwartz, Peter
Nathaniel Pitcher, Corporal	Hahn, John	Shennemow, James
George Keizor or Raizor, Corporal	Hasses, Andrew	Shuman, John
Bradly Mowry, Musician	Hasses, George	Shuman, Joseph
Caleb Howard, Musician	Hasses, Henry	Sides, Charles
	Heabner, Charles	Sides, Lorin
Privates.	Hebbard, Isaac	Speer, Joshua
Allen, Duty	Howard, William	Sproul, James
Barnes, Benjamin	Keen, Charles	Sproul, Thomas
Barnes, James	Keizor, George	Swetland, Charles
Barns, Jacob	Kuhn, Jacob	Taylor, Godfrey
Bartlett, John	Kuhn, Paul	Taylor, Philip
Benner, Christopher	Kuhn, Peter	Vinal, John
Benner, George	Lash, Casiniah	Wade, Levi
Benner, Jacob	Melvin, Amos	Waldo, Michel
Benner, John	Mink, Andrew	Wallice, Saul
Benner, Philip	Mink, George	West, Matthias
Brown, Hector	Mink, John	White, James
Burket, Henry	Mink, John, 3d	Willet, Thomas
Burket, Jacob, 2d	Mink, Philip	Winslow, Ezekiel
Burket, John	Mink, Philip, 2d	Winslow, Jacob
Burket, John, 3d	Newbit, Adam	

Capt. C. Miller's Company, Lieut. Col. S. Thatcher's Regiment.
From Sept. 4 to Sept. 10, 1814. Raised at Waldoboro. Service at Camden.

Rank and Name.	Privates.	
Charles Miller, Captain	Acron, Charles	Kalah, George
Jacob Ludwing, Lieutenant	Acron, George	Kalah, John
Thomas Simmons, Ensign	Acron, John	Kalah, Joseph
	Arnold, Benjamin	Kinsel, John
John Brown, Sergeant	Benner, Charles, 2d	Labi, John
Saul Morse, Sergeant	Benner, Frederic	Lash, John
Saul A. Thomas, Sergeant	Bonneman, John	Light, Francis
Daniel Simpson, Sergeant	Brock, John	Miller, Charles
Daniel Blake, Corporal	Chase, John	Miller, Frank
Martin Dennett, Corporal	Demuth, Charles	Miller, John
John Freeman, Corporal	Demuth, John	Moody, William
Jacob Barker, Corporal	Demuth, Philip	Overlock, George
Christian Holter, Musician	Fish, William, Jr.	Schenck, Andrew
James Simmons, Musician	Groton, Joseph	Schwartz, Jacob, 4th
	Hahn, George	Schwartz, John M.
	Head, John B.	Sides, John
	Hill, Philip	Umberhind, Charles

Capt. L. Andrews' Company, Lieut. Col. S. Thatcher's Regiment.
From Sept. 5 to Sept. 8, 1814. Raised at Warren. Service at Camden.

Rank and Name.		
Lemuel Andrews, Captain (absent)	Crawford, Malcomb	Rogers, Joshua
Oliver Copeland, Ensign	Crawford, William	Russell, Amasa
	Creighton, James	Russell, Rufus
	Dunbar, Jesse	Skinner, Alexander
William Montgomery, Sergeant	Farrington, Isaac	Skinner, Ebenezer
Stephen C. Burgess, Sergeant	Farrington, John	Skinner, James
Peter Fuller, Sergeant	Hodges, John	Skinner, Joseph
Archibald Crawford, Corporal	Howard, Thomas	Skinner, Thomas
Samuel Connce, Corporal	Hunnewell, Calvin	Snow, Ansel
Abner Farrington, Corporal	Jones, John	Spear, Saul
Thomas Starrett, Musician	Jones, Lewis	Stall, Henry
Miller Martin, Musician	Kirkpatrick, John	Starret, Charles
	Laurence, Jeremiah D.	Starret, James
Privates.	Laurence, Joshua	Starret, Lewis
Cobb, Nathaniel	Leach, Enoch	Starret, William
Cobb, Rowland	Libbey, Samuel	Sumner, Charles
Comery, Mathew	Maxey, Smith	Swift, Zipha
Copeland, Charles	Montgomery, Robert	Thomas, John
Crawford, Alexander	Parker, Josiah	Wetherbee, Charles
Crawford, Joseph	Payson, John	

Capt. L. Andrews' Company, Lieut. Col. S. Thatcher's Regiment.
From Nov. 3 to Nov. 7, 1814. Raised at Warren. Service at Camden.

Rank and Name.	Jeremiah D. Lawrence, Corporal	Farrington, Abner
Lemuel Andrews, Captain	Miller Martin, Musician	Farrington, Isaac
Benjamin Andrews, Lieutenant		Fogerty, Samuel
Peter Fuller, Ensign	*Privates.*	Harrington, John
	Bogs, Joshua	Hodgkins, John
Cyrus Eaton, Sergeant	Cobb, Nathaniel	Jones, John
Archibald Crawford, Sergeant	Conry, Mathias	Kellock, Charles
Samuel Connce, Sergeant	Copeland, Charles	Laurence, Joshua
Calvin Heminway, Sergeant	Crawford, Joseph	Laurence, Shuman
Alexander Crawford, Corporal	Crawford, Malcom	Leach, Enoch
Roland Cobb, Corporal	Crawford, William	Leach, Jerathmalel
Zipha Swift, Corporal	Creighton, James	Libbey, Samuel

Capt. L. Andrews' Company, Lieut. Col. S. Thatcher's Regiment — Concluded.

Privates — Concluded.
Payson, John
Russell, Amasa
Russell, Rufus
Skinner, Alexander
Skinner, Ebenezer

Skinner, James
Skinner, Joseph
Skinner, Thomas
Spear, Saul
Stall, Henry
Starret, Charles

Starret, James
Starret, Lewis
Starret, William L.
Sumner, Charles

Capt. J. Fuller's Company, Lieut. Col. S. Thatcher's Regiment.
From Nov. 3 to Nov. 7, 1814. Raised at Warren. Service at Camden.

RANK AND NAME.
Jonathan Fuller, Captain
Marshall Wilber, Lieutenant
John M. Paskell, Ensign

Alexander Kellock, Sergeant
Joseph Bucklin, Sergeant
Charles Robinson, Sergeant
Hugh Anderson, Sergeant
George Weston, Corporal
Jonathan G. Benson, Corporal
Edward Weston, Musician
Alexander Anderson, Musician

Privates.
Anderson, Joshua
Blake, John W.
Boggs, James
Brown, Robert
Conce, Rufus
Condy, Daniel

Copeland, Amasa
Copeland, Bois
Copeland, Moses
Crawford, James
Cushman, Ezra
Davis, Israel
Davis, Osman
Dickey, David
French, Saul
French, William
Fuller, James
Hysler, Peter
Kellock, Adam
Lamson, William
Libbey, George
Libbey, Hatwell
Libbey, Henry
Libbey, Isaac
Libbey, James
Libbey, Oliver
McCollum, Andrew

McCollum, Archibald
McCollum, John
Robinson, Richard
Sidensparder, George
Sidensparder, John
Skinner, Isaac
Skinner, John
Spear, Alexander
Spear, David
Spear, Hugh
Spear, Isaac
Standish, James
Standish, John
Standish, William
Still, Philip
Sumner, Saul
Vaugh or Vaughan, Daniel
Vose, John
Vose, Seth
Young, Alexander
Young, William

Capt. J. W. Lindley's Company, Lieut. Col. S. Thatcher's Regiment.
From Nov. 3 to Nov. 7, 1814. Raised at Union. Service at Camden.

RANK AND NAME.
John W. Lindley, Captain
Harvey Maxey, Lieutenant
Saul Stone, Ensign

David Robbins, Sergeant
Peter W. Robbins, Sergeant
Fisher Hart, Sergeant
Nathan Packard, Sergeant
Jacob Townsend, Musician
John Hart, Musician
Spencer Mero, Musician

Privates.
Carrid, Nathan
Chase, Calvin
Gay, David
Gay, Obed
Hills, Joel
Hills, Reuben, 2d
Irish, Ichabod
Law, Benjamin L.
Litterall, James
Maxey, Waterman
Morse, Jonathan

Robbins, Ebenezer
Simons, Moses
Simons, Ziba
Stone, Ebenezer
Taylor, John
Taylor, Thomas
Wintworth, Saul
Young, Aaron
Young, David

Capt. M. Robinson's Company, Lieut. Col. S. Thatcher's Regiment.
From Nov. 3 to Nov. 7, 1814. Service at Cushing.

RANK AND NAME.
Moses Robinson, Captain

Privates.
Bradford, Isaiah
Burton, Isaac
Burton, William
Davis, Francis
Elwell, Samuel
Gay, John
Gilchrist, Matthew
Harthorn, Samuel
Henderson, Dunbar
Henderson, William
Hyler, Herman
Hyler, William
Jameson, Thomas
Karsons, James

Kerby, Robert
Killeran, Arthur F.
Killeran, Thomas C.
Killeran, William
Malcomb, Andrew
Malcomb, William
McCarter, Isaac
McCarter, James
McCarter, John
McCarter, Robert
McIntire, John
Miller, Jonah
Norton, Darius
Norton, Jabez
Page, William, Jr.
Rivers, Thomas
Robinson, Archibald
Robinson, Benjamin

Robinson, Charles
Robinson, Cornelius
Robinson, E.
Robinson, Jacob
Robinson, John
Robinson, John L.
Robinson, John W.
Robinson, Marlboro
Robinson, Simon
Seavey, Thomas
Smith, Martin
Smith, Thomas
Vose, William
Willey, Robert
Willey, William
Young, James

Lieut. L. Soule's Detachment, Lieut. Col. S. Thatcher's Regiment.
From Oct. 5 to Nov. 11, 1814. Raised at Waldoboro. Service at Friendship.

RANK AND NAME.
Levi Soule, Lieutenant

James F. Paskel, Sergeant
Edward Gay, Sergeant
John Pitcher, Corporal
Frederic Bradford, Corporal

Privates.
Arnold, Thomas
Benner, Frederic
Boggs, James, 2d
Brown, Hector
Butler, Flavel
Conner, Charles
Conner, Charles, Jr.

Cook, F.
Dolhims, Paul
Enghly, John
Esenby, Charles
Ewell, Charles
Heaborn, Charles
Hill, Samuel, 2d
Jones, Lines
Keizor, George
Larmand, Joshua
Larrance, Shuman
Lash, Jacob
Lash, John
Lincoln, Lot
Lincoln, Lot, 2d
Maxey, Smith

Meservy, Charles
McBeath, Henry
McIntire, Robert
McLellen, James
Morton, Isaac
Moses, Oliver
Robinson, Alexander
Seavey, Thomas
Shannemon, James
Snow, Ansel
Waldo, Michell
Wetherbee, Charles
Willy, Peleg
Wilson, Theodore

Ensign J. McIntire's Detachment, Lieut. Col. S. Thatcher's Regiment.
From Sept. 5 to Oct. 6, 1814. Service at Cushing.

RANK AND NAME.
John McIntire, Ensign

Thomas Killeran, Sergeant
Eleazer Gay, Corporal

Privates.
Bradford, Isaiah
Davis, Francis
Gage, William
Gilchrist, Joseph
Killeran, Arthur T.

Malcom, William
Parson, William
Rivers, David
Robinson, John L.
Robinson, John W.

MASSACHUSETTS VOLUNTEER MILITIA IN THE WAR OF 1812.

Lieut. Col. C. Thomas' Regiment.
From June 20 to June 22, and Sept. 10 to Sept. 29, 1814. Service at Bath.

FIELD AND STAFF.
Charles Thomas, Lieutenant Colonel, Brunswick
Thomas S. Estabrooks, Major, Brunswick
Nathaniel Poors, Major, Brunswick
William Sewall, Adjutant, Brunswick
Nathaniel Badger, Adjutant, Brunswick

Silas H. Dodge, Quartermaster, Brunswick
Charles Thomas, Jr., Paymaster, Brunswick
Jacob Herrick, Chaplain, Durham
Jonathan Page, Surgeon, Brunswick
Moses Holbrook, Surgeon's Mate, Bath

NONCOMMISSIONED STAFF.
Martin Anderson, Sergeant Major
John Dunning, Quartermaster Sergeant
John E. Coombs, Musician

Capt. R. D. Dunning's Company, Lieut. Col. C. Thomas' Regiment.
From June 20 to June 22, and Sept. 10 to Sept. 29, 1814. Raised at Brunswick. Service at Bath.

RANK AND NAME.
Robert D. Dunning, Captain
John Owen, Lieutenant
John Coburn, Ensign

Epha Brown, Sergeant
Aaron Dunning, Sergeant
John Dunning, 3d, Sergeant
Joseph Noyes, Sergeant
Isaac O. Robertson, Corporal
Joshua Herrick, Corporal
John Brown, Corporal
David Shaw, Corporal
Samuel Given, Musician
Edward Eaton, Musician

Privates.
Baker, Zacharias
Bradley, Foster
Brown, Gardner, Jr.
Clark, John, 2d
Davis, Joseph W.
Dinsmore, James
Dunlap, Robert
Dunning, Joseph N.
Ellet, James
Flood, Henry
Fuller, Ira
Graffam, Thomas
Graves or Groves, John
Hall, Neal
Hammond, James R.
Hunt, William

Kidder, Jonathan
Lock, Abraham
Moore, Richard
Moulton, Samuel
Mullen, Thomas
Mustard, William
Noyes, James
Osgood, Theodore
Owen, Saul
Ross, James, 3d
Sampson, Alexander
Shaw, John
Titcomb, John F.
Toothaker, John
Wing, Calvin
Woodside, George

Capt. E. Warren's Company, Lieut. Col. C. Thomas' Regiment.
From June 20 to June 22, and Sept. 10 to Sept. 29, 1814. Raised at Durham. Service at Bath.

RANK AND NAME.
Ebenezer Warren, Captain
Francis Harmon, Lieutenant
William Newell, Ensign

Zebulon York, Sergeant
Ebenezer Roberts, Sergeant
Henry Warren, Sergeant
William Gerrish, Sergeant
Joshua Gerrish, Corporal
John Fairfield, Corporal
Lemuel Nichols, Corporal
Ivory Warren, Corporal
Israel Newell, Corporal
James Woodbury, Musician

Privates.
Adams, Andrew, Jr.
Beal, Joseph
Bennet, Francis
Blithin, Andrew
Blithin, John
Booker, James
Cushin, James
Cushin, Quincy
Davis, William
Duran, Nathaniel
Dyer, James
Dyer, Richard

Farr, John
Fifield, Israel
Gerrish, Benjamin
Gerrish, Charles
Gerrish, James
Gerrish, John
Gerrish, Moses
Goodwin, Samuel
Harmon, Isaiah
Harmon, Robery
Harmond, Daniel
Harrington, William
Hebbert, Timothy M.
Herrick, Jacob, 3d
Higgins, Reuben
Hoyt, John, 3d
Hoyt, Joseph
Johnson, William
Knight, Francis
Knight, Parker
Littlefield, George
Maxwell, James
Merrill, Jabez
Milcolm, Joseph
Mitchell, Peter
Moses, Benjamin M.
Newell, John
Nichols, James
Orr, Clement

Osgood, Aaron, Jr.
Osgood, David, Jr.
Osgood, Moses
Osgood, Nathaniel, Jr.
Osgood, Saul G.
Pierce, Seth
Potterfield, William
Rouck, John
Rouck, William
Runnels, Thomas
Snow, Ebenezer
Snow, Moses
Snow, Simeon
Stetson, Charles
Stetson, Isaac
Strout, Ebenezer
Sylvester, Job, 3d
Sylvester, Joseph
Thomas, Theophilus
Tracy, Saul
True, Benjamin
Vining, Benjamin
Vining, William
Wagg, Saul
Warmal, Henry
Warren, Rufus
Wesson, Stephen

Capt. J. Dustin's Drafted Company, Lieut. Col. C. Thomas' Regiment.
From June 27 to July 11, 1814. Service at Bath.

RANK AND NAME.
Joseph Dustin, Captain
Nathaniel Todd, Lieutenant
John Dunning, Ensign

Zebulon York, Sergeant
Nathaniel Merryman, Sergeant
Stephen Foss, Sergeant
Nathan Farrow, Sergeant
David Cowing, Corporal
Jesse Mersevey, Corporal
Josiah Farrow, Corporal
John Lord, Corporal
Henry Sampson, Musician
John Given, Musician

Privates.
Adams, Andrew
Alexander, John
Bisbee, Studly
Bragdon, John
Cannon, John
Chase, Judah
Cook, Barnabas
Coombs, Asa, Jr.
Coombs, Joseph
Coombs, William

Dinsmore, Charles
Doughty, Jacob
Douglas, William
Dunlap, Ebenezer
Dunlap, Ezekiel
Eaton, Abel
Eaton, John
Estes, John
Farr, John
Furbush, Isaac
Furbush, John
Gowell, Charles
Grant, Benjamin
Gray, John
Hanscom, James
Harridan, Andrew
Hill, Rowland
Hinkley, William
Hunter, Timothy
Irish, James
Kimball, Dean
Mallett, William, Jr.
Mariner, John, 3d
Maxwell, Noble
McIntosh, Nathan
McKinney, William
Metcalf, Benjamin

Mitchell, A.
Morse, Ephraim
Peterson, Africa
Purrington, Isaac
Ransom, David
Roak, William
Ross, Robert, Jr.
Sawyer, Samuel
Scaley, Sylvester
Sennett, Hugh
Smart, William, 2d
Smith, James
Snow, Ebenezer
Spark, James, Jr.
Stanwood, Samuel
Stoddard, Jeremiah
Strout, Ebenezer
Tarr, Joseph
Tolman or Totman, Elias
Varney, William
Webber, Stephen
Welsh, Daniel
Whitney, Abizer
Wilson, James, 1st
Wilson, James, 2d
Woodward, James
Woodward, Joseph

Capt. J. Dustin's Commanding Drafted Company, Lieut. Col. C. Thomas' Regiment.
From July 9 to July 27, 1814. Service at Bath.

RANK AND NAME.
Joseph Dustin, Captain
Nathaniel Todd, Lieutenant
John Dunning, Ensign

Zebulon York, Sergeant
Henry Jordan, Sergeant
Benjamin Whitney, Sergeant
Abizer Whitney, Sergeant
Joshua Gerrish, Corporal
James Farrow, Corporal
David Hannaford, Corporal
Benjamin Alexander, Corporal
Cornelius Thompson, Musician
James Woodbury, Musician

Privates.
Adams, John
Barnes, Charles
Bragdon, Nathaniel
Campbell, Adam
Carr, Joseph
Coombs, Asa
Coombs, Joseph, Jr.
Coombs, William S.
Donnell, Abel
Dunlap, Martin

Eastman, Kingsbery
Eaton, Leonard
Elliott, James, 2d
Farr, Simeon
Frazier, James
Gardner, John
Gilbert, Lee
Given, David
Gowbert, Nicholas
Grant, Unite
Hannaford, William
Hewey, Jonathan
Hopkins, Isaac
Jack, Joseph
Jackson, William
Jaques, Aaron
Jones, John
Jordan, Robert
Kilgore, William
Knight, Stephen
Larrabee, William
Libby, Jonathan
Mariner, Thomas
Mayhew, Zacheus
McKenney, William
Means, John
Michaels, William

Miller, Stephen
Mitchell, Dummer
Morse, Adam
Newell, John
Page, Samuel
Patten, William
Peterson, Benjamin
Plummer, Daniel
Potter, John, 2d
Potter, Robert
Pratt, Samuel
Preble, William
Robertson, John
Shirtliff, William
Sinclair, John
Smith, Edward
Snow, Isaac
Snow, Moses
Stafford, Edward
Starbird, John
Thomas, William
Thompson, Peltiah
Trask, Abiezer
Varney, Enoch
Weymouth, David
Wheeler, Joseph
Witham, Benjamin

MASSACHUSETTS VOLUNTEER MILITIA IN THE WAR OF 1812.

Capt. W. Torrey's Company, Lieut. Col. C. Thomas' Regiment.
From July 25 to Aug. 6, 1814. Raised at Bath. Service at Bath.

RANK AND NAME.
William Torrey, Captain
Elias Statten, Lieutenant
John W. Stinson, Ensign

Joseph W. Marsh, Sergeant
William R. Webb, Sergeant
Thomas H. Gage, Sergeant
Benjamin Brown, Sergeant
Peleg Bradford, Corporal
Christopher A. Brown, Corporal
George Bowe, Corporal
Samuel Owen, Corporal
James Dunning, Musician
Robert Simpson, Musician

Privates.
Alexander, Hugh
Alexander, James
Allen, Micah
Anderson, John
Arnold, Ebenezer
Aubins, George
Badger, Joseph
Barton, John
Blasdell, Jonathan
Blin, Joshua
Bowman, Samuel G.
Brown, Elisha

Brown, William
Card, Joseph
Card, Thomas, Jr.
Delano, Joshua
Drummond, Ezekiel
Estes, John
Gatchell, Aaron
Gerrish, Charles
Gerrish, Moses
Hagan, Thomas
Haley, James
Haley, Thomas
Hall, William
Harding, Nehemiah
Hatch, Davis
Higgins, Reuben
Hilton, Alfred
Innis, Samuel
Knight, Francis
Lambard, James
Lemont, Robert
Marston, Daniel
McManners, James, Jr.
Merriman, Thomas
Owen, Jeremiah
Parks, John D.
Porter, Rufus R.
Preble, John
Purrington, John, Jr.

Purrington, Nathaniel
Reed, Charles
Robinson, Jeremiah
Ryan, Charles
Sayward, Luther
Sewall, Charles
Shaw, Joseph
Skofield, Jacob
Spea, David
Sprague, Oakman
Springer, David T.
Sylvester, Marlborough
Tarr, Benjamin
Thomas, Ephraim
Ticket, Vinson
Todd, Thomas
Trott, David
Vining, Ammi
Wade, Caleb
Walker, David
White, James
Witham, Ammon
Wormwood, Jotham

Waiters.
Crooker, Robert
Drummond, Alexander

Capt. W. Webster's Company, Lieut. Col. C. Thomas' Regiment.
From Sept. 7 to Sept. 13, 1814. Raised at Durham. Service at Bath.

RANK AND NAME.
William Webster, Captain
Paul Snow, Lieutenant
John Dunning, 2d, Ensign

James Merryman, Sergeant
Joseph Badger, Sergeant
Simeon Hopkins, Jr., Sergeant
Rufus Bisbee, Sergeant
Jesse Maservey, Corporal
Cornelius Toothaker, Corporal
Edmund Dow, Corporal
John Fifield, Corporal
Joshua Robinson, Musician

Privates.
Barringdon, William
Beal, Joseph
Bennet, Francis
Blake, Samuel
Blanchard, Josiah
Blithen, John
Booker, James
Bradly, Foster
Chase, Enoch
Cox, Isaac
Crowell, John

Curtis, James
Cushing, Quincy
Doughty, Stephen
Dresser, Ebenezer
Dunning, Thomas
Estham, James
Gripps, John, Jr.
Hasbrook, Israel
Hoyt, Joseph
Hunt, William, 2d
Jones, Joshua
Larrabee, William
Larrabee, William, Jr.
Levit, Caleb
Levitt, George
Littlefield, Ward
Matthews, Samuel
McLellan, Alexander
Merritt, Henry
Merryman, Benjamin
Merryman, Michel, Jr.
Milcher, John
Morris, Joseph
Morse, James
Nichols, Samuel
Orr, David
Orr, William

Parker, Amos
Parker, Nathaniel
Parsley, Eliphalet
Peters, Simon
Peterson, Benjamin
Peterson, Benjamin, 2d
Plummer, Jeremiah
Pollard, George
Purinton, Joshua
Reed, William
Roberts, Samuel, Jr.
Rourk, John
Sawyer, Samuel
Simpson, Lewy, Jr.
Simpson, Matthew
Skofield, John
Snow, Simeon
Stanwood, David, 3d
Stilkey, George
Stover, David
Stutson, Isaac
Sylvester, William
Toothaker, Isaac
Toothaker, Seth
Webster, William

Capt. R. T. Dunlap's Company, Lieut. Col. C. Thomas' Regiment.
From Sept. 10 to Sept. 29, 1814. Raised at Brunswick. Service at Bath.

RANK AND NAME.
Richard T. Dunlap, Captain
Richard McMannas, Lieutenant

Davis Stanwood, 2d, Sergeant
William Titcomb, Sergeant
Nathaniel Merryman, Sergeant
Joseph Badger, Sergeant
Benjamin Titcomb, Jr., Sergeant (?)
Henry Merritt, Corporal
Saul Owen, Corporal
Alfred Clark, Corporal
Jeremiah O'Brian, Corporal
Isaac Cox, Corporal
Samuel Moore, Musician
Odiorne Lovejoy, Musician

Privates.
Blake, Samuel
Bowker, Washington
Carey, Alanson
Caswell, Wilber
Clark, John
Cowing, Daniel
Cox, James
Curtis, Joshua
Curtis, William

Dailey, Silas
Eaton, Abner
Eaton, Daniel, Jr.
Elliot, James, 2d
Given, Thomas
Grant, John
Grant, Unite
Gray, John
Groves, Thomas
Hand, Hammond
James, William
Kimball, Joseph
Kinkade, David
Lambert, James
Lemont, Adam
Litchfield, Ward
Littlefield, James
Lovell, John
Lovell, Simeon
Lunt, Joseph
Lunt, Josiah
McLellan, Alexander
McMannas, Charles
McMannas, Richard, 2d
Merriman, Thomas, 2d
Merriman, Timothy
Merritt, Jesse

Milcher, Samuel, 3d
Minot, George
Morse, Lemuel
Morse, Paul
Moses, Benjamin
Otis, James
Owen, Jeremiah
Ransom, David
Rodick, William
Ross, John
Ross, Robert, 2d
Ross, William
Ryan, Charles
Simpson, William
Skofield, James
Sloan, Robert
Snow, Abiezer
Stanwood, Philip
Starbird, William, Jr.
Taylor, Phineas
Thomas, Ephraim
Thompson, Peltiah
Toothaker, Abraham
Toothaker, Alexander
Toothaker, Isaac
Turner, James
Woodard, Martin

Capt. J. Dustin's Company, Lieut. Col. C. Thomas' Regiment.
From Sept. 10 to Sept. 29, 1814. Raised at Brunswick. Service at Bath.

RANK AND NAME.
Joseph Dustin, Captain
William Pennell, Lieutenant
John Dunning, Ensign

Benjamin Brown, Sergeant
Thomas Given, Sergeant
James Dunning, 2d, Sergeant
Jazariah Lewis, Sergeant
Benjamin Alexander, Corporal
Jesse Meservey, Corporal
Charles Anderson, Corporal
Thomas Dunning, Corporal
John Given, 3d, Musician
Robert Simpson, Musician

Privates.
Blasdell, Jonathan
Chase, George
Cripps, John
Curtis, Abiezer

Curtis, Calvin
Curtis, Melzer
Given, Benjamin
Given, David, Jr.
Given, John, 2d
Gould, Joseph
Graffam, Samuel
Hodgdon, Jeremiah
Hunt, William, 2d
Mariner, John, 3d
Michaels, William
Miller, Stephen
Miller, William, 3d
Minot, Vincent
Morse, Adam
Morse, Anthony, Jr.
Morse, James
Morse, Joseph, Jr.
Mosely, William
Parsley, Eliphalet
Pennell, Jacob

Pennell, Robert
Scofield, Jacob
Simpson, Lewis
Simpson, Mathew
Stanwood, Benjamin
Stanwood, David
Stanwood, James, 3d
Stanwood, Judah, 1st
Stanwood, Judah, 2d
Stanwood, Robert
Stevens, Reuben
Stilkey, George
Woodside, Robert
Woodside, Stinson
Woodside, William
Woodward, Nathan

Waiters.
Blanchard, Josiah
Dustan, Dunning

Capt. D. Johnson's Company, Lieut. Col. C. Thomas' Regiment.

From Sept. 10 to Sept. 29, 1814. Raised at Harpswell. Service at Bath.

RANK AND NAME.
David Johnson, Captain
Peleg Curtis, Lieutenant
David Curtis, Ensign

James Merryman, Sergeant
Benjamin Randall, Sergeant
Isaac Sylvester, Sergeant
James S. Wier, Sergeant
Ebenezer Curtis, Corporal
Thomas Merryman, Corporal
John Reed, Jr., Corporal
Simeon Orr, Corporal
James Dunning, Musician
Jacob Merryman, Musician
Fryeholt Eastman, Musician

Privates.
Alexander, Hugh
Alexander, Isaac
Alexander, Joseph
Allen, Ephraim, Jr.
Barston, Robert
Bibber, Cortney

Booker, Daniel, Jr.
Clark, David
Curtis, James
Curtis, Paul, Jr.
Curtis, Simeon
Douglass, George
Ewing, James, Jr.
Ewing, John
Gardner, Robert
Hearsey, John
Hodgkins, Benjamin
Ingalls, John N.
Jordan, William
Kemp, Silas
Matthews, Samuel
Merryman, James, 3d (D.)
Merryman, John
Merryman, Mitchell, Jr. (D.)
Merryman, Samuel
Merryman, Waitsdel
Merryman, William
Orr, David
Orr, William
Perry, David

Sinnet, Hugh (D.)
Skofield, Samuel
Stephens, William H.
Stover, Daniel
Stover, David
Stover, John
Stover, Joseph
Stover, Joshua
Stover, Paul (D.)
Sylvester, John
Sylvester, Marlborough, Jr.
Sylvester, William
Thomas, Jesse (D.)
Tinkham, Richard
Toothaker, David
Webber, Charles
Wheeler, John
Wheeler, Simeon
Wilson, John

Waiters.
Blake, John
Blasland, William
Clerk, Paul

Capt. P. Jordan's, Jr., Company, Lieut. Col. C. Thomas' Regiment.

From Sept. 10 to Sept. 29, 1814. Raised at Brunswick. Service at Bath.

RANK AND NAME.
Peter Jordan, Jr., Captain
Isaac Woodward, Lieutenant

Josiah T. Tappin, Sergeant
Henry Jordan, Sergeant
Rufus Bisbee, Sergeant
Jordan Snow, Sergeant
Thomas Mariner, Corporal
Caleb Levit, Corporal
Benjamin Peterson, Corporal
Benjamin Gatchell, Corporal
Joseph Mariner, Musician
John Peterson, Musician

Privates.
Bisbee, Sturdly
Coombs, Joseph, Jr.
Coombs, Samuel
Cotton, Levi

Cowing, David, Jr.
Crawford, Charles
Crawford, John, Jr.
Crowell, John
Curtis, John
Danforth, Enoch
Davis, Miab
Donnel, Abel
Doughty, Jacob G.
Doughty, Stephen
Easter, John
Farrin, Winthrop, Jr.
Gatchell, Aaron
Harding, Nehemiah
Hildreth, Hosea
Holbrook, John
Holmes, William
Hyde, Jude
Jordan, Abijah
Jordan, Jesse

Larrabee, Ephraim
Larrabee, James
Larrabee, Joseph W.
Lewis, Nathan
Linscot, Abijah
Linscot, Abraham
Linscott, Joseph
Low, Samuel
Mann, Joseph
Mariner, Unight
Milcher, John
Peters, Simon
Pollard, George
Smiley, David
Thomas, William
Wallas, John
Winslow, Job
Woodward, Ebenezer
Woodward, John
Woodward, Samuel

Capt. S. Snow's Company, Lieut. Col. C. Thomas' Regiment.

From Sept. 10 to Sept. 29, 1814. Raised at Harpswell. Service at Bath.

RANK AND NAME.
Stephen Snow, Captain
Paul Snow, Lieutenant
William Merritt, Ensign

Stephen Merritt, Sergeant
Jonathan Holbrook, Sergeant
Elisha Coombs, Sergeant

William Thomas, Sergeant
Samuel Toothaker, Corporal
Cornelius Toothaker, Corporal
Kingsbury Eastman, Corporal
Simeon Hopkins, Corporal
Daniel Sawyer, Musician
Josiah Green, Musician

Privates.
Alexander, John
Aubins, George
Aubins, Humphry
Coombs, Jesse
Dingly, Spencer
Dresser, Ebenezer
Eastman, James

Capt. S. Snow's Company, Lieut. Col. C. Thomas' Regiment — Concluded.

Privates — Concluded.	Purington, Joshua	Snow, Samuel
Holbrook, Israel	Purington, Nathaniel	Toothaker, John
Hopkins, Elisha	Rich, Benjamin	Wilson, Alexander
Kemp, Timothy	Rich, David	Wilson, Seth
Leavitt, George	Rich, Isaac, Jr.	
Loring, James	Ridly, Mark, Jr.	*Waiters.*
Merritt, Isaac	Small, Israel	Blackmore, James
Merritt, Samuel	Snow, Isaiah, Jr.	Blake, Samuel
Otis, Samuel, Jr.	Snow, Jesse	Lunt, Josiah
Prior, Leonard P.	Snow, Jesse, Jr.	

Capt. W. Webster's Company, Lieut. Col. C. Thomas' Regiment.

From Sept. 13 to Sept. 29, 1814. Raised at Durham. Service at Bath.

RANK AND NAME.	Fabin, Thomas	Miller, David, Jr.
William Webster, Captain	Gross, Reuben	Nichols, Samuel, Jr.
Elias States, Lieutenant	Herriden, Andrew	Nichols, Thomas
Samuel Roberts, Ensign	Hunnewell, Andrew	Parker, Amos
	Hunnewell, Benjamin	Parker, Nathaniel
Jeremiah Dingly, Sergeant	Hunnewell, John	Proctor, Elijah
Thomas Waterhouse, Sergeant	Hunnewell, Moses	Proctor, George
Luther Plummer, Sergeant	Hunnewell, Robert	Putney, Samuel
John Stackpole, Sergeant	Jones, Joshua, Jr.	Rice, Daniel
Nathaniel Bragdon, Corporal	Lambert, Isaac	Rice, George
Edmund Dow, Corporal	Larabee, John	Roberts, Reuben
John Mitchell, Corporal	Larabee, Jonathan	Roberts, Samuel, Jr.
Joshua Robinson, Musician	Larabee, Josiah	Roberts, Thomas
	Larabee, Nathaniel	Sawyer, Samuel
Privates.	Larabee, Thomas	Skinner, Samuel
Austin, Thomas	Larabee, William	Stackpole, Samuel
Blethen, Simeon	Larabee, William, Jr.	Stoddard, Jeremiah
Bowe, David	Libbey, Jonathan	Strout, James
Bowe, George	Libby, Dennis	Strout, Jonathan
Bragdon, Ephraim	Libby, Moses	Ticket, Joshua
Bragdon, George	Libby, William, Jr.	Ticket, Rushworth
Bragdon, John, Jr.	Martin, Isaac	Vining, Ammi
Brown, Jeremiah	McKenney, Charles	Ward, Samuel
Dingley, John	McKenney, Jedediah	Webster, William, Jr.
Dyer, Micah	McKenney, William	Wilber, Nathaniel
Ellis, John	Merrill, Oland	Wilbur, Benjamin

Lieut. Col. Jacob Ulmer's Regiment.

From Sept. 2 to Sept. 21, 1814. On the morning of September 2 General Gosselin, under cover of the British fleet at anchor in the bay, landed with 600 troops and took possession of Belfast.

FIELD AND STAFF.	William Salmon, Adjutant, Belfast	NONCOMMISSIONED STAFF.
Jacob Ulmer, Lieutenant Colonel, Lincolnville	Chauncey C. Chandler, Surgeon, Belfast	Benjamin Stevens, Sergeant Major
Noah Miller, Major, Northport	Charles Hall, Surgeon's Mate, Belfast	George Ulmer, Quartermaster Sergeant
Thomas Cunningham, Major, Belfast		Thomas Osborne, Drum Major
		Samuel Jackson, Fife Major

MASSACHUSETTS VOLUNTEER MILITIA IN THE WAR OF 1812.   301

Capt. A. Campbell's Company, Lieut. Col. J. Ulmer's Regiment.
From Sept. 2 to Sept. 21, 1814. Service at Belfast.

RANK AND NAME.
Amos Campbell, Captain
Washington Webster, Lieutenant
Nicholas Phillips, Lieutenant

Ansell Lothrop, Sergeant
Jacob Cunningham, Sergeant
John H. Conner, Sergeant
David Patterson, Sergeant

Privates.
Bartlet, John
Bean, Hezekiah
Brice, Robert
Brickmor, George
Bruse, George W.
Cunningham, Benjamin
Farrow, Simon
Gray, Luther

Knowlton, George
Mason, John
Miller, John
Pitcher, Calvin
Ward, Simon
Whittier, Porter

Capt. J. Dow's Company, Lieut. Col. J. Ulmer's Regiment.
From Sept. 2 to Sept. 21, 1814. Raised at Prospect. Service at Belfast.

RANK AND NAME.
Jonathan Dow, Captain
James Field, Lieutenant
Nathaniel Munsey, Ensign

David Calcost, Sergeant
Simon Lampheer, Sergeant
James Black, Sergeant
John George, Sergeant
Joseph Ames, Corporal
James Leach, Corporal
James Curtis, Corporal
William Treat, Corporal

Privates.
Ames, Henry
Black, Alexander
Black, James
Block, Henry
Block, John
Block, John, 2d
Calcost, Chase
Carr, Berry
Carter, James
Curtis, William
Ewel, Joseph
Fowler, James
Fowler, John
George, Stephen

Hopkins, Smith
Lampheer, Elisha
Mathews, Samuel
Mushern, Peter
Nickerson, Joseph
Pike, Robert
Saunders, Samuel
Savery, Jotham
Smart, Daniel
Smart, Ephraim K.
Smart, Richard
Tole, John
Tole, Stacy
Tripp, Jesse
Weed, William

Capt. T. Dunton's Company, Lieut. Col. J. Ulmer's Regiment.
From Sept. 2 to Sept. 21, 1814. Raised at Lincolnville. Service at Belfast.

RANK AND NAME.
Timothy Dunton, Captain
Isaac Wyman, Lieutenant

Isaac Morey, Sergeant
Elisha Tilden, Sergeant
Ellison Annis, Sergeant
William Toothaker, Sergeant
Samuel Moody, Corporal
George Smith, Corporal
Thomas Frohawk, Corporal
David Wyman, Musician

Privates.
Alexander, Samuel
Bridge, John
Brown, Elisha
Chapman, Francis

Crocker, David
Cunningham, Saul
Cunningham, William
Dagget, Thomas
Davis, Aaron
Dolloff, Jacob
Dolloff, John P.
Dolloff, Malichi
Donnell, Joseph T.
Dow, Joseph
Eames, Nathaniel
Frohawk, Jonathan
Frohawk, Solomon
Gorden, Michael
Gray, Reuben
Grear, James
Hamilton, Simon
Hemmingway, Benjamin

Hemmingway, Joshua
Hemmingway, Sylvanus
Hodgdon, Isaac
Jackson, Nathaniel
Meservy, Charles
Pottle, Joseph, Jr.
Robinson, Stephen
Silas, Samuel
Smith, Joseph
Smith, Obed
Tharron, Nathan
Tilden, Isaac
Veasey, Stephen
Walker, William
Weymouth, John
Weymouth, Pierce
Whittier, Thomas
Whittier, Thomas, Jr.

Capt. J. Frye's Company, Lieut. Col. J. Ulmer's Regiment.
From Sept. 2 to Sept. 21, 1814. Raised at Northport. Service at Belfast.

RANK AND NAME.
Jonathan Frye, Captain
David Allen, Lieutenant

John Collier, Sergeant
David Knowles, Sergeant
Reuben Braynard, Sergeant
Thomas Barrow, Sergeant
George Harvey, Corporal
Richard Lear, Corporal
Daniel Richardson, Corporal
Richard Whiting, Corporal

Privates.

Calef, Allen
Clark, Isaac
Clark, Jacob
Clark, Jonathan, Jr.
Collier, Roland
Cross, Josiah
Davis, Phineas
Drinkwater, Ammi
Drinkwater, James
Drinkwater, Micajah, Jr.
Drinkwater, Nathaniel
Drinkwater, West
Drinkwater, William
Duncan, John, Jr.
Duncan, Kingsbury
Duncan, Samuel
Elwell, Thomas
Gardner, Henry
Hall, Cornelius
Hopkins, Peter
Joseph, Peter
Josselyn, Abraham
Knight, George
Knowles, John
Miller, Thomas
Parkhurst, Elisha
Pendleton, Jonathan
Pendleton, William
Pitcher, Job
Rhoades, James, Jr.
Rhodes, Jacob
Rhodes, Jacob L.
Robson, Benjamin
Smith, John, Jr.
Thomas, Tilden
Watson, Simon

Capt. R. Kelsey's Company, Lieut. Col. J. Ulmer's Regiment.
From Sept. 2 to Sept. 21, 1814. Service at Belfast.

RANK AND NAME.
Robert Kelsey, Captain
Shephard Blanchard, Lieutenant
Joshua Nickerson, Ensign

William Durham, Sergeant
James Houston, Sergeant
John McKeen, Sergeant
Robert L. Eels, Sergeant
Daniel Bracket, Corporal
Charles Gordon, Corporal
Jesse Basford, Corporal
John Houston, Corporal

William H. Oraskey, Musician
William Griffin, Musician

Privates.

Ames, John
Bryer, Moses
Cooxford, John
Corinby, Miles
Cunningham, James
Davis, Eleazer
Eels, Seth W.
Fowler, Miles
French, Abram
Gilmore, John, 2d
Lane, Cornelius
Nickerson, Salithiel
Patterson, Elisha
Patterson, George
Patterson, John
Patterson, Robert
Patterson, Robert, 3d
Philbrook, Urel
Ross, Hugh
Ryon, John, Jr.
Shute, John
Stephenson, Jerome

Capt. J. Mahoney's Company, Lieut. Col. J. Ulmer's Regiment.
From Sept. 2 to Sept. 21, 1814. Service at Belfast.

RANK AND NAME.
James Mahoney, Captain
Simon Morse, Lieutenant
Amon Dalie, Ensign

Abner Heal, Sergeant
James Thomas, Sergeant
Robert Moody, Sergeant
Philip Thomas, Sergeant
Joseph Marriner, Corporal
James Mathews, Corporal
Nehemiah Richards, Corporal
Daniel Heal, Corporal
David Pottle, Corporal

Privates.

Brown, Ephraim
Brown, Saul
Calderwood, George
Clay, Richard
Dean, John
Dean, Thomas
Duncan, Isaac
Dunton, Abner
Dunton, Josiah
Farnham, Jeremiah
Fletcher, Francis
Fletcher, Nathan
Gray, John
Heal, Chesley, 2d
Heal, John
Heal, John, Jr.
Heal, Peter
Heal, William
Lamb, Benjamin
Lurch, John
Marriner, Stephen
Mathews, Levi
McKinney, Thomas, Jr.
Miller, Ephraim
Miller, Israel
Milliken, Abner, Jr.
Moody, William
Norton, John
Paine, Saul
Pottle, Daniel
Price, John
Prince, John
Robbins, Lewis
Spaulding, Asa
Thomas, Charles
Thomas, Cornelius
Thomas, Royal
Trussel, Joshua
Upham, Abijah
Wadsworth, Abiah
White, George
Young, Sedate

Capt. P. Pendleton's Company, Lieut. Col. J. Ulmer's Regiment.

From Sept. 2 to Sept. 21, 1814. Raised at Prospect. Service at Belfast.

RANK AND NAME.
Phineas Pendleton, Captain
Henry Hitchborn, Lieutenant
John F. Ewers, Ensign

Isaac Berry, Sergeant
Daniel Lancaster, Sergeant
Simon Porter, Sergeant
Joseph Ellis, Sergeant
Alexander Staples, Corporal
Peleg Griffin, Corporal
Ephraim Colson, Corporal
Josiah Soule, Musician
Joseph Berry, Musician

Privates.

Bassick, William
Berry, John
Berry, Jonathan
Block, Alexander
Bonnell, Thomas
Campbell, John
Carrie, David
Cleverly, Joseph

Clifford, Nathaniel
Colcard, Benjamin
Colcard, John
Cousins, John
Cousins, Nathaniel
Dickey, John
Eustis, Jacob
Eustis, James
Fletcher, Simon
French, Joel
French, Josiah
French, Samuel
French, Zitham, 2d
Goodall, David
Grout, Elisha
Harding, Samuel
Harriman, Benjamin
Harriman, Elisha
Kneeland, Edward
Lackey, Simon
Lamphere, John
Lancaster, Nathan
Mudger, John
Park, Berry

Park, John
Park, Saul
Park, Thomas
Partridge, Edward
Partridge, Thomas
Pavil, Hickborn
Rendell, James
Shute, Berry
Shute, Thomas
Smith, Samuel
Smith, Richard
Staples, James, 2d
Staples, Jotham, 2d
Staples, Jotham, 3d
Staples, Miles
Staples, William, 2d
Stover, James
Sweetser, Jeremiah
Treat, Amos
Treat, James
Treat, Robert
Woodbury, Samuel

Capt. J. Stetson's Company, Lieut. Col. J. Ulmer's Regiment.

From Sept. 2 to Sept. 21, 1814. Raised at Lincolnville. Service at Belfast.

RANK AND NAME.
Josiah Stetson, Captain
Paul H. Stevens, Lieutenant
Joseph Palmer, Ensign

William Eckley, Sergeant
Jacob S. Adams, Sergeant
John Wade, Sergeant
John Green, Sergeant
John Studley, Jr., Musician

Privates.

Adams, Alfred
Dean, Nathan
Decrow, Israel

Decrow, John
Decrow, John, Jr.
Dunbar, Richard
Flynn, Thomas
Foster, Charles
Jameson, Ebenezer
Jameson, Samuel
Kidder, William
Knight, Enoch
Knight, Nathan
Marriner, John E.
Meader, Ebenezer
Morse, Isaac
Ordway, David
Palmer, Bozabel

Palmer, Nathaniel
Parker, Elisha
Prescott, Jeremiah
Prescott, John
Prescott, Joseph
Reed, John D.
Rogers, A. Wales
Smith, Asa
Spaulding, Robert
Spaulding, Stephen
Spring, William
Sylvester, Philip
Thomas, Joseph, Jr.

Capt. N. Swan's Company, Lieut. Col. J. Ulmer's Regiment.

From Sept. 2 to Sept. 21, 1814. Raised at Belfast. Service at Belfast.

RANK AND NAME.
Nathan Swan, Captain
Ralph C. Johnson, Ensign

Alfred Sawyer, Sergeant
Jeremiah Swan, Sergeant
Benjamin Munroe, Sergeant
Joshua Adams, Sergeant
Ebenezer Williams, Corporal
Lewis Bean, Corporal

James Holmes, Corporal
Benjamin Poor, Corporal

Privates.

Bean, Josiah
Bracket, Joshua
Brown, Parker
Brown, Samuel
Cochran, Robert B.
Colburn, Ebenezer

Crea, John
Derby, Andrew
Dolouph, John
Douglas, James
Dunham, David
Dunham, Jonathan
Emery, Robert
Fletcher, Samuel
Frederick, William
French, Jacob

Capt. N. Swan's Company, Lieut. Col. J. Ulmer's Regiment — Concluded.

Privates — Concluded.
French, Samuel
Frost, Benjamin, Jr.
Homes, John
Homes, Peter
Johnson, Daniel, Jr.
Kellock, James
McFarland, Andrew

Merrill, John
Miller, James, Jr.
Moor, John
Murch, Zebulon
Quimby, Jonathan
Peety, Samuel
Rowe, Peter
Ryder, Richard

Sawyer, Aaron
Stevens, Jonathan
Wentworth, Stephen
Whitaker, Joseph
White, William, Jr.
Winslow, Peter

Capt. E. Williams' Company, Lieut. Col. J. Ulmer's Regiment.
From Sept. 2 to Sept. 21, 1814. Raised at Swanville. Service at Belfast.

RANK AND NAME.
Ebenezer Williams, Captain
Amariah Dodge, Lieutenant
Ebenezer Cunningham, Ensign

Joseph Stuart, Sergeant
Joseph Staples, Sergeant
Joseph Curtis, Sergeant
John Curtis, Sergeant
John Young, Corporal
William Lord, Corporal
William Bowdin, Corporal
Hezekiah Staples, Corporal
Isacker Thistle, Musician
William Dodge, Musician

Privates.
Batchelder, Daniel
Batchelder, Joseph
Bowden, John
Chase, Elisha
Curtis, Benjamin
Curtis, Moses
Curtis, Phineas E.
Doak, James
Eames, Samuel
Elles, William
Fowler, John H.
Houston, Thomas
Landfist, John
Nash, Amasa

Nickerson, Joshua
Nickerson, Nathaniel
Nickerson, Reuben
Nickerson, Samuel
Nickerson, William
Spencer, Ichabod
Sukins, Josiah
Thomson, Alexander
Trefehern, John
Tyler, Ebenezer
Wall, John
Warren, Benjamin
West, Peter

Lieut. Col. J. Waugh's Regiment.
From Sept. 14 to Sept. 24, 1814. In camp at Waterville, awaiting orders.

FIELD AND STAFF.
James Waugh, Jr., Lieutenant Colonel, Starks
John G. Neil, Major, Norridgewock
Joseph Lock, Major, Brownfield
John Wyman, Quartermaster, Canaan
James Young, Paymaster, Starks
James Bowen, Surgeon, Canaan
Joseph Batchelder, Surgeon's Mate, Norridgewock

NONCOMMISSIONED STAFF.
David Waugh, Sergeant Major
Eli Weston, Jr., Quartermaster Sergeant
Levi Bigelow, Drum Major

Waiters.
Boise, Bartholomew
Cayford, ——
Cayford, John E.
Jewett, Joshua

Capt. D. Beedy's Company, Lieut. Col. J. Waugh's Regiment.
From Sept. 13 to Sept. 24, 1814. Raised at Industry. In camp at Waterville, awaiting orders.

RANK AND NAME.
Daniel Beedy, Captain
James Thompson, Lieutenant
Josiah Blackstone, Ensign

Daniel Luce, Sergeant
Moses True, Sergeant
John Russell, Sergeant
Peter W. Willis, Sergeant
James Eveleth, Corporal
Robert Thompson, Corporal

Trueman Allen, Corporal
Joseph Ames, Corporal
William Johnson, Musician
Job Swift, Musician

Privates.
Allen, Harrison
Allen, Sylvanus
Atkinson, James
Atkinson, Thomas M.
Benson, Matthew

Bradbury, John S.
Brooks, Benjamin
Burges, Benjamin
Butler, Josiah
Church, Silas
Clark, Humphrey
Collins, James
Collins, Lemuel, Jr.
Crawford, Benjamin T.
Crumton, George
Davis, Cornelius

MASSACHUSETTS VOLUNTEER MILITIA IN THE WAR OF 1812. 305

Capt. D. Beedy's Company, Lieut. Col. J. Waugh's Regiment — Concluded.

Privates — Concluded.
Davis, James
Drue, Elisha
Ellis, William
Eveleth, Joseph
Goodrich, Jonathan
Hays, Jacob
Hildreth, David, Jr.
Hobby, James
Howes, Alvin
Howes, Lemuel, Jr.
Johnson, Dyrenus

Johnson, Henry
Look, Valentine
Luce, Arvin
Luce, Benjamin
Luce, David
Luce, Rowlin
Meader, Henry
Morse, Caleb
Norton, Peter
Norton, Saul
Pike, Joshua
Pressy, Moses

Remick, Francis
Remick, True
Robbins, Amial
Rogers, Thomas
Shaw, Daniel
Smith, Henry
Standley, James
Swift, Benjamin
Swift, Ebenezer
White, James
Williamson, Ebenezer

Capt. G. Gray's Company, Lieut. Col. J. Waugh's Regiment.
From Sept. 13 to Sept. 24, 1814. Raised at Starks. In camp at Waterville, awaiting orders.

RANK AND NAME.
George Gray, Captain
Abraham Greenleaf, Lieutenant
Matthew Taylor, Ensign

John Sawyer, Sergeant
Eleazer Snell, Sergeant
Sewall Waugh, Sergeant
Samuel Taylor, Corporal
James Wood, Corporal
William Ladd, Jr., Corporal
Moses Bickford, Musician
Elijah Dutton, Musician
William Meader, Musician
Henry Bickford, Musician

Privates.
Bearce, Holmes
Beedy, Ephraim

Burgess, Elijah
Caulking, Ebenezer
Dutton, Josiah
Dutton, Josiah, Jr.
Dutton, Mason
Fish, Elisha K.
Fish, Nathan
Fisk, Ebenezer
Folsom, William E.
Forbes, Samuel
Frederick, Joseph, Jr.
Frederick, Valentine
Frederick, William
Greaton, Leonard
Hilton, Joshua
Hilton, Theophilus
Ingalls, John
Lovejoy, Abiel
Lovejoy, Joseph

Lovejoy, William
Macomber, Joseph
Mancey, Andrew D.
Maxwell, Daniel
Morrell, Joseph
Nichols, Joel
Nichols, John
Skillings, John
Sterry, Edward L.
Taylor, Joel
Taylor, John
Taylor, Joseph
Waugh, Elijah
Waugh, Thomas
Whitcomb, Nathaniel

Capt. J. Greenleaf's Company, Lieut. Col. J. Waugh's Regiment.
From Sept. 13 to Sept. 24, 1814. Raised at Starks. In camp at Waterville, awaiting orders.

RANK AND NAME.
John Greenleaf, Captain
John Marshall, Lieutenant
Joseph Greenleaf, Ensign

Thomas Williamson, Sergeant
Anthony Greenleaf, Sergeant
Joseph Holbrook, Sergeant
Levi Greenleaf, Sergeant
William Boyinton, Corporal
John Witham, Musician
John Chapman, Musician

Privates.
Albee, Samuel
Boyinton, George
Chapman, James
Chapman, John
Chapman, Samuel
Collins, John
Dickinson, James

Dulcy, James
Dunlap, Guy
Emery, Nathaniel
Fish, Eleazer
Fish, John
Fish, Samuel
Frizzle, Benjamin
Gray, Ebenezer
Gray, John
Green, David
Green, Stephen
Greenleaf, Ebenezer
Greenleaf, Stephen
Hankinson, David
Hilton, John
Holbrook, John
Holbrook, Richard
Jones, William
Joy, Abijah
Kimball, David
Kimball, Nicholas

Leeman, Alexander
Leeman, Samuel
Martin, William
McFadden, John
Pomeroy, Benjamin
Pomeroy, Jeremiah
Sheaffe, Richard
Snell, James
Taylor, Benjamin
Toccusey, Mayhew
White, Abijah
White, William
Williams, John
Williamson, Stephen
Williamson, Sylvanus
Witham, William
Young, James
Young, Joshua
Young, Robert

Capt. D. Flanders' Company, Lieut. Col. J. Waugh's Regiment.

From Sept. 14 to Sept. 24, 1814. Raised at Cornville. In camp at Waterville, awaiting orders.

RANK AND NAME.
Daniel Flanders, Captain
Daniel Collins, Lieutenant
Abram P. Tilton, Ensign

Dudley S. Fogg, Sergeant
Peter Malbon, Sergeant
Samuel True, Sergeant
Josiah Morrell, Sergeant
Elijah Smith, Musician
Benjamin McDaniell, Musician

Privates.
Butler, Benjamin
Collins, Barnard
Collins, Daniel
Currier, Ephraim, 1st
Currier, Ephraim, 2d
Dellof, David
Flanders, Jacob
Flanders, Jonathan
Flanders, Moses
Flanders, Thomas
Flanders, William
Fogg, Joshua
Fogg, Josiah
Folsom, James
Folsom, Rufus
Green, Benjamin
Griffin, Job
Hilton, Daniel
Hilton, John
Judkins, Benjamin
Judkins, Levi
Judkins, Peter
Kemp, James
Lammas, Murry
Lammas, Samuel
Lewis, Isaac
Lewis, Sherebiah
Lumbard, Daniel
Malbon, Nathaniel
Marsh, Aaron
Morrell, Henry
Morrell, John
Morrill, Micajah
Perkins, David
Sanborn, Levy
Smith, David
Smith, Elkins
Smith, Trueworthy
Smith, William
Stoddard, Demeric
Trefelhen, Abraham
Trefelhen, Hanover
Weymouth, Samuel
Whittemore, Nathan
Whittier, Joseph
Whittier, Nathaniel
Whittier, William
Woodman, Joshua

Waiter.
Currier, Phineas

Capt. I. Holt's Company, Lieut. Col. J. Waugh's Regiment.

From Sept. 14 to Sept. 25, 1814. Raised at Canaan. In camp at Waterville, awaiting orders.

RANK AND NAME.
Isaac Holt, Captain
Christopher H. Gerald, Lieutenant
Levi Tuttle, Ensign

Joseph Patten, Sergeant
Benjamin Eaton, Sergeant
David Mayson, Sergeant
Dudly Blake, Sergeant
Samuel Watson, Corporal
Stephen Watson, Corporal
Eli Tuttle, Corporal
Benjamin Chase, Corporal
David Kendall, Musician
Samuel Wheeler, Musician
Jonas Wheeler, Musician

Privates.
Adams, John
Ames, Eliakim
Ames, Isaac F.
Annis, John
Booker, Charles
Booker, Jacob
Brown, James
Brown, Reuben
Brown, William
Burrill, Hull
Burrill, Humphry
Buzzell, Elisha
Buzzell, Joseph
Carson, Aaron
Clark, Benjamin
Corson, John
Corson, Nahum
Curtis, James
Dane, Levi
Dudley, John
Emery, Benjamin
Emery, Jonathan
Fairbanks, Benjamin
Flood, Edward L.
Foster, Daniel
Frieze, George
Frost, Eliot
Gardner, Ebenezer
Gardner, Thomas
Gerald, Daniel F.
Gerald, David S.
Goodrich, Isaac
Goodridge, David
Goodridge, Ebenezer
Goodridge, Oliver
Gould, George F.
Grace, James
Grace, William
Gray, William
Hall, Isaac
Hall, Lemuel
Hamstead, Timothy
Herring, Andrew
Hobbs, Stephen
Hobby, George
Horson, Thomas
Hutcherson, William
Jenkins, Joseph
Kincaid, David
Lambert, David
Littlefield, John
Mayson, William
McGoon, Joseph
McKenney, Andrew
McKenney, William
Partman, Daniel
Powers, Adam
Powers, Jonathan
Pratt, Jacob
Rhines, George T.
Rhines, Moses
Ricker, Trustram
Roberson, Thomas
Row, Caleb
Sanborn, Newell
Sergent, Simon G.
Shaw, Nathaniel
Sinclair, Jonathan
Small, Daniel
Smith, Abraham
Smith, Gilman
Soule, William
Southard, Stephen
Stewart, John
Swain, Dudly S.
Waldron, Isaac
Walker, Edward
Waymouth, John
Webb, Asa
Webb, John
Whetcher, William
Whidden, James, 2d
Whidden, James, 3d
Whitman, John
Wyman, John

Waiter.
Kimball, Jacob

MASSACHUSETTS VOLUNTEER MILITIA IN THE WAR OF 1812.

Capt. J. Patten's Company, Lieut. Col. J. Waugh's Regiment.
From Sept. 14 to Sept. 24, 1814. Raised at Norridgewock. In camp at Waterville, awaiting orders.

RANK AND NAME.
Joseph Patten, Captain
Calvin Heald, Lieutenant
Melzar Lindsey, Ensign

Joseph Adams, Sergeant
Robert Cook, Sergeant
Oliver C. Blunt, Sergeant
Thomas Greenleaf, Sergeant
Lemuel Adams, Corporal
John Taylor, Corporal
John Brown, Jr., Corporal
Joseph Wither, Corporal
John Emerson, Musician
John Loring, Jr., Musician

Privates.
Ames, Jonas
Baston, Joseph
Bowden, Theodore
Bridges, John
Brown, Nahum
Chaffin, Nathan
Chandler, David
Cook, Isaac

Crumbie, David G.
Davis, Jonathan
Davis, Pruel, Jr.
Dinsmore, William
Fairbrother, James, Jr.
Fairbrother, Lovel
Farnham, Ralph
Fletcher, Amos
Harding, Benjamin
Hastings, Amos
Hibberd, Jonathan, Jr.
Hook, Joseph
Kidder, Isaac, Jr.
Kumpton, Charles T.
Leeman, Eli
Leighton, Asa
Leighton, Luther
Longly, Benjamin
Longly, Joseph
Mantor, Daniel
Mantor, Daniel, 2d
Marston, Roby
Maxim, Andrews
Nutting, Abijah
Nutting, Royal

Parker, Edmund, Jr.
Pease, Charles
Pierce, Isaac
Pratt, Joseph
Robbins, John
Rogers, William
Sawyer, Levi
Smith, Liba
Spaulding, Arthur
Spaulding, Union
Stinson, Saul
Streeter, Daniel
Sylvester, Saul I.
Tarbell, William
Taylor, James
Vichere, Asa
Washburn, Ephraim
Weston, George B.
Whitney, John
Whitton, John
Witham, Isaac
Witham, Thomas
Woodman, Daniel

Capt. N. Russell's Company, Lieut. Col. J. Waugh's Regiment.
From Sept. 14 to Sept. 24, 1814. Raised at Skowhegan. In camp at Waterville, awaiting orders.

RANK AND NAME.
Nathaniel Russell, Captain
George Porter, Lieutenant
Levi Wyman, Ensign

Stephen Hartwell, Sergeant
Joseph Cleveland, Sergeant
Elijah Wyman, Sergeant
John W. Weston, Sergeant
Solomon Stewart, Jr., Musician
Joseph David, Musician

Privates.
Abel, Wyman, or Wyman, Abel
Allen, Daniel
Allen, Eliphalet
Austin, Daniel
Brown, Thomas
Clark, John
Cleveland, James
Cook, Richard
Emerson, Daniel R.
Emery, Joseph, 3d

Fletcher, William
Hartwell, Benjamin
Hearl, John
Higgins, Nathaniel
Holman, Levi
Holway, Freeman
Honeywell, Thomas
Ireland, David
Jewett, Joshua
Kelly, Sylvanus
Lander, Jesse
Mason, Abijah
Mason, David
Mayo, Seth
Moor, Nathan
Moore, John
Parker, Jonathan
Parkham, David
Parkham, Simeon
Pennell, John
Pratt, George
Pratt, Whitcomb
Sawyer, Nathaniel

Smith, Lemuel
Southard, John
Spear, Nehemiah
Stewart, Asa
Stilson, Amos
Tinkham, Andrew
Webb, Joseph B.
Webb, Samuel
Weston, Daniel
Weston, Ensebus
Weston, Jonas
Weston, Stephen
Wheeler, Amos
Wheeler, Edward W.
Wheeler, Perley
White, James
White, Nathaniel
White, William
Wood, John
Wyman, Abel, or Abel, Wyman
Wyman, Joseph

Capt. E. Works' Company, Lieut. Col. J. Waugh's Regiment.

From Sept. 14 to Sept. 24, 1814. Raised at Mercer. In camp at Waterville, awaiting orders.

RANK AND NAME.
Elias Works, Captain
Saul Williamson, Lieutenant
Cyrus True, Ensign

Martin Burr, Sergeant
Luther Burr, Sergeant
John Thompson, Sergeant
Thomas Fletcher, Sergeant
Robinson Gilman, Corporal
Ransford Smith, Corporal
Daniel Kimball, Corporal
George Riggs, Corporal
Rufus Works, Musician
Jonathan Charles, Musician
Benjamin Rollins, Musician

Privates.
Allen, Daniel
Arnold, John
Arnold, William
Atkins, Sylvanus
Baldwin, Seth
Bean, Ebenezer

Boyington, John
Boyington, Joshua
Branch, Daniel
Bump, Alson
Burr, John
Chapman, Amasa
Chapman, Thomas
Cromwell, Oliver
Croswell, Thomas
Cummings, Asa (D.)
Day, Daniel
Drew, Levi
Dudley, James
Elliot, Daniel
Ellis, John
Gordon, Josiah
Green, Asa
Greenleaf, Seth
Horson, Benjamin
Jacobs, George
Jacobs, Theodore
Jewell, Jacob
Jewell, William
Kimball, Nehemiah

Leathers, Levi
Lombard, Cornelius, Jr.
Merriam, Ephraim
Quimby, Stephen
Quimby, Thomas
Riggs, Starbird
Rollins, John
Rowe, Ebenezer
Russell, Leonard
Sawyer, Josiah
Sawyer, Otis
Stevens, William
True, James
Vose, Ebenezer
Weaver, Phillip
Welts, Amos
Welts, David
Whitcomb, Levi
Whittier, Moses
Wiley, Samuel
Willard, Amasa
Williamson, James
Works, Clark

Sergt. J. Baker's Guard, Lieut. Col. E. Cutter's Regiment.

From June 29 to July 2, 1814. Service at Wiscasset.

RANK AND NAME.
John Baker, Sergeant

Privates.
Babcock, Benjamin
Beith, Jeremiah

Campbell, John
Floyd, John
Kenney, John
Lewis, Joseph
Light, Andrew
Pinkham, Francis

Reed, Samuel
Rust, William
Smith, Francis
Williams, Samuel
Wylie, Benjamin

Lieut. O. Walker's Detachment of Guards.

From June 9 to June 29, 1814. Service at Kennebunk Landing.

RANK AND NAME.
Oliver Walker, Lieutenant

William Perkins, Sergeant
Bartholomew Huff, Sergeant

Privates.
Adams, Joseph
Brown, Benjamin

Coes, Benjamin
Fairfield, James
Hammond, Abner
Huff, Nicholas
Lord, Sumner
Merrett, Edwin
Merrill, Benjamin
Perkins, Ezra
Perkins, Francis

Perkins, Israel
Perkins, Joseph
Perkins, Joseph, 2d
Staples, John
Stone, Abner
Stone, Adam
Stone, Jonathan
Ward, Israel

Lieut. G. Wheelwright's Detachment of Guards, under Supervision of Gen. Ichabod Goodwin.

From June 29 to July 9, 1814. Raised at Wells. Service at Kennebunkport.

Rank and Name.	Privates.	
George Wheelwright, Lieutenant	Barnard, Josiah H.	Gooch, Daniel
	Bragdon, George	Hubbard, Dimon, Jr.
Samuel Ross, Sergeant	Butland, John, 3d	Littlefield, Samuel
Daniel Wise, Jr., Sergeant	Currier, Edmund	Lord, David
James Brown, Corporal	Drown, Joseph	Michel, William
Archibald Hamilton, Corporal	Emery, Isaac, Jr.	Osborne, James
	Emery, Thomas	Patten, Robert
	Gilpatrick, William	Tripp, Benjamin
	Gooch, Abijah	Witham, John, Jr.

Lieut. G. Wheelwright's Roll of Detached Guard, under Supervision of Gen. Ichabod Goodwin.

From June 29 to July 29, 1814. Stationed at Kennebunkport.

Rank and Name.	Privates.	
George Wheelwright, Lieutenant	Barnard, Josiah H.	Gooch, Daniel
	Bragdon, George	Hubbard, Dimon
Samuel Ross, Sergeant	Butland, John	Littlefield, Samuel
Daniel Wise, Jr., Sergeant	Currier, Edmund	Lord, David
James Brown, Corporal	Drown, Joseph	Mitchell, William
Archibald Hamilton, Corporal	Emery, Isaac, Jr.	Osborn, James
	Emery, Thomas	Patten, Robert
	Gilpatrick, William	Tripp, Benjamin
	Gooch, Abijah	Witham, John

Lieut. O. Walker's Detachment of Guards, under Supervision of Gen. Ichabod Goodwin.

From July 9 to Aug. 8, 1814. Raised at Kennebunk. Service at Kennebunkport.

Rank and Name.	Privates.	
Oliver Walker, Lieutenant	Coes, Benjamin	Noble, Amariah
	Emery, Philip	Perkins, Francis
Ephraim Mitchell, Sergeant	Hubbard, Benjamin	Ricker, Levi
Nahum Littlefield, Sergeant	Leach, Jotham	Robinson, Thatcher
Robert Patten, Corporal	Littlefield, Nicholas	Stackpole, John
Joshua Bragdon, Corporal	Lord, Dummer	Treadwell, Joshua
	Merrill, Benjamin	Williams, Benjamin
	Mitchell, James	Winn, Josiah

Lieut. D. Maxwell's Detachment of Guards, under Supervision of Gen. Ichabod Goodwin.

From Aug. 8 to Sept. 8, 1814. Raised at Wells. Service at Kennebunkport.

Rank and Name.	Privates.	
David Maxwell, Lieutenant	Boston, Ivory	Leach, Asa
	Bragdon, George	Littlefield, Benjamin
Robert Patten, Sergeant	Brown, Benjamin	Littlefield, John
Jacob Low, Sergeant	Getchell, Benjamin	Miller, James
Aaron Littlefield, Corporal	Hatch, John, Jr.	Perkins, Francis
John Butland, 3d, Corporal	Johnson, John L.	Perkins, Israel
	Kimball, Jonathan	Perkins, Luther
		Treadwell, Joshua

Lieut. G. Wheelwright's Detachment of Guards, under Supervision of Gen. Ichabod Goodwin.
From Sept. 8 to Oct. 3, 1814. Raised at Wells. Service at Kennebunkport.

Rank and Name.	Privates.	
George Wheelwright, Lieutenant	Brown, John	Hutchins, John
	Cleaves, Merchant	Morrison, Nathan
Ephraim Mitchell, Sergeant	Currier, Nathaniel	Osborne, John
Joseph Lord, Sergeant	Downing, Joshua	Perkins, George
Ithamy Hatch, Corporal	Getchell, Benjamin	Shackley, Daniel, Jr.
Benjamin Coes, Corporal	Getchell, Joseph	Ward, Israel
	Goodwin, John	West, William
	Hatch, Elisha, Jr.	Wilds, Nathaniel

Sergt. A. Tobey's Detachment, Colonel Sherwin's Regiment.
From Sept. 13 to Sept. 24, 1814. Raised at Sidney. Service at Augusta.

Rank and Name.	Atwood, William	Hoxie, Allen
Ansel Tobey, Sergeant	Bates, Elijah	Jones, John, Jr.
John Bates, Sergeant	Bates, James	Lander, James
Allen Jones, Sergeant	Bates, Joshua	Lawrence, Henry
Ellis Burgess, Sergeant	Bates, Silas	Nye, Alden
George Nye, Corporal	Bowman, Benjamin	Nye, Cornelius
Elihu Lawrence, Corporal	Cannon, Nathan	Nye, Ezra
Lemuel Tobey, Jr., Corporal	Cleveland, Timothy	Nye, Jonathan
Joseph Nye, Corporal	Davis, Benjamin	Sawyer, Joseph
Joshua Nye, Musician	Davis, Joseph	Snell, David
Charles Coffin, Musician	Davis, Walter	Tibbetts, George
	Fisk, Eliab	Tobey, Ansel
Privates.	Fuller, Asa	Tobey, Nathaniel
Allen, Ansel	Gibbs, Nathan	Young, Moses
Allen, Moses	Gibbs, Reuben	
Atwood, Heman	Holway, Joseph	

Lieut. L. Soule's Guard, Lieut. Col. E. Thatcher's Regiment.
From June 30 to July 15, 1814. Service at Waldoboro.

Rank and Name.	Privates.	
Levi Soule, Lieutenant	Stall, John	
	Wallace, Charles	
Charles Hebner, Corporal	Winchepan, Isaac	

Sergt. J. Blunt's Detachment, Lieut. Col. E. Thatcher's Regiment.
From June 29 to July 4, 1814.

Rank and Name.	Clark, Alexander	Hawley, Roger
James Blunt, Sergeant	Coombs, Saul	McKown, Samuel W.
	Goudy, Amos	Miller, Robert
Privates.	Goudy, John	Miller, Saul
Boyd, James	Hatch, Alexander	Sprowl, John
Boyd, Robert	Hatch, John	Varney, James

Sergt. F. Bradford's Guard, Lieut. Col. S. Thatcher's Regiment.
From Sept. 4 to Oct. 6, 1814. Service at Friendship.

Rank and Name.	Privates.	
Frederic Bradford, Sergeant	Card, George	Cordon, William, Jr.
Edward Gay, Corporal	Condon, Saul	Lowry, Benjamin, Jr.
	Cook, Francis	Morse, Oliver
	Cook, James, 2d	Morton, Isaac
	Cook, Zenas	Park, Oliver

Corp. C. Hebner's Guard.
From June 30 to July 15, 1814. Stationed at Waldoboro.

Rank and Name.	Privates.	
Charles Hebner, Corporal	Stall, John Wallace, Charles Winchenpaw, Isaac	

Corp. N. Pitcher's Guard.
From June 30 to July 7, 1814. Stationed at Waldoboro.

Rank and Name.	Privates.	
Nathaniel Pitcher, Corporal	Clark, John Hofer, George Howard, Samuel	Mink, Charles Vinal, John

Sergt. I. Sylvester's Guard, under Lieut. Col. C. Thomas' Command.
From July 13 to Sept. 25, 1814. Service at Harpswell.

Rank and Name.	Privates.	
Isaac Sylvester, Sergeant Jesse Snow, Corporal	Curtis, John Perry, Robert Rich, David Small, Israel	Snow, Jesse, Jr. Snow, Saul Stover, John Stover, Joshua

Sergt. J. S. Tompson's Guard.
From July 25 to Aug. 24, 1814. Service at Fort Edward, York Harbor. ("Sea Fencibles.")

Rank and Name.	Privates.	
John S. Tompson, Sergeant	Donnell, Henry Donnell, Nathaniel Gillman, George Harman, James	Lindsey, Samuel McDaniel, James Storer, Samuel, 3d Varrell, Solomon, Jr.

Sergt. J. S. Tompson's Detached Guard, from Capt. Isaac Lyman's Company.
From July 26 to Sept. 23, 1814. Service at Fort Edward, York Harbor. ("Sea Fencibles.")

Rank and Name.	Privates.	
John S. Tompson, Sergeant	Blaisdell, David Donnell, Nathaniel Goodwin, Abiel McIntire, Charles	Moody, Charles Varrell, Rufus Young, John, Jr. Young, Joseph

Sergt. A. Gregory's Guard.
From July 21 to Sept. 1, 1812. Raised at Eastport. Service at Eastport.

Rank and Name.	Privates.	
Abijah Gregory, Sergeant Lewis Putnam, Sergeant Jery Chase, Sergeant William Frost, Sergeant Alexander Todd, Musician Gaius Perkins, Musician *Privates.* Bell, Philip Bennet, Job K.	Buck, John Cushing, John M. Delesdernier, John, substitute for Alanson T. Rice, Aug. 13 to Sept. 1 Delesdernier, William Ellis, Nathaniel Fosdick, Nathaniel F., Aug. 20 to Sept. 1 Fowler, Asa George, Jacob Green, Thomas, Jr. Kimball, William	King, Benjamin, Jr., Aug. 13 to Sept. 1 Moore, Samuel Newcomb, Robert Prince, Joseph, Aug. 1 to Sept. 1 Rice, Alanson T., substituted by Delesdernier, John Rollins, Samuel Thayer, Silas, Aug. 13 to Sept. 1 Tredwell, Thomas Wilson, Nathaniel

Sergt. J. Marr's, Jr., Guard of Lieut. S. S. Fairfield's Detachment.

From Aug. 25 to Sept. 23, 1814. Service at Biddeford.

RANK AND NAME.
James Marr, Jr., Sergeant

Privates.
Bradden, Isaac
Chase, Abel
Chick, S. James
Davis, Ezra, 3d

Durgin, Benjamin
Edgecomb, John
Furlong, Patrick
Knox, Shadrach
Lord, Daniel
Moeds, Artemas
Patten, Nathaniel
Pitts, Benjamin

Robinson, George
Smith, Israel
Strout, George
Webber, Edmund
Wentworth, John
Woodward, William

Sergt. J. Lowell's Guard, under Supervision of Maj. Lemuel Weeks.

From Nov. 26, 1814, to Jan. 23, 1815. Service at Fort Burrows, Fish Point, Portland, "for the protection of the forts, ordnance, and munitions of war, and other property belonging to the Commonwealth."

RANK AND NAME.
John Lowell, Sergeant
Asa Erskine, Corporal

Privates.
Brown, Stephen
Butterfield, Leonard
Crockett, Richard

Davis, John, Jr.
Gray, George
Ham, William
Hartshorn, William
Henly, John
Lamb, Seth
Merrow, Samuel
Miller, George

Morrison, Samuel
Nason, Abraham
Newbegin, James
Pierce, Joseph
Roberts, Daniel
Smith, John
Wyer, Peter M.

Capt. J. Brown's Company, Lieut. Col. H. Moore's Regiment.

From Aug. 12, 1812, to February, 1813. This company evidently belongs to some regiment of the regular army or the United States Volunteers.

RANK AND NAME.
James Brown, Captain
Amasa Davis, Lieutenant

Thomas Self, Sergeant
Isaac Winshall, Sergeant
Lewis Stenrod, Sergeant
Joseph Hawkins, Sergeant
Mathias Spangler, Corporal
Peter Patterson, Corporal
Daniel Bain, Corporal
Samuel Jennings, Corporal

Privates.
Binear, Lewis
Bowman, Daniel
Crawford, Joseph

Cummins, John
Cummins, Samuel
Curtis, Joshua
Dains, Jacob
Fuller, William
Gormand, John
Hammon, Zeeth
Huges, William
Ingalls, Abraham
Jay, George
Lewis, William
Linn, Joseph
Marshall, Simon
McCully, Patrick
McKee, Thomas (died)
Monotony, Isaac
Newburn, William

Owens, Thomas
Parker, George
Parkinson, John
Pearse, Jonathan
Pilby, James
Pilby, Moses
Poke, William
Rainey, John
Reasoner, Benjamin
Ross, William
Sawyer, George
Swank, George
Taylor, Thomas
White, Benjamin
Workman, Benjamin
Wright, Robart B.

Capt. S. Watson's Company, Lieut. Col. P. Osgood's Regiment.

From Sept. 18 to Oct. 18, 1812. Raised at Boston. Service at Boston. (Record states not part of Massachusetts militia.)

RANK AND NAME.
Samuel Watson, Captain

Daniel McMichael, Sergeant

Privates.
Coon, George
Coon, Jacob
Coon, John

Gass, William
McClure, James
McClure, James, 2d
McClure, Samuel
McClure, Thomas
Myrick, John
Oldfield, Jonathan
Riddle, William
Robins, Elisha

Sent, Daniel
Sent, Jacob
Sent, John
Sent, John, 2d
Speers, Duncan
Speers, William
Stout, Jacob
Watson, Amaziah

INDEX.

INDEX

INDEX.

[Numerals enclosed in parenthesis indicate repetitions of name on page designated by preceding number.]

A

Abbey, Abner, 43
Abbey, Adolphus, 46
Abbot, Abiel, 31
Abbot, Asa, 151
Abbot, Elias, 138
Abbot, Enos, 218
Abbot, Ephraim, 132
Abbot, George, 9, 135, 188
Abbot, Holtin, 218
Abbot, Isaac, 151
Abbot, J., 218
Abbot, Joel, 151
Abbot, John, 10, 218, 220, 239
Abbot, Micah, 151
Abbot, Moses, 218
Abbot, Nathaniel, 34, 38
Abbot, Nathaniel F., 218
Abbot, Samuel, 33
Abbot, Silas, 151
Abbot, Stephen, 35, 151, 281
Abbot, Timothy, 218
Abbott, Abel B., 150
Abbott, Abial, 263
Abbott, Benjamin, 100
Abbott, Daniel, 118, 178
Abbott, David, 8
Abbott, Ebenezer, 42, 261
Abbott, Edmund, 213
Abbott, Enos, Jr., 261
Abbott, Farnum, 261
Abbott, George, 183 (2), 184, 236
Abbott, Jacob, 100
Abbott, James, 40, 87
Abbott, Jeduthan, 100
Abbott, John, 180, 245, 259
Abbott, Jonathan, 88
Abbott, Joseph, 23, 244
Abbott, Joshua, 41, 82
Abbott, Lewis, 91
Abbott, Micah, 255
Abbott, Moses, 151, 261
Abbott, Nathan, Jr., 100
Abbott, Nathaniel, 21, 68, 79, 158 (2), 261
Abbott, Nehemiah, 13, 14
Abbott, Reuben, Jr., 180
Abbott, Samuel, 263
Abbott, Samuel L., 7
Abbott, Saul, 132, 140
Abbott, Stephen, 35, 37 (2), 90, 150, 236, 277
Abbott, Thomas, 245
Abbott, William, 39, 70, 116, 259
Abbott, William T., 10
Abel, William, 65
Abel, Wyman, 307
Abell, Jehiel, 231
Abon, James, 118
Aborn, Ebenezer, 117
Aborn, Samuel, 117
Aborns, Benjamin, 6
Acass, Benjamin, 219
Achorn, John, 204, 205

Achorn, Michel, 204
Achorn, Philip, 204, 205
Acly, Saul, 213
Acorn, Michel, 200
Acres, George, 24, 39, 77
Acres, Thomas, 25, 39
Acron, Charles, 292
Acron, George, 289, 292
Acron, John, 292
Acron, Joseph, 289
Adams, Adam, 232 (2)
Adams, Alfred, 303
Adams, Amos, 118, 138
Adams, Andrew, 296
Adams, Andrew, Jr., 295
Adams, Asa, 64
Adams, Augustus, 243
Adams, Benjamin, 91, 160
Adams, Casner, 42, 89
Adams, Charles, 23, 70, 80, 84, 155
Adams, Daniel, 162 (2), 163, 235
Adams, David, 272
Adams, David R., 183, 184, 188, 191
Adams, Eben, 17
Adams, Ebenezer, 93
Adams, Ebenezer W., 286, 290
Adams, Eli, 17, 278, 281
Adams, Ely, 20
Adams, Etheiner, 84
Adams, Ezekiel, 13, 14
Adams, Gamaliel, 129
Adams, George, 132
Adams, Giles, 16
Adams, H., 19
Adams, Hanson H., 17
Adams, Henry, 164 (2), 166, 221, 254
Adams, Henry K., 78
Adams, Ichabod, 45
Adams, Ira, 136, 137
Adams, Isaac, 13, 14, 85, 109, 219, 225
Adams, Isaac, 2d, 85
Adams, Isaac A., 104
Adams, Jacob S., 303
Adams, James, 93, 183, 184, 188, 232 (2), 290
Adams, Jephthah H., 227, 283
Adams, John, 17, 80, 140, 149, 220, 241, 242, 296, 306
Adams, Jonas, 101
Adams, Joseph, 17, 26, 96, 134, 140, 145, 173, 269, 307, 308
Adams, Joseph, Jr., 26
Adams, Joseph N., 26
Adams, Joshua, 303
Adams, Josiah, 100
Adams, Josiah H., 100
Adams, Lemuel, 266, 307
Adams, Levi, 82
Adams, Lot, 74, 137
Adams, Moses, 162 (2), 218
Adams, Moses, Jr., 219, 231
Adams, Nathan, 155, 156, 261
Adams, Nathaniel, 6, 22, 169, 281

Adams, Nehemiah, 90
Adams, Nicholas G., 21
Adams, Peter, 96
Adams, Richard, 16, 21
Adams, Robert, 210
Adams, Samuel, 23, 71, 74, 101, 112, 185, 284
Adams, Samuel, Jr., 183, 184, 188
Adams, Samuel G., 217
Adams, Samuel R., 6, 21
Adams, Saul, 98, 140
Adams, Solomon, 147
Adams, Stephen, 16, 93
Adams, Thomas, 58, 86, 89
Adams, Walter B., 93
Adams, Whiting, 90
Adams, William, 10, 89
Adams, William D., 83, 111
Adams, Winthrop, 13, 14
Adation, Joseph, 178
Addington, Francis, 82
Addington, Francis M., 86
Additon, John, 168
Aderton, John, 232
Adle, Christopher, 282
Agers, John, 36
Agge, Jacob, 133
Agraull, Roswell, 33
Agrey, John, Jr., 274
Agry, Thomas, 249
Aiken, James G., 110
Aiken, John, 82
Aikin, John, 78
Ainsworth, Kenslow, 43
Ainsworth, Luther, 44
Airs, Jonathan S., 40
Akens, Elihu, 127
Akens, James, 127
Akins, Benjamin, 127
Akins, Job, 127
Akins, Job, Jr., 127
Akins, John, 129, 133
Akley, William, 236
Albee, Samuel, 305
Alber, John, 190
Alber, Samuel, 66
Albert, Ivory C., 129
Albra, Samuel, 268
Alcher, Daniel, 132
Alcock, John, 26
Alden, Alexander, 223, 224, 257
Alden, Amasa, 49
Alden, Benjamin, Jr., 168
Alden, Charles, 269
Alden, Cyrus, 97
Alden, Daniel, 9, 53, 177, 260
Alden, Earl, 52, 102
Alden, Ebenezer, 55, 57
Alden, Elijah, Jr., 53
Alden, Ezra, 97
Alden, Ezra, 2d, 49
Alden, Gardner, 173
Alden, Hosea, 39

INDEX.

Alden, Isaac, 9, 86
Alden, Isaiah, 103
Alden, Jesse, 158
Alden, John, 79
Alden, John A., 69
Alden, Jonathan, 67, 97
Alden, Leustin, 218
Alden, Lot, 136
Alden, Oliver, 51
Alden, Oliver H., 54
Alden, Peter O., 148
Alden, Rufus, 52
Alden, Seth, 53, 58
Alden, Silas, 272
Alden, Thomas, 51
Aldrich, Cromwell, 146
Aldrich, Eaton, 91
Aldrich, Hendrick, 259
Aldrich, Henry, 222
Aldrich, Hosea, 54, 66
Aldrick, Willis, 98
Alexander, Benjamin, 296, 298
Alexander, Campbell, 228
Alexander, David, 148
Alexander, Elisha, 232 (2)
Alexander, Hugh, 297, 299
Alexander, Isaac, 299
Alexander, James, 155, 226, 231, 297
Alexander, Jeduthan, 151
Alexander, Jeremiah, 244
Alexander, John, 39, 155, 296, 299
Alexander, Joseph, 39, 146, 299
Alexander, Robert, 85
Alexander, Samuel, 3, 301
Alexander, William, 231
Alexander, William T., 94
Alger, Ansel, 49
Alger, Daniel, 92
Alger, George, 94
Alger, Howard, 49
Alkerson, Joseph, 116
Allbee, Benjamin, 186
Allbee, John, 186, 187
Allen, ———, 27
Allen, Abel, 260
Allen, Abner, 13, 14
Allen, Abraham, 55
Allen, Abram, 4
Allen, Alden, 58, 73, 75
Allen, Alexander, 46
Allen, Alpheus, 177
Allen, Amos, 36
Allen, Ansel, 263, 310
Allen, Anthony, 58
Allen, Asa, 23, 53, 224, 259
Allen, Barney, 161
Allen, Barziliel, 49
Allen, Benjamin, 63, 175, 260, 285
Allen, Benjamin J., 44
Allen, Charles, 63, 131
Allen, Charles J., 4
Allen, Chester, 4
Allen, Clother, 102
Allen, Daniel, 36, 47, 49, 97, 228, 230, 307, 308
Allen, Daniel P., 31
Allen, Datus T., 223, 259
Allen, David, 66, 129, 141, 210, 302
Allen, Duty, 291
Allen, Eaton, 59
Allen, Ebenezer, 65
Allen, Edmund, 225
Allen, Edward F., 77

Allen, Eliab, 147 (2)
Allen, Eliphalet, 307
Allen, Elisha, 212, 255, 269
Allen, Elisha, 2d, 61
Allen, Ephraim, 101
Allen, Ephraim, Jr., 299
Allen, Ezra, 276
Allen, Ezra, Jr., 117
Allen, Gardner, 55
Allen, George, 185, 187
Allen, Green, 63
Allen, Harrison, 304
Allen, Harvey, 32
Allen, Henry, 5, 34, 38
Allen, Hiram, 32
Allen, Ichabod, 168, 170, 281
Allen, Ignatius, 229
Allen, Isaac, 8, 212, 251
Allen, Isaac, 1st, 150
Allen, Isaac, 2d, 150
Allen, Isaiah, 98
Allen, Jacob, 56, 251
Allen, James, 84, 93, 177, 259
Allen, James, 2d, 177
Allen, Jesse, 155, 156, 187, 190
Allen, John, 32, 55, 56, 57, 60, 63, 127, 134,
  140, 150, 161, 187, 206, 225 (2), 228, 235,
  256, 282
Allen, John P., 36, 99
Allen, Joseph, 36, 67, 131, 152, 261
Allen, Joseph B., 170
Allen, Joshua, 255
Allen, Joshua C., 210
Allen, Josiah, 33
Allen, Lemuel, 44
Allen, Levi, 96, 176
Allen, Lewis, 10, 90, 276
Allen, Libbeus, 176
Allen, Luther, 147 (2)
Allen, Mack, 13
Allen, Major, 63
Allen, Marston, 69, 111
Allen, Martin, 41
Allen, Micah, 249, 297
Allen, Morton, 57
Allen, Moses, 228, 251, 263, 310
Allen, Nathan, 112, 256
Allen, Noah, 160
Allen, Ophie, 90
Allen, Otis, 47, 139, 223, 225
Allen, Paul, 209, 225
Allen, Reuben, 80, 83, 97, 259
Allen, Rufus, 55, 57, 119
Allen, Samuel, 15, 45, 97, 188, 253
Allen, Samuel, 2d, 188
Allen, Samuel R., 7, 110
Allen, Sanders, 44
Allen, Solomon, 253
Allen, Stephen, 224
Allen, Sylvanus, 304
Allen, Theophilus, 269
Allen, Thomas, 23, 36, 223
Allen, Thompson, 85
Allen, Tilly, 42, 89
Allen, Trueman, 304
Allen, Verona S., 53
Allen, Warren, 55, 57, 97, 127
Allen, Waters, 46
Allen, Willard, 13, 73, 151
Allen, William, 49, 73, 81, 120, 123, 131, 138,
  159, 169, 175, 178, 213, 219
Allen, Winthrop, 227, 282

Allen, Zacheus, 75, 76
Allen, Zacheus M., 58
Allen, Zadoc, 256
Allen, Ziba, 46
Alley, Benjamin, 117 (2)
Alley, Ephraim, Jr., 183
Alley, Henry, 21
Alley, Isaac, 162, 164
Alley, Jacob, 183
Alley, John, 185
Alley, John, Jr., 183
Alley, John, 3rd, 183
Alley, Joseph, Jr., 116
Alley, Lewis, 116
Alley, Nathan, 117
Alley, Richard, 2, 108
Alley, Solomon, Jr., 116
Alley, Thomas, 259
Alley, William, 116, 183
Allin, John, 55
Allison, Walter H., 115
Ally, John, 267
Alvord, Alvin, 45
Alvord, Elisha, 67
Alvord, Luther, 44
Alvord, Samuel, 67
Alvord, Sewall, 44
Alwood, William, 102
Amberry, Thomas H., 197, 204
Amby, Benjamin, 89
Amedy, John, 96
Ames, Austin, 45
Ames, Benjamin, 50
Ames, Charles, 49, 91
Ames, Doyal, 181
Ames, Ebenezer, 280
Ames, Eliakim, 266, 306
Ames, Gideon, 4
Ames, Henry, 301
Ames, Isaac, 98, 229, 280
Ames, Isaac F., 266, 306
Ames, Jacob, 68, 228
Ames, John, 50, 151, 153, 302
Ames, Jonas, 83, 266, 306
Ames, Joseph, 268, 301, 304
Ames, Moses, 23, 77
Ames, Nathaniel, 49, 50
Ames, Noyes, 226
Ames, Peter, 90, 136, 137
Ames, Phineas, 156, 157 (2)
Ames, Ralph, 225
Ames, Rufus, 229, 282
Ames, Samuel, 101, 222
Ames, Saul, 254
Ames, Simeon, 2
Ames, Theron, 50
Ames, Thomas, 37
Ames, Waldo, 49
Ames, William, 74
Amis, Solomon, Jr., 257
Amory, Rufus G., 111
Amory, Rufus G., Jr., 69
Amsden, David, 47
Amsden, Ephraim, 90
Amus, Jonas, 80
Anable, Barnabus, 65
Anable, David, 36
Anderson, Abraham, 211
Anderson, Alexander, 289, 293
Anderson, Archibald, 289
Anderson, Charles, 298
Anderson, Daniel, 65

INDEX.

Anderson, David, 65
Anderson, Ephraim, 276
Anderson, Ezra, 211, 259
Anderson, George, 209
Anderson, Hugh, 289, 293
Anderson, Jacob, 234
Anderson, James, 161, 169, 217, 277, 285, 286 (2), 288
Anderson, John, 170, 297
Anderson, Joshua, 69, 289, 293
Anderson, Lloyd, 255
Anderson, Martin, 295
Anderson, Montgomery, 255
Anderson, Otis, 167
Anderson, Robert, 166, 219
Anderson, Samuel, 174, 211
Anderson, Stephen, 11
Anderson, Thomas, 240, 278
Anderson, Timothy, 150
Anderson, William, 120, 121, 124 (2), 182, 184, 270
Andrew, James, 198
Andrews, Abel, 14, 246
Andrews, Alonzo, 29
Andrews, Amos, 152, 254
Andrews, Arthur, 147 (2)
Andrews, Asaph, 51
Andrews, Benjamin, 14, 292
Andrews, Charles, 14
Andrews, Daniel, 138
Andrews, Daniel H., 225
Andrews, Dean, 253
Andrews, Ebenezer, 89, 161, 170, 246
Andrews, Elisha, 32, 269
Andrews, Elisha, Jr., 269
Andrews, Ephraim, 233
Andrews, Erastus, 67
Andrews, George, 23, 78
Andrews, Ichabod, 169
Andrews, Isaac, 154
Andrews, Isaac W., 132
Andrews, Isacher, 152
Andrews, Jacob, 152
Andrews, James, 199, 201, 202
Andrews, John, 7, 36, 55, 91, 167, 170
Andrews, John H., 135
Andrews, Jonathan, 272
Andrews, Lemuel, 292 (2)
Andrews, Lescom, 222
Andrews, Lloyd, 252
Andrews, Loved, 253, 257
Andrews, Lucius, 222, 259
Andrews, Luman, 32
Andrews, Manassah, 259
Andrews, Moses, 16
Andrews, Nathaniel, 53, 132
Andrews, Otis, 169, 281
Andrews, Philip, 126
Andrews, Reuben, 169
Andrews, Rodolphus, 64
Andrews, Samuel, 14, 25, 158, 212, 251
Andrews, Samuel, Jr., 267
Andrews, Saul, 138
Andrews, Seth, 285, 286
Andrews, Stephen, 27, 114
Andrews, Thomas, 36, 138
Andrews, William, 5, 86, 257
Andrews, Zephaniah, 52, 57
Angel, Jeremiah, 30
Angells, Asa, 60
Angier, John, 41

Annable, Benjamin, 139 (2)
Annis, Ellison, 301
Annis, George, 266
Annis, John, 207, 306
Annis, Moses, 117
Annis, Robert, 202, 207, 208, 209
Annis, Rollins, 265
Anthoine, Amos, 255
Anthoyn, John, 211
Applebee, Hawley, 244
Appleton, B. B., 68
Appleton, Charles, 78, 81, 109
Appleton, Charles J., 69
Appleton, Daniel, 36, 37
Appleton, Daniel, Jr., 269
Appleton, Henry K., 68, 79, 112, 115
Appleton, James, 10
Appleton, Joseph, 264, 266
Appleton, Moses, 261, 265
Appleton, Thomas, 68
Appleton, William, 26
Appling, William, 128
Apthorp, James, 33
Arbuckle, John, 34
Archer, George, 137
Archer, Henry G., 161
Ardeton, Nathaniel B., 153
Areas, James, 225
Arey, Joseph, 104, 105 (2), 106, 107
Arf, George, 289
Arlean, James, 267
Armin, William B., 82
Armington, Ambrose, 61
Armington, George, 61
Armington, Joseph, 2d, 61
Arms, Ralph, 66
Arms, Thomas C., 52
Armsby, Amos, 146
Armsby, Mathias, 28
Armstrong, Elias, 278
Armstrong, George W., 26
Armstrong, James, 26, 39
Armstrong, John, 221
Armstrong, William, 25
Arno, Ezekiel, 170
Arno, Isaac, 170, 277
Arno, Zacheus, 170
Arnold, Benjamin, 292
Arnold, Ebenezer, 297
Arnold, Elisha, 31
Arnold, James, 268
Arnold, John, 199, 200, 203, 209, 277, 308
Arnold, John, Jr., 170
Arnold, Jonathan, 33
Arnold, Joseph, 100
Arnold, Josiah, 33
Arnold, Leonard, 29
Arnold, Lewis, 45
Arnold, Nathaniel T., 91
Arnold, S., 218
Arnold, Samuel, 30, 88, 226, 282
Arnold, Spencer, 179
Arnold, Thomas, 29, 227, 282, 290, 294
Arnold, William, 179, 199, 202, 308
Arnoly, Lemuel M., 55
Arns, Ezekiel, 277
Arras, James, 233
Arras, Thomas L., 233
Arrington, Joseph, 133
Arus, Ezekiel, 277
Arsas, Patrick, 233
Ashford, Robert, 230

Ashley, Abraham, 56, 58
Ashley, Abraham, 2d, 56
Ashley, Bishop, 56
Ashley, Henry, 29
Ashley, John, 4
Ashley, Leonard, 56
Ashley, Luther, 53
Ashley, Simeon, 56
Ashley, Tabor, 56
Ashley, Thomas, 56, 130
Ashley, William, 58
Ashton, Elisha V., 82
Ashton, William, 117
Askins, James, 193
Askins, John, 190, 193
Askins, Richard, 193
Askins, William, 193
Aspinwall, Samuel, 24
Aspinwall, William, 4
Athan, Benjamin, 201 (2), 202
Athan, John, 201 (2), 203
Athean, Frederick W., 110
Athearn, Cyrus, 24
Athearn, Frederic, 7
Athern, William, 248
Atherton, Abel, 242
Atherton, Abel W., 145, 165 (2), 241
Atherton, Charles, 241, 242
Atherton, Ebenezer, 275
Atherton, Ezra, 257
Atherton, John, 257
Atherton, Marshall, 88
Atherton, Peter, 162, 164
Atherton, Thomas, 162, 164
Atkins, Ansel, 275
Atkins, Benjamin, 28
Atkins, Edward, 85, 87
Atkins, Eleck, 272
Atkins, Henry, 287
Atkins, James, 139
Atkins, John, 138, 272, 277
Atkins, Joseph, 106 (2), 107
Atkins, Nathaniel, Jr., 278
Atkins, Rowland W., 118
Atkins, Sylvanus, 308
Atkins, Thomas N., 275
Atkinson, Benjamin, 17, 278
Atkinson, Enoch, 224, 259
Atkinson, Henry, 277, 281
Atkinson, James, 181, 304
Atkinson, Jonathan, 155
Atkinson, Samuel, 51
Atkinson, Thomas M., 304
Atley, William 4
Attis, Daniel, 64
Attis, George, 64
Atwell, George, 21
Atwill, Amos, 117
Atwill, Jesse L., 116
Atwood, Benjamin, 216
Atwood, Bradbury C., 243
Atwood, Ebenezer, 215
Atwood, Ephraim, 59
Atwood, Francis, 51
Atwood, Heman, 310
Atwood, Isaac, 213
Atwood, James, 151
Atwood, Jesse, Jr., 216
Atwood, Job, 252, 255
Atwood, John, 98, 233
Atwood, Joseph, 62
Atwood, Joshua, 52

INDEX.

Atwood, Levi, 128
Atwood, Nathaniel, 261
Atwood, Pelham, 103
Atwood, Phineas, 33
Atwood, Richard, 23
Atwood, Samuel, 21, 51
Atwood, Saul, 15
Atwood, Warren, 128
Atwood, William, 40, 52, 310
Atwood, Zacheriah, 20
Auben, Greenleaf, 82
Aubin, John, 90
Aubin, Joseph, 19
Aubin, Joshua, 110
Aubin, Samuel, 8
Aubins, George, 297, 299
Aubins, Humphry, 299
Aubray, Benjamin, 42
Auker, John, 3d, 138
Auld, Jacob, 145, 284
Auld, James, 284, 287
Auld, William, 284, 287
Aush, Solomon, 224
Austin, Aaron, 100, 202 (2), 204
Austin, Abiathar, 61
Austin, Abner, 82
Austin, Asa, 224
Austin, Buck, 252
Austin, Chester, 31
Austin, Daniel, 222, 307
Austin, Ebenezer, 257
Austin, Edward, 156, 157
Austin, Henry, 169
Austin, Jacob, 159
Austin, John, 177, 264
Austin, Jonah, Jr., 211
Austin, Josiah, 184
Austin, Minion, 256
Austin, Nahum, 264
Austin, Palmer, 59
Austin, Richard, 82
Austin, Robert, 240
Austin, Samuel, 85
Austin, Solomon, 59
Austin, Stephen, 167
Austin, Thomas, 24, 300
Austin, William, 25, 41, 138, 211
Austin, William B., 84
Averill, Daniel I., 148
Averill, Ezekiel, 184, 188
Averill, James, 184, 187
Averill, John, 244
Averill, William, 184, 188
Averit, Asa, 276
Avery, Benjamin, 13, 14
Avery, Ephraim, 44
Avery, James E., 7
Avery, Jeremiah, 215
Avery, John, 193
Avery, Philip, 130
Avery, Samuel, 113 (2)
Avery, Thomas, 172
Avery, Worster, 67
Avis, Thomas, 25
Axdell, Thomas, 33
Ayer, Asa, 150
Ayer, Benjamin, Jr., 180
Ayer, Hazen, 181
Ayer, Jacob, 149
Ayer, James, 184, 188
Ayer, John S., 180
Ayer, Joseph W., 40

Ayer, Moses, 8
Ayer, Samuel, 101
Ayer, William, 184, 185, 188
Ayers, Benjamin, 64
Ayers, Calvin, 45
Ayers, Charles, 87
Ayers, David, 17
Ayers, Ebenezer, 33
Ayers, Fisher, 90
Ayers, James, 191, 244
Ayers, Joseph, 85
Ayers, Lucius, 47
Ayers, Moses, 30, 68, 265
Ayers, Parly, 93
Ayers, Thomas, 38, 70, 77
Ayers, Will, 68
Ayling, Henry, 70
Ayling, Thomas, 70
Ayres, Francis, 39
Ayres, John, 13, 14, 39
Azel, Gurney, 91

B

Babb, Alexander, 221
Babb, Charles, 246, 256
Babb, David, 221
Babb, George, 189, 221
Babb, George, Jr., 220
Babb, Henry, 221, 246
Babb, Henry, Jr., 221
Babb, James, 85, 173
Babb, James, Jr., 219
Babb, John, 173, 218
Babb, Joseph, 273
Babb, Mark, 221
Babb, Nathaniel, 15, 184
Babb, Samuel, 149, 218
Babb, Solomon, 16
Babber, Abijah, 2d, 62
Babbidge, Benjamin, 132 (2)
Babbidge, John P., 138
Babbidge, William, 137
Babbitt, Crockett, 62
Babbitt, Isaac, 62
Babcock, ——, 27, 114
Babcock, Abel, 41
Babcock, Alpheus, 82
Babcock, Benjamin, 183, 308
Babcock, David, 276
Babcock, Elisha, 141
Babcock, Isaac, 55
Babcock, James, 66, 129
Babcock, Jesse, 276
Babcock, Jonathan, 276
Babcock, Joseph, 36
Babcock, Josiah, 40
Babcock, Nathan, 149
Babcock, Samuel H., 82
Babcock, William, 271
Babon, Reuben, 88
Babson, James, 12
Babson, John, 185
Babson, John, Jr., 182
Babson, Nathaniel, 13
Bachelder, Amos, 116
Bachelder, Ephraim, 212, 244
Bachelder, John, 21, 35
Bachelder, Jordan P., 250
Bachelder, Joseph, 85
Bachelder, Joshua, 137
Bachelder, Josiah, 85
Bachelder, Levi, 250

Bachelder, Nathaniel, 135
Bachelder, Rufus, 212
Bachelder, Timothy, Jr., 250
Bacheldor, George, 38
Bacheldor, Joseph, 119
Bacheler, Samuel, 262
Bachellor, Joseph, 265
Bacholor, Cornelius, 38
Bachelor, Gilman, 279
Bachelor, John, 290
Backliff, Benjamin, Jr., 187, 190
Backus, Andrew, 59
Backus, Calvin, 74
Backus, Heman, 74
Backus, Joshua, 74 (2)
Backus, Thomas, 74
Bacon, Bela, 90
Bacon, Benjamin, 32, 33, 250
Bacon, Columbus, 263
Bacon, Ebenezer, 131
Bacon, George, 32
Bacon, Henry, 42, 89, 131
Bacon, Jabes, 277
Bacon, James, 173, 246
Bacon, John, 84
Bacon, Jonathan, 66
Bacon, Joshua B., 7
Bacon, Josiah, 277, 281
Bacon, Judah, 25
Bacon, Lary, 278
Bacon, Micah, B., 70, 79
Bacon, Michael, 29
Bacon, Nathaniel, 212
Bacon, Oris, Jr., 131
Bacon, Robert, 27
Bacon, Samuel, 32
Bacon, Stephen, 158
Bacon, Thomas, 161
Bacon, Timothy, Jr., 165, 166, 173
Bacus, Herman, 73
Badcock, J., 218
Bader, Charles, 133
Badger, Barber, 113 (2)
Badger, Daniel, 14, 64
Badger, Jonathan, 39
Badger, Joseph, 297 (2), 298
Badger, Nathaniel, 295
Badger, Philip, 264
Badger, Thomas, 24, 28
Badgers, Samuel, 69
Badry, Joseph, 280
Baggs, David, 42
Bagley, Green, 238, 265
Bagley, John, 10
Bagley, Levi, 181
Bagley, Moses, 123, 124
Bagley, Samuel, 119, 122
Bagnall, Benjamin, 131
Bagnall, Joseph, 128
Bailey, Aaron, 118
Bailey, Abner R., 89
Bailey, Amos, 213
Bailey, Aretas, 178
Bailey, Charles, 1, 103
Bailey, Daniel, 15, 25
Bailey, David P., 271
Bailey, Ebenezer, 167
Bailey, Frederic, 218
Bailey, Gad, 1, 103
Bailey, Gideon, 109
Bailey, Henry, 42, 89
Bailey, Jacob, 271

INDEX. 319

Bailey, James, 271
Bailey, James P., 164 (2), 166, 220
Bailey, Jeremiah, 218
Bailey, John, 23, 42, 145, 213, 227
Bailey, Joseph, 83, 149, 164 (2), 166, 167 (2), 171, 221, 261
Bailey, Levi, 213
Bailey, Lewis J., 26
Bailey, Luther, 178
Bailey, Moses, 19, 124 (2), 159
Bailey, Nathaniel, 27
Bailey, Neser, Jr., 222
Bailey, Otis, 67
Bailey, Philip, 248
Bailey, Reuben, 213
Bailey, Richard, 184, 188
Bailey, Richard G., 221
Bailey, Samuel, 11, 175, 221
Bailey, Samuel, Jr., 218
Bailey, Samuel, 3d, 15
Bailey, Tappan, 15
Bailey, Thomas, 6
Bailey, Whitman, 167
Bailey, William, 227
Baily, Abner, 15
Baily, Adolphus, 43
Baily, Arctus, 260
Baily, Cushing, 24
Baily, Daniel C., 15
Baily, Hudson, 260
Baily, James, 15
Baily, John, Jr., 276
Baily, John W., 179
Baily, Joseph, 277
Baily, Joshua, 36
Baily, Luther, 260
Baily, Micajah, 276
Baily, Nathan, 276
Baily, Oliver, 226
Baily, Thadeus, 179
Baily, Thomas, 6
Baily, Whitman, 277
Baily, Zebina, 88
Bain, Daniel, 312
Baird, Aaron S., 32
Baird, John, 178
Baird, Samuel, 32
Baird, William, 225
Bairon, Joseph, 284
Baker, Abel, 28 (2), 226
Baker, Abel P., 23, 77
Baker, Abijah, 105 (2), 107
Baker, Abner, 230
Baker, Alexander, 60, 242
Baker, Amariah, 262
Baker, Amasa, 212
Baker, Andrew, 28
Baker, Asa, 14, 191
Baker, Azariah, 185
Baker, Barnabus, 72
Baker, Benjamin, 211, 239
Baker, Benoni, 104, 105 (2), 106
Baker, Burton, 31
Baker, Caleb, 230
Baker, Charles, 244
Baker, Clark, 228
Baker, Daniel, 60, 131, 155, 226
Baker, David, 26, 62, 216, 268
Baker, Davis, 131
Baker, Edmund, 72
Baker, Edward, 160
Baker, Elijah, 131, 154, 211

Baker, Elisha, 229
Baker, Enos, 17
Baker, Francis, 69
Baker, George, 22
Baker, George S., 30
Baker, Gideon, 15
Baker, Henry, 182
Baker, Henry A., 182
Baker, Ivers, 4
Baker, Jabez, 72
Baker, James, 53, 78, 268
Baker, Jeremiah, 162, 215
Baker, John, 35 (2), 149 (2), 183, 185, 191, 230, 308
Baker, Jonathan, 148, 237
Baker, Joseph, 51
Baker, Joshua, 249
Baker, Levi, 171
Baker, Matthew, 30
Baker, Miles C., 30
Baker, Moses, 216
Baker, Nathaniel, 72, 216, 261
Baker, Oliver, 239
Baker, Richard, 216
Baker, Ruel, 86
Baker, Samuel, 197, 215, 258
Baker, Saul, 233
Baker, Silas, 5
Baker, Snow, 156, 157 (2)
Baker, Solomon, 158
Baker, Stephen, 34, 38, 180
Baker, Sylvanus, 125
Baker, Sylvester, 131
Baker, Thomas, 242, 283
Baker, Walker, 32
Baker, William, 13, 78, 79, 86, 227, 282, 283
Baker, William M., 26
Baker, Zachariah, 239, 295
Baker, Zenos, 60, 230
Balch, Benjamin, 135, 137, 138
Balch, Daniel, 125
Balch, Saul, 137
Balch, William, 39, 79, 121, 124
Balcom, Thaddeus, 5
Balcomb, John, 159
Balcomb, Lima, 237
Baldwin, Abel, 68, 79
Baldwin, Augustus, 66
Baldwin, Cyrus, 25
Baldwin, Cyrus, Jr., 39, 278
Baldwin, Davis, Jr., 88
Baldwin, Ephraim, 31
Baldwin, Jaheil, 33
Baldwin, King, 46
Baldwin, Nahum, 227
Baldwin, Phineas P., 23, 114
Baldwin, Seth, 308
Baldwin, Stephen, 31
Baley, Winslow C., 53
Balk, Daniel, 122
Ball, Daniel, 70, 272
Ball, Ebenezer, 24
Ball, Eli, 44
Ball, Francis, 44
Ball, George, 65
Ball, James, 48
Ball, John, 118, 268
Ball, Jonathan, 28
Ball, Josiah, 3
Ball, Levi, 184
Ball, Milton, 31
Ball, Phinehas, 94

Ball, Russell, 68
Ball, Stephen, 65
Ball, Thomas, 26, 77
Ballan, Seth, 222
Ballard, Alva, 66
Ballard, Calvin, 275
Ballard, Daniel, 271
Ballard, David C., 24
Ballard, Dela F., 274
Ballard, Frederick, 283
Ballard, George, 23, 86
Ballard, Henry, 132
Ballard, Orin, 66
Ballard, William, 162
Ballard, Zelotes, 66
Ballister, Joseph, 7
Ballou, Ebenezer M., 85
Ballou, James, 85
Ballou, Rufus, 48
Banan, Charles, 236
Bancroft, Alpheus, 45
Bancroft, Ebenezer, 114
Bancroft, Jacob, 253, 255
Bancroft, Joseph, 253
Bancroft, Lyman, 66
Bancroft, Stephen, 139 (2)
Bancroft, Thomas, 139 (2)
Bancroft, Timothy, 39
Banett, Daniel, 99
Banford, Jeremiah, 152, 255
Bangs, Alkanah, 267
Bangs, Amos, 67
Bangs, David, 29
Bangs, Dean, 153
Bangs, Edward D., 94
Bangs, Ezekiel, 154
Bangs, George, 241
Bangs, Isaac, 7, 113
Bangs, Martin, 2
Bangs, Silvanus, 270
Bangs, Thomas G., 28
Banister, John B., 84, 114
Banks, James, 170
Banks, John, 225
Banks, Richard, 225
Banks, Thomas G., 28
Banney, Isaac, 281
Banney, Luther, 31
Bannia, David, 69
Bannington, Edward, 27
Bannister, John, 113 (2)
Bannister, Liberty, 91
Bannister, Samuel, 26
Banny, Josiah, 53
Banskins, Thomas, 164, 166
Banton, Joseph, 180
Barber, Benjamin, 18
Barber, Caleb, Jr., 190
Barber, Ebenezer, 3
Barber, Elias, 259
Barber, Fisher, 27, 86
Barber, Hamlet, 96
Barber, James, 100
Barber, John, 23, 86
Barber, Joseph, Jr., 100
Barber, Lawrence, 4
Barber, Oliver, 2
Barber, Robert, 66
Barber, Samuel, 23, 86
Barber, Samuel, Jr., 33
Barber, Thomas, Jr., 30
Barbor, James, 5

INDEX.

Barbour, David, 154
Barbour, John, 220
Barden, John, 54
Barden, R., 54
Bardon, Randolphus, 52
Bardotte, Joseph, 146
Barhall, Gilman, 278
Barker, Bamos, 189
Barker, Caleb, 232 (2)
Barker, Caleb, Jr., 187
Barker, Clark, 283
Barker, David, 79, 166, 277
Barker, Ezra, 244
Barker, George, Jr., 6
Barker, Gideon, 188, 190
Barker, Henry, 213
Barker, Jacob, 280, 292
Barker, Jacob W., 100
Barker, Jairus, 33
Barker, James, 162, 163
Barker, Jedediah, 71
Barker, Jeremiah, 137
Barker, John, 213, 226
Barker, John W., 185, 188, 191
Barker, Jonah, 265
Barker, Jonathan, 252
Barker, Joseph, Jr., 103
Barker, Jotham, 267
Barker, Nathan, 34, 258
Barker, R. M., 190
Barker, Richard M., 186 (2), 187
Barker, Samuel, 63, 185, 187, 299
Barker, Samuel, 3d, 257
Barker, Simeon, 269
Barker, Stephen, 181, 213
Barker, Timothy, 160
Barker, Turner, 156, 157 (2)
Barker, Wendell R., 85, 109
Barker, William, 21, 37, 257
Barley, John R., 6
Barley, Timothy, 100
Barlow, Anson, 180
Barlow, Cornelius, 29
Barlow, Heman, 45
Barlow, John, 4
Barlow, Samuel, 145
Barmester, Samuel, 86
Barnaby, Benjamin, 161
Barnaby, Nathan, Jr., 45
Barnam, David, 88
Barnard, Edward, 109, 157
Barnard, Emery, 30
Barnard, Horace, 77
Barnard, Jacob, 8
Barnard, Joel, 90, 222
Barnard, John, 239, 285, 286 (2), 288
Barnard, Jonah G., 7
Barnard, Josiah, 28, 239
Barnard, Josiah H., 309 (2)
Barnard, Lucas, 195
Barnard, Robert M., 7
Barnard, Silas, 222
Barnard, Thomas, 290
Barnes, Abel, 198, 202, 207, 208 (2)
Barnes, Amos, 94, 198, 199, 201, 202
Barnes, Benjamin, 156, 217, 234, 291
Barnes, Charles, 296
Barnes, Cornelius, 149
Barnes, Daniel, 32
Barnes, Ebenezer, 45
Barnes, Edmund, 156
Barnes, Edward, 157

Barnes, Elisha, 32
Barnes, Elkanah, 131
Barnes, Elnathan, 32
Barnes, Harvey, 44
Barnes, Henry, 232
Barnes, James, 178, 242, 291
Barnes, John, 39, 80, 117
Barnes, Joseph, 32
Barnes, Nathan, 44
Barnes, Peletiah, 166
Barnes, Robert, 232
Barnes, Russell, 29
Barnes, Stephen, 128
Barnes, Thomas, 25, 28
Barnes, William, 131
Barnet, Josiah M., 82
Barney, Ezra, 128
Barney, Griffin, 1
Barney, James O., 60
Barney, John, 98
Barney, John C., 77
Barney, Jonathan, 24, 52, 80, 114
Barney, Lyman, 62
Barney, Oliver, 92
Barneywell, Edward, 241
Barns, Henry, 232
Barns, Jacob, 291
Barns, John, 21, 23
Barns, Nathaniel, 67
Barns, Samuel, 215
Baroler, William, 179
Barr, John, Jr., 135
Barr, John S., 138
Barr, Phineas, 64
Barr, Robert, 135
Barr, Simeon, 64
Barr, William, 135, 137
Barrees, Peletiah, 277
Barrell, Elias, 1
Barrell, Elisha, 1, 103
Barrell, Pascal, 178
Barrell, William, 178
Barret, Archer, 33
Barret, Benjamin, 164, 166
Barret, Elba C., 33
Barret, Levi, 261
Barrett, Benjamin, 93, 164
Barrett, Calvin, 274
Barrett, Daniel, 202
Barrett, Daniel, Jr., 198, 208
Barrett, David, 11
Barrett, George S., 13, 14
Barrett, Henry, 188
Barrett, John, 13, 14
Barrett, Joseph, 123, 178
Barrett, Nathaniel, 117
Barrett, Nathaniel, 198, 202, 207, 208 (2), 209
Barrett, Otis, 29
Barrett, Royal C., 30
Barrett, Thomas, 238
Barrett, William, 91
Barrill, Bill, 39
Barringdon, William, 297
Barrington, Edward, 39
Barrington, Henry, 89
Barron, Charles, 234
Barron, John, 210
Barron, Oliver, 86
Barron, William L., 255
Barrow, Thomas, 302
Barrows, Ansel, 178
Barrows, Asa, 146, 150

Barrows, Buel, 175
Barrows, Charles, 128
Barrows, Cornelius, 175, 260
Barrows, George, 51, 175
Barrows, Gifford, 61
Barrows, Jabez, 175
Barrows, Job C., 175
Barrows, Job H., 260
Barrows, John, 158
Barrows, Joseph, 128
Barrows, Joshua, 223
Barrows, Robert, 65
Barrows, Ruel, 176
Barrows, Rufus, 91
Barrows, Samuel, 202
Barrows, Saul, 198, 201
Barrows, Simeon, 259
Barrows, Stephen, 198, 201, 202, 209
Barrows, Stillman, 102
Barrows, Sylvanus, 52
Barrows, Thomas, 52
Barrows, Wheaton, 53
Barrows, William, 44
Barry, Aaron, 224
Barry, Daniel, 264
Barry, James, 66
Barry, John, 246
Barry, Jonathan, 133
Barry, Oliver, 136
Barry, Stephen, 151
Barry, Thomas, Jr., 68
Barry, William, 42, 87
Bars, Ebenezer N., 93
Bars, Hiram, 93
Barsley, John, Jr., 131
Barsley, Joseph, 131
Barston, Robert, 299
Barstow, Alexander, 193, 196
Barstow, Benjamin, 195
Barstow, James, 194
Barstow, John, 159
Barstow, Joseph, 136, 137
Barstow, Nathaniel, 193
Barter, Benjamin, 183, 184, 188, 191
Barter, Benjamin A., 149
Barter, George, 42, 77, 89
Barter, John, 183, 184, 186, 188, 191
Barter, John, Jr., 186
Barter, John, 4th, 183, 184, 188
Barter, Samuel, 183, 184, 188
Barter, Samuel, 2d, 183
Barter, Samuel, 3d, 188
Bartlet, Alexander, 45
Bartlet, Charles, 16, 218
Bartlet, David, 16, 223
Bartlet, Edward M., 92
Bartlet, Eli, 21
Bartlet, Freeborn, 261
Bartlet, George, 84
Bartlet, Gideon, 21
Bartlet, Isaac, 16
Bartlet, Israel, 16
Bartlet, James, 15
Bartlet, Jason B., 286
Bartlet, John, 301
Bartlet, Joseph B., 21
Bartlet, Joshua, 280
Bartlet, Lazarus, 65
Bartlet, Luther, 65
Bartlet, Robert, 243
Bartlet, Saul, 280
Bartlet, Stephen, 20

INDEX. 321

Bartlet, Sylvanus, 255
Bartlet, Tilden, 251
Bartlet, William, 15, 16, 19, 21
Bartlett, Alfred, 65
Bartlett, Alva, 45
Bartlett, Amasa, 216
Bartlett, Bailey, Jr., 98
Bartlett, Benoni, 4
Bartlett, Charles, 20
Bartlett, Clement, 253
Bartlett, Cutting, 89
Bartlett, David, 49, 181, 259
Bartlett, Devereux D., 6
Bartlett, Ebenezer, 257
Bartlett, Edward, 147
Bartlett, Elkanah, 128
Bartlett, Flavel, 147
Bartlett, Ira, 223
Bartlett, J. W., 152
Bartlett, James, 272
Bartlett, Jason, 290
Bartlett, Jedediah, 30
Bartlett, Jeremiah, 215
Bartlett, John, 6, 22, 170, 201 (2), 203, 291
Bartlett, Jonathan, 175, 181, 220, 260
Bartlett, Joseph B., 6
Bartlett, Joshua, 281
Bartlett, Knot, 197, 203
Bartlett, Lemuel, 252
Bartlett, Lemuel, 2d, 252, 255
Bartlett, Levi, 158
Bartlett, Mailchi, 252
Bartlett, Malachi, 255
Bartlett, Martin, 87
Bartlett, Moses, 15
Bartlett, Nathaniel, 6, 22
Bartlett, Noah, 46
Bartlett, O. Timothy, 281
Bartlett, Ozias, 224
Bartlett, Peter, 22
Bartlett, Richard, 17, 197, 203, 204
Bartlett, Richard M., 19
Bartlett, Robert, 6
Bartlett, Rufus, 215, 238, 265
Bartlett, Rufus, Jr., 252
Bartlett, Samuel, 173
Bartlett, Samuel K., 117
Bartlett, Seth, 182, 191
Bartlett, Sylvanus, 252
Bartlett, Thomas, 203, 204, 206
Bartlett, William, 6, 22
Bartol, Ammi, 153
Bartol, Barnabus, 145
Bartol, John, 21
Bartol, Samuel, 209
Barton, Augustus, 45
Barton, Enoch, 195, 197
Barton, Gideon, 179
Barton, Henry, 78
Barton, Herman C., 267
Barton, Hernand C., 236
Barton, Isaac, 284
Barton, Jacob, 258
Barton, John, 192, 193, 248, 288, 297
Barton, John, Jr., 183
Barton, Joseph, 47, 181
Barton, Josiah, 46
Barton, Nathan, 238
Barton, Phinehas, 47
Barton, Samuel, 44
Barton, Solomon N., 75
Barton, William, 30, 213

Basford, David, 251
Basford, Jesse, 302
Basford, Jonathan, 213
Basford, Joseph, 213
Basford, Reuben, 170
Basley, John, 101
Bass, Charles, 23, 109
Bass, Elias, 70
Bass, George, 28
Bass, Gillan, 80, 86
Bass, Moses, 24
Buss, William W., 23
Basset, Abner, 230
Basset, Benjamin, 237
Basset, Cornelius, 30
Basset, Daniel, 96
Basset, Heli, 230
Basset, Jabez, 237
Basset, Joseph, 237
Basset, Lewis, 230
Bassett, Adolphus, 30
Bassett, Caleb, 51
Bassett, Charles, 74
Bassett, Christopher, 19
Bassett, Cyrus, 51
Bassett, Daniel, 11
Bassett, David, 59
Bassett, Jabez, 237
Bassett, Jeremiah, 62
Bassett, John, 73, 74
Bassett, Jonathan, 51
Bassett, Joseph, 51, 121, 265
Bassett, Josiah, 51
Bassett, Keith, 51
Bassett, Lewis, 235
Bassett, Nathan, 73, 76
Bassett, Nathaniel, 17, 129
Bassett, Peres, 130
Bassett, Samuel T., 6
Bassett, Saul, 90
Bassett, Thomas, 71
Bassett, William, 51, 73
Bassett, William, Jr., 76
Bassey, Thomas, 264
Bassford, David, 255
Bassford, Nathaniel, 234
Bassick, William, 303
Basson, John, 82
Basto, Israel, 240
Baston, Joseph, 307
Baston, William, 261
Batchelder, Abraham, 271
Batchelder, Asa, 273
Batchelder, Daniel, 304
Batchelder, George, 226
Batchelder, George, 2d, 34
Batchelder, Henry, 34, 38
Batchelder, James, 116, 272
Batchelder, John, 139, 154, 286
Batchelder, Jonathan, 34
Batchelder, Joseph, 122, 304 (2)
Batchelder, Joshua, 117, 136
Batchelder, Levi, 249
Batchelder, Lewis, 286
Batchelder, Nathaniel, 34, 38, 116, 139, 140
Batchelder, Philip, 271
Batchelder, Phinehas, 228
Batchelder, Samuel, 116, 250
Batchelder, Samuel E., 155
Batchelder, William, 133, 136, 170
Batchelder, Winthrop, 34, 89
Batcheldore, Joseph, 19

Bates, Asa, 67, 263, 266
Bates, Benjamin, 102, 131
Bates, Benjamin, 2d, 102
Bates, Caleb, 102, 128
Bates, Clement, 127
Bates, Cotton, 102
Bates, Cyrus, 178
Bates, Daniel, 49, 65
Bates, Dexter, 54
Bates, Dexter B., 33
Bates, Edmund, 27
Bates, Elijah, 170, 263, 310
Bates, Elnathan, 102
Bates, Ezekiel, 54, 101
Bates, Frederic, 232
Bates, Henry, 4, 82, 168
Bates, Ira, 23
Bates, Isaac, 131, 268
Bates, Israel, 186
Bates, Jacob, 43
Bates, Jacob H., 98
Bates, James, 65, 86, 102, 232, 263, 310
Bates, Jared, 190
Bates, Jesse, Jr., 102
Bates, John, 102, 175, 260, 267, 310
Bates, John B., 128
Bates, Joseph, 168, 281
Bates, Joshua, 310
Bates, Levi, Jr., 168
Bates, Mordicai, 101
Bates, Moses, 130
Bates, Nathan, 65, 226
Bates, Nathaniel N., 89
Bates, Newcomb, 42, 88
Bates, Orrick, 65
Bates, Paddock, 130
Bates, Phineas, 42
Bates, Phineas B., 45
Bates, Reuben, 167
Bates, Samuel, 236, 267
Bates, Silas, 263, 310
Bates, Simeon, 30
Bates, Solomon, 271
Bates, Stephen, 24, 114
Bates, Sylvester, 44
Bates, William, 43, 98, 102, 153
Bath, Daniel, 46
Bath, Edmund, 46
Bathrick, Jonathan, 5
Bation, Mula, 119
Batles, Briggs, 205
Batten, Abraham, 166
Batten, John, 150
Battice, Joseph, 15
Battin, John, 138
Battle, Daniel, 282
Battle, Ebenezer, 47
Battle, James, 280
Battle, William, 283
Battles, Benjamin, 71, 75
Battles, Joseph, 42, 88
Battles, William, 50
Batts, John, 280
Batts, Robert, 280
Baxter, Charles, 131
Baxter, Francis, 33
Baxter, John C., 90
Baxter, Joseph, 27
Baxter, Robert, 126
Baxter, Rufus, Jr., 26
Baxter, Samuel, 3d, 191
Baxter, Solomon S., 26

INDEX.

Baxter, Thomas M., 7
Baxton, Charles, 35
Baxton, Edward, 165, 166
Bayles, Alexander, 37
Bayles, Ichabod, 34
Bayley, Charles, 182
Bayley, Job, 79
Bayley, John, 77
Bayley, Joseph, 249
Bayley, Moses, 19, 120 (2), 121 (2)
Bayley, Thomas, 17
Bazlin, Sargent, 285
Beach, Apolus, 65
Beach, Atwater, 30
Beach, Geriel, 45
Beach, Henry, 30
Beach, Joseph, 134
Beal, David, 92, 147 (2)
Beal, Ebenezer, 235
Beal, Edward, 162, 163
Beal, George, 42
Beal, Harvey, 268
Beal, Henry, 181
Beal, Ira, 176
Beal, Isaac, 23, 42, 88
Beal, Joseph, 295, 297
Beal, Martin, 109
Beal, Nathaniel, 9
Beal, William, 233
Beal, Woodman, 149
Beale, Caswell, 84
Beale, Charles, 101
Beale, Daniel, 227, 282
Beale, George, 101
Beale, Levi, 83, 110
Beale, Lewis, 110
Beales, George, 261
Beales, Isaac N. C., 77
Beals, Alexander, 24
Beals, Asa, 49
Beals, Caleb, 30
Beals, Jarvis, 153
Beals, John, 167
Beals, Lemuel, 27
Beals, Levi, 69, 80
Beals, Luther, 222, 259
Beals, Martin, 80
Beals, Samuel, 222
Beals, Saul, 212
Beals, Zacheus, 232
Beals, Zenas, 175
Beamos, Elisha, 285
Bean, Abiather, 253, 257
Bean, Abner, 258
Bean, Abram, 236
Bean, Asa, 278, 279
Bean, Daniel, 237, 267
Bean, Daniel, Jr., 257
Bean, Ebenezer, 229, 308
Bean, Edward, 279
Bean, Franklin, 278
Bean, Greenleaf, 224
Bean, Henry, Jr., 6
Bean, Hezekiah, 301
Bean, Ira A., 161
Bean, Isaac, 145
Bean, Israel, 223
Bean, Ivory, 268
Bean, James, 224, 254
Bean, Jeremiah, 181, 193, 229
Bean, Jesse, 257
Bean, John, 241, 271

Bean, Jonathan, 181
Bean, Joseph, 181
Bean, Joshua, 281
Bean, Josiah, 303
Bean, Jude, 141
Bean, Kimball, 257
Bean, Levi, 264
Bean, Lewis, 303
Bean, Lyman, 228
Bean, Manly, 278, 281
Bean, Milton, 278
Bean, Moses, 125, 280
Bean, Nathan, 152, 181
Bean, Nathaniel, 152, 229, 254, 257, 282
Bean, Oliver, 278
Bean, Samuel, 223
Bean, Samuel, 2d, 152
Bean, Saul, 152
Bean, Simeon, 69
Bean, Simon, 239
Bean, Smith, 278
Bean, Thomas, 150
Bean, Thomas, Jr., 152
Bearce, Asa, Jr., 175, 257
Bearce, Benjamin, 95
Bearce, Ebenezer, 193
Bearce, Ford, 49
Bearce, Gideon, Jr., 175
Bearce, Holmes, 305
Bearce, Homer, 128
Bearce, Isaac, 175, 287
Bearce, John, 193, 258
Bearce, Levi, 176
Bearce, Oliver, 210
Bearce, Samuel, 193
Bearce, Saul, 78
Beard, Samuel, Jr., 178
Beard, Stephen, 41
Bears, Hezekiah, 277
Bears, Josiah, 277
Bears, Moses, 125
Bearse, David, 278, 281
Bearse, Thomas, 74
Beck, Frederick, 70
Beck, Thomas, 262
Becker, Joseph H., 291
Becket, David, 138
Becket, Jeremiah, 208
Becket, John, 201
Becket, Joseph H., 288 (2)
Becket, William, 138
Beckett, John, 132, 138, 198, 199
Beckland, Rodney, 23
Beckley, Francis, 257
Beckwith, Chauncey, 29
Beebe, Robert, 257
Beede, Aaron, 268
Beedy, Daniel, 304
Beedy, Ephraim, 305
Beel, James, 247
Beel, Samuel H., Jr., 248
Beel, Zacheus, 232
Beeman, Charles, 161
Beeman, Daniel, 242
Beeman, Ezra, 242, 246
Beeman, Samuel, 241
Beeman, Stephen, 211
Been, William, 10
Beers, John B., 86
Becton, John, 23
Begram, Charles, 90
Beith, Jeremiah, 308

Belcher, Benjamin, 29
Belcher, Comfort, 99
Belcher, Curtis, 29
Belcher, Eliphalet, 42, 89
Belcher, Jeremiah, 42, 89
Belcher, John, 26, 68
Belcher, John H., 28
Belcher, Joseph, 29
Belcher, Richard, 158
Belcher, Samuel, 27
Belcher, Solomon, 53
Belcher, William, 8, 23, 100
Belders, Silas, 32
Belding, Amos, 67
Belding, Aretus, 4
Belding, Chester, 96
Belding, Hezekiah, 4
Belding, Salmon, 45
Belding, Samuel, 67
Belding, Stephen, 179
Belford, Davis, 244
Beliter, Thomas, 160
Belknap, Samuel A., 83
Belknap, Zedekiah, 261
Bell, David, 79, 86
Bell, David W., 85
Bell, Edward, 25, 26, 79
Bell, George, Jr., 160
Bell, Jeremiah, 247
Bell, John, Jr., 257
Bell, Philip, 8, 311
Bell, Robert, 224, 259
Bell, Samuel, 25
Bell, William, 28, 41, 79, 221, 243, 261
Bell, William B., 244
Bell, William D., 25, 79
Bellington, Nathaniel, 49
Bellows, Elijah, 98
Bellows, Jesse, 43
Bellows, Newell, 91
Belnap, Charles, 289
Below, Leonard, 47
Bemant, Anson, 64
Bemis, Amos, 151, 254
Bemis, Charles, 115
Bemis, David, 90, 146
Bemis, Francis, 146, 150
Bemis, Isaac, 79
Bemis, James, 146, 150
Bemis, Joel, 27, 86
Bemis, Jonathan, 146 (2), 150
Bemis, Jonathan, Jr., 150
Bemis, Joseph, 254
Bemis, Luke, 93
Bemis, Reuben, 80
Bemis, Samuel, 82
Bemis, Thaddeus, Jr., 152, 254
Bench, Joseph, 135
Benchard, Seneca B., 44
Bender, Jacob, 24
Benedict, Sylvester, 32
Benet, Elisha, 283
Benige, George, 26
Benjamin, Billy, 223, 254, 259
Benjamin, Charles, 223
Benjamin, John, 40, 268
Benjamin, Samuel, 277, 281
Benner, Charles, 2d, 292
Benner, Christopher, 291
Benner, Frederic, 292, 294
Benner, George, 291
Benner, Henry, 276

INDEX. 323

Benner, Jacob, 291
Benner, James, 194
Benner, John, 291
Benner, Joshua, 194
Benner, Nathaniel, 276
Benner, Philip, 291
Bennery, Luke, 64
Bennet, Andrew H., 209
Bennet, Archelaus C., 87
Bennet, Asa, 291
Bennet, Barsillai, 87
Bennet, Calvin, 44
Bennet, Charles, 55
Bennet, Daniel, 162, 164
Bennet, David, 27, 78
Bennet, Eben, 44
Bennet, Elisha, 290
Bennet, Elisha, Jr., 228
Bennet, Francis, 295, 297
Bennet, Henry, 213
Bennet, Isaac, 103, 252, 256
Bennet, Israel, 29, 33
Bennet, Jacob, 52, 54, 87
Bennet, Jeremiah, 58, 212
Bennet, Jesse, 87
Bennet, Job K., 311
Bennet, John, 31, 38, 47, 110, 186
Bennet, Jonathan, 274
Bennet, Michael, 58
Bennet, Moses, 213
Bennet, Noah, 213
Bennet, Robert G., 38
Bennet, Saul, 286, 290
Bennet, Thomas, 75, 94
Bennet, William, 228
Bennett, Abraham, 52
Bennett, Asa, 285
Bennett, Benjamin, 91
Bennett, Charles, 57
Bennett, Daniel, 183
Bennett, George, 126
Bennett, James, 43, 80, 110
Bennett, James H., 24
Bennett, John, 34, 183, 263
Bennett, Joseph, 130, 244
Bennett, Moses, 70
Bennett, Ralph R., 44
Bennett, Robert G., 34
Bennett, Samuel G., 269
Bennett, Thomas, 30, 71
Bennett, William, 259
Bennett, William L., 148
Benney, James, 2
Benney, John, 178
Benning, Joseph, 218, 244
Benskins, Thomas, 164
Benson, Aaron L., 286, 288
Benson, Aaron S., 285, 286
Benson, Ansel, 52
Benson, Artemas, 130
Benson, Asa, 52, 223
Benson, Caleb, 175
Benson, Consider, 66
Benson, Cyrus, 51
Benson, Henry, 65
Benson, Hosea, 223
Benson, Jared, 98
Benson, John, 52
Benson, Jonah, 51
Benson, Jonathan, 51
Benson, Jonathan G., 289, 293
Benson, Joseph, 178, 259

Benson, Leonard, 178, 259
Benson, Linus, 52
Benson, Matthew, 304
Benson, Nathan, 51
Benson, Samuel, 214, 253
Benson, Seth, 51, 251, 255
Benson, Sullivan, 259
Benson, William, 154
Bent, Adam, 70
Bent, Avery, 85
Bent, Isaac, 229
Bent, Joseph, 59, 61
Bent, Otis, 251, 255
Bent, Samuel, 51, 103
Bent, Zenos, 51
Bentlet, John, 119
Bently, Caleb, 30
Bently, Eliphalet, 30
Benton, Burnham, 180
Benton, William, 29
Berbeck, John, 23
Berbeck, William, 23
Bergin, Ebenezer, 261
Bernard, Horace, 23
Bernard, Isaac, 156
Bernard, Jonathan, 258
Berry, Abraham, 172
Berry, Allen, 229
Berry, Andrew, 273
Berry, Andrew B., 275
Berry, Arthur, 275
Berry, Benjamin, 147 (2), 174
Berry, Charles, 176
Berry, Daniel, 266
Berry, David, 269, 275
Berry, Edward, 18
Berry, Ephraim, 269
Berry, George, 2d, 15
Berry, George W., 90
Berry, Henry, 151
Berry, Isaac, 83, 303
Berry, Jeremiah, 204, 205 (2)
Berry, John, 140, 165, 166, 168, 172, 243, 303
Berry, John, Jr., 134, 140, 172
Berry, Jonathan, 139, 141, 196, 303
Berry, Joseph, 77, 167, 180, 303
Berry, Josiah, 231, 275
Berry, Levi, 152, 164 (2), 166, 172, 251, 255
Berry, Mial, 150
Berry, Morrill, 256
Berry, Nathaniel, 172
Berry, Obediah, 176, 257
Berry, Oliver, 133, 134, 140
Berry, Peletiah, 255
Berry, Peter, 176
Berry, Richard, 191
Berry, Robert, 172
Berry, Rufus, 227, 269, 282
Berry, Samuel, 220
Berry, Solomon, 263
Berry, Thomas, 150, 219
Berry, Timothy, 35, 175
Berry, William, 134, 140, 151, 177, 250, 254
Berry, Zebedee, 172
Berry, Zebulon, Jr., 172
Berry, Zoath, 125
Bert, Simeon, 56
Bert, Sylvester, 56
Beson, Saul, 138
Besse, Anthony, 146, 150

Besse, Asa, 126
Besse, Caleb, 252
Besse, David, 281
Besse, Elijah, 90
Besse, Elisha, 280
Besse, John, 252
Besse, Lathrop, 56
Besse, Nathaniel, 55, 57
Besse, Samuel, 279, 280
Besse, Seth, 175
Besse, Warren, 251
Besse, Woodin, 278, 281
Besser, David, 277
Bessey, Ephraim, 239
Bessey, Martin, 63
Besson, Jonathan, 138
Bettes, Jacob, 171
Beverly, Joel, 8
Beseley, Edward S., 43
Bibber, Cortney, 299
Bickford, Aaron, 146, 233
Bickford, Abijah, 263, 267
Bickford, Andrew, 12
Bickford, Charles, 188
Bickford, David, 134, 135
Bickford, George, 156, 157
Bickford, Gideon, 244
Bickford, Henry, 262, 267, 305
Bickford, Hesekiah, 254
Bickford, John, 69, 187, 190
Bickford, Joshua, 135, 140
Bickford, Moses, 262, 305
Bickford, Samuel, 262 (2)
Bickford, Silas, 14
Bickford, Thomas, 138
Bickford, William, 152, 190, 191, 233
Bickford, William, 2d, 187
Bickmore, Benjamin, 206 (2)
Bickmore, Charles, 240
Bickmore, John, 240
Bickmore, Samuel, 180
Bickmore, Solomon, 285, 288, 291
Bicknell, Cyrus, 175
Bicknell, David, 175
Bicknell, Lovell, 96
Bicknell, Randall, 9
Bicknell, Samuel, 9
Bicknell, Thomas, 102
Bicknell, William, 53
Bidwell, Barnabus, 33
Biffing, Alanson, 114
Bigelow, David, 5, 102
Bigelow, Isaac, 5
Bigelow, John, 222
Bigelow, Levi, 304
Bigelow, Luther, 91, 93
Bigelow, Thomas, 115
Bigelow, William H., 115
Biglow, John, 86
Billings, Alanson, 25
Billings, Asa, 65
Billings, Benjamin, 4
Billings, Charles, 47
Billings, Christopher, 47
Billings, Daniel, 257
Billings, Dudley, 99
Billings, Ebenezer, 39, 68
Billings, Elijah, 27
Billings, Ephraim, Jr., 100
Billings, Ezekiel F., 84
Billings, Jabes, 23
Billings, James, 93

Billings, Joel, 4, 228
Billings, John, 88
Billings, Nathaniel, 42
Billings, Paul H., 5
Billings, Phinny, 94
Billings, William, 278
Billings, Zebina, 66
Billington, Francis, 52
Billington, Isaac, 147 (2)
Billington, Job, 278
Billington, Nathaniel, Jr., 280
Billington, Seth, 280 (2)
Bills, Jason, 286, 290
Bincar, Lewis, 312
Bingham, Delwina L., 36
Bingham, Parsons, 147
Bingham, Pliney, 99
Bingham, Preston, 147
Binney, Amos, 23
Binney, Elkanah, 102
Binney, Samuel, 191
Birchard, James H., 45
Bird, Alpheus, 85
Bird, Bayley, 91
Bird, Daniel, 118
Bird, Eli, 64
Bird, James, 28
Bird, John, 146
Bird, John, 2d, 146
Bird, Nelson, 30
Bird, Robert L., 28
Bird, Samuel S., 226
Bird, Shippin, 176
Bird, William, 176, 226, 257
Birt, Ebenezer, 9
Birt, William, 259
Birtch, Stanton, 129
Bisbee, Calvin, 178
Bisbee, Chandler, 49
Bisbee, Daniel, 178
Bisbee, Luther, 178, 259, 299
Bisbee, Moses, 257
Bisbee, Rufus, 297
Bisbee, Studly, 296
Bisbee, Sturdly, 299
Bisbey, Isaac, 59
Bisby, Ansel, 251
Bisby, Hopstill, 251
Bisby, J., 82
Bishop, Asa, 212
Bishop, Daniel, 127
Bishop, George, 220
Bishop, Hersey, 179
Bishop, James, 42, 79, 89, 168
Bishop, Jesse, 278
Bishop, John, 13, 14
Bishop, Joseph, 130, 168
Bishop, Nathan, 273
Bishop, Paul, 19
Bishop, Squire, Jr., 279
Bishop, Zenos, 52
Bismore, David, 127 (2)
Bissel, Israel, 33
Bissel, William B., 279
Bissell, Harvey, 23
Bissell, Jabez F., 3
Bissell, John W., 66
Bissell, Oliver, 66
Bisson, Israel, 36, 37
Bither, Benjamin, 240
Bither, Elisha, 240
Bither, Peter, 239

Bixby, Amasa, 284
Bixby, Asa, 87
Bixby, John, 221, 267
Bixby, Rufus, 284
Bixby, William, 221
Bixley, David, 90
Black, Aaron, 155
Black, Alexander, 301
Black, Asa, 85
Black, Bannon, 31
Black, Benjamin, 188
Black, Charles H., 19
Black, David, 74
Black, Edmund, 179
Black, Edward, 161
Black, Henry, 226
Black, James, 264, 301 (2)
Black, John, 162 (2)
Black, Joshua, 179
Black, Samuel, 32
Black, Saul, 212
Black, William, 19, 69
Blackburn, Benjamin, 68
Blackburn, Timothy, 25
Blackington, Benjamin, 204
Blackington, James W., 197, 203
Blackinton, Benjamin, 205, 206
Blackinton, David, 54
Blackinton, Fisher, 54
Blackinton, Virgil, 54
Blackman, Bradley, 217
Blackman, Eliphalet, 276
Blackman, Henry B., 158
Blackman, Jacob, 42, 89
Blackman, James, 231
Blackman, Samuel, 78
Blackman, Thomas, 68, 79
Blackmore, James, 300
Blackner, Sear, 45
Blacksten, Benjamin, 229
Blackstone, Benjamin, 220, 282
Blackstone, Ebenezer, 227, 282
Blackstone, Josiah, 266, 304
Blackstone, Robert, 220
Blackstone, Samuel, 209
Blackstone, William, Jr., 227
Blackwell, Alfred, 145
Blackwell, Alvin, 236
Blackwell, Ansel, 280
Blackwell, Benjamin, 71
Blackwell, Dennis, 153
Blackwell, Eli, 153
Blackwell, Ellis, 71
Blackwell, James, 161
Blackwell, Levi, 52
Blackwell, Micah, 130
Blackwell, Sylvanus, 278, 281
Blackwell, William, 224
Blackwood, James, Jr., 161
Blagden, Alexander, 186 (2)
Blagden, Charles, 186 (2), 187, 190
Blagden, James, 186 (2), 187, 190
Blagdon, Alexander, 184
Blagdon, Charles, 186, 268
Blagdon, John, 214
Blagge, T. W. T., 28
Blair, Alexander, 188
Blair, Eben, 271
Blair, James, Jr., 249
Blair, John, 188
Blair, Joshua, 188, 191
Blair, Lemuel, 276

Blair, M. D., 87
Blair, Reuben, 253
Blair, Robert, 153
Blair, Samuel, 188
Blair, Thomas, 249
Blaisdell, Daniel, 266
Blaisdell, David, 311
Blaisdell, Ivory, 228
Blaisdell, John, 35 (2)
Blaisdell, John, 3d, 20
Blaisdell, Nicholas, 122
Blaisdell, William R., 166
Blake, Alfred, 62
Blake, Barnum, 91
Blake, Benjamin, 155, 257
Blake, Billing, 214
Blake, Bradbury, 228
Blake, Charles, 214
Blake, Daniel, 158, 292
Blake, Dudley, 306
Blake, Ebenezer, 271
Blake, Edward, 61, 151
Blake, Edwin, 7
Blake, Eliphalet, 252
Blake, Ephraim, 173, 213, 256
Blake, Henry, 70, 221
Blake, Ira, 275
Blake, Jacob, 233
Blake, James, 70, 77
Blake, James, Jr., 221
Blake, James H., 59, 78, 81
Blake, Jespar, 17
Blake, John, 152, 213, 254, 262, 280, 299
Blake, John S., 170, 277
Blake, John W., 289, 293
Blake, Jonathan, 93
Blake, Judson, 54
Blake, Lemuel, 7
Blake, Nathaniel, 26, 39, 147, 172, 258
Blake, Pascal P., 169
Blake, Richard, 252, 255, 256
Blake, Samuel, 71, 158 (2), 173, 220, 225, 246, 297, 298, 300
Blake, Samuel B., 54
Blake, Samuel S., 169
Blake, Seth, 155
Blake, Solomon, 214
Blake, Stephen, 252, 255
Blake, Thomas, 40
Blake, Walter, 286
Blake, William, 23, 24, 60, 68, 85, 87, 114, 152, 179, 198, 199, 202, 207, 220, 233, 254
Blake, Zebulon, 233
Blaming, Saul, 229
Blanchard, Alexander, 271
Blanchard, Amos, 4
Blanchard, Asa, 85, 275
Blanchard, Benjamin, 155
Blanchard, Cyrus, 212
Blanchard, Daniel, 117, 138
Blanchard, David, 77, 86
Blanchard, Edward, 23
Blanchard, Eli, 49
Blanchard, Elisha, 70, 77
Blanchard, Ellis, 267
Blanchard, Ezra, 101
Blanchard, Farwell, 151
Blanchard, Hezekiah, 7
Blanchard, Jabez, 187, 190
Blanchard, Jacob, 212
Blanchard, James T., 77
Blanchard, Jeremiah, 19

INDEX. 325

Blanchard, John, 271
Blanchard, John R., 99
Blanchard, Jonas, 263, 267
Blanchard, Joseph, 170
Blanchard, Josiah, 70, 77, 85, 115, 297, 298
Blanchard, Lemuel, 23, 114
Blanchard, Leonard, 271
Blanchard, Moses, 228
Blanchard, Nathan, 86, 156, 157 (2)
Blanchard, Nathaniel, 21, 69, 86, 116
Blanchard, Nehemiah, 40
Blanchard, Oliver, 92
Blanchard, Ozias, 219
Blanchard, Samuel, 23, 42, 77, 87, 89, 219
Blanchard, Samuel J., 118
Blanchard, Samuel T., 135, 140
Blanchard, Shephard, 302
Blanchard, Solomon, 230
Blanchard, Theophilus, 275
Blanchard, Thomas, 42
Blanchard, William, 102, 173, 230, 246
Blanden, John, 39
Blandin, Benjamin, 54
Blandin, Jesse, 60
Blandin, Noah, 10
Blanding, Christopher, 98
Blaney, Ambrose, 84
Blaney, Benjamin, 68, 87
Blaney, Jonathan, 117
Blaney, Joseph, 78, 101, 111 (3), 112
Blaney, William, 28
Blank, Franklin, 279
Blankenship, George, 130
Blankenship, James, Jr., 130
Blankenship, Jared, 130
Blankenship, Stephen, 119
Blankinburgh, John, 161
Blany, A., 287
Blark, Bannon, 31
Blasdell, Abner, 244
Blasdell, Andrew B., 53
Blasdell, Christian, Jr., 250
Blasdell, Christopher, 249
Blasdell, Daniel, 262
Blasdell, Jonathan, 297, 298
Blasdell, Nicholas, 119
Blasdell, Samuel, 228
Blasdell, Sanbourn, 74
Blasdil, Sanbourn, 215
Blasedell, Samuel, 262, 282
Blasland, Gideon, 69
Blasland, William, 299
Blaswell, Thomas, 282
Blatchford, John, 10
Blatchford, Joseph, 161
Bleathen, Job, 233
Bleather, Levi, 248
Blen, Gilmore, 188
Blen, Harrison, 188
Blen, James, 195, 197
Blen, John, 188
Blethen, Increase, 233
Blethen, Reuben, 233
Blethen, Simeon, 300
Blew, John, 170
Blin, Joshua, 297
Blinn, Gilmore, 186
Blish, Charles, 74
Blish, George, 74
Blish, Joseph, 276
Blish, William, 153
Bliss, Alfred, 61

Bliss, Benjamin W., 93
Bliss, Caleb, 61
Bliss, David, 66
Bliss, Ebenezer, 4
Bliss, Elijah, 6
Bliss, George, 1
Bliss, Hartwell, 5
Bliss, Jacob, 1, 43
Bliss, Josiah S., 129
Bliss, Leonard, 30
Bliss, Levi, 2, 108
Bliss, Obed, 271
Bliss, Oliver, 2d, 61
Bliss, Samuel, 32
Bliss, Simeon, 32
Bliss, Stephen, 4
Bliss, William, Jr., 129
Blithen, John, 297
Blithin, Andrew, 295
Blithin, John, 295
Block, Alexander, 303
Block, Henry, 301
Block, John, 301
Block, John, 2d, 301
Blodget, David, 276
Blodget, Lyman, 64
Blodget, Nathaniel, 276
Blodget, William, 44
Blodgett, Elias, 93
Blodgett, Enos, 39
Blodgett, Isaac, 81
Blodgett, Jacob, 41
Blodgett, William, 85
Blogett, Benjamin, 46
Blood, Abel, 201 (2), 203
Blood, Asa, Jr., 67
Blood, Faron, 88
Blood, Joel, 204, 205 (2)
Blood, Nathan, 137
Blood, Peres, 99
Blood, Reuben, 3
Blood, Richard, 86
Blood, Simon, 285, 286, 288
Bloom, William, 247
Blossom, Alden, 145
Blossom, Ansel, 170, 276
Blossom, Benjamin, 73
Blossom, Josiah, 74
Blossom, Levi, 55, 57, 127
Blossom, Samuel, 73
Blossom, Saul, 76
Blunt, Ebenezer, 286, 290
Blunt, Isaac, 116
Blunt, James, 287, 310
Blunt, Jesse, 228, 282
Blunt, John W., 272
Blunt, Mark S., 284
Blunt, Oliver C., 307
Blunt, Samuel, 193
Blye, William, 228, 282
Boardman, Francis, 138
Boardman, James, 140
Boardman, Jeremiah, 118
Boardman, John, 135, 138
Boardman, Leonard, 280
Boardman, Saul, 289
Boardman, Savillan, 30
Boardman, Stephen, 20, 201 (2), 202
Boardman, Thomas, 20, 22, 23
Boardman, William, 19, 78, 82, 118
Bobbins, Samuel, 103
Boddely, John, 20

Boddershall, Doan, 216
Boddershall, Fredoni, 216
Boden, Simpson, 87
Bodfish, Alvin, 74
Bodfish, David, 74
Bodfish, Ebenezer, 74
Bodfish, Joseph, 74
Bodfish, Josiah, 74
Bodfish, Oliver, 74
Bodfish, Prince, 74
Bodfish, William, 261, 266
Bodfish, William, Jr., 262, 266
Bodge, Benjamin, 108
Bodge, John, 211
Bodin, Charles, 136
Bodlear, John, 24
Bodrey, Nathan, 103
Bodwell, Bailey, 252, 255
Bodwell, John, 8
Bodwell, Nathaniel, 252, 255
Bodwell, Samuel, 8
Bogart, Amos, 175
Boggs, David, 101
Boggs, Ephraim, 285, 286, 288
Boggs, James, 289, 293
Boggs, James, 2d, 289, 294
Bogs, Joshua, 292
Bohanan, Amariah, 160
Bohanan, Daniel, 160
Bohonon, John E., 36
Boies, Bartholomew, 304
Boker, Cyrian, 251
Boland, John, 184
Boland, Joseph, 184
Bolden, John, 249
Bolden, Joseph, 182 (2)
Boldin, Sargent, 145
Bolding, Asher, 64
Boler, Bebani, 274
Bolster, Alvin, 252
Bolten, Daniel, 211
Bolten, Saul, 211
Bolton, Elijah, 276
Bolton, Elisha, 276
Bolton, Gamaliel, 31
Bolton, James, 3d, 276
Bolton, John, 62
Bolton, Royal, 165, 166
Bolton, Thomas, 165, 166, 171
Bolton, Walter, 276
Bolton, William, 171, 263
Boman, Ransom, 43
Bomphroy, Lewis, 44
Bond, George, 71
Bond, Henry, Jr., 192, 195
Bond, Hollis, 216
Bond, James, 64
Bond, John, 95, 153, 271
Bond, Lucius, 46
Bond, Phineas, 39
Bond, Samuel, 269
Bond, Thomas, 42, 89
Bond, William, 25, 195
Bonds, Samuel, 159
Boney, Lebbeus, 260
Boney, Ward, 244
Bonn, Caleb, 33
Bonndy, Thomas, 6
Bonnell, Thomas, 303
Bonneman, John, 292
Bonner, John, 24, 84, 176
Bonner, Philip, 70

INDEX.

Bonney, Asa, 259
Bonney, Ichabod, Jr., 178
Bonney, Isaac, 276
Bonney, James, 277
Bonney, John, 176, 257
Bonney, Marshall, 252
Bonney, Moses, 178
Bonney, Thomas, 178
Bonney, William, 49
Booder, William, 162
Boodry, Benjamin G., 62
Boodry, Benjamin S., 59
Boohr, John, 162
Booker, Beniah, 231
Booker, Charles, 266, 306
Booker, Daniel, Jr., 299
Booker, Jacob, 167, 281, 306
Booker, James, 272, 295, 297
Booker, John B., 183
Booker, Joseph, Jr., 183
Booker, Nicholas, 272
Boone, Benjamin, 29
Booth, Abiel P., 102
Booth, Elijah, 43, 93
Booth, Elisha, 45
Booth, Russ N., 63
Booth, Russell, 1
Booth, Thomas S., 57
Boothbay, John, 233
Boothby, Arthur, 155
Boothby, Asa, 155
Boothby, Cyrus, 167
Boothby, Daniel, 167
Boothby, Enoch, 269
Boothby, George, 170
Boothby, Isaac, 167
Boothby, Nathaniel, 170, 246
Boothby, Nathaniel, 2d, 170
Boothby, Samuel, 174, 222, 269
Boothby, Samuel, 2d, 174
Boothby, Stephen, 167, 277
Boothe, Isaac, 286, 290
Bootman, Elias, 15
Borden, Biscum, 56
Borden, Japtha, 52
Borden, Stephen, 56, 57
Borden, Thomas, 56
Borland, Samuel, 195
Bornwell, Timothy, 160
Boslear, Jesse, 127
Boston, George, Jr., 130
Boston, Ivory, 309
Boston, John, 151
Boston, Joseph, 238, 245
Boston, Timothy, 243
Boston, William, 152
Boswell, Isaac, 8
Boswell, William, Jr., 239
Boswort, J. P., 229
Bosworth, Augustus, 52
Bosworth, Benjamin, 64
Bosworth, Daniel, 161
Bosworth, David, 212
Bosworth, Elijah, 89
Bosworth, Elisha, 44
Bosworth, Harvey, 46
Bosworth, Hesekiah F., 94
Bosworth, Howard, 92
Bosworth, James, 62
Bosworth, Jesse, 64
Bosworth, Lewis, 51, 103
Bosworth, Lyman, 31
Bosworth, Noah, 225, 259

Bosworth, Oliver, 31
Bosworth, Sherman, 29
Bosworth, Stacy, 5
Bosworth, William, 128, 178, 259
Bosworth, Zadock, 44
Bosworth, Zenas, 285
Bothwell, James, 152, 261
Bott, Linch, 132, 140
Bott, Lynch, 140
Botten, Ebenezer, 94
Bottom, Abisha, 215
Bottom, Eliab, 87
Bottom, Solomon, 162, 215
Botton, William, 140
Bouetlier, John, 77
Boughton, Jonathan W., 31
Boughton, Joy C., 32
Boughton, Stephen, 32
Boulter, Daniel, 174
Boulter, John, 174
Boulter, Nathaniel, 174
Boulter, Samuel, 174
Bourk, Charles, 230
Bourk, Cyrus, 230
Bourk, Thomas, 230
Bourk, William, 247
Bourn, Caleb, 259
Bourn, Stephen, 61
Bourne, Abner, 76, 77
Bourne, Allen, 55
Bourne, Alvin, 71
Bourne, Barah, 75
Bourne, Barnabus, 72
Bourne, Benjamin, 125
Bourne, Caleb, 177
Bourne, David, 72
Bourne, East, 52
Bourne, Elijah, 72
Bourne, Elisha, 71, 73, 75
Bourne, Elisha, 2d, 73
Bourne, Elisha, 3d, 73, 76
Bourne, Ephraim, 28
Bourne, Ezra L., 73
Bourne, Freeman, 76
Bourne, Henry, 75
Bourne, Isaac, 76
Bourne, Jarvis, 72
Bourne, John, 75
Bourne, Lemuel, 71, 75
Bourne, Leonard, 52
Bourne, Nathan, 71
Bourne, Nathaniel, 72
Bourne, Newcomb, 95
Bourne, Samuel, 73
Bourne, Timothy, 75
Bouse, Benjamin, 80
Bouster, John, 16
Boutell, David, 98
Boutwell, Levi, 45
Boutwell, Sewall, 41
Boutzell, William, 5
Bow, William S., 44
Bowans, Jonas, 82
Bowdage, Horace, 85
Bowden, John, 304
Bowden, Simeon, 79
Bowden, Theodore, 307
Bowden, Thomas, 14
Bowdin, Frank, 179
Bowdin, William, 304
Bowdly, Samuel, 68
Bowdoin, Simpson, 81

Bowe, David, 300
Bowe, George, 297, 300
Bowe, Nathaniel, 219
Bowen, Amos, 286, 290
Bowen, Charles, 3
Bowen, Chester, 31
Bowen, Ezra, 286, 290
Bowen, James, 304
Bowen, John, 32
Bowen, Jonathan, 61, 84
Bowen, Levi, 60
Bowen, Martin, 58
Bowen, Silas, 60
Bowen, Uriah, 53
Bowen, William C., 47
Bower, Alexander, 231
Bower, Henry, 202
Bowerman, William, 187, 190
Bowers, Artemas, 48
Bowers, Charles, 69
Bowers, Dennison T., 89
Bowers, George, 60
Bowers, Henry, 198, 207, 208 (2), 209 (2)
Bowers, John, 48
Bowers, John, Jr., 207
Bowers, Joseph, 202
Bowers, Levi, 83
Bowers, Luther, 83
Bowers, Samuel, 199
Bowker, Benjamin, 103
Bowker, Charles, 39, 68
Bowker, Cyprian, 251
Bowker, David, 130
Bowker, Gershom, 82
Bowker, James, 5, 249, 250
Bowker, Joel, 135, 137
Bowker, John, 116
Bowker, Joshua, 103
Bowker, Lazarus, 249, 250
Bowker, Lemuel, 111
Bowker, Washington, 298
Bowler, Caleb, 22
Bowler, Cobb, 6
Bowler, James, 6, 22
Bowler, John, 117
Bowler, Joseph, 180
Bowler, Nathaniel, 117
Bowler, Samuel, 117
Bowley, Benjamin, 229
Bowley, George, 200
Bowley, Michel, 200
Bowley, William, 202
Bowlin, John, 216
Bowlin, Peter, 216
Bowly, Ephraim, Jr., 201 (2), 203
Bowly, George, 201, 203
Bowly, William, 201 (2)
Bowman, Benjamin, 310
Bowman, Daniel, 312
Bowman, Edward, 275
Bowman, James, 275
Bowman, John, 91, 180
Bowman, Joshua, 241, 242
Bowman, Samuel, 41
Bowman, Samuel G., 249, 297
Bowton, Joseph, 180
Boxworth, Elijah, 42
Boyd, Elisha, 44
Boyd, George M., 183
Boyd, James, 145, 310
Boyd, John, 268
Boyd, Robert, 217, 310

INDEX. 327

Boyd, Samuel, 183
Boyd, Thomas, 184, 188
Boyden, Alexander, 60, 99
Boyden, Amos, 48
Boyden, Daniel, 97
Boyden, David, 64, 66, 98
Boyden, Ezekiel, 46
Boyden, Harvey, 97
Boyden, Israel, 67
Boyden, Jabes, 85
Boyden, Jason, 97
Boyden, Nathaniel, 67
Boyden, Ozel, 46
Boyden, Warren, 97
Boyington, John, 308
Boyington, Joshua, 282, 308
Boyington, Methuselah, 89
Boyinton, George, 305
Boyinton, William, 305
Boyle, Ichabod, 34
Boyle, John, 285
Boyle, Thomas, 60
Boylston, Samuel, 4
Boynton, Abel, 155
Boynton, Amos, 100
Boynton, Benjamin, 100
Boynton, David, 90, 196
Boynton, Ebenezer A., 170, 277
Boynton, Elijah, 8
Boynton, Ellis, 117
Boynton, George, 268
Boynton, Hugh M., 170
Boynton, Isaac, 269
Boynton, Jeduthan, 182
Boynton, John, 184, 196, 268
Boynton, John, Jr., 184, 188, 191
Boynton, John, 3d, 188, 191
Boynton, Joseph, 275
Boynton, Joseph W., 217
Boynton, Joshua, 136, 141, 229
Boynton, Moses, 170
Boynton, Nathan, 192, 196
Boynton, Nathaniel, 133, 217
Boynton, Oliver, 180
Boynton, Richard, 192
Boynton, Robert, 217
Boynton, Rufus, 196
Boynton, Samuel H., 39
Boynton, Stephen, 78, 82, 138
Boynton, William, 152, 268
Boynton, William, Jr., 254
Brabock, William, 5
Brace, James, Jr., 138
Brack, Benjamin, 184
Brackenridge, Allenbert, 46
Bracket, Anthony, 211
Bracket, Daniel, 302
Bracket, Enoch, 211
Bracket, Joshua, 303
Bracket, Peter, 150
Bracket, Richard, 87
Bracket, William, 211
Brackett, Abraham, 261, 274
Brackett, Alfred, 246
Brackett, Daniel, 164 (2), 166, 171
Brackett, David, 245
Brackett, Ebenezer, 245
Brackett, Elijah, 246
Brackett, Enoch, 258
Brackett, Ephraim, 164 (2), 166, 220
Brackett, Hiram, 239
Brackett, James, 239

Brackett, Jeremiah, 207
Brackett, John, 98, 212
Brackett, John, Jr., 46
Brackett, Joseph, 155
Brackett, Joshua, 44, 193, 289
Brackett, Joshua, 2d, 289
Brackett, Moses, 238, 265
Brackett, Nathan, 238
Brackett, Nathan A., 122
Brackett, Nathaniel, 150
Brackett, Richard, 27
Brackett, Silas, 219
Brackett, Thomas, 195, 197
Brackett, William, 158
Brackett, Zachariah, 158, 220
Brackett, Zachariah, Jr., 220
Brackinridge, John, 31
Brackly, John, 280
Brackly, William, 280
Bradberry, Andrew, 243
Bradberry, John, 218
Bradburn, Peter, 39
Bradbury, Andrew, 174, 260
Bradbury, Charles, 83, 145
Bradbury, David, 177
Bradbury, David, Jr., 282
Bradbury, Eben, 17
Bradbury, Elijah, 152
Bradbury, Emery, 162
Bradbury, Enos, 176
Bradbury, Ezra, 149
Bradbury, Jacob, 176, 257
Bradbury, John, 210
Bradbury, John S., 268, 304
Bradbury, Joseph, 228
Bradbury, Jotham, 228, 283
Bradbury, Osgood, 210
Bradbury, Samuel, 229
Bradbury, Silas, 277, 281
Bradbury, William, 209
Bradbury, Wyman, 197, 203, 204
Bradeen, Isaac, 312
Braders, John B., 79
Bradford, Abraham, 198, 199, 200, 202, 208
Bradford, Andrew, 153, 243
Bradford, Asa, 178
Bradford, Benjamin, 175, 260
Bradford, Benjamin W., 128
Bradford, Calvin, 176
Bradford, Charles, 145
Bradford, David, 72, 131, 176
Bradford, Davis, 61
Bradford, Dura, 150
Bradford, Ephraim, 177
Bradford, Ethelbert, 150
Bradford, Frederic, 288, 291, 294, 310
Bradford, Frederick, 285, 288
Bradford, Freeman, 178
Bradford, Henry, 31
Bradford, Hiram, 145
Bradford, Isaiah, 287, 294 (2)
Bradford, James, 291
Bradford, James, Jr., 128
Bradford, John, 36, 37 (2), 95
Bradford, John R., 28
Bradford, Joseph, 207
Bradford, Josiah, 131, 287
Bradford, Lemuel, 131
Bradford, Luther, 128
Bradford, Mallone, 58
Bradford, Martin, 153, 177
Bradford, Nelson, 84, 109

Bradford, Peleg, 249, 297
Bradford, Prince, 128
Bradford, Samuel, 176, 259
Bradford, Stephen, 178
Bradford, William, 237
Bradford, William B., 28
Bradin, Isaac, 155
Bradish, Henry, 44
Bradlee, Ebenezer, 84
Bradlee, Hezekiah, 89
Bradley, Caleb, 41
Bradley, David, 151
Bradley, Foster, 295, 297
Bradley, H., 139
Bradley, Harrison, 17
Bradley, Jeremiah, 151
Bradley, Jesse, 193
Bradley, Joseph, 100
Bradley, Joseph T., 110
Bradley, Moses P., 229, 282
Bradley, Samuel B., 31
Bradley, Thomas, 27, 113 (2)
Bradley, William, 186 (2), 187 (2), 190
Bradley, Wingate, 227
Bradly, Caleb, 218
Bradly, Ebenezer C., 32
Bradly, Monson, 32
Bradly, Thomas, 78
Bradly, William, 135
Bradman, George, 176
Bradshaw, Andrew, 71
Bradshaw, James, 136
Bradshaw, Jesse, 42, 89
Bradshaw, John, 133
Bradstreet, Aaron, 180
Bradstreet, Ezekiel, 10
Bradstreet, Moses, 180
Bradstreet, Nathaniel, 10, 116
Bradstreet, William, 275
Bradway, William, 2d, 44
Bragden, Jeremiah, 228
Bragdon, Arthur, 155
Bragdon, Daniel, 150, 152, 232
Bragdon, Ephraim, 173, 300
Bragdon, George, 300, 309 (3)
Bragdon, J. R., 245
Bragdon, Jeremiah, 283
Bragdon, John, 296
Bragdon, John, Jr., 300
Bragdon, Joseph, 274
Bragdon, Joshua, 309
Bragdon, Nathaniel, 172, 296, 300
Bragdon, Simeon, 154
Bragdon, Solomon, 164, 165, 166
Bragdon, Stephen, 227
Bragg, Daniel, 237
Bragg, David, 237
Bragg, Ingalls, 218, 261
Bragg, Isaac, 237
Bragg, James, 153, 172
Bragg, James F., 218
Bragg, John, 262
Bragg, John, Jr., 266
Bragg, Nathan, 237
Bragg, Nathaniel, 237
Bragg, Nathaniel, 3d, 238
Bragg, Royal, 238
Bragg, Shubal, 261
Bragg, Stephen, 239
Bragg, Thomas, 218
Bragg, William, 125, 131, 239, 284, 287
Brailey, Amos, 264, 266

Brailey, James, 264
Brailey, Russell, 264, 266
Brailey, William, 264
Brainard, Benjamin, 229
Brainard, Josiah, 227
Brainerd, Austin, 43
Brainerd, Hosea, 43
Brainerd, Josiah, 282
Brainerd, William, 227
Braley, Hattal, 159
Braley, Job, 56
Braley, Jonathan, 56
Braley, Silas, 53
Braman, Thomas, 126
Bramhead, James, 273
Bramhead, Orin, 273
Bramhead, Reuben, Jr., 273
Bramin, Andrew, 54
Bramin, Sylvanus, 54
Bran, Simon, 265
Branch, Benjamin, Jr., 262
Branch, Daniel, 308
Branch, Nathaniel, 274
Branch, Palmer, 262, 267
Branch, Samuel, 237
Branch, Tibbetts, 262
Branchder, John, 244
Brand, Abel, 119
Brand, Samuel, 265
Branding, Noah, 9
Brannigum, Samuel, 232
Brannum, Stephen, 77
Branscomb, James, 146
Branscomb, John, 227
Brasure, Joseph, 179
Brattle, Jesse, 183
Brattle, William W., 94
Brause, Adam, 288
Brawn, Rufus, 185
Bray, Aaron, 213
Bray, Benjamin, 213
Bray, Daniel, 13, 14, 132, 177
Bray, Edmund, 6
Bray, Edward, 11, 21, 211
Bray, Edwin, 11
Bray, Eli, 90
Bray, Ezekiel, 265
Bray, Henry, 225
Bray, James, 17
Bray, Jeremiah, 11
Bray, John, 138
Bray, Libbeus, 177
Bray, Moses, 13, 14
Bray, Nathaniel, 213
Bray, Oliver, 153, 246
Bray, William B., 159
Braynard, Golden, 84
Braynard, Reuben, 302
Brayton, B., 99
Brayton, David, 61
Brazer, William G., 87
Brazier, Elijah R., 109
Brazier, Isaac K., 78, 81, 109, 110, 111
Brazier, T. K., 112
Brazier, Thomas, 78
Brazier, William G., 81
Brebner, Archibald, 226
Breed, Allen, 117
Breed, Amos, 116, 117
Breed, Andrew, Jr., 117
Breed, Joseph, 117
Breed, Josiah, 141

Breed, William, 117
Breen, Joseph, 183
Brentnall, Thomas, 287
Brett, Ezra, 158
Brett, Lenos, 50
Brett, Martin, 252, 255
Brett, Samuel, 50
Brett, Seneca, 252
Brett, Simeon, 150
Brett, William, Jr., 70
Bretton, Ira, 59
Brew, Cornelius, 58
Brewer, Abijah, 48
Brewer, Ebenezer, 213
Brewer, Edward, 209
Brewer, Edwin, 31
Brewer, Henry, 48
Brewer, Isaac, 197, 204
Brewer, James, 209
Brewer, James, Jr., 212
Brewer, John, 4, 193
Brewer, Joseph, 93
Brewer, Reuben, 3d, 212
Brewer, Samuel, 183
Brewster, Benjamin, 156, 204, 205
Brewster, Ira, 198
Brewster, John, 125 (2)
Brewster, Martin, Jr., 128
Brewster, Milton, 65
Brewster, Morgan, Jr., 168
Brewster, William, 65, 198, 199, 201
Briant, Alvin, 30
Briant, Barton, 30
Briant, Levi, Jr., 176
Briant, Micah, 128
Briant, Nehemiah, 239
Briant, Reuben, 196
Briant, William, 160
Briar, William, 287
Brice, Edward, 2d, 184
Brice, Robert, 301
Brice, William, 3d, 145
Brick, Jonas, 94
Brick, Levi, 39
Brick, Lewis, 39
Brick, Moses, 67
Bricket, Nathan A., 18
Brickett, Jonathan, 152
Brickett, Moody, 15
Brickett, Nathan A., 124
Brickmor, George, 301
Bridge, Charles, 94
Bridge, Jesse C., 161
Bridge, John, 301
Bridge, Mathew, 23, 34, 38
Bridge, William, 26
Bridgeman, George, 2
Bridgeman, Oliver, 4
Bridgeman, Theodore, 4
Bridges, Jesse, 284
Bridges, John, 149, 307
Bridges, Joseph, 197, 203, 204
Bridges, Josiah, 152
Bridges, Kingsbury, 197, 203, 204, 207
Bridges, Moses, 161
Bridges, Philip, Jr., 6
Bridges, Thomas, 6, 22
Bridgham, Calvin, 175
Bridgham, Cyrus, 176
Bridgham, Joseph, Jr., 161
Bridgham, Luther, 175
Bridgham, Samuel, 175

Bridgham, Thomas W., 166, 281
Bridgham, William, 209
Bridgman, Cephas, 92
Bridgman, Spencer, 64
Brier, Elihu, Jr., 183
Brier, Jesse, 183
Brier, Samuel, 183
Brierhurst, Thomas, 155
Brigford, James, 80
Briggs, Abel, 56
Briggs, Abiather, 102
Briggs, Abner, 42, 138
Briggs, Alanson D., 59
Briggs, Asa, 49
Briggs, Bartlett, 104
Briggs, Benjamin, 182
Briggs, Bennet, 51, 59, 61
Briggs, Charles, 59, 177, 260
Briggs, Cornelius, 83
Briggs, Daniel, 110, 176, 177, 260
Briggs, David, 167
Briggs, Edmund, 59
Briggs, Elijah, 130
Briggs, Elisha, 129
Briggs, Elkanah, 66
Briggs, Enos, 240
Briggs, Ezra, 221
Briggs, Frederick, 62
Briggs, George, 225
Briggs, Hart, 178
Briggs, Hathaway, 62
Briggs, Henry, 98, 104
Briggs, Isaac, 103
Briggs, James, 42, 89
Briggs, John, 70, 96, 177, 178, 222, 243, 254, 255, 271
Briggs, John, Jr., 57
Briggs, John W., 182, 184
Briggs, Joseph, 57, 101
Briggs, Judson, 102
Briggs, Lemuel, 47
Briggs, Lewis, 95, 128
Briggs, Luther, 251
Briggs, Melbone, 102
Briggs, Nathaniel, 178
Briggs, Peter, 41, 59
Briggs, Rufus, 47
Briggs, S., 51
Briggs, Samuel, 178
Briggs, Saul, 138
Briggs, Seth, 79
Briggs, Silas P., 62
Briggs, Simeon, 271
Briggs, Spencer, 126
Briggs, Thomas, 65, 153
Briggs, Weston, 63
Briggs, William, 167
Briggs, Zephaniah, 53
Brigham, Aaron, 212
Brigham, Artemas, 225
Brigham, Asa, 5
Brigham, Athemar, 225
Brigham, Benjamin, 91
Brigham, Briant, 257
Brigham, Daniel, 212
Brigham, Dexter, 91
Brigham, George, 250
Brigham, Ithamar, 258
Brigham, Jabez, 3
Brigham, John, 2
Brigham, Jonathan, 86
Brigham, Joseph, 91

INDEX.

329

Brigham, Josiah, 100
Brigham, Lambert, 47
Brigham, Levi, 23, 257
Brigham, Lovel, 48
Brigham, Luther, 257
Brigham, Nathaniel, 91
Brigham, Otis, 91
Brigham, Pierpont, 91
Brigham, Samuel, 91, 151
Brigham, Stephen B., 48
Brigham, Sylvanus, 91
Brigham, Tilly, 24
Brigham, William, 250
Bright, Coleman W., 154
Bright, James, 23
Bright, Jonathan, 39
Bright, Josiah, Jr., 100
Bright, Samuel, 77
Bright, Thomas, 21, 138
Bright, William, 140
Brightman, Henry, 63
Brightman, Jeremiah, 63 (2)
Brightman, Nathan, 55
Brightman, Samuel, 63
Brigs, Samuel, 128
Brimejohn, William, 281
Brimison, William, 169
Brimmer, Daniel, 34
Brimmer, William, 34
Brinkall, Jonas, 93
Brinney, Joshua, 82
Brinngion, Samuel, 232
Brintnall, Benjamin, 108
Brintnall, Charles, 23
Brintnall, Nathaniel, 113, 114
Britt, Silas H., 95
Britton, H. G., 18
Britton, Joshua, 60
Broad, Amos, 152
Broad, Daniel, 221
Broad, Ephraim, 221
Broad, Joseph, 218
Broad, Silas, 218
Broad, Thaddeus, 239
Broad, Thomas, 218
Broad, William, 85, 218
Broaders, John, 25
Broadstreet, David, 212
Broadstreet, Ebenezer, 179
Broadstreet, John, 239
Broadstreet, Nathaniel, 179
Broadstreet, Thomas, 180
Brock, John, 292
Brock, John, Jr., 251
Brock, Leonard, 251
Brocklebank, John, 42, 89
Brockway, Simelious, 67
Bromade, Abram, 26
Brooker, William, Jr., 234
Brookhouse, Benjamin, 133
Brookhouse, Daniel, 133
Brookhouse, Daniel W., 21
Brooking, John, 122
Brookings, James, 276
Brookings, John, 125
Brookins, Calvin, 32
Brookins, Henry, 276
Brookins, Nathan, 249
Brookins, Samuel, 11, 13
Brooks, Abijah, 87
Brooks, Amos, 67, 95
Brooks, Anson, 29

Brooks, Anthony, 160
Brooks, Barker, 41
Brooks, Benjamin, 5, 21, 304
Brooks, Charles, 136, 137, 189, 242, 256
Brooks, Dickerson, 93
Brooks, Ebenezer, 47
Brooks, Francis, 240
Brooks, George, 151
Brooks, Gideon, 245
Brooks, Isaac, 99
Brooks, Jacob, 88
Brooks, Jacob L., 255
Brooks, John, 141, 160, 182, 210, 216, 276
Brooks, Joseph, 1, 47, 185
Brooks, Joseph, Jr., 104
Brooks, Lyman, 31
Brooks, Michel L., 87
Brooks, Nathaniel, 103
Brooks, Nathaniel W., 78, 81, 87
Brooks, Noah, 198, 202, 207, 208 (2)
Brooks, Samuel, 136, 270
Brooks, Saul, 132
Brooks, Theodore, 77
Brooks, Thomas, 86
Brooks, Thomas, Jr., 132, 189
Brooks, William, 137, 152, 169, 262
Brooks, William M., 136
Broughton, Charles, 83
Brow, Joseph, 224
Brown, Aaron, 177
Brown, Abijah, 3
Brown, Abner, 44 (2), 167
Brown, Abraham, 6, 22, 35 (2), 134, 135, 169 285
Brown, Abram, 281
Brown, Ailam, 22
Brown, Alfred, 64, 65
Brown, Alpheus, 30
Brown, Alvin, 30
Brown, Amaziah, 268
Brown, Ambris, 168
Brown, Amos, 8
Brown, Andrew, 36, 37, 275
Brown, Artemus, 99, 178, 260
Brown, Artimas H., 3
Brown, Asa, 8
Brown, Asa, Jr., 238
Brown, Asaph, 257
Brown, Averis M., 33
Brown, Benjamin, 6, 15, 33, 93, 180, 199, 200, 297, 298, 308, 309
Brown, Benjamin, Jr., 134, 135
Brown, Caleb, 164 (2), 165
Brown, Charles, 12, 34, 48, 83, 86, 224
Brown, Christopher, Jr., 161
Brown, Christopher A., 249, 297
Brown, Consider, 148
Brown, Daniel, 80, 83, 110, 275
Brown, Daniel C., 227, 282
Brown, Daniel E., 50
Brown, David, 9, 13, 61, 138, 149, 172, 212, 234, 274
Brown, Ebenezer, 26
Brown, Edward, 3
Brown, Edward T., 132
Brown, Eldad, 28
Brown, Eli, 5
Brown, Elijah, 80
Brown, Elihu, 67
Brown, Elijah, 185, 227, 283
Brown, Eliphalet, 229 (2)
Brown, Elisha, 248, 297, 301

Brown, Elisha, Jr., 219
Brown, Emery, 49
Brown, Enoch, 134, 135
Brown, Epha, 295
Brown, Ephraim, 10, 13, 14, 133, 187, 302
Brown, Ephraim, Jr., 211
Brown, Ezekiel M., 231
Brown, Gardner, Jr., 295
Brown, George, 61, 135, 137
Brown, George W., 56
Brown, Hammon, 229
Brown, Hammond, 283
Brown, Hector, 291, 294
Brown, Henry, 64, 249
Brown, Herman, 257
Brown, Ira, 80, 82
Brown, Isaac, 33, 69, 79, 180, 203, 206
Brown, Isaac, Jr., 49, 238
Brown, Isaiah, 32
Brown, J., Jr., 19
Brown, Jabez, 257
Brown, Jackson, 219
Brown, Jacob, 246, 256, 282
Brown, James, 8, 29 (2), 36, 44, 87, 96, 201, 202, 211, 223, 230, 259, 271, 275, 306, 309 (2), 312
Brown, James B., 28, 64, 85
Brown, James P., 198, 208
Brown, Jeddo, 96
Brown, Jeffry B., 227
Brown, Jeremiah, 231, 268, 300
Brown, Jesse, 88, 211, 230
Brown, John, 2, 14 (2), 18, 20, 21, 27, 30, 39, 47, 68, 80, 83, 86, 99, 180 (2), 211, 227, 239, 246, 267, 279, 292, 295, 310
Brown, John, Jr., 240, 265, 307
Brown, John, 3d, 138, 145, 225, 284
Brown, John B., 7
Brown, John H., 195
Brown, John O. W., 16
Brown, Jonas, 83, 88
Brown, Jonas A., 150, 151
Brown, Jonathan, 137, 190, 238
Brown, Joseph, 20, 41, 77, 87, 211, 212, 224, 271
Brown, Joseph, Jr., 118
Brown, Joseph, 3d, 19
Brown, Josiah, 117, 174, 257
Brown, Levi, 173, 212
Brown, Lewis, 91
Brown, Luke, 238
Brown, Luther, 30
Brown, Marshall, 118
Brown, Matthew, 232, 235
Brown, Moses, 15, 177, 259
Brown, Moses, Jr., 21
Brown, Nahum, 307
Brown, Nathan, 20, 279
Brown, Nathaniel, 13, 81, 148, 238, 271, 276
Brown, Nathaniel, 2d, 275
Brown, Nicholas, 268
Brown, Oak P., 50
Brown, Odel, 3
Brown, Orlando, 19, 121, 124
Brown, Parker, 303
Brown, Paul, 207
Brown, Paul H., 34
Brown, Peter, 22, 195
Brown, Phileman, 61
Brown, Phineas, 81
Brown, Reuben, 5, 225, 306
Brown, Reuben, Jr., 212

INDEX.

Brown, Rex, 31
Brown, Richard, 6, 167
Brown, Robert, 35 (2), 148, 293
Brown, Rowland G., 67
Brown, Rufus, 47
Brown, Samuel, 19, 88, 98, 125, 167, 173, 183, 186, 209, 221, 253, 279, 303
Brown, Samuel, Jr., 121
Brown, Samuel, 3d, 6
Brown, Samuel G., 282
Brown, Samuel L., 111
Brown, Samuel N., 50
Brown, Saul, 9, 139 (2), 141, 230, 302
Brown, Saul, Jr., 279
Brown, Simeon, 222, 258, 259
Brown, Solomon, 168
Brown, Stephen, 219, 312
Brown, Sylvanus, 131
Brown, Thomas, 10, 18, 87, 120, 123, 141, 158, 307
Brown, Thomas, 3d, 6, 22
Brown, Thurston, 59
Brown, Uziel, 130
Brown, Walter, 18, 21
Brown, Walter B., 160
Brown, Warren, 94
Brown, Willard, 87
Brown, William, 13, 14, 17, 27, 39, 46, 47, 89, 98 (2), 116, 138, 145, 198, 199, 201 (2), 202, 207, 216, 271, 275, 297, 306
Brown, William, Jr., 248
Brown, William D., 90
Brown, Zenas, 87
Brownell, Benjamin, 63, 129
Brownell, Daniel, 56
Brownell, George, 56, 264
Brownell, Perry, 63
Brownell, Thomas, 63
Browning, Benjamin, 30
Browning, Clark, 141
Browning, George, 141
Browning, John, 141 (2)
Browning, Stephen, 141
Brownserville, Gilbert, 56
Brownserville, Joseph, 56
Brownseville, John, 56
Brownson, William A., 44
Bruce, Barnard, 191
Bruce, Calvin, 81
Bruce, Cyrus, 24
Bruce, David, 69
Bruce, Elijah, 2
Bruce, George, 23
Bruce, George W., 301
Bruce, James, 66
Bruce, John, 244
Brudin, Elnathan, 27
Bruge, Isaac, 65
Brumade, Abraham, 78
Brunett, John, 24
Brunsen, Smissen, 67
Brush, Amasa, 65
Brush, James, 2d, 46
Bryan, Robert, 97
Bryant, Abel, 173, 260
Bryant, Abraham, 221
Bryant, Amos, 175, 260
Bryant, Anchiel, 4
Bryant, Arodus, 252
Bryant, Azel, 130
Bryant, Bela, 58
Bryant, Benjamin, 192

Bryant, Cephas, 95
Bryant, Christopher, 251, 255
Bryant, David, 237, 267
Bryant, Eliphalet, 170
Bryant, George, 4, 176, 192, 195
Bryant, Henry, 199, 200, 203
Bryant, Hezekiah, 150
Bryant, Ichabod, 252, 255
Bryant, Ichabod, Jr., 252
Bryant, Isaac, 51
Bryant, Isaac, 2d, 103
Bryant, Jacob, 101, 179
Bryant, James, 178, 259
Bryant, James, Jr., 243
Bryant, Job, 78
Bryant, John, 101, 195
Bryant, Levi, 51, 103
Bryant, Luther, 206
Bryant, Lyman, 101
Bryant, Nathaniel, 80, 83, 194
Bryant, Nehemiah, 178, 179
Bryant, Oliver, 50
Bryant, Pelham, 176, 254, 257
Bryant, Reuben, 195
Bryant, Samuel, 95, 195, 251, 255
Bryant, Saul, 101
Bryant, Seth, 51, 265
Bryant, Solomon, 251
Bryant, Solomon, Jr., 255
Bryant, Thomas, 48, 69, 85, 222
Bryant, Timothy, 224
Bryant, William, 96, 179, 199, 200, 203
Bryant, Zebulon, 252, 255
Bryant, Zimrie, 179
Bryer, Moses, 302
Bryre, John, 231
Bryrehurst, Thomas, 156
Bubier, Mark, 169
Buck, Abner, 65
Buck, Arimiah, 62
Buck, Asa, 161
Buck, Daniel, 252
Buck, Elisha, 251, 254, 257
Buck, Isaac, 65
Buck, James, 251, 255
Buck, Jesse, 65
Buck, John, 311
Buck, John, 3d, 251
Buck, Jonathan, 251
Buck, Moses, 251
Buck, Samuel, 251
Buck, Simeon, 176, 257
Buck, Simon I., 183
Buck, Thomas, 37
Buck, William, 122
Buck, Zebediah, 261
Bucker, Daniel, 215
Buckingham, Joseph F., 68
Buckland, Daniel, 4
Bucklin, B., 60
Bucklin, David W., 60
Bucklin, Jonas, 200
Bucklin, Joseph, 280, 293
Bucklin, Mark, 198, 202
Bucklin, Robert, 198, 199, 200, 208
Buckman, Arad, 47
Buckman, Asa, 68, 220
Buckman, Asahel, 90
Buckman, Ben, 160
Buckman, John, 21, 34, 213
Buckman, Joses, 26
Buckminster, William, 239

Buckmond, Jacob, 46
Bucknam, David, 115
Bucknam, John, Jr., 220
Bucknam, Spencer, 114
Bucknam, William, 233
Bucknell, Andrew B., 150, 152
Bucknell, Benjamin, 152
Bucknell, John, 152
Bucknell, John, Jr., 212
Bucknell, Stephen, 102
Budd, Nathaniel, 32
Budge, Benjamin, 2
Buel, Arthur, 32
Buffington, Benjamin, 59
Buffington, John, 34
Buffington, Mason, 56
Buffington, Stephen, 60
Buffum, H. F., 87
Buffum, Henry, 82
Buffum, James R., 132
Bugbee, Chester, 54
Bugbee, Nehemiah, 4
Bugbee, Robert, 159
Bugbee, William, Jr., 159
Bugnon, George, 275
Buker, David, 231
Buker, Samuel, 232
Bulkley, Samuel, 9
Bull, Briggs, 85
Bull, Epaphras, 28 (2)
Bull, George, 65
Bull, William, 80, 85
Bullard, Besoled, 279
Bullard, Charles, 111
Bullard, Chester, 99
Bullard, David, 279 (2)
Bullard, Eleazer, 33
Bullard, George, 77
Bullard, Isaac, 24
Bullard, Joseph, 252
Bullen, Daniel, 146, 150
Bullen, John R., 146, 150
Bullen, Joseph, 85
Bullen, Warren, 229
Bulling, Joshua, 229
Bullock, Ezra, 60
Bullock, James, 62, 132
Bullock, Rufus, 10
Bullock, Samuel W., 61
Bullock, William, 31
Bump, Alson, 308
Bump, Andrew, 52
Bump, Josephus, 52
Bump, Thomas, 52
Bump, Warren, 53
Bumpas, Calvin, 259
Bumpas, Jesse, 175, 260
Bumpas, Samuel, 175
Bumpas, Silas, 175, 260
Bumpas, William, 175
Bumpus, Admiral, 126
Bumpus, Alden, 175
Bumpus, Benjamin, 126
Bumpus, Braddock, 71
Bumpus, Calvin, 224
Bumpus, Eliphalet, 126
Bumpus, Lenus, 112
Bumpus, Luther, 278
Bumpus, Samuel, 52
Bumpus, Seth, 55
Bumpus, Thomas, 51
Bunce, Frederic, 64

INDEX. 331

Bunce, Richard, 64
Bundell, Daniel, 160
Bunker, Benjamin, 34
Bunker, Elisha, 21
Bunker, Francis, 268
Bunker, Isaac, 197, 203, 204
Bunker, Joseph, 268
Bunker, Nathan, 236
Bunker, Nathaniel, 36, 37, 234
Bunker, Robert, 268
Bunnel, John, 50
Bunt, Sabin, 44
Buntin, Joseph, 19
Burbank, Asa, 29, 152, 261
Burbank, Benjamin, 271
Burbank, Caleb, 139 (2),
Burbank, Eleaser, 264
Burbank, Isaac, Jr., 57
Burbank, Isaiah, 255
Burbank, Israel, Jr., 152
Burbank, Jesse S., 280
Burbank, John, 170
Burbank, Samuel, 51
Burbank, Samuel S., 261
Burbank, Silas, 264, 266
Burbank, Stephen, 261
Burbank, Thomas, 57
Burbank, Walter, 51
Burbant, Jonathan M., 19
Burbeck, Henry, 78
Burbeck, William, 114
Burches, Lewis, 79
Burchmore, Stephen, 137
Burchstead, Allen, 35 (2)
Burchstead, George, 34, 38
Burchsted, John, 39
Burdaken, Joseph, 84
Burden, Holder, 55
Burden, James, 55
Burden, William, 274
Burdett, Ebenezer, 84
Burdett, James, 5
Burdett, Stephen, 116
Burding, Thomas, 190
Burding, Winslow, 186, 187, 190
Burdish, Lodowick, 141
Burdish, William, 98
Burdit, Henry, 84
Burdit, James W., 84
Burdon, Thomas, 136
Burge, Lorenzo, 113
Burge, Seth, Jr., 250
Burgon, Isaac, 150, 151
Burges, Abial, 36
Burges, Abial, Jr., 36
Burges, Amasa, 36
Burges, Benjamin, 304
Burges, David, 36
Burges, David, Jr., 36
Burges, Josiah, 274
Burgess, Anson, 71, 75
Burgess, Charles, 223
Burgess, Covel, 75
Burgess, David, 2d, 237
Burgess, Ebenezer, 223, 259
Burgess, Elias, 263
Burgess, Elijah, 305
Burgess, Elisha, 278
Burgess, Ellis, 267, 310
Burgess, Jabez, 75
Burgess, Jacob, 71
Burgess, James, 73, 76, 264, 278

Burgess, John, 128
Burgess, Josiah D., 52
Burgess, Perez, 73
Burgess, Peter, 75
Burgess, Richard, 237
Burgess, Samuel, 223, 239, 267
Burgess, Seth, Jr., 249
Burgess, Stephen, 53, 292
Burgess, Thomas, 75, 222
Burgess, William, 41, 278
Burgess, Zadock, 239, 267
Burghart, Henry W., 31
Burghart, Josiah, 31
Burk, Charles, 247
Burk, Franklin, 67
Burk, Nathan, 60
Burk, William, 18, 119
Burke, Thomas, 266
Burket, Henry, 291
Burket, Jacob, 2d, 291
Burket, John, 291
Burket, John, 3d, 291
Burkis, Lewis, 68
Burks, Thomas, 264
Burley, Jonathan, 90
Burley, Moses, 179
Burley, Paul, 184
Burlingame, Allen, 33
Burlingame, Humphrey, 30
Burlingham, C. F., 269
Burlingham, C. T., 269
Burlingham, Carpenter J., 269
Burlinham, Levi, 30
Burly, Josiah, 88
Burnal, Newton, 64
Burnall, William, 212, 258
Burnam, Nathaniel, 90
Burnell, David, 173
Burnell, Thomas, 212
Burnes, Jacob, 287
Burnes, James, 120, 123
Burnes, Patrick, 161
Burnes, Thomas, 197
Burnes, William, Jr., 197
Burnet, Almond, 291
Burnett, Bela, 4
Burnett, Nathan, 221
Burnett, Samuel, 258
Burnham, Abraham, 2
Burnham, Amos, 243
Burnham, Andrew, 25
Burnham, Andrew M., 12
Burnham, Benjamin, 221
Burnham, Benjamin M., 13
Burnham, Bohemia, 261
Burnham, Ebenezer, 170
Burnham, Elisha, 14
Burnham, Enoch, 250
Burnham, Ezra, 14
Burnham, Ira, 218, 261
Burnham, Isaac, 14, 68
Burnham, Jedediah, 261
Burnham, Jeremiah, 119
Burnham, John, 170, 218, 240
Burnham, Jonathan, 172
Burnham, Joshua, 13, 14
Burnham, Joseph, 117
Burnham, Moses, 15
Burnham, Nathan, 30
Burnham, Richard, 170
Burnham, Ruel, 65
Burnham, Samuel, 170

Burnham, Simeon, 258
Burnham, Solomon, 185
Burnham, Thomas, 2d, 170
Burnham, William D., 18
Burns, George, Jr., 165, 166, 242
Burns, James, 275
Burns, John, 268, 286, 290
Burns, Martin, 268
Burns, Michael, 112
Burns, Thomas, 195
Burns, William, 153, 192, 212
Burp, Joseph, 117
Burpee, Joseph, 140
Burr, Alanson, 214
Burr, David C., 271
Burr, Elijah, 65
Burr, Jehiel, 32
Burr, John, 101, 308
Burr, Laban, 96
Burr, Luther, 308
Burr, Martin, 308
Burr, Peres, 173
Burr, Theophilus, 80
Burr, William, 57
Burrage, George H., 78
Burrell, Abram, Jr., 237
Burrell, Asa, 102, 239
Burrell, Benoni, 261
Burrell, Ebenezer, Jr., 116
Burrell, Jacob, 230
Burrell, James, 21, 118, 237
Burrell, John, 24, 96, 261
Burrell, Joseph, 100, 266
Burrell, Josiah, 261
Burrell, Nathaniel, 116
Burrell, Noah, 261
Burrell, Seth, 2d, 100
Burrill, Anthony, 16
Burrill, Benoni, 266
Burrill, Bill, 27
Burrill, Daniel, 50
Burrill, Ebenezer, 27
Burrill, Elijah G., 138
Burrill, Hull, 306
Burrill, Humphrey, 306
Burrill, James, 16
Burrill, John, 26, 114, 118
Burrill, Joseph, Jr., 27
Burrill, Josiah, 266
Burrill, Josiah G., 138
Burrill, Nathan, 98
Burrill, Patrick, 16
Burrill, Robert, 42
Burrill, Samuel, 118
Burrill, William, 118
Burroughs, Edward, 112
Burroughs, John, 28
Burroughs, Stephen, 28
Burroughs, Walter, 9
Burroughs, William, 113, 114
Burrows, Stephen, 15, 199
Bursly, Lemuel, 227
Burt, Alanson, 59
Burt, Daniel, 53, 161
Burt, Ebenezer, 4, 10
Burt, Francis, 29, 43
Burt, George, 62
Burt, Henry, 4
Burt, John, 56
Burt, John M., 24, 114
Burt, Nathaniel, 62
Burt, Royal, 59

INDEX.

Burt, Simeon, 55
Burt, Sylvester, 55
Burt, William, 177
Burton, Charles, 37
Burton, Davis, 217
Burton, Ebenezer, 238
Burton, Frederic, 285, 287
Burton, Isaac, 288, 294
Burton, James, 32
Burton, James, Jr., 271
Burton, Joel, 217
Burton, Matthew, 284, 288
Burton, William, 64, 288, 294
Burwell, Benjamin, 201 (2)
Burwell, Jason, 65
Burwell, Thomas, 229
Bush, Daniel W., 27
Bush, Edward, 31
Bush, Henry W., 94
Bush, Hezekiah, 33
Bush, Milo, 31
Bush, Samuel, 183
Bush, William, 20
Buskirk, L. V., 161
Buss, Henry, 282
Bussby, Heman, 74
Bussby, Josiah, 74
Buswell, John, 17, 161
Butcher, Daniel, 273
Butchmore, Stephen, 135
Butland, John, 309
Butland, John, 3d, 309 (2)
Butler, Aaron, 26, 114
Butler, Abijah, 94
Butler, Adams, 93
Butler, Amos, 39, 88
Butler, Benjamin, 147, 306
Butler, Brackett, 285, 286 (2), 288
Butler, Briggs, 204, 205, 206
Butler, Charles, 18, 120, 123
Butler, Daniel, 29
Butler, David, Jr., 73
Butler, Davis, 72
Butler, E., 12
Butler, Ebenezer, 44
Butler, Elezer, 33
Butler, Elijah, 29, 280
Butler, Eliphalet, 90
Butler, Ezra A., 283
Butler, Flavel, 294
Butler, George, 200, 204, 205, 249
Butler, George, 2d, 204
Butler, Ivory, 171
Butler, James, 250
Butler, John, 73, 121 (2), 124 (2), 249, 250, 290
Butler, John, 2d, 290
Butler, Joseph, 227, 280
Butler, Joshua, 217
Butler, Josiah, 304
Butler, Leonard B., 205
Butler, Levi, 205
Butler, Martin, 286
Butler, Merrill, 78, 82
Butler, Minor, 3
Butler, Moses, 147
Butler, Moses S., 2d, 147
Butler, Nehemiah, 149
Butler, Obed, 75, 76
Butler, Philip, 21, 89, 119, 120, 122, 123, 125 (2)
Butler, Richard, 10
Butler, Samuel, 2, 108, 147 (2), 200, 211

Butler, Simeon, 88
Butler, Stephen, 29
Butler, Thomas, Jr., 249, 250
Butler, Walter, 12
Butler, Wentworth, 245
Butler, William, 69, 79, 147, 156, 161
Butman, Benjamin, 36, 37, 241, 242
Butman, Benjamin, Jr., 6
Butman, Frederick B., 213
Butman, Henry, 241
Butman, John, 6, 14, 18
Butman, Joseph, 6
Butman, Samuel, 213
Butman, Thomas, 6
Butmore, Jeremiah, 29
Butnam, John, 22
Butnam, William, 37, 38
Butterfield, Aaron, 229, 283
Butterfield, Asa, 283
Butterfield, Benjamin, 101
Butterfield, Daniel, 229
Butterfield, Ebenezer, 227
Butterfield, Henry, 147
Butterfield, J. P., 227
Butterfield, Jacob W., 227
Butterfield, James, 229, 283
Butterfield, Jesse, 174
Butterfield, John, 24, 101, 178, 228
Butterfield, Jonathan, 228
Butterfield, Joseph, 41, 147
Butterfield, Josiah, 274
Butterfield, Leonard, 220, 246, 312
Butterfield, Levi, 66
Butterfield, Philip, Jr., 227
Butterfield, Stephen R., 48
Butterfield, Thomas, 65
Butters, Daniel, 286
Butters, Flavel, 286
Butters, Joshua, 26
Butters, Timothy S., 152
Butterworth, Shubal, 44
Buttrick, Cyrus, 87
Butts, Abraham, 263
Butts, Nathaniel, 33
Butts, Samuel, 115
Butts, Stephen, 33, 63
Buxton, Charles, 35
Buxton, Ebenezer, 239
Buxton, Edmund, 289
Buxton, Joseph, 212
Buzzel, Nathaniel, 243
Buzzell, Daniel, 162
Buzzell, Elisha, 266, 306
Buzzell, Joseph, 306
Byram, Charles, 272
Byran, ——, 90
Byrnes, Martin, 159

C

Cabbott, John C., 87
Cabot, John O., 70
Cabot, Richard C., 84
Cade, Asa, 33
Cade, Daniel, 33
Cadwell, Abel, 30
Cadwell, Daniel, 119
Cadwell, Stephen, Jr., 43
Cady, Curtis, 30
Cahn, James, 273
Cahoon, Asa, 246
Cahoon, Smalley, 72
Cain, Daniel, 101

Cain, David, 180, 238
Cain, Edward, 39
Cain, Henry, 180
Cain, John P., 113 (2)
Cain, Moses, 33
Caine, John, 145
Cajer, Oliver, 94
Calcost, Chase, 301
Calcost, David, 301
Calder, William, 26
Calderwood, Esekiel, 207 (2), 208
Calderwood, George, 302
Calderwood, John, 193
Calderwood, Thomas, 192, 193
Caldwell, Alexander, 17
Caldwell, Benjamin, 15
Caldwell, Daniel, 276
Caldwell, Ebenezer, 6, 49
Caldwell, Edward P., 26
Caldwell, Elijah, 250, 255
Caldwell, James, 65, 79, 90
Caldwell, John, 7, 24, 49, 134, 135
Caldwell, Stephen, 275
Caldwell, Timothy, 46
Caldwell, William, 17
Calef, Allen, 302
Calef, Josiah, 268
Calf, Thomas, 114
Califf, Jedediah T., 258
Calins, Ezra, 4
Call, Abraham, 24
Call, Charles, 120 (3), 121, 122, 123 (3), 124 (2)
Call, David, 187
Call, James, 191
Call, James, Jr., 190
Call, Jonathan, 188
Call, Jonathan, Jr., 19
Call, Moses, 20
Call, Nathan, 156, 157
Call, Philip, 187, 190, 191
Call, Reuben, 240
Call, Richard, 187, 190
Call, Samuel, 187, 191, 217
Call, Saul, 190
Call, William, 187, 190
Call, William, Jr., 187
Callahan, Joseph, 42, 89
Callendar, William, 82
Callender, Charles, 68
Callender, Chester, 31
Callum, Ebenezer, 133, 136
Cally, William, 239
Calton, Frederic M., 113
Cambell, Charles, 87
Cambridge, Frederic, 78
Cambridge, Frederick, 70
Cameron, John, 183, 185, 188
Cameron, William, 183, 188
Cammett, Dudley, 242
Cammett, John, 242
Cammett, Jonathan, 239
Campbell, Abijah, 214
Campbell, Adam, 230, 296
Campbell, Alexander, 248, 260
Campbell, Amos, 301
Campbell, Benjamin, 220
Campbell, Charles, 176
Campbell, Collins, 226
Campbell, Daniel, 216, 276, 278, 281
Campbell, Duncan, 34
Campbell, Elijah, 248
Campbell, George, 15, 231

INDEX. 333

Campbell, James, 3, 18, 119, 120 (5), 121 (2), 122 (3), 123 (5), 124 (3), 125 (3), 145, 231, 284
Campbell, John, 80, 82, 183, 184, 189, 246, 303, 308
Campbell, Joshua, 222
Campbell, Joshua T., 98
Campbell, Moses, 235
Campbell, Nathaniel, 87, 231
Campbell, Robert, 248
Campbell, Samuel, 226
Campbell, Thomas, 184
Campbell, William, 248
Campbell, Xerxes, 169
Canady, Alexander, 52
Canady, Zebulon, 53
Canfield, Roderick H., 33
Canney, Benjamin, 244
Cannon, Cable L., 130
Cannon, Cornelius, 2
Cannon, James, 1, 32
Cannon, John, 296
Cannon, Nathan, 263, 267, 310
Capen, ——, 27
Capen, Alexander, 160
Capen, David, 86
Capen, Edmund, 69
Capen, John, 5, 26, 78, 114
Capen, Phineas, 85
Capen, Thomas, 70, 244
Capen, Timothy, 257
Capen, Uriah, 223, 257
Capers, Simeon, 85
Capron, Collins, 98
Capron, Joshua, 48
Carby, Robert, 288
Card, Achus, 141
Card, Dominicus, 162, 164
Card, Francis, 231
Card, George, 288 (2), 291, 310
Card, Jeffrey, 141
Card, Jelly, 141
Card, Jeremiah, 162, 163
Card, John, 285, 291
Card, Joseph, 249, 297
Card, Joshua, Jr., 249
Card, Seth, 156
Card, Simeon, 268
Card, Thomas, 249
Card, Thomas, Jr., 297
Card, Thurston, 249
Card, Walter, 249
Card, William, 141, 153
Cardeff, Philip, 82
Cardwell, Francis, 252
Carew, Joseph, 43
Carey, Alanson, 298
Carey, Archer, 93
Carey, Cassander, 178
Carey, Edward, 248
Carey, Ephraim, 97
Carey, Esra, 178
Carey, George, 84
Carey, James, 15
Carey, James, Jr., 148
Carey, John, 134, 140
Carey, John S., 252
Carey, Joseph W., 140
Carey, Josiah D., 68
Carey, Lenos, 50
Carey, Luther, 50
Carey, Martin, 50

Carey, Simeon, 50
Carey, Thomas, 134, 140
Carey, William H., 95
Cargill, Daniel, 189
Cargill, Donald, 186
Cargill, William, 184, 186
Carl, Asa, 240
Carl, Jonathan, 238
Carl, Nathaniel, 240
Carl, Robert, 240
Carle, Dexter, 94
Carle, James, 198, 200 (2), 207, 208
Carle, John, 198, 202, 207, 208 (2)
Carle, Rufus, 200, 202
Carleton, Albert, 246
Carleton, William, 182, 197
Carlisle, Amos, 186
Carlisle, George, 179, 245
Carlton, Albert, 239
Carlton, Benjamin, 100, 156, 157
Carlton, Charles C., 149
Carlton, Daniel, 141
Carlton, Francis, 139
Carlton, Henry, 282
Carlton, Isaac, 68
Carlton, Jeremiah, 184, 188
Carlton, John, 15, 19, 217, 249
Carlton, John G., 249
Carlton, Jonathan, 156, 157
Carlton, Joseph, 136, 137
Carlton, Martin, 77
Carlton, Nathaniel, 190
Carlton, Roderick M., 113, 114
Carlton, Samuel, Jr., 190
Carlton, Stephen, 185
Carlton, Thomas, 48, 239
Carlton, William, 78, 82, 110
Carman, John, 111
Carman, Luther, 260
Carmon, Luther, 175
Carner, William, 133
Carnes, David G., 81, 87
Carnes, Edward, 26
Carnes, William, 136
Carney, Benjamin B., 24, 114
Carney, James, 203, 204
Carpenter, Abel, 98
Carpenter, Abijah, 60
Carpenter, Andrew, 270
Carpenter, Calvin, 60
Carpenter, Daniel, 99
Carpenter, Darius, 98
Carpenter, Ebenezer, 53
Carpenter, Elisha, 30
Carpenter, Francis, 90
Carpenter, George W., 65
Carpenter, James, 41
Carpenter, John, 251
Carpenter, Jonathan, 61
Carpenter, Joseph, 61
Carpenter, Joshua, 223, 254, 260
Carpenter, Levi, 32
Carpenter, Miles, 33
Carpenter, Nathan, 61
Carpenter, Nathaniel, 30
Carpenter, Samuel, 61, 80, 90, 270
Carpenter, William, 60
Carpenter, Wooster, 98
Carr, Berry, 301
Carr, Daniel, 186 (2), 187, 190, 277
Carr, George, 275
Carr, James, 60, 283

Carr, John, 87, 120, 121, 124 (2), 228, 283
Carr, Joseph, 181, 296
Carr, Joseph, Jr., 231
Carr, Joshua, 274
Carr, Josiah, 180
Carr, Macarus, 181
Carr, Richard, 162
Carr, Richey, 179
Carr, Samuel, Jr., 274
Carr, William M., 238
Carr, Wingate, 274
Carrid, Nathan, 290, 293
Carrie, David, 303
Carriel, Nathaniel, 286
Carrier, Samuel, 46
Carrington, John, 46
Carrol, David, 258
Carrol, William, 34
Carroll, George, 1
Carroll, John, 22, 169
Carrul, Jonathan, 286
Carry, Alpheus, 2
Carsen, Seward, 267
Carsley, Ebenezer, 258
Carsley, Seth, 211
Carsley, William C., 211
Carson, Aaron, 161, 306
Carson, James, 279
Carson, Moses, 278
Carter, Amos H., 244
Carter, Asa, 141
Carter, Benjamin, 36, 165 (2), 170
Carter, Brigham, 67
Carter, Charles, 32
Carter, David K., 161
Carter, Dennis M., 41
Carter, Enoch, 12, 41
Carter, Ephraim, 5, 192
Carter, George, 117, 122, 125
Carter, Harry, 46
Carter, Isaac, 161
Carter, Jacob, 275
Carter, James, 162, 163, 301
Carter, John, 5, 26, 67
Carter, John M., 288
Carter, Jonathan, 181
Carter, Joseph, 11
Carter, Joseph W., 5
Carter, Miles, 31
Carter, Nathan, 38, 153
Carter, Peter, 244
Carter, Richard, 2d, 170
Carter, Rufus, 170
Carter, Samuel F., 32, 151
Carter, Thomas, 170
Carter, Timothy, 78, 81
Carter, Willis, 63
Carver, Amos, 223, 259
Carver, Eleazer, 167
Carver, Eleazer, Jr., 277
Carver, Isaac, 209
Carver, John, 168, 277
Carver, Josiah, 52
Carver, Nathan, 290
Carver, William, 167
Carvill, Joseph, 169, 277
Carvill, Sewell, 169, 277
Cary, Anslem, 168
Cary, Francis, 97
Cary, Luther, 168
Casdiff, William, 147
Case, Ambrose, 282

INDEX.

Case, B., 67
Case, Hiram, 33
Case, Isaac, 55
Case, John, 227, 253, 257
Case, Pardon, 63
Case, William, 56 (2), 160
Casey, John, 94
Cash, Francis, 219
Cash, Jacob, 173
Cash, James, 6
Cash, John, Jr., 258
Cash, Stephen, 164, 165, 166, 219
Cask, James, 22
Caskman, William, 275
Cass, John, Jr., 98
Cass, Moses, 17
Cass, Robert, 12
Cassell, James, 69
Cassell, John, 39
Cassidy, Henry, 128 (2)
Cassin, David, 229
Castle, John, 23
Castner, Charles, 291
Castner, Frederic, 291
Caswell, Abraham, 62
Caswell, Alanson, 129
Caswell, Benjamin, 52
Caswell, Daniel, 61
Caswell, Darius, 61
Caswell, Elijah, 52
Caswell, George, 52, 54
Caswell, George, 2d, 59
Caswell, Ira, 1
Caswell, Job, 177, 260
Caswell, John, 257
Caswell, John, Jr., 168
Caswell, Joshua, 85
Caswell, Lewis, 25
Caswell, Libbeus, 212, 258
Caswell, Nathaniel, 53
Caswell, Noah, 41, 177, 257
Caswell, Otis, 177
Caswell, Philip, 59
Caswell, Richard, 6, 22, 60
Caswell, Thomas, 52
Caswell, Wilber, 298
Caswell, William, 150, 178
Cate, Benijah, 187, 190
Cate, Daniel, 182, 192
Cate, Joseph, 24
Cathcart, Oliver T., 65
Catland, Robert, 193, 196
Catlin, Hezekiah, 30
Catlin, John, 181
Catlin, Joseph S., 33
Catlin, Richard, 181
Caton, Rufus, 2
Caul, Ira, 66
Caulking, Ebeneser, 305
Caunnet, Peter, 227
Causwell, Allen, 243
Cavendish, John, 116
Cayford, ——, 304
Cayford, John E., 304
Center, Jacob, 258
Chace, Aaron, Jr., 59, 62
Chace, Benjamin, 52
Chace, Edmund, 57
Chace, Gilbert, Jr., 57
Chace, Giles G., 59
Chace, Holder, 57
Chace, Increase, 62

Chace, Isaac, 283
Chace, James, 57, 59, 231
Chace, James, Jr., 62
Chace, John, 63, 212
Chace, Levi, 56
Chace, Michael, 57
Chace, Samuel, 57
Chace, Simeon, 57
Chace, Wanton, 80
Chace, Welcome W., 281
Chadborn, James, 211
Chadborn, Zebedee, 253
Chadbourn, Benjamin, 245, 258
Chadbourn, Elijah, 270
Chadbourn, Humphrey A., 152
Chadbourn, James, 167
Chadbourn, John, 162, 167
Chadbourn, John W., 152
Chadbourn, Joshua, 246
Chadbourn, Thomas, 10
Chadbourn, Timothy, 165, 246
Chadbourne, Ira, 269
Chadbourne, Nathan, 170
Chadburn, Daniel G., 162
Chadburn, Francis, 237
Chadburn, Humphry A., 261
Chadburn, Joshua, 165, 166
Chadburn, Levi, 239, 244
Chadburn, Timothy, 165
Chadwell, John, 165 (2), 243
Chadwick, Barnabus, 72
Chadwick, Charles, 130
Chadwick, Daniel, 3
Chadwick, David, 72
Chadwick, Dean, 90
Chadwick, Elijah, 72
Chadwick, George, 243
Chadwick, James, 74
Chadwick, James W., 285, 288, 291
Chadwick, John, 138
Chadwick, Lot, 179
Chadwick, Oliver, 72
Chadwick, Richard, 241
Chadwick, Samuel, 72
Chadwick, Samuel C., 130
Chadwick, Saul, 138
Chadwick, Sylvanus, 237
Chadwick, Thatcher, 130
Chadwick, Thomas, 241, 242
Chadwick, Thomas A., 83
Chadwick, William, 241
Chaffee, Lewis, 61
Chaffee, Noah, 98
Chaffee, Walker, 61
Chaffen, John, 100
Chaffer, Alvin, 43
Chaffer, Freeborn M., 44
Chaffin, Comfort F., 53
Chaffin, John, 251
Chaffin, Lester, 60
Chaffin, Nathan, 307
Chaffin, Robert, 60
Challis, Enoch, 9
Chalmer, Peter, 161
Chalmers, James, 239
Chalmers, John, 239
Chalmers, Scotland, 239
Chamberlain, Aaron, Jr., 257
Chamberlain, Amos, 42, 89
Chamberlain, David, 68, 110
Chamberlain, Earle, 246 (2)
Chamberlain, Enoch, 39

Chamberlain, John, 8, 152, 257, 267
Chamberlain, Jonathan, 97
Chamberlain, Joshua, 162, 164, 165, 166, 172 (2), 174
Chamberlain, Obediah, 42, 89
Chamberlain, Pickman, 161
Chamberlain, Samuel J., 48
Chamberlain, Stephen, 42, 89
Chamberlain, William, 172, 193, 196, 246, 266
Chamberlin, Aaron, Jr., 177
Chamberlin, Abija, 49
Chamberlin, Asa, 15
Chamberlin, Benjamin, 271
Chamberlin, Daniel, 134, 140
Chamberlin, Edward, 91
Chamberlin, Eli, 91
Chamberlin, Ezekiel, 100
Chamberlin, Gad, 30
Chamberlin, Hazen, 133, 137
Chamberlin, Henry, 132, 140
Chamberlin, Ira, 287
Chamberlin, Jason, 91
Chamberlin, John, 93
Chamberlin, Joseph, 49, 133, 136, 139, 218
Chamberlin, Joseph B., 100
Chamberlin, Joshua, 213
Chamberlin, Louis, 49
Chamberlin, Nathaniel, 118
Chamberlin, Philip, 150
Chamberlin, Samuel, 91
Chamberlin, Saul, 132
Chamberlin, Silas, 34
Chamberlin, Solomon K., 29
Chamberlin, Thomas, 128
Chamberlin, Timothy, 132
Chamberlin, William, 117, 243, 262
Chambers, Eli, 61
Chambers, Prescott, 27
Champion, Reuben, 43
Champney, Joseph, 14, 69
Champney, William I., 69
Champus, John D., 204
Chancy, John, Jr., 228
Chancy, Josiah, 228
Chancy, William, 228
Chandler, Alfred, 277, 281
Chandler, Benjamin, 26, 28, 79, 132, 140, 250, 254
Chandler, Charles, 100
Chandler, Chauncey C., 300
Chandler, Daniel, 227, 268
Chandler, David, 43, 283, 307
Chandler, Ebeneser, 24, 100
Chandler, Eliphalet, 100
Chandler, Ephraim, 128
Chandler, Ezekiel, 55, 57
Chandler, George, 222
Chandler, Henry, 79
Chandler, Ichabod, 176
Chandler, Ira, 128
Chandler, Isaac, 155
Chandler, Jacob, 26, 78
Chandler, Jeremiah, 254
Chandler, Joel, 209
Chandler, John, 8, 152, 254, 280
Chandler, John F., 176
Chandler, John T., 176
Chandler, Jonathan, 176, 260
Chandler, Joseph, 146
Chandler, Joseph D., 141
Chandler, Levi, 158
Chandler, Moses, 147, 150, 228, 283

INDEX. 335

Chandler, Nathan, 128, 152
Chandler, Nathaniel, 131, 176
Chandler, Noah, 280
Chandler, Phineas, 176, 260
Chandler, Reuben, 176
Chandler, Samuel, 45, 227, 273
Chandler, Seth, 260
Chandler, Stephen, 160, 176, 186, 260
Chandler, Thomas, 109
Chandler, William, 63, 209
Chandler, William H., 134
Chandler, Zebedee, 176
Chandley, Jeremiah, 151
Channing, Henry, 28
Chany, Josiah, 283
Chapel, Jonathan, 29
Chapin, Aaron, 28, 43
Chapin, Asaph, 43
Chapin, D., 69
Chapin, Eli, 5
Chapin, Enoch, 4
Chapin, Frederic, 67
Chapin, Gorham, 66
Chapin, Isaac, 43
Chapin, James, 45
Chapin, Josiah, 215
Chapin, Leonard, 5
Chapin, Libbeus, 4
Chapin, Olden, 43
Chapin, Philip, 4
Chapin, Quartus, 43
Chapin, Theodore, 43
Chapin, Thomas, 64
Chaples, John, 206, 285
Chaplin, Daniel, Jr., 257
Chaplin, Jacob, 258
Chapman, Abraham, 195
Chapman, Amasa, 268, 308
Chapman, Anthony, 195
Chapman, Asa, 46
Chapman, Benjamin, 11, 135, 196
Chapman, Caleb, 46
Chapman, Daniel, 194
Chapman, David, 67
Chapman, Edward, 34
Chapman, Elijah, 43
Chapman, Ephraim, 195
Chapman, Francis, 301
Chapman, Henry, 16
Chapman, Isaac, 34, 37, 67
Chapman, Israel, 192, 193, 195
Chapman, Jacob, 195
Chapman, James, 305
Chapman, Jedediah, 64
Chapman, Jesse, 192, 195
Chapman, John, 70, 77, 192, 195, 305 (2)
Chapman, Joseph, Jr., 195
Chapman, Michael, 195
Chapman, Nathan, 194, 196
Chapman, Nathaniel, 6, 21, 195
Chapman, Nathaniel, Jr., 195
Chapman, Orris, 195
Chapman, Ralph, 197, 203, 204, 206
Chapman, Robert, 195
Chapman, Robert, Jr., 195
Chapman, Samuel, 268, 305
Chapman, Saul, 136
Chapman, Stephen, 194
Chapman, Thomas, 192, 308
Chapman, Thomas, Jr., 195
Chapman, Timothy, 257
Chapman, William, 194

Chappell, Richard S., 94
Chappels, James, 145
Chardon, James, Jr., 69
Charles, Isaac, 151
Charles, James, 151
Charles, John, Jr., 152
Charles, Jonathan, 308
Charles, Simeon, 152, 254
Charles, Timothy, 152, 254
Charlton, Jeremiah, 191
Chase, Abel, 155, 218, 312
Chase, Abner, 162, 177, 257
Chase, Allen, 55
Chase, Amos, 16, 174
Chase, Andrew, 191
Chase, Arnold, 62
Chase, Arthur, 261, 266
Chase, Benjamin, 34, 37, 306
Chase, Benjamin I., 242
Chase, Caleb S., 241, 242
Chase, Calvin, 290, 293
Chase, Charles, 20, 21, 176
Chase, Daniel, 15, 18, 176, 242
Chase, Daniel P., 48
Chase, David, 158, 165, 166
Chase, Edmund, 90, 159
Chase, Eli, 41
Chase, Eliphalet, 213
Chase, Elisha, 304
Chase, Enoch, 151, 297
Chase, Enos, 4
Chase, Gardner, 129
Chase, George, 298
Chase, Gideon, 152
Chase, Henry, 16
Chase, Hull, 151
Chase, Israel, 55
Chase, Jacob, 16, 136, 137
Chase, James, 165, 166, 222, 254, 262, 270
Chase, J., Jr., 19
Chase, Jery, 311
Chase, Joel, 268
Chase, John, 15, 116, 217, 225, 292
Chase, John, Jr., 20, 231
Chase, John W., 242
Chase, Jonathan, Jr., 210
Chase, Joseph, 55, 123, 176, 258
Chase, Joseph F., 120
Chase, Joseph T., 19
Chase, Joshua, 177
Chase, Josiah, 16, 118
Chase, Judah, 231, 296
Chase, Luther, 77
Chase, Moses, 210, 237, 270
Chase, Moses, 3d, 17
Chase, Nahum, 234
Chase, Nathaniel, 169, 281
Chase, Noah, 215
Chase, Perkins, 287
Chase, Peter, 177, 260
Chase, Plummer, 138
Chase, Robertson, 55, 57
Chase, Samuel, 118, 149
Chase, Saul, 18
Chase, Seth S., 151
Chase, Sheffield, 60
Chase, Thomas, 15, 215, 220
Chase, Thomas H., 15
Chase, Timothy, 238
Chase, Welcome U., 277
Chase, William, 20 (2), 93, 186, 189, 191
Chase, William, Jr., 21

Chase, William J., 8
Chatty, John, 261
Cheaney, Abner N., 16
Cheaney, Jonathan, 16
Cheaver, Benjamin, 2d, 34
Cheaver, Jacob, 38
Cheaver, James, 138
Cheaver, Joseph, 34
Cheaver, Nathaniel, 34
Cheaver, Samuel, 36
Cheaver, William P., 37
Check, Moses, 213
Cheeseman, Abel, 45
Cheeseman, Saul, 45
Cheever, Charles, 113
Cheever, Frederick, 117
Cheever, Henry, 112
Cheever, John, 27, 39, 117
Cheever, Joseph, 27, 38, 138
Cheever, Joshua, 117
Cheever, William, 14, 26, 84, 90, 118, 139
Cheevers, Aaron, 89
Cheevers, Joshua, 70
Cheevers, Philip, 89
Chenery, William, 257
Cheney, Moses, 27
Cheney, Thomas, 42
Cheney, William, 40, 223
Cherrne, Abner, 234
Chesbrock, Elihu, 46
Chesley, Benjamin, 250
Chesley, Isaac, 221
Chesley, Jonathan, 228, 255
Chesley, Sawyer, Jr., 228
Chick, Abraham, Jr., 217
Chick, Abram, 161
Chick, Elias, 167
Chick, Joseph, 273
Chick, S. James, 312
Chick, Samuel, 245
Chick, Silas, 285, 287
Chick, Thomas, 245
Chickering, Daniel, 100
Chickering, Hartshorn, 88
Chickering, Isaac, 100
Chickering, John, 19, 20, 100
Chickering, Oliver, 48
Chickering, Samuel, 100
Chickering, Shubal, 3
Chicks, James S., 155
Child, Daniel, 222
Child, Gardner, 224
Child, James, 98
Child, James L., 236
Child, John W., 98
Childs, Amasa, 47
Childs, Amos, 2
Childs, Barnabus, 72
Childs, Benjamin, 32, 88
Childs, Caleb, 78, 90
Childs, Calvin, 72
Childs, Charles H., 115
Childs, David H., 44
Childs, Ephraim, 224
Childs, Howland, 224
Childs, Isaac, 110
Childs, James, 131
Childs, John, 72
Childs, Jonas, 32
Childs, Jonathan, 64, 68
Childs, Joseph, 72, 88
Childs, Nathaniel, 87

336   INDEX.

Childs, Oliver, 276
Childs, Oliver L., 98
Childs, Reuben P., 89
Childs, Robert, 274
Childs, Robert P., 42
Childs, Samuel, 98, 131
Childs, Saul, 66
Childs, Stephen, 32
Childs, Thomas, 70, 72
Childs, Timothy, 77
Childs, Willard, 99
Childs, William, 224
Chilson, Ichabod, 96
Chilson, John, Jr., 96
Chilson, Joshua, Jr., 96
Chin, Robert B., 6
China, Stephen P., 180
Chipman, Anthony, 10
Chipman, Barnabas, 131
Chipman, George, 51
Chipman, John, 139
Chipman, John, Jr., 133
Chipman, Saul, 137
Chipman, Seth, 256
Chipman, Simeon, 252
Chipman, Walter, 131
Chisam, James, 249
Chisholm, Daniel B., 274
Chism, Ephraim, 156
Chism, John, Jr., 156, 157
Chism, William, 156, 157 (2)
Chittenden, Israel, 47
Choat, Abram, 185, 190
Choat, Robert, 181
Choat, Rufus, 179
Choate, Aaron, 2d, 274
Choate, Adoniram, 11
Choate, Benjamin, 165, 221
Choate, Henry, 34, 38
Choate, Humphrey, 13, 14
Choate, John, 132, 137
Choate, Jonathan, 119, 122
Choate, Josiah, 153
Choate, Moses, 228
Choate, Solomon, 9
Chote, Aaron, 2d, 274
Chote, Benjamin, 164, 166
Chote, James, 263
Chrispin, William, 132
Christopher, George, 160
Chubb, Thomas, 85
Chubbuck, Eleazer, 101
Chubbuck, Henry, 41, 68
Chubbuck, Levi, 40
Church, Charles, 141
Church, David, 271
Church, Isaac S., 58
Church, James, 55, 57, 266
Church, John, 47
Church, Jonathan, 45
Church, Joseph, 2d, 186
Church, Luther, 276
Church, Randall, 262
Church, Samuel, Jr., 276
Church, Silas, 304
Church, Stephen P., 34
Church, William, 78
Churchill, Alfred, 128
Churchill, Artemas, 64
Churchill, Bela, 251
Churchill, Benjamin, 255
Churchill, Eleazer, 49

Churchill, Hosea, 128
Churchill, Jabez, 225
Churchill, Jacob, 128
Churchill, Jesse, 42
Churchill, Joseph, 39
Churchill, Lewis, 128
Churchill, Mathew, 251
Churchill, Moses, 31
Churchill, Nathan, 131
Churchill, Peleg, 128 (2)
Churchill, Peres, 252
Churchill, Rufus, 96, 101, 274
Churchill, Samuel, 3
Churchill, Seth, 128
Churchill, Seymour, 32
Churchill, Shepherd, 251
Churchill, Sprague, 146, 150
Churchill, William, 252, 255
Churchill, Zadoc, 95
Churchward, Timothy, 136, 137
Churchwell, Levi, 69
Cilly, Cuttin, 133
Cilly, Cutting, 135, 137
Cinklee, Ebenezer, 169
Cladd, Peter, 36
Clafford, Peter, 138
Claflen, Otis, 90
Claflin, David, 70
Claflin, Hartford, 126
Claftin, Leonard, 30
Claghorn, Ahaz, 64
Claghorn, Benjamin, 65
Claghorn, John W., 25
Claiton, John, Jr., 283
Clampton, Samuel, 45
Clap, Artemus, 68
Clap, Benjamin, 77
Clap, Eleaser, 67
Clap, Joel, 67
Clap, Luther C., 67
Clap, Martin, 77
Clap, Nehemiah, 77
Clap, Quartus, 67
Clap, Seth, 29
Clapp, Amasa, 64
Clapp, Artemus, 39
Clapp, Azariah, 67
Clapp, Benjamin, 81
Clapp, Billings, 217
Clapp, Bradish, 97
Clapp, Charles, 247
Clapp, Curtis, 97
Clapp, Daniel, 4
Clapp, Edward, 23
Clapp, Enos, 89
Clapp, Ezekiel, 78, 81
Clapp, Francis, 82
Clapp, Francis W., 80
Clapp, Frederic, 28
Clapp, Galen, 28
Clapp, George L., 64
Clapp, James, 67
Clapp, Jarvis, 7
Clapp, John, 1, 40, 104
Clapp, Jonathan, 86
Clapp, Lemuel, 92
Clapp, Martin, 21
Clapp, Moses, 89
Clapp, Nathaniel, 103, 195
Clapp, Nehemiah, 82
Clapp, Richard, 64
Clapp, Robert, 46

Clapp, Silas, 89
Clapp, Warren, 97
Clapp, Zebediah, 64
Claridge, Stephen, 246
Clark, Abijah, 32
Clark, Abner, 42, 67, 89, 286
Clark, Abraham S., 10
Clark, Alanson, 4
Clark, Alexander, 195, 310
Clark, Alfred, 298
Clark, Allen, 4
Clark, Amasa, 67, 196
Clark, Amos, 120
Clark, Anson K., 67
Clark, Artherton, 269
Clark, Asa, 57, 284
Clark, Atkins, 2
Clark, Benjamin, 193, 306
Clark, Benjamin, Jr., 26
Clark, Benjamin F., 7
Clark, Benjamin H., 1, 103
Clark, Benjamin R., 160
Clark, Cephas, 4, 90
Clark, Chandler, 280
Clark, Charles, 192, 276
Clark, Charles C., 139 (2)
Clark, Christopher, 4, 141
Clark, Consider, 128
Clark, Cyrus, 175
Clark, David, 57, 127, 194, 299
Clark, Davis, 55
Clark, Ebenezer, 84, 133, 136
Clark, Edson, 93
Clark, Edward, 14, 67
Clark, Eli, 280
Clark, Elias, 141
Clark, Eliphalet, 45
Clark, Elisha, 129, 180, 193, 229, 237
Clark, Elisha T., 52
Clark, Enos, 123
Clark, Ephraim, 192
Clark, Ephraim, 3d, 237
Clark, Ezekiel, 58, 286, 290
Clark, Ezra, 182, 184
Clark, Francis, 209
Clark, Francis G., 135, 137
Clark, Freeman, 65
Clark, G. W., 84
Clark, Gardner, 141
Clark, George, 129, 241
Clark, George, Jr., 11
Clark, George W., 80
Clark, Gershon, 240
Clark, Harry, 29
Clark, Henry, 10, 15, 53
Clark, Henry, Jr., 10
Clark, Henry A., 159
Clark, Humphrey, 304
Clark, Isaac, 112, 302
Clark, Isaac, Jr., 276
Clark, Israel, 36, 37
Clark, Jacob, 115, 152, 302
Clark, James, 26, 66, 84, 156, 157 (2), 162, 217, 242
Clark, James, Jr., 199, 200
Clark, Jason, 48
Clark, Joel, 146
Clark, John, 7, 13, 29, 49, 66, 119, 134 (2), 135, 137, 162 (2), 180, 193 (2), 195, 206, 216, 217, 220, 223, 224, 225, 259 (2), 287, 291, 298, 307, 311
Clark, John, Jr., 195, 206, 221

INDEX. 337

Clark, John, 2d, 295
Clark, John H., 128
Clark, John R., 173
Clark, John T., 17
Clark, Jona, 159
Clark, Jonathan, 37, 276
Clark, Jonathan, Jr., 302
Clark, Joseph, 5, 57, 186, 203, 210, 236, 264, 287, 290
Clark, Joseph H., 4, 168, 281
Clark, Joshua, 9, 263, 269
Clark, Josiah, 161, 199, 200
Clark, Julius, 85
Clark, Justin, 4
Clark, Lemuel, 80, 82
Clark, Leonard, 3
Clark, Lucius, 4
Clark, Mason, 93
Clark, Michael, 33
Clark, Moses I., 10
Clark, Nathan, 155, 162 (2), 187, 190
Clark, Nathan, Jr., 184, 186
Clark, Nathan T., 33
Clark, Nathaniel, 26, 78, 128, 160, 193
Clark, Nathaniel, Jr., 160
Clark, Nicholas, 192
Clark, Norman, 257
Clark, Oliver, 7
Clark, Oramel, 29
Clark, Peleg, 1, 130
Clark, Peter, Jr., 272
Clark, Peter O., 218
Clark, Philip, 67
Clark, Phincy, 46
Clark, Porter, 6
Clark, Ralph, 66
Clark, Ralph C., 45
Clark, Richard, 26, 53
Clark, Robert, 217
Clark, Roswell, 46
Clark, Russell, 30
Clark, Samuel, 8, 23, 32, 121, 123 (2), 124, 145, 186 (2), 224, 263, 281
Clark, Samuel, Jr., 193, 231
Clark, Samuel L., 10
Clark, Saul, 20, 259
Clark, Selah, 45
Clark, Sereno, 4
Clark, Seth, 241, 242
Clark, Shubal, 42
Clark, Sidenham, 4
Clark, Simeon, 53
Clark, Smith, 147
Clark, Solomon, 275
Clark, Stephen, 141
Clark, Thaddeus, 4, 67
Clark, Theophilus, 116
Clark, Thomas, 25, 26, 239, 240
Clark, Thomas B., 39
Clark, Thomas L., 10
Clark, Warren, 88, 102
Clark, West, 194
Clark, Willard, 62
Clark, William, 8, 12, 14, 62, 160, 178, 183, 184, 188, 206, 272
Clark, William, 2d, 14
Clark, William C., 4, 10, 206
Clark, William M., 272
Clark, Zenas, 29
Clarke, Lovell, 5
Clarkson, Richard P., 213
Clary, David, 179

Clary, James, 179
Clary, John, 196
Clary, Moses, 42
Clary, Robert, Jr., 196
Clary, Timothy, 179
Clausen, Luther J., 222
Claver, John, 274
Claxton, Philip, 36, 37
Clay, Benjamin, 161, 254
Clay, Daniel, 272
Clay, Enoch, 42
Clay, George, 161
Clay, Job, Jr., 180
Clay, John, 240
Clay, Jonathan, 180
Clay, Richard, 272, 302
Clay, Samuel, 275
Clay, Stephen, 180
Clay, William, 171
Clayton, Joseph, 34
Cleary, Caleb, 279
Cleary, John, 192
Cleasby, Tilly H., 182, 284, 287 (2)
Cleaver, John, 77
Cleaves, Abraham, 265
Cleaves, Benjamin, 38
Cleaves, Charles, 252
Cleaves, Humphrey, 252
Cleaves, Merchant, 310
Cleaves, Nathaniel, 38
Cleaves, William P., 36
Cleavis, William P., 148
Cleek, James, 244
Clemens, Hill, 215
Clemens, John, 215
Clemens, Luther, 47
Clemens, Saul, 134, 135
Clement, Cyrus, 239
Clement, Tilly, 245
Clement, Job, 181
Clements, Eleazer, 173
Clements, Ephraim, 21
Clements, Henry, 21
Clements, Jeremiah, 221
Clements, John, 173
Clements, Moses, 3
Clements, Rufus, 228
Clemmons, Prentice, 217
Clenne, John, 6
Clerk, James, 169, 242
Clerk, Paul, 299
Clerk, Samuel, 169
Clesley, Joseph, 84
Cleveland, Benjamin, 46
Cleveland, George, 141
Cleveland, Ira, 5
Cleveland, James, 307
Cleveland, John, 261
Cleveland, Joseph, 307
Cleveland, Josiah, 31
Cleveland, Timothy, 263, 267, 310
Cleverly, Ebenezer, 39
Cleverly, Jonathan, 101, 102
Cleverly, Joseph, 303
Cleverly, Lewis, 100
Cleves, Samuel, 139
Cliff, James, 138
Clifford, Andrew, 191
Clifford, David, 15, 267
Clifford, Ebenezer, 185, 186
Clifford, John, 185, 252, 263, 267

Clifford, Jonathan F., 251, 255
Clifford, Nathaniel, 303
Clifford, Peter, 196
Clifford, Prince, 261
Clifford, Richard, 263
Clifford, Spencer, 185
Clifford, William, 191
Clifford, William, 3d, 183
Cline, Hugh, 31
Close, Jacob, 289
Close, William, 289
Cloudman, Nathan, 252
Clough, Aaron, 81
Clough, Andrew, 138
Clough, Asa, 170
Clough, Benjamin, 83, 165 (2)
Clough, Daniel, 279 (2), 280
Clough, David, 198, 199, 201, 202, 208, 244
Clough, Elijah, 282
Clough, James I., 282
Clough, John, 212
Clough, Joseph, 184, 186, 188
Clough, Jonathan, 279
Clough, Josiah R., 218, 220
Clough, Samuel, 6, 156, 157
Clough, Saul, 22, 156
Clough, Simon, 277
Clough, William, 88, 133, 136
Clouse, George, 289
Cloutman, George, 6, 136, 137
Cloutman, Henry, 6
Cloutman, John, 198, 207, 208
Cloutman, Joseph, 132, 134, 135
Cloutman, Saul, 138
Clover, John, 6
Clowes, Philip, 39
Cluff, Nathaniel, 244
Clute, Daniel, 258
Coadin, William, 288
Coames, Josiah, 285
Coates, Benjamin, 116
Coats, Elisha, 5
Coats, Erastus, 64
Coats, Jesse, 5
Coats, John, 116
Cobb, Allanson, 71
Cobb, Asa, 220
Cobb, Benjamin, 131
Cobb, Chandler, 210
Cobb, Churchill, 252, 255
Cobb, Cyrus, 234, 252, 255
Cobb, David, 67, 170
Cobb, David George Washington, 162
Cobb, Eaton, 96
Cobb, Ebenezer, 62, 210, 290
Cobb, Eleazer, Jr., 131
Cobb, Elisha, 241
Cobb, Enoch, 154
Cobb, Enos, 69
Cobb, Elijah, 104
Cobb, Garvis, 53
Cobb, George, 153, 221
Cobb, Isaac, 131, 154
Cobb, James, Jr., 220
Cobb, John, 67, 172, 247, 264
Cobb, Jonathan, 102, 131
Cobb, Joseph, 153, 164, 165, 166
Cobb, Josiah, 69, 79, 130
Cobb, Lemuel, 216, 221
Cobb, Levi, 220
Cobb, Matthew, 131
Cobb, Nathaniel, 292 (2)

INDEX.

Cobb, Otis, 51
Cobb, Peter, Jr., 220
Cobb, Philip, 211
Cobb, Prentiss, 131
Cobb, Richard, 131, 220
Cobb, Robert, 241
Cobb, Roland, 292
Cobb, Rowland, 292
Cobb, Samuel H., 215
Cobb, Saul, 234
Cobb, Silvanus, Jr., 210
Cobb, Smith W., Jr., 241
Cobb, Stephen, 178, 243, 259
Cobb, Thomas, 181
Cobb, William, 131, 162, 214
Cobb, William, Jr., 220
Cobb, William D., 23
Cobbert, Joseph, 99
Cobbington, Jacob, 103
Cobble, Alanson, 95
Coburn, Blanchard, 88
Coburn, Frederick, 250
Coburn, George, 239
Coburn, Hiram, 81
Coburn, Isaiah, 167, 281
Coburn, Jephtha, 229
Coburn, Jeremiah, 255
Coburn, John, 295
Coburn, Jonas, Jr., 259
Coburn, Manly, 229, 282
Coburn, Moses, 261
Coburn, Peter, 178
Coburn, Phineas, 167, 281
Coburn, Reuben, 169
Coburn, Samuel, 178
Coburn, Silas, 178
Cochran, David, 184, 186, 189, 191
Cochran, Jacob, 278
Cochran, James, 47
Cochran, Nathaniel, 227
Cochran, Osgood, 278
Cochran, Robert B., 303
Cochran, Samuel, 160, 191
Cochran, Timothy, 158
Cochran, William, 184, 186, 191
Codd, Thomas, 193
Codding, Josiah, 42, 89
Coding, Abial, 53
Codman, Edward P., 241
Codman, George, 81
Codman, Henry, 84
Coe, Job, 31
Coes, Benjamin, 308, 309, 310
Coff, William, 210
Coffin, Abner, 35
Coffin, Charles, 39, 263, 310
Coffin, David, 269 (3)
Coffin, David, Jr., 20
Coffin, David N. B., 271
Coffin, Enoch, 89
Coffin, George, 19
Coffin, Grindal, 180
Coffin, Henry, 1
Coffin, James, 167
Coffin, John, 18
Coffin, John, 2d, 16
Coffin, Joseph, 16, 98
Coffin, Moses, 121, 124
Coffin, Naphtali, 224, 257
Coffin, Nathaniel, 18, 241
Coffin, Peleg, 59
Coffin, Saul, 17

Coffin, Simeon, 225
Coffin, Stephen, 184, 186 (2), 187, 190
Coffin, Thomas, 209
Coffin, Tristram, 13, 153
Coffin, Valentine C., 126
Coffin, William, 10
Coggeshall, Charles, 1
Coggeshall, Hayden, 1
Coggin, Benjamin W., 160
Coggins, Samuel, 161
Coggins, Simeon, 192
Coggshall, John, 54
Cogswell, David, 9
Cogswell, George, 8
Cogswell, Henry T., 99
Cogswell, John, 268
Cogswell, Moody, 90
Cogswell, Stephen, 205
Coher, William, 17
Coit, Thomas C., 82
Cok, Charles, 19
Colbath, James, Jr., 228
Colbey, John, 281
Colbrook, Isaac, 173
Colburn, Charles, 81, 110, 115
Colburn, David, 40
Colburn, Ebenezer, 303
Colburn, Jeraghmeel, 251
Colburn, Lemuel, 81
Colburn, Nathaniel, 5, 98
Colburn, Prescott, 41
Colburn, William, 40, 188
Colburne, John, 271
Colburne, Joseph, 271
Colby, Ebenezer, 257, 271
Colby, Eli, 162, 164
Colby, Elias, 234
Colby, Harry, 265
Colby, Hartley, 265
Colby, Henry, Jr., 189, 191
Colby, Israel, 258
Colby, J., 189
Colby, Jacob, 152
Colby, James, Jr., 234
Colby, John, 169
Colby, Joseph, 151
Colby, Philip, 119, 122
Colby, Robert, 151
Colby, Thomas, 206
Colcard, Benjamin, 303
Colcard, John, 303
Colcord, David, 151
Colcord, Wilson, 261
Cole, Abel, 271
Cole, Alden, 53
Cole, Asa, 107
Cole, Asahel, 244
Cole, Augustus, 103
Cole, Braddock, 103
Cole, Calvin, 251
Cole, Charles, 120
Cole, Consider, 64
Cole, Cyprian, 250
Cole, Daniel, 244
Cole, Eli, 244
Cole, Elisha, 104, 105 (2), 106, 107
Cole, Ephraim, 50, 104, 105 (2), 106, 107
Cole, Freeman, 51
Cole, Gale, 277
Cole, George, 210, 259
Cole, James, 52, 108, 118, 128, 236, 251, 255
Cole, Jeremiah, 166

Cole, Job, 251
Cole, Joel, 104, 105 (2), 106, 107
Cole, John, 41, 104, 105, 106, 107, 159, 244
Cole, Jonathan, 250
Cole, Joseph, 34, 41, 65, 127, 171, 216, 251, 255 (2)
Cole, Levi, 250, 255
Cole, Moses, 18
Cole, Nathan, 178, 260
Cole, Nathaniel, 60
Cole, Nathaniel S., 90
Cole, Richard, 6, 22 (2)
Cole, Robert, 269
Cole, Sampson, 251
Cole, Samuel, 52, 53, 54
Cole, Samuel, Jr., 166
Cole, Samuel, 2d, 102
Cole, Seth, 70, 77, 87, 162, 214
Cole, William, 11, 22 (2), 52, 61, 176
Cole, Zackariah M., 36
Coleman, Daniel T., 16
Coleman, Elijah B., 59
Coleman, James, 83
Coleman, John, 240
Coleman, Louden, 33
Coleman, Samuel, 33
Colfield, Anthony D., 138
Coll, Abram, 291
Coll, James, 291
Collamer, Davis, 195
Collamer, Nathaniel, 195
Collamore, Alpheus, 286, 290
Collar, Aaron, 80
Coller, Aaron, 85
Coller, David, 148
Collerton, William W., 65
Colley, ———, 19
Colley, John, Jr., 219
Colley, Johnson, 83
Colley, Joshua, 220
Colley, Roger, 44
Colley, William, 133
Colley, William, Jr., 219
Collidge, Aaron, 77
Collie, Edward, 86
Collier, Ebenezer, 280
Collier, Edward, 86
Collier, Isaac, 21, 132
Collier, John, 21, 302
Collier, Jonathan, 86
Collier, Roland, 302
Collier, William, 232
Collins, Aaron, 199, 200, 202
Collins, Barnard, 134, 135, 266, 306
Collins, Charles, 13, 14, 244
Collins, Daniel, 29, 217, 306 (2)
Collins, Daniel D., 260
Collins, Dixy, 133
Collins, James, 83, 265, 275, 304
Collins, James P., 12
Collins, John, 305
Collins, Joseph W., 212
Collins, Lemuel, Jr., 304
Collins, Moses, 217
Collins, Robert, 138
Collins, Samuel, 275
Collins, Saniar, 44
Collins, Sylvanus, 46
Collins, Thomas, 55
Collins, William, 17, 199, 200, 202
Collis, Abel, 48
Collomore, Davis, 197

INDEX.

Collomore, Enoch, 103
Collomore, Nathaniel, 196
Colman, Ebenezer, 71
Colman, Elijah B., 62
Colman, Frederick, 173
Colman, Joshua, 82
Colson, Bolter, 65
Colson, David, 162, 215
Colson, Ephraim, 303
Colting, Elijah D., 109
Colton, William, 251
Colvard, James, Jr., 215
Combey, David C., 266
Combs, Abner, 231
Combs, David, 264
Combs, Zebulon, 232
Comee, Aaron, 99
Comee, Lyman, 99
Comery, Mathew, 292
Comfort, Richard, 240
Comins, Charles, 217
Commings, Benjamin, 179
Commings, John, 179
Complete, Dennis, 39
Comstock, Jonathan, 66
Comstock, Joshua, 30
Comstock, Silas, 30
Comston, Henry V., 172
Con, James, 230
Con, John, 178, 274
Con, Joseph, 230
Conan, Samuel, 283
Conant, Aaron, 94
Conant, Abraham, 201 (2), 203
Conant, Andrew, 49
Conant, Asa, 80
Conant, Benjamin, 150
Conant, Daniel, 88
Conant, Daniel, Jr., 221
Conant, Edward, 164, 165, 166, 221
Conant, Ezra, 35 (2), 37
Conant, Farwell, 94
Conant, Galand, 51
Conant, Hooper, 178
Conant, Isaac, 201 (2), 202
Conant, Jabes, 69
Conant, Jacob, 91
Conant, James, 93, 100
Conant, Jedediah K., 283
Conant, Joel, 83, 84, 100
Conant, John, 82, 100
Conant, John A., 97
Conant, Joseph, 5
Conant, Josiah, 45
Conant, Lot, 93
Conant, Marcus, 178
Conant, Marshall, 27
Conant, Oliver, 232 (2), 235
Conant, Paul, 100
Conant, Peter C., 88
Conant, Samuel, 27, 100, 221
Conant, Sylvanus, 51
Conce, Rufus, 289, 293
Conclin, Isaac, 200
Condee, George, 285
Conden, Saul, 78
Conden, William, 285
Conden, William, 2d, 285
Conder, Joseph, 70
Condon, Saul, 288, 310
Condon, William, 288
Condy, Daniel, 289, 293

Cone, David, 238
Cone, Isaac, 238, 265
Cone, Mathew H., 44
Cone, Oliver, 238
Cone, Samuel, Jr., 238
Congdon, Benjamin, 141
Conhord, James, 161
Conkey, John, 45
Conkey, John S., 47
Conkey, William, 47
Conn, John, 271
Connant, Ebeneser, 99
Connant, Silas, 99
Connce, Samuel, 292 (2)
Conner, Charles, 285, 294
Conner, Charles, Jr., 294
Conner, David Y., 271
Conner, John, 115
Conner, John H., 301
Conner, Richard C., 83
Connor, Jeremiah, 240
Connor, John, 2
Connor, Richard C., 87
Connor, William, 20
Connry, Mathias, 292
Conter, William, 9
Converse, Boswell, 93
Converse, Jeremiah, 96
Converse, Jesse, 96
Converse, Joshua, 80
Converse, Phineas, 46
Converse, Robert, 140
Convis, Rufus, 86
Conway, Frederic, 200
Conwise, Joshua, 81
Cony, Hartson, 280
Cook, Abijah, 86
Cook, Asa, 47, 129
Cook, Barnabas, 296
Cook, Charles, 18, 19, 121
Cook, Charles, 3d, 124
Cook, Corey, 69
Cook, Cornelius, 285, 288, 291
Cook, Cory, 79
Cook, Daniel, 92
Cook, David, 80, 83, 184
Cook, Elijah, 288 (2), 291
Cook, F., 294
Cook, Francis, 288, 291, 310
Cook, George, 213
Cook, Horatio G., 244
Cook, Isaac, 307
Cook, James, 42, 44, 89, 135, 136, 137, 140, 148, 213, 288, 291
Cook, James, 2d, 288, 291, 310
Cook, James M., 244
Cook, John, 71, 128, 258
Cook, John, 2d, 96
Cook, John L., 75
Cook, John M., 134, 140
Cook, John W., 41
Cook, Jonathan, 87, 100, 182
Cook, Joseph, 18, 47, 60, 268
Cook, Joseph, Jr., 261
Cook, Josiah, 3
Cook, Julius, 64
Cook, Kingman, 49
Cook, Levi, 131
Cook, Lincoln, 148
Cook, Moses, 29
Cook, Nathaniel, 261, 266

Cook, Noah, 98
Cook, Otis, 85
Cook, Peleg B., 128
Cook, Reuben, 85, 92
Cook, Richard, 255, 307
Cook, Robert, 58, 307
Cook, Robert, Jr., 128
Cook, Roswell, 92
Cook, Russell, 45
Cook, Saul, 230
Cook, Seth B., 68, 78, 110
Cook, Simeon, 101
Cook, Stephen W., 98
Cook, Thomas D., 18
Cook, Zenas, 291, 310
Cookson, Abram, 180
Cookson, John, 180
Cookson, Joseph, 180
Cookson, Josiah, 240
Cookson, Reuben, 240
Cookson, William, 186, 190
Cool, Jacob, 263
Cooland, Daniel, Jr., 180
Coolbroth, Ebenezer, 261
Coolbroth, Edward, 149, 242, 244
Coolbroth, Joseph, 170
Coolbroth, Rufus, 170, 246
Cooledge, Jonathan, 19
Cooledge, Joseph, 223
Cooledge, Moses, 222
Coolege, Amos, 70
Cooley, Alvin, 30
Cooley, Aretus, 44
Cooley, Ariel, 4
Cooley, Asher, 44
Cooley, Caleb, 43
Cooley, Charles, 44
Cooley, Chester, 50
Cooley, Festus, 44, 46
Cooley, Jacob, 43
Cooley, John B., 43
Cooley, John S., 41
Cooley, Jonathan, Jr., 46
Cooley, Samuel, 4
Cooley, Titus, 4
Cooley, William, 4
Coolidge, Charles, 24
Coolidge, Francis, 90
Coolidge, James, 26, 79
Coolidge, Merrick, 48
Coolidge, Rufus, 66
Coolidge, Samuel, 66
Coolidge, Thomas B., 272
Coolidge, William C., 109
Coolige, William, 242
Coolrath, James, 152
Coolridge, James, 94
Coolridge, John, 94
Coolridge, Lewis, 80
Coolridge, William, 92
Coombs, A. G., 197, 203
Coombs, Abizer, 203, 204
Coombs, Albion, 206
Coombs, Archelaus J., 197
Coombs, Asa, 200, 296
Coombs, Asa, Jr., 235, 296
Coombs, Benjamin, 172, 214
Coombs, David, 152, 234, 248, 267
Coombs, Elisha, 299
Coombs, Elnathan, 102
Coombs, Ephraim, 74
Coombs, George, 197, 203, 204

INDEX.

Coombs, Jesse, 299
Coombs, John, 169, 234
Coombs, John, 2d, 234
Coombs, John E., 295
Coombs, Joseph, 233, 235, 296
Coombs, Joseph, Jr., 296, 299
Coombs, Joshua, 232, 280
Coombs, Samuel, 145, 234, 299
Coombs, Saul, 310
Coombs, Simeon, 53
Coombs, Thomas, 234, 235
Coombs, William, 233, 296
Coombs, William S., 296
Coombs, Zebulon, 232
Coon, George, 312
Coon, Jacob, 312
Coon, John, 312
Cooper, Alexander, 190, 191
Cooper, Benjamin, 53
Cooper, George B., 156, 159
Cooper, Henry, 276
Cooper, James A., 188
Cooper, James M., 184, 191
Cooper, Jesse, 84
Cooper, John, 26, 27
Cooper, Leonard, 189
Cooper, Leonard, Jr., 276
Cooper, Nicholas, 198, 202, 208 (2)
Cooper, Noah, 54
Cooper, Peter, 276
Cooper, Richard, 128, 244
Cooper, William P., 77
Cooxford, John, 302
Copeland, Amasa, 289, 293
Copeland, Axel H., 49
Copeland, Bois, 289, 293
Copeland, Charles, 49, 292 (2)
Copeland, Elias, Jr., 70
Copeland, Horatio, 95
Copeland, John, 28, 289
Copeland, Jonathan, 27, 49
Copeland, Joseph, 214, 286 (2)
Copeland, Joseph, Jr., 288
Copeland, Martin, 51, 60
Copeland, Moses, 39, 289, 293
Copeland, Nathaniel, 200, 201, 203
Copeland, Oliver, 292
Copeland, Royal, 189
Copeland, Rufus, 289
Copeland, Seth, 28
Copeland, William, 83, 104, 214
Copeton, Samuel, 9
Coops, William, 244
Corbett, Isaac M., 249
Corbett, John, 5
Corbett, Thomas, 28
Cordon, William, Jr., 310
Corey, Daniel, 147
Corinby, Miles, 302
Corkins, Ephraim, 268
Corliss, David, 223, 257
Corliss, Ebenezer, Jr., 212
Cormerais, John, 24
Cornell, Abner, 63
Cornell, James, 56
Cornell, Solomon, 56
Cornell, Thomas T., 56
Cornforth, Leonard, 264
Corning, Peter, 36, 37
Corning, Samuel, 88, 130
Cornish, Benjamin, 6
Cornish, Henry, 232

Cornish, Humphrey, 232
Cornish, William, 51, 214
Cornwell, Christopher, 56
Cornwell, John, 130
Corrin, Elijah, 46
Corrington, Jacob, 51
Corry, Ebenezer M., 242
Corry, George, 70
Corry, John, 149
Corsing, Richard, 130
Corson, John, 268, 306
Corson, Nahum, 306
Corson, William, 252, 255
Corthel, Robert, 209
Corthell, Theophilus, 103
Corthill, Isaiah, 101
Cory, Avory, 69
Cosset, Lothrop, 128
Cost, George, 36
Cost, Nash D., 1
Costelow, John, 188
Cotelle, John, 74
Cotes, James S., 21
Cothel, Hosea, 26
Cothern, John, 189
Cothern, Robert, 185
Cothran, William, 283
Cothrel, Robert, 208
Cothrell, Jonathan, 198
Cothrell, Robert, 198
Cotterill, Jonathan, 202
Cotterill, Robert, 202
Cottle, John, 179
Cottle, Lot, 227, 282
Cotton, Alex, 113 (2)
Cotton, Asa, 213
Cotton, Ebenezer, 249, 250
Cotton, Eliphalet, 201 (2)
Cotton, John S., 61
Cotton, Joseph, 165, 166, 173
Cotton, Levi, 299
Cotton, Preserved, 57
Cotton, Richard, 3
Cotton, Thomas J., 128
Cotton, William, 109, 153, 255
Cottrill, John, 146
Cottrill, Oliver, 30
Couch, Elijah, 274
Couch, George, 146
Couch, John, 20
Couch, Moses, 67
Couch, William, 18
Coudin, Saul, 291
Coudin, William, 291
Coulson, Jonathan J., 215
Courllard, Henry, 217
Courson, Isaac, 245
Cousens, Abraham, 155
Cousens, Jeremiah, 244
Cousens, Jesse, 217
Cousins, Alexander, 170
Cousins, Ebenezer, 281
Cousins, John, 303
Cousins, Joseph, 269
Cousins, Nathaniel, 303
Cously, Caleb C., 78
Coutman, Henry, 118
Covall, Joshua, 282
Covel, Benjamin B., 129
Covel, Caleb, 80
Covel, Charles, 129
Covel, Elisha, 32

Covell, Eli, 75
Covell, Israel, 226
Covell, Joel, 94
Covell, Solomon, 214
Coverly, Samuel, 84
Cowan, George, 214
Cowan, Isaac, Jr., 271
Cowan, Jacob, 214
Cowan, James, 267
Cowan, Jonathan, 214
Cowden, Samuel, 81
Cowell, Isaac, 244
Cowell, Saul, 140
Cowen, Job, 49
Cowen, Thomas, 237
Cowen, William, 55
Cowen, Zena, 55
Cowin, Charles, 30
Cowin, Isaac, 88
Cowing, Calvin, 155
Cowing, Cornelius, 69
Cowing, Daniel, 298
Cowing, David, 296
Cowing, David, Jr., 299
Cowing, Francis, 249, 250
Cowing, Isaac, 229
Cowing, Thomas, 233
Cowles, Enos, 4
Cowllard, Joseph, Jr., 247
Cown, Thomas, 265
Cox, Alexander, 193
Cox, Arthur, 193
Cox, Benjamin, 117, 118
Cox, Edward, 257
Cox, Ezra, 181
Cox, George, 272
Cox, Isaac, 297, 298
Cox, James, 6, 22, 285, 286 (2), 288, 298
Cox, John, 34, 37, 38, 159, 178, 203, 259, 287
Cox, Joseph, 134, 140
Cox, Nathaniel, 231
Cox, Samuel, 69
Cox, Thomas, 2
Cox, William, 192, 193
Coy, Cyrus, 252, 255
Coy, Henry, 175
Coy, Judson, 2
Coy, Nathan, 282
Cozens, Nathaniel, 238
Crabbe, Austin, 62
Crabtree, Agreen, 219
Crabtree, David, 203
Crabtree, Eleazer, 219
Crabtree, Samuel, 201, 203
Crabtree, Saul, 200
Crafts, David, 192
Crafts, Moses, 177
Crafts, Moses M., 223
Crafts, Samuel, Jr., 175
Crafts, Thomas, 64
Crafts, Zibeon, 177
Crague, Ezekiel, 210
Crague, James, 211
Crague, John, Jr., 211
Crague, Josiah, 211
Craig, Elias, Jr., 279, 281
Craig, Enoch, Jr., 283
Craig, Freeman, 263, 266
Craig, George, 162
Craig, John O., 278, 281
Craig, Peter, 278

INDEX. 341

Craige, George, 213
Crain, Samuel, 264
Cram, Daniel, 152, 171, 271
Cram, James, 181
Cram, John, 13, 153
Cram, Stephen, 271
Cram, Varnum, 226
Cram, Wear, 174
Cram, William, 272
Crandall, Caleb, 77
Crandall, John, 138, 141
Crandall, Soltner, 268
Crane, Abijah, 182 (2), 184, 186
Crane, Allen, 217
Crane, Ashabel, 174
Crane, Boyne, 201 (2), 203
Crane, Daniel, 261
Crane, Elisha C., 117
Crane, George, 27
Crane, James, 181
Crane, Jesse, 39
Crane, John, 261
Crane, John, 2d, 146
Crane, Joseph, 184, 186 (2), 190
Crane, Joshua, 28, 111
Crane, Lazra, 28
Crane, Levi G., 62
Crane, Nathan, 80, 83, 110
Crane, Obediah, 280
Crane, Reuben, 278
Crane, Richard, 42, 89
Crane, Robert, 161
Crane, Shadrack, 280
Crane, Silas, 92
Crane, William, 29, 70, 289
Crapo, Briggs, 52, 130 (2)
Crapo, William, 130
Craps, Abel, 55
Craps, Asa, 55
Craps, Briggs, 52
Craps, Reuben, 56
Crasbury, Samuel B., 118
Craw, John, 126
Crawford, Alexander, 292 (2)
Crawford, Archibald, 292 (2)
Crawford, Benjamin T., 280, 304
Crawford, Charles, 299
Crawford, James, 289, 293
Crawford, John, 273
Crawford, John, Jr., 209
Crawford, Joseph, 292 (2), 312
Crawford, Lawrence, 156, 159
Crawford, Malcom, 292
Crawford, Malcomb, 292
Crawford, Robert, 273
Crawford, William, 93, 220, 292 (2)
Crea, John, 303
Creasey, John, 2d, 35
Creasey, Jonathan, 2d, 35
Creasy, Benjamin, 2d, 35
Creasy, James, 34, 38
Creasy, John, 35, 173
Creasy, Jonathan, 2d, 35 (2)
Creasy, Jonathan, 3d, 35
Creesy, Joseph, Jr., 173
Creesy, Noah, 38
Crehone, Elisha, Jr., 99
Crehore, Lewis, 40
Crehore, Timothy, 93
Creighton, James, 292 (2)
Creighton, John, 285, 286, 288
Cremer, Edward, 109

Cresey, John, 219
Cresey, Michel, 16
Cressey, John, 64
Cressey, Samuel, 120, 121
Cresy, Samuel, 122
Cresy, Samuel, 124
Crichet, Nathaniel, 2
Cripps, John, 298
Crisam, James, 250
Crispin, William, 140
Crocker, Abiather, 74
Crocker, Abner, Jr., 74
Crocker, Alexander, 72
Crocker, Alvin, Jr., 74
Crocker, Arthur, 74
Crocker, Asa, 24, 131
Crocker, Avery, 276
Crocker, Barnabas, 74
Crocker, Barret, 276
Crocker, Benjamin, 185
Crocker, Bethuel, 74
Crocker, Calvin, 74
Crocker, Canaan, 56
Crocker, Charles, 260
Crocker, Cornelius, 131
Crocker, David, 74, 301
Crocker, David, 2d, 74
Crocker, Ebenezer, 50
Crocker, Enoch, 74
Crocker, Ezra, 74
Crocker, George, 62, 73, 74, 76
Crocker, Hamlin, 74
Crocker, Heman, 74
Crocker, Henry, 72
Crocker, Isaac, 74
Crocker, James, 85, 149, 207, 280
Crocker, James, 39, 73 (2), 243
Crocker, Joseph, 3d, 74
Crotker, Josiah, Jr., 74
Crocker, Lemuel, 74
Crocker, Loring, 131
Crocker, Moses, 74
Crocker, Nimphus, 74
Crocker, Prince, 74
Crocker, Robert, 81
Crocker, Rodney, 30
Crocker, Rufus, 74, 125
Crocker, Samuel, 226
Crocker, Thacker, 74
Crocker, Thomas, 207, 255
Crocker, Waldron, 235
Crocker, Warren, 278, 281
Crocker, Watson, 74
Crocker, Zacheus, 74 (2)
Crocker, Zenas, 74
Crocket, John, 234
Crocket, Joseph, 211
Crocket, Mark, 211
Crockett, Andrew, 173
Crockett, Asa, 197, 203, 204
Crockett, David, 205, 256
Crockett, David, Jr., 204, 206
Crockett, Ephraim, 252
Crockett, Henry, 165, 166, 174
Crockett, John, 244, 259
Crockett, John, Jr., 171
Crockett, Joseph, 178, 243
Crockett, Joshua, 253
Crockett, Knot, 200, 204
Crockett, Lewis, 252
Crockett, Nathaniel, 173
Crockett, Oliver, 204, 205

Crockett, Richard, 168, 225, 246, 312
Crockett, Robert, 200, 204
Crockett, Samuel, 158, 178, 252
Crockett, Silas, 172
Crockett, Thomas, 204, 205
Crockett, William, 160
Crofts, John, 83
Cromer, Charles, 289
Cromer, Cornelius, 289
Crompton, George, 268
Cromwell, Moses, 191
Cromwell, Oliver, 308
Crooker, Alden, 176
Crooker, Comfort, 176
Crooker, Francis, 183
Crooker, Hatch, 186
Crooker, Isaac, 159
Crooker, Isaac, 3d, 177
Crooker, Joseph, 159
Crooker, Noah, 247
Crooker, Philip, 287
Crooker, Robert, 249, 297
Crooker, Samuel D., 248
Crooker, Thomas, 252
Crooker, William, 176, 249
Crops, John, 5
Crosby, Abel, 104
Crosby, Abial, 105 (2)
Crosby, Ebenezer, 148
Crosby, Edmund, 106 (2), 107 (2), 108
Crosby, Ephraim G., 198, 199, 200, 208
Crosby, Harvey, 41
Crosby, Isaac, 85
Crosby, James, 215, 236
Crosby, Joel, 236
Crosby, John, 42, 65, 89
Crosby, Joseph, 104, 105 (2)
Crosby, Joshua, 43, 105 (2), 106, 107
Crosby, Jotham, 248
Crosby, Logan, 46
Crosby, Manson, 265
Crosby, Nathaniel, 104, 105, 263
Crosby, Obed, 104, 105
Crosby, Theophilus, 67
Crosby, William, 236, 265
Crosier, Andrew, 33
Crosier, Jason, 33
Cross, Aaron, 132, 136, 153
Cross, Amos H., 241, 242
Cross, Charles, 137
Cross, Ebenezer, Jr., 257
Cross, George, 241
Cross, Heaton, 18
Cross, Hector, 120, 123
Cross, Henry, 132
Cross, Isaac, 133, 136
Cross, Jesse, 250
Cross, John, 5, 26
Cross, Joseph, 136, 141
Cross, Joshua, 137
Cross, Josiah, 302
Cross, Leonard, 241, 242
Cross, Lyman, 44
Cross, Nathaniel, 240
Cross, Nathaniel, Jr., 242
Cross, Ralph, 17
Cross, Saul, 137, 240
Cross, William, 141, 146, 240
Crossman, Abner, 40
Crossman, Benjamin, 39
Crossman, Daniel, 66
Crossman, Ebenezer S., 60

342 INDEX.

Crossman, Elisha, 9, 10
Crossman, John O., 59
Crossman, Rufus, 62
Crossman, William, 59
Crossman, William H., 59
Croswell, James, 61
Croswell, Thomas, 308
Crouch, Daniel, 8
Crouch, Elwin, 75
Crouch, Levi, 8
Crowel, Michael, 179
Crowell, Adinah, 72
Crowell, Ariel, 90
Crowell, Arnold, 275
Crowell, Asa, 179
Crowell, Benjamin, 72, 272
Crowell, Daniel, 237
Crowell, David, 108, 135, 137, 237, 267
Crowell, Ebenezer, Jr., 67
Crowell, Elbridge, 237
Crowell, Elisha, 272
Crowell, Hiram, 264
Crowell, Isaiah, 264
Crowell, Jabez, 265
Crowell, Jabish, 237
Crowell, John, 297, 299
Crowell, John, Jr., 237
Crowell, Miller, 264
Crowell, Samuel, 13, 14
Crowell, Seth, 264, 267
Crowell, William, 72, 215
Crowley, Jacob, 54
Crowley, Jeremiah, 233
Crowninshield, Benjamin, 140
Crowninshield, Benjamin W., 136
Cruff, William, 6
Crumbell, Moses, 189
Crumbell, Simeon, 189
Crumbie, David G., 307
Crumby, Benjamin, 36
Crumby, John, 36
Crummet, John, 237
Crummet, Saul, 274
Crumton, George, 304
Cruse, John, 68
Cudworth, Benjamin, 130
Cudworth, Elijah, 128
Cudworth, Israel, 103
Cudworth, John D., 57
Cudworth, William, 129
Culvert, Richard, 271
Cumings, Samuel S., 148
Cumins, David, 290
Cummer, John, 280
Cummings, Aaron, 257
Cummings, Alexander, 27
Cummings, Asa, 47, 308
Cummings, Daniel, 251
Cummings, Daniel, Jr., 251
Cummings, Francis, 257
Cummings, George, 57
Cummings, George W., 251
Cummings, Isaac, 225
Cummings, James, 20, 227
Cummings, John, 55, 174, 250, 259
Cummings, Joseph, 210, 263, 266
Cummings, Luther, 27, 114
Cummings, Moses, 252
Cummings, Oliver, Jr., 178
Cummings, Philip, 286
Cummings, Samuel, 24, 262, 263
Cummings, Samuel S., 235

Cummings, Simeon, 174, 250
Cummings, Thomas, 85, 109, 191
Cummings, William, 57, 219, 225
Cummins, Ebenezer, 168
Cummins, Howard, 61
Cummins, Jacob, 231
Cummins, James, 52
Cummins, John, 168, 312
Cummins, Lloyd, 60
Cummins, Oliver, 259
Cummins, Samuel, 312
Cunningham, Alexander, 186, 189
Cunningham, Asa, 180
Cunningham, Benjamin, 301
Cunningham, Charles, 111, 186, 189
Cunningham, Daniel, 196
Cunningham, Ebenezer, 304
Cunningham, Henry, 83, 189
Cunningham, Isaac, 189
Cunningham, Jacob, 301
Cunningham, James, 83, 302
Cunningham, Jesse, 55, 57
Cunningham, John, 180
Cunningham, John, Jr., 11
Cunningham, Mark, 273
Cunningham, Rufus, 183, 185, 191
Cunningham, Samuel, 180, 189
Cunningham, Saul, 189
Cunningham, Simon, 180
Cunningham, Thomas, 70, 78, 184, 189, 300
Cunningham, Timothy, 180
Cunningham, William, 183 (2), 185, 186, 188, 196, 301
Currier, Adoniram, 11
Currier, Benaiah, 8
Currier, Benjamin, 176, 260
Currier, Daniel, 36
Currier, David, 8
Currier, Edmund, 230, 309 (2)
Currier, Edward, 20, 121 (2), 123, 124
Currier, Ephraim, 1st, 306
Currier, Ephraim, 2d, 306
Currier, James S., 287
Currier, John, 277, 280
Currier, Jonathan, 118
Currier, Jonathan, Jr., 277
Currier, Joseph, 187, 190
Currier, Joseph H., 18
Currier, Matthew, 123
Currier, Matthew, Jr., 20
Currier, Morrel, 274
Currier, Nathaniel, 310
Currier, Nathaniel, Jr., 123
Currier, Phineas, 306
Currier, Samuel, 18, 45, 276
Currier, William, 185, 284
Currill, David, 211
Currin, Isaac, 159
Currin, Jabin, 4
Curry, Cadwalder, 242
Curry, Edward, 241
Curry, Zenas, 64
Curtis, Aaron, 94
Curtis, Abel, 233
Curtis, Abiezer, 298
Curtis, Abner, 168
Curtis, Alfred, 111
Curtis, Ashley, Jr., 175
Curtis, Barnabas, 32
Curtis, Barstow, 234
Curtis, Benjamin, 13, 14, 70, 80, 86, 304
Curtis, Calvin, 198, 199, 202, 298

Curtis, Charles, 68 (2), 181, 251, 255
Curtis, Chauncey, 31
Curtis, David, 26, 215, 299
Curtis, Ebenezer, 299
Curtis, Edmund, 1
Curtis, Edward, 3, 103
Curtis, Gershom, 167
Curtis, Gideon, 233
Curtis, James, 162, 193, 196, 202, 208 (2), 209, 216, 297, 299, 301, 306
Curtis, James, Jr., 216
Curtis, Jay, 32
Curtis, Jesse, 6, 22
Curtis, Job, 1, 104
Curtis, John, 1, 9, 39, 60, 61, 80, 103, 216, 299, 304, 311
Curtis, Joseph, 304
Curtis, Joshua, 43, 298, 312
Curtis, Lebbeus, 5
Curtis, Lemuel, 1, 104, 215
Curtis, Leonard, 31
Curtis, Levi, 1, 103, 127, 234
Curtis, Libeus, 168
Curtis, Lincoln, 168
Curtis, Luther, 1, 104
Curtis, Melzer, 298
Curtis, Morton, 251
Curtis, Moses, 304
Curtis, Nahum, 95
Curtis, Nathaniel, 1, 24, 103, 136
Curtis, Nehemiah, 21
Curtis, Noah, Jr., 251
Curtis, Obadiah, 233
Curtis, Paul, Jr., 299
Curtis, Peleg, 299
Curtis, Peter, 193
Curtis, Philip, 78, 108
Curtis, Phineas E., 304
Curtis, Reuben, Jr., 103
Curtis, Robert, 1, 103, 167
Curtis, Robert H., 6
Curtis, Rufus, 9, 101, 193
Curtis, Samuel, 30, 68, 70, 76, 128, 130, 192, 209, 215
Curtis, Seth, 103, 251
Curtis, Shadrach B., 103
Curtis, Simeon, 215, 299
Curtis, Stephen, 1, 209, 265
Curtis, Thaddeus, 88, 98
Curtis, Theodore, 209
Curtis, Theophilus, 70
Curtis, Thomas S., 29
Curtis, William, 13, 95, 104 (2), 165, 193, 298, 301
Curtis, William B., 168, 281
Curtis, William T., 113, 114
Curtis, Wright, 98
Curtiss, Elijah S., 27
Curwen, Samuel, 98
Cushin, James, 295
Cushin, Quincy, 295
Cushing, Abner, 86
Cushing, Adam, 42, 101
Cushing, Allen, 42
Cushing, Bela, 108
Cushing, Benjamin, 128, 130
Cushing, Brackly, 92
Cushing, Caleb, 140
Cushing, David, 2, 102
Cushing, David L., 39
Cushing, Eleazer, 40
Cushing, Ensign, 42

Cushing, George, 82
Cushing, Harvey, 89
Cushing, Henry, 83
Cushing, James, 248 (2)
Cushing, John, 42, 65, 84, 92, 101, 102, 134, 140, 233
Cushing, John, 2d, 42, 101
Cushing, John M., 311
Cushing, Joseph, 6, 22, 243
Cushing, Laban, 93
Cushing, Leavitt, 78
Cushing, Levi L., 80, 84
Cushing, Loammi, 153
Cushing, Loring, 98, 248
Cushing, Martin, 80, 85, 169
Cushing, Nathaniel, 130
Cushing, Quincy, 297
Cushing, Rufus, 209
Cushing, Samuel, 81, 82
Cushing, Seth, Jr., 128
Cushing, Stephen, 23
Cushing, Thomas, 33, 248
Cushing, Thomas, 2d, 102
Cushing, Thomas, 3d, 102
Cushing, William, 80
Cushing, Ziba, 102
Cushman, Abel, 291
Cushman, Alexander, 79
Cushman, Andrew, 155, 167, 253, 257
Cushman, Andrew, Jr., 277
Cushman, Artemas, 167
Cushman, Bartholomew, 250
Cushman, Caleb, 251
Cushman, Daniel, 128
Cushman, Ebeneser, 146
Cushman, Elkanah, 129
Cushman, Ezra, 289, 293
Cushman, George, 51, 103
Cushman, Gideon, Jr., 175
Cushman, Heman, 129
Cushman, Isaac, 58, 233, 260
Cushman, Isaac, Jr., 175
Cushman, Isaac, 3d, 102
Cushman, Jabez, 213
Cushman, James, 103
Cushman, John, 257
Cushman, Kenelam, 182
Cushman, Kineland, 182
Cushman, Levi, 178, 259
Cushman, Lewis, 233
Cushman, Nathaniel, 175
Cushman, Obed, 127
Cushman, Reuben, 175
Cushman, Richard, 53
Cushman, Robert, 129
Cushman, Samuel, 53
Cushman, Saul, 209
Cushman, Seneca, 289
Cushman, Simeon M., 46
Cushman, Thomas, 181
Cushman, Wendam, 184
Cushman, Zebedee, Jr., 253, 257
Cushman, Zenas, 2d, 103
Cusick, Henry, 33
Cutler, Abner, 204, 205, 206
Cutler, Amos, 26, 79, 86
Cutler, Artemus, 101
Cutler, Ezra, 26, 79
Cutler, Isaac, 48
Cutler, James, 23, 26
Cutler, John, 26
Cutler, Leonard, 41

Cutler, Liberty, 8
Cutler, Lyman, 47
Cutler, Nahum, 70
Cutler, Nathan, 280
Cutler, Pliny, 81
Cutler, Richard, 101
Cutler, Solomon, 6
Cutler, William, 26
Cutter, Benjamin, 90
Cutter, Eber, 46
Cutter, Ezekiel, 182
Cutter, James, 101
Cutter, Leonard, 7
Cutter, Levi, 101
Cutter, Oliver, 69, 79
Cutter, Samuel, 24, 114
Cutter, Simon, 219
Cutter, Solomon, 6
Cutting, Cyprian, 46
Cutting, John, 286
Cutting, Lewis, 7
Cutting, Samuel, 82
Cutting, William, 101
Cuttings, Mark, 88
Cutts, Oliver, 245
Cutts, Samuel, 271

D

Dade, Isaac, 11
Dadman, William, 29
Dadman, William, 2d, 29
Dadmun, Willard, 8
Dagget, Daniel D., 176
Dagget, Samuel, 290
Dagget, Thomas, 301
Dagget, William, 286, 290
Daggett, Aaron, 168
Daggett, Benjamin, 61
Daggett, Carlos, 88
Daggett, Edmund, 286
Daggett, Elihu, 54
Daggett, Frederick, 287
Daggett, Henry, 265, 286, 290
Daggett, James, 180
Daggett, John, 2d, 60
Daggett, Levi, 60
Daggett, Plemington, 280
Daggett, Saul, 286
Daggett, Timothy, 60
Daggett, William, 283
Dailey, Joseph, 99
Dailey, Noah, 67
Dailey, Silas, 298
Daily, Cornwell, 31
Daily, Joseph, 65
Daily, Warren, 222
Daily, William, 31
Dain, Ebenezer, 233
Dain, William, Jr., 233
Dains, Jacob, 312
Dakin, Shearabiah, 226
Daland, Benjamin, 137
Daland, John, 133, 136
Dale, Moses, 269
Daley, Daniel, 223
Dalie, Amos, 302
Dallas, Stephen, 215
Dally, Daniel, 259
Dalrymple, James, 29
Dalrymple, William, 8
Dalton, Eleaser, 139
Dalton, James, 7, 110

Dalton, Jesse, 145
Dalton, John, 82
Dalton, Joseph, 132 (2), 133
Dalton, William A., 234
Damaron, Joshua, 264
Damaron, Samuel, 264
Dame, Abraham, 70
Dame, Nathan, 77
Damerell, Samuel S., 39
Damerin, Samuel, 246
Dammen, Nisbet, 169
Dammon, Jonathan, 255
Damon, Abel, 46
Damon, Abiah, 127
Damon, Elijah, 103
Damon, Ezra, 100
Damon, Gale, 103
Damon, George, 47
Damon, Israel, 285, 287
Damon, James, 104
Damon, Jonathan, Jr., 251
Damon, Joseph, 1, 251
Damon, Joshua, 285, 287
Damon, Piam, 1
Damon, Priam, 104
Damon, Samuel, 3, 116
Damon, Samuel H., 118
Damond, Josiah, 39
Damoth, Jacob, 289
Dana, Elisha, 9
Dana, George, 7, 112, 113
Dana, Joseph, 47
Dana, Luther, 241, 242
Dana, Richard, 146
Dana, Thomas, 146
Dana, William J., 25
Dane, Asa, 285, 287
Dane, Levi, 306
Dane, Nathan, 69, 91
Danford, Enock, 122
Danford, Jeremiah, 36
Danford, Moses, 228
Danford, William, 36
Danforth, Asa, 10
Danforth, Charles, 126
Danforth, Enoch, 119, 299
Danforth, Isaac, 84, 88, 148, 235
Danforth, John, 116
Danforth, Josiah, 180
Danforth, Nathaniel, 54, 180
Danforth, Stephen, 180
Dangy, Martin, 44
Daniel, John, 122
Daniel, Joseph G., 8
Daniel, Libeus, 5
Daniels, Amos, 98
Daniels, David, 262
Daniels, Elbridge G., 98
Daniels, Isaac, 42
Daniels, James, 146
Daniels, Jeremiah, 85
Daniels, Joel, Jr., 86
Daniels, Joseph, 146
Daniels, Moses, 35
Daniels, Moses, Jr., 98
Daniels, Nathaniel, 80, 109
Daniels, Riley, 98
Daniels, Simeon, 252
Daniels, Smith, 98
Danielson, Otis S., 244
Danks, Eliakim, 44
Danks, Ruel, 46

344 INDEX.

Dannel, Jonathan, 188
Darby, Evander, 46
Darland, John, 8
Darley, Erastus, 44
Darlin, Michel C., 141
Darling, Benjamin, 32, 113, 114
Darling, Darius, 103
Darling, David, 88
Darling, Edmund, 270
Darling, Elakin, 25
Darling, George L., 173
Darling, John, 47, 79, 82, 110
Darling, Joseph, 78, 83
Darling, Newton, 98
Darling, Samuel, 68
Darling, William, 45
Darling, Zelick, 47
Darr, Ebenezer, 224
Darr, Ebenezer, Jr., 224
Darra, Lewis, 60
Darracott, George, 113 (2)
Dart, Elijah, 31
Dary, Allen, 10
Dary, Jesse, 198
Dascomb, Thomas, 70
Dascomb, Thomas R., 111
Dasy, Daniel, 251
Dauble, Elijah, 257
Davee, William, 128
Davenport, Anthony, 125
Davenport, Benjamin, 247, 270
Davenport, Charles, 19
Davenport, Daniel, 47
Davenport, Darius, 225
Davenport, Elijah, 277
Davenport, Francis, 39
Davenport, Isaac, 82
Davenport, Israel, 80
Davenport, Noah, 223
Davenport, Thomas, 132, 140
Davenport, William, 18, 120, 123
Davenson, Peter, 87
David, James, 39
David, John, 113 (2)
David, Joseph, 307
David, William, 249
Davids, John, 119
Davidson, John, 69, 111 (3)
Davidson, Thomas, 101
Davidson, William, 196
Davis, Aaron, 45, 301
Davis, Aaron, Jr., 251
Davis, Aaron A., 275
Davis, Abel, 5, 43, 48
Davis, Amasa, 312
Davis, Amos, 44, 79, 159
Davis, Asa, 237
Davis, Barney, 61 (2)
Davis, Barzilla, 131
Davis, Benesley, 91
Davis, Benjamin, 175, 211, 213, 225, 256, 267, 285, 288, 291, 310
Davis, Charles, 18, 86, 119, 122, 123 (2), 262
Davis, Charles S., 266
Davis, Christopher, 63
Davis, Christopher S., 220
Davis, Cornelius, 304
Davis, Daniel, 12, 172, 180 (2), 244, 283
Davis, Daniel G., 77
Davis, David, 61, 139 (2)
Davis, Ebenezer, 70, 79, 100
Davis, Edward, 149, 220

Davis, Edward S., 131
Davis, Eleazer, 302
Davis, Elias, 82, 179 (2), 210
Davis, Elias, Jr., 12
Davis, Ephraim, 153
Davis, Ethan, 79
Davis, Ezra, 162, 163
Davis, Ezra, 3d, 155, 312
Davis, Francis, 288, 294 (2)
Davis, Francis, Jr., 75
Davis, Francis, 2d, 288
Davis, Francis H., 12
Davis, Frederic, 79
Davis, Frederick, 68, 221
Davis, Gardner, 291
Davis, George, 12, 94, 131, 154, 288
Davis, George W., 63
Davis, Gideon, 211, 213
Davis, Heald, 184
Davis, Henry, 80, 84
Davis, Humphrey, 63
Davis, Isaac, 150, 174, 177
Davis, Isaac D., 111
Davis, Isaiah, Jr., 72
Davis, Israel, 154, 181, 289, 293
Davis, Jabez, 31
Davis, Jacob, 175, 272
Davis, James, 15, 55, 87, 193, 196, 221, 228, 229, 231, 305
Davis, James D., 111
Davis, James W., 218
Davis, Job, 72
Davis, John, 12, 13, 34, 37, 45, 60, 61, 90, 98, 118, 134, 138, 139 (2), 148, 161, 169, 210, 255, 261, 272, 275, 277, 280
Davis, John, Jr., 75, 131, 246, 312
Davis, John, 2d, 16
Davis, John H., 12
Davis, Jonathan, 233, 276, 280, 307
Davis, Jonathan B., 100
Davis, Joseph, 60, 63, 131, 159, 213, 217, 257, 263, 310
Davis, Joseph, 3d, 72
Davis, Joseph G., 111
Davis, Joseph H., 176
Davis, Joseph W., 85, 295
Davis, Joshua, 115, 181
Davis, Joshua, Jr., 88
Davis, Josiah, 171, 210
Davis, Lane, 210, 260
Davis, Lanson, 116
Davis, Levi, 47
Davis, Lewis B., 69, 78
Davis, Luther, 47, 76, 100, 173
Davis, Malorhia, Jr., 72
Davis, Miah, 299
Davis, Moses, 256, 269
Davis, Nathaniel, 56, 67, 75, 76, 171
Davis, Nicholas, 193
Davis, Noah, 75, 76, 174
Davis, Nymphus, 131
Davis, Oliver, 16, 48
Davis, Osman, 293
Davis, Patrick, 249, 250
Davis, Paul, 57
Davis, Peter, 21, 48
Davis, Philip, 63
Davis, Phineas, 302
Davis, Pruel, Jr., 307
Davis, Reuben, 79
Davis, Richard, 16, 138, 288
Davis, Robert, 225, 266, 284, 288, 291

Davis, Robert, 2d, 291
Davis, Robert S., 39
Davis, Rodney, 45
Davis, Samuel, 25, 39, 72, 175, 225, 238, 252
Davis, Saul, 15, 149, 209, 231
Davis, Simeon, 175, 221
Davis, Solomon, 6, 175
Davis, Stephen, 73, 176, 257
Davis, Thomas, 13, 20, 22, 26, 72, 76, 85, 198, 223, 259, 278, 291
Davis, Thomas, 3d, 75
Davis, Thomas H., 5
Davis, Timothy, 28, 118, 213
Davis, Timothy R., 12
Davis, Walter, 72, 267, 310
Davis, William, 18, 30, 76, 77, 80, 90, 111, 117, 120, 123, 134, 136, 140, 145, 149, 151, 169, 176, 193, 199, 200, 203, 213, 226, 250, 256, 295
Davis, William N., 28 (2), 77
Davis, William P., 241, 242
Davis, Zebedee, 56
Davis, Zebulon R., 10
Davis, Zimri, 115
Davison, James G., 215
Davison, John, 109, 115, 270
Davison, Pliney, 14
Davol, Allen, 56
Davol, Benjamin, 56
Davol, Davis, 56
Davol, Gideon, 63
Davol, Joseph, 63
Davol, Pardon, 63
Davol, Peter, 56
Davy, Solomon, 260
Davy, Thomas, 151
Dawbin, James, 255
Dawbin, William, 255
Dawes, Bela, 225, 258
Dawes, Harrison, 84
Dawsett, John, 242
Day, Abraham, 241
Day, Alexander, 251
Day, Alfred, 44
Day, Alpheus, 195
Day, Benjamin, 262
Day, Daniel, 158, 192, 308
Day, David, 21, 48
Day, Dependence, 244
Day, Eben, 195
Day, Ebenezer, 244
Day, Eli, 67
Day, Eliheu, 180
Day, Elijah, 192, 195
Day, Ezekiel, 244
Day, Francis, 158
Day, George, 176, 257
Day, Henry, 169, 244
Day, Henry, 2d, 244
Day, Horace, 44
Day, Hosea, 44
Day, Jabez, 152
Day, Jabez C., 254
Day, Jacob, 45, 167, 282
Day, James, 95, 109, 244
Day, Jeremiah, Jr., 97
Day, Joel, 44
Day, John, 95
Day, Jonathan, 269
Day, Jonathan F., 228
Day, Josiah, 97

INDEX. 345

Day, Levi, 271
Day, Moses, 162, 164, 273
Day, Nathaniel, 90, 273
Day, Porter, 43
Day, Robert, 192, 244
Day, Samuel, 66, 152
Day, Spencer, 4
Day, Stephen P., 101
Day, Thomas, 163, 164
Day, William, 11, 168, 195, 244, 281
Day, William A., 168
Deacons, Jonathan, 6
Deadman, William, 96
Dean, Abial F., 62
Dean, Abijah, 54
Dean, Abraham, 253
Dean, Allen, 61
Dean, Alonzo, 73, 76
Dean, Barnard, 54
Dean, Barsilla, 10
Dean, Benjamin, 62, 203, 204, 206
Dean, Benjamin, Jr., 57
Dean, Chandler, 59
Dean, Charles, 53
Dean, Cornelius, 59
Dean, D. E., 209
Dean, Ebenezer, 57, 268
Dean, Edmund, 251, 255
Dean, Eliah, 59
Dean, Enos, 9, 10
Dean, Faxon, 110
Dean, George, Jr., 132
Dean, Gilbert, 59
Dean, Gulliver, 60
Dean, Henry C., 253
Dean, Isaiah, 214, 253
Dean, Israel, 206
Dean, Jesse S., 214
Dean, Job, 59
Dean, Joel W., 59
Dean, John, 57, 302
Dean, John, Jr., 179
Dean, John, 2d, 57
Dean, John G., 162
Dean, Jonas, 206
Dean, Jonathan, 62
Dean, King, 57
Dean, Lemuel, 87
Dean, Linus, 59, 61
Dean, Monroe, 73
Dean, Nathan, 10, 303
Dean, Obadiah, 162
Dean, Robert, 162
Dean, Samuel, 81, 202
Dean, Saul, 208
Dean, Simeon, 39, 54
Dean, Thaddeus, 84
Dean, Thomas, 38, 41, 77, 134, 135, 224, 302
Dean, Timothy, 86
Dean, Trueman, 214
Dean, William, 30, 60, 162, 200, 203, 204
Dean, William I., 60
Dean, William S., 60
Dean, Zebulon, 167
Deane, Asa, 62, 146
Deane, Daniel, 62
Deane, Edward, 90
Deane, Joseph, 62
Deane, Samuel, 62
Dearborn, Asa, 240, 265
Dearborn, Benjamin, 225, 272

Dearborn, David, 169
Dearborn, Dudly, 277
Dearborn, Ebenezer S., 170
Dearborn, Edward, 80
Dearborn, Frederic W., 169
Dearborn, Jacob, 162
Dearborn, John, 234, 235, 240, 246
Dearborn, John M., 113 (2), 114
Dearborn, Josiah, 170, 246
Dearborn, Math, 68
Dearborn, Richard, 83
Dearborn, Samuel, 83
Dearing, John, 180
Dearing, John, Jr., 171
Dearing, Samuel, 234
Dearing, Saul, 212
Dearing, William, 180
Debble, Sylvanus, 30
Deblois, James, 115
Decker, Abraham, Jr., 183, 188
Decker, Amos, 238
Decker, David, 258
Decker, Ebenezer, 183, 184, 188
Decker, Isaac, 184, 186 (2), 187, 190
Decker, Israel, 184
Decker, James, 183, 188
Decker, John, 183, 185, 186, 188, 190
Decker, John, Jr., 174
Decker, John M., 186, 187, 190
Decker, Joseph, 196
Decker, Joshua, Jr., 238
Decker, Spencer, Jr., 189
Decker, Stephen, 261, 266
Decker, Thomas, Jr., 183, 185, 186, 188
Decker, Thomas, 3d, 188
Decker, William, 185, 263, 277
DeCoster, Chandler, 225, 259
DeCoster, Jacob, 175
Decoster, James, 68, 79
Decoster, Samuel, 175
DeCoster, Roger, 175
DeCoster, Thomas, 178
Decrow, Israel, 303
Decrow, John, 303
Decrow, John, Jr., 303
Dedman, Jeduthan, 39
Deering, James, 151
Deering, John, 246, 257
Deering, Joshua L., 158
Deering, Robert, 251
DeForest, Sydney, 70
Degno, John, 243
Deland, Abial, 259
Deland, Ezekiel, 243
Deland, Jonathan T., 135
Deland, Joseph, 94
Deland, Robert, 140
Deland, William, 259
Delands, David, 116
Delano, Abel, 224
Delano, Albert, 249
Delano, Benjamin, 212
Delano, Bradford, 249
Delano, Calvin, 224
Delano, Ebenezer, 55, 57, 221, 249
Delano, Ephriam, 55, 57
Delano, Ezekiel, 252, 255
Delano, Henry, 55, 57, 127
Delano, John, 50, 58
Delano, John C., 249
Delano, John R., 94

Delano, Joseph, 55, 57, 127
Delano, Joshua, 249, 297
Delano, Leonard, 224
Delano, Nathaniel, 221
Delano, Peleg, 249
Delano, Reuben, 55, 57
Delano, Richard, 58
Delano, Rufus, 225
Delano, Samuel, 259
Delano, Seth, Jr., 150
Delano, Warren, 55, 57
Delano, William, 131, 224
Delant, Ezekiel, 212
Delesdernier, John, 311
Delesdernier, William, 311
Delesderwin, William, 161
Delesdiner, Lewis F., Jr., 160
Dellawey, Samuel, 26
Dellingham, Thomas R., 209
Dellof, David, 306
Delly, Joseph E., 211
Demares, John, 122
Demars (?), John, 119
Demerit, Ebenezer, 181
Deming, John E., 78
Demmean, Louis, 64
Demmean, Zeneas, 64
Demmick, Lot, 76
Demming, John, 30
Demming, Jonathan E., 68
Demmings, Gordon, 55
Demnicn, Nathan, 64
Demon, Jeremiah, 94
Demon, Samuel, Jr., 46
Demoranois, Phineas, 33
Demoransville, Josiah, 56
Dempsey, William, 34
Demuth, Charles, 292
Demuth, John, 292
Demuth, Philip, 292
Denerson, Solomon, 233
Deniston, Joseph, 276
Dennat, Samuel, 234
Dennen, Samuel, 13, 14
Dennet, Charles, 16
Dennet, John, 146, 150
Dennet, Joseph, 220
Dennett, Martin, 292
Dennett, Reuben, 245
Dennett, Samuel, 174
Dennett, Samuel G., 269
Dennett, William, 148
Dennie, Thomas, 110
Dennin, Job, 11
Dennin, Peter, 213
Dennin, Samuel, 256
Denning, Thomas, 112
Dennis, Amos, 20
Dennis, Amos, Jr., 179
Dennis, Archibald S., 6
Dennis, Benjamin, 180
Dennis, David, Jr., 195
Dennis, Erasmus, 6
Dennis, Foster S., 84
Dennis, John, 22, 273
Dennis, Jonas, 6
Dennis, Peleg, 56
Dennis, Thomas, 7, 14, 146
Dennis, William, 12, 128
Dennison, Abner, 225
Dennison, Ammi, 212
Dennison, Andrew, 225

INDEX.

Dennison, Caleb, 209
Dennison, David, 12
Dennison, Isaac, Jr., 12
Dennison, James, 13
Dennison, John, 66, 209
Dennison, Jonah, 14
Dennison, Nathan, 66
Dennison, Simeon, 256
Dennison, William, Jr., 120
Denny, Daniel, 91
Densmore, Ephraim, 186, 188
Densmore, Thomas, 284
Densmorr, Asa, 194
Denton, John, 114
Denton, William, 24
Deny, Morgan, 45
Derby, Andrew, 303
Derby, George, 60, 135
Derby, James, 135
Derby, Martin, 42
Derby, Richard, 132
Derby, Samuel B., 132
Derham, Joseph, 269
Deriggs, Marvel, 75
Derrick, Thomas F., 38
Derry, Jesse, 202
Detson, William, 71
Deven, Francis, 209
Devenport, Anthony, 122
Devenport, Isaac, 5
Devenport, Nathaniel, 146
Devens, John, 23
Deverall, Samuel, 24, 41
Deveraux, Humphrey, 139
Deveraux, Thomas, 137
Devereaux, Elisha S., 6, 22
Devereaux, Humphrey, 141
Devereux, Benjamin, 6
Deveroux, Thomas, 136
Devett, Medad, 65
Dewey, Charles, 43
Dewey, Henry, 31
Dewey, Paul, 46
Dewey, Ralph, 46
Dewey, William, 70
Dewing, Cheney, 91
Dewing, Elijah, 96
Dewing, Ephraim, 91
Dewing, Timothy, 83, 87, 110
Dewing, Warren, 42, 89
Dexter, Aaron, 79
Dexter, Amasa, 280
Dexter, David, 148 (2)
Dexter, Ephraim, 75, 76
Dexter, Gideon, 130, 239
Dexter, James, 25
Dexter, John, 93
Dexter, Jonathan, 130
Dexter, Leonard, 24
Dexter, Luke, 130
Dexter, Nathan, 47
Dexter, Nathaniel, 100
Dexter, Thomas, 183
Dexter, Timothy, 114
Dexter, William, 9
Dexter, Zenas, 26
Dexter, Zenos, 162
Dibble, Daniel, Jr., 46
Dickenson, Giles, 64
Dickenson, John, 182
Dickenson, Jonathan, 64
Dickenson, Oliver, 182

Dickerman, Benjamin, 91
Dickerman, Caleb, 139
Dickerman, Daniel T., 95
Dickerman, Samuel, 22, 50
Dickerson, Darius, 14
Dickerson, James, 268
Dickerson, John, 186
Dickey, Darius, 226
Dickey, David, 290, 293
Dickey, Ephraim, 25, 114
Dickey, James, 289
Dickey, John, 303
Dickey, William, 215, 239
Dicky, Elijah, 215
Dickinson, Abijah, 47, 182
Dickinson, Abijah, Jr., 182
Dickinson, David, 5
Dickinson, Elihu, 92
Dickinson, Elisha, 92
Dickinson, Enos, 47
Dickinson, Epaphras, 67
Dickinson, Ira, 81
Dickinson, James, 305
Dickinson, John, 33, 182
Dickinson, John, 3d, 47
Dickinson, Jonathan, 47
Dickinson, Joseph, 182 (2), 184
Dickinson, Josiah, 92
Dickinson, Leonard, 47
Dickinson, Obediah, 77, 82
Dickinson, Oliver, 182
Dickinson, Samuel, 92
Dickinson, Sylvanus, 92
Dickman, Samuel, 6
Dickson, Caleb W., 45
Dickson, Joseph, 101
Dickson, Shedrick, 169
Dike, Bela C., 50
Dike, Fuller, 259
Dike, Samuel, Jr., 50
Dill, Enoch, 219
Dill, Joseph, 169
Dill, Josiah, 169
Dill, Thomas, 177
Dill, William, 166, 229, 277
Dillanse, Caleb, 263
Dillaway, John, 78
Dillaway, Samuel, 79
Dillaway, Thomas, 78
Dillingham, Albert A., 271
Dillingham, Alvan, 164
Dillingham, Alvin, 164
Dillingham, Anson, 263
Dillingham, Asa, 77
Dillingham, Barnard, 198, 202
Dillingham, Benjamin, 55, 57, 127, 208
Dillingham, Benjamin P., 202, 209
Dillingham, Cornelius, 150
Dillingham, Henry, 24
Dillingham, Job, 47
Dillingham, John, Jr., 176
Dillingham, John B., 73, 76
Dillingham, Joseph P., 271
Dillingham, Josiah, 208
Dillingham, Josiah, Jr., 198, 208
Dillingham, Lemuel, 58, 73
Dillingham, Oliver, 165
Dillingham, Seth, 81
Dillingham, Simeon, 76
Dillingham, Simon, 73
Dimmick, David, 75
Dimmick, David, Jr., 71

Dimmick, Frederic, 75
Dimmick, Frederick, 71
Dimmick, Henry, 73
Dimmick, John, 73
Dimond, Benjamin, 42
Dimond, David, 70
Dinger, Jeremiah, 269
Dingley, John, 233, 300
Dingley, Nathan, 236
Dingly, Jeremiah, 300
Dingly, Spencer, 299
Dinsdell, William, 241
Dinsmore, Andrew, 155
Dinsmore, Charles, 233, 296
Dinsmore, James, 176, 295
Dinsmore, Nathaniel, 39
Dinsmore, Prince, 234
Dinsmore, Samuel, 230, 263, 266, 278, 281
Dinsmore, Thomas, 155
Dinsmore, William, 307
Discom, Thomas, 149
Ditson, John, 69
Ditson, William, 78, 88
Dival, John, 3d, 48
Divol, James, 5
Divol, Levi, 94
Dix, Benjamin A., 133, 136
Dix, John, 21, 138, 244
Dix, Jonas, 16
Dixie, John, 6
Dixie, Woodward, 6
Dixon, Edward, 23
Dixon, Francis, 118
Doak, James, 304
Doak, John, 118
Doak, Michael, 6, 22
Doan, Edward, 166, 215
Doan, Isaac W., 191
Doan, Joseph, Jr., 125
Doane, Amos, 215
Doane, Asa, 219, 259
Doane, Asia, 246
Doane, Beriah, 104, 105 (2), 106, 107
Doane, Charles, 259
Doane, Dennis, 215
Doane, Edward, 164, 165, 259
Doane, Elihu, 216
Doane, Ephraim, 216
Doane, George B., 76, 77
Doane, Isaac W., 182
Doane, Joseph, 216
Doane, Joshua, 58, 104, 105 (2), 106, 107
Doane, Lewis, 104, 105, 106, 107
Doane, Samuel, 106
Doane, Timothy, 105
Doane, Timothy, Jr., 104, 105, 107
Doane, William, 216
Doane, Zenas, 106
Doart, Samuel, 136
Dobbin, William, 246
Dobbins, James, 246
Dobbins, James, Jr., 220
Dobbins, William, 220, 246
Doble, Aaron, 176
Doble, Phineas, 178
Doble, Solomon, 259
Dobler, Benjamin, 6
Dockendorf, Solomon, 287 (2)
Dockhan, Stephen B., 138
Dockindoff, Walter, 177
Dockindorf, Thomas, 195
Dodd, Asa, 12

INDEX. 347

Dodd, Benjamin, 6, 23, 68, 77
Dodd, John, 12, 78, 82
Dodd, Silas, 68
Dodd, Thomas, 6
Dodge, A., 132
Dodge, Alexander, 193
Dodge, Amariah, 304
Dodge, Andrew, 35
Dodge, Azor, 34 (2)
Dodge, Benjamin, 193, 215
Dodge, Daniel, 10, 185, 189
Dodge, Dudley, 35 (2)
Dodge, Ebenezer, 183
Dodge, Endicott F., 182
Dodge, Enoch, 185
Dodge, Enos, 21
Dodge, Francis, 193, 196
Dodge, Havilah, 14
Dodge, Hesekiah, 161
Dodge, Isaac, 84, 193
Dodge, Israel, 14
Dodge, James, 193
Dodge, Jesse, 34, 38
Dodge, John, 14, 18, 35, 36, 120, 122, 138, 147, 164, 165, 166, 183, 185, 225
Dodge, John, Jr., 18, 193
Dodge, John, 2d, 183, 185
Dodge, Jonathan, 212
Dodge, Jonathan, 3d, 34
Dodge, Joseph, 189
Dodge, Josiah, 118, 193, 196
Dodge, Josiah, Jr., 134, 135
Dodge, Judah, 138
Dodge, Levi, 34
Dodge, Mathew, 212
Dodge, Moses, 184, 186, 189, 191
Dodge, P., 139
Dodge, Peter, 180
Dodge, Robert, 35 (2)
Dodge, Samuel, 34, 38, 121, 123 (2), 124, 183, 185, 213
Dodge, Saul, 20
Dodge, Silas H., 295
Dodge, Simon, 192
Dodge, Thomas, 34, 36, 67
Dodge, Thomas, 3d, 37
Dodge, Warren, 185
Dodge, Washington, 193
Dodge, William, 11, 14, 35, 161, 304
Dodge, William B., 133, 139
Doe, Andrew, 237, 267
Doe, Asa, 275
Doe, Charles, 210
Doe, David, 237, 265
Doe, Dearborn, 244
Doe, Henry, 244
Doe, John, 239
Doe, John, 2d, 239
Doe, Jonathan, 237, 239, 267
Doe, Joshua, 271
Doe, Nathaniel, Jr., 239
Doe, Simeon, Jr., 271
Dogett, Frederick, 145
Dogget, George, 261
Doggett, Eliphalet, 52
Doggett, Joseph, 130
Doggett, William, 13
Dohl, Benjamin, 64
Doland, Benjamin, 136
Doland, Benjamin, 2d, 136
Dole, Benjamin, 139
Dole, Cyrus, 183

Dole, Daniel, 269
Dole, Enoch, 15, 16, 17
Dole, Greenleaf, 15
Dole, Henry, 270
Dole, Jacob, 16
Dole, John, 20, 85
Dole, John, 2d, 184, 188
Dole, Joseph, 87, 109
Dole, Richard, 225
Dole, William, 139
Dolhiner, Paul, 289, 294
Dolibber, William, 22
Dolibe, William, 6
Doll, Cyrus, 185
Doll, Ebenezer, 274
Doll, Joseph, 109
Dollbier, Charles, 280
Dolley, Ammisabad, 241
Dolloff, David, 261, 279 (2)
Dolloff, Jacob, 301
Dolloff, John, 279
Dolloff, John P., 301
Dolloff, Malichi, 301
Dolly, Daniel, 219
Dolly, John, 210
Dolly, Joseph, 252
Dolly, William, 219
Dolouph, John, 303
Domony, John, 33
Donald, Henry M., 246
Donaldson, Alexander, 138
Donaldson, George, 75
Done, Nathan, 91
Donell, Frederic W., 18
Doney, Benjamin, 47
Donham, Daniel, 51
Donham, John F., 131
Donion, Henry, 119
Donnel, Abel, 299
Donnel, Kingsbury, 247
Donnell, Abel, 296
Donnell, Benjamin, 233
Donnell, Charles, 84
Donnell, Henry, 311
Donnell, Jeremiah, 247
Donnell, Joseph T., 301
Donnell, Jotham, 184, 191
Donnell, Nathaniel, 311 (2)
Donnell, Timothy, 149
Donnett, C. M., 24, 114
Donniel, Frederic, 21
Dook, John, 6
Dor, Samuel, 180
Dorn, Ebenezer, 1st, 259
Dorn, Ebenezer, 2d, 259
Dorr, Ebenezer, 224
Dorr, Ebenezer, Jr., 224
Dorr, Nathan, 78
Dorr, Richard M., 261, 265
Dorrison, Levi, 64
Dorset, Samuel, 241
Doten, Ebenezer, 128
Doten, Silas, 255
Doten, Stephen, 128
Doty, James, 74
Doty, Joseph, 18
Doty, Nathaniel, 126
Doty, Paul, 181
Doubty, John M., 256
Doughty, Elias, 266
Doughty, Elijah, 236
Doughty, Jacob, 296

Doughty, Jacob G., 299
Doughty, Stephen, 297, 299
Douglas, Barnabas N., 130
Douglas, James, 303
Douglas, Randal, 161
Douglas, William, 296
Douglas, Zebedee, 272
Douglass, Abraham, 215
Douglass, Benjamin, 129
Douglass, Daniel, 57
Douglass, Elisha, 155, 215
Douglass, Francis, 244
Douglass, George, 55, 299
Douglass, John, 155, 211
Douglass, Joseph, 271
Douglass, Randal, 217
Douglass, William, 2, 115
Dove, George, 40
Dovell, William, 150
Dow, Aaron, 248
Dow, Abram, 154
Dow, Amos, 24, 214
Dow, Benjamin, 132
Dow, Daniel, 93
Dow, Ebeneser, 272
Dow, Edmund, 297, 300
Dow, Evan, 28 (2)
Dow, Jabez, 153
Dow, Jabez, Jr., 171
Dow, James, 16
Dow, John, 184, 186 (2), 187 (2), 190, 191, 192, 196
Dow, Jonathan, 301
Dow, Jones, 28
Dow, Joseph, 150, 171, 180, 184, 187, 190, 191, 229, 301
Dow, Moses, 87, 239
Dow, Orem, 229
Dow, Stephen, 69
Dow, Thomas, 145
Dow, Zenas, 93
Dowd, Asahel, 33
Dowd, Noah, Jr., 33
Dowd, Sylvester, 33
Dowe, Levi, 266
Dowe, Stephen, 64
Dowley, Thomas, 117
Downer, Daniel, 15
Downing, Amos, 177
Downing, Frederic, 57
Downing, John, 57, 167
Downing, John, Jr., 117
Downing, Joshua, 57, 310
Downing, Smith, 117
Downing, Warren, 60
Downs, Elisha, 274
Downs, Jabez, 33
Downs, Jesse, 79
Downs, Joshua, 216
Downs, Paul, 216
Downs, Phineas, 216
Downs, Thomas, 264, 266
Dows, Kennel, 265
Dowst, Oxum, 283
Dowst, Samuel, 138
Dowty, Elias, 262
Doyl, Felix, 11
Doyle, Patrick, 196
Drake, Alpheus, 175
Drake, Codding, 168, 281
Drake, Daniel, 91
Drake, David, 53

348 INDEX.

Drake, Elijah, 60
Drake, Enoch, 53
Drake, Enos, 53, 177, 257
Drake, Ephraim, 178
Drake, Isaac, 53
Drake, James, 199
Drake, Jehiel, 67
Drake, Jesse, 28, 112, 286, 290
Drake, John, 251, 286, 290
Drake, Jonathan, 60
Drake, Joseph, 251
Drake, Lemuel, 213
Drake, Lincoln, 95
Drake, Martin, 50, 176, 257
Drake, Nathaniel, 177, 260
Drake, Reuben, 95
Drake, Richard, 240
Drake, Simeon, 60
Drake, Stephen, 251, 255
Drake, Stimson, 65
Drake, Warren, 239
Drake, Washington, 239, 265
Drake, William, 53, 240
Drake, Zenas, 95
Draper, James, 88
Draper, Lorenzo, 7, 91
Drayton, John, 69
Drayton, Thomas A., 69
Dresser, Daniel, 217
Dresser, Ebeneser, 297, 299
Dresser, Edmund, 269
Dresser, Elijah, 212, 254
Dresser, Frederic, 152, 254
Dresser, James, 255
Dresser, Job, 152
Dresser, John, 178, 243, 260
Dresser, Jonathan, 152
Dresser, Joseph, 165, 166, 246
Dresser, Joseph P., 221
Dresser, Levi, 152, 254
Dresser, Mark, 241
Dresser, Nehemiah C., 151, 254
Dresser, Otis, 32
Dresser, Richard, 221
Dresser, Rufus, 283
Dresser, Stephen, Jr., 152, 254
Dresser, Tyrus, 178
Drew, Aaron, 149
Drew, Asa, 149
Drew, Atwood, 128
Drew, Benjamin, 268
Drew, Charles, 131
Drew, Cornelius, 176
Drew, Ebeneser, 129
Drew, Elisha, 268
Drew, Israel, 268
Drew, Job, 81
Drew, John, 226, 244 (2)
Drew, John, Jr., 53
Drew, John B., 279
Drew, Josiah, 176
Drew, Lazarus, 129
Drew, Levi, 308
Drew, Lewis, 176, 257
Drew, Nicholas, 126
Drew, Reuben, Jr., 129, 131
Drew, Robert, 244
Drew, Samuel, 245
Drew, Stephen, 257
Driggs, Manual, 76
Drinkwater, Ammi, 302
Drinkwater, Bradford, 242

Drinkwater, James, 302
Drinkwater, John R., 212
Drinkwater, Micajah, Jr., 302
Drinkwater, Nathaniel, 302
Drinkwater, Sewall, 242
Drinkwater, Tristram, 212
Drinkwater, West, 302
Drinkwater, William, 255, 302
Driver, Andrew, 36
Driver, Solomon, 2d, 36
Driver, Stephen, 138
Drody, Allen, 73, 76
Drody, Samuel, 73
Droell, Peter, 150
Droely, Samuel, 76
Drool, John, 63
Drout, John, 224, 259
Drown, John J., 61
Drown, Joseph, 309 (2)
Drown, Royal P., 98
Drue, Elisha, 305
Druherst, Henry, 78
Drummond, Alexander, 249, 297
Drummond, Alexander, Jr., 250
Drummond, Clark, 236
Drummond, David, 248
Drummond, Esekiel, 247, 297
Drummond, Parker, 249
Drummond, Patrick, 250
Drury, Joseph, 94
Drury, Nathan, 39
Ducker, David, 259
Dudley, Aaron, 276
Dudley, Benjamin, 281
Dudley, Daniel, 252
Dudley, Elihu, 234
Dudley, Gilman, 264, 266
Dudley, James, 214, 268, 274, 308
Dudley, John, 87, 266, 306
Dudley, Joseph, 38, 228
Dudley, Josiah, 251, 255
Dudley, Moses, 159, 251
Dudley, Samuel B., 132
Dudley, Silas, 41
Dudly, Henry, 282
Dudly, Joseph, 243
Dudly, Moses, 255
Dudly, Nathan, 175
Dudly, Saul, 282
Duff, Royal, 48, 77
Duff, William, 2, 77, 108
Dugate, David, 80, 84
Dugen, Thomas, 232
Duggin, Thomas, 232
Duley, James, 248, 305
Duley, Patrick, 248
Dummer, Joseph O., 146
Dummer, Joshua, 16
Dummer, Samuel, 16
Dunan, David, Jr., 128
Dunbar, Amasa, 10
Dunbar, Amos, 1, 103
Dunbar, Charles, 49
Dunbar, Eliab, 49
Dunbar, Hosea, 39, 88
Dunbar, Isaac, 4, 162
Dunbar, Jacob, 238
Dunbar, Jesse, 194, 292
Dunbar, John, 44, 194
Dunbar, John W., 125
Dunbar, Joseph, 97, 194, 196
Dunbar, Josiah, Jr., 45

Dunbar, Martin, 49
Dunbar, Peleg, 42
Dunbar, Peter, 85
Dunbar, Richard, 303
Dunbar, Salmon, 91
Dunbar, Seth, 85
Dunbar, Silas, 50
Dunbar, Simeon, 50
Dunbar, Simeon, 2d, 50
Dunbar, Thomas, 97
Dunbar, William, 29
Duncan, Abner, 189
Duncan, Andrew, 189
Duncan, Daniel, Jr., 189
Duncan, Isaac, 302
Duncan, John, Jr., 189, 302
Duncan, Joseph, 186, 189
Duncan, Kingsbury, 302
Duncan, Samuel, 302
Duncan, Samuel W., 98
Duncan, Simon, 189
Duncan, Stephen, 189
Duncan, Tillotson, 130
Duncan, William, 132, 140
Dunean, Jason, 94
Dunham, Braddish, 30
Dunham, Calvin, 52
Dunham, David, 303
Dunham, Ebeneser, 175
Dunham, Eleaser, 251, 255
Dunham, Gamaliel, 31
Dunham, George, 214
Dunham, George L., 1
Dunham, Jacob, 128
Dunham, James, 235
Dunham, James, Jr., 175
Dunham, Jesse, 214
Dunham, John, 41, 214
Dunham, John F., 128
Dunham, Johnson, 148
Dunham, Jonathan, 303
Dunham, Josiah, 2
Dunham, Lemuel, 225
Dunham, Samuel, 61, 71, 75, 251
Dunham, Selva, 251
Dunham, Thomas, 114
Dunham, Witham, 148
Dunkam, William, 53
Dunklee, Jesse, 90
Dunks, Gershom, 67
Dunlap, Alexander, 44
Dunlap, Ebeneser, 231, 296
Dunlap, Esekiel, 184, 188, 230, 296
Dunlap, Guy, 305
Dunlap, Isaac, 235
Dunlap, John, 230
Dunlap, John I., 234
Dunlap, John, 2d, 236
Dunlap, Joseph, 148
Dunlap, Martin, 235, 296
Dunlap, Richard T., 298
Dunlap, Robert, 230, 295
Dunn, Daniel, 210
Dunn, Eliphalet, 224
Dunn, Isaiah, 253
Dunn, James, 213
Dunn, Jeremy, 264
Dunn, Jonathan, 23
Dunn, Joshua, Jr., 229
Dunn, Josiah, 3d, 213
Dunn, Moses, 269 (2)
Dunn, Nathaniel, 264, 266

INDEX. 349

Dunn, Richard, 278
Dunn, Samuel, 84, 223
Dunnaway, Daniel, 11
Dunnell, Joseph, Jr., 269 (2)
Dunnell, Moses, 186
Dunning, Aaron, 295
Dunning, Andrew, 160
Dunning, David, 166
Dunning, James, 161, 297, 299
Dunning, James, 2d, 298
Dunning, John, 295, 296 (2), 298
Dunning, John, 2d, 297
Dunning, John, 3d, 295
Dunning, Joseph N., 295
Dunning, Joshua, 233
Dunning, Robert, 215, 225
Dunning, Robert D., 295
Dunning, Thomas, 297, 298
Dunphe, Elvin, 91
Dunsmore, Asa, 196
Dunsmore, Samuel, 68
Dunster, Henry, 48
Dunt, Micajah, 20
Duntlin, John, 8
Dunton, Abner, 302
Dunton, Daniel, 23, 191
Dunton, Isaac, 201, 202
Dunton, Israel, 190
Dunton, James, 215
Dunton, John, 25
Dunton, Josiah, 302
Dunton, Peter, 80
Dunton, Simon, 191
Dunton, Thomas, 87
Dunton, Timothy, 301
Dunttin, Nathaniel, 83
Dunum, Charles, 126
Dupee, Lewis, 111, 113 (2)
Duran, Nathaniel, 295
Durang, Daniel, 183
Durant, Charles, 90
Durant, Clark, 45
Durant, Edward, 138
Durell, Joseph, 268
Durell, Peter, 146
Durell, William, 146
Duren, James, 221
Duren, John, 41, 221
Durfer, Thomas, 129
Durfry, Harvey, 29
Durgen, Leavit, 261
Durgen, Nicholas, 15
Durgin, Abraham, 270
Durgin, Benjamin, 154, 155, 312
Durgin, John, 153
Durgin, Joseph, 153
Durgin, Joshua, 269
Durham, James, 215
Durham, William, 302
Durham, Witham, 148
Durong, John, 14
Durphy, Elijah, 283
Durphy, Peleg, 99
Durrell, Daniel, 113 (2)
Durwage, Francis S., 70
Dusenbury, James, 254
Dustan, Dunning, 298
Dustin, Charles M., 275
Dustin, Farnham, 257
Dustin, Joseph, 296 (2), 298
Duston, Jesse, 261
Dutch, George, 211

Dutch, Robert, 160
Dutch, Samuel, 152, 254
Dutton, Asa, 264
Dutton, David, 178, 259
Dutton, Elijah, 305
Dutton, Ephraim, 271
Dutton, Gideon, 217
Dutton, James, 278, 281
Dutton, John, 262
Dutton, Josiah, 268, 305
Dutton, Josiah, Jr., 305
Dutton, Mason, 305
Dutton, Samuel, 162 (2)
Dutton, Stephen, 224
Dwell, Peter, 150
Dwell, William, 150
Dwelley, Barzaleel, 255
Dwelling, Warren, 56
Dwelly, Barzilla, 252
Dwight, Charles, 4
Dwight, John, 4
Dwight, John W., 4
Dwight, Peregrine, 4
Dwight, Pliney, 4
Dwight, Simeon, 4
Dwight, Solomon, 204, 205 (2), 206
Dwinal, Aaron, 233
Dwinal, Andrew, 159
Dwinal, Isaac, 159
Dwinal, Jacob, 159
Dwinal, Simeon, 233
Dwinel, David, 10, 227
Dyer, Abijah, 149
Dyer, Andrew, 258
Dyer, Arthur, 218
Dyer, Asa, 268
Dyer, Barzilla, 169
Dyer, Benjamin, 210, 221
Dyer, Brackett, 202
Dyer, Caleb, 219
Dyer, Chadbourne, 164, 165
Dyer, Chadburn, 166
Dyer, Charles, 203, 204, 206, 207, 256
Dyer, Christopher, 219, 229
Dyer, Clark, 158
Dyer, Clement J., 221
Dyer, Daniel, 51, 275
Dyer, Darius, 32
Dyer, David, 102, 162
Dyer, Ebenezer, 2, 221
Dyer, Edward, 221
Dyer, Elkanah, 169
Dyer, Elliot, 219
Dyer, Enos H., 221
Dyer, Ezekiel, 49, 218, 219
Dyer, George, 79
Dyer, Gideon B., 227
Dyer, Henry, 181, 221
Dyer, Henry B., 126
Dyer, Israel, 219
Dyer, Jacob, 49, 65
Dyer, James, 43, 154, 219, 225, 295
Dyer, James, Jr., 226
Dyer, Jesse, 219
Dyer, John B., 233
Dyer, John S., 226
Dyer, Jonah, 221
Dyer, Joshua, 243
Dyer, Joseph, 155
Dyer, Leonard, 221
Dyer, Micah, 300

Dyer, Moses, 262
Dyer, Nathaniel, 216
Dyer, Paul, 271
Dyer, Reuben, 219, 221, 229, 282
Dyer, Reuben H., 221
Dyer, Richard, 295
Dyer, Robert, Jr., 221
Dyer, Samuel, 63, 160, 219
Dyer, Sherborn, 221
Dyer, Silas G., 222
Dyer, Stephen, 42, 102
Dyer, Stephen, Jr., 160
Dyer, Sylvanus, 149, 246
Dyer, Timothy, 172
Dyer, Willis, 225
Dyke, Fuller, 224
Dyke, Nathaniel, 223, 259
Dyke, Samuel, 212
Dyre, Bezilla, 277
Dyre, Elkanah, 277

E

Eames, Daniel, 29, 247
Eames, John, 195
Eames, Joseph, 118
Eames, Mydad, 29
Eames, Nathaniel, 233, 301
Eames, Nimrod, 265
Eames, Peter, 118
Eames, Robert, 118
Eames, Samuel, 227, 304
Eames, Saul, 261
Eames, William, 238, 267
Earl, Thomas, 1
Earle, Hiram, 160
Earle, Joseph, 61
Earline, Josiah C., 212
Ears, Charles, 115
Eason, Alden, 66
Eastburn, Peleg, 49
Easter, John, 299
Eastman, Benjamin, 271
Eastman, David, 272
Eastman, Enos, 180
Eastman, Fryeholt, 296
Eastman, Haynes, 261
Eastman, James, 152, 299
Eastman, John, 153, 204, 206
Eastman, Joseph, 92, 152, 160, 254
Eastman, Kingsbery, 296
Eastman, Kingsbury, 299
Eastman, Nathaniel, 272
Eastman, Peter, 45
Eastman, Philip, 47, 151
Eastman, Robert, 148
Eastman, Saul, 92
Eastman, Solomon, 152
Eastman, Thomas, 158
Eastman, Timothy, 223, 259
Eastman, William, 244, 275
Easty, Jeremiah, 139 (2)
Easty, Solomon, 273
Eaton, Aaron, 269
Eaton, Abel, 29, 235, 296
Eaton, Abner, 298
Eaton, Alfred, 53
Eaton, Barnabus, 49
Eaton, Barzilla, 53
Eaton, Benjamin, 306
Eaton, Charles, 13, 236
Eaton, Cyrus, 292
Eaton, Daniel, Jr., 298

INDEX

Eaton, Darius, 46
Eaton, Ebenezer, 26, 39
Eaton, Edward, 295
Eaton, Enoch, 234
Eaton, Enos, 52
Eaton, Ezra, 25, 77
Eaton, Henry M., 160
Eaton, Isaac, 228
Eaton, Israel, 54
Eaton, James, 169
Eaton, Jeremiah, 20, 228
Eaton, John, 93, 228, 296
Eaton, Jonathan, 15
Eaton, Joseph, 96, 155
Eaton, Josiah, 94
Eaton, Justice, 43
Eaton, Leonard, 235, 296
Eaton, Lowell, 283
Eaton, Nathan, 24
Eaton, Robert W., 8
Eaton, Rowell, 228
Eaton, Rufus, 108, 109
Eaton, Samuel, 177, 260
Eaton, Samuel A., 28
Eaton, Seth, 53
Eaton, Simeon, 152
Eaton, Solomon, 53, 54
Eaton, Tappan, 283
Eaton, Thaddeus, 77
Eaton, Thomas, 3
Eaton, Topham, 227
Eaton, William, 3, 41, 152, 234
Eaton, William G., 34, 38
Eaton, Ziba, 51, 54
Eayres, Joseph, 28
Eayrs, Henry, 118
Eckley, David, 83
Eckley, William, 303
Eddy, Apollus, Jr., 62
Eddy, Daniel, 46
Eddy, Ebenezer, 217
Eddy, Elijah, 54
Eddy, Ezra, 51, 103
Eddy, Ira, 46
Eddy, John, 46, 55
Eddy, Lyman, 54
Eddy, Nathaniel, 51
Eddy, Sylvanus, 42, 89
Eddy, William, 86, 161
Eddy, William S., 51
Eddy, Zebulon, 67
Eddy, Zenas B., 42
Eddy, Zenos D., 89
Edes, Benjamin, 87
Edes, Benjamin F., 83
Edes, Gideon, 209
Edes, Samuel, 70
Edgar, George R., 28
Edgarton, Benjamin W., 67
Edgcomb, Daniel, 165, 222, 259
Edgcomb, Dedymus, 222
Edgcomb, Didimus C., 259
Edgcomb, Eliphalet C., 244
Edgcomb, Gibbens, 2d, 171
Edgcomb, Gideon, Jr., 165
Edgcomb, Isaac, 228
Edgcomb, James, 223
Edgcomb, Job, 312
Edgcomb, John, 155, 170
Edgcomb, Joseph, 174, 247
Edgcomb, Levi, 244
Edgcomb, Robert, 171

Edgcomb, Thomas, 149, 272
Edgcomb, Walter, 152
Edgcumb, Daniel, 164
Edgcumb, Gideon, Jr., 164
Edge, Asa, 30
Edgecomb, Daniel, 166
Edgecomb, Gideon, Jr., 166
Edgell, Benjamin, 94
Edgerly, Peter, 141
Edminster, John, 52, 55
Edminster, Lemuel, 57
Edmonds, Nathaniel, 115
Edmunds, Elijah, 92
Edmunds, Lot, 118
Edmunds, Walter, 204, 205
Edmunds, William, 18, 27
Edney, John N., 13
Edson, Allen, 51
Edson, Barnabus, 91
Edson, Benjamin, 41
Edson, Charles, 49
Edson, Daniel, 60
Edson, David, 91
Edson, Jesse, 49
Edson, Jonah, 97
Edson, Jonathan, 50
Edson, Josiah, 129
Edson, Nathaniel, 49
Edson, Noah, 92
Edson, Pliney, 49
Edson, Robert, 90
Edward, Richard, 225
Edward, Samuel, 38
Edwards, Abraham A., 88
Edwards, Asa, 130
Edwards, Asa, Jr., 72
Edwards, Asa B., 35 (2)
Edwards, Benjamin, 35 (2), 37, 87
Edwards, Caleb, 211
Edwards, Calvin, 173
Edwards, Cypron I., 271
Edwards, Elisha, 67
Edwards, Ephraim, 258
Edwards, Ezra, 35
Edwards, John, 72, 180
Edwards, Joseph, 135, 140
Edwards, Joshua, 134, 135
Edwards, Nathaniel, Jr., 212
Edwards, Ralph, 67
Edwards, Robert, 35 (2)
Edwards, Samuel, 173
Edwards, Stephen, 258
Edwards, Walter, 206
Edwards, William, 2, 173
Eels, Pitkin, 31
Eels, Robert L., 302
Eels, Seth W., 302
Eels, William, Jr., 225
Eggan, Simmons, 195
Eggleston, Elisha, 70
Egleston, Eli, 46
Egleston, Frederic, 31
Egleston, George, 67
Elder, Francis, 174
Elder, Hanson, 240
Elder, Jacob, 243
Elder, John, 45
Elder, Joseph, 18, 121, 124
Elder, Morrill, 210
Elder, Reuben, 221
Elder, Reuben, Jr., 171
Elder, Samuel, 2

Elder, Samuel, Jr., 171
Elder, Simon, 173
Elder, William, 3, 150, 154
Eldred, David, 75, 76
Eldred, Levi, 276
Eldred, Michell, 271
Eldred, William, 73
Eldredge, Daniel, 244
Eldredge, Freeman, 43
Eldredge, Joseph, 41
Eldridge, Bartlett, 131
Eldridge, Benjamin, 72
Eldridge, Ebenezer, 174
Eldridge, Eli, 67
Eldridge, Ephraim, 74
Eldridge, Ezekiel, 72
Eldridge, Hereziah, Jr., 216
Eldridge, Isaac, 54
Eldridge, John, 64, 125
Eldridge, Nathaniel, 72
Eldridge, Obediah, 106 (2), 107 (2), 108
Eldridge, Oliver, 23
Eldridge, Richard, 127
Eldridge, Samuel, 72
Eldridge, Seth, 216
Eldridge, Simeon, 72
Eldridge, Thomas, 106, 107 (2), 108
Eldridge, Ward, 72
Eldridge, West D., 37
Eliot, John, 25, 113, 114
Elkins, Josiah, 279
Elkins, Saul, 279
Elkins, Thomas, 22
Ellenwood, Jacob, 252
Ellery, Benjamin, 9
Ellery, Joseph, 13
Ellery, William, 14
Elles, William, 304
Ellet, Jacob, 231
Ellet, James, 295
Ellet, Stephen, 231
Ellingwood, Abraham, 85
Ellingwood, Benjamin, 117
Ellingwood, Chester, 44
Ellingwood, Ezra, 34
Ellingwood, Herbert, 34, 38 (2)
Ellingwood, John, 34
Ellingwood, John, Jr., 38
Ellingwood, Joseph, 217
Ellingwood, Ralph, 216
Elliot, Andrew, 34, 38
Elliot, Asiel, 59
Elliot, Daniel, 308
Elliot, Dummerston, 47
Elliot, Enoch, 234
Elliot, James, 36
Elliot, James, 2d, 298
Elliot, John, 36, 37, 224
Elliot, Moses, 178
Elliot, William, 6, 22, 192
Elliott, Andrew, 8, 193
Elliott, Ephraim L., 28
Elliott, Henry, 28
Elliott, James, 37, 195, 197
Elliott, James, 2d, 296
Elliott, Josiah, 153, 246
Elliott, Nathaniel, 41
Elliott, Simon, 195
Elliott, Simon, Jr., 197
Elliott, William, 197
Ellis, Abner, 71, 73, 75
Ellis, Arden, 223

INDEX. 351

Ellis, Ardin, 259
Ellis, Bartlet, 75
Ellis, Bartlett, 71
Ellis, Benjamin, 30, 56, 265
Ellis, Charles, 71, 112
Ellis, Clark, 5
Ellis, Cyrus, 103
Ellis, Ebenezer, 85, 222, 263
Ellis, Elisha, 26, 236
Ellis, Freeborn, 284
Ellis, George, 52
Ellis, Gideon, 75, 223
Ellis, Helita, 18
Ellis, Isaac, 176
Ellis, Ivory, 228, 282
Ellis, James, 59, 75
Ellis, Jason, 86
Ellis, Jesse, 71, 75
Ellis, Joel B., 270
Ellis, John, 262, 263, 267, 268, 300, 308
Ellis, John, Jr., 44
Ellis, Jonathan, 263, 267
Ellis, Jonathan S., 223
Ellis, Joseph, 129, 181, 303
Ellis, Josiah, 71
Ellis, Josiah, Jr., 73
Ellis, Levi, 71
Ellis, Martin, 224
Ellis, Micah, 71, 75
Ellis, Moses, 26, 65
Ellis, Nathan, 72
Ellis, Nathaniel, 311
Ellis, Oran, 167
Ellis, Philip, 224
Ellis, Robert, 262, 266,
Ellis, Samuel, 262
Ellis, Simeon, 85
Ellis, Southworth, 51
Ellis, Stephen, 161
Ellis, Thomas, 1, 71, 75
Ellis, Watson, 1
Ellis, Willard, 97
Ellis, William, 65, 71, 263, 305
Ellms, Nathaniel, 104
Ellsworth, David, 135
Elmes, Abner, 271
Elmes, Daniel, 103
Elmes, Elijah, 271
Elmes, John, 103, 198, 199, 202
Elmes, Thomas, 271
Elmes, William, 103, 182 (2)
Elms, John, 2
Elsworth, Hezekiah, 45
Elsworth, Joseph, 283
Elwell, Athiel, 269
Elwell, Caleb, 11
Elwell, David, 10, 259
Elwell, Elias, Jr., 13
Elwell, Hezekiah, 221
Elwell, Isaac, 14, 225
Elwell, Jabez, 154
Elwell, John, 250, 258
Elwell, Joseph, 165
Elwell, Othiel, 269
Elwell, Robert, 84
Elwell, Samuel, 166, 294
Elwell, Saul, 284, 288
Elwell, Solomon, 12
Elwell, Thomas, 47, 302
Elwell, William, 13, 14
Ely, Henry, 44
Ely, Osly, 44

Emerson, Asa, 232 (2)
Emerson, Benjamin, 115, 215
Emerson, Charles, 19, 21, 119, 122
Emerson, Cyrus B., 141
Emerson, Daniel, 101, 214
Emerson, Daniel R., 307
Emerson, David, 117
Emerson, Ebenezer, 41
Emerson, Elias, 93
Emerson, Ephraim, 117
Emerson, George S., 68
Emerson, George W., 151
Emerson, Henry, 98
Emerson, Isaac, 258, 263
Emerson, Jacob, 150, 151
Emerson, James, 96
Emerson, Jeremiah, 85, 87
Emerson, John, 84, 307
Emerson, Jonathan, 8
Emerson, Jonathan, 2d, 8
Emerson, Joseph, 185
Emerson, Joshua, 258
Emerson, Loring, 117
Emerson, Nathan, 98, 215
Emerson, Oliver, 117
Emerson, Phineas, 77
Emerson, Robert, 69
Emerson, Rufus, 262
Emerson, Stephen, 214
Emerson, Theodore, 211
Emerson, William, 39, 249
Emery, Benjamin, 306
Emery, Caleb, 261
Emery, Daniel, 214
Emery, Elijah, 165, 166, 171, 246
Emery, Eliphalet, 15
Emery, Eliphalet H., 116
Emery, George, 244
Emery, Haven, 269
Emery, Hosea, 215
Emery, Isaac, 171
Emery, Isaac, Jr., 309 (2)
Emery, Jacob, 15
Emery, James, 171, 254, 261
Emery, Joel, 88, 245
Emery, John, 197, 204, 206, 219
Emery, John, Jr., 214
Emery, Jonah, 197, 203
Emery, Jonas, 70, 215
Emery, Jonathan, 306
Emery, Joseph, 213
Emery, Joseph, 3d, 307
Emery, Josiah, 204
Emery, Moses, 20
Emery, Nathaniel, 305
Emery, Nicholas, 15
Emery, Paul, 16
Emery, Peter, 80
Emery, Philip, 309
Emery, Robert, 303
Emery, Samuel, 153, 261
Emery, Samuel, 2d, 261
Emery, Saul, 136, 137
Emery, Silas, 268
Emery, Simon, 215
Emery, Stephen M., 15
Emery, Thomas, 309 (2)
Emery, William, 149, 165, 166, 242, 253
Emes, Clark, 78
Emes, Isaac, 50
Emmerson, Hazen, 262
Emmerson, Mirick, 211

Emmerson, Nathaniel, 211
Emmerson, Seth, 211
Emmerston, Jeremiah, 69
Emmons, Benjamin, 249
Emmons, John, 33, 180
Emmons, Jonathan, 69
Emmons, Lewis, 33
Emmons, Samuel F., 69
Emmons, Thomas, 28, 248
Emory, William, 215
Endicott, Nathan H., 34
Endicott, Samuel, 129, 135
Endicott, Samuel, Jr., 134
Endicott, William, 78
Engby, Jacob, 194
Enghly, John, 294
England, John, 16
Engley, Jacob, 196
English, Aaron, 44
English, Philip, 136 (2)
Ensign, Thomas, 119
Erskine, Asa, 153, 246, 312
Erskine, Christopher, 50
Erskine, George, 145, 153
Erskine, John, 145, 186 (2), 187 (2), 190
Erskine, Robert, 278
Erskine, Thomas, 184, 188
Erskins, John, 3d, 196
Erskins, William, 196
Ervin, Joseph, 133
Erving, Ernest A., 136
Erving, Henry, 287
Escot, John, 36
Escot, Philip, 36
Esenby, Charles, 294
Estabrook, Charles G., 131
Estabrooks, Endor, 101
Estabrooks, Thomas S., 295
Esterbrook, Henry, 65
Estes, George, 261
Estes, John, 257, 296, 297
Estes, Samuel G., 87
Estes, Thomas, 33
Estes, William, 245, 256
Estey, Aaron, 273
Estey, Joseph, 70
Estham, James, 297
Esty, David, 31
Ettis, Levi, 125
Eustace, George, 257
Eustace, Joseph, 136
Eustace, Thomas, 257
Eustace, William, 259
Eustis, George, 223
Eustis, Jacob, 303
Eustis, James, 303
Eustis, Joseph, 84, 133
Eustis, Thomas, 223
Evans, Benjamin, 176
Evans, David, 59
Evans, Ephraim, 181
Evans, Gilbert, 178
Evans, Henry H., 254
Evans, Jacob, 150, 151
Evans, James, 21, 117
Evans, John, 151, 244, 254
Evans, John, Jr., 21
Evans, Jonathan, 152
Evans, Joseph, 57
Evans, Joseph, 2d, 57
Evans, Josiah, 246
Evans, Nathaniel, 168

INDEX

Evans, Richard, 18, 120, 121, 123
Evans, Robert, 124, 164 (2), 165
Evans, Samuel, 96
Evans, Thomas, 267
Evans, William, 41, 56, 57, 127
Evarts, John, 29
Eveleth, Asa, 45
Eveleth, David, 213
Eveleth, Francis, 136
Eveleth, James, 256, 304
Eveleth, Joseph, 268, 305
Eveleth, Joseph, Jr., 132
Eveleth, Moses, 210, 256
Eveleth, Perkins, 210
Eveleth, Saul, 141
Evens, Josiah, 172
Evens, Nathaniel, 237
Evens, Thomas, 237
Everden, James, 9
Everden, William, 9
Everett, Aaron, 28, 112
Everett, Charles, 98
Everett, Daniel, 99
Everett, David, 197, 204 (2)
Everett, George, 99
Everett, Joel, 54, 99
Everett, John, 265
Everett, John B., 252
Everett, Leonard, 99
Everett, Nathan, 99
Everett, Noble, Jr., 126
Everett, Silas, 54
Everett, William, 39, 69
Everson, Ephraim, 129
Everson, Levi, 128
Everson, Timothy, 51, 103
Ewel, Joseph, 301
Ewell, Charles, 294
Ewell, Nathan, 291
Ewen, William, 232
Ewer, Abram, 74
Ewer, Alvin, 73
Ewer, Barnabus, 131
Ewer, Benjamin, 74
Ewer, John, Jr., 239, 267
Ewer, Lemuel, 73, 74
Ewer, Shubel, 74
Ewers, John F., 303
Ewers, Moses, 63
Ewin, William, 232
Ewing, James, Jr., 299
Ewing, John, 299
Ewing, Shirley, 7
Ewing, Thomas A., 39

F

Fabin, Thomas, 300
Fabins, Benjamin, 133, 136
Fabins, Ilar, 171
Fabins, John, 139
Fabins, Samuel, 133, 136
Fabins, William, 133
Faerman, Orrin, 64
Fairbanks, Asa, 273
Fairbanks, Benjamin, 266, 306
Fairbanks, Columbus, 273
Fairbanks, David, 277, 281
Fairbanks, Dennis, 147 (2)
Fairbanks, Elias, 259
Fairbanks, Enos, 147 (2)
Fairbanks, Franklin, 277
Fairbanks, Gerry, 24

Fairbanks, James, 147 (2)
Fairbanks, Jesse, 147 (2)
Fairbanks, Joel, 150
Fairbanks, John, 70, 77, 147 (2)
Fairbanks, John, Jr., 200
Fairbanks, Levi, 277, 281
Fairbanks, Pliney, 39
Fairbanks, Silas, 85
Fairbanks, Stephen, 68
Fairbrother, James, 266
Fairbrother, James, Jr., 307
Fairbrother, Lovel, 307
Fairfield, Abraham, 116
Fairfield, James, 308
Fairfield, Jedediah, 237
Fairfield, John, 78, 295
Fairfield, Samuel, 138
Fairfield, Seth S., 149, 154 (2), 155
Fairservice, John, 184
Fairservice, Thomas, 186
Fairwell, Daniel, 64
Fales, Abijah, 97
Fales, Alwood, 205
Fales, Asa, 205
Fales, Atwood, 200, 205
Fales, David, 284
Fales, Elisha, 204, 205, 206
Fales, Ensebins, 204, 205 (2)
Fales, James, 99
Fales, James, 3d, 156
Fales, Joshua, 99
Fales, Lewis, 97
Fales, Nathan, 198, 202
Fales, Nathaniel, 205
Fales, Nathaniel, Jr., 205
Fales, Nehemiah, 99
Fales, Noyes, 285, 286 (2), 288
Fales, Shepherd, 51
Fales, Stephen, 99
Fales, Waterman, 156, 157
Fall, Aaron, Jr., 267
Fall, Ebeneser, 149, 262
Fall, John, 245
Fall, Samuel, 272
Fall, Stephen, 234, 236
Falls, Hiram, 86
Fanie, Joseph, 103
Faning, Pliney, 267
Fanington, Thomas, 27
Fannin, Daniel, 153
Fanning, Chester, 94
Fanning, John B., 84
Far, Samuel, 140
Fargo, Thomas, 31
Farless, James, 132
Farless, Thomas, 132
Farley, Charles, 244
Farley, Ebenezer, 193
Farley, James, 136, 137
Farley, John, 29
Farley, John D., 15
Farley, John Dennis, 20
Farmer, Asa, 88
Farmer, James, 164 (2), 165
Farmer, John, 108
Farmer, Joseph, 51
Farmer, Samuel, 68
Farmer, Thomas, 128
Farmer, William, 183, 185, 188
Farmington, Benjamin, 224
Farmington, Daniel, 214
Farmington, Silas, 214

Farnam, John, 174
Farnes, John, 34
Farnham, Abiel, 151
Farnham, Benjamin, 184, 239
Farnham, David, 194
Farnham, Ebeneser, 145, 285
Farnham, Isaac, 264
Farnham, Jeremiah, 302
Farnham, John, 183, 285, 287
Farnham, Jonathan M., 141
Farnham, Joseph, 183
Farnham, Joshua, 239, 249
Farnham, Moses, 149, 264
Farnham, Ralph, 307
Farnham, Rufus, 239, 267
Farnham, Samuel, 145, 264 (2), 285
Farnham, Warren, 44
Farnham, William, 285, 287
Farnsworth, Chephas, 237
Farnsworth, David B., 77
Farnsworth, James D., 88
Farnsworth, John, 291
Farnsworth, Jonathan, 8
Farnsworth, Oliver, 24
Farnsworth, Robert, 291
Farnsworth, Rufus, 87
Farnsworth, Thomas, 40
Farnsworth, William, 8
Farnum, Edwin, 8
Farnum, Jedediah, 8
Farnum, Joseph, 254
Farnum, Merrill, 261
Farnum, Samuel, 214, 261
Farnum, Thomas, 24
Farr, John, 36, 295, 296
Farr, Samuel, 66, 198, 202
Farr, Simeon, 280, 296
Farr, Willard, 8
Farrar, Amos D., 99
Farrar, John, 201
Farrar, Saul, 259
Farrar, Thomas, 252, 255
Farrder, Timothy, 6
Farrell, Gideon, 270
Farrell, Laurence L., 85
Farren, Richard, 230
Farrie, John, 113
Farrin, John, 234
Farrin, William, 230, 234
Farrin, Winthrop, Jr., 299
Farrington, Abner, 292 (2)
Farrington, Benjamin, 214, 218, 261
Farrington, Daniel S., 85
Farrington, Ebenezer, 15, 139
Farrington, Elijah, 5
Farrington, Eliphalet, 149
Farrington, Isaac, 292 (2)
Farrington, Jabez, 224
Farrington, Jacob, 151, 218
Farrington, Jesse, 99
Farrington, John, 292
Farrington, Jonathan, 152
Farrington, Joshua, 111 (2), 112 (2)
Farrington, Martin, 223
Farrington, Nathan, 85
Farrington, Philander, 218, 261
Farrington, Philip, 152
Farrington, Samuel, 152
Farrington, Stephen, 152
Farrington, Thomas, 151
Farris, Hezekiah, 253
Farris, Thomas, 34, 37, 38 (2)

INDEX.

Farris, William, 175
Farriss, Benjamin, 239
Farriter, J., 70
Farron, Samuel, 225
Farrow, Bela, 251
Farrow, David, 251
Farrow, Edward, 195
Farrow, Jacob, 230
Farrow, James, 234, 296
Farrow, John, 234
Farrow, Josiah, 234, 296
Farrow, Nathan, 234, 251, 296
Farrow, Nathaniel, 1, 104
Farrow, Reuben, 234
Farrow, Simon, 301
Farrow, Thomas, 180
Farrow, Timothy, 22
Farrow, William, 195
Farwell, Absolom, 149
Farwell, Cyrus, 99
Farwell, Ebenezer, 240, 265
Farwell, Hannibal, 237, 265
Farwell, Henry, 175
Farwell, Isaac, 101
Farwell, Jacob, 101
Farwell, Jeremiah, 237, 265
Farwell, Luther, 83, 84
Farsar, Adoniram, 87
Fassett, Alexander, 280
Fassett, John, 148
Fast, Walter, 269
Faught, James, 237
Faught, Nathaniel, 237, 267
Faught, Philip, 262
Faught, Samuel, 262
Faunce, Allen, 129
Faunce, Ezra, 129
Faunce, James, 51, 127
Faunce, Tilden, 131
Faunce, William, 73
Faunce, Zenas, 129
Favor, Isaac, 87
Favot, Jacob, 212
Favours, Peter, 284, 287
Faxon, Charles, 275
Faxon, Nathaniel, 23, 112
Faxton, Luther, 97
Fay, Briah, 100
Fay, Elihu, 91
Fay, Jesse, 198, 199, 202, 207
Fay, Joel, 68
Fay, John, 39, 117
Fay, Nehemiah, 95
Fay, Silas, 84
Fay, William, 44, 91
Fay, Winsor, 28
Faye, John, 285
Fearing, Charles, 96
Fearing, Cushing, 24, 114
Fearing, Moses T., 126
Fears, James, 11
Fedwell, David, 30
Fegan, Joseph I., 186, 190
Fegan, Joseph J., 187
Felch, Isaac, 269
Felch, Samuel, 278
Fellows, Aaron, 228
Fellows, Benjamin, 39, 69, 77
Fellows, Isaac, 228, 268
Fellows, John, 228
Fellows, Moses, 277
Fellows, William, 276

Felson, Gilbert, 285
Felt, David, 111, 113 (2), 114
Felt, Ephraim, 132
Felt, Jonathan W., 159
Felt, Joseph, 133, 136 (2), 140
Felt, Nathaniel, 133, 136
Felt, Thomas, 6
Felton, Cornelius C., 15
Felton, Francis, 22
Felton, Luther, 68
Felton, Oliver, 44
Fenderson, Benjamin, 170, 246
Fenderson, James, 171
Fenno, John, 2, 26, 39
Fenno, John W., 132
Fenno, Joseph, 94
Fenno, William, 48, 82, 94
Fenring, Lincoln, 94
Fenton, Elisha, 4
Ferdinan, Samuel, 90
Ferguson, Alexander, 245
Ferguson, James, 33
Ferguson, John, 238
Ferguson, Jonathan, 213
Ferguson, William, 213
Fermin, David, 78
Fern, James, 118
Fernal, William, 139
Fernald, Joseph, 256
Fernald, Mark, 162
Fernald, Solomon, 285
Ferrald, Edmund, 213
Ferrald, Samuel, 176
Ferrill, John, 260
Ferrin, Eben, 2d, 236
Ferrin, John, 236
Ferrin, Rufus, 155, 156
Ferrin, William, 236
Ferry, Thomas, 77
Fessenam, Ebenezer, 150
Fessenden, Arthur, 84
Fessenden, Benjamin, 24, 114
Fessenden, Ebenezer, 151
Fessenden, John, 243
Fessenden, Jonathan, 151
Fessenden, Moses, 68, 79
Fessenden, Samuel, 73, 210
Fessenden, Stephen, 82
Fessenden, Thomas, 73, 125
Fessenden, William, 73, 76, 150, 151
Fetton, Oliver, 44
Fickett, Ephraim, 243
Fickett, Ezra, 172
Fickett, Nathaniel, 187 (2), 190
Fickett, Samuel, 164, 165, 166
Field, Abiather, 62
Field, Alpheus, 219
Field, Amasa, 97
Field, Ansel, 146, 150
Field, Benjamin, 262
Field, Charles, 53, 70
Field, Ebenezer, 42
Field, Elias, 214
Field, Galen, 251
Field, George, 24, 239, 267
Field, Horace, 60
Field, James, 86, 89, 301
Field, John, 42, 50, 89, 149, 269
Field, Jonathan, 61
Field, Joseph, 2, 27, 169, 274
Field, Josiah, 23, 164, 165, 219

Field, Michael, 218
Field, Nathaniel, 219
Field, Peter, 214
Field, Rowlin, 65
Field, Sharon, 3
Field, Silas, 25
Field, Simeon, 219
Field, Solomon, 53
Field, Stephen, 135, 145, 219, 241, 242
Field, Thomas, 45
Field, Thomas, Jr., 46
Field, Waldo, 50
Field, William A., 100
Field, Zibron, 251
Fielder, John, 34
Fielder, Knott, 34, 38, 90
Fielder, William, 34, 38, 90
Fields, John, 158
Fields, Josiah, 166
Fields, Libbeus, 99
Fife, James, 236
Fife, Nathan, 77
Fife, Silas, 85
Fifield, Benjamin, 152, 254
Fifield, E. O., 68
Fifield, Ebenezer, Jr., 282
Fifield, Israel, 295
Fifield, John, 297
Fifield, Jonathan F., 152
Fifield, Wire, 282
Figes, William, 13
Fiket, Nathaniel, 161
Files, Ebenezer, Jr., 173
Files, Ebenezer S. S., 173
Files, Nathaniel, 171
Files, Robert, Jr., 171
Fillbrock, Jonathan, 153
Fillbrock, Simon, 153
Fillbrooks, Simpson, 261
Fillebrown, Asa, 24
Fillebrown, James, 24
Fillebrown, James, Jr., 278
Fillebrown, John, 98
Fillebrown, Leonard, 101
Fillebrown, Luther W., 278
Fillebrown, Thomas, 272, 278
Fillebrown, William, 272
Finch, Eleen, 84
Fincks, Thomas, 30
Finn, James, 190
Finney, Clark, 128
Finney, Elkanah, 128 (2)
Finney, Ephraim, 128
Finney, George, 128
Finney, John, 20, 121
Finney, Robert, 128
Finney, Seth, 128
Finsome, Thomas, 210
Firbish, Abraham, 167
Firbish, John, 167
Firbush, Isaac, 234
Firbush, John, 234
Firmin, Davis, 68
Fish, Abraham, 73, 76
Fish, Alexander, 65
Fish, Anson R., 74
Fish, Asa, 74
Fish, Benjamin, 167
Fish, Braddock, 74
Fish, Calvin, 130
Fish, Charles, Jr., 47
Fish, Chipman, 73, 74

354   INDEX.

Fish, Church, 291
Fish, Daniel, 73, 76
Fish, David, 74 (2)
Fish, Edward, 72, 130
Fish, Eleazer, 268, 305
Fish, Eliab, Jr., 267
Fish, Eliakim, 24
Fish, Elisha, 263
Fish, Elisha K., 305
Fish, Ephraim, 73, 74
Fish, Francis, 75
Fish, I., Jr., 167
Fish, Isaiah, 73, 76
Fish, J., Jr., 167
Fish, James, 73, 76
Fish, James C., 163 (2)
Fish, Jesse, 74
Fish, John, 180 (2), 268, 305
Fish, Lemuel, 74
Fish, Lemuel, Jr., 73
Fish, Moody, 73, 76
Fish, Nathan, 72, 305
Fish, Nathan, 2d, 72
Fish, Nathaniel, 192
Fish, Otis, 75
Fish, Peleg, 266
Fish, Prince, 74
Fish, Reuben, 74
Fish, Rufus, 72
Fish, Russel, 214
Fish, Samuel, 305
Fish, Saul, 291
Fish, Seth, 167
Fish, Silas, 73
Fish, Simeon, 74, 192
Fish, Simeon, Jr., 74
Fish, Theodore, 74 (2)
Fish, Thomas, 74
Fish, Timothy, 72
Fish, William, 167
Fish, William, Jr., 277, 292
Fish, Zadoc, 128
Fish, Zenas, 74
Fisher, Aaron, 64, 90
Fisher, Alexander R., 214
Fisher, Alvin, 28
Fisher, Benjamin, 23
Fisher, Daniel, 53
Fisher, Elias, 86
Fisher, Elijah, 222, 259
Fisher, Ephraim C., 3
Fisher, Everett, 95
Fisher, Gardner, 162
Fisher, Grinsell, 222
Fisher, Isaac, 33
Fisher, Jabez, 24, 25
Fisher, James, 2d, 90
Fisher, Jeremiah, 247
Fisher, Joel, 215
Fisher, John, 222
Fisher, John, Jr., 234
Fisher, Loren, 47
Fisher, Luther, 90
Fisher, Mathias, 188
Fisher, Nahum, 91
Fisher, Oliver, 24
Fisher, Peter, Jr., 90
Fisher, Salem, 45
Fisher, Thomas, 234
Fisher, William, 234
Fisher, William, Jr., 70
Fishley, Benjamin, 132, 140

Fisk, Asa, 46
Fisk, Calvin, 72
Fisk, David, 48, 59
Fisk, Dexter, 65
Fisk, Ebenezer, 305
Fisk, Eliab, 310
Fisk, George, 60
Fisk, Henry, 101
Fisk, James, 72
Fisk, James J., 75
Fisk, James C., 163
Fisk, Jonas, 80
Fisk, Martin, 66
Fisk, Peleg, 262
Fisk, Perez, 129
Fisk, Seth, 65
Fiske, Abel, 201 (2), 203
Fiske, Abijah, 95
Fiske, Eben, 113
Fiske, James J., 7
Fiske, John, 198, 199, 201, 202
Fiske, Richard, 29
Fiske, Sewall, 115
Fiskett, Joseph, 173
Fitch, Amos, 25
Fitch, Andrew, 271
Fitch, David, 275
Fitch, George, 212
Fitch, Hardy E., 55, 57
Fitch, Henry, 180
Fitch, Solomon P., 65
Fitch, Timothy, 145
Fitch, William, 264
Fitts, Ephraim, 247
Fits, Nathaniel, 120, 124
Fits, Richard, 209
Fits, William, 23
Fitzgerald, Andrew, 291
Fitzgerald, John, 238
Fitzgerald, William, 78, 238
Flagg, Abel, 3
Flagg, Adonijah, 156
Flagg, Amos, 3
Flagg, Asa, 94
Flagg, Chandler, 67
Flagg, David, 234
Flagg, Edward, 90, 117
Flagg, Elijah, 3
Flagg, Ephraim, 10
Flagg, George, 238
Flagg, Isaac, 203
Flagg, Isaac, Jr., 201
Flagg, John, 231
Flagg, John, 2d, 3
Flagg, Levi, Jr., 48
Flagg, Luke, 47
Flagg, Marshall, 4
Flagg, Timothy, 98
Flagg, William, 214, 226
Flagg, William B., 25
Flanders, Charles, 16, 20, 125 (2)
Flanders, Daniel, 289, 306
Flanders, Enoch, 20
Flanders, Jacob, 306
Flanders, John, 19, 120, 123
Flanders, John C., 248
Flanders, Jonathan, 306
Flanders, Joseph, 12
Flanders, Moses, 306
Flanders, Nathaniel, 19, 20, 123
Flanders, Nathaniel S., 120
Flanders, Nehemiah, 19, 21, 121, 123, 124 (3)

Flanders, Nehemiah, Jr., 120, 121 (2)
Flanders, Samuel, Jr., 248
Flanders, Thomas, 306
Flanders, William, 19, 121, 125, 306
Flavers, John, 120
Fletcher, Abner, 229
Fletcher, Amos, 133, 136, 307
Fletcher, Asa, 268
Fletcher, Atwood, 280, 281
Fletcher, Benjamin, 178, 259
Fletcher, David, Jr., 276
Fletcher, Eleazer, 94
Fletcher, Francis, 302
Fletcher, Gardner, 41
Fletcher, Henry, 2, 108
Fletcher, Jacob, 155
Fletcher, James, 100
Fletcher, Jeromiah, Jr., 227
Fletcher, Joel, 284
Fletcher, John, 100
Fletcher, John S., 100
Fletcher, Joseph, Jr., 276
Fletcher, Lemuel, 227
Fletcher, Levi, 279
Fletcher, Nathan, 302
Fletcher, Phineas P., 88
Fletcher, Porter, 88
Fletcher, Robert, 237
Fletcher, Robert D., 276
Fletcher, Samuel, 303
Fletcher, Simon, 303
Fletcher, Thomas, 308
Fletcher, Timothy, 2, 108
Fletcher, William, 236, 307
Fletcher, Zachariah, 210
Fling, Nathan, 278
Flinn, John, 39
Flint, Amos, 100
Flint, Benjamin, 96, 192, 195
Flint, Daniel, 93, 99, 194. 228, 283
Flint, David, 6
Flint, Edward, 99
Flint, Elias, 133
Flint, Elijah, 253
Flint, Farman, 211
Flint, Isaac, 250
Flint, James, 211, 243
Flint, Jeremiah, 10
Flint, Jesse, Jr., 195
Flint, Joseph, 141, 195
Flint, Nathaniel, 151, 200
Flint, Nehemiah, 99
Flint, Nehemiah, Jr., 99
Flint, Silas, 99
Flitner, Thomas, 271
Flood, Edward L., 306
Flood, Henry, 295
Flood, Joseph, 171
Flood, Luther, 255
Flood, Samuel, 255
Flood, William, 269
Florance, John, 133
Florence, Charles, 118
Flower, Horner, 44
Flowers, Enos, 29
Flowers, James, 29
Flowers, William, 36
Floyd, Abijah, 27, 112
Floyd, Enoch, 16
Floyd, Enos, 17
Floyd, George, 10
Floyd, Henry, 261

INDEX. 355

Floyd, John, 183, 185, 188, 191, 308
Floyd, John, 2d, 27, 112
Floyd, Michael, 153
Floyd, Moses, 17
Floyd, Nathaniel, 172, 229, 282
Floyd, Patrick, 15
Floyd, Samuel, 27, 149, 229
Floyd, Saul, 282
Floyd, Silas, 15
Floyd, Thomas, 27, 112
Floyt, Charles, 110
Fluent, Nathan, 241
Fly, Daniel, 194
Fly, Isaac, Jr., 221
Fly, John, 239
Fly, William, Jr., 185
Flynn, Thomas, 303
Foard, William, 250
Fobes, Alpheus, 51
Fobes, Ansell, 108
Fobes, Billings, 252
Fobes, Joshua, 2d, 49
Fobes, Reed, 51
Fobes, Silas A., 33
Fog, Henry, 231
Fogerty, Dennis, 200, 206
Fogerty, Samuel, 292
Fogerty, Saul, 288
Fogg, Abel, 209
Fogg, Abner, Jr., 172
Fogg, Benjamin, 169, 212
Fogg, Daniel, 174, 256
Fogg, David, 171
Fogg, Dudley S., 306
Fogg, George, 174
Fogg, George W., 170
Fogg, Hesekiah, 269
Fogg, John, 172
Fogg, Jonathan, 170
Fogg, Joseph, 172, 188, 211
Fogg, Joshua, 306
Fogg, Josiah, 172, 306
Fogg, Moses, 172
Fogg, Nathan, 170
Fogg, Newell, 170
Fogg, Peleg B., 147 (2)
Fogg, Royal, 170
Fogg, Saul, 209, 213
Fogg, Walter, 168
Fogg, William, 169, 245, 281
Fogler, Charles, 198, 200, 202
Fogler, John, 290
Folds, Solomon, 91
Foles, Asa, 205
Foles, Atwood, 205
Foles, Elisha, 205
Foles, Ensebins, 205
Foles, Nathaniel, 205
Folger, George F., 5
Folinsby, Charles, 194
Folk, Abraham, 45
Follansbee, Charles, 196
Follansbee, Enoch, 15
Follansbee, John, 15, 98
Follansbee, Joseph, 89, 271
Follansbee, Nathan, 19
Follansbee, Newman, 15
Follansbee, William, 89
Follet, Daniel, 29
Follet, Simon, 33
Follett, Otis, 158
Follinsbe, Daniel K., 226

Follinsbee, Benjamin, Jr., 275
Folsom, Benjamin, 228
Folsom, Bradbury C., 272
Folsom, Dudley, 170
Folsom, Eliphalet, 230
Folsom, George, 254
Folsom, Henry, 192, 195
Folsom, Jacob, 230
Folsom, James, 192, 196, 306
Folsom, Jeremiah, 280, 281
Folsom, John, 272
Folsom, Joseph, 161
Folsom, Peter, 228
Folsom, Rufus, 306
Folsom, Samuel, 84 (2), 229, 260, 268
Folsom, Tristram, 271
Folsom, Warren, 280
Folsom, William E., 305
Fooler, George, 291
Foot, Barnard, 89
Foot, Bernard, 122
Foot, David, 247
Foot, Enos, 43
Foot, Erastus, 32, 197
Foot, J. L., 18
Foot, James, 21
Foot, Stephen, 283
Foote, Enoch, 247
Forbes, Asra, 176
Forbes, Charles, 134, 135, 138
Forbes, Daniel, 252
Forbes, Dexter, 91
Forbes, Elias, 91
Forbes, Henry, 45
Forbes, Holland, 91
Forbes, Samuel, 305
Forbisher, William, 26
Forbus, Amasa, 220
Forbus, Thomas, 231
Forbush, Abel, 100
Forbush, Chancy, 93
Forbush, Richard, 2d, 228
Force, Nathaniel, 240
Ford, Burnett, 70
Ford, Daniel, 4
Ford, Daniel A., 9
Ford, David, 102
Ford, Forbes, 229
Ford, Gideon, 192, 196
Ford, Henry, 238
Ford, Isaac, 279
Ford, James, 34, 38, 238, 267
Ford, James, Jr., 278
Ford, John, 32, 65, 278, 281
Ford, Joseph, 9
Ford, Joshua, 178
Ford, Luther, 66
Ford, Michael, 104
Ford, Obadiah, 259
Ford, Packard, 45
Ford, Samuel B., 76, 77
Ford, Samuel D., 18
Ford, Seth, 178
Ford, Seth H., 45
Ford, Stephen, 112, 169, 277
Ford, William, 196, 215, 249
Foreman, Amos, 18, 121, 124
Forest, Francis, 116
Forgate, John, 66
Forgett, Aseph, 66
Forrester, Amariah, 29
Forrester, Charles, 136

Forrester, J., 111
Forrester, John, 41
Forrester, Jonathan, 81
Forrester, Levi, 82
Forrester, Thomas H., 136
Forward, George, 4
Fosdick, Nathaniel F., 311
Fosdick, Willard, 229
Foskitt, Robert M., 66
Foss, Asa, 278
Foss, Charles, 280
Foss, Cyrus, 167, 277
Foss, Daniel, 169, 281
Foss, Ebeneser, 174
Foss, Eliakim, 278
Foss, Ezekiel, 172
Foss, George, 278, 281
Foss, Gustavus, 278
Foss, Hiram, 169, 281
Foss, Joel, 238
Foss, John, 165, 166, 174
Foss, John S., 164, 165, 166
Foss, Jonathan, 171
Foss, Joseph, 222
Foss, Lemuel, 269
Foss, Levi, 167, 277
Foss, Nathaniel, 221
Foss, Nichols, 246
Foss, Pelatiah, 171
Foss, Rufus, 269
Foss, Sampson, 159
Foss, Samuel, 6, 22
Foss, Shepherd, 213
Foss, Stephen, 233, 296
Foss, Thaddeus, 167
Foss, Thomas, 225
Foss, Walter, 25
Foss, William, 170
Fosse, William, 273
Fosset, Henry, 286
Fossett, Alex, 193
Fossett, Alexander, 287
Fossett, George, 193
Fossett, Henry, 193
Fossett, Henry, 3d, 192
Fossett, James, 193
Fossett, Samuel, 192
Fossett, Thomas, 193
Fossitt, Amasiah, 41
Fossitt, Henry, 290
Foster, Aaron, 36, 179
Foster, Abijah, 176, 257
Foster, Adams, 71
Foster, Alex, 193
Foster, Amos, 196, 199, 207, 208, 253
Foster, Asa, 261
Foster, Benjamin, 77, 85, 141, 232 (2), 247, 265
Foster, Brad, 270
Foster, Charles, 10, 83, 303
Foster, Cyrus, 41
Foster, Daniel, 147, 306
Foster, Daniel, Jr., 20
Foster, David, 9
Foster, Ebeneser, 27, 227, 282
Foster, Edward, Jr., 97
Foster, Eliab, 110
Foster, Elijah, 9
Foster, Elisha, 48
Foster, Enoch, 41
Foster, Ezra, 37
Foster, Forris D. A., 249
Foster, Francis, 206 (2)

INDEX.

Foster, Freeman, 147 (2)
Foster, Hesekiah, 36, 37
Foster, Isaac, 81, 244
Foster, Isaac P., 138
Foster, Isacker O., 36, 37
Foster, Israel, 36, 37 (2)
Foster, Israel, 2d, 36
Foster, James, 34, 38, 42, 68, 88, 148
Foster, Jeremiah, 36, 37, 200, 206, 257
Foster, Jeremiah, 4th, 36
Foster, Jesse, 133
Foster, John, 10, 26, 77, 78, 139(2), 192, 193, 235
Foster, John B., 138, 139
Foster, John H., 36
Foster, Jonathan, 36, 37
Foster, Jonathan, 2d, 36, 37
Foster, Joseph, 34
Foster, Joseph, Jr., 179
Foster, Joseph, 3d, 231
Foster, Joseph L., 37
Foster, Josiah, 4th, 37
Foster, Micah, 128
Foster, Michael, 176
Foster, Michel, 257
Foster, Moses, 210, 273
Foster, Moses B., 76, 77
Foster, Nathan, 125, 181, 261
Foster, Nathan, Jr., 253
Foster, Nathaniel, 36, 37, 223
Foster, Oliver, 273
Foster, Peter, 3
Foster, Philip H., 231
Foster, Richard, 206
Foster, Rufus, 40, 66, 87
Foster, Samuel, 43
Foster, Samuel, 2d, 37
Foster, Saul, 210
Foster, Seth, 34, 222, 274
Foster, Solomon, 18
Foster, Stephen A., 21, 132
Foster, Thomas, 34, 181, 193, 269
Foster, Thomas E., 100
Foster, Thomas W., 85
Foster, Timothy, 100, 168
Foster, Wadsworth, 273
Foster, William, 83, 90
Fountain, John, 195
Fountaine, Barna, 206
Fourd, Nathan, 196
Fowell, John, 25
Fowl, Robert L., 146
Fowl, Saul, 10
Fowle, Benjamin, Jr., 147
Fowle, Charles, 82
Fowle, George M., 28
Fowle, Henry, 113, 182
Fowle, Isaac, 41
Fowle, John, 42, 84, 85, 109
Fowle, Joseph, 39
Fowle, Parker, 82
Fowle, Samuel, 115
Fowle, William, 68, 83, 114
Fowle, William B., 85
Fowler, Abraham, 134
Fowler, Asa, 311
Fowler, Calvin, 31
Fowler, Clark, 3
Fowler, Daniel, 237
Fowler, David, 258
Fowler, Ebenezer, 186
Fowler, Hugh, 256
Fowler, James, 30, 301

Fowler, John, 3, 301
Fowler, John H., 304
Fowler, Jonathan, 189
Fowler, Joseph, 241
Fowler, Miles, 302
Fowler, Nathan, 240, 267
Fowler, Philip, 244
Fowler, Royal, 46
Fowler, Samuel R., 277
Fowler, Simeon, 216
Fowler, Thomas, 240
Fowler, Timothy, 36
Fowler, Warham, 32
Fowles, Ebeneser, 189
Fox, Ebenezer, 132, 140
Fox, Ephraim, 152
Fox, George, 242
Fox, Harvey, 31
Fox, Hubbard, 32
Fox, Israel, 67, 238
Fox, John, Jr., 153
Fox, Jonathan, 153
Fox, Joseph, Jr., 118
Fox, Joshua, 231
Fox, Josiah, 4
Fox, Nathaniel, 151
Fox, Richard, 28
Fox, Stephen R., 16
Foxcroft, Joseph E., 209
Foy, Henry, 231
Foy, John, 243
Foy, Samuel, 247
Foye, Henry, 149
Foye, Hollis, 179
Foye, James, 274
Foye, John, 145, 179
Foye, Joseph, 179
Foye, Nathaniel, 168
Foye, Thomas, 77
Foye, William, 138, 179
France, Stephen, 40
Francis, Bartholomew, 6, 22
Francis, Charles, 59
Francis, Edward B., 59
Francis, Elisha, 56
Francis, George, 35, 71, 90
Francis, James, 19, 22, 114, 122, 125
Francis, John, 69, 77, 167
Francis, Math, 68
Francis, Thomas, Jr., 167
Francisco, Peter, 29
Frank, Alpho, 210
Frank, James, Jr., 210
Frank, Josiah, 210
Frank, Levi, 252
Frank, Thomas, 177
Frank, William, 219
Fraser, Charles, 59
Fraser, Reuben, 62
Frasier, James, 233
Frasier, Marvin, 31
Frasure, James, 235
Fray, Samuel, 31
Frazer, John, 131
Frazer, Robert, 46
Frazier, Hugh, 117
Frazier, James, 296
Frazier, Joseph, 213
Frazier, Thomas, 213
Frederick, Henry, 129
Frederick, Joseph, Jr., 305
Frederick, Valentine, 268, 305

Frederick, William, 268, 303, 305
Freeman, Abner, 106
Freeman, Allen, 167, 217, 277
Freeman, Asa, 60
Freeman, Barnard, 125
Freeman, Benjamin, 104, 105 (2), 107, 108
Freeman, Benjamin B., 87
Freeman, Charles, 153, 271
Freeman, Daniel, 158, 175
Freeman, David, 173
Freeman, Ebenezer, 146, 147 (2)
Freeman, Edmund, 73, 104, 105 (2), 107, 108
Freeman, Edward, 76
Freeman, Enoch, 161
Freeman, Freeman, 60
Freeman, George, 163, 164
Freeman, Henry, 165, 166
Freeman, Hesekiah, 106, 107 (2), 108
Freeman, Isaac, 167, 277
Freeman, James, 130, 221
Freeman, James, Jr., 216
Freeman, Jared, Jr., 30
Freeman, John, 10, 55, 71, 292
Freeman, John B., 26
Freeman, Jonathan, 104, 105 (2), 106, 107, 211
Freeman, Joseph, 105, 107, 108, 273
Freeman, Joshua, 104, 105 (2), 106, 107, 174
Freeman, Josiah, 51, 107, 108 (2), 172
Freeman, Nathan, 173
Freeman, Nathaniel, 26, 107, 221, 240
Freeman, Nathaniel, Jr., 221
Freeman, Oran, 95
Freeman, Philip, 23
Freeman, Reuben, 163, 215, 240, 265
Freeman, Reuben, Jr., 163, 164
Freeman, Reuben, Sr., 164
Freeman, Richard, 239
Freeman, Rodolphus, 65
Freeman, Samuel, 162, 167, 177, 217
Freeman, Saul, 257
Freeman, Seth, 106 (2), 107 (2)
Freeman, Stephen, 53, 224
Freeman, Thomas, 162, 216
Freeman, Timothy, 213
Freeman, Trueman, 60
Freeman, William, 7, 271
Frees, Abraham, 265
Freese, Abraham, 163
Freese, George, 163
Freese, Isaac, 163
Freese, Abraham, 163, 238
Freese, George, 163
Freese, Isaac, 163
French, Abel, 227
French, Abram, 302
French, Alfred M., 10
French, Amos, 87
French, Benjamin, 153, 253
French, Benjamin C., 62
French, Chancy, 33
French, Charles, 24, 78, 178
French, Cyrus, 61
French, Daniel, 51, 88
French, David, 101, 102
French, Dearborn, 228
French, Ebeneser, 39, 280
French, Ebeneser, Jr., 229
French, Edmund, 146
French, Eli, 237
French, Ephraim, 126
French, Ephraim, Jr., 60
French, Ezra, 98

INDEX.

French, George G., 61
French, Gilbert, 41
French, Henry, 150
French, Isaac, 102, 273
French, Jacob, 153, 303
French, James, 61, 158, 250, 255
French, Joel, 303
French, John, 6, 36, 109, 211, 246, 258
French, Jonathan, 53
French, Jones, 58
French, Joseph, 39, 59, 68, 181
French, Josiah, 303
French, Leonard, 4
French, Levi, Jr., 280
French, Moses, 28
French, Nathan, 181
French, Nehemiah, 41, 227, 282
French, Noah, 82
French, Othaniel, 26
French, Othniel. Jr., 2, 79
French, Otis, 65
French, Reuben, 42, 89
French, Samuel, 303, 304
French, Saul, 290, 293
French, Stephen, Jr., 102
French, Sylvanus, 50
French, Uriah, 100
French, William, 23, 25, 224, 230, 283, 290, 293
French, Zithan, 2d, 303
Fretoe, James, 6
Frickett, Henry, 219
Frickett, Moses, 219
Frickett, Nathaniel, 219
Frickett, Samuel, 219
Friend, Daniel, 38
Friend, Joseph, 35
Friend, Richard, 9
Friend, Samuel, 35 (2)
Friend, William, 20
Friets, Jacob, 8
Friese, George, 306
Frink, Andrew, 98
Frink, Ichabod, 43
Frink, Lyman, 33
Frink, Samuel, 220
Frisbee, Austin S., 258
Frissel, Lemuel, 33
Frissel, Socrates, 33
Frith, Joseph, 182
Frizzle, Benjamin, 305
Frogg, George W., 277
Frohawk, Jonathan, 301
Frohawk, Solomon, 301
Frohawk, Thomas, 301
Frost, Aaron, 160
Frost, Aaron, Jr., 280
Frost, Andrew P., 218
Frost, Antipas, 90
Frost, Asa, 101
Frost, Benjamin, 173
Frost, Benjamin, Jr., 304
Frost, Charles, 173
Frost, Coleman, 83
Frost, Daniel, 43
Frost, Daniel H., 174
Frost, David, 29
Frost, Dominicus, 173
Frost, Edmund, 250, 255, 277
Frost, Eliot, 306
Frost, Elisha, 29
Frost, Enoch, 252

Frost, Gardner, 234
Frost, George, 280
Frost, George D., 256
Frost, Henry, 256
Frost, Horace, 29
Frost, Howard, 8
Frost, Isaac, 101
Frost, Isaac, Jr., 246
Frost, Jacob, 151, 155, 156
Frost, Joel, 101
Frost, John, 261
Frost, Joseph, 268
Frost, Josiah, 215
Frost, Luther, 173
Frost, Mason, 173
Frost, Moses, 261
Frost, Noah, 278
Frost, Peter, 252, 258
Frost, Richard M., 280
Frost, Robert, 252
Frost, Samuel, 162, 245, 264
Frost, Samuel A., 116
Frost, Samuel J., 226
Frost, Thomas, 159, 226
Frost, William, 155, 156, 173, 220, 246, 252, 257, 311
Frost, Winthrop, 215
Frothingham, Caleb, 21, 133
Frothingham, Charles, 28
Frothingham, Henry, 18
Frothingham, Isaac C., 115
Frothingham, J. M., 241
Frothingham, James, 116
Frothingham, Nathaniel, 137
Frothingham, Richard S., 139
Frothingham, Thomas, 77
Frothingham, Thomas, Jr., 69
Fruthy, James, 161
Fry, Ebenezer, 139
Fry, John, 230
Fry, Jonathan, 137, 178
Fry, Robert, 181
Fry, William, 136
Frye, Benjamin, 244
Frye, Eben, 10
Frye, Frederic, 150, 152
Frye, Isaac, 151
Frye, James, 158 (2), 291
Frye, John, 158, 265
Frye, John N., 137
Frye, John W., 135
Frye, Jonathan, 259, 302
Frye, Joseph, 145
Frye, Joshua, 20
Frye, Rolen, 240
Frye, Rowland, 265
Frye, Samuel, 90, 100
Frye, Samuel, 3d, 100
Frye, William, 151
Fuliton, Benjamin, 35
Fullam, Boylston, 83
Fullam, Daniel, 83
Fullam, Jacob, 5, 83
Fuller, Aaron, 251, 259
Fuller, Abraham, 224, 259
Fuller, Adam, 241
Fuller, Artemas, 178
Fuller, Asa, 310
Fuller, Barnabas, 175, 260
Fuller, Benjamin, 73, 76
Fuller, Calvin, 99
Fuller, Calvin B., 61

Fuller, Charles, 87, 224, 259
Fuller, Consider, 103, 251
Fuller, Constant, 236
Fuller, Daniel, 10, 72, 85
Fuller, David, 271
Fuller, Ebenezer, 26, 129
Fuller, Eleazer, 72, 129
Fuller, Elisha, 53
Fuller, Elisha D., 87
Fuller, Ezra, 224
Fuller, Ezra, Jr., 259
Fuller, Freeman, 251
Fuller, George, 131, 291
Fuller, Harvey, 251
Fuller, Henry W., 270
Fuller, Hilton, 224
Fuller, Ira, 253, 295
Fuller, Isaac, 44, 259
Fuller, Isaac, Jr., 225
Fuller, Isaiah, 146
Fuller, Jackson, 224
Fuller, James, 65, 74, 138, 206, 290, 293
Fuller, Joel, 251
Fuller, John, 55, 57, 65, 199, 200, 203, 224, 284, 287
Fuller, John B., 224, 259
Fuller, John S., 51
Fuller, John T., 103
Fuller, Jonathan, 53, 289, 293
Fuller, Joseph, 10, 31, 87, 126, 224, 259
Fuller, Joseph, Jr., 73, 76
Fuller, Josiah, Jr., 129
Fuller, Matthias, 74
Fuller, Moses, 161
Fuller, Nathan, 134, 140
Fuller, Nathaniel, 257
Fuller, Nathaniel, Jr., 253
Fuller, Norman, 31
Fuller, Oliver, 119, 223
Fuller, Oliver, Jr., 257
Fuller, Peter, 292 (2)
Fuller, Robert, Jr., 175
Fuller, Samuel, 73, 76, 129, 195, 197, 222, 275
Fuller, Seth, 109, 110
Fuller, Simon, 286
Fuller, Thomas, 74, 129, 271, 277, 279
Fuller, William, 51, 282, 312
Fuller, William, Jr., 271
Fuller, William C., 281
Fullerton, Henry, 163 (2)
Fullerton, James, 284, 287
Fullerton, John, 145, 284, 287
Fulliton, Benjamin, 35
Fullman, Samuel, 68
Fulton, Samuel B., 80, 81
Furber, Jonathan, 237
Furbish, John, 281
Furbush, Daniel, 48
Furbush, David, 244
Furbush, Elisha, 162
Furbush, Isaac, 296
Furbush, John, 296
Furbush, Stephen, 228, 282
Furbush, Sylvester, 8
Furguson, Charles, 218
Furlong, Henry, 20
Furlong, Patrick, 155, 312
Furlong, Thomas, 250
Furnald, Jacob, 125
Furnald, Joseph, 18, 121
Furnald, Thomas, 120, 123, 244

358   INDEX.

Furnald, Tristram, 244
Furness, Nathaniel, 28
Furness, Nathaniel H., 78

G

Gabriel, John, 2, 26
Gaffield, Abram, 266
Gaffney, William, 13
Gage, A., 38
Gage, Asmon, 34
Gage, Daniel, 229
Gage, John, 161, 215
Gage, Josiah, 241
Gage, Nathaniel, 117
Gage, Philip, 47
Gage, Prince, 125
Gage, Reuben, 267
Gage, Seth, 264
Gage, Thomas H., 247, 297
Gage, William, 34, 294
Gahan, John, 249
Gailor, Amhurst, 54
Gale, David, 65
Gale, Isaac, 83
Gale, James, 135, 137
Gale, John, 68, 90
Gale, Luther, 86
Gale, Noah, 82, 110
Gale, Richard, 137
Gale, Stephen, 65, 138
Gale, Thomas, 6, 22
Gale, Will, 68
Galee, Ephraim, 90
Galen, Richard, 162
Gall, Abraham, 66
Gall, Daniel, 20, 21
Galland, Robert, 132
Gallison, Henry, 244
Gallison, John, 7
Galord, Israel, 92
Galt, John, 126
Galvin, George I., 221
Gamage, Daniel, 193
Gamage, Ebenezer, 12
Gamage, John, 152
Gamage, Joshua, 150, 193
Gamage, Joshua, Jr., 152
Gamage, Nathaniel, 84, 109
Gamage, Samuel G., 12
Gamage, Thomas, 193
Gamage, William, 181, 193
Gammage, Stephen, 13
Gammar, Perkin, 225
Gammon, Edmund, 174
Gammon, Ephraim, 52
Gammon, James, 165 (2), 173
Gammon, John, 221
Gammon, Moses, 252
Gammon, Nathaniel, 176, 256, 257
Gammon, Robertson, 257
Gammon, Robinson, 176
Gammon, Samuel, 225, 235
Gammon, Stephen, 252
Gammon, Thomas, 176
Gammon, William, 58
Gammon, Wilmot, 253, 257
Gammons, Perkins, 259
Ganbert, Nicholas, 230
Gane, Enoch, 180
Gannet, Joseph, 49
Gansley, Andrew, 84
Gant, Ira, 66

Garcebon, Peter, 234
Garcelon, Ammi, 169
Garcelon, Daniel, 169
Garcelon, James, 169
Garcelon, Mark, 169
Garcelon, Samuel, 169
Garcelon, William, 169
Garden, Alpheus, 40
Gardiner, John, 146
Gardiner, Luke, 274
Gardner, A., Jr., 161
Gardner, Abel, 6, 21
Gardner, Anthony, 40
Gardner, Benjamin, 135, 137, 141, 226
Gardner, Calvin, 96
Gardner, Constant, 42
Gardner, David, 241, 254
Gardner, David M. 244
Gardner, Ebenezer, 306
Gardner, Edward, 129
Gardner, Giles, 117
Gardner, Henry, 302
Gardner, Ira, 251
Gardner, Israel, 183
Gardner, John, 21, 34, 38, 134, 135, 139 (2), 235, 260, 296
Gardner, John, 3d, 132
Gardner, John, 4th, 21
Gardner, John F., 118
Gardner, Joseph, 19, 137
Gardner, Josiah, 39
Gardner, Lemuel, 43 (2)
Gardner, Nicholas, 6
Gardner, Oakman, 80
Gardner, Peres, 42, 101
Gardner, Quincy, 42
Gardner, Robert, 20, 120, 121 (3), 123, 124 (2), 125 (3), 138, 299
Gardner, Sanders, 9
Gardner, Simon, 84
Gardner, Thomas, 24, 306
Gardner, Thomas G., 8
Gardner, Timothy, 44
Gardner, William, 81, 250
Gareslon, Mark, 277
Garet, Edward, 135, 137
Garet, Jonathan, 135
Garet, W. M., 135
Garet, William, 137
Garey, Elbridge, 159
Garfich, Elisha, 93
Garfield, Cooper, 99
Garfield, Moses, 93
Garland, Benjamin, 163 (2)
Garland, Edward, 163 (2)
Garland, Francis, 69
Garland, Hiram R., 42, 89
Garland, John, 213
Garland, Josiah, 163
Garland, Josiah, Jr., 163
Garlin, Aaron, 237
Garlin, Thomas, 237
Garner, Abner, 91
Garner, Richard, 211
Garney, Gridley, 101
Garney, Thomas, 6
Garrett, Joseph, 132, 140
Garrison, Joseph, 95
Garry, Benjamin, 285
Garshee, William, 59
Gaspeld, Silas, 32
Gass, William, 312

Gatchell, Aaron, 297, 299
Gatchell, Benjamin, 299
Gatchell, Daniel, 281
Gatchell, Ephraim, 261
Gatchell, John, 235
Gatchell, John S., 230
Gatchell, Simmons, 230
Gates, Eneas, 87
Gates, Henry, 94
Gates, Joel, 3
Gates, John, 93, 196
Gates, Joshua, 3
Gates, Lemuel, 81
Gates, Levi, 3
Gates, Levi, 2d, 3
Gates, Noah, 87
Gates, Oliver, 3
Gates, Saul, 43
Gates, Silvanus, 109
Gates, Sylvanus H., 24, 114
Gatley, Charles, 28
Gatt, Thomas, 123
Gault, Benjamin, 39
Gavitt, Jonathan, 138
Gavitt, Saul, 140
Gay, Abner, 27
Gay, Amos B., 86
Gay, Benjamin, 100
Gay, David, 258, 290, 293
Gay, Ebenezer, 95
Gay, Edward, 291, 294, 310
Gay, Eleazer, 288, 294
Gay, Harvey, 272
Gay, Ichabod, 85
Gay, Isaac, 264
Gay, Isaac, Jr., 284
Gay, Jabez, 281
Gay, Job, 284
Gay, John, 294
Gay, Jonah, 285, 291
Gay, Joseph, 29
Gay, Leonard, 90
Gay, Martin, 126
Gay, Obed, 290, 293
Gay, Phineas, 85
Gay, Seth, Jr., 272
Gay, Thomas, 28, 272
Gay, Timothy, 26
Gay, Willard, 86
Gay, William, 94
Gayney, Seth, 159
Gear, Hezekiah, 31, 119
Gear, Joshua W., 112
Gearfield, Alvis, 39
Gears, Ebenezer, 47
Geary, Saul, 96
Geasy, Benjamin, Jr., 96
Geer, Ebenezer, 47
Gelatt, John, 55, 58, 127
Gellinan, John, 277
Gelston, Hugh, 83
Gelusha, Abijah, 271
Gening, Nathaniel, 40
Gennerson, Samuel, 40
Gennings, Joseph, 227
Genthmer, John, 194
Genthmer, Samuel, 194
Genthmer, Charles, 287
Genthners, John, 195
Genthnor, John, 289
Gentleman, Joseph, 245
Gentner, Benjamin, 205 (2)

INDEX. 359

Gentner, David, 200, 205
Gentner, Samuel, 196
George, Benjamin, 136, 140
George, Francis, Jr., 167
George, Henry, 217
George, Jacob, 311
George, John, 198, 199, 200, 202, 208, 229, 300
George, Nathaniel, 8
George, Stephen, 301
George, Thomas, 161
George, William, 8, 80, 109, 229
Gerald, Christopher H., 306
Gerald, Daniel F., 306
Gerald, David F., 266
Gerald, David S., 306
Gerand, Peter, 80
Gerard, Peter, 132
Gere (?) Silsby, 5
Gerrish, Benjamin, 295
Gerrish, Charles, 295, 297
Gerrish, Enoch, 20
Gerrish, Franklin, 20
Gerrish, J. M., 242
Gerrish, James, 295
Gerrish, John, 20, 295
Gerrish, Joseph, 120, 122
Gerrish, Joseph M., 241
Gerrish, Joshua, 295, 296
Gerrish, Mayo, 20
Gerrish, Moses, 295, 297
Gerrish, Obediah, 254
Gerrish, Rufus B., 156
Gerrish, Rufus H., 157
Gerrish, William, 295
Gerry, Benjamin, 287
Gerry, Eldridge, 88
Gerry, James, 85
Gerry, Jesse, 208
Gerry, John, 180
Gerry, John O., 90
Gerry, Morgan, 245
Gerry, Nathaniel, 134, 140
Gerry, Richard, 180
Gerry, Samuel, 32, 85
Getchell, Abel, 263
Getchell, Abial, 239, 267
Getchell, Asa, 236
Getchell, Benjamin, 265, 309, 310
Getchell, Calvin L., 263
Getchell, Daniel, 168
Getchell, David, 237
Getchell, Edmund, Jr., 239
Getchell, Elihu, Jr., 239
Getchell, Ephraim, 265
Getchell, George, Jr., 190
Getchell, Howard, 265
Getchell, Howard H., 239
Getchell, Hugh, 230
Getchell, Isaac, 245
Getchell, John, 232 (2)
Getchell, Joseph, 310
Getchell, Otis, 158
Getchell, Peter, 148
Getchell, Samuel H., 171
Getchell, Stephen, 236
Getchell, William, 236
Getchell, Winslow, 232 (2)
Gevlin, Nathaniel, 214
Gevlin, Peter, 214
Gevlin, Richard, 214
Geyer, Frederick W., 25, 110
Geyer, George, 78

Geyer, James W., 79
Geyer, John J., 68
Geyer, Joseph, 68, 111
Geyer, Joseph W., 112
Geyer, Samuel, 68
Geyer, Saul, 291
Gibbens, Vassall, 28
Gibbons, Daniel L., 81, 86
Gibbs, Alex H., 7, 113
Gibbs, Alrich, 174
Gibbs, Andrew, 52
Gibbs, Barnabus, 71, 75
Gibbs, Caleb, 75
Gibbs, Caleb, Jr., 71
Gibbs, Cromwell, 39
Gibbs, Daniel, 205 (3)
Gibbs, Dennis, 264
Gibbs, Ezra, Jr., 210
Gibbs, Frank, 224
Gibbs, Freeman, 71
Gibbs, Heman, 173
Gibbs, James, 285
Gibbs, Jesse, 211
Gibbs, John, 224, 259
Gibbs, Jonathan, 71
Gibbs, Joshua, 126 (2)
Gibbs, Josiah, 71, 73, 75
Gibbs, Nathan, 310
Gibbs, Nathan B., 71, 73, 75
Gibbs, Pelham, Jr., 75
Gibbs, Pelham E., 52
Gibbs, Pitham, Jr., 71, 73
Gibbs, Reuben, 263, 310
Gibbs, Robert, 71, 73, 75
Gibbs, Rufus, 71
Gibbs, Samuel, 75, 207
Gibbs, Seth, 126
Gibbs, William, 126
Gibson, Abel, 151
Gibson, Andrew, 267
Gibson, Isaac, 41
Gibson, John, 133, 268
Gibson, Nathaniel, 77
Gibson, Peter, 190
Gibson, Samuel, 119, 120, 121, 122, 123, 124, 150, 152, 267
Gibson, Saul, 238
Gibson, Simeon, 112
Giddings, Aarod, 12
Giddings, Francis, 85
Giddings, Henry, 14
Gidly, Benjamin, 63
Gidly, John, 63
Gifford, Abiather, 76
Gifford, Adam, 74
Gifford, Adams, 56
Gifford, Alden, 55, 73
Gifford, Alfred, 73
Gifford, Asa, 73
Gifford, Bassett, 73
Gifford, Benjamin, 127
Gifford, Bethuel, 75, 76
Gifford, Cook, 63
Gifford, David, 56, 102
Gifford, Elihu, 63
Gifford, George, 56, 127
Gifford, Isaac, 56
Gifford, Jesse, 76
Gifford, Jesse, Jr., 75
Gifford, Job, 56
Gifford, John, 238
Gifford, Jonah, 53

Gifford, Jonathan, 1, 55
Gifford, Joseph, 240
Gifford, Joseph, Jr., 262
Gifford, Obed, 55, 58
Gifford, Pardon, 56, 63
Gifford, Paul, 55, 126
Gifford, Peleg, 56
Gifford, Prince, 130
Gifford, Reuben, 58, 63
Gifford, Rossiter, 73
Gifford, Rufus, 116
Gifford, Shubal, 58
Gifford, Silas, 71
Gifford, Warren, 56
Gifford, William, 263
Gifford, Zacheus, 56
Gilbert, Alvah, 168
Gilbert, Bailey, 168, 281
Gilbert, Benjamin, 11
Gilbert, Charles, 129
Gilbert, Charles D., 168
Gilbert, Coleman, 91
Gilbert, George, 45
Gilbert, James, 264
Gilbert, John, 78, 82
Gilbert, Josiah, 178
Gilbert, Judson, 86
Gilbert, Lee, 233, 296
Gilbert, Levi, 147 (2)
Gilbert, Marcus, 147 (2)
Gilbert, Reuben, 91
Gilbert, Samuel, 59
Gilbert, Samuel P., 11
Gilbert, Samuel R., 226
Gilbert, Thomas, 66
Gilbert, Warren, 45
Gilbreth, John, 226
Gilchrist, Alexander, 206 (3)
Gilchrist, Hugh, 181
Gilchrist, James, 288
Gilchrist, James, 2d, 288
Gilchrist, Joseph, 39, 288, 294
Gilchrist, Joseph L., 205 (2)
Gilchrist, Mathew, 294
Gilchrist, Robert, 206
Gilchrist, Samuel, 206
Gilchrist, Saul, 206
Gilchrist, William, 181
Giles, Magra, 66
Giles, William, 11
Gilford, Elijah, 242
Gilford, James, 242
Gilford, Samuel, 67
Gilinan, Zebulon, 284
Gilkey, James, 259
Gilkey, John, 280
Gilkey, Reuben, 173
Gilkey, Samuel, 173
Gill, James B., 40
Gill, Michel, 79
Gill, Nathan, 8
Gill, William, 274
Gillet, Cephas, 44
Gillet, Eliphalet, 270
Gillet, Jonathan A., 64
Gillet, Marcus, 139 (2)
Gilley, James, 276
Gilley, John, 6
Gilley, William, 163, 164
Gillman, George, 311
Gillman, John, 164, 165
Gillman, Thomas, 27

INDEX

Gillpatrick, Jacob, 154
Gillpatrick, Riggs, 179
Gillson, Alexander, 210
Gillson, Sutton, 98
Gillson, Timothy, 64
Gilman, Bela, 280
Gilman, Benjamin, 279
Gilman, Dennis, 280
Gilman, Ebeneser, 174, 255
Gilman, Eliphalet, 163 (2)
Gilman, Eliphalet F., 34, 38
Gilman, Esekiel, 226
Gilman, George G., 87
Gilman, Henry, 133, 136
Gilman, James, 47
Gilman, John, 117, 151, 153, 166, 169, 219
Gilman, John H., 170
Gilman, John T., 88
Gilman, Jonathan, 156
Gilman, Joseph, 280, 281
Gilman, Moses, 228
Gilman, Nathan, 279
Gilman, Robert, 169
Gilman, Robinson, 268, 308
Gilman, Samuel, 238
Gilman, Smith, 181
Gilman, Thomas, 77
Gilman, Warren, 161
Gilman, William, 71, 112
Gilmore, Abraham, 30
Gilmore, John, 2d, 302
Gilmore, John D., 62
Gilmore, Melvin, 95
Gilmore, Miller, 286
Gilmore, Rufus, 213, 286
Gilmore, Samuel, 201, 202
Gilmore, Turner, 41
Gilmore, Willard, 290
Gilmour, Joseph, 138
Gilpatrick, Christopher, 234
Gilpatrick, David, 180
Gilpatrick, John, 161, 180
Gilpatrick, Nathaniel, 234
Gilpatrick, Samuel, 169, 269
Gilpatrick, Thomas, 180, 234, 275
Gilpatrick, William, 309 (2)
Gilson, Amos, 60
Gilson, James, 87
Gilson, John, 116
Gilson, Jonas, 87
Ginn, William R., 163
Gipson, William, 215
Girdler, Lewis, Jr., 6
Girdler, William, 14
Girdley, George, 13
Given, Benjamin, 298
Given, David, 184, 296
Given, David, Jr., 298
Given, Ebeneser, 169
Given, John, 169, 296
Given, John, 2d, 298
Given, John, 3d, 298
Given, Samuel, 295
Given, Thomas, 298 (2)
Givens, David, 191
Givens, Ebeneser, 237
Givin, David, 186
Givings, John, 34
Givins, James, 179
Givum, James, 134
Glass, Charles, 50
Glass, Consider, 131

Glass, Esekiel, 210
Glass, John, 184, 186 (2), 187, 190
Glass, Moses, 271
Glass, Nathaniel, 131
Glass, Nehemiah, 271
Glazier Abram F., 94
Glazier, Joseph, 243
Glazier, Reuben, 47
Glazin, Perley, 46
Gleason, Abijah, 64
Gleason, Artemas, 48
Gleason, Bryant, 264
Gleason, Ira, 63
Gleason, James, 3
Gleason, Joel, 3, 88
Gleason, Josiah, 87
Gleason, Reuben, 3
Gleason, Silas, 161
Glidden, Arnold, 191
Glidden, Charles, 190
Glidden, David, 180
Glidden, John, 21, 239
Glidden, John, Jr., 194
Glidden, John C., 240
Glidden, Jonathan, 136
Glidden, Joseph, 141, 192, 194
Glidden, Moses, 180
Glidden, Nathaniel, Jr., 194
Glidden, Robert, 90, 116
Glidden, William, 193
Glines, Daniel, 261
Glines, John, 17
Glines, Timothy, 261
Glody, David, 126
Glover, Cook O., 136
Glover, Eaton, 25
Glover, Elisha, 100
Glover, George, 132
Glover, Ichabod, 135
Glover, James, 81
Glover, John H., 133
Glover, Joseph, 175
Glover, Joshua, 223
Glover, Josiah, 100
Glover, Nathaniel, 178
Glover, William, 24
Gloves, Levi G., 91
Gloyd, Spencer, 50
Glynn, John, 110
Glynn, Moses, 10
Goady, William, 31
Gobert, John, 155
Godard, Asa, 3
Godard, Nathaniel, 93
Goday, William, 14
Goddard, Cyrus, 103
Goddard, David, 261
Goddard, Ebeneser, 227
Goddard, Elias, 26, 78
Goddard, Jonah, 48
Goddard, Lyman, 48
Godding, Andrew R., Jr., 210
Godding, John, 156
Godfrey, Albert, 50
Godfrey, Albert W., 60, 161
Godfrey, Asa, 91
Godfrey, Benjamin, 213
Godfrey, David, 54
Godfrey, John, 233
Godfrey, Joseph, 70, 261
Godfrey, Rufus, 61
Godfrey, William, 61

Godfry, Joseph, 77
Goff, Asahel, 61
Goff, Charles, 78
Goff, Isaac, 62
Goff, James, 177, 257, 260
Goff, Nathaniel, 60
Goff, Robert, 59
Goff, Robert S., 70
Goff, William, 83
Goffield, Thomas, 25
Going, James, 87
Going, Samuel, 180
Gol, Edward, 179
Gold, Samuel, 24
Golden, John, 169
Golder, William, 169
Golding, Peter, 159
Goldsborough, Asa, 14
Goldsbuck, Adam, 78
Goldsmith, David, 268
Goldsmith, George W., 79
Goldsmith, John, 36
Goldsmith, Joseph, 116
Goldsmith, Samuel, 36, 37
Goldsmith, Zacheus, 230
Goldthwait, Benjamin, 85
Goldthwait, Esekiel, 141
Goldthwait, George W., 85
Goldthwait, Jacob, 271
Goldthwait, John, 274
Goldthwait, Luther, 141
Goldthwait, Moses, 6, 21
Goldthwait, Samuel, 172
Goldthwait, Timothy, 274
Goldthwait, William, 274
Goldthwaite, John, 90
Goldthwight, Thomas, 269
Gooch, Abijah, 309 (2)
Gooch, Daniel, 309 (2)
Goodale, Nathan, 132
Goodale, Paul, 3
Goodall, David, 303
Goodall, Esekiel, 146
Goodall, Jacob, 47
Goodall, John, Jr., 211
Goodall, Rufus, 47
Goodell, Abner, 66
Goodell, Samuel, 219
Goodenough, Thomas, 65
Goodenow, Nathan, 194
Goodhue, Ira, 213
Goodhue, Isaac, 133
Goodhue, James, 122, 132
Goodhue, James S., 89, 119
Goodhue, Jeremiah, 132, 140
Goodhue, Manassah, 211
Goodhue, Richard, 242
Goodin, Moses, 215
Gooding, Isaac, 224
Gooding, Nathaniel, 272
Goodman, Otis, 43
Goodman, Sylvester, 92
Goodnow, Elisha, 29
Goodnow, Elmer, 95
Goodnow, Isaac, 95
Goodnow, Jonas, 29
Goodnow, Rufus, 88
Goodnow, William, 91, 152
Goodrich, Aaron, 30
Goodrich, Anson B., 31
Goodrich, David, 15
Goodrich, Isaac, 306

INDEX. 361

Goodrich, James T., 26, 78
Goodrich, John, 85
Goodrich, Jonathan, 305
Goodrich, Joseph, 77
Goodrich, Joseph, Jr., 12
Goodrich, Noah, 238
Goodridge, Benjamin, 9, 268
Goodridge, David, 306
Goodridge, Ebenezer, 306
Goodridge, John, 265
Goodridge, Joshua, 258
Goodridge, Oliver, 306
Goodridge, Sewall, 3
Goodspeed, Benjamin, 2d, 74
Goodspeed, Charles, 74
Goodspeed, Charles H., 74
Goodspeed, David S., 131
Goodspeed, Elias, 2
Goodspeed, Ervin, 74
Goodspeed, Ezra, 74
Goodspeed, Harrison, 73
Goodspeed, John, 74
Goodspeed, Jonathan, 74
Goodspeed, Joseph, 74 (2)
Goodspeed, Levi, 74
Goodspeed, Luther, 73, 76
Goodspeed, Reuben, 213
Goodspeed, Rowland, 74
Goodspeed, Silas, 74
Goodspeed, Thomas, 74
Goodspeed, Walley, 74
Goodwin, Abiel, 311
Goodwin, Amos, 17
Goodwin, Andrew, 271
Goodwin, Benjamin, 187, 191, 245
Goodwin, Benjamin, 2d, 245
Goodwin, Caleb, 238
Goodwin, Charles, 53, 128, 131
Goodwin, Daniel, 17, 186, 188, 271
Goodwin, David S., 188
Goodwin, Ebenezer, 272
Goodwin, Edmond, 154
Goodwin, Edmund, 149
Goodwin, Ephraim, 19, 119, 122
Goodwin, Francis L. B., 216
Goodwin, George, 62
Goodwin, Henry, 245
Goodwin, Hiram, 245
Goodwin, James, 271, 272
Goodwin, Jedediah, 238
Goodwin, John, 6, 20, 146, 245, 310
Goodwin, Joseph, 17, 151
Goodwin, Josiah, 17
Goodwin, Levi, 20, 272
Goodwin, Major, 17
Goodwin, Miles, 238
Goodwin, Nathaniel, 17
Goodwin, Nehemiah, 217
Goodwin, Samuel, 156, 157, 188, 191, 225, 295
Goodwin, Saul, 17, 156
Goodwin, Simeon, 149
Goodwin, Simeon, Jr., 271
Goodwin, Thomas, 17, 21, 80, 245
Goodwin, Uriah, 2
Goodwin, William, 90, 216, 245, 269
Goof, Squier, 41
Gookin, Samuel, 164 (2), 165
Gookin, Thomas, 39
Goold, Abner, 211
Goold, James, 212
Goold, John, 233
Goold, Jonathan, 167, 255

Goold, Moses, 233
Goold, Noah, 255
Goold, Robert, 225
Goold, Thomas F., 225
Gordan, Daniel, 282
Gordan, Jabez, 269
Gordan, John, 150
Gordan, Newell, 228
Gordan, Simeon, 228
Gordan, Thomas, 2d, 228
Gordan, William, 23
Gorden, Ithnal, 279
Gorden, Michael, 301
Gorden, Robert, 124, 280
Gordon, Alexander, 278
Gordon, Amos, 269
Gordon, Charles, 19, 120, 123, 302
Gordon, Daniel, 179, 227, 228, 280, 282
Gordon, Emanuel, 24
Gordon, George, 15, 168
Gordon, Henry, Jr., 152
Gordon, John, 24, 26
Gordon, John, Jr., 152
Gordon, Jonathan, 71, 168, 281
Gordon, Joseph, 152, 228 (2), 254
Gordon, Josiah, 308
Gordon, Luther, 282
Gordon, Manly, 26
Gordon, Newal, 283
Gordon, Robert, 18, 121
Gordon, Stephen, 125 (2)
Gordon, Thomas, 271
Gordon, Timothy, 16
Gordon, William, 54
Gore, Christopher, 7, 25
Gore, Christopher, Jr., 69
Gore, James, 24, 114
Gore, Jeremiah, 7, 113
Gore, John, 81, 243
Gore, Watson, 7, 112
Gorham, Benjamin, 252, 255
Gorham, Charles, 131
Gorham, David, 193
Gorham, George, 81
Gorham, James, 57
Gorham, John, 87, 125, 131
Gorham, John, Jr., 131
Gorham, Nathaniel, 131
Gorham, Sylvanus, 131
Gorham, Thomas, 81
Gorham, William, 178
Gormand, John, 312
Gormin, John D., 77
Gorton, James, 181
Gorum, Charles, 44
Goss, Benjamin C., 229, 282
Goss, Enos, 47
Goss, Francis, 138
Goss, George, 256
Goss, James, 10
Goss, Joseph, 132
Goss, Leonard, 83
Goss, Philemon C., 256
Goss, William, 6, 101, 256
Goss, William, Jr., 11
Gott, Eliab, 163, 164
Gott, George, 12
Gott, James, 12
Gott, Nathaniel, 163, 164
Gott, Solomon, 11
Gott, William, Jr., 248, 278
Gouch, James, 28

Gouch, Russell, 99
Goudy, Amos, 287, 310
Goudy, John, 287, 310
Gould, Aaron, 180
Gould, Abner, 243, 246
Gould, Abraham J., 98
Gould, Andrew, 252, 255
Gould, Asa, 70, 77, 167
Gould, Benjamin, 229
Gould, Crowell, 265
Gould, Daniel, 156, 157
Gould, David, 280
Gould, Ebenezer, 270
Gould, Edmund, 135
Gould, Edward, 145
Gould, Eleazer, 242
Gould, Eli, 167, 277
Gould, Elijah, 268
Gould, Emerson, 137
Gould, Franklin, 161
Gould, Frederick, 113 (2)
Gould, George, 112
Gould, George F., 306
Gould, Jacob, 25
Gould, James, 104, 107, 132, 237
Gould, John, 15, 215, 227, 236, 283
Gould, Jonathan, 211
Gould, Joseph, 64, 298
Gould, Josiah, 221, 227, 283
Gould, Lemuel, 264
Gould, Levi, 278
Gould, Moses, 180
Gould, Nathan, 211, 234
Gould, Nathaniel, 3
Gould, Nathaniel, Jr., 216
Gould, Nathaniel W., 147
Gould, Nehemiah, 239, 265
Gould, Noah, 252
Gould, Oliver, 226
Gould, Peletiah, 277
Gould, Peltiah, 167
Gould, Reuben, 70
Gould, Robert, 158, 167
Gould, Rufus, 167
Gould, Samuel, 15, 218, 265, 278
Gould, Silas, 5, 84
Gould, Simeon, 167
Gould, Stephen, 155
Gould, Thomas, 81, 104, 107
Gould, Thomas, Jr., 104
Gould, Thomas F., 165, 166
Gould, William, 167, 218, 256
Gould, William, 2d, 191
Gould, Zadock, 240
Goulder, Arnold, 245
Gouldsberry, Joseph, 34, 38
Gove, Caleb, 169
Gove, Elijah, 185, 191
Gove, James, 185
Gove, John, 78, 243
Gove, Peter, 163 (2)
Gove, Solomon, 282
Gove, Solomon, Jr., 220
Gove, Stephen, 70
Goward, Israel, 53
Gowbert, Nicholas, 296
Gowdey, John, 118
Gowel, John, 232
Gowel, William, 232
Gowell, Charles, 235, 296
Gowell, James, 177, 260
Gowell, John, 232

INDEX.

Gowell, Joseph, 178
Gowell, William, 232, 259
Gowen, Alpheus, 245
Gowen, James, Jr., 220
Gowen, John, 199, 203, 245
Gowen, Levi, 220
Gowen, Moses, 220
Gower, John, 200
Gower, Richard, 276
Gower, William, 230
Gowin, Asa, 181
Gowin, Ebenezer, Jr., 181
Gowin, Joseph, 179
Gowin, Nathan, 149
Gowin, Nathaniel, 181
Grace, Aaron, 225
Grace, James, 306
Grace, Richard P., 160
Grace, Thomas, 171
Grace, William, 306
Graffam, Caleb, 211
Graffam, David, 167
Graffam, James, 172
Graffam, Jeremiah, 172
Graffam, Peter, 212, 220, 255
Graffam, Samuel, 298
Graffam, Thomas, 168, 295
Graffan, Daniel, 222
Graffan, Jacob, 200, 204
Graffan, Thomas, 255
Graffum, Daniel, 259
Grafton, Benjamin, 288
Grafton, David, 286, 290
Grafton, George W., 132
Grafton, Joseph D., 7
Gragg, Jacob, 87
Gragg, Moses, 99
Graham, Aretus, 5
Graham, George, 87, 261
Graham, Jeremiah, 265
Graham, John, 199, 200, 203, 219, 258
Graham, William, 46
Grammar, Seth, 2, 26
Grammer, Seth, 79
Grandey, Eri, 43
Granger, George W., 45
Granger, Parley, 93
Grant, Andrew, 213
Grant, Asa, 225
Grant, Benjamin, 154, 234, 270, 296
Grant, Charles, 84, 271
Grant, Christopher, 266
Grant, Daniel, 214
Grant, Elijah, 161
Grant, George, 8
Grant, Isaac, 256
Grant, John, 6, 22, 31, 46, 84, 109, 139, 268, 298
Grant, Joseph, 27, 35 (2), 137, 220
Grant, Joshua, 267
Grant, Josiah, 217
Grant, Judin, 217
Grant, Moses, 7
Grant, Nathaniel, 216
Grant, Samuel, 217, 228, 275
Grant, Stephen, 167, 215
Grant, Stephen, Jr., 217
Grant, Thomas, 6, 36, 183, 245
Grant, Unite, 296, 298
Grant, Watts, 209
Grant, William, 149, 216
Grant, William B., 275
Grass, John, 103

Grass, Lewis, 104
Grate, Samuel, 63
Graves, Andrew, 220
Graves, Asa, 8
Graves, Blaney, 6, 22 (2)
Graves, Christopher, 6, 22
Graves, Daniel, 231
Graves, Eben, 231
Graves, Issacher, 45
Graves, Jacob, 231
Graves, John, 6, 40, 96, 295
Graves, Johnson, 234
Graves, Joseph, 4
Graves, Josiah D., 4
Graves, Justus, 96
Graves, Levi, 231
Graves, Lomous, 64
Graves, Moses, 231
Graves, Newell, 66
Graves, Orlando, 67
Graves, Perea, 96
Graves, Phinna, 96
Graves, Rodney, 94
Graves, Rolin, 96
Graves, Samuel, 3, 6, 22, 231
Graves, Thomas, 234
Graves, True G., 21, 125
Graves, Truel G., 125
Graves, William, 6, 96, 266
Graves, Wrotus, 96
Gray, Aaron, 161, 169
Gray, Abel, 48
Gray, Abraham, 153
Gray, Asa, 23
Gray, Benjamin, 71
Gray, Charles, 174, 196
Gray, Chester, 45, 47
Gray, Daniel, 151, 234, 237
Gray, David, 212, 238
Gray, Ebenezer, 268, 305
Gray, Ezekiel, 89
Gray, Francis, 84, 115
Gray, Frederick, 16
Gray, George, 174, 246, 305, 312
Gray, Harrison, 28, 112
Gray, Henry, 28, 183, 185, 188
Gray, James, 170, 190, 234, 238, 277
Gray, James, Jr., 212, 276
Gray, Jeremiah, 70
Gray, Jesse, 169, 281
Gray, Job, 129
Gray, John, 132, 161, 268, 290, 298, 302, 305
Gray, John, 3d, 140
Gray, Jonathan, 237
Gray, Joseph, 153, 169
Gray, Joseph W., 97
Gray, Joseph Y., 274
Gray, Joshua, 170, 265
Gray, Josiah, 191
Gray, Leverett, 197, 204
Gray, Levi, 231
Gray, Luther, 301
Gray, Mark, 276
Gray, Moses, 249
Gray, Nathan, 170
Gray, Nathaniel, 237
Gray, Pardon, 272
Gray, Patrick, 67
Gray, Reuben, 301
Gray, Robert, 160
Gray, Samuel, 25, 50, 165, 166, 185, 188, 225, 237, 262

Gray, Saul, 132, 140, 183, 280
Gray, Solomon, 148, 236
Gray, Stephen, 169, 281
Gray, Thomas, 186, 189
Gray, Thomas, Jr., 184
Gray, Thomas N., 170
Gray, Uriah, 148
Gray, Uriah H., 224
Gray, William, 35 (2), 278, 285, 287, 306
Gray, William, Jr., 13
Grear, James, 301
Greaton, Leonard, 305
Greaves, John, 90
Greeley, Benjamin, 18
Greeley, Daniel, 180
Greeley, Eben B., 146
Greeley, John, 274
Greeley, Joseph, 279
Greeley, Nathaniel, 121, 125
Greeley, Philip, 137
Greeley, Samuel, 275
Greeley, William, Jr., 255
Greely, Henry, 282
Greely, Jacob, 3d, 180
Greely, Nathaniel, 20
Greely, Samuel, 282
Greely, Stephen, 180
Green, Abel, 88
Green, Andrew, 28
Green, Asa, 308
Green, Axel, 141
Green, Benjamin, 76, 149, 306
Green, Clark, 24
Green, Daniel, 149, 263
Green, Daniel P., 64
Green, David, 74, 233, 305
Green, Ebenezer, 73
Green, Edward, 72
Green, Elisha, 76
Green, Gardner, 148
Green, George, 267
Green, Guy, 147
Green, Henry, 244
Green, Hosea, 93
Green, Isaac, 70
Green, James, 100, 117, 233
Green, Jarvis, 72
Green, Jeremiah, 60
Green, Jesse, 219
Green, Job W., 113 (2)
Green, John, 20, 22, 27, 87, 123 (2), 255, 265, 303
Green, John, Jr., 149
Green, John, 3d, 225
Green, Jonathan, 212
Green, Joseph, 91, 171
Green, Josiah, 299
Green, Lawson H., 32
Green, Littlebridge, 141
Green, Luther, 39
Green, Nathan, 139
Green, Oliver, 42, 89
Green, Robert S., 243
Green, Samuel, 94
Green, Samuel R., 85
Green, Saul, 101
Green, Simeon, 54
Green, Stephen, 27, 268, 305
Green, Stephen, 2d, 268
Green, Stuart, 173
Green, Thomas, 6, 39, 72
Green, Thomas, Jr., 311

INDEX.

Green, Ware, 174
Green, William, 28, 151
Greenlaw, Eben, 193
Greenlaw, Thomas Alexander, 193
Greenleaf, Abner, 15
Greenleaf, Abraham, 305
Greenleaf, Abram, 268
Greenleaf, Anthony, 305
Greenleaf, Benjamin, Jr., 184, 186 (2)
Greenleaf, Charles, 18
Greenleaf, Ebenezer, 189, 305
Greenleaf, Edmund, 14
Greenleaf, George, 19
Greenleaf, Jacob, 17
Greenleaf, John, 19, 268, 305
Greenleaf, Joseph, 229, 282, 305
Greenleaf, Levi, 305
Greenleaf, Seth, 308
Greenleaf, Spencer, 182 (2), 186
Greenleaf, Stephen, 252, 305
Greenleaf, Thomas, 268, 307
Greenleaf, Westbrook, 189
Greenleaf, William, 9, 150, 251
Greenlow, Alexander, 192
Greenlow, Joseph, 192
Greenough, Jonathan M., 84
Greenough, Moses, 182 (2), 184, 186
Greenough, Parker, 15
Greenough, Thomas M., 98
Greenough, William, 7, 112
Greenwood, Henry, 98
Greenwood, John, 158
Greenwood, Mason, 258
Greenwood, Nathaniel, Jr., 258
Greenwood, Thadeus, 218, 252, 255
Gregg, Stephen, 79
Greggs, Nathaniel, 39
Gregory, Abijah, 311
Gregory, Esbon, 30
Gregory, Eshon, 30
Gregory, Isaac, 3
Gregory, Israel, 207, 208
Gregory, James, 22
Gregory, John H., 6, 21
Gregory, Joseph, 22
Gregory, Joseph, Jr., 6
Gregory, Uriah, 115
Gregory, William, 208
Gregory, William, 3d, 199, 207
Grenald, Philip, 180
Grey, Francis, 191
Grey, Henry, 191
Grey, Thomas, Jr., 191
Grice, Caleb E., 110
Gridler, Benjamin, 6
Gridler, Lewis, Jr., 6
Gridley, Jeremiah, 63
Gridley, William, 114
Gridley, William, Jr., 25
Griffin, Amos, 11
Griffin, Davis, 12
Griffin, Dudly, 139 (2)
Griffin, Edward, 279 (2)
Griffin, Eliphalet, 14
Griffin, Hardwick, 222
Griffin, Henry, 12
Griffin, Isaac, 167
Griffin, Jacob, 17, 20, 119, 120, 121, 122 (2), 124, 125 (2)
Griffin, Job, 306
Griffin, Joseph, 212
Griffin, Leonard, 241, 242

Griffin, Mark, 17
Griffin, Nathaniel, 138, 241
Griffin, Peleg, 303
Griffin, Robert, 119, 122
Griffin, Simon, 212
Griffin, Tristram, 13, 14
Griffin, William, 272, 302
Griffith, Ellis, 52
Griffith, Hezekiah, 259
Griffith, John, 222
Griffiths, John, 259
Grigg, Stephen, 66
Griggs, Thomas, 40
Grimage, William, 192
Grimes, Joseph, 183
Grinat, Daniel B., 290
Grind, Joseph, 20
Grinnel, Daniel B., 286
Grinnel, Samuel S., 286
Grinnell, Isaac, 47
Grinnell, Remington, 55, 58
Grinnell, William F., 84
Grinol, Wilson, 141
Gripps, John, Jr., 297
Griswald, Philo, 32
Gross, Andrew, 217
Gross, Jacob, 101
Gross, James, 161
Gross, John, 1
Gross, Lewis, 1, 104
Gross, Reuben, 300
Gross, William, 224, 258
Grossman, Henry, 79
Grossman, John G., 80
Groton, Joseph, 292
Groton, Leonard, 268
Groton, Zenas, 194
Grout, Elisha, 303
Grout, Joshua, 136
Grove, Jeremiah S., 45
Grove, Samuel, 30
Grovenor, Lewis, 7
Grover, Asahel, 258
Grover, Benjamin, Jr., 249
Grover, Calvin, 99
Grover, Ebenezer, Jr., 11
Grover, Elias, 258
Grover, James, 231, 258
Grover, James, Jr., 258
Grover, John, 12, 231
Grover, John, Jr., 183
Grover, Jonathan, 210
Grover, Joseph, 231
Grover, Josiah, 12, 150
Grover, Josiah, Jr., 67
Grover, Nehemiah, 12
Grover, Peter, 258
Grover, Samuel, 232 (2)
Grover, William, 150
Grover, Zebulon P., 256
Groves, Ansel, 3
Groves, John, 87, 295
Groves, Joseph, 167, 186, 190
Groves, Merritt, 65
Groves, Orlando, 67
Groves, Parley F., 91
Groves, Thomas, 298
Growman, Henry F., 112
Grubb, William, 82, 110
Grunlow, Joseph, 194
Grush, Philip, 14, 34, 38

Guffield, Abraham, 262
Guild, Abner, 99
Guild, Freedom, 99
Guild, George, 28
Guild, Horace, 97
Guild, James, 90
Guild, Lewis, 97
Guild, Nathaniel, 95
Guilford, Aaron, 139
Guilford, Benjamin, 149
Guilford, David, 266
Guilford, Samuel, 27
Guill, Daniel, 10
Guillam, Benjamin, 30
Guillow, David, 66
Gullifer, David, 262
Gullifer, John, Jr., 262
Gullifer, Peleg, 262
Gulliver, John, 7
Gulliver, Joseph, 153
Gulliver, Lemuel, 217
Gulliver, Samuel, 59
Gulliver, Spencer, 85
Gulliver, Stephen, 70, 85
Gulliver, Thomas, 217
Gunlan, Ebenezer, 192
Gunn, Frederic, 31
Gunn, Willard, 65
Gunsmith, John, 62
Guptil, Nathaniel, 160
Guptil, Robert, 160
Guptil, Thomas, 160
Gurdler, William, 36
Gurley, William, 14
Gurney, Alpheus, 81 (2)
Gurney, Chandler R., 50
Gurney, David, 273
Gurney, Edward, 202, 255
Gurney, Elisha, 200
Gurney, Ephraim, 56
Gurney, Gridley, 96
Gurney, Heman, 75
Gurney, Lemuel, 175
Gurney, Levi, 260
Gurney, Melvin, 92
Gurney, Samuel B., 250, 255
Gurney, Seth, 49
Gurney, Thomas, 175
Gurnsey, Thomas, 71
Gustin, Robert M., 179
Gustin, Thomas, 172
Guy, Edward, 288
Guy, Jesse, 145
Guy, Jonah, 288
Gwin, David, 189
Gwin, Saul, 231
Gwin, William, Jr., 148
Gwiney, Elisha, 199
Gwinn, James, 135
Gyer, John, 285
Gyer, Martin, 285
Gyer, Martin, Jr., 285

H

Hach, Daniel, 62
Hackelton, James, 192, 193
Hacker, Edmund, 237
Hacket, Elijah, 213
Hacket, George, 52
Hacket, Joseph, 59
Hackett, Barnabus, 159
Hackett, James, 256

INDEX.

Hackett, John, 167, 277
Hackett, Richard, 283
Hackett, Salmon, 176
Hackett, Simeon, 280
Haddock, Henry, 32
Hadley, Charles, 68
Hadley, Moses, 84
Hadley, Samuel, 68
Hadley, Samuel D., 114
Hadley, Samuel S., 150
Hadley, Sewell, 98
Hadlock, William, 219
Hadly, Moses, 83
Hadoway, John T., 28
Hafford, James, 129
Haffords, James, 126
Hagan, John, 247
Hagan, Michael, 247
Hagan, Thomas, 297
Hagar, Ezekiel, 290
Hagar, James, 68
Hagar, Samuel, 42
Hagar, Sewel, 290
Hagar, William, 68
Hagen, Joseph, 85
Hagen, Samuel, 172
Hager, Charles, 289
Hager, Ezekiel, 286
Hager, Joseph, 77
Hager, Martin, 66
Hager, Reuben, 66
Hager, Saul, 286
Hager, Sewel, 286
Hagerty, George, 69
Haggens, Aaron, 270
Hagget, Amos, 185
Hagget, Ebenezer, 191
Hagget, Ebenezer, Jr., 191
Hagget, Isaac, 274
Haggett, Daniel, 184, 186 (2)
Haggett, Ebenezer, 189
Haggett, William, 185, 191, 243
Hahn, George, 292
Hahn, John, 291
Haiden, William, 235
Hail, William, 31
Hallend, Henry, 28
Hailey, Matthew, 186
Haines, William, 259
Hains, Daniel, 44
Hains, Peleg, 278
Hale, Christopher, 99
Hale, Daniel, 36
Hale, Enoch, Jr., 270
Hale, George, 220
Hale, Henry, 36
Hale, James, 37
Hale, John, 141, 227, 282
Hale, Jonathan, 135
Hale, Joshua, 3
Hale, Moses, 18
Hale, Nathan, 70, 79
Hale, Nathaniel, Jr., 211
Hale, Otis, 48
Hale, Saul, 99
Hale, William, 123, 124
Hales, William, 12
Haley, Abner, 148
Haley, Abraham, 149
Haley, James, 148, 153, 235, 247, 297
Haley, John, 2d, 236
Haley, Joshua, 234

Haley, Peletiah, Jr., 234
Haley, Peletiah, 2d, 236
Haley, Samuel, 169
Haley, Seth, 64
Haley, Thomas, 247, 297
Haley, William, 269
Hall, Aaron, 27, 87
Hall, Aaron, Jr., 263
Hall, Abiel, 193, 244
Hall, Abijah, 252, 255
Hall, Alexander, 196
Hall, Alva, 30
Hall, Amos, 217
Hall, Andrew, 176, 200, 257
Hall, Anthony, 197, 204
Hall, Archibald, 206 (2)
Hall, Arial, 31
Hall, Atherton, 67
Hall, Barsilla, 49
Hall, Benjamin, 8, 23, 39, 133, 136, 140, 285, 286 (2), 289
Hall, Benjamin, Jr., 258
Hall, Benjamin W., 17, 149
Hall, Benoni, 31
Hall, Bryant, 44
Hall, Charles, 20, 120, 258, 300
Hall, Charles B., 99
Hall, Cornelius, 302
Hall, Cyprian, 146
Hall, Cyrus, 274
Hall, Daniel, 88, 194, 258
Hall, Daniel, Jr., 194, 196
Hall, David, 99, 177, 253
Hall, Ebenezer, 51, 149, 196
Hall, Ebenezer, Jr., 101
Hall, Elijah, 45, 86, 194
Hall, Elijah C., 178
Hall, Eliphalet, 16
Hall, Enoch, 17
Hall, Enoch B., 8
Hall, Ephraim, 150, 196
Hall, Ezekiel, 131, 193
Hall, Ezekiel, Jr., 99
Hall, Ezekiel C., 77
Hall, Ezekiel O., 88
Hall, Frederic N., 146, 150
Hall, Frye, 202, 207, 208
Hall, George, 31, 33, 54, 64, 219, 241
Hall, Gorham, 131
Hall, Harvey, 194
Hall, Henry, 1, 30, 219, 246
Hall, Irial, 238
Hall, Isaac, 62, 169, 173, 181, 194, 196, 206 (2), 248, 258, 281, 306
Hall, Israel, 134, 135
Hall, James, 117, 194, 287, 290
Hall, James, Jr., 194, 196
Hall, James, 3d, 192
Hall, Jason, 82, 110
Hall, Jeremiah, 212, 268
Hall, Jesse, 192, 196
Hall, John, 34, 38, 67, 90, 131, 145, 173, 176, 257
Hall, John, 2d, 232 (2)
Hall, John B., 13, 14, 118
Hall, John G., 237
Hall, John H., 243
Hall, Joseph, 62, 73, 76, 95, 192, 196, 207, 208, 209 (2)
Hall, Josiah, 97, 164, 165, 166, 219
Hall, Josiah R., 222
Hall, Judah, 42

Hall, Kimball, 251, 255
Hall, Lemuel, 232, 306
Hall, Levi, 171
Hall, Luman, 30
Hall, Luther, 155, 156, 275
Hall, Mark, 194
Hall, Marks, 196
Hall, Martin, 155
Hall, Moses, 136, 140, 174, 219
Hall, Nathan, 29, 52, 282
Hall, Nathaniel, 158
Hall, Neal, 295
Hall, Noah, 251
Hall, Oliver, 16, 29, 174
Hall, Oliver, Jr., 274
Hall, Percival, 93
Hall, Perley, 151
Hall, Peter, 206
Hall, Peter, Jr., 200
Hall, Reuben, 51
Hall, Richard, 229
Hall, Robert, 148, 196, 219
Hall, Samuel, 102, 206 (2), 247
Hall, Solomon, 252
Hall, Spencer, 138
Hall, Stephen, 77, 194, 212, 252
Hall, Stephens, 196
Hall, Sylvanus, 51, 178
Hall, Thomas, 20, 65, 253, 255
Hall, Timothy, 26, 66, 192, 194 (2), 230
Hall, Willard, 97, 212
Hall, William, 3, 7, 17, 20 (2), 23, 27, 101, 112, 123, 145, 235, 290, 297
Hall, William, 2d, 7
Hall, Winslow, 73, 76
Hall, Zachariah, 23
Hall, Zenas, 178, 196, 259
Hallet, Avory, 235
Hallet, Ezekiel, 74
Hallet, John, 264
Hallet, Soule, 237
Hallet, William S., 237
Hallets, Hansard, 125
Hallett, Elisha, 264
Hallett, Isaiah, 264
Hallett, John, Jr., 131
Hallett, Joseph B., 261
Hallett, Joseph M., 265, 267
Hallett, Watson F., 265
Hallis, Benjamin, 2
Hallowell, James, 116, 179
Hallowell, Joel, 179
Hallowell, John, 116, 179
Hallowell, William, 179
Hally, James, 154
Halmer, Benjamin, 17
Ham, Enoch, 240, 265
Ham, Israel, 233
Ham, James, 169
Ham, Jeremiah, 243
Ham, Joel, 247
Ham, John, 166, 217
Ham, Joseph, 120, 123
Ham, Moses, 139 (2)
Ham, Reuben, 279 (2)
Ham, Rufus, 168
Ham, Samuel, 245
Ham, Thomas, 166, 230, 277
Ham, William, 236, 280, 281, 312
Hambelly, Thomas, 204
Hamblet, John P., 243
Hamblin, Barnabus, 130

INDEX. 365

Hamblin, Charles, 173
Hamblin, Cyrus, 173
Hamblin, Eliphalet, 257
Hamblin, Enoch, 173
Hamblin, Ichabod, 244
Hamblin, Isaac, 173
Hamblin, Joseph, 74
Hamblin, Joseph, 3d, 173
Hamblin, Nathaniel, 126, 173
Hamblin, Reuben, 55, 58
Hamblin, Samuel, 211
Hamblin, Saul, 236
Hamblin, Simeon, 130
Hamden, Benjamin, 151
Hamden, Ebenezer, 151
Hamden, Levi, 253
Hamilton, Aaron, 234
Hamilton, Adam R., 67
Hamilton, Alexander, 133, 136
Hamilton, Archibald, 309 (2)
Hamilton, Asa, 227
Hamilton, Edward, 270
Hamilton, Jacob, 245
Hamilton, John, 79, 169
Hamilton, Lemuel, 162, 214
Hamilton, Luther, 32
Hamilton, Oliver, 281
Hamilton, Patrick, 32
Hamilton, Richard, 270
Hamilton, Sewall, 94
Hamilton, Silas, 45, 179
Hamilton, Simon, 301
Hamilton, Squire, 47
Hamilton, William, 81, 82, 227, 282
Hamilton, William F., 179
Hamlet, Jonathan, 42, 88
Hamlin, Barnabus, 72
Hamlin, Benjamin, 74
Hamlin, Charles, 74
Hamlin, Daniel, 74
Hamlin, Ellis, 74
Hamlin, George, 274
Hamlin, Isaac, 224
Hamlin, Isaiah, 237
Hamlin, John, 271
Hamlin, John, Jr., 74
Hamlin, Josiah, 237
Hamlin, Nathaniel, 74
Hamlin, Peres, 262
Hamlin, Reuben, 72
Hamlin, Seth, 72, 74
Hamlin, Shubal, 74
Hamlin, Silvanus, 72
Hamlin, Solomon, 72, 227
Hamlin, Thomas, 73, 76
Hamlin, Winslow, 74
Hamm, Robert, 147
Hammatt, Abraham, 80
Hammett, Charles, 85
Hammett, William B., 83
Hammon, Benjamin, 146
Hammon, Chester, 4
Hammon, Frederick, 237
Hammon, Gamaliel, 4
Hammon, Moses, 146
Hammon, Pliney, 4
Hammon, Samuel, 228
Hammon, Timothy, 108
Hammon, Zeeth, 312
Hammond, Abner, 308
Hammond, Andrew, 34, 37, 38
Hammond, Barnabus, 55, 57

Hammond, Bela, 153
Hammond, Benjamin, 129 (2)
Hammond, Caleb, 53, 58
Hammond, Charles, 130
Hammond, Daniel, 58
Hammond, David, 138, 250
Hammond, Elihu, 58
Hammond, Elisha, 53
Hammond, Enoch, 251
Hammond, Frederick, 103
Hammond, Freeman, 127
Hammond, Isaiah, 75, 76
Hammond, Israel, 130
Hammond, Jacob, 153
Hammond, James, 55, 58, 127
Hammond, James R., 295
Hammond, John, 52, 132
Hammond, John L., 138
Hammond, Joseph, 154
Hammond, Loring, 96
Hammond, Michael, 55
Hammond, Michel, 58
Hammond, Paul, 224, 263
Hammond, Robert, 76
Hammond, Samuel, 55, 75, 76
Hammond, Samuel H., 283
Hammond, Seth, 280
Hammond, Shubal, 52
Hammond, Sylvanus, 280
Hammond, Thomas, 70, 77, 218
Hammond, Thomas B., 242
Hammond, Thomas P., 6
Hammond, Timothy, 2
Hammond, William, 70, 213, 256
Hammond, Wilson, 58
Hammonds, John, Jr., 6
Hammot, Consider H., 84
Hamon, John, 29
Hámond, David, 250
Hampson, John, 6
Hamstead, Timothy, 306
Hamstead, Nathaniel, 133
Hanby, Patrick, 193
Hanchet, Frederic, 43
Hanck, Theophilus, 9
Hancock, Henry, 70
Hancock, John, 264
Hancock, Lewis, 225
Hancock, William, 25, 48
Hand, Hammond, 298
Hand, Hollobert, 30
Hand, Joseph, 274
Handen, Levi, 253
Handley, James, 30
Handly, Henry, 200
Handson, Joseph, 87
Handy, Abisha, 275
Handy, Calvin, 71
Handy, Daniel, 220
Handy, David, 60
Handy, Jabes, 130
Handy, James, 262
Handy, James H., 56, 266
Handy, Lemuel, 239, 265
Handy, Otis, 60
Handy, Richard, 239
Hanes, Reuben, 148
Hanes, Samuel, 27
Hanford, Edward, 198, 199, 207 (3)
Hanford, Solomon, 261
Hankinson, David, 305
Hanly, Henry, 206

Hanly, John, 287
Hanly, Roger, 287
Hannaford, David, 296
Hannaford, William, 296
Hannell, John, 265
Hanniford, Davis, 235
Hanniford, William, 235
Hannon, Philip, 169
Hannum, Sydney, 45
Hannums, Gove, 47
Hannums, Henry, 47
Hanover, William, 271
Hanscom, Charles, 271
Hanscom, Henry, 271
Hanscom, James, 296
Hanscom, John, 174
Hanscom, Joseph, 231
Hanscom, Lewis, 173
Hanscom, Samuel, 245
Hanscomb, Aaron, 211
Hanscomb, Benjamin, 230
Hanscomb, James, 232 (2)
Hanscomb, John, 234
Hanscomb, John, Jr., 269
Hanscomb, Joseph, 269
Hanscomb, Moses, 164, 165, 166, 275
Hanscomb, Nathan, 211
Hansel, Robert, 99
Hansell, William, 39, 79
Hanson, Alpheus, 245
Hanson, Andrew H., 237
Hanson, Caleb, 267
Hanson, Caleb, Jr., 237
Hanson, Daniel, Jr., 269
Hanson, Ebenezer, 167
Hanson, Elijah, 269
Hanson, Hiram, 233
Hanson, Humphrey, 254
Hanson, James, 239
Hanson, Joshua, 237
Hanson, Josiah, 242
Hanson, Michael, 269
Hanson, Moses, 243
Hanson, Naphtali, 167
Hanson, Nathan, 174
Hanson, Nehemiah, 264
Hanson, Samuel, 25, 237
Hanson, Stephen, 269 (2)
Hanson, Thomas, 266, 270
Hapgood, Benjamin, 85
Hapgood, Ephraim, 78, 83
Hapgood, Nathaniel, 100
Hapgood, Oliver, Jr., 258
Hapgood, Samuel, 69
Hapgood, Sprout, 258
Hapgood, William, 152, 254
Hapworth, William, 60
Hard, Daniel, 136
Harden, Alfred, 60
Harden, Charles, 39, 194
Harden, Freeman, 205 (2)
Harden, Jabes, 51
Harden, Jesse, 216
Harden, John C., 97
Harden, Noah, 97
Harden, Simeon, 54
Harden, Thomas, 97
Harden, Ward, 51
Harden, William, 243
Hardin, Amariah, Jr., 240, 265
Hardin, Eddy, 60
Hardin, Harlow, 272

INDEX.

Hardin, Joseph, 87
Hardin, Pelham, 272
Harding, Abijah, 67
Harding, Alpheus, 63
Harding, Austen, 215
Harding, Benjamin, 266, 307
Harding, Charles, 196
Harding, Daniel F., 182
Harding, David, 173
Harding, Isaac, 284
Harding, James, 171
Harding, Jesse, 284
Harding, John, 3d, 174
Harding, Joseph, 165, 166, 174, 193, 246 (2)
Harding, Nathaniel, Jr., 229, 282
Harding, Nehemiah, 249, 282, 297, 299
Harding, Pliny, 86
Harding, Reed, 214
Harding, Richard C., 148
Harding, Robert, 174
Harding, Rufus, 41
Harding, Samuel, 303
Harding, Seth, Jr., 174
Harding, Simeon, 72
Harding, Simon, 269
Harding, Thomas, 40
Harding, William, 171
Hardy, ——, 82
Hardy, Benjamin, 8, 214
Hardy, Daniel, 160
Hardy, Dudley, 124
Hardy, Dudly, 120
Hardy, John, 6, 22, 90
Hardy, Jonathan, 33, 151
Hardy, Joshua, 78 (2), 113, 114
Hardy, Moses, 227, 283
Hardy, Nathaniel, 8
Hardy, Noah, 87
Hardy, Phineas, 14
Hardy, Stephen, 240
Hardy, Stephen G., 151
Hardy, Temple, 133, 141
Hardy, William, 79
Hare, James S., 136, 137
Hare, Mack, 245
Harem, William, 8
Harford, George, 248
Harford, Ira, 90
Harford, Lewis, 248
Harford, Solomon, 153
Harford, William, 248
Hariden, Andrew, 145
Hariman, James, 215
Harkness, John, 198, 199, 207 (2)
Harkness, William, 198, 199, 201, 202, 208
Harley, Caleb, 189
Harley, Joseph, 88
Harley, Robert, 186, 189
Harlow, Amariah, 128
Harlow, Amasiah, 131
Harlow, Asa, 95, 176, 260
Harlow, Asaph, 109
Harlow, Benjamin, 52
Harlow, Branch, 102
Harlow, David, 252
Harlow, Ebeneser, 177
Harlow, Ellis, 51
Harlow, Ezra, 52
Harlow, Freeman, 206
Harlow, Gideon, 129
Harlow, Henry, 242
Harlow, Hosea, 177

Harlow, Ichabod, 129
Harlow, Isaac, 223
Harlow, Ivory, 223
Harlow, Jabez, 267
Harlow, James, 176, 257
Harlow, John, 90
Harlow, Josiah, 51, 234
Harlow, Lazarus, 244
Harlow, Lewis, 47, 51
Harlow, Nathaniel, 128
Harlow, Samuel, 232
Harlow, Stephen, 51
Harlow, Sylvanus, Jr., 239
Harlow, Thomas, 239
Harlow, Tisdale, 95
Harlow, William, 223, 259
Harlow, Zacheus, 39, 68
Harlton, Ebeneser, 150
Harman, George, 164
Harman, James, 311
Harmon, Amos, 33
Harmon, Benjamin, 173
Harmon, Daniel, 172, 174
Harmon, Daniel, 3d, 172
Harmon, Dummer, 171
Harmon, Elias, 171, 210
Harmon, Francis, 295
Harmon, George, 163, 242
Harmon, Hiram, 33
Harmon, Isaiah, 295
Harmon, Israel, 174
Harmon, James, 165, 166, 225, 246
Harmon, James, Jr., 269
Harmon, James, 2d, 166
Harmon, John, 154
Harmon, John M., 172, 246
Harmon, John S., Jr., 172
Harmon, Jonathan, 164, 165, 246, 255, 269 (2)
Harmon, Jonathan, 3d, 172, 246
Harmon, Leander, 211
Harmon, Levi, 233
Harmon, Levi M., 172
Harmon, Luke, 33
Harmon, Moses, Jr., 172
Harmon, Pelatiah, 269
Harmon, Richard, 172
Harmon, Robert, 172, 210, 295
Harmon, Rufus, 174, 258
Harmon, Simon, 279
Harmon, Stephen, 172, 246, 269
Harmon, Thomas, 164, 165, 166
Harmon, William, 225, 246
Harmon, Zachariah, 2d, 171
Harmond, Daniel, 205
Harnden, Benjamin, 254
Harnden, Elbridge, 254
Harnden, Lemuel W., 249
Harper, Eliot, 283
Harper, Samuel, 218
Harper, Samuel, Jr., 269
Harper, William, 163, 164
Harraden, Andrew, 12
Harriden, Andrew, 296
Harriden, Robert, 90
Harriman, Benjamin, 303
Harriman, Dudley, 181
Harriman, Ebeneser, 273
Harriman, Elisha, 303
Harriman, John, 9

Harriman, Levi, 273
Harriman, Thomas, 179
Harrin, Oliver, 85
Harrington, Amasa, 101
Harrington, Asa, 101
Harrington, Charles, 39, 78, 156, 157
Harrington, Dana, 91
Harrington, Edward, 79, 82
Harrington, Eli, 92
Harrington, Elisha, 25, 79, 81, 86
Harrington, Emery, 48
Harrington, Ephraim, 70
Harrington, Israel, 185
Harrington, Jacob, 5
Harrington, James, 191, 198, 202
Harrington, Jeremiah, 30
Harrington, Job, 191
Harrington, John, 139, 185, 292
Harrington, Jonas, 99, 139
Harrington, Josiah, 198, 202, 209
Harrington, Leonard, 115
Harrington, Moses, 115
Harrington, Nathaniel, 86
Harrington, Nicodemus, 30
Harrington, Schuyler, 48
Harrington, Seneca, 3
Harrington, Thomas, 48
Harrington, William, 295
Harrington, William B., 39
Harrington, Wyman, 39, 68
Harris, Abial, 9
Harris, Abraham, 104
Harris, Amariah, 251
Harris, Amos, 176
Harris, Asa, 97
Harris, Caleb, 276
Harris, Charles, 34
Harris, Elijah, 70
Harris, Enos, 213
Harris, Ephraim, 70, 213
Harris, Heman, 93
Harris, Herman, 277, 279
Harris, Humphrey, 93
Harris, Isaac, 2, 70
Harris, James, 70, 206 (2)
Harris, James, Jr., 11
Harris, John, 6, 11, 22, 85, 89, 113 (2), 134 (2), 150, 182 (2), 191, 193
Harris, John, Jr., 100
Harris, John A., 47
Harris, Jonathan, 37
Harris, Joseph, 6, 70, 73, 75, 281
Harris, King, 3
Harris, Leach, 224
Harris, Martin, 177, 256
Harris, Moses, 136
Harris, Nathaniel, 167, 245
Harris, Nathaniel S., 92
Harris, Obediah, 277
Harris, Oliver, 83
Harris, Pliny, 230
Harris, Reuben, 148
Harris, Richard, 167
Harris, Richard D., 277
Harris, Robert, 70
Harris, Robert, 3d, 22
Harris, Robert, 4th, 6
Harris, Samuel, 188
Harris, Samuel, Jr., 183, 185
Harris, Stephen, 242
Harris, William, 4, 6, 22, 87, 97, 139 (2), 183, 185, 188

INDEX.

Harris, William C., 25
Harrison, James W., 161
Harriss, James, 71
Harriss, Joseph, 71
Harrod, William, 87
Harryman, Eliakim, 180
Harsey, Sylvanus, 91
Hart, Charles, 67
Hart, Daniel, 90
Hart, Ephraim, 206
Hart, Fisher, 290, 293
Hart, Gamaliel, 129
Hart, Hartfield, 117
Hart, Jacob, 214
Hart, James, 199, 200
Hart, John, 266, 293
Hart, John, 3d, 206
Hart, John F., 286
Hart, Joseph, 26, 48, 132, 140
Hart, Martin, 90
Hart, Russell, 214
Hart, Samuel, 206
Hart, Seth, 62
Hart, William, 160, 206
Hartford, William, 245
Harthern, John, 191
Hartshorn, Ashbel, 217
Hartshorn, Caleb, 24, 114
Hartshorn, Daniel, 97
Hartshorn, David, 217
Hartshorn, David, 2d, 217
Hartshorn, Fisher, 99
Hartshorn, George, 99
Hartshorn, James, 78
Hartshorn, John, Jr., 190
Hartshorn, Joseph, 69, 217
Hartshorn, Josiah, 217
Hartshorn, Oliver S., 242
Hartshorn, Oliver T., 241
Hartshorn, Otis, 97
Hartshorn, Richard, 97
Hartshorn, Rolan, 78
Hartshorn, Rolin, 69
Hartshorn, Samuel 288, 294
Hartshorn, Saul, 284, 288
Hartshorn, Silas, 217
Hartshorn, William, 246, 254, 312
Hartson, Preston, 110
Hartwell, Benjamin, 307
Hartwell, Daniel, 49
Hartwell, Daniel L., 49
Hartwell, Jonas, 42
Hartwell, Peter, 64
Hartwell, Stephen, 307
Hartwell, Thomas, 24, 114
Harvey, Barnabus, 62
Harvey, Benjamin, 13
Harvey, David, 59
Harvey, Elijah, Jr., 46
Harvey, George, 44, 302
Harvey, James, 27, 41
Harvey, James, 2d, 41
Harvey, John, 132
Harvey, Joseph, 13
Harvey, Leonard, 62
Harvey, Nathaniel, 30
Harvey, Samuel, 89
Harvey, Stephen, 150
Harvey, William, 236
Harwood, Andrew, Jr., 46
Harwood, Benjamin B., 45
Harwood, Ebenezer, 14

Harwood, Murvel, 33
Harwood, Nathaniel, 91
Harwood, Otis, 235
Harwood, Richard, 203
Harwood, Thomas, 155
Harwood, William, 30
Hasbrook, Israel, 297
Hascall, Benjamin, 95
Hascall, David, 290
Hascall, Saul, 95
Hase, Benjamin J., 119
Haseltine, Arad, 195
Haseltine, Ebenezer, 151
Haseltine, John, 272
Haselton, Asel, 172
Haselton, Daniel C., 276
Haselton, Jonathan, 136
Haselton, Joseph, 277, 281
Hasey, Jacob, 176, 260
Hasey, Joseph, 176, 260
Hashley, Stephen S., 48
Hask, Samuel, 243
Haskell, Abiah, 84
Haskell, Amasa, 224
Haskell, Asa, 177, 259
Haskell, Benjamin, 11, 13, 14, 237, 267
Haskell, Benjamin, Jr., 174
Haskell, Caleb, 225
Haskell, Calvin, 80
Haskell, Charles, 12, 206, 207
Haskell, Charles C., 210
Haskell, Daniel, 210
Haskell, David, 20, 286
Haskell, Ebenezer, 256
Haskell, Edward, 118
Haskell, Enoch, 20
Haskell, George, 221
Haskell, H. B., 123
Haskell, Humphrey B., 120
Haskell, Isaac, 271
Haskell, Israel, 3, 280
Haskell, Jacob, 13, 14, 278
Haskell, James, 11, 36, 37, 210
Haskell, Jeremiah, 114
Haskell, Jesse, 1
Haskell, John, 10, 37, 204 (2), 213, 285, 286 (2), 288
Haskell, John W., 118
Haskell, Jonathan, 11
Haskell, Joseph, 20, 48, 54, 88
Haskell, Joshua, 208
Haskell, Lemuel, 11
Haskell, Levi, 13, 81, 174
Haskell, Luther, 80
Haskell, Mathew, 118
Haskell, Nathan, 153
Haskell, Nathaniel, 41, 57, 221
Haskell, Nathaniel, Jr., 221
Haskell, Nathaniel, 2d, 41
Haskell, Parsons, 258
Haskell, Peleg, 256
Haskell, R., 82
Haskell, Rufus, 158
Haskell, Samuel, 34
Haskell, Samuel, Jr., 258
Haskell, Samuel H., 256
Haskell, Seth, 52
Haskell, Seth L., 225
Haskell, Thomas, 204 (2), 222
Haskell, William, 36, 37, 135, 153, 176, 210, 237
Haskell, Zelotes, 177, 260

Hasket, Elias, 195
Haskett, Isaiah, 177
Hasking, Samuel, 160
Haskins, Clark, 56
Haskins, Eben, 59
Haskins, Ebenezer, 62, 221
Haskins, Edmund, 12
Haskins, Elijah, 45
Haskins, Gideon, 52
Haskins, Henry, 61
Haskins, John, 9, 57, 66
Haskins, Joshua, 54
Haskins, Levi, 52
Haskins, Matthew, 267
Haskins, Nathaniel, 59, 61
Haskins, Orrin, 29
Haskins, Samuel, 146
Haskins, Thomas, 11, 71
Haskins, William, 59, 149
Haskins, William B., 11
Haskins, William P., 59, 61
Haslett, William, 136, 140
Hassack, Daniel, 242
Hassam, John, 176
Hasses, Andrew, 291
Hasses, Charles, 289
Hasses, George, 291
Hasses, Henry, 291
Hasses, William, 289
Hassum, John, 176
Hastings, Amos, 307
Hastings, Charles, 82
Hastings, Daniel, 23
Hastings, Daniel, 2d, 77
Hastings, Ebenezer, 3
Hastings, Ezra, 25
Hastings, James, 101
Hastings, John, 88, 93
Hastings, Joseph, 3, 262
Hastings, Josiah, 90
Hastings, Lewis, 83
Hastings, Matthew, 262
Hastings, Mitchell, 67
Hastings, Nathan, 39
Hastings, Nathaniel, 23
Hastings, Oliver, 64, 86
Hastings, Orrissimus, 66
Hastings, Samuel, 153
Hastings, Simeon, 3
Hastings, Thaddeus, 85
Hastings, Thomas, 29
Hastings, William, 18, 91, 120, 123, 195
Hasty, Benjamin, 155
Hasty, Daniel, 170
Hasty, Dominicus, 155
Hasty, Hiram, 171
Hasty, John, 260
Hasty, Joseph, 170, 172, 205
Hasty, Nathaniel, 243, 260 (2)
Hasty, Samuel, 171
Hasty, William, 23, 174
Hatch, Abiel, 181
Hatch, Alexander, 192, 287, 310
Hatch, Allen, 73, 75, 78, 87
Hatch, Anslem, 76
Hatch, Benjamin, 72
Hatch, Charles, 196
Hatch, Chesley, 177
Hatch, Clift, 80, 84
Hatch, Colman, 72
Hatch, Crowell, 195
Hatch, Daniel, 62

Hatch, Darius, 249
Hatch, David, 194, 297
Hatch, Davis, 75
Hatch, Dunham, 72
Hatch, Ebenezer, 72, 73, 230
Hatch, Elihu, 73, 230
Hatch, Elijah, 194, 196
Hatch, Eliphalet, 72
Hatch, Elisha, 73
Hatch, Elisha, Jr., 310
Hatch, Ephraim, Jr., 276
Hatch, Ezra, 237
Hatch, Foster, 73, 76
Hatch, Frederic, 193, 196
Hatch, Henry, 159
Hatch, Isaac, 72
Hatch, Isaiah, 72
Hatch, Ithamy, 310
Hatch, Jacob, 38, 167
Hatch, James, 50, 65
Hatch, Job, 75
Hatch, John, 34, 64, 68, 72, 151, 169, 219, 287, 310
Hatch, John, Jr., 309
Hatch, Jonathan, 190
Hatch, Joseph, 221
Hatch, Joshua, 25, 39
Hatch, Josiah, 167
Hatch, Levi, 178
Hatch, Luriel, 75
Hatch, Luther, 49
Hatch, Mark, 179
Hatch, Mathew, 75
Hatch, Moses, Jr., 72
Hatch, Nathaniel, 173
Hatch, Nehemiah, 268
Hatch, Oaks, 192, 194
Hatch, Reuben, 72, 283
Hatch, Robinson, 76
Hatch, Roswell, 76
Hatch, Samuel, 52, 104, 167, 281
Hatch, Silas, 73
Hatch, Silvanus, 72, 75, 76
Hatch, Stephen, 160
Hatch, Sylvanus, 276
Hatch, Thacher L., 75
Hatch, Thomas, 194
Hatch, William, 223
Hatch, Zacheus, 193
Hatchman, John, 81
Hathaway, Anson, 41, 59
Hathaway, Bailey, 224
Hathaway, Benjamin, 33, 62
Hathaway, Benjamin S., 55
Hathaway, Biarush, 59
Hathaway, Braddock, 57, 229
Hathaway, Chancy, 33
Hathaway, Charles, 30, 127, 129
Hathaway, Clothier, 60
Hathaway, Cushman, 49
Hathaway, Daniel, 52, 57
Hathaway, David F., 56
Hathaway, Eli, 222, 259
Hathaway, Elijah, 52
Hathaway, Elkanah, 62
Hathaway, Ennis, 57
Hathaway, Enoch, 57
Hathaway, Enos, 41
Hathaway, Ephraim, 57
Hathaway, Ezra, 127, 129, 229, 283
Hathaway, Gideon, 41
Hathaway, Gideon, 2d, 41

Hathaway, Gilbert, 224
Hathaway, Henry P., 57
Hathaway, Isaac, 55
Hathaway, Jason, 57
Hathaway, Job, 59, 61, 62
Hathaway, John, 6
Hathaway, Joseph, 6
Hathaway, Joseph, 2d, 57
Hathaway, Joshua, 128, 131
Hathaway, Lazarus, 252
Hathaway, Lemuel, 59, 61
Hathaway, Leonard, 59
Hathaway, Lot, 57
Hathaway, Luther, 59
Hathaway, Lynde, 57
Hathaway, Malbon, 57
Hathaway, Martin, 1
Hathaway, Michael, 57, 58
Hathaway, Morrell, 129
Hathaway, Nicholas, 58
Hathaway, Noah, 57
Hathaway, Nobles E., 52, 102
Hathaway, Peleg, 33, 130
Hathaway, Philip, 57
Hathaway, Philip P., 57
Hathaway, Richard, 251
Hathaway, Robert, 261
Hathaway, Salathiel, 102
Hathaway, Seebra, 49
Hathaway, Silas, 53, 54, 57
Hathaway, Stephen, 6
Hathaway, Thomas, 55, 101, 126
Hathaway, William, 55, 62, 133
Hathaway, Wilson, 30
Hathorn, Alexander, 206
Hathorn, James, 202
Hathorn, John, Jr., 187
Hathorn, Samuel, 235
Hathorn, Seth, 247
Hathorn, Seth, Jr., 249
Hathorne, James, 198, 199
Hathwait, Francis, 69
Hathway, James, 22
Hathway, Joseph, 22
Hathway, William, 22
Haven, Ashel, 29
Haven, Calvin, 84
Havener, Joseph, 205 (2)
Havers, John, 120
Hawes, Benjamin, 139 (2)
Hawes, Burnard, 265
Hawes, Caleb, 47, 86
Hawes, David, 267
Hawes, Ebenezer, 240, 267
Hawes, Edward W., 79
Hawes, Herman, 289
Hawes, Isaiah, 267
Hawes, James, 86, 267
Hawes, John, 153, 169
Hawes, Joseph, 86
Hawes, Lemuel, 268
Hawes, Lewis, 125
Hawes, Luther, 92
Hawes, Noyes P., 290
Hawes, Otis, 286
Hawes, Prince, 81
Hawes, Robert, 206
Hawes, Seth, 239, 267
Hawes, Stephen, 139
Hawes, Thomas, 240
Hawes, Whiting, 290
Hawes, William, 69

Hawes, William B., 78
Hawk, John, 32
Hawk, Sheppard, 255
Hawkes, Benjamin, Jr., 132
Hawkes, John B., 285, 286, 289
Hawkes, Thomas, 90
Hawkes, William, Jr., 6
Hawkins, Henry, 224, 259
Hawkins, Joseph, 312
Hawks, Dan, 176
Hawks, Daniel, 118, 176
Hawks, Ezra, 24, 77
Hawks, Isaac, 67
Hawks, John, 47, 116
Hawks, John B., 286
Hawks, Nathan, Jr., 118
Hawks, Rufus, 67
Hawks, Thomas, 116
Hawks, William, 22
Hawland, William, 53
Hawley, Roger, 310
Hawley, William, 239
Haws, Daniel, 33
Haws, Daniel G. H., 24
Haws, David, 237
Haws, Edward W., 23, 25
Haws, James, 237
Haws, Joseph, 25
Haws, Lot, 127
Haws, Moses, 274
Haws, Stephen, 139
Hay, Jonathan, 96
Hay, Joseph, 113
Hay, Richard, 134 (2)
Hay, Thomas, 70, 109, 111
Hay, William, 40
Hayden, Artemas, 39
Hayden, Benjamin, 24
Hayden, Charles, Jr., 236, 265
Hayden, Daniel, 236
Hayden, Ebenezer, 56
Hayden, Elijah, 42
Hayden, Esekial, 85
Hayden, Freeman, 104, 105 (2), 106, 107
Hayden, Henry, 80, 81
Hayden, Jacob, 46
Hayden, James, 265, 266
Hayden, John, 79, 81, 87
Hayden, Jonathan, 265
Hayden, Lewis, 224
Hayden, Lewis G., 257
Hayden, Luther, 42
Hayden, Lyman, 88
Hayden, Peleg, 81, 87
Hayden, Peter, 42, 89
Hayden, Richard V., 236, 267
Hayden, Robert, 108
Hayden, Samuel, 100
Hayden, Solomon, 100
Hayden, Thomas, 65
Hayes, Abraham, 135
Hayes, David, 218
Hayes, Dennis, 253, 257
Hayes, George H., 224
Hayes, John, 135, 222
Hayes, Samuel, 159
Hayford, Benjamin, 54
Hayford, Gustavus, 225
Haynes, David, 234
Haynes, Francis, 223
Haynes, Francis F., 259
Haynes, George, 78, 81

INDEX. 369

Haynes, John, 90 (2), 261, 284
Haynes, Josiah, 66
Haynes, Timothy, 211
Haynes, William, 200, 201, 203, 258
Hayood, Josiah, 88
Hayrus, Jonathan, 44
Hays, Asa, 25
Hays, George, 241
Hays, Jacob, 305
Hays, John, 3d, 225
Hays, Pierpont, 96
Haysen, Daniel C., 15
Hayson, John, 87
Hayte, Elna, 82
Hayward, Aaron, 135
Hayward, Albert, 158
Hayward, Alvin, 158
Hayward, Ansel, 49, 78
Hayward, Arnold, 79
Hayward, Calvin, 51
Hayward, Cyrus, 51
Hayward, Edson, 51
Hayward, Erastus, 51
Hayward, Independent, 39
Hayward, Ira, 50
Hayward, Israel, 196
Hayward, Jacob, 49
Hayward, James, 39, 100
Hayward, Jeremiah, 51
Hayward, John, 47, 79
Hayward, John, Jr., 99
Hayward, Joseph, 51, 99
Hayward, Joshua, 60
Hayward, Josiah, 117
Hayward, Lewis, 5
Hayward, Luther, 49
Hayward, Moses, 100
Hayward, Nahum, 95
Hayward, Nathaniel H., 113
Hayward, Otis, 91
Hayward, Samuel, 24, 42, 101, 114
Hayward, Seth, 51
Hayward, Thomas C., 82
Hayward, Tiba, 51
Hayward, Timothy, 264
Hayward, Timothy B., 267
Hayward, Waldo, 50
Haywood, Aaron, 100, 134
Haywood, Eli, 49
Haywood, Luther, 100
Haywood, Saul, 238
Haywood, Simeon, 211
Haseltine, Arad, 192
Haseltine, Harry, 192
Haseltine, Samuel, 149
Haselton, Leonard, 9
Haselton, Saul, 134, 135, 152
Heabner, Charles, 291
Heaborn, Charles, 294
Head, Asa, 151
Head, James, 289
Head, John B., 292
Head, Nathaniel, 151, 254
Head, Uriah, 129
Head, William, 72
Headley, Joseph, 81
Heagen, Richard, 248
Heal, Abner, 302
Heal, Chesley, 2d, 302
Heal, Daniel, 302
Heal, Gilbert, 231
Heal, James, 189, 276

Heal, John, 302
Heal, John, Jr., 302
Heal, Peter, 198, 208, 302
Heal, William, 302
Heald, Calvin, 307
Heald, Cyrus, 284
Heald, James, 236
Heald, Jonas, 267
Heald, Joseph, 236
Heald, Josiah, 80, 83, 150
Heald, Odiorne, 238, 267
Heald, Samuel, 152
Heald, Simeon, 236
Heald, Thatcher, 268
Heald, Thomas, 39, 284
Heald, Washington, 236, 267
Healey, James H., 200, 205
Healey, Nathaniel, 68, 79
Healey, Pearley, 65
Healy, Jeremiah, 94
Healy, Kalsey, 284
Healy, Tildston, 205
Healy, Tildton, 205
Healy, Tilson, 207
Heard, Daniel, 140
Heard, James, 182, 186, 287
Heard, John, 68, 111, 245, 270
Hearl, John, 307
Hearsey, Caleb, 28
Hearsey, Isaac, 211
Hearsey, Jacob, 87
Hearsey, James, 283
Hearsey, John, 299
Hearsey, Levi, 213
Heart, Elias, 87
Heart, Harvey, 199
Heart, James, Jr., 88
Heartwell, Jonas, 88
Heath, Aaron, 156, 157
Heath, Abner, 31
Heath, Abram, 228
Heath, Asa, 170, 262
Heath, Dudly, 15
Heath, Ebeneser, 31
Heath, Enoch, 156, 157 (2)
Heath, Hows, 161
Heath, Isaac, 190
Heath, Isaac, Jr., 190
Heath, James, 184, 188, 191
Heath, John, 31, 69, 84, 157 (2)
Heath, John G., 161
Heath, John R., 2
Heath, John W., 150, 151
Heath, Jonathan, 161, 185, 191
Heath, Joshua, 41
Heath, Justin, 242
Heath, Richard, 15, 162 (2)
Heath, Samuel, 165, 166, 233
Heaton, Isaac, 180
Heaton, Samuel, 254
Heats, Ezra, 31
Heavens, Pierce, 119
Hebard, Davison, 271
Hebbard, Isaac, 291
Hebbert, Timothy M., 295
Hebner, Charles, 287, 310, 311
Heddon, George, 234
Hedge, Barna, 287
Hedge, Barris, 285
Hedge, George, 148
Hedge, Seth, 237
Hedges, Josiah, 9

Hefford, James, 127
Held, Benjamin, 178
Held, Benjamin, Jr., 178
Held, Israel, 178
Helmes, Peter Y., 29
Heman, Joshua, 73, 76
Heman, William, 73, 76
Hemenway, Adam, 29
Hemenway, Elias, 29
Hemenway, Jason, 64
Hemenway, Josiah, 33
Hemenway, Martin, 48
Hemenway, William, 64
Hemingway, Israel, 88
Heminway, Calvin, 292
Heminway, Micajah, 3
Hemmenway, Benjamin, 26
Hemmingway, Benjamin, 301
Hemmingway, Joshua, 301
Hemmingway, Sylvanus, 301
Henderson, Dunbar, 284, 288, 294
Henderson, Howard, 7
Henderson, John, 265
Henderson, Joseph, 10, 206
Henderson, Luther, 85
Henderson, Moses, 233
Henderson, Nathan, 162
Henderson, Samuel, 132
Henderson, Saul, 140
Henderson, Thomas, 233
Henderson, William, 206, 288, 294
Hendley, Henry W., 68
Hendley, James, 69, 78
Hendly, John, 100
Hendrick, Stephen, 47, 67
Hendricks, John, 55, 58
Henery, James, 24
Henford, Richard L., 118
Henley, Henry, 79
Henley, John, 261
Henly, James, 243
Henly, John, 246, 312
Henman, John, 21, 132
Hennaford, William W., 257
Henry, George, 155
Henry, James, 155
Henry, John, 222, 234, 261
Henry, Joseph, 196
Henry, Orrin, 29
Henry, Robert, 196
Henry, Samuel, 45
Henry, Samuel, Jr., 233
Henry, William, 29, 83, 114
Henshaw, David, 26
Henshaw, Ebeneser, 85
Henshaw, Samuel, 2
Hensler, George, 134, 140
Henson, Moses, 269
Hentry, Saul F., 139
Hentton, William, 277
Herbert, George, 163
Herbon, Henry, 132
Herd, Moses, 197, 204
Herd, Oliver, 204
Herd, Robert, 204 (2), 206
Hermon, Samuel, 258
Herrick, Amos, 161
Herrick, Benjamin, 212
Herrick, Daniel, 243, 271
Herrick, George W., 34, 37, 38
Herrick, Hallibut, 164
Herrick, Henry, 36, 37

370 INDEX.

Herrick, Hollibut, 164, 165
Herrick, Isaac, 98
Herrick, Israel, 167
Herrick, Jacob, 295
Herrick, Jacob, 3d, 295
Herrick, John, 11
Herrick, John, 2d, 34
Herrick, Jonathan, 2d, 34, 38
Herrick, Joseph, 11, 12
Herrick, Joseph, Jr., 281
Herrick, Joseph, 2d, 167
Herrick, Joshua, 295
Herrick, Moses, 177
Herrick, Samuel, 80
Herrick, Thomas F., 34
Herrick, Thomas P., 2d, 34
Herrick, William, 38
Herrick, William, 3d, 37
Herrick, William, 4th, 34
Herriden, Andrew, 300
Herriman, John, 190
Herring, Andrew, 306
Herring, John, 253
Herrington, Asa, 46
Herrington, Ebenezer, 92
Herrington, James, 208 (3)
Herrington, Josiah, 207, 208 (2)
Herris, John, Jr., 167
Herris, Joseph, 167
Herron, James, 40
Hersey, Abel, 134, 135
Hersey, Abisha, 283
Hersey, Amos, 175
Hersey, Caleb, 258
Hersey, Charles, 42
Hersey, Ebenezer, 40
Hersey, Elias, 241
Hersey, Israel, 164, 165, 166, 246, 255
Hersey, James, Jr., 178
Hersey, Jesse, 226
Hersey, John, 177
Hersey, Lewis, 84
Hersey, Moses, 150
Hersey, Noah, 99
Hersey, Noah, Jr., 177
Hersey, Noaman, 112
Hersey, Simeon, 178
Hersey, Welcome, 141
Hershel, Ebenezer D., 233
Hersum, John, 260
Hervey, Darius, 59
Hervey, Frederic, 59
Hervey, James, 80
Hervey, Robert, 193
Hervy, David, 19
Hervy, Eliphalet, 80
Hesselton, John, 10
Hesum, John, 260
Hovins, Nathan, 99
Hewens, Elijah, 32
Hower, William Y., 110
Hewes, David, 214
Hewes, Elijah, 214
Hewes, John, 90
Hewes, William G., 7
Howett, Harvey, 202
Hewett, John, 198, 202, 209
Hewett, Samuel, 156
Hewett, Waterman, 198
Hewett, William, 201 (2), 203
Hewey, David, 234
Hewey, Jonathan, 236, 296

Hewey, Jonathan, Jr., 234
Hewey, Joseph, Jr., 234
Hewey, Samuel, 234
Hewey, Thomas, 234
Hewins, Abel, 70
Hewins, James, 158
Hewins, Whiting, 70
Hewiston, Benjamin, 17
Hewitt, Daniel, 3
Hewitt, Harvey, 201
Hewitt, John, 207
Hewitt, Richard, 59
Hewitt, Waterman, 208
Hewitt, Harvey, 198
Howlot, Westly, 32
Hows, Elihu, 102
Hewson, Robert, 3
Heywood, Reuben, 5
Hibbard, Billy, 29 (2)
Hibbard, Daniel, 180
Hibbard, John, 245
Hibbard, Joseph, 133
Hibbard, Samuel, 6
Hibberd, Jonathan, Jr., 307
Hickey, Dennis, 82
Hicks, Benjamin, 250
Hicks, Ephraim, 171
Hicks, George, 209
Hicks, James, 220
Hicks, John, 42
Hicks, Joseph, 63
Hicks, Nathaniel, 171
Hicks, Samuel, 219
Hicks, William, 221
Hicock, George, 119
Hicock, Moses, 119
Hierl, John, 154
Higbee, Lemuel, 118
Higerman, Ira, 65
Higgin, Timothy, 234
Higgins, Aaron, 105, 106, 107
Higgins, Abiather, 104
Higgins, Abisha, 107
Higgins, Asa, 104, 105, 106, 107
Higgins, Barnabas, 173
Higgins, Benjamin, 105 (2), 106, 214
Higgins, Carney, 105 (2), 107
Higgins, Charles, 104, 106
Higgins, Cyrus, 214
Higgins, Dyer, 233
Higgins, Elinkim, 104, 106
Higgins, Elisha, 105, 107, 215, 220
Higgins, Enos F., 173
Higgins, Hezekiah, 104, 105
Higgins, Jabez, 104
Higgins, James, 105, 106 (3), 107 (2), 108
Higgins, James, Jr., 104, 105, 107
Higgins, James, 2d, 215
Higgins, Jeremiah, 234, 236
Higgins, John, Jr., 220
Higgins, Jonathan, 198, 202, 208 (2)
Higgins, Joseph, 248
Higgins, Josiah, 162
Higgins, Judah, 106 (2), 107, 108
Higgins, Knowles, 104, 105 (2)
Higgins, Levi, 65
Higgins, Luther, 65
Higgins, Misha, 215
Higgins, Moses, 104, 105 (2), 106, 107
Higgins, Nathan, 55, 262
Higgins, Nathaniel, 129, 307
Higgins, Philip, Jr., 248

Higgins, Reuben, 295, 297
Higgins, Richard, 104, 105, 106, 107
Higgins, Richard, Jr., 107
Higgins, Samuel, 213, 248
Higgins, Samuel C., 173
Higgins, Seth, 214
Higgins, Simeon, 247
Higgins, Simeon, Jr., 248
Higgins, Simon, 104
Higgins, Simon, Jr., 105 (2), 106, 107
Higgins, Sylvanus, 104, 105 (2), 106, 107
Higgins, Thomas, 104, 105 (2), 106, 107, 220, 262
Higgins, William, 215
Higgins, Zacheus, 174
High, John, 6, 22
Hight, Humphrey, 171
Higsbee, Lemuel, 21
Hilbourn, Robert, 253
Hilder, Josiah, 94
Hildreth, Alvan, 141
Hildreth, David, Jr., 305
Hildreth, Hosea, 299
Hildreth, Jonathan, 5
Hildreth, Nathaniel, 36
Hildreth, Robert, 271
Hiler, Simeon, 108
Hiler, Stephen G., 2
Hiler, Thomas, 26
Hiler, William H., 2, 108
Hill, Aaron, 90
Hill, Abram, 215
Hill, Alexander, 251
Hill, Amos, 36, 37, 90, 96, 152
Hill, Amos S., 266
Hill, Barnum, 51
Hill, Bela, 97
Hill, Benjamin, 36
Hill, Bezar, 97
Hill, Charles, 133, 136, 137, 139, 250, 255
Hill, Chase, 174
Hill, Consider, 252, 255
Hill, Daniel, 68, 151, 152
Hill, Daniel, Jr., 209 (2)
Hill, David, 21, 132
Hill, Ezekiel, 229, 283
Hill, George, 32, 149, 241
Hill, Henry, 133, 138
Hill, Ira, 39
Hill, James, 223
Hill, Jeremiah, 245
Hill, John, 16, 89, 93, 252, 258
Hill, John W., 113
Hill, Jonathan, 42, 96, 264
Hill, Josiah, 97, 271, 290
Hill, Josiah, Jr., 154, 253, 255
Hill, Leonard, 9, 10
Hill, Levi, 30
Hill, Miles, 100
Hill, Nathaniel, 152, 271
Hill, Nelson, 245
Hill, Obediah, 16
Hill, Oliver C., 160
Hill, Philip, 292
Hill, Ralph, 161
Hill, Reuben, 252
Hill, Richard, 129, 138
Hill, Robert, 137
Hill, Rowland, 296
Hill, Samuel, 23, 77, 101, 113 (2), 114, 269 (2)
Hill, Samuel, Jr., 270
Hill, Samuel, 2d, 294

Hill, Samuel B., 69
Hill, Simon, 138
Hill, Thomas, 35 (2), 48, 160, 255, 258
Hill, Thomas, Jr., 252
Hill, W. D., 26
Hill, William, 77, 114, 151, 100, 176, 257, 279
Hill, Woodbury, 115
Hillen, Benjamin, 179
Hiller, Jonathan, 55, 58 (2)
Hiller, Levi, 58
Hilliard, Henry, 59
Hillis, Francis, 130
Hillman, Erastus B., 96
Hillman, George, 26, 87
Hillman, Jethro, 278
Hillman, Justin, 64
Hillman, Presberry, 64
Hills, Charles, 16
Hills, Edmun, 15
Hills, Eliphalet, 15
Hills, Joel, 290, 293
Hills, Joshua, 17
Hills, Josiah, 286
Hills, Reuben, 290
Hills, Reuben, 2d, 293
Hills, Saul, 290
Hilt, Daniel, 201 (2), 203
Hilt, Freeman, 198, 208
Hilt, Philip, 201 (2), 203
Hilt, William, 198, 202, 208 (3)
Hilton, Alfred, 249, 297
Hilton, Amos, 36
Hilton, Andrew, 156, 157 (2)
Hilton, Daniel, 151, 285, 287, 306
Hilton, Daniel, Jr., 271
Hilton, Ebenezer, 265
Hilton, Edgar, 208
Hilton, Elisha, 265
Hilton, Ellis, 285, 286
Hilton, James, 196
Hilton, John, 268, 305, 306
Hilton, Joseph, 184
Hilton, Joseph, Jr., 188
Hilton, Joshua, 182, 305
Hilton, Moses, 151, 244, 285, 287
Hilton, Nathan, 151
Hilton, Peter, 82
Hilton, Rufus, 285, 287
Hilton, Samuel, 243
Hilton, Simeon, 265
Hilton, Theophilus, 305
Himer, Joseph A., 72
Himman, Ebenezer, 141
Hinckley, Benjamin, 131
Hinckley, Charles, 131
Hinckley, Edmund, 235
Hinckley, Isaac, 131
Hinckley, John, 235
Hinckley, Josiah, 131
Hinckley, Lot, 131
Hinckley, Matthew, 235
Hinckley, Otis, 131
Hinckley, Samuel, 234, 236
Hinckley, Samuel W., 235
Hinckley, Stotham, 46
Hinckley, William, 131
Hind, Chapman, 259
Hinds, Asher, 3
Hinds, Benjamin, 192, 195, 197, 238
Hinds, Chipman, 177
Hinds, Edward, 103
Hinds, Leonard, 53, 103

Hinds, Nimrod, 266
Hinds, Owen, 272
Hine, Thaddeus, 177
Hinfield, Richard L., 116
Hingman, Samuel, 102
Hinkle, Abraham, 74
Hinkley, Aaron, 169
Hinkley, Abner, 72
Hinkley, Alanson, 224, 260
Hinkley, Ariel, 274
Hinkley, Barnard, 274
Hinkley, Benjamin, 146, 169, 281
Hinkley, Ebenezer, 275
Hinkley, Ebenezer C., 214
Hinkley, Edmund, 75, 233
Hinkley, Elijah, 72
Hinkley, Enoch, 283
Hinkley, Ezekiel, 148
Hinkley, Holmes, 146
Hinkley, Jacob, 169
Hinkley, James, 148
Hinkley, John, 233
Hinkley, John N., 84, 109
Hinkley, Levi, 272
Hinkley, Matthew, 148
Hinkley, Nathaniel, 233
Hinkley, Obed, 275
Hinkley, Owen, 272
Hinkley, S., 125
Hinkley, Shubel, Jr., 274
Hinkley, Thomas, 233
Hinkley, Thomas W., 233
Hinkley, William, 233, 296
Hinkly, James, 74
Hinkly, John, 248
Hinkly, Joseph, 282
Hinkly, Samuel, 220
Hinkly, William, 74, 215, 248
Hinton, John, 188
Hinton, William, 188
Hintoon, John, 191
Hiscock, Benjamin, 195
Hiscock, Daniel, 283
Hiscock, Enos, 283
Hiscock, James, 194
Hiscock, Jesse, 229
Hiscock, John, 195, 229
Hiscock, Peres, 194
Hiscock, Richard, 193
Hiscock, Thomas, Jr., 283
Hiscock, William, 192, 195
Hiscock, William, Jr., 195
Hisey, John, 257
Hitchborn, Alexander, 70, 79
Hitchborn, Henry, 303
Hitchcock, Asher, 4
Hitchcock, Chancy, 46
Hitchcock, Daniel, 4
Hitchcock, Eaton, 44
Hitchcock, Ebenezer M., 45
Hitchcock, Eleazer, 43
Hitchcock, Gad, 209
Hitchcock, George K., 4
Hitchcock, Heber, 4
Hitchcock, Josiah, 4
Hitchcock, Obed, 64
Hitchcock, Walter, 4
Hitchings, Benjamin, 134
Hitchings, Jesse, 117
Hitchings, Joseph, 263
Hitchings, Nathaniel, 138
Hitchins, Benjamin B., 118

Hitchins, Benjamin T., 118
Hitchins, Ichabod, 152
Hitchins, John, 118
Hitchins, Samuel, 7, 22
Hitchman, Solomon, 130
Hiter, Stephen, 26
Hito, Samuel C., 179
Hix, Daniel, 60
Hix, Samuel, 197, 204 (2)
Hoadlett, Charles, 157
Hoar, Charles, 94
Hoar, Job, Jr., 53
Hoar, John, 43
Hoar, Joseph, 101
Hoar, Lot, 25
Hoar, Stephen, 53
Hoar, William, 53, 174
Hoard, Cromwell, 59
Hoard, Elias, 55
Hoard, Gilbert, 61
Hoard, Jarvis, 61
Hoard, Stephen, 68
Hobart, Calvin, 78
Hobart, Hawks, 2d, 101
Hobbard, Joseph, 136
Hobbs, Amos, 224
Hobbs, Charles, 202
Hobbs, Daniel, 80, 83
Hobbs, Ebenezer, 198, 202, 208 (2)
Hobbs, George, 266
Hobbs, Isaac, 258
Hobbs, Jeremiah, 132, 253
Hobbs, Jeremiah, Jr., 253
Hobbs, John, 39, 244, 258
Hobbs, John L., 23, 84
Hobbs, Jonathan, 219
Hobbs, Joseph, 268
Hobbs, Josiah, 218, 222
Hobbs, Micah, 203
Hobbs, Nathan, 79
Hobbs, Nathaniel, 23, 245
Hobbs, Robinson, 253, 260
Hobbs, Stephen, 306
Hobby, George, 306
Hobby, James, 305
Hobert, Henry, 99
Hobert, Joseph, 49
Hobert, Nehemiah, 91
Hobert, Seth, 187
Hobert, Thomas, 19
Hobert, William, 86
Hobin, Richard, 216
Hobson, Moses, 134, 135, 136, 140
Hobson, Samuel, 14, 270
Hobson, William, 270
Hock, Jacob, 289
Hock, John, 289
Hodgden, Benjamin, 183
Hodgden, Moses, 252
Hodgden, Saul, 132
Hodgdon, Abraham, 259
Hodgdon, Benjamin, 185, 188, 191, 192
Hodgdon, Caleb, 189
Hodgdon, Elijah, 264
Hodgdon, Isaac, 301
Hodgdon, Israel, 176
Hodgdon, James, 169
Hodgdon, Jeremiah, 298
Hodgdon, John, 163, 164, 176, 189, 191, 283
Hodgdon, John, Jr., 189
Hodgdon, Joseph, 189, 267

INDEX.

Hodgdon, Joseph, 2d, 189
Hodgdon, Joshua, 245
Hodgdon, Moses, 255
Hodgdon, Robert, 138
Hodgdon, Samuel, 194, 245
Hodgdon, Saul, 140
Hodgdon, Stephen, 252
Hodgdon, Thomas, 189, 191
Hodge, Benjamin, 92
Hodge, Charles, 19
Hodge, David, 210, 260
Hodge, Ezra, 274
Hodge, George, 92
Hodge, Jacob, 2
Hodge, James, 156, 157
Hodge, John, 182
Hodge, John M., 225, 260
Hodge, Joseph, 137, 176, 260
Hodge, Nathaniel, 18, 120, 122
Hodge, S. S., 122, 125
Hodge, Stephen, 10
Hodges, Adoniram, 10
Hodges, Barnam, 126
Hodges, Benjamin, 146
Hodges, Ezra, 165, 166
Hodges, Gamaliel, 140
Hodges, George, 10, 138, 243
Hodges, George A., 132
Hodges, Henry B., 54
Hodges, John, 292
Hodges, Joseph, 10
Hodges, Joseph W., 54
Hodges, Josiah, 10
Hodges, Otis, 99
Hodgkins, Benjamin, 249, 299
Hodgkins, Chipman, 150
Hodgkins, David, 13, 14, 145
Hodgkins, Ebenezer, 177
Hodgkins, Francis, 196
Hodgkins, Frank, 194
Hodgkins, Henry, 11
Hodgkins, Isaac, 13
Hodgkins, Israel, 255
Hodgkins, James, 194
Hodgkins, John, 13, 292
Hodgkins, John, Jr., 249
Hodgkins, Jonathan, 169
Hodgkins, Joseph, 14
Hodgkins, Nathaniel, 242
Hodgkins, Samuel, 148
Hodgkins, Samuel B., 148, 235
Hodgkins, Thomas, 134, 140
Hodgkins, True, 229
Hodgkins, William, 12
Hodgman, Amos, 230, 232
Hodgman, Asa, 230
Hodgman, Buckley, 198, 199, 207
Hodgman, David, 280
Hodgman, Job, 208 (2)
Hodgman, Job, Jr., 197
Hodgman, Thomas, 160, 202
Hodgdon, Abraham, 224
Hodgdon, John, 224
Hodgdon, Samuel C., 224
Hodsden, Daniel, 261
Hodsdon, Israel, Jr., 211
Hodsdon, James, 281
Hodsdon, Samuel, 275
Hodsdon, Thomas, 154
Hofer, George, 311
Hoffman, Peter, 78
Hogan, Andrew, 250

Hogan, Charles, 232
Hogan, James, 247
Hogan, John, 232 (2)
Hogan, Thomas, 249
Hogan, William, 232 (2)
Hogen, Charles, 235
Hogin, Andrew, 249
Hoit, Samuel, 168
Holbrook, Aaron, 2d, 96
Holbrook, Abisur, 249
Holbrook, Caleb, 42, 89
Holbrook, Calvin, 214
Holbrook, Cephas, 96
Holbrook, Charles, 84
Holbrook, Clark, 90
Holbrook, D., 101
Holbrook, Dan, 42, 102
Holbrook, Daniel, 97, 126
Holbrook, Edmund, 71
Holbrook, Elias, 42, 88
Holbrook, Eliphalet, 86
Holbrook, Elisha, 42, 102
Holbrook, Ellis, 96
Holbrook, Henry, 86
Holbrook, Israel, 300
Holbrook, James, 42
Holbrook, Jennet, 253, 257
Holbrook, Jesse, 148, 249
Holbrook, John, 25, 101, 265, 299, 305
Holbrook, Jonathan, 299
Holbrook, Joseph, 23, 305
Holbrook, Joshua, 102
Holbrook, Josiah D., 30
Holbrook, Moses, 295
Holbrook, Otis, 48
Holbrook, Reuben, 92, 209
Holbrook, Richard, 92, 305
Holbrook, Royal, 23
Holbrook, Samuel, 68, 80
Holbrook, Seth, 96
Holbrook, Solomon, 182 (3)
Holbrook, Sylvanus, 78
Holbrook, William, 42
Holbrook, Zadoc, 42
Holcomb, Edmund, 46
Holden, Abel, 8
Holden, Daniel, 7, 147
Holden, Ebenezer, 39, 71
Holden, Jabes, 60
Holden, James, 41, 48
Holden, Jonas, 93
Holden, Moses, 109
Holden, Obed, 67
Holden, Thomas, 23
Holden, William, 96
Holdes, Steven, 229
Holdridge, Ira, 32
Holland, Cornelius, 222, 254
Holland, John, 39, 169
Holland, John G., 40
Holland, Samuel, 222
Holland, Thomas, 69
Holland, Thomas, 2d, 70
Holland, William, 40, 80, 81
Holley, Horace, 68
Hollis, Daniel, 28, 80
Hollis, David, 80, 81, 87, 256
Hollis, Ebenezer, 39
Hollis, Garnet, 42
Hollis, Hosea, 101
Hollis, Joseph, 77
Hollis, Samuel, 229

Hollis, Solomon, 210
Hollis, Stephen, 65
Hollis, Thomas, 42, 89, 229
Hollis, William, 68, 78, 83, 98, 109 (2), 110, 111 (3), 112
Hollister, Henry, 29
Holloway, James, 7
Holly, William, 112
Holman, Abner, 224, 259
Holman, Daniel, 224
Holman, Ebenezer, 222
Holman, John, 84, 109
Holman, Jonathan, 222
Holman, Levi, 307
Holman, Richard, 48, 77
Holman, Samuel, 48, 132
Holman, Thomas J., 88
Holmes, Abner, 59
Holmes, Alvah, 257
Holmes, Andrew, 131
Holmes, Asa, 177
Holmes, Bartlet, 128
Holmes, Bradford, 129
Holmes, Caleb, 225
Holmes, Charles I., 93
Holmes, Ebenezer, 59, 253, 257, 263
Holmes, Eleaser, 243
Holmes, Eliphalet, Jr., 54
Holmes, Francis, 129
Holmes, George, 117
Holmes, Horace, 94
Holmes, J. G., 230
Holmes, James, 303
Holmes, John, 119, 264, 285
Holmes, John, 2d, 171
Holmes, Jonathan, 225
Holmes, Joseph, 9
Holmes, Joseph W., 71
Holmes, Josiah, 129
Holmes, Josiah N., 112
Holmes, Miles, 257
Holmes, Nathan, 128
Holmes, Nathaniel, Jr., 129
Holmes, Nathaniel B., 113 (2)
Holmes, Nye, 129
Holmes, Oliver, 55, 58, 80
Holmes, Pearley, 83
Holmes, Peter, 128
Holmes, Rufus, 59
Holmes, Salmon, 257
Holmes, Samuel, 170
Holmes, Samuel, Jr., 90
Holmes, Solomon, 253
Holmes, Stephen, 112
Holmes, Thomas, 52
Holmes, William, 9, 55, 58, 60, 64, 171, 299
Holt, Amasa, 67
Holt, Amos, 86
Holt, Enoch, 90
Holt, Herman, 257
Holt, Isaac, 238, 266, 306
Holt, Jonas, 3
Holt, Jonathan, 66
Holt, Joseph, 257
Holt, Saul, 2d, 66
Holt, Stephen, 163 (2)
Holt Timothy A., 258
Holt, William, 34, 161
Holter, Christian, 292
Holton, Asaph, 39
Holton, Elias, 3
Holton, Euclid, 286

INDEX. 373

Holton, Henry, 84
Holton, Jeremiah, 145, 284, 287
Holton, John, 3
Holton, Lucius, 3
Holway, Freeman, 307
Holway, Joseph, 267, 310
Holway, William, 73, 76
Holyoke, John, 216
Homan, Benjamin, 6, 7, 21
Homan, John, 218
Homan, Joseph, 7
Homan, Nathaniel, 22
Homan, Philip C., 22
Homan, Samuel, 6, 21
Homan, William, 7, 22
Homans, Stephen, 34, 38
Homas, Benjamin, 6
Hombs, Lymond, 46
Homer, John, 87, 263, 267
Homer, William, 83
Homes, Francis, 2
Homes, John, 27, 304
Homes, Miles, 176
Homes, Peter, 304
Hondlett, Charles, 156, 157
Hondlett, Francis, 156, 157
Hondlett, George, 156, 157
Hondlett, James, 156, 157
Hondlett, Philip, 156
Honeywell, Thomas, 307
Honor, Oliver, 11
Hood, Billings, 150
Hood, Charles, 28
Hood, Christopher, 265
Hood, George S., 59
Hood, James, 62
Hood, John, 60 (2), 116
Hood, Otis, 150
Hood, Peter, 160
Hood, Willard, 62
Hood, William, 269
Hood, William C., 62
Hook, John, 217
Hook, Joseph, 307
Hooker, Benning, 270
Hooker, John, 7, 22
Hooker, Philip, 7
Hooker, Revereius, 272
Hooker, Richard, 20
Hooker, William, 42
Hoole, Joseph, 242
Hooper, Edward, 10
Hooper, Eleaser, 36 (2), 37
Hooper, Gamaliel, 47
Hooper, Henry, 255
Hooper, Isaac, 51
Hooper, Isaac S., 167
Hooper, Jacob, 6, 21
Hooper, James, 250
Hooper, John, 7, 22, 36
Hooper, Joseph, 36, 51
Hooper, Leander, 31
Hooper, Levi, 265
Hooper, Mathew, 10
Hooper, Robert, 12
Hooper, Simeon, 49
Hope, George S., 83
Hopkins, Allen, 163 (2), 214
Hopkins, Andrew, 52
Hopkins, Asa, 104
Hopkins, Benjamin, 215
Hopkins, Bradford, 196

Hopkins, Chandler, 240
Hopkins, Charles, 198, 208 (2), 209
Hopkins, Constant, 80
Hopkins, Curtis, 104, 105 (2), 106, 107
Hopkins, Daniel, 139 (2)
Hopkins, Elisha, 300
Hopkins, Ephraim, 216
Hopkins, Freeman, 23, 114
Hopkins, Isaac, 233, 235, 296
Hopkins, James, 215
Hopkins, John, 54, 90, 232 (2), 270
Hopkins, Joshua, 106, 229
Hopkins, Joshua, Jr., 107, 108
Hopkins, Josiah, 215
Hopkins, Nathan, 198, 202, 208 (2)
Hopkins, Peter, 302
Hopkins, Redfield, 160
Hopkins, Richard, 198, 202, 208 (2), 209, 240
Hopkins, Robert, 180
Hopkins, Samuel, 113, 270
Hopkins, Simeon, 299
Hopkins, Simeon, Jr., 297
Hopkins, Smith, 301
Hopkins, Theodore, 240
Hopkins, Thomas R., 28
Hopkins, William, 189
Hopkinson, Theophilus, 229
Hopkinson, William, 272
Hoppin, Daniel, 115
Hoppin, John B., 160
Hopping, William, 88
Hord, Nehemiah, 229
Horle, Joseph, 241
Horn, Andrew, 291
Horn, Benjamin, 266
Horn, David, 218
Horn, Frederick, 195
Horn, James, 244
Horn, Joseph, 191
Horn, Mishach, 245
Hornan, John, 218
Horne, Ephraim B., 15
Horne, William, 237
Horrey, Calvin, 90
Horsefield, Timothy, 125
Horsey, Welcome, 141
Horsley, Oralana, 66
Horson, Benjamin, 308
Horson, Thomas, 306
Horsum, Oliver, 245
Horton, Asahel, 61
Horton, Aseph, 86
Horton, Barnet, 61
Horton, Benjamin, 134, 135, 137, 138
Horton, Benjamin, Jr., 69
Horton, J., 19
Horton, James, 288
Horton, James M., 67
Horton, John, 60, 79, 90
Horton, Joshua, 288
Horton, Moses, 252
Horton, Samuel, 7, 22
Horton, Samuel, Jr., 6
Horton, Simeon, 59
Hosea, Richard, 23
Hosea, Samuel, 78
Hosei, Clark, 30
Hosford, Arad, 65
Hosley, James, 3
Hosman, Nathan, 65
Hosmer, Anthony, 198, 207 (2), 208
Hosmer, Castalio, 41

Hosmer, Charles, 6, 198, 202, 208 (2)
Hosmer, Cyrus, Jr., 99
Hosmer, David, 39
Hosmer, Hammon, 80
Hosmer, Hammond, 68
Hosmer, Jesse, 6
Hosmer, John, 6
Hosmer, Jonathan, 100
Hosmer, Joseph, 5
Hosmer, Josiah W., 202, 208, 209
Hosmer, Nathaniel, 41
Hosmer, Pearley, 99
Hosmer, Samuel, 217
Hosmer, Silas, 100
Hosnal, John I., 230
Houghton, Asa, 48
Houghton, Evelio, 290
Houghton, Henry, 3
Houghton, Jason N., 39
Houghton, Jesse, 90
Houghton, John, 116
Houghton, Millard, 48
Houghton, Phinehas, 48
Houghton, Ralph, 38, 40
House, Allen, 280
House, Caleb, 2d, 177
House, Eleazer, 180
House, Eleazer G., 78
House, H., 167
House, John, 168
House, Joshua, 177
Houston, Alexander, 287
Houston, James, 302
Houston, John, 302
Houston, Joseph, 256
Houston, Samuel, 145
Houston, Thomas, 304
Hoverman, Peter, 87
Hovey, Aaron, 69
Hovey, Alfred, 289
Hovey, Ebeneser, 101
Hovey, George, 226
Hovey, Isaac, 229
Hovey, Ivory, 285, 286, 288
Hovey, Rufus P., 99
Hovey, Samuel, 42
How, Abraham, 9
How, Amos, 5
How, Daniel, 151, 241
How, Edward F., 3
How, Jeremiah, 178
How, Jesse, 178
How, Joel, Jr., 192
How, John, 241
How, Joseph, 241
How, Marcus, 196
How, Nathan, 244
How, Nathaniel, 97
Howard, Aaron, 136, 140
Howard, Abel, 52
Howard, Abiazer, 164, 165
Howard, Abijah, 7
Howard, Abner, 220
Howard, Almond, 225
Howard, Amasa, 44
Howard, Amos, 64, 96
Howard, Asa, 216
Howard, Asaph, 53, 177, 257
Howard, Austin, 50
Howard, Barnabus, 53, 91
Howard, Barnard, 69
Howard, Benjamin, 55, 58

INDEX.

Howard, Benjamin B., 49
Howard, Caleb, 49 (2), 287, 290, 291
Howard, Calvin, 41, 126
Howard, Charles, 49, 95
Howard, Cyrus, 50
Howard, Daniel, 59, 280
Howard, Daniel C., 187, 190
Howard, David, 49
Howard, Ebenezer, 93
Howard, Edward C., 49
Howard, Ethan, 95
Howard, George, 95
Howard, Gideon, 50
Howard, Henry, 53, 153
Howard, James, 128
Howard, John, 43, 62, 127, 136, 137, 217, 261
Howard, John D., 113 (2), 114
Howard, Johnson, 41
Howard, Jonathan, 67
Howard, Josephus, 149
Howard, Joshua, 118, 225, 246
Howard, Lewis, 50
Howard, Libbeus, 237
Howard, Lina, 49
Howard, Moses, 34, 37, 38
Howard, Nathaniel, 121, 125
Howard, Oliver, 50
Howard, Oliver, Jr., 50
Howard, Otis, 50
Howard, Penos, 224
Howard, Peter, 102
Howard, Pliney, 49
Howard, Richard, 201 (2)
Howard, Ruell, 270
Howard, Samuel, 275, 311
Howard, Samuel B., 149
Howard, Sidney, 49, 50
Howard, Simeon, 49
Howard, Stillman, 167
Howard, Thomas, 58, 95, 292
Howard, Warren, 95
Howard, William, 20, 55, 58, 176, 291
Howard, Zenas, 262, 267
Howard, Zepheon, 236
Howard, Ziba, 49
Howard, Zuriel, 2
Howe, Alvin, 79, 83
Howe, Asor, 49
Howe, Benjamin L., 182
Howe, Calvin W., 99
Howe, Daniel, 254
Howe, Eleazer G., 81
Howe, George, 83
Howe, Henry, 40, 69
Howe, Isaac, 2, 25
Howe, Jacob, 23, 79
Howe, Jesse, 259
Howe, Joel, 182
Howe, John, 7, 23, 77, 113, 261, 283
Howe, Joseph N., 24
Howe, Joshua, 50
Howe, Marius, 287
Howe, Otis, 83, 261
Howe, Philip, 8
Howe, Richard, 24
Howe, Richard S., 114
Howe, Samuel, 128
Howe, Seneca, 151
Howe, Thomas, 40
Howe, Thomas, Jr., 24
Howell, Robert, 15
Howes, Alvin, 305

Howes, Edmond, 268
Howes, Lemuel, Jr., 305
Howes, Loring, 26, 87, 112
Howes, Samuel, 24
Howes, William, 67, 71
Howill, Levi, Jr., 282
Howlan, Jabes, 31
Howland, Abraham, 231
Howland, Asa, 63
Howland, Benjamin, 231
Howland, Benjamin I., 80
Howland, Benjamin J., 83
Howland, Bradford, 63
Howland, Charles, 128
Howland, Daniel, 63
Howland, David, 129
Howland, Eastman, 63
Howland, George, 231
Howland, Henry, Jr., 128
Howland, Ichabod, 97
Howland, Isaac, 30, 193
Howland, James, 1, 73, 76
Howland, Jason, 74
Howland, John, 63, 231
Howland, John, Jr., 129
Howland, Jonathan, 129
Howland, Joseph, 30, 74, 94, 262
Howland, Joshua, 63
Howland, Lloyd, 1
Howland, Malichi, 57
Howland, Pardon, 63
Howland, Samuel, 59
Howland, Seth, 57
Howland, Stephen, 276
Howland, Timothy, 55
Howland, Walter, 63
Howland, William, 56, 128
Howland, Wing, 1
Howlet, Sylvester, 46
Hows, David, 282
Hows, E. O., 27
Hows, George P., 27
Hoxie, Allen, 310
Hoxie, Barrett, 266
Hoxie, John, 73, 76, 215
Hoyt, Chase, 11
Hoyt, Daniel, 14
Hoyt, Elna, 80
Hoyt, George, 230
Hoyt, John, 18, 121, 125, 179
Hoyt, John, 3d, 295
Hoyt, John C., 63
Hoyt, John H., 12, 282
Hoyt, John T., 243
Hoyt, Joseph, 15, 295, 297
Hoyt, Levi, 282
Hoyt, Moses, 20
Hoyt, Samuel, 19
Hoyt, Stephen, 276
Hoyt, William, 241
Hubbard, Allen, 46
Hubbard, Benjamin, 42, 309
Hubbard, Cyrus, 99
Hubbard, Daniel W., 119
Hubbard, Darius, 88
Hubbard, Dimon, 309
Hubbard, Dimon, Jr., 309
Hubbard, Elijah, 45
Hubbard, Hawly, 31
Hubbard, John, 31, 230, 283
Hubbard, Jonathan, 47, 99
Hubbard, Joseph, 149

Hubbard, Leroy, 262
Hubbard, Luroy, 266
Hubbard, Moses, 279
Hubbard, Nathan, 244
Hubbard, Noah, 263, 266
Hubbard, Noah Dyer, 45
Hubbard, Orrin, 31
Hubbard, Richard, 279 (2)
Hubbard, Silas N., 42
Hubbard, Stephen, 245
Hubbard, Thomas, 42, 159
Hubbard, Walter, 31
Hubbard, Warwick, 152, 254
Hubbell, Deodatus, 30
Hubberd, Samuel, 31
Hubert, George, 164
Huchins, Daniel, 243
Huckings, Jonathan, 183
Hudson, Barzilla, 23, 76
Hudson, Benjamin, 242
Hudson, Charles, 87
Hudson, Henry, 18
Hudson, Isaac, 49
Hudson, John, 90, 118
Hudson, Miles, 49
Hudson, Nathan, 117
Hudson, Samuel, 238
Hudson, Thomas, 82
Hudson, Thomas B., 21
Hueston, Nathaniel, 128
Huff, Bartholomew, 308
Huff, Daniel, 185
Huff, George, 185, 191
Huff, Moses, 2d, 183, 185
Huff, Moses, 3d, 185
Huff, Nathaniel, 231
Huff, Nicholas, 308
Huff, Noah, 180
Huff, Samuel, 148, 231, 235
Huff, Saul, 185, 191
Huffin, William, 9
Huger, Samuel, 89
Huges, William, 312
Huggins, William, 31
Hughs, James, 116
Hulet, Lewis, 33
Huley, John, 234
Hulin, William, 138
Hull, Abraham, 63
Hull, George, 84, 113, 114
Hull, Perkins, 226
Hull, Robert C., 63
Hull, Samuel, 63
Hull, William, 14, 63, 121
Human, John, Jr., 71
Humble, David, 50
Hume, William, 263, 267
Humes, John, 162
Humphreville, Ambrose, 30
Humphrey, Ebenezer, 42, 102, 195, 196
Humphrey, Jesse, 195
Humphrey, John, 61, 199, 200, 203, 256
Humphrey, John, 3d, 256
Humphrey, Lemuel, 102
Humphrey, Moses L., 40
Humphrey, Stephen, 42
Humphrey, William, 102
Humphreys, Jacob, 192
Humphreys, Leavitt, 40
Humphries, Edward, 7
Humphries, Jacob, 193
Humphries, John, 6, 23, 86

INDEX.

Humphries, Richard, 27
Humphries, Thomas, 23
Humphry, Ebenezer, 88
Humphry, Levi, 110
Hunewell, Nathaniel, 211
Hunnaford, William, 224
Hunneford, William, 148
Hunnewell, Andrew, 300
Hunnewell, Barnabus, 268
Hunnewell, Benjamin, 300
Hunnewell, Calvin, 292
Hunnewell, James, 182 (2)
Hunnewell, John, 300
Hunnewell, Jonathan, 94
Hunnewell, Joseph, 219
Hunnewell, Josiah, 172, 246
Hunnewell, Moses, 300
Hunnewell, Peter, 85
Hunnewell, Phineas, 266
Hunnewell, Robert, 300
Hunnewell, William, 98
Hunt, Arad, 119
Hunt, Asa, 102, 214
Hunt, Benjamin B., 141
Hunt, Charles, 18
Hunt, Daniel, 60, 136, 173
Hunt, David, 133, 184, 188
Hunt, David, Jr., 210
Hunt, Ebenezer, 54
Hunt, Elias, 15
Hunt, Ellsworth, 3
Hunt, Enoch, 39
Hunt, Francis, 278, 281
Hunt, Frederic, 48
Hunt, Horace, 48
Hunt, Israel, 210
Hunt, Jacob, 218
Hunt, James, 173
Hunt, Jeremiah, 148
Hunt, John, 30, 32, 39, 45, 50, 71, 80, 84, 87, 148, 248, 287, 291
Hunt, John M., 39 (2)
Hunt, Joseph, 10, 173
Hunt, Josiah, 4
Hunt, L., 53
Hunt, Lawrence, 9
Hunt, Martin, 85
Hunt, Moses, 10
Hunt, Nathaniel P., 24, 25
Hunt, Noah I., 227
Hunt, Oliver, 10
Hunt, Samuel, 7, 42, 102, 112
Hunt, Sherabish, 41
Hunt, Silas, 30
Hunt, Simon, 80, 83, 199, 202, 207
Hunt, Solomon, 79
Hunt, Thomas, 39
Hunt, Timothy, 77, 110
Hunt, William, 7, 22, 39, 88, 295
Hunt, William, Jr., 248
Hunt, William, 2d, 297, 298
Hunt, William H., 70
Hunter, Adams, 231
Hunter, Alexander, 231
Hunter, Arthur, Jr., 231
Hunter, Bela, 70
Hunter, Benjamin, 231
Hunter, Charles, 231
Hunter, David, 231, 238, 265
Hunter, Ely, 40
Hunter, James, 238
Hunter, John, 55, 190

Hunter, Lithgo, 231
Hunter, Robert, 235, 255
Hunter, Samuel, 231
Hunter, Thomas, 3d, 231
Hunter, Timothy, 296
Hunter, William, 193, 231
Hunting, Bela, 41
Hunting, Jabez F., 42, 89
Hunting, John, 77, 93
Hunting, Joseph, 93
Huntington, Benjamin, 68
Huntington, John, 272, 273
Huntington, Richard, 4
Huntington, Timothy, 230
Huntington, William, 273
Huntoon, David, 278, 281
Huntoon, John, 186 (2), 187
Huntoon, Jonathan G., 146
Huntress, James, 245
Huntress, Nathaniel, 245
Huntress, Samuel D., 152
Huntress, Saul D., 254
Hupper, William, 206
Hurd, Abel, 88
Hurd, Alvin, 106 (2), 107 (2), 108
Hurd, Benjamin, 106 (2), 107 (2), 108
Hurd, Hiram, 240
Hurd, Luther, 106 (2), 107 (2), 108
Hurd, Moses, 145
Hurd, Samuel, 31
Hurd, Zenas, 106, 107 (2), 108
Hurland, James, 69
Hurley, George, 84
Hurley, James, 40
Hurley, John L., 82
Huse, John, 18, 120, 123
Huse, Jonathan, 289
Huse, Joseph, 289
Huse, Nathaniel, Jr., 167
Hussey, Benjamin, 194, 196
Hussey, Ebenezer, 264
Hussey, Elijah K., 228, 282
Hussey, James, 272
Hussey, Job, Jr., 192
Hussey, John, 194 (2), 272
Hussey, Joseph, 195
Hussey, Lemuel, 196
Hussey, Nathaniel, 194
Hussey, Obed, 272
Hussey, Reuben, 263
Hussey, Richard, 184, 186 (2), 187, 190, 191
Hussey, Richard, 2d, 228
Hussey, Robert, 228, 282
Hussey, Samuel, 194, 263, 267
Hussey, William, 228, 239
Hussy, Job, Jr., 194
Huston, Alexander, 220
Huston, Thompson, 220
Hustin, Josiah, 145
Hustin, Rufus, 158
Huston, Daniel, 194
Huston, Elijah, 256
Huston, James, 194
Huston, John, Jr., 194
Huston, Joseph T., 287
Huston, Lewis, 220
Huston, Paul, 220
Huston, Robert, 154, 174, 194, 246
Huston, Saul, 283
Huston, William, 194, 219, 287
Hutchason, John, 262
Hutcherson, John, 169

Hutcherson, William, 306
Hutchings, Andrew, 183, 185, 186, 188
Hutchings, Baker, 194
Hutchings, Henry, 196
Hutchings, John, 160, 183, 185, 188
Hutchings, Jonathan, 183
Hutchings, Samuel, 183
Hutchings, Saul, 185
Hutchings, Thomas, 196
Hutchings, Thomas, Jr., 194
Hutchings, William, 42, 89, 196
Hutchingson, John, 140
Hutchins, David, 265
Hutchins, Ichabod, 254
Hutchins, Isaiah, 176
Hutchins, John, 92, 151, 184, 188, 246, 248, 310
Hutchins, Jonathan, 161, 176, 177, 260
Hutchins, Joseph, 92
Hutchins, Moses, 254
Hutchins, Moses, Jr., 152
Hutchins, Purley, 79
Hutchins, Samuel, 225
Hutchins, Solomon, 193
Hutchins, William, 148
Hutchinson, Asa, 228, 283
Hutchinson, Daniel, 176, 260
Hutchinson, Ebenezer, 227, 282
Hutchinson, Ephraim B., 26
Hutchinson, Henry, 175
Hutchinson, Isaac, 168, 281
Hutchinson, Israel, 136, 273
Hutchinson, James, 150, 230, 273 (2)
Hutchinson, John, 134, 267, 279, 285
Hutchinson, John, Jr., 178
Hutchinson, Joseph, 26, 80, 87, 282
Hutchinson, Luther, 279
Hutchinson, Matthew, 174
Hutchinson, Robert, 179
Hutchinson, Samuel, 238, 273
Hutchinson, Stephen, 176
Hutchinson, Thomas, 26, 101, 138
Hutchinson, William, 138, 271, 273
Hutler, Simon, 290
Hutlesom, Henry, 127
Hutlestone, Henry, 127
Hutson, Thomas B., 133
Huttlestone, Henry, 41, 127
Huttlestone, Thomas, 55, 58
Hutton, Joseph, 192
Huzzey, Richard, 245
Huzzy, John, 149
Hyatt, Benjamin, Jr., 20
Hyde, Aaron, 28
Hyde, Amasa, 83
Hyde, Asa, 109
Hyde, John W., 84
Hyde, Jonathan L., 241, 242
Hyde, Jude, 299
Hyde, Michel S., 77
Hyde, Nathaniel, 85, 109
Hyde, Samuel, 24
Hyde, Zina, 247
Hyer, George, 195
Hyer, John, 60
Hyler, Hannce, 284
Hyler, Herman, 294
Hyler, Jacob, 284
Hyler, John, 284
Hyler, William, 284, 288, 294
Hysler, Peter, 290, 293

INDEX.

I

Ide, Ebenezer, 60
Ide, Ephraim, 98
Ide, Newman, 98
Idle, Aruna, 53
Idle, Harvey, 33
Idle, Rowland, 216
Idle, Stephen, 216
Ilsey, Wade, 15, 20
Ilsey, William, 15
Ilsley, Nathaniel, 219
Imbener, Edward, 270
Ingalls, Aaron, 151
Ingalls, Abraham, 312
Ingalls, Asa, 211
Ingalls, B., 60
Ingalls, Benjamin, 79
Ingalls, David, 82
Ingalls, Francis, 3d, 258
Ingalls, Gardner, 258
Ingalls, Isaiah, 211
Ingalls, Jacob, Jr., 116
Ingalls, James, 133, 136
Ingalls, John, 7, 22, 116, 305
Ingalls, John N., 299
Ingalls, Jonathan B., 116
Ingalls, Joseph, 7, 22, 118
Ingalls, Loammi, 255
Ingalls, Nathaniel, 90, 133, 136
Ingalls, Nehemiah, 221
Ingalls, Royal, 41
Ingalls, Samuel, 60, 258
Ingalls, Saul, 3d, 212
Ingalls, Sergent, 135, 140
Ingalls, Spofford, 211
Ingalls, Stephen, 81
Ingalls, Thomas, 133, 136
Ingalls, William, 23, 118, 255
Ingersol, David P., 32
Ingersoll, Daniel B., 255
Ingersoll, George H., 133
Ingersoll, Isaac P., 109
Ingersoll, James, 84
Ingersoll, Jonathan, 94
Ingersoll, Joshua, 13, 14
Ingersoll, Peter, 220
Ingersoll, Sargent, 139 (2)
Ingeway, Philip, 25
Ingham, Amasa, 280
Ingraham, Artemas, 43
Ingraham, Barnard, 197, 204 (2)
Ingraham, Coit, 197, 204 (2), 206
Ingraham, Elias, 54
Ingraham, G. T., 243
Ingraham, Isaac, 197, 204 (2), 206
Ingraham, Jabel, 54
Ingraham, John, 185, 204 (2)
Ingraham, Joseph, 205
Ingraham, Joseph, Jr., 206
Ingraham, Josiah, 197, 204
Ingraham, Josiah, 3d, 204
Ingraham, Nathaniel, 64
Ingraham, William, 244
Ingram, Joseph, 243
Inman, Allin, 161
Inman, Marcy, 161
Innis, Samuel, 247, 297
Insly, Benjamin, 243
Ireland, David, 307
Ireland, James, 69
Ireland, Jonathan, 71, 78
Ireland, Samuel, 230
Ireland, Thomas, 132
Ireland, William H., 70
Ireson, Benjamin, 22, 118
Irish, Benjamin, 171
Irish, Cornelius, 286, 290
Irish, Ebenezer, 223, 259
Irish, Elisha, 174
Irish, Elkanah, 260
Irish, Ichabod, 290, 293
Irish, Jacob, 171
Irish, James, 296
Irish, James, Jr., 145
Irish, Joseph, 176, 260
Irish, Joshua, 225, 260
Irish, Levi, 199, 200, 203
Irish, Samuel, 255
Irish, Simeon, 175
Irish, Stephen, 152, 225, 254
Irish, William, 225, 259
Irving, Edward, 69
Irving, John, 241
Isaacs, James, 138
Isham, L., 119
Isley, Paul, 17
Isley, William, 90
Ives, Peter S., 117
Ivry, Elijah, 205

J

Jack, Andrew, Jr., 231
Jack, Andrew, 3d, 231
Jack, David, 27, 112, 114
Jack, Jacob, 234
Jack, James, 153
Jack, John, 148, 278
Jack, Joseph, 233, 235, 278, 296
Jack, Robert, 230
Jack, Samuel, 155, 234
Jack, Samuel, Jr., 278
Jack, Saul, 234
Jack, Thomas, 275
Jackett, Nathaniel, 57
Jackins, David, 182 (2), 186
Jackins, Saul, 278
Jackman, James, 161, 268
Jackman, John, 161
Jackman, Joseph N., 16
Jackman, Mathias, 3d, 16
Jackman, Noah, 16
Jackman, Richard, 17
Jackman, Samuel, 16
Jackman, William, 21
Jackson, Aaron, 233
Jackson, Abraham, 225
Jackson, Alexander, 29, 193, 195, 240
Jackson, Alexander, 2d, 239
Jackson, Amasa, 40
Jackson, Antyrhas, 89
Jackson, Barnard, 50
Jackson, Bartholomew, 116
Jackson, Benjamin, 146, 170, 271
Jackson, Boston, 254
Jackson, Daniel, 79
Jackson, David, 162
Jackson, Edmund, 1, 55
Jackson, Elijah, 224, 257, 275
Jackson, Francis, 85, 106, 211
Jackson, George, 232
Jackson, Godfrey, 153
Jackson, Henry, 20, 123 (2), 176
Jackson, Isaac, 94
Jackson, Jacob, 146, 150
Jackson, James, 150
Jackson, John, 51, 163, 164, 239, 267, 277
Jackson, Jonathan, 111
Jackson, Joseph, 146, 176, 222, 260 (2)
Jackson, Lemuel, 146, 210
Jackson, Michael, 167, 281
Jackson, Nathaniel, 196, 223, 301
Jackson, Samuel, 125 (2), 196, 244, 250 (2), 300
Jackson, Solomon, 33
Jackson, Stephen W., 70
Jackson, Sylvanus, 146
Jackson, Thomas, 193, 219, 256
Jackson, William, 181, 231, 258, 296
Jacob, Abraham, 11
Jacob, Benjamin H., 117
Jacob, Francis, 31
Jacob, James, 280
Jacob, John, 84
Jacobs, Benjamin R., 104
Jacobs, Daniel, 263
Jacobs, David C., 84
Jacobs, Edward, 1, 103
Jacobs, George, 306
Jacobs, James H., 103
Jacobs, Josiah, 263
Jacobs, McConn, 200
Jacobs, McCowan, 199, 203
Jacobs, Peter, 101
Jacobs, Samuel, 197
Jacobs, Stephen, 1
Jacobs, Theodore, 268, 308
Jacobs, Walter, 130
Jacobs, William, 245
Jacobson, Mathias, 134, 135
Jacques, Enoch, 15
Jamerson, Paul, 207
Jamerson, Thomas, 284
Jamerson, William, 196
James, Allen, 74
James, Benjamin, 263
James, Daniel S., 274
James, Ebenezer, 11
James, Elisha, 215
James, Enoch, 65
James, George, 32
James, Horatio, 47
James, John, 25
James, John, Jr., 1, 104
James, Joshua, 104
James, Thomas P., 7
James, William, 100, 190, 191, 298
Jameson, Ebenezer, 303
Jameson, Jeremiah, 285
Jameson, John, 138, 204, 234, 236
Jameson, Levi, 131
Jameson, Paul, 205
Jameson, Robert, 197
Jameson, Samuel, 194, 303
Jameson, Thomas, 288, 294
Jameson, William, Jr., 273
Jamison, John, 280
Jamison, Peter, 201 (2), 203
Jamison, Thurston W., 285, 288
Janes, Eaton, 94
Janes, Henry, 94
Janes, Libbeus, 150
Janes, Robert, 160
Jannevar, George, 47
Janvim, Joseph, 17
Jaques, Aaron, 232, 296
Jaques, E., 82

INDEX.

Jaques, Henry C., 15
Jaques, Johnson, 232
Jaquis, Aaron, 232
Jaquis, Johnson, 232
Jaquith, Andrew, 238, 265
Jaquith, Josiah, 29
Jaquith, Moses, 82
Jaquith, Parker, 116
Jarulson, Mark, Jr., 277
Jarvis, Denning, 7
Jarvis, Edward, 217
Jarvis, Francis, Jr., 99
Jarvis, John, 106 (2), 107 (2), 108, 126
Javery, Ephraim, 66
Javim, Joseph, 17
Jay, Charles, 86
Jay, George, 312
Jay, William, 23
Jaynes, Charles, 15
Jaynes, Moody, 15
Jaynes, Moses, 15
Jeffards, Alpheus, 30
Jeffers, Ebeneser, 125
Jeffers, William, 39
Jeffords, Rufus, 221
Jelason, Job, 230
Jelason, William, 230
Jellison, Jack, 163
Jellison, John, 162 (2)
Jellison, Stephen, 245
Jellison, Zacharius, 163
Jemes, Joseph, 185
Jenkins, Abner, 75, 76, 170, 277
Jenkins, Bailey, 104
Jenkins, Baily, 74
Jenkins, Charles, 39, 75, 131
Jenkins, Dennis, 278
Jenkins, Elijah, 77
Jenkins, Eliphalet, 74
Jenkins, Ellis, 74
Jenkins, Gridley, 9
Jenkins, Henry, 205
Jenkins, Joseph, 69, 72, 92, 266, 306
Jenkins, Joshua, 72
Jenkins, Josiah, 173
Jenkins, Lemuel, 74, 92
Jenkins, Merritt, 9
Jenkins, Nathan, 74
Jenkins, Nathaniel, Jr., 2, 74
Jenkins, Noble, 39
Jenkins, Peres, 74
Jenkins, Peres T., 103
Jenkins, Philip, Jr., 170
Jenkins, Samuel, 69, 72, 74, 79, 170, 277
Jenkins, Solon, 25, 41
Jenkins, Southworth, 64
Jenkins, Weston, 73
Jenks, George F., 53
Jenks, Henry, 200, 205 (2)
Jenks, John, 204, 205
Jenks, Jeremiah, 45
Jenks, Robert, 69
Jenks, William, 30, 247
Jenne, Benjamin, 55
Jenne, David, 55
Jenne, Israel, 55
Jenne, Jonathan, 55
Jenne, Luther, 55
Jenne, Nathaniel, 55
Jennes, Joseph, 183
Jenney, Edward, 58
Jenney, Isaac, 28

Jenney, Jeduthan, 58
Jenney, Joseph, 58
Jenney, Joseph H., 55
Jenney, Joseph L., 1
Jenney, Samuel, 58
Jenney, Stephen, 7
Jenning, John H., 105
Jennings, Alexander, 167
Jennings, Bartlett, 118
Jennings, Benjamin, 24
Jennings, Charles, 232
Jennings, Franklin, 167
Jennings, Henry, 278
Jennings, Ira, 64
Jennings, John, 2, 167
Jennings, John H., 164, 225
Jennings, John J., 164
Jennings, Joseph, 2, 108
Jennings, Lewis, 278
Jennings, Perry, 129
Jennings, Samuel, 281, 312
Jennings, Samuel, Jr., 278
Jennings, William, 82, 87
Jennis, Francis, 214
Jennison, Asa, 23, 114
Jennison, William, 122
Jepson, Ebenezer, 167
Jerald, John, 85
Jeune, Benjamin, 58
Jeune, David, 58
Jeune, Israel, 58
Jeune, Jonathan, 58
Jeune, Luther, 58
Jeune, Nathaniel, 58
Jewel, Thomas, 249
Jewell, Enoch, 261
Jewell, Gould, 275
Jewell, Jacob, 308
Jewell, Jesse, 279
Jewell, Jesse, Jr., 279
Jewell, John, 228, 254
Jewell, John, Jr., 258
Jewell, Joseph, 228, 273
Jewell, Joshua A., 8
Jewell, Lewis, 258
Jewell, Nathaniel, 169
Jewell, Robert, 170
Jewell, Samuel, 215
Jewell, William, 308
Jewet, David, 16
Jowet, Isaiah, 16
Jewet, Robert, 16
Jewett, Benjamin, 188, 191
Jewett, Daniel, 151, 256
Jewett, David, 169, 281
Jewett, Eliphalet, 14
Jewett, Ephraim, 151
Jewett, George, 271
Jewett, Ivers, 93
Jewett, J. S., 242
Jewett, Jacob, 179
Jewett, James, 156, 157 (2), 176
Jewett, Jeremiah, 184, 188, 191
Jewett, John, 133, 156, 157 (2), 264, 279
Jewett, Joseph, 40, 190, 191, 241
Jewett, Joseph S., 172
Jewett, Joshua, 266, 304, 307
Jewett, Josiah, 27
Jewett, Luther S., 172
Jewett, Moses, 189, 190, 271
Jewett, Moses, Jr., 191
Jewett, Nathaniel, 69, 184, 188, 191

Jewett, Nathaniel G., 151
Jewett, Samuel, 69
Jewett, Solomon, 68, 87
Jewett, Stephen, 274
Jewett, Thomas, 14
Jewett, Washington, 279, 282
Jewett, William, 151
Jewitt, Joseph, 80
Jewitt, William, 79
Jillson, Amos, 53
Jillson, David, 53
Jinket, Asa, 66
Johnson, Abel, 19, 41
Johnson, Adam, 230
Johnson, Albert, 117
Johnson, Alfred, 278
Johnson, Amory, 85
Johnson, Amos, 29
Johnson, Andrew, 152, 256
Johnson, Asa, 150, 151, 269
Johnson, Asa, Jr., 212
Johnson, Benjamin, 177
Johnson, Benjamin B., 116
Johnson, Benjamin F., 158
Johnson, Benjamin G., 122, 125
Johnson, Calvin, 5, 278
Johnson, Charles, 135, 137
Johnson, Daniel, 170, 216, 275, 277, 278
Johnson, Daniel, Jr., 304
Johnson, David, 213, 244, 254, 299
Johnson, David, 2d, 213
Johnson, Derring, 256
Johnson, Doremus, 268
Johnson, Dyrenus, 305
Johnson, E., 137
Johnson, Ebenezer, 161
Johnson, Edmund, 26, 135
Johnson, Eleaser, Jr., 19
Johnson, Elijah, 95
Johnson, Ellis, 86
Johnson, Ephraim, 192, 216
Johnson, Gardner, 94
Johnson, George, 117, 171, 198, 199, 200, 225
Johnson, George W., 87
Johnson, Gerah, 40
Johnson, Green, 19
Johnson, Henry, 236, 305
Johnson, Hesekiah, 159
Johnson, Hugh M., 66
Johnson, Isaac, 158, 216
Johnson, Jacob, 48, 230
Johnson, James, 8, 82, 152, 195, 256, 276
Johnson, Jasper, 225
Johnson, Job, Jr., 159
Johnson, Joel, 48
Johnson, John, 22, 40, 69, 79, 135, 151, 157 (4), 159, 259
Johnson, John L., 218, 309
Johnson, John R., 116
Johnson, Jonathan, 19
Johnson, Joseph, 187, 190, 275, 283
Johnson, Josiah, 157
Johnson, Lebina, 49
Johnson, Legree, 116
Johnson, Levi, 146, 276
Johnson, Lewis, 86
Johnson, Luther, 94
Johnson, Mark, 145
Johnson, Mark A., 41
Johnson, Mathew, 134
Johnson, Milton, 70
Johnson, Moses, 40

Johnson, Nath, 25
Johnson, Oliver, 53, 171
Johnson, Parker, 91
Johnson, Patten, 29
Johnson, Paul, Jr., 161
Johnson, Philip, Jr., 19
Johnson, Ralph C., 303
Johnson, Reuben, 90
Johnson, Robert, 273
Johnson, Rowland, 188
Johnson, Samuel, 115, 116, 117, 133, 136, 159, 189
Johnson, Samuel G., 187
Johnson, Samuel M., 98
Johnson, Saul, 133, 140, 277, 281
Johnson, Sidney, 49
Johnson, Stephen, Jr., 5
Johnson, Thomas, 42, 121, 122, 124, 125, 149, 216, 246
Johnson, Timothy, 25, 79, 100
Johnson, Walter, 5, 256
Johnson, Willard, 27
Johnson, William, 7, 9, 46, 48, 67, 164, 165, 166, 193, 221, 268, 295, 304
Johnson, William B., 271
Johnson, William G., 187, 191
Johnson, William H., 24
Johnson, William P., 19
Johnson, William W., 22
Johnson, Zacheriah, 27, 79
Johnston, George, 202
Johnston, James, 195
Johnston, Jonathan, 8
Johnston, Josias, 3
Johnston, Jotham, 245
Johnston, William, 174, 195
Joiner, Seymour, 31
Jones, Abijah, 177
Jones, Abner, 178, 260
Jones, Adonijah, 31
Jones, Alexander, 192, 196
Jones, Alexander, Jr., 196
Jones, Alexander H., 29
Jones, Alfred, 150
Jones, Allen, 310
Jones, Apollus, 224
Jones, Asa, 178
Jones, Asa, Jr., 74
Jones, Asia, 257
Jones, Barnum, 150
Jones, Belcher, 234
Jones, Benjamin, 74, 198, 199, 201, 202
Jones, Benjamin, Jr., 74, 177, 196
Jones, Butler, 164, 165, 166
Jones, Chad F., 253
Jones, Charles, 130, 163, 164
Jones, Crowel, 198, 199
Jones, Crowell, 201, 202
Jones, Cyrus, 76, 115, 217, 243
Jones, Daniel, 84, 109, 110, 111, 266
Jones, David, 25, 40, 80
Jones, Ebenezer, 245
Jones, Edward, 165, 166
Jones, Elijah, 214
Jones, Ephraim, 26, 41
Jones, Ezekiel, 81
Jones, Ezekiel S., 288, 291
Jones, Francis, 73
Jones, Francis F., 73, 76
Jones, Frederic W., 5
Jones, Galen, 150
Jones, Gardner, 196

Jones, George, 23, 190
Jones, Hawkes, 196
Jones, Henry, 74, 150, 241, 242
Jones, Herman, 9
Jones, Hiram, 225
Jones, Ira, 150
Jones, Isaac, 115, 177, 234, 281
Jones, Israel, 168
Jones, Jacob, 214
Jones, James, 6, 32, 41, 100, 170, 194, 196, 287
Jones, Jedediah, 74
Jones, Jeremiah, 246
Jones, Jeremiah R., 218
Jones, Jesse, 193
Jones, Joel, 210
Jones, John, 25, 74, 87, 88, 135, 137, 141, 145, 169, 172, 194, 206, 226, 229, 231, 272, 292 (2), 296
Jones, John, Jr., 310
Jones, John, 2d, 196, 271
Jones, John R., 87
Jones, Jonathan, 164, 165, 166
Jones, Joseph, 74
Jones, Joseph Q., 74
Jones, Joshua, 297
Jones, Joshua, Jr., 300
Jones, Josiah, 2
Jones, Kinsley, Jr., 180
Jones, Lemuel H., 160
Jones, Lewis, 292
Jones, Lines, 294
Jones, Merena, 74
Jones, Micajah, 74
Jones, Michael, 196
Jones, Moses, 101
Jones, Nathan, 30, 50, 75
Jones, Nathaniel F., 278
Jones, Peleg G., 60
Jones, Richard, 260, 264, 266
Jones, Richmond, 178
Jones, Robinson, 76
Jones, Rufus, 192
Jones, Russell, 33
Jones, Samuel, 33, 70, 172, 206 (2), 264
Jones, Samuel C., 263
Jones, Samuel F., 214
Jones, Samuel T., 12
Jones, Shadrack, 145, 196
Jones, Silas, 100, 224
Jones, Silvanus, 75, 76
Jones, Simeon, 209
Jones, Simon, 33, 96, 191
Jones, Solomon, 43
Jones, Stephen, 4, 159, 220, 222
Jones, Stephen, Jr., 75
Jones, Sullivan, 258
Jones, Sylvester, 178
Jones, Sylvester, Jr., 278
Jones, Theodore, 163
Jones, Theodore, Jr., 164
Jones, Thomas, 40, 75 (2)
Jones, Thomas, Jr., 199, 200, 203
Jones, Tilden, 177
Jones, Timothy, 31
Jones, William, 27, 160, 180, 181, 192, 206, 277, 305
Jordan, Abijah, 299
Jordan, Abraham, 221, 246, 253, 256, 272
Jordan, Abram, 165 (2)
Jordan, Allen, 173
Jordan, Andrew, 233
Jordan, Asa, 243

Jordan, Benjamin, 163, 211, 234, 235, 251, 272
Jordan, Benjamin, Jr., 164
Jordan, Charles, 218 (2), 252, 256
Jordan, Clement, 221
Jordan, Curtis, 212
Jordan, Daniel, 221
Jordan, David, 211
Jordan, Dominicus, 234
Jordan, Eben, 197, 204
Jordan, Ebenezer, 200, 212
Jordan, Ebenezer, Jr., 197
Jordan, Edward, 258
Jordan, Elias, 179
Jordan, Elijah, 65, 150, 228, 252, 255, 282
Jordan, Elijah, Jr., 251
Jordan, Elliot, 222
Jordan, Ephraim, 199, 200
Jordan, Ezekiel, 242
Jordan, George, 212
Jordan, Henry, 83, 296, 299
Jordan, Ignatius, 222
Jordan, Isaac, 163, 164
Jordan, Israel, 222
Jordan, Jabez, 269
Jordan, James, 201 (2), 203, 222, 258
Jordan, James, Jr., 210
Jordan, James H., 151
Jordan, Jeremiah, 272
Jordan, Jesse, 299
Jordan, John, 218, 221, 253
Jordan, John G., 163, 164
Jordan, Jonathan, 71
Jordan, Joseph, 40, 163, 164
Jordan, Josiah, 213
Jordan, Levi, 225
Jordan, Marks, 258
Jordan, Nathaniel, 169
Jordan, Nathaniel, Jr., 222, 258
Jordan, Nathaniel, 4th, 222
Jordan, Nathaniel, 5th, 222
Jordan, Peter, Jr., 299
Jordan, Richard, 221
Jordan, Robert, 155, 234, 296
Jordan, Roger, Jr., 211
Jordan, Rufus, 222
Jordan, Samuel, 155, 156, 222, 234, 252
Jordan, Saul, 211
Jordan, Solomon, 163
Jordan, Solomon, Jr., 164
Jordan, Stephen F., 164
Jordan, Stephen T., 163
Jordan, Thomas, 221, 222
Jordan, Valentine, 234
Jordan, Wales, 258
Jordan, Walter, 163, 222
Jordan, Walter, Jr., 164
Jordan, William, 209, 222, 256, 299
Jordan, William, Jr., 256
Jordan, Winter, 222
Jordan, Woodbury, 221
Jorden, John, 40
Jorden, William, 77
Jose, Jonathan, 170
Joseph, George, 65
Joseph, Peter, 302
Joslin, Eleazer, 103
Joslin, Marquis F., 95
Joslin, William, 133
Joslyn, Eleazer, 1
Joslyn, Elias, Jr., 5
Joslyn, Oran, 1

INDEX.

Joslyn, Peter, 208
Joslyn, Waterman, 128
Joss, Oliver, 282
Josselyn, Abraham, 302
Josselyn, Alden, 279 (2)
Josselyn, John D., 279
Josselyn, Harvey, 279
Josselyn, Martin, 279 (2)
Josslyn, Samuel, 78
Josslyn, William, 90
Jostlin, Marquis F., 129
Jostrum, Henry, 32
Joy, Abijah, 273, 305
Joy, Alfred, 162 (2)
Joy, Benjamin, 181
Joy, Cyrus, 43
Joy, David, 40, 101
Joy, Elisha, 84
Joy, Ivory H., 163, 164
Joy, James, 238
Joy, John, 135, 137
Joy, John G., 162 (2)
Joy, Love, 162 (2)
Joy, Samuel, 79, 163
Joy, Samuel, Jr., 163
Joy, Temple, 162 (2)
Joy, Thomas, 91
Joy, William, 110
Joyce, David T., 103
Joye, Joseph, 134, 140
Judd, Jabez, 32
Judkins, Abraham, 271
Judkins, Asa, 278
Judkins, Benjamin, 306
Judkins, Calvin, 104
Judkins, David, 278
Judkins, Elisha, 279 (2)
Judkins, Jacob, 278, 281
Judkins, Joel, 279
Judkins, Joel, Jr., 278
Judkins, John, 278
Judkins, Levi, 306
Judkins, Moses, 32
Judkins, Peter, 306
Judkins, Richard, 282
Judkins, Thomas, 253
Judkins, Zacheus, 271
Jumper, Ezekiel, 219
Jumper, John, 11
Jumper, Joseph, 165, 166, 197, 204 (2), 219, 246
Justin, Phineas W., Jr., 154

K

Kahler, Jeremiah, 39
Kalah, George, 292
Kalah, John, 292
Kalah, Joseph, 292
Kanavan, John, 272
Kanservice, Thomas, 189
Karner, Plinny, 31
Karsons, James, 294
Kates, Edmund, 239
Kating, John, 199, 200, 203
Kavanaugh, Edward, 193
Keag, Thomas, 245
Kean, James, 274
Kean, John, Jr., 274
Keating, Charles, 113
Keating, James, 186, 190
Keating, John, 197, 200, 203
Kebbe, Isaac, 5

Koel, Luther, 248
Keen, Abraham, 71, 73, 75
Keen, Andrew, 178
Keen, Charles, 274, 291
Keen, Cyrus, 178
Keen, Daniel, 178, 198, 199, 201, 202, 209
Keen, Edward, 178
Keen, Elisha, 198
Keen, Ephraim, 194
Keen, Freeman, 73, 178
Keen, Howlen, 195
Keen, Jacob, 177
Keen, James, 194, 198, 199, 202
Keen, John, 71, 75
Keen, John, Jr., 177
Keen, Josiah, 177
Keen, Judah, 178
Keen, Mark, 192, 195
Keen, Meshack, 178
Keen, Nathan, 81
Keen, Robert M., 203
Keen, Robert S., 209
Keen, Samuel, 194
Keen, Shadrick, 136
Keen, Trueman, 71
Keen, Wait, 195
Keene, Ebenezer, 58
Keene, Edward, 260
Keene, Elisha, 208
Keene, Francis, 251, 255
Keene, Jarius, 160
Keene, John, Jr., 200
Keene, Joseph, 58
Keene, Joshua, 253
Keene, Judah, Jr., 259
Keene, Nathaniel, 175
Keene, Prince, 179
Keene, Reuben, 58
Keene, Seth, 253
Keene, Shadrack, 251, 255
Keene, Snow, Jr., 175
Keene, William, 216
Keep, James, 32
Kees, Elijah, 223
Keet, Thomas, 65
Kehew, Aaron, 87
Kehew, John, 133
Keiler, George, 2d, 291
Keint, Martin, 86
Keith, Aberdeen, 53, 102
Keith, Abner, 49
Keith, Asa, 234
Keith, Austin, 49
Keith, Benjamin, 51
Keith, Benjamin H., 91
Keith, Caleb, 51
Keith, Cyrus, 49, 52
Keith, Daniel, 53
Keith, Ephraim, 49
Keith, Foster A., 102
Keith, Friend, 181
Keith, George, 91
Keith, Heman, 97
Keith, Ichabod, 49
Keith, Isaac, 49
Keith, Israel, 52, 54
Keith, James, 110, 111 (2)
Keith, Jeremiah, 53
Keith, John, 49
Keith, Joseph, 175
Keith, Lemuel, 95
Keith, Lewis, 49

Keith, Martin, Jr., 102
Keith, Nathaniel, 70
Keith, Oliver, 49
Keith, Orrin, 51
Keith, Otis, 51
Keith, Parden, 49
Keith, Parley, 97
Keith, Peres, 49
Keith, Pliney, 257
Keith, Pliny, 177
Keith, Quincy, 159
Keith, Seth, 32, 49
Keith, Solomon, 49
Keith, Sylvanus, 51
Keith, Sylvester, 49
Keith, Thaxter, 91
Keith, Timothy, 213
Keith, William, 54
Keith, Zephaniah, 49
Keiser, George, 287
Keiser, John, Jr., 273
Keisor, George, 291 (2), 294
Keisor, Philip, 291
Kelgore, Caleb, 233
Kelley, Amos, 58
Kelley, Andrew, 26
Kelley, Phineas, 147
Kelley, Samuel, 240
Kelley, William, 83
Kelliher, Samuel, 268
Kelloch, Benjamin, 145
Kellock, Adam, 290, 293
Kellock, Alexander, 289, 293
Kellock, Benjamin, 285, 286, 289
Kellock, Charles, 292
Kellock, Hance, 206
Kellock, Haunce, 206
Kellock, James, 59, 304
Kellock, John, 206
Kellock, John, 2d, 206
Kellock, Joseph, 204, 206
Kellock, Matthew, 206
Kellock, Moses, 205 (2), 206
Kellock, Samuel, 289
Kellock, Saul, 285, 286 (2)
Kellock, William, 206 (2)
Kellog, Auren, 33
Kellog, David, 47
Kellog, Giles C., 43
Kellog, Hawley, 43
Kellog, James M., 241
Kellogg, Ezekiel F., 159
Kellogg, Jonathan, 95
Kellogg, Joshua, 47
Kellogg, Phineas, 119
Kellum, Phineas, 189
Kelly, Amos, 55
Kelly, Christopher, 134, 135
Kelly, David H., 155
Kelly, Isaac, 146, 284
Kelly, Jacob, 227
Kelly, Jeremiah, 75
Kelly, John, 183, 212, 248
Kelly, John O., 39
Kelly, Joseph, 147 (2)
Kelly, Josiah, 67
Kelly, Moses, 227
Kelly, Nathaniel, 163 (2)
Kelly, Shubael, 37
Kelly, Shubal, 36
Kelly, Sylvanus, 307
Kelly, Thomas, 248

INDEX.

Kelly, Warren, 75
Kelly, William, 21, 160, 161
Kelsey, Robert, 302
Kelton, Elihu, 86
Kelton, Jason, 86
Kemill (?), John, 32
Kemp, David, 171
Kemp, Eben, 256
Kemp, Eleazer, 87
Kemp, Francis, 87
Kemp, James, 306
Kemp, Jonas, 87
Kemp, Jonathan, 171
Kemp, Joseph, 13, 14
Kemp, Laurence, 65
Kemp, Silas, 299
Kemp, Timothy, 300
Kempton, Daniel, 55, 58
Kempton, David, 1
Kempton, Elijah, 55, 58
Kempton, Isaac, 1
Kempton, Nathan, 55, 58
Kempton, Stephen, 55, 58
Kempton, Thomas, 129
Kempton, William, 54
Kempton, William N., 129
Kenard, Aleut, 80
Kendal, Calvin, 29
Kendal, Nathan, 203
Kendal, Samuel, 203, 209
Kendall, Amasa, 29
Kendall, Artemas, 83
Kendall, Bezaleel, 258
Kendall, Calvin, 66
Kendall, Charleville, 201 (2)
Kendall, Daniel, 201
Kendall, David, 5, 306
Kendall, Gains, 44
Kendall, Horace, 91 (2)
Kendall, Hubbard, 94
Kendall, James, 49
Kendall, Jonas, 262, 266
Kendall, Jonathan, 215
Kendall, Joseph, 258
Kendall, Loammi, 38, 85
Kendall, Nathaniel, 201
Kendall, Peter, 88
Kendall, Samuel, 88, 92, 201
Kendall, Saul, 202
Kendall, Thomas, 81
Kendall, Thomas B., 113
Kendall, William, 162
Kendell, Charleville, 202
Kendell, Thomas, 28
Kendrick, Stephen, 25
Kenester, Edward, 135
Kenfield, Chester, 47
Keniston, Daniel, 245
Keniston, Thomas, 284
Kennard, Aleut, 68
Kennard, Alpheus, 245
Kennard, Michael, 81
Kennard, William, 85
Kennedy, Alexander, 192, 196
Kennedy, Andrew, 283
Kennedy, James, 274
Kennedy, John, 196
Kennedy, Nicholas, 196
Kennedy, Robert, 186, 189, 191
Kennedy, Thomas, Jr., 184
Kennedy, William, 183, 189, 196, 283, 289
Kennedy, William, 3d, 186
Kenney, Benjamin, 216

Kenney, Benjamin, W. 241
Kenney, Charles, 275
Kenney, Edward, 39, 163, 186
Kenney, Gilman, 275
Kenney, Henry M., 221
Kenney, John, 183, 217, 308
Kenney, John H., 81
Kenney, Jonathan, 58
Kenney, Levi, 162
Kenney, Samuel, 221
Kenney, Thomas, 206 (3)
Kenney, William, 221
Kenney, Woodman, 275
Kennison, David, 256
Kennison, Hugh, 245
Kennister, Edward, 134
Kennister, John, 254
Kenniston, David, 162
Kenniston, Henry, 205
Kenniston, Theodore, 205 (2)
Kenny, Edward, 154
Kenny, Elisha, 260
Kenny, Henry, 284
Kenny, Jesse, 107, 138
Kenny, John, 106, 107 (2), 108
Kenny, Moses, 139
Kenrick, Henry, 106 (2), 107, 108
Kenrick, John, 104, 105 (2), 106, 107
Kensly, Henry, 68
Kent, Barker, 284, 281
Kent, Benjamin, 19, 119, 122
Kent, Charles, 90
Kent, Ebenezer, 185
Kent, Elisha, 278
Kent, Ezekiel, 208
Kent, Frederick A., 146
Kent, Gains, 44
Kent, Henry, 20, 282
Kent, Hezekiah, 115
Kent, James, 48
Kent, John, 16, 61
Kent, John, 2d, 61
Kent, John S., 281
Kent, John T., 280
Kent, Joseph, 183, 185, 188
Kent, Joseph, 2d, 17
Kent, Josiah, 36
Kent, Justin, Jr., 241
Kent, Martin, 80, 86
Kent, Nathaniel, 278, 281
Kent, Noah, 58
Kent, Richard, 216
Kent, Samuel, 4
Kent, Stillman, 216
Kent, William, 216
Kentfield, Elias, 45
Kentfield, Smith, 44
Kepler, Jeremiah, 23
Kerby, Eleazer, 127
Kerby, Every, 126
Kerby, George, 126
Kerby, Robert, 294
Kerr, William, 68
Ketchum, Elihu, 30
Ketchum, Solomon, 30
Ketson, Richard, 241
Kettle, Andrew, 68
Kettle, John, 186
Kettle, Jonathan, 27
Kettle, Samuel, 113, 114
Keun, James, 78
Keyes, Albert, 32

Keyes, Elisha, 48
Keyes, Imla, 8
Keyes, James, 100
Keyes, Lewis, 40
Keyes, Luther, 64
Keys, Jonas T., 160
Keys, Tyler, 181
Keser, Luther, 256
Kidder, Cyrus, 284
Kidder, Elkanah, 45
Kidder, Ephraim, 24
Kidder, Isaac, 266
Kidder, Isaac, Jr., 307
Kidder, John, Jr., 239, 267
Kidder, Jonathan, 295
Kidder, Jonathan, Jr., 66
Kidder, Joseph, 271
Kidder, Moses, 38
Kidder, Saul, 239
Kidder, Stephen, 68
Kidder, William, 303
Kidlon, Charles, 154
Kiff, Ephraim, 206
Kilber, David, 33
Kilber, Phineas, 33
Kilborn, Ebenezer, 258
Kilborn, John, 212
Kilborn, Robert, 257
Kilborn, Samuel, 176
Kilborne, George, Jr., 20
Kilborne, Robert, 20
Kilbourn, Ira, 159
Kilbourn, Ivory, 241
Kilbourn, John, 258
Kilbourne, Nathaniel, 274
Kilbreth, James, 225
Kilburn, Alva, 94
Kilburn, Isaac, 98, 257
Kilburn, Jedediah, 20
Kilburn, John, 160
Kilby, Daniel, 161
Kilby, John, 161
Kilby, Nathaniel, 133
Kilby, Thomas, 209
Kilby, William, Jr., 161
Kilgore, Andorus, 251
Kilgore, Andrew, 255
Kilgore, Elihu, 258
Kilgore, Gabriel, 258
Kilgore, Joseph, 152, 261
Kilgore, William, 235, 296
Kilham, Daniel, 134
Kilham, Eliab, 81
Kilham, George W., 9
Killeran, Arthur F., 294
Killeran, Arthur S., 288
Killeran, Arthur T., 294
Killeran, Thomas, 294
Killeran, Thomas C., 294
Killeran, William, 294
Killsa, John K., 156
Killsa, William, 205
Killsea, Enoch, 287
Killsea, Moses, 287
Killser, William, 206
Killay, John, 194
Killy, Phineas, 147
Kilpatrick, Joseph, 235
Kilsa, William, 205
Kimbal, Phineas, 233
Kimball, ——, 27
Kimball, Abel, 69

INDEX. 381

Kimball, Abiel, 115
Kimball, Ansel, 279
Kimball, Asa, 46
Kimball, Benjamin, 229
Kimball, Benjamin, Jr., 170
Kimball, Caleb, 154
Kimball, Charles, 90, 239, 241, 242
Kimball, Clark, 90
Kimball, Cook, 146
Kimball, Daniel, 149, 154, 161, 308
Kimball, David, 305
Kimball, Dean, 148, 235, 296
Kimball, Dudley, 133, 139
Kimball, Ebenezer, 138
Kimball, Edmund, 6, 7
Kimball, Ephraim, 152
Kimball, George, 184, 188, 290
Kimball, Hazen, 8
Kimball, Heber, 147 (2)
Kimball, Henry, 90, 185, 275
Kimball, Iddo, 205, 206
Kimball, Isaac, 254
Kimball, Isaiah, Jr., 258
Kimball, Israel, Jr., 258
Kimball, Jacob, 306
Kimball, James, 161, 241, 242
Kimball, Jeremiah, 258
Kimball, John, 84, 97, 101, 149
Kimball, John S., 146
Kimball, Jonathan, 11, 110, 309
Kimball, Jonathan C., 136, 140
Kimball, Joseph, 152, 298
Kimball, Josiah, 136, 140
Kimball, Moses, 119, 122
Kimball, Nathan, 9, 259
Kimball, Nathaniel, 14, 134 (2), 138, 224, 225
Kimball, Nehemiah, 308
Kimball, Nicholas, 305
Kimball, Phineas, 95
Kimball, Robert, 14
Kimball, Stephen, 6
Kimball, Timothy, 195
Kimball, William, 133, 136, 152, 230, 311
Kimball, William, Jr., 18
Kimbel, Iddo, 290
Kimbol, Daniel, 173
Kincade, James, 276
Kincaid, David, 306
Kincaid, Patrick, 148
Kincaid, Samuel, Jr., 190
Kincaid, William, 190, 191
Kindell, Elisha, 65
Kindricks, Seth, 154
Kineson, Job, 263
King, Adverdas, 210
King, Amasa, 277
King, Amos, 21, 66
King, Benjamin, 50, 53, 59, 186, 196, 277, 281
King, Benjamin, Jr., 311
King, Bernard, 147 (2)
King, Cyrus, 172
King, David, 202, 207, 208, 270
King, Ebenezer, 119
King, Elijah, Jr., 62
King, Gedney, 84
King, Grinfill H., 177
King, Henry, 222, 259
King, Isaac, 52, 61, 277
King, Isaac, Jr., 59
King, James C., 132
King, Jason, 169, 281
King, John, 61

King, Jonathan, 59, 130
King, Joseph, 23, 86
King, Lyman, 33
King, Moses, 191
King, Nathan, 59, 61, 87
King, Nathaniel, 134
King, Obed, 51, 103
King, Samuel, 48, 59, 138, 170
King, Seth, 87
King, William, 66, 71, 73, 75, 78
King, Wilson, 56
Kingman, Abner, 40
Kingman, Asa, 40
Kingman, Benjamin, 50
Kingman, Ebenezer, 98
Kingman, Edward, 41
Kingman, Elias H., 81
Kingman, Henry, 60
Kingman, Jabez, 50
Kingman, Martin, 50
Kingman, Mathew, 106
Kingman, Simeon, 104
Kingman, Thomas, 133
Kingman, William, 210
Kingsbury, Emmons, 214
Kingsbury, Fisher, 118
Kingsbury, John, 216
Kingsbury, Nathan, 214
Kingsbury, Samuel, 87
Kingsbury, William, 31, 216
Kingsley, Asahel, Jr., 177
Kingsley, Ellis, 70
Kingsley, Hall, 60
Kingsley, Justin, 177
Kingsley, Silas, 206
Kingsly, Martin, 260
Kinison, David B., 151
Kinison, John, Jr., 151
Kinkade, David, 298
Kinkley, Edward, 71
Kinner, Richard, 6
Kinneston, Henry, 206
Kinneston, Theodore, 205, 206
Kinney, Edward, 185
Kinney, Jacob, 58
Kinney, John, 185, 188
Kinney, Jonathan, 55
Kinney, Phineas, 58
Kinniston, Henry, 205
Kinsbury, Benjamin, 84
Kinsbury, Daniel, 135
Kinsel, John, 203, 292
Kinsell, John, 199
Kinsley, Unite, 52
Kinsman, Arnold, 36
Kinsman, Daniel, 275
Kinsman, Joseph, 12
Kinsman, Samuel, 14
Kinsman, Thomas F., 260
Kinston, Abner, 16
Kinston, Tappan, 16
Kinyon, Charles, 66
Kirby, Noah, 63
Kirby, Stephen, 56
Kirby, William, 56
Kirk, William, 240
Kirkland, Ichabod, Jr., 44
Kirkpatrick, John, 292
Kirky, John, 248
Kito, Samuel C., 179
Kitsfield, Asa, 36
Kitsfield, Thomas H., 36

Kitteridge, Job, 33
Kittle, John, 84
Kittle, Porter, 84
Kittredge, Asaph, 134
Kittredge, Ingalls, 278
Kittredge, Joseph, 134
Kittredge, Nahum, 41
Kittredge, William, 81
Kloot, William, 18, 20, 121 (3), 124 (2), 125
Knap, Edward, 59
Knap, Jacob, 20
Knap, Job, 59
Knap, Joseph, Jr., 18
Knapp, Abiather, 10
Knapp, Aurin K., 33
Knapp, Charles, 167
Knapp, Elijah, 167
Knapp, Elijah, 2d, 167
Knapp, Ephraim, 62
Knapp, Isaac, 134, 135
Knapp, Joseph, 120, 121, 122, 124 (2), 125
Knapp, Moses, 217
Knapp, Russel, 44
Knapp, Samuel, 119, 122
Knapp, William, 65
Kneeland, Aaron, 14
Kneeland, Edward, 303
Kneeland, John, 14
Kneeland, Moses, 258
Kneeland, Samuel, 24, 83
Kneeland, Simeon, 258
Knight, Aaron, 133, 140, 220
Knight, Abel, 64
Knight, Abner, 209, 220
Knight, Abraham, 243, 256, 258
Knight, Adam, 222
Knight, Alexander, 154
Knight, Amos, 20, 36, 220
Knight, Apolius, 211
Knight, Artemas, 64
Knight, Asa, 218
Knight, Benjamin, 22, 25, 189
Knight, Charles, 11, 220, 246
Knight, Coleman W., 154
Knight, Colman W., 173
Knight, Dan, 185
Knight, Daniel, 133, 183, 188, 196, 211, 225, 231
Knight, David, 221
Knight, Ebenezer, 225
Knight, Eliphalet, 152
Knight, Elliott, 3
Knight, Enoch, 228, 252, 303
Knight, Ephraim, 220
Knight, Francis, 278, 281, 295, 297
Knight, George, 48, 68, 173, 174, 246, 302
Knight, Henry, 96, 160, 221
Knight, Isaac, 220, 251, 255
Knight, Jacob, 220
Knight, James, 13, 14, 17, 36, 38, 40, 240
Knight, James P., 13, 14
Knight, Joel, 160
Knight, John, 17, 151, 154, 170, 183, 220
Knight, John, Jr., 211
Knight, John A., 145, 284
Knight, John T., Jr., 220
Knight, Jonathan, 270
Knight, Joseph, 17
Knight, Josiah, 220
Knight, Levi, 220
Knight, Manasseh, 81
Knight, Moses, 17, 256

Knight, Nathan, 211, 303
Knight, Nathaniel, 211, 220, 225
Knight, Noyes, 151
Knight, Oliver, 220
Knight, Parker, 295
Knight, Peter, 211
Knight, Peter M., 154
Knight, Reuben, 220
Knight, Richard, 154
Knight, Robert, 242
Knight, Rowland, 221
Knight, Samuel, 6, 22, 44, 220, 225, 242, 245, 261
Knight, Samuel, Jr., 6
Knight, Saul, 211
Knight, Silas, 17
Knight, Simon, 219
Knight, Solomon, 219, 268
Knight, Stephen, 154, 164 (2), 166, 189, 220, 225, 296
Knight, Theophilus, 221
Knight, Thomas, 153, 189, 258
Knight, Tristram, 254
Knight, Wentworth, 41
Knight, Westbrook, 160
Knight, William, 10, 17, 141, 154, 164, 165, 166, 225, 278
Knight, Winchester, 119, 122
Knight, Winslow, 153, 165, 166
Knight, Winthrop, 69
Knight, Zebulon, 220
Knock, Reuben, 270
Knowland, James, 73
Knowles, Aaron, 254
Knowles, Abiather, 162, 215
Knowles, Amos, 227
Knowles, Daniel, 31
Knowles, David, 279, 302
Knowles, David, 2d, 279
Knowles, Henry, 106 (2), 107 (2), 108
Knowles, John, 302
Knowles, Jonathan, 215, 278
Knowles, Jonathan, Jr., 60
Knowles, Nathan, 27
Knowles, Samuel L., 228
Knowles, Seth, 106 (2), 107 (2), 108
Knowles, Silas, 259
Knowles, William, 268, 279
Knowls, John, 282
Knowls, John C., 228, 283
Knowls, Jonathan, Jr., 282
Knowls, Joseph, 282
Knowls, William, 282
Knowlton, Alvin, 257
Knowlton, Asa, 10
Knowlton, Azor, 11
Knowlton, Benjamin, 21, 36, 37, 249
Knowlton, Caleb, 36
Knowlton, David, 192, 195
Knowlton, Ebenezer, 36, 37, 228
Knowlton, Ephraim, 64
Knowlton, Friend, 67
Knowlton, George, 301
Knowlton, Henry, 145
Knowlton, Isacker, 37
Knowlton, John, 167, 194, 196, 277
Knowlton, John, Jr., 12
Knowlton, Jonathan, Jr., 282
Knowlton, Joseph, 192, 194, 227
Knowlton, Joshua, 177
Knowlton, Levi, 89
Knowlton, Mark, 34, 38

Knowlton, Michael, 21
Knowlton, Moses, 14
Knowlton, Nathaniel, 25
Knowlton, Roswell, 45
Knowlton, Samuel, 227
Knowlton, Washington, 194
Knox, Amos P., 254
Knox, Chadwick, 155
Knox, Eli, 224
Knox, James, 224, 260
Knox, Jeremiah, 224
Knox, Joshua, 224, 260
Knox, Page, 152
Knox, Shadrach, 312
Knutsford, John, 11
Knutsford, Thomas, 11
Knutsford, William, 11
Kranska, Jason, 260
Krating, James, 190
Kuhn, George, 289
Kuhn, Jacob, 291
Kuhn, Paul, 291
Kuhn, Peter, 291
Kumpton, Charles T., 307
Kuscot, Jeremiah W., 213

L

Labi, John, 292
Labroke, Jacob, 251
Labroke, Nicholas, 251
Lackey, Asor O., 7
Lackey, Simon, 303
La Crois, Ferdinand, 276
Lacy, Patrick, 186
Lad, John, Jr., 44
Lad, Nathan, 44
Ladd, Benjamin, 279 (2)
Ladd, Dutty, 182
Ladd, Jesse, 279, 280
Ladd, John, 15
Ladd, Paul, 147 (2)
Ladd, Samuel G., 146
Ladd, Simeon, Jr., 278, 281
Ladd, Thomas, 123, 270
Ladd, William, 268, 270
Ladd, William, Jr., 305
Laighton, David, 279
Laighton, Joseph, 279
Laighton, Samuel, 279
Laighton, Silas, 279
Laighton, Simeon, 279
Laighton, Thomas, 279
Laighton, Timothy, 279
Lain, Abraham C., 228
Lain, Charles, 216
Lain, Daniel, 216
Lain, Elijah, 216
Lain, John, 216
Lain, Samuel W., 130
Lain, Silas, 216
Laine, Matthias, 228
Laiten, Samuel, 181
Laiten, Saul, 181
Laiton, George, 186
Laiton, John, 28 (2)
Laiton, Joseph, 184, 188
Lake, David, 19
Lake, Enos, 38, 41
Lake, Ephraim E., 99
Lake, George, 41
Lake, Philip D., 46
Lakeman, Jedediah, 146

Lakeman, Joseph, 34
Lakeman, Robert M., 135
Lakeman, Solomon, 173
Lakeman, Thomas, Jr., 146
Lakeman, William, 14
Lalley, Daniel, 78
Laman, Henry, 189
Lamb, Benjamin, 302
Lamb, Chester, 65
Lamb, David, 109
Lamb, James, 160
Lamb, John, 65, 221
Lamb, Richard, 211
Lamb, Seth, 153, 246, 312
Lamb, Solomon, 256
Lamb, William, 41, 80, 256
Lambard, James, 297
Lambert, Abraham, 23
Lambert, Abraham T., 77
Lambert, Daniel, 217
Lambert, David, 206, 306
Lambert, Gideon, 2, 108
Lambert, Isaac, 300
Lambert, James, 298
Lambert, John, 219, 267
Lambert, John L., 255
Lambert, Joseph, 217
Lambert, Levi G., 283
Lambert, Saul, 138
Lambert, Seth, 212
Lambert, Solomon, 125, 266, 268
Lambert, Thomas, 14, 233
Lamberton, James F., 46
Lamberton, Reuben, 46
Lammas, Murry, 306
Lammas, Samuel, 306
Lammond, Alexander, 285, 286
Lamphear, Robert S., 66
Lampheer, Elisha, 301
Lampheer, Simon, 301
Lamphere, John, 303
Lamprell, Simon, 22
Lampson, Benjamin, 134, 135
Lampson, Ephraim, 183, 191
Lampson, Jonathan, 93
Lamson, Alfred, 131
Lamson, Asa, 135, 137
Lamson, Benjamin, 28
Lamson, George, 34
Lamson, John, 7
Lamson, Joseph, 74, 135
Lamson, Nathaniel, 34
Lamson, Rufus, 133
Lamson, Samuel, 64
Lamson, William, 34, 293
Lancaster, Bartlet, 271
Lancaster, Christopher, 155, 156
Lancaster, Daniel, 303
Lancaster, James, Jr., 237
Lancaster, John, 217
Lancaster, Joseph, 237
Lancaster, Joseph, Jr., 233
Lancaster, Levi, 217
Lancaster, Nathan, 303
Lancaster, Robert, 237
Lancaster, Thomas, 16, 227, 265, 282
Lancaster, William, 217
Lance, John, 23
Lancey, Samuel F., 28
Lancton, Matthew R., 119
Land, Saul, 16
Lander, Aaron, 169

INDEX.

Lander, Abraham, 264
Lander, Ansel, 281
Lander, Edward, 132
Lander, James, 267, 310
Lander, Jesse, 307
Lander, Moody, 264
Lander, Warren, 136
Lander, William, 135
Landerkin, John, 183
Landerkin, Richard, 2d, 183
Landers, Abiel, 60
Landers, Ansel, 168
Landers, Bathuel, 72
Landers, Caleb I., 29
Landers, Freeman, 168
Landers, James, Jr., 180
Landers, Lot, 177, 257
Landers, William, 40
Landfest, Abraham, 167
Landfist, John, 304
Landis, Daniel W., 49
Landon, Luther, 32
Lane, A., 9
Lane, Allen, 10
Lane, Alpheus, 167
Lane, Alphonso F., 242
Lane, Amos, 260
Lane, Andrew, 12
Lane, Anthony, 79, 82
Lane, Benjamin, 177
Lane, Calvin, 9, 10
Lane, Charles, 96
Lane, Cornelius, 302
Lane, Daniel, 54, 126
Lane, David, 10, 230
Lane, Elias, 168
Lane, Elijah, 278
Lane, Eliphalet, 277
Lane, Ezekiel, 243
Lane, George, 10, 12, 84
Lane, George, Jr., 11
Lane, Isaac, 10
Lane, Isaiah, 10
Lane, Jeremiah, 279
Lane, John, 7, 138, 100, 167, 247, 250, 255, 277, 278, 280
Lane, Jonathan D., 9
Lane, Joseph, 3d, 11
Lane, Josiah, 210
Lane, Lemuel, 29
Lane, Levi, 258
Lane, Mack, 12
Lane, Marshall, 128
Lane, Michel, 179
Lane, Moses, 265
Lane, Nathan, 160
Lane, Nathaniel, 213
Lane, Nehemiah, 213
Lane, Samuel, 12, 25
Lane, Serchwell B., 228
Lane, Silas, 260 (2)
Lane, Solomon, 12
Lane, Stephen, 13, 14, 269 (2)
Lane, William, 10, 129, 160, 235
Lane, William H., 279 (2)
Lanfer, James, 180
Lanford, Abraham, 277
Lang, Charles, 14
Lang, John, 149
Lang, Levi, 212
Langley, Edmund, 263
Langley, Levi, 6, 7

Langsford, Andrew, 11
Laning, James, 50
Lanman, Nathaniel, 128
Lannanan, Barnard, 13
Lanter, John, 195
Lapham, Calvin, 229, 283
Lapham, Isaac, 275
Lapham, James, 271
Lapham, Thomas, 127
Lapham, William, 104
Lappand, Abial, Jr., 177
Lapsell, Edwin, 154
Larabee, Dennis, 256
Larabee, John, 240, 300
Larabee, Jonathan, 300
Larabee, Josiah, 300
Larabee, Nathaniel, 300
Larabee, Richard, 98, 212
Larabee, Thomas, 300
Larabee, William, 300
Larabee, William, Jr., 300
Larcom, Andrew, 37
Larcom, Henry, 34
Larcon, Andrew, 36
Larder, William, 137
Larkin, John, 131
Larmand, Joshua, 294
Larmond, Alexander, Jr., 288
Larmond, George, 286, 288
Larmond, James, 286
Larned, Abel, 271
Laroach, Stephen, 259
Larock, John, 136
La Rogue, Benjamin, 70
Laroke, William, 5
Larrabee, Ammi, 168, 281
Larrabee, Benjamin, 96, 174, 225
Larrabee, Daniel, 172
Larrabee, Ephraim, 299
Larrabee, Isaac, 172
Larrabee, Isaac, Jr., 174
Larrabee, James, 299
Larrabee, John, 85, 265
Larrabee, John, Jr., 168
Larrabee, Joseph, 172, 243
Larrabee, Joseph W., 299
Larrabee, Josiah, 117, 166
Larrabee, Philip, 173
Larrabee, Richard, 109
Larrabee, Samuel, 140, 155
Larrabee, Seth, 186, 190
Larrabee, William, 296, 297
Larrabee, William, Jr., 297
Larrance, Shuman, 294
Larrock, John, 133
Lary, John, 172
Lasell, Israel, 150
Lash, Casiniah, 291
Lash, Jacob, 289, 294
Lash, John, 292, 294
Lasher, David W., 30
Laske, Stephen, 101
Laskey, James, 22
Laskey, Joseph, 121, 124 (2)
Lasky, James, 35 (2)
Lasky, Joseph, 18, 20, 120
Lasley, Richard, 243
Lassall, Joshua, 202
Lassel, Jeremiah, 208
Lassel, John, 203
Lassell, Israel, 151
Lassell, John, 199, 201 (2)

Lassell, Joshua, Jr., 201 (2)
Latham, Abial, 260
Latham, Barzillia, 176, 257
Latham, D., 49
Latham, Galen, 258
Latham, M., 33
Lathrop, Beza, 49
Lathrop, Cyrus, 53
Lathrop, Ebenezer, 131
Lathrop, Erastus, 45
Lathrop, Howard, 290
Lathrop, James, 27
Lathrop, John, 288
Lathrop, John P., 28
Lathrop, Salmon, 54
Lathrop, Samuel, 180
Lathrop, Stillman, 27
Lathrop, Wells, 4
Laton, David, 279
Laton, Simon, 279
Lattimore, Nicholas, 20
Laughton, Asa, 266
Laughton, Ebenezer, 275
Laughton, Hannibal, 3
Laughton, John, 68
Laughton, Jonathan, 201, 202
Laughton, Luther, 266
Laughton, Samuel, 83
Laughton, William, 24
Lauman, Samuel, 131
Laurence, Charles, 275
Laurence, Edmund, 88
Laurence, Ephraim, 210
Laurence, Henry, 78
Laurence, James, 272
Laurence, Jeremiah D., 292
Laurence, John, 209, 247
Laurence, Jonas, 86
Laurence, Joshua, 292 (2)
Laurence, Salmon, 8
Laurence, Samuel, 86, 209
Laurence, Shuman, 292
Laurence, Simeon, 271
Laurence, Simon S., 258
Laurence, William, 76, 275
Laurence, Zadock, 8
Lavell, Benjamin, 75
Law, Benjamin L., 290, 293
Law, John, 239, 275
Law, Reuben, 229
Lawney, Nathaniel, 226
Lawrence, Abbott, 7, 110, 113
Lawrence, Abel, Jr., 132
Lawrence, David, 57, 71
Lawrence, Ebenezer, 267
Lawrence, Elihu, 310
Lawrence, Elijah, 101
Lawrence, Ephraim, 75, 76
Lawrence, Freeman, 63
Lawrence, Henry, 47, 73, 74, 267, 310
Lawrence, Horatio G., 94
Lawrence, Isaac, 40
Lawrence, Jacob, 101
Lawrence, James, 267
Lawrence, Jeremiah D., 292
Lawrence, John, 73
Lawrence, Jonas, 101
Lawrence, Joseph, 75
Lawrence, Lewis, 138
Lawrence, Millard, 48
Lawrence, Noah, 224
Lawrence, Owen, 71

384 INDEX.

Lawrence, Peleg, 73, 74, 75, 76
Lawrence, Robert, 63
Lawrence, Shadrack, 75
Lawrence, Shubel, 72
Lawrence, Silas, Jr., 73
Lawrence, Solomon, 73, 76
Lawrence, Thomas, 73, 94
Lawrence, William, 25, 74, 160, 267
Lawrence, Zeno, 74
Laws, James, 93
Lawson, William, 20
Lawton, Abel, 77
Lawton, James, 78, 127, 180
Lawton, Jonathan, 179
Lawton, Robert, 41
Lawton, Thomas, 60
Layer, Henry, 180
Layer, Martin, 180
Layne, Elias, 281
Layne, Samuel, 167
Layton, Thomas, 192
Lazell, Alvah, 67
Lazell, James, 285
Lazell, Martin, 49
Lazell, Reuben, 46
Lazell, Saul, 285
Lazell, Warren, 86
Leach, Amasa, 47
Leach, Asa, 309
Leach, Charles, 101, 102
Leach, Daniel, 36, 37
Leach, Elijah, 176
Leach, Eliphalet, 43
Leach, Enoch, 292 (2)
Leach, Finney, 128
Leach, George, 132
Leach, Hardy, 132
Leach, Henry, 81
Leach, James, 211, 256, 301
Leach, Jerathmalel, 292
Leach, John, 149
Leach, Jonathan, 258
Leach, Jotham, 309
Leach, Levi, 49
Leach, Mark, 252, 255, 256
Leach, Peleg, 49
Leach, Samuel, 128
Leach, Seth, 49
Leach, Simeon, 95
Leach, Stephen, 95
Leach, Thomas, 83, 129
Leach, William, 34
Leadbetter, Gurdon A., 70
Leadbetter, Luther, 167
Leadbetter, Thomas, 224, 259
League, William, 133
Lean, John, 164
Lear, Philip, 219
Lear, Richard, 302
Learnard, Benjamin, 283
Learnard, Elisha, 26
Learneard, William, 28
Learned, Benjamin, 229
Learned, William, 109
Leatch, Hosea, 54
Leathe, Benjamin, 93
Leathe, James, 96
Leatherby, Samuel, 180
Leatherland, William, 14
Leathers, Aaron, 168
Leathers, Asa, 184, 186
Leathers, Benjamin, 90

Leathers, Levi, 308
Leathers, Obednego, 245
Leavers, John, 85
Leavis, Hugh M., 166, 246
Leavit, Albert, 150
Leavit, Josiah, 212
Leavitt, Aaron, 101
Leavitt, Abraham, 171
Leavitt, Bracet, 270
Leavitt, Charles, 40, 136, 137
Leavitt, Cushman, 104
Leavitt, David, 238
Leavitt, Edward, 171
Leavitt, George, 300
Leavitt, Hinskin, 171
Leavitt, Isaac, 101, 177
Leavitt, James, 2d, 171
Leavitt, Jesse, 177
Leavitt, John C., 102
Leavitt, Joseph, 246
Leavitt, Mark, 171
Leavitt, Martin, 96
Leavitt, Samuel, Jr., 96
Leavitt, William, 241, 249
Leavy, Eli, 170
Leavy, John, 163
Leballister, Thomas, 179
Lebanon, William, 252
Le Barn, Roderic, 31
Le Baron, Isaac, 128
Le Baron, Joseph, 52
Le Baron, Lazarus, 52
Le Baron, Ziba, 52
Le Barron, Jepthah, 102
Le Barron, Joshua, 102
Le Barron, Ziba, 102
Lebetter, Daniel, 138
Leeran, John, 7
Ledbetter, James, 181
Ledbetter, John, 181
Ledbetter, Samuel, 179
Lee, Aaron, 13, 14
Lee, Andrew, 14, 36, 141
Lee, Asa, 80
Lee, Benjamin, 21
Lee, Charles, 250 (2)
Lee, Cyrel, 78
Lee, Cyrus, 99
Lee, David, 60
Lee, Edward, 14
Lee, Ezra, 47
Lee, Harmon B., 65
Lee, Henry, 96
Lee, I., 36
Lee, John, 21
Lee, John, 2d, 38
Lee, Joseph L., 138
Lee, Joshua, 136
Lee, Larkin F., 36
Lee, Larkin T., 37
Lee, Nathan, 13, 14
Lee, Nathaniel, 36
Lee, Nathaniel B., 11
Lee, Oliver, 82
Lee, Reuben, 3
Lee, Richard, 6
Lee, Stephen, 276
Lee, Washington, 83
Lee, William, 5
Lee, William C., 250 (2)
Leeds, John, 206 (2)
Leeds, Samuel, 78

Leeland, Abner, 285, 287
Leeman, Alexander, 305
Leeman, Eli, 307
Leeman, Jacob, 227
Leeman, Samuel, 305
Leeman, Thomas, 265
Leeran, William, 22
Le Favor, Nathaniel, 243
Lefavor, Thomas, 134
Lefavour, Thomas, 34, 37, 135
Legrove, William, 211
Lehorn, John, 206
Leigh, Benjamin, 17
Leigh, Robert, 119, 122
Leighton, Andrew, 158, 164, 166
Leighton, Asa, 307
Leighton, Charles, 81
Leighton, Chesley, 219, 225
Leighton, Daniel, 225, 228, 246, 253, 265, 272
Leighton, Edward, 154
Leighton, Ezekiel, 164, 165, 166, 219
Leighton, Francis, 88
Leighton, George, 41, 80, 158, 191
Leighton, George W., 161
Leighton, Hatwell, 160
Leighton, Isaac, 154
Leighton, Jeremiah, 225
Leighton, John, 160, 268
Leighton, Joseph, 225
Leighton, Levi, 153, 228
Leighton, Luther, 307
Leighton, Mordecai, 228, 283
Leighton, Nathaniel, 158
Leighton, Peletiah, 228
Leighton, Peter, 228
Leighton, Reuben, 153, 246
Leighton, Richard, 17
Leighton, Robert, 165, 166, 251, 255
Leighton, Samuel, 160, 268
Leighton, Thaddeus, 154
Leighton, Thomas, 211, 219
Leighton, Tobias, 11
Leighton, William, 212
Lekeman, Richard M., 137
Lelan, Lewis, Jr., 179
Leland, Aaron, 87
Leland, Amasa, 94
Leland, Ebenezer, 99
Leland, Lemuel, 33
Leland, Lowell, 48
Leland, Sherman, 161
Lelland, Joseph M., Jr., 241
Loman, David, 272
Lemaster, George, 22, 83
Lemon, David, 27
Lemond, Alexander, 159
Lemond, Oliver, 159
Lemont, Adam, 298
Lemont, Robert, 249, 297
Lena, Ebenezer, 70
Lenan, John, 6
Lenant, William, 39
Leniken, Daniel, 286
Lennison, Asa, 23
Lenolds, Joshua, 32
Lenox, Patrick, 189
Lenox, Patrick, Jr., 184
Lenox, Robert, 191
Lenox, Thomas, 189
Leonard, Abner, 52, 54
Leonard, Alanson, 46
Leonard, Alford, 59

Leonard, Ansel, 51
Leonard, Azza, 91
Leonard, Benjamin, 52
Leonard, Caleb, 263
Leonard, Charles F., 51
Leonard, David, 90
Leonard, Ebenezer, 59
Leonard, Elijah, 41
Leonard, George, 54
Leonard, Gideon, 52
Leonard, Gilbert, 59
Leonard, Ichabod, 126
Leonard, Isaac, 274
Leonard, Isam, 51
Leonard, Jacob, 251, 255
Leonard, James B., 115
Leonard, Jesse, 30
Leonard, John, 34, 67
Leonard, Juber, Jr., 44
Leonard, Lewis, 59
Leonard, Micah, 51
Leonard, Nahum, 49
Leonard, Samuel, 29, 51 (2), 54
Leonard, Seth, 51
Leonard, Solomon, 42, 60, 62
Leonard, Spencer, 51
Leonard, Thomas, 25
Leonard, Watson, 47
Leonard, William, 64
Leonard, William D., 249
Leonard, William S., 51
Leonard, Zadock, 62
Lerow, Charles, 23
Lerow, Lewis, 26
Leroy, Job, 68
Leru, Shubal, Jr., 281
Lesley, Amasa, 262, 266
Lessett, Robert, 239
Lester, John, 4
Lesure, Thomas, 161
Levans, Charles, 214
Levens, Elkanan W., 67
Leverett, Gad, 88
Leverett, John, 84
Levi, Morris, 59
Levins, Charles, 46
Levit, Caleb, 297, 299
Levit, Charles B., 116
Levitt, George, 297
Lewey, Jacob, 164
Lewin, Nathan, 60
Lewis, Aaron, 61, 62, 97, 116
Lewis, Alonzo, 21, 118
Lewis, Amos, 23
Lewis, Andrew, 180
Lewis, Asa, 264
Lewis, Augustus I., Jr., 141
Lewis, Benjamin, 46, 239
Lewis, Blaney, 116
Lewis, Charles, 96, 236, 265
Lewis, Dana, 137
Lewis, Daniel, 2, 118
Lewis, David, 30, 75, 76
Lewis, Ebenezer, 238
Lewis, Ebenezer, 2d, 238
Lewis, Edmund, 28
Lewis, Edward, 44, 153
Lewis, Edward C., 117
Lewis, Elijah, 53
Lewis, Elijah N., 96, 102
Lewis, Elisha, 102, 239
Lewis, Fletcher, 73

Lewis, Frederick, 276
Lewis, George, 26, 79
Lewis, Giles, 185
Lewis, Gills, 183
Lewis, Henry, 7, 112 (2), 113, 116, 270
Lewis, Hiram, 93
Lewis, Hugh M., 243
Lewis, Isaac, 97, 266, 306
Lewis, Isaiah, 72
Lewis, James, 8, 72, 251
Lewis, Jason, 97
Lewis, Jazariah, 298
Lewis, Jesse, 125, 152
Lewis, John, 23, 38, 97, 191
Lewis, John, Jr., 183
Lewis, John, 2d, 183
Lewis, John, 3d, 188
Lewis, Joseph, 23, 79, 186, 256, 308
Lewis, Joseph, 2d, 183
Lewis, Lemuel, Jr., 185
Lewis, Lyman, 1
Lewis, Mark, 89
Lewis, Meric, 8
Lewis, Morgan, 153
Lewis, Moses, 111 (2), 112
Lewis, Nathan, 299
Lewis, Nathaniel, 75, 76
Lewis, Noah, 153, 261
Lewis, Peter S., 118
Lewis, Reuben, 276
Lewis, Samuel, 99, 128, 185, 186, 239
Lewis, Samuel, Jr., 183
Lewis, Samuel H. B., 173
Lewis, Saul, 183, 188
Lewis, Saul, Jr., 188
Lewis, Seth, 131
Lewis, Sherebiah, 306
Lewis, Simon P., 141
Lewis, Stephen, 184
Lewis, Stephen, Jr., 183, 188
Lewis, Thatcher, 73
Lewis, Thomas, 72, 235, 241
Lewis, Thomas, Jr., 242
Lewis, Timothy, 62
Lewis, William, 180, 264, 312
Lewis, William, Jr., 267
Lewis, William R., 69
Lewrader, Benjamin, 275
Libbey, Abner, 172
Libbey, Alexander, 290
Libbey, Amos, Jr., 172
Libbey, Andrew, 172, 210
Libbey, Benjamin, 210
Libbey, Cyprus, 172
Libbey, Daniel, 172, 262
Libbey, Daniel, 3d, 172
Libbey, Dennis, 172
Libbey, Ebenezer, 168
Libbey, Eliakim, 172
Libbey, Elias, 245
Libbey, Enos, 166, 255
Libbey, George, 172, 290, 293
Libbey, Hatwell, 293
Libbey, Hatwil, 290
Libbey, Henry, 290, 293
Libbey, Isaac, 290, 293
Libbey, Jacob, 290, 293
Libbey, James, 155, 172, 210, 254, 290
Libbey, Jedediah, 210
Libbey, Jedediah C., 210, 256
Libbey, Jeremiah, 245
Libbey, Joab, 210

Libbey, John, 245
Libbey, John A., 172
Libbey, Jonathan, 300
Libbey, Joseph, 158 (2)
Libbey, Joseph, 3d, 172
Libbey, Josiah, 209
Libbey, Luke, 172
Libbey, Morris, 172
Libbey, Nathaniel, 172
Libbey, Oliver, 290, 293
Libbey, Parker, 172
Libbey, Philip, 168
Libbey, Reuben, 168, 172
Libbey, Rufus, 172
Libbey, Samuel, 169, 214, 258, 292 (2)
Libbey, Sewall, 172
Libbey, Sherborn, 172
Libbey, Sherburn, 165
Libbey, Shirley, 172
Libbey, Simon, Jr., 172
Libbey, Solon, 245
Libbey, Stephen, 172
Libbey, Theodore, 119
Libbey, Theophilus, 153
Libbey, Thomas, 168, 211
Libbey, Thomas, Jr., 172
Libbey, William, 210, 256, 286, 290
Libbey, William, Jr., 256
Libbey, Zenos, 172
Libby, Andrew, Jr., 172
Libby, Asa, 272
Libby, Benjamin, 172, 173
Libby, Daniel, 85, 221, 236
Libby, Daniel, Jr., 173
Libby, Daniel, 3d, 172
Libby, Darius, 174
Libby, David, 177, 239
Libby, Dean S., 240
Libby, Dennis, 300
Libby, Ebenezer, 239, 281
Libby, Elisha, 153
Libby, Elliott, 174
Libby, Enoch, 232
Libby, Enos, 165, 243
Libby, Ephraim, 172
Libby, Hanson, 153
Libby, Hugh, 243
Libby, Isaac, 219
Libby, James, 171
Libby, James, Jr., 155
Libby, Jethro, Jr., 171
Libby, Joel, 174, 193
Libby, John, 153
Libby, John, Jr., 172
Libby, John T., 219
Libby, Jonathan, 224, 296
Libby, Joseph, 164, 165, 166
Libby, Josiah, 166
Libby, Lemuel, 174
Libby, Levi, 238
Libby, Luther, Jr., 172
Libby, Moses, 300
Libby, Moses, Jr., 172
Libby, Nahum, 236
Libby, Parmenio, 155
Libby, Peter, 263
Libby, Richard, 172, 246
Libby, Richard, 3d, 172
Libby, Robert, Jr., 172
Libby, Rufus, 234
Libby, Samuel, 272
Libby, Samuel K., 172

INDEX.

Libby, Saul, 239
Libby, Sewall, 171
Libby, Sherburn, 165
Libby, Simon, 243
Libby, Solomon, 173, 272
Libby, Stephen, 155
Libby, Stephen, Jr., 153
Libby, Thomas, 153, 246
Libby, Timothy, 170
Libby, Tobias, 153
Libby, Walter, 171
Libby, William, 155
Libby, William, Jr., 300
Light, Adam, 289
Light, Andrew, 185, 308
Light, Francis, 292
Light, George, 289
Light, James, 145, 285
Light, Peter, 180
Lilla, Caleb, 243
Lilley, John, 28, 164, 166
Lillie, Daniel, 80
Lilly, Daniel, 87
Lilly, John, 165
Lilly, John, Jr., 171
Lilly, Jonathan W., 26
Lilly, Theodore, 122
Lily, Gardner, 29
Linch, Daniel, 182 (2), 184
Linch, John, 182 (2)
Linekin, Daniel, 200
Lincoln, Abel, 10
Lincoln, Abijah, 59
Lincoln, Alanson, 48
Lincoln, Ambrose, 62
Lincoln, Amos, 83
Lincoln, Anslen, 82
Lincoln, Benjamin, 54
Lincoln, Charles, 24, 50, 114
Lincoln, Christopher, 26, 273
Lincoln, Cornelius, 40
Lincoln, Cotton, 174
Lincoln, Danforth, 59
Lincoln, Daniel, 81, 83, 199, 203, 209, 290
Lincoln, Ebenezer M., 9, 10
Lincoln, Elijah, 59, 82, 83
Lincoln, Enoch, 225
Lincoln, Esekiel, 26, 69, 205
Lincoln, Ezra, 69
Lincoln, George, 23, 25
Lincoln, Gershon, 212
Lincoln, Hawks, 28
Lincoln, Henry, 41
Lincoln, Isaac, 190
Lincoln, Isaac W., 200, 205 (2)
Lincoln, James M., 79
Lincoln, Jaras, 39
Lincoln, John, 41, 173
Lincoln, John C., 160
Lincoln, John M., 153
Lincoln, John W., 94
Lincoln, Lemuel, 69, 199, 200
Lincoln, Leonard, 90
Lincoln, Lewis, 25
Lincoln, Lot, 290, 294
Lincoln, Lot, 2d, 294
Lincoln, Luther, 47, 157
Lincoln, Michell, 93
Lincoln, Nathan, 56
Lincoln, Nehemiah, 39, 50
Lincoln, Nephaniah, 59
Lincoln, Nicholas H., 62

Lincoln, Peleg, 199, 200, 209
Lincoln, Peres, W., 12
Lincoln, Peter, 77
Lincoln, Pruel, 97
Lincoln, Robert, 62
Lincoln, Rufus, 126, 167
Lincoln, Russell, 28
Lincoln, Seth, 60, 63
Lincoln, Stephen, 93
Lincoln, Tisdale, 10
Lincoln, Warren, 62
Lincoln, William, 263
Lincoln, William L., 202
Lincoln, Zenas, 42, 102
Lindley, John W., 290, 293
Lindsay, James, 265
Lindsay, Nathaniel, Jr., 6
Lindsey, Alfred, 198, 202, 208 (2)
Lindsey, David, 168
Lindsey, George, 200, 204
Lindsey, Ichabod, 209
Lindsey, Ira, 168
Lindsey, James, 167
Lindsey, John, 61, 204
Lindsey, Joseph, 7
Lindsey, Melzar, 307
Lindsey, Nathaniel, 7
Lindsey, Robert B., 168
Lindsey, Samuel, 311
Linekin, Benjamin, 206
Linekin, James, 206
Linen, Andrew, 248
Linen, James, 248
Lines, John, 42, 89
Ling, Josiah, 165
Lingfield, William, 23
Link, John, 32
Linn, James, 179
Linn, Joseph, 312
Linnell, Benjamin, 104 (2), 105 (3), 106, 107
Linnell, Elisha, 107
Linnell, Elisha, Jr., 171
Linnell, Isaac, 104, 105 (2), 106, 107
Linnell, Israel, 106 (2), 107 (2), 108
Linnell, Jonathan, 104
Linnell, Joseph, 107
Linnell, Joseph, Jr., 107
Linnell, Josiah, 104, 106
Linnell, Josiah, Jr., 105 (2)
Linnell, Russell, 104, 105, 107
Linnell, Samuel, 106, 107, 108, 246
Linnell, Solomon, 104, 106
Linning, Bryant, 215
Linscot, Abijah, 299
Linscot, Abraham, 299
Linscot, Elijah, 196
Linscot, Elisha, 149
Linscot, Ephraim, 196
Linscot, Jacob, 245
Linscot, Jeremiah, 196
Linscot, Thomas, 196
Linscot, William, 195, 196
Linscott, Andrew D., 228
Linscott, Jacob, 228
Linscott, John, 245
Linscott, Joseph, 179, 290
Linscott, Samuel, 228
Linscott, William, 245
Linsey, Ephraim, 152
Linsey, James M., 90
Linsey, John, 204
Linus, Dana, 135
Liscom, John, 219

Liscom, William, 118
Liscomb, John, 246
Liscomb, John G., 24
Liscomb, Thomas D., 217
Lisner, Charles, 180
Lisner, George, 180
Liswell, Thomas, Jr., 44
Litchfield, Abner, 77
Litchfield, Barnard, 103
Litchfield, Benjamin, 286, 290
Litchfield, Ensign, 64
Litchfield, Hersey, 79
Litchfield, Isaac, 103
Litchfield, James, 103
Litchfield, Luther, 166
Litchfield, Marshall, 103
Litchfield, Milton, 103
Litchfield, Noah, 169
Litchfield, Peres, 103
Litchfield, Simeon, 81
Litchfield, Stephen, 103
Litchfield, Ward, 298
Litchfield, Zacheus, 166
Lithgow, Alfred, 157 (2)
Litterall, James, 290, 293
Little, Alexander, Jr., 193
Little, Charles, 195
Little, Daniel, 133, 136
Little, Ebenezer, 25
Little, George, 16, 21
Little, Henry, 226
Little, Henry, Jr., 193
Little, Hugh, 193
Little, Isaac, 63
Little, Jacob T., 145
Little, John, 15, 193
Little, John William, 52
Little, Joseph, 9, 217
Little, Luther, 130
Little, Michael, 17
Little, Nathaniel, 247
Little, Ophert, 34
Little, Samuel, 145
Little, Stephen, 17, 149
Little, Stephen M., 15
Little, Thomas, 193, 194, 196
Little, William, 196
Little, William M., 145
Littlefield, Aaron, 309
Littlefield, Adams, 29
Littlefield, Benjamin, 309
Littlefield, Calvin A., 234
Littlefield, Daniel, 217
Littlefield, Enoch, 176, 260
Littlefield, Ephraim, 167, 281
Littlefield, Frederic, 2
Littlefield, Frost, 264
Littlefield, George, 295
Littlefield, Ivory, 167
Littlefield, James, 298
Littlefield, Jeremiah, 217, 274
Littlefield, John, 2, 306, 309
Littlefield, Joseph, 148
Littlefield, Joshua, 177
Littlefield, Laphael, 107
Littlefield, Luther, 277
Littlefield, Moses, 5, 148, 235
Littlefield, Nahum, 309
Littlefield, Nathaniel, 245
Littlefield, Nicholas, 309
Littlefield, Peletiah, 152
Littlefield, Robert, 217

INDEX. 387

Littlefield, Samuel, 78, 233, 253, 264, 309 (2)
Littlefield, Story, 167
Littlefield, Ward, 297
Littlefield, William B., 274
Littlefield, Zacheus, 277
Littlehall, Sargent, 7
Littleton, John, 42
Livermore, Nathaniel, 86
Livermore, Stephen G., 3
Livermore, William, Jr., 146
Livin, Samuel B., 179
Livingston, Alexander, 20
Lloyd, Frederic, 70, 80
Lloyd, John, 14
Lloyd, Peter, 44
Lobdell, George, 129
Lobdell, Stetson, 218 (2)
Lock, Abraham, 295
Lock, Benjamin B., 42, 89
Lock, Ebenezer, 220
Lock, Joel, 6
Lock, Jonathan, 23
Lock, Joseph, 304
Lock, Low, 86
Lock, Luther, 258
Lock, Nathan, 83
Lock, Nathaniel, 219, 256
Lock, Thomas, 261
Locke, Abel, 101
Locke, Davis, 101
Locke, Peter, 101
Locke, William, 24
Lockwood (?), Stephen, 31
Lolson, John, 215
Lombard, Allen, 158
Lombard, Charles, 264
Lombard, Cornelius, Jr., 308
Lombard, Edward, 72
Lombard, Harding, 169
Lombard, James, 12, 211
Lombard, John, 155, 237
Lombard, Joseph, 130, 246, 258
Lombard, Joseph, Jr., 174
Lombard, Lemuel, 264
Lombard, Richard, 121, 256
Lombard, Wentworth, 169
Lombard, William, 74
Londborn, J., 234
Long, Charles, 13
Long, Darius, 225, 258
Long, David, 65
Long, Elijah, 211, 246, 255
Long, John, 2
Long, Joseph, 70
Long, Josiah, 165 (2)
Long, Lemuel, 164, 165, 166
Long, Michel, 206
Long, Samuel, 21
Long, William, 83
Longfellow, Dearborn, 276
Longfellow, Green, 179
Longfellow, Jonas, 180
Longfellow, Stephen, 179
Longley, George W., 257
Longley, Loren, 67
Longley, Luther, 67
Longley, Thomas, 24, 63, 114, 168
Longly, Benjamin, 307
Longly, Edmund, 8
Longly, Joseph, 307
Look, John, 67
Look, Valentine, 266, 305

Looker, Marshall, 70, 111
Loomis, Daniel, 30
Loomis, Jonathan C., 96
Loomis, Russell, 4
Lord, Abraham, 35 (2), 212
Lord, Ammi, 134, 135, 136, 140
Lord, Benjamin, 135, 242
Lord, Charles, 271
Lord, Daniel, 14, 155, 269, 312
Lord, David, 135, 140, 251, 309 (2)
Lord, Dummer, 309
Lord, Elihu, 271
Lord, Hiram, 275
Lord, Ichabod, 245
Lord, Isaac, 264, 275
Lord, Jacob, 153
Lord, James, 151, 220, 260, 269
Lord, Jeremiah, 245
Lord, Job, 151, 180
Lord, Job C., 254
Lord, John, 235, 236, 264, 266, 269, 296
Lord, Joseph, 14, 212, 272, 310
Lord, Joseph H., 141
Lord, Josiah, 135, 140
Lord, Lemuel, 86
Lord, Levi, 153
Lord, Mark, 85
Lord, Nahum, 174
Lord, Nathan, 164, 165, 166
Lord, Peter, 240
Lord, Philip, 134, 135, 136, 140
Lord, R., 82
Lord, Samuel, 26, 39, 46, 154, 220, 245, 252
Lord, Samuel D., 34
Lord, Sumner, 308
Lord, Temple, 245
Lord, William, 86, 119, 256, 263, 304
Lord, William G., 154
Loring, Benjamin, 82, 109
Loring, Caleb, 81
Loring, Calvin, 243
Loring, Charles, 212
Loring, Charles D., 247
Loring, Daniel, 2
Loring, David, 125, 158, 256
Loring, David R., 147
Loring, Elijah, 131
Loring, Ezekiel, 242
Loring, Freeman, 81
Loring, Friend, 244
Loring, George, 244
Loring, Henry, 79, 82, 122, 125
Loring, Hollis C., 115
Loring, Irvin C., 147
Loring, Isaac, 159
Loring, James, 300
Loring, John, 23, 34
Loring, John, Jr., 307
Loring, Joseph, 79
Loring, Joshua, 40, 129, 131
Loring, Josiah, 70
Loring, Lemuel, 180
Loring, Levi, 128
Loring, Peter, Jr., 159
Loring, Samuel, 41
Loring, Thomas, 178
Loring, William, 68, 78, 82, 178
Loring, William P., 99
Lose, William, 245
Lothrop, Ansell, 301
Lothrop, Daniel, 3d, 170
Lothrop, Elijah, 223

Lothrop, Howard, 95
Lothrop, Ira, 167
Lothrop, Isaac, 95
Lothrop, John, 291
Lothrop, Joshua, 95
Lothrop, Lovet, 168
Lothrop, Lovit, 281
Lothrop, Solomon, 168
Lothrop, Sullivan, 168
Lothrop, Thomas, 167
Lothrop, Tisdale, 24
Loud, Alexander, 42
Loud, Asa, 25, 80
Loud, Daniel, 42
Loud, Eben, 42
Loud, Ebenezer, 102
Loud, Edward, 94
Loud, Ephraim, 162
Loud, Esau, 91
Loud, John, 92
Loud, Joseph, 102
Loud, Perez, 42
Loud, Samuel, 101
Loury, Benjamin, 285
Loury, William, 31
Love, Alva, 165
Love, George, 183, 185, 188
Love, James, 242
Love, John, 183, 185, 188
Love, John, Jr., 185
Lovejoy, Abiel, 15, 305
Lovejoy, Albert, 267
Lovejoy, Benjamin, 218
Lovejoy, Boswell, 116
Lovejoy, Ebenezer, 279
Lovejoy, Ebenezer O., 279
Lovejoy, Enoch, 197, 203
Lovejoy, Isaac, 253
Lovejoy, Isaac F., 253
Lovejoy, Isaac T., 253
Lovejoy, Jacob, 223, 259
Lovejoy, Jesse, 279
Lovejoy, John, 237, 285, 286, 289
Lovejoy, Joseph, 262, 305
Lovejoy, Nathaniel, Jr., 237
Lovejoy, Odiorne, 298
Lovejoy, Orlando, 100
Lovejoy, Perkins, 23
Lovejoy, Peter, 279
Lovejoy, Samuel, 267, 271
Lovejoy, Stephen, 262, 267
Lovejoy, William, 268, 305
Lovel, David, 216
Lovel, John, 182
Loveland, Joshua, 29
Loveland, Thomas C., 5
Lovell, Archibald C., 197, 204
Lovell, Benjamin, 250
Lovell, Charles, 75
Lovell, Colton, 42
Lovell, Cotton, 42, 102
Lovell, David, 102
Lovell, Ezekiel, 75
Lovell, James, 42, 89, 287
Lovell, John, 211, 250, 298
Lovell, Joseph, 20
Lovell, Mark, 176
Lovell, Moses, 261
Lovell, Oliver, 227, 282
Lovell, Samuel, 41, 52, 102, 287
Lovell, Simeon, 298
Lovell, Thomas, 261

INDEX.

Lovell, William, 71
Loverage, Ethan, 67
Lovering, John, 86
Lovering, Nathaniel, 273
Lovett, Augustus, 36, 37
Lovett, Benjamin, 137, 269
Lovett, Edmond, 37
Lovett, Edmund, 36, 37
Lovett, Ephraim, 197, 204 (2), 206
Lovett, Isaac, 37
Lovett, Israel, 34
Lovett, Jeremiah, 34
Lovett, John, 78
Lovett, Jordan, 206
Lovett, Joseph, 4th, 34, 38
Lovett, Josiah, 2d, 36, 37
Lovett, Pyam, 34, 38
Lovett, Rufus, 171
Lovett, Samuel P., 34, 38
Lovett, Stephen, 90
Lovett, William B., 34, 38
Lovewell, Luther, 222, 260
Lovis, Calvin, 79, 82
Lovis, Thomas, 82
Low, Asa, 217
Low, Beulah, 149
Low, David, 11, 16, 28, 251, 263, 265
Low, Elijah, 217
Low, Ephraim, 245
Low, George, 28
Low, Isaac, 13
Low, Ivory, 264
Low, Jacob, 309
Low, James, 11
Low, John, 26, 156, 267
Low, Joseph H., 82
Low, Justin, 254
Low, Justus, 211
Low, Lewis, 81, 109, 110
Low, Moses, 16
Low, Nathaniel, 11, 245
Low, Nicholas, Jr., 210
Low, O. Thomas, 282
Low, Richard, 118, 133, 136
Low, Robert, 276, 281
Low, Samuel, 26, 28, 299
Low, Solomon, 113, 114
Low, Stephen, 239
Low, Thomas, 161
Low, William, 156
Low, William, Jr., 10
Low, William H., 132
Lowd, Nathaniel, 43
Lowe, John, 82, 85
Lowe, John W., 13
Lowe, Joseph, 78
Lowell, Abner, 184, 248
Lowell, Archibald C., 197, 204, 206
Lowell, Benjamin, 162
Lowell, Benjamin, Jr., 215
Lowell, Charles, 76, 77, 184
Lowell, David, 74, 190, 191
Lowell, Edward, 169
Lowell, George, 218
Lowell, James, 167, 188, 215
Lowell, John, 153, 182, 184, 223, 312
Lowell, John P., 153
Lowell, Jonathan, 166
Lowell, Jonathan, Jr., 165, 171
Lowell, Jonathan A., 180
Lowell, Joseph, 21
Lowell, Moses, 153

Lowell, Reuben, 153
Lowell, Richard, 174
Lowell, Rufus, 181
Lowell, Samuel, 215
Lowell, Stephen, 171, 248
Lowell, Thomas, 153
Lowell, William, 169
Lower, John, 86
Lowers, Nathaniel, 185
Lownsbury, Benjamin, 46
Lowry, Benjamin, 288, 291
Lowry, Benjamin, Jr., 310
Lowry, Calvin, 265
Lowry, William, 265
Lucas, Abijah, 129
Lucas, Alden, 128
Lucas, Ansel, 57
Lucas, David, 177, 260
Lucas, Ephraim, 40
Lucas, George W., 44
Lucas, Isaac, 129
Lucas, Ivory, 128
Lucas, Oliver, 225, 259
Lucas, Willard, 225
Lucas, William, 33, 59
Luce, Alsatt, 278
Luce, Arvin, 305
Luce, Benjamin, 268, 305
Luce, Daniel, 304
Luce, David, 305
Luce, Ezekiel, 282
Luce, Helron, 277
Luce, Rowlin, 305
Luce, Samuel, 229
Luce, Shubal, Jr., 277
Luce, Thadeus, 286, 290
Luce, Thomas, 278
Luckey, Asor, 22
Luckforth, Robert, 199, 203, 207
Ludden, Jacob, 177, 260
Ludwing, Godfrey, 289
Ludwing, Jacob, 292
Ludwing, James, 289
Ludwing, Joseph, 289
Luffingwell, Andrew, 64
Lufkin, Caleb, 19
Lufkin, David, 19
Lufkin, Jacob, 80
Lufkin, Josiah, 11
Lufkin, Michael, 11
Lufkin, Moses, Jr., 12
Lufkin, Samuel, 12
Lufkin, Seth S., 212
Lufkin, Thomas, 13, 14
Lufkin, William, 14
Lufkin, Zebulon, 11
Lufta, Edmund, 83
Luke, Eleazer, 224
Luke, George, 96
Lukin, Charles, 25
Lul (?), Jonathan, 36
Lull, John, 14
Lumbard, Abial, 46
Lumbard, Abiram, 44
Lumbard, Daniel, 306
Lumbard, David, 46
Lumbard, Erastus, 44
Lumbard, Harding, 281
Lumbard, Lyman, 44
Lumbard, Thomas, 249
Lumbard, Thomas, Jr., 71
Lumber, Calvin, 224

Lumber, Peter, 177
Lumber, Thomas, 60
Lumber, William, 150
Lummis, Warren, 78
Lummus, John, 14
Lunds, Ebenezer, 185
Lundy, Ebenezer, 183, 188
Lunt, Bartholomew, 220
Lunt, Benjamin, 15
Lunt, Daniel A., 15
Lunt, Isaac, 243
Lunt, John, 148, 160, 161, 211, 219, 220, 246, 259
Lunt, Joseph, 125, 160, 273, 298
Lunt, Joseph, Jr., 122
Lunt, Joshua, 219, 220
Lunt, Josiah, 298, 300
Lunt, Lane, 219
Lunt, Nathan, 219
Lunt, Nathaniel, 220
Lunt, Peter, 218
Lunt, Richard, 17
Lunt, Samuel, 20
Lunt, Saul, 17
Lunt, Simeon I., 271
Lurch, Hardy, 139
Lurch, John, 302
Lurvey, William, 11
Luscomb, Andrew, 22, 133
Luscomb, Henry, 136
Luther, Abraham, 60
Luther, Chelsey, 260
Luther, David, 60
Luther, Harron, 62
Luther, John, 60
Luther, Joseph, 60
Luther, Levi, 60
Luther, Obediah, 60
Luther, Royal, 59
Luther, Wheaton, 60
Lydston, William, 231
Lydstone, John, 230
Lydstone, Roby, 235
Lye, Joseph, 117
Lyford, Dudly, 279
Lyford, Joseph, 224
Lyford, Levi, 266
Lyford, Oliver S., 224
Lyford, Samuel, 224, 259
Lyman, George, 82
Lyman, Horace, 5
Lyman, Joel, 67
Lyman, Joel M., 44
Lyman, Saul, 45
Lyman, Serano, 64
Lyman, Thadeus, 68
Lyman, Thomas, 3, 65
Lyman, William, 33
Lyms, Luther, 2
Lynch, John, 3, 184, 186
Lynde, Nathaniel, 91
Lyndes, Stephen, 28
Lynes, Samuel, 108
Lynfield, William V., 87
Lynfield, Zeno, 87
Lynn, John, 3
Lyon, Abner, 68
Lyon, Alpheus, Jr., 272
Lyon, Benjamin, 69
Lyon, Elon, 274
Lyon, James, 7
Lyon, Mathew, 160

INDEX.

Lyon, Nathan, 67
Lyon, Tabor, 158
Lyon, Thomas, 7, 22
Lyons, Joshua, 95
Lyons, Samuel, 2
Lyons, Thomas, 22

M

Mabson, Ezra, 33
Mace, Benjamin H., 230
Mace, Fayette, 283
Mace, James, 69
Mace, John, 14, 18, 40, 78
Mace, Joshua, 17, 125 (2)
Macintyre, Joseph, 138
Mack, David, Jr., 43
Mackay, James, 262
Mackay, William, 84
Mackentosh, Peter, 84
Mackie, Andrew, 256
Macomber, Joseph, 305
Macomber, William, 278
Macuen, John, 40
Macumber, Allen, 63
Macumber, Asa, 52
Macumber, Bradford, 59
Macumber, Bryant, 1
Macumber, Ebenezer, 95
Macumber, Elisha, 127
Macumber, Ephraim, 56
Macumber, Ezra, 10, 126
Macumber, Gideon, 52
Macumber, John, Jr., 60
Macumber, Joseph, 52
Macumber, Josiah, 126
Macumber, Josiah R., 52
Macumber, Nathaniel, 52, 65
Macumber, O., 41
Macumber, Paul, 65
Macumber, Samuel, 56
Macumber, Venus, 62
Macy, Samuel, 78
Madden, James, 5
Madden, Jonathan, 162
Maddock, George, 286
Maddocks, Amos, 163
Maddocks, Benjamin, 163
Maddocks, Benjamin, Jr., 163
Maddocks, James, 218
Maddocks, Nathan, 164
Maddocks, Nathaniel, 228, 283
Maddocks, Samuel, 163
Maddox, Benjamin, 163
Maddox, Benjamin, Jr., 163
Maddox, Henry, 253
Maddox, Jonathan, 162
Maddox, Pelsgrave, 183, 188
Maddox, Samuel, Jr., 163
Magoon, Ephraim, 273
Magoon, James, 43, 80
Magoon, John, 273
Magoon, Joseph, 267
Magoun, Elisha, 103
Magowan, Elias, 1, 103
Magowan, Elisha, 1
Magown, Joseph, 17
Magown, N. S., 25
Magrath, Thomas B., 109
Magregory, Alpheus, 170
Magroth, Thomas, 84
Maguire, Patrick, 87
Mahen, William, 161

Mahoney, James, 302
Mahoney, Thomas, 248
Mahoon, James, 161
Maibury, Isaac, 225
Main, David, 43
Maine, David, 89
Maine, Jacob, 263
Maines, William, 281
Maining, John, 180
Mains, Jacob, 267
Mains, James McCobb, 249
Mains, John, 230
Mains, Joseph, 248
Maintosh, Thomas, 89
Majory, John, 219
Malbon, Nathaniel, 306
Malbon, Peter, 306
Malcolm, Robert, 250
Malcom, Andrew, 284
Malcom, David, 189
Malcom, William, 294
Malcomb, Andrew, 294
Malcomb, David, 186
Malcomb, Michael, 70
Malcomb, Robert, 250
Malcomb, William, 294
Malce, Philip, 155
Mallard, Abraham, 3
Mallard, Moses, 65
Mallay, Jeremiah, 234
Mallery, Samuel, 30
Mallet, Collamore, 231
Mallet, John, 232
Mallet, Samuel, 234
Mallet, Solomon, 260
Mallet, William, 2
Mallot, William, Jr., 231
Mallett, James B., 285
Mallett, James G., 286
Mallett, Thomas, 22
Mallett, Thomas S., 289
Mallett, William, Jr., 296
Mallon, James, 31
Malone, Benjamin, 265
Maloon, Samuel, 281
Maloon, Simon, 281
Malthy, Seth M., 2
Man, Benjamin, 180
Man, Isaac, 155
Man, Jacob, 214
Mancey, Andrew D., 305
Manchester, Calvin, 63
Manchester, James, 63
Manchester, John, 163, 164
Manchester, Joseph, 33
Manchester, Stephen, 211
Manchester, William, 63
Mander, Woodbery F., 11
Manes, Sargent, 248
Manes, William, 168
Mange, Henry, 243
Mankin, Andrew, 205
Manley, Austin, 33
Manley, John, 32
Manley, Joseph N., 33
Manley, Josiah B., 31
Manlon, Henry, 128
Manly, Galen, 50
Manly, Hayward, 50
Manly, Solomon, 50
Mann, Andrew, 200
Mann, Ariel, 270

Mann, Arnold, 94
Mann, Edmund, 173
Mann, Fisher, 225
Mann, Frederick, 7
Mann, Isaiah, 83
Mann, Jacob, 39
Mann, James, Jr., 155
Mann, Jason, 94
Mann, Joseph, 42, 99, 299
Mann, Levi, 48
Mann, Richard, 98
Mann, Samuel, 97
Mann, Seth, 66
Mann, Thomas, 40, 103, 128
Mann, William, 11, 36, 97, 112
Mann, William B., 111 (3)
Mannel, Samuel, 63
Manner, Joseph, 219
Manning, James, Jr., 88
Manning, John, 198, 199, 201, 202
Manning, Joseph B., 14
Manning, Richard, 141
Manning, Robert, 137
Manning, Samuel, 82
Manning, Sylvester, 205 (2), 206
Manning, William, 38
Mannings, Samuel B., 87
Mans, Eleazer, 212
Mans, John, 2d, 236
Mansfield, Amos, 118
Mansfield, Asa, 152
Mansfield, Benjamin, 133, 140
Mansfield, Daniel, 116
Mansfield, Ephraim, 117, 118
Mansfield, James, Jr., 132
Mansfield, John, 117, 118 (2), 138
Mansfield, Jonathan, 118
Mansfield, Nathaniel, Jr., 118
Mansfield, Nathaniel B., 21, 133
Mansfield, Rufus, 118
Mansfield, Samuel, 133, 136
Mansfield, Thomas, 118
Mansfield, William, 116, 208, 209
Mansin, Thomas, 28
Mansir, Ebenezer B., 26
Mansise, John A., 21
Manson, George W., 276
Manson, James, 215, 225
Manson, Joseph, 270
Manson, Robert, 247
Manson, Samuel, 247
Manton, James, 265
Manton, Lewis, 170
Mantor, Daniel, 307
Mantor, Daniel, 2d, 307
Manuel, James, 178
Manuel, John, 223
Marble, Abner P., 102
Marble, Baldwin, 222
Marble, Charles, 57
Marble, David, 225
Marble, Elijah, 85
Marble, Ira, 222, 259
Marble, James, 288
Marble, Jerome, 291
Marble, Joel, 93
Marble, John, 88
Marble, Jones, 66
Marble, Stephen, 93
March, Benjamin, 174
March, Henry, 286, 290
March, John S., 149
March, Mathias, Jr., 171

INDEX.

March, Moses, 174
March, Nathaniel, 18, 119, 121, 125
March, Samuel, 153
Marchant, Barua, 73
Marchent, Nathaniel, 237
Marcy, Thomas, 192
Marden, George, 239
Marden, James, Jr., 179
Marden, John, 152
Marden, Jonathan, 179
Marden, William, 17, 20, 121, 124
Marean, Enoch, 174
Marean, John, 171
Mareun, Josiah, 166
Margatt, Asa, 163
Margatt, David, 163
Margatt, David, Jr., 163
Margatt, Moses, 163
Margrige, William, 228
Mariner, James, 243
Mariner, John, 219
Mariner, John, 3d, 296, 298
Mariner, Joseph, 299
Mariner, Thomas, 296, 299
Mariner, Unight, 299
Mark, Abel, 67
Marker, Philip, 134
Markoe, Philip, 135
Marks, John, 141
Marn, Sylvester, 93
Maroney, Joseph, 160
Maroney, Peter, 160
Maroney, Samuel, 160
Marque, Philip, 138
Marr, James, Jr., 312
Marr, John, 234
Marr, John, Jr., 180
Marr, Rufus, 169
Marriner, John E., 303
Marriner, Joseph, 302
Marriner, Stephen, 302
Marrow, William, 133
Marrows, Daniel, 277
Marrs, Cyrus, 222
Marrs, James, 221
Marrs, John, Jr., 235
Marrs, Oliver, 245
Mars, Alexander, 248
Mars, Dennis, 248
Mars, Eleazer, 212
Mars, George, 287
Mars, Isaiah, 248
Mars, James, 248
Mars, Richard, 248
Mars, Thomas, 248
Marsh, Aaron, 306
Marsh, Apollus, 4
Marsh, Asa, 47
Marsh, David, 23, 222, 259
Marsh, Elias, 93
Marsh, Eliphas, 64
Marsh, Elisha, 100
Marsh, Ephraim, 113 (2)
Marsh, Ephraim, Jr., 114
Marsh, Foster, 46
Marsh, George, 243
Marsh, Henry, 179
Marsh, J. M., 249
Marsh, Joseph, 2d, 47
Marsh, Joseph W., 297
Marsh, Lemuel, 45
Marsh, Lewis, 92

Marsh, Moses, 45, 92
Marsh, Moses M., 235
Marsh, Nathaniel, 122
Marsh, Peletiah, 258
Marsh, Richard K., 93
Marsh, William, 40, 244
Marshall, Aaron, 175, 260
Marshall, Abraham, 96
Marshall, Enoch, 239, 272
Marshall, Isaac, 154, 274
Marshall, James, 88
Marshall, James W., 37, 38
Marshall, Joel, 269
Marshall, John, 15, 36, 37, 147 (2), 175, 200, 206, 305
Marshall, Jonathan, 171
Marshall, Josiah, 39
Marshall, Moses, 43, 89, 255
Marshall, Nathaniel, 171
Marshall, Samuel, 68, 109, 274
Marshall, Simon, 312
Marshall, William, 111, 116, 145, 158, 285
Marson, Benjamin, 276
Marson, George, 179
Marson, James, 276
Marson, Samuel, 276
Marson, Stephen, 188
Marsters, Andrew, 82
Marsters, Robert, 69
Marstein, Samuel, 218
Marston, Charles, 75
Marston, Clement, 75
Marston, Daniel, 209, 249, 297
Marston, Ebeneser, 219
Marston, Edward, 132
Marston, Elisha, 279 (2)
Marston, Ephraim, Jr., 219
Marston, Henry, 131
Marston, James, 271, 272
Marston, James B., 69, 79
Marston, James M., 252
Marston, John, 132, 155
Marston, John C., 99
Marston, Jonathan, 166
Marston, Joseph, 153
Marston, Nathaniel, 271
Marston, Nimphus, 75
Marston, Peter, 220
Marston, Philbrick, 278
Marston, Prentice, 75
Marston, Roby, 307
Marston, Samuel, 176
Marston, Thomas, 212
Marston, William, 153, 216
Martin, Abner, 174
Martin, Ambrose, 60
Martin, Andrew, 36
Martin, Arnold, 3d, 7
Martin, Charles, 41
Martin, Chester, 47
Martin, David, 61, 212, 268
Martin, Ebeneser, 118
Martin, Esekiel, 40
Martin, Isaac, 80, 90, 115, 300
Martin, Israel, 60
Martin, James, 7, 22
Martin, James P., 24, 114
Martin, Jesse, 179
Martin, John, 27, 136, 199, 200, 202, 212, 256
Martin, Jonathan B., 118
Martin, Josiah, 165
Martin, Knott, 6, 22

Martin, Lewis, 277
Martin, Lindel, 52
Martin, Mason, 57
Martin, Miller, 292 (2)
Martin, Nathaniel, 209, 212, 242, 256
Martin, Oliver, 7
Martin, Petty, 90
Martin, Robert, Jr., 176
Martin, T., 36
Martin, Thomas, 1, 6, 7, 21 (2), 200, 206
Martin, William, 159, 305
Martin, William, Jr., 82, 195
Martindale, Cyrus, 66
Martis, Anthony, 68
Marvel, John, 62
Marvel, Joseph, 169
Marvin, Benjamin, 277
Marvin, Reuben, 280
Marvin, Whitman, 87
Marvin, William, 45
Maryfield, William, 198
Maservey, Jesse, 297
Maservy, Roger, 225
Mason, Aaron, 28
Mason, Abijah, 266, 307
Mason, Abraham, 200
Mason, Asa, 274
Mason, Asa, Jr., 274
Mason, Comer, 69
Mason, Cyrus, 99
Mason, Daniel, 100, 191
Mason, David, 307
Mason, Ebeneser, 261
Mason, Ephraim, 171
Mason, George, 30
Mason, Gideon, 254
Mason, Hezekiah, 57
Mason, Isaac, 30, 60, 154
Mason, Jabez, 40
Mason, James, 61, 171
Mason, Jeremiah, 241
Mason, Joel, 77
Mason, John, 25, 69, 78, 152, 161, 167, 301
Mason, Jonathan, 66
Mason, Joseph, 171
Mason, Martin, 167
Mason, Moses, 174, 275
Mason, Nathan, 65, 245
Mason, Nathaniel, 215, 256, 260
Mason, Peletiah, 245
Mason, Philip, 62
Mason, Reuben, 178, 260
Mason, Richard, 149, 171
Mason, Samuel, 97, 120
Mason, Samuel, Jr., 171
Mason, Samuel R., 271
Mason, Stephen, 149, 271
Mason, Thomas, 84, 109, 212
Mason, W. S., 120
Mason, Willard, 177
Mason, William, 46, 47, 120, 121, 123, 124, 159
Mason, William B., 63
Mason, William C., 41
Mason, William J., 122
Mason, William S., 89
Massy, Samuel, 2
Master, George L., 81
Masters, William, 83
Masting, Edward, 40
Masting, John B., 90
Masting, Richard, 40

INDEX. 391

Mastings, Joseph, 89
Mastins, Joseph, 43
Masury, John, 21
Masury, Joseph, 35
Mateson, Amos, Jr., 29
Mathews, Abiezer, 156
Mathews, Charles, 127
Mathews, Dan, 185
Mathews, Daniel, 183, 188, 206
Mathews, David, 91
Mathews, Ebenezer, 158
Mathews, James, 302
Mathews, John, 185
Mathews, Joseph, 96, 183, 185, 188
Mathews, Levi, 302
Mathews, Samuel, 301
Mathews, William, 183
Matison, Mathew, 7
Matoon, Isaac, 230
Matoon, John, 29
Matoon, Samuel, 281
Matoon, Simon, 281
Matthews, Abeizer, 155
Matthews, Anthony, 197
Matthews, Constant, 257
Matthews, Constine, 176
Matthews, George, 82
Matthews, Jabez, 257
Matthews, John, 262
Matthews, John, Jr., 176, 257
Matthews, Jonathan, 158
Matthews, Samuel, 172, 176, 297, 299
Matthews, Thomas, 151
Matthews, Winslow, 237
Mattocks, James, 203
Mattocks, Pelsgrove, 191
Mattoon, Elijah, 3
Mattoon, Noah D., 1
Maxey, Harvy, 290, 293
Maxey, Smith, 287, 292, 294
Maxey, Waterman, 290, 293
Maxfield, James, 199, 200, 202
Maxfield, Robert C., 212
Maxfield, Thomas, 1
Maxfield, Warren, 1
Maxfield, William, 199, 200
Maxfield, William M., 203
Maxim, Abraham, 178
Maxim, Andrew, 307
Maxim, Benjamin, 282
Maxim, Jacob, 278
Maxim, Nathan, 251
Maxim, Seth, 277
Maxim, Silas, 252
Maxim, Silas, Jr., 255
Maxim, Thomas, 129
Maxson, Benjamin, 276
Maxson, James, 276
Maxson, Samuel, 276
Maxum, Caleb, 102
Maxwell, Alex P., 64
Maxwell, Daniel, 305
Maxwell, David, 274, 309
Maxwell, George, 230
Maxwell, James, 222, 295
Maxwell, James B., 147
Maxwell, John, 230
Maxwell, Joseph, 163, 241, 242, 281
Maxwell, Marshall, 154
Maxwell, Matthew, 222
Maxwell, Noble, 296
Maxwell, Richard, 234

Maxwell, Robert, 155, 156
Maxwell, Seth, 245
Maxwell, Solomon, 234
Maxwell, Stephen, 164, 165, 166, 222, 246, 260
Maxwell, Thomas, 232 (2), 235
Maxwell, William, 222, 230
Maxy, Elijah, 36, 37
May, Chauncy, 94
May, David, 40
May, Henry E., 29
May, John, 50
May, Jully, 54
May, Lemuel, 54
May, Moses, 36
May, Saul, 46
Mayall, John, 233
Mayberry, Abraham, 174
Mayberry, Benjamin, 209
Mayberry, Josiah, 261
Maybery, Josiah, 152
Maybury, Ezekiel, 256
Maybury, Foster, 210
Maybury, Francis, 211
Maybury, Harvey, 211
Maybury, Jordan, 210
Maybury, Oliver, 211
Maybury, Robert M., 211
Maybury, Thomas, 211
Mayer, Charles, 188
Mayer, George, 188
Mayer, Louis, 185
Mayers, John, 157 (2)
Mayhew, Andrew B., 283
Mayhew, Augustus, 84
Mayhew, Francis, 226
Mayhew, Frederic, 1
Mayhew, Hatch, 76
Mayhew, Holmes, 67
Mayhew, John, 251
Mayhew, Nathaniel, 251
Mayhew, Thomas, 242
Mayhew, Zacheus, 296
Maynard, Cornelius D., 172
Maynard, Ebenezer, 92
Maynard, Edward, 93
Maynard, Ephraim, 91
Maynard, Gardner, 3
Maynard, John, 5
Maynard, Jonathan, 46
Maynard, Joseph, 68, 268
Maynard, Leonard, 92
Maynard, Levi, 239
Maynard, Moses Gill, 92
Maynard, Silas, 92
Maynard, Simon, 268
Maynard, William, 33
Mayo, Abner, 104, 105 (2), 106, 107
Mayo, Asa, 24
Mayo, Asaph, 104, 107
Mayo, Ebenezer, 274
Mayo, Edmund, 174
Mayo, Enos, 65
Mayo, Ephraim, 272
Mayo, Hayes, Jr., 214
Mayo, Israel, Jr., 215
Mayo, James, Jr., 215
Mayo, Jonathan, 106
Mayo, Nathaniel, Jr., 215
Mayo, Obed, 274
Mayo, Robert, 104, 105 (2), 106, 107
Mayo, Samuel, 79

Mayo, Seth, 131, 266, 307
Mayo, Simeon, 215
Mayo, Simon, 107 (3)
Mayo, Theophilus, 104, 105 (2), 106
Mayo, Theophilus, Jr., 107
Mayo, Thomas, 106, 215, 258
Mayo, Uriah, Jr., 106
Mayson, Abraham, 201, 203
Mayson, David, 306
Mayson, Uriah, 166
Mayson, William, 306
McAllister, Archibald, 181
McAllister, Isaac, 152
McAllister, James, 113 (2), 114
McAllister, John, 152, 254
McAllister, Joseph, 197, 204
McAllister, Richard, 181
McAlvin, William, 41
McAuly, Obed, 53
McBeath, Henry, 294
McBurns, Mark, 217
McCalister, Joseph, 204
McCaller, James, 284
McCardy, Daniel, 180
McCarter, Isaac, 294
McCarter, James, 294
McCarter, John, 294
McCarter, Robert, 294
McCarther, Robert, 284
McCarthney, William, 13, 14
McCarthy, James, 138
McCarty, James, 189
McCaslin, Adam, 161
McCaslin, Reuben, 161
McCausland, Alexander, 272
McCausland, Andrew, 275
McCausland, Charles, 146
McCausland, Jeremiah, 146
McCausland, John, 275
McCauslin, Henry, 272
McCauslin, James, 272
McClain, John, 199
McCleary, Isaac, 81
McCleary, John, 113, 114
McClemen, William, 113 (2)
McCleod, Charles, 64
McClucley, Joseph, 27
McClure, Bartholomew, 68
McClure, David, 83
McClure, James, 312
McClure, James, 2d, 312
McClure, Robert, 79
McClure, Samuel, 312
McClure, Thomas, 312
McCobb, Andrew, 196
McCobb, David G., 162
McCobb, Ephraim, 183, 287
McCobb, John, 185
McCobb, Joseph, 183
McCobb, Paul, 284, 287
McCobb, William, 193, 284, 287 (2)
McCollum, Andrew, 290, 293
McCollum, Andrew, 2d, 290
McCollum, Archibald, 290, 293
McCollum, John, 290, 293
McComber, John, 199
McCorison, William, 165
McCornison, Isaac, 270
McCorrison, William, 164
McCorriston, William, 166
McCown, Robert, 249

McCoy, Daniel, 64
McCrate, Thomas, 156
McCrelles, Reuben, 21
McCrillis, Andrew, 89, 277
McCrusen, Lemuel, 173
McCulley, John, 283
McCully, Andrew, 52
McCully, John, 229
McCully, Patrick, 312
McCumber, Ira, 59
McCumber, John, 200
McCurdy, Jesse, 23, 77
McCurdy, Robert, 275
McDaniel, James, 311
McDaniel, Jeremiah, 215
McDaniel, John, 160
McDaniel, Major, 235
McDaniel, Matthew, 215
McDaniel, Michell, 25
McDaniell, Benjamin, 306
McDaniels, Benjamin, 266
McDetton, Hugh, 165
McDonald, Alexander, 92
McDonald, Charles, 210
McDonald, James, 171
McDonald, John, 240
McDonald, Joseph, 171
McDonald, Michael, 39
McDougal, Thomas, 174
McDurmit, George W., 96
McEntire, Daniel, 140
McEntire, Samuel F., 139
McFadden, Abner, 194
McFadden, Abraham, 192
McFadden, John, 230, 305
McFadden, Saul, 248
McFadden, Thomas, 248
McFarland, Abel, 30
McFarland, Andrew, 181, 304
McFarland, Duncan, 23
McFarland, Elisha, 25
McFarland, Ephraim, 284, 287
McFarland, J. C., 112
McFarland, John, 145, 181, 284, 287
McFarland, John, 2d, 145
McFarland, John C., 8
McFarland, Robert, 29
McFarland, Thomas, 2, 263
McFarland, Walter, 29
McFarland, William, 153, 234
McFarley, Robert, 116
McFurlin, Elijah, 41
McFarlin, Robert, 243
McFellan, Warren, 235
McField, Duncan, 159
McGaffey, David, 226
McGaffey, James, 281
McGaffy, Andrew, 279
McGaffy, George, 279
McGaffy, James, 279
McGill, Benjamin, 148
McGill, Joseph, 174
McGill, William, 171
McGlauflin, David, 160
McGlauflin, William, 160
McGoon, Joseph, 306
McGoon, Josiah, 275
McGowen, Lot, 75
McGowns, Lot, 71
McGowns, Samuel, 60
McGrath, Richard, 217
McGray, Samuel, 209

McGuire, Henry, 192, 193
McGuire, James, 192
McGuire, John, 256
McInney, Benjamin, 248
McInney, Matthew, 248
McInney, Matthew, Jr., 248
McIntire, Charles, 311
McIntire, Daniel, 136
McIntire, Ebenezer, 151
McIntire, Flint, 93
McIntire, Henry, 248
McIntire, Isaiah, 248
McIntire, James, 39
McIntire, Jeremiah, 21
McIntire, John, 294 (2)
McIntire, Jonathan, 48
McIntire, Nathaniel, 78
McIntire, Robert, 284, 294
McIntire, Thomas, 145
McIntosh, Elisha, 99
McIntosh, Francis, 83
McIntosh, Henry, 227, 285, 286 (2), 289
McIntosh, John, 46
McIntosh, Joseph, 211
McIntosh, Nathan, 235, 296
McIntosh, Thomas, 43
McIntosh, William, 88
McIntyer, Palmer, 289
McIntyer, Thomas, 289
McIntyre, David, 213
McIntyre, Palmer, 285, 286
McIntyre, Samuel, 236
McIntyre, Solomon, 213
McIntyre, Thomas, 285, 286
McKechnie, Alexander, 153
McKeckner, John M., 262
McKee, Thomas, 312
McKeen, John, 302
McKellar, Archibald, 219
McKeller, Isaac, 198, 208 (2)
McKellock, Archibald, 206
McKenneson, William, 212
McKenney, Aaron, 240
McKenney, Andrew, 306
McKenney, Benjamin, 171
McKenney, Brooks, 148
McKenney, Charles, 300
McKenney, Charles P., 210
McKenney, Daniel, 184, 186, 256
McKenney, Daniel, Jr., 182
McKenney, Enoch, 243
McKenney, George, 145, 239
McKenney, Humphrey, 155
McKenney, Jedediah, 209, 300
McKenney, John, 170, 287
McKenney, Jonathan, 210
McKenney, Moses, 172
McKenney, Philemon, 171
McKenney, William, 254, 256, 296, 300, 300
McKenny, Daniel, 287
McKenny, William, 267
McKenzie, John, 163, 164
McKenzie, William, 163, 164
McKinney, Alexander, 240
McKinney, Henry, 248
McKinney, Lot, 234
McKinney, Matthew, 250
McKinney, Solomon, 270
McKinney, Thomas, Jr., 302
McKinney, William, 296
McKinstry, William, 15
McKissick, Aaron, 153

McKissick, Moses, 153
McKown, John, 182
McKown, Samuel W., 310
McKown, William, 185, 193
McKunnison, Lemuel, 154
McLain, Alexander, 199, 203
McLain, Jesse, 280
McLain, John, 200
McLain, William, 199, 200
McLane, Edward, 83
McLane, John, 202
McLane, Joseph, 23
McLane, Thomas, 72
McLaughlin, Abraham, 237, 267
McLaughlin, Benjamin, 237
McLaughlin, Daniel, 178, 260
McLaughlin, George, 265
McLaughlin, Jacob, 237
McLaughlin, James, 172
McLaughlin, John, 239, 243, 265
McLaughlin, Miller, 128
McLaughlin, Robert, Jr., 172
McLaughlin, Thomas, 181
McLaughlin, William, 172
McLean, Alexander, 200
McLean, Ephraim, 197, 203
McLean, Robert, 184 (2), 188
McLeavis, Hugh, 246
McLelan, George, 245
McLelan, William, 3
McLellan, Alexander, 297, 298
McLellan, David, 173
McLellan, Elkanah, 272
McLellan, George, 200
McLellan, James, Jr., 174
McLellan, John, 173
McLellan, Joseph, Jr., 242
McLellan, Nathaniel, 231
McLellan, Robert, 173
McLellan, Samuel, 170
McLellan, Thomas, 173
McLellan, William, 284
McLellan, William, Jr., 174
McLelland, Alexander, 243, 244
McLelland, Joseph, 153
McLellen, Elihu, 242
McLellen, James, 294
McLemer, William, 79
McLenan, Ephraim, 204
McLenan, George, 204
McLintock, William, 64
McLucas, Abraham, 246
McLucas, James, 152
McMahon, Thomas, 248
McMannas, Charles, 298
McMannas, Richard, 298
McMannas, Richard, 2d, 298
McManners, Daniel, 240
McManners, James, Jr., 297
McManus, Hugh, 265
McManus, John, Jr., 235
McMaster, Adams, 16
McMaster, Henry, 47
McMichael, Daniel, 312
McMichel, David, 194
McMichel, James, Jr., 194
McMillan, John, 225
McMiller, Fryling, 161
McMurphy, Henry H., 206
McMurphy, Neill, 249
McMurphy, Robert, 206 (2)
McNally, Arthur, 265

INDEX.   393

McNeal, Francis, 58
McNear, James, 193
McNear, John, 194
McNear, Samuel, 186, 189, 191
McNelly, Elijah, 44
McNelly, James, 238
McNull, Vryling S., 237
McOldpine, Moses, 152
McPherson, Paul, 275
McPheters, William, 161
McPhetres, Robert, 217
McQuillan, William, 173
McQuillin, David P., 160
McQuillium, John, 174
McRogers, James, 230
McWales, John, 96
Meacham, Philip, 45
Meachum, Selalan, 44
Meacom, Ebeneser, 34, 38
Mead, Hiram A., 30
Mead, Nathaniel, 78
Mead, William, 81, 111
Meade, Henry, 268
Meade, Levi, 267
Meade, Nathaniel, 70
Meader, Benjamin, 272
Meader, Ebeneser, 303
Meader, Henry, 305
Meader, William, 305
Meads, Freeman, 48
Meads, Ira, 4
Means, John, 296
Means, Nicholas, 256
Mears, Jeremiah P., 287
Mears, John, 287
Mears, Zebediah, 41
Mocom, Robert, 87
Medar, Daniel, 163, 164
Meder, Edward, 233
Meeds, Artemas, 155, 312
Meeker, Medad, 84, 110
Meeks, Benjamin, 192
Meeks, Ephraim, 192
Meeks, John, 192
Meguire, Nathaniel, 153
Meheren, Allen, 42
Meiggs, Jonathan, 73
Meigs, Asa, 74
Meigs, Eliphalet, 74
Meigs, Jonathan, 74
Meigs, Josiah, 74
Meigs, Seth, 74
Melcher, Abner, 235, 236
Melcher, George, 25
Mellen, James, 32
Mellen, Joseph, 88
Mellen, Joshua N., 48
Mellon, Alanson, 250
Melvin, Amos, 291
Melvin, Benjamin, 240
Melvin, Daniel, 267
Melvin, James F., 5
Melvin, John, 6, 198, 200, 202, 282
Melvin, Samuel, 6
Mendall, Moses, 130
Mendall, Samuel, 130
Mentser, Andrew, 110
Merchant, Chester, 87
Merchant, Daniel, 11
Merchant, Ebeneser, 264
Merchant, Edward, 264
Merchant, Nathaniel, 265, 267

Mercy, Joseph, 23
Mercy, Leonard, Jr., 147
Meriam, Oliver, 0
Mero, Jesse, 27
Mero, Lemuel, 27, 79
Mero, Martin, 205
Mero, Spencer, 290, 293
Merrell, George W., 188
Merrell, James W., 213
Merrett, Aaron, 69
Merrett, Benjamin, 104
Merrett, Consider, 104
Merrett, Edwin, 308
Merriam, Abraham, 85
Merriam, Amos, 5
Merriam, Artemas, 81, 110
Merriam, Benjamin, 95
Merriam, Ephraim, 308
Merriam, George, 98
Merriam, Jacob, 80, 81
Merriam, Jacob P., 39
Merriam, Jesse, 95
Merriam, John, 98
Merriam, John C., 39
Merriam, Rubus, 95
Merrick, Barnabus, 228
Merrick, Joseph, 85, 90
Merrick, William, 78
Merrifield, Samuel, 272
Merrifield, William, 264
Merrihew, Edmund, 58
Merrihew, Stephen, 58
Merril, Levi, 166
Merrill, Abel, 230
Merrill, Abel, Jr., 178, 260
Merrill, Abraham, 169, 263
Merrill, Alexander, 220, 255
Merrill, Amasiah, 166
Merrill, Amos, 168
Merrill, Asa, 169, 277
Merrill, Benjamin, 308, 309
Merrill, Benjamin, 3d, 168
Merrill, Calvin, 150
Merrill, Charles, 15, 219
Merrill, Daniel, 12, 177, 271
Merrill, David, 176, 178, 260
Merrill, Davis, 162
Merrill, Edmund, 90, 219, 253
Merrill, Edward, 209, 254, 260
Merrill, Eliphalet, 238
Merrill, Enoch, 16 (2), 178, 194, 253
Merrill, Enos, 244
Merrill, Ephraim, 220
Merrill, Ephraim, Jr., 220
Merrill, Ezekiel, 169, 275
Merrill, Earn, 220
Merrill, Francis, 242
Merrill, Frederick, 219
Merrill, George U., 183
Merrill, George W., 191
Merrill, Giles, 210, 220
Merrill, Giles, Jr., 175
Merrill, Humphrey, 177, 252
Merrill, Isaiah, 152
Merrill, J. A., 23
Merrill, Jabes, 177, 295
Merrill, Jabes, 2d, 177
Merrill, Jacob, 16, 20, 168
Merrill, James, 19, 67, 121, 148, 160
Merrill, James C., 70
Merrill, Jedediah, Jr., 167
Merrill, Jeremiah, 177, 213, 220

Merrill, Joel, 225
Merrill, John, 16, 152, 168, 169, 194, 196, 241, 253, 254, 256, 266, 277, 304
Merrill, John, 2d, 281
Merrill, John, 4th, 20
Merrill, Jonathan, 141, 149, 222
Merrill, Joseph, 170, 195, 219, 241, 242, 244, 250, 259
Merrill, Joseph C., 124
Merrill, Joshua, 170
Merrill, Joshua, Jr., 220
Merrill, Josiah, 220
Merrill, Justus, 94
Merrill, Laban, 15
Merrill, Lane, 219
Merrill, Levi, 164, 165, 211, 246
Merrill, Levi, Jr., 168, 175
Merrill, Levi, 3d, 168, 281
Merrill, Luther, 177, 219
Merrill, Moses, 82, 152, 175, 218, 254
Merrill, Nahum, 173
Merrill, Nathan, 149
Merrill, Nathaniel W., 220
Merrill, Oland, 300
Merrill, Peter, Jr., 239
Merrill, Reuben, 171, 220, 246, 255
Merrill, Reuben, 3d, 220
Merrill, Richard, 167, 224
Merrill, Rufus, 260
Merrill, Samuel, 16, 168, 194, 224, 225, 268, 269, 274
Merrill, Saul, 212
Merrill, Seward, 173
Merrill, Sidney, 85, 111
Merrill, Simon, 191
Merrill, Solomon, 219
Merrill, Stephen, 170
Merrill, Thomas, Jr., 194
Merrill, Thomas, 3d, 16
Merrill, Timothy, 164, 165, 166, 219
Merrill, William, 219, 253, 272
Merrill, William, 3d, 16
Merrill, Zachariah, 220
Merrill, Zeriah, 177
Merriman, Nathaniel, 204
Merriman, Thomas, 228, 297
Merriman, Thomas, 2d, 298
Merriman, Timothy, 298
Merrit, Daniel, 224
Merrit, Isaac, 47
Merrit, John S., 223
Merrit, Joseph, 129
Merritt, Aaron, 77, 111
Merritt, Daniel, 130
Merritt, Dexter, 103
Merritt, Francis, 7, 22 (2)
Merritt, Henry, 297, 298
Merritt, Isaac, 300
Merritt, James L., 103
Merritt, Jesse, 298
Merritt, Joshua, 25, 40
Merritt, Noah, 68
Merritt, Samuel, 300
Merritt, Stephen, 299
Merritt, William, 299
Merrow, Samuel, 312
Merry, Daniel, 28, 112
Merry, David, 183
Merry, Hadlock, 33
Merry, Joseph, 185, 280
Merry, Robert D. C., 26
Merry, Samuel, 264

Merry, Stephen, 263
Merryfield, Arnold, 40
Merryfield, Lewis, 3
Merryfield, Richard, 153, 261
Merryman, Benjamin, 297
Merryman, Jacob, 299
Merryman, James, 297, 299
Merryman, James, 3d, 299
Merryman, John, 299
Merryman, Michel, Jr., 297
Merryman, Mitchell, Jr., 299
Merryman, Nathaniel, 296, 298
Merryman, Samuel, 299
Merryman, Thomas, 299
Merryman, Waitsdel, 299
Merryman, William, 299
Merservey, Barnet, 199
Merservey, George, 199, 200
Merton, Nathaniel, 173
Mesemal, John, 159
Mesener, Joseph, 270
Mesener, Rufus, 270
Meserve, Daniel, 187, 190
Meserve, Elisha, 187, 190
Meserve, Reuben, 187, 190
Meserve, Silas, 155
Meservey, Andrew, 172
Meservey, Barrett, 200, 203
Meservey, Charles, 265
Meservey, Ephraim, 35
Meservey, George, 202
Meservey, Jesse, 296, 298
Meservey, John, 200, 203, 212
Meservey, John, Jr., 172
Meservey, Joseph, 170
Meservey, Martin, 199, 200, 202
Meservey, Nathaniel, 172, 194
Meservey, Thomas, Jr., 172
Meservey, William, Jr., 172
Meservy, Charles, 294, 301
Meservy, Curtis, 220
Meservy, Ephraim, 34
Meservy, John, 34
Meservy, Joseph, 35
Messenger, Timothy, 79
Messer, Leonard, 97, 98
Messer, Samuel, 3
Messinger, Daniel, 28, 68
Messinger, Ebenezer, 85
Metcalf, Benjamin, 235, 236, 296
Metcalf, Eliab W., 98
Metcalf, Elial W., 97
Metcalf, Gorham, 272
Metcalf, Harvey, 65
Metcalf, James, 198, 202, 208
Metcalf, Jesse, 201 (2), 203
Metcalf, John, 66
Metcalf, Joseph, 208, 272
Metcalf, Junier, 60
Metcalf, Silas, 93
Metcalf, Tuel, 233
Mew (?), William P., 270
Mexton, Daniel, Jr., 44
Michaels, George, Jr., 265
Michaels, William, 162, 296, 298
Michel, William, 309
Michels, James, 238
Micholds, Zadock, 45
Mickell, Thomas, 24
Midberry, John, 61
Middleton, William, 18, 120, 123
Mighalls, Jesse, 245

Milcher, George, 80
Milcher, John, 297, 299
Milcher, Samuel, 3d, 298
Milcher, William, 192
Milcher, William, Jr., 194
Milcolm, Joseph, 295
Miles, Abner, 27
Miles, Caleb, 230
Miles, Erastus, 260
Miles, Joel, 269
Miles, John, 269
Miles, Jonah, 48
Miles, Reuben, 6
Miles, William, 82
Milford, Joshua, 131
Milikin, Phinehas, 243
Millard, Job, 55
Miller, Amos, 85
Miller, Apollus, 222
Miller, Auiden, 102
Miller, B. V. H., 40
Miller, Benjamin, 214
Miller, Caleb, 245
Miller, Charles, 292 (2)
Miller, Collins, S. 29
Miller, Cyrus, 3
Miller, Daniel, 272
Miller, David, Jr., 300
Miller, Ebenezer, 57
Miller, Ephraim, 302
Miller, Frank, 292
Miller, George, 193, 242, 246, 312
Miller, Henry, 214
Miller, Hosea, 44
Miller, Israel, 302
Miller, Jacob, 147
Miller, Jacob, Jr., 147
Miller, James, 36, 67, 93, 214, 309
Miller, James, Jr., 304
Miller, Jesse, 69
Miller, Job, 133
Miller, John, 8, 80, 110, 112, 113, 292, 301
Miller, John, Jr., 214
Miller, Jonah, 294
Miller, Joseph, 23, 286, 290
Miller, Joseph, 2d, 286
Miller, Loring, 52
Miller, Nathan, 62
Miller, Nathaniel, 270
Miller, Noah, 300
Miller, Parker, 125
Miller, Robert, 310
Miller, Robert, Jr., 214
Miller, Robert H., 152
Miller, Rodolphus, 92
Miller, Samuel, 53, 287
Miller, Samuel, Jr., 33
Miller, Saul, 310
Miller, Stephen, 296, 298
Miller, Thomas, 302
Miller, Timothy, 214
Miller, William, 33, 193
Miller, William, 3d, 208
Millet, Charles, 138
Millet, David, 176, 260
Millet, Israel, 256
Millet, John, 211
Millet, Jonathan, 138 (2)
Millet, Samuel, 176, 227
Millet, Simeon, 176
Millett, Solomon, 176
Millett, Benjamin, 13, 14

Millett, Isaac, 9
Millett, Israel, 253
Millett, John, 167
Millett, Samuel, 14
Millett, Samuel R., 13
Millett, Thomas, 13, 14
Millett, Zebulon P., 167
Milliken, Abner, Jr., 302
Milliken, Abraham, 171
Milliken, Alexander, 172
Milliken, Allan, 163 (2)
Milliken, Allison, 172
Milliken, Benjamin, 171, 212
Milliken, Cyrus, 172
Milliken, Ezekiel, 212
Milliken, Isaac, 171
Milliken, Jacob, 170
Milliken, John, 176
Milliken, John M., 221, 246
Milliken, John M., Jr., 172
Milliken, Joseph, 171
Milliken, Josiah, 256
Milliken, Moses, 181
Milliken, Samuel, 162 (2)
Milliken, Simeon, 162 (2), 164, 171
Milliken, Thomas, Jr., 172
Milliken, Thomas, 3d, 172
Milliken, William, 29, 172
Millions, Ebenezer, 171
Millis, Charles, 81
Mills, Asa C., 274
Mills, Benjamin, 9
Mills, Elligood, 149
Mills, George, 68
Mills, James, 206 (2)
Mills, Jeremiah, 169
Mills, Job, 31
Mills, John, 48
Mills, Richard, 264 (2)
Mills, Simeon, 31
Mills, William, 270
Miltemore, James, 16, 23
Miltemore, John, 16
Milton, Ephraim, 26
Milvin, Benjamin, 162
Mimey, Peter, 147
Miner, Daniel, 31
Miner, Robert, 205
Mink, Andrew, 291
Mink, Charles, 311
Mink, George, 291
Mink, John, 291
Mink, John, 3d, 291
Mink, Philip, 291
Mink, Philip, 2d, 291
Minon, Reuben, 260
Minor, Noble F., 30
Minot, George, 208
Minot, James, 264
Minot, John, 220
Minot, Vincent, 208
Minott, George, 43, 89
Minott, William, 99
Mirick, Ebenezer, 61
Mirick, Joseph, 207 (2), 209
Mirrick, Ebenezer, 59
Mirrick, Jacob B., 44
Mirrick, Joseph, 198, 199
Mitchel, Stuben, 205
Mitchell, A., 296
Mitchell, Alex, 81
Mitchell, Alexander, 80

INDEX.

Mitchell, Ammi, 209, 235
Mitchell, Andrew, 218, 266
Mitchell, Arthur, 51
Mitchell, Benjamin, 240, 249
Mitchell, Caleb, 51, 247
Mitchell, Charles, 213, 222, 233, 259
Mitchell, Christopher, 213, 219
Mitchell, Cushing, 97
Mitchell, Daniel, 212
Mitchell, Daniel, Jr., 212
Mitchell, Dolphin, 65
Mitchell, Dummer, 206
Mitchell, Dummer, Jr., 232
Mitchell, Ebenezer, 131
Mitchell, Edmund, 225
Mitchell, Edward, 209
Mitchell, Eliphalet, 95, 148
Mitchell, Elisha, 51
Mitchell, Emesiah, 169
Mitchell, Ephraim, 309, 310
Mitchell, Gardner, 28
Mitchell, George, 97
Mitchell, Israel, 210
Mitchell, James, 170 (2), 222, 244, 309
Mitchell, Jeremiah, 212, 215
Mitchell, Jesse P., 155
Mitchell, Job, 210
Mitchell, Joel, 209
Mitchell, John, 153, 213, 300
Mitchell, Jonathan, 51, 228, 283
Mitchell, Joseph, 148, 166, 240
Mitchell, Joseph, 2d, 240
Mitchell, Joseph, 4th, 265
Mitchell, Joshua, 170, 221, 241
Mitchell, Josiah, 172, 277
Mitchell, Josiah, Jr., 170
Mitchell, Leonard, 95
Mitchell, Lovell, 228
Mitchell, Mathew, 171
Mitchell, Milby, 213
Mitchell, Nahum, 177
Mitchell, Nathaniel, 153, 209, 249
Mitchell, Peleg, 218
Mitchell, Peter, 295
Mitchell, Phineas, 28
Mitchell, Reuben, 241, 242
Mitchell, Robert, 171, 209, 230
Mitchell, Robert G., 26
Mitchell, Samuel, 153, 171, 228
Mitchell, Samuel H., 130
Mitchell, Seth, 55, 58, 209
Mitchell, Simon W., 49
Mitchell, Stuben, 205 (2)
Mitchell, Theodore, 49
Mitchell, Thomas, 168, 286
Mitchell, Thomas A., 290
Mitchell, Thomas K., 4
Mitchell, Timothy, 212
Mitchell, William, 19, 23, 87, 168, 281, 309
Mitchell, Zachariah, 171
Mitchell, Zenas, 257
Mitts, Samuel, 87
Mixer, William, 252
Mixter, Charles, 25
Mixter, Joseph, 253
Mobbins, Arunah, 290
Mobbins, Isaac C., 205
Mobbins, Shepherd, 205
Moffat, Alvan, 2
Moffat, Stephen, 258
Moffatt, James, 188
Moffett, James, 184

Molineax, John, 198, 202, 207, 208 (2)
Monarch, Daniel, 162 (2)
Monk, Alfred, 251
Monk, William, Jr., 237, 265
Monotony, Isaac, 312
Monroe, Benjamin L., 1
Monroe, Cyrus, 128
Monroe, James, 252
Monson, John, 96
Monson, Zebina, 2
Monsul, John, 274
Montague, Heman, 92
Montague, Stephen, 92
Montford, David, 258
Montford, Joshua, 258
Montgomery, James, 183
Montgomery, John, 206 (2)
Montgomery, Nathaniel, 145, 284, 287
Montgomery, Robert, 180, 292
Montgomery, Samuel, 183
Montgomery, William, 183, 292
Moody, Charles, 15, 226, 311
Moody, Clement, 179
Moody, D., 69
Moody, Daniel, 155, 171, 194, 196
Moody, David, 41, 193, 196
Moody, Dudley, 147 (2)
Moody, Elias, 234
Moody, Enoch, 164 (2), 165, 174, 242, 268
Moody, Enos, Jr., 45
Moody, Ezekiel, 194
Moody, James, 134, 135, 265
Moody, James, Jr., 171
Moody, Jeremiah, Jr., 276
Moody, John, 20, 173, 179, 180, 244, 246, 276
Moody, John, Jr., 172, 194
Moody, Jonathan, 220
Moody, Joseph, 172
Moody, Lemuel, Jr., 242, 246
Moody, Lemuel, 2d, 165
Moody, Levi, 276
Moody, Nathan, 233
Moody, Nathaniel, 177, 260
Moody, Richard, Jr., 194
Moody, Robert, 251, 302
Moody, Rufus, 172
Moody, Samuel, 68, 220, 233, 301
Moody, Samuel, 2d, 166
Moody, Simon, 155
Moody, Spencer, 44
Moody, William, 16, 171, 221, 276, 292, 302
Moody, William, Jr., 242
Moon, Abner, 163
Moon, Amos, 32
Moon, Robert, 141
Moony, William, 193
Moor, John, 304
Moor, John R., 80
Moor, Nathan, 307
Moore, Aaron, 268
Moore, Abiel, 153
Moore, Abner, 163
Moore, Asa, 45, 85, 224, 259
Moore, Augustus, 84, 109
Moore, Bailey, 286
Moore, Baly, 290
Moore, Benjamin, 163
Moore, Benjamin, Jr., 163
Moore, Cephas, 87
Moore, Charles, 275
Moore, Collins, 262
Moore, Cornelius, 163

Moore, Daniel, 265
Moore, Ebenezer, 262
Moore, Ebenezer, Jr., 272
Moore, Edward, 163
Moore, Edward, Jr., 163
Moore, Eli, 4
Moore, Elisha, 135, 137
Moore, Enoch M., 229
Moore, George W. G., 30
Moore, Heman, 265
Moore, Henry, 48
Moore, Henry F., 230
Moore, Herbert, 236
Moore, Humphry, 261
Moore, J., 191
Moore, James, 206
Moore, John, 13, 41, 238, 253, 265, 268, 272, 307
Moore, John, 2d, 272
Moore, John, 3d, 45
Moore, John R., 109
Moore, John W., 266
Moore, Jonathan, 91, 184
Moore, Joshua, 83
Moore, Josiah, 230
Moore, Jotham, 163 (2)
Moore, Nathan, 167, 262
Moore, Oliver, 237, 267
Moore, Peletiah, 244
Moore, Phinehas, 94
Moore, Pliny, 33
Moore, Richard, 289, 295
Moore, Robert, 237, 271
Moore, Samuel, 167, 265, 267, 298, 311
Moore, William, 19, 178, 185, 275
Moore, Wyatt, 163
Moore, Wyatt, Jr., 163
Moores, Joseph A., 48
Moores, Thomas, 271
Moores, Tristram, 271
Moors, Jonathan, 178
Moors, Solomon, 258
Moote, William, 288
Morcut, Benjamin, 59
More, Ezekiel, 214
More, Levi, 273
More, Moses, 18
Morefield, Eliakim, 233
Moreland, James, 141
Moreson, Thomas, 19
Moreton, Major, 173
Moreton, Mathias, 253
Moreton, Richard, 253
Morey, Daniel, 10
Morey, Ichabod, 128
Morey, Isaac, 301
Morey, John, 140
Morey, Philip, 196
Morey, Silas, 42
Morgan, Ammi, 272
Morgan, Apollus, 3
Morgan, Benjamin, 135, 137
Morgan, Chancy, 44
Morgan, Daniel L., 68
Morgan, David, 275
Morgan, Horace, 66
Morgan, Jacob, 36
Morgan, James, 160
Morgan, John, 33, 37, 210
Morgan, Obadiah, 3
Morgan, Paul, 193
Morgan, Ralph, 45

INDEX.

Morgan, Samuel D., 250
Morgan, Saul H., 44
Morgan, Solomon, 175, 260
Morgan, Thomas, 7
Morgan, Tolford, 194
Morgridge, John, 230
Moriarty, John, 141
Morland, John, 182
Morley, Horatio, 44
Morley, John, 46
Morley, William, 33
Morn, Thomas, 92
Morning, Samuel, 95
Morrel, John, 229
Morrel, Joseph, 229
Morrell, Amariah, 277
Morrell, Benjamin, 211
Morrell, Daniel, Jr., 230
Morrell, Elijah, 259
Morrell, Henry, 306
Morrell, Horace F., 29
Morrell, Jedediah, 237
Morrell, John, 306
Morrell, John, Jr., 21
Morrell, Jonathan, 212
Morrell, Joseph, 20, 305
Morrell, Josiah, 306
Morrell, Nathan, 154
Morrell, Phineas, 245
Morrell, Stephen, 230, 262
Morrill, Ebenezer, 64
Morrill, Elijah, 224
Morrill, Henry D., 158
Morrill, Humphries, 260
Morrill, John, 277
Morrill, John A., 269
Morrill, Joseph, 224
Morrill, Josiah, 153, 282
Morrill, Micajah, 306
Morrill, Pelatiah, 273
Morrill, Samuel, 282
Morrill, Saul, 277
Morris, Caleb Dudley, 89
Morris, Daniel, 9
Morris, Edward, 43
Morris, Emery, 35
Morris, Francis, 158
Morris, Hezekiah, 64
Morris, John, 153
Morris, Joseph, 297
Morris, Samuel, 224
Morrison, Alexander, 278, 282
Morrison, David, 67
Morrison, Dependence, 238
Morrison, Elijah, 265
Morrison, Henry, 19, 28 (2), 120, 121, 124 (2)
Morrison, James, 258
Morrison, John, 159, 227, 250 (2) 280
Morrison, Jonathan, 183
Morrison, Joseph, 162 (2)
Morrison, Michel, 89
Morrison, Montgomery, 278, 279
Morrison, Nathan, 310
Morrison, Nathaniel, 148, 235
Morrison, Parson, 250
Morrison, Richard, 148
Morrison, Samuel, 224, 243, 246, 312
Morrison, Thomas, 125 (2)
Morrison, William, 159, 223, 259
Morrou, Daniel, 282
Morroug, Jonathan, 137
Morrow, James, 81, 84

Morrow, Joseph, 244
Morrow, Milton, 158
Morry, Ichabod, 179
Morse, Aaron, 147 (2)
Morse, Adam, 296, 298
Morse, Amos, 99
Morse, Anthony, 13
Morse, Anthony, Jr., 298
Morse, Barnet, 213,
Morse, Benjamin, 210
Morse, Bezaleel, 239
Morse, Caleb, 268, 305
Morse, Calvin, 211
Morse, Charles, 115, 202, 229
Morse, Cyrus, 98
Morse, Dana, 79
Morse, Daniel, 223, 257
Morse, David, 31, 222
Morse, David, Jr., 260
Morse, Ebenezer, 267, 285, 288, 291
Morse, Elias, 222, 259
Morse, Elijah, 91, 237, 248, 265, 279 (2), 285, 288
Morse, Ephraim, 148, 296
Morse, Esdias, 248
Morse, Esom, 11
Morse, Francis, 155, 248
Morse, George, 213
Morse, Hazen, 28
Morse, Henry, 177, 260
Morse, Isaac, 202, 208 (2), 303
Morse, James, 186, 192, 205 (2), 297, 298
Morse, Jeremiah, 36, 37
Morse, Jesse, 68
Morse, Joel, 170
Morse, John, 211
Morse, John, Jr., 258
Morse, John G., 3
Morse, Jonah, 285 (2), 288, 291
Morse, Jonathan, 9, 168, 293
Morse, Joseph, 17, 183, 185, 249, 250, 279, 287
Morse, Joseph, Jr., 298
Morse, Justin, 90
Morse, Lemuel, 148, 298
Morse, Leonard, 282
Morse, Lyman, 88
Morse, Marner, 258
Morse, Merrill, 18, 120, 123
Morse, Moses, 13, 14, 290
Morse, Nathan, 46
Morse, Nathaniel, 285, 287
Morse, Nathaniel, 2d, 154
Morse, Newbury, 262, 266
Morse, Oliver, 95, 285, 288, 291, 310
Morse, Oris, 223
Morse, Paul, 298
Morse, Peter, 17
Morse, Richard, 155, 156
Morse, Robert, 89
Morse, Russel, 93
Morse, Samuel, 36, 39, 51, 288
Morse, Saul, 285, 291, 292
Morse, Seth, 146, 150
Morse, Simon, 302
Morse, Spencer, 54
Morse, Swan, 53
Morse, Sylvester, 69
Morse, Thomas, 192, 222
Morse, Walter, 286
Morse, William, 9, 155
Morse, William, Jr., 273
Morse, Winslow, 248

Morse, Zebulon, 239
Morse, Zebulon, Jr., 265
Morss, Amos, 15
Morss, Joseph, 15
Morss, Moses, 15
Morss, Saul, 15
Morthy, Joseph, 104
Morton, Amasa, 90
Morton, Arnold, 96
Morton, Caleb, 174
Morton, Cornelius, 285
Morton, Cornelius D., 277
Morton, Daniel, 123
Morton, David, 133
Morton, David, Jr., 171
Morton, Elkanah, 161
Morton, Ephraim, Jr., 147
Morton, George, 122, 147
Morton, Isaac, 285, 287, 288, 294, 310
Morton, Jacob, 174, 246
Morton, James, 121, 174, 285
Morton, James, Jr., 193
Morton, Job, 175
Morton, John, 171, 175, 291
Morton, Joseph, 174
Morton, Joshua, 291
Morton, Josiah, 131
Morton, Josiah, 2d, 285
Morton, Major, 165, 166
Morton, Moses, 97, 120, 122
Morton, Nathaniel, 160, 241
Morton, Simon, 210
Morton, Sylvester, 96
Morton, Thomas, 174, 193, 195
Morton, Timothy, 55, 58, 175
Morton, William, 3, 174, 193, 280
Morton, Zebulon, 147
Mosely, William, 298
Moses, Benjamin, 298
Moses, Benjamin M., 295
Moses, Daniel, 226
Moses, Henry, 241
Moses, Joseph, 268
Moses, Joshua, 58
Moses, Liberty B., 3
Moses, Oliver, 294
Moses, Silas, 172
Moses, Timothy, Jr., 145
Mosher, Brice, 227
Mosher, Caleb, 263
Mosher, Elihu, 129
Mosher, Elijah, 228
Mosher, Elisha, 228
Mosher, Ephraim, 228
Mosher, George W., 228
Mosher, Gideon, 55
Mosher, Holden, 55
Mosher, Rauen, 129
Mosher, Reuben, 63
Mosher, Richard, 55
Mosher, Samuel F., 174
Mosher, William, 237
Moshier, David, 264
Moshier, Elisha, 228
Moshier, Stephen, 266
Mosley, Thomas D., 94
Mosman, Rufus, 27
Mossman, Aaron, 145
Mossman, William, 205 (2)
Motherwell, Thomas, 249
Mott, Joshua, 70
Moulton, Abel, 45
Moulton, Abiel, 45

Moulton, Bartholomew, 139 (2)
Moulton, Benjamin F., 174
Moulton, Daniel, 15
Moulton, Daniel, 4th, 172
Moulton, David, 141
Moulton, Enoch, 241, 242
Moulton, George, Jr., 120
Moulton, James, 223
Moulton, John, 153, 174, 269
Moulton, John, 3d, 172
Moulton, Jonathan, 7, 18, 122
Moulton, Jonathan, Jr., 22, 120
Moulton, Joseph, 133, 136
Moulton, Mace, 45
Moulton, Moses, 118
Moulton, Oliver, 274
Moulton, Perley, 47
Moulton, Reuben S., 172
Moulton, Reuben T., 246
Moulton, Robert, 172
Moulton, S., 261
Moulton, Samuel, 295
Moulton, Thomas, 172
Moulton, William, 16, 25, 167
Mountford, Charles, 25
Mountford, Daniel, Jr., 242
Mountford, George, 219
Mountford, James, 242
Mounts, Stephen, 154
Movars, Jacob, 100
Movers, John, 275
Movers, Timothy, 275
Mowatt, Henry, 15
Mower, Isaac, 167, 281
Mower, Thomas, 167
Mowing, Abraham, 114
Mowry, Abraham, 25
Mowry, Bradly, 291
Moyer, John, 157 (2)
Moyes, James, 243
Muchmore, John, 210
Muchmore, Joseph, 245
Muckford, Samuel, 22
Mudge, Daniel L., 117
Mudge, Enoch, 213
Mudge, Joseph, 116
Mudge, Samuel, 21
Mudget, John, 303
Mudgett, Abraham, 213
Mudgett, Edmund, 213
Mudgett, Levi, 162
Mudgett, Nathaniel, 213
Mudgett, Stephen, 226
Mudgett, Thomas, Jr., 275
Muffit, Abraham, 45
Muffitt, Aquilla, 212
Mugford, Ezra, 211
Mugridge, William, 217
Muk (?), Jacob, 7
Mullen, Stephen, 231
Mullen, Thomas, 295
Mullet, George, 93
Mullett, John, 115
Mulliken, Alexander, 34
Mulliken, Allen, 163
Mulliken, Jonathan, 274
Mullin, Daniel, 265
Mulloy, Edward, 155
Mulloy, Thomas, 155
Muloon, Samuel, 166
Mumfad, Edmund, 210
Muncy, Edward, 43

Mune, Nathaniel, 97
Muney, Edward, 80
Munger, Daniel, Jr., 44
Mungo, Elias, 65
Munn, Seth, 66
Munrad, Edmund, 116
Munro, George, 8
Munro, John, 8, 127
Munro, Nathan, 8
Munro, Nathaniel, 98
Munroe, Benjamin, 129, 303
Munroe, Benjamin, Jr., 61
Munroe, Benjamin S., 104
Munroe, Charles, 93
Munroe, Ebenezer, 93
Munroe, Harris, 98
Munroe, Isaac, 10
Munroe, James, 205
Munroe, Martin, 205 (2)
Munroe, Nathan, 99
Munroe, Thaddeus, 94
Munroe, Thomas, 42
Munroe, William, 204, 206
Munsey, Isaac, 184, 186 (2), 187, 190
Munsey, Nathaniel, 301
Munsey, Reuben, 186, 190
Munsey, Samuel, 186, 187, 191
Munsey, Saul, 190
Murch, Aaron, 169
Murch, Ebenezer, 240
Murch, Ephraim, 113
Murch, John, 275
Murch, Josiah, 240
Murch, Walter, 162, 214
Murch, William, 163, 164
Murdock, Hollis, 48
Murdock, Isaac, 69
Murdock, James, 48, 175
Murdock, Luther, 52
Murdock, Samuel, 48
Murdough, Robert, 239
Murphy, George, 151
Murphy, John, 196
Murray, Adam, 245
Murray, Amos, 168
Murray, Benjamin, 162
Murray, Calvin, 46
Murray, Hiram, 245
Murray, Ivory, 245
Murray, James, 183
Murray, John, 81, 91
Murray, Samuel, 183
Murry, Amos, 281
Murry, Joshua, 263
Murry, Robert, 189
Murry, Thadeus, 83
Murry, Trueworthy, 148
Mury, Benjamin, 213
Musham, Caleb, 52
Musham, Ebenezer, 52
Musham, Joseph, 52
Musham, Samuel, 52
Mushern, Peter, 301
Mustard, James, 156
Mustard, Joseph, 231
Mustard, William, 295
Mute, John, 186 (2), 187, 190
Muzzy, Daniel, 174
Muzzy, John, 24, 110, 114
Muzzy, Lewis, 85
Muzzy, William, 174

Myer, Timothy, 108
Myer, William, 187
Myer, William Otis, 110
Myers, Lewis, 190
Myers, Louis, 187
Myers, Stephen, 187, 190
Myers, William, 190
Myltic, James, 241
Myrick, Ebenezer, 58, 127
Myrick, John, 55, 312
Myrick, Joseph, 79, 215
Myrick, Josiah, 194
Myrick, Lot, 192
Myrick, Reuben, 215
Myrick, Samuel, 106 (2), 108
Myrick, Solomon, 214
Myrick, Stephen, 175
Myttic, James, 241

N

Nance, John W., 77
Nanscomb, Nathaniel, 213
Napp, Elijah, 129
Nash, Alexander, 25, 91
Nash, Amasa, 102, 304
Nash, Asa, 102
Nash, Church, 194
Nash, David, 181
Nash, Eleazer, 289
Nash, Elias, 43
Nash, James, 50, 79
Nash, John, 102, 213
Nash, John P., 102
Nash, Joseph, 263
Nash, Lemuel, 177
Nash, Leonard, 43
Nash, Levi, 26, 102
Nash, Martin, 102
Nash, Micah, 43
Nash, Nathaniel, 82
Nash, Oliver, 195
Nash, Peter, 276
Nash, Samuel, 194, 260, 271
Nash, Timothy, 102
Nash, William, Jr., 271
Nash, Zebulon, 128
Nash, Zichri, 102
Nason, Abraham, 174, 246, 312
Nason, Abraham, Jr., 164
Nason, Abram, Jr., 165
Nason, Joel, 25
Nason, John, 226
Nason, Joseph, 163 (2)
Nason, Nathaniel, 177
Nason, Nathaniel, Jr., 177
Nason, Robert, 164
Nason, Samuel, 123, 177
Nason, Samuel, Jr., 177
Nason, Simon, 270
Nason, Uriah, 165
Nathan, Stephen, 20
Nayson, Abraham, Jr., 166
Neal, Andrew, 229
Neal, Barker, 182, 191
Neal, John, 42, 268, 282
Neal, Jonathan, 140
Neal, Jonathan, 4th, 136
Neal, Joseph, 136, 139, 140
Neal, Joseph, Jr., 271
Neal, Samuel, 224, 273
Neal, William, 233
Neale, Benjamin, 243

Neale, John, 102
Neall, John, 62
Neall, Lemuel, 275
Nealley, John, 215
Nealley, Joseph, 215
Neaton, Harvey, 184
Need, Amariah, 61
Need, Ivory, 274
Needham, Abner, 47
Needham, Benjamin, 136, 137
Needham, David, 116
Needham, Evi, 253
Needham, John, 252, 253, 255
Needham, Jonathan, 47
Needham, Joseph, 66
Needham, Joseph P., 27
Needham, Samuel, 100
Negus, Aaron, 33
Negus, Abel, 60
Neil, John G., 304
Nelson, Alex, 118
Nelson, Alexander, 253
Nelson, Calvin, 94
Nelson, Charles, 180
Nelson, Cyrus, 52, 54
Nelson, D., 16
Nelson, David, 40, 70, 90, 184, 188, 191
Nelson, Ebenezer, Jr., 131
Nelson, Eli, 184
Nelson, Elis, 188
Nelson, Ezra, 5
Nelson, Henry, 5
Nelson, Ichabod, 66
Nelson, Jacob, 277
Nelson, James, 2, 33, 148
Nelson, John, 53, 179
Nelson, Jonathan, 179
Nelson, Moses, 67
Nelson, Nathaniel, 129
Nelson, Peter, 25
Nelson, Samuel, 5, 273
Nelson, Seth, 224
Nelson, William, 102, 118, 238
Nesmith, Adam, 138
Nesmith, John, 99
Nettleton, Edward, 3
Nevens, Hugh, 210
Nevens, Robert, 210
Nevers, Jonathan, 160
Nevins, Amasiah, 226
Nevins, Davis, 166
New, Jesse, 90
Newbegin, James, 174, 312
Newbegin, John, 212
Newbegin, Jonathan, 245
Newbegin, Solomon, 174
Newbert, John, Jr., 200
Newbit, Adam, 291
Newbit, Christopher, 291
Newbit, John, 291
Newbit, Michel, 2d, 291
Newbit, Michel, 3d, 291
Newburn, James, 246
Newburn, William, 312
Newbury, Isaac, 29
Newcomb, Archelaus, 221
Newcomb, Briant, 62
Newcomb, Bryant, 133, 136
Newcomb, Charles, 24, 87
Newcomb, Daniel, 145, 286, 288
Newcomb, Edward, 27
Newcomb, Elisha, 211, 258

Newcomb, Francis, 42
Newcomb, Henry, 161
Newcomb, Henry K., 63
Newcomb, John, 100
Newcomb, Loring, 25
Newcomb, Lucius, 44
Newcomb, Peter, 162, 215
Newcomb, Robert, 311
Newcomb, Samuel, 42, 66, 73, 221
Newcomb, Thomas, 53, 98
Newcomb, William, 12
Newel, Zebulon, 233
Newell, Dudley, 137
Newell, Ebenezer, 198
Newell, George, 272
Newell, Gustavus, 178
Newell, Harrington, 88
Newell, Israel, 295
Newell, John, 295, 296
Newell, Joseph L., 94
Newell, Montgomery, 8, 110
Newell, Nathan, 184
Newell, Reuben, 47, 90
Newell, Saul, 62
Newell, William, 295
Newhall, Aaron, 3d, 116
Newhall, Benjamin, 118
Newhall, David, 118
Newhall, Dudley, 135
Newhall, Ebenezer, 59, 118
Newhall, Edward, 117
Newhall, Frederick, 118
Newhall, George, 117, 132
Newhall, Isaac M., 118
Newhall, James, 116, 118 (2)
Newhall, Jedediah, Jr., 118
Newhall, John, 28, 117
Newhall, John B., 118
Newhall, John B. L., 118
Newhall, Joseph, Jr., 117
Newhall, Josiah, 116, 117
Newhall, Merritt, 5
Newhall, Otis, 116
Newhall, Philip, 7
Newhall, Samuel, 117, 118
Newhall, Samuel P., 97
Newhall, Seaver, 8
Newhall, Thomas, 115
Newhall, William, 49
Newhall, William G., 117
Newhall, Wright, 117
Newland, John C., 53
Newlet, John, Jr., 199, 203
Newman, Andrew, 71
Newman, Benjamin, 9, 124
Newman, Benjamin, Jr., 17, 121
Newman, Daniel, 274
Newman, Ebenezer, 48, 220
Newman, George L., 28
Newman, John, 12, 119, 122
Newman, Josiah, 222
Newman, Nathan, 61
Newman, Thomas, 27, 277
Newman, William, 178
Newton, Abraham, 222
Newton, Arnold, 59
Newton, Asahel, 66
Newton, Daniel H., 3
Newton, Edward, 41
Newton, Elmer, 93
Newton, Foster, 91
Newton, Foye, 84

Newton, Henry, 66
Newton, Holdworth, 218
Newton, Hollsworth, 261
Newton, Jacob, 222
Newton, Lambert, 251
Newton, Levi, Jr., 222
Newton, Luther, 39
Newton, Martin, 83
Newton, Willard, 93
Newton, Winthrop, 218, 261
Nezenhy, John, 160
Nicholas, Alexander, 25
Nicholas, George, 83
Nicholas, John, Jr., 250
Nicholas, William, 135
Nichols, Aaron, 85
Nichols, Alexander H., 78
Nichols, Benjamin, 10, 139, 231
Nichols, Charles, 193
Nichols, Daniel S., 45
Nichols, David F., 102
Nichols, Eaton, 221
Nichols, Ebenezer B., 109
Nichols, Edmund, 16
Nichols, George, 109, 141, 189, 216
Nichols, Henry, 2, 133, 140
Nichols, Isaac, 42
Nichols, James, 20, 64, 217, 295
Nichols, Jesse, 39
Nichols, Joel, 305
Nichols, John, 7, 41, 57, 109, 117, 133, 138, 186, 305
Nichols, John, Jr., 250
Nichols, John, 3d, 48
Nichols, Joseph, 250 (2)
Nichols, Joseph P., 137
Nichols, Joshua, 45
Nichols, Lemuel, 295
Nichols, Martin, 241
Nichols, Nicholas, 249, 250
Nichols, Samuel, 297
Nichols, Samuel C., 25
Nichols, Samuel, Jr., 300
Nichols, Stephen, 267
Nichols, Thadeus, 82
Nichols, Thomas, 5, 89, 300
Nichols, Thomas O., 27
Nichols, Thomas P., 112
Nichols, William, 34, 57, 140, 153
Nicholson, John, 128, 208, 209
Nicholson, Jonathan, 29
Nicholson, Thomas, 6, 7, 22
Nickels, Thomas, 193
Nickerson, Aaron, 216
Nickerson, Absalom, 107
Nickerson, Constant, Jr., 278
Nickerson, Daniel, 162
Nickerson, Eliphalet, 216
Nickerson, Enos, 72
Nickerson, Ephraim, 280
Nickerson, Exdras, 230
Nickerson, Huberd, 215
Nickerson, James, 87
Nickerson, Jesse, 216
Nickerson, John, 216
Nickerson, Joseph, 210, 301
Nickerson, Joshua, 302, 304
Nickerson, Michel, 41
Nickerson, Nathaniel, 106 (2), 107 (2), 108, 304
Nickerson, Nehemiah, 265
Nickerson, Reuben, 304

INDEX.

Nickerson, Salithiel, 302
Nickerson, Samuel, 304
Nickerson, Theophilus, 216
Nickerson, Thomas, 280
Nickerson, Warren, 216
Nickerson, William, 304
Nickerson, Yates, 226
Nickery, David, 240
Nickery, Joel, 240
Niebbs, Moses, 237
Nightingale, Asa, 43, 80
Nightingale, Ebenezer, 66
Nightingale, Ellis, 71, 73, 75
Nightingale, George, 100
Nightingale, Solomon, 100
Nightingale, William, 71
Nights, George, 160
Niles, Benajah, 178
Niles, David, 115
Niles, Jeremiah, 234
Niles, Jesse, 115
Niles, John, 271, 272
Niles, Nathan, 177
Niles, Stephen H., Jr., 244
Niles, Robert H., 234
Nims, James, 64
Nims, Samuel P., 64
Nivens, William, 27
Noble, Alva, 46
Noble, Amariah, 309
Noble, Benjamin, 275
Noble, Christopher, 284
Noble, Daniel, 100, 252 (2)
Noble, David, 31, 46, 252, 256
Noble, Edmund, 46
Noble, Eleaser, 262
Noble, Ezekiel, 31
Noble, George, 84, 226
Noble, Henry, 31
Noble, Hezekiah, 46
Noble, Isaac, 85, 164, 165, 166
Noble, Jesse, 73
Noble, John, 211, 258
Noble, Joseph, 139, 211, 242, 262
Noble, Nathan, 260
Noble, Nathan, Jr., 253
Noble, Paul, 31
Noble, Reuben, 44
Noble, Samuel, 148
Noble, Simeon, 253, 255
Noble, Simon, 253
Noble, Stephen, 226, 234
Noble, Thomas, 262
Noble, Webber, 171
Nobles, Walter, 47
Nock, David, 245
Noice, Joseph C., 153
Nolan, Harvey, 97
Nolen, Christopher, 220
Nolen, Spencer, 70
Noles, Nehemiah, 223
Norcot, John, 32
Norcross, Daniel, 146
Norcross, Elisha, 26
Norcross, James B., 229
Norcross, Nathaniel, 40
Norcross, Robert C., 275
Norcross, Thomas, 146
Norcut, Daniel, 52
Norcutt, Ansell, 51
Norcutt, Zebina, 51
Nordiss, Edward, 135

Nordiss, Henry, 135
Norris, Benjamin, 280
Norris, Ebenezer, 280
Norris, Edward, 3d, 137
Norris, Emery, 35
Norris, Ephraim, 280
Norris, Ezra, 269
Norris, George W., 109
Norris, Grafton, 278
Norris, Henry, 137
Norris, Jeremiah, 132
Norris, Jesse, 82
Norris, John, 269
Norris, Jonathan C., 146
Norris, Joshua, 278
Norris, Otis, 274
Norris, Shephard H., 272
Norris, Shepherd, 29
Norris, Simeon, 224, 274
Norris, William, 224
Norris, Woodin, Jr., 280
North, Edmund, 15
North, Elijah, 220.
Northey, Roger, 190
Northond, John, 16
Northway, Friend, 45
Norton, Allen, 55
Norton, Asa, 54
Norton, Bassett, 283
Norton, Benjamin, Jr., 50
Norton, Daniel, 123
Norton, Darius, 284, 288, 294
Norton, Ebenezer, 273
Norton, George, 122
Norton, George, Jr., 89, 119
Norton, George W., 227
Norton, Harvey, 33
Norton, Hobson, 224
Norton, Isaac, 280
Norton, Jabez, 284, 288, 294
Norton, Jacob, 237
Norton, James, 123, 283
Norton, John, 24, 302
Norton, John L., 131
Norton, Joseph, 237
Norton, Joseph, Jr., 227
Norton, Mayhew, 227
Norton, Milford B., 274
Norton, Moses, 89, 119, 122
Norton, Nathaniel, 238
Norton, Peter, 283, 305
Norton, Samuel, 50
Norton, Samuel B., 227
Norton, Saul, 280, 305
Norton, Simeon, Jr., 44
Norton, Simon, 7
Norton, Thaxter, 97
Norton, Thomas, 93, 237
Norton, Timothy, 175
Norton, William, 243, 275
Norton, William B., 20
Norton, Winthrop, 283
Norton, Zachariah, 237
Norton, Zebulon, 224
Norwood, Abraham, 199
Norwood, Charles, 13, 14
Norwood, Daniel, 12
Norwood, Elias, 13, 14
Norwood, Isaac, 206
Norwood, Jacob, 206
Norwood, Joshua, 153
Norwood, Moses, 161

Norwood, Nathaniel, 161
Norwood, Samuel, 200
Norwood, Saul, 206
Norwood, Thomas, 36, 118
Norwood, William, 36, 133, 161
Nott, Oliver, 45
Nottage, Henry, 230
Notway, Joseph, 74
Nourse, Reuben, 47
Nourse, Stephen, 34, 38
Nowell, James, 13, 14, 80, 82, 117
Nowell, John, 233
Nowell, Mack, 245
Nowell, Silas, 20
Nowell, Simon, 244
Noyce, Daniel, 201 (2)
Noyce, Enoch, 145
Noyes, Abiel, 195
Noyes, Abraham, 21, 134
Noyes, Alva, 50
Noyes, Amos, 219
Noyes, Amos, Jr., 20
Noyes, Bela, 253
Noyes, Benjamin, 196
Noyes, Benjamin, Jr., 50
Noyes, Daniel, 16, 184, 196, 207
Noyes, David, 220
Noyes, Ebenezer, 19, 121, 124
Noyes, Enoch, 15
Noyes, Henry, 285
Noyes, Isaac, 192, 196, 271
Noyes, Jacob, 20, 50, 116, 123
Noyes, Jacob, Jr., 123
Noyes, James, 92, 295
Noyes, John, 15, 17, 21, 134, 196, 209, 235, 252
Noyes, John M., 20
Noyes, John P., 242
Noyes, Joseph, 26, 295
Noyes, Joshua, 16, 141
Noyes, Lincoln, 134
Noyes, Merrill, 220
Noyes, Merrit, 43
Noyes, Michel, 141
Noyes, Moses, 126
Noyes, Nathan, 220
Noyes, Nathaniel, 99, 203, 219
Noyes, Peter, 17, 175, 257
Noyes, Reuben, 219
Noyes, Robert, 19, 241
Noyes, Robert H., 120
Noyes, Robert K., 123
Noyes, Samuel, 24, 99, 147 (2)
Noyes, Saul, 99
Noyes, Silas, 220
Noyes, Simeon, 135
Noyes, Stephen, 243
Noyes, Stillman, 223
Noyes, Thomas, 15, 182 (2), 184, 191
Noyes, William, 15
Noys, Samuel, 275
Nubbs, Amos, 237
Nudd, Moses, 78
Nugan, Thomas, 22
Nurse, Newel, 29
Nute, John, 186 (2), 187
Nute, Saul, 213
Nutt, Ashley, 199, 202
Nutt, William, 159, 198, 199, 200, 201, 202, 208
Nutter, Alexander, 163 (2)
Nutter, Charles, 153, 261
Nutter, George, 79, 160

INDEX.

Nutter, Jacob, 270
Nutter, James, 160, 162
Nutter, John, 160, 182, 191
Nutter, Nathan, 241
Nutting, Abijah, 307
Nutting, Buckley, 40
Nutting, George, 284
Nutting, J., 70
Nutting, James, 250
Nutting, Royal, 307
Nutting, Samuel, 27
Nutting, Silas B., 284, 288
Nutting, Zacheriah, 66
Nye, Abraham, 73, 76
Nye, Abraham W., 73, 76
Nye, Alden, 267, 310
Nye, Alvin, 72
Nye, Ansel, 274
Nye, Benjamin, 72, 126
Nye, Bethuel, 73 (2), 76
Nye, Charles, 73, 76, 146
Nye, Cornelius, 310
Nye, Daniel B., 71, 75
Nye, David, 71
Nye, Ebenezer, 73
Nye, Edmund, 73, 76
Nye, Edward, 73 (2), 76
Nye, Ervin, 72
Nye, Ezra, 263, 267, 310
Nye, Francis, 72, 75, 76
Nye, George, 310
Nye, Heman, 73, 76
Nye, Holmes, 73, 76
Nye, Isaac, 73, 129
Nye, James, 55, 58 (2), 72
Nye, Jonathan, 310
Nye, Joseph, 32, 263, 310
Nye, Joseph, 3d, 73, 125
Nye, Joshua, 72, 73, 310
Nye, Josiah, 73, 76
Nye, L., 75
Nye, Nathan, 73
Nye, Nathaniel, 71, 73, 76
Nye, Obed B., 73
Nye, Pardon, 58
Nye, Parker, 75
Nye, Paul, 72, 73, 76, 217
Nye, Prince, 72
Nye, Robinson, 273
Nye, Samuel, 71, 72, 73, 76
Nye, Shubal, 72
Nye, Solomon, 71
Nye, Stephen, 72, 125
Nye, Sturgis, 262
Nye, Thomas, 76
Nye, Thomas S., 73 (2)
Nye, Timothy, 75, 76
Nye, Warren, 73
Nye, Willard, 75
Nye, William, 55, 57, 58, 73
Nye, Zenas, 76
Nye, Zenas, 2d, 73 (2)
Nyles, Sands, 32

O

Oakes, Edward, 283
Oakes, Eli, 161
Oakes, John, 12
Oakes, Simeon, 266
Oakman, Tobias, 216
Oaks, George, 7
Oaks, Joshua, 136

Oaks, Thomas, 134 (2)
Oaks, William, 67
Oarsley, Seth, 211
Obeon, Simeon, 213
Ober, Daniel, 14
Ober, Isaac, 37
Ober, Joseph, 36, 37
Ober, Oliver, 34
Ober, Samuel, 34, 38, 116
Ober, Samuel, 2d, 37
Ober, William, 35, 138
O'Brian, Jeremiah, 298
Obrian, John, 205
Obrian, John, Jr., 205
Obrine, Charles, 188, 191
Obrine, James, 188
Obrine, John, 43
Obrine, William, 191
Obrine, William, Jr., 188
Oddell, John, 213
Odell, James, 135, 137
Odell, John, 162
Odell, Thomas, 135
Odell, William, 90
Oden, George, 110
Odgson, Robert, 21
Odin, George, 8
Odion, George, 25
Ogier, Abraham, 209
Ogier, Andrew, 209
Ogier, Joseph, 198, 207, 208
Ogier, Peter, 202, 208, 209
Ogier, Robert, 199, 207, 208 (2)
Ogil, Joseph, 202
Ohlin, John, 268
Oldfield, Jonathan, 312
Oldham, Daniel, 178
Oldham, John, 127
Oldham, Thaddeus, 178
Oldham, Thomas, 129
Olds, Cheny, 91
Olds, Ephraim, 31
Olds, George, 91
Olds, James, 161
Olds, John, 43
Olds, Jonathan, 45, 91
Olds, Levi, 65
Olds, Luther, 30
Olds, Moses, Jr., 46
Olds, Nathaniel, 65
Olds, Zardeus, 44
Olis, Rodolphus, 67
Oliver, Alexander, 248
Oliver, Benjamin P., 118
Oliver, Charles, 68, 80, 112
Oliver, Daniel, 84, 91, 145
Oliver, David, 248 (2)
Oliver, David, 2d, 248
Oliver, David S., 117
Oliver, Ebenezer, 81
Oliver, Ebenezer, Jr., 26
Oliver, Ensebius, 248
Oliver, Ephraim, 217
Oliver, George, 248
Oliver, Henry, 248
Oliver, Henry, Jr., 248
Oliver, Henry J., 113
Oliver, Isaiah, 248
Oliver, Jacob, 145, 248 (2)
Oliver, James, 235
Oliver James S., 39
Oliver, James T., 100

Oliver, John, 212, 235, 248, 258
Oliver, John B., 118
Oliver, Jonathan, Jr., 194
Oliver, Nathaniel, Jr., 248
Oliver, Richard, 248
Oliver, Robert, 78
Oliver, Royal, 86
Oliver, Samuel, 195
Oliver, Thomas, 248
Oliver, Thomas, Jr., 248
Oliver, Turner, 248
Oliver, Wadsworth, 248
Oliver, William, 35, 138, 248
Oliver, William P., 230
Oliver, William Y., 248
Olvine, John, 90
Olmsted, Francis, 32
Olmsted, Sunard, 32
Omans, James, 55
Omey, Wilbourn, 58
Omond, Robert, 77, 111
O'Neal, Joseph, 100
Onions, Othniel, 75
Oraskey, William H., 302
Oraston, William, 161
Orbeton, Isaac, 198, 199, 201, 202
Orcutt, Benjamin, 86
Orcutt, Eber, 31
Orcutt, Elijah, 217
Orcutt, Gershom, 49
Orcutt, Hosea, 90
Orcutt, John, 95, 217
Orcutt, Levi, 118
Orcutt, Micah, 43, 89
Orcutt, Moses, 49
Orcutt, Samuel, 40
Ordney, John, 16
Ordward, John, 16
Ordway, Benjamin, 2d, 16
Ordway, David, 303
Ordway, James, 16
Ordway, Moses, 16, 19, 120, 122
Ordway, Nathaniel, 16
Ordway, Peter, 16
Ordway, Richard, 16
Ordway, Samuel, 20
Ordway, Stephen, 18
Ordway, William, 15
O'Rea, David N., 195
Orf, George, 289
Orgin, Isaac, 21
Orgin, Isaac, Jr., 21
Orgins, Isaac, 117
Oriment, John, 36
Ormsbury, Daniel, 32
Ormsby, Daniel, 275
Ormsby, Elijah, 31
Ormsby, George, 41
Ormsby, John, 32
Ormsby, Royal, 31
Ormsby, Samuel, 60
Ormsby, William, 61
Orn, James, 185
Orn, William, 183, 185, 188
Ornan, Thomas, 58
Orne, Edward, 132
Orne, John, 81
Orne, Jonathan, 7
Orne, Joshua, 7
Orr, Clement, 295
Orr, David, 297, 299
Orr, Gershom, 234

INDEX.

Orr, Hector, 49
Orr, Simeon, 209
Orr, William, 297, 299
Orrs, John, 234
Orvin, William, 161
Osborn, Alpheus, 47
Osborn, Asa, 37
Osborn, Cyrus, 263
Osborn, Ezra, 136
Osborn, George, 24
Osborn, Isaac, 47
Osborn, James, 139, 309
Osborn, John, 28 (2), 100, 127
Osborn, Jonathan, 135
Osborn, Levi, 47
Osborn, Luther, 39
Osborn, Martin, 97
Osborn, Sylvester, 30
Osborn, William, 262
Osborne, Aaron, 141
Osborne, George, 266
Osborne, James, 309
Osborne, John, 310
Osborne, Thomas, 300
Osburn, Benjamin, 32
Osburn, Cyrus, 87
Osgood, Aaron, Jr., 295
Osgood, Alexander, 218
Osgood, Apollus, 3
Osgood, Asa, 261
Osgood, Asa, Jr., 152
Osgood, David, Jr., 295
Osgood, Dean, 254
Osgood, Eliphalet, 148
Osgood, Francis, 145
Osgood, Hazen, 235
Osgood, Isaac, 150, 151
Osgood, James, 150, 151
Osgood, Jeremiah, 136
Osgood, John, 15
Osgood, Jonathan, 3, 148
Osgood, Joseph, 197
Osgood, Joshua B., 225
Osgood, Luther, 66
Osgood, Moses, 295
Osgood, Nathaniel, Jr., 295
Osgood, Peter, 76, 77
Osgood, Robert, 254
Osgood, Robert B., 21
Osgood, Samuel, 148
Osgood, Saul G., 295
Osgood, Silas, 66, 209
Osgood, Stephen, 272
Osgood, Theodore, 295
Osgood, Thomas, 243
Osgood, Thomas D., 243
Ostin, John, 179
Osyer, Thomas, 197
Othcoor, John H., 247
Otherman, Henry, 79
Otis, David, 155
Otis, Ensign, 168, 277
Otis, Howland, 103
Otis, James, 298
Otis, John, 193
Otis, Rodolphus, 65
Otis, Samuel, Jr., 300
Otis, Seth B., 91
Otis, Simon, 169
Otis, Thomas, 182, 186
Otis, Welcom, 97
Otis, William, 40, 193

Overlock, George, 289, 292
Overlock, Godfrey, 145
Overlock, Jacob, 180, 291
Overlock, John, 180, 289
Overlock, John, 2d, 289
Overlock, Joseph, 291
Overlock, Joseph, Jr., 180
Overlock, Martin, 180
Owen, Abisha, Jr., 274
Owen, Benjamin, 235
Owen, Chauncey, 23
Owen, Ebenezer, Jr., 243
Owen, Elijah, 46, 270
Owen, Gideon, 168
Owen, Hiram, 31
Owen, Jeremiah, 297, 298
Owen, John, 231, 275, 295
Owen, John, 2d, 148
Owen, Nathaniel, 85
Owen, Philip, 148
Owen, Philip, Jr., 148
Owen, Samuel, 297
Owen, Saul, 295, 298
Owen, Shimmel, 273
Owen, Thomas, 233
Owen, William, 249, 269
Owens, Benjamin, 148
Owens, Ira, 31
Owens, Thomas, 312
Oxton, William, 198, 199, 201, 202 (2), 207
Oxton, William, Jr., 199
Osier, Barker, 195
Osier, Thomas, 195

P

Pach, William, 24
Packard, Adam, 50
Packard, Ambrose, 50
Packard, Asa, 49, 250
Packard, Bela, 50
Packard, Benjamin, 203
Packard, Benjamin, Jr., 197, 204, 207
Packard, Bewel, 89
Packard, Buel, 43
Packard, Caleb, Jr., 278
Packard, Cyrus, 260
Packard, Daniel, 50, 198, 199, 201, 202
Packard, David, 50, 197, 200, 204
Packard, David, 2d, 50
Packard, Elathan, 176
Packard, Elijah, 47
Packard, Eliphalet, 176, 257
Packard, Ephraim, 195, 211
Packard, Ezra, 50
Packard, Galen, 50
Packard, George, 119, 123
Packard, Hesekiah, 50, 182
Packard, Isaac, 50, 175, 204 (2), 206
Packard, James, 198, 199, 201, 202
Packard, Jason, 50
Packard, Jedediah, 9, 60
Packard, Jesse, 50
Packard, John, 176, 198, 199, 200, 202, 206
Packard, Jonathan, 176, 257
Packard, Joseph S., 50
Packard, Joshua, Jr., 278, 282
Packard, Josiah, 178, 260
Packard, Lewis, 175
Packard, Lincoln, 50
Packard, Luke, 50
Packard, Matthew, 177

Packard, Mayo, 49
Packard, Moses, 176
Packard, Nathan, 293
Packard, Nathaniel, 237, 278
Packard, Nehemiah, 159
Packard, Othenial, 43
Packard, Othniel, 89
Packard, Pardon, 51
Packard, Robert, 262, 266
Packard, Samuel, 47, 49, 176, 199, 200, 202
Packard, Saul, 198, 208
Packard, Shepard, 251, 255
Packard, Stephen, 177, 251, 255
Packard, Sullivan, 50
Packard, Sylvanus, 81
Packer, Edward, 19, 121, 124, 125
Packer, George, 19, 21, 120 (2), 121, 122 (2), 124 (3)
Packer, James, Jr., 90
Packer, Samuel, Jr., 251
Paddelford, James, 59
Paddock, Eddino, 57
Paddock, Joseph, 52, 54
Paddock, William, 78
Page, Benjamin, 24, 100
Page, Charles, 43, 89, 264
Page, Daniel, 183
Page, Daniel G., 2
Page, David, 271
Page, Ebenezer, 262, 266
Page, Edward H., 148
Page, Elijah, 259
Page, Ezekiel, 228
Page, Ezra, 262
Page, Francis, 262
Page, Henry, 16
Page, Insley, 17
Page, Jacob, 81
Page, James, 216, 264, 266
Page, James B., 59
Page, James W., 194
Page, Jeremiah, 282
Page, Jesse, 269
Page, John, 18, 70, 77, 82, 109, 150, 151, 179, 194, 229, 234, 264
Page, John A., 278, 279
Page, John C., 275
Page, Jonathan, 85, 295
Page, Joseph, 161
Page, Larkin P., 86
Page, Lewis, 264
Page, Moses, 224, 229
Page, Newell, 153
Page, Peter, 262
Page, Richard, 15, 30
Page, Rufus K., 270
Page, Samuel, 256, 264, 266, 276, 282, 296
Page, Samuel L., 135
Page, Saul, 132, 229
Page, Sewal, 279, 282
Page, Thaddeus, 26
Page, Timothy, 86, 199
Page, Timothy, Jr., 275
Page, William, 216, 288
Page, William, Jr., 288, 294
Page, Woodberry, 139
Page, Woodbury, 139
Paget, George, 224
Pain, Nathaniel, 274
Pain, Samuel, 233
Paine, Aldrich, 171
Paine, Alexander, 164, 165, 166

INDEX.

Paine, Alva, 98
Paine, Barney, 43
Paine, Charles, 209, 256
Paine, Francis, 22
Paine, Frederick, 236
Paine, Ira, 65
Paine, James, 62, 90
Paine, John, 240, 283
Paine, John K., 171
Paine, Jonathan, 171
Paine, Joseph, 171
Paine, Joshua, 171, 234
Paine, Josiah, 226
Paine, Leonard, 41
Paine, Levi, 45
Paine, P. Francis, 7
Paine, Parney, 89
Paine, Paschal, 61
Paine, Richard, 60, 160, 171, 173
Paine, Rufus, 94
Paine, Samuel, 43, 89, 174
Paine, Saul, 302
Paine, Stephen, 171
Paine, Thomas, 28, 160, 173, 259
Paine, Thomas, Jr., 170
Paine, Wales, 94
Paine, William, 171
Paine, William, Jr., 173
Paine, Zebulon A., 171
Paison, Paul, 191
Palfrey, Andrew, 138
Palfrey, George, 24
Palfrey, Richard, 134, 135
Palfrey, Thomas, 132
Palfrey, Warwick, 138, 141
Pall, Peter, 63
Palmenter, William, 24
Palmer, Alexander, 192, 195
Palmer, Amos, 279
Palmer, Asher, 198, 200, 202
Palmer, Bozabel, 303
Palmer, Braddock S., 218
Palmer, Charles, 287
Palmer, Daniel, 205 (3)
Palmer, David, 58
Palmer, Elijah, 273
Palmer, Elisha, 184, 188
Palmer, Enoch, 141
Palmer, Ephraim, 192, 195
Palmer, George, 84
Palmer, Gideon, 63
Palmer, Isaac, 63
Palmer, James, 191
Palmer, Jeremiah, 8
Palmer, John, 90, 161, 184, 188, 195, 273, 275
Palmer, Jonathan, 62, 184, 188
Palmer, Joseph, 226, 303
Palmer, Moses, 254
Palmer, Moses, Jr., 13
Palmer, Nathaniel, 200, 202, 208, 209, 291, 303
Palmer, Richard, 209
Palmer, Samuel, 1st, 276
Palmer, Samuel, 2d, 276
Palmer, Silas, 162
Palmer, Stephen, 139
Palmer, William, 184, 186, 188, 265, 274
Palmeter, Caleb, 237
Palmeter, Calvin D., 94
Palmeter, Joseph, 237
Palmeter, William, 31
Palton, David, 67
Panchard, Benjamin, 90

Papoon, Solomon, 7
Pappoon, Solomon, 22
Parcher, Daniel, 167
Pardee, Benjamin, 19
Parce, Jabez W., 256
Parish, Daniel, 65
Park, ———, 70
Park, Benjamin, 303
Park, Caleb, 32, 257
Park, Caleb, Jr., 222
Park, Isaac, 20
Park, John, 303
Park, Joshua, 222
Park, Moody, 82
Park, Oliver, 310
Park, Saul, 303
Park, Thomas, 303
Park, William, 24, 59, 115
Parker, Amos, 297, 300
Parker, Amos B., 70
Parker, Andrew, 9
Parker, Artemas, 29
Parker, Asa, 96
Parker, Avery, 1, 129
Parker, Bela, 4
Parker, Benjamin, 72, 90, 174
Parker, Benjamin M., 23
Parker, Caleb E., 153
Parker, Calvin, 72, 130
Parker, Cyrus, 48
Parker, David, 75, 80, 263, 267
Parker, Davis, 23
Parker, Ebenezer, 118
Parker, Eber, 40, 68
Parker, Edmund, Jr., 307
Parker, Edward, 20, 28, 259
Parker, Edward T., 83
Parker, Elias, 94
Parker, Elijah, 55
Parker, Elinda, 119
Parker, Elisha, 274, 303
Parker, Ephraim, 73
Parker, Fry, 156
Parker, George, 21, 72, 312
Parker, Giles, 94, 119
Parker, Isaac, 69, 72, 159
Parker, Jacob, 168, 281
Parker, James, 227, 271, 282
Parker, John, 58, 233
Parker, John A., 78
Parker, Jonas L., 8
Parker, Jonathan, 83, 307
Parker, Joseph, 8, 52, 75, 152, 223, 240, 254, 265, 267
Parker, Joshua, 75
Parker, Josiah, 88, 292
Parker, Josiah, Jr., 75
Parker, Kendall, 155
Parker, L., 42
Parker, Lemuel, 87
Parker, Levi, 88
Parker, Luther, 58, 215
Parker, Moses, 198, 200, 202, 208, 209
Parker, Nathan, 58
Parker, Nathaniel, 297, 300
Parker, Nehemiah, 28
Parker, Oliver, 216, 285, 291
Parker, Peter, 83
Parker, R. H., 84
Parker, Robert, 247
Parker, Robert H., 79
Parker, Samuel, 24, 111, 174

Parker, Samuel H., 113
Parker, Saul, 47
Parker, Seth, 75
Parker, Silas, 3
Parker, Silvanus, 72
Parker, Simeon, 239, 267
Parker, Simon, 285, 291
Parker, Sturges, 75
Parker, Thomas, 96, 274
Parker, Thomas G., 79
Parker, Timothy, 76, 118
Parker, Timothy, Jr., 117
Parker, Walter, 88
Parker, Ward M., 75
Parker, Washington, 8
Parker, William, 36, 79, 83, 88, 118, 149 (2), 247
Parker, William A., 87
Parker, Zachariah, 168
Parker, Zacheus, 263
Parkham, David, 307
Parkham, Simeon, 307
Parkhurst, Alexander, 5
Parkhurst, Elisha, 240, 302
Parkhurst, Horace, 98
Parkhurst, Jonathan, 179
Parkhurst, Nathan, 240
Parkill, Stephen, 30
Parkinson, John, 312
Parkman, Charles, 91
Parkman, Elias, 8
Parkman, George, 76
Parkman, Nathaniel, 108
Parkman, Samuel, 111, 112
Parkman, Samuel S., 111
Parkman, William, 209
Parks, ———, 84
Parks, Artemas, 48
Parks, Caleb, 257
Parks, Charles, 46
Parks, Chetham, 230
Parks, Daniel, 156 (2)
Parks, Ebenezer, 139
Parks, Edward, 223
Parks, James, 31, 156
Parks, Jesse, 48
Parks, John, 68
Parks, John D., 249, 297
Parks, Leonard, 80, 81, 110
Parks, Richard, 156 (2)
Parks, Royal M., 81
Parks, Thomas I., 230
Parks, William C., 28
Parlen, Almond, 178
Parlen, Ira, 178
Parlen, Oliver, 178
Parlin, Abel, 268
Parlin, Almond, 260
Parlin, Oliver, 260
Parmely, Benjamin, 65
Parmenter, Silas, 5
Parmer, Elnathan, 197
Parmer, Joseph, 46
Parmeter, Dexter, 60
Parris, Elias, 53
Parris, Enos, 102
Parris, John, 23
Parris, Orren, 49
Parris, Thomas, 49
Parrish, Ambrose, 129
Parrot, William, 161
Parrott, Benjamin, 118
Parshley, William, 249

INDEX. 403

Parshly, Ezekiel, 247
Parlsey, Eliphalet, 297, 298
Parson, Hiram, 282
Parson, Joseph T., 210
Parson, William, 40, 294
Parsons, Amos, 66, 163 (2)
Parsons, Charles, 241
Parsons, Daniel, 225
Parsons, David, 12, 16
Parsons, Davis, 65
Parsons, Eben, 12
Parsons, Ebenezer, 11
Parsons, George, 117, 223, 255
Parsons, George W., 92, 244
Parsons, Guy, 182, 191
Parsons, Haso, 4
Parsons, Henry, 83
Parsons, Jacob, 10
Parsons, James, 288
Parsons, Jeremiah, 227
Parsons, John, 13, 14, 45, 109
Parsons, John, Jr., 256
Parsons, John, 4th, 11
Parsons, Jonah, 3d, 13
Parsons, Jonathan, 14
Parsons, Joseph, 20
Parsons, Nathaniel, 229, 282
Parsons, Nicholas G., 13
Parsons, Samuel, 16, 23, 149
Parsons, Stephen, 65
Parsons, Theodore, 4
Parsons, Thomas, 13, 14, 79
Parsons, Timothy, 65
Parsons, William, 69, 287, 288
Parsons, Winthrop, 13
Parth, Abraham, 135
Partman, Daniel, 306
Partridge, David, 226
Partridge, Edward, 303
Partridge, Hiram, 48
Partridge, Ichabod, 186, 190
Partridge, James, 205 (2)
Partridge, John S., 92
Partridge, Joseph, 196
Partridge, Philip, 96
Partridge, Samuel, 48
Partridge, Thomas, 303
Partridge, William, 272
Partridge, William W., 92
Paskel, James F., 294
Paskell, James, 289
Paskell, John M., 289, 293
Patch, Abijah, 26
Patch, Abraham, 140
Patch, David, 134
Patch, Levi, 178
Patch, Reuben, 12
Patch, William, 36
Patch, William, 2d, 37
Pate, James N., 176
Patrick, Benjamin, 151, 256
Patrick, Charles, Jr., 173
Patrick, Stephen, 173
Patrick, William, 137
Patridge, Joseph, 221
Pattee, Arthur S., 25
Pattee, Benjamin, 247
Pattee, Samuel, 247
Patten, Actor, 235
Patten, Adams, 231
Patten, Daniel, 6, 22
Patten, David, 111

Patten, George F., 231
Patten, Hugh, 234
Patten, James B., 231
Patten, Joel B., 39, 71
Patten, John, 27
Patten, John H., 22
Patten, Joseph, 265, 306, 307
Patten, Matthew, 231
Patten, Moses B., 216
Patten, Nathaniel, 154 (2), 155, 312
Patten, Robert, 309 (4)
Patten, Thomas, 26
Patten, William, 231, 236, 296
Patten, William, Jr., 235
Patterson, Aaron, 270
Patterson, Abraham, 256
Patterson, Adolphus, 4
Patterson, Benjamin, 243, 246
Patterson, David, 185, 186, 301
Patterson, Elias, 189, 191
Patterson, Elisha, 235, 302
Patterson, George, 302
Patterson, H., 135
Patterson, Hans, 137
Patterson, James, Jr., 116
Patterson, John, 302
Patterson, John M., 270
Patterson, Nathan, 270
Patterson, Peter, 312
Patterson, Richard, 270
Patterson, Robert, 152, 254, 302
Patterson, Robert, 3d, 302
Patterson, Samuel, 185, 187
Patterson, Saul, 190
Patterson, Sylvanus, 64
Patterson, William, 154, 185, 270
Pattey, William, 83
Patton, Hugh, 236
Patton, James, 214
Patton, John, 214
Patton, Samuel, 215
Patty, John, 49
Paul, Dean, 59
Paul, Isaac, Jr., 59
Paul, Jacob W., 287
Paul, James, 204, 229
Paul, Micah, 62
Paul, Michall, 31
Paul, Oliver, 229
Paul, Samuel, 168
Paul, William, 211
Pavil, Hickborn, 303
Pavol, David, 63
Payen, Lemuel, 86
Payn, Burnell, 33
Payne, Abraham, 57
Payne, Calvin, 57
Payne, Ebenezer, 117
Payne, Ezra, 70
Payne, Henry, 57
Payne, Solomon, 57
Payne, William, 69
Payson, Asa, 200, 201, 203
Payson, Ephraim, 203
Payson, Ephraim, Jr., 199, 200
Payson, Hartwell, 286
Payson, John, 292, 293
Payson, Leonard, 81
Payson, Noah, 203
Payson, Noyce, 200
Payson, Noyes, 199
Payson, Silas, 182, 191

Payson, Sion, 201, 202
Peabody, Aaron, 7, 112
Peabody, Asa, 258
Peabody, Chandler, 93
Peabody, Ebenezer, 83, 87
Peabody, Francis, 9
Peabody, George, 18
Peabody, Isaac, 9
Peabody, John, 76, 110
Peabody, Joseph, 132
Peabody, Oliver, 265
Peabody, Stephen, 286, 290
Peabody, Stephen H., 121, 124
Peabody, Webster, 134, 135, 136, 140
Peach, John, 22
Peacock, Benjamin, 272
Peacock, Edward, 272
Peacock, James, 272
Peak, Clark, 161
Peaks, William, 103
Pealer, David, 82
Pearce, Abiel, 181
Pearce, Anson, 53
Pearce, Crocker, 256
Pearce, Elias, 181
Pearce, Ephraim, 96
Pearce, George W., 9
Pearce, Isaac, 61
Pearce, Jonah, 60
Pearce, Malitiah H., 53
Pearce, Pardon, 63
Pearce, Pason, 274
Pearce, Robert, 98
Pearce, Seth, 8
Pearce, William, 167
Pearl, Benjamin, 261
Pearl, Dimond, 153, 261
Pearl, Joseph, 254
Pearly, John, 116
Pearse, Jonathan, 312
Pearsey, Gilmore, Jr., 250
Pearson, Aaron, 97
Pearson, Abel, 16
Pearson, Abner, 18
Pearson, Amos, 14, 78
Pearson, Andrew, Jr., 181
Pearson, Charles, 19, 121, 124
Pearson, David, 17
Pearson, Henry, 16, 20
Pearson, Henry S., 241, 242
Pearson, Ira, 35
Pearson, Joseph, 136, 140
Pearson, Nathaniel, 15
Pearson, Paul, 184, 188
Pearson, Robert, 7, 19, 20, 22
Pearson, Samuel, 68
Pearson, Thomas, 18, 25, 124
Pearson, Thomas, Jr., 121
Pearson, William, 28
Pearsons, Joseph, 87
Pearsons, Thomas, 87
Pearsons, William, 78
Pearster, William, 154
Peart, Jacob, 37, 38
Peary, John N., 161
Peary, Moses, 151
Peary, Stephen, 151
Peas, Barsilla, 73
Peasby, Abial, 190
Peasby, John, 190
Pease, Alexander, 199
Pease, Charles, 44, 307

INDEX.

Pease, Elijah, 31, 229
Pease, George, 199, 200, 202
Pease, Henry M., 199, 200, 202
Pease, James, 20, 121, 125
Pease, Lemuel, 47
Pease, Lewis, 221, 244
Pease, Mark, 151
Pease, Nathan, Jr., 199, 200, 203
Pease, Palatiah, 199
Pease, Shubal M., 199, 200, 203
Pease, Thomas, 239
Pease, Warren, 227
Peaslee, Abiel, 191
Peaslee, Jonathan, Jr., 196
Peaslee, Nathan, 2d, 191
Peasley, Ezekiel, 190
Peasley, James, 190
Peasley, Nathan, Jr., 190
Peasley, Oliver, 186
Peasly, Daniel, Jr., 190
Peasly, Jonathan, Jr., 192
Peavey, John, 199, 200
Peavey, Samuel, 238
Pebbles, Charles, Jr., 222
Pebbles, James, 222
Peck, Benoni, 93
Peck, Chaney, 93
Peck, Edward, 61
Peck, Erasmus R., 60
Peck, George, 41
Peck, James, 31
Peck, Jason, 60
Peck, Jonathan, 9, 60
Peck, Oliver C., 10
Peck, Philip W., 271
Peck, Samuel, 90
Peck, William, 60, 61
Pecker, George W., 89
Peckham, David, 283
Peckham, Silas, 59
Peckham, William, 55
Peckman, William, 58
Pedrick, Benjamin, 7
Pedrick, John, 134, 135
Pedrick, John B., 7, 22
Pedrick, William, 7, 22
Peel, Josiah, 140
Peel, Robert, 138
Peel, Robert, Jr., 134
Peety, Samuel, 304
Peirce, Calvin, 64
Peirce, Henry, 134
Peirce, Isaac, 53
Peirce, Jonathan, 136
Peirce, Leonard, 161
Peirce, Parker H., 25
Peirce, Robert, 225
Pelfrey, Jonathan, 80
Pelham, Thomas, 110
Pellon, John, 16
Pelton, Joel, 190
Pender, Isaac, 43, 89
Pendleton, Alexander, 203
Pendleton, Arthur, 198, 199, 200, 207
Pendleton, Henry, 198, 200, 202, 207, 209
Pendleton, Hiram, 62
Pendleton, Jonathan, 302
Pendleton, Phineas, 308
Pendleton, William, 302
Pendley, James, 252
Penfield, Nathan, 174
Pengres, William, 151

Penley, James, 255
Penley, William, 253
Penly, William, 257
Pennel, Isaac, 273
Pennel, James, 210
Pennel, Joshua, 235, 236
Pennel, Thomas, 210
Pennell, Jacob, 209, 298
Pennell, John, 307
Pennell, Joseph, 177, 265
Pennell, Josiah, 244
Pennell, Robert, 298
Pennell, Thomas, 148
Pennell, William, 298
Penney, Arba, 267
Penney, Daniel, 264
Penney, John, 264
Pennington, Daniel, 171
Pennington, Elisha, 96
Penny, Aaron, 256
Penny, Benjamin, 217
Penny, Ephraim, 153
Penny, George, 263
Penny, Ichabod, 54
Penny, John, 54, 245
Penny, John, Jr., 262
Penny, Levi, 104
Penny, Nehemiah, 263
Penny, Stephen, 253
Penny, Thomas, 180
Pennyman, James, 70
Pens, Robert, 133
Pepper, Abner, 45
Pepper, Ashbel, 93
Pepper, Benjamin, 115
Pepper, Jacob, 93
Pepper, Phiney, 44
Pepper, Simon, 107
Perce, Jonathan, 133
Perea, James, 281
Percifal, Freeman, 73
Percifal, John, 73, 74
Percifal, Timothy, 74
Percival, Isaac, 75
Percival, James, 40
Percival, Trueman, 167
Percy, Arthur, 248
Percy, Ellis, 248
Percy, Gilmore, 248
Percy, Levi, 1
Percy, Nathaniel, 248
Percy, William, 231
Perd, James, 188
Pere, Charles, 167
Pere, James, Jr., 167
Perham, Hiram, 48
Perham, Jotham, 251
Perham, Lemuel, 251
Perham, Seled, 167
Perham, Silas, 227
Perkins, Alden, 55, 58
Perkins, Andrew L., 274
Perkins, Andrew S., 267
Perkins, Anthony, 19
Perkins, Benjamin, 77
Perkins, Caleb, 66
Perkins, Daniel, 137, 193, 194, 197
Perkins, David, 306
Perkins, Ebenezer, 175
Perkins, Ebenezer, Jr., 193
Perkins, Edmund, 40
Perkins, Edward, 117

Perkins, Eleazer, 175
Perkins, Eliphalet, 272
Perkins, Elisha, 141
Perkins, Enoch, 235
Perkins, Enoch, 2d, 235
Perkins, Enos, 81
Perkins, Ephraim, 199, 200
Perkins, Ezra, 308
Perkins, Francis, 308, 309 (2)
Perkins, Gaius, 311
Perkins, George, 36, 37, 57, 310
Perkins, Henry, 53
Perkins, Horace, 67
Perkins, Ignatius, 64
Perkins, Isaiah, 253
Perkins, Israel, 116, 308, 309
Perkins, Jacob, 133, 183
Perkins, James, 160, 176
Perkins, Jesse, 245
Perkins, John, 20, 59, 64, 134, 137, 140, 214, 215, 269
Perkins, John C., 52
Perkins, John H., 109
Perkins, John M., 180
Perkins, Jonathan, 135, 271, 275
Perkins, Jonathan S., 9
Perkins, Joseph, 195, 257, 308
Perkins, Joseph, Jr., 253
Perkins, Joseph, 2d, 308
Perkins, Joseph H., 158
Perkins, Levi, 235, 236
Perkins, Luther, 253, 257, 309
Perkins, Moses, 14, 177, 260
Perkins, Nahum, 148, 245
Perkins, Nathan, 52, 277
Perkins, Nathaniel, 14, 119, 122, 179
Perkins, Nathaniel T., 279
Perkins, Noah, 57, 154
Perkins, Oliver, 253
Perkins, Russell, 4
Perkins, Samuel, 148, 184
Perkins, Silva, 54
Perkins, Simeon, 252
Perkins, Stephens, 14, 217
Perkins, Thomas, 140
Perkins, Thomas S., 199, 200
Perkins, William, 186, 187, 190, 308
Perkins, Zalli, 53
Perkins, Zebediah, 187
Perley, Abraham, 210
Perley, Daniel, 211
Perley, Henry, 116
Perley, Isaac, 210
Perley, John, 209
Perley, Porter, 258
Perley, Saul, 211
Perley, Thomas, 212
Perly, David, 94
Perly, Francis, 277
Permenter, Joseph, 65
Perrin, George, 84
Perry, Arthur, 32, 71
Perry, Ather, 75
Perry, Benjamin, 66, 275
Perry, Benjamin F., 253
Perry, Bethure, 262
Perry, Caleb, 252
Perry, Caleb E., 41
Perry, Charles, 79
Perry, David, 197, 204 (2), 206, 215, 299
Perry, Dimon, 159
Perry, Ebenezer, 26, 262

INDEX. 405

Perry, Edmund, 280
Perry, Edward, 9, 62
Perry, Elijah, 128
Perry, Elisha, 228
Perry, Ezra, 32
Perry, Franklin, 280
Perry, Gad, 177, 257
Perry, George, 22, 26
Perry, Gideon, 1, 103
Perry, Heman, 71, 75
Perry, Henry, 156
Perry, Isaac, 27
Perry, Israel, 172, 198
Perry, Jabes, 41
Perry, James, 71, 101, 145, 252
Perry, James M., 231
Perry, Jeduthan, 48
Perry, John, 43, 58, 80, 81, 89, 101, 127, 181, 198, 252, 256, 280
Perry, Jonah, 94
Perry, Joseph, 250 (2), 252
Perry, Joseph, Jr., 255
Perry, Joshua, Jr., 252
Perry, Josiah, 5
Perry, Lemuel, 10
Perry, Levi, 177, 228
Perry, Little, 7
Perry, Luke, 94
Perry, Maish, 256
Perry, Mark, 250 (2)
Perry, Miles, 80, 83
Perry, Mitaliah, 71
Perry, Nathan, 1
Perry, Nathaniel, 129
Perry, Otis, 52, 156
Perry, Phineas, 72
Perry, Phinehas, 56, 75
Perry, Prince, 72, 75
Perry, Robert, 231, 311
Perry, S., 84
Perry, Salathiel, 126
Perry, Samuel, 54, 66
Perry, Seth, 262
Perry, Sheldon, 23 (2), 26, 28, 68, 82, 114
Perry, Silas, 72
Perry, Simeon, 141
Perry, Solomon, 72, 75
Perry, Stephen, 53, 72, 73
Perry, Thomas, 177, 198, 199, 200, 208, 250
Perry, William, 209, 244, 269
Perry, Zacheus, 72
Perry, Zenas, 262
Perry, Zoath, 125
Perseval, Zenas, 240
Persley, John, 231
Person, Aaron, 176
Persons, Daniel, 260
Persons, Quartus, 45
Persons, Thaddeus, 67
Persons, William, Jr., 253
Pervin, Meshack, 136
Peters, Andrew, 163, 164
Peters, Horace, 40
Peters, Joseph, 90
Peters, Richard, 17
Peters, Simon, 297, 299
Peterson, Alfred, 279
Peterson, Africa, 296
Peterson, Benjamin, 233, 296, 297, 299
Peterson, Benjamin, 2d, 297
Peterson, Charles, 129
Peterson, Clark, 129

Peterson, Daniel, 155
Peterson, George, 131
Peterson, John, 40, 112 (2), 299
Peterson, Nathaniel, 131
Peterson, Thomas, 84
Peterson, William, 283
Petingel, Holmes, 201 (2)
Petingill, Asa, 88
Pettee, Asa, 9
Pettee, Oliver, 99
Pettee, Seth, 86
Pettee, Simon, 99
Pettegrow, Francis, 160
Pettegrow, Nahum, 160
Pettengale, Samuel, 30
Pettengill, Cuttin, 17
Pettengill, David, 17
Pettengill, Eaton, 177
Pettengill, Moses, 17
Pettengill, Nathaniel, 17
Pettes, John, 248
Pettingill, Abraham, 283
Pettingill, Ansel, 276
Pettingill, Arcadus, 168, 281
Pettingill, Benjamin, 158, 170
Pettingill, Benjamin, Jr., 89
Pettingill, David, 148
Pettingill, Elisha, 279 (2)
Pettingill, Ethan, 260
Pettingill, Harvey, 168
Pettingill, Harvy, 277
Pettingill, Howard, 276
Pettingill, Jacob, 211
Pettingill, John, 168, 170, 281
Pettingill, John, Jr., 168
Pettingill, Jonathan, 18
Pettingill, Joseph, 168
Pettingill, Mark, 280
Pettingill, Moses, 14
Pettingill, Nathan, 255
Pettingill, Nathaniel, 166, 277
Pettingill, Real, 168
Pettingill, Sumner, 148, 235
Pettis, Benjamin, 61
Pettis, Daniel, 61
Pettis, Ezekiel, 2d, 61
Pettis, Silas, 55
Pettis, Thomas, 61
Petty, Asa, 56
Petty, Benjamin, 56
Petty, Elias, 56
Petty, John, 133
Petty, Joseph, 79
Petty, Martin, 90
Petty, Moses, 56
Petty, Nathan, 56
Petty, Pardon, 56
Petty, Philip, 56
Petty, Silas, 56
Petty, Stephen, 56
Petty, Thomas, 56
Pettyplace, William, 138
Peva, James, 184
Pew, Richard, 14
Pew, William, 9
Pheland, Gad, 45
Phelps, Aaron G., 46
Phelps, Africa, 48
Phelps, Benjamin, Jr., 45
Phelps, Daniel, 32
Phelps, Edward, 96
Phelps, George, 3, 44, 159

Phelps, Jacob, Jr., 116
Phelps, John, 5, 87
Phelps, Jonah, 160
Phelps, Joseph, 10
Phelps, Julius, 4
Phelps, Leonard, 29
Phelps, Lilly, 23
Phelps, Nathan, 32
Phelps, Simeon, 45
Phelps, Theodore, 9
Phelps, Thomas, 3
Phelps, Timothy, 27
Phelps, William, 4, 160
Phelps, William B., 274
Philbrick, Benjamin, 158
Philbrick, Caleb P., 165, 166
Philbrick, David, 158
Philbrick, Elias, 282
Philbrick, James, 171, 191
Philbrick, John, 174
Philbrick, Joseph, 179
Philbrick, Moses, 228
Philbrick, Nathan S., 281
Philbrick, Walter W., 281
Philbrick, William, 274
Philbrook, Ebenezer, Jr., 190
Philbrook, Elias, 280
Philbrook, James, 190
Philbrook, Jeremiah, 204
Philbrook, Jerry, 197
Philbrook, John, 280
Philbrook, Nathaniel S., 280
Philbrook, Urel, 302
Philbrook, W. W., 280
Philbrooks, John, 188
Philip, Ichabod S., 6
Philip, Leonard, 19
Philips, Asa, 93
Philips, Baytus, 57
Philips, Benjamin C., 81
Philips, David, 59, 61
Philips, David A., 7
Philips, Edward, 224
Philips, Ephraim, 59
Philips, Ira, 55
Philips, Isacah, 61
Philips, Joel, 64
Philips, John, 62
Philips, Joseph, 7
Philips, Nathaniel, 7, 21, 62, 80, 84
Philips, Pierce, 57
Philips, Richard, 6
Philips, Robert, 7
Philips, Saul, 260
Philips, Sawyer, 64
Philips, Serrannus, 59
Philips, Seth, 242
Philips, Surannus, 62
Philips, Thomas, 7, 170
Philips, William, 7
Philips, William B., 65
Phillip, William K., 78
Phillips, Amasa, 53
Phillips, Amos, 167
Phillips, Charles E., 165, 166
Phillips, Cyrus B., 50
Phillips, Daniel H., 90
Phillips, Edmund, 259
Phillips, Elisha, 31
Phillips, George, 125
Phillips, Harvey, 64
Phillips, Henry, 163 (2)

INDEX.

Phillips, Ichabod, 21
Phillips, James, 14, 161
Phillips, John, 22
Phillips, Joseph, 22
Phillips, Nathaniel, 109
Phillips, Nicholas, 301
Phillips, Otis, 178, 260
Phillips, Reuel, 257
Phillips, Richard, 22, 90
Phillips, Ruel, 176, 254
Phillips, Samuel, 41, 69
Phillips, Seth, 241
Phillips, Silas, 60
Phillips, Southerland, 239
Phillips, Thomas, 82, 92, 257
Phillips, William, 22, 263
Phillips, Zacheus, 33
Philpot, Andrew, 269
Philpot, Moses, 269
Philpot, Richard, 269
Phinney, Abner, 72
Phinney, Alexander, 173
Phinney, Asa, 72
Phinney, Braddock, 72
Phinney, Calvin, 32
Phinney, Coleman, 173
Phinney, Ebeneser, 72
Phinney, Edward, 72, 75
Phinney, Elisha, 72
Phinney, Gershom, 76
Phinney, Isaiah, 75
Phinney, Jabes, 72, 75
Phinney, Jason, 95
Phinney, John, 72, 123, 158 (2), 273
Phinney, Joseph, 70
Phinney, Josiah, 72
Phinney, Nathan, 173
Phinney, Nathaniel, 173
Phinney, Robinson, 72
Phinney, Thomas, 74
Phinny, David, 75
Phinny, Gersham, 73
Phinny, Josiah, 73
Phippen, Abraham, 133, 140
Phippen, Hardy, 138
Phippen, Robert, 137
Phipps, James, 67
Phipps, Joseph, 139 (2)
Phipps, William K., 82
Phlinn, John, 27
Piatt, Laban, 102
Piatt, Matthew, 102
Piatt, William, 102
Pickard, Daniel, 214
Pickard, David, 276
Pickard, Ephraim, 34
Pickard, James, 185
Pickard, Joshua, 216
Pickard, Nathaniel, 14
Pickard, Samuel, 14
Pickard, Thomas, 34
Pickard, Thomas, Jr., 276
Pickens, David, 229
Pickens, John, Jr., 229
Pickens, Leonard, 229
Pickering, Stephen, 139 (2)
Picket, Joseph, 89
Picket, Moses, 22
Pickett, Benjamin, 31
Pickett, John, 34
Pickett, John, Jr., 31, 38
Pickett, Joseph, 31

Pickett, Josiah, 34
Pickett, Richard, 34 (2), 38
Pickett, Thomas L., 34
Pickham, Philip, 56
Pickins, Silas, 53
Pickins, Zacheus, 53
Pickman, Benjamin S., 113
Pickman, Benjamin T., 7
Pickman, Levi, 20
Pidge, Palemon, 62
Pidgin, Benjamin, 19, 120 (2), 121, 123, 124 (2)
Pierce, Abraham, 1, 256
Pierce, Alden, 47
Pierce, Asa, 276
Pierce, Benajah, 52
Pierce, Benjamin, 129
Pierce, Benjamin F., 3
Pierce, Benjamin I., 153
Pierce, Benjamin T., 261
Pierce, Besalcel, 200
Pierce, Bezzilla, 197, 204
Pierce, Charles, 278
Pierce, Clothier, 59
Pierce, Comfort, 60
Pierce, Cyrus, 228
Pierce, Daniel, 210, 233
Pierce, Darius, 60
Pierce, David, 183, 185, 188, 213 (2), 217
Pierce, Dennis, 130
Pierce, Eaton, 53
Pierce, Ebeneser, Jr., 66
Pierce, Edward B., 183, 188
Pierce, Eli, 102
Pierce, Elijah, 40
Pierce, Eliphalet, 52, 102
Pierce, Elisha, 52, 59
Pierce, Emery, 27
Pierce, Enoch, 17
Pierce, Enos, 102
Pierce, Ephraim, 133
Pierce, Freeman, 52
Pierce, George, 103, 134, 135
Pierce, George P., 133, 136
Pierce, George T., 140
Pierce, George W., 183, 185, 188
Pierce, Gilbert, 52
Pierce, Hach, 60
Pierce, Hollis, 3
Pierce, Hopkins, 245
Pierce, Isaac, 226, 268, 307
Pierce, Israel, 60
Pierce, Israel, 3d, 60
Pierce, Jacob, 185
Pierce, James, 3, 93, 269
Pierce, James W., 13
Pierce, John, 24, 27, 51, 62, 68, 82
Pierce, John, Jr., 153
Pierce, Jonathan, 8, 52, 87
Pierce, Joseph, 53, 93, 165, 166, 246 (2), 253, 312
Pierce, Josiah, 33, 153
Pierce, Lambert, 39
Pierce, Levi, 54, 258
Pierce, Lewis, 38
Pierce, Luther, 67, 115, 179
Pierce, Nathan, 62
Pierce, Nathan, Jr., 181
Pierce, Nathaniel, 217, 268
Pierce, Nicholas, 18, 269
Pierce, Oliver, 170
Pierce, Peter H., 52
Pierce, Preserved, 61

Pierce, Robert, 43
Pierce, Rowland, 52
Pierce, Russell, 55
Pierce, Samuel, 26, 58, 153, 169, 174, 213 (2)
Pierce, Seth, 295
Pierce, Silas, 27, 93
Pierce, Silas, 2d, 52
Pierce, Stephen, 245
Pierce, Sylvester, 183, 185, 188
Pierce, Thacker, 53
Pierce, Thomas, 30, 34, 38, 65, 90, 183, 188, 278
Pierce, Thomas H., 43, 89
Pierce, Timothy, 96
Pierce, William, 33, 36, 37, 48, 60, 261
Pierce, Zadoc, 65
Pierce, Zadock, 51
Pierson, John, Jr., 252
Pike, Barnabas, 119
Pike, Benjamin, 7, 85
Pike, Charles, 9
Pike, Daniel, 120, 121, 123, 124
Pike, Elisha, 67, 87, 179
Pike, Hugh, 138
Pike, Jabes, 89
Pike, Jacob, 133, 136, 211
Pike, James, 223
Pike, James T., 18
Pike, Jesse, 271
Pike, Job K., 151
Pike, John, 153
Pike, John, Jr., 252
Pike, Joseph, 18, 124
Pike, Joseph, Jr., 121
Pike, Joshua, 305
Pike, Leonard, 64
Pike, Moses, 16
Pike, Moses F., 41
Pike, Nathaniel, 47, 245, 252
Pike, Parley F., 198, 202
Pike, Perley F., 208
Pike, Perly F., 208, 209
Pike, Richard, 83
Pike, Robert, 160, 301
Pike, Samuel, 151, 252
Pike, Samuel D., 221
Pike, Saul, 254
Pike, Stephen, 9
Pike, William, 81
Pilby, James, 312
Pilby, Moses, 312
Pilgrim, Israel, 44
Pilkin, Edward, 92
Pillsbury, Amos, 15
Pillsbury, Charles, 19
Pillsbury, Daniel, 15, 122, 123, 171
Pillsbury, John, 15, 170
Pillsbury, Joshua, 219
Pillsbury, Silas, 139
Pillsbury, Thomas, 219
Pillsbury, Tristram, 108, 171
Pillsbury, William C., 122
Pilsbury, Amos, 275
Pilsbury, Charles, 119, 120
Pilsbury, Daniel, 119, 120
Pilsbury, Enoch, 100
Pilsbury, George, 236
Pilsbury, Isaac, 275
Pilsbury, John, 197, 204 (2), 206
Pilsbury, Johnson, 198, 199
Pilsbury, Johnston, 202
Pilsbury, Joseph, Jr., 197, 204 (2)

INDEX.

Pilsbury, Nathan, 197, 203, 204
Pilsbury, Nathan, Jr., 206
Pilsbury, Nathaniel, 197, 204
Pilsbury, William, 274
Pilsbury, William C., 89, 119
Pincin (?), Elias, 104
Pincin (?), Perez, 104
Pincer, Benjamin, 97
Pingree, Daniel R., 119
Pingree, Hezekiah, 256
Pingree, Hoyt, 256
Pingree, Parker, 151
Pingree, William, 260
Pingrey, David R., 122
Pingrey, Hezekiah, 253
Pingrey, Hoyt, 253
Pingrey, Samuel, 253
Pingrey, Stephen, Jr., 253
Pingrey, William, 253
Pinkham, Abraham, 262
Pinkham, Amos, 180
Pinkham, Andrew, 170
Pinkham, Benjamin, 284
Pinkham, Cornelius, 54
Pinkham, Ebenezer, 58
Pinkham, Francis, 308
Pinkham, Ichabod, 183, 185, 188
Pinkham, Isaac, 183, 185, 189
Pinkham, James, 279
Pinkham, John, 180, 183, 262, 284, 287
Pinkham, Nathan, 147, 183, 189, 191
Pinkham, Nathaniel, 185, 272
Pinkham, Otis, 43
Pinkham, Reuben, 267
Pinkham, Samuel, 183, 185, 189
Pinkham, Solomon, 183, 189
Pinkham, Thomas, 183, 185, 189
Pinkham, Walter, 262
Pinkham, William, 225
Piper, Alexander H., 101
Piper, David, 216
Piper, Gilman, 35
Piper, Joseph, 18
Piper, Moses, 111
Piper, Peletiah, 245
Piper, Samuel, 290
Piper, Silas, 100, 230
Piper, Stephen, 244
Piper, Thomas, 169
Piper, Thomas S., 277
Pishon, Frederic, 266
Pishon, Isaac, 161
Pishon, Reuben, 262, 266
Pitcher, Calvin, 301
Pitcher, David, 2
Pitcher, Earle, 9
Pitcher, James, 291
Pitcher, Job, 302
Pitcher, John, 291, 294
Pitcher, Nathaniel, 291, 311
Pitcher, Robert P., 64
Pitcher, Samuel, 125
Pitman, Benjamin, 139
Pitman, John, 28
Pitman, Joshua, 79
Pitman, Joshua, Jr., 25
Pitman, Michel, 132
Pitman, Saul, 139
Pitsinger, John, 64
Pitsinger, Jonathan, 64
Pitsley, Abraham, 57
Pitsley, Alexander, 57

Pitsley, Francis, 57
Pitsley, James, 57
Pitt, Adam, 263
Pitt, William, 285, 287
Pitte, Joseph, 102
Pittee, John, 220
Pittee, Nathaniel, Jr., 96
Pitts, Adam, 266
Pitts, Benjamin, 155, 312
Pitts, Ichabod, 263
Pitts, John, 59, 270
Pitts, Lindall, 69
Pitts, Philip, 224
Pitty, Joseph, 26
Pixley, Edmund, 31
Place, Charles, 186, 191
Place, Henry, 1
Place, Joseph, 59
Place, Joshua, 195
Place, Samuel, 60
Plaisted, Andrew, 173
Plaisted, Ichabod, Jr., 272
Plaisted, Joseph, 269
Plaisted, Roger, 172
Platts, Moses, 5
Plimpton, Asa, 99
Plimpton, Daniel, 97
Plimpton, Elias, 97
Plimpton, Elijah, 99
Plimpton, Henry, 97
Plimpton, John, 90
Plimpton, Ziba, 97
Plumer, Ezra, 27
Plummer, Aaron, 181, 233, 239
Plummer, Abraham, 172
Plummer, Arthur, 272
Plummer, Benjamin, 272
Plummer, Christopher, 171
Plummer, Daniel, 157, 179, 219, 232, 296
Plummer, David, 17, 169
Plummer, Eber, 12
Plummer, Edward, 210
Plummer, Elliot, 210
Plummer, Enoch, 19, 196
Plummer, Henry, 9
Plummer, Isaac, 233
Plummer, Isaac, Jr., 171
Plummer, Isaiah, 17
Plummer, Jeremiah, 184, 188, 297
Plummer, John, 157 (2), 169, 192, 195, 239, 281
Plummer, Joseph, 17, 18
Plummer, Joshua, 80, 90, 115, 172
Plummer, Josiah, 258
Plummer, Lemuel D., 148
Plummer, Luther, 300
Plummer, Major, 221
Plummer, Micajah, 12
Plummer, Michael, 154
Plummer, Moses, 9, 27, 114, 148, 165, 166, 172, 218, 234, 256
Plummer, Moses, Jr., 172
Plummer, Moses I., 243
Plummer, Nathan, 122, 125
Plummer, Nathaniel, 15, 148, 188
Plummer, Stephen, 17
Plummer, Thomas, 18, 243
Plummer, Timothy, 215
Plummer, Tristram, 19, 121, 124
Plummer, William, 17, 169, 281
Plummer, William, Jr., 17
Poke, Benjamin, 279

Poke, William, 312
Poland, John, 145, 192
Poland, Nehemiah, 192, 195
Poland, Oliver, 138
Poland, Sylvanus, 225, 260
Polin, David, 138
Pollan, John, 181
Pollard, Amos F., 24, 80
Pollard, Barton, 267
Pollard, Charles, 78, 275
Pollard, George, 23, 146, 297, 299
Pollard, Henry D., 239, 267
Pollard, John, 38
Pollard, Jonathan, 149
Pollard, Levi, 236, 267
Pollard, Oliver, 225
Pollard, Stephen, 159
Pollard, William, 236, 237, 267
Polley, Asahel, 232
Pollock, George, 82
Pollock, Neal, 82
Polly, Amos, 48
Polly, Asahel, 232
Polly, Jacob, 48
Polly, Joseph, 93
Polly, Luther, 5
Polly, William, 232
Pollyes, William, Jr., 242
Poltusky, John, 157 (2)
Pomeroy, Benjamin, 305
Pomeroy, Jeremiah, 305
Pomery, William, 162
Pomroy, Aaron, 67
Pomroy, Andrew, 214
Pomroy, Arad, 133, 136
Pomroy, Arad H., 214
Pomroy, Barry G., 287
Pomroy, Isaac, 30
Pomroy, James, 30
Pomroy, Joseph, Jr., 214
Pomroy, Richard, 220
Pomroy, Samuel, 45
Pomroy, Spencer, 67
Pomroy, William, 214
Pond, ——, 47
Pond, Asa A., 163, 164
Pond, Benjamin, 27, 97
Pond, Caleb, 242
Pond, Jasper, 163, 164
Pond, Jemotis, Jr., 86
Pond, Jeremiah, 48
Pond, John A., 97
Pond, Jones, 5
Pond, Labin, 162 (2)
Pond, Lewis, 86
Pond, Loring, 214
Pond, Moses, 39
Pond, Preston, 5
Ponno, John, 114
Pool, Aaron, 12
Pool, Abinther, 55
Pool, Abram H., 11
Pool, Daniel, 50
Pool, David, 176
Pool, Eben, 10, 12
Pool, Ebenezer, 193, 220
Pool, Francis, 11, 12
Pool, George P., 283
Pool, Henry, 25
Pool, Isaac, 185
Pool, James, Jr., 12
Pool, John, 11, 49, 95

408   INDEX.

Pool, John, 4th, 11
Pool, Joshua, 9, 12
Pool, Major, 55
Pool, Moses, 11
Pool, Oliver, 95
Pool, Peres, 126
Pool, Samuel H., 192
Pool, Samuel P., 176
Pool, Solomon, Jr., 12
Pool, William, 12, 43
Pool, William, Jr., 50
Pool, Zebulon, 11
Poole, Abijah, Jr., 149
Poole, Asa, 253
Poole, James, Jr., 243
Poole, Samuel P., 257
Pooler, John, 266
Poor, Amos, 152
Poor, Benjamin, 16, 303
Poor, Daniel, 100
Poor, David, 16
Poor, Eben, 16
Poor, Edward, 218
Poor, Edward L., 261
Poor, Edward S., 261
Poor, Eliphalet, 16
Poor, Enoch, 16
Poor, Henry, 100
Poor, Isaac, 18, 26, 119, 122
Poor, James, 21
Poor, John, 16
Poor, Samuel, 16
Poor, Thomas, 16
Poor, Thomas, 2d, 9
Poor, Timothy, 100
Poor, William, 150, 152
Poore, Andrew, 48
Poors, Nathaniel, 295
Pope, Calvin J., 26
Pope, Cornelius, 55
Pope, Ebenezer, 84
Pope, Edward, 54, 242
Pope, Edward, Jr., 97
Pope, Enos, 55, 58
Pope, Freeman, 55, 57, 127
Pope, Ichabod, 4
Pope, Jesper, 140
Pope, Joseph, 8, 113
Pope, Joseph H., 125
Pope, Lervin, 73, 76
Pope, Loring, 55
Pope, Ralph, 84
Pope, Seth, 73
Pope, Silas, 55, 58
Pope, Stephen, 31
Pope, Thomas, 92
Porter, Aaron, 31, 135, 137
Porter, Alfred, 9
Porter, Amasa, 280
Porter, Asa, 39, 216
Porter, Asael, 151
Porter, Asahel, 96, 254
Porter, Benjamin, 83, 112, 202, 212, 216
Porter, Calvin, 280
Porter, Charles, 26, 251
Porter, David, 151, 213, 254
Porter, Ebenezer, 29
Porter, Edward, 80
Porter, Edward J., 111
Porter, Eleazer A., 99
Porter, Elijah, 43, 89
Porter, Elisha, 92

Porter, Ezra, 191
Porter, Ezra, Jr., 182 (2)
Porter, George, 307
Porter, Harvey, 146
Porter, Henry, 57
Porter, James, 228, 262
Porter, Jeremiah, 34
Porter, Jeremy, 283
Porter, Job, 7
Porter, John, 19, 34, 35 (2), 79, 230, 251, 255
Porter, Jonathan, 64, 242
Porter, Josiah, 40
Porter, Nehemiah, 258
Porter, Rufus, 243, 246, 256
Porter, Rufus K., 249
Porter, Rufus R., 297
Porter, Samuel, 43
Porter, Simon, 303
Porter, Stephen, 230
Porter, Stewart, 241
Porter, Thomas, 7, 25
Porter, Tyler, 212, 213
Porter, Warren, 9
Porter, William L., 68
Porterfield, J., 247
Porterfield, James, 218 (2)
Porterfield, William, 218
Poshard, Abraham, 262
Poshard, David, 262
Post, Enoch, 197, 204 (2)
Post, Ezekiel, 197, 204 (2), 206
Post, Horace, 29
Post, Peter, 18
Post, Richard H., 117
Post, Stephen, 198, 199, 200, 202
Post, Zachariah, 204
Post, Zacheus, 197
Pote, Samuel, 226
Potter, Aaron, 185, 190
Potter, Alexander, 226, 273
Potter, Ambrose, 64
Potter, Amos, 273
Potter, Asa, 78, 258
Potter, Bailey, 272
Potter, Benjamin, 14, 35, 232 (2)
Potter, Briggs, 66
Potter, Charles, 247
Potter, Collins, 247
Potter, Daniel, 157, 260
Potter, David, 24, 69, 109, 226, 230, 247
Potter, Edward, 91
Potter, Elijah, 132
Potter, Ezekiel, 190
Potter, George, 56
Potter, Hugh, Jr., 272
Potter, James, 232 (2)
Potter, James B., 231
Potter, Jeremiah, 273
Potter, Jesse, 139 (2), 231, 232
Potter, John, 232, 242, 247
Potter, John, 2d, 232, 296
Potter, Joseph, 232 (2), 234
Potter, Joshua, 56
Potter, Nathaniel, 139 (2), 235
Potter, Peleg, 30
Potter, Philip, 56, 215
Potter, Reuben, 230
Potter, Robert, 230, 296
Potter, Saul, 231
Potter, Simeon, 272
Potter, Solomon, 150
Potter, Stephen, 156 (2)

Potter, Thomas, 132, 234
Potter, William, 247, 273
Potter, William, Jr., 214
Potter, William S., 148
Potterfield, William, 295
Pottle, Benjamin, 159
Pottle, Daniel, 302
Pottle, David, 186, 190, 302
Pottle, David, Jr., 230
Pottle, John, 159
Pottle, Jordan, 182 (2), 184
Pottle, Joseph, Jr., 301
Pottle, Moses, 159
Pottle, Richard, 159
Pottle, Samuel, 276
Pottle, William, 159
Potts, William H., 138
Pousland, John, 35 (2)
Pousland, John, 3d, 34, 38
Pousland, Joseph, 34, 90
Pousland, William, 34
Powell, John, 149
Power, Robert, Jr. 248
Powers, Adam, 306
Powers, Asa, 66
Powers, Calvin, 151
Powers, Daniel, 160
Powers, Francis, 68
Powers, Gideon, Jr., 227
Powers, Hosmer, 227
Powers, Isaac, 211
Powers, James, 68, 79
Powers, Joel C., 119
Powers, John, 22, 95, 115
Powers, John G., 84
Powers, Jonathan, 71, 257, 306
Powers, Levi, 68, 111
Powers, Moore, 224
Powers, Paul, 148
Powers, Robert, 235
Powers, Thomas, 22, 155
Pratt, Aaron, 42
Pratt, Aaron, Jr., 33
Pratt, Abner, 102, 250
Pratt, Amasa, 53
Pratt, Amos, 96
Pratt, Andrew, 58
Pratt, Asa, 102, 218, 238
Pratt, Asel, 95
Pratt, Barnabus, 175
Pratt, Barney, 61
Pratt, Benajah, 253
Pratt, Benjamin, 51 (2), 230
Pratt, Benjamin C., 1, 103
Pratt, Caleb, 42, 102
Pratt, Calvin, 182
Pratt, Charles, 101, 129, 168, 221
Pratt, Church, 177, 260
Pratt, Cushing, Jr., 218
Pratt, Daniel, 177, 260
Pratt, David, 27
Pratt, David, Jr., 79
Pratt, Ebenezer, 47, 62
Pratt, Eberdeen, 256
Pratt, Edward, 2
Pratt, Elihu, 52, 102
Pratt, Elijah, 51, 86
Pratt, Eliphas, 86
Pratt, Enoch, 40, 102
Pratt, Enos, 59
Pratt, Ephraim, 66
Pratt, George, 82, 307

Pratt, Gideon, 42, 102
Pratt, Greenleaf, 53
Pratt, Henry, 218
Pratt, Herriman, 40
Pratt, Isaac, 112
Pratt, Jabez, 168
Pratt, Jacob, 266, 306
Pratt, James, 62, 65, 100, 179
Pratt, James, Jr., 238
Pratt, Jared, 49
Pratt, Jedediah, 146, 150
Pratt, Jesse, 130
Pratt, John, 241
Pratt, John N., 57
Pratt, Jonathan, 47, 88
Pratt, Joseph, 41, 118, 266, 307
Pratt, Joseph W., 70, 110
Pratt, Joshua, 128
Pratt, Josiah, 33, 65
Pratt, Jotham, 25
Pratt, Laban, 40, 102
Pratt, Lemuel, 90
Pratt, Lewis, 102
Pratt, Luther, 58
Pratt, Mather, 42
Pratt, Micah, 4
Pratt, Nathan, 51, 92
Pratt, Nathan G., 274
Pratt, Nathaniel, 118, 128
Pratt, Noah, 44, 92
Pratt, Obed, 81
Pratt, Oliver, 27, 272
Pratt, Orthnell, 107
Pratt, Othniel, 277
Pratt, Paul, 26, 229, 282
Pratt, Phineas, 81
Pratt, Reuben, 6
Pratt, Robert, 50
Pratt, Robert B., 58
Pratt, Samuel, 27, 231, 296
Pratt, Seneca, 255
Pratt, Seth, 51, 162
Pratt, Silas, 45, 67
Pratt, Solomon, 43
Pratt, Stephen, 253, 255, 259
Pratt, Stillman, 95
Pratt, Thomas, 26, 27, 52, 92, 103, 115
Pratt, Tillson, 129
Pratt, Uri, 32
Pratt, Vincent, 239
Pratt, Washington, 27
Pratt, Whitcomb, 307
Pratt, William, 97, 102, 175, 237
Pratt, Zebedee, 253, 257
Pratt, Zerobabel, 103
Pratt, Zerubabel, 51
Pray, Abraham, 146, 150
Pray, Alexander, 256
Pray, Charles, 230
Pray, David P., 83
Pray, Edmund, 148, 235
Pray, George, 42, 102
Pray, James, 100, 245
Pray, Jonathan, 146
Pray, Joseph, 112
Pray, Peter, 100
Prebble, Daniel, 276
Prebble, David, 185
Prebble, James, 274
Prebble, Jeremiah, 179
Prebble, John, 181, 234
Prebble, Joseph, 276

Prebble, Zebulon, 234
Preble, Ebenezer, 256
Preble, Jeremiah, 230
Preble, John, 149, 256, 297
Preble, John, Jr., 247
Preble, Joseph, 231
Preble, Nehemiah, 7, 22
Preble, Richard, 231
Preble, William, 191, 231, 296
Prentice, George, 48
Prentice, Jesse, 237
Prentice, Loammi, 44
Prentice, Philo, 237
Prentice, Saul, 237
Prentis, Amos, 101
Prentis, Henry, 253
Prentis, John, 22
Prentiss, Caleb, 6
Prentiss, George W., 182
Prentiss, John, 7
Prentiss, Jonathan C., 98
Prentiss, Joshua, 6, 7
Prentiss, Joshua, 3d, 22
Prenton, Jonathan, 136
Presbrey, Asa, 62
Presbury, Charles, 122
Prescot, Abel, 282
Prescot, Adonijah, 229
Prescot, Jedediah, 230
Prescot, Joseph, 282
Prescot, Simon M., 228
Prescot, Solomon, 260
Prescot, William, 282
Prescott, Abel, 39, 229
Prescott, Adonijah, 283
Prescott, Asa, 37
Prescott, Benjamin B., 273
Prescott, Elisha, 158
Prescott, Jason, 147 (2)
Prescott, Jedediah B., 170, 283
Prescott, Jeremiah, 303
Prescott, John, 8, 93, 303
Prescott, Jonathan, 228, 271
Prescott, Joseph, 170, 303
Prescott, Levi, 85
Prescott, Moses, 198
Prescott, Nathan A., 122
Prescott, Newell, 147 (2)
Prescott, Oliver, 125
Prescott, Oliver, Jr., 122
Prescott, Peter, 135, 137
Prescott, Samuel, Jr., 226
Prescott, Solomon, 178
Prescott, Stephen, 147 (2), 275
Prescott, Thomas, 8
Pressey, John, 20
Pressey, Thomas J., 236
Presson, Emerson, 66
Presson, Tristram, 227, 282
Pressy, Moses, 305
Pressy, Thomas, Jr., 267
Preston, David, 133, 136
Preston, Hiram, 229
Preston, Ira, 90
Preston, Isaac, Jr., 36
Preston, John, 225
Preston, Jonathan, 133, 136
Preston, Joshua, 80, 83
Preston, Michael, 85
Preston, Nathaniel, 29
Preston, Richard, 36, 37
Preston, Samuel, 31

Preston, Samuel H., 4
Prews, Alfred, 229
Prey, Eliphalet, 275
Pribble, Aris, 183, 189
Pribble, Daniel, 276
Pribble, David, 183, 189
Pribble, Joseph, 183, 185, 189, 276
Prible, Nehemiah, 6
Priblet, Abraham, 190
Price, David, 75
Price, Ephraim, 140
Price, Isaac, 76
Price, John, 302
Price, Jonathan, 227
Price, Stephen, 129
Price, William, 133, 136
Prichard, Asa, 199
Prichard, Benjamin, 273
Prichard, Jacob, 18, 121
Prichard, Stephen, 119
Prichard, Thomas, 195
Prichard, William, 7
Prickard, John, 3
Pride, Henry, 153
Pride, John, 220
Pride, John, Jr., 218
Pride, Josiah, 258
Pride, Peter, 36, 220
Pride, Peter, Jr., 37
Pride, Samuel, 220
Pride, Thomas, 220
Priest, David, 263
Priest, Isaac D., 24, 114
Priest, Joel, 238
Priest, Josiah, 239
Priest, Libbeus, 48
Priest, Reuben, 239
Priest, Timothy, 240
Priest, William, 180
Prime, Henry, 136
Prime, Saul, 47
Prince, Amariah, 9
Prince, Amos, 226
Prince, Benjamin, 158
Prince, Benjamin D., 159
Prince, Charles, 26
Prince, Cushing, Jr., 212
Prince, Daniel N., 116
Prince, David M., 133
Prince, David N., 139
Prince, Ebenphom, 134, 135
Prince, George, 220, 246
Prince, Isaac, 210, 252
Prince, Job, 251, 255
Prince, John, 22, 154, 302
Prince, John, 2d, 36
Prince, John, 3d, 37
Prince, Joseph, 256, 311
Prince, Joshua, 6
Prince, Noyes, 220
Prince, Reuben, 219
Prince, Samuel, 18, 120, 122
Prince, Saul, 47
Prince, Sewell, 165, 166
Prince, William, 256
Prince, William H., 122, 125, 134, 140
Princin, William, 49
Prindel, John, 65
Prine, John O., 305
Prine, Robert, 89
Pringe, William, 4
Prior, Leonard P., 300

INDEX.

Prisher, Joel, 161
Pritchard, Jacob, 124
Pritchard, Stephen, 89, 122
Pritchard, Thomas, 90
Procter, Caleb, 58
Proctor, Benjamin, 139
Proctor, Charles, 221
Proctor, Daniel, 41
Proctor, David, 211
Proctor, Demmack, 13, 14
Proctor, Ebenezer, 139 (2), 174
Proctor, Elijah, 300
Proctor, Frederic, 220
Proctor, George, 139, 300
Proctor, Hadley, 139
Proctor, Humphrey, 11, 36
Proctor, Isaac, 229
Proctor, Jeremiah, 199, 200
Proctor, John, 6, 7, 9, 25, 114, 116, 170, 258
Proctor, John, 3d, 6
Proctor, Joseph, Jr., 7
Proctor, Perley, 10
Proctor, Richard, 221
Proctor, Samuel A., 221
Proctor, Thorndike, 138
Proctor, Uriah, 2, 223
Proctor, William, 28, 132
Proctor, Willoughby, 139 (2)
Proud, James, 129
Prout, Dominicus I., 172
Prout, Harris, 44
Prouty, Artemas, 7
Prouty, Jonas, 84, 109
Prouty, Samuel, 42
Prowd, Samuel, 129
Pruttlebury, Thomas, 161
Puffer, James B., 85
Puffer, Jesse, 87
Puffer, Josiah, 87
Puffer, Otis, 85
Pulcifer, Jonathan, 226
Pulcifer, Nathaniel, 9
Pullen, Dexter, 264
Pullen, Gilbert, 179
Pullen, Greenleaf, 158
Pullen, Larnead, 278
Pullen, Lemuel, 153
Pullen, William, 264
Pullin, James, 273
Pulsifer, Eps, 36
Pulsifer, Francis, 137
Pulsifer, John, 11, 14
Pulsifer, John A., 13
Pulsifer, Jonathan, 213
Pulsifer, William, 14
Purington, Elisha, 226
Purington, Joshua, 300
Purington, Nathaniel, 300
Purinton, Joshua, 297
Purkett, Henry F., 87
Purkins, Daniel, 263
Purkins, Ephraim, 237
Purkitt, Henry, 80
Purrington, Abiaser, 231
Purrington, Humphrey, 232
Purrington, Isaac, 231, 296
Purrington, James, 55, 230
Purrington, John, Jr., 247, 297
Purrington, Nathaniel, 234, 247, 297
Purrington, William, 234
Purrinton, Charles, 232
Purrinton, Humphrey, 232

Purvis, William, 258
Purviss, J., 138
Pushard, John G., 188
Putman, Daniel, 215
Putman, Jacob, 261
Putman, Jeremy, 34
Putman, Jesse, 261
Putman, John, 22
Putman, Joseph, 17
Putman, Saul, 139
Putman, Silas, 215
Putman, Stephen, 261
Putman, William, 34, 66, 140
Putnam, Charles, 3
Putnam, Daniel, 8
Putnam, Elbridge, 21
Putnam, Henry, 100
Putnam, James, 81
Putnam, Jesse, 9
Putnam, John, 12, 19, 121, 124
Putnam, John C., 8
Putnam, John J., 113
Putnam, Lewis, 24, 311
Putnam, Samuel, 63
Putnam, Saul, 63
Putnam, Simeon, 95, 223
Putnam, William, 22, 34, 136
Putney, Samuel, 300

Q

Quance, Thomas, 92
Quarles, John, 140
Quarter, John, 132
Questrom, Oliver, 116
Quier, Benjamin, 35
Quiggle, Elias, 53
Quiles, Isaac, 46
Quillon, John P. M., 135, 137
Quimby, Benjamin, 167, 221, 281
Quimby, Benjamin F., 221
Quimby, Benjamin M., 81
Quimby, Charles, 221
Quimby, Daniel, 13, 14
Quimby, Hiram, 165, 166, 226
Quimby, Jacob, 254
Quimby, James, 279
Quimby, John, 167, 228, 279
Quimby, Jonathan, 304
Quimby, Joseph, 154
Quimby, Simeon, 221
Quimby, Stephen, 308
Quimby, Thomas, 308
Quinby, Hiram, 164
Quinby, John, 252, 255, 278, 281
Quiner, Benjamin, 21
Qunion, Abraham, 24, 28
Quinn, George, 169
Quinn, John, 22
Quinnam, Daniel, 182, 192
Quint, Luther, 265
Qurley, Stephen, 268

R

Race, George, 186
Race, George, Jr., 183
Rachlyft, Nelson, 241
Rackley, Benjamin, 168, 281
Rackley, Stephen, 168
Rackliff, George, 174
Racklifft, Charles F., 20
Racklyft, Charles, 124
Racklyft, Charles F., 19

Racklyft, Edmund, 19
Radcliff, Benjamin J., 240
Radcliff, Henry, 235
Radcliff, Nelson, 242
Radcliff, William, 183, 248
Radford, Daniel, 244
Radford, John, 133, 136
Raines, Miles, 138
Rainey, John, 312
Rairdon, Timothy, 247
Raitt, Alexander, 245
Raitt, John, 245
Raizor, George, 291
Rallings, John W., 146
Ralph, Daniel, 24
Ramsdale, Joseph, 4
Ramsdale, Reuben, 87
Ramsdale, Shadrack, 21
Ramsdel, Abner, 227
Ramsdel, Joshua, 277
Ramsdel, Samuel, 210
Ramsdell, Bartholomew, 127
Ramsdell, Benjamin, 22
Ramsdell, Isaac, 128, 160
Ramsdell, John, 127
Ramsdell, Joshua, 168
Ramsdell, Reuben, 81
Ramsdell, Robert, 256
Ramsdell, Shadrach, 21
Ramsdell, William, 87, 168
Ramsden, Job, 53
Ramsey, Blanchard, 178
Ramsey, Charles, 16
Rand, Aaron, 78
Rand, Barzilla, 170
Rand, Benjamin, 174
Rand, Bradbury, 226
Rand, Charles, 78
Rand, Daniel, 15
Rand, David, 251
Rand, Ebenezer, 141
Rand, Ezra, 118
Rand, Henry J., 173
Rand, Isaac, 18
Rand, James B., 218
Rand, John, Jr., 183, 185, 189
Rand, John B., 173
Rand, Joseph, 66
Rand, Nathaniel, 41, 88, 174
Rand, Philemon, 172
Rand, Robert C., 218
Rand, Rufus, 173
Rand, Stephen, 183, 189
Rand, Watson, 225
Rand, William, 127, 183, 189, 238
Rand, William M., 113, 114
Randal, Kinicum, 241
Randal, Michel, 129
Randal, Thomas, 57
Randall, Alvin, 3
Randall, Apollos, 49
Randall, Barney, 53
Randall, Benjamin, 49, 164, 165, 166, 232, 247, 272, 299
Randall, Benjamin R., 22
Randall, Caleb, 53, 237
Randall, Clement, 178
Randall, Elijah, 47, 95
Randall, Elvins, 53
Randall, Ezra, 261
Randall, Ezra, Jr., 167
Randall, James, 58, 167, 172, 277

INDEX. 411

Randall, John, 230
Randall, John M., 21
Randall, Joseph, 23, 77
Randall, Joseph H., 154
Randall, Joshua, 49
Randall, Lewis, 45
Randall, Nathan, 53
Randall, Nathaniel, 49
Randall, Nelson, 180
Randall, Prosper, 3
Randall, Reuben, 267
Randall, Samuel, 104, 139, 223, 259
Randall, Saul, 133
Randall, Thomas, 240
Randall, William, 7, 134, 140, 230, 245
Randall, William, Jr., 231
Randell, Edward, 48
Randell, Joseph, 117
Randell, Joshua, 30
Randell, Timothy, Jr., 229, 283
Randell, William, 217, 270
Randell, William P., 116
Randlett, Daniel, 7
Randlett, Moses, 170
Randlett, Samuel, 147
Randol, Elisha, 47
Ranell, Joseph, 130
Rankin, Samuel, 156
Rankin, Thomas, 228
Ranking, Joshua, 245
Rankins, Andrew, 206
Rankins, Constance, 199
Ranlet, Henry, 181
Ranlett, Daniel, 271
Ranlett, David, 180
Ranlett, Samuel, 147
Ransom, David, 296, 298
Rantoul, William, 138
Rasebrook, Eleaser, 280
Rathbon, Nathaniel, 32
Rathbon, Samuel, 32
Raviel, Ebenezer, 217
Rawson, Allen, 48
Rawson, Ebenezer, 250
Rawson, Emor, 146
Rawson, George, 2
Rawson, Jonathan, 32
Rawson, Mark B., 251
Rawson, Nathaniel W., 146, 150
Rawson, Samuel, 146
Rawson, Zebina, 108
Ray, Caleb, 96, 102
Ray, Charles, 96
Ray, Gideon, 37
Ray, Heman, 99
Ray, Jonathan, 167, 221, 277
Ray, Levi, 81
Ray, Thomas, 96
Ray, William, 170
Raymon, William, 112
Raymond, Benjamin, 57, 233
Raymond, Benjamin, 2d, 34, 38
Raymond, Daniel, 33
Raymond, Ezekiel, 235
Raymond, Francis, 69
Raymond, James, 231
Raymond, James G., 30
Raymond, Joel, 115
Raymond, John G., 35
Raymond, Josiah, 34, 38
Raymond, Levi, 51
Raymond, Solomon, 125

Raymond, Stephen, 23
Raymond, Thomas, 82, 280
Raymond, William, 34, 38
Raymond, William, Jr., 280
Raymond, Zenos, 52, 102
Rayner, John, 28
Raynes, John, 229
Raynolds, Benjamin, 160
Raynolds, John W., 160
Raynolds, Jonathan, 160
Raynolds, Jotham G., 160
Razor, Charles, Jr., 180
Razor, Jacob, 180
Rea, Ebenezer, Jr., 36, 37
Rea, Gideon, 36, 37
Read, Dean H., 57
Read, George, 88
Read, Gideon, 59
Read, Howard, 88
Read, Ichabod, 167
Read, Jacob H., 167
Read, John, 57, 146
Read, Nathaniel, 88
Read, Oliver, 167
Read, Robert, 138
Read, Russell H., 281
Read, Samuel, 41
Read, William, 88
Read, William V., 214
Reading, Ebenezer, 160
Reading, Joseph, 59, 160
Readington, Samuel, 263
Readington, Silas, 263
Readington, William, 263
Real, Michael, 215
Reasoner, Benjamin, 312
Record, Andrew, 252
Record, Calvin E., 260
Record, David, 176
Record, Domineas, 176
Record, Ebenezer, 176
Record, Elisha, 177, 260
Record, Ezekiel, 176
Record, Isaac, 224, 255
Record, Isaac, Jr., 252
Record, Jonathan, Jr., 176
Record, Lewis, 176
Record, Owen, 63
Record, Samuel, 176
Record, Saul, 254
Record, Simon, Jr., 176
Record, Thomas, 176, 177
Record, Timothy, 176
Records, Calvin E., 178
Reddell, Thomas, 129
Redding, Joseph, 52, 87
Reding, Joseph, 80
Redlen, Charles, 226
Rodman, Benjamin, 40
Reed, Aaron, Jr., 113, 114
Reed, Abel, 50, 192
Reed, Abiah, 92
Reed, Abiel, 195
Reed, Alden, 55
Reed, Alexander, 284, 287
Reed, Amariah, 59
Reed, Amos, 83, 115
Reed, Andrew, 183, 185, 189, 247
Reed, Andrew, 2d, 185
Reed, Andrew, 4th, 185
Reed, Asa, 229
Reed, Augustus, 85

Reed, Benjamin, 3, 23, 24 (2), 114
Reed, Benjamin, Jr., 239, 267
Reed, Bethuel, 42, 88
Reed, Caleb, 21
Reed, Charles, 65, 249, 298
Reed, Daniel, 212, 276
Reed, David, 16, 40, 48, 50,, 94, 121, 124, 283
Reed, Denny, 248
Reed, Edmund, 81
Reed, Elijah, 53
Reed, Elisha, 39
Reed, Ephraim, 116
Reed, Ezekiel, 49
Reed, Francis, 61
Reed, Frederic, 185
Reed, George, 25, 79, 85, 158, 170, 277
Reed, George W., 59, 62
Reed, Gideon, 61
Reed, Goddard, 92
Reed, Henry, 145, 284, 287
Reed, Holtin, 134
Reed, Ichabod, 277
Reed, Isaac, 40, 41, 276
Reed, Isaac G., 289
Reed, Jacob, 260
Reed, Jacob, Jr., 177
Reed, James, 26, 56, 183
Reed, James B., 234
Reed, Jared, 49
Reed, Jason, 45, 274
Reed, Joel, 249, 286
Reed, John, 183, 185, 189, 247
Reed, John, Jr., 299
Reed, John, 2d, 185
Reed, John A., 53
Reed, John D., 303
Reed, John H., 39
Reed, John M., 183, 185, 189, 249
Reed, Jonathan, 59, 283
Reed, Joseph, 9, 57, 61, 134, 185, 190
Reed, Joshua, 61
Reed, Lemuel, 55
Reed, Lemuel B., 55
Reed, Littleton, 215
Reed, Lott, 41
Reed, Louis, 65
Reed, Luke, 53
Reed, Lyman, 25
Reed, Nathan, 52, 54
Reed, Nathaniel, 10
Reed, Noah, 60, 61
Reed, Otis, 53, 88
Reed, Paul, 183, 185, 186, 189
Reed, Paul, Jr., 183, 189
Reed, Paul, 2d, 185
Reed, Paul M., 183
Reed, Perrin, 239
Reed, Peter, 228
Reed, Quincy, 2, 80
Reed, Reason, 48
Reed, Reuben, 23, 212
Reed, Robert, 284, 287
Reed, Robert, Jr., 249
Reed, Robert, 3d, 185
Reed, Robert, 4th, 185
Reed, Roswell, 8
Reed, Russell H., 167
Reed, Samuel, 249, 308
Reed, Samuel P., 9
Reed, Samuel R., 166
Reed, Samuel W., 239
Reed, Seth, 43, 89

INDEX.

Reed, Simeon, 92, 96
Reed, Solomon, 54, 64
Reed, Sylvanus, 81, 86
Reed, Thomas, 61, 102, 126, 226
Reed, Ulrich, 249
Reed, Weston, 63
Reed, William, 24, 42, 59, 62, 100, 102, 114, 127, 163 (2), 220, 284 (2), 287, 297
Reed, William H., 214
Reed, William M., 183
Reed, Zachariah, 31
Reen, Robert, 200
Reeves, Isaac, 196
Reeves, Richard, 206
Reeves, Samuel, 68
Reigns, Samuel, 181
Reivry, Silas, 33
Remick, Benjamin, 218
Remick, Enoch, 245
Remick, Francis, 305
Remick, James, 248
Remick, John, 16, 243
Remick, Samuel H., 81
Remick, True, 305
Remington, Hutchins, 245
Rendal, Eliphalet, 16
Rendell, James, 303
Renmow, Thomas, 45
Renney, Moses, 139
Renow, Richard, 7
Reswick, Field, 64
Reubier, Mark, 277
Revice, Isaac, 192
Revice, William, 192
Rex, John, 41, 80
Reynard, John, 1
Reynolds, Abel, 22
Reynolds, Abraham, 55
Reynolds, Adna, 236
Reynolds, Alden, 66
Reynolds, Andrew, 117
Reynolds, Benjamin, 55
Reynolds, David P., 97
Reynolds, Edward, 262
Reynolds, Ichabod, 177, 260
Reynolds, Joel, 7
Reynolds, John, 6, 7, 21
Reynolds, Joshua, 51
Reynolds, Luther, 262
Reynolds, Micah, 2d, 57
Reynolds, Noah, 55
Reynolds, Parmenus, 238, 265
Reynolds, Philip, 55
Reynolds, Samuel, 83
Reynolds, Thadeus, 56
Reynolds, Thomas, 50, 262
Reynolds, Wilbour, 57
Reynolds, William, 25, 55, 69, 77
Reynolds, William H., 6, 21
Reynolds, Zapher, 176
Rhines, George T., 306
Rhines, Moses, 306
Rhoades, James, Jr., 302
Rhoads, Daniel, 160
Rhoads, Ellis, 85
Rhodes, Allen, 117
Rhodes, Jacob, 302
Rhodes, Jacob L., 302
Rhodes, John, 7
Rhodes, Rufus, 236
Rhodes, Stephen, 99
Rhodes, Thomas, 117

Rhodes, Washington, 98
Riant, Joseph, Jr., 283
Rice, Abner, 81
Rice, Alanson T., 311
Rice, Baxter, 218
Rice, Benjamin S., 3
Rice, Calvin, 209
Rice, Cheney, 91
Rice, Colver, 67
Rice, Cyrus, 217
Rice, Daniel, 300
Rice, David, 39, 162
Rice, Ebeneser, 160
Rice, Eber, 152
Rice, Edmund, 90
Rice, Elihu, 31
Rice, Ephraim, 61
Rice, George, 300
Rice, Henry, 71
Rice, Horace, 5
Rice, James, 264
Rice, Jesse, 91
Rice, John, 87, 91, 174
Rice, Joseph, 93, 174
Rice, Josiah, 3
Rice, Lemuel, 174
Rice, Loammi, 48
Rice, Lovell, 3
Rice, Micajah, 87
Rice, Moses, 66, 173
Rice, Nathan, 290
Rice, Nathan D., 286
Rice, Nathaniel, 81, 174
Rice, Noah, 286, 290
Rice, Oliver, 227
Rice, Peter, 94
Rice, Phineas, 172
Rice, Ransom, 45
Rice, Reuben, 93
Rice, Rufus, 8, 110, 113, 209
Rice, Samuel, 227, 243
Rice, Samuel, Jr., 171
Rice, Samuel H., 4
Rice, Solomon, 23
Rice, Stephen, 29
Rice, Thomas, 160
Rice, Timothy R., 94
Rice, Warren, 182
Rice, William, 24, 65, 158
Rich, Benjamin, 300
Rich, David, 81, 87 (2), 223, 260, 300, 311
Rich, Elisha, 66
Rich, George, 31
Rich, Isaac, 85
Rich, Isaac, Jr., 300
Rich, Isaiah, 215
Rich, Israel, 174
Rich, James, 161
Rich, John, 48, 79
Rich, Obediah, 41, 79
Rich, Moses, 54
Rich, Samuel, 45
Rich, Sylvanus, 215
Richard, Ebeneser, 242
Richard, James, 270
Richard, John, 222
Richard, Joseph, 88
Richard, Robert, 198
Richard, Thomas, 103
Richard, Turner, 276
Richard, Willard, 244
Richards, Abel, Jr., 90

Richards, Asa, 207 (2)
Richards, Benjamin, 31, 195
Richards, Daniel, 145, 168, 197, 277
Richards, Dodipher, 201 (2), 203, 209
Richards, Edward, 283
Richards, George, 53
Richards, Isaac, 197
Richards, Isaac, Jr., 129
Richards, Isaac D., 23
Richards, Jacob, 40, 275
Richards, James, 102, 192, 195
Richards, Jeremiah, 278
Richards, Jesse, 40
Richards, Joel, 99
Richards, John, 68, 133, 136, 168, 194, 273
Richards, Joseph, 21, 42, 69, 195, 275
Richards, Mason, 99
Richards, Nathaniel, 23, 77, 168
Richards, Nehemiah, 302
Richards, Oliver, 278, 279
Richards, Paul, 192, 195
Richards, Pearl, 201 (2), 203, 209
Richards, Peter, 70
Richards, Phineas, 29
Richards, Reuben, 8, 23, 110
Richards, Robert, 199, 200, 202, 203, 208 (2)
Richards, Rufus, 85
Richards, Samuel, 219, 273
Richards, Stephen, 138
Richards, Thomas, 54, 100
Richards, Timothy, 195
Richards, Walter, 133, 136
Richards, William, 99, 198, 220
Richards, William, Jr., 273
Richardson, Aaron, 153
Richardson, Abiathar, 195
Richardson, Abijah, 230
Richardson, Adam, 223
Richardson, Alford, 145
Richardson, Allen, 98, 100
Richardson, Alpheus, 96
Richardson, Amos, 151, 230
Richardson, Andrew, 238, 267
Richardson, Andrew J., 8
Richardson, Anthony W., 263
Richardson, Asa, 38, 82, 138
Richardson, Benjamin, 54, 70, 163 (2)
Richardson, Bodwell, 41
Richardson, C. C., 9
Richardson, Charles, 44
Richardson, Cornelius, 230
Richardson, Daniel, 236, 302
Richardson, David, 15, 163 (2), 174
Richardson, Eben, 265
Richardson, Ebeneser, 116, 236, 267
Richardson, Edmund, 133
Richardson, Eleaser F. F., 84
Richardson, Elisha, 51
Richardson, Ephraim, 41, 138
Richardson, Ezekiel, 224
Richardson, Ezra, 192, 195
Richardson, George, 82, 151, 163 (2)
Richardson, Henry, 15, 153, 273
Richardson, Henry, Jr., 262
Richardson, Hugh, 163 (2)
Richardson, Isaac, 133, 155, 163 (2)
Richardson, Israel, 87, 116, 238, 267
Richardson, James, 135, 137, 163 (2)
Richardson, James B., 84
Richardson, James P., 26
Richardson, Jeffrey, 8
Richardson, Joel, 267

INDEX. 413

Richardson, John, 25, 70, 78, 89, 116, 138, 170, 277
Richardson, John, Jr., 15
Richardson, Jonathan, 272
Richardson, Joseph, 209
Richardson, Joshua, 42, 152, 254
Richardson, Josiah, 82, 88, 224
Richardson, Lewis, 45
Richardson, Loammi, 39
Richardson, Luke, 68, 77
Richardson, Luther, 152, 242
Richardson, Maraite, 89
Richardson, Moses, 60, 117
Richardson, Nathan, 25, 87
Richardson, Nathaniel, 96, 163 (2)
Richardson, Oliver, 262
Richardson, Parker, 139 (2)
Richardson, Peter, 39
Richardson, Philip, 151
Richardson, Pliney, 47
Richardson, Richard, 163 (2), 272
Richardson, Robert, 138, 238, 267
Richardson, Rufus, 47, 250, 255, 273
Richardson, Samuel, 77, 96, 113 (2), 236, 238
Richardson, Saul, 212
Richardson, Seth, 240, 267
Richardson, Seth, 2d, 267
Richardson, Sheron, 87
Richardson, Silas, 60, 167, 264
Richardson, Smith, 157
Richardson, Stephen, 93, 133, 157, 163, 175, 260
Richardson, Stephen, Jr., 163 (2)
Richardson, Stephen, 3d, 163
Richardson, Stephen, 4th, 163
Richardson, Thomas, 41, 48, 117, 155, 272
Richardson, Varnum, 60
Richardson, Whitney, 45
Richardson, William, 87, 96, 170, 238, 247
Richardson, Zacheriah, 167
Richman, Kingman, 60
Richmond, Abraham, 57
Richmond, Allen, 51
Richmond, Alpheus, 131
Richmond, Apollus, 54
Richmond, Atwood, 218
Richmond, Benjamin, 54
Richmond, Benjamin D., 62
Richmond, Bess, 59
Richmond, Eliab, 253
Richmond, Elias, 52
Richmond, George, 61
Richmond, Henry, 61
Richmond, Hercules, 52
Richmond, Isaac, 57
Richmond, Israel, 222
Richmond, James, 51
Richmond, John, 46
Richmond, John C., 41
Richmond, King, 62
Richmond, Leonard, 150
Richmond, Nathaniel, 61
Richmond, Oliver, 95, 129
Richmond, Samuel, 57
Richmond, Seth, 33
Richmond, Theodore, 59
Richmond, William, 52, 61
Rickens, Henry, 102
Rickens, James, 102
Ricker, Ephraim, 176, 257
Ricker, George, 264
Ricker, George, 2d, 264
Ricker, Hiram, 244

Ricker, Ichabod, 152
Ricker, Jacob, 245
Ricker, John, 244
Ricker, Levi, 245, 309
Ricker, Moses, 267
Ricker, Nathaniel, 245
Ricker, Richard, 245
Ricker, Rufus, 264
Ricker, Samuel, 169
Ricker, Theodore, 245
Ricker, Tobias, 176
Ricker, Trustram, 306
Ricker, Winthrop, 219
Rickerson, Nehemiah, 240
Ricketson, Cook, 126
Ricketson, Gilbert, 62
Rickford, Abraham, 85
Rickford, Lewis, 2
Rickman, Abiel, 51
Riddle, Anthon, 67
Riddle, William, 312
Rideout, Jacob, 231
Rideout, John H., 232 (2)
Rideout, Johnson, 232 (2), 277, 282
Rideout, Wanton, 235
Rideout, William, 232
Rider, Atkins, 217
Rider, Benjamin, 130
Rider, Chapman, 52
Rider, Ebeneser, 125
Rider, Elisha, 45
Rider, Ezra, 95
Rider, Francis, 216
Rider, Henry, 55
Rider, Isaac, 52
Rider, John, 45
Rider, John B., 286, 288
Rider, John D., 286
Rider, Joseph, 140
Rider, Lot, 216
Rider, Richard, 217
Rider, Robert, 52
Rider, Robert, Jr., 102
Rider, Samuel, 52
Rider, Samuel, Jr., 217
Rider, Seth, 61, 161
Rider, Standish, 52
Rider, Stephen, 217
Rider, William, 216
Ridgway, James, 280
Ridgway, John, 109
Ridgway, Joseph, 15, 78
Ridlen, Joseph, 270
Ridley, Daniel, 233, 278, 282
Ridley, George, Jr., 231
Ridley, Mark, 235
Ridley, Matthias, 278
Ridley, Samuel, 278
Ridley, Thomas, 109
Ridley, William, 233
Ridlon, Charles, 154
Ridly, Mark, Jr., 300
Riggs, George, 308
Riggs, Jacob, 244
Riggs, Jeremiah, 154
Riggs, John, 12
Riggs, John L., 253
Riggs, Joshua, 13
Riggs, Moses, 247
Riggs, Samuel, 183
Riggs, Saul, 185
Riggs, Starbird, 306

Riggs, Stenford, 268
Riggs, Stephen, 154
Riggs, Thomas, 13, 14, 218
Riggs, Thomas M., 180
Riggs, William S., 212
Riggs, Wintworth, 13
Right, Timothy, 85
Riker, Moses, 263
Riley, David, 40
Riley, Micah, 87
Rinds, Samuel, 162
Rines, Benjamin, 153
Rines, George, 266
Rines, Thomas, 179
Ring, Aaron, 185
Ring, Daniel, 138, 273
Ring, David, 198, 202
Ring, Jesse, 67
Ring, John, 226
Ring, Martin, 212
Ring, Nathaniel, 24, 114
Ring, Samuel, 85
Ring, Thomas, 232
Ring, William, 273
Rino, Joseph, Jr., 183, 189
Rion, Nathaniel, 86
Ripley, Aaron, 199, 200, 203
Ripley, Abraham, 203
Ripley, Archalaus, 199, 200, 203
Ripley, Charles, 28
Ripley, David, 129
Ripley, Elijah, 66
Ripley, Ezra, 66
Ripley, F. W., 2
Ripley, Isaiah, 95
Ripley, James, 192, 196
Ripley, James W., 225
Ripley, Joseph, 212, 261
Ripley, Justin, 96
Ripley, Levi, 60
Ripley, Lorenzo, 25
Ripley, Naum, 181
Ripley, Peter, 96, 199, 200, 203, 207
Ripley, Phineas, 32
Ripley, Ransom, 252
Ripley, Robert, 27
Ripley, Samuel, 83, 87
Ripley, Simeon, 273
Ripley, Sylvanus, 129
Ripley, Thomas, 199, 200, 203, 212
Ripley, Uriah, 251
Ripley, William, 251
Ripley, Zenas, 129
Riply, Daniel, 289
Ripner, James, 55
Rising, Abram, Jr., 46
Risley, Chester, 67
Risly, John, 237
Ritcher, Andrew, 217
Ritchie, Thomas, 217
Ritchinson, Joshua, Jr., 271
Rittal, Francis, 188
Rittal, Francis, Jr., 191
Rittal, James, 188
Rittal, John, 188
Rittal, William, 187, 191
Rittall, James, 186
Rivers, David, 287, 288, 294
Rivers, Robert, 205, 207
Rivers, Thomas, 288, 294
Roach, James K., 256
Roach, Samuel, 83

INDEX.

Roak, Daniel, 145
Roak, William, 296
Roakes, David, 285
Roakes, James, 200, 203
Robards, George, 11
Robards, Thomas, Jr., 12
Robason, Charles, 198, 202
Robbins, Abither, 188
Robbins, Amial, 305
Robbins, Ammial, 268
Robbins, Anselm, 131
Robbins, Arunah, 205 (2)
Robbins, Asa, 147
Robbins, Asa, Jr., 147
Robbins, Avery, 205
Robbins, Benjamin, 131, 273
Robbins, Calvin, 253, 257
Robbins, Chaney, 287
Robbins, Charles, 128, 276
Robbins, Cheney, 285
Robbins, Cyrus, 147
Robbins, Daniel, 13, 14
Robbins, David, 135, 136, 140, 290, 293
Robbins, Ebenezer, 290, 293
Robbins, Edward, 181
Robbins, Elias, 188, 191
Robbins, George, 100
Robbins, George W., 100
Robbins, Harvey, 199
Robbins, Henry, 41, 128, 200
Robbins, Hildreth, 229
Robbins, Isaac C., 205 (3)
Robbins, James, 20
Robbins, Jeremiah, 160
Robbins, Jesse, 131
Robbins, Joel, 289
Robbins, John, 17, 229, 307
Robbins, John A., 128, 131
Robbins, John G., 202
Robbins, John P., 286, 290
Robbins, Jonathan, 48
Robbins, Joseph, 97, 100, 227
Robbins, Joshua, 153
Robbins, Joshua S., 101
Robbins, Lebbeus, 253
Robbins, Lemuel, 53
Robbins, Leonard, 265
Robbins, Lewis, 302
Robbins, Luther, 167
Robbins, Moses, 53
Robbins, Nathaniel, 277
Robbins, Oliver, 178, 273
Robbins, Peter W., 290, 293
Robbins, Reuben, 167, 281
Robbins, Rufus, 128
Robbins, Shepard, 205 (3)
Robbins, Thomas, 84, 139
Robbins, William, 13, 70, 168
Robbinson, George, 199
Robbinson, John, 70
Robbinson, Joshua, 200
Robbinson, Micah, 183
Roberson, Joseph, 160
Roberson, Marcus, 97
Roberson, Thomas, 306
Roberts, Aaron, 36, 247
Roberts, Alanson, 3
Roberts, Andrew, 36
Roberts, Benjamin, 258
Roberts, Daniel, 246, 256, 312
Roberts, David P., 36, 37
Roberts, David W., 30

Roberts, Ebenezer, 295
Roberts, George, 7, 181
Roberts, Gilman, 215
Roberts, Jacob, 11
Roberts, James, 13, 14, 37
Roberts, James W., 244
Roberts, John, 26, 79 (2), 151, 245
Roberts, John A., 16
Roberts, Joseph, 137, 243, 272
Roberts, Joseph, Jr., 171
Roberts, Joseph A., 44
Roberts, Joshua, 174
Roberts, Lemuel, 272
Roberts, Levi, 278
Roberts, Mark, 235, 236
Roberts, Nathaniel, 243
Roberts, Reuben, 149, 219, 256, 300
Roberts, Richard, 33
Roberts, Richard S., 80, 85
Roberts, Rufus, 98
Roberts, Samuel, 43, 88, 149, 174, 300
Roberts, Samuel, Jr., 297, 300
Roberts, Saul, 89
Roberts, Seth, 176
Roberts, Theodore, 11 (2)
Roberts, Thomas, 245, 300
Roberts, Vinson, 218
Roberts, William, 136, 140, 163 (2), 221
Robertson, Archibald, 284
Robertson, Benjamin, 97
Robertson, George, 181, 200
Robertson, Isaac O., 295
Robertson, Jacob G., 115
Robertson, James G., 48
Robertson, John, 15, 80, 168, 172, 296
Robertson, Robert, 110
Robertson, Smith, 87
Robertson, Thomas, 181
Robeson, Charles, 208
Robie, Joseph, 89, 241
Robie, Thomas, 173
Robie, Toppan, 173
Robings, Jedediah, 88
Robins, Elisha, 312
Robins, Shepherd, 207
Robinson, Abial, 59
Robinson, Alexander, 121, 125, 252, 255, 284, 294
Robinson, Alvan, 254
Robinson, Alvin, 53, 178
Robinson, Andrew, 206, 207
Robinson, Archibald, 196, 288, 294
Robinson, Asa, 66, 146, 260
Robinson, Asa, Jr., 178
Robinson, Benjamin, 239, 284, 288, 294
Robinson, Bonny, 30
Robinson, Braddock, 72
Robinson, Bryant, 148
Robinson, Calvin, 75
Robinson, Chancy, 45
Robinson, Charles, 181, 196, 208, 284, 288, 289, 293, 294
Robinson, Charles, Jr., 179
Robinson, Charles, 2d, 288
Robinson, Cornelius, 284, 294
Robinson, Daniel, 279
Robinson, Daniel A., 12
Robinson, Daniel C., 25
Robinson, David, 76
Robinson, Davis, 75
Robinson, E., 294
Robinson, Eben D., 193

Robinson, Ebenezer, 69
Robinson, Edward, 184, 188, 288
Robinson, Elijah, 54, 75, 239
Robinson, Elisha, 76
Robinson, Ephraim, 206, 284
Robinson, Ezekiel, 72, 272
Robinson, Fall, 223
Robinson, Gain, 164 (2)
Robinson, Gaine, 165
Robinson, George, 21, 117, 155, 203, 312
Robinson, Godfrey, Jr., 62
Robinson, Henry, 284
Robinson, Isaac, 75, 76, 214
Robinson, Jacob, 27, 284, 288, 294
Robinson, Jacob G., 77
Robinson, James, 158, 193
Robinson, James, Jr., 196
Robinson, Jeremiah, 249, 297
Robinson, John, 72, 145, 180, 190, 191, 206 (2) 214, 263, 272, 284, 288, 294
Robinson, John, 2d, 62
Robinson, John, 3d, 284
Robinson, John L., 288, 294 (2)
Robinson, John W., 294 (2)
Robinson, Jonathan, 279
Robinson, Joseph, 73, 76, 180, 206
Robinson, Joseph, Jr., 178
Robinson, Joshua, 199, 202, 297, 300
Robinson, Josiah, 51, 103
Robinson, Kilburn G., 158
Robinson, Lyman, 25
Robinson, Mabbry, 284
Robinson, Marlboro, 294
Robinson, Moses, 279 (2), 284, 288, 294
Robinson, Nathaniel, 76, 182, 184, 185, 186, 276
Robinson, Nathaniel B., 179
Robinson, Peter, 72, 238
Robinson, Richard, 290, 293
Robinson, Robert, 41, 196
Robinson, Robert M., 181
Robinson, Robert V., 288
Robinson, Rowland, 76
Robinson, Samuel, 234, 253
Robinson, Seth, 72
Robinson, Silvan, 76
Robinson, Simeon, 62
Robinson, Simon, 284, 288, 294
Robinson, Smith, 25
Robinson, Stephen, 178, 271, 301
Robinson, Stephen R., 259
Robinson, Sylvanus, 75
Robinson, Thaddeus, 2
Robinson, Thatcher, 309
Robinson, Thomas, 76, 89, 270
Robinson, Thomas D., 247
Robinson, Timothy, 31
Robinson, Wentworth, 267
Robinson, West, 224
Robinson, Whiting, 236
Robinson, William, 14, 192, 196, 273, 284, 285, 286 (2), 287, 289, 290
Robinson, William E., 272
Robinson, Winthrop, 267
Robinson, Woodberry, 242
Robinson, Yarby, 284
Robinson, Yardley, 288
Robison, Charles, 208
Robison, Eli, 212
Robison, Joseph, 212
Robison, Richard, 215
Robison, Robert, 192

INDEX.

Robison, Samuel, 262
Robson, Benjamin, 302
Roby, Henry, 182
Roby, Henry, Jr., 191
Roby, Samuel, 227
Rockleff, Samuel, 181
Rockliff, Charles F., 121
Rockton, Jonas, 179
Rockwell, Joseph W., 31
Rockwood, Benjamin, 86
Rockwood, Levi, 5
Rockwood, Peter, 5
Rockwood, Thomas, 3
Rod, Solomon, 53
Rodberd, Thomas S., 227
Roddin, Joseph, 118
Rodgers, George, 63
Rodgers, John, 26
Rodgers, Nathaniel, 140
Rodgers, William, 24
Rodick, William, 298
Rodliff, William, 60
Rodman, Thomas, 2
Roe, Benjamin, 88
Roe, Rufus, 145
Rogers, A. Wales, 303
Rogers, Aaron, 17
Rogers, Abner, 15
Rogers, Allen, 215
Rogers, Asa, 47, 106, 107, 108
Rogers, Beniah, 89
Rogers, Charles, 121, 125, 153
Rogers, Daniel, 16
Rogers, David, 15, 84
Rogers, Ebenezer, 104, 105 (2), 106, 107
Rogers, Edward, 165, 166, 174, 246, 256
Rogers, Eldred, 84
Rogers, Eleazer, Jr., 108
Rogers, Enoch, 145, 179
Rogers, Ezekiel, 15
Rogers, Foster, 106 (2), 107
Rogers, Francis, 248
Rogers, George, 19, 155, 231, 248
Rogers, Gideon, 15
Rogers, Gideon, Jr., 30
Rogers, Henry, 21, 217
Rogers, Hesekiah, Jr., 106, 107 (2)
Rogers, Hugh, 231, 235
Rogers, Isaac, 108
Rogers, Israel, 104, 105 (2), 106, 107
Rogers, James, 15, 104, 105 (2), 106, 107
Rogers, James G., 250 (2)
Rogers, John, 48, 100, 161, 209, 214, 264, 279
Rogers, John, Jr., 154, 231
Rogers, John J., 5
Rogers, Jonathan, 104
Rogers, Joseph, 15
Rogers, Joseph, Jr., 179
Rogers, Joseph L., 108
Rogers, Joshua, 46, 64, 106 (2), 107, 211, 292
Rogers, Joshua, Jr., 107
Rogers, Knowles, 216
Rogers, Levi, Jr., 176
Rogers, Luke, 6
Rogers, Luther, 57
Rogers, Michel, 21
Rogers, Moses, 193
Rogers, Nathaniel, 12, 20, 248
Rogers, Oliver, 15
Rogers, Peter, 7
Rogers, Reuben W., 17
Rogers, Richard, 133

Rogers, Richard S., 132
Rogers, Samuel, 6, 7, 9, 22, 106, 107, 181
Rogers, Samuel L., 250
Rogers, Saul H., 250
Rogers, Sears, 108
Rogers, Seth, 106 (2), 108
Rogers, Shubal, 106, 107 (2)
Rogers, Shubel, 108
Rogers, Silas, 18
Rogers, Silvanus, 131
Rogers, Smith, 217
Rogers, Stephen, 128
Rogers, Sylvanus, 128
Rogers, Theodore, 15
Rogers, Thomas, 15, 93, 226, 305
Rogers, Thomas, Jr., 105 (2), 106, 107
Rogers, Timothy, 12, 104, 106, 107
Rogers, Tully, 106 (2), 107
Rogers, Uriah, 106, 107, 108
Rogers, William, 4, 16, 17, 231, 307
Rogers, William A., 132
Rogers, Zacheus, 125
Rogers, Zenas, 106 (2), 107 (2), 108
Rokes, John, 290
Roler, Jacob, 289
Roler, Jacob, 2d, 289
Roler, Jacob, 3d, 289
Roler, Jacob L., 289
Roler, John, 289
Roler, John W., 289
Roler, Paul, 289
Rolf, Moses, 17
Rolf, Nathaniel, 261
Rolf, Samuel, 261
Rolfe, Benjamin, 149, 173
Rolinger, Jonathan, 279
Rollins, John, 232
Roller, Pisquale, 13, 14
Rollings, Aaron, 148
Rollings, John, 229
Rollins, Aaron, 181
Rolline, Benjamin, 268, 308
Rollins, Daniel, 198, 199, 201, 202
Rollins, David, 198, 202, 208 (2), 233, 235
Rollins, Edward, 181
Rollins, Elias, 188
Rollins, Eliphalet, 180
Rollins, Enoch W., 158
Rollins, Ephraim, 192
Rollins, Frank, 192, 195
Rollins, Freeman, 266
Rollins, George, 239, 267
Rollins, Ichabod, 179
Rollins, Jacob S., 159
Rollins, James, 237
Rollins, Job, 275
Rollins, John, 232, 264, 266, 273, 308
Rollins, John, Jr., 195
Rollins, Jonathan, 264
Rollins, Joseph, 235
Rollins, Joseph, Jr., 282
Rollins, Moses, 159, 239
Rollins, Nathaniel, 187, 190, 239, 267
Rollins, Robert, 195
Rollins, Samuel, 239, 311
Rollins, Thomas, 239, 267
Rollins, Valentine, 264
Rollins, William, 195, 204
Rolph, Daniel, 77
Rondlet, Philip, 157
Ronney, Sewall, 46
Rood, Aaron, 32

Rood, Augustus, 60
Rooks, Joseph, 217
Root, Luther, 47
Root, Solomon, 45
Root, Whiting, 119
Rope, Joseph, 135
Roper, Benjamin, 134, 135
Roper, Henry, 134
Roper, John, 13, 14
Roper, John, 2d, 14
Roper, Saul, 136
Ropes, Ebenezer, 138
Ropes, Henry, 21, 134
Rose, Asa, Jr., 168
Rose, Calvin, 46
Rose, Christopher, 46
Rose, Gideon, 80
Rose, Joseph, 59
Rose, Seth, 168
Ross, Benjamin, 182, 271
Ross, Charles, 114
Ross, Daniel, 194
Ross, Frederick, 14
Ross, Hugh, 302
Ross, James, 3d, 295
Ross, James D., 84
Ross, Jesse, 177
Ross, John, 90, 194, 197, 246, 298
Ross, Jonathan, 211
Ross, Joseph, 198, 199, 201, 202, 278
Ross, Moses, 89
Ross, Robert, Jr., 296
Ross, Robert, 2d, 298
Ross, Samuel, 194, 197, 309 (2)
Ross, Saul, 197
Ross, Stephen, 198, 208
Ross, Thomas, 241
Ross, Wentworth, 236
Ross, William, 26, 90, 194, 298, 312
Ross, Zebulon, 30
Rost, Horace, 29
Rouck, John, 295
Rouck, William, 295
Roulston, Michel, 86
Roulston, Michel, Jr., 87
Round, David P., 61
Round, Theodore, 245
Rounds, Abner, 251, 257
Rounds, John, 212
Rounds, Mark, 154
Rounds, Stephen, 152
Rounds, Sylvester, Jr., 60
Roundy, Amos, 238
Roundy, David, 238
Roundy, Israel W., 34, 38
Roundy, Jonathan, 7
Roundy, Samuel, 265
Roundy, Stephen, 34, 38
Roundy, Thomas, 22
Rounsville, Silas, 57
Rourk, John, 297
Rouse, James, 28
Rouse, William, 247
Row, Caleb, 306
Row, Joseph, 119
Rowe, Allen, 117
Rowe, Amos, 117
Rowe, Anthony, 70, 78
Rowe, Asa, 264
Rowe, Benjamin, 81, 83, 84, 175, 260
Rowe, Benjamin, Jr., 11 (2)
Rowe, Caleb, 264, 266

INDEX.

Rowe, Daniel, 11, 212
Rowe, Eben, 11
Rowe, Ebeneser, 268, 308
Rowe, Elisha, 217, 264, 266
Rowe, George, 11
Rowe, Gilbert A., 256
Rowe, Isaac, 11
Rowe, James, 179
Rowe, Job, 11
Rowe, John, 168, 281
Rowe, Jonas W., 96
Rowe, Jonathan, 210
Rowe, Joseph, 175, 253
Rowe, Joshua, 210
Rowe, Lewis, 282
Rowe, Moses, 210, 256
Rowe, Peter, 304
Rowe, Rufus, 188
Rowe, Samuel, 175, 252, 256
Rowe, Saul, 210
Rowe, Stephen, 265
Rowe, William, 14
Rowe, William, Jr., 263
Rowe, William D., 116
Rowe, Zacheus, 178
Rowe, Zebulon, 210
Rowell, Jacob, 181
Rowell, James, 217
Rowell, Jesse, 196
Rowell, John, 224
Rowell, Jonathan, 265
Rowell, Moses, 170
Rowell, Thomas, 183, 185, 189
Rowlen, Luther, 46
Rowley, Erastus, 29
Rowley, Thomas, 67
Rowse, Isaac, 24, 114
Rowse, James, 28
Royal, Jacob, 145
Royal, John, 252
Royal, Peter, 199, 202
Royal, Samuel, 210
Royal, William, 256
Royal, Winthrop, 212
Royal, Woodis, 262
Royse, Silas, 83
Ruddock, Amos, 68, 80
Rue, Benjamin, 134, 135
Ruff, Adam, 81
Rugg, Elisha, 24, 114
Rugg, William, 5
Ruggart, Abel, 214
Ruggles, Fordyce, 47
Ruggles, John, 98
Ruggles, Levi, 84
Ruirdon, Samuel, 247
Ruirdon, William, 247
Rumery, Edward, 149
Rummonds, John, 34, 38
Rummonds, Robert, 34
Rumney, Benjamin, 80, 81
Rumwell, Joseph, 24
Rundel, Reuben, 237
Rundell, Martin, 50
Rundlet, Charles, 156, 157
Rundlet, Oak, 184
Rundlet, Oaks, 186
Rundlett, Oaks, 189
Runnalls, Valentine, 136
Runnel, Isaac, 260
Runnels, Daniel, 240
Runnels, Eliphalet, 90

Runnels, Isaac, 154
Runnels, Isaac E., 260
Runnels, Job, 244
Runnels, Saul, 242
Runnels, Thomas, 295
Runney, William, 160
Runville, Alexander, 44
Rupp, Adam, 80, 110
Rush, John, 247
Rush, Peleg, 247
Rush, Samuel, 12
Rushley, John, 10
Russ, Henry, 227
Russ, John, 226
Russ, Robert, 84
Russell, Abraham, 161
Russell, Abram G., 280
Russell, Amasa, 292, 293
Russell, Asa, 10
Russell, Benjamin, 136
Russell, Benjamin G., 83
Russell, Calvin, 268
Russell, Chandler, 258
Russell, Charles, 45
Russell, Cyrus, 115
Russell, Daniel, 178
Russell, Ebeneser, 43
Russell, Edward, 25, 145
Russell, Elijah, 160
Russell, Ephraim, 82, 223
Russell, Francis, 60, 253
Russell, George, 71, 193
Russell, Humphrey, 55
Russell, Isaac, 278
Russell, Jacob, 223
Russell, Jacob M., 259
Russell, James, 88, 193
Russell, Jeremiah, 194, 223
Russell, Job, 48
Russell, John, 7, 22, 33, 60, 84, 117, 223, 304
Russell, John M., 212
Russell, Jonas, 114
Russell, Joseph, 22, 37, 113, 181
Russell, Lemuel, 55, 58
Russell, Leonard, 306
Russell, Luther, 266
Russell, Nathaniel, 208, 246, 283, 307
Russell, Otis, 84
Russell, Peleg, 291
Russell, Philemon R., 101
Russell, Pliny, 66
Russell, Prince, 127
Russell, Richard, 150
Russell, Robert, 192, 193
Russell, Rufus, 292, 293
Russell, Samuel, 67, 79, 114, 200, 208
Russell, Samuel, Jr., 209
Russell, Saul, 17, 66
Russell, Saul, Jr., 198
Russell, Solomon, 80
Russell, Solomon L., 67
Russell, Stephen, 53
Russell, Stoddard, 155
Russell, Sylvanus, 39
Russell, Thomas, 90, 129, 283
Russell, Valentine, 140
Russell, William, 14, 101, 133, 136, 150, 193
Russell, Ziba, 266
Rust, Henry, 254
Rust, Henry, Jr., 250
Rust, Isaac, 192, 193
Rust, Israel, Jr., 11

Rust, Moses, 14
Rust, Robert, 109
Rust, Samuel, 11
Rust, William, 183, 308
Rust, William C., 13
Ruswell, Benjamin, 202
Ruth, Josiah, 157
Ruth, William, Jr., 50
Rutnam, Austin R., 94
Ryan, Charles, 297, 298
Ryanson, Ebeneser, 242
Ryder, Daniel, 47
Ryder, John D., 285
Ryder, Richard, 304
Ryers, John, 243
Ryerson, William, 250, 254
Ryon, John, Jr., 302
Ryther, Alpha, 65
Ryther, Erastus, 66

S

Sabells, Thomas, 88
Sabine, Hezekiah, 30
Sabor, David, 138
Sacket, Daniel, 29
Sacket, Gad, 4
Sacket, Israel, 46
Sacket, Roy, 119
Sacket, Thomas, 33
Sadder, Silas, 29
Safford, Daniel, 69, 223
Safford, David, 139 (2)
Safford, John, 223
Safford, Joshua, 138
Safford, Moses, 271
Safford, Nathan, 168
Safford, Nathaniel, 132
Safford, Reuben, 203
Safford, Reuben, Jr., 201
Safford, Samuel, 15
Safford, Thomas, 3, 21
Sagar, Robert, 155
Sage, Dennis, 33
Sage, Ira, 31
Sage, John, 32, 134 (2)
St. John, Caleb, 44
Selby, James, 247
Salisbury, Abijah, 43
Salmon, John, 28
Salmon, William, 300
Saltmarsh, Seth, 134, 140
Saltonstall, Richard, 132
Sampreel, Simon, 7
Sampson, Abel, 168
Sampson, Abraham, 93
Sampson, Ahira, 211
Sampson, Alexander, 295
Sampson, Hazel, 168
Sampson, Henry, 230, 231, 296
Sampson, Isaac, 42
Sampson, Isaiah, 176
Sampson, Jacob, 223, 230
Sampson, James, Jr., 231
Sampson, John, 104, 159, 241
Sampson, Joseph, 104, 280
Sampson, Joshua, 320
Sampson, Josiah, Jr., 75
Sampson, Micah, 75, 76
Sampson, Morse, 223
Sampson, Nathaniel, 225
Sampson, Oliver, 168
Sampson, Philip, 41

INDEX.

Sampson, Robert, 168
Sampson, Rufus, 231
Sampson, Samuel, 66
Sampson, Seth, 58, 60, 127
Sampson, Thomas, 103, 235
Sampson, William, 186, 234, 272
Samson, Davis, 240
Samson, George, 38
Samson, John, 53
Samson, Stephen, 55
Samson, Thomas, 53
Sanborn, Asa, 174
Sanborn, Benjamin, 174, 211
Sanborn, Bradbury, 235
Sanborn, Coffin, 160
Sanborn, Daniel, Jr., 212
Sanborn, David, 40, 250, 255
Sanborn, David, Jr., 212
Sanborn, James, Jr., 165
Sanborn, John, 162, 191, 250, 256
Sanborn, John, Jr., 166
Sanborn, Jonathan, 168
Sanborn, Joseph, 171
Sanborn, Levi, 266
Sanborn, Levy, 306
Sanborn, Lewis, 256
Sanborn, Moses, 226, 281
Sanborn, Nathaniel, 258
Sanborn, Newell, 266, 306
Sanborn, Paul, 209
Sanborn, Peter, 170
Sanborn, Stephen, Jr., 282
Sanborn, William, 218
Sanborne, John, 188
Sanborne, Mark, 135, 137
Sanborne, Moses, 135
Sanbourn, Abiather, 215
Sanburn, Daniel, 87
Sand, Saul, 16
Sandborn, Jonathan, 220
Sandburn, Jonathan V., 149
Sandburn, Joseph, 226
Sandburn, Seth, 226
Sandburn, Stephen, 229, 230
Sanders, Abiel, 72
Sanders, Abraham, 74
Sanders, Asa, 88
Sanders, George, Jr., 226
Sanders, George W., 258
Sanders, Jedediah, 15
Sanders, John, 81, 87
Sanders, Levi, 5
Sanders, Peter, 30
Sanders, Robinson G., 75
Sanders, Stephen, 110
Sanders, Thomas M., 136
Sanders, William, 223
Sanderson, Allen, 64
Sanderson, Amos, 70, 86
Sanderson, Benjamin, 117
Sanderson, Elijah, 64
Sanderson, Elisha, 110
Sanderson, Jacob, 115
Sanderson, James, 64
Sanderson, John, 37, 101
Sanderson, Lodi, 82
Sanderson, Luther, 83
Sanderson, Nathan, 82
Sanderson, Saul, 46
Sanderson, Seth, 98
Sanderson, Stephen, 151
Sandes, Marcellus, 29

Sandey, Edward A. H., 132
Sandford, Daniel, 145
Sandford, James, 233
Sandford, John, Jr., 231
Sandford, Josiah, 232
Sandford, Nathaniel, 234, 236
Sandford, Thomas, 56
Sandford, William G., 76, 230
Sands, Ephraim, 160
Sands, Isaac, 35 (2), 37, 154
Sands, James, 269
Sands, Samuel, 269
Sands, Stephen, 35 (2)
Sands, Thomas, 152, 269
Sands, William, 152
Sandwood, Samuel, 137
Sanford, Alonzo, 4
Sanford, Charles, 76
Sanford, Daniel, 179
Sanford, Henry, 179
Sanford, John, Jr., 247
Sanford, Paul, 127
Sanford, Samuel, 68, 75, 80
Sanford, Saul, 53
Sanford, William, 156 (2)
Sanger, John, 246
Sanger, Joseph, 42, 242
Sanger, Samuel F., 51
Sanger, Zebulon, 275
Santer, Noah S., 211
Sargant, William, 279
Sargent, Andrew, 13, 14
Sargent, Benjamin, 246, 259
Sargent, Benjamin C., 13, 14
Sargent, Charles, 11
Sargent, David, 111
Sargent, Dudley, 12
Sargent, Edward, 13, 14
Sargent, Epes, 9
Sargent, George, 14
Sargent, Hall B., 88
Sargent, James, 68
Sargent, Joel, 26
Sargent, John, 275
Sargent, Jonathan, 12, 89
Sargent, Joseph F., 254
Sargent, Leonard A., 198, 208 (3)
Sargent, Levi, 21
Sargent, Lewis, 273
Sargent, Montgomery, 36
Sargent, Moses, 181
Sargent, Oliver, 13, 14
Sargent, Roger, 13, 14
Sargent, Samuel, 80, 118
Sargent, Samuel, Jr., 12
Sargent, Solomon, 24
Sargent, Stephen, 15
Sargent, Thomas, 86, 183
Sargent, William, 15, 279
Sargent, Winthrop, 9
Sartel, Amos, 209
Sartell, Amos, 200, 207
Sarter, David B., 229
Satchel, William, 17
Satchwell, William, 137
Saul, Joseph, 133, 140
Saul, Joshua, 280
Saul, Thomas, 136
Saul, Zebel, Jr., 129
Saulsbury, Abijah W., 89
Saunders, Edward, 132
Saunders, Joseph, 75

Saunders, Kendal P., 78
Saunders, Samuel, 301
Saunders, Simeon, 11
Saunders, William, 21, 113 (2)
Saur, Moses, 210
Savage, Abraham, 182 (2), 191
Savage, Charles, 265
Savage, Daniel, 285
Savage, Daniel, Jr., 276
Savage, David B., 271
Savage, Edward, 69
Savage, Isaac, 271
Savage, Isaac, Jr., 274
Savage, James, 263, 276
Savage, John, 158, 263
Savage, Joseph, 249
Savage, Robert, 265
Savage, Rufus, 191
Savery, Aaron, 222
Savery, Abijah, Jr., 223
Savery, Archibald, 222
Savery, Jotham, 301
Savery, Phineas, 126
Savery, Samuel, 126 (2)
Savil, John, 100
Savil, Samuel, 42
Savill, John, 77
Saville, William, 10
Savory, Harvy, 29
Savory, William, 129
Sawin, Esekiel, 70
Sawtell, Calvin, 23
Sawtell, Elnathan, 198
Sawtell, Henry, 48
Sawtell, Joseph, 84
Sawtell, Nathaniel, 2d, 177
Sawtelle, Abel, 262
Sawtelle, Asa, 263
Sawtelle, Benjamin, 266
Sawtelle, John, 262
Sawtelle, Moses, Jr., 266
Sawyer, Aaron, 304
Sawyer, Abel, 89
Sawyer, Alfred, 303
Sawyer, Anthony, 242
Sawyer, Asa, 220
Sawyer, Asaph, 70
Sawyer, Benjamin, 220
Sawyer, Charles, 13
Sawyer, Daniel, 299
Sawyer, David F., 219
Sawyer, Dean, 172
Sawyer, Ebenezer, 256, 269 (2)
Sawyer, Elisha, 219
Sawyer, Enos, 212
Sawyer, Ephraim, 219
Sawyer, Ezra, 167
Sawyer, George, 312
Sawyer, Henry, 172
Sawyer, Isaac, 173
Sawyer, Ivory, 219
Sawyer, Jacob, Jr., 227
Sawyer, James, 14, 174, 217, 220
Sawyer, James D., 252
Sawyer, John, 15, 40, 174, 220, 226, 282, 305
Sawyer, John, Jr., 219, 220
Sawyer, John G., 48
Sawyer, Jonas, 48
Sawyer, Jonathan, 71
Sawyer, Joseph, 212, 233, 241, 310
Sawyer, Joseph M., 220
Sawyer, Joshua, 48, 220

Sawyer, Josiah, 308
Sawyer, Justum, 270
Sawyer, Leonard, 229
Sawyer, Levi, 211, 307
Sawyer, Luke, 265
Sawyer, Mark, 220
Sawyer, Michael, 270
Sawyer, Moses, 28, 213, 219
Sawyer, Nathan, 255
Sawyer, Nathaniel, 133, 140, 219, 266, 283, 307
Sawyer, Otis, 308
Sawyer, Phinehas, 3
Sawyer, Reuben, 213, 251
Sawyer, Samuel, 66, 273, 296, 297, 300
Sawyer, Saul, 15, 134, 135
Sawyer, Simon, 88
Sawyer, Thaddeus, 168
Sawyer, Thomas, 66
Sawyer, Thomas, Jr., 220
Sawyer, Thomas B., 26, 79
Sawyer, Tristram, 154
Sawyer, William, 13, 242
Sayer, Frederick, 98
Sayward, James, 197, 204 (2), 207
Sayward, Joseph, 197, 203, 204
Sayward, Joseph S., 9
Sayward, Luther, 297
Sayward, William, 9, 12
Scales, John, 227
Scammon, Eliakim, 276
Scammon, John F., 268
Scammon, Samuel, 154
Scates, Joseph, 135, 137
Schenck, Andrew, 292
Scholdfield, Elisha, 31
Schwartz, Jacob, 291
Schwartz, Jacob, 4th, 292
Schwartz, John M., 292
Schwartz, Peter, 291
Scolfield, Jacob, 298
Scott, Aretus, 96
Scott, Daniel, 48, 80, 83, 271
Scott, David, 64
Scott, Elhanan, 86
Scott, Ephraim, 46
Scott, Isaac, 27
Scott, James, 24, 27
Scott, John, 19, 242, 271
Scott, Lewis, 66
Scott, Nathaniel, 70
Scott, Peter, 243
Scott, Samuel, 160
Scott, William, 279
Scott, Zorah, 66
Scovy, Solomon, Jr., 187
Scranton, Amos, 66
Scribner, Daniel, 257
Scribner, Harvey, 211
Scribner, Jonathan, 211, 228
Scribner, Joseph, 210, 211, 258
Scribner, Rufus, 8
Scribner, Samuel, 16
Scribner, Samuel G., 174
Scudder, Charles, 8
Scudder, Palmer, 29
Scudder, William, 262
Sculley, William, 165, 166
Scurl, Wareham, 67
Seabury, Dodge, 105
Seabury, George, 105
Seabury, George, Jr., 105

Seabury, Josiah, 159
Seabury, Millet, 129
Seabury, Pearce, 63
Seagar, Charles H., 46
Seagraves, Joseph, 63
Seague, Nathaniel, 133
Seague, Thomas, 133
Sealey, Sylvester, 296
Sealy, Edward, 15
Seaman, Job, 30
Seame, John G., 162
Seamore, Benjamin, 128
Sear, John, 163
Searl, Jerry, 44
Searle, Ephraim, 70
Searles, Joseph, 82
Searles, Sylvester, 233
Searls, Stephen, 133, 137
Sears, Abner, 67
Sears, Alfred, 32
Sears, Eleaser, 128
Sears, John, 130, 271
Sears, Josiah, 95
Sears, Oliver S., 52
Sears, Peter, 80, 81, 110
Sears, Sylvester, 67
Sears, Thomas, 132
Seaton, James, 83
Seaver, Benjamin, 62, 71
Seaver, Caleb, 173
Seaver, Joseph, 48
Seaver, Peter, 69, 79
Seaver, Thomas, 141
Seavers, William, 81
Seavery, Nathaniel, 206
Seavery, Samuel, 62
Seavey, Daniel, 206
Seavey, David, 62
Seavey, Gideon, 285, 289
Seavey, James, 184, 244
Seavey, Michel, 184
Seavey, Nathaniel, 171, 207
Seavey, Solomon, 171
Seavey, Solomon, Jr., 184
Seavey, Thomas, 284, 294 (2)
Seavey, Thomas B., 247
Seavey, William, 2d, 171
Seavry, Gideon, 286
Seavy, David, 243
Seavy, Rufus, 241
Seavy, Thomas, 288
Seaward, Nathaniel B., 37
Sedgley, James, 282
Sedgley, Joseph, 231
Sedgley, Samuel, 217
Sedgley, Stephen, 231
Sedgly, Daniel, Jr., 216
Sedgly, James, 277
Seekel, Job, 61
Seekell, John, 2d, 62
Seeley, John, 159
Seeman, Ebenezer, 2
Segar, Henry, 116
Segar, John, 116
Segar, Philip S., 21
Segars, Martin, 29
Segars, Philip L., 117
Segers, Henry, 91
Seigars, Ebenezer, 188
Seigars, John, Jr., 187, 191
Sekins, Benjamin, 179
Sekins, Ezekiel, 41

Selange, James, 117
Self, Thomas, 312
Sellars, John, 44
Semes, John, 163
Semond, Samuel, 140
Sennett, Hugh, 296
Sent, Daniel, 312
Sent, Jacob, 312
Sent, John, 312
Sent, John, 2d, 312
Sepl, Joshua, 57
Sergeant, David, 11
Sergeant, John, 235
Sergent, Levi, 135
Sergent, Simon G., 306
Serill, William, 255
Sessions, Robert, 44
Sevars, Benjamin, 22
Sevens, Nathaniel, 229
Severance, Benjamin, 216
Severance, John, 217
Severance, Joseph, 216
Severance, Reuben, 217
Severance, Rufus, 16
Severance, Samuel, 217
Severens, Rodney, 81
Severs, Henry, 269
Sevey, Jacob, 163
Sevey, James, 182 (2)
Sevey, John, 182, 191
Sevey, Michel, 182 (2)
Sevey, Solomon, Jr., 182
Sewall, Benjamin, 182
Sewall, Charles, 276, 297
Sewall, Daniel, 240, 267
Sewall, David, 187
Sewall, Henry, 228, 283
Sewall, Jason, 182
Sewall, Jotham, Jr., 226
Sewall, Moses, 146
Sewall, Oliver, 228
Sewall, Rufus, 185
Sewall, Samuel, 182
Sewall, Stephen, 277
Sewall, Thomas R., 8
Sewall, William, 247, 295
Sewall, William B., 145, 241, 242
Seward, John, Jr., 240
Sewards, Nathaniel B., 36
Sewell, Charles, 247
Sewell, Dummer, Jr., 228
Sewell, Joshua, 227
Sewell, Samuel, 118
Sewell, William, 271
Sexton, Orin B., 41
Seymour, Friend, 27, 77
Seyross, Francis, 6
Shackley, Daniel, 244
Shackley, Daniel, Jr., 310
Shackley, Joseph, 53, 245
Shacksford, William, 2
Shadbourn, Isaac, 2
Shadman, John, Jr., 213
Shaites, Edmund, 71
Shales, William, 78
Shane, William, 226
Shannemon, James, 294
Shannon, M., 136
Shattuck, Calvin, 4, 87
Shattuck, David, 187
Shattuck, Henry, 9
Shattuck, Jacob W., 44

INDEX. 419

Shattuck, Jesse, 09
Shattuck, Noah, 87, 88
Shattuck, Samuel, 165 (2)
Shattuck, Thomas, 66
Shattuck, Walter, 88
Shaw, Abisha M., 55, 158
Shaw, Abraham, 58
Shaw, Advardis, 238
Shaw, Advertis, 265
Shaw, Alvin, 97
Shaw, Amos, 150, 176
Shaw, Bela, 220
Shaw, Benjamin, 52
Shaw, Benjamin, 2d, 129
Shaw, Brackley, 43, 92
Shaw, Cassine D., 62
Shaw, Charles, 9
Shaw, Coburn, 54
Shaw, Daniel, 35 (2), 92, 171, 223, 305
Shaw, Davenport, 85
Shaw, David, 212, 295
Shaw, Eben, 53
Shaw, Ebenezer, 53, 227, 239
Shaw, Ebenezer, Jr., 174
Shaw, Ebenezer, 2d, 92
Shaw, Eber, 66
Shaw, Edward, 260
Shaw, Eli, 53
Shaw, Eliab, Jr., 158
Shaw, Elijah, 51
Shaw, Elisha, 52, 54, 66
Shaw, Enoch, 174
Shaw, Francis, 238, 253
Shaw, Freeman, 265
Shaw, Gains, 102
Shaw, George, 52, 55, 58, 146
Shaw, George M., 90
Shaw, Gilman, 229
Shaw, Isaac, Jr., 273
Shaw, James, 58, 248, 262
Shaw, Jesse, 84, 109, 177
Shaw, Job, 223, 259
Shaw, Joel, 53
Shaw, John, 39, 52, 66, 86, 91, 102, 169, 274, 281, 295
Shaw, John A., 108
Shaw, John M., 281
Shaw, John P., 226
Shaw, Joseph, 46, 95, 129, 219, 227, 249, 282, 297
Shaw, Joshua, 53
Shaw, Joshua, Jr., 103
Shaw, Leonard, 65
Shaw, Levin, 99
Shaw, Luke, 237
Shaw, Marshall, 103
Shaw, N., 50
Shaw, Nathaniel, 50, 243, 306
Shaw, Nathaniel T., 86
Shaw, Oliver, 61, 86
Shaw, Orin, 158
Shaw, Peter, 174
Shaw, Richard, Jr., 258
Shaw, Samuel, 31, 51, 61, 95, 103, 176, 199, 200, 202, 226
Shaw, Sargent, Jr., 174
Shaw, Silas, 102
Shaw, Solomon, 65, 146, 150
Shaw, Sullivan, 53
Shaw, Thomas, 51, 55, 58, 110, 233
Shaw, Walter, 44
Shaw, William, 18, 19, 52, 55, 58, 120, 123, 243, 275

Shaw, William H., 216
Shaw, William W., 31
Shaw, Zacheriah, 64
Shaw, Zephaniah, 53
Shea, David, 247
Shea, Nicholas, 247
Shead, Oliver, 159
Sheafe, William, 150, 242
Sheaffe, Richard, 305
Shearer, Pierce, 45
Shearer, Reuben, 205
Shearman, Allen, 1
Shearman, C., 63
Shearman, Emery, 90
Shearman, James, 33
Shearman, John, 33
Shearman, John, 3d, 130
Shearman, John A., 63
Shearman, Joseph, 33, 185
Shearman, Seth, 33
Shearman, Stephen, 55, 126
Shearman, Uriah, 55
Shearman, William, 63, 185
Shed, James, 80
Shed, John, 254, 258
Shed, Josiah, 274
Shed, Pierce, 181
Shed, Samuel, 25
Shed, Samuel A., 83
Shed, Silas, 253
Shehan, Benjamin, 154
Shehan, Daniel, 138
Shelby, Libeus, 59
Shelden, Saul, 136
Sheldon, Alva, 66
Sheldon, Daniel, 30
Sheldon, Israel, 66
Sheldon, John, 182 (2), 191
Sheldon, Joshua, 35
Sheldon, Nathaniel W., 145
Sheldon, Samuel H., 138
Sheldon, Webb, 184
Sheldon, William, 87
Sheldron, Fred, 187
Shelley, Libeus, 62
Shelly, Seth, 62
Shennemow, James, 290
Shepard, James, 25
Shepard, Jonathan, 116
Shepard, S. W., 138
Shepard, Thomas, 83
Sheperd, Thaddeus, 290
Sheperdson, Arema, 3
Sheperdson, Elijah, 3
Shepherd, Artemas, 277
Shepherd, Charles, 271
Shepherd, Cheney, 48
Shepherd, Edward, 82
Shepherd, Green, 253
Shepherd, Nathan, 286
Shepherd, Samuel, 64
Shepherd, Sterry, 65
Shepherd, Theodore, 46
Shepherd, Thomas R., 42
Shepherdson, Amos, 65
Shepherdson, Lovell, 30
Sheppard, Cullever, 196
Sheppard, Davis, 192
Sheppard, Francis, 196
Sheppard, James, Jr., 196
Sheppard, Samuel, 196
Sheppard, William, Jr., 196

Shepperd, Silas, 59
Sherburn, Elias, 280
Sherburn, George, 245
Sherburn, James, 275
Sherer, Joseph, 64
Sherkley, Ephraim, 55
Sherman, Aaron, 189
Sherman, Almarine, 198, 199, 207
Sherman, Earl, 47
Sherman, Ebenezer, 129
Sherman, Elisha, 183
Sherman, Ephraim, 5
Sherman, Isaac, 52
Sherman, James, 24, 81
Sherman, Job, 30
Sherman, John, 31, 183
Sherman, Joseph, 183, 198, 200
Sherman, Joseph, Jr., 45, 202
Sherman, Nathan, 51, 197
Sherman, Nathan, Jr., 204 (2), 207
Sherman, Peleg, 126
Sherman, Reuben, 87
Sherman, Robert, 63, 284
Sherman, Samuel, 99
Sherman, Solomon, 32
Sherman, Thomas, 131
Sherman, Thomas B., 128
Sherman, William, 63
Sherman, Willis, 52, 54
Sherman, Zacheus, 129
Sherrill, John, 29
Sherry, Wiman, 264
Shertley, Ephraim, 58
Sherwin, Elnathan, 261, 265
Sherwin, Richard, 108
Sherwood, Orson, 94
Sheverick, Turner, 103
Shibles, Simon, 205 (2), 207
Shillaber, Benjamin, 135, 137
Shillaber, John, 132
Shillaber, William, 160
Shilton, Richard, 165
Shingon, Elisha, 141
Shinkle, John, 32
Shipe, Charles, 247
Shiple, Danforth, 8
Shipley, Jonathan, 167
Shipley, Oliver, 87
Shippee, Amasa, 64
Shippee, Reuben, 64
Shirley, Arthur, 241, 242
Shirley, John, 7, 22
Shirley, Jonathan, 150, 151
Shirley, Joshua, 241, 242
Shirley, William, 151
Shirtliff, Alva, 252, 255
Shirtliff, Isaac, 230
Shirtliff, William, 230, 296
Shiverick, Foster, 76
Shiverick, Nathaniel, 73, 76
Shiverick, William, 73
Shoates, William, 71
Shoney, Benjamin, 179
Shoney, Edmund, 179
Shoney, James, 179
Shorey, Benjamin, 137
Shorey, James, 153, 267
Shorey, Samuel, 79, 266
Shorry, Daniel, 239
Shorry, Urban, 258
Short, Charles, 18
Short, Daniel, 30

420   INDEX.

Short, George, 18
Short, Henry, 17
Short, Joseph, Jr., 18
Short, Nicholas, 20
Short, Samuel, 51
Short, Sewell, 15
Shreve, Isaac, 139 (2)
Shuman, Andrews, 136
Shuman, John, 291
Shuman, Joseph, 291
Shumway, Asa, 68
Shumway, Edward, 48
Shumway, Ellis, 43, 89
Shurtliff, Abiel, 52, 102
Shurtliff, Barnabas, 129
Shurtliff, Ebeneser, 129
Shurtliff, William, 52
Shurts, Moody, 271
Shute, Aaron, 16
Shute, Berry, 303
Shute, Jacob, 27
Shute, John, 302
Shute, Samuel, 171
Shute, Thomas, 303
Sibley, Benjamin, F., 217
Sibley, Isaac, 3
Sibley, Jacob, 286
Sibley, Jonas, 92
Sibley, Joseph, 137
Sibley, Nathaniel, 48
Sibley, Timothy, 217
Sibly, Alva, 29
Sibly, David, 214
Sibly, John, 32
Sibly, Joseph, 133
Sidelinger, Charles, 181, 195
Sidelinger, George, 289
Sidelinger, Jacob, 145, 194
Sidelinger, John, 181, 194
Sidelinger, Peter, 192
Sidelinger, Samuel, 194
Sidensparder, George, 290, 293
Sidensparder, John, 290, 293
Siders, Daniel, 193, 197
Siders, Martin, 41
Sides, Charles, 289, 291
Sides, John, 292
Sides, Lorin, 291
Sides, Philip, 289
Sienett, Stephen, 98
Sikes, James, 46
Sikes, Shardat, 29
Silas, Samuel, 301
Silliway, Joseph, 19
Silloway, David S., 89
Silloway, Joseph, 85, 120 (2), 121, 123, 124, 125 (2)
Silloway, William, 20
Silloway, Daniel, 15
Silsbee, John, 282
Silsbee, Nathaniel, 118
Silsbee, Nathaniel S., 138
Silsbee, Samuel, 138
Silsbee, William, 138
Silsbee, Zachariah F., 134
Silsbee, Zacheus F., 135
Silsby, Isaac, 98
Silsby, Phinehas, 48
Silver, Isaiah, 8
Silver, James, 138
Silver, John P., 90
Silvester, Joseph, 1

Silvester, Thomas, 130
Simmonds, Joshua, 69
Simmonds, Lemuel, 131
Simmons, Benjamin, 63, 199, 203
Simmons, Charles W., 103
Simmons, Daniel, 260, 275
Simmons, Ebeneser, 127
Simmons, George, 43, 89, 198, 199, 201 (3), 202, 203
Simmons, James, 129, 292
Simmons, Jedediah, 199, 200, 203
Simmons, John, 9
Simmons, Joseph, 47
Simmons, Lemuel, 128
Simmons, Levi, 181
Simmons, Luke, 68
Simmons, Martin, 128
Simmons, Moses, 282
Simmons, Nathan, 59
Simmons, Noah, 131
Simmons, Oliver, 209
Simmons, Oliver, Jr., 199
Simmons, Peabody, 200, 203
Simmons, Reuben, 42
Simmons, Russell, 60
Simmons, Samuel, 153
Simmons, Thomas, 62, 292
Simmons, Weston, 128
Simmons, William, 129
Simmons, Zebedee, 291
Simonds, Andrew, 14, 36
Simonds, Ebeneser F., 32
Simonds, Elijah, 48
Simonds, Isaac W., 115
Simonds, John J., 225
Simonds, Joseph, 24
Simonds, Reuben, 9
Simonds, Samuel, 226
Simonds, Shepherd, 84
Simonds, Solomon, 100
Simonds, William, 3
Simons, James, 87
Simons, Moses, 290, 293
Simons, Silas, 87
Simons, Thomas, 90
Simons, Ziba, 290, 293
Simonton, Abraham, 197, 205 (2)
Simonton, Benjamin, 192, 193
Simonton, James, 243, 255
Simonton, John, 197, 202, 204 (2), 208, 242
Simonton, John, Jr., 207
Simonton, John, 2d, 204
Simonton, Thomas, 219
Simonton, William, 198, 199
Simpson, Andrew, 77
Simpson, Benjamin, 2, 108
Simpson, Charles, 85
Simpson, Daniel, 7, 23, 80, 83, 113, 292
Simpson, Joshua, 270
Simpson, Lewis, 298
Simpson, Lewy, Jr., 297
Simpson, Mathew, 298
Simpson, Matthew, 297
Simpson, Paul R., 261
Simpson, Robert, 65, 157 (3), 184, 189, 297, 298
Simpson, Robert, Jr., 184
Simpson, Thomas, 148
Simpson, William, 184 (2), 187, 188, 189, 261, 278, 282, 298
Simpson, William, Jr., 186
Sinclair, James, 290

Sinclair, Benjamin, 170
Sinclair, Ebeneser, 281
Sinclair, James, 168, 286
Sinclair, John, 233, 296
Sinclair, John M., 180
Sinclair, Jonathan, 306
Sinclair, Robert, 80, 81
Sinclair, William, 200, 281
Sinderson, John, 244
Singer, Jesse, 77
Singleton, George, 80, 82
Sinkley, Nathaniel, 233
Sinnet, Hugh, 299
Sisson, Benjamin, 56, 61
Sisson, Charles, 115
Sisson, Daniel, 56
Sisson, Edward, 63
Sisson, George, 56
Sisson, John, 129
Sisson, Joseph, 63
Skeels, Anias, 17
Skeery, William, 138
Skerry, Chipman, 134
Skerry, Ephraim, 135
Skerry, John, 134
Skerry, John, Jr., 140
Skiff, Abraham, 53
Skiff, Russell, 31
Skillen, Alexander, 219
Skillen, Daniel, Jr., 219
Skillen, Isaac, 219
Skillen, Lemuel, 219
Skillen, Rufus, 219
Skillen, William, 219
Skillen, Zebulon, 219
Skillin, Dennis, 172
Skillin, Enoch, 172
Skillin, James, 239
Skillin, Josiah B., 172
Skillin, Lemuel, 166
Skilling, Edward, Jr., 210
Skillings, Benjamin, 173
Skillings, Isaac, 212
Skillings, James, 212
Skillings, John, 211, 243, 258 (2), 305
Skillings, Joseph, 210
Skillings, Josiah, 172
Skillings, Lemuel, 164, 165
Skillings, Reuben, 212
Skillings, Samuel, 210
Skillings, Simon, 226
Skilton, Richard, 164 (2)
Skinner, Alexander, 292, 293
Skinner, Alfred, 54
Skinner, Charles, 70
Skinner, David, 223, 259
Skinner, Ebeneser, 292, 293
Skinner, Freeman, 166
Skinner, Herbert, 54
Skinner, Isaac, 293
Skinner, Jacob, 116
Skinner, James, 292, 293
Skinner, John, 22, 46, 290, 293
Skinner, Joseph, 118, 292, 293
Skinner, Loring, 54
Skinner, Peter, 210
Skinner, Samuel, 300
Skinner, Solon, 60
Skinner, Thomas, 292, 293
Skinner, Zophar, 10
Skofield, Jacob, 297
Skofield, James, 298

INDEX. 421

Skofield, John, 297
Skofield, Samuel, 299
Slade, Isaac, 2
Slade, John, 2, 108
Slade, William, 274
Slater, Alanson, 31
Slater, Andrew, 3
Slater, Samuel, 3
Slayton, Charles, 45
Sleavry, John, 163
Sleeper, Chase S., 226
Sleeper, Jere, 204 (2)
Sleeper, Jesse, 197, 204 (2)
Sleeper, Nathan, 166, 290
Sleeper, Nathaniel, 286
Sleeper, Samuel, 226
Sleet, James, 90
Slemmon, Andrew, 136
Slemmon, Hezekiah, 216
Slemon, William, 221
Sloan, Francis, 26
Sloan, John, 267
Sloan, Robert, 298
Slocken, Amos, 118
Slocum, Charles, 126
Slocum, Charles C., 46
Slocum, Ebenezer, 134
Slocum, Ebenezer, Jr., 134
Slocum, Frederic, 63
Slocum, Giles, 63
Slocum, Lemuel S., 30
Slocum, Otis, 117
Slocumb, Frederic, 96
Sloper, Noah, 221
Slover, Charles, 285
Small, Asa, 220
Small, Benjamin, 155, 160
Small, Daniel, 209, 210, 240, 250 (2), 307
Small, David, 155
Small, Ebenezer, 169, 270
Small, Edward, 155
Small, Elisha, 229
Small, Ephraim, 249, 270
Small, Francis, 155, 231, 258
Small, Humphrey, 155
Small, Isaac, 48, 106, 155, 170, 240, 277
Small, Israel, 225, 300, 311
Small, James, 155, 156, 177, 229, 233, 235, 253
Small, Jeremiah, 256
Small, Joel, 166
Small, John, 221, 232, 250, 256, 257
Small, John, 2d, 232
Small, John S., Jr., 221
Small, Jonathan, 197, 204, 231
Small, Joseph, 181, 221
Small, Joshua, 155
Small, Levi, 210
Small, Mark, 232
Small, Nathan, 238
Small, Nathaniel C., 155
Small, Nehemiah, 160
Small, Peter, 220
Small, Phineas, 236, 267
Small, Reuben, 172
Small, Samuel, 152, 155
Small, Saul, 260
Small, Simeon, 210
Small, Stephen, 232 (2)
Small, Tailor, 232 (2)
Small, Thomas, 233
Small, William, 155

Small, Zacheriah, 106, 107 (2), 108
Smalley, Anthony, 72
Smalley, Archelaus, 206
Smalley, Isaac, 206 (2)
Smalley, James, 72
Smallidge, Jeremiah, 69
Smallpeace, Robert, 84, 110
Smally, Joshua, 207
Smart, Anthony, 243
Smart, Daniel, 301
Smart, Ephraim K., 301
Smart, Ira, 261
Smart, Jacob, 181
Smart, Jeremiah, 224, 259
Smart, Jonathan, 181, 240, 265
Smart, Levi, 240
Smart, Nehemiah, 226
Smart, Richard, 240, 301
Smart, Robert, 230
Smart, William, 232
Smart, William, 2d, 232, 296
Smart, Winthrop, 226
Smead, Elihu, 4
Smodly, Joseph, 30
Smethhurst, Benjamin, 21
Smiler, Francis, 262
Smiley, David, 299
Smiley, Dean M., 274
Smiley, Joseph, 153
Smiley, Lemuel, 266
Smith, Aaron, 64, 149
Smith, Aaron, 3d, 14
Smith, Abial, 169
Smith, Abiathar, 131, 208
Smith, Abiather, 156, 159, 198
Smith, Abiel, 211
Smith, Abner, 46
Smith, Abraham, 153, 306
Smith, Adolphus, 3
Smith, Amasa, 33, 44, 272
Smith, Amerith, 44
Smith, Amos, 258
Smith, Andrew, 40
Smith, Ansel, 102
Smith, Anson, 46
Smith, Anthony, 19
Smith, Antipas, 252
Smith, Archibald, 233
Smith, Artemus, 153
Smith, Asa, 5, 86, 152, 256, 303
Smith, Ashley, 64
Smith, Barnabas, 1
Smith, Benjamin, 9, 33, 116, 129, 210, 235, 244, 263
Smith, Benjamin, Jr., 131, 258
Smith, Benjamin W., 135, 137
Smith, Bowen, 278
Smith, Bradbury, 280
Smith, Bradwell, Jr., 66
Smith, Caleb, 15, 132, 173
Smith, Carpenter, 278, 282
Smith, Charles, 13, 75, 135, 276, 281
Smith, Charles, Jr., 233
Smith, Charles W., 14
Smith, Chester, 67
Smith, Christopher, 128
Smith, Cicero, 70
Smith, Clark, 147
Smith, Clement, 270
Smith, Cyrus, 24, 114
Smith, Daniel, 17, 18, 65, 77, 89, 115, 163 (2), 214, 215, 273

Smith, David, 12, 268, 306
Smith, David P., 283
Smith, Dennis, 92
Smith, Dudley, 184, 185, 186 (2), 187, 190
Smith, Ebenezer, 52, 93, 211
Smith, Edward, 296
Smith, Eleazer, 147 (2)
Smith, Elijah, 53, 86, 92, 163 (2), 213, 229, 306
Smith, Eliphalet, 9
Smith, Elisha, 67, 106, 107 (2), 108, 126
Smith, Elkins, 306
Smith, Elliot, 133, 140, 178, 260
Smith, Enoch, 30
Smith, Ephraim, 17, 122, 123 (2)
Smith, Ephraim I., 119, 120 (3), 121 (2)
Smith, Ephraim J., 124 (3)
Smith, Ezekiel, 36
Smith, Francis, 183, 189, 308
Smith, Gad, Jr., 96
Smith, George, 46, 133, 137, 169, 233, 278, 283, 301
Smith, George G., 113 (2)
Smith, George T., 173
Smith, George W., 28
Smith, Gilman, 306
Smith, Glisson, 67
Smith, Harry, 31
Smith, Hatevil H., 177
Smith, Henry, 10, 146, 165 (2), 216, 241, 242, 305
Smith, Hoel, 19
Smith, Hubbel, 31
Smith, Hugh, 272
Smith, Ichabod, 204
Smith, Increase, 127
Smith, Ira, 77
Smith, Isaac, 1, 75, 107 (2), 230, 233, 272
Smith, Isaac W., 37
Smith, Israel, 129, 155, 177, 312
Smith, J. E., 2
Smith, Jabes, 33
Smith, Jacob, 131, 169
Smith, Jacob, Jr., 215
Smith, Jacob S., 173
Smith, James, 15, 47, 118, 132, 138, 158, 170, 210, 215, 231, 233, 238, 245, 258, 265, 278, 296
Smith, James, Jr., 45
Smith, James A., 181
Smith, James B., 230
Smith, James C., 85
Smith, James P., 22
Smith, James S., 6
Smith, Jasiel, 227
Smith, Jeremiah, 97, 153, 235
Smith, Jesse, 32, 46
Smith, Jesse, Jr., 132
Smith, Joab, 46
Smith, Joel, 18, 28, 271
Smith, John, 27, 28, 41, 50, 161, 174, 213, 214, 218, 230, 234, 246 (2), 249, 256, 258, 266, 270, 273, 275, 278, 281, 312
Smith, John, Jr., 12, 26, 181, 280, 302
Smith, John, 2d, 270
Smith, John H., 278, 282
Smith, John L., 11
Smith, John M., 238, 266
Smith, John P., 33
Smith, John T., 170
Smith, John W., 244, 275
Smith, Jonathan, 80, 243, 283

INDEX.

Smith, Joseph, 5, 73, 83, 106, 107, 108, 134, 140, 151, 154 (2), 195, 203, 215, 231, 243, 245 (2), 258, 280, 284, 301
Smith, Joseph, Jr., 75
Smith, Joseph B., 50, 135, 137
Smith, Joseph S., 146
Smith, Josiah, 1, 86, 106, 107 (2), 108, 162
Smith, Justin, 96
Smith, Justus, 67
Smith, Lebina, 67
Smith, Lemuel, 162, 215, 307
Smith, Lemuel, 3d, 17
Smith, Levi, 94
Smith, Lewis, 91
Smith, Liba, 307
Smith, Lorenzo, 92
Smith, Luke, 90
Smith, Mace, 224
Smith, Mack, 174
Smith, Mager, 64
Smith, Mark, 69
Smith, Marshall, 258
Smith, Martin, 25, 33, 45, 77, 294
Smith, Mathew, 45
Smith, Mathias, 75
Smith, Michel, 44
Smith, Moses, 238, 244
Smith, Myrick, 230
Smith, Nathan, 149, 229, 233, 280, 282, 287
Smith, Nathaniel, 10, 13, 30, 82, 132, 162, 231
Smith, Nathaniel, Jr., 162
Smith, Nehemiah, 34, 38
Smith, Nicholas, 244
Smith, Nicholas, Jr., 251
Smith, Noah, 154
Smith, Nowell, 24, 81, 114
Smith, Obed, 301
Smith, Oliver, 70, 99
Smith, Otis, 43
Smith, Parsons, 158
Smith, Pelatiah, 254
Smith, Peter, 99, 261
Smith, Philo, 33
Smith, Phineas, 48, 64, 77
Smith, Pitts, 97
Smith, Pliney, 27
Smith, Ralph, 82
Smith, Ransford, 308
Smith, Reuben, 132, 268, 282
Smith, Revel, 190
Smith, Richard, 5, 17, 204, 205, 263, 303
Smith, Richard T., 258
Smith, Rind, 187
Smith, Robert, 79, 80, 84, 96, 109
Smith, Ruel, 185
Smith, Rufus, 23
Smith, Russell, 46
Smith, Sabinas, 33
Smith, Samuel, 20, 24, 25, 64, 79, 89, 94, 98, 147, 171, 263, 264, 275, 276, 279, 303
Smith, Samuel, Jr., 215, 231
Smith, Samuel E., 156
Smith, Samuel G., 185, 189, 191
Smith, Samuel W., 230
Smith, Sardius, 48
Smith, Saul G., 183
Smith, Saul W., 15
Smith, Silas, 211
Smith, Simon, 116
Smith, Stephen, 36, 66, 245, 274
Smith, Stillman, 9, 10
Smith, Stinson, 276

Smith, Sylvanus, 131
Smith, Taylor, 106, 107
Smith, Theophilus, 151
Smith, Thomas, 14, 87, 90, 132, 161, 174, 230, 284, 294
Smith, Thomas, Jr., 154
Smith, Thomas B., 55
Smith, Timothy, 25
Smith, Trueworthy, 306
Smith, Tustin, 18
Smith, Tyng, 221
Smith, Walden, 280
Smith, Walter, 66
Smith, Warren, 33
Smith, Wilber, 62
Smith, William, 20, 33, 56, 66, 92, 106 (2), 107, 108, 117, 118, 133, 137, 139, 154, 172, 212, 224, 233, 240, 241, 242, 246, 263, 266, 276, 278, 285, 307
Smith, William, Jr., 172, 270
Smith, William, 2d, 285
Smith, William G., 84
Smith, William H., 158, 252, 255
Smith, Zenas, 217
Smith, Zenos, 9, 268
Smithers, Gamaliel, 7, 22
Smothers, Benjamin, 133
Smullen, Joseph, 233
Snell, Abel, 55
Snell, Appleton, 262
Snell, Benjamin, Jr., 51
Snell, Besar, 267
Snell, Beser, 273
Snell, Caleb, 150
Snell, Chadrick, 286
Snell, David, 267, 290, 310
Snell, Edward, 237
Snell, Eleaser, 178, 305
Snell, Henry, 56
Snell, James, 56, 305
Snell, Jeremiah, 50
Snell, Job, 213
Snell, John, 56, 212
Snell, Leonard, 55
Snell, Matthew, 50
Snell, Moses, 260
Snell, Moses, Jr., 178
Snell, Oliver, 50
Snell, Robert, 213
Snell, Samuel, 50
Snell, Shadrack, 290
Snelling, Christopher, 25, 77
Snelling, Enoch H., 28
Snelling, Ephraim, 26, 79
Snelling, Henry, 86
Snelling, John, 26, 134, 140
Snelling, Moses, 14
Snelling, Nathaniel G., 26
Snelling, Samuel G., 26
Snipe, Charles, 247
Snipe, John, Jr., 247
Snow, Abiather, 106 (2), 108
Snow, Abieser, 298
Snow, Amasa, 24
Snow, Ambrose, 197, 204 (2)
Snow, Ansel, 287, 292, 294
Snow, Benjamin, 130, 216, 247
Snow, Caleb, 29
Snow, Charles, 49
Snow, Daniel, 49, 54, 117, 217
Snow, David, 49
Snow, Dean S., 104

Snow, Ebeneaer, 59, 295, 296
Snow, Edmund, 106
Snow, Edmund, Jr., 104, 105 (2), 107
Snow, Edward, 217
Snow, Elisha, 199
Snow, Elnathan, 105, 106, 107
Snow, Ephraim, 41, 130 (2), 217
Snow, Ezekiel, 72
Snow, Fletcher, 107
Snow, Freeman, 216
Snow, George, 91
Snow, Gideon S., 106 (2), 107 (2), 108
Snow, Harding, 226
Snow, Harry C., 217
Snow, Henry, 252
Snow, Henry C., 162
Snow, Hercules, 75
Snow, Herman, 3d, 107
Snow, Hiram, 245
Snow, Isaac, 232 (2), 235, 296
Snow, Isaiah, Jr., 300
Snow, Israel, 197, 200, 204 (2), 216
Snow, Jacob, 65
Snow, James, 130, 151, 256
Snow, Jesse, 105, 107, 300, 311
Snow, Jesse, Jr., 229, 300, 311
Snow, John, 25 (2), 79, 114, 232 (2), 297
Snow, John M., 197
Snow, John P., 7
Snow, Jonas, 48
Snow, Jonathan, 104, 105 (2), 106 (2), 107, 232 (2)
Snow, Jordan, 299
Snow, Joseph, 152, 217, 254
Snow, Joshua, 261
Snow, Knowles, 127
Snow, Larkin, 25
Snow, Levi, 224, 260
Snow, Linus, 59
Snow, Loami, 58
Snow, Loring, 31
Snow, Luther, 105
Snow, Martin, 83
Snow, Micajah, 214
Snow, Moses, 295, 296
Snow, Nathan, 53
Snow, Nathaniel D., 159
Snow, Paul, 299
Snow, Paul M., 226
Snow, Phares, 171
Snow, Prince, 106
Snow, Robinson, 130
Snow, Royal, 25, 79
Snow, Samuel, 104, 300
Snow, Samuel, Jr., 7
Snow, Saul, 311
Snow, Silas, 152, 254
Snow, Simeon, 295, 297
Snow, Sprague, 50
Snow, Stephen, 299
Snow, Thatcher, 105 (2), 106
Snow, Thomas, 7, 22, 68
Snow, Tilley, 27
Snow, William, 5, 197, 204 (2), 207, 216, 248
Snow, William, Jr., 173
Snowden, William, 83
Snowman, Charles, 149
Soal, Asa, 45
Soames, David, 184
Sole, Joshua, 222
Sollanus, Francis, 90
Somerby, Arthur, 20, 121, 123

INDEX.

Somerby, Enoch, 20
Somerby, Profit, 69
Somerby, Robert, 83
Somerby, Thomas, 119, 120, 123
Somerby, Thomas, Jr., 19, 122
Somerby, William, 120 (2), 122, 123
Somerby, William, Jr., 120
Somersby, Robert, 86
Somersby, William, 89
Somes, Burley, 287
Somes, David, 187
Somes, Isaac, 12
Somes, John G., 41, 79
Somes, Joseph, 9
Somes, Nehemiah, 182, 184, 285, 287
Somes, Simeon, 184, 188
Soper, Alexander, 223, 260
Soper, Gad, 223, 260
Soper, Jesse, 228, 283
Soper, Nathaniel, 222
Soper, Oliver, 59
Sotherly, William, 258
Soul, David, 249
Soule, Aaron, 177
Soule, Abraham, 271
Soule, Alexander, 257
Soule, Barnabas, 209, 226
Soule, Benjamin, 212
Soule, Besa, 259
Soule, Bezai, 223
Soule, Cornelius, 209
Soule, Daniel, 209
Soule, David, 263
Soule, Emory, 209
Soule, Ezekiel, 179
Soule, Ezra, 51
Soule, George, 267
Soule, Isaac, 51 (2), 63, 209, 212
Soule, Jabez, 95
Soule, James, 209
Soule, James, Jr., 253
Soule, John, 49, 179, 212
Soule, John, Jr., 51, 103
Soule, Joseph, 179, 223
Soule, Joseph E., 209
Soule, Josiah, 126, 303
Soule, Levi, 289, 294, 310
Soule, Nathan, 97
Soule, Nathaniel, 90
Soule, Peletiah, 263
Soule, Philander, 264
Soule, Phineas, 212
Soule, Robert, 210
Soule, Rufus, 227, 282
Soule, Samuel, 212, 260
Soule, Samuel W., 177
Soule, Sylvanus, 1
Soule, Thomas, 51
Soule, Timothy, 209
Soule, William, 51, 306
Southack, Ciprian, 79
Southack, James G., 80
Southack, Joseph D., 114
Southack, Joseph G., 113
Southack, Robert G., 113
Southard, Constant, 168, 281
Southard, John, 307
Southard, Joslin, 274
Southard, Stephen, 306
Souther, Asa, 42
Souther, Daniel, 64
Souther, Isaiah, 84

Souther, Moses, 87
Souther, Nathan, 42
Southerland, Alexander, Jr., 233
Southerland, Benjamin, 233
Southerlin, George, 149
Southward, John, 184
Southward, John, Jr., 183, 188
Southward, Leonard, 52, 54
Southwarth, Lewis, 77
Southwick, Daniel, 3d, 98
Southwick, James, 116
Southwick, John, 118, 133, 140
Southwick, Joseph, 138
Southworth, Apollos, 86
Southworth, Edward, 51
Southworth, Lewis, 26
Southworth, Richard, 134, 135
Southworth, Thomas, 52, 68
Southworth, William, 54
Soveraigh, Joseph, 245
Soyer, Joseph, 108
Spafford, Henry, 9
Spafford, John, 285, 286
Spalding, John, 250
Spangler, Mathias, 312
Sparahawk, John, 133
Sparhawk, John, 7
Sparhawk, John, Jr., 6
Spark, James, Jr., 296
Sparks, David, 64
Sparrow, Benjamin, 162, 216
Sparrow, Bradford, 60
Sparrow, Godfrey, 105
Sparrow, Harvey, 105 (3), 106, 107
Sparrow, Isaac, 104, 105 (2), 106, 107
Sparrow, Joel, 105, 106, 107
Sparrow, John, 105
Sparrow, Jonathan, 266
Sparrow, Joshua, 162, 216
Sparrow, Joshua R., 105 (3), 106, 107
Sparrow, Josiah, 105, 106, 215
Sparrow, Samuel, 105 (2), 106, 107
Sparrow, Seth, 105, 106
Sparrow, Stephen, 240
Sparrow, William, 223
Sparrowhawk, Charles, 40
Sparrowhawk, John, 137
Spaulding, Andrew, 238
Spaulding, Arthur, 307
Spaulding, Asa, 302
Spaulding, Daniel, 284
Spaulding, George, 8
Spaulding, Jonas, 251
Spaulding, Joseph, 10
Spaulding, Luther, 141
Spaulding, Maurice, 48
Spaulding, Oliver, 19
Spaulding, Otis, 284
Spaulding, Robert, 159, 303
Spaulding, Samuel, 8
Spaulding, Stephen, 303
Spaulding, Sylvester, 266
Spaulding, Sylvester G., 262
Spaulding, Union, 307
Spaulding, William, 251, 259
Spes, David, 297
Spead, Robert, 24
Spear, Alexander, 290, 293
Spear, Daniel, 28
Spear, Daniel B., 100
Spear, David, 293

Spear, Edward, 285, 286 (2), 289
Spear, Elkanah, 204, 205
Spear, Gershom, 79, 81
Spear, Gideon, 286
Spear, Hugh, 293
Spear, Isaac, 42, 290, 293
Spear, Israel, 272
Spear, James, 204, 205
Spear, John, 199
Spear, Joseph C., 28
Spear, Joshua, 78
Spear, Lemuel B., 2
Spear, Mark, 145
Spear, Nehemiah, 307
Spear, Robert, 234
Spear, Rufus, 200, 205, 207
Spear, Saul, 292, 293
Spear, Stephen, 65
Spear, Thomas, 81, 234, 272
Spear, William, 24, 47, 145
Spearen, Joseph, 238
Spearen, William, 238
Spearer, Reuben, 200
Spears, Asa, 169
Spears, George, 235
Spears, Ivory, 273
Spears, William, 273
Speed, Amos, 87
Speed, Benjamin, 180
Speed, David, 231
Speed, Joseph, 179
Speed, Robert, 2, 180
Speer, Joshua, 291
Speers, Duncan, 312
Speers, William, 312
Spelman, Lyman, 46
Spelman, O., 43
Spencer, Andrew, 217
Spencer, Augustus, 32
Spencer, Benjamin, 217
Spencer, D. S., 269 (2)
Spencer, Erastus, 33
Spencer, Ichabod, 304
Spencer, Isaac, 217 (2)
Spencer, James, 239
Spencer, Jesse, 119
Spencer, Job, 28
Spencer, John, 160, 269 (2)
Spencer, Moses, 217
Spencer, Theron, 32
Spencer, William, 150, 171, 181
Spendergast, Thomas, 16
Spilinger, Jeremiah, 213
Spiller, Amos, 243
Spiller, Daniel, 18
Spiller, Job, 140
Spiller, John, 179
Spiller, John, Jr., 258
Spiller, Joseph, 179
Spiller, Moses, 136, 140
Spiller, Samuel, 239, 267
Spiner, Rex, 238
Spinney, Caleb, 248
Spinney, David, 248
Spinney, Ephraim, 235
Spinney, George, 250
Spinney, Jeremiah, 248
Spinney, John, 245
Spinney, Joseph, 245
Spinney, Nicholas, 248
Spinney, Richard, 248

Spinney, S. R., 245
Spofford, Charles, 156
Spofford, David, 234
Spofford, Enoch W., 109
Spofford, Greenlief, 234
Spofford, Henry, 100
Spofford, Moody, 234
Spofford, Thomas, 100
Spooner, Abner, 39
Spooner, Benjamin, 58, 147
Spooner, John, 58
Spooner, Joshua, 55
Spooner, Lemuel, 55, 58
Spooner, Micah, 56
Spooner, Nathaniel, 55
Spooner, Noah, 55, 58
Spooner, Samuel, 91
Spooner, Shubal, 147
Spooner, Thomas, 58
Spooner, William, 113
Sprague, Abijah, 289
Sprague, Amos, 42, 102
Sprague, Benjamin, 51
Sprague, Charles, 71, 78
Sprague, Elbridge, 258
Sprague, Elkanah, 170, 277
Sprague, Hosea, 69, 78
Sprague, Isaac, 25, 167
Sprague, Isaac S., 78
Sprague, J., 69
Sprague, Jairus, 96
Sprague, James, 41, 160
Sprague, Jeremiah, 70
Sprague, John, 67, 160
Sprague, Jonathan, 71, 78
Sprague, Josiah, 272
Sprague, Luther, 129
Sprague, Martin, 96
Sprague, Mathew, 2
Sprague, Matthew, 108
Sprague, Moses, 167, 281
Sprague, Nathaniel, 148
Sprague, Nelson, 248
Sprague, Noah, 199, 200, 203
Sprague, Oakman, 249, 297
Sprague, Peleg, 148
Sprague, Peter, 274
Sprague, Samuel, 41
Sprague, Stephen G., 283
Sprague, William, 85
Sprague, William, Jr., 167, 281
Sprague, Zebedee, 92
Spratt, David, 237
Spratt, George, 237, 266
Spratt, James, 237
Spratt, Nathaniel, 237, 265
Spring, Alpheus, 152
Spring, Ephraim, 48
Spring, Isaac, 152, 261
Spring, Jacob, 240
Spring, John, 45, 268
Spring, Lebee G., 160
Spring, Lewins, 18
Spring, Samuel, 18
Spring, William, 236, 303
Springer, Abraham, 183
Springer, Benjamin, 275
Springer, David T., 249, 297
Springer, Elisha, 231
Springer, Gideon, 274
Springer, Jacob, 275
Springer, James, 273, 274, 275

Springer, John, 156 (2), 274
Springer, Mark, 275
Springer, Samuel, 159
Springer, Stephen, 156, 274
Springer, Thomas, 230
Springer, Tillinghast, 274
Springer, William, 2d, 275
Springer, William, 3d, 275
Sproul, James, 192, 291
Sproul, John, 192, 287, 310
Sproul, Thomas, 291
Sproul, William, 192 (2), 287
Sprout, Ezra, 45
Sprowl, Amos, 193
Sprowl, Cornelius, 194
Sprowl, James, 192 (3), 194
Sprowl, John, 193 (2)
Sprowl, John, Jr., 193
Sprowl, Thomas, 194, 199
Sprowl, William, 193, 194, 199
Spurr, Oliver, 211
Spurr, William, 26
Squire, Abel, 44
Squire, Benjamin, 4
Squire, Charles, Jr., 45
Squire, Jesse, 47
Squire, John, 45
Squire, Peter, 44
Squire, Solomon, Jr., 45
Squire, Thomas, 45
Squire, William, 45
Squires, Josiah, 94
Squires, Zebina, 44
Stacey, Benjamin, 9
Stacey, George, 116, 225, 246
Stacey, John, 110
Stackpole, ——, 204
Stackpole, Absalom, 245
Stackpole, Cornelius, 233
Stackpole, Elias, 276
Stackpole, John, 300, 309
Stackpole, Joseph, 239
Stackpole, Joseph, Jr., 276
Stackpole, Nathan, 276
Stackpole, Samuel, 300
Stackpole, Samuel, Jr., 239
Stackpole, Stephen, 245
Stackpole, William, 239, 267, 286, 288
Stacy, Alfred, 45
Stacy, Charles C., 126
Stacy, George, 165 (2)
Stacy, John, 6, 177, 182, 191, 260
Stacy, John, Jr., 12
Stacy, Jordan, 152
Stacy, Oliver, 152
Stacy, Samuel, 7
Stacy, William, 182, 191
Stafford, Amherst, 268
Stafford, Edward, 233, 296
Stafford, Isaac, 268
Stafford, James, 127
Stafford, John, 289
Stafford, Jonathan, 129
Stafford, Lilly, 63
Stafford, William, 64
Stagpole, John, 263
Stahl, Jacob, 145
Stain, Emerson, 280
Stain, Samuel, 282
Stain, Saul, 280
Stall, Henry, 292, 293
Stall, Jacob, 285, 286, 289

Stall, John, 310, 311
Stall, John G., 19
Stall, Samuel, 1
Stallard, Thomas, 20, 125
Stamford, Aaron, 149
Standish, David, 290
Standish, Ephraim, 289
Standish, James, 293
Standish, John, 290, 293
Standish, John C., 53
Standish, Joseph, 51, 103
Standish, Miles, 50
Standish, Thomas, 129
Standish, William, 290, 293
Standish, William, 2d, 290
Standley, Andrew, 37
Standley, Benjamin, 2d, 38
Standley, Benjamin, 3d, 34
Standley, David, 36, 37
Standley, James, 305
Standley, John, 36
Standley, John, Jr., 37
Standley, Phineas, 23
Standley, S., 7
Standley, Stephen, 37
Standley, Thomas, 34
Standley, William, 37
Standley, Zacheriah M., 37
Stanford, David, 257
Stanford, Israel, 219
Stanford, Jeremiah, 222
Stanford, William, 172
Stanforth, Warren, 234
Stanhope, Asahel R., 66
Stanhope, Rudolphus, 159
Stanley, David, 3d, 35
Stanley, Edward, 211
Stanley, Elisha, 153, 261
Stanley, Harmon, 54
Stanley, James, 268
Stanley, Leonard, 263
Stanley, Nathan, 265
Stanley, Samuel, 47
Stanley, Thomas H., 245
Stanley, Waterman, 277
Stanly, George, 54
Stanly, Hugh, 149
Stanly, Lemuel, 282
Stanly, Miller, 54
Stanly, Morrell, 282
Stanly, Nathan, 236
Stanmon, Gersham, 33
Stannard, Winthrop, 219
Stannels, John, 154
Stanton, John, 242
Stanton, Palmer, 45
Stanton, Peleg, 32
Stanwood, Benjamin, 15, 298
Stanwood, Daniel, 119, 120 (2), 122, 123
Stanwood, David, 122, 298
Stanwood, David, 3d, 297
Stanwood, Davis, 298
Stanwood, James, 235
Stanwood, James, 3d, 298
Stanwood, Judah, 1st, 298
Stanwood, Judah, 2d, 298
Stanwood, Philip, 298
Stanwood, Robert, 14, 298
Stanwood, Samuel, 219, 233, 296
Stanwood, Saul, 89, 133
Stanwood, Thomas, 148
Stanwood, William, 18, 71

INDEX.

Staple, Daniel, 283
Staple, Hosea, 233
Staple, Isaac, 233
Staple, William, 283
Staples, Ai, 174
Staples, Alexander, 303
Staples, Allen, 59
Staples, Andrew, 253
Staples, Carrol, 149
Staples, Charles, 48, 150
Staples, Daniel, 59, 61
Staples, Daniel, Jr., 212
Staples, David, 209, 253
Staples, Eliphalet, 59, 61
Staples, Frost, 213
Staples, Gilbert, 57
Staples, Hesekiah, 304
Staples, Isaac, 342
Staples, James, 155, 211
Staples, James, 2d, 303
Staples, James N., 78, 82
Staples, Jeremiah, 253
Staples, John, 308
Staples, Joseph, 270, 304
Staples, Josiah, 177, 210
Staples, Jotham, 2d, 303
Staples, Jotham, 3d, 303
Staples, Luther, 178
Staples, Miles, 303
Staples, Moses, 257
Staples, Nathaniel, 222, 228
Staples, Noah, 59
Staples, Oliver, 172, 245
Staples, Paul, 62
Staples, Peter, 118
Staples, Richard, 164, 165, 166, 213
Staples, Robert, 234
Staples, Samuel, Jr., 173
Staples, Seth, 62, 178
Staples, Simon, 253, 257
Staples, Timothy, 245
Staples, William, 58, 155, 245
Staples, William, 2d, 303
Starbird, James, 223
Starbird, John, 232, 296
Starbird, John, Jr., 221
Starbird, Joshua, 218
Starbird, Levi, 218
Starbird, Robert, 210 (2)
Starbird, William, 210, 218
Starbird, William, Jr., 298
Starboard, James, 260
Starboard, Samuel, 231
Stark, Justus, 96
Starkey, Amasa, 239
Starkey, Cyrus, 54
Starkey, Milton, 54
Starkweather, Joseph, 65
Starling, Solomon, 177
Starr, James, 225
Starr, James B., 274
Starr, Samuel, 66
Starr, William, 86
Starret, Charles, 292, 293
Starret, James, 292, 293
Starret, Lewis, 292, 293
Starret, William, 292
Starret, William L., 293
Starrett, Calvin, 180
Starrett, Thomas, 292
Start, Ebenezer, 198, 199, 207

Starte, Ebenezer, 200
Staten, Samuel, 169
States, Elias, 300
Statten, Elias, 297
Stearnes, Amos, 29
Stearnes, Charles, Jr., 258
Stearnes, Curtis, 81
Stearnes, John, 81
Stearnes, Phineas, 251
Stearnes, William, 133
Stearns, Artemas, 3
Stearns, Benjamin, 19
Stearns, Calvin, 3
Stearns, Daniel, 216
Stearns, Edwin, 99
Stearns, Elijah, 160
Stearns, Ezekiel, 184, 187, 189
Stearns, Franklin, 286
Stearns, Isaac, 101
Stearns, John, 252, 255
Stearns, John S., 152
Stearns, Jonas, 115
Stearns, Moses, 41
Stearns, Nathaniel, 101
Stearns, Phineas, 255
Stearns, Silas, 115
Stearns, Theodore, 252
Stearns, Thomas, 252
Stearns, William, 197
Stearns, William, Jr., 139
Stebbins, Abiel, 45
Stebbins, Asa, 33, 46
Stebbins, Benjamin, 43
Stebbins, Erasmus, 45
Stebbins, Harvey, 4
Stebbins, Henry, 4
Stebbins, Ithemer, 4
Stebbins, James, 45
Stebbins, Judah, 68
Stebbins, Obed W., 46
Stebbins, Quartus, 4
Stebbins, Rook, 245
Stebbins, Samuel, 26, 92
Stebbins, Samuel H., 4
Stebbins, Saul, 70
Stebbins, Thomas, 145
Stebbins, Timothy, 40
Stebbins, Zenos, 4
Stedman, Calvin, 24
Stedman, Ebenezer, 4
Stedman, Edward P., 46
Stedman, Elijah, 84
Stedman, John, 175
Stedman, Samuel W., 175
Steel, Robert, 99
Steele, Ephraim B., 40
Steele, Ephraim P., 26
Steele, James, 150, 254
Steele, James, Jr., 111
Steele, Samuel, 259
Steen, Elisha, 46
Stenchfield, Ephraim, 213, 256
Stenchfield, John, 256
Stenchfield, William, 213, 234
Stenrod, Lewis, 312
Stephen, Jesse, 46
Stephen, Oliver, 70, 80
Stephens, Benjamin, 213, 264
Stephens, Cyrus, 67
Stephens, Hilton, 40
Stephens, James, 283

Stephens, John, 18, 195, 197
Stephens, Lewis, 90
Stephens, Sampson, 88
Stephens, Samuel, 145
Stephens, Solomon, 46
Stephens, Thomas, 26, 195, 211, 264
Stephens, Tilton, 25
Stephens, William, 81
Stephens, William H., 299
Stephenson, David, 45
Stephenson, Francis, 200, 201, 203
Stephenson, Jerome, 302
Stephenson, Jesse, 160
Stephenson, Martin, 25
Stephenson, Peter, 24
Stephenson, Priest P., 159
Stephenson, William, 39
Sterling, John, 150
Sterns, Benjamin, 152
Sterns, David, 215
Sterns, Ezra, 65
Sterns, Franklin, 285, 286, 288
Sterns, Levi, 215
Sterry, Edward L., 305
Stetson, Abel, 178
Stetson, Abner, 193
Stetson, Ansel, 55, 58
Stetson, Charles, 295
Stetson, Elijah, 167
Stetson, Elisha, 223, 277
Stetson, Elisha C., 127
Stetson, Elisha H., 194
Stetson, Ephraim, 178, 260
Stetson, Gideon, 160
Stetson, Hervey, 177
Stetson, Hesekiah, Jr., 178
Stetson, Isaac, 295
Stetson, John, 197
Stetson, Joshua, 1, 104
Stetson, Josiah, 303
Stetson, Melzar, 104
Stetson, Michel, 58
Stetson, Mitchell, 55
Stetson, Nathaniel, 127
Stetson, Oliver, 92
Stetson, Silas, 58
Stetson, Smith, 1
Stetson, Stephen, 167, 277
Stetson, Turner, 167
Stetson, William, 130, 133, 137
Stetson, Zenas, 178, 259
Stevens, Aaron, 223
Stevens, Aaron, Jr., 272
Stevens, Alexander, 111
Stevens, Atherton H., 80, 84
Stevens, Benjamin, 71, 146, 220, 279, 300
Stevens, Calvin, 171
Stevens, Charles, 218
Stevens, Daniel, 236, 255, 264, 273, 274
Stevens, Daniel W., 89
Stevens, David, 221
Stevens, Ebenezer, 181, 240
Stevens, Eleazer, 251
Stevens, Elihu, 228
Stevens, Elijah, 6
Stevens, Eliphalet, 273
Stevens, Enoch, 100, 218, 261
Stevens, Ephraim, 66
Stevens, Ezra, 178, 259, 278
Stevens, George W., 205 (3), 207
Stevens, Guy, 31

INDEX.

Stevens, Harvey, 158
Stevens, Ira, 33
Stevens, Isaac, 220
Stevens, Jacob, 240, 280
Stevens, James, 2, 41, 188, 218, 283
Stevens, Jeremiah, 223
Stevens, Joel, Jr., 253
Stevens, John, 31, 123, 150, 151, 173, 266, 271, 280, 282, 286, 290
Stevens, John, 2d, 280
Stevens, John H., 118
Stevens, Jonathan, 211, 253, 264, 265, 266, 304
Stevens, Joseph, 152, 220, 253
Stevens, Joshua, 280
Stevens, Joshua A., 220
Stevens, Joshua B., 83
Stevens, Josiah, 54, 221, 250
Stevens, Mark, 189
Stevens, Micah, 130
Stevens, Michel, 20
Stevens, Michell, 17
Stevens, Moses, 17, 21, 251, 273
Stevens, Nathaniel, 90, 205 (2), 221
Stevens, Nathaniel B., 205
Stevens, Paul H., 303
Stevens, Reuben, 298
Stevens, Rufus, 167
Stevens, Samuel, 13, 75, 91, 226
Stevens, Samuel, Jr., 251
Stevens, Saul, 18, 90
Stevens, Seth, 55, 58
Stevens, Simeon, 108
Stevens, Thomas, 29, 40, 114, 264, 273
Stevens, Thomas, Jr., 168
Stevens, Timothy, 86, 277, 282
Stevens, Timothy L., 279
Stevens, Tristram C., 218
Stevens, William, 8, 16, 151, 182 (3), 221, 226, 271, 308
Stevens, William, Jr., 264
Stevens, Zacheriah B., 220
Stevenson, Nathaniel D., 113, 114
Steward, Joseph R., 21
Steward, William M., 283
Stewart, Amos, 66
Stewart, Asa, 307
Stewart, Charles, 86, 240
Stewart, Daniel, 283
Stewart, George, 237
Stewart, James, 73, 255
Stewart, John, 5, 92, 306
Stewart, Joseph, 211, 234
Stewart, Robert, 184
Stewart, Simon, 41
Stewart, Solomon, 211
Stewart, Solomon, Jr., 307
Stewart, Stephen, 245
Stewart, Wentworth, 165, 174, 264, 266
Stickney, Amos, 146
Stickney, Benjamin, 38, 170
Stickney, Benjamin, Jr., 146
Stickney, Charles, 17, 136
Stickney, David, 146
Stickney, Enoch, 122, 125
Stickney, Jacob, 19
Stickney, Jeremiah, 99
Stickney, John, 24, 100, 134
Stickney, Jonathan, 34, 38
Stickney, Joseph, 19, 34, 121
Stickney, Josiah, 124

Stickney, Nicholas, 243
Stickney, Paul, 146
Stickney, Richard, 136
Stickney, Samuel, 159
Stickney, Thomas, 179
Stickney, Timothy, 159
Stickney, William, 89, 134 (3), 135, 228, 283
Sticky, Richard, 140
Stiffin, Charles, 271
Stiles, Enoch, 211
Stiles, Jacob, 211
Stiles, Joseph, 16
Stiles, Moses, 9
Stiles, Nathan, 258
Stiles, Stephen, 210
Stilfin, James T., 186
Stilkey, George, 297, 298
Still, Philip, 293
Still, Roger, 46
Still, William, 31
Stillman, Daniel, 13, 14
Stilphin, Cornelius, 188, 191
Stilphin, James L., 188
Stilphin, Lewis, 191
Stilphin, Louis, 188
Stilson, Amos, 307
Stilson, Lemuel, 266
Stimpson, Amos, 165, 166, 173
Stimpson, Charles, 226
Stimpson, Ebenezer, 168
Stimpson, George, 48, 81, 115
Stimpson, John, 28, 165, 166
Stimpson, Joseph, 269
Stimpson, Reuben, 78, 93, 111
Stimson, John, 90, 173, 233
Stimson, Nathaniel, 203
Stinchfield, Ebenezer, 168
Stinchfield, Ezekiel G., 168, 277
Stinchfield, Ezra, 168
Stinchfield, John, 227
Stinchfield, Moses, 153
Stinchfield, Solomon B., 168
Stinchfield, Stephen, 258
Stinchfield, Thomas, 227
Stine, Isaac, 172
Stinson, Abiel, 233
Stinson, Alfred, 249
Stinson, Charles, 277
Stinson, David, 268
Stinson, Eben, 247
Stinson, Eben, Jr., 247
Stinson, Frederick, 249
Stinson, James, 247, 285, 287
Stinson, James, Jr., 247
Stinson, John, 3d, 247
Stinson, John N., 269
Stinson, John W., 249, 297
Stinson, Mark, 233
Stinson, Nathaniel, 201 (2)
Stinson, Samuel, 148, 235, 247
Stinson, Saul, 307
Stinson, Stephen, 247
Stinson, Thomas, Jr., 249
Stinson, William, 148 (2), 187 (2), 235
Stinson, William, Jr., 184, 186, 190
Stirling, John, Jr., 151
Stock, Caleb P., 3
Stockbridge, Thomas, 43, 80
Stocken, Samuel, 176
Stocking, Austin, 46

Stocking, Herod, 67
Stocking, Ralph, 94
Stockman, Jesse, 231
Stockman, John, 11, 12, 243
Stockman, William, 210
Stockwell, Caleb, 217
Stockwell, Charles, 47
Stockwell, Isaac, 93
Stockwell, Jonathan, 93
Stockwell, Joseph, 70, 93
Stockwell, Reuben, 93
Stockwell, Simeon, 93
Stockwell, Tarrant, 93
Stoddar, Thomas, 84
Stoddard, Amos, 272
Stoddard, Ananias, 102
Stoddard, Bartlett, 23
Stoddard, Bela, 84
Stoddard, Calvin, 272
Stoddard, Daniel, 96
Stoddard, Demeric, 306
Stoddard, Henry, 55, 58 (2)
Stoddard, Hosea, 80
Stoddard, Ichabod, 40, 102
Stoddard, Isaiah, 102
Stoddard, Jacob T., 145
Stoddard, Jeremiah, 296, 300
Stoddard, Jesse, 43
Stoddard, John, 82
Stoddard, John, 2d, 82
Stoddard, Joshua, 96
Stoddard, Levi, 42
Stoddard, Lot, 40
Stoddard, Luther, 96, 102
Stoddard, Matthew, 102
Stoddard, Obediah, 12, 117
Stoddard, Reuben, 47
Stoddard, Samuel, 40
Stoddard, Stephen, Jr., 96
Stoddard, Thomas, 40, 101, 125
Stoddard, William, 40, 61
Stodder, Caleb, 102
Stodder, Hosea, 85
Stoder, Elijah, 88
Stoker, George, 116
Stokes, Bachus N., 118
Stone, Aaron, 118
Stone, Abijah, 92
Stone, Abner, 308
Stone, Abraham, 88
Stone, Adam, 308
Stone, Alfred, 148
Stone, Amos, 93
Stone, Ansel, 274
Stone, Archelus, 173
Stone, Asa, 85
Stone, Benjamin, 42, 94, 116, 134, 135
Stone, Buckley, 98
Stone, Daniel, 120, 123, 158
Stone, Ebenezer, 290, 293
Stone, Ephraim, 229, 283
Stone, Ephraim, Jr., 229
Stone, Ezra, 25, 34, 37, 87
Stone, Harvey, 46
Stone, Isaac, 7, 22, 90, 93, 139, 172
Stone, Israel O., 34, 38
Stone, James, 48, 190
Stone, John, 20, 116, 224, 270, 280
Stone, John S., 32
Stone, Jonathan, 308
Stone, Jonathan, Jr., 173

INDEX.

Stone, Joseph, 7, 22, 85
Stone, Joshua, 83, 116
Stone, Levi, Jr., 8
Stone, Moses, 222, 274
Stone, Nathaniel, 7, 85, 187
Stone, Nehemiah, 22
Stone, Samuel, 39
Stone, Saul, 290, 293
Stone, Seth, 93
Stone, Simeon, 7, 22, 214
Stone, Stephen, 7
Stone, Theophilus, 66
Stone, Thomas, 92
Stone, Thomas, Jr., 278
Stone, Thomas B., 17, 121, 124
Stone, William, 121, 124, 212, 258, 274
Stone, Windsor, 5
Stone, Zachariah, 34, 38, 240
Storer, Elias, 286 (2), 289
Storer, J., 152
Storer, Jedediah, 234
Storer, John, 153, 241, 286, 289
Storer, Joseph, 218
Storer, Samuel, 3d, 311
Storey, Amos, 11
Storey, David, 9
Storey, Isaac, 21
Storey, Miles, 94
Story, David, 231
Story, Franklin, 138
Story, Frederick W., 7
Story, Isaac, 6
Story, Stephen, 231
Stout, Christopher, 219
Stout, Enoch, 240
Stout, Jacob, 312
Stout, Nathaniel, 257
Stout, Peter B., 146
Stout, Peter B., 2d, 146
Stover, Caleb, 206
Stover, Charles, 232 (2)
Stover, Daniel, 299
Stover, David, 297, 299
Stover, George D., 241
Stover, James, 303
Stover, John, 183, 185, 189, 285, 299, 311
Stover, Joseph, 20, 299
Stover, Joshua, 299, 311
Stover, Paul, 299
Stover, Samuel, 185, 186, 189
Stover, Saul, 183
Stovers, Experience, 159
Stow, Benjamin, 95
Stow, Stephen, 94
Stow, William M., 247
Stowe, Samuel, 48
Stowel, Davis, 65
Stowell, Benjamin, 69
Stowell, Daniel, Jr., 252
Stowell, Eliakim, 42
Stowell, George, 115
Stowell, Isaiah, 24, 40, 78
Stowell, John, 69, 71, 78, 115
Stowell, Lewis, 250
Stowell, Rufus, 252
Stowell, Samuel, 94
Stowell, Seth, 96
Stowell, Thomas, 2, 70, 78
Stowell, William, 112
Stowell, William E., 48
Stowers, John, 227

Strange, John, Jr., 57
Strange, Joseph, 56
Strange, Lot, 56
Stranger, Edward, 129
Stratter, George W., 194
Stratton, Alpheus, 48
Stratton, Austin, 239
Stratton, Calvin, 3
Stratton, Charles, 239, 267
Stratton, David, 163 (2)
Stratton, Ebenezer, 239
Stratton, Elisha, 115
Stratton, George W., 197
Stratton, Henry, 65, 115
Stratton, James, 239
Stratton, Ness, 239
Stratton, Paul, 239
Stratton, Roswell, 3
Stratton, Thomas, 115
Street, Edmund, 19
Streeter, Daniel, 307
Streeter, Kellog, 46
Streeter, Samuel, 65
Streeter, Vintin, 284
Stricking, Oliver, 218
Strickland, David, 66
Strickland, John, 223
Stricklin, Emery, 47
Strobridge, Ebenezer, 53
Strobridge, Henry, 102
Strong, Asahel, 4
Strong, Chester, 5
Strong, Cotton, 81
Strong, Elihu, 67
Strong, Elisha, 67
Strong, Gennbeth, 4
Strong, Horatio, 64
Strong, Huit S., 67
Strong, James, 94
Strong, Job S., 67
Strong, Jonathan, 67
Strong, Noble, 67
Strong, Paul, 64
Strong, Russell, 67
Strong, Seth, 5
Strong, Simeon, 47
Strout, Anthony, 222
Strout, Daniel, 200
Strout, Ebenezer, 210, 295, 296
Strout, Elisha, 270
Strout, George, 155, 219, 221, 312
Strout, George, Jr., 174
Strout, Isaac, 256
Strout, James, 222, 260, 300
Strout, Jonathan, 219, 300
Strout, Joseph, 270
Strout, Joshua, 136, 223
Strout, Lemuel, 260
Strout, Nathaniel, 223
Strout, Nehemiah, 213
Strout, Prince, 258
Strout, Samuel, 270
Strout, Saul, 210
Strout, Solomon, 270
Strout, William, 169, 281
Strow, Benjamin, 83
Stuart, Joseph, 304
Stuart, Joseph B., 37
Stuart, Niles, 171
Stuart, Richard, Jr., 275
Stuart, Robert, 182 (2)

Stuart, Silas, 113
Stuart, Solomon, 174
Stuart, Wentworth, 166
Stubborn, John, 181
Stubbs, Bradbury S., 226
Stubbs, Eben, 216
Stubbs, Edward, 216
Stubbs, Nathan, 223, 259
Stubbs, Richard, 216
Studley, Andrew, 36
Studley, Gideon, Jr., 103
Studley, John, 240, 267, 291
Studley, John, Jr., 303
Studley, Jonathan, 36
Studley, Warren, 24
Studley, William, 36
Studley, Zackariah M., 36
Studly, Gideon, 1
Studly, Nathaniel, 195
Studson, Elisha, 192
Sturdavant, Samuel, 129
Sturdavant, Winslow, 129
Sturdavant, Zedock, 129
Sturdevant, Andrew, 278
Sturdevant, Bernard, 153
Sturdevant, Croade, 51
Sturdevant, David, 273
Sturdevant, Francis, Jr., 175
Sturdevant, James, 102, 260
Sturdevant, John, 175, 280
Sturdevant, Joseph, 175
Sturdevant, Joseph, Jr., 251
Sturdevant, Moses, 279
Sturdevant, Nathan, 280
Sturdevant, Nathaniel, 175
Sturdevant, Samuel, 50
Sturdevant, Seth, 272
Sturdevant, William, 270
Sturdevant, Zenos, 275
Sturdivant, Joshua, 40
Sturdivant, William, 281
Sturdley, Ebenezer, 72
Sturgess, Ebenezer G., 173
Sturgess, Joseph, 173
Sturgis, Davis, 132
Sturgis, Jackson, 132
Sturgis, Samuel, 32
Sturgiss, Heman, 237
Sturgiss, Robert, 32
Sturtavant, Luther, 128
Sturteford, Jonas, 239
Sturtevant, Caleb, 95
Sturtevant, Joshua, 102
Sturtevant, Samuel, 3
Sturtevant, Ward, 95
Stutley, Daniel, 238
Stuts, Eben, 162
Stuts, Edad, 162
Stutson, Charles, 148
Stutson, Harvey, 148
Stutson, Isaac, 297
Stutson, John, 195
Stutson, Oliver, 102
Stutson, Peleg, 50
Stutson, Thaddeus, 66
Suckforth, Philip, 145
Suckforth, Robert, 199, 200, 203
Sukins, Josiah, 304
Suller, William, 145
Sullivan, Dennis, 271
Sullivan, George, 7

INDEX.

Summer, Samuel, 203
Summer, Saul, 290
Summer, Seth, 290
Summers, Ezra, 79
Summers, Samuel, 100
Sumner, Alexander B., 2, 108
Sumner, Amos, 70, 111
Sumner, Benjamin, 80, 85, 215
Sumner, Charles, 292, 293
Sumner, Clark, 5
Sumner, Emory, 5
Sumner, George, 138
Sumner, Hoten, 167
Sumner, John W., 37
Sumner, Lemuel, 50
Sumner, Michel, 17
Sumner, Samuel, 199, 200, 209
Sumner, Saul, 293
Sumner, Seth, 71
Surner, John, 138
Sutton, George, 270
Sutton, Richard, 149
Swain, Dudly S., 306
Swain, Jacob, 19
Swain, Samuel, 94
Swain, Walter P., 106, 107, 108
Swaine, Nathaniel, 117
Swallow, Ezra, 42, 88
Swallow, Thomas, 88
Swan, Aaron, 134, 140
Swan, Amos M., 80
Swan, Benjamin, 134, 140, 274
Swan, Duty, 54
Swan, Edward, 275
Swan, Farwell, 255
Swan, Foxwell, 250
Swan, Frederic, 229
Swan, Gideon, 251
Swan, Henry, 101
Swan, Jeremiah, 214, 303
Swan, John, 134, 140
Swan, Joseph, 134, 140
Swan, Nathan, 303
Swan, Nathaniel, 134, 140
Swan, Samuel, 140
Swan, Samuel, Jr., 134
Swan, Saul, 134
Swan, Stephen, 101
Swan, Thomas, 134, 140
Swan, Timothy, 28
Swan, William, 240, 241, 254
Swan, William, Jr., 251
Swank, George, 312
Swanton, William, 249, 276
Swasey, Ambrose, 212
Swasey, John, 138
Swasey, Joseph, 136
Swasey, Samuel, 20, 120, 123
Sway, Joseph, 137
Sway, Stephen, 61
Sweat, Gardner, 246
Sweat, John, 150
Sweat, Joshua, 246
Sweat, Moses, 3d, 246
Sweat, Moses, 4th, 246
Sweat, Samuel, 158, 246
Sweat, William, 169
Sweeney, William, 134, 135
Sweet, Adam, 210
Sweet, Arnold, 265
Sweet, Benjamin, 165, 166
Sweet, David, 171

Sweet, Ellis, 276, 281
Sweet, George, 30, 172
Sweet, Jabez, 27
Sweet, James, 220, 255
Sweet, Jesse, 227, 283
Sweet, John, 22
Sweet, Jonathan, 120, 122
Sweet, Joseph, 176
Sweet, Joshua, 220
Sweet, Josiah, 257
Sweet, Lemuel, 190
Sweet, Lewis, 220
Sweet, Mark P., 40
Sweet, Moses, 3d, 220
Sweet, Newton, 10
Sweet, Samuel, 30, 219
Sweet, Samuel, Jr., 146
Sweet, Stephen, 7, 22, 82
Sweet, Stephen, Jr., 221
Sweet, Sylvester, 32
Sweet, Thomas, 10
Sweet, Werborn A., 226
Sweet, William, 9, 10, 17, 99, 126
Sweet, William B., 82
Sweet, Winborn A., 282
Sweet, Zebediah, 283
Sweetland, James, 201 (2), 203, 206, 207
Sweetland, Seth, 273
Sweetland, Wace, 201
Sweetzer, Benjamin, 172
Sweetzer, Benjamin G., 19
Sweetser, Charles, 117 (2)
Sweetser, Charles B., 68, 80
Sweetser, Jeremiah, 303
Sweetser, John, 115
Sweetser, John, Jr., 172
Sweetser, Joshua, 25
Sweetser, Levi, 212
Sweetser, Oliver, 118
Sweetser, Richard, 263
Sweetser, Salathiel, 212
Sweetser, Saul, 212
Sweetser, Silas, 48
Sweetser, William, 263
Sweeser, Samuel, 96
Swet, Josiah, 256
Swet, Richard, 22
Swetland, Charles, 291
Swett, Clark, 171
Swett, James, 225
Swett, John, 100
Swett, Joshua, 246
Swift, Abraham, 72
Swift, Alden, 72, 75
Swift, Alfred, 279 (2)
Swift, Allen, 72
Swift, Alvin, 75
Swift, Asaph, 76
Swift, Benjamin, 27, 305
Swift, Caleb, 252
Swift, Charles D., 55, 58
Swift, Clark, 72
Swift, David, 8
Swift, Eben, 132
Swift, Ebeneser, 268, 305
Swift, Ellis, 72, 75
Swift, Ezekiel, 72
Swift, Heman, 75
Swift, Henry, 8
Swift, Herman, 73
Swift, Isaac, 51
Swift, James, 72, 75

Swift, Jiah, 169
Swift, Job, 304
Swift, John, 76, 251, 255
Swift, John, Jr., 72
Swift, Jonathan, 252
Swift, Joseph, 51, 103, 236
Swift, Joseph, Jr., 178
Swift, Levi, 71
Swift, Luman, 71
Swift, Nathaniel, 72
Swift, Oliver, 75
Swift, Reuben, 55
Swift, Ruel, 51
Swift, Samuel, 252, 255
Swift, Thomas, 71, 72, 76
Swift, Thomas, Jr., 72
Swift, William, 55, 72, 75, 83, 88, 258
Swift, Zipha, 292 (2)
Swinson, Peter, 12
Switcher, Timothy, 45
Swombly, John, 248
Sykes, Artemus, 194
Sylvester, Abner, Jr., 209
Sylvester, Amos, 180
Sylvester, David, 179, 264
Sylvester, Ebeneser, 181
Sylvester, Gustavus, 50
Sylvester, Isaac, 299, 311
Sylvester, James, 90
Sylvester, Job, 3d, 295
Sylvester, John, 27, 28, 42, 264, 280, 299
Sylvester, Joseph, 103, 239, 264, 295
Sylvester, Luke, 181
Sylvester, Marlborough, 297
Sylvester, Marlborough, Jr., 299
Sylvester, Massey, 168
Sylvester, Philip, 303
Sylvester, Richard, 90
Sylvester, Saul I., 307
Sylvester, Samuel, 12
Sylvester, Turner, 248
Sylvester, William, 8, 284, 297, 299
Symmes, Edmund, 115
Symmes, Thomas, 109
Symms, William, 8
Symonds, Daniel, 118
Symonds, Ebeneser, 134
Symonds, Ebeneser, Jr., 140
Symonds, Ephraim, 134, 140
Symonds, George, 137
Symonds, Jesse, 151
Symonds, John, 101, 134
Symonds, John, 3d, 140
Symonds, John D., 134
Symonds, Jonathan, Jr., 140
Symonds, Joseph, 134, 140, 258
Symonds, Nathaniel, 134, 140
Symonds, Samuel, 134, 140
Symonds, Stephen, 134, 140
Symonds, Thomas, 140
Symonds, Thomas, Jr., 134
Symonds, Thorndike, 134, 140
Symonds, William, 69
Symons, Saul, 136

T

Tabbot, John B., 62
Tabbott, Nathaniel, 18
Taber, Edward, Jr., 127
Taber, Gideon, 127
Taber, James, 58

INDEX.

Taber, Jeduthan, 55, 57, 58
Taber, John, 55, 58
Taber, Joseph, 55, 58
Taber, Noel, 129
Taber, Pardon, 58
Taber, Peter, 56
Taber, Philip, 56
Taber, Reuben, 55, 57
Taber, Samuel, 55, 58
Taber, William, 58
Tabor, David, 21, 138
Tabor, Jeduthan, 41
Tabor, Lloyd, 41
Taft, Amasa, 5
Taft, Elisha, 24, 114
Taft, Ellis, 5
Taft, John, 64
Taft, Leonard, 5
Taft, Lyman, 30
Taft, Wales, 181
Taggart, James, 42
Taggart, Rufus, 64
Taggerd, Henry, 83
Tailor, Ebenezer, 54
Tainter, Benjamin, 216
Tait, George, 218
Talbot, Baily, 212
Talbot, Joel, 39
Talbot, John, 23
Talbot, Nathaniel, 18, 40
Talbot, Simeon, 209
Talbott, George, 70, 78
Talbott, John, 100
Talcott, William, 147
Tallman, Scott J., 249
Tallman, Stephen, 63
Tallman, William T., 40
Talmage, Calvin, 44
Talpy, Oliver, 146
Talum, Henry, 136
Tannatt, Abram G., 28
Tanner, Anthony, 245
Tanner, Ebenezer, 224
Tanner, Joshua, 74
Tapley, Aaron, 9
Tapley, Asa, 21, 278
Tapley, Jesse, 116
Tappan, Benjamin, 36, 37
Tappan, Ebenezer, Jr., 36
Tappan, Edward, 7
Tappan, Jeremiah P., 19
Tappan, Thomas P., 89
Tappan, William, 13
Tappin, Josiah T., 299
Tappin, Luther, 212
Tarbell, Abel, 88
Tarbell, Benjamin, 239
Tarbell, Josiah, 237
Tarbell, Nathaniel, 118
Tarbell, Saul, 239
Tarbell, Thomas, 82
Tarbell, William, 240, 307
Tarbelly, Joseph, 88
Tarbox, Adriel, 44
Tarbox, Daniel, 213
Tarbox, Eleazer, Jr., 272
Tarbox, James, 270
Tarbox, John, 270
Tarbox, Jonathan, 270
Tarbox, Jordan, 185, 189
Tarbox, Lemuel, 253
Tarbox, Nathaniel, 272

Tarbox, Philip, 234
Tarbox, Samuel, 118, 189, 270
Tarbox, Samuel, Jr., 270
Tarbox, Saul B., 272
Tarbox, Stephen, 242, 269
Tarbox, William, 149, 210
Tarbox, William, 3d, 116
Tarbox, Zachariah, 272
Tarr, Aaron, 248
Tarr, Andrew, 216
Tarr, Benjamin, 297
Tarr, Benjamin, Jr., 248
Tarr, Benjamin, 3d, 248
Tarr, Charles, 12
Tarr, Christopher, 190
Tarr, Clark, 235, 236
Tarr, David, Jr., 11
Tarr, Ebenezer, 11
Tarr, Francis, Jr., 11
Tarr, Francis P., 11
Tarr, Henry, 12
Tarr, Jabez, Jr., 12
Tarr, James, 12, 248
Tarr, John, 198, 202, 208 (2)
Tarr, Jonathan, Jr., 11
Tarr, Jordan, 248
Tarr, Joseph, 296
Tarr, Joseph, Jr., 11, 248
Tarr, Joshua, 11
Tarr, Moses, 12
Tarr, Nathaniel, 12, 208 (2)
Tarr, Paul, 231
Tarr, Robert, 12
Tarr, Samuel, 208
Tarr, Seth, Jr., 248
Tarr, Solomon, 11
Tarr, Willard, 8
Tate, Richard, 6
Tate, William, 2, 235
Taylor, Abner, 240
Taylor, Abram, 240
Taylor, Amasa, 105, 107
Taylor, Andrew, 138
Taylor, Ansel, 67, 284
Taylor, Arial, 4
Taylor, Asa, 107, 181
Taylor, Augustus, 33, 48
Taylor, Benjamin, 231, 305
Taylor, Calvin, 88
Taylor, Chester, 8, 65
Taylor, Daniel, 77, 83
Taylor, Daniel D., 94
Taylor, David, 65, 105, 106
Taylor, Dennis, 207
Taylor, Ebenezer, 3
Taylor, Elias, 176, 264
Taylor, Elias, Jr., 266
Taylor, Eliphalet, 10
Taylor, Elisha, 88
Taylor, Elisha T., 182
Taylor, Einathan, 239
Taylor, Ephraim, 93, 193
Taylor, George, 45, 138
Taylor, Godfrey, 291
Taylor, Henry, 29
Taylor, Henry W., 91, 94
Taylor, Ira, 33
Taylor, Isaac, 48, 107
Taylor, James, 64, 214, 224, 266, 272, 277, 307
Taylor, Joel, 268, 305
Taylor, John, 3, 47, 105, 106 (3), 231, 264, 280, 282, 293, 305, 307

Taylor, John, Jr., 240
Taylor, John S., 180
Taylor, Joseph, 18, 305
Taylor, Joshua, 107, 225
Taylor, Josiah, 268
Taylor, Jotham, 245
Taylor, Kensalear, 119
Taylor, Levi E., 44
Taylor, Lucius, 45
Taylor, Mathew, 268
Taylor, Matthew, 305
Taylor, Moses A., 25
Taylor, Nathan, 17
Taylor, Noah, 44
Taylor, Obediah, 245
Taylor, Owen, 43
Taylor, Philip, 291
Taylor, Phineas, 298
Taylor, Richard, 105, 106, 107
Taylor, Rodolphus, 65
Taylor, Rowland, 213
Taylor, Rufus, 65
Taylor, Samuel, 82, 282, 305
Taylor, Samuel, 3d, 179
Taylor, Saul, Jr., 278
Taylor, Saul G., 274
Taylor, Simeon, 49, 75
Taylor, Solomon, 81
Taylor, Thomas, 167, 290, 293, 312
Taylor, Thomas, Jr., 277
Taylor, William, 4, 46, 212, 282
Taylor, Zebulon, 212
Taylor, Zoath, 104, 106, 107
Teague, Asa, 229
Teague, Isaac, 226
Teague, John G., 140
Teague, Jonathan, 136
Teague, Joseph, 193
Teague, Nathaniel, 133
Teague, Richard, 134, 135
Teague, Thomas, 133, 140
Teague, William, 140
Tebbetts, Greenleaf, 245
Tebbitts, James, 268
Teel, George, 71
Teel, Nathaniel, 25, 79
Teele, Ammi, 101
Teele, Benjamin, 101
Teele, Samuel P., 101
Teele, Thomas H., 101
Tefferin, William, 245
Tell, Thomas M., 5
Tell, Warren, 61
Temple, Benjamin, 64
Temple, Ebenezer, 67
Temple, Ebenezer, Jr., 231
Temple, Isaac, 159
Temple, John, 29
Temple, Joseph, 234
Temple, Levi, 181
Temple, Luther, 268
Temple, Solomon, 64
Temple, Stephen, 181
Tenison, William, 18
Tenney, Benjamin T., 15
Tenney, Cookam T., 16
Tenney, John, 258
Tenney, Joseph, 5
Tenney, Moses, 27, 81
Tenney, Samuel, 146
Tenney, Saul, 15
Tenney, William, 5

INDEX.

Tenny, Simon, 95
Tent, Isaac, 84
Terrell, Isaac, 9, 264
Terrell, Orrin, 65
Terrill, George, 26
Terry, Edmund S., 46
Terry, Elias, 58
Terry, James, 57
Terry, Joseph, 57
Terry, Sanford, 58
Terry, Silas, 57
Tery, Reuben, 64
Tewksberry, Isaac, 15
Tewksbury, Andrew, 108
Tewksbury, Bill, 27
Tewksbury, H., 27
Tewksbury, Henry, 112
Tewksbury, James, 220
Tewksbury, John, 3d, 27
Tewksbury, Thomas, 27, 112
Tewksbury, Washington, 27
Thacher, George, Jr., 154
Tharron, Nathan, 301
Thatcher, Ebeneser, 284
Thatcher, Edmund, 267
Thatcher, Elisha, 181
Thatcher, James, 132
Thatcher, John, Jr., 132
Thatcher, Peleg, 132
Thatcher, Samuel, 289
Thaxter, Duncan McB., 96
Thaxter, Gridley, 9
Thaxter, Jonathan, 2
Thayer, Aaron, 90
Thayer, Abiather, 59
Thayer, Abijah, 49
Thayer, Abner, 150, 178
Thayer, Alvin, 263, 267
Thayer, Asaph, 25
Thayer, Barnabus, 262, 267
Thayer, Bela, 40
Thayer, Benjamin, 92
Thayer, Charles, 86
Thayer, Daniel, 262
Thayer, David, 42, 86, 102
Thayer, Earl, 49
Thayer, Eli, 2
Thayer, Elihu, 100
Thayer, Elijah, 66
Thayer, Elisha, 216
Thayer, Ezra, 54
Thayer, Gideon F., 28
Thayer, Isaac, 83
Thayer, Jairus, 96
Thayer, Jechonias, 68
Thayer, Jesse, 32, 95
Thayer, Job, 42
Thayer, John, 251
Thayer, John C., 141
Thayer, John W., 86
Thayer, Jonathan, 54
Thayer, Loring, 24
Thayer, Lyman, 47
Thayer, M., 60
Thayer, Martin, 96
Thayer, Nathaniel, 3
Thayer, Peter, 253
Thayer, Randall, 42
Thayer, Reuben, 47
Thayer, Rufus, 5
Thayer, Samuel, 65
Thayer, Savil, 66

Thayer, Silas, 64, 311
Thayer, Simeon, 65, 95
Thayer, Stephen, 210, 236
Thayer, Sylvester, 59
Thayer, Thompson, 98
Thayer, Washington, 70, 111
Thayer, Wyman, 25, 87
Thayer, Zacheriah, 60
Thayne, Luther, 45
Theobald, George, 157 (2)
Theobald, Philip E., 182
Thing, Isaiah, 273
Thing, Jonathan, 273
Thing, John, 275
Thing, Joseph, 273
Thing, Levi, Jr., 275
Thissell, Nehemiah, 37
Thissell, Samuel M., 37
Thistle, Andrew, 79
Thistle, Ezra, 215
Thistle, Isacker, 304
Thistle, Nehemiah, 36
Thistle, Samuel M., 36
Thomas, Amos, 165, 166
Thomas, Andrew, 62
Thomas, Arnold, 56
Thomas, Benjamin, 220
Thomas, Charles, 295, 302
Thomas, Charles, Jr., 295
Thomas, Consider, 148
Thomas, Cornelius, 302
Thomas, Cyrus, 117
Thomas, Daniel, 52, 223
Thomas, Eben, 204
Thomas, Ebeneser S., 127
Thomas, Edward, 198, 202, 208 (3)
Thomas, Eleaser, 52
Thomas, Eliab, 51
Thomas, Elias, 30
Thomas, Eliphalet, 52
Thomas, Elisha, 75, 223
Thomas, Enoch, Jr., 53
Thomas, Ephraim, 52, 297, 298
Thomas, Ezra, 103
Thomas, George, 148
Thomas, Harvey C., 51
Thomas, Hesekiah, 33
Thomas, Isaac, 52, 168
Thomas, Israel, 51
Thomas, Jacob, 51, 90
Thomas, James, 102, 185, 189, 302
Thomas, James, Jr., 103
Thomas, Jedediah, 225
Thomas, Jeremiah, Jr., 51, 103
Thomas, Jesse, 299
Thomas, Job, 172
Thomas, John, 40 (2), 50, 70, 86, 181, 231, 244, 252, 262, 266, 292
Thomas, John W., 243
Thomas, Jonah, 262
Thomas, Joseph, Jr., 303
Thomas, Joseph M., 17
Thomas, Lathrop, 52
Thomas, Levi, 128
Thomas, Levi, 2d, 52
Thomas, Lewis, Jr., 259
Thomas, Martin, 168, 281
Thomas, Melzer, 285
Thomas, Micah, 222
Thomas, Nathan, 282
Thomas, Nathan, Jr., 280
Thomas, Nathaniel, 222, 223, 259

Thomas, Norton, 195
Thomas, Otis, 52
Thomas, Peres, 52
Thomas, Philip, 302
Thomas, Richard, 33
Thomas, Royal, 302
Thomas, Saul A., 292
Thomas, Seneca, 52
Thomas, Theophilus, 295
Thomas, Tilden, 302
Thomas, Walter, 52
Thomas, William, 87, 171, 189, 191, 199, 223, 296, 299 (2)
Thomas, William N., 52
Thomas, Winslow, 52, 102
Thomas, Zonas, 51
Thomb, John, 256
Thomb, William, 114
Thombs, Amos, Jr., 174
Thombs, Eli, 173
Thombs, George, 175
Thombs, George, Jr., 173
Thombs, George W., 218
Thombs, James, 173
Thombs, Job, 218
Thombs, Joseph, 246
Thombs, Michael, 23
Thombs, Stephen, 175
Thombs, Thomas, 175
Thombs, William, 27, 266
Thomes, Nathaniel, 145
Thomes, William, 158
Thornhill, Thomas, 160
Thompson, Aaron, 169
Thompson, Abel, 232 (2)
Thompson, Abijah, 232 (2)
Thompson, Abraham, 51
Thompson, Adam, 95
Thompson, Alexander, 26, 79, 235
Thompson, Amasa T., 2, 108
Thompson, Amos, 7, 22
Thompson, Andrew, 133, 137
Thompson, Archibald, 28, 112
Thompson, Asa, 47, 95, 219
Thompson, Asel W., 96
Thompson, Bartholomew, 245
Thompson, Benjamin, 36, 169, 192, 193, 194, 234, 235
Thompson, Caleb, 153
Thompson, Cephas, 95
Thompson, Charles, 6, 230
Thompson, Charles D., 22
Thompson, Cornelius, 230, 296
Thompson, Cyrus, 225
Thompson, Daniel, 95, 193
Thompson, Daniel O., 283
Thompson, David, 170, 183, 185, 189, 231
Thompson, David, 3d, 53
Thompson, Eben, 197, 204
Thompson, Ebeneser, 207
Thompson, Ebial, 54
Thompson, Edward, Jr., 212
Thompson, Eli, 96
Thompson, Eliab, 95
Thompson, Ephraim, 194, 197
Thompson, Ezra, 95
Thompson, Galen, 259
Thompson, George, 19, 103
Thompson, Giles, 95
Thompson, Gilmore, 176, 257
Thompson, Hannibal, 176
Thompson, Hesekiah B., 230

INDEX. 431

Thompson, Hiram, 54
Thompson, Ichabod, 181
Thompson, Isaac, 181, 280
Thompson, Israel, 181
Thompson, Jabez P., 95
Thompson, Jacob, 90, 175
Thompson, James, 60, 82, 94, 235, 266, 269, 286, 290, 304
Thompson, Jeremiah B., 236
Thompson, Jesse, 95
Thompson, Joel, 284, 287
Thompson, John, 7, 14, 15, 22, 93, 102 (2), 149 (2), 186, 200, 225, 227, 238, 247, 260, 290, 308
Thompson, John A., 233
Thompson, Jonathan, 7, 176
Thompson, Joseph, 5, 64
Thompson, Joseph A., 133, 137
Thompson, Joshua, 154, 181, 245
Thompson, Jotham, 166
Thompson, Luther, 47
Thompson, Moses, 98, 181
Thompson, Nathaniel, 211
Thompson, Nehemiah, 95 (2), 128
Thompson, Oliver, 245
Thompson, Peltiah, 296, 298
Thompson, Phineas, 233
Thompson, Robert, 162, 181, 216, 304
Thompson, Samuel, 40, 150, 170, 184, 188, 191, 234
Thompson, Samuel, Jr., 183
Thompson, Samuel, 2d, 236
Thompson, Saul, 235
Thompson, Stephen, 64
Thompson, Thomas, 11, 169, 181
Thompson, Ussa, 223
Thompson, Ward, 95
Thompson, Warren, 217
Thompson, Willard, 66
Thompson, William, 8, 14, 108, 113, 152, 155, 181, 183, 184 (2), 186, 187, 188, 190, 191, 202, 212
Thompson, William J., 171
Thompson, Zadoc, 95
Thompson, Zeba, 95
Thompson, Zebulon, 95
Thoms, Benjamin, 212
Thoms, John, 212
Thomson, Alexander, 304
Thomson, Isaac, 129
Thomson, Jacob, 3d, 129
Thomson, James, 54
Thomson, John, 199, 203
Thomson, Jonathan, 22
Thomson, Richard L., 22
Thomson, Ward, 129
Thomson, William, 200
Thorn, Benjamin, 226
Thorn, Eleaser, 256
Thorn, Israel, 3d, 175
Thorn, John, 171
Thorn, Joseph, 175
Thorn, Simeon, 226
Thorn, Thomas, 224
Thorn, William, 256
Thorndick, John M., 290
Thorndike, Ebenezer, 198, 199, 200, 207
Thorndike, Israel, 83, 198, 199, 207
Thorndike, J. W., 198, 199, 202, 207, 208
Thorndike, Jeremiah, 69
Thorndike, John M., 286
Thorndike, William, 34, 38

Thorner, Jacob, 22
Thorning, Isaac, 39
Thornton, Joshua, 238
Thornton, Thomas, 268
Thornton, William, 277
Thorp, Reuben, 178
Thorp, Titus, 32
Thorpe, Aurin, 33
Thoyts, Simeon, 209
Thracker, James, 49
Thrasher, Asahel, 60
Thrasher, Cyrus, 91, 103
Thrasher, Ebenezer, 219
Thrasher, Elkanah, 59, 62
Thrasher, George, Jr., 128
Thrasher, Harlow, 93
Thrasher, James, 88
Thrasher, Joseph, 257
Thrasher, Noah, 62
Thrasher, Robert, 164, 165, 166, 219, 258
Thrasher, Samuel, 93
Thunnell, George, 245
Thunnell, John, 245
Thunnell, Samuel, 245
Thurber, Edward, 4
Thurle, Abraham, 146
Thurlo, Richard, 210
Thurlow, Amos, 251, 255
Thurlow, James, 17, 221
Thurlow, John, 16
Thurlow, Joseph, 17
Thurlow, Joshua, 235
Thurlow, Parker G., 16
Thurlow, Robert, 150
Thurlow, Samuel, 16
Thurrell, Jacob, 231
Thurrell, John, 230
Thurston, Benjamin, 27, 79
Thurston, Daniel, 9, 171
Thurston, David, 93
Thurston, David, Jr., 256
Thurston, Ebenezer, 170
Thurston, Ezekiel, 241, 242
Thurston, John, 213
Thurston, John B., 128
Thurston, John P., 241, 242
Thurston, Joseph, 11
Thurston, Philo, 90
Thurston, William, 10, 220, 277
Thwing, James, 271
Thwing, Thomas, 23
Tibbets, Eli, 154
Tibbets, Enoch, 233
Tibbets, Ephraim, 153
Tibbets, Giles, 145, 284
Tibbets, Henry, 181
Tibbets, Isaac, 185
Tibbets, James, 185, 272
Tibbets, Jesse L., 282
Tibbets, John, 233
Tibbets, Mark, 183
Tibbets, Nathaniel, 183, 185
Tibbets, Paul, 233
Tibbets, Samuel, 284, 287
Tibbets, William, 272
Tibbetts, Abraham, 171
Tibbetts, Benjamin, 180
Tibbetts, David, 193
Tibbetts, Ephraim, 193, 244
Tibbetts, George, 310
Tibbetts, Ichabod, 161
Tibbetts, Isaac, 183, 189, 247

Tibbetts, Jesse L., 226
Tibbetts, John, 161, 229
Tibbetts, Joseph, 183
Tibbetts, Mark, 183, 189
Tibbetts, Nathaniel, 188, 191
Tibbetts, Samuel B., 193
Tibbetts, Timothy, 154
Tibbetts, William, 217
Tibbits, Aaron, 15
Tibbits, John, 216
Tibbits, Moses, 194
Tibbitts, Ephraim, 264
Tibbitts, George, 263
Tibbitts, John, 264
Tibbitts, John, 2d, 264
Tibbitts, Moses, 264
Tibbitts, Samuel, 152
Tibbitts, Samuel, Jr., 193
Ticket, Joshua, 300
Ticket, Rushworth, 300
Ticket, Vinson, 297
Tidd, Charles, 7, 110, 113
Tidd, Ebenezer G., 101
Tidd, Jacob, 83
Tiffany, Henry, 66
Tiffts, John, 33
Tilden, Christopher, 40, 81, 82, 110
Tilden, Convers, 132
Tilden, Elisha, 301
Tilden, Isaac, 301
Tilden, John, 130
Tilden, Jonathan, 99
Tilden, Joseph, 108
Tilden, Luther, 104
Tilden, Robert, 89
Tilden, Thomas, 81
Tileston, Charles, 71
Tileston, Ezra B., 28
Tileston, James, 84
Tileston, O. C., 84
Tileston, Otis, 84
Tilestone, Euclid, Jr., 70
Tiller, James, 185
Tillinghast, George, 25, 114
Tillitson, Daniel, 33
Tillotson, Samuel, 46
Tillson, Ephraim, 95
Tilson, Gilbert, 145, 285, 286 (2), 289
Tilson, John, 223
Tilson, Robert, 223
Tilton, Abraham, 191
Tilton, Abram P., 306
Tilton, Amos, 278
Tilton, Daniel, 20
Tilton, Greenleaf, 16
Tilton, Jeremiah, 264
Tilton, John, 129, 193
Tilton, Josiah, 169, 281
Tilton, Stephen, 19
Tilton, William, 65
Tilton, William P., 28
Tiltson, Ephraim, Jr., 129
Timpson, George, 154
Tiney, John, 20
Tingley, Samuel, 53
Tinker, John, 162 (2)
Tinker, Joseph, 163, 164
Tinker, Nehemiah, 65
Tinkham, Abiel W., 241, 242
Tinkham, Amasa, 170
Tinkham, Andrew, 307
Tinkham, Asa, 51

INDEX

Tinkham, Caleb, 52, 103
Tinkham, Cornelius, 52
Tinkham, Cyrus, 103
Tinkham, Ebenezer, 51
Tinkham, Enoch, 103
Tinkham, Enos, 51
Tinkham, Ephraim, 43, 89, 130
Tinkham, George W., 51
Tinkham, Harvey, 51
Tinkham, Isaac, 54
Tinkham, John, 51, 52, 54
Tinkham, Josiah, 51
Tinkham, Levi, 51, 103
Tinkham, Orren, 52
Tinkham, Otis, 89
Tinkham, Paddock, 52
Tinkham, Richard, 299
Tinkham, Seth, 90
Tinkham, Spencer, 184, 186 (2), 187, 190
Tinkham, Sylvanus, 51
Tinney, William, 85
Tinny, Henry, 210
Tirrel, William, 177
Tirrell, David, 86
Tirrell, Ebenezer, 41, 69, 80
Tirrell, Ezra, 77
Tirrell, George, 26
Tirrell, Gideon, 70, 80
Tirrell, Henry, 65
Tirrell, Joseph, 70
Tirrell, Loring, 25
Tirrell, Luther, 176
Tirrell, Noah, 102
Tirrell, Thomas, 100
Tirrell, Thomas, Jr., 65
Tirrill, George, 100
Tisdale, Barney, 8
Tisdale, Dean, 243
Tisdale, Mace, 70
Tisdale, Seth, 53
Titcomb, Benarah, 15
Titcomb, Bendiah, Jr., 212
Titcomb, Benjamin, 220, 266
Titcomb, Benjamin, Jr., 298
Titcomb, Edward, 19
Titcomb, Enoch, 212
Titcomb, George, 220
Titcomb, Isaac, 251
Titcomb, Jeremiah, 258
Titcomb, John, 15
Titcomb, John F., 295
Titcomb, John H., 20
Titcomb, Jonathan, 20
Titcomb, Josiah, 16
Titcomb, Paul, 19
Titcomb, Reuben, 220
Titcomb, Samuel, 220
Titcomb, William, 298
Titcomb, William, Jr., 220
Titus, Conly, 290
Titus, Horatio, 45
Titus, Samuel, 99, 169
Tivers, Joshua, 34
Tobey, Ansel, 310 (2)
Tobey, Curtis, 126
Tobey, Elisha, 58
Tobey, Ezra, 76
Tobey, Isaac, 184
Tobey, John, 72
Tobey, Lemuel, 154
Tobey, Lemuel, Jr., 310
Tobey, Nathaniel, 286, 310

Tobey, Samuel F., 56
Tobey, Sylvanus, 191
Tobey, Tristram, 75
Tobey, William, 56, 154
Tobey, Zimri, 75
Tobey, Zimri H., 76
Tobin, Benjamin, 225, 260
Tobin, John, 226
Tobin, Joseph, 223
Toby, Ansel, 263
Toby, Elias, 276
Toby, Elisha, 54
Toby, Ezra, 73
Toby, Hylon, 32
Toby, James, 71
Toby, John, 71
Toby, Joseph, 180
Toby, Nathaniel, 200
Toby, Sylvanus, 188
Toby, Sylvester, 184
Toby, Thomas H., 213
Toby, Tristram, 72
Toceusey, Mayhew, 305
Todd, Alexander, 311
Todd, Francis, 18
Todd, George, 8, 110, 243
Todd, Jeremiah, 138
Todd, John, 81, 148
Todd, John M., 160
Todd, Nathan, 12
Todd, Nathaniel, 248, 296 (2)
Todd, Samuel, 149
Todd, Thomas, 20, 123, 241, 244, 249, 297
Todd, Wallingford, 89
Todd, William, 226
Tolbert, Enoch, 86
Tolbert, Joseph, 86
Tole, Benjamin, 173
Tole, John, 301
Tole, Levi, 221
Tole, Samuel, 192, 196
Tole, Stacy, 301
Tole, Theophilus, 241
Tollman, Timothy, 32
Tolly, Daniel, 86
Tolman, Benjamin, 103, 119
Tolman, Calvin, 156, 157
Tolman, David, 156
Tolman, Edward, 43, 89
Tolman, Elias, 231, 296
Tolman, Elijah, 43, 89
Tolman, Elliot, 156
Tolman, Enos, 42, 88
Tolman, Isaac, 163
Tolman, James, 201 (2), 203
Tolman, Jeremiah, 276
Tolman, Jesse, 82
Tolman, Joseph, 295 (2)
Tolman, Joseph C., 104
Tolman, Josiah, 156
Tolman, Nathan, 202
Tolman, Robert P., 70
Tolman, Samuel, 104, 198, 199, 201, 202, 274
Tolman, Shepard, 205 (2)
Tolman, Stephen, 42, 88
Tolman, William, 71, 78
Tolman, William F., 26
Tombs, Dexter, 86
Tombs, Michel, 86
Tomlinson, Fabian, 93
Tomlinson, John, 188
Tomlinson, Paul, Jr., 194

Tomlison, John, 184
Tompkins, Lemuel, 24
Tompkins, Nathaniel, 63
Tompkins, Tillinghast, 129
Tompkins, William, 2
Tompson, John S., 311 (2)
Tompson, Robert, 273
Tonus, Amos, 213
Tool, Andrew, 145, 284
Toothaker, Abraham, 298
Toothaker, Alexander, 298
Toothaker, Charles, 148
Toothaker, Cornelius, 297, 299
Toothaker, David, 299
Toothaker, Ephraim, 233
Toothaker, Gideon, 235
Toothaker, Isaac, 297, 298
Toothaker, John, 295, 300
Toothaker, Joseph, 233
Toothaker, Samuel, 299
Toothaker, Seth, 297
Toothaker, William, 148, 301
Topliff, Benjamin, 78, 113, 114
Topliff, James, 69, 78, 111 (3), 112
Toppen, Benjamin, Jr., 20
Tor, Vincent, 90
Tornning, Thomas, 154
Torrence, Levi, 161
Torrener, Levi, 214
Torrey, David, 104
Torrey, George, 104
Torrey, James, 102
Torrey, John, 3, 28, 102
Torrey, Joseph, 25
Torrey, Nathaniel, 113 (2)
Torrey, Silas, 102
Torrey, William, 249, 297
Torry, Benjamin, 86, 101
Torry, Ebenezer, 24
Torry, Elijah, 205, 207
Torry, Haviland, 128
Torry, Isaac, 128, 222
Torry, Martin, 99
Torry, Nathan, 33
Torry, Noah, 101
Torry, Saul, 86
Torsey, John A., 160
Totman, Elias, 296
Totman, Joseph, 232
Totman, Thomas V., 92
Totsman, John, Jr., 3
Tourtellot, Eaton, 98
Tourtellot, Nathaniel, 163
Tourtellot, Stephen, 98
Tower, Alexander, 42
Tower, Benjamin, 40
Tower, Benjamin C., 40
Tower, Ezekiel, 65
Tower, Henry, Jr., 114
Tower, Jonas, 40
Tower, Lewis, 263
Tower, Luther, 65
Tower, Obediah, 65
Tower, Rufus, 79
Tower, Stephen, 263
Towers, Nathaniel, 191
Towl, Benjamin, Jr., 147
Towl, Ivory, 170
Towl, Jonathan, 180
Towl, Robert L., 146
Towle, Abner, 129, 174
Towle, Benjamin, Jr., 147

INDEX. 433

Towle, Israel, 63
Towle, Jonathan, 28
Towle, Josiah, 109
Towle, Levi, 221
Towle, Robert, 170
Towle, Samuel, 269
Towle, Thomas, 266
Towles, Thomas, 264
Town, Amos, 253
Town, Edmund, 109
Town, Elijah, 134, 139, 140
Town, Jacob, 141
Town, Jonathan, 83
Town, Joshua, 138
Town, Salem, 91
Town, Samuel, 134, 140, 268
Town, Solomon, 45
Town, Solomon D., 104
Town, Stephen, 141
Towne, Arad, 66
Towne, Edmund B., 85
Towne, Elijah, 139
Towne, Israel, 4
Towne, John, 272
Towne, Jonathan, 110
Towne, Thomas, 272
Towner, Ouvin, 65
Townes, Abner, 231
Townes, Samuel, 148
Towns, Daniel, 9, 100
Towns, Elisha, 229
Towns, John, 40
Towns, Joseph, 273
Towns, Samuel, 21
Towns, Thomas, 223, 231, 259
Towns, William, 230
Townsend, Avery, 53
Townsend, Benjamin, 232 (2)
Townsend, Burt, 150
Townsend, Daniel, 117
Townsend, Daniel, Jr., 116
Townsend, David, 50, 262
Townsend, David, Jr., 25
Townsend, Ellis, 74
Townsend, Ezekiel, Jr., 9
Townsend, Gara, 163
Townsend, George, 220
Townsend, Henry, 48, 77
Townsend, Hosea, 33
Townsend, Isaac, 286, 290
Townsend, Jacob, 116, 154, 293
Townsend, James, 244
Townsend, Jerva, 163
Townsend, Jesse, 232 (2)
Townsend, John, 116, 118
Townsend, Nathaniel, 243
Townsend, Otis, 251, 255
Townsend, Penn, 138
Townsend, Peres, 232
Townsend, Reuben, 93
Townsend, Robert, 264
Townsend, Samuel, 40, 88, 101, 202
Townsend, Solomon, 150
Townsend, Stephen, 239
Townsend, Terize, 232
Townsend, Thayer, 150
Townsend, Thomas, 222, 259
Townsend, William, 99, 209
Townson, Abijah, 100
Townson, Robert, 100
Towzer, William, 138
Tozer, William, 161

Tozier, Jeremiah, 3d, 153
Tozier, Jonathan E., 153
Tozier, Levi, 170
Tozier, Simeon, 267
Tozier, William, 267
Tracy, Henry, 46
Tracy, Horace, 94
Tracy, Nathaniel, 228
Tracy, Saul, 295
Tracy, Solomon, Jr., 228
Tracy, William, 94
Trafford, Joseph, 126
Trafton, Benjamin, Jr., 62
Trafton, George, 149
Trafton, Ivory, 245
Trafton, Jacob, 207
Trafton, Jeremiah, 153
Trafton, Joseph, 220
Trafton, Joshua, 211
Trafton, Samuel G., 60
Trafton, Thomas, 248
Trafton, Zacheus, 245
Traill, John, 6
Train, Oliver, 78
Trask, Abiezer, 296
Trask, Alvin, 153
Trask, Benjamin, 38
Trask, Benjamin, 2d, 34
Trask, D., 157
Trask, Daniel, 80, 183, 185
Trask, David, 179, 196
Trask, Ebeneser, 34, 38, 263, 266
Trask, Edward, 35 (2)
Trask, Enoch, 139 (2)
Trask, Enos, 192, 196
Trask, George, 34
Trask, Isaac, 35
Trask, Israel, 34, 35
Trask, James, 69, 146, 279
Trask, John, 7, 34, 38, 44, 179, 229
Trask, John, Jr., 229
Trask, Jonathan, 157, 196
Trask, Joseph, 133, 140
Trask, Joshua, 133
Trask, Nathaniel, 34, 38
Trask, Oliver, 34
Trask, Thomas, 196
Trask, William, 145, 183
Trask, William, Jr., 185
Trask, William, 2d, 145
Travers, Saul, 254
Treadwell, Ephraim, 136, 137
Treadwell, Jabez, 135, 140
Treadwell, Jacob, 216
Treadwell, John, 25
Treadwell, Jonathan, 254
Treadwell, Joshua, 309 (2)
Treadwell, Samuel, 134
Treadwell, William, 136, 137
Treat, Amos, 303
Treat, Ezra, 216
Treat, James, 303
Treat, John, 180
Treat, Richard, 165, 166, 173, 246, 257
Treat, Robert, 303
Treat, Thomas, 32
Treat, William, 101, 301
Treats, James, 243
Tredwell, Thomas, 311
Trofeheren, John, 304
Trefelhen, Abraham, 306
Trefelhen, Hanover, 306

Trefry, Samuel S., 6
Trevett, Robert, 182 (2)
Trevett, Saul, 216
Tribeau, Francis, 91
Tribou, Adna, 252
Tribou, Alpha, 212
Trickerman, Robert, 129
Trickey, David, 218
Trickey, Joseph, 256
Trickey, William, 218
Trim, John, 160
Tripe, Thomas, 245
Tripp, Aaron, 127
Tripp, Abel, 53
Tripp, Allen, 63 (2)
Tripp, Benajer, 63
Tripp, Benjamin, 56, 309 (2)
Tripp, Carmi, 63
Tripp, Duray, 56
Tripp, Ebeneser, 56
Tripp, Elihu, 56
Tripp, Ezekiel, 1
Tripp, Gilbert, 58
Tripp, Henry, 63
Tripp, Howard, 56
Tripp, Ishmael, 127
Tripp, James, 55, 58, 63
Tripp, Jesse, 301
Tripp, Job, 56, 63
Tripp, Joseph, 63
Tripp, Lemuel, 58
Tripp, Nathaniel, 56, 261
Tripp, Philip, 56
Tripp, Rufus, 56
Tripp, Stephen, 1st, 56
Tripp, Stephen, 2d, 56
Tripp, Stephen, 3d, 56
Tripp, Sylvanus, 55, 58
Tripp, Thomas, 55, 58
Tripp, Timothy, 58
Tripp, Weston, 56
Tripp, William, 55, 56, 58 (2), 126
Trivett, Benjamin, 216
Trobridge, Luther, 88
Troop, Alexander, 271
Troop, William, 271
Trott, Charles, 249
Trott, David, 249, 297
Trott, John, 212
Trott, Samuel, Jr., 249
Trow, Bartholomew, 97
Trow, Charles, 9
Trowbridge, Henry, 25
Trowbridge, James, 91
Trowbridge, John, 156 (2)
Trowent, Samuel, 195
True, Abner, 238
True, Benjamin, 295
True, Cyrus, 308
True, Ezekiel, 19, 119, 122, 181
True, Jacob L., 256
True, James, 308
True, John, 228, 272, 283
True, Jonathan, 210, 326
True, Moses, 181, 304
True, Paul, 181
True, Philip, 177
True, Samuel, 234, 256, 306
True, Thurston W., 170
True, William, 246, 257, 273
Truell, Abiather, 251
Truell, Ebeneser, 251

INDEX.

Trueman, John, 51, 75
Trueman, Keen, 75
Trueman, Samuel, 40
Trueman, Thomas, 114
Trueman, William, 2, 81
Truesdale, A. W., 120, 123, 125
Truesdale, Artemas W., 124
Truesdall, Artemas W., 121 (2)
Truett, George, 153, 261
Trueworthy, Daniel, 240
Trueworthy, Jacob, 240
Trueworthy, Jeremiah, 214
Trufant, Seth, 147
Trull, Elijah, 88
Trull, Joel, 26, 87, 114
Trull, Micah, 151, 254
Trull, Silas, 258
Truman, Joshua, 73
Truman, Thomas, 113
Truman, William, 73
Trumbull, J., 151
Trumbull, James, 69
Trumbull, John, 98
Trumbull, John W., 82
Trumbull, Nathaniel, 136
Trumbull, Peter, 40
Trumbull, Samuel, 151
Trumbull, W., 140
Trundy, William, 222
Trus, John, 212
Trusdall, Artemas W., 19
Trussel, Joshua, 302
Truwargy, Nathaniel, 162
Tryon, Elijah, 66
Tubbs, Elias, 175
Tubbs, Elisha W., 62
Tubbs, Isaac, 65
Tubbs, Samuel, 252, 256
Tuck, Enos, 283
Tuck, Hugh, 179
Tuck, Jesse, 276, 281
Tuck, John, 37, 38
Tuck, John, 2d, 38
Tuck, Levi, 36, 37, 278, 279
Tuck, Samuel, 272, 279
Tuck, Saul G., 179
Tuck, William, 283
Tucker, Amasa, 178
Tucker, Benjamin, 205 (2)
Tucker, Chandler, 40
Tucker, Daniel, 48, 236
Tucker, Daniel E., 234
Tucker, David, 26, 149, 222
Tucker, Devenport, 269
Tucker, Ebenezer, 213
Tucker, Isaac, 13, 94
Tucker, Jacob, 13
Tucker, James B., 241, 242
Tucker, Jesse, 271
Tucker, John, 7, 22, 70, 85, 223, 260
Tucker, John, Jr., 70
Tucker, Jonas, 222
Tucker, Joseph, 22, 136, 140
Tucker, Lyman, 2, 108
Tucker, Nathan, 51
Tucker, Nicholas, 6, 22, 163 (2)
Tucker, Pascal, 33
Tucker, Peter, 117
Tucker, Richard H., 186, 187
Tucker, Samuel, 106
Tucker, Samuel, Jr., 251
Tucker, Saul, 255

Tucker, Stephen, 266
Tucker, Thomas, 7, 22
Tucker, William, 7, 13
Tucker, Woodard, 24
Tuckerman, John T., 26, 79
Tuckerman, Stephen, 273
Tuckerman, William, 129
Tuell, Gilbert, 178
Tufts, Aaron, 111, 114
Tufts, Asa, 88
Tufts, Benjamin S., 4
Tufts, Caleb, 83
Tufts, David, Jr., 117
Tufts, Edmund, 81
Tufts, Fitch, 68
Tufts, Francis, 195
Tufts, Gardner, 2
Tufts, John, 227
Tufts, John, Jr., 27, 210
Tufts, Mathias, 108
Tufts, Samuel, 115, 116
Tufts, Seth, 115
Tufts, Simeon, 150
Tufts, Thomas, 86
Tufts, Walter, 94
Tufts, William, 88 (2), 227
Tukesbury, Benjamin, 209
Tukey, Benjamin, 165 (2), 193, 241, 242, 246
Tukey, Charles, 244
Tukey, Daniel, 149
Tukey, David, 149
Tukey, James, 243
Tukey, John, 258
Tukey, Samuel, 256
Tukey, William, 189
Tupper, Enoch, 126
Tupper, Hiram, 28
Tupper, Joseph, 18
Tupper, Lathrop, 27
Tupper, Lothrop, Jr., 132
Tupper, Peleg, 131
Tupper, Samuel, 264 (2)
Tupper, Spencer, 45
Turnbull, James, 194
Turnbull, John, 79
Turnbull, Nathaniel, 140
Turnbull, Robert, 192, 104
Turnbull, William, 194
Turner, Abel, 13, 104
Turner, Abiel, Jr., 177
Turner, Alpheus, 168
Turner, Alvan, 175
Turner, Artemas, 253
Turner, Asa, 264
Turner, Barker, 216
Turner, Barnabas, 115
Turner, Benjamin, 104, 168
Turner, Benjamin, Jr., 180
Turner, Bradish, 222
Turner, Briggs, 156, 157
Turner, Burrell D., 116
Turner, Calvin, 78
Turner, Charles, 256
Turner, Christopher, 278, 282
Turner, Daniel, 97, 228, 282
Turner, David, 2d, 180
Turner, Elijah B., 103
Turner, Enos, 225
Turner, Fobes, 39, 148
Turner, Gideon, 184, 187, 189
Turner, Henry, 113 (2)
Turner, Hezekiah, Jr., 90

Turner, Hollis, 180
Turner, Isaac, 251
Turner, Jacob, 278
Turner, James, 187, 191, 298
Turner, Jesse, 131, 251
Turner, John, 21, 138, 278, 289
Turner, John, Jr., 12
Turner, Jonathan, 47
Turner, Joseph, 168, 251, 281
Turner, Lemuel, 228
Turner, Leonard, 13
Turner, Levi, 251, 257
Turner, Luther, 1, 104, 251
Turner, Nathan, 180
Turner, Nathaniel, 189
Turner, Obediah, 168
Turner, Oliver, 178, 260
Turner, Samuel, 104
Turner, Samuel D., 6, 7, 21
Turner, Seth, 39
Turner, Silas, 284
Turner, Simeon, 168
Turner, Solomon, 228
Turner, Stephen, 60
Turner, Walter, 72
Turner, Zadoc, 65
Turrell, Francis, 258
Turrell, Kingman, 42
Turrier, John B., 162
Turrill, Job, 86
Turrill, Vincent, 86
Turwagry, Nathaniel, 162
Tutlow, Richard, 6
Tutt, Richard, 7
Tuttle, Cyrus, 159
Tuttle, Daniel, 177
Tuttle, Edward, 25
Tuttle, Eli, 306
Tuttle, Israel, 27
Tuttle, Jedediah, 2
Tuttle, John, 24, 31, 263
Tuttle, John W., 26
Tuttle, Jonathan, 268
Tuttle, Josiah, 148
Tuttle, Lebbeus, 226
Tuttle, Levi, 306
Tuttle, Reuben, 226, 262
Tuttle, Richard 6
Tuttle, Samuel, 117
Tuttle, Saul, 280
Tuttle, Sewell E., 162 (2)
Tuttle, Simon, 48
Tuttle, Thomas, 118
Tuttle, William, 177, 209
Tuttle, Worster, 161
Twambly, Arch, Jr., 215
Twambly, Nathaniel, 217
Twambly, Samuel F., 215
Twambly, Solomon, 215
Twambly, William, 243
Twining, Barnabus, 106, 107
Twining, Barnabus, Jr., 105 (2)
Twining, Prince, 106
Twining, Prince, Jr., 105 (2), 107
Twisden, Ebenezer L., 22
Twist, Joshua, 21
Twist, William, 139 (2)
Twitchel, John, 29
Twitchel, Josiah, 205
Twitchell, Asa, 258
Twitchell, Benjamin M., 95
Twitchell, David, 95, 252

INDEX.

Twitchell, Eleazer, 257
Twitchell, George, 95
Twitchell, John, 95, 181, 252, 255
Twitchell, Mark, 226
Twitchell, Moses, 252
Twitchell, Nathan F., 257
Twitchell, Sylvanus, 258
Twombly, Amos, 165
Twombly, Ezekiel, 245
Twombly, John, 248
Twombly, Solomon, 226
Twombly, William, 166, 213
Tyler, Abel, 198, 199, 207 (2)
Tyler, Abraham, 258
Tyler, Amos, 33
Tyler, Andrew, Jr., 213
Tyler, Benjamin, 9
Tyler, Chester, 29
Tyler, Coburn, 199, 202, 207
Tyler, Cutter, 48
Tyler, Daniel, Jr., 171
Tyler, Dudley, 199, 202, 207
Tyler, Ebenezer, 304
Tyler, Elijah, 67
Tyler, Isaac, 30, 210
Tyler, James, 171, 210
Tyler, John, 32
Tyler, Joseph, 258
Tyler, Moses, 27, 93
Tyler, Richard, 39
Tyler, Samuel, 152, 199, 207
Tyler, Saul, 150, 207
Tyler, Simeon, 208, 210
Tyler, Simeon, Jr., 199, 207
Tyler, Timothy, 145
Tyler, William H., 122, 125
Tylor, Simeon, 198
Tylor, Timothy, 179
Tyrrel, Benjamin, 65, 102
Tyson, Saul, 198

U

Uland, Edmund C., 224, 259
Ulmer, Andrew, 205 (2)
Ulmer, George, 300
Ulmer, Henry, 207
Ulmer, Jacob, 300
Ulmer, John, 204, 205
Ulmer, John, Jr., 206
Ulmer, Martin, 198, 200, 202, 206
Ulmer, Philip, 156
Umberhind, Charles, 292
Underhill, John, 8
Underwood, Arad, 39
Underwood, George, 134, 135
Underwood, John, 220
Underwood, Joseph H., 276
Underwood, Levi, 44
Underwood, Russell, 2
Underwood, William, 63
Upham, Abijah, 302
Upham, Amos, 70
Upham, James, 56
Upham, Joel, 91
Upham, Pliny, 91
Upton, Edward, 138
Upton, Eliab, 90
Upton, Elias, Jr., 67
Upton, Francis, 253
Upton, John, 117
Upton, Josiah, Jr., 67
Upton, Micah, 253

Upton, Reuben, 41
Upton, Robert, 133
Upton, Samuel, 137
Upton, Saul, 133
Upton, Stephen, 66
Upton, Sturgis, 46
Usher, Robert, 256
Usher, Scilly G., 258

V

Vainey, Andrew, 153
Valentine, Andrew, 7
Valentine, Benjamin, 7, 22
Valentine, Benjamin T., 22
Valentine, Gilbert, 221
Valentine, John, 252, 255
Valentine, Jonathan, 81, 82, 109
Valentine, Joseph, 97, 221
Valentine, Lowell, 221
Valentine, Lynde, 217
Vanderford, Charles, 133, 137
Van Esch, Simon Zward, 118
Vanhorn, Harvey, 44
Van Ness, Abraham, 31
Van Sailer, Jarret, 88
Varell, Jeremiah, 213
Varman, Ralph, 233
Varner, Charles, 194
Varner, George, 194, 197
Varner, Henry, 194
Varner, John, 194
Varney, Andrew, 261
Varney, Enoch, 235, 236, 296
Varney, James, 245, 310
Varney, Jedediah, 238
Varney, Loring, 244
Varney, Silas, 239
Varney, Solomon, 262
Varney, William, 296
Varnum, David, 196
Varnum, Phineas, 149
Varnum, Samuel, Jr., 238
Varnum, William, 145
Varny, Isaac W., 287
Varny, James, 287
Varrell, John, 260
Varrell, Rufus, 311
Varrell, Solomon, Jr., 311
Varrell, William M., 217
Vaugh, Daniel, 290, 293
Vaughan, Andrew, 54
Vaughan, Cushman, 52, 54
Vaughan, Daniel, 52, 54, 293
Vaughan, Ebenezer, 53, 103
Vaughan, George, 54
Vaughan, Jabez, 51
Vaughan, James, 79, 109 (2), 110, 111
Vaughan, Jonathan, 130
Vaughan, Peter, 52
Vaughan, Sylvanus, 52
Vaughn, James, 82
Vaughn, Pettey, 275
Vaughn, William O., 275
Vaughn, Zenos, 224, 260
Veasey, Stephen, 301
Veasie, Eli, 25
Veasie, Elijah, 27
Veasie, Saul, 236
Veisey, George, 81
Vent, James, 133
Verney, William, 231
Verril, John, 256

Verrill, Ezekiel, 177
Verrill, John, 176, 177
Verrill, Samuel, 3d, 177
Verrill, Samuel, 4th, 176
Verry, James, 35 (2)
Very, James, 139
Very, Joseph, 243
Very, Robert, 139
Very, Saul, 10
Very, William, 139 (2)
Vezie, Stephen, 100
Vial, Burrill, 86
Vial, James, 39
Viat, Elias, 88
Vibber, William, 67
Vichere, Asa, 307
Vickere, Joseph, 284
Vickery, Benjamin, 22
Vickery, Benjamin B., 7
Vickery, Daniel, 129
Vickery, Joel, 266
Vickery, Nathaniel, 210
Vickery, William, 7, 20
Vicory, Robert, 139
Videto, Jasper, 251, 255
Vila, Joseph, 84
Viles, Joseph, 280
Vilner, Peter, 80
Vinal, John, 42, 291, 311
Vinal, John S., 102
Vinal, Joseph, 291
Vinal, Seth, 115
Vinal, Simeon, 89
Vinall, Levi, 103
Vinall, Simeon, 43
Vinall, William, 103 (2)
Vincent, Abner, 58
Vincent, David, 64
Vincent, Isaac, 58
Vincent, John, 30
Vincent, Joseph, 40, 78, 86
Vincent, Joseph, Jr., 64
Vincent, Matthew, 14
Vincent, Samuel, 79, 87
Vincent, Samuel, Jr., 71
Vincent, Saul, 78
Vincent, Thomas, 35
Vincent, William, 285
Viney, David, 188
Viney, Samuel, 184, 186, 187 (2)
Viney, Saul, 190
Vinica, Hiram, 48
Vining, Ammi, 297, 300
Vining, Benjamin, 295
Vining, Daniel, 145
Vining, Ebed, 92
Vining, Ezra, 50
Vining, James, 86
Vining, Joseph, 92
Vining, William, 295
Vinion, Lothrop, 64
Vinning, Benjamin, 40
Vinson, Samuel, 26
Vinton, Abel, 69
Vinton, David, 4
Vinton, John, 42
Vinton, Josiah, 27
Vinton, M. M., 28
Virgin, Jeremiah W., 242
Virgin, John, 261
Vlesie, Jesse, 212
Vogle, John S., 2

Volage, Nathaniel, 282
Vosburg, Nathaniel, 31
Vose, David, 285, 286 (2), 289
Vose, Eben, 268
Vose, Ebenezer, 308
Vose, Isaac, 28
Vose, James W., 69
Vose, Jeremiah, 111
Vose, John, 40, 86, 284, 288, 290, 293
Vose, Reuben, 69
Vose, Samuel, 89
Vose, Seth, 290, 293
Vose, Thomas, 159
Vose, Thomas, Jr., 159
Vose, Tristram, 82
Vose, William, 40, 71, 259, 284, 294
Vosmas, John, 233
Vosmus, Isaac, 210
Vowland, Jabez, 75

W

Wadder, Andrew C., 22
Wade, Abner, 231
Wade, Amos, 62
Wade, Caleb, 249, 298
Wade, George F., 85
Wade, James, 274
Wade, John, 24, 42, 303
Wade, Leonard, 197, 203, 204
Wade, Levi, 2, 108, 262, 291
Wade, Lewis, 59
Wade, Lorin, 264
Wade, Luther, 231
Wade, Nathaniel, 103
Wadey, Henry, 127
Wadleigh, Benjamin, 15
Wadleigh, Benjamin H., 17, 121, 124
Wadleigh, William, 186, 188
Wadsworth, Aaron, Jr., 272
Wadsworth, Abiah, 302
Wadsworth, Cephas, 129
Wadsworth, Isaac, 42
Wadsworth, Jesse, 223
Wadsworth, John, 270
Wadsworth, Kenophon, 32
Wadsworth, Peleg, Jr., 153
Wadsworth, Peleg, 3d, 153
Wager, William, 148
Wagg, James, 198, 202, 208 (2), 209
Wagg, Saul, 295
Wagg, William P., 256
Wagner, Jacob, 199, 200, 202
Wagner, John, 289
Wagner, William, 289
Wainright, Thomas, 11
Wait, Abraham, 64
Wait, Ashial, 67
Wait, Chester, 33
Wait, David, 48
Wait, Edward, 154
Wait, Elmer, 3
Wait, Enos, 64
Wait, Gersham, 222
Wait, Harvey, 222
Wait, James, 67
Wait, Joel, 64
Wait, Niles, 224
Wait, Oliver, 27, 40
Wait, Solomon, 154
Wait, Stephen, Jr., 242
Wait, Thomas, 25
Wait, Tyler, 222, 259
Waite, Abraham, 152

Waite, Daniel, 226
Waite, George, 256
Waite, James, 259
Waite, John, Jr., 220
Waite, Josiah, 94
Waite, Otis, 91
Waite, Thomas, 46
Wakefield, James, 148
Wakefield, Jeremiah, 275
Wakefield, William, 133
Walch, Abraham, 139
Walch, Ebenezer, 18
Walcot, Silas, 86
Walcut, Silas, 6
Walden, Abijah, 118
Walden, Benjamin, 30
Walden, Daniel, 134, 135
Walden, Ephraim, 3
Walden, Joseph, 134, 135
Waldo, Edward, 137
Waldo, Henry L., 77
Waldo, Henry S., 76
Waldo, Jonathan, 141
Waldo, Michel, 291
Waldo, Michell, 294
Waldo, William, 81
Waldow, Edward, 135
Waldron, Daniel, 276
Waldron, Isaac, 306
Waldron, Nathaniel, 220
Waldron, Richard, 251
Waldron, Timothy W., 247
Wales, Cyrus, 92
Wales, John, 135, 226
Wales, Joseph, 100
Wales, Nathaniel, 49
Wales, Samuel, 92, 233
Wales, William, 92
Walker, Aaron, 4
Walker, Abraham, 191
Walker, Abram, 184, 188
Walker, Asa, 93, 229
Walker, Bartoll, 227
Walker, Benjamin, 88, 151, 227
Walker, Charles, 121, 124, 218, 252, 255
Walker, Daniel, 251
Walker, David, 89, 249, 297
Walker, Dependence, 149
Walker, Ebenezer, 152
Walker, Edward, 306
Walker, Elijah, 224
Walker, Elisha, 59
Walker, Ephraim W., 98
Walker, Ezekiel, 241, 242
Walker, Gardner, 221
Walker, George, 9, 10, 98, 145, 224
Walker, George, Jr., 59
Walker, Gideon, 89
Walker, Henry, 130
Walker, Hezekiah, 4
Walker, Horace, 4
Walker, Isaac I., 172
Walker, Jacob I., 30
Walker, James, 265
Walker, James P., 210
Walker, Jason, 224
Walker, John, 127, 170, 171, 213, 250 (2), 256, 265, 277, 283
Walker, John, Jr., 152
Walker, John B., 93
Walker, Jonathan, 229
Walker, Joseph, 229, 239

Walker, Joseph C., 258
Walker, Joshua, 230
Walker, Josiah, 93
Walker, Lewis, 60
Walker, Micah, 252
Walker, Nathan, 106 (2), 107
Walker, Nathaniel, 148
Walker, Oliver, 308, 309
Walker, Orin H., 48
Walker, Osgood, 229, 283
Walker, Peter, 150
Walker, Richmond, 59
Walker, Ripley, 66
Walker, Robert, 59, 151, 171
Walker, Samuel, 48, 66, 220
Walker, Saul, 59
Walker, Simeon, 61, 270, 284
Walker, Solomon, 23
Walker, Supply, 254
Walker, Timothy, 267
Walker, William, 188, 251, 301
Walker, Zeph, 59
Walkup, Thomas, 66
Wall, Benjamin, 197
Wall, David, 206, 276
Wall, Ephraim, 206, 207
Wall, John, 304
Wallace, Alexander, 248
Wallace, Charles, 310, 311
Wallace, Eli, 248
Wallace, Elisha F., 138
Wallace, Francis, 248
Wallace, Isaac, 250
Wallace, James, 181
Wallace, John, 90, 248
Wallace, John, Jr., 250
Wallace, Samuel, Jr., 250
Wallace, William, 248
Wallace, Zachariah, 248
Wallas, John, 299
Wallby, Ichabod, 215
Wallen, John, 36
Walley, John, 35
Wallice, John, 289
Wallice, Saul, 291
Wallice, William, 289
Wallis, Bartholomew, 34, 38
Wallis, Caleb, 34
Wallis, Chancey, 86
Wallis, Ebenezer, 38
Wallis, Ebenezer, 2d, 34, 38
Wallis, Ebenezer, 3d, 34
Wallis, Ezekiel, 102
Wallis, Henry, 34, 38
Wallis, Israel, 34
Wallis, Jeremiah, 81, 87
Wallis, John, 163 (2), 221
Wallis, Jonathan, 13
Wallis, Joseph, 278, 282
Wallis, Josiah H., 34
Wallis, Levi, 34, 92, 221
Wallis, Levy, 168
Wallis, Mordecai L., 81
Wallis, Nathaniel, 34, 38
Wallis, Noah, 66
Walsh, William, Jr., 156
Walter, George, 197
Walter, Harvey, 29
Walter, Samuel, 19
Walter, Sylvester, 33
Walton, Charles, 98
Walton, John, 201

INDEX. 437

Walton, Moses, 228
Walton, Rufus, 279
Walton, Saul, 279
Walton, Simeon, 255
Walton, William, 290
Walts, Samuel, 194
Ward, Andrew, 138 (2)
Ward, Artemas, 46
Ward, Benjamin, 129, 215
Ward, Benjamin C., 8
Ward, Eliab, 129
Ward, Elihu, 31
Ward, Ephraim, 49
Ward, Ezekiel, 171
Ward, George A., 132
Ward, George H., 138
Ward, Isaac J., 24
Ward, Israel, 308, 310
Ward, Jacob, 93
Ward, John, 34, 37, 38, 40, 42, 79, 82, 215, 216
Ward, Jonas, 66
Ward, Jonathan, 138, 150, 151, 210, 215
Ward, Joseph, 95
Ward, Joshua, 232
Ward, Josiah, 232
Ward, Julius, 44
Ward, Lemuel, 226
Ward, Nathaniel, 137, 215
Ward, Nehemiah, 209, 237, 266
Ward, Richard, 7, 110, 112, 113, 137
Ward, Roswell, 64
Ward, Royal, 68
Ward, Samuel, 237, 267, 300
Ward, Saul, 138
Ward, Simeon, 46
Ward, Simon, 301
Ward, Stephen, 134, 140
Ward, Thomas, 26, 263
Ward, Thomas, Jr., 237
Ward, William, 238, 267, 275
Ward, Wiswell, 112
Warden, William P., 189
Wardwell, Jeremiah, 216
Wardwell, Samuel, Jr., 256
Ware, Aratus, 137
Ware, Benjamin, 190, 191
Ware, David, 191
Ware, Everett, 186, 190
Ware, Galen, 98
Ware, George, 38, 86
Ware, James, 5
Ware, Joseph, 186, 190
Ware, Joshua, 69
Ware, Josiah, 215
Ware, Lewis, 170, 277
Ware, Nathan, Jr., 190
Ware, Thomas, 40
Ware, Timothy, 190
Ware, Vinal, 286
Ware, Warren, 216
Wares, Jonathan, 165 (2)
Warf, Oliver, 180
Warfield, Horace, 46
Wargatt, Asa, 163 (2)
Wargatt, David, 163 (2)
Wargatt, David, Jr., 163
Wargatt, Davis, 163
Wargatt, Moses, 163 (2)
Waring, James, 139 (2)
Warlow, Benjamin, 67
Warmal, Henry, 295
Warner, Alvin, 64

Warner, Caleb, 132
Warner, Daniel, 93, 134, 135
Warner, George, 32
Warner, Henry, 65
Warner, James, 254
Warner, John, 7, 22, 132, 289
Warner, Johnson, 225
Warner, Jonathan, 48
Warner, Joseph, 138
Warner, Joseph H., 89
Warner, Luther, 96
Warner, Nathaniel, 19, 120, 122
Warner, Newton, 64
Warner, Oliver, 92
Warner, Simeon, 50
Warner, Stephen, 111 (2)
Warner, Thaddeus, 44
Warner, Theodore S., 82
Warner, William, 13, 242
Warren, Abijah, 258
Warren, Abraham, 243
Warren, Andrew, 52, 267
Warren, Benjamin, 129, 304
Warren, Caleb, 151
Warren, Charles W., 94
Warren, Cyrus, 5, 50
Warren, Daniel, 54
Warren, David, 174
Warren, Ebenezer, 295
Warren, Edmund, 233
Warren, Galen, 50
Warren, George, 116, 117
Warren, Gilbert, 261
Warren, Henry, 113, 241, 295
Warren, Isaiah, 150, 151
Warren, Ivory, 295
Warren, James, 51, 59, 151
Warren, James, 3d, 171
Warren, John, 91, 240, 251, 255, 285, 287
Warren, Joseph, 267
Warren, Josiah, 101
Warren, M., 243
Warren, Marshall, 223
Warren, Nathan, 115
Warren, Nathaniel, 152, 221, 254
Warren, Nathaniel M., 277
Warren, Nathaniel W., 170
Warren, Nehemiah, 115
Warren, Peleg, 258
Warren, Peltiah, Jr., 170
Warren, Phineas, 145
Warren, Richard, Jr., 340
Warren, Robert, 164, 165, 166, 218
Warren, Rufus, 295
Warren, Samuel, 29, 87
Warren, Samuel, Jr., 251
Warren, Stephen, 111
Warren, Sylvanus, 54
Warren, Thomas, 241
Warren, Willard, 92
Warren, William, 67, 149, 158
Warrick, Paul, 25
Warriner, Justin, 4
Warriner, Solomon, 2
Warriner, W. B., 28
Warriner, Walter, 4
Warriner, Warren, 44
Warwell, Joseph, 163
Washburn, Benjamin, 53, 67, 273
Washburn, Calvin, 62
Washburn, Cyrus, 178
Washburn, David, 234

Washburn, Eli, 253, 257
Washburn, Eliab, 4, 39
Washburn, Ephraim, 307
Washburn, Herman, 97
Washburn, Hosea, 268
Washburn, Isaac, 253
Washburn, James, 176, 223
Washburn, Job, 205 (2)
Washburn, Joseph, 4, 95, 176
Washburn, Josiah, 50
Washburn, Lettice, 30
Washburn, Levi, 97
Washburn, Linus, 54
Washburn, Luther, 103
Washburn, Martin, 223, 259
Washburn, Moses, 129
Washburn, Nahum, 91
Washburn, Nathan, 53
Washburn, Peleg, 175
Washburn, Reuel, 129
Washburn, Roland, 52
Washburn, Samuel, 78, 109
Washburn, Sears, 51
Washburn, Seth, 51
Washburn, Stephen, 175, 260
Washburn, Stillman, 56
Washburn, Thomas, 51, 53, 54
Washburn, Zalmana, 237
Wason, Uriah, Jr., 171
Waste, Noah, 55
Waston, Eaton, 5
Watchman, Ebenezer, 212
Wate, Reuben, 56
Waterhouse, Ai, 172
Waterhouse, Alexander, 222
Waterhouse, Benjamin, 233
Waterhouse, Daniel, 85, 211
Waterhouse, David, 174
Waterhouse, Elias, 233, 244
Waterhouse, Ezekiel, 272
Waterhouse, George, 274
Waterhouse, Isaac, 274
Waterhouse, James, 223
Waterhouse, John, 170, 245
Waterhouse, Joseph, 166, 172, 225
Waterhouse, Joseph H., 164, 165, 218
Waterhouse, Josiah, 171
Waterhouse, Richard, 159
Waterhouse, Robert, 31
Waterhouse, Samuel, 219
Waterhouse, Samuel, Jr., 256
Waterhouse, Thomas, 300
Waterhouse, Timothy, 213, 237, 265
Waterhouse, William, 154
Waterhouse, William H., 173
Waterhouse, Zebulon, 210
Waterhouse, Zenus, 233
Waterman, Benson, 129
Waterman, Daniel, 213
Waterman, George, 30
Waterman, Grey, 177
Waterman, Henry, 198, 199, 201, 202, 208
Waterman, Jabes, 256
Waterman, John, 253
Waterman, Jonah, 177, 198, 199, 201, 202
Waterman, Joseph, 52, 199, 202
Waterman, Joseph, Jr., 209
Waterman, Joseph S., 39
Waterman, Levi, 69
Waterman, Martin, 128
Waterman, Noah, 224
Waterman, Noah, Jr., 260

INDEX.

Waterman, Otis, 50
Waterman, Thomas, 104, 256
Waterman, Townsend, 30
Waterman, William, 268
Waters, Clark, 69
Waters, Gardner, 222, 260, 276
Waters, Isaac, 222
Waters, Israel, 259
Waters, James, 77, 194
Waters, John, 96, 110, 134, 135, 137, 195, 213
Waters, Lewis, 224
Waters, Nathaniel, 48
Waters, Nathaniel B., 189, 191
Waters, William, 189
Waters, William, Jr., 184, 187
Waters, William D., 30
Watkins, Andrew, 111
Watkins, Jacob S., 258
Watson, Alexander, 270
Watson, Amasiah, 312
Watson, Asa, 27
Watson, David, 28, 279 (2)
Watson, Ebenezer, 252
Watson, Greenleaf C., 173
Watson, Henry, 279
Watson, James, 145, 279
Watson, John, 165 (2), 241, 242
Watson, Jonathan, 116, 266, 268
Watson, Joseph, 61, 172, 278, 279
Watson, Joseph, 3d, 279
Watson, Josiah M., 282
Watson, Nathaniel, 285
Watson, Richard, 278
Watson, Samuel, 306, 312
Watson, Saul, 233
Watson, Simeon, 251
Watson, Simon, 302
Watson, Stephen, 306
Watson, Stephen P., 253
Watson, Thomas B., 261
Watson, Thomas G., 152
Watson, William, 263
Watton, John, 198, 199
Watts, Andrew, 278
Watts, Daniel C., 118
Watts, Freeman, 169
Watts, George, 200, 206
Watts, Isaac, 118
Watts, John, 200, 206
Watts, Moses, 200, 206
Watts, Nathaniel, 169
Watts, Samuel L., 108
Watts, William, 206
Waugh, David, 304
Waugh, Elijah, 305
Waugh, George, 279
Waugh, James, Jr., 304
Waugh, John, 278, 282
Waugh, Samuel, 282
Waugh, Sewall, 305
Waugh, Thomas, 305
Waymouth, John, 306
Waymouth, Robert, 166
Wead, Stephen, 63
Weatherbee, Jabes, 99
Weatherbee, Oliver, 100
Weatherbee, William B., 83
Weatherby, Henry C., 86
Weatherhold, John, 67
Weathern, Arthur, 182
Weaver, Phillip, 308
Webb, Asa, 306

Webb, Benjamin, 187, 220
Webb, Daniel, 94
Webb, David, 246
Webb, Ebenezer, 193
Webb, Eli, 218
Webb, George, 218
Webb, Gustavus, 257
Webb, James, 221
Webb, John, 38, 82, 240, 266, 306
Webb, John, 2d, 34
Webb, Jonathan, 134 (2), 138
Webb, Joseph, 27, 79, 114
Webb, Joseph B., 307
Webb, Joshua, 186, 187, 189
Webb, Kier, 221
Webb, Nathan, 35 (2)
Webb, Nicholas B., 16
Webb, Pearson, 240
Webb, Robert, 160
Webb, Samuel, 138, 263, 307
Webb, Seth, 171
Webb, Stephen, 103, 172
Webb, Thomas, 138
Webb, Thomas B., 133
Webb, Walter, 78
Webb, William, 132, 138, 158, 210, 212
Webb, William H., 249
Webb, William R., 297
Webb, Winslow, 224
Webber, Aaron, 220
Webber, Amos, 241
Webber, Amos S., 149, 246
Webber, Asa, 159
Webber, Benjamin, 36, 38, 195, 197
Webber, Charles, 237, 265, 299
Webber, Daniel, 237
Webber, Daniel, Jr., 158
Webber, Edmund, 155, 312
Webber, Elias, 272
Webber, George, 240
Webber, Henry, 133, 136, 140
Webber, Ignatius, Jr., 13
Webber, Israel, 34, 230
Webber, John, 71, 183, 185, 189 (2), 191, 213, 247, 266
Webber, John P., 34
Webber, Joseph, 14, 230, 233
Webber, Josiah, 35
Webber, Kimball, 47
Webber, Loring, 233
Webber, Nathaniel, 194
Webber, Samuel, 216, 228, 233
Webber, Stephen, 233, 296
Webber, Stephen, Jr., 233
Webber, Sylvanus, 237, 266
Webber, William, 29
Webbs, John, 2d, 21
Webster, Amos, 46
Webster, Andrew, 261
Webster, Benjamin, 149, 209
Webster, Charles, 116
Webster, Daniel, 217
Webster, David, 185
Webster, Elijah, 217
Webster, George, 12
Webster, James, 57, 161
Webster, John, 27, 83, 112, 217
Webster, John W., 97
Webster, Joshua, 11
Webster, Josiah, 150, 152
Webster, Lyman, 32
Webster, Nathan, 83

Webster, Nathaniel, 173, 243
Webster, Owen, 44
Webster, Peter E., 141
Webster, Stephen, 183, 185 (2), 189
Webster, Thomas, 201 (2), 203, 210
Webster, Washington, 119, 122, 301
Webster, Whitely, 258
Webster, William, 297 (2), 300
Webster, William, Jr., 300
Weed, Benjamin, 216
Weed, Henry, 182, 186
Weed, James, 201 (2), 203
Weed, Jonathan, 30
Weed, Moses, 35, 216
Weed, Nathan, 216
Weed, Warren, 7
Weed, William, 301
Weeden, Daniel, 11
Weeks, Amasa, 90
Weeks, Benjamin, 196, 256
Weeks, Braddock, 238
Weeks, Caleb, 66
Weeks, Charles, 239
Weeks, Daniel, 194, 242
Weeks, Daniel, Jr., 196
Weeks, David, 263
Weeks, David S., 145
Weeks, Ebenezer, 226
Weeks, Edward, 217
Weeks, Ephraim, 196, 237
Weeks, Ezra, 226
Weeks, Henry, 249
Weeks, Isaac, 210
Weeks, John, 196, 237, 256
Weeks, Joseph, 195, 196 (2), 210
Weeks, Joseph, Jr., 196
Weeks, Joshua F., 149
Weeks, Josiah G., 196
Weeks, Samuel, 226
Weeks, Samuel P., 252
Weeks, Thomas, Jr., 196
Weeks, William, 148, 158, 173
Weeks, Zenos, 75
Weighmont, Timothy, 276
Welch, Charles, 229, 282
Welch, Edward, 148, 169
Welch, Elijah, 227
Welch, George, 241
Welch, Jacob, 283
Welch, James, 219
Welch, John, 38, 250 (2)
Welch, John A., 40, 68
Welch, Jonathan, 149
Welch, Jonathan C., 20
Welch, Joseph, 28, 219
Welch, Lawrence, 145
Welch, Lemuel, 219
Welch, Mark, 234
Welch, Moses, 245
Welch, Otis, 147
Welch, Reid, 148
Welch, Richard, 250 (2)
Welch, William, 17, 205
Welcomb, John, 159
Welcome, Stephen, 168, 281
Welcome, Timothy, 176
Weld, Joseph, 89
Weld, Nathaniel, Jr., 247
Weld, Timothy, 167
Weld, William, 83
Weldbore, Adam, 224
Welden, Isaac, 127

INDEX. 439

Welden, Peter L., 31
Welden, Solomon, 135
Wellam, Phineas, 186, 187
Wellborn, Stephen, 127
Weller, Andrew, 70
Weller, Percy, 29
Welles, Theodore S., 78
Welling, Michell, 14
Wellington, Alden, 223
Wellington, Darius, 101
Wellington, Elijah, 224, 259
Wellington, Erastus, 267
Wellington, Joel, 239, 267
Wellington, Levi, 94
Wellington, Thaddeus, 138
Wellman, Bartholomew, 116
Wellman, Benjamin, 289
Wellman, Gilbert, 195
Wellman, James, 266
Wellman, Jedediah, 200, 202
Wellman, Oliver, 139
Wellman, Samuel, 195
Wellman, Samuel E., 139 (2)
Wellman, Stephen, 139 (2)
Wellman, Timothy, 138 (2)
Wells, Abner, 66
Wells, Albigence, 48
Wells, Allen, 61
Wells, Caleb T., 80
Wells, Charles, 69
Wells, Daniel, 20, 125
Wells, Daniel, Jr., 21, 125
Wells, David, 268
Wells, Ebenezer, 28
Wells, George, 83
Wells, Israel, 64
Wells, James, 228
Wells, John, 14
Wells, John, Jr., 20
Wells, Joseph, 14
Wells, Moses, 134, 135
Wells, Nathaniel, 134, 135, 275
Wells, Nathaniel B., 14
Wells, Otis, 44
Wells, Peaslee, 285, 286
Wells, Peasley, 286, 288
Wells, Philip, 141
Wells, Pliny, 64
Wells, Richard, 19, 121, 125
Wells, Robert, 264
Wells, Stephen, 90, 279
Wells, Theodore, 69
Wells, William, 264
Welman, James, 264
Welman, Jedediah, 199
Welman, John, 264
Welsh, Daniel, 235, 296
Welsh, James, 138
Welts, Amos, 308
Welts, David, 308
Wendall, Jacob, Jr., 70
Wendell, Charles J., 82
Wentworth, Andrew, 275
Wentworth, Daniel, 154
Wentworth, David, 275
Wentworth, Enoch, 245
Wentworth, Gant, 216
Wentworth, Hiram, 8, 112, 113
Wentworth, James, 28
Wentworth, John, 82, 148, 268, 270, 312
Wentworth, Jonathan, 240
Wentworth, Joseph, 17

Wentworth, Lemuel, 199
Wentworth, Mark, 228
Wentworth, Noah, 272
Wentworth, Oliver, 86
Wentworth, Paul, 250, 255
Wentworth, Samuel, 152
Wentworth, Saul, 290
Wentworth, Spencer, 86
Wentworth, Stephen, 304
Wentworth, Thomas, 224, 259, 269 (2)
Wentworth, Timothy, 239
Wentworth, Tobias, 198, 202, 208 (2), 209
Wentworth, William, 213, 254
Wenzell, Henry, 84
Wescoat, Weston, 61
Wescot, William, 212
Wescott, James, 171
Wescott, John, 175
Wescott, John, Jr., 171
Wescott, Joseph, 158
Wescott, Reuben, Jr., 173
Wescott, William, 174, 246
Wesson, Russell, 92
Wesson, Stephen, 295
West, Amos, 2d, 61
West, Asa, 226
West, Bartlett, 216
West, Benjamin, 69
West, Charles C., 273
West, Ebenezer, 224
West, Edward, 132
West, Edward B., 58
West, Enos, 215
West, James, 112
West, John, 79, 184, 186, 187, 190
West, John P., 1
West, Joseph, 8, 36, 37, 113, 191, 226
West, Lloyd, 46
West, Luther, 226
West, Matthias, 291
West, Nathaniel, 133
West, Peter, 304
West, Richard, 1
West, Samuel, 55, 58, 74
West, Shubal, 275
West, Stephen, 129
West, Stephen, Jr., 74
West, Thomas, 37, 55, 58, 136, 211
West, Thomas, Jr., 99
West, William, 55, 57, 162, 216, 273, 310
Westoot, Charles, 218
Western, Henry, 40
Westgate, Daniel, 53
Westgate, Horace, 53
Westgate, Jonathan, 102
Westgate, Joseph, 102
Westgate, Obed, 53
Westgate, Weston, 59, 61
Westgate, William, 53, 57
Weston, Abner, 53
Weston, Amos, 217
Weston, Asahel, 68
Weston, Coomer, 128
Weston, Cyrus, 284
Weston, Daniel, 51, 52, 88, 197, 307
Weston, Eaton, 5, 91
Weston, Edward, 293
Weston, Eli, Jr., 304
Weston, Eliphalet, 41
Weston, Eliphas, 195, 197
Weston, Enoch, 56
Weston, Ensebus, 307

Weston, Ephraim, 101, 118
Weston, George, 290, 293
Weston, George B., 307
Weston, Jacob, Jr., 155, 156
Weston, James, 211
Weston, John, 129, 210, 258
Weston, John W., 307
Weston, Jonas, 307
Weston, Joshua, 195
Weston, Josiah, 253
Weston, Liberty, 77
Weston, Luther, 21
Weston, Melzar, 129
Weston, Samuel, 118
Weston, Sasson, 217
Weston, Seth, 52
Weston, Stephen, 129, 284, 307
Weston, Theodore, 290
Weston, Thomas F., 129
Wetharbee, Elijah G., 88
Wetherbee, Charles, 292, 294
Wetherbee, Elijah G., 160
Wetherbee, John, 71
Wetherbee, John H., 28
Wetherbee, Jonas, 28, 110
Wetherbee, Jude, 258
Wetherbee, Simon P., 71
Wetherbee, William B., 81
Wethercox, Jacob, 68
Wetherell, Charles, 54
Wetherell, George, 10
Wetherell, John, 73
Wetherell, Rufus, 135
Wetherell, Samuel B., 284
Wetherell, Zelotes, 126
Wethern, Benjamin, 147
Weyer, Henry, 70
Weymouth, Archibald, 235
Weymouth, David, 296
Weymouth, H., 234
Weymouth, John, 245, 301
Weymouth, John S., 210
Weymouth, Moses, 148
Weymouth, Nathan, 234
Weymouth, Nathaniel, 234
Weymouth, Pierce, 301
Weymouth, Robert, 164, 165, 219, 246
Weymouth, Samuel, 266, 280, 306
Weymouth, Solomon, 266
Weymouth, Stephen, 211
Weymouth, Thomas, 234
Weymouth, Walter, 169
Whalen, Daniel, 56
Whalen, Jonathan, 56
Whales, George, 244
Whalking, Jacob, 48
Wharf, Eliphalet, 244
Wharf, Nathaniel, 256
Wharff, Joseph, 273
Wharffey, William, 13
Whealor, Simeon, 190
Wheaton, Elisha, 171
Wheaton, Godfrey, 241, 242
Wheaton, Humphrey, 181
Wheaton, John, 98
Wheaton, Jonathan, 62
Wheaton, Samuel, 61
Wheeden, John, 28
Wheedon, Daniel, 56
Wheedon, John, 58
Wheeldon, Ebenezer, 217
Wheeler, Abner, 100

Wheeler, Abraham, 33, 43, 89
Wheeler, Amos, 9, 307
Wheeler, Artemus, 99
Wheeler, Calvin, 3, 56
Wheeler, Cyrus, 5, 68, 264
Wheeler, Daniel, 66
Wheeler, David, 2, 78, 206, 207 (2), 261, 265
Wheeler, Dewey, 65
Wheeler, Edward T., 228
Wheeler, Edward W., 307
Wheeler, Elisha, 5
Wheeler, Francis, 5
Wheeler, George, 228, 283
Wheeler, Harvey, 33
Wheeler, Henry, 83
Wheeler, Jestus, 30
Wheeler, Joel, 94
Wheeler, John, 222, 231, 299
Wheeler, Jona, 82
Wheeler, Jonas, 198, 208 (2), 209, 266, 306
Wheeler, Jonathan, 100
Wheeler, Joseph, 26, 164, 165, 166, 221, 296
Wheeler, Josiah, 93, 116
Wheeler, Milton, 30
Wheeler, Moses, Jr., 11
Wheeler, Nathaniel, 62, 71, 164, 165, 166, 221
Wheeler, Noah, Jr., 99
Wheeler, Perley, 307
Wheeler, Phineas, 99
Wheeler, Reuben, 35, 94
Wheeler, Samuel, 71, 123, 258, 306
Wheeler, Samuel, Jr., 120
Wheeler, Saul, 18
Wheeler, Simeon, 66, 168, 191, 299
Wheeler, Simeon H., 6
Wheeler, Simon, 231
Wheeler, Solomon, 45
Wheeler, Stephen, 101
Wheeler, Thomas, 134
Wheeler, Thomas, 2d, 99
Wheeler, Timothy, 99
Wheeler, Wheaton, 60
Wheeler, William, 71, 100, 231, 261
Wheeler, William D., 94
Wheeler, Zacheus, 66
Wheelock, Cephas, 27
Wheelock, Josiah, 66
Wheelock, Paul, 69
Wheelock, Samuel, 24, 114
Wheelright, Ebenezer, 19, 120, 122
Wheelright, George, 68
Wheelright, James, 77
Wheelright, Jeremiah, 19
Wheelright, Robert, 182 (2)
Wheelwright, George, 309 (2), 310
Wheelwright, John, 70, 184
Whelden, Peter, 267
Whelden, S., 125
Whelock, Manning, 65
Whelwell, William, 69
Whetcher, William, 306
Whotely, John, 237
Whetten, Thomas, 286
Whicher, Ezekiel, 27
Whidden, Asa, 275
Whidden, Daniel, 42
Whidden, James, 266
Whidden, James, 2d, 266, 306
Whidden, James, 3d, 306
Whidden, Rendol, 275
Whiden, David, 151
Whiden, John, 151

Whipple, Charles, 19
Whipple, David, 266
Whipple, Henry, 141
Whipple, John, 30
Whipple, Jonathan, 133, 136, 149
Whipple, Larnard, 53
Whipple, Stephen, 10
Whitacer, Nathaniel, 61
Whitaker, James, 95, 304
Whitaker, Joel, 61
Whitaker, Paul, 66
Whitaker, Silas, 95
Whitaker, Stewart F., 234
Whitaker, William, 95
Whitcher, Artemas, 306
Whitcomb, Ebenezer, Jr., 201 (2), 203
Whitcomb, Ira, 203
Whitcomb, John, 64, 203, 212, 266
Whitcomb, Joseph, 5
Whitcomb, Josiah, 5
Whitcomb, Laban, 70
Whitcomb, Levi, 2, 268, 306
Whitcomb, Nathaniel, 305
Whitcomb, Oliver, 186 (2), 187, 190, 191
Whitcomb, Paul, 258
Whitcomb, Samuel, 86
Whitcomb, Silas, 66
White, Aaron, 261, 282
White, Abiather, 59
White, Abijah, 62, 305
White, Alanson, 93, 95
White, Alexander, 47
White, Alfred, 56
White, Ambrose, 273
White, Amos, 48
White, Aneyl, 48
White, Ansel, 58
White, Asa, 9, 24, 53, 59, 90, 226, 275
White, Asaph, 126
White, Augustine, 214
White, Augustus, 54
White, Bartlett, 182 (2), 184
White, Benjamin, 54, 60, 94, 228, 271, 274, 312
White, Cyrus, 1, 52, 103
White, David, 43, 89, 92
White, Ebenezer, 2, 106, 272
White, Elijah, 2d, 236
White, Eliot, 41
White, Enos, 94
White, Ezra, 58
White, Farman, 30
White, Ferdinand E., 68
White, Francis, 187
White, Freeborn, 64
White, Gardner, 64
White, George, 41, 56, 80, 273, 302
White, Gideon, 231
White, Harris, 64
White, Henry, 133, 222
White, Henry, Jr., 10
White, Horatio, 210
White, Hosea, 253
White, Howe, 60
White, Isaac, 62, 231, 247
White, Isaac, Jr., 129
White, James, 42, 57, 187, 222, 247, 264, 284, 291, 297, 305, 307
White, Jarvis, 30, 61
White, Jeremiah, 48, 86
White, Jesse, 182, 191
White, Jesse, Jr., 182
White, Job, 56, 92, 154

White, Joel, 223
White, John, 22, 38, 48, 57, 62, 63, 71, 78, 181, 232, 240, 247, 254, 280
White, John B., 181
White, John R., 181
White, Jonathan, 54
White, Joseph, 25 (2), 64, 67, 157 (2), 179
White, Joseph G., 182 (2)
White, Josiah, 80, 93
White, Lazarus, 273
White, Levi, 129
White, Lewis, 224
White, Linus, 168
White, Loring, 50
White, Luther, 56
White, Malachi, 57
White, Mark, 174
White, Martin, 53
White, Moses, 139 (2), 273
White, Nathaniel, 43, 89, 307
White, Nicholas, 63
White, Obediah, 27
White, Phineas, 58
White, Samuel, 40, 62, 217
White, Samuel, Jr., 57
White, Samuel F., 118
White, Saul, 45
White, Solomon, 53, 174
White, Stephen, 138
White, Stephen B., 84, 138
White, Thomas, 2, 97, 100, 108, 274
White, Thomas B., 18, 120, 123
White, Timothy, 273
White, Walter, 10
White, William, 24, 58, 61, 99, 161, 232, 247, 284, 305, 307
White, William, Jr., 304
White, Willis, 53
Whitefield, George, 55, 58
Whitefield, Humphrey, 58
Whitehead, John, 252
Whitehouse, Daniel, 240
Whitehouse, Daniel O., 24
Whitehouse, David, 194
Whitehouse, Ebenezer, 176
Whitehouse, Ephraim, 256
Whitehouse, Hanson, 7
Whitehouse, Isaac, 263
Whitehouse, James, 196
Whitehouse, John, 192, 196, 212, 245
Whitehouse, Nathaniel, 263
Whitehouse, Robert, 262
Whitehouse, Stephen, 194
Whitehouse, Thomas, 240, 263, 265
Whitehouse, William, 196
Whiten, Isaac, 50
Whitham, Asa, 256
Whitham, Benjamin, 150
Whitham, Ebenezer, Jr., 256
Whitham, Jerry, 197
Whitham, Thomas, 213
Whiting, Ansel, 43
Whiting, Asa, 37, 38
Whiting, Benjamin, Jr., 128
Whiting, Caleb, 60
Whiting, Clement, 254
Whiting, David, 68
Whiting, Eben, 8
Whiting, Ebner E., 3
Whiting, Eleazer, 92
Whiting, Ephraim, 126, 128, 131
Whiting, George, 70

INDEX. 441

Whiting, Isaac, 99
Whiting, Jabez, 82
Whiting, James, 152, 254
Whiting, John, 3, 50, 99
Whiting, John T., 54
Whiting, Jonathan, 273
Whiting, Joseph, 94, 128
Whiting, Justus, 1, 103
Whiting, Kimball, 23
Whiting, Melsar, 129
Whiting, Nathan, 82
Whiting, Oliver, Jr., 152, 254
Whiting, Ozias, 1, 103
Whiting, Richard, 302
Whiting, Samuel, Jr., 224
Whitley, Benjamin, 238
Whisley, William, Jr., 238
Whitly, William, 267
Whitman, Alexander, 97
Whitman, Daniel, 51, 65
Whitman, Ebenezer, 91
Whitman, Eli, 151
Whitman, Gilbert, 97
Whitman, Jacob, 251
Whitman, James, 215
Whitman, Jeptha, 33
Whitman, Jesse, 44
Whitman, John, 28, 244, 266, 306
Whitman, Joseph, 75
Whitman, Joshua, 176
Whitman, Martin, 97
Whitman, Nathan, 50
Whitman, Samuel, 150
Whitman, Thomas, 97
Whitman, William, 48
Whitman, Zachariah G., 80, 81
Whitmarsh, Charles, 243
Whitmarsh, Jacob, 91
Whitmarsh, John, 253, 258
Whitmarsh, Lot, 50
Whitmarsh, Nathan, 65
Whitmarsh, Thomas, 49
Whitmore, Abraham, 231
Whitmore, Benjamin, 211
Whitmore, Edmund, 54
Whitmore, Enoch, 93
Whitmore, Francis, 247
Whitmore, Isaiah C., 249
Whitmore, Jacob, 233
Whitmore, James C., 247
Whitmore, John, 71
Whitmore, John W., 50
Whitmore, Joseph, 89
Whitmore, Major, 256
Whitmore, Nathaniel, 70
Whitmore, William, 17, 118, 247
Whitmore, William, Jr., 174
Whitney, Abiezer, 235, 296
Whitney, Abizer, 296
Whitney, Abner, 95
Whitney, Abraham, 235
Whitney, Adam, 158, 175
Whitney, Alexander, 226
Whitney, Andrew, 280
Whitney, Benjamin, 233, 296
Whitney, Calvin, 205 (2)
Whitney, Christopher A., 280
Whitney, Daniel, 80, 83, 109
Whitney, Ebenezer, 280
Whitney, Edmund, 173
Whitney, Eli, 173

Whitney, Elisha, 45, 71, 78
Whitney, Ephraim, 152, 254
Whitney, Frost, 213
Whitney, George W., 212, 256
Whitney, Hains, 205 (2)
Whitney, Hanes, 205
Whitney, Haynes, 207
Whitney, Henry, 182
Whitney, Israel, 83
Whitney, Jacob, 26, 47, 95
Whitney, Jacon, 83
Whitney, James, 40, 212, 280
Whitney, Jason, 110
Whitney, John, 40, 83, 100, 266, 290, 307
Whitney, Jonathan, 77, 80, 235
Whitney, Joseph, 84, 159, 168
Whitney, Joshua, 160
Whitney, Levi, 83, 171
Whitney, Lewis, 90
Whitney, Luke, 94
Whitney, Luther, 164, 165, 166, 173
Whitney, Nathan, 233
Whitney, Peter, 233
Whitney, Reuben, 174
Whitney, Salmon, 80, 85
Whitney, Samuel, 100
Whitney, Seth, 94
Whitney, Silas, 80, 83
Whitney, Stephen, 43, 89
Whitney, Theodore, 78
Whitney, William, Jr., 175
Whiton, Elisha, 32
Whiton, Hanks, 102
Whiton, Isaiah, 102
Whiton, Job S., 96
Whiton, Theophilus, 101
Whittemore, Amos, 40
Whittemore, Bernard, 26
Whittemore, Gamaliel, 148
Whittemore, Gershom, 101
Whittemore, Hill, 266
Whittemore, John, 138, 175
Whittemore, Joseph, 101, 119, 120, 122 (2)
Whittemore, Joshua, 86
Whittemore, Levi, 175, 260
Whittemore, Major, 174, 246
Whittemore, Nathan, 306
Whittemore, Roswell, 270
Whittemore, Samuel, Jr., 175
Whittemore, Stephen, 135
Whittemore, William, 175
Whittemore, William D., 148
Whitten, Daniel, 212
Whitten, Ebenezer, Jr., 181
Whitten, Israel, 267
Whitten, Joseph, 235, 236
Whitten, Paul, Jr., 181
Whitten, Thomas, 274
Whittidge, Henry T., 138
Whittier, Abel, 229, 279
Whittier, Benaiah, 282
Whittier, Benjamin, 228, 283
Whittier, Clark, 228
Whittier, David W., 228, 283
Whittier, James, 186 (2), 187, 190
Whittier, Jonathan, 282
Whittier, Joseph, 179, 282, 306
Whittier, Josiah, 228, 282, 283
Whittier, Levi, 280
Whittier, Moses, 14, 306
Whittier, Nathaniel, 147 (2), 229, 306

Whittier, Peter, 41
Whittier, Porter, 301
Whittier, Reuben, 179
Whittier, Thomas, 301
Whittier, Thomas, Jr., 301
Whittier, William, 279 (2), 306
Whittington, Francis, 139
Whittington, Samuel, 34, 43
Whistle, James, 138
Whittlesly, Charles, 32
Whittlesly, Solomon, 32
Whittlesy, Heman, 32
Whitton, John, 307
Whitton, Robert, 68
Whittridge, John, 35
Whitwell, Samuel, 83
Whood, Samuel, 17
Whorf, Nathaniel, 213
Wibly, William, 195
Wicker, David, 16
Wickford, Hilles, 263
Wicks, Charles, 75, 76
Wicks, Enoch, 196
Wicks, Henry, 75, 76
Wicks, John, 73
Wicks, Thomas, 75, 76
Wicks, William, 3d, 75, 76
Widen, John, 83
Widger, Thomas, 22
Widger, William, 7, 22
Wiely, John, 117
Wier, George, 25
Wier, Henry, 78
Wier, James S., 299
Wier, Robert, 211
Wiggin, Asa, 141
Wiggin, Eaton, 246
Wiggin, James, 237
Wiggin, James D., 137
Wiggin, John, 181
Wiggin, Thomas D., 137
Wiggins, Charles, 239
Wiggins, Daniel, 279 (2)
Wiggins, James, 237
Wiggins, John, 212
Wiggins, John D., 133
Wiggins, Nathaniel, 256
Wiggins, Pierce L., 137
Wiggins, Samuel, 212, 255
Wiggins, Thomas D., 133
Wiggins, Thomas L., 137
Wight, Harris, 67
Wight, Willard, 64
Wightman, Melvin, 178
Wilber, Charles, 95
Wilber, Daniel, 62
Wilber, Elijah, 54
Wilber, Isaiah, 95
Wilber, James, 99
Wilber, Jason, 95
Wilber, Jonathan, 41
Wilber, Joseph, 95
Wilber, Marshall, 260, 263
Wilber, Nathaniel, 209
Wilber, Samuel, 62
Wilber, Stephen, 62
Wilber, William A., 62
Wilbour, Charles, 56
Wilbour, Daniel, 60
Wilbour, Derius, 57
Wilbour, Elkanah, 56

Wilbour, Ephraim, 149
Wilbour, Joshua, 59
Wilbour, Stephen, 127
Wilbour, Ziba, 126
Wilbur, Abiathar, 99
Wilbur, Barrick, 50
Wilbur, Benjamin, 300
Wilbur, Caleb, 263
Wilbur, David, 263
Wilbur, George, 50
Wilbur, Isaac, 50
Wilbur, Joel, 54
Wilbur, John, 66
Wilbur, Josiah, 54
Wilbur, Otis, 61
Wilbur, Seth H., 61
Wilbur, William, 59
Wilbur, Zera, 59
Wilbur, Ziba, 61
Wilby, William, 195
Wilcoat, Joseph, 40
Wilcocks, Loven, 32
Wilcocks, Lyman, 32
Wilcocks, William, 32
Wilcot, Joseph, 24
Wilcott, George, 108
Wilcox, Abner, 63 (2)
Wilcox, Allen, 125
Wilcox, Benjamin B., 92
Wilcox, Cyrenus, 64
Wilcox, David, 67
Wilcox, Henry, 62
Wilcox, Jeheel, 30
Wilcox, Jonathan, 58
Wilcox, Joseph, 129
Wilcox, Samuel, 31
Wild, Benjamin, 83
Wild, Eben, 8
Wild, Elijah, 42
Wild, Frederic, 24
Wild, John, 9, 26
Wild, John, Jr., 60
Wild, Joseph, 43
Wild, Timothy, 281
Wilde, Calvin, 5
Wilde, William Cobb, 275
Wilder, Bela, 161
Wilder, Beniah, 52
Wilder, Calvin, 104
Wilder, Calvin D., 1
Wilder, Darius, 182
Wilder, David, 94
Wilder, Ebenezer, 3
Wilder, Eleazer, 68, 80
Wilder, Ephraim, 248
Wilder, George, 91
Wilder, Isaac, 94
Wilder, James, 101
Wilder, John, 248
Wilder, John N., 84
Wilder, Lewis, 71, 78
Wilder, Nahum, 94
Wilder, Nathaniel, 40, 54
Wilder, Oren, 161
Wilder, Reuben D., 1
Wilder, Samuel, Jr., 248
Wilder, T., 3d, 161
Wilder, Titus, 3
Wildes, Francis, 248
Wilds, Earl, 47
Wilds, Nathaniel, 310

Wiley, Aaron, 216
Wiley, Adam, 206
Wiley, Alexander, Jr., 185
Wiley, America, 152
Wiley, Jacob, 117
Wiley, James, 140, 286
Wiley, John, 152, 194, 284
Wiley, Peleg, 286
Wiley, Robert, 284
Wiley, Samuel, 47, 48, 96, 308
Wiley, William, 50
Wilie, Alexander, Jr., 183
Wilie, James, 285, 286
Wilie, Robert, 183
Wilkes, Joseph, 92
Wilkie, George, 5
Wilkie, Henry, 5
Wilkins, Asa, 81
Wilkins, Darius, 253
Wilkins, David, 10, 167, 281
Wilkins, Isaac, 47
Wilkins, Jacob, 7
Wilkins, James C., 40
Wilkins, Jason, 35, 38
Wilkins, Jeremiah, 82
Wilkins, John, 82
Wilkins, John G., 134, 140
Wilkins, Stephen, 166
Wilkins, Sylvester, 35 (2)
Wilkinson, John, 57
Wilkinson, Richard, 193
Wilkinson, Samuel, 245
Wilkinson, Thomas, 78
Willard, Amasa, 308
Willard, Asa, 227
Willard, Bartlett, 75
Willard, Caleb, 93
Willard, Daniel, 222, 246
Willard, David, 5
Willard, Ephraim, 25, 27
Willard, George, 70, 78
Willard, John, 81, 83, 217, 219
Willard, Nathaniel, 229
Willard, Samuel, 219
Willard, Simon, 25
Willes, George, 71
Willes, Preserved, 205
Willet, Thomas, 291
Willets, John, 229
Willett, Benjamin, 167
Willey, Charles, 240
Willey, James, 27, 112
Willey, John, 287
Willey, Robert, 288, 294
Willey, William, 288, 294
Williams, Abisha, 65
Williams, Abner, 64
Williams, Abraham, 12, 19, 80
Williams, Alpheus, 30
Williams, Ambrose, 80, 81
Williams, Asa, Jr., 274
Williams, Benjamin, 59, 62, 197, 204, 309
Williams, Benjamin, Jr., 204, 240
Williams, C. M., 27
Williams, Caleb, 13, 38
Williams, Charles, 113 (2)
Williams, Cornelius, 213
Williams, Daniel, 171, 276
Williams, Drury, 66
Williams, Dwelly, 95
Williams, Ebenezer, 303, 304

Williams, Ebenezer B., 271
Williams, Eleazer W., 84
Williams, Eli, 62
Williams, Elijah, 248
Williams, Enoch, 62
Williams, Enos, 59
Williams, Ephraim, 94
Williams, Erastus, 32
Williams, George, 51, 138, 156, 169
Williams, Greenfield, 53
Williams, Grusham, 62
Williams, Gustavus, 220
Williams, Harvey, 109
Williams, Henry, 284, 287
Williams, Horace, 32
Williams, Isaac, 32, 83, 102
Williams, Isaac, 3d, 64
Williams, Jabez, 129
Williams, Jacob, 60
Williams, James, 79, 81, 156 (2), 183, 185, 189, 231, 248, 272
Williams, Jason, 97
Williams, John, 8, 12, 24, 56, 86, 116, 133, 305
Williams, John, Jr., 54, 138
Williams, Johnson, 160
Williams, Jonathan, 197, 204 (2)
Williams, Joseph, 36, 37, 54, 66, 68, 165, 166, 171
Williams, Joseph, 2d, 166
Williams, Joseph L., 165
Williams, Joshua, 45
Williams, Joshua H., 40, 70
Williams, Josiah, 49, 68
Williams, Kanson, 64
Williams, Larned, 95
Williams, Lewis, 95, 278, 282
Williams, Luther, 88
Williams, Martin, 96
Williams, Moses, 273
Williams, Nathaniel, 12
Williams, Noah, 40
Williams, Peres, 49
Williams, Peter, 165, 166, 173, 204 (2)
Williams, Philip, 178
Williams, Philo, 62
Williams, Robert P., 8, 110
Williams, Rufus, 54
Williams, Samuel, 4, 43, 89, 233, 308
Williams, Saul, 46, 185, 308
Williams, Seth, 95
Williams, Silas, 41
Williams, Stephen, 62, 64, 134, 135, 280
Williams, Stephen W., 63
Williams, Thomas, 59, 113, 114, 169, 248, 268
Williams, Thomas R., 132, 140
Williams, Tillson, 40
Williams, Tyler, 119
Williams, Warren, 64
Williams, William, 13, 14, 32, 62, 230
Williams, William, Jr., 90
Williams, William C., 28 (2)
Williams, Zebedee, 62
Williamson, Abraham, 226
Williamson, Calvin, 39
Williamson, Ebenezer, 305
Williamson, George, 271
Williamson, James, 308
Williamson, Samuel S., 205
Williamson, Saul, 308
Williamson, Stephen, 305
Williamson, Sylvanus, 268, 305

Williamson, Thomas, 268, 305
Williamson, Warren, 227
Willing, Abraham, 101
Willington, Alding, 259
Willington, Edmund, 3
Willis, Abial, 40
Willis, Abiel, 25
Willis, Alden, 64
Willis, Benjamin, 77, 133, 140
Willis, Cyrus, 41
Willis, Daniel, 17
Willis, Daniel, Jr., 50
Willis, Ephraim, 50
Willis, George, 41
Willis, Hopestill, 39
Willis, Isaiah, 146
Willis, James, 50, 177, 288
Willis, Jesse, 6
Willis, John, 45, 49
Willis, Joseph, 257
Willis, Martin, 49
Willis, Nathan, 8
Willis, Peter W., 304
Willis, Seth, 252
Willis, Sumner, 10
Willis, Wendall, 75
Willis, Wendell D., 72
Willis, William, 52
Willis, William B., 68, 112
Willison, John, 134
Williss, Benjamin, 191
Williston, Caleb, 87
Williston, James, 24, 40, 77
Williston, Samuel, 24
Willman, Thomas, 215
Willmanhouser, Frederick, 195, 197
Willmarth, Henry, 33
Willmoth, Ephraim, 30
Wills, Benjamin, 189
Willson, Actor, 232
Willson, Andrew, 232 (2)
Willson, James, 232 (2)
Willson, William, 232
Willy, James, 134
Willy, Peleg, 294
Wilmanhouser, Charles, 195
Wilmarth, Benoni, 10
Wilmarth, Foster, 32
Wilmarth, Seth, 54
Wilmarth, Thomas, Jr., 60
Wilmer, David, 92
Wilmot, Benoni, 126
Wilmot, Orlando, 148
Wilmouth, David, 66
Wilson, Abel, 88
Wilson, Actor, 232
Wilson, Adam, 235
Wilson, Alexander, 300
Wilson, Amos, 180
Wilson, Andrew, 88
Wilson, Asa, 118
Wilson, Benjamin, 27, 48
Wilson, Caleb, 103
Wilson, Calvin, 32
Wilson, Charles, 39, 138
Wilson, Cyrus, 158
Wilson, David, 227, 282
Wilson, Earl, 258
Wilson, Eliphalet, 61
Wilson, Ephraim, 212, 267
Wilson, Ephraim, Jr., 236
Wilson, Francis, 45

Wilson, George, 154
Wilson, Goen, 220
Wilson, Gowen, 259
Wilson, Hammond, 55
Wilson, Henry, 78, 220
Wilson, Hugh, 3, 230
Wilson, Humphrey, 235, 236
Wilson, Increase, 220
Wilson, James, 235 (2), 236
Wilson, James, 1st, 296
Wilson, James, 2d, 296
Wilson, Jason, 2
Wilson, Jesse, 23, 77
Wilson, John, 2, 35, 37, 38, 63, 64, 79, 135, 161, 226, 235, 266, 299
Wilson, John, Jr., 234
Wilson, John, 4th, 148
Wilson, John H., 235, 236
Wilson, Jonathan, 133, 136, 137 (2), 197
Wilson, Joseph, 121, 124, 151
Wilson, Joseph, Jr., 17
Wilson, Lemuel, 240
Wilson, Leonard, 209
Wilson, Levi, 158
Wilson, Luke, 236
Wilson, Mark, 224
Wilson, Moses, 186, 187, 189
Wilson, Nathaniel, 93, 139 (2), 311
Wilson, Otis, 64
Wilson, Robert, 133, 272
Wilson, Samuel, 30, 118, 231, 235, 236, 267
Wilson, Samuel, 2d, 231
Wilson, Samuel G., 185
Wilson, Samuel N., 160
Wilson, Seth, 300
Wilson, Theodore, 294
Wilson, Thomas, 234, 236
Wilson, Walter H., 180
Wilson, Willard, 98
Wilson, William, 13, 14, 21, 101, 206, 233
Wilson, William K., 18
Wilton, James, 195
Wilton, Joseph, 195
Wimbleton, Charles, 36, 37
Winchel, Erastus, 31
Winchempan, Jacob, 180
Winchenpan, Daniel, 288
Winchenpan, Henry, 288
Winchenpan, John, 288
Winchenpaw, Henry, 289, 291
Winchenpaw, Isaac, 311
Winchepan, Isaac, 310
Winchester, Alden, 44
Winchester, Bancroft, 21, 139
Winchester, Benjamin, 214
Winchester, Benjamin P., 279
Winchester, Charles, 214
Winchester, Solomon W., 182
Winchester, William D., 9
Wing, Allen, 148
Wing, Alvan, 75
Wing, Alvin, 72
Wing, Baker, 103
Wing, Barker, 1
Wing, Caleb, 168
Wing, Calvin, 278, 295
Wing, Charles, 63
Wing, David, 63, 228
Wing, Ezekiel, 239, 266
Wing, Jabes, 253
Wing, James, 168, 239, 278
Wing, Joshua, 277, 282

Wing, Latham, 63
Wing, Lot, 72, 75
Wing, Moses, 281
Wing, Moses, Jr., 276
Wing, Nathaniel, 72
Wing, Noah, 277
Wing, Obed, 223, 278
Wing, Samuel, 280
Wing, Saul, 65
Wing, Seneca, 53
Wing, Stephen, 56, 239
Wing, Stephen, 2d, 56
Wing, William, 75
Wingate, Edmund, 213
Wingate, Frederick, 274
Wingate, Harrison, 227
Wingate, Simon, 201, 203
Winn, Erastus, 133
Winn, Japheth, 238
Winn, John, 138, 256
Winn, Joseph, 266
Winn, Josiah, 309
Winn, William, 238
Winnick, William B., 41
Winshall, Isaac, 312
Winshall, William, 215
Winshell, Robert, 231
Winship, Amos, 84
Winship, Benjamin, 66, 236, 267
Winship, Daniel, 171
Winship, Jonas, 243
Winship, Meyers, 25
Winship, Oliver, 90
Winship, Stephen, 25, 155
Winship, Thomas, 254
Winship, William, 86
Winslow, Adam, 158
Winslow, Barnabas, 57
Winslow, Charles, 84
Winslow, Consider, 249
Winslow, David, 221
Winslow, Ebenezer, 220
Winslow, Edward, 52, 54
Winslow, Ephraim, 57
Winslow, Ezekiel, 291
Winslow, Gilbert, 57, 224
Winslow, Henry, 289
Winslow, Isaac, 86
Winslow, Jacob, 212, 256, 291
Winslow, Job, 299
Winslow, John, 167, 194, 196
Winslow, Joseph, 194
Winslow, Joshua, 56
Winslow, Josiah, 129, 194
Winslow, Leonard, 91
Winslow, Miles, 221
Winslow, Nathan, 104
Winslow, Nathaniel, 194, 196
Winslow, Nicholas, 147
Winslow, Peter, 304
Winslow, Philip, 210
Winslow, Prince, 227, 282
Winslow, Reuben, 192
Winslow, Richard, 56
Winslow, Samuel, 249
Winslow, Snow, 194
Winslow, Thomas, 2d, 224
Winslow, William, 57 (2), 148, 158, 220, 246
Winslow, William P., 80
Winslow, Zenas, 128
Winston, John, 40
Winter, Alden, 248

444 INDEX.

Winter, Joseph, 45, 259
Winton, John, 82
Wintworth, James, 194
Wintworth, John, 194, 197, 217, 293
Wintworth, John, 2d, 194
Wintworth, Joshua, 216
Wintworth, Saul, 194
Wintworth, Theophilus, 51
Wipphen, Joseph B., 117
Wire, James, 145
Wire, Joseph, 232 (2)
Wise, Daniel, Jr., 309 (2)
Wise, John, 14, 78
Wise, Jonathan, 111
Wise, Peter M., 246
Wise, William, 42
Wishington, Newell, 68
Wiston, Liberty, 24
Wiswall, Andrew, 68
Wiswell, Benjamin, 110, 111 (2)
Wiswell, Benjamin P., 111 (2)
Wiswell, David, 45
Wiswell, Edward, 66
Wiswell, James, 41
Wiswell, Jesse, 37
Wiswell, Joseph, 243
Wiswell, Lovell, 96
Wiswell, Payne, 52, 112 (2)
Wiswell, Richard, 241
Wiswell, Thomas, 25, 40, 217
Witham, Aaron, 210
Witham, Ammon, 297
Witham, Amnon, 249
Witham, Asa, 265
Witham, Benjamin, 204, 296
Witham, Daniel, 168
Witham, Dunham, 148
Witham, Durham, 148
Witham, Ebenezer, 167, 229
Witham, Henry, Jr., 12
Witham, Isaac, 307
Witham, James, 263
Witham, Jerre, 204
Witham, Jesse, 262
Witham, John, 210, 226, 305, 309
Witham, John, Jr., 309
Witham, Jonathan, 83
Witham, Joseph, 11
Witham, Joshua, 282
Witham, Josiah, 192, 196
Witham, Jotham, 216
Witham, Mark, 12
Witham, Nathaniel, 12
Witham, Samuel, 148
Witham, Thomas, 307
Witham, William, 13, 14, 305
Witham, William C., 210
Withee, Samuel, 267
Withee, Zachariah, 284
Withen, George, 9
Wither, George, 93
Wither, Joseph, 307
Witherell, Ivory, 277
Witherell, James, 170
Witherell, John, 72, 75
Witherell, Joshua, 42
Witherell, Nathaniel, 59, 61
Witherell, Thomas, 169, 281
Witherell, William, 169
Witherspoon, Robert, 209
Withertca, William, 242
Withey, John, 116

Withington, Alpheus M., 40
Withington, E., 82
Withington, Enos, 79
Withington, Joseph, 28
Withington, Phineas, 86
Withington, Samuel, 23, 89
Withington, William, 246
Withum, Joshua, 227
Witt, Archibald, 94
Witt, Charles, 289
Witt, Daniel, 252, 255
Witt, John, 252, 257
Witt, John W., 289
Witt, Sewell, 180
Witt, William, 46, 180
Wittemore, Stephen, 134
Witter, Abraham, 33
Wittington, William, 101
Woddell, Nathaniel, 56
Wodis, Edward, 93
Wolcott, Calvin, 141
Wolcott, Francis, 47
Wolcott, Josiah, 26
Wolcott, Oliver, 56
Wolcott, Samuel, 33
Wolcott, Solomon, 176
Wolcott, William, 176
Wois, Benjamin, 194
Wolsgrover, George, 285
Woltsgrove, Christopher, 288
Woltsgrover, Christopher, 285
Wood, Aaron, 133, 139
Wood, Absalom, 253, 257
Wood, Alba, 51
Wood, Alden, 47, 87
Wood, Alonzo, 275
Wood, Amos, 16
Wood, Barnabas, 43, 89
Wood, Benjamin, 136
Wood, Benjamin, Jr., 66
Wood, Butler, 236
Wood, Charles, 129
Wood, Collins, 67
Wood, Daniel, 23
Wood, Earl, 257
Wood, Ebenezer, 29, 67, 99
Wood, Edward, 39, 175
Wood, Elihu, 55, 58
Wood, Elihu, Jr., 127
Wood, Eliphalet, 230
Wood, Ezekiel, 65
Wood, Ezra, 52
Wood, George, 35, 38, 56, 240, 266
Wood, Harvey, 52
Wood, Heman, 225
Wood, Henry, 118, 222, 240
Wood, Ichabod, 2d, 52, 54
Wood, Israel, 257
Wood, J., 19
Wood, Jacob, 138
Wood, James, 56, 120, 121 (2), 124 (3), 154, 270, 305
Wood, James L., 257
Wood, Jedediah, 88
Wood, Jeremiah, 52
Wood, Jesse, 39
Wood, John, 13, 14, 48, 95, 159, 275, 277, 307
Wood, John F., Jr., 283
Wood, Jonathan, 18, 121, 124, 216
Wood, Jonathan, Jr., 96
Wood, Jordan, 266
Wood, L., 129

Wood, Levi, 52
Wood, Lewis, 69
Wood, Lorenzo, 52, 54
Wood, Manning, 215
Wood, Martin, 96
Wood, Nathan, 99, 271
Wood, Nehemiah, 23
Wood, Obadiah, 263
Wood, Obed, 273
Wood, Pelham, 52
Wood, Peter, Jr., 51
Wood, Philander, 50
Wood, Ralph, 263
Wood, Ransom T., 51, 103
Wood, Richard, 58
Wood, Russell, 129
Wood, Sampson, 280
Wood, Samuel, 102, 121, 124, 235
Wood, Samuel M., 91
Wood, Saul, 236, 290
Wood, Simeon, 51
Wood, Solomon, 260
Wood, Stephen, 133
Wood, Sylvanus, 54
Wood, Sylvanus T., 52
Wood, Theo, 124
Wood, Thomas, 9, 52, 58, 121 (2), 124, 266
Wood, Thomas C., 145
Wood, Timothy, 223
Wood, Waterman, 75
Wood, William, 19, 35, 38, 58, 120, 124, 165, 166, 260
Wood, William, Jr., 246
Wood, Wyman, 81
Wood, Zacheriah, 202, 208 (2)
Wood, Zacheus, 198, 208
Wood, Zenos, 52
Woodard, Amos, 275
Woodard, Daniel, 274, 275
Woodard, Daniel, 2d, 275
Woodard, Elkanah, 128
Woodard, James, 40
Woodard, Jesse, 48
Woodard, John, 25
Woodard, Joseph, 233
Woodard, Lemuel, 233
Woodard, Martin, 298
Woodard, Michael, 275
Woodard, Samuel, 173
Woodard, Theodore, 8
Woodard, William, 233
Woodard, Zebra, 60
Woodberry, Amos, 272
Woodberry, Andrew, 37
Woodberry, Benjamin, 35
Woodberry, Elisha, 37
Woodberry, Elliot, 37
Woodberry, Freeborn, 37
Woodberry, George, 35
Woodberry, Gideon, 36, 37
Woodberry, Hugh, 272
Woodberry, Jacob, 35, 38
Woodberry, Jeremiah, 37
Woodberry, Joel, 35
Woodberry, Joseph, 35, 37, 38
Woodberry, Larkin, 35
Woodberry, Mark, 37
Woodberry, Moses, 21, 35
Woodberry, Peter, 35, 219
Woodberry, Richard, 37
Woodberry, Robert, 35
Woodberry, Samuel, 35, 37, 38

INDEX. 445

Woodberry, Stephen, 37
Woodberry, Thomas, 3d, 35 (2)
Woodberry, True, 272
Woodberry, Warren, 36
Woodberry, Willoughby, 37
Woodberry, Zebulon, 35
Woodbery, Israel, 194
Woodbery, William, 2d, 35 (2)
Woodbridge, ———, 18
Woodbridge, Benjamin, 184, 187, 189
Woodbridge, Benjamin, Jr., 186
Woodbridge, Harry, 184
Woodbridge, Henry, 187, 189, 191
Woodbridge, Hodge, 157 (3)
Woodbridge, James, 184, 187
Woodbridge, Oliver, 226
Woodbridge, Paul D., 237
Woodbridge, Samuel G., 22
Woodbridge, Thomas, 187, 189
Woodbridge, William, 184, 188, 191
Woodbury, Andrew, 36
Woodbury, Asa, Jr., 12
Woodbury, Benjamin, 35, 256
Woodbury, Collins, 251
Woodbury, Ebeneser, 220
Woodbury, Edward, 83, 233
Woodbury, Epes, Jr., 11
Woodbury, Gideon, 38
Woodbury, Israel, 219
Woodbury, James, 295, 296
Woodbury, Jeremiah, 36
Woodbury, John, 83, 87, 146
Woodbury, Jonas, 195
Woodbury, Larken, 220
Woodbury, Obediah, 9
Woodbury, Peter, 11
Woodbury, Philemon, 210
Woodbury, Samuel, 303
Woodbury, Stephen, 36
Woodbury, Willard H., 159
Woodbury, William, 256
Woodbury, William A., 146
Woodbury, Willoby, 38
Woodcock, Ari, 273
Woodcock, George, 266
Woodcock, Isaac, 239
Woodcock, James, 273
Woodcock, Manson, 58
Woodcock, Matthew, 273
Woodcock, Nathan, 285, 286 (2), 289
Woodcock, Patrick, 285, 286 (2), 289
Woodcock, Timothy, 43, 89
Wooderson, James, 75
Woodfellow, James, 40
Woodford, Chauncy, 220
Woodland, William, 47
Woodman, Amos, 166, 279
Woodman, Archibald, 215
Woodman, Benjamin, 151, 216, 226, 254
Woodman, Daniel, 307
Woodman, David, 89
Woodman, Enoch, 254
Woodman, Isaac, 269 (2)
Woodman, Jabes, 176, 260
Woodman, James, 269
Woodman, James, Jr., 269
Woodman, Jeremiah, 164, 165, 166
Woodman, Joseph, 16
Woodman, Joseph, 3d, 120
Woodman, Joshua, 154, 306
Woodman, Josiah, 123
Woodman, Levi, 270

Woodman, Merrill, 175
Woodman, Moses, 213
Woodman, Nathan, 268
Woodman, Nathaniel, 18, 121, 125, 226
Woodman, Peter, 67
Woodman, Rufus, 223
Woodman, Samuel, 212
Woodman, Saul, 16
Woodman, Stephen, 16
Woodman, Stephen G., 164
Woodman, Timothy, 35 (2)
Woodman, William, 178, 269 (2), 270
Woodruff, Henry, 32
Woodruff, John, 250
Woods, Daniel, 41
Woods, Henry, 279
Woods, John, 146
Woods, John, Jr., 48
Woods, Jonathan, 61
Woods, Nehemiah, 79
Woods, Sampson, 282
Woods, Samuel, 8, 84
Woods, William, Jr., 173
Woodside, George, 295
Woodside, Robert, 298
Woodside, Stinson, 298
Woodside, William, 298
Woodsman, Daniel, Jr., 239
Woodsom, Daniel, 164, 166, 219
Woodsom, Gideon, 219
Woodson, Abijah, 212
Woodson, Daniel, 165
Woodson, Daniel, Jr., 267
Woodward, Benjamin, 5
Woodward, Caleb, 90
Woodward, Cyrn, 148
Woodward, Davis, 167
Woodward, Ebeneser, 299
Woodward, Ephraim, 227
Woodward, George, 97
Woodward, Isaac, 299
Woodward, James, 193, 296
Woodward, John, 194, 299
Woodward, Joseph, 69, 270, 296
Woodward, Josiah, 160
Woodward, Levi, 186, 187, 190
Woodward, Mark, 65
Woodward, Nathan, 298
Woodward, Robert, 59
Woodward, Samuel, 59, 92 231, 299
Woodward, Smith, 78
Woodward, Timothy, 226
Woodward, William, 312
Woodwell, Gideon, 17
Woodwell, John, 17
Woodworth, Benjamin, 266
Woodworth, James, 31, 234
Woodworth, John, 278, 279
Woodworth, Stephen G., 163
Woolcot, Lyman, 47
Woolcot, Solomon, 260
Woolcott, Hasall, 67
Woolcott, Stephen, 67
Wooldridge, John, 7
Wooldridge, Samuel G., 7
Woolly, Jonathan, 32
Woorster, Benjamin, 88
Wooster, John, 275
Worcester, Alexander, 245
Worcester, Alpheus, 68
Worcester, Clement, 245
Worcester, Eldad, 41

Worcester, James, 177
Worcester, Lemuel, 275
Worcester, Samuel, 27
Wordell, Benjamin, 56
Wordell, George, 56
Wordell, Gershom, 56
Wordell, John, 56
Wordell, Peleg, 56
Wordell, Perry, 56
Worden, Isaac, 141
Work, David, 231
Work, Stephen, 44
Work, William, 236, 250, 255
Workman, Benjamin, 312
Works, Clark, 308
Works, Elias, 308
Works, Henry, 229
Works, Rufus, 308
Wormstead, Benjamin, 7
Wormstit, Saul, 10
Wornwood, Ithamar, 245
Wornwood, Jotham, 249, 297
Wornestead, Benjamin, 22 (2)
Worray, John, 155, 156
Worster, Nathan, 31
Worster, Thomas, 174
Worthen, John, 179
Worthen, Jonathan, 179
Worthen, Lewis, 240
Worthen, Nathan, 179
Worthen, Samuel, 180, 267
Worthing, Benjamin, 145
Worthington, Anthony, 69
Worthington, Joel, 44
Worthington, Ransford, 44
Worthington, Theodore, 44
Worthington, William, 211
Worthley, Daniel, 283
Worthy, Oramee, 31
Wortman, William, 161
Wotten, Samuel, 185
Wovel, Silas, 94
Wridington, Thomas, 126
Wright, Almond, 64
Wright, Artemas, 8
Wright, Bela, 8
Wright, Benjamin, 75
Wright, Calvin, 4
Wright, Christopher, 241
Wright, David, 31
Wright, Ebeneser, 88
Wright, Edmund, Jr., 23
Wright, Edward, 6
Wright, Elan, 45
Wright, Elias, 179
Wright, Erastus, 46
Wright, Gaius, 47
Wright, George, 21, 138
Wright, Henry, 3
Wright, Heron, 46
Wright, Isaac, 229, 282
Wright, James, 35, 38, 170
Wright, Jason, 99
Wright, Joel, 4, 47, 87, 88
Wright, John, 27, 59, 166, 261
Wright, John H., 96
Wright, Jonathan, 169
Wright, Joseph, 170
Wright, Josiah, 192, 283
Wright, Lang, 166
Wright, Nathan, 253, 257
Wright, Nathaniel, 94

INDEX.

Wright, Parker, 8
Wright, Peter, 7, 22
Wright, Phineas, 166
Wright, Reuben, 249
Wright, Robert B., 312
Wright, Samuel, 253, 257
Wright, Saul, 47
Wright, Simeon, W., 33
Wright, Simon, 84
Wright, Sylvester, 44
Wright, Warren, 179
Wright, Will, 68
Wright, William, 46
Wright, Woodbridge S., 94
Wright, Zebedee, 129
Wright, Zebulon, 170, 277
Wrightington, John, 1
Wyatt, Simon, 14
Wyatt, Thomas, 119, 120 (4), 122 (3), 123 (3), 124
Wyer, George, 77
Wyer, Nathaniel, 125
Wyer, Peter, 154
Wyer, Peter M., 312
Wyer, William, 260
Wyett, George, 69
Wylie, Alex, 145
Wylie, Alexander, Jr., 189
Wylie, Benjamin, 151, 308
Wylie, John, Jr., 183
Wylie, Robert, 185
Wylie, Robert, 3d, 183
Wylie, Robert, 4th, 189
Wylie, William, 284, 287
Wyly, America, 254
Wyly, John, Jr., 254
Wyman, Abel, 307
Wyman, Alpheus, 27
Wyman, Asa, 98
Wyman, Baily, 251
Wyman, Daniel, 90, 240
Wyman, David, 80, 85, 248, 264, 301
Wyman, Elijah, 307
Wyman, Ephraim, 248
Wyman, Ezekiel, Jr., 237
Wyman, F., 248
Wyman, Fairfield, 240, 266
Wyman, Isaac, 301
Wyman, Jacob, 146
Wyman, James, 265
Wyman, John, 78, 154, 224, 304, 306
Wyman, John, 2d, 90, 266
Wyman, Jonathan, 114
Wyman, Joseph, 82, 307
Wyman, Lemuel, 22, 212
Wyman, Levi, 307
Wyman, Luke, 7
Wyman, Marbick, 68
Wyman, Maverick, 80
Wyman, Oliver, 274
Wyman, Percy, 248

Wyman, Richard, 88
Wyman, Samuel, 99
Wyman, Simeon, 24
Wyman, Starkey, 262
Wyman, Stephen, 249
Wyman, William, 82, 224, 236, 240
Wyman, Zacheus, 85
Wyman, Zebedee, 240
Wymard, William, 228
Wymer, Oliver, Jr., 274
Wynn, Sylvanus, 138
Wythe, Jones, 3d, 98

Y

Yale, Isaac, 93
Yates, George, 197
Yates, James, 196, 197
Yates, Josiah, 175
Yates, Thomas, 197
Yates, William, 250, 255
Yatt, Thomas, 123
Yatte, Thomas, 119
Yeates, George, 192, 195
Yeates, George W., 195
Yeates, James, 195
Yeates, James, 2d, 195
Yeates, John, 195
Yeates, Thomas, 195
Yeates, William, Jr., 250
Yeates, Zinas, 195
Yeaton, Harvey, 186, 188
Yeaton, James, 264
Yeaton, Joseph, 159
Yeaton, Philip, Jr., 229
Yeaton, Samuel, 264
Yerbey, John, 160
Yetten, Joseph, 153
Yetton, Ebenezer, 274
York, Abel, 181
York, Archibald, 161
York, Ebenezer G., 220
York, Ezekiel, 215
York, Jacob, Jr., 175
York, John, 174
York, Joseph, 164, 166, 174, 213
York, Joshua, 175
York, Lewis, 266
York, Reuben G., 220
York, Samuel G., 220
York, Simon, 181
York, Stephen, 213, 226
York, Thomas, 10
York, William, 220
York, William, Jr., 220
York, Zebulon, 295, 296 (2)
Young, Aaron, 278, 293
Young, Alexander, 290, 293
Young, Amos, 250
Young, Andrew, 76
Young, Anson, 154, 290
Young, Asa, 131, 250, 255, 263

Young, Bango, 214
Young, Benjamin, 114, 176, 179, 223, 277, 285, 286 (2), 289
Young, Bradford, 182, 184
Young, Charles, 250
Young, Christopher, 177, 257
Young, David, 290, 293
Young, David I., 160
Young, Dudley, 276
Young, Dudley D., 233
Young, Edward, 193
Young, Eli, 276
Young, Elps, 12
Young, Enos, 171, 246
Young, Ephraim, 103
Young, Gideon, 130
Young, Harvey, 201
Young, Hezekiah, 149
Young, Isaac, 174, 223, 257
Young, Jacob, 279
Young, James, 18, 119, 122, 207, 284, 287, 288, 294, 304, 305
Young, Jedediah, 107, 108
Young, Jeremiah F., 160
Young, John, 20, 106 (2), 126, 149, 208, 212, 218, 227, 276, 282, 287, 304
Young, John, Jr., 182, 311
Young, John C., 177
Young, Johnson, 196
Young, Jonathan, 106 (2), 107 (2), 108, 126, 276, 279
Young, Jonathan F., 106 (2), 107, 108
Young, Jonathan S., 126
Young, Joseph, 68, 88, 276, 311
Young, Joshua, 182, 184, 251, 305
Young, Lewis, 154
Young, Moses, 176, 224, 267, 310
Young, Moses, Jr., 224
Young, Moses, 2d, 259
Young, Nathaniel, 105 (3), 107, 252
Young, Oliver, 276
Young, Reuben, 214
Young, Richard, 154, 225, 245
Young, Robert, 305
Young, Rowland, 275
Young, Sedate, 302
Young, Servant, 270
Young, Stephen, 193
Young, Thomas, 126
Young, William, 19, 36, 37 (2), 207, 211, 252, 290, 293
Young, Zebulon, Jr., 214
Young, Zenas, 107, 108
Younglove, George, 31

Z

Zall(?), Simon, 51
Zenas, John, 106
Zumon, Levi, 109

INDEX.

Home Stations of Companies, Detachments, and Guards who responded to the Call of the Governor.

MASSACHUSETTS.

Abington, 9
Abington and Vicinity, 92
Acton and Vicinity, 100
Adams, 30, 33
Andover, 8, 100
Ashburnham and Vicinity, 93
Attleborough, 53, 54
Barnstable, 104, 131
Bedford and Vicinity, 86
Belchertown, 4
Belchertown and Vicinity, 45
Bellingham, 96
Boston, 7, 23, 24, 27, 68, 69, 70, 77, 78, 79, 80, 81, 82, 83, 84, 312
Boston and Vicinity, 41
Bridgewater, 49, 50, 51
Bridgewater and Vicinity, 97
Brookfield and Vicinity, 91
Cambridge and Vicinity, 98, 101
Canton and Vicinity, 85
Charlemont and Vicinity, 67
Chelsea, 27, 112
Concord, 5
Concord and Vicinity, 99
Danvers, 9
Dartmouth, 63
Dedham and Vicinity, 99
Dorchester, 88
Dorchester and Vicinity, 42
Dover and Vicinity, 90
Easton, 60, 95
Fairhaven, 55
Falmouth, 74, 75, 76
Foxborough, 99
Freetown, 56, 57
Gardner and Vicinity, 94
Gloucester, 9, 10, 11, 12, 13, 14
Goshen and Vicinity, 65
Granville and Vicinity, 45
Greenfield and Vicinity, 66
Groton, 8
Groton and Vicinity, 87, 88
Hadley and Vicinity, 92
Hancock, 30
Haverhill and Vicinity, 98
Hingham and Vicinity, 40, 43
Ipswich, 14
Lancaster and Vicinity, 3
Lee and Vicinity, 32
Lenox and Vicinity, 29
Leominster, 5
Lynn, 116, 117
Lynn and Vicinity, 21
Lynnfield, 117
Mendon, 47
Mendon and Vicinity, 98
Middleborough, 51, 52, 53, 54, 102
Middleton, 103
Milford and Vicinity, 5
Milton and Vicinity, 39
Monson and Vicinity, 44
New Bedford, 55, 129
New Braintree, 93
Newbury, 15, 16, 17
Newburyport, 17, 19, 20, 89, 119, 123
New Marlborough, 31, 33
New Salem, 95

New Salem and Vicinity, 66
Newton and Vicinity, 39
Northampton and Vicinity, 67, 92
Northborough and Vicinity, 91
Northfield, 3
Norton and Vicinity, 10
Orleans, 104, 108
Otis and Vicinity, 31
Pelham and Vicinity, 47
Pittsfield, 94
Quincy and Vicinity, 100
Raynham, 62
Rehoboth, 61
Rehoboth and Vicinity, 98
Royalston and Vicinity, 93
Sandwich, 71, 73, 74, 75, 76
Scituate, 104
Shrewsbury, 48
Shutesbury and Vicinity, 65
Somerset, 60
Springfield, 4, 43
Springfield and Vicinity, 44
Stockbridge and Vicinity, 32
Stoneham, 96
Stowe and Vicinity, 64
Taunton, 59, 60, 61, 62
Walpole and Vicinity, 97
Waltham and Vicinity, 101
Ware and Vicinity, 46
Westborough and Vicinity, 91
Westfield, 46
Westport, 56, 63
Weymouth, 101, 102
Whately, 96
Williamsburgh and Vicinity, 64
Worcester, 3
Worcester and Vicinity, 94

MAINE.

Albany, 257
Albion and Vicinity, 267
Alna, 156, 157, 184, 188
Augusta, 271, 274, 276
Bangor, 217
Bath, 148, 155, 247, 297
Belfast, 303
Belgrade, 264
Bethel, 257
Bingham and Vicinity, 268
Boothbay, 183, 184, 188, 191, 284, 287
Bowdoin, 155, 231, 232, 236
Bowdoinham, 230, 232, 234
Brewer, 162, 209, 214
Bridgton, 211, 212
Bridgton and Vicinity, 258
Bristol, 192, 193, 195, 197, 287
Brownfield, 152
Brunswick, 148, 295, 298, 299
Buckfield, 176, 251
Bucksport, 215
Buxton, 269
Calais, 160
Camden, 198, 199
Canaan, 306
Canaan and Vicinity, 266
Cape Elizabeth, 219, 221, 225
Chesterfield, 228
China, 237

Clinton, 238
Cornville, 306
Cushing, 284
Danville, 256
Dearborn, 262
Denmark, 151
Dixfield, 222
Dixmont, 213
Dresden, 187, 190, 191
Durham, 295, 297, 300
Eastport, 161, 311
Eddington, 216, 217
Ellsworth, 162, 163
Fairfax, 239
Fairfield, 261
Falmouth, 154, 158, 219, 220, 221
Farmington, 227, 282
Farmington and Vicinity, 283
Fayette, 279
Frankfort, 216, 217
Freedom and Vicinity, 180
Freeport, 209
Friendship, 291
Fryeburg, 151 (2)
Gardiner, 272, 275
Georgetown, 247, 248
Greenwood, 250
Gorham, 158, 171, 173
Gray, 210
Greene, 167
Greene and Vicinity, 168
Hallowell, 146, 158, 272, 274, 275
Hampden, 214, 215
Harpswell, 299
Hartford, 223, 225
Hebron, 175, 253
Hiram, 152
Hope, 199, 200, 201, 203
Industry, 304
Jay, 223, 224
Jefferson, 195, 196
Kennebunk, 155, 309
Leeds, 167
Leeds and Vicinity, 168
Lewiston, 166, 169
Lewiston and Vicinity, 277
Limington, 270
Lincolnville, 301, 303
Lisbon, 233, 234
Litchfield, 230, 271, 273
Livermore, 222, 223, 224, 259
Lubec, 161
Mercer, 308
Minot, 159, 175, 176, 177
Minot and Vicinity, 257, 260
Monmouth, 147, 169, 170
Monroe, 215
Montville, 180, 181
Newcastle, 189, 193, 194
New Gloucester, 153, 159, 210, 213, 256
New Sharon, 226
New Vineyard, 280
Nobleborough, 192, 194, 195, 196
Norridgewock, 284, 307
North Palermo, 179
Northport, 302
Norway, 252, 253
Orrington, 216

INDEX.

Palermo, 180
Paris, 146, 251, 252, 255
Paris and Vicinity, 150
Phippsburg, 249
Pittstown, 276
Porter, 254
Portland, 149, 158, 241, 242, 243, 244, 246
Prospect, 301, 303
Readfield, 278, 279, 281, 282
Robinstown, 159
Rome, 228
Rumford and Vicinity, 261
Saco, 154, 155
Scarborough, 170, 172
Scarborough and Vicinity, 246
Sidney, 262, 263
Sidney and Vicinity, 266, 267

Skowhegan, 307
South Montville, 181
Standish, 171, 174
Starks, 305
Starks and Vicinity, 268
St. George, 206 (2)
Sumner, 178
Swanville, 304
Thomaston, 156, 203, 204, 205, 285, 286, 288
Topsham, 148, 231, 234, 235
Turner, 159, 177, 178
Turner and Vicinity, 150
Union, 286, 290, 293
Vassalborough, 153, 237, 239, 265
Vienna, 229
Waldoboro, 289, 291, 292, 294
Wales and Vicinity, 169

Warren, 289, 292, 293
Washington, 180
Waterville, 263, 264
Wayne, 278, 280
Wells, 309, 310
Westbrook, 218, 221
Whitefield, 190
Wilton, 227, 229, 283
Windham, 211
Windsor, 179
Winslow, 236
Winthrop, 273, 277
Winthrop and Vicinity, 158
Wiscasset, 182, 186, 187, 190, 285, 287
Woodstock, 251
Yarmouth, 212

www.ingramcontent.com/pod-product-compliance
Lightning Source LLC
Chambersburg PA
CBHW071233300426
44116CB00008B/1022